THE UNITED STATES

The United

THE HISTORY OF A REPUBLIC

PRENTICE-HALL, INC.   ENGLEWOOD CLIFFS, NEW JERSEY

SECOND EDITION

States

Richard Hofstadter

Columbia University

William Miller

Author, A New History of the United States

Daniel Aaron

Smith College

Maps by Hagstrom Company, Inc.

Picture Editor: Gabriele Wunderlich

Design by Walter Behnke

C

Current printing (last digit):

15   14   13   12   11   10   9   8   7   6   5   4   3

Preface

This first revision of *The United States: The History of a Republic*—after ten years of nationwide use—is in many respects a new book. Those teachers who have used *The United States* in the past will discover, on a mere perusal of the new edition, the freshness of the entire work—from the first three chapters which present a thoroughly reconsidered approach to the age of discovery, the aboriginal peoples, the epoch of colonization and the maturation of the English colonies, to the last four on the modern temper and the modern generation. A more thorough examination, we feel certain, will only deepen the impression made by a quick look.

It is to the new student, nevertheless, even more than to the experienced teacher, that this new edition of *The United States* is principally addressed. The authors are aware of how often many students have encountered courses in American History in high school or preparatory school and even in elementary school. It is our hope and intention in this book to open up the subject of American History even for such students and not to close it as so many textbooks do.

Each generation, as it approaches maturity, rewrites the history of the past. Its vantage point has become different from that of earlier generations. Its perspective has been altered by its own experience; its hopes have changed shape because of frustrations in some areas, fulfillment in others. This book was written—and more pertinently, revised—to provide a synthesis of American History for this generation.

Throughout the book the authors have sought to keep clear their awareness that America is and always has been part of the world and a force in it, that our national experience is most illuminatingly viewed in the context of Western Civilization and world-wide movements. We have enlarged and we hope strengthened all sections dealing with foreign relations, and in particular this new edition contains expanded discussions of relations with Latin America and Canada. Immigration, voluntary and forced, can profitably be viewed as part of American relations with the rest of the world; and the place of "ethnic groups" in American life, from the first Germans and Irish who made their way against the established order, is newly elaborated. The history of the Negro in America has likewise been given fresh consideration—in the colonial period, the revolutionary age, and the Jacksonian era, as well as in the more familiar Old South, New South, and the northern cities of the twentieth century.

The authors also have sought to support their belief that history is more than politics and public policy. This new edition, like the old, encompasses those aspects of life and action that emerge from aesthetic experience, intellectual tradition, and human values. In the new edition the chapters on economic and social organization as well as those on literature and the arts are somewhat more closely integrated with the main thread of political narrative and analysis. But we have tried not to neglect the reverse relationship as well: Historians today study politics with perceptions sharpened and awareness deepened by knowledge of the economy and social structure, and by familiarity with the philosophy, religion, and creative arts through which a people and a nation arrive at self-realization.

In writing this revised edition the authors have not hesitated to draw on their own other works, joint and individual, to enhance the presentation. At the same time, this new edition contains much fresh contemporary detail to help convey a feeling for the life of the past and an appreciation of historical personages. A special feature of the new edition is the consideration given to the lasting impact of such living documents as the Declaration of Independence, the Constitution, and the Emancipation Proclamation.

All the maps in this new edition have been redrawn for clarity and simplicity and to make the most advantageous use of color. Many of the maps, like many of the illustrations, are new. The suggested Readings at the end of each chapter, and the General Readings at the end of the book, have been rewritten to reflect here, as in the text itself, significant advances in American scholarship.

The authors wish to express their appreciation of the favorable reception of the first edition and especially to thank those who took the trouble to call attention to errors in it. These they have made every effort to correct. They also wish to acknowledge the comments they received from those asked to read the first edition with the new edition in view. Professor Arthur P. Dudden has supplied a most helpful teacher's manual and student workbook. It is a great pleasure once more to be able to thank Wilbur E. Mangas and his staff, particularly Mrs. Nancy Hall, and Edgar P. Thomas of Prentice-Hall for the most generous consideration, sometimes under the most trying conditions. Prentice-Hall itself has stinted nothing in the planning and production of this volume, to the advantage of the reader as well as the authors.

R.H.   W.M.   D.A.

Contents

Maps

xviii

THE UNITED STATES

CHAPTER ONE

At about a quarter to five in the morning, a half hour before dawn on Friday, August 3, 1492, the pull of the moon began to draw the waters of the Atlantic Ocean back from their crest on the Rio Tinto at the little port of Palos in Andalusia in Spain.

As the tide ran out to sea that morning, it carried from the security of Palos harbor three fated ships, *Niña, Pinta,* and *Santa Maria.* Aboard *Santa Maria,* flagship of this fleet, sailed the "Captain-General" in command, long-faced, hawk-nosed Christopher Columbus, an aging mariner many thought mad. His destination was "the lands of India," a storied realm of wealth and power

The Discovery of America by Europeans

somewhere to the east of the Mohammedan world that sorely menaced Christendom. His route: "I should not go by land, the usual way, to the Orient," Columbus the Genoese told his royal backers, King Ferdinand and Queen Isabella of Spain, but by water, westward, "by the route to the Occident, by which no one to this day knows for *sure* that anyone has gone."

His ships, Columbus said himself, were "well furnished with much provision and many seamen." The season was sounder than he knew for an ocean voyage on the course he proposed to follow. The morning of departure his sails hung limp in the windless air, but by eight o'clock the river tide had floated his small ships to the sea where they caught a strong breeze.

By sunset on the first day officers and men lost sight, over the curving rim of the earth, of dear, familiar shores, visible havens from the unknown terrors of the deep that claimed so many of the seagoing clans. But Columbus' mariners, seasoned in ocean navigation, knew, or thought they knew, something of what lay ahead and did not worry yet.

Six days out, 660 miles "South and by West" of Palos, the little fleet reached the Canary Islands, already owned and settled by Spain. These islands cluster just off Africa's turbulent western coast at 28° north latitude. On this very parallel, Columbus believed, lay Cipangu—Japan—the richest part, according to the information he trusted most, of "the lands of India" he sought.

Columbus and his men rested in the Canaries for a month while their ships underwent needed repairs and supplies were replenished. The Captain-General fell in love with the lady ruler of the island of Gomera, Doña Beatriz de Peraza. But Columbus loved his mission more than his mistress, and in the early hours of the morning of September 6, his prayers said and his vessels bulging with fresh wood and water, wine, biscuit, and cheese, he weighed anchor at San Sebastián, Doña Beatriz' pleasant port.

For nearly 48 hours Columbus' fleet stood becalmed off the fiery, 12,000-foot volcano on the island of Tenerife, tallest in the Canaries. Then, at 3 A.M. Saturday, September 8, as the commander recorded, "the wind come fair" from the Northeast, and he set his bold new course: *Oeste: nada del noroeste, nada del sudoeste*—"West: nothing to the northward, nothing to the southward."

The next day he did something bolder still. What this was he put down in the privacy of his Journal, in the third person, as was his practice: "he decided to reckon less than he made," to doctor the log, that is, "so that if the voyage were long the people," as he called the crew, "would not be frightened and dismayed." The people, that Sunday morning and afternoon, still could see the westernmost of the Canaries, the island of Ferro, and lofty Tenerife breathing smoke. By dusk, each last point of land had faded out. By nightfall, the three small ships bobbed alone on the uncharted sea, their crews, mostly Spanish, restive under a foreign captain they did not fully trust.

Thirty days out, having doubled all known records for ocean sailing beyond sight of the shore, *Santa Maria*'s people mutinied. This was October 10. The very uneventfulness of the lengthening voyage had overstrained the nerves of sailors made idle by the easy passage. Only Columbus' promise to turn back if no land were raised in three days quieted the crew. Then, just past 2 A.M. on October 12, the deadline nearing, *Pinta*'s lookout called, *"Tierra! Tierra!"*

After three false landfalls on recent days, this cry in the night awakened mixed feelings in the men. But a light in the distance on an island in the Bahamas had indeed been sighted six miles off. As soon as daylight made debarkation safe on this engaging gateway to the New World—"all is so

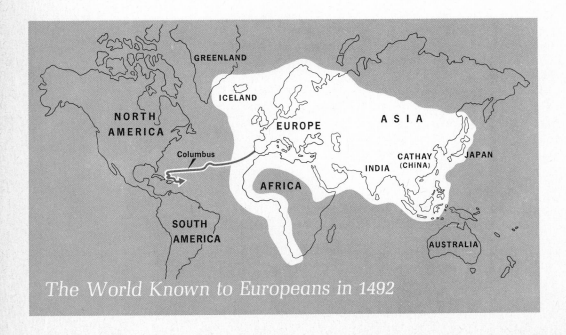

The World Known to Europeans in 1492

green that it is a pleasure to gaze upon it," wrote the Captain-General in his Journal—the momentous "Landing of Columbus" took place.

"To the first island which I found," Columbus later wrote home to his sovereigns, "I gave the name 'San Salvador,' in remembrance of the Divine Majesty, Who had marvellously bestowed all this; the Indians call it 'Guanahaní.'" Today a British possession, this island is officially and perhaps more appropriately known as Watling's Island after the English buccaneer who settled there in the seventeenth century.

Soon, "I found very many [other] islands," Columbus added in his letter to Ferdinand and Isabella, "filled with innumerable people, and I have taken possession of them all for their Highnesses, done by proclamation and with the royal standard unfurled, and no opposition was offered to me."

Columbus' hosts, during his first few weeks of exploration, were the mild Arawaks, as pleasing to gaze upon as the land itself and "so guileless and so generous with all that they possess, that no one would believe

it who has not seen it. They refuse nothing . . . if it be asked of them; on the contrary, they invite any one to share it and display as much love as if they would give their hearts."

Columbus was quick, on this fateful first contact, to return native kindness with aggression: "As soon as I arrived in the Indies, in the first island which I found, I took some of the natives by force, in order that they might learn and might give information of whatever there is in these parts." When he then mended his manners, it was not without ulterior motives of enduring consequence: "I gave them a thousand handsome good things, which I had brought, in order that they might conceive affection for us and, more than that, might become Christian and be inclined to the love and service of Your Highnesses and of the whole Castilian nation, and strive to collect and give us of the things which they have in abundance and which are necessary to us."

I. *The New World before Columbus*

THE CHALLENGE
OF INDIAN CULTURE

When we say, "Columbus discovered America," we mean only that his voyage across the Atlantic Ocean in 1492 first opened the New World to permanent occupation by people from Europe, itself a complex and challenging term perhaps most usefully defined by the geographer, Derwent Whittlesey, as "the habitat of western civilization, a dynamic society not paralleled in any other part of the earth, until Europeans carried their expansive mode of life overseas."

Before Columbus charted the course for his ambitious rivals in the age of Europe's Renaissance, "America" certainly had been discovered two or three times and may have been discovered many more. The most re-

cent estimates place the arrival of the earliest known settlers—Columbus was the first to name these tawny Mongoloids, Indians—about 40,000 years ago. These people, or more properly this mixture of peoples, having moved eastward across Asia over thousands of years (while others, somehow differently mixed and grown fatefully fair in complexion, were moving into European lands) apparently first crossed from Siberia to Alaska by way of the ancient land bridge, whose long existence modern science recently established. Melting ice submerged this bridge after the Indian trek began, and later comers for countless generations presumably negotiated narrow Bering Strait.

With the conspicuous exception of the Eskimos, the newcomers gradually spread southward in pursuit of the big game on

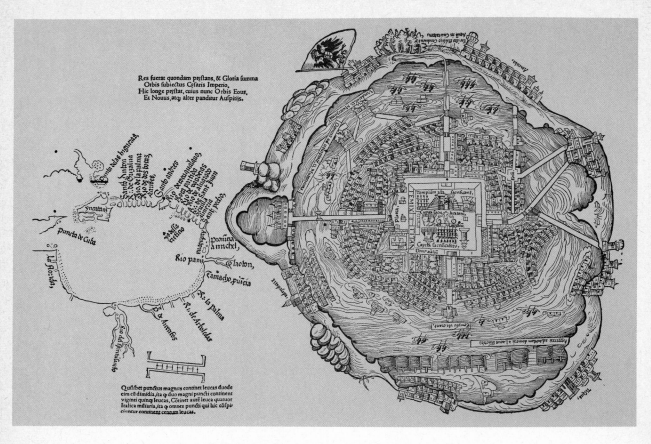

Plan of the Aztec city, Tenochtitlan, Mexico City, which was situated on two islands in Lake Texcoco. Causeways and aqueducts linked the city with the mainland. The large square in the center of the city, enclosed by a stone wall, contained temples used for human sacrifices to Aztec gods.

which they chiefly lived. Some settled permanently on the high plains of what is now the arid Southwest of the United States. Here, until a great climatic change occurred about 8,000 B.C., a lush forest afforded ample greenery on which mammoths, wild bison, antelopes, and mountain goats fed. This fare thinned out farther west where a "desert culture" developed. For thousands of years small desert groups, occasionally finding shelter in mountain caves where their traces have been preserved, eked out the big game with smaller carnivores such as coyotes, gophers, bobcats, and rats, and more significantly, with plant food. After 8,000 B.C., with the forests of the high plains dying because of the dwindling water supply, the plains Indians also turned to scrub plants for their principal food supply. Some 2,000 years later they

were successfully gathering, preserving and planting seeds, and cultivating regular crops with crude tools of wood and stone.

As early, according to recent findings, as 12,000 B.C., husbandry had also begun in the "valley of Mexico," where the largest numbers of Indians had settled down after the southward trek. The stable society husbandry made possible turned Mexico, and neighboring Guatemala and Honduras, into the "heartland of Middle America." Here, and in Peru on the South American mainland, during the early centuries of the Christian era in Europe, which we call the Dark Ages, Indian culture flowered.

Widespread if disconnected disasters seem to have disrupted many areas of Indian life in the century or two before the catastrophic European invasion. These included earthquakes and epidemics, prolonged

6

droughts and dynastic civil wars, and helped prepare the ground for the Europeans' success among the dark worshipers of the Sun in Heaven, who innocently welcomed white men coming from the direction of the Sun's rising as the true children of the Gods. Yet, even in the years of their decline, when they first were encountered by the Spanish *conquistadores* (see p. 17), the Aztecs of Mexico, the Incas of Peru, the Mayas of Guatemala and Yucatán astonished the newcomers with their wealth and artistry; and to this day their accomplishments, and those attributed to predecessor peoples they themselves had mastered, challenge the mind and heart.

Bernal Díaz del Castillo, who fought with Cortez in all his campaigns and wrote the best account of *The Discovery and Conquest of Mexico,* conveys the characteristic wonder of his countrymen on their first triumphant march across the American mainland:

During the morning, we arrived at a broad Causeway and continued our march towards Iztapalapa, and when we saw so many cities and villages built in the water and other great towns on dry land and that straight and level Causeway going towards Mexico [City], we were amazed and said that it was like the enchantments they tell of in the legend of Amadis [the most popular chivalric romance of the age], on account of the great towers and temples and buildings rising from the water, and all built of masonry. And some of our soldiers even asked whether the things that we saw were not a dream. . . .

And then when we entered the city of Iztapalapa, the appearance of the palaces in which they lodged us! How spacious and well built they were, of beautiful stone work and cedar wood, and the wood of other sweet scented trees, with great rooms and courts, wonderful to behold, covered with awnings of cotton cloth.

When we had looked well at all this, we went to the orchard and garden, which was such a wonderful thing to see and walk in. . . . Then the birds of many kinds and breeds which came into the pond. I say again that I stood looking at it and thought that never in the world would there be discovered other lands such as these. . . . Of all these wonders that I then beheld today all is overthrown and lost, nothing left standing.

Even Bernal Díaz' English editor shares the white man's tendency to discredit the achievements of "savages," to which Cortez' companions' own eyes testified: "It could not have failed to make a vivid impression on the Spaniards, who, it must be remembered, . . . had seen nothing better during the twenty-five years of exploration of America than the houses of poles and thatch of Indian tribes, none of whom had risen above the state of barbarism." Yet, when Albrecht Dürer, the great German artist, saw the trophies sent from Mexico by Cortez for the coronation at Aix-la-Chapelle of Charles I of Spain as Holy Roman Emperor, his enchantment matched that of Bernal Díaz del Castillo, and he wrote in his diary:

Also did I see the things which one brought to the King out of the new Golden Land: . . . all sorts of marvelous objects for human use which are much more beautiful to behold than things spoken of in fairy tales. . . . In all the days of my life I have seen nothing which so rejoiced my heart as these things, . . . and I marveled over the subtle genius of these men in strange countries.

For all the stunning beauty of their environment—the sturdy causeways, for example, and the enchanting ponds and lakes and canals of Mexico were man-made parts of intricate irrigation systems—the Aztecs were a brutal and terrifying people, much given to human sacrifice. And yet the desolation Bernal Díaz mentions was wrought by the Spanish, not by the savages, by the Christians, not by the children of darkness.

The Incas of Peru, inheritors, like the Aztecs, of an earlier advanced culture, were at least the Aztecs' equal in building and design. In imperial and social organization and administration, they were far ahead. At the time of the Spanish invasion, the Inca empire stretched along the western coast of South America from 2° north to 37° south latitude and included much of modern Ecuador, Peru, Bolivia, and Chile, all bound together by roads and runners the Romans would have admired. Nor were their rulers lacking the consciousness of power. When urged by Pizarro's chaplain, on his way to the conquest of Cuzco, the glittering Inca capital, to accept Christ as his Lord, the Pope as his master, and Emperor Charles as his monarch, the reigning Inca sovereign, Atahuallpa, replied:

I will be no man's tributary. . . . Your emperor may be a great prince; I do not doubt it, when I see that he has sent his subjects so far across the waters; and I am willing to hold him as a brother. As for the Pope of whom you speak, he must be crazy to talk of giving away countries which do not belong to him. For my faith, I will not change it. Your own God, as you say, was put to death by the very men whom he created. But mine, my God still lives in the heavens and looks down upon his children.

In the "classic age" of their "Theocratic Period," which seems to have ended catastrophically about 900 A.D., the Mayas, possessors of the third great Indian culture, were the uncontested masters of the science of the sky. Their gods were many and were associated with the peaceful pursuit of husbandry. Their efficiency in cultivation supplied the wherewithal for the support of priestly learning, and especially the learning that had to do with the weather, the seasons, the round of the year. Mayan priests specialized in astronomy, to which mathematics was the key. Abstract thought itself was the key to mathematics. The Mayas' brilliant achievements along all these lines culminated, before the end of the seventh century, A.D., in their extraordinary 365-day calendar, one better than Europeans generally would have for a thousand years. The quality of Mayan thinking has prompted western historians to think of them as the Greeks, as they think of the imperial Incas as the Romans, and the marauding Aztecs as the Assyrians, of pre-Columbian America. Mayan triumphs in art serve only to underscore the Grecian theme. Only nowadays is pre-Columbian art being transferred from natural history museums, where they were preserved mainly as arti-facts, to the galleries that house the aesthetic treasures of civilization.

This Grecian theme—in fact, it is but a metaphor of European-oriented men—can easily be overdone. The Indians of Mexico and Peru had a high civilization all their own. The Aztecs are said to have known of the wheel, yet to have used it for no productive purpose. They and others also practiced metallurgy, but only for ornaments, not arms. The Mayas in particular probably had many of what we call advanced ways and ideas, including a system of written notation for which we have yet to find the

Amulet; an example of Mayan pre-Columbian art.

Rosetta Stone. Invading Spanish soldiers, fearful of retribution, destroyed Mayan cities as they destroyed those of Mexico and Peru. So also, in the 1560's, intrusive Spanish missionaries, fearful of the Devil's words, burned almost all the Mayan books. Such desecration heightens the challenge of understanding, as its record heightens the challenge of shame, among those who are keenly aware today of the barbarism of Europe's own culture as well as of its blessings and beauty.

Indian Mexico and Peru, at their peak, held a population (possibly 30 million) almost as great as that of western Europe at the time of the Renaissance; and their principal cities, despite much controversy over their precise size, far outdistanced contemporary Paris and London. The simple fact that such populations and urban concentrations were adequately fed for centuries alone testifies to the technological standards and political stability of what we may appropriately call the old New World.

From Mexico and Peru, long before the white man's arrival, aboriginal peoples had spread once more far into the temperate zones, north and south. The farther they moved from their great heartland, like Europeans from their Mediterranean havens, generally speaking the cruder and harsher their culture seems to have become.

Yet, even as far north as the St. Lawrence River Valley the earliest explorers from overseas marveled at the cities they encountered. One such was Cartier's Hochelaga, the site of modern Montreal, of which the Frenchman reported to his king in 1535, how impressed he was by "the immense numbers of peoples living there" and "their kindness and peacefulness." Ralph H. Brown, in his *Historical Geography of the United States,* remarks that "it has often been suggested, among other explanations, that originally the name 'Canada' signified a place of large Indian lodges." Brown goes on to describe the "underestimation of the extent to which the Indians had been engaged in agriculture," the frequency of Indian towns farther south, and the "Indian old fields" so commonly encountered and so zealously coveted for their open spaces by the first English settlers in what was to become the eastern United States.

Of the Indians in the rest of the future United States something new is being discovered almost every day as archaeological remains in the great river basins are exposed by the rush to develop hydroelectric power and establish flood control. And most of what is being discovered tends to undermine the myth of Indian savagery by which the first white settlers, on each new advance into fresh territory, comforted themselves and assuaged their guilt.

Of these same Indians, John Collier, a

former Commissioner of Indian Affairs, wrote in 1947: "At the time of the discovery, the region that is now the United States contained some one million Indians, . . . formed within more than six hundred distinct societies. . . . These societies existed in perfect ecological balance with the forest, the plain, the desert, the waters, and the animal life. . . . At the time of the white arrival there was no square mile unoccupied or unused."

By their step-by-step resistance to encroachment for almost three hundred years these Indians are said by some to have hardened the fighting qualities in the American character. Their more peaceful contributions to the American civilization include the canoe and the snowshoe, the white potato, the tobacco leaf that was to become the first staple of the English mainland colonies, and Indian corn, that remarkable man-made hybrid, which remains to this day the staple of much of the Middle West.

CONTACTS THAT FAILED
TO ENDURE

While America was developing in isolation a still mystifying civilization of its own, other parts of the world were themselves much more restless than our casual inattention to them suggests. For our own purposes we will refer here only to activities in the Far East and the far North.

For hundreds of years, while Europe slumbered, China developed the most advanced civilization on earth and was to bequeath to the West such basic instrumentalities for its own later expansion as the compass, gunpowder and printing. One climax of Chinese achievement was reached in the opening decades of the fifteenth century when seven tremendous seagoing expeditions, each of fifty huge junks manned by some 25,000 hands, sailed westward to India, Siam, the Persian Gulf and the Red Sea, and even visited east Africa. These expeditions dwarfed the pitiful little Portuguese ventures which at the same time were so painfully seeking the way around West Africa in search of the fabled East (see p. 15).

Why, with their infinite resources and virtuosity, did these Chinese fail to press on into the vast unknown, while the impoverished Europeans of the same period would be stopped by nothing in their unprecedented expansive thrust? No doubt the fact that Europe in the fifteenth century was "on the make," as we say, while China felt it "had it made," suggests some part but hardly all of the explanation. At any rate, centuries before these awesome excursions of the Ming emperors, and far in advance of the white man, modest Chinese and Japanese fishermen, swarming on the north Pacific, may easily have been blown by the prevailing west winds to California, Oregon, or British Columbia, and even as far south as the jutting coast of modern Ecuador.

The white man himself may have reached the Atlantic shores of North America as early as the ninth century. At that time, an Irish Christian hermit sect that had inhabited Iceland for hundreds of years was violently dislodged by invading pagans from Scandinavia. Proven navigators of great skill and possessors of seaworthy craft, these Irishmen could have fled to the New

World island we know as Greenland and even to Labrador.

Even more significant than their possible destination was the known cause of their removal. In the middle of the ninth century the great Viking epoch began and the northern sea routes, east and west of Scandinavia, became alive with the Norsemen's "long ships." The Swedes staked out vast holdings on the Baltic Sea. The Danes moved into England. The Norwegians ventured into all these regions but monopolized the "vestervegen," the "westward way"—to Iceland and beyond. They first visited Iceland in 860 and within ten years had made it a flourishing settlement.

Beyond Iceland lay the forbidding expanse of Greenland. Only 200 miles beyond Greenland lay the outermost reaches of modern Canada. Greenland won its name late in the tenth century when Erik the Red, a wily Norseman expelled from the Iceland republic for disrupting the peace, tried to lure settlers to its barren wastes. His deception worked well. Greenland was settled from Iceland in 986 and became a colony of Norway in the thirteenth century, when its population had reached a peak of about 4,000. For reasons still hidden, white men in Greenland lost all contact with Eu-

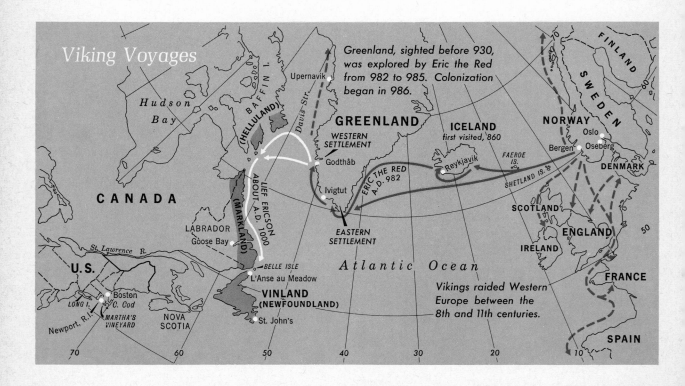

Viking Voyages

Greenland, sighted before 930, was explored by Eric the Red from 982 to 985. Colonization began in 986.

Vikings raided Western Europe between the 8th and 11th centuries.

rope fifty years or more before 1492. When John Davis visited the great island in 1585 and gave his name to the strait that separates it from Baffin Island, he found the white man extinct. Not until the eighteenth century was well along did white settlers return.

Around the year 1000, Leif Ericsson, son of Erik the Red, set out from Greenland to explore the American mainland coast he had learned of some years earlier from a less enterprising Norse captain, Bjarni Herjulfsson, who had missed his Greenland anchorage and probably sighted Labrador before turning back. Leif may have sailed as far south as Massachusetts, but modern evidence makes that most doubtful. The land he first sighted probably was Baffin Island, which he named Helluland, land of flat stones. Sailing southward, he next sighted forested Labrador, which he called Markland, or woodland. Sailing southward still another two days, he and his companions came ashore at last at the place they called Vinland, "in accordance with the good things they found in it."

Vinland, for centuries, sorely tried the historian's imagination. Thought to have been a vine land, a land of grapes, its location was pressed as far south as an historian's patriotic impulse might dictate. In 1964, however, its most likely location was fixed. Not a land of grapes, but a land of grass, as its Norse etymology indicates, "Vinland the Good" was named by thankful Greenlanders for its lovely grazing lands. Leif and his company remained there a year, and left artifacts that have been dug up in recent years. These voyagers were followed by Leif's brother, Thorvald, who first encountered the hostile natives, whom he called Skraelings, or screechers, and died at their hand. Next came Thorfinn Karlsefni, at the head of an expedition of three ships with 160 settlers and livestock and tools. For three years Karlsefni struggled to establish a colony, but the Skraelings far outnumbered them and eventually drove them back to Greenland. The place was the little fishing village known today as L'Anse au Meadow, the bay of the meadow,

at the northernmost tip of the island of Newfoundland.

By the time of Columbus even this certain discovery and attempted settlement of America by Europeans had been lost to memory—except simply as one more strand in the richly embroidered tales of other worlds by which the medieval imagination was possessed.

FORESHADOWINGS
IN MIND AND SPIRIT

These tales of other worlds, and certain morsels of truth which they contained, went back to the Old Testament story of the Garden of Eden and to pagan Homer and the classic Greeks. As part of the mythology and learning of western culture, they were more important in motivating Columbus and his successors than the hazy discoveries of the more recent past.

Almost 2,500 years before Columbus, the poet Homer, in the story of Odysseus, placed the Elysian Fields—the *earthly* paradise—on the river Oceanus, "at the world's end where all existence is a dream of ease." Thereafter, successive Mediterranean civilizations took heart from visions of new Edens across the western ocean, visions that materialized at last in the United States.

Four hundred years after Homer, the philosopher Plato wrote of the lost island of Atlantis, once the site, he said, of an ideal commonwealth just beyond the Strait of Gibraltar. For a full millennium and more, few would sail beyond this Strait, "where Hercules his landmarks set as signals," as Dante wrote in the thirteenth century, "that no man farther onward should adventure." As long as men failed to disprove the existence of Atlantis, Plato's pleasing myth or invention grew ever more real to the European mind.

During the Middle Ages, imaginary Atlantic lands multiplied, and two in particular exercised an enduring spell. One was St. Brendan's isle of contentment, the discovery and domicile of a sixth-century Irish monk, which adorned even the most authentic maps of the ocean until as late as the middle of the eighteenth century. The second was the Island of the Seven Cities, also known in Columbus' time as Antilia, where each of seven Christian bishops, fleeing the Mohammedan invasion of Spain in the eighth century, was said to have built a gilded town, one more lovely than another. From it comes the name Antilles, given derisively to the Caribbean islands by some of Columbus' own mariners who were skeptical that they were in fact in the West *Indies,* as their captain claimed.

The peak of medieval misdirection was reached in that popular fourteenth-century phantasmagoria, *The Travels of Sir John Mandeville,* which Columbus and his men knew well. Replete with fables of ants the size of hounds guarding hills of gold, and of monstrous chameleons that fed on air, this work also described, and described truly for all one knew, an "Indian" archipelago of no less than 5,000 islands strung out from Asia almost to the western sea, "And man may well prove by experience and subtle compassment of wit," wrote the author of *The Travels of Mandeville,* "that a man might go by ship all about the world above and beneath . . . and turn again to his country. . . . And always he should find men, lands and isles,"while circumnavigating the globe.

THE REACH
OF GEOGRAPHIC SPECULATION
The morsels of "experience and wit" in *Mandeville* and similar medieval concoctions themselves derived largely from the geographical learning of antiquity which the Arabs preserved and enlarged. This learning Europe began to regain in Columbus' early years, when it was given greater currency than ever before by the spread of printing and by the growing secular interests of scholars and scientists upon which the printers fed.

As early as the fourth century B.C., Aristotle's mathematical proofs had caused most learned Greeks to agree that the earth

was more or less a sphere. By then, too, commerce and war with neighboring Mediterranean lands had familiarized even ordinary Greeks with the nearest borders of three continents—Europe, Asia and Africa. In 327-325 B.C. Alexander the Great's armies crossed northern India almost to Tibet. This exploit pushed Greek knowledge of the inhabited world well over 1,500 miles eastward and opened up more distant vistas of Oriental marvels which thereafter held the minds of Europeans enthralled.

The Greeks called familiar territory the *oekumene,* or the known world, or the "Old World," the name which itself gave rise to the use of "New World" for Columbus' discoveries. The farther the *oekumene* was extended, the more interested did the Greeks become in the size of the whole sphere and the extent of its watery parts. Directing much of their thinking was the principle of symmetry, or balance, the first general principle in the history of geographical science.

Aristotle himself argued from the occurrence of elephants in both Africa and India, and from the assumed difficulty of carrying them by sea from one place to the other, that the watery surface of the sphere was limited and the ocean passage from the western bulge of Africa to the eastern extremity of Asia was short. This conclusion sailed through the ages on Aristotle's immense authority as a seer, until it was quoted often and energetically by Columbus himself.

Since most Greeks agreed that land was heavier than water, and that these elements must nevertheless balance one another by weight, it followed from the belief in a small watery surface that the heavier land surface of the sphere must be smaller still. By such a process of reasoning Aristotle reached a second long-lived geographical conclusion: that the short ocean passage from Africa to Asia was uncluttered by islands. The land mass known to the Greeks in Europe, Africa, and Asia, he said, was ample to balance all the water on the sphere.

For all his authority, Aristotle's reasoning about the occurrence of elephants and the absence of islands did not go unchallenged even in his own time. There were Greeks who held that since there was a habitable land mass on the one surface of the sphere known to them, there must be at least its antipode on the opposite side, there must be at least that "world above" balanced by the "world beneath" which *Mandeville* in fact recalled. And indeed, said some, there may be a number of unknown lands, each in balance with one another, and hence a very much larger ocean than Aristotle spoke of with water enough to balance all.

The principle of balance also led certain Greeks to divide the sphere latitudinally into five climatic zones—two frigid zones balancing each other at the poles; a broad torrid zone girdling the center; and between the torrid zone and each frigid zone, two temperate zones in balance in the northern and southern latitudes. These Greeks and most of their followers for almost 2,000 years held that the frigid zones were too cold and that the torrid zone was too hot to sustain life even if there were land. But about the north temperate zone where they themselves lived they were willing to make bold non-Aristotelian predictions. Eratosthenes, who lived and wrote in Alexandria during the third century B.C., was responsible for one of the most remarkable of these prognostications:

If the extent of the Atlantic Ocean were not an obstacle, we might easily sail from Iberia [Spain] to India, on the same parallel. . . . It is quite possible that within the same temperate zone there may be two or even more inhabited earths.

Eratosthenes was a brilliant mathematician who calculated the circumference of the sphere at 25,000 miles, almost precisely right. A successor of his in Alexandria in the second century B.C., Hipparchus by name, was the first to divide the sphere by parallels of latitude and meridians of longitude and to attempt to locate habitable points on it in terms of degrees. A third Alexandrian, known to us as Ptolemy, who lived in the second century A.D., made what

may have been the very first atlas of the world employing the method Hipparchus developed.

Ptolemy's atlas accompanied his work on world geography, which reflected much of the ancient Greek tradition, corrected, as he thought, by all the evidence he could gather from the itineraries of sailors and the reports of travelers. But many of Ptolemy's corrections proved to be erroneous. Most significant for the future was his espousal of the idea of a sphere much smaller than that of Eratosthenes. This led him to calculate each of the sphere's 360 degrees as itself much smaller than it was in reality. Ptolemy also brought west Africa and east Asia far too close to each other.

These errors, embalmed in the geographical writings he absorbed while preparing for his "enterprise of the Indies," were to prove irresistible to Columbus. Indeed, so possessed was he by his notion of finding a short sea route to the Orient that he even improved on Ptolemy. He was encouraged to take this step by a more recent source to whose accuracy on virtually every point modern scholarship has testified except the one point on which Columbus most relied. This source was Marco Polo's "Travels."

On his return to his native Venice in 1298, after nearly thirty years in China in the service of the Great Khan, Polo published his famous book only to be scoffed at by his countrymen for the Oriental wonders he reported. Copies of Polo's work had been out of circulation for a century and a half when it was reprinted for the first time in 1477 and immediately devoured by all aspiring navigators, Columbus among the first. Polo reserved his choicest language for the wonders of Japan, which he never actually visited and of whose extent his knowledge remained vague.

By indefensible manipulations of fanciful Arabic evidence, Columbus compulsively shrank each short Ptolemaic degree by 10 per cent. And on the basis of Polo's second- and third-hand information, he stretched Asia no less than 30 degrees nearer West Africa, so that, as S. E. Morison writes, "Japan almost kissed the Azores." Columbus' calculations, in fact, placed Japan almost precisely where he made his Bahamas landfall.

II. *The Expansion of Europe*

THE MENACE OF MOHAMMEDANISM

Columbus was about thirty years old, a veteran Atlantic sailor and ship captain in Portuguese service, when he first sought the support of the Portuguese king early in the 1480's for his great ocean voyage to the East. Columbus was in the right place at the right time for the promotion of his enterprise. Vast historical changes had already assured the Atlantic primacy over the Mediterranean in Europe's future, and Portugal, at land's end, primacy over Europe's other maritime nations in Atlantic navigation. At the heart of these historical changes lay the menace of Mohammedanism, or Islam, to Christianity.

Spain, of which Portugal was long a part, had been the first Christian country to succumb to the Mohammedan invasion of Europe from north Africa in the eighth century. Thereafter, Mohammedanism spread ever farther south in Africa, ever farther east in Asia, and ever farther north in Europe itself, gradually absorbing the legends, lore, and learning of the world from captured Persians, Hindus, Jews, Moors, Egyptians, Greeks and others. Within the vast expanse of Islam by the end of the tenth century lay most of the great cities known to man: Cairo and Alexandria, Bagdad, Damascus and Antioch, Tabriz, Samarkand and Jerusalem. In such cities, known collectively in Europe as the Levant, or the land of the rising sun, were to be found the luxuries of the yet more distant East, whence they would be distributed more deeply into Islam and poorer Christendom.

The Christian reaction began early in the eleventh century when, with the encouragement of the Pope, the Italian republic of Pisa expelled the Mohammedans from the island of Sardinia. The Christian offensive gained its strongest momentum with the start of the Crusades in 1096, and reached a peak three years later when holy Jerusalem was regained.

The Crusades solidified the authority of the Roman popes in Christendom and solidified the leadership of the Italian city-states in the Mediterranean trade. Pisa, Genoa, and Venice in particular profited from carrying pilgrims eastward from Europe to Jerusalem and from carrying westward from the Levant the spices, silks, gems, tapestries, and other exotic wares which Europe's upper classes had learned to love.

By the thirteenth century, however, Christianity's crusading spirit had spent itself, Jerusalem had once again fallen to the Mohammedans, and the onslaught of Islam on Europe from the east had taken on renewed force under the leadership of the Turks. The Levantine trade was so hard hit by this reversal of fortune that Pisa, Genoa, and Venice engaged in suicidal wars among themselves in their efforts to hold on to a worthwhile share of it. And the rest of Europe, with prices of Oriental goods soaring because of the disruption of the traditional lines of supply, began to yearn for new routes to the Indies which would somehow circumvent the formidable Turkish strongholds.

PORTUGAL TAKES THE LEAD

As early as 1291 two brothers, Ugolino and Vadino Vivaldo of Columbus' native Genoa, embarked on what may have been the first deliberate effort to reach the East by sailing west. There seems little doubt that they perished on the voyage. Early in the next century, other Italians, Spaniards, and Frenchmen, beginning to explore the western coast of Africa, discovered and occupied the Canaries, the somewhat more westerly Madeiras, and ultimately the still more westerly Azores. But it remained for the Portuguese, after 1415, to begin that systematic collection of geographic information which dissipated the ancient fears of the "green sea of gloom," as the Arabs described the Atlantic, and transformed that ocean into a great path of adventure and commerce, not least the commerce in Negro slaves whom the Portuguese first introduced into Europe in 1442.

Portugal had freed herself from Spain in 1140 and had rid herself of the last Mohammedan enclave (while retaining much of the ancient learning that the Mohammedans had preserved) in 1249. Thereafter, while consolidating their territory at home, her rulers prepared to pursue the Mohammedans in Africa itself. This policy was stimulated by the legend of Prester (that is, Priest) John, which began to spread through beleaguered Europe late in the twelfth century. Prester John was said to be a mighty Christian potentate somewhere in the heart of Islam who had withstood Mohammedan expansion and might help the Europeans subdue the infidel. The Portuguese quest for him was intensified when the House of Avis took the throne in 1385 and assumed greater importance than ever after 1415 when Portuguese forces invaded Africa and took the Moroccan seaport of Ceuta across from Gibraltar, from the Mohammedans.

Thenceforth, Prince Henry, son of King John I and famous in history as Henry the Navigator, gave African exploration a tremendous impetus. In 1488, many years after Prince Henry's death, of course, and after Prester John had proved to be nothing more than an Abyssinian native chieftain, Bartholomeu Diaz at last rounded *Cabo Tormentoso,* the Cape of Storms, at the southernmost tip of Africa and thereby opened the first all-water route from Europe to the Indies. So impressed was the king of Portugal with the prospects afforded by this feat that he promptly renamed the

treacherous neck of land "Cape of Good Hope."

Nine years after Diaz' voyage a flotilla of four Portuguese ships under Vasco da Gama sailed for Calicut from Lisbon and returned in 1499 laden with spices and jewels. Da Gama's voyage marked the end of Levantine supremacy in the Oriental trade, the eclipse of the Italian merchants, and the decline of the Mediterranean. The Portuguese, moreover, soon drove the Mohammedan merchants from the Indian Ocean itself, destroyed their navy, and reduced their strongholds at the sources of supply for Oriental goods.

In 1500, on a voyage to the Orient, a Portuguese captain, Pedro Alvarez Cabral, found himself on the New World shore,

Fifteenth-century portrait of Henry the Navigator.

promptly claimed it for his native land under the name of "Terra de Vera Cruz," and proceeded on his journey. Cabral's men had discovered on the land a tree with bright red wood similar to the "brazil" wood long imported from the Far East for the making of red dye, and soon the place he found became known as Brazil, and brazil-wood became its principal product. But Portuguese interest in the New World languished until, half a century later, other European nations showed a growing interest in Brazil. It was in the Orient that the Portuguese made their major effort and created an empire that lasted, at least in fragments, to our own day.

SPAIN'S GAMBLE

If Columbus was in the right place at the right time when he first broached his enterprise of the Indies in Portugal, he offered all the wrong reasons for his daring idea. Portugal's mariners, by the 1480's, simply by their own venturesome-ness, had long since proven Ptolemy wrong on so many points that her maritime experts were wholly disenchanted with him and all other Greek authorities. Marco Polo, moreover, had no standing with them at all. Columbus's proposition thus was promptly laughed out of court. When he persisted in offering it, he gradually won the reputation for madness that henceforth clung to him.

Columbus left Portugal in 1485 to try his luck in Spain, but here he found King Ferdinand and Queen Isabella altogether engaged in ridding their own country, after 700 years, of the last Mohammedan strong-holds in Granada. Columbus was back in Portugal when the news of Diaz' success reached Lisbon and killed what little interest might have lingered there in his own bolder scheme. He next tried the kings of England and France without success, and finally the rulers of Spain once more, where, in 1490, the royal experts judged his plan "impossible and vain and worthy of rejection."

When Ferdinand and Isabella succeeded at last, in January, 1492, in expelling Islam from Granada, they moved immediately by means of the Inquisition and by expulsion and execution to wipe out all other non-Catholic elements in the Spanish population, including the Jews who had helped immensely in financing the long wars. Driven thus to dissolve in blood and misery the sources of their wealth and power at home, Ferdinand and Isabella were all the better prepared to listen once more to Columbus' project for converting the "princes and people" of "the Indies" to the holy faith and diverting their fabled wealth to Spain's own purposes.

In April, 1492, they capitulated to the importunings of Columbus' influential friends, granted him his coveted title, "Admiral of the Ocean Sea," and began to equip his fleet. Every ship carrying refugee Jews had been ordered by Ferdinand and Isabella to leave Spain by August 2, 1492. S. E. Morison, in his admirable biography of Columbus, suggests that that is why he may have waited until the following day to set sail himself under a brighter omen. Even so, the same tide that bore *Niña, Pinta,* and *Santa Maria* so hopefully toward such golden isles as the Admiral might "discover and acquire by his labor and industry," also bore the last of some hundreds of thousands of Spanish Jews toward Italy and other hostile refuges, whence many of them eventually moved to eastern Europe.

We know now what Columbus found. After a few months spent in exploring the Caribbean, where the climate constantly reminded the Admiral of "spring in Andalusia," he left some of his men behind in Hispaniola, modern Haiti, and returned to Spain with a few gold nuggets and a few red Indians to prove the success of his venture. None of the Indians survived the voyage. In September, 1493, he set sail once more with 1,500 settlers for his islands in the Ocean Sea and for further exploratory work. Columbus made two later voyages to America, in 1498 and again in 1502, only four years before his death. His search, on these visits, was for a passage through the tantalizing barrier just beyond which,

16

he continued certain, must lie Japan, those islands he was really after.

Naturally, he found no passage. Not until Magellan's men, in the service of Spain, circumnavigated the globe in 1519-1522 did the truth become known about how enormously long was the westward passage to the East—as Eratosthenes and other Greeks had foretold. But Columbus, nevertheless, had his compensations. When he was assailed by doubts that he had in fact reached Japan (as he was, indeed, from his very first sight of the naked island natives who, as he wrote, "were a people very deficient in everything"), his faith in the Lord's apparently altered purpose continued firm. During his third visit in 1500 Columbus wrote from America: "God made me the messenger of the new heaven and the new earth of which He spoke in the Apocalypse by St. John, after having spoken of it by the mouth of Isaiah, and He showed me the spot where to find it." During the same visit he also referred to "those lands which I have recently discovered, and where I believe in my soul the earthly paradise is situated."

So little trust did Ferdinand and Isabella place in the Admiral's claims to have found Japan, that in 1493 they had the Pope, himself a Spaniard, divide the world beyond the *oekumene* between themselves and the Portuguese. The next year, in the Treaty of Tordesillas, Spain and Portugal agreed on the specific boundary separating their portions of the sphere. Portugal, in effect, got the Orient and Spain the New World, except for the region that was to become Brazil (see p. 16). Spain soon encouraged others beside Columbus to occupy her claim, to search out its limits, convert its inhabitants, and uncover its wealth.

One of the first to sail under her colors was a Florentine, Amerigo Vespucci, who in 1497 began a series of voyages on which he explored the American coastline southeast from Mexico all the way to Brazil. Historians now feel that he well earned the fame that attached to his name ever since a German geographer, in 1507, first called the new world, "America."

SPANISH ASCENDANCY IN THE NEW WORLD

More useful to Spain than the navigators who followed Columbus under her flag in seeking the passage to India were many of her old *conquistadores.* Freed now from fighting the Mohammedan at home, they would establish Spain's ascendancy over the Indian and the land in the New World.

Soon after Columbus' first discoveries, these rough opportunists lorded it over Hispaniola. Using it as a base they extended their grasp to Jamaica in 1509, Cuba in 1511, and Puerto Rico in 1512, thereby completing Spain's occupation of the Greater Antilles. By then rumors of great wealth on the mainland had begun to exert their charm, and the *conquistadores,* disappointed with their rewards in the islands, left the Lesser Antilles to later adventurers and embarked on their conquest of Central America, Mexico, and Peru.

The first Spanish settlement on the American mainland was made in Panama in 1508 by Alonzo de Ojeda. In 1513 Vasco Nuñez de Balboa worked his way across the Panama isthmus to sight the Pacific, and Ponce de Léon began his quest for the fountain of youth in Florida. But the two greatest exploits were yet to come. The first was the conquest of the Aztecs of Mexico, beginning in 1519, by Hernando Cortez and his mighty horsemen. The second, beginning in 1528, was the yet more cruel conquest of the Incas of Peru by the brutal Francisco Pizarro. Here, at last, was the wealth Spain sought, stored up in hoards more magnificent than any European could imagine, and at hand for her superior arms to claim.

From Mexico and Peru, their appetites sharpened by the finds of their superiors, other *conquistadores* set out to discover hoards of their own, but with little success.

Tough Hernando de Soto led his men on a fruitless search through the gloomy forests from Florida to the Mississippi River, which he discovered in 1541 only to die on its banks of fever. In the same year Francisco de Coronado, seeking the mythical Seven Cities of Cibola and the gold they held, began his broad explorations of the American Southwest which he disgustedly called the "great American desert," a description which helped retard settlement there for 300 years. On the water, moreover, Spanish ship captains, by 1600, had ranged as far

among the people there. At the same time, Spain's own purpose was the extraction of gold and silver. Her obligation to the Pope worked sufficiently on the consciences of her rulers for them to send active missionaries overseas; and these missionaries themselves sometimes proved to be great humanitarians. The most notable of them was Bartolomé de Las Casas, who devoted his life to combating the enslavement and extermination of the Indians. But other missionaries soon fell themselves into the ways of the *conquistadores,* and like

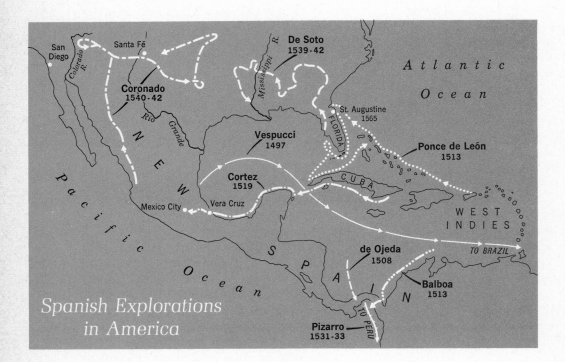

Spanish Explorations in America

south as Chile and Argentina and as far north and west as the shores of upper California.

Long before other Atlantic nations challenged her in the New World, Spain had already established a vast empire in the West Indies and on the Spanish Main. The Spanish regime was in many respects inflexible and harsh. The papal bull of 1493, which had confirmed Spain's right to the New World (see p. 17). stated explicitly that the sole purpose of the grant was the propagation of Christianity

them disdained both the scruples of the Crown and the censure of the Church. Indeed, the priesthood itself became one of the most exploitive of the Spanish castes and eventually controlled more than half the land of the empire.

The principal instrument of early Spanish exploitation was the *encomienda,* which Columbus himself introduced into Hispaniola and which still colors the land and labor practices of many Latin American countries. Under this system each deserving conqueror was entrusted with a given number of Indians whose work he could command in exchange for his care of their souls. Under a supplementary system, the *repartimiento,* the Indians could be gathered up in one section and transported to another. Both the *encomienda* and the *repartimiento* became in fact deadly systems of enslavement on lordly fiefs run by men who cared little enough for their own souls not to be hampered by concern for the souls of natives.

It is true that many Indians, like the fierce Caribs whom Columbus himself encountered on West Indian islands he visited on his later voyages, as well as mainland Aztecs, Incas, and Mayas, resisted and sometimes withstood enslavement, just as did many fierce tribes of Negroes who scared off the slave trade's Iberian minions in Africa. But it is also true that other Africans first were introduced into the New World by *conquistadores* who, having literally depopulated entire islands (they called them "useless," for their lack of gold) by carrying off the aborigines as short-lived bondsmen, required a continually replenished labor supply to "strive to collect and give us," as Columbus said, "the things which . . . are necessary to us."

One of the lasting myths of the Negro's past is that he took docilely to enslavement, a myth fed largely by the contrasting myth of the Indian's brave preference for extinction. But in those tropical regions where they were most numerous, millions of Indians were extinguished (and additional millions and their descendants were repressed) *by* enslavement; and in the same regions many of those Negroes successfully carried into slavery first chilled their captors with the menace of servile revolts.

By the 1540's the reign of the *conquistadores* was drawing to a close. In the islands the precious metals they sought never were found in quantity. When they turned to the land itself for wealth, first in ranching and then in staple agriculture, their unfitness as managers left poor and discontented those who did not take off for the mainland. On the mainland, in turn, *conquistadores* got rich on the hoards they captured, but most of them failed in their efforts to

augment their finds by organizing systematic production in the mines from which the hoards had come. These failures hastened the more thorough-going intervention of the Crown in the New World. The Crown had thought of intervening even earlier, when the mariners of rival nations had begun to pirate Spanish ships carrying the royal share of New World treasure on the high seas.

Under the reorganized official regime, the great gold and silver mines of Mexico and Peru began to add some $30 million a year to the currency of world trade. Yet commercial cattle-raising, especially for the production of hides, and commercial agriculture, especially sugar- and tobacco-growing, soon challenged mining as the major source of wealth and eventually surpassed it. In each of these activities the *encomienda* system lasted almost to the close of the eighteenth century, its frightful abuses in no way mitigated by the aristocrats and bureaucrats in the mother country under whose dominion it had fallen, nor by the Spanish-born officials who ran things in the New World.

These officials quickly imposed their own cultural institutions in America. In 1544 the first New World printing press was set up in Mexico City. Its initial publication was a *Compendium of Christian Doctrine, "en lengua Mexicana y Castellana."* In 1551, the first New World universities were opened in Mexico City and Lima. Shortly thereafter imposing cathedrals were to be found in important coastal cities, while all over the land hundreds of monasteries plied their business of saving souls. Still, the progress of Europeanization, if discernible at all, was slow. In 1595, for example, the Viceroy of New Spain, Luis de Velasco II, wrote for the benefit of his successor: "The two Republics, of Spaniards and Indians, of which this Kingdom consists are so repugnant to each other . . . that it seems that the conservation of the former always means the oppression and destruction of the latter."

III. *National Rivalry in America*

If the menace of Islam underlay the extension of Portuguese and Spanish power to the most distant habitable regions of the globe, a religious revolution within Christendom itself fostered the *permanent settlement* of Europeans in the New World, and especially in its northern parts.

This religious revolution, which we call the Reformation, began in Germany in 1517 when the Catholic monk, Martin Luther, posted on the church door in Wittenberg the ninety-five "theses" in which he asserted that men were saved by faith alone and not by works. Luther's stand suggested that, between man and God, the mediation of the priesthood was unnecessary. Luther aimed at a drastic reformation of the Church, not its abolition, but his doctrine pointed toward the radical notion of the priesthood of all believers, and it soon became clear that it was inconsistent with the very structure of the Roman Catholic establishment. After the Pope excommunicated Luther in 1521 he won the support of many German princes and Scandinavian rulers who had their own quarrels with Rome and "protested" the Pope's efforts to crush the reform movement.

In 1536, almost twenty years after Luther's revolt, John Calvin, harried from his native France to Geneva, published his *Institutes of the Christian Religion* which pushed the claims of the religious rebels beyond Luther's assertions. Calvin maintained that only a few choice spirits, the "visible elect," were preordained by God to enjoy the "Covenant of Grace." Only these few vessels of Christ, he said, were endowed with the requisite faith to rule the world, God's creation. Thus, under suitable circumstances, inferior magistrates might be justified in leading the people against the authorities of the state. In Geneva, Calvin himself promptly took over the government and afforded his zealous followers elsewhere a model of a purified or "puritan" regime. Although Calvinism was in theory undemocratic, it strengthened the cause of individual freedom by insisting on the privacy of religious experience, by making all "callings" honorable, by giving layman a vital role in church government, and by teaching that the authority of the state was limited by a higher, divine law concerned with the individual soul.

On religious grounds Calvinism was as much a menace to the papacy as Lutheranism. On political grounds it was far more of a menace than Lutheranism to those monarchs who remained, in the Calvinists' estimation, impure and Godless men even though the Pope had given them his blessing. Chief among these monarchs was Charles I, who became King of Spain in 1516. Three years later Charles also became the Holy Roman Emperor, and thereby suzerain of all the German princes and chief protector of the Roman popes. Charles also became the principal enemy of France, whose territory his Spanish and German holdings virtually hemmed in and many of whose great nobles would soon become "Huguenots," or "confederates" of Calvin.

As early as 1521 Charles swore to Pope Leo X that in undertaking to crush the Lutheran heresy he would not spare his "dominions, friends, body, blood, life, and soul." The next year he began to impose the Spanish Inquisition on his subjects in non-Spanish lands. In 1534 Charles approved the creation by the Spanish monk, Ignatius Loyola, of the Society of Jesus, composed of the famous Jesuits whose task was to help reclaim Europeans and convert the heathen masses to the old religion. And yet Protestantism—as Lutheranism, Calvinism, and other rising sects—spread far in Europe. Outside of Germany and France, most irritating to Charles was the infection of his Dutch subjects in the Spanish Netherlands with the most virulent brand of Calvinism, and the infection of England

20

with what became known as Anglicanism. Anglicanism was a local brand of Protestantism which was declared the state religion of England in 1534 after Henry VIII, in defiance of the Pope, annulled his marriage to Charles' aunt, Catherine of Aragon, and was excommunicated.

In 1556, worn out in the service of the popes, Charles retired to a monastery and left the immense burden of his crusade against the Reformation to his son, who ruled Spain and the other extensive Hapsburg holdings as Philip II. Philip also claimed to be King of England, for in 1554 he had married Queen Mary, the Catholic daughter of Henry VIII and Catherine. Between them, Philip and Mary restored Catholicism in England, the Queen earning notoriety as "Bloody Mary" for executing some 300 Protestants. When Mary died in 1558, Philip immediately tried to marry her successor, her half-sister Elizabeth, but Elizabeth rejected both Philip and his faith.

In 1563 Elizabeth strengthened the position of Anglicanism in England by subscribing to the Thirty-nine Articles of religion, which made clearer and more specific the differences between the new Church of England and the old Church of Rome. By taking this step Elizabeth severed the attachment of the many English Catholics to the throne. She also weakened the loyalty of the growing numbers of English Calvinists who wished to go much farther than the Thirty-nine Articles in eliminating the last vestiges of Romanism in English belief and worship. "To cast contempt and more upon the[se] sincere servants of God," William Bradford writes in his *Of Plymouth Plantation,* the stirring account of the first English Calvinist settlement in America (see p. 52), their enemies at this time "opprobriously . . . imposed upon them that name of Puritans, which is said the Novatians [an obscure early sect] out of pride did . . . take unto themselves."

These religious divisions in her island—which were profound enough eventually to lead to civil war—tempered Elizabeth's policies in many ways. And yet having declared unequivocally for her own brand of

Protestantism at home, she soon offered to aid anti-Catholics elsewhere in Europe. Elizabeth especially aided the Dutch, who had revolted against Philip in 1568. In 1570, the Pope excommunicated her and absolved English Catholics of allegiance to her.

Spain and England now became more bitter enemies than ever, and the "scepter'd isle" at last turned her attention to mastery of the seas. The principal lures on the seas were the Spanish galleys carrying the wealth of Mexico and Peru to Philip's treasury for the support of his Catholic armies. The most magnificent catch of all was made by Francis Drake in *Golden Hind.* Weighing anchor in 1577, Drake spent the next three years on the water raiding the Atlantic and Pacific coasts of the Spanish Main, the Spanish New World islands, and Spanish shipping on the two great oceans. He returned home in 1580 with £1,500,000 in American gold and silver, a portion of which went to Elizabeth, a shareholder in the venture. When "Queen Bess" knighted the raider, Philip swore vengeance.

The final insult came in 1587, when Elizabeth was forced by the urging of her council, her Parliament, and most of her people, to order the execution of her Catholic cousin, Mary, Queen of Scots. Twenty years earlier, Mary had been forced by the Calvinists in her own country to abdicate, and she sought refuge in England. There she repaid Elizabeth's calculated hospitality—the better to keep an eye on Mary—by conspiring constantly with Philip's English friends to help him grasp the throne.

Philip now declared open war on England and in 1588 sent forth the grand Armada with which he hoped to destroy Elizabeth, proceed to victory over the stubborn Dutch, and assist the Catholic party in France to crush the Huguenots. But Sir Francis Drake's defeat of the Spanish Armada in 1588 with the assistance of the bold Dutch "water beggars" frustrated Philip's plans and initiated his decline.

The year after the Armada's defeat the wars between Catholic and Protestant forces in France ended in victory for the Huguenot Henry of Navarre, who as Henry IV became the first Bourbon king. To placate the French Catholics, Henry returned to the Catholic Church in 1593. But this was a political not a religious step. In 1598 Henry issued the famous Edict of Nantes offering an exceptional degree of religious liberty to the Huguenots with whom his heart remained. Along with the Protestant English and Dutch he was soon to establish his own claims to New World lands in defiance of Catholic Spain's monopoly.

POLITICAL AND ECONOMIC
NATIONALISM

Protestantism so rapidly transformed so much of sixteenth-century Europe largely because Catholicism itself had fallen on evil days. The failure of the late Crusades against Islam had placed the papacy at once in debt and on the defensive. As calls for funds on Catholic rulers grew more frequent and burdensome, their resistance to paying matched in ingenuity and intensity the popes' importunities. One reason why the Reformation itself began in Germany was that the popes were forced increasingly to seek their funds from the German people on whom, as subjects of the Holy Roman Empire, they had the most direct claim. Methods so crude and corrupt were used to wring money from the Germans that they became profoundly disenchanted with the materialism of their priests and their religion. This widespread popular discontent with Rome made all the more practical the lust of the German princes themselves for the vast lands of the Church, and for control of Church offices and income. For similar reasons the spark of the German Reformation quickly engulfed much of the rest of Europe.

As sides were drawn, other always volatile elements—ancient feudal family rivalries, dynastic ambitions of rising clans, greed for commercial monopolies—fed the flames. The very nature of European civilization was altered with extraordinary speed. Great new nations emerged out of the bloody chaos of contending principalities. New national armies incurred heavy costs not only in establishing the new monarchs but also in protecting and extending their hegemony. To meet these costs the monarchs sought new national taxes and loans. These, in turn, could be most effectively obtained by abating the old Church doctrine against high profits and interest.

One of the most obvious sources of high profits in still largely agricultural communities was improved land use. Such improvement often entailed the dislodging of many small husbandmen and the combination of their fields into extensive estates producing cash crops. The removal of families from the land supplied many new hands for commercial and early industrial enterprises, for the growing national armies and navies, and for settlement in colonial outposts overseas. Improved land use and commerce in cash crops, in turn, made available the wherewithal for heavy-interest loans to royalty, and also for investment in colonial enterprises. Naturally these enterprises were usually promoted and manned in newly Protestant countries by those in revolt against Roman Catholic ideas and institutions. In England in particular, in the opening decades of Elizabeth's reign, a strong new impulse was given to the modernization of society. In keeping with emerging "mercantilist" theories of national competition (see p. 66), the commercialization of agriculture, the development of mining and manufacturing, the improvement of facilities for domestic commerce all were speeded up. The object was to make the Protestant Queen "a prince of power" by promoting English self-sufficiency to the extent that nature and improved technology permitted. At the same time, every national advantage was sought in extending foreign trade.

Much else, of course, in what we may justly call the New World of Europe fostered the development of the New World in America. Even in Catholic lands, with the resurgence of interest during the Renaissance in classic society and the imperial grandeur of Rome, the very idea of empire grew more attractive. The attack of Protestant thinkers, in turn, on the mysticism, not to say the superstition of the old Church strengthened the rising spirit of secularism and science, including the science of discovery. Discovery itself raised profound questions about the origins of strange beasts and people which the Bible inadequately accounted for. Such questions culminated in the Darwinian theories of evolution and the science of anthropology. This concern with empire, secular thought, and scientific study spread across Europe after the fifteenth century; but it most deeply altered life in the new maritime (as against the old Mediterranean) nations of the north, especially France, the Netherlands and England.

THE WAY OF THE FRENCH

The French launched their activities in the New World as early as 1520 when their vessels began probing the coasts of Brazil and putting men ashore to cut up cargoes of brazilwood. Soon they were landing missionaries as well. But the main result of their labors here was to heighten Portuguese resistance to all foreign interlopers. The French themselves were evicted from Brazil in 1615.

The French had better luck against the Spanish. As early as 1523, more than half a century before Drake in *Golden Hind* (see p. 21), a French corsair, Jean Fleury, intercepted Spanish galleys carrying the gold and silver of the New World to the treasury of Charles V. The next year, Francis I of France sent Giovanni Verrazano to North America in search of the northwest passage to the Indies. Verrazano explored the coast from Newfoundland to North Carolina, to which Dutch mapmakers, mocking Spanish claims to the whole New World, soon gave the name "New France." In 1534 Jacques Cartier, on a mission similar to Verrazano's, began the exploration of the Gulf and River of St. Lawrence and thereby strengthened French claims to the sites of future Quebec and Montreal.

Soon after Cartier's expedition, France was ravaged by religious wars and explora-

tion ceased for almost 75 years. But freelance French corsairs continued so to harass Spanish shipping from the New World that Spain, in 1565, was forced to set up a base at St. Augustine, Florida, from which to combat the marauders. This was the first European settlement on land that was to become part of continental United States. Far to the north other Frenchmen on fishing voyages to Newfoundland had begun exchanging precious bits of metal for the rich pelts the native red men would bring to the shore. The trade in fur (soon enlarged by the exchange of brandy and guns as well as scraps of iron) became the staple of New France after exploration and settlement were resumed under the leadership of Samuel de Champlain.

Champlain's voyages to America were supported by private French capitalists who hoped to make a good thing of the fur trade. Champlain himself, however, was more interested in exploration than in business. In 1603 he made his first visit to the area of Cartier's explorations and ascended the St. Lawrence river to the Lachine (or China) rapids. From 1604 until its abandonment in 1607, Champlain was the leading figure in the little colony established at modern Annapolis Royal, Nova Scotia. During these years he accurately charted the Atlantic Coast as far south as future Plymouth harbor and Cape Cod. But Champlain yearned to return to the St. Lawrence region, and there, in 1608, he built a fort at Quebec, the foundation of the first permanent French colony in North America. The next year, in company with friendly Huron Indians, he ascended the Richelieu River to the lovely lake in New York State which bears his name. Here, French arms helped the Hurons defeat their bitter enemy, the Iroquois; but the victory cost the French the undying enmity of the formidable New York tribes which so vitally affected later French history in the New World (see p. 94). By 1615, Champlain himself had penetrated westward to Lake Huron. Thereafter, he sent out other pathfinders, and when he died in 1635, the French were in a position to dominate the entire Great Lakes area.

By then, however, there had never been more than a hundred Frenchmen in New France at any one time, and Quebec threatened to go the way of Annapolis Royal. Beginning in the 1620's, Cardinal Richelieu tried to infuse French colonization with a new vitality under government direction; but he had no better luck than the private capitalists, and in 1663 Louis XIV took personal charge of overseas activity. Louis, however, kept his governor, his intendant (really an independent spy on the governor), and his bishop on such short tether from Versailles that an American policy adapted to New World conditions could not be worked out.

If the French failed as settlers, however, they performed brilliantly as empire-builders. The spearheads of French expansion after Champlain were the Jesuit fathers to whom Richelieu had given a monopoly of American inland activity as part of his policy of central control. The Jesuits performed such exceptional feats of conversion and exploration, especially from their mission on Lake Michigan, that in June, 1671, the "Great Intendant," Jean Talon, ordered a regal ceremony at Sault Ste. Marie to be attended by the chiefs of 14 tribes and their retinues. Here the French flag was raised and French claims were made to all the known lands of Canada and "all other countries, rivers, lakes and territories, contiguous and adjacent thereunto, as well discovered as to be discovered, which are bounded on the one side by the Northern and Western Seas and on the other side by the South Sea, including all its length and breadth."

The Jesuit explorers did well for the Quebec regime, but not well enough to justify their obstructionist tactics in times of crisis against less pious Frenchmen who, in fact, could not be kept out of the woods and the West. The most daring of these were the famous *coureurs de bois*—outlaws of the bush, as Parkman branded them—who were given their first formal encouragement to infringe on the Jesuit monopoly in 1654.

Much romantic nonsense has been written about the *coureurs de bois,* inspired no doubt by stories of the readiness with which they threw off the restraints of civilization and took on Indian women and Indian ways. In reality, most of the *coureurs* had shed the restraints of civilization before they ever entered the woods. Their success in gathering furs from the red men was only less remarkable than their willingness to travel great distances to virgin country and their imagination in seeking safe routes back. Once they had penetrated as far as Lake Superior in 1659, one of the outlets that most enticed them was Hudson Bay (see p. 26), and when the French administration in Quebec would not countenance any bypassing of the St. Lawrence citadel, the *coureurs* showed their contempt for officialdom by offering their trade to the English. The English grasped the opportunity and in 1670 formed the Hudson's Bay Company to exploit it.

A second outlet that fired the imagination was the Mississippi River. In 1672 Talon named the great *coureur,* Louis Joliet, to explore the Mississippi to its mouth. In December that year he agreed to allow the Jesuit Father, Marquette, to accompany Joliet "as chaplain and Christian spokesman." In the spring of 1673, Joliet and Marquette reached the Mississippi via the Wisconsin River. They then proceeded down the Father of Waters until they learned from the Indians that "the Mississippi River discharged into . . . the Mexican Gulf, and not to the east in Virginia . . . or to the west in California." Joliet and Marquette had traveled as far south as Arkansas, and, fearful of falling into Spanish hands, they then turned back.

They were followed by the most daring of French explorers, the *coureur,* Robert Cavelier, Sieur de La Salle, who not only made the journey down the Mississippi all the way to the Gulf, but also claimed the entire Mississippi Valley for the King of

France, in whose honor he named it Louisiana. This solemn event took place on April 9, 1682 (see p. 96).

THE WAY OF THE DUTCH

Although the French corsairs led the way in attacking Spain, the Dutch far outdid them in pirating Spanish gold. The Dutch had other capabilities as well. Many Jews who had been exiled from Spain in 1492 found opportunities in Holland to use their industrial, commercial, and financial skills. Strengthened by these versatile capitalists, the Dutch developed their own manufactures, fisheries, trade centers, and banks. Splendidly situated between booming Scandinavia, which was supplying Europe with much of its timber and naval stores, and booming France and England, which were exporting wines, woolens, and coal, the Dutch became the middlemen on the northern, as the Italians once had been on the southern water routes.

Once the Portuguese had opened their direct trade with the Orient, moreover, the Dutch worked out an agreement with them to meet their ships at sea in order to pick up and speed the delivery of Oriental wares to the northern countries. They also were licensed to serve as carriers between Lisbon and Brazil. When Portugal fell to Spain once more in 1580, the Dutch were engaged in their own successful revolution against Spain. This revolution they carried on now against Portugal too and soon dominated Oriental and Brazilian traffic.

In 1602 the Dutch created the Dutch East India Company to consolidate their Oriental interests. Its record of dividend payments is probably the most spectacular in business annals and it endowed the nation, in addition, with a Far Eastern empire that remained intact until 1949.

In 1609 the Dutch East India Company sent Henry Hudson in *Half Moon* to make its own futile search for the elusive northwest passage. Hudson entered the river which now bears his name by way of New York harbor, and, finding it salt, proceeded hopefully northward. His search failed; but while anchored in the vicinity of modern Albany he entertained a band of Mohawks of the great Iroquois nation and made them gifts of "firewater" and firearms. The friendship of the Iroquois helped the Dutch in their contest with the French, which began in 1614 when another Dutch party established Holland's first fur-trading post near Albany. The English inherited Iroquois good will when they ousted the Dutch from North America (see p. 64). In April, 1610, this time in the employ of English adventurers, Hudson set forth on his last voyage, on which he discovered Hudson Bay.

On the model of the East India Company, the Dutch, in 1621, also created a West India Company to extend their grip on Portuguese Brazil and break the Spanish Caribbean monopoly. The Dutch gained their first successes in Brazil in 1630 and by 1637 controlled 1,200 miles of coastal lands on which they grew brazilwood, tobacco, and above all, sugar cane. When, in 1640, Portugal rewon her independence from Spain, Brazilian Catholics were shocked by a Portuguese-Dutch agreement recognizing Dutch holdings. They revolted against both the Portuguese and the Dutch, and by 1654, faced with crises elsewhere, the Dutch completed their withdrawal, taking with them their slaves, their tools, and their invaluable knowledge of sugar production.

By 1630 the Dutch West India Company had also smashed Spanish shipping in the Caribbean and largely taken charge of the carrying trade there themselves. They also had begun their occupation of islands in the Lesser Antilles, with Curaçao as their main base. Dutch victories over the Spanish permitted the English and the French to grasp Lesser Antilles islands too, the British making their earliest settlements on St. Kitts, Barbados, and Nevis, the French theirs on Martinique and Guadeloupe.

The attraction of these and neighboring islands lay initially in their value as bases for smuggling and piracy; but the English

Contemporary engraving shows Petrus Plancius, leading Dutch geographer in the employ of the Dutch East India Company, instructing Company navigators.

settlers on the islands soon tried to make a go of it by growing tobacco for the European market. The Virginia variety, however, had already proved of higher quality (see p. 45). The Dutch watched the islanders' losing struggle with concern, and in order to keep full the holds of their own vessels in the Caribbean trade they began, as early as 1637, to teach the English and the French the intricacies of sugar-growing and manufacture. The Dutch also supplied them with capital and equipment and with the slaves who soon displaced the white workers and laid the foundation for the heavy Negro concentration in the population of these islands to this day. After 1650 sugar produced by slave labor on large plantations made the islands in the Lesser Antilles the most precious of New World colonies.

In 1626 the Dutch West India Company purchased Manhattan Island from the local braves as a base for its own fur-trade operations already begun at New Amsterdam. The Company promptly extended its claims up the Hudson Valley and outward to Hartford on the Connecticut River, to Camden on the Delaware, and to Long Island. In 1629 it made its first great grants of land along the Hudson to the patroons who were expected to bring in permanent tenants. In 1638, when the first Scandinavians in America established New Sweden in the vicinity of the Delaware, the Company for a few years took no steps to dislodge them.

In 1638, flouting mercantilist theory (see p. 66), the Dutch opened New Amsterdam to mariners of all nations. This step alone showed that the Dutch, a nation of a mere 2.5 million souls, had begun to over-reach themselves; but long after they surrendered New Amsterdam to the English in 1664 they remained a power to reckon with elsewhere.

26

The French and the Dutch exposed the weakness of Spain's hold on America, but it was England that most effectively contested Spanish claims and most successfully colonized the northern hemisphere.

In 1497, Henry VII, the first of the Tudor line, who established the modern national monarchy in England by his victory in the War of the Roses 12 years earlier, sent out John Cabot, a naturalized Venetian, to seek the fabled northwest passage to Asia. Upon Cabot's single visit to Labrador, England's New World claim long rested. Almost a century later, in 1576, the Cathay Company, formed to develop English trade with China, sent Martin Frobisher on the first of his three voyages duplicating Cabot's quest, but nothing came of them except reinforcement of English reluctance to chase this will-o'-the-wisp any longer. Drake's voyage in *Golden Hind* in 1577 (see p. 21) confirmed the greater value of chasing Spanish galleys.

While Elizabethan sailors were scourging the seas, Elizabethan soldiers dreamed their own dreams of adventure and wealth. Walter Ralegh was the greatest of them, but it was his half-brother, Humphrey Gilbert, who in 1578 obtained from Elizabeth the first charter for a North American settlement. Gilbert was not without ambitions to emulate Drake; nor had the lure of the northwest passage altogether died in him. His path-breaking goal was a permanent North American base for his endeavors.

The outcome of Gilbert's first voyage remains a mystery. While returning from Newfoundland with high hopes on his second voyage in 1583, his ship went down. Ralegh then took up the mission, only to exhaust his fortune on three profitless expeditions. On the first of these, in 1584, his captains made their landfall in the vicinity of Roanoke Island, to which, on their return with enchanting reports, Ralegh gave the name Virginia for the virgin queen, Elizabeth. Ralegh's second expedition in 1585 included a group of intended settlers who sailed home after one year, having found neither gold nor the "South Sea."

Ralegh's third effort, his most serious attempt at colonization, was launched in 1587, when he sent 120 persons to Virginia under the leadership of John White. Once he had landed his passengers and selected the site for their settlement, White sailed home for supplies. On his return to Virginia in 1590 he found the settlement deserted, and no one really knows its fate.

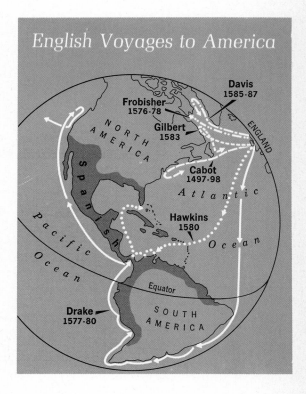

In later years, in a desperate effort to recoup his personal fortune at Spain's expense. Ralegh abandoned North America for the Spanish Main where he vainly sought gold in "Guinea." His and Gilbert's work, meanwhile, was taken up by their friend, Richard Hakluyt the younger, who, beginning in 1589, promoted the establishment of permanent colonies overseas as the way to relieve the growing economic crisis in England, especially the growing unemployment, following the outbreak of the Spanish war two years before (see p. 21).

Hakluyt's *Voyages,* numerous publications in which he gathered every scrap of information he could find about foreign lands, revealed much of the outside world to his insular countrymen. Hakluyt argued persuasively for a North American settlement as a source of raw materials for English industry, a market for English goods, and an attraction for the "able men" who now "pestered" English prisons. When Hakluyt wrote, the English statute books listed some 400 capital crimes. Many felons in the sixteenth century—given the choice of deportation or death—preferred the perils of the newly discovered world to the mysteries of that "undiscovered country" from which (as Shakespeare reminded them) no one ever returned.

But not all Englishmen who eventually left for the New World acted from such desperate motives. Some dutifully followed the injunction to "marry this land, a pure virgin, to thy kingly son Christ Jesus." For others less concerned with converting the heathen, "a Land more like the Garden of Eden than any part else of all the earth," offered another congenial challenge. Reports of exotic animals and plants, variations in climate, unusual customs and rare "objects for contemplation" also whetted the appetite for adventure. Prospects of new Inca and Aztec hoards, moreover, continued to sharpen the greed of "right worthy" promoters as well as the avarice of the settlers they sent out.

Readings

* Asterisk indicates that book is available in paperback.

A stimulating study of the emergence of western civilization against the background of world history is W. H. McNeill, *The Rise of the West* (1963). The new world of Europe, from which emerged the impulse to seek new worlds overseas, is the subject of R. L. Reynolds, *Europe Emerges: Transition Toward an Industrial World-Wide Society 600-1750* (1961). On this theme see also Derwent Whittlesey, *Environmental Foundations of European History* (1949). More conventional are two books by E. P. Cheyney: *The European Background of American History 1300-1600** (1904); and *The Dawn of a New Era 1250-1453 ** (1936). The best introductions to the Renaissance and Reformation are to be found in G. R. Potter, ed., *The Renaissance 1493-1520* (1957); and G. R. Elton, ed., *The Reformation 1520-1559* (1958).

Digging into the earth for archeological survivals is going on as actively as the exploration of space. New findings are often presented in authoritative fashion in such magazines as *Scientific American* and *National Geographic.* Examples from the first include W. C. Haag, "The Bering Strait Land Bridge" (January, 1962); R. S. MacNeish, "The Origins of New World Civilization" (November, 1964); and B. J. Meggers and Clifford Evans, "A Transpacific Contact in 3000 B.C." (January, 1966). Of special interest in the second is Helge Ingstad, "Viking Ruins Prove Vikings Found the New World" (November, 1964). The background for the discovery and settlement of Vinland is perhaps best supplied in Gwyn Jones, *The Norse Atlantic Saga* (1964). R. A. Skelton, T. E. Marston and G. D. Painter, *The Vinland Map and the Tartar Relation* (1965), adds suggestive information.

George Kubler, *The Art and Architecture of Ancient America* (1962), is authoritative. Excellent on the Aztecs and Mayas is M. D. Coe, *Mexico* (1962), and on the Incas, J. A. Mason, *The Ancient Civilizations of Peru** (1961). Still valuable on pre-Columbian culture are the many works by those classical American historians, W. H. Prescott and Francis Parkman. Most germane here are Prescott's *History of the Conquest of Mexico*

(3 vols., 1843), and *History of the Conquest of Peru* (2 vols., 1847), both abbreviated in paperback editions; and Parkman's Introduction on "Native Tribes" in his *The Jesuits in North America in the Seventeenth Century* (2 vols., 1867). This Introduction is reproduced in the excellent one-volume edition of excerpts from Parkman, *The Parkman Reader* (1955), edited by S. E. Morison. A contemporary classic on the first Spanish invasion of the American mainland is Bernal Díaz del Castillo, *The Discovery and Conquest of Mexico,* * edited in a satisfactory one-volume edition by I. A. Leonard (1956). Cortez' own dispatches from Mexico are available in I. R. Blacker and H. M. Rosen, *Conquest* * (1962). Of unusual interest is M. Leon-Portilla, *The Broken Spears, the Aztec Account of the Conquest of Mexico* (1962). Of the many general works on the Indians, the following three offer varied fare: John Collier, *Indians of the Americas* * (1947); R. M. Underhill, *Red Man's America* (1953); and P. S. Martin, G. L. Quimby and Donald Collier, *Indians Before Columbus* (1947). W. E. Washburn, *The Indian and the White Man* * (1964) is an invaluable anthology.

J. E. Gillespie, *A History of Geographical Discovery 1400-1800* (1933), is a good short introduction. A. P. Newton, ed., *Travel and Travellers of the Middle Ages* (1930); and Boies Penrose, *Travel and Discovery in the Renaissance 1420-1620* * (1960), are excellent on the background for Columbus' adventure. C. E. Nowell, *The Great Discoveries and the First Colonial Empires* * (1954), is a short, authoritative survey. The outstanding biography of Columbus is S. E. Morison, *Admiral of the Ocean Sea* (2 vols., 1942). A good, brief treatment is Morison's *Christopher Columbus, Mariner* * (1956). The best edition of Columbus' own writings and related materials is S. E. Morison, ed., *Journals and Other Documents on the Life and Voyages of Christopher Columbus* (1963). J. B. Brebner, *The Explorers of North America 1492-1806* * (1933), is indispensable for the opening of the continent. R. H. Brown, *Historical Geography of the United States* (1948), is excellent on the character and use of the land.

On Portugal and her empire, useful introductions are supplied in C. E. Nowell, *A History of Portugal* (1952); Elaine Sanceau, *Henry the Navigator* (1947); and two short works by C. R. Boxer: *Four Centuries of Portuguese Expansion 1415-1825* (1961); and *Race Relations in the Portuguese Colonial Empire 1415-1825* (1963). On the Spanish empire, besides Prescott, see J. H. Parry, *The Spanish Seaborne Empire* (1966); F. A. Kirkpatrick, *The Spanish Conquistadores* * (1934); and L. B. Simpson, *The Encomienda in New Spain* (1950). A. P. Newton, *The European Nations in the West Indies 1493-1688* (1933), is invaluable for Spain and her rivals. See also J. H. Parry and P. M. Sherlock, *A Short History of the West Indies* (1963). On the great event of 1588, see Garrett Mattingly, *The Armada* * (1959).

On France in the New World, in addition to Parkman, see W. B. Munro, *Crusaders of New France* (1920), and G. M. Wrong, *The Rise and Fall of New France* (2 vols., 1928). On the expansion of Holland see C. R. Boxer, *The Dutch Seaborne Empire: 1600-1800* (1965), and George Masselman, *The Cradle of Colonialism* (1963).

The background for English expansion is presented in numerous works by J. A. Williamson, of which three are most relevant: *Maritime Enterprise 1485-1558* (1913), *The Age of Drake* (1938), and *Sir Francis Drake* * (1962). Extracts from Richard Hakluyt's twelve volumes of "Voyages" are presented in the excellent one-volume "World's Classics" edition edited by Janet Hampden (1958). D. W. Waters, *The Art of Navigation in England in Elizabethan and Early Stuart Times* (1958), is the standard work on its subject. A. L. Rowse, *The England of Elizabeth* * (1951), and *The Expansion of Elizabethan England* * (1955), are modern histories that capture the spirit of the age. Rowse's *The Elizabethans and America* (1959) is excellent on the early attempts at colonization. His *Sir Walter Ralegh, His Family and Private Life* (1962), is the most authoritative biography.

CHAPTER TWO

In July, 1603, a few months after James I became King of England, Sir Walter Ralegh was locked up in the Tower of London for treason. His personal fortunes had sunk as low as the fortunes of his colonial enterprises in North America almost twenty years earlier, but he still clung to his old hopes for Virginia which he expressed as late as 1602; "I shall yet live to see it an English nation."

When Ralegh at last was executed under his old sentence in 1618, Virginia had indeed become an English colony. But the English *nation* Ralegh had in mind was a far grander enterprise than the feeble settle-

An

English Nation

ment that had been planted at Jamestown in 1607. This settlement tried in every way to emulate the Spanish *conquistadores,* and it was to be a disastrous failure for a generation. Ralegh's idea had been not to emulate but to evict the Spanish. He would so develop the economy of his territory that the "shipping, victual, munition, and transporting of five or six thousand soldiers may be defrayed." With this force he would march on and conquer New Spain. Ralegh's Virginia was to be nothing less than the New World itself, unshared, unpartitioned, a mighty imperial accession.

Ralegh, as we know, failed in his grand design. New Spain prospered, and fragments of the New World were to remain under Spanish rule until the eve of the twentieth century. New France, in turn, continued to occupy most of the northern part of North America until the English took it in 1763. A mere twenty years later, the English themselves were driven out of what was to prove the gateway to the richest region of the Western Hemisphere by the rebellious inhabitants of their own "plantations," assisted by the French, who were eager to return.

And yet Ralegh's hopes for Virginia were not altogether unfulfilled. Although surrounded by foreign enemies and inhabited by many foreign peoples, the American colonies became an "English nation" in language, law, and tradition. Indeed, they quickly became more English than the English in those very qualities which helped distinguish the English from their continental rivals other than the Dutch—nonconformism in religion, representative government, economic and social opportunity for the common man. For a generation before the permanent settlement of America, all these social aspirations suffered grievous setbacks in England, which themselves impelled people to migrate overseas. Certain old obstacles to their realization were carried to America, and new ones appeared here. Yet, virtually from the start of mainland settlement, Englishmen in America began to demand individual liberty, self-government, and equality with their betters, and gradually attained these objectives. They took such pride in their new "system," as they came to call it, that as late as the 1890's, Ralegh's vision of the New World with "but one flag and one country" continued to animate America's expansive policy (see chapters 12 and 23).

I. *The English at Home*

THE CHALLENGE
OF THE UNDERWORLD

In the English nation under the Tudors, royal power had been built on the breakup of feudal institutions (see p. 22). The cause of the Crown was advanced by self-serving commoners like Wolsey and Thomas Cromwell under Henry VIII and Walsingham and the Cecils under Elizabeth, men who by sheer ability dominated the Privy Council. In keeping with the spirit of the times, these men seized opportunity arising from their closeness to the monarch to feather their nests and those of their own sycophants out of the new royal offices and emoluments.

Many others besides the Crown, its councillors, and its favorites at Court profited hugely from the modernization of society (see p. 22); but the lot of the majority steadily worsened until, in Elizabeth's time, destitution stalked the land. Respectable farmers dislodged by the enclosure movement, rural tenants and laborers, village artisans and shopkeepers often grew so weak from want that before they could stand up to be whipped for begging without a license, "they had need to be relieved with foode." Their ranks were swelled by monks and friars evicted from fallen monasteries and mendicant orders, by clowns and players from broken baronies, by poor university students bereft of church support. Drilled to a degree by military personnel cast off from great houses and mariners and fighters discharged armed but penniless in port after overseas campaigns, this "rowsey rabblement of rakehells" became "a nation within a nation," often holding respectable elements at bay.

Under enactments of the 1560's and 1570's, known collectively as the Elizabethan Poor Laws, anyone without property, aged fourteen or older, on being caught in "the roguish trade of life" and refusing to work for the parish as punishment at lawful wages, was to be "grievously whipped and burnt through the gristle of the right ear with a hot iron." For a third offense he could be put to death. In later years the scope and severity of these laws were increased. Yet "the roguish nation" multiplied until it became the gravest social concern of the kingdom. Children were born into it as the only life they would ever know, "to take the basest and most poorest shape," as Shakespeare wrote in *King Lear,* "that ever penury, in contempt of man, brought near to beast." Laws were also enacted to force such children to train for useful employment and to serve long apprenticeships from which there was no legal escape. But many refused to be bound to labor.

Thousands of boys and beggars eventually were transported to Virginia and other colonies, along with English laws explicitly reenacted in America for their control. But bound labor short of outright slavery proved even harder to manage and constrain in a free and open land.

THE MIRROR OF IRELAND

Besides the unnerving challenge of the underworld and the spread of want, the shadow of Spanish power, the menace of Catholic ambition, continued to hang over Elizabeth's island like an eternal London fog. For a generation the Queen's self-made soldiers of fortune—Hawkins, Drake, Gilbert, Ralegh—had dazzled the populace with daring exploits. Beyond the treasure they brought from their Spanish victims on the sea (and from others under any flag, including their own, if the truth be told), they had given a welcome thrust to the throne which knew well the value of heroes in holding the hearts of the people. Yet final victory eluded them and their Queen before they died, soured, or retired. Worse, for all the booty of its most sensational prizes, privateering—and piracy—paid the Queen and her captains, on the average, little more than the cost of fitting out and putting to sea, and the growing distress in the kingdom was aggravated by rising wartime taxes, untimely harvest failures, and the hazards to trade of privateering itself. The drain on Elizabeth's funds for her last disastrous wars in Ireland, which broke out in 1598, forced her to call parliaments to extract yet additional "subsidies" from subjects sick of fighting and yearning for her end.

For thirty years now, mainly because the Queen had so arbitrarily fought all efforts to bring about Calvinist religious reforms by means of legislation, Parliament had been nourishing its own independence and developing opposition tactics. Among these tactics was that of trying to force the Queen to bargain for funds by yielding on other issues. Out of concern for the people's temper, the Parliament of 1601 in particular was more carefully packed than usual with the Queen's minions, yet the mounting rebelliousness that was soon to decide the

Stuarts' fate (see p. 41) was apparent from the start. A provocative issue this time was that of "patents" of monopoly bestowed by the Queen and her councillors on their favorites, who thereby pushed up the people's cost of living and closed the door of opportunity to ordinary entrepreneurs, most of them now of the Puritan persuasion. The right of the Queen to grant these patents independently of Parliament was also questioned, thereby lifting the curtain once again on the fateful constitutional issue, whether men or laws were supreme.

As the monopolies granted since the last session were being read off in the House, a crowd was found milling about the lobby and the stairs in an unheard of demonstration to bring pressure on the members to withstand the Queen's "prerogative." Elizabeth eventually was voted her subsidies for continuing the Irish war, but not before she promised "her careful reformation," in accordance with which no new monopolies "should be . . . put into execution but such as should have a trial according to the law for the good of her people."

Ireland, as so often in English history, soon disclosed more about the character of the reign. Gleaming on England's open flank to the sea, the Emerald Isle for centuries loomed as a temptation both to England and her enemies. In Elizabeth's time, persistent attempts were made to plant Protestant colonies there, as in America, to relieve land hunger and unemployment at home and to strengthen the throne abroad. These attempts, combined with rash programs of conversion, had led only to grim guerrilla warfare, with occasional wild uprisings ferociously put down (by Gilbert, Ralegh, and perhaps even John Smith of Virginia fame), when the full-scale rebellion of 1598 broke out, inviting Spanish intervention and conquest. The young Earl of Essex, the Queen's newest favorite, was sent to crush the Irish in time-honored fashion. He proceeded to botch the mission in a way that aroused the Queen's suspicions and mistrust. Soon after his recall, seething with her reproaches and stripped of his lucrative offices and especially of his monopoly of sweet wines, Essex led a mad revolt against Elizabeth in London's streets, which cost him his head in 1601 and the Queen her reason for living. When the Irish rebellion finally was suppressed by Lord Mountjoy in the spring of 1603, Elizabeth was dead.

Mountjoy proceeded to impose on the Irish countryside the "peace of the grave," dislodging and dismembering the people with the traditional malignity that made the English approach to the Indians of North America almost seem humane. "It has been said," writes G. M. Trevelyan, in his classic *History of England,* "that the Elizabethan eagles flew to the Spanish Main while the vultures swooped down on Ireland; but they were in many cases one and the same bird. . . . They saw in America and Ireland two new fields of equal importance and attraction, where private fortunes could be made, public service rendered to their royal mistress, and the cause of true religion upheld against Pope and Spaniard."

"THE PRINCE'S POWER AND THE FREEDOM OF ENGLISHMEN"

Much is often made of "the English birthright," of the "Liberties, Franchises, and Immunities," as the first Virginia charter put it in 1606, of English subjects living under the rule of law and not of men. That these are more than mere phrases history attests. Yet we are not to confuse them, or even the aspirations they suggest, with the egalitarian concepts of our own day, however liberal the tradition they inspired, especially in America.

The reign of the Tudors, brought to a close by Elizabeth's death, remained a despotism with a long roll of martyrs to conscience, to conviction, and to convenience. Many troublesome books were burned publicly, their possessors executed, their authors expelled from the country. Freedom of expression meant no more than the Commons' right to introduce legislation not proposed by the Crown, and it usually was denied. Freedom of assembly and of petition were considered seditious goals. Religious dissidents were persecuted mainly on political grounds, the numerous Catholics (except under "Bloody Mary") as agents of a foreign foe, the growing number of Puritans as enemies of monarchy; but these were grounds enough to kill the bloom of toleration.

Toward the end of her reign, Elizabeth herself conducted a virtual reign of terror against Catholics, no doubt in self-defense against heightened Spanish intrigue. In 1583, with her appointment of John Whitgift as Archbishop of Canterbury, the head of the Church of England, she also set in motion what became a perpetual "Romish Inquisition" against Puritan "traitors," which frightened her own Privy Council. The more determined Puritans now were driven underground—both the Presbyterians, who still clung to their hope of obtaining reforms *within* the Church of England; and the Separatists, the more radical minority, who broke away from the Church and its control to meet in independent congregations, "as near the primitive pattern of the first churches," in William Bradford's words, as "the light of the gospel" revealed it.

The Tudors, moreover, created and freely employed exceptional agencies of administration whose potentiality for repression the Stuarts were only the more carelessly to explore. They also tried to undermine popular forums which, by exercising their capacity for resistance, were to grow strong enough to throw the unfortunate Stuarts out.

Henry VII, beginning as early as 1497, became the first English ruler to make a formal instrument of authority of the "Court of Star Chamber," where torture could be used in secret hearings to wring confessions from political challengers, and cruel punishments imposed without indictments, juries, or cross-examination. Henry VIII extended Star Chamber proceedings to offenders against his proclamations, to which his malleable parliaments gave statutory standing after 1540. Attempting to influence juries in England was "accounted very violent, tyrannical, and contrary to the liberty and custom of the realm." Yet, country juries misbehaving under Elizabeth "were many times commanded to appear in star chamber, or before the privy council for the matter," where their ignorance or prejudice was corrected. From her own first parliament in 1559, Elizabeth extracted the establishment of the Court of High Commission, with secret inquisitorial and judicial powers in religious cases equivalent to those of Star Chamber in political ones. Whitgift made this court almost as brutal a weapon against nonconformists as the notorious Laud himself under Charles I (see p. 42). In 1566, Elizabeth told the French ambassador that the three parliaments she had already called were sufficient for any reign. The nagging need for money compelled her to summon ten more sessions, but these were fewer and shorter than England had grown accustomed to even under earlier Tudor monarchs.

By and large, among Englishmen still habituated to doffing the cap, bending the knee, and prostrating themselves in supplication, the Tudors' was a popular despotism satisfying, however imperfectly, the deep yearning for domestic peace. It may fairly be said of Elizabeth in particular—comely, gracious, clever, confident—that she ruled more by "progresses" than by "prerogative." Elizabeth owned numerous palaces, rallying points of national pride. And she was constantly on the move across the country from one palace to another, her living presence filling such pride to overflowing. Each of her "progresses" was an act of state, meticulously well thought out. No one knew better than the Tudors, as a contemporary of Elizabeth said, that "in pompous ceremonies a secret of government doth much consist." To the people, she said herself, "no music is so sweet as the affability of their prince." Yet even Elizabeth wore out her welcome, especially among Puritans who never tasted "the affability of their prince," and who hated "pompous ceremonies."

Near the end of Elizabeth's reign, Puritans probably made up a majority of the kingdom. With their friends in the Commons, mainly lawyers and justices of the peace aroused to the defense—really, the revolutionary extension—of their privileges by the Queen's intransigence in religious matters, they certainly commanded an overwhelming majority of Parliament. When the drive for a Presbyterian order was at its height in 1593 and her own repressive measures were most vicious, Elizabeth told the Commons: "I see many overbold with God Almighty, making too many subtle scannings of His blessed will, as lawyers do with human instruments. . . . If I were not certain that mine were the true way to God's will, God forbid that I should live to prescribe it to you." Such sentiments sat very poorly even with her own carefully selected members of the House.

By the time of Elizabeth's death, Parliament had fashioned itself into a well-tempered instrument of opposition to all pretensions to absolutism. Above all, the frequency of its meetings within a short span of time toward the end of the reign had brought many of the same members together again and again. They developed an *esprit de corps,* an institutional self-consciousness, a realization of their role as the voice of the popular will. This deepening appreciation of their character strengthened the members' determination to gain the initiative in legislation. For this purpose they extended and refined the practice of submitting the Crown's proposals to committees, a powerful device by which members could gather free of Crown surveillance and examine independently not only what the Queen asked but alternative proposals of their own. The Speaker of the House, nominally elected by the members, was in fact a Crown designee whose responsibility it was so to run the sessions that the Queen's business won full and swift approval and nothing else came up. The committee system made the Speaker's position increasingly difficult until the House gained the power freely to choose its own Speaker, one responsive to the members, not the Crown. But that step lay in the future when Elizabeth's heirs, her Stuart cousins, foreigners to England and foreigners with strong leanings toward absolutist Spain and France, turned English despotism into tyranny. When that happened, Parliament twice cut them down.

THE STUART SUCCESSION

When Elizabeth succeeded "Bloody Mary" on the English throne in 1558, no question agitated Englishmen more deeply than that of the new Queen's marriage, so that she might soon give birth to a legitimate Protestant heir. Indeed, the momentous issue of freedom of speech in Parliament arose largely over the right of the members to remind the Queen of her obligation in this respect, especially from the religious point of view, and her determination to forbid their interference. Once Elizabeth had passed the age of child-bearing, the succession gnawed all the more at England's heart. Once she had grown old, even her closest councillors sharpened their watchfulness, their eyes cocked on one another and on the likely successor to the throne.

Elizabeth's own secret choice was James VI of Scotland, son of Mary, Queen of Scots, whom she herself had executed (see p. 21). To prepare James, Elizabeth had long engaged in secret correspondence, tutoring him in English ways. In one letter she observed, "There is risen a sect of perilous consequences, who would have no kings but a presbytery. . . . Suppose you I can tolerate such scandals!" No one had had a harder time at the hands of presbyteries than James himself, who came to the throne of Scotland at the age of one in 1567, when his mother, amidst scenes of murder, abduction, attempted flight, imprisonment, and escape, was forced to abdicate by the followers of John Knox (see p. 21). James' own early years were spent in terror of warring Protestant groups; and while he was well trained in Calvinism as befitted a Scottish

king, he disavowed with the full fervor of his soul that part of the doctrine, stated in the words of Knox himself to Mary: "If . . . princes exceed their bounds, Madam, they may be resisted and even disposed."

Whatever else Elizabeth attempted to teach James about England seems never to have taken hold. James' Calvinism commended him the more readily to many Puritans who, having grown sick of combating a woman's wiles, were eager to have a king. Catholics, on the other hand, despaired. It was a weird Catholic plot, the Bye Plot, to capture and dispose of James in 1603, that somehow implicated Ralegh and got him thrust into the Tower by James for treason. Yet Puritans, as it turned out, had as much to fear from James as Catholics; and England herself more to fear than both. Yet the Stuarts did have a chance to win English hearts.

THE RESUMPTION
OF THE AMERICAN ENTERPRISE

It is difficult to grasp today the ecstasy of relief in monarchies when the succession is effected peaceably, especially in time of war and with no direct heir available, and the surge of love for a new ruler, fed by awe for the Crown and the quieting of anxiety. On his own royal progress from Scotland to take the throne Elizabeth had held too long, James was greeted with adulation by thousands all along the way. His own repulsive countenance, build, gear, and gait gave a twinge to those accustomed to Tudor beauty in kings and queens. When a purse snatcher was caught working the crowds, James ordered him instantly hanged without a trial, an awful augury. Yet only the most amiable demonstrations floated him and his entourage to London.

James' peaceful accession brought a welcome lull in the bitter border wars with Scotland which ravaged the northern frontier. When his assumption of the throne was followed in 1604 by his making peace at last with Spain, and this peace was followed with new commercial treaties, the reign enjoyed an unprecedented expansion of trade which further gilded its prospects.

During the great surge of mercantilist economic expansion in the early years of Elizabeth's reign (see p. 22), the joint-stock company, a device borrowed from the Dutch especially for distant trading, had come into general use in England. Joint-stock companies, by selling shares to those rising on the economic scale and accustoming themselves to the long-term risks of far off ventures, could quickly amass far larger capital funds than most individuals had at their disposal. Anyone with money could subscribe to company stock, participate in the profits, and even gain a voice in management—features that favorably distinguished joint-stock enterprises from the traditional trading gilds with their prohibitive fees and tests, and the hated monopolies by which court favorites ate out the substance of the country.

In the early decades of Elizabeth's reign, joint-stock companies had extended English commerce to Russia, Scandinavia, and the Levant, even to Africa and the Orient. America itself remained as yet too formidably Spanish, too hazily exotic, to attract any but the most adventurous soldiers and sailors; yet even Gilbert and Ralegh, once they had run through the private funds available to them, each had bartered certain commercial privileges in their patents to experienced joint-stock promoters in London who undertook to raise new funds and fresh supplies for another try. This try was long deferred because of Elizabeth's interminable Spanish war. James' peace with Spain in 1604 led to its spectacular revival.

Joint-stock undertakings in America followed directly upon the voyage to the Maine coast in 1605 of Captain George Waymouth in search of a refuge for Catholics who had already aroused James' ire (see p. 38). In Maine, Waymouth kidnapped five Indians, an act local tribes were to hold against all later white visitors, and when he displayed them in London on his return, having trained them to talk of the wonders of their native land, they caused a sensation. Sir Ferdinando Gorges, one of the organizers of the Virginia Company of Plymouth late in 1605 or early the next year (the records

are lacking), declared that "this accident" of the red men's arrival "must be acknowledged the means under God of putting on foot and giving life to all our plantations."

One of those to whom Ralegh had bartered commercial privileges in Virginia in 1589 was Thomas Smith, probably the leading merchant in London. In 1600, on the organization of the great joint-stock enterprise, the English East India Company, Smith was elected its first governor. Sir Thomas, as he became on being knighted in 1603, almost certainly was one of the promoters of the second Virginia Company chartered in 1605 or 1606, the Virginia Company of London. In any case he quickly assumed a leading role in its direction. The possibility of finding a short route to China by way of Virginia rivers, an objective dear to his East India Company, no doubt contributed to his enthusiasm for the venture.

The Virginia Company of Plymouth never fulfilled its promise (see p. 43). The Virginia Company of London, having got Jamestown started in 1607, was thoroughly reorganized under a new charter in 1609. Despite Sir Thomas Smith's heroic efforts at home and those of Captain John Smith in America, it also failed (see p. 45). But before its demise in 1624, the Virginia Company of 1609 had done more than establish the English permanently in the New World. Its joint-stock organization set the pattern for self-government in all future English "corporate" colonies. The joint-stock company governor was the prototype of the provincial governor, the directors the prototypes of his "assistants" or council, the shareholders or "freemen" the prototypes, in the aggregate, of the "General Court" or "assemblie." Self-government in the "proprietary" colonies to be established on princely grants to royal favorites was more closely derived from the example of Parliament, especially as it increasingly asserted its independence of the Crown, the equivalent of the colonial proprietor.

The release of mercantile energies during the early years of James' reign was fostered by the Privy Council under the leadership of Robert Cecil, Elizabeth's able Secretary of State who had helped smooth the way for James' accession and was retained in his post until his death in 1612. Cecil's revival of expansive mercantilism promoted what may be called the *colonizing* activity of the nation, the staking out of English outposts in many parts of the world like the one Ralegh first intended a generation earlier in America. James himself, and Charles after him, secured the permanence and profitability of colonies, particularly in America, by promoting the *settlement*—the flight, really—of large numbers of Englishmen overseas. The Stuarts accomplished this by forfeiting every good hope for their reign from their first contact with the people.

James believed in the divine right of kings, a convenient belief for Protestant rulers after breaks such as Henry VIII had had with the Pope. Elizabeth herself, as we have seen (p. 35), said that she knew God's will better than anyone and could be trusted to enact it. But she also acknowledged the scope of the law and the dangers of over-stepping it. James was a logician who thought divine right could admit of no ifs or buts.

Even in the midst of James' first "progress" from Scotland to London, spokesmen for a thousand reform clergymen placed in his hand the "Millenary Petition" requesting alterations in Church of England doctrine and worship far milder than those which had driven Elizabeth to extremities. In January, 1604, James yielded sufficiently to call a conference at Hampton Court to consider the petition and, as was his wont, he argued patiently with the members before smiting them with the full fury of his wrath. "If you aim at a Scottish Presbytery," he cried, "it agreeth as well with monarchy, as God with the Devil." The reformers had expressed no such aim, but grasping his hat to signalize the end of the confer-

ence, James shouted: "If this be all your party hath to say, I will make them conform themselves or else harry them out of the land."

Shortly thereafter, hundreds of reform clergymen were evicted from their livings, and thousands more, for conscience sake, embraced the Puritan position. The radical Separatists themselves recognized the bleakness of their plight and began preparations for their exodus to Holland and eventually to a haven in the New World (see p. 52). On the other hand, the royalist clergy took to announcing their own divinity and infallibility, a position sustained by ecclesiastical courts, including the Court of High Commission. Royalist judges, in turn, assented to ecclesiastical court encroachments on the jurisdiction of the common-law courts. In self-defense, common-law lawyers were impelled ever more strongly toward nonconformist ranks.

James spent as little time dallying with the Catholics as he had with the Protestant reformers. Under Elizabeth, the Catholics had been the hunted pariahs of the realm. James' own goal in the Spanish peace was to bring an end to Spanish subversion of the Catholic underground in England. This accomplished, he even restored diplomatic relations with the Pope and gave other signs of toleration. Having thus drawn Catholics out of hiding, he promptly conjured up the old blood-curdling fears, to which, indeed, Catholic leaders had given some substance. As early as February, 1604, the royal reaction began, and Catholics found themselves worse off than ever. Certain Catholic leaders began forming the elaborate Gunpowder Plot in which Guy Fawkes and others planned to blow up both the King and Parliament, initiate a civil war, and call Spain in to restore order. The great explosion was planned for December, 1605, but the plot was uncovered in November, when Fawkes and his co-conspirators were arrested and soon tried, convicted and hanged.

For fifteen years, Catholics knew no more peace in England; and like the radical Protestants, they turned their eyes to refuges abroad. The official condition of the English Catholics improved after the outbreak of the Thirty Years' War on the Continent in 1618, when James, by an elaborate exercise in king-craft, tried to save Protestant regimes, including that of his son-in-law in Germany, from Spanish aggression by pushing the marriage of his son Charles to the Spanish Infanta. To give James' plan a better odor, English royalty and its friends began to cultivate eminent Catholics again and to conciliate others. The rest of the country, however, saw through James' scheme. The projected family tie with Spain could only result in the resumption of Spanish power in England. Popular detestation of this policy was manifested by heightened violence against Catholics all across the land and in the deepening hostility of Protestant subjects to the King.

James himself realized that England's safety could not be left to the marriage project alone; to put the country on a war footing he was forced to call on Parliament for funds. The session that opened in January, 1621, was the first formal one in ten years, and it soon made James sorry that he had not tried to govern another ten years without it. Although England did not engage in the Thirty Years' War, the conflict brought a halt to the great period of trade expansion. The depression that followed intensified the impulse to leave England even among those not irreversibly impelled to go by defeat in the struggle for law and liberty.

THE VICTORY OF LAW DEFERRED

Elizabeth's successive parliaments had gained their strength from the growing strength of their members. As Tudor society became more complex, the scope of legislation broadened, and the responsibilities of justices of the peace, in particular, were gradually extended to include the administration of many new laws. Numerous justices resisted the new responsibilities and "went to grass." But others, especially those elected to Parliament and who helped make the new laws, gained greater respect and even reverence for the whole legal tra-

dition of the community. The great difference between Elizabeth's parliaments and those under James and Charles was the strengthening of this tradition by the common-law lawyers and judges, whose own work gained in force from contending against Stuart claims to absolutism.

The greatest of the common-law lawyers and judges was Sir Edward Coke, royalist enough to serve both Elizabeth and James, but legalist enough to combat both. The tenor of Coke's lifelong thinking is evident in his report of a case in 1605, when he was James' Attorney-General. The King had justified his interference with a lay court that had been reluctant to yield the case to an ecclesiastical court, as the King desired. "Then," writes Coke:

the king said that he thought the law was founded upon reason, and that he and others had reason as well as the judges. To which it was answered by me that . . . His Majesty was not learned in the laws of his realm of England and causes which concern the life or inheritance or goods or fortunes of his subjects; they are not to be decided by natural reason, but by the artificial reason and judgement of the law, which law is an act which requires long study and experience before that a man can attain cognizance of it; and that the law was the golden . . . measure to try the causes of his subjects. . . . With which the king . . . said that then he should be under the law, which was treason to affirm.

Without Coke's own "long study and experience" it is doubtful that the English common law could have been carried to America. Much of the strength of the common law lay in its antiquity, which went back at least to the reign of Henry II in the twelfth century. Its weakness lay in the inconsistencies that grew up in the precedents over the centuries and in the many localities in which the common-law courts functioned. In 1600, Coke started publishing the thirteen volumes of his *Reports* of common-law cases, taken down "while the matter was . . . almost yet sounding in the ear,"

Parliament in session in the reign of James I. The prisoner kneeling at the bar is being admonished by the Speaker.

and yet buttressed by precedents "beyond the memory or register of any beginning." These *Reports,* like Coke's own influential decisions, teem with references to ancient statutes and rulings painfully dug up. They made the common law viable just when America herself was on the verge of settle-

ment. Coke's *Institutes,* which he began to publish in 1628, went even deeper. In them, for the first time, the great documents from Magna Carta on were exhumed, and printed in full or extensively excerpted. Coke's tendentious glosses upon them underscored the supremacy of the law and the majesty

40

of its tradition as against the wilfulness of chance holders of the throne, especially such as James and Charles.

James had inherited large war debts from Elizabeth. He also came to the throne with obligations to many backers. Insecure in his new eminence, he sought, furthermore, to enlist the support of many courtiers with lavish grants. His hunger for funds had forced James in his early years as King to call session after session of Parliament; but the members would yield little without the certainty that their growing list of grievances, especially on religious and legal issues, would be corrected. In the meantime, they added new institutional devices, such as sitting as the "committee of the whole house," the better to develop their own programs without interference from Speaker or Clerk. The first such committee assembled in 1607. Smaller special committees also were set up to unearth precedents, like Coke's own, to support Parliament's increasingly radical tendency.

The struggle between Crown and Commons deepened when James, and Charles after him, deprived of funds by the House, began to reach out for other sources of income. Among the tastiest of these were the "impositions," or duties, on imported goods, which had grown greatly in value during the economic boom. James, moreover, frequently raised the duties by proclamation, and those who protested too strongly were haled before the Court of Star Chamber and might have an ear cut off for their impudence. The Commons, in 1610, reminding James that "without advice or counsel of Parliament" he had "in time of peace set both greater impositions and more in number than any of your noble ancestors did ever in time of war," went on to assert its own power of the purse. It asked that "a law be made to declare that all impositions set upon your people . . . save only by common consent in parliament, . . . shall be void." The House also asked for restraints on the Court of High Commission and other ecclesiastical courts.

In a rage, James dissolved this Parliament

in 1611. When a new Parliament in 1614 presented even stronger religious and legal demands in exchange for "supplies" for the king, James not only dissolved it immediately, but sent four of its leading members to the Tower. With his new chief minister, George Villiers, whom he made Duke of Buckingham, James now ruled without restraint until the wartime Parliament of 1621. Impositions soared; peerages were sold for huge sums; new monopolies were granted to the rich. At the same time, economies so ruined the navy that Turkish pirates enslaved English seamen in the Channel itself, while the Dutch captured much of London's trade.

Never had England suffered under a more corrupt regime, and when Parliament met in 1621 it made its first order of business the punishment of those responsible. A fifteenth-century law had been found empowering the Commons to impeach offenders against the commonwealth for trial in the Lords. Parliament now reached for the most conspicuous of the officers of state, the Lord Chancellor, Sir Francis Bacon. Bacon spent no time preparing a defense: "I do plainly and ingenuously confess that I am guilty of corruption." He had, in fact, been thrown to the wolves by the even more corrupt men around the King, and on conviction was let off with light punishment.

Having stretched its power in domestic affairs, the Parliament of 1621 reached for power in foreign affairs as well. It denounced the Spanish marriage proposal and petitioned for war with Spain and the guarantee of a Protestant marriage for Prince Charles. James received the petition with threats of imprisonment for its bearers. The Commons then resolved:

That the liberties, franchises, privileges and jurisdictions of Parliament are the ancient and undoubted birthright and inheritance of the subjects of England; and that the arduous and urgent affairs concerning the King, state, and defence of the realm, and of the Church of England, . . . are proper subjects and matter of council and debate in Parliament. And that in the handling and proceeding of those businesses every member of the House hath, and of right ought to have, freedom of speech to propound, treat, reason, and bring to conclusion the same.

The King demanded the Journal of the House, ripped out the resolution, and dissolved the session.

When Charles I succeeded James in 1625, Buckingham embarked on military and maritime adventures to regain mercantile support. But these were such costly failures that the Crown itself was brought into ever worse repute and Parliament into outright rebellion. Parliament's refusal to vote money for further adventures like Buckingham's brought Charles at last to the policy of "forced loans," with refusal to lend carrying with it the penalty of imprisonment without trial. A compliant clergy attempted to aid Charles by declaring nonpayment of taxes and loans a sin. This reminder of papal corruption completed the mortification of the Puritans who had already become alarmed by the sincere efforts of Charles' new Archbishop, William Laud, to reform the Church of England. Unfortunately, Laud's reforms went directly opposite to those the Puritans themselves demanded, bringing in many Roman innovations to attract worshippers who did not in fact have Christ in their hearts. Laud, at the same time, intensified the persecution of nonconformists.

In 1629, Parliament, with Sir John Eliot to the fore, proposed the famous "Three Resolutions" to Charles, demanding that the King declare "as a capital enemy to this kingdom and commonwealth" not only he who lays and he who pays taxes "not being granted by Parliament," but he also who "shall bring in innovation in religion." Charles rejected the Resolutions. When Parliament voted them anyway, Charles dissolved the body, not to recall it until April, 1640, when he again needed funds to suppress an uprising of Scotch Presbyterians. This "Short Parliament" was immediately dissolved when it insisted on reforms first. By then no less than 70,000 Englishmen had migrated to the West Indies and North America.

A settlement with the Scots committed Charles to still further outlays, and in November, 1640, he called the fateful "Long Parliament," which resisted his demands, raised its own army, touched off the Civil War, and paved the way for the dictatorship of Oliver Cromwell. Before any of this, the "Long Parliament," in May, 1641, passed two revolutionary measures. One required the convening of Parliament every three years even without a call from the Crown. The second forbade the dissolution of this Parliament without its consent.

The "Long Parliament" held office until the Restoration in 1660. During its turbulent career, Cromwell welded his army of "Roundheads" into an irresistible force. Soon after Parliament ordered the beheading of the King in 1649, Cromwell became Lord Protector of the Commonwealth, as the kingdom came to be called. In the Commonwealth period, the flow of dissenters to America slackened, and only a few royalists were prepared to leave England, joyless and austere though the land now seemed, for the uncertainties of the New World.

II. *The Rude Beginnings on the Chesapeake*

SURVIVAL IN VIRGINIA

The petition of the promoters of the two Virginia companies seeking a royal patent for the renewal of the Virginia enterprise (see p. 37) was submitted to King James in September, 1605. Thereafter, it received the careful attention of the Privy Council which worked out the details for "so noble a Work," as they said, sometimes in consultation with the petitioners. Before the King's great seal was affixed to the final draft of the charter, in April, 1606, it was studied by the Attorney-General, Sir Edward Coke himself, who is credited with having seen to it that the "Liberties, Franchises, and Immunities" of Englishmen at home were expressly to be carried with them overseas; and likewise, that the limitations and obligations of the law were not to be evaded there. Coke may also have been largely responsible for the charter provision creating a royal council of thirteen appointed by the King and responsible only to him to oversee the whole enterprise. The charter also provided that each of the two distinct colonies it projected should have its own council of thirteen to see to details of administration.

Under the charter of 1606, the Virginia Company of London obtained the right to settle at any point between 34° and 41° north latitude; the Virginia Company of Plymouth at any point between 38° and 45°, the Crown considering this region "either appertaining to us, or . . . not now actually possessed by any *Christian* Prince or People." The borders of the two companies overlapped, but they were required to make their first "Plantations and Habitations" at least 100 miles from one another. Each was granted the land 50 miles north and south of its first settlement, extending 100 miles inland and 100 miles out to sea.

The merchants of Plymouth outdid their rivals in getting underway. Their first expedition set sail in August, 1606, only to fall prey to Spaniards in the West Indies. In May and June, 1607, Sir Ferdinando Gorges dispatched two ships, one of them carrying Waymouth's pilot, to the region of Waymouth's visit (see p. 37), and there, on the Sagadohoc River, the lower Kennebec today, the Plymouth Company's first and only colony endured one "extreme, unseasonable and frosty" winter and quit. Thereafter, fishermen from all expansionist nations of Europe regularly visited the Maine coast but established no lasting bases.

In December, 1606, meanwhile, *Susan Constant, Godspeed,* and *Discovery,* with 160 men, all under the command of Captain Christopher Newport, an experienced West Indian buccaneer, had quietly weighed anchor for the London Company, and on April 26, 1607, sighted "the Bay of Chesupiac," or Chesapeake. Landing amidst "faire meddows and goodly tall Trees," a scouting party under Newport immediately fell into a skirmish with the Indians. A few days later, the expedition sailed some 50 miles up the river they named the James and chose a site they named Jamestown, one well situated for defense. The settlers had been warned not to "plant in a low or moist place, because it will prove unhealthfull." But, fearing an assault from the sea more than malaria and bad water, they ignored the warning and suffered the consequences. When Newport returned to England after two months in Virginia, he took many of his original passengers back with him. Of the 104 or 105 who remained to make the settlement, more than half perished during the first summer, most of them the victims of fluxes and fevers.

Following its plan to settle Virginia gradually, the company sent Newport out again in October, 1607, with 120 more settlers, and still again the next year with 70, but their fate was no better than that of the first contingent. In 1610 there were only 60 persons living in Jamestown, and Virginia was on the verge of going the way of Sagadohoc. Indeed, in June, 1610, the despairing bitter-enders, one of their number having been tortured and executed for cannibalism, were afloat toward the sea hoping for some fishing craft to pick them up and take them home to England. Then the heralds of a substantial fleet under Thomas West, Lord De la Warr, suddenly appeared on the James. The refugees were ordered back to Jamestown, "which appeared," as one of the newcomers observed, "rather than as the ruins of some ancient fortification, than that any people living might now inhabit it."

Virginia's plight had many causes, the basic ones being confusion of purpose and ignorance of conditions other than climate and terrain. Sir Thomas Smith and his colleagues in London hoped that the Virginia settlers might discover the elusive route to China, establish trade with the Indians, and develop gold, copper, and iron mines. But none of these grandiose hopes was realized. During the bleak winter of 1608-09, the "starving time," only the efforts of Captain John Smith had held the colony together. Smith was as interested in gold and China as anyone, but he also had an appreciation of the necessity of hard work that escaped his superiors in London and most of the "decayed gentlemen" they sent out. Work meant building shelters, planting food, seeing to fortifications, before the quest for metallic and commercial wealth could begin. It meant trying to befriend the Indian, elicit his assistance, implement his recommendations. For all his exertions and example, Smith failed to arouse his fellow-settlers even to look to their survival.

The company's policies helped as little as its goals. The company, for example, held on to all the land itself and required the settlers to work it for the common store. This system probably was essential to security during the precarious first years in a strange country, but it also helped to kill incentive. The London council, furthermore, provided that Virginia should be run by a council of seven there, with a president at its head. But the president had no power except to preside at meetings. Thus authority, sorely needed if only to keep order, was wholly lacking. Smith took authority upon himself; but the gentlemen of early Virginia looked down their noses at the rough soldier. Nevertheless, when Smith himself was injured in 1609 and left Virginia for good, the "starving time" grew worse than ever. His own explorations in search of the river to the South Sea, moreover, aroused the suspicions even of the most helpful Indians who realized that the Englishmen had come not only to trade metal for corn, but to take their land as well. "It is true," said De la Warr's emissary in 1610, that the Indian was "as fast killing without as the famine and pestilence within."

The Virginia Company council in London gradually learned of Virginia's travail from those who fled home with Newport after his successive visits and by other means. They knew, as one said, that "the eyes of all Europe are looking upon our endeavours to . . . plant an English nation there, . . . to the end that we may thereby be secured from being eaten out of all profits of trade by our more industrious neighbours." As the first step in their "great effort" to improve their enterprise, the London Company applied successfully for a new charter in 1609, terminating their association with the Plymouth Company, abolishing the royal council overseeing their activities, and setting them up as a thoroughgoing joint-stock enterprise with the right and power to govern as well as to trade. The new charter also greatly enlarged the company's boundaries north and south and extended its grant across the entire continent.

Armed with this new patent, the company immediately launched a strong promotional campaign for subscribers to the stock which quickly brought it almost seven hundred shareholders, including some of the richest and most ancient companies in London as well as 650 individuals. It also launched the biggest expedition to America before the "great migration" to Massachusetts Bay (see p. 55). This expedition of six ships with some 800 passengers, again under Captain Newport, set forth on May 15, 1609. The new Governor, De la Warr, was to leave shortly after. Difficulties delayed his arrival in Virginia for almost two years, but it was the group under his deputy, Sir Thomas Gates, that reached the vicinity of Jamestown in time to turn back the last desperate refugees. In place of the wrangling council in Virginia, the company now gave the new governor the absolute power of a military commander over settlers who were treated like prisoners. This was another mistake, however justified it may have seemed. The "starving time" did not end under the new regime, for the colonists were to suffer privations for another decade. But Virginia's economic future was assured between 1612 and 1614 when the settlers discovered a new cash crop—tobacco, a variety imported from Trinidad proving more satisfactory than the bitter native plant. John Rolfe is credited with being the first to experiment with commercial tobacco in Virginia. The momentous consequences of his discoveries were deepened after 1619, when the first Negro slaves accidently were landed in the colony by a Dutch privateer just when its hunger for field hands was sharpened. In 1618, Virginia sent 30,000 pounds of tobacco to England. By 1627, she was shipping 500,000 pounds a year.

Until 1619, the Virginia Company paid little attention to the comforts and desires of the colonists. Soon after the arrival of a new governor in 1619, however, a proclamation declared "that those cruel lawes by which we had soe longe been governed were now abrogated," and that the settlers would henceforth be governed "by those free lawes" under which the king's subjects lived in England. The company parceled out land to the "ancient planters" (those who had arrived before 1616) and to later settlers who had paid their own way. This policy, declared John Rolfe,

. . . giveth all greate content, for now knowing their owne landes, they strive and are prepared to build houses & to cleer their groundes ready to plant, which giveth . . . them greate incouragement, and the greatest hope to make the Colony florrish that ever yet happened to them.

Under the "head-right" system, introduced at this time, the company turned over 50 acres of land to any person who transported himself to the colony and stuck it out for three years. Later, the head of a family could claim an additional 50 acres for any dependent or servant he brought with him. Some men made a business of importing colonists, and acquired large tracts of land in this way.

On the model of the company government itself in England the directors now also "granted a general assemblie should be helde yearly once, whereat were to be present the Govr and Counsell with two Burgesses from each plantation freely to be

elected by the inhabitants thereof; this assembly to have the power to make and ordaine whatsoever lawes and orders should by them be thought good and proffittable for our subsistance." This liberal policy was carried out on July 30, 1619, when the New World's first representative assembly (later known as the House of Burgesses) met at Jamestown.

Despite these political and social improvements, the whole Virginia enterprise

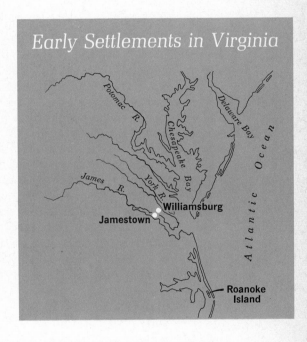

Early Settlements in Virginia

continued to languish. A frightful Indian massacre in 1622 dissipated much of the hope aroused by the tobacco staple and the liberalized conditions in Virginia. The difficulties in America only heightened the problems of the company itself in London. A royal investigation of the company in 1623 revealed some melancholy statistics: Of the 6,000 colonists who had taken part in the colonial adventure since 1606, about 4,000 had died. The Virginia enterprise had been a financial failure as well. Investors had put £200,000 into the venture, gaining not a single pound in return.

Early Settlements in Maryland

BALTIMORE'S CHARTER BOUNDARY OF 1632

40°

Patapsco R.

Susquehanna R.

Delaware R.

Severn R.

Potomac R.

Patuxent R.

Bay

St. George's R.

Preston

Mattapony

St. Mary's

VIRGINIA

Chesapeake

The apparent failure on all sides prompted the Crown to take up the company's charter in 1624 and make Virginia into the first royal colony. With the change, the new governmental system itself also seemed to be in jeopardy. A royal governor was sent to rule, and no meetings of the assembly were held again until 1628. Not before 1639 did the king accept the assembly's right to permanent existence under the governor; but thereafter, especially under the administration of Sir William Berkeley, beginning in 1642, the executive, council, and assembly system became fixed. Berkeley's suppression of an Indian uprising in 1644 brought almost thirty years of peaceful relations with the red men.

THE MARYLAND REFUGE

Maryland, first settled in 1634, was truly a "sprout from Virginia," but an unwanted and unwelcome one of entirely different parentage.

Maryland's founder, Sir George Calvert, had long nourished great ambitions for his family, which were encouraged by James I, who knighted him in 1617. Following Elizabethan precedents, James, for services rendered, also granted Calvert vast domains wrung from the Irish and in 1625 made him an Irish peer as Baron Baltimore of Baltimore. Calvert's interest in America went back at least as far as the chartering of the Virginia Company, to whose shares he had subscribed. In 1622, James granted him the whole of Newfoundland with virtual regal powers there, and in 1625, after he acknowledged his conversion to Catholicism, Calvert attempted to make the settlement already underway in the province a refuge for his co-religionists.

Calvert hated the Newfoundland weather and in 1629, after his northern enterprise had foundered, he visited Jamestown where he was suspected of having characteristically grand designs on the land. In any case, his religion supplied ample excuse for his being ordered out of the settlement. When, in 1632, Calvert was indeed granted land in their region, the Virginians felt their suspicions sufficiently confirmed to make the most resolute protests to Charles I, now king. Charles yielded to the extent of moving Calvert's grant north of the Potomac, whence it extended all the way to the fortieth parallel. Calvert named his new holding Maryland, after Charles' Queen, Henrietta Maria. When he died later in the year, his charter was reconfirmed to his son, the second Lord Baltimore. For years, Virginians carried on a private war to regain Maryland and on one occasion, in 1644, temporarily drove out the governor.

Cecilius Calvert, the second Lord Baltimore, began the settlement of Maryland in November, 1633, when he sent out his brother, Leonard, and 300 persons in *Ark* and *Dove*. Their instructions were to deal fairly with the Indians, and soon after their arrival at the mouth of the Potomac in March, 1634, they purchased a healthful and accessible tract which they named St. Mary's. Their consideration for the red men spared the newcomers the terrors of war during the critical early period; orders from the Crown to the governor of Virginia to supply the new colony with grain, along with supplies brought in by Plymouth and Massachusetts traders (see p. 51), also spared it the terrors of starvation. Once they had looked to their own subsistence, most of the colonists began to raise tobacco in competition with Virginia and soon enjoyed a modest prosperity.

Maryland was the first of the so-called "proprietary" colonies among the English mainland settlements. The others all came after the restoration of the Stuarts to the throne in 1660 (see p. 61) and reflected, as did the establishment of Maryland itself, the persistence of feudal as against commercial motivations for colonization among aristocrats to whom the Stuarts were indebted.

As the proprietor's charter required, Leonard Calvert laid out the new colony in manors of from 1,000 to 3,000 acres, each under a manor lord, usually a Catholic. The lords were themselves privileged to "subinfeud" their land to lesser vassals. Both small and large landholders, to be "quit" of traditional feudal obligations to the proprietor, were obliged to pay him a "quit-rent" in money, amounting to 2 shillings per hundred acres, annually. The manors were expected to be self-sufficient in traditional feudal ways, with local government taken care of by traditional baronial courts. But manors, in fact, seldom were set up on this basis, and only the quit-rent provision survived.

Calvert's charter, like his father's earlier ones in Ireland and Newfoundland, gave the proprietor "free, full and absolute power" to make laws that even a King could not review. At the same time it required that he act, "with the advice, assent and approbation of the Freemen of the . . . Province," who were to be assembled from time to time by the proprietor or his heirs, "in such sort and form as to him or them shall be best." The first Maryland assembly was convened in 1635, and while no record remains of its proceedings, it was not long before future ones found it increasingly difficult to give their "assent and approbation" to certain of the proprietor's notions. At the same time, the proprietor, endowed personally with all military, judicial, and executive prerogatives, and with a council like the Privy Council in England to assist him in his work, found it difficult to heed the assembly's "advice." In the first assembly of which there is a record of the proceedings, that of 1637, freemen and council sat together and only the council's proposals were taken up. But Parliament's own recent

gains in initiative and independence served as models to colonial delegates in Maryland as elsewhere. The assembly insisted on proposing and adopting its own measures. By 1650, the elected house was separated from the council and Maryland had a bicameral legislature which gradually asserted its superior authority.

The Baltimores realized from the start that most English Catholics fleeing persecution at home would seek refuge in Catholic countries in Europe and that in Maryland, as elsewhere in America, most settlers would be Protestants. Thus while Catholics were offered a place to go to freely if they wished, the proprietors warned them from the outset that, "no scandall nor offence" be given to Protestants. The Baltimores' great hope was to create an atmosphere of toleration which, by avoiding the grim example of religious conflict in Europe, would foster peace and prosperity in America. This hope was realized for some years. When Virginia's loyalty to the Crown in the 1640's led to increasing harassment of Puritans in that colony, however, Maryland, in 1648 invited hundreds of them to come to her. Rightly fearful of Puritan tyranny now, against the Catholic minority in Maryland, the reigning Lord Baltimore, in 1649, sent over his "Act Concerning Religion," justly famous as his "Toleration Act," which the Maryland Assembly promptly approved. Under this act, anyone who used reproachful epithets like "heretic," "popish priest," or "Puritan," was to be severely punished. Although the Toleration Act made the denial of the Trinity a capital offense, it nonetheless advanced the cause of conscience by requiring the hostile Christian denominations to suffer one another peacefully.

Despite attempts to negotiate with the Puritan rulers in England after 1649, the Baltimores lost control of their colony. From 1650 to 1657, the Puritan element managed Maryland's affairs. In 1654, the assembly repealed the Toleration Act, and in 1655 a force of 200 men under the proprietor's deputy-governor was routed by a troop of Puritan planters during a brief civil war. But the anti-proprietary group exercised authority for only a few years, and by 1657 Baltimore had regained his privileges. The Calverts ruled unchecked until 1691, when Maryland became a royal colony, and so it remained until it was returned to the Calverts in 1715.

ESTABLISHING
THE PLANTATION SYSTEM

The early settlements in Virginia and Maryland, whatever their political and legal differences, were drawn into an economic unit by Chesapeake Bay. Together, these settlements provided the English with their first firm foothold on America's "moving frontier."

The marshy coastal plain that became known as the tidewater region of the Chesapeake settlements was threaded by countless navigable streams along which the first "planters" extended their estates. Ocean-going vessels could sail right up to plantation wharves, making it unnecessary for the planters to send their tobacco to export centers. This geographic circumstance helps account for the development of a society of independent plantations and smaller farms more or less sufficient to themselves, often uncooperative and difficult to administer. For more than a century this society did not "have any one place of Cohabitation . . . that may reasonably bear the Name of a Town."

By 1650, while subsistence farms remained common in the Chesapeake region, and beaver and other fur-bearing game continued to be trapped or shot, the basic unit of production had become the independent tobacco farm. Before the end of the seventeenth century, large one-crop plantations had become common even inland, their owners established as the dominant class and as models for the ambitious. Those who had not graduated to planter status were already being pushed ever more deeply into the interior where they might grow some tobacco to market for the small amounts of cash they needed, but where hunting and subsistence agriculture remained the principal occupations.

The extraordinary rapidity with which tobacco, unlike sugar, for example, wore out the soil, combined with "the Ambition each Man had of being Lord of a vast, tho' unimproved Territory," led the more far-sighted planters themselves to push the frontier ever westward. The very laws designed to check them, moreover, merely improved their opportunities. Theoretically, the "head-right" system (see p. 45) should have peopled the wilderness with small landholders; actually, it played into the hands of the private speculators and colonial officials, many of whom obtained head-rights by the baldest frauds. By law, land granted under the system had to be put under cultivation within three years. But since this proviso was usually ignored, and since land taxes were hard to collect on the frontier, it was easy for those who grasped the land to withhold it from the market as long as they liked.

Most of the newcomers to the Chesapeake country once the plantation system got under way were Englishmen sent over as indentured servants or contract laborers. In the typical contract made before sailing with company or planter agents at home, each person agreed to work for a fixed period (usually five to seven years) in payment for his passage. During this time he would be forbidden to marry, and violation of this and other restrictions might lengthen his term of indenture. Convicts supplied another source of contract labor, as did beggars and rogues kidnapped in English slums, and child apprentices often coerced into leaving for America by administrators of the poor laws at home. Those who survived the hideous ordeal of the Atlantic voyage and the hard years of servitude, sometimes became rich and respected citizens. Runaways, moreover, were frequent where the abundance of free land on the frontier fired men with ambition to strike out for themselves.

After 1660 the widely held theory that

England was overpopulated was abandoned and the flow of servants from the home country declined until, by 1689, there were few new arrivals. This change only aggravated the situation on the plantations where the need for labor was always greater than the supply. It also strikingly raised the demand for Negro hands. As late as 1670, Virginia counted only 2,000 Negroes in a population of 40,000, and the ratio in Maryland was even smaller. During the next thirty years the number of Negroes in the Chesapeake settlements multiplied five or six times, much faster than the number of whites. Maryland legislation, almost from the start of settlement, made important distinctions between white servants and Negro "slaves." In Virginia, Negroes first were subject to the same laws as white servants, but legal differentiations against the Negro began to be made in 1630 and by 1661 Virginia recognized slavery for life. After 1669, strict laws were passed controlling slave activities. In 1671 Virginia law lumped the slave with "sheep, horses and cattle" as property, his body freely subject to the master's whip, his life to the master's whim. Slave-owning itself, as much as land-owning, became the cachet of aristocratic standing and conceit.

Tobacco brought wealth to Chesapeake planters after the West Indies gave up tobacco for sugar-growing in the middle of the seventeenth century. But Chesapeake prosperity throughout the colonial period remained subject to all the hazards of unregulated one-crop systems, especially those dependent for markets on ocean shipping which was likely to be disrupted by war. One of the worst hazards was over-production, which periodically would glut the market and depress prices. At a low point in 1661, the Virginia Assembly forbade planting for one year. But many Virginians refused to bow to dictation. Those, moreover, who did hold their tobacco off the market found Marylanders taking advantage of this fortuitous scarcity, to "pour into England all they can make, both good and bad without Distinction," thereby giving Chesapeake tobacco a bad name in the bar-

gain. Governor Berkeley tried to wean the planters over to such varied crops as hemp and silk and grapes, and to the manufacture of cloth and wine. He even sent expeditions once more, "to make Discoveries . . . amongst the Indians" of ways to diversify Virginia's economy, but to no avail. When the assembly's ban ran out, "All the people relaps'd again into the Disease of planting Tobacco."

BACON'S REBELLION

The commitment of the Chesapeake planters to this one-crop system, which was so demanding in land for expansion, so vulnerable to distant contingencies, so inviting to undesirable controls, brought into focus all the grievances that culminated in Bacon's Rebellion in Virginia in 1676. By then, the Virginia frontier had been pushed only some fifty miles inland, and this slow penetration had helped keep the general peace with the Indians of the region, who served as buffers between the colony and unfriendly tribes in the interior, for thirty years. Yet the pressure on the red men was mounting. In 1671 and again in 1673 expeditions sent out by the most influential Virginia fur traders and land speculators had for the first time pierced the Appalachian barrier. These explorations greatly enlarged the Virginians' vision of empire; but they also sent a quiver of dismay through the Indian nations whose country they trespassed upon, nations whose territory had already been infiltrated by unwelcome aborigines from broken tribes in the North and East fleeing before the Englishman's well-known land hunger. This land hunger was already manifesting itself increasingly on Virginia's own moving frontier of settlement, where the day-to-day encroachment on Indian towns and farms as well as enslavement of Indian captives, were making the tribesmen wild with frustration and fear. Hardened Virginians themselves had already learned to shoot first, "it matters not whether they be Friends or Foes Soe they be Indians."

In Maryland, the Susquehannocks, far up at "the head of the Bay," had played a role similar to that of the friendly tribes of Virginia, guarding the northern reaches of the colony from the aggressive Iroquois League (see p. 94). By 1674, however, Maryland had made grants of land to planters far up the Susquehanna Valley and, in anticipation of the spread of settlement, had signed a treaty with the Senecas, members of the Iroquois League most hostile to the Susquehannocks just south of them. Thus tied to the English, the Senecas promptly made war on the betrayed Susquehannocks and drove them southward where they met the usual hostile reception from the local braves, themselves, as we have said, now in an exceptionally excitable state.

Food shortages soon drove Indians to raid frontier plantations in Maryland with accompanying atrocities. In September, 1675, a combined force of Maryland and Virginia militia failed in an attempt to wipe out the Susquehannocks, who then poured across the Potomac in wild roving bands that became the scourge of the Virginia frontier as far south as the James River. Frontier planters, flying eastward, demanded that Governor Berkeley send a new force sufficiently strong to destroy all the rampaging braves. Berkeley at first agreed to do so. When he then countermanded his orders, the frontiersmen's own anger, well warmed by all their older grievances, took fire.

These grievances arose out of rising taxes levied in a manner discriminatory toward the inland settlers for purposes against which they were strongly opposed. One such purpose was the development of Jamestown into a city suitable for the effective administration of the navigation laws regulating the tobacco trade and other English measures. There were, at the same time, purposes which inland settlers strongly favored, such as protection against the Indians, for which little action was taken. Well-founded suspicions that public funds were being misappropriated by the self-serving elite further soured the spirit of the times; and since this elite was still beholden to the proud Governor for its place and privileges, the mounting dissatisfaction soon focused on Berkeley himself. He had in fact failed to call a single election of Burgesses since 1661, and ruled with his congenial friends of long standing, "the very persons our complaints do accuse," Bacon said, in explaining why there was no hope for redress by more constitutional means.

Berkeley's defense was that the militia could never find the Susquehannocks who melted into the forest, and that any serious attempt to do so must only stir the more distant tribes to unite to drive the white man once and for all into the sea. He had before him the grim experience of New England, only a few months earlier, when twelve towns were utterly destroyed during King Philip's War before the Indian power was broken (see p. 59). Berkeley tried instead to conciliate Virginia's traditionally friendly nearby braves, a policy with which the assembly, meeting in March, 1676, most reluctantly complied. Berkeley's shilly-shallying gave the firebrand, Nathaniel Bacon, his chance.

A young aristocrat with a short, shady past, Bacon was in his twenties when he arrived in Virginia as recently as 1674 and set himself up on more than 1,000 acres of fine land in the interior up the James. Berkeley, forty years his senior, was his cousin by marriage, and within a year of Bacon's arrival had given him a coveted seat on the Governor's Council. Bacon, however, was far from all gratitude. The country, he said, wanted dead, not friendly, Indians; and he demanded that Berkeley grant him a military commission to do the job against the red men that the Governor had mishandled. When Berkeley angrily refused, Bacon set himself up as the leader of the anti-Berkeley party, collected a force of willing volunteers, and led them in successful raids. For his pains, Berkeley formally branded him a "rebel."

When Bacon arrived in Jamestown to

take his seat in the House of Burgesses after an election which Berkeley had called in order to seek a vote of confidence for himself, Berkeley had him arrested and placed under parole. When the Governor again refused Bacon's request for a military commission, the rebel rallied 500 men and terrorized Berkeley into granting it. This was in June, 1676. The House of Burgesses itself, at that time, with no assistance from the firebrand himself, proceeded to enact what became known as "Bacon's Laws," which aimed at liberalizing suffrage and office-holding requirements and procedures relating to taxation.

When Bacon, commissioned, again left Jamestown to suppress a new Indian outbreak on the frontier, the Governor once more named him a traitor subject to being hanged, and tried with little success to raise an army against him. A further attempt by Berkeley to regain control brought Bacon back to Jamestown in September, when he captured and burned the capital. When Bacon died suddenly of dysentery in October, 1676, the rebel force disintegrated. Berkeley regained control, and before King Charles' commissioners arrived to relieve him of his office he had executed 23 of Bacon's followers.

Bacon was not the "Torchbearer of the Revolution," as he has been painted. If his rebellion did in fact hasten the Revolution, which, it must be recalled, did not begin for another hundred years, it could only be because of the impetus it gave to the tightening of English control on colonial expansiveness. When news of the uprising

first reached England in September, 1676, 1,100 soldiers under Colonel Herbert Jeffreys were promptly shipped out to Virginia to restore order. Jeffreys himself was to take over as Lieutenant-Governor. This military force, one of the very first sent to America, with a military man placed in charge of the colony, showed the determination of the Stuarts to bring the far-off freemen to book. The policy in relation to the Indians, henceforth, was to keep the Americans away from them, the land the settlers already held, it was said in 1677, "being more than they either will or can cultivate to profitt." Beyond that, the hope of peaceful relations was surrendered, the goal of conversion to Christianity abandoned, the policy of swift extermination rejected as too costly in money and men. Indian and white man both knew that the aborigines' hold on the land was sure to be broken. In 1682, when Jeffreys' force was recalled after the Virginia Assembly refused to bear the cost of it, the formal policy was adopted that was to be followed along the whole course of the moving frontier: It was acknowledged that the Indian would never yield peacefully; to reduce the hazards of retaliation to the minimum, the system of frontier rangers was initiated. These rangers, armed and mounted at their own expense, rode regular patrols to learn of menacing Indian movements and to warn the settlers to prepare for attacks.

III. *The Puritan Colonies of New England*

THE PILGRIMS OF PLYMOUTH

While the first English settlers were struggling at Jamestown and the first French at Quebec, the country between these outposts engaged the active attention of adventurers from the New World and the Old. In 1614, Captain John Smith, in the employ of London merchants still in quest of gold and copper mines, sailed to

the northern reaches of Virginia, brought back fish and furs instead, and a map from which, in 1616, the name New England first was given to the region.

Although New England was to become a land of family farms, Congregational villages, and town-meeting government, the most grandiose early schemes for it, like those in Maryland, were feudal in character. The leading spirit behind these schemes was Sir Ferdinando Gorges of the Plymouth Company, who in 1620, along with some forty aristocrats, petitioned the king for a charter for the Council of New England to supplant the Plymouth Company, and a new land grant reaching from present-day Philadelphia to Newfoundland and from the Atlantic to the Pacific. The plan to divide this empire into fiefs for the aristocratic subscribers never materialized, but after 1622 Sir Ferdinando himself was busy laying out vast estates between the Merrimack and Kennebec rivers.

Almost on the very day in November,

1620, that the Council of New England won its charter, a much more homely group bound for Virginia in the ship, *Mayflower,* accidentally made their landfall off the council's shores at Cape Cod. They were a mixed group of 102 persons, 35 of them from among the most dedicated of Separatists who had fled from persecution in England in 1608 and 1609 to a refuge granted them in the Netherlands. By 1617 they had grown disenchanted with life in a foreign country and had decided that their best hope "was to live as a distinct body by themselves" on the virgin land of the New World.

Captain John Smith and his map of New England. 1614.

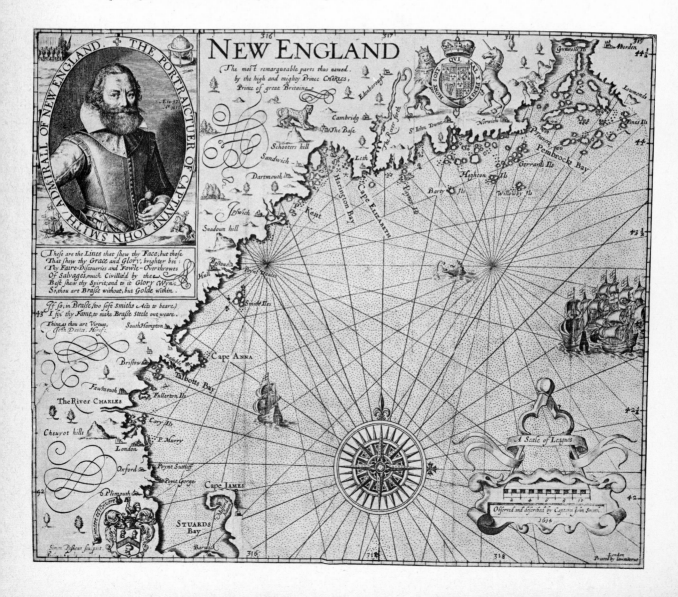

Three years of the most disheartening dickering passed before the Pilgrims could set out for America. When they did, it was with the financial backing of a group of London merchants who sent with them a rough company of some 60 "strangers"— artisans, indentured servants, and soldiers, including John Alden and Captain Miles Standish. These merchants had obtained a grant from the Virginia Company for a colony of their own. In return for their backing and the promise of continuing supplies, the settlers agreed to work together for seven years for the promoters. At the end of this period such profits as had been made were to be divided equally between the Londoners and the American community.

The mainstay of the Pilgrim group during the voyage and their first governor after they landed was the deacon, John Carver. Only second to him was William Bradford, his successor as governor on Carver's death from overwork in 1621. On finding themselves off Cape Cod in November, 1620, Carver and his colleagues decided to forego Virginia and to seek a suitable site in the region where God had led them. This decision made, they felt the urgency to form "a combination . . . before they came ashore, being the first foundation of their government in this place." Why they did this is well told by Bradford in his *Of Plymouth Plantation.* This "combination," Bradford writes, was

. . . occasioned partly by the discontented & mutinous speeches that some of the strangers amongst them had let fall from them in the ship—That when they came ashore, they would use their own liberty; for none had power to command them, the patent they had being for Virginia, and not for Newengland, which belonged to another Government. . . . And partly that such an act by them done . . . might be as firm as any patent, and in some respects more sure.

This "combination" was the memorable Mayflower Compact, the autonomous instrument of government by which the 41 members of the expedition who signed it on November 11,

. . . do by these presents solemnly and mutually in the presence of God and one of another, Covenant and Combine ourselves together into a Civil Body Politic, for our better ordering and preservation . . . ; and by virtue hereof to enact, constitute and frame such just and equal laws, . . . as shall be thought most meet and convenient for the general good of the Colony.

It was December 11 before the voyagers' searching party under Carver found Plymouth harbor, already so named by John Smith, "and marched into the land and found divers cornfields and little running brooks." On December 25, Christmas day to many but not to the Pilgrims who denounced it as another Romish "corruption" since men did not know when Christ was born, the main body "began to erect the first house for common use." That first winter half the colonists died, and only the friendship and tutelage of Squanto and his Indian friends, "a spetiall instrument sent by God for their good," preserved the remainder for another year. The Indians' own strength for possible resistance had been depleted three years before by a vicious plague that destroyed a third of their number, a visitation, the newcomers said, by which "divine providence made way for the quiet and peaceable settlement of the English in those nations." In November, 1621, the ship *Fortune* came with provisions to augment the first crops. Her arrival inspired the first Thanksgiving feast, a celebration which reduced supplies once more.

The Pilgrims by 1626 felt sufficiently well established to buy out the London investors who themselves had made no profit from the venture. This step severed all effective connection with the mother country, and the specific means by which the purchase was completed in effect established the colony as a joint-stock corporation. Those who subscribed to the purchase price, 53 men in the settlement and five friends in England, became freemen of the corporation and the colony. In 1628, when there were still fewer than 300 persons in Plymouth, each head of a family among the freemen received 20 acres of cleared land as his share. When Massachusetts Bay was settled in 1630 (see p. 55), the Council of New England confirmed Plymouth's right to its own territory, whose boundaries were now set for the first time.

In 1636, when new towns had been added to Plymouth and problems of government had grown more complex, the colony adopted the "Great Fundamentals," the first basic system of laws originating in the English colonies. These "Fundamentals" instituted a system of representative government in place of the arbitrary, informal rule of the Pilgrim founders. They prescribed the formation of a general court or unicameral legislature to which the freemen of each town might elect two deputies from among themselves, who would sit with the governor and his assistants. In Plymouth, as elsewhere in the corporate colonies, the rank of freeman was gradually extended to non-shareholders. In Plymouth, as in Massachusetts Bay, those aspiring to this rank had to survive the strictest examination by the divines, and those found "insufficient or troublesome" were rejected.

Until 1691, when it was absorbed into Massachusetts Bay, the Pilgrim community led an austere but independent existence, sustained chiefly by trade in fish and fur. "Let it not be grievous to you," one of their friends wrote from England, that "you have been but the instruments to break the ice for others; the honor shall be your's till the world's end."

THE COMMONWEALTH OF MASSACHUSETTS

The Pilgrims of Plymouth made up only a small minority of the Separatist exiles from England early in the seventeenth century. The Separatists themselves made up only a small minority of the whole body of Puritans, most of whom remained, in their own estimation, the only loyal members both of the kingdom and the Church of England. But even these Puritans felt by 1629, in the words of the lawyer, John Winthrop, that God was "turning the Cup toward us also, & because we are the last our portion must be, to drink the very dregs that remain." The following March, under Winthrop's direction, the Great Migration "to inhabit and continue in New England" began.

The Puritans had been anticipated in New England not only by the Pilgrim Fathers but also by a group of settlers on Cape Ann sent out in 1624 by promoters from Dorchester. When the promoters abandoned the project in 1626, forty or fifty of the newcomers, led by Roger Conant, established a settlement of their own at Naumkeag, soon renamed Salem. In 1628 a number of Puritan merchants and others, organized as the New England Company, obtained the rights of the Dorchester promoters and sent to Salem a vanguard of 40 Puritan settlers under John Endecott, who became governor there. They strengthened their title to the land by obtaining a patent from the Council of New England for the territory between the Charles and the Merrimack rivers. In 1629 the New England Company was reorganized as the Massachusetts Bay Company with a new charter from the king confirming its land title, which included the Salem settlement.

This company's charter resembled those granted to other trading companies. The colony was to be administered by a governor, a deputy-governor, and a council of assistants elected by the freemen sitting as its general court or "assemblie." It neglected, however, to specify the company's official residence or to declare that the colony must be administered from England. Winthrop, named governor of the company, and his colleagues hungrily seized upon this oversight to transfer the whole enterprise to Massachusetts, where, as Cotton Mather later explained, "we would have our posterity settled under the pure and full dispensation of the gospel; defended by rulers who should be ourselves." By winter, 1630, a thousand picked settlers had been landed in Massachusetts, and radiating from Boston, the Puritan capital, seven other towns were laid out. Within a decade, 25,000 persons had journeyed to the commonwealth. Winthrop and his colleagues, however, struggled manfully to keep control in the godly minority he headed.

This minority was so small at the start that when Winthrop, in October, 1630, ordered the government of the commonwealth to be set up, it was found that the provision of the charter requiring *eighteen* assistants, all of whom must be freemen, could not be met, for there were as yet not that many shareholders of the company in the colony. In order to proceed, some who were not freemen promptly were named assistants, and this tiny group constituted the full general court as well. Since the general court alone was empowered by the charter to make others freemen, the self-perpetuating nature of the oligarchy was obvious from the outset.

Before the end of the year, popular pressure compelled the general court to enlarge the number of freemen. At the same time, however, contrary to the charter, which required quarterly meetings of the court, the assistants limited its meetings to one a year. They also restricted the court's duties to electing the governor and assistants, who would then exercise all the powers of government, including the laying and collecting of taxes and the distribution of undivided land. In 1631 the assistants declared that no one could become a freeman who was not a member of a Puritan church—a difficult position to attain here as in Plymouth. Three years later the assistants ruled that no new church could be started without their consent.

These regulations were so harsh that petitioners demanded that Winthrop show them the charter under which they were imposed. Winthrop knew his administration had gone beyond its charter rights, and after unlocking and displaying the document he acknowledged the privileges and powers of the general court set forth in it. At the same time, rather than permit all the new freemen to sit in the general court, where they would easily outvote the free-

men who served as assistants, the latter made the court a representative body made up of themselves and two or three deputies elected by the freemen of each town. By 1644, the number of deputies even under this system had become too large for the assistants. They now divided the court into two houses, one of deputies and one of assistants, each with power to veto the acts of the other, a power the deputies in fact already had by their majority in the old court.

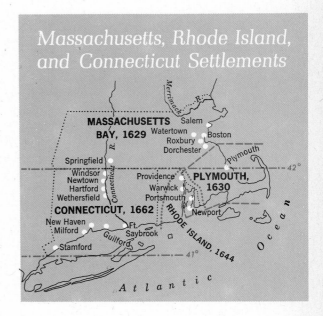

Massachusetts, Rhode Island, and Connecticut Settlements

By an act of 1635, the general court adopted the historic measure giving the freemen of the separate towns unprecedented freedom in town government. This act inaugurated the general town meeting at which, to this day in many small communities, the entire body of voters acts directly on such important matters as schools, roads, water supply, and police. But here, too, there was a catch at the time. Since only Puritan church members could be freemen under the law of 1631 (see above), this measure in effect extended the power of the oligarchy over localities, and did not mitigate at all the growing conflict for control of the Bible Commonwealth itself between the self-perpetuating "visible elect" and the less religious visibly successful.

As early as May, 1635, the visibly successful also began to press Winthrop to prepare and publish an explicit code of laws, "whereby," as the general court put it later, "we may manifest our utter disaffection to arbitrary government." The oligarchy managed to withstand the petitioners for thirteen years. When at last the general court published the great "Book of the General Lawes and Libertyes concerning the Inhabitants of the Massachusets" in 1648, it acknowledged that public laws made by self-governing freemen were to take precedence over the laws of God, as in the Mosaic code. Even so, the court said, "we had opportunity put into our hands . . . to frame our civil Polities, and Laws according to the rules of his most holy word whereby each do help and strengthen other (the Churches the civil Authoritie, and the civil Authoritie the Churches)" and the opportunity was not missed.

The year 1648 saw another momentous event in the running conflict between the "elect" and the others, with the elect again having their way. This event was the promulgation of the Cambridge Platform. On learning that Oliver Cromwell in England had received Baptists, Quakers, and members of other radical sects into his "New Model" Army, the General Court of Massachusetts that year called a synod, or general court of Puritan clergymen, to meet at Cambridge expressly to sever all remaining ties with Presbyterianism at home. Lest Cromwell's "pernicious errors" seep into Massachusetts, the synod went on to confirm the unity of church and state in the commonwealth and to make the secular government the explicit agent for enforcing the religious and moral decrees of the Puritan—now the Congregational—clergy. The "dictatorship of the visible elect," in Perry Miller's phrase, soon became known as "the New England Way."

The appeal to the force of the state seemed gradually to diminish Puritanism's moral strength. When the Anglican Church was re-established in England on the restoration of the Stuarts in 1660, and thus enjoyed a revival in America as well, those tired of Puritan engrossment found a welcome escape within the Anglican structure. Aware of this competition, and fearful of an English investigation of their "tyranny" under the New England Way, the Massachusetts General Court and the Congregational general synod in 1662 agreed to the "Half-Way Covenant," under which those who preferred not to run the rigors of seeking membership in the Congregational Church might now become freemen and participate equally with the elect in civic affairs. They might also have their children baptized into the Covenant of Grace.

Winthrop warned that New England's marked material success (see p. 59) would make the colonists "fall to embrace this present world and prosecute our carnall intentions." Yet Yankee merchants quickly came to the support of churches which, of course, were built in Massachusetts from the first. They also supported the college that was organized in 1636 to train the "learned clergy" of the future and gentlemen as well. In 1638, John Harvard, no stranger to wealth as it was judged at the time, bequeathed the new college his library and half his estate and since then it has borne his name. In 1642 and again in 1647, the general court, noting that "one chief point of that old deluder, Satan, [was] to keep men from a knowledge of the Scriptures . . . by keeping them in an unknown tongue," adopted legislation to further public education to insure that all might read and even "to fit youths for the university." This legislation proved ineffective (see p. 118); but it established the principle of compulsory public education new to the English-speaking world and served as an inspiration to other New England settlements.

THE RADICALS
OF RHODE ISLAND

Concession came hard to the leaders of Massachusetts Bay. In earlier times they used harsher means to deal with what Winthrop once called, "the seditious and undermineing practices of hereticall false brethren."

Among the first of the "false" was Roger Williams, the founder of Rhode Island, "a man," to quote Bradford, "having very many precious parts, but very unsettled in judgment." Williams was a Separatist who arrived in Massachusetts in 1631 after having encountered the wrath of Archbishop Laud at home. In Massachusetts he raised embarrassing issues—by asserting, for example, that the Bay colony had no just claim to Indian lands. He also denied that the Puritan rulers, or any others, had the right to compel men to engage in religious observances.

The magistrates insisted that "the powers that be are ordained by God . . . and they that resist shall receive to themselves damnation." Williams repudiated this doctrine not as a secular liberal but simply as a deeply religious man who doubted that "Judges are God upon earthe." The Puritan leaders recognized the dangerous undercurrent of his thinking and decided he would have to leave. Threatened with deportation to England, Williams, in the winter of 1635, fled to the region of Narragansett Bay. The following spring he established his own community there, which he called Providence, the foundation of later Rhode Island.

Three years later a second Rhode Island community was started by another refugee from Massachusetts, Anne Hutchinson. The sharp-witted wife of a mild Puritan merchant, Mrs. Hutchinson had moved from practical discussions of midwifery in Boston to more touchy analyses of sermons she heard on Sundays. Her incautious speculations soon split the town. Behind the jargon of Puritan theology lay an all-important question: Was it possible for a person to know that he had received the grace of God directly and to bypass scripture, ministerial authority, or logic? Anne Hutchinson insisted that it was. Immediately her enemies in Boston were convinced that Satan, not God, was the source of her inspiration, and the more she talked, the more certain they

became that she was "deluded by the Devil." In 1638 the magistrates ordered her expelled. Early the following year, on being excommunicated, she left Massachusetts for Rhode Island with her husband and children, and there founded a town, which later was called Portsmouth. On her husband's death in 1642 she moved to New York, near present-day New Rochelle, where she and her household were massacred by Indians in 1643.

By then, four loosely federated settlements existed in Rhode Island, and to insure their title to the land Williams sought a charter from Parliament, which he received in 1644. Under this charter, Rhode Island was organized with a corporate government similar to that of Massachusetts, with the privilege of electing its own governor. When a new charter was obtained from Charles II in 1663 and Rhode Island became a royal colony, it still retained its old governmental autonomy.

For many years, Rhode Island was the only colony in which all Christian sects enjoyed "liberty in religious concernments," as the charter put it, including the liberty to vote, whether a church member or not. Perhaps such libertarianism lay behind the attitude of the other New England colonies, which continued to regard Rhode Island as "Rogues' Island"—"the receptacle of all sorts of riff-raff people, and . . . nothing else than the latrina of New England."

THE EXPANSION
OF NEW ENGLAND

By 1643, Puritan settlements had spread beyond Rhode Island, westward to the Connecticut River, southward to Long Island Sound, and northward to New Hampshire and Maine. The Moses of the exodus into the fertile Connecticut Valley in the late 1630's was the Reverend Thomas Hooker, whose congregation had grown dissatisfied with the poor land around the village of Newtown (Cambridge). Hooker himself was too powerful and ambitious a man to be content with a subordinate role in Massachusetts affairs. Moreover, he was among those disturbed by the absence in Massachusetts of a codified body of law, a situation not rectified until 1648 (see p. 56).

The Fundamental Orders of Connecticut, drawn up in 1639 by delegates from the newly established towns of Hartford, Wethersfield, and Windsor, has been hailed as "the first written constitution of modern democracy." Actually, it was not democratic in our sense of the word, and it followed rather closely the Puritan theory of civil government and the implementation of the theory in the corporate charter of Massachusetts Bay. The Fundamental Orders dispensed with religious qualifications for citizenship so long as the candidate was "acceptable," but in effect only good Puritans were acceptable. Under its provisions, a general assembly or court was established to which each town might send four deputies. The general assembly chose a governor each year, and no governor could serve two years consecutively. It also elected a group of assistants to function as an upper house with the right (after 1645) to veto the legislation of the deputies. Similar patterns of government took form in the New Haven settlement on Long Island Sound, founded by the Reverend John Davenport and Theophilus Eaton in 1638, and in the nucleus of other towns that affiliated themselves with New Haven (1643-56). There was no relaxation of Puritan orthodoxy, and church membership continued to be a prerequisite for the franchise. Connecticut emerged as a separate colony in 1662, when, like Rhode Island the next year, it obtained a charter from the Crown which joined New Haven with the river towns. Like Rhode Island, although it now became a royal colony, Connecticut retained the right to elect its own governor.

The colonies of New Hampshire and Maine began as illegal settlements on the tracts of Captain John Mason and Sir Ferdinando Gorges, who between them owned all the land between the Merrimack and Kennebec rivers. Even though the two proprietors neglected to do anything themselves to develop their holdings, small settlements began to spring up here and there across the countryside. The gradual occupation of the New Hampshire area by Massachusetts emigrants foreshadowed its absorption into the Bay Colony in 1644. Charles II detached it again in 1679, and New Hampshire became a royal province. The Massachusetts penetration of Maine proceeded along the same lines, and after the death of Gorges in 1668 it was officially joined to Massachusetts.

The Puritans in Massachusetts like the Pilgrims in Plymouth, at first had encountered the smallest and least thickly settled Indian tribes of the entire eastern coast. These were mainly of the Algonquian culture, and their total number, as we have seen (p. 53), had already been reduced from about 25,000 to 16,000 by the fierce plague of 1616-17. Although they had had many unhappy experiences with English and other fishermen and traders before the Puritan settlements were established, these Indians were content to be friendly with the newcomers and, as in Virginia, first looked upon them as possible allies for their own forces in the constant tribal rivalries.

When the French and the Dutch, as well as the English, began to compete with one another after 1620 for Indian allies in the fur trade, the rivalry among the eastern tribes grew more intense. The rapid expansion of Massachusetts Bay in the 1630's soon added to the Indians' anxieties. The Puritans usually acquired Indian territory by fair purchase treaties, but the Indians, with no knowledge of private property or its laws, failed to understand what they had surrendered. Soon Indian raids on white frontier settlements changed the Puritan attitude from one of peaceful attempts to convert the red men to fearful retaliation.

The most important of the early Indian wars in New England saw the extermination of the Pequots, who dominated the Rhode Island and Connecticut areas around Long Island Sound. The Pequots were "Mohicans," not Algonquians. Their name, in fact, means "destroyer" in the Algon-quian tongue. In July, 1636, some Pequot tribesmen murdered a New England trader in their area, and the next spring a Con-necticut force set out for revenge. The Yan-kees routed the tribesmen, burned their main camp near present-day Stonington, Connecticut, and chased the remnants of the tribe to the vicinity of New Haven, where men converging from Plymouth, Massachusetts Bay, and northern Connecti-cut slaughtered them.

After describing the "stink and stench" of the Pequots burning, Bradford writes: "But the victory seemed a sweet sacrifice and they (the English) gave praise thereof to God." They also realized that the Indian, as well as the French and Dutch, menace was greater than they thought and that their efforts against the Pequots, successful though they proved, were poorly coordi-nated. In an effort to strengthen their re-sistance to the common danger, and also to promote their common interests, Massachu-setts Bay, Plymouth, Connecticut, and New Haven joined together in 1643 to form "The Confederation of the United Col-onies of New England," the first of a series of colonial efforts to work together. The very fact that the New Englanders set up the confederation was evidence that they felt perfectly capable of negotiating with the French and Dutch without consulting the mother country. The confederation re-fused to admit Rhode Island, whose lands were coveted by the other settlements as strongly as they detested her principles. Maine's petition for entrance also was turned down. According to the agreement, each of the four colonies elected two rep-resentatives who determined Indian policy, negotiated with foreign powers, and arbi-trated differences among themselves.

Although the confederation had lan-guished by the middle 1660's, its sternest test lay ahead. In June, 1675, a number of revived local tribes, organized in a confed-eration of their own under the Wampanoag chieftain, King Philip, attacked settlements around Plymouth. Soon a full-scale war was in progress between the braves and the New

England Confederation and other New England colonies. This war lasted a full year. About 500 Yankees lost their lives and more than 40 towns were pillaged and burned. At least 1,000 Indians also per-ished, but the survivors escaped to Canada and aided the French in further bedeviling northern New England.

In 1684 the confederation finally broke up. Massachusetts' overbearing behavior and her refusal on occasion to submit to majority rule may have speeded its end.

NEW ENGLAND'S
MATERIAL FOUNDATIONS

The New England countryside, with the exception of the Connecticut and Merrimack valleys, was less fertile than the Chesapeake region. As the years passed, small farms and compact villages grew up among the New England hills. When a group of settlers wanted to establish a new town (for, unlike the Virginians, the New Englanders planned their expansion be-forehand), they obtained permission from the general court to settle a new block of land of approximately six square miles ad-joining an older one. The settlers laid out the main street, the village green, the cen-trally located church, the school, the town lots, and fields or strips adjacent to the village. All freemen were eligible to draw for the town lots and to make use of the undistributed woods and meadows. The richer settlers sometimes got additional lots, but even the most favored never received more than two or three times as much land as the poorest.

This system of establishing new towns carried with it certain disadvantages, no-tably that the original proprietors retained control over the future distribution of un-divided land. This power set them apart from the late-comers who along with land-less and voteless tenants and laborers soon formed a disgruntled majority. Disputes be-tween the old settlers and the new often

New England cod fishermen.

ended with the latter moving west to newer settlements, and gradually the old New England system of planned expansion broke down. By 1725, in New England as well as in the colonies farther south, townships were being sold to speculators instead of to communities of settlers. During most of the seventeenth century, however, the New England plan of settling the new country worked effectively, and it insured that the culture of the region was carried to new frontiers more or less intact.

About 85 per cent of New England settlers during this period engaged in subsistence agriculture and home industry. The more ambitious 15 per cent, finding the land intractable, had turned to the water. Fishing off the banks of Newfoundland became so important in the Massachusetts economy that the cod was placed on the commonwealth's coat of arms. Enough fish were caught for export to the West Indies and elsewhere, along with foodstuffs and timber, and all together nurtured a class of Yankee merchants as sharp and self-important as any in the world. Commerce, like fishing, greatly stimulated shipbuilding; and Yankee ships were at once so seaworthy and so cheap they were soon being built for foreign as well as domestic sale. As early as 1644 iron was being smelted in Massachusetts, and rum was being distilled from West Indian molasses. New England craftsmen also made many of the commodities needed in the colony, such as furniture, silverware, pottery, hardware, and tools, articles which the Yankees, who did not have a big export staple such as the southerners had in tobacco, could not easily pay for abroad.

IV. *The Completion of Mainland Colonization*

THE CAROLINAS AND GEORGIA

While England was torn by civil war and problems of the Cromwellian Protectorate from 1640 to 1660 (see p. 42), emigration to America practically ceased. With the restoration of the Stuarts in the person of Charles II in 1660, new men came into power with claims on the new king and designs on the New World. During the following three-quarters of a century seven new colonies, most of them established by such men, and all growing from proprietary grants, completed the roster of those that became the United States.

The first of the Restoration colonies was called Carolina and extended from the southern boundary of Virginia to the borders of Spanish Florida and as far westward as the continent itself. This princely domain was granted by Charles II in 1663 to eight of his friends who had been instrumental in placing him on the throne. Among them were rich men who had made their fortunes in sugar-growing in Barbados. Since England by this time had altered its views about excess population at home, and indeed, in 1660, explicitly forbade the migration of skilled artisans, these men proposed to people their land in America with tenants from the West Indies and elsewhere in the New World. On the model of the similar proprietorship in Maryland, they also expected further to enrich themselves by collecting quit-rents from their tenants.

As early as 1653, Virginia had permitted some of her own more intractable settlers actually to occupy the northern area of the Carolina grant around Albemarle Sound as buffers against the Spanish and the Indians. In 1664 the new proprietors named a governor for this area. Albemarle, as it was now formally called, continued to draw Virginia malcontents who resisted control as successfully as their soil resisted cultivation. Poor access to the sea further contrived to keep the settlers poor. As in Virginia, their main crop was tobacco and their main outlets were in the Old Dominion itself. When, in 1679, Virginia forbade any further importation of the Albemarle leaf, the growers began to dispose of it to bold Yankee traders who carried it directly to the European continent in defiance of the English navigation acts then in force (see p. 68).

In addition to such smugglers, Albemarle became the haunt of pirates who preyed on Spanish shipping, of runaway slaves, defaulting debtors, and other discreditable persons. After 1691, when it acquired the name of North Carolina, this region was looked upon by the aristocrats of Virginia and South Carolina as a "lubberland," the home of paper-money agitation and other economic heresies as well as distasteful political equality and religious toleration.

The Carolina "Lord Proprietors" began the settlement of the more southerly parts of their domain around the Cape Fear River in 1665 when they brought in the first contingent of Barbadians from among those who had been squeezed off the land by the growth of great sugar plantations in the island. The proprietors provided these settlers with a government under liberal "Concessions and Agreements," which granted them liberty of conscience and generous representation in a one-house legislature. Within two years this experiment failed; many of the Barbadians returned to the island, the rest scattered elsewhere.

In 1668 Sir Anthony Ashley Cooper, who had emerged as the leader among the proprietors, persuaded the famous philosopher, John Locke, to become secretary of the group and devise a framework of government deliberately designed to "avoid erecting a numerous democracy." The result was the remarkable document known as, "The Fundamental Constitutions of Carolina," which made the Maryland manorial plan seem a model of practical wisdom. How much Locke himself contributed to the provisions for a hereditary nobility of "seignors," each endowed with 12,000 acres, and lesser "landgraves," "caciques" and "lords of the manor," is debatable. The Fundamental Constitutions also provided for a governor to be appointed by the proprietors in England, and a one-house legislature made up of the great landholders and of deputies (owners of at least 500 acres) elected by freeholders (owning at least 50 acres).

In the succeeding years, about fifty great estates actually were set up, few of them, however, on a hereditary basis. As settlement proceeded, the Fundamental Constitutions gradually were liberalized, a bicameral legislature was established, and the lower house, here as elsewhere in the English colonies, assumed ever greater powers. By the end of the century, the Fundamental Constitutions had been wholly superseded in practice. In 1721 South Carolina was proclaimed a royal colony and in 1729, when the proprietors at last yielded their charter to the Crown, North Carolina attained the same status. In South Carolina, the aristocratic spirit of the Fundamental Constitutions persisted. Property qualifications for office-holding and voting there, for example, became among the highest in the British mainland empire.

The first settlement under the Fundamental Constitutions was begun in March, 1670, off Port Royal Sound, with the arrival

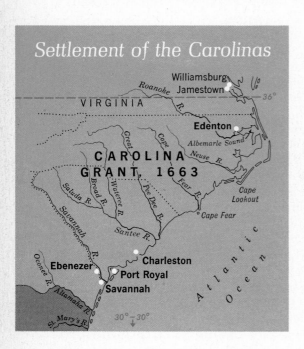

Settlement of the Carolinas

of an expedition of Englishmen augmented by Barbadians and other West Indians picked up on the way. Fear of the Spanish this far south prompted a northward move a month later to the Ashley River. Twenty-five miles up the river Charles Towne was begun. In 1680, the town was moved to its present site where the Ashley and Cooper

rivers meet. A successful war in 1671 against the Kusso Indians, thought to be conspiring with the Spanish against the new settlement, led to the enslavement of captured braves, an experiment which soon led to Indian wars simply to provide more captives for this slave trade (see p. 83). By 1680 South Carolina traders had spread as far south as the Savannah River. A war that year with the Westos of the region convinced the red men that they had better cooperate with the Charles Towne traders in supplying furs, deer hides, and other skins, as well as more captive Indians. This traffic rapidly was converting Charles Towne into a flourishing trading post. Its cosmopolitan populations grew after 1685, when Louis XIV resumed persecution of the Huguenots and French Protestant refugees flooded in.

In the 1690's rice became South Carolina's export staple, the plantation system spread, and Negro slavery, with many harsh aspects more characteristic of the West Indies than the mainland, fed the sense of superiority among the masters, as it did in Virginia. The large landholders held firm to the reins of government in Charles Towne (as Charleston was called until 1783), where most of them lived as absentee landlords. In the eighteenth century (see p. 83), absenteeism only made more bitter the usual conflicts between grandees and frontier settlers.

Spain, outraged by the formation of South Carolina on her borders, was furious when in 1732 George II granted the unsettled southernmost part of Carolina, reclaimed by the Crown in 1729, to a group of British philanthropists whose spokesman was the reformer, James Oglethorpe. The next year, Oglethorpe landed the first hundred settlers of Georgia, as he called his grant, above the mouth of the Savannah River, where they established the town of Savannah.

The Crown regarded Georgia as a military outpost; the proprietors hoped to make it an asylum for Englishmen imprisoned for debt. Oglethorpe himself envisioned a community of small farmers who might also comprise a yeoman militia. No person, the trustees ruled, could own more than 500 acres, and the land could be passed on only to male heirs. Slavery was prohibited, for both humanitarian and strategic reasons, and the importation of rum and brandy was banned. The trustees had unrealistically planned an economy based on the production of wine and silk, neither of which required slave labor. They felt that Negroes would be a military hazard if the Spaniards ever succeeded in inducing them to revolt against their masters.

These regulations did not sit well with the mixed group of Welsh, Scots, English, and Germans who had come to Georgia to improve their fortunes. These Georgians found active supporters among the South Carolinians who gradually infiltrated the colony and soon made it their satellite. The ban on the importation of rum was removed in 1742, and after 1749 slavery was permitted and rice-planting spread. Three years later Georgia became a royal colony. By then parliament itself had appropriated more than £135,000 to further Georgia's

humanitarian and imperialistic future. The humanitarian phase now passed. Spain herself never conceded Georgia's existence, and not until the United States purchased Florida from Spain in 1819 was the incendiary southern border of Georgia defined.

NEW YORK AND NEW JERSEY

In the 1660's, while the expansion of New England encroached on New France in the north, and the establishment of the Carolinas encroached on New Spain in the south, England's principal maritime rival, the Dutch, with their colony of New Netherland, split England's growing mainland empire in two. New Netherland, with forts at Albany and Kingston and the thriving town of nearly 10,000 at New Amsterdam on Manhattan Island, dominated the whole range of the Hudson Valley. Her allies, the Iroquois, moreover, dominated the country west of the Hudson, radiating from the Mo-

The tip of Manhattan Island, New Amsterdam, 1660.

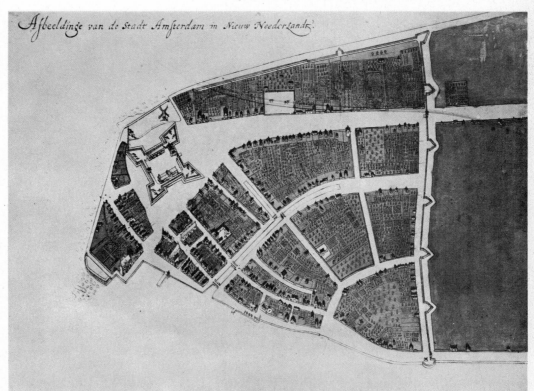

hawk Valley, so that together they controlled the first great gateway to the West south of the St. Lawrence River. New Netherland also extended east of the Hudson to the Connecticut River and southwest to the Delaware, but the Dutch did little to develop the distant reaches of their claim. In 1655 they extinguished the settlement of New Sweden on the Delaware, but otherwise evicted few squatters.

The English in the later seventeenth century certainly coveted the expanse of Dutch territory. Yet their main quarrel with the Dutch in America, as in Europe and Asia, arose from the latter's free-wheeling infringement upon the sea-going traffic the English now tried increasingly to keep for themselves. Dutch ships, like England's own and those of the upstart Puritans of Massachusetts as well, sailed everywhere for cargo and markets. To check Dutch traffic on American waters, the English, in 1664, decided to expel the Dutch from America.

In March, 1664, with Parliament's consent, Charles II granted to his brother, the Duke of York, all the territory between the Connecticut and the Delaware rivers. In April, the Duke commissioned Colonel Richard Nicolls, with a force of four frigates, to secure the grant. Nicolls reached New Amsterdam at the end of August and within ten days, without resistance, Governor Peter Stuyvesant capitulated. The Dutch at home retaliated by declaring war on England. When they made peace in 1667 they acknowledged the loss of New Amsterdam, but during the renewal of the war they recaptured New York, as New Amsterdam had been renamed, in 1673. When the new war ended the next year, the Dutch finally gave up the town for good.

Four new English colonies were carved from the Dutch mainland empire—New York, New Jersey, Pennsylvania and Delaware. Until 1683, New York was ruled as the Dutch had ruled it, with an absolute governor and council, and with the same unfortunate results. In 1683 a new governor, Colonel Thomas Dongan, arrived in New York with instructions to create an elected assembly privileged to meet every three years and to enact provincial taxes. By the time this assembly held its first meeting in 1686, the Duke of York had ascended the throne as James II and had made New York a royal colony. When the assembly's legislative efforts reached him for approval, he rejected them, restored the absolute rule of governor and council, and ordered the assembly dissolved.

New York had to wait a few years yet, and to endure a violent rebellion in the bargain, before it joined the other colonies in enjoying a representative government (see p. 70). Not until well into the eighteenth century, moreover, did New York begin to take advantage of its unparalleled harbor and rich inland soil to develop its economy.

In 1664, Colonel Nicolls, who had become James' governor in New York for four years following the capitulation of Peter Stuyvesant, tried to strengthen the colony by inviting English Puritans from eastern Long Island to settle in its southeasterly portion between the Hudson and the Delaware. To make his invitation more appealing, Nicolls offered them their own representative assembly. Many Long Islanders accepted the invitation and thereby offset the preponderance of Netherlanders already living in the northwesterly part of this region.

Unbeknown to Nicolls, James himself in 1664 had granted the whole region from the Hudson to the Delaware to two of his aristocratic friends, Sir George Carteret and John, Lord Berkeley, who proceeded to name it New Jersey, after the Isle of Jersey where Carteret had once served as governor. All James had granted them was the soil and the right to quit-rents from it; but on no greater authority than Nicoll's own, Carteret and Berkeley in 1665 offered their settlers a set of "Concessions and Agreements" modeled on the liberal ones issued that same year in Carolina (see page 61). They also named Philip Carteret, a relative of Sir George, as governor. The Dutch in the northwesterly section accepted the new proprietors and their government; the Puritans in the southeasterly section resisted them.

In 1674 Berkeley and Carteret divided their holdings, Berkeley taking the northwesterly portion which he promptly sold to a group of Quakers. In 1676 this division was formalized by the creation of West Jersey (Berkeley's portion), and East Jersey (Carteret's). On Carteret's death in 1680, a second group of Quaker proprietors bought East Jersey from his estate and under their liberal control the Jerseys became a haven for the persecuted. The Puritans continued to resist Quaker rule until the Crown reunited East and West Jersey in 1702, giving it one representative assembly under the governor of New York. New Jersey did not have a royal government of its own until 1738.

PENNSYLVANIA AND DELAWARE

In 1681, William Penn, who had been largely responsible for the liberal government of West Jersey, acquired a charter from Charles II that enabled him to found a colony of his own. The son of an aristocratic and wealthy British admiral, Penn, at this time thirty-seven years old, had been infected with Quaker ideas as a young boy. Despite the attempts of his angry father to make him renounce the principles of what was then a despised sect, he held onto them doggedly throughout his life.

Like other dissenters, the Quakers rejected the ritual and hierarchical organization of the Anglican Church, but they also rejected the Calvinism of the Puritans. George Fox (1624-91), the founder of the Religious Society of Friends, as the Quakers called themselves, was a mystic who felt himself divinely commissioned to preach the new creed: that man's love for God could best be shown by man's love for man, and that salvation was possible for all. Every Quaker regarded himself as a member of the priesthood, since all men possessed the "inner light" that enabled them to hear God's voice. The radical egalitarianism of the Quakers—their refusal to swear oaths, to fight, to accept class distinctions— seemed a threat to the existing order, and they were savagely persecuted both in Europe and America. And yet they prospered through their diligence and frugality.

After the death of his father, Penn set out to fulfill his dream of providing a refuge for his persecuted brethren. In exchange for a debt Charles II had owed his father, Penn in 1681 obtained a grant to a large area in the Delaware region north of Maryland that had once been part of New Netherland but that lay outside the Duke of York's original proprietorship. To "Sylvania"— Penn's name for his forest-covered province —the King attached the prefix "Penn" in honor of his old friend, the Admiral.

The terms of Penn's charter did not give him the sweeping powers enjoyed by the early proprietors, for British officials had begun to check colonial pretensions to self-rule. Nevertheless, Penn laid down a plan of government that was certainly the most liberal in the colonies and perhaps in the world. It called for a two-chambered parliament, both houses to be elected by the freemen. The upper house would propose legislation; the lower house would ratify or reject it. Since the ownership of a small amount of land or the payment of taxes entitled a man to vote, suffrage was widely held. Only the Rhode Islanders could claim so liberal a franchise.

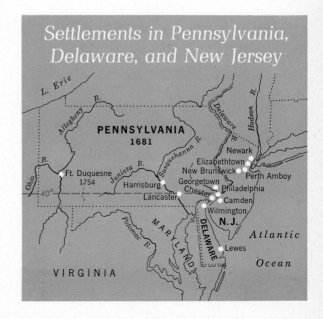

Settlements in Pennsylvania, Delaware, and New Jersey

Even though Penn's government and humane legal code proved attractive to settlers, non-Quakers in the colony fought his administration from the start. Moreover, boundary disputes with New York and Maryland, together with charges in 1692 that he favored the cause of the exiled James II, made his position insecure. In 1692, he in fact lost his charter, and his colony was directed for the next two years by the governor of New York. In 1694, the Crown restored the proprietary government, but Penn remained in England until 1699. Though disgusted with his enemies, Penn liberalized his government even further. The "Charter of Privileges" granted in 1701 reduced proprietary authority to a minimum and made the assembly the real law-making body, although subject to vetoes by the governor; it also gave partial self-government to the counties west of the Delaware that once had belonged to the Swedes. Delaware itself, though granted to Penn in 1682, was officially detached from Pennsylvania in 1701 and its first legislature met in 1704. Until the Revolution, however, Delaware had the same governor as Pennsylvania.

The immediate success and extraordinary progress of Pennsylvania indicate how much practical wisdom the colonists had accumulated since the days of Jamestown and Plymouth. Penn carefully selected the site for Philadelphia before the first settlers had even arrived, and he laid out his city with foresight. By making friends with the Indians, he insured an interval of peace that lasted for 75 years. That his province turned out to be fertile and that its beginnings happened to coincide with religious persecutions on the Continent, were, of course, accidental. But Penn skillfully took advantage of his opportunities. He circulated a prospectus for his colony in England and on the Continent and persuaded hundreds of German sectarians from the Rhineland to migrate. Colonists of all faiths were attracted by Penn's guarantee of complete religious toleration for anyone who worshiped God. By 1689, there were 12,000 settlers in Pennsylvania. A flourishing trade quickly sprang up with the West Indies, where Pennsylvania's pork, beef, wheat, and flour were in great demand. Pennsylvania soon became the richest colony in North America (see p. 83). Ironically, the proprietor did not share in the colony's good fortune. Penn, who returned to England in 1701, was ruined by a dishonest steward and landed in a debtor's prison for a short time. The province was mortgaged to trustees in 1708. Penn died in 1718.

v. *Consolidation of the Imperial System*

THE SPIRIT OF MERCANTILISM

The permanent settlement of the mainland colonies, their economic growth, political maturity, and strategic expansion, all occurred within the framework of the emerging British mercantilist system. Of course, many of the colonists went largely untouched by this system. Perhaps as many as nine out of every ten mainland settlers lived on subsistence farms. On these farms families grew their own corn and grain, raised their own meat, wove their own cloth, built much of their own furniture, and made many of their own tools. If they had surplus crops to dispose of, they often bartered them locally for such commodities as salt, iron, and ammunition, which they could not make at home. Thus the vast majority of Americans in all sections shared an independence of the market, of the fluctuating value of money, of the ups and downs of international trade. But they also lived outside the mainstream of economic growth and international tension which carried the world onward and from time to time also caught up even the most isolated in problems of government, war, and rebellion.

The mercantilist system was one in which economic activity was organized and controlled—insofar as organization and control could be applied—for the advantage not of the individual but of the rising national state. Spain, Portugal, France, the Netherlands, and England all lived under some sort of mercantilist system from the fifteenth to the nineteenth century. Such a system, indeed, was the means by which each of these states mobilized its economic resources behind its national aims. Since these aims usually were in conflict and often led to war, one of the fundamental goals of the mercantilist system was to preserve and enlarge a nation's gold supply by which armies and navies were supported. The rush to America in the sixteenth and seventeenth centuries was strongly motivated, as we have seen, by the quest for gold hoards and gold mines.

Where there was little or no gold, as in the English mainland colonies, bullion was sought through the regulation of trade. Stated simply, colonies were useful for selling raw materials cheaply to the mother country and buying her manufactures dearly, thereby giving the mother country a favorable edge in the exchange which, by further exchange elsewhere, she could convert into gold. An important corollary of this mode of exchange, lest gold be paid out to foreigners for services, was the requirement that commodities going in either direction be carried in national or colonial ships. Lest gold also be paid to foreigners for goods, another corollary of the mercantilist system was the granting of bounties to colonial settlers to encourage the production of critical commodities. The British, for example, paid Americans bounties for producing hemp for ships' ropes, for refining tar for pitch, for cutting timber for ships' masts, and for growing indigo for the manufacture of dyes.

The mercantilist system worked best in connection with overseas colonies that produced great agricultural staples—such as the tobacco of Virginia and Maryland and the sugar of the West Indian islands. The planters of these staples found a protected market for their products in the mother country. They were also granted extensive credit for the manufactures they bought. British exporters, assured of payment in marketable crops each year, as we have

seen (p. 48), encouraged the colonial planters to live well.

The mercantilist system had fewer attractions to the merchants of the Middle colonies and fewest of all to those of New England who had to roam the world in their ships to get sufficiently ahead in their transactions to earn money for the good life. Earn it they did, but in ways that brought little benefit to the mother country.

ADMINISTRATION
OF THE NAVIGATION ACTS

As early as 1620 the English ordered that Virginia tobacco, although its principal users were on the Continent, must be exported exclusively to England in English bottoms. Subsequent "navigation acts" placed additional colonial products under similar mercantilist restrictions. The system was enlarged under Cromwell in the early 1650's, when Dutch carriers took advantage of English internal conflicts to encroach on English overseas trade. After the restoration of the Stuarts in 1660, the Crown was urged to tighten the reins on its New World settlements in order to improve the revenues of the kingdom. Heretofore, only occasional parliamentary committees were charged with the responsibility for administering the navigation acts, and little real attention had been paid to their enforcement. Early in the 1660's, Charles II created a "civil list" of crown employees to give full time to colonial regulation, while Parliament stiffened the navigation code.

One of the new measures was the Navigation Act of 1660, re-enacted by the first regular Restoration Parliament in 1661, which provided that no goods or commodities could be brought to or sent out of any English colony except in ships that were owned by Englishmen and operated by an English master with a crew at least three-fourths English. This requirement worked no hardship on the colonials, because the term "English" was always understood to include English subjects in the colonies. The act also required that certain "enumerated articles"—chiefly sugar, tobacco, indigo, and cotton-wool—that were grown or manufactured in the colonies be sold only to England or to another colony. Among the first enumerated articles only tobacco was of major importance, but other items were added from time to time. This measure was intended to keep other countries from obtaining commodities from the colonies, but the mother country had no intention of harming the trade of the colonies themselves. To assure the colonials the full benefit of the English market, the act forbade the growing of tobacco in England and the importing of tobacco from foreign countries into England.

In 1663, another Navigation Act was passed to give English merchants a monopoly of colonial trade, and this one affected the colonists more seriously. It required, with a few exceptions (salt, wine from Madeira and the Azores, and provisions, horses, and servants from Scotland and Ireland), that all European goods destined for the colonies be shipped by way of English ports and on English ships. Import and export duties were charged on this transshipment, but a system of rebates enabled the colonists to buy foreign goods coming by way of England about as cheaply as Englishmen could buy them at home. The colonial merchants, none the less, complained that the measure was a serious limitation and inconvenience, since in some cases the required stop-over in England added an extra leg to the return voyage from the Continent. They began to violate the Act of 1660, with its enumerated articles, by shipping directly to European ports, and to violate the Act of 1663 by smuggling European goods directly back to the colonies without stopping at England.

Parliament passed a third Navigation Act, which became effective in 1673, in an attempt to stop up some of the loopholes. Colonial shippers, for example, would pretend that they were taking enumerated articles to another colonial port, but after having cleared that port they would strike out for Europe, carrying their illegal cargoes with them. To stop this easy practice, the Act of 1673 assessed duties in the colonies *at the port of clearance,* unless the captain would bind himself to take the cargo to England. In order to collect these new export duties, a staff of officials was set up in the colonies and before long a good deal of friction had developed between the colonials and the royal officials. One of the most meddlesome of these officers was Edward Randolph, who harassed the New Englanders for many years after 1676.

After the Restoration, much of the authority to make recommendations on colonial policy and colonial trade had been granted to the Committee for Trade and Plantations of the Privy Council, more commonly known as the Lords of Trade. As early as 1664, a royal commission had been sent to investigate infringements of crown authority in Massachusetts. Finally, convinced by Randolph's charges against the colonials, the Privy Council annulled Massachusetts' charter and made plans to overhaul the entire system of colonial administration. The annulment occurred in 1684. In 1685, James II became king and in the following year began to consolidate all the northern colonies into one administrative unit, called the "Territory and Dominion of New England." This "Dominion" included all the New England colonies, together with New York and East and West New Jersey—an unwieldy realm administered from Boston by the stubborn and dictatorial Sir Edmund Andros, James' governor.

Andros abolished the colonial assemblies and even tried to force the colonists to worship in the Anglican Church. No one could have reconciled Massachusetts to these steps, but Andros made matters even worse by the insolence with which he offended Yankee sentiments. Everyone felt threatened by his policies, especially by his attempt to undermine the validity of the Massachusetts land titles. In 1687, Massachusetts sent her leading minister, Increase

Mather, to England to try to retrieve the charter and effect Andros' recall.

THE GLORIOUS REVOLUTION
IN ENGLAND AND AMERICA

Edward Randolph and Sir Edmund Andros were not the only members of the Stuart "civil list" to incite the Americans. Both Charles II and James II filled colonial offices with indigent court favorites to help them make or recoup their fortunes at the Americans' expense. Others sent over were royal zealots, inquisitors who boldly overrode colonial liberties as well as those of English merchants in the colonial trade. Before long, these merchants so tired of James' administrators and of the King himself that they joined with others in forcing James to abandon the throne and flee to France in 1688. Most of these others were aroused by James' militant Catholicism. On taking the throne in 1685, James was forced to put down a Puritan revolt under the Duke of Monmouth, after which he suppressed dissenters with such zeal that Anglicans themselves took fright. He also flouted the Test Act of 1673, which prohibited all but Anglicans from holding public office in England, by placing many Catholics in positions of power. Such actions shook even royalist Tories who believed in the doctrine of the divine right of kings. When James fathered a son in June, 1688, the dire menace of a new Catholic succession chilled the English soul, and Tories and Whigs together drove James out.

A parliamentary committee itself now boldly invited William of Orange, the Dutch Protestant husband of James' daughter Mary, to England. After some months devoted, as a historian has put it, to "decently covering up the unpleasant rents in the fabric of the constitution," the reign of William and Mary, or of William III, began in February, 1689. At that time, Parliament also adopted the "Bill of Rights," opening with an array of accusations against James II foreshadowing those arrayed against George III by the Americans in July, 1776. The famous "Bill" then proceeded to set forth the rights of Englishmen under the law. No Catholic could henceforth occupy the throne. Dissenters might worship openly as they pleased, but public office remained closed to them and to others not subscribing to the communion of the Church of England.

Such was the peaceful "Glorious Revolution," which, at least for English constitutional theory during the life of the new rulers, seemed to give the elected representatives of the "people" superiority over their "elected" king. As elaborated by John Locke (see p. 120), this theory became one of the pillars of the colonists' own argument later, that since they did not participate in the election of parliamentary representatives in England, their allegiance must be only to their own local "parliaments" and the king *these* parliaments chose to recognize.

On learning of James' abdication, the Puritans of Massachusetts, even before news of the Glorious Revolution reached America, conducted a bloodless revolution of their own. In April, 1689, an armed band of Boston citizens marched against Andros, forced him to seek refuge in a fort, and aroused the public to such a high pitch of feeling against him that he capitulated and went to jail. An ad hoc "council" of the general court ruled Massachusetts until the Commonwealth was brought under a new royal charter in 1691. This charter reflected the failure of Increase Mather's mission. No longer would Massachusetts elect its own governor. Henceforth, he would be appointed by the Crown. His council would be elected by the general court, subject to the governor's veto. General court legislation itself was to be subject to review in England. The new charter ended Plymouth's independent existence. Along with Maine it was incorporated in Massachusetts Bay. Andros' downfall in Massachusetts had prompted Connecticut and Rhode

Island to resume their old regimes which they were now permitted to continue.

In New York, meanwhile, Andros' deputy, Francis Nicholson, resigned on learning of his superior's plight. In May, 1689, Jacob Leisler, a German trader in Manhattan since its Dutch days, took advantage of Nicholson's absence to call upon neighboring counties and towns to set up a representative government for the first time. Backed by dissident elements who were alarmed by rumors of a French invasion and a Catholic conspiracy, Leisler managed civil affairs vigorously and efficiently for several months. But by disregarding a message he had intercepted from the Crown ordering Nicholson to conduct colonial affairs until new authorities took over, he gave support to the charges of his enemies that he was a revolutionist and a usurper. When in March, 1691, Leisler resisted the deputy William III sent over, he was captured and soon tried and sentenced to death along with seven of his men. Leisler and his son-in-law, his closest follower, were hanged in May. The others were pardoned by the Crown, which proceeded to bring order to New York, as elsewhere, with the establishment of royal and representative government there.

THE ENGLISH SYSTEM
AFTER 1696

William III brought with him to England his traditional continental rivalry with the Catholic French, which was only intensified by Louis XIV's hospitality to the ousted James II. As early as 1689, this rivalry flared up in the War of the League of Augsburg, the opening conflict in the world wars of the eighteenth century over the domination of North America as well as other regions (see p. 97). To strengthen his position at home, William III undertook to strengthen the Anglican establishment. To strengthen his position in the New World he enlarged, as we have seen, the number of royal colonies and in other ways strengthened the position of the royal governors. Starting in 1696, he also re-vamped the administration and extended the reach of the navigation system.

As the Crown's chief representative in the colonies, the royal governor came to possess broad powers. He could summon and dissolve assemblies, veto their legislation, appoint minor officials. The upper house, or council, served as his advisory board, with executive, legislative, and judicial functions. Except in Massachusetts, it was chosen from among leading colonials by the Board of Trade in England. But since the governor's recommendations influenced the board in its choice of council members, his friendship counted much to the wealthy and capable colonials who sought his favors. With all his dignity and authority, however, the governor found himself caught between colonial and royal crossfire. As the symbol and spokesman of the Crown, he was expected to follow instructions from England that reflected the rigid policies of British officialdom, the interests of British merchants, and decisions of the Board of Trade which were made thousands of miles away from the scene of their application. Yet at the same time he had to respect the needs of the colony and keep from offending its leaders, among whom he had to live. The job called for remarkable tact, a genius for knowing when to compromise and when to stand firm, but even the best of governors gradually lost their primacy to the colonial assemblies (see p. 91).

The changes in the navigation system after 1696 did little to improve the governors' prospects of good relations with the Americans. In May, that year, the Stuarts' old administrative agency, the Lords of Trade (see p. 68), was supplanted by the Lords Commissioners of Trade and Plantations, commonly known as the Board of Trade. With the Privy Council, it administered colonial relations until the Revolution. New parliamentary navigation acts then strengthened the board's hand. New customs offices were to be set up in each colony, with customs officials given the same powers as those in England, including access to "writs of assistance" by which they could invoke constabulary aid in forcing their way into suspect private premises. Offenders against the new navigation code were henceforth to be tried in new admiralty courts. Manned by royal, not provincial, judges, these courts could try colonial merchants without juries. The admiralty courts became one of the most detested of all English institutions. The navigation code itself also was strengthened by the "enumeration" of more commodities which had to be shipped exclusively to England. Parliament also began to ban the exportation to England of colonial wheat, flour, and fish which competed with England's own. Starting with the Wool Act of 1699, moreover, colonial craftsmen were forbidden to export and later even to make many manufactured goods in which English merchants were thus given a monopoly.

And yet the colonies prospered. The modern reader may easily imagine that English regulation of American affairs was more burdensome to the colonies than it actually was. Smuggling and other modes of evasion went largely unpunished. American as well as English merchants, moreover, benefited from the exclusion of the Dutch and others from the imperial trade and from protection from enemies on the sea. To draw up a balance sheet of the gains and losses of American membership in the Empire would be difficult. What seems certain, however, is that the apparatus of colonial regulation and control schooled the Americans first in the arts of evasion and then in the defiance of authority. Although on principle they accepted most of the regulations of the old colonial system, in practice they were extremely uneasy about conforming with the demands of any external authority. These demands grew harsher as Britain's costly wars with the French approached their showdown phase, and the friction engendered by mounting British pressure on the colonies went far to rekindle the spirit of independence that had been so marked in the early settlements.

Readings

Asterisk indicates that book is available in paperback.

The works of A. L. Rowse cited at the end of the Readings for Chapter 1 afford a stirring introduction to the English background of American settlement. S. T. Bindoff, *Tudor England* * (1950), and G. M. Trevelyan, *England Under the Stuarts* (1904), are scholarly general accounts. J. E. Neale, *Queen Elizabeth* * (1934), is probably the best biography. Neale, *Elizabeth I and Her Parliaments* (2 vols., 1958), is excellent on parliamentary development. C. D. Bowen, *The Lion and the Throne, The Life and Times of Sir Edward Coke 1552-1634* * (1957), helps carry this story through early Stuart years. William Haller, *The Rise of Puritanism* * (1938), and C. H. and Katherine George, *The Protestant Mind of the English Reformation 1570-1640* (1961), are good introductions to the religious controversy. They may be supplemented by C. V. Wedgewood, *The King's Peace 1637-1641* (1955). M. St. Clare Byrne, *Elizabethan Life in Town and Country* * (rev. ed., 1961), is illuminating on social conditions. A. V. Judges, ed., *The Elizabethan Underworld* (1930), is a scholarly anthology of Tudor and early Stuart tracts and ballads. Charles Wilson, *England's Apprenticeship 1603-1763* (1965), opens with an able survey of the early Stuart economy. Wallace Notestein, *The English People on the Eve of Colonization* (1954), affords a useful summary of many facets of English life.

The first three volumes of C. M. Andrews, *The Colonial Period of American History* * (4 vols., 1934-1938), afford the most satisfactory extended account of American settlement. The fourth volume is excellent on England's commercial and colonial policy. The standard single-volume account of the colonial period is C. P. Nettels, *The Roots of American Civilization* (1938). Three books by T. J. Wertenbaker cover the social history of the early colonial period under the general title, *The Founding of American Civilization*. These are *The Old South* (1942), *The Middle Colonies* (1938), and *The Puritan Oligarchy* * (1947).

W. F. Craven, *The Southern Colonies in the Seventeenth Century 1607-1789* (1949), is outstanding on Virginia and her neighbors. P. L. Barbour, *The Three Worlds of Captain John Smith* (1964), is the best biography, with much illuminating material on early Virginia. G. F. Willison, *Behold Virginia* (1952), is an informal but scholarly account. T. J. Wertenbaker, *The Shaping of Colonial Virginia* (1958 ed.), is an intensive study of the "origin and development of social classes of the Old Dominion." It should be supplemented with the essays by Mildred Campbell and Bernard Bailyn in the exceptional collection, J. M. Smith, ed., *Seventeenth Century America, Essays on Colonial History* * (1959). Louis B. Wright's modern edition (1947) of Robert Beverley, *The History and Present State of Virginia* (first published in 1705), affords us an invaluable early account, especially of Indian relations. W. E. Washburn, *The Governor and the Rebel: A History of Bacon's Rebellion in Virginia* (1957), stresses the importance of these relations in this much misunderstood event. A. E. Smith, *Colonists in Bondage: White Servitude and Convict Labor in America 1607-1776* (1947), is the standard study of this important subject. V. W. Crane, *The Southern Frontier 1670-1732* * (1929), is excellent on early Carolina history, for which see also Readings for Chapter 3.

William Bradford, *Of Plymouth Plantation 1620-1647* (in the S. E. Morison edition, 1952), is the best work on its subject. A useful modern account is G. F. Willison, *Saints and Strangers* * (1945). Of Perry Miller's many indispensable works on Massachusetts Bay and its satellites, the following may be selected for mention: *The New England Mind, The Seventeenth Century* * (1939); *The New England Mind, From Colony to Province* * (1953); and *Orthodoxy in Massachusetts 1630-1650* (1933). Perry Miller and T. H. Johnson, eds., *The Puritans* * (1938), is an excellent anthology of Puritan writing. Perry Miller, *Errand into the Wilderness* * (1956), is a collection of the author's essays on many aspects of colonial and New England life. J. T. Adams, *The Founding of New England* * (1921), is strongly anti-Puritan. Its biases may be corrected in S. E. Morison, *Builders of the Bay Colony* * (1930). E. S. Morgan, *The Puritan Dilemma: The Story of John Winthrop* * (1958), is a somewhat disenchanted biography. Other biographies of note are O. E. Winslow, *Master Roger Williams* (1957), and Edith Curtis, *Anne Hutchinson* (1930). A. T. Vaughan, *New England Frontier, Puritans and Indians 1620-1675* (1965), is a well-written study of Puritan attitudes and actions. G. L. Haskins, *Law and Authority in Early Massachusetts* (1960), affords an excellent introduction to the American legal tradition. Bernard Bailyn, *The New England Merchants in the Seventeenth Century* * (1955), is a useful supplement to the still valuable older study by W. B. Weeden, *Economic and Social History of New England 1620-1789* (2 vols., 1890). Land policy in early New England and elsewhere in the English colonies is analyzed authoritatively in Marshall Harris, *Origin of the Land Tenure System in the United States* (1953). E. N. Hartley, *Ironworks on the Saugus* (1957), is illuminating on early New England industry. The struggle between God and Mammon in seventeenth century Massachusetts comes clear in Bernard Bailyn, ed., *The Apologia of Robert Keayne, The Self-Portrait of a Puritan Merchant* (1964).

Two special studies help broaden the picture of early New York: J. R. Reich, *Leisler's Rebellion, A Study of Democracy in New York 1664-1720* (1953), and A. W. Trelease, *Indian Affairs in Colonial New York, The Seventeenth Century* (1960). F. B. Tolles, *Quakers and the Atlantic Culture* (1960), is a short, scholarly introduction to the background and early history of Pennsylvania. Tolles' *Meeting House and Counting House, The Quaker Merchants of Colonial Philadelphia 1682-1763* * (1948), is outstanding on

God and Mammon in Pennsylvania. C. O. Peare, *William Penn* (1957), is a useful biography. F. B. Tolles and E. G. Alderfer, *The Witness of William Penn* (1957), is an excellent anthology of Penn's writings. J. E. Pomfret, *The Province of West New Jersey 1609-1702* (1956), is a scholarly unraveling of early Jersey history.

On British colonial regulation, in addition to C. M. Andrews, cited at the head of these Readings, the standard older works are those by G. L. Beer, *The Origins of the British Colonial System 1578-1660* (1908), and *The Old Colonial System* (2 vols., 1912). L. H. Gipson, *The British Empire before the American Revolution* (11 vols., 1936-1965), is a monumental modern account. Special studies of importance for the early period include L. A. Harper, *The English Navigation Laws, A Seventeenth Century Experiment in Social Engineering* (1939); and Maurice Ashley, *Financial and Commercial Policy Under the Cromwellian Protectorate* (rev. ed., 1962). M. G. Hall, *Edward Randolph and the American Colonies 1676-1703* (1960), is a valuable study of the most persistent of British inquisitors. M. G. Hall, L. H. Leder, and M. G. Kammen, *The Glorious Revolution in America, Documents on the Colonial Crisis of 1689* * (1964), is an illuminating anthology.

CHAPTER THREE

In 1614, Captain John Smith had written of North America:

As for the goodness and fine substance of the land, we are for the most part yet altogether ignorant of them, but only here and there where we have touched or seen a little, the edges of those large dominions which do stretch themselves into the main, God doth know how many thousand miles.

By the time Georgia was settled in 1733 (see p. 62), the English and the world had gained a better if still imperfect notion of America's dimensions and a better yet still incomplete understanding of how to live within them.

Expansion
in North America

The earliest settlers had approached the shores of the New World pitifully ill-equipped for its rigors. We have spoken of the agonies of Jamestown and of the "humorous ignorances" of the Pilgrims of Plymouth, to quote John Smith once more, which "caused them for more than a year to endure a wonderful deal of misery with infinite patience . . . thinking to find things better than I advised them." During the next century, the English crossed the ocean in greater numbers to clinch their hold on 1,200 miles of the Atlantic seaboard. The Atlantic itself formed a bridge to the culture and commodities of the Old World.

It also provided a path of communication among all the settlements of the New World, from Labrador to the Caribbean islands and the Spanish Main. And the English seaboard merchants became the principal organizers of this New World unity. More and more, New France and the Caribbean islands came to depend for their very food and materials for shelter, as well as for their trade, largely upon Yankee, Yorker, and Quaker coasting vessels, irregular though their sailings were.

Well to the west of this first range of well-established settlements the rivers then known to most Americans began their course to the sea. Beyond the "fall line" of these rivers, where cataracts two hundred feet high dramatically signaled a halt to upstream navigation, the Susquehanna Valley in Pennsylvania and the "Great (Shenandoah) Valley" of Virginia tied the "back parts" of the British mainland "plantations" together (see map, p. 78). In the eighteenth century, immigrants by the thousands with no particular provincial loyalties settled in these valleys, and visitors like the Baptist circuit-rider James Ireland marveled at the "common state of sociability" in which the numerous sects and nationalities seemed to live there. By the 1750's, issues of church administration, participation in politics, law enforcement, and commercial growth, all indicated the need for freer intercourse between this hinterland and the cities and harbors of the seaboard. Forward-looking Americans like the Washingtons and Jeffersons of Virginia, the Norrises, Morrises, and Franklins of Pennsylvania, had begun to press for east-west roads and bridges to link up the natural north-south routes.

Here, then, by the middle of the eighteenth century, was a new land among the settled regions of the world, clearly marked off by natural boundaries, and a new people, a million and a quarter strong, with a common official language, a common legal tradition, a common Protestant heritage. To these new "Americans" of the eighteenth century the country beyond the Appalachians still loomed as a trackless wilderness so densely wooded that the sun itself seldom penetrated the foliage beneath whose cover lurked wild brave and beast and terrifying creatures of the mind. Yet as we know, this land too was far from empty, and when, after 1768, permanent settlers at long last penetrated the region (see p. 128), "they found weatherbeaten trails," as J. B. Bartlett writes in his fine study of *The Explorers of North America,* "skilful, knowledgeable guides, and Indians who had dealt with the white man for a century."

When the war for this wilderness of North America finally was fought out between Britain and France in the middle of the eighteenth century, the British mainland settlements, a new nation despite themselves, were to play an American rather than a British role. In a sense, the American Revolution was a late phase of this war which red men, Spaniards, Frenchmen, and Britons had been waging intermittently for more than a hundred years and which, in fact, did not finally flicker out until the end of the Indian wars on the plains following the American Civil War (see Chapter 18).

I. *The New American Population*

EXTRAORDINARY GROWTH
AND SPREAD

Britain's ultimate success in North America sprang largely from the astonishing growth of her mainland colonies, which already gave many in Europe cause for wonder and alarm. After 1700 the population of these colonies almost doubled every 25 years. In round numbers the 200,000 people in 1688 had grown to about 1,800,000 in 1750. At that time, there were but 65,000 Europeans in New France.

The most densely populated mainland colonies were in the South, which in 1750 contained some 700,000 inhabitants. Of this total, 300,000 were Negro slaves, most of them West Africans carried over in British and colonial slave ships. Approximately a half-million people lived in New England at this time, and some 400,000 in the Middle colonies, which were expanding at the fastest rate. The high birth rate among the white colonists accounts in large part for the remarkable population growth—it has been estimated that the average colonial family increased by one child every two years. Immigration from the British Isles and from continental countries, and to a lesser degree from the West Indies, helped swell the total.

Before the 1680's, America had been a catch-all for Europe. Swedes, Finns, Netherlanders, French Huguenots, and Spanish and Portuguese Jews, together with a sprinkling of more exotic nationalities, had all settled in the British colonies. Thereafter, by far the largest numbers came from Germany and Northern Ireland. Most of the new arrivals settled first on William Penn's welcoming domains (see p. 66) and gradually filtered into the vast stretch of territory between the Allegheny foothills and the southern lowlands, spreading some 600 miles southwestward from the Maryland-Pennsylvania boundary.

THE GREAT GERMAN INFLUX

Continuous German immigration began in 1683, when small groups of Mennonites and Quakers, harassed elsewhere for their radical Christianity, established Germantown, near present-day Philadelphia. During the next three decades other radical German Protestants founded such Pennsylvania towns as Bethlehem, Lititz, and Nazareth. These early German immigrants were mainly well-educated people, who paid for their own passage, brought property with them from the Old World, and bought land on their arrival. They built substantial communities where many of the original buildings still stand.

These first German settlers are to be distinguished from the poorer, conservative Lutherans and German-Reformed groups, the so-called "church people," who poured into Pennsylvania in the eighteenth century, mainly from the Rhine Valley. For a hundred years after 1618 the Rhine Valley had been the battleground in religious and dynastic wars, and the peasants there were periodically despoiled by military foragers and feudal overlords. When they learned through advertisements of promoters or the reports of friends of a country where there were no feudal obligations and where land was plentiful, they responded eagerly to the call.

Most of these church people were too poor to pay their way to America, and came

mainly as "redemptioners," one of the various forms of "white servitude." The "indentured servants" who were first shipped to Virginia and Maryland early in the seventeenth century had made contracts with the joint-stock companies or proprietary agents abroad to work in the colonies in exchange for their passage across the ocean (see p. 48). The "redemptioners" of the eighteenth century sold themselves to ship captains or "soul brokers" in European ports. As their numbers grew, the voyage itself, because of overcrowding and related conditions, became even more horrible than on slave ships, and it is estimated that on the average a third of the redemptioners died at sea. The contracts or "indentures" of those landed in America were sold to the highest bidders. Thereafter, their situation was the same as the earlier "white servants." The usual term was from four to seven years, at the expiration of which the servant was to receive "freedom dues," usually fifty acres of land, tools and clothing, and perhaps a bit of cash to get started on his own. The evidence suggests that these duties were often withheld or, when granted, that the servant sold off his land for a pittance in ready money. On the other hand, runaways were frequent and often went unapprehended. Many of the German redemptioners gradually occupied the rich farmland of the Lehigh, Susquehanna, and Cumberland valleys. When they reached less fertile lands in the north, they swung down into the Shenandoah Valley. German immigration reached its high point between 1749 and 1754 when to the dismay of the English colonists who feared they might be engulfed, over 5,000 Germans were arriving in American ports every year.

The Germans did their best to preserve in America the way of life they had known at home. They hoped to develop their farms in the quiet valleys, cultivate their traditional domestic arts, embrace their religion in purity and peace. But the village pattern they had known in Germany could **not** be sustained in Pennsylvania. They were forced, instead, into the more isolated lives of independent farmers that were to become characteristic of the moving frontier. Nevertheless, they held tenaciously to their homesteads and, as the open spaces filled up around them, they gradually resumed their intensive farming methods, industrious practices, and traditional ways.

Their influence on both the agricultural and industrial development of Pennsylvania thus became profound. The Germans were celebrated throughout the colonies for their rich gardens and orchards, for their stout barns and well-tended livestock, and for their sturdy self-sufficiency. Many skilled craftsmen, both German and Swiss, had settled in the Pennsylvania interior, where they introduced their techniques for knitting, weaving, shoemaking, and carving. German artisans developed the famous long rifle, which was first manufactured in Lancaster and was later adopted by other frontiersmen. Perhaps more important innovations were the iron stove and the Conestoga wagon. The stove was a vast improvement over the heat-wasting open hearth of the English-style dwelling, and the new wagon was a durable, efficient vehicle for carrying inland produce to the seaboard.

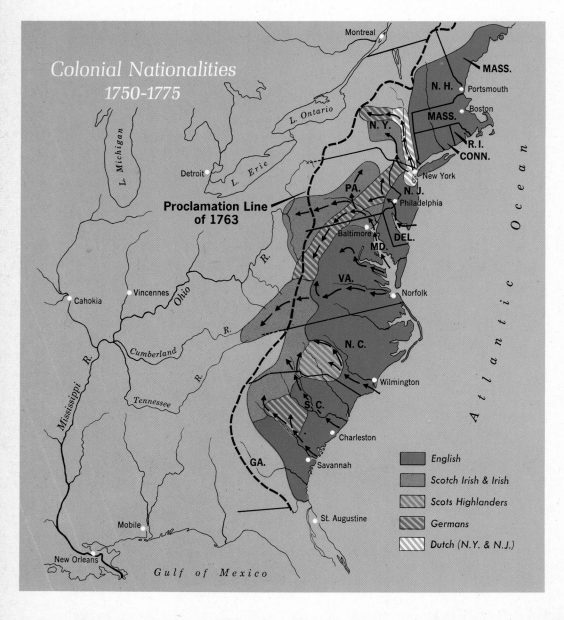

Colonial Nationalities
1750-1775

Proclamation Line
of 1763

English
Scotch Irish & Irish
Scots Highlanders
Germans
Dutch (N.Y. & N.J.)

Ulstermen from Northern Ireland, preceded by small numbers of Irish Quakers, began to emigrate at about the same time as the Germans. Of lowland Scot origin, the Ulstermen had settled in Northern Ireland during the reign of James I. Here they had prospered as farmers and small manufacturers until discriminatory laws shut off the English markets for their linen and woolen products. As Presbyterians, moreover, they resented having to pay taxes to support the official Anglican Church.

A few Ulstermen had trickled over to America from Northern Ireland during the Puritan revolution, but parliamentary legislation between 1660 and 1718 provoked a mass exodus. For example, to protect English farmers and the woolen interests, Parliament excluded Ulster meat, dairy products, and woolens from England and the colonies. The final blow came when British absentee landlords raised the rents of their Irish tenants. Around 1718, thousands of Scotch-Irish turned their backs on Europe for the New World, and they continued to come by the shipload in succeeding decades. After distressing receptions in New England, they, like the Germans, turned to Pennsylvania, from where they pushed farther and farther into the interior, southward and westward. By 1750, they were heavily concentrated in the Cumberland Valley and in the Carolina back country, as well as in southwestern Pennsylvania.

Like the Germans, most of the Scotch-Irish first came as redemptioners and served as indentured servants. They were, however, usually flinty, aggressive solitaries, more prone than others to become runaways and to set out on their own before their terms expired. They took easily to frontier life and made up for their indifference to the arts by their zeal in warfare and their passion for politics. Later they distinguished themselves as ministers, teachers, statesmen, and soldiers, and formed a hard core of anti-British sentiment on the eve of the Revolution.

II. *The Mature Southern Colonies*

THE TIDEWATER

Throughout the colonial period, most of the population of the Chesapeake region, of tidewater Virginia and Maryland, and of adjacent parts of North Carolina, remained of English extraction. Here, although grain and other food crops were widely grown, the economy was based on the production and export of tobacco. The Carolina low country, extending southward to the Savannah River and inland about 60 miles, was settled later than the Chesapeake region, and for reasons of climate, crops, and the origins of its colonists, differed from it in its culture.

The Chesapeake planters, under the social and political leadership of an elite group of large landholders maintained close ties with England and aped the manners of her aristocracy. The Carters, Lees, Byrds, Randolphs, and Fitzhughs of Virginia, and the Carrolls, Dulanys, and Galloways of Maryland, lived in solid Georgian mansions with well-proportioned rooms filled with fine imported furniture. They also hired able American artisans to carry out the plans of English architects and the designs of foreign cabinet-makers. The evidence of colonial craftsmanship may be seen today in the Byrd mansion, "Westover," and in the stylish town houses of Annapolis.

Observers noted that the Chesapeake gentry were an outdoor people, fonder of fox-hunting and horse-racing and long house parties than of polite learning. Some of them boasted large libraries—William Byrd II, for example, who even made a practice of reading many of the old works he

To his Excellency James Glen, Esq, Capt General, Governor & Commander in Chief in and over his Majesty's Province of South Carolina, and Vice Admiral within the same. This Prospect of CHARLES-TOWN is most humbly Inscribd by his much Obliged humble Servant B: Roberts.

Charleston, South Carolina, around 1735, looking across the Cooper River.

owned, and Robert Carter of a later generation with his collection of some 1,500 books. But these men were exceptions. What reading the planters did usually dealt with practical subjects like law, medicine, commerce, and surveying. They respected education, at least for their own class, and many sent their sons abroad for sound classical instruction. But they feared rusticity and inelegance more than ignorance. The dancing master was as much in demand as the tutor.

Although highly conscious of their rank and thoroughly undemocratic in their dealings, the Chesapeake planters took the management of their tobacco plantations seriously. Yet, as in the seventeenth century (see p. 48), they continued to be misled by their own pretensions, to splurge on fine

imports supplied on credit by their British agents, and generally to live above their means. Land, which represented their greatest wealth, was also their downfall. "Such amazing property," observed Philip Fithian, tutor to the Carters in their heyday, "no matter how deeply it is involved [in debt], blows up the owners to an imagination, which is visible to all." They "live up their suppositions," a Londoner remarked, "without providing against Calamities and accidents." The slave system reinforced the sense of mastery arising from majestic land holdings.

From the 1730's to the 1750's the price of Virginia tobacco soared. Rising prices for their staple also put a premium on the planters' land. In this period, the Chesa-

80

CHARLES TOWN or METROPOLIS of the Province of South Carolina, is pleasantly Situated between Coopers & Ashley Rivers, which form a spacious & convenient Harbour, & floods in 32.45 of N. Latitude, & of W.L. from London, & Climate of Carolina, formerly called Florida... [caption text, partially illegible]

peake gentry enjoyed their "golden age,"
the age of "the gauntlet and the glove," in
which the myth of southern chivalry and
romance took firm root. Yet few indeed
could afford for long the high life of cavaliers, the expenditures for clothes, carriages,
and body slaves, mansions, parks, and wine.
Eventually, the Virginians' debts for gaudy
imports grew so calamitously high that Governor Francis Farquier remarked in 1766
that their "Blood . . . is soured by their
private distresses." To those who crashed,
the West loomed more beguilingly than ever
as a refuge or new springboard to success.

Of all the mainland colonies, South Carolina was closest to the West Indian settlements in character. As we have seen (p.
61), many of its early settlers had come
from Barbados and from among the Huguenots of the French West Indian islands as
well as from France herself. In 1740, the
cultivation of indigo was introduced into
South Carolina from the West Indies with
the support of a crown bounty (after 1748)
because of its importance as a dye in England's growing textile industry. Production
increased rapidly under this official encouragement and, together with rice, indigo
provided the Carolinians with incomes less
subject to price fluctuations and competition than tobacco.

South Carolina, in the middle of the
eighteenth century, was the only mainland
colony in which Negroes outnumbered
whites, another West Indian characteristic,
and they did so by three to one. The whites

81

below the 2,000 leading families, moreover, were the most depressed on the continent, showing the lowest literacy rate and the strongest antagonism to the ruling group. The Carolina planters were characteristically absentees, leaving management of the land and the slaves to overseers. They themselves spent their summers in Newport, Rhode Island, or abroad. For much of the rest of the time, they lived in Charleston, the leading city, and perhaps the only genuine *city* in the entire South.

What helped give eighteenth-century Charleston its exotic charm was its architecture, also borrowed from the West Indies —the pastel-shaded brick and stucco houses embellished with wrought-iron balconies and gates, and lush private gardens. Handsome churches and public buildings lent an added dignity. Clustered around the wharves were wholesale and retail establishments, warehouses, and business offices— evidence of Charleston's commercial vigor.

In Carolina, unlike the Chesapeake country, debt among the nabobs was rare. "The planters are full of money," Henry Laurens, one of the richest of them, observed in 1750. At the same time, the concentration of wealth in Charleston seems to have supplied an unusually strong impulse for further accumulation and display. "Their whole lives," said the *South Carolina Gazette,* of the planters on the eve of the Revolution,

are one continued Race in which everyone is endeavoring to distance all behind him; and to overtake or pass by, all before him; everyone is flying from his inferiors in Pursuit of his Superiors. . . . Every Tradesman is a Merchant, every Merchant is a Gentleman, and every Gentleman one of the Noblesse. We are a Country of Gentry. . . . We have no such Thing as a common People among us: Between Vanity and Fashion, the Species is utterly destroyd.

THE "BACK PARTS"

The back country of the Chesapeake settlements began to fill up after 1730. A generation later, the overflow occupied the "back parts," as they were called, of South Carolina and Georgia. On the eve of the Revolution, about 250,000 persons—free Negroes and slaves, and a mixed white population made up of Germans, Scots, Scotch-Irish, English Quakers, and migrants from the tidewater itself—had displaced most of the aborigines of the region and developed a society of their own.

Although the entire back country at first offered a paradise for hunter and trapper, a mixed subsistence agriculture producing cereals, potatoes, fruits, and meat, as well as flax and hemp, gradually developed in the Chesapeake back parts. Life was hard for these pioneer husbandmen, whose families lived in crude log shanties that afforded very little shelter. As population grew, however, trade itself expanded and living conditions improved. Even before midcentury, such thriving crossroads communities as Fredericksburg and Hagerstown in Maryland, Martinsburg and Winchester in Virginia, and Charlotte in North Carolina, had been built, each with its grist mills, country stores, bakers, masons, carpenters, coopers, brickmakers, and weavers.

The "back parts" of the Carolina country were more isolated and much rougher. It must have been particularly hard on settlers fresh from Ulster or German villages to spend lonely years in a country still ringing with the cries of wolves and panthers. Malaria was endemic here and only added to the difficulty of facing the prospect of unending labor to clear the land. Many settlers soon fell back into the nomadic life from which civilization had worked for centuries to raise mankind. They became herdsmen of wild swine and cattle, often stolen from the red men. Itinerant clergymen reported with dismay how the people in this region dwelt together in "Concubinage, swapping their wives as Cattel, and living in a State of Nature, more irregularly and unchastely than the Indians." A few, nevertheless, found this life so satisfactory that they made fortunes out of meat and skins and tallow. Such men became a regular back country gentry living on the most extensive cattle ranges on the entire mainland. Most others, however, continued their slide on the social scale into the life of primitive huntsmen on the prowl for elusive game, including Indians.

As early as 1708, South Carolina alone had half as many Indian as Negro slaves (see p. 62), and their number was not inconsiderable. The whole colony that year counted 9,500 persons, of whom Negroes made up 2,900, and Indian slaves 1,400. Soon, Carolina Indians were being shipped all the way to New England and the West Indies. Verner W. Crane, in *The Southern Frontier,* writes of this period that, "Yankee merchants and masters, before they became great purveyors of blacks from Guinea to the plantation colonies, had made acquaintance with the slave-trade in their trafficking from Carolina to Boston and Newport."

Gradually, tidewater institutions, both legal and political, were imposed on the "back parts" of Maryland and Virginia, although the incompleteness of tidewater control was shown even as late as 1863, when the West Virginians seceded from the slave-holding and slave-breeding East. Resistance to Charleston domination in hinterland South Carolina and Georgia was even stronger. Throughout the eighteenth century, the back parts of these colonies complained frequently of the "mixt Multitude" of "white-collar parasites" from Charleston, the "mercenary tricking Attornies, Clerks, and other little Officials," who came to prey upon them, taking full advantage of their poor knowledge of English, their ignorance, their friendlessness. "Finding . . . they were only amus'd and trifled with," they said at last, "all Confidence of the Poor in the Great is destroy'd and . . . will never exist again." In the Revolution, when the Carolina planters themselves fought the British, the non-English back parts, Anglophobe though they were to the marrow, chose to fight the planters. And yet, their very Indian wars, their pursuit of Indian slaves, by bringing them into confrontation with the French in Louisiana and the Spanish in Florida, worked to develop the idea of empire and the hunger for the whole continent, unaware though they remained of its true extent.

III. *The Middle Colonies*

PENNSYLVANIA

During the eighteenth century the Middle colonies attracted the largest number of immigrants, and formed the most heterogeneous part of British North America. Pennsylvania, the newest, quickly became the largest of the Middle colonies. By 1755, Philadelphia, her leading town, had 28,000 inhabitants and had passed Boston for first place among colonial cities. Though Quakers then no longer were a majority in Philadelphia, the Quaker merchants comprised the city's wealthiest group and dominated the whole settlement. Their wealth stemmed largely from their extensive trade, the profits from which they invested in mining and manufacturing enterprises, and especially in urban and forest land.

The Quakers' religious beliefs, like the Puritans', inspired the thrift, industry, and reliability essential to business success. The persecution of the Friends for their beliefs both in Europe and America had scattered them over the western world, a circumstance they also turned to commercial advantage. Frederick B. Tolles, the historian of colonial Quaker life, writes:

There were Quakers in most of the ports with which Philadelphia had commercial relations. A number of them, like the Hills in Madeira, the Lloyds in London, the Callenders in Barbados, the Wantons in Newport, and the Franklins in New York, were related by marriage to the leading Quaker families of Philadelphia. . . . The intelligence which they received through their correspondence and from itinerant "public Friends" . . . from Nova Scotia to Curaçao and from Hamburg to Lisbon . . . was chiefly concerned with prices current and the prosperity of Truth.

The industrious farmers Penn brought to

the back country of his colony, in turn, supplied the Philadelphia merchants with excellent grain and other staples for export and a thriving market for imported goods. Philadelphia shipyards turned out vessels the equal of any in the world, and their captains were second to none, especially in evading the British Navigation Acts. The Quakers' refusal on religious grounds to take oaths was a particular thorn in the flesh to British officials.

Before the end of the seventeenth century, rich Quaker merchants had already begun to turn Anglican in order to escape from having to report their private affairs publicly at the Friends' meetings. Others soon became known as "wet Quakers," a term whose origin is unknown but whose meaning was clear; they had grown too sophisticated to be true believers and had fallen off from their religious observances. Still others, drawn perhaps by their traditional attachment to "Laborious Handicrafts," became involved with Newtonian science and experimentation. Among the more interesting imports of the Philadelphia merchants were the books, instruments, and mixtures of the science of the day. Such men frequently became Deists, for whom God was but the "Heavenly Engineer." Far from unknown among the educated planters of Virginia and the intellectuals of New England, Deism flourished in Philadelphia, and its greatest New World apostle was Philadelphia's leading citizen, Ben Franklin (see p. 114).

The liberal government that William Penn had created for his settlement was, by the early years of the eighteenth century, already on the way to being corrupted by his absentee successors. The rising Quaker merchants grew most vocal in attacking the regime and in proposing the strengthening of the local assembly at the expense of the proprietors. After 1740 the struggle quickened between the proprietary party (which stood for centralized authority in the hands of the governor and council) and the popular party (composed of city merchants and property-holding farmers). Liberal suffrage laws and the sup-

port of the German element enabled the anti-proprietary Quaker party to outmaneuver the deputies of the Penns.

For a time, the assembly enjoyed the confidence of all sections of the colony. But in 1754 its failure to protect the frontier from Indian raids the frontiersmen themselves had inspired by land-grabbing and violence brought the assembly under attack. Actually, the assembly did not object to appropriating funds for frontier defense, but it insisted that the proprietors share the expense by accepting a tax on their lands. A deadlock resulted until the proprietors agreed to put up £5,000 for the defense of the colony and the assembly voted the necessary funds. The Pennsylvania frontier, nevertheless, continued right up to the Revolution to be the scene of bloodshed as the "thirst for large tracts of land . . . prevailed with a singular rage" among the grandees, and the hunger for space at the red man's expense remained unappeased among the frontier settlers.

NEW JERSEY AND NEW YORK

Travelers passing through New Jersey in the eighteenth century sometimes stopped long enough to comment on its natural beauty, its prosperity, or the succulence of its oysters. But there was little more to detain the curious, who usually hastened on to New York. Jerseyites, to a degree, felt the same way about their settlement. In the 1750's about 70,000 people lived in New Jersey, and many of them looked upon it as a "keg tapped at both ends," the colony transporting its surplus hemp, grain, flax, hay, and Indian corn either to New York or Philadelphia for shipment overseas.

The movement of Yankee Puritans from Long Island to East Jersey, which had begun while the Dutch still held New Netherland, was perhaps the most significant of early inter-colonial migrations (see p. 64). The cultural influence of New England continued strong in East Jersey, particularly in the towns of Newark, Elizabeth, and Woodbridge. But elsewhere in the colony by the eighteenth century the old New England ways were modified and the transplanted village community, with its town meetings and its close social and religious supervision, had broken down. The influence of neighboring Pennsylvania thereafter grew stronger, and the farm became the basic unit rather than the village. The New England influence persisted, however, in the Georgian farmhouses, inns, and churches.

Nature endowed New York City with the finest harbor in the Atlantic world, yet its growth was far slower than that of Philadelphia, Boston, or Charleston. Patroon control of the Hudson Valley (see p. 26) and Indian control of the interior were partly responsible for New York's low state. Until 1720, the pirate taint also held back the development of legitimate trade. New York merchants liked pirate goods, which they could buy cheap and sell dear. Pirate crews also were good customers when they came ashore. A pirate rendezvous, however, offered no attraction to legitimate captains and shippers who could easily ply an active trade elsewhere. Early in the 1700's, New York's governor pressed London for vessels swift enough to "destroye these vermin who have hitherto made New York their nest of safety." But a quarter of a century passed before effective action was taken. Thereafter, Yorkers entered more vigorously into competition with the Yankees to the north and the Quakers to the south and earned a growing share of American, West Indian, and world trade.

At mid-century, New York City boasted 13,000 inhabitants, many of them living in houses, as a visitor then said, "more compact and regular, and in general higher built" than those of Philadelphia, "most of them after the Dutch model with their gravell ends fronting the street." Otherwise, the city had begun to lose many of its Dutch features, and the Dutch language itself was less commonly heard. The absence of a Dutch press or a Dutch colonial literature left the dying culture with few supports, and the opening of King's College in 1754 made it certain that English speech and culture would predominate.

Having noticed the decline of Dutch influence in New York City, travelers sailing north by sloop were the more sharply struck by its persistence in the Hudson Valley. The voyage up the Hudson was punctuated by stops at small settlements like Poughkeepsie. Long before Washington Irving exploited the romance and mystery of this region, visitors experienced delicious shudders as they surveyed the solitary river scenery "where nothing presents but huge precipices and inaccessible steeps, where foot of man never was." At the end of this scenic route was Albany, where the Dutch language remained the predominant one as late as the 1740's.

Lying open to Indian raiders from French Canada, Albany kept the look of a frontier outpost until the French were defeated in 1763 (see p. 101). Wooden palisades enclosed the town. In its center stood a square stone fortress manned by 300 of the king's troops. But the domestic architecture was comfortable enough. Observers spoke of the "superstitiously clean" look of the wood and brick houses, their ends characteristically facing the streets.

Their chambers and rooms are large and handsome [wrote a contemporary]. They have their beds generally in alcoves, so that you may go thro' all the rooms of a great house and never see a bed. They affect pictures much, particularly scripture history, with which they adorn their rooms. They set out their cabinets and *buffets* much with china. Their kitchens are likewise very clean, and they hang earthen or delft plates and dishes around the walls, in manner of pictures.

Eighteenth-century travel accounts often mention "the avarice, selfishness, and immeasurable love of money" of the Albany Dutch. They were even charged with trading with the enemy when Indian war-parties led by the French were burning New England settlements (1702-1706). But this materialism and particularism was not unusual in the colonies.

The Hudson Valley between New York City and Albany was the only part of the entire province that was well settled as late as 1750. Yet even here the landscape was characterized by huge primeval tracts owned by a few rich men. From the start of the eighteenth century, British governors of New York, emulating the Dutch patroon system, rewarded their favorites with land grants ranging from 50,000 to a million acres. As a result, the richest land was monopolized by owners who sometimes paid nothing but a token tax on their property and thus had small incentive to sell. They leased occasional tracts to tenant farmers. Otherwise, bona-fide settlers were discouraged. "Squatters," however, took advantage of the unpatrolled country. Between 1720 and 1756 New York's population grew from 30,000 to 85,000, much of the increase occurring in the Hudson Valley. When, in later years, the patroons tried to collect rents from families that had squatted here for generations, they were resisted with spirit.

IV. *Eighteenth-Century New England*

RHODE ISLAND

Eighteenth-century Boston was regarded by many as the most impressive and the most English city in the colonies. Many roads led to Boston, but the most common way from the Middle colonies, or at least from New York, was to sail out Long Island Sound to New London, Connecticut, or to cross over from Long Island itself by ferry. From New London, most travelers would stop first at Newport, Rhode Island, the fifth largest city in the colonies, and one already renowned among vacationists for its pleasing and healthful climate. Planters from the Carolinas and the West Indies were coming to Newport as early as the 1730's to escape the tropical heat. Bishop Berkeley, the famous English philosopher, lived here between 1720 and 1731, and Newport was the home of one of America's

Portrait of Isaac Royall and family, by Robert Feke, who delineated the silks and satins of the New England and Pennsylvania aristocracy.

first artists, Robert Feke, whose portraits tell us so much about the values and aspirations of the New England and Pennsylvania aristocracy. The magnificence of Newport's private and public buildings rivaled those of Boston, Philadelphia, and Charleston. In Peter Harrison, the town could claim the most distinguished American architect who introduced the classical temple form that was eventually adopted everywhere in the colonies. King's Chapel in Boston (1749-1754) is perhaps Harrison's most famous structure, but other fine examples of his work are Christ Church in Cambridge, Massachusetts (1759-1761), and the Touro Synagogue (1759-1763) in Newport itself.

Approximately 7,000 people lived in Newport in the 1750's and many of them lived off what we, today, would call the tourist trade. But the city was also a flourishing port. Its shippers, like those of the rest of seaboard New England, engaged in supplying the West Indies with foodstuffs, timber, and African slaves, and carrying away sugar and molasses for the manufacture of rum. As a British customs man said of Yankees generally, Newporters were careful "to keep their ships in constant employ, which makes them trye all ports to force a trade."

Yet Rhode Island had still to live down its reputation for radicalism that it had earned in Roger Williams' day. "The private people," declared one English visitor, "are cunning, deceitful, and selfish; they live almost entirely by unfair and illicit trading." Dr. Alexander Hamilton, who visited the colony in 1744, decided that Rhode Island, with its "rural scenes and pretty frank girls," was the most agreeable place he had struck in his travels, but he had to admit that the people had "as bad a character for chicane and disingenuity as any of our American Colonies."

MASSACHUSETTS

The city of Boston, if not yet the "hub of the universe," was the heart of Massachusetts, as Massachusetts was the heart of New England. Even prejudiced observers from other sections, who came with preconceived notions about the "enthusiastical" or "canting" Yankees, were amazed by the richness and graciousness of Boston's upper-class life and the general comfort of the rest of the people. North of Boston such ports as Salem, Marblehead, and Gloucester, which much later were to supply many of the "proper Bostonians" of the Victorian era were already enjoying a thriving trade. But the capital of the commonwealth, with over 15,000 people in 1750, the best harbor, and the biggest hinterland markets, was still far ahead of the other towns and growing faster.

Boston's commercial prosperity had begun, as we have seen (p. 60), virtually from the beginning of settlement there. Her merchants were quick to take all the advantage they could of England's wars with the Dutch which, in the seventeenth century, diverted the vessels of the two greatest commercial nations of the time from the world's trading routes. Early in the eighteenth century, it was peace rather than war that gave the strongest impetus to Boston's prosperity, especially the Peace of Utrecht of 1713 (see p. 98). In the West Indies, the growing demand for all necessities sent prices and profits soaring. By the terms of the Peace of Utrecht, Britain obtained Newfoundland and Nova Scotia from France, and the vast fisheries of their waters were opened to Yankee enterprise. At the same time, Nantucket whalers began to sail far from their home waters on long voyages to the Arctic Ocean and Brazilian shores. "Farming the sea," as the Yankees said, was itself procreative. The demand for more and better ships promoted such land-based businesses as rope- and sail-making. These drew artisans from nearby and foreign towns, and their growing number fostered new home and business construction. Agriculture in the surrounding countryside also felt the surge of prosperity as town populations had to be fed. New road-building gave its own impetus to growth and speeded the exchange of goods.

As in Pennsylvania and the South, so in Massachusetts wealth enlarged the demands of nature. Calvin, it is true, warned the Saints "perpetually and resolutely [to] exert themselves to retrench all superfluities and to restrain luxury." He particularly commanded the "elect" to "give an account of thy stewardship." But by the eighteenth century, the richest Puritans, like the richest Quakers, had moved away from the old religion to the more congenial Anglican communion, where there was no requirement to make "a public relation of their experiences." King's Chapel, the first Anglican Church in Boston, was opened in 1688, and there, as in their new brick mansions on Beacon Hill, the "visible elect" might display God's bounty without having to disclose how it fell to their lot.

Boston's "codfish aristocracy" and its emulators in other Yankee ports now affected swords, satins, and sturdy English broadcloths. In the country, comfortable "colonial" homes replaced the rude structures of pioneer days, and the gentry drank and dressed as befitted their new substance and standing. The requirement that all Puritan residences be within half a mile of the town church remained but a faint reminder of narrower times, and with its passing went the stringency of religious observance, the strength of the public school plan. Boston and other towns merely breathed easier for the change.

Self-indulgence gave still another impetus to trade; but Massachusetts had no staple that was wanted where the luxuries she craved originated. Problems involving the navigation system (see p. 67) only enlarged the challenge to Yankee ingenuity on the sea. In resolving their problems, Yankee merchants were not constrained by conscience or by consciousness of crime. Like others, they engaged in much illicit traffic, and some did not scruple about practicing sheer piracy. New England's most lucrative legitimate voyages involved the so-

called slave-trade triangle, in which Bostonians gained their full share. The American South was usually supplied with slaves by British or southern ships, although Rhode Islanders also participated in this part of the slave traffic. On the typical Boston slaving voyage, Boston rum was carried to Africa to pay for or otherwise obtain the human cargo. The Africans then were carried to the British West Indies, a passage the brutality of which defies exaggeration. In the West Indies, precious coin was taken on along with the molasses for the production of more rum, and so around once more. When British West Indian sugar production began to fall off, Boston captains took to visiting "closed" French and Spanish islands to pick up their molasses. In 1733, Parliament yielded to the protestations of France and Spain as well as British West Indian planters and adopted the Molasses Act, prohibiting mainland merchants from trading with the foreigners. This was a blow Yankee merchants knew well how to parry. Smuggling became at once a common and a fine art. When Britain, in 1764, decided to strengthen the enforcement of the Molasses Act, Yankee resistance quickly took on a revolutionary tinge (see p. 131).

Distant commerce has always involved a strong element of risk. To reduce the risk, Yankee merchants often installed their brothers, sons, and in-laws as their agents in foreign lands. In Britain itself they turned, when they could find them, to relatives who had resisted the lures of the New World. Family connections failing, they, like the Quakers, sought out their co-religionists. As a last recourse, in Dutch or Spanish, French or Portuguese ports, they employed their own countrymen to look after their interests. Characteristically, family businesses were enlarged and family ties multiplied by intermarriage among mercantile families. In this way, wealth was consolidated; yet a strong start could be made with little capital and the established elite itself was pleased to make room for proven competitors, especially when it had daughters to provide for.

To the west, north, and south of Boston, simpler ways persisted, even though the conservatives thought that the new settlements springing up everywhere in the first third of the eighteenth century displayed a shocking disregard for authority. These "ungospelized" plantations, according to Cotton Mather, were "the very Brothel houses of Satan," and the inhabitants in the hinterlands were said to be "Indianizing" themselves. But to the outsider, the New England villages still seemed remarkable for their tidiness and decency.

Living frugally in simple frame houses, tilling an indifferent soil, the New England farmers developed into the tough, uncommunicative (though sometimes garrulous) American stereotype. Travelers thought them too democratic and careless of social distinctions. "They seem to be a good substantial Kind of Farmers," remarked one visitor, "but there is no break in their Society; their Government, Religion, and Manners all tend to support an equality. Whoever brings in your Victuals sits down and chats to you." When they did "chat," moreover, their superior education compared to that of rurals farther south, soon became evident. One observer from the South seemed surprised that these people, who looked "rather more like clowns, than the riff-raff of our Maryland planters," should discuss matters "that in our parts would be like Greek, Hebrew, or Arabick."

Actually, however, the plain people of New England, especially in Massachusetts, did not condone unlimited democracy, and they observed their own social distinctions. The large landowners in southern and western New England were the acknowledged leaders, along with the ministers, physicians, and innkeepers. The church meeting enforced a practical social discipline, and what often seemed like loose behavior (for example, the courtship custom known as "bundling" or "tarrying") simply illustrated rural innocence.

The Yankee, tight with his money yet philanthropic for the public good, loyal to his neighbors but regarding the world beyond his village as fair game, gradually became a kind of colonial paradox. He was admired for his industry and his institutions, but disdained for his shrewdness. Though deeply conservative and wary of sudden change, he was susceptible to emotional appeals in religion and to heresies in politics and economics.

v. *The Spirit of Provincial Politics*

THE BONDS
OF SOCIAL INTERCOURSE

When John Adams of Massachusetts, while attending the Continental Congress in Philadelphia in 1774, first saw in the flesh well-horsed, saber-rattling southerners with their flashy body slaves, he suffered the greatest anxiety of his life. He hastened to write home to his wife how he dreaded "the consequences of this dissimilitude of character" between Yankees and planters, and added that, "without the utmost caution on both sides, and the most considerate forbearance with one another, . . . they will certainly be fatal."

Long before Adams' unsettling experience it had become apparent to many in America and abroad that a country so diverse geographically and culturally, as the American mainland colonies had become, was not likely to unify itself. Idiom, custom, and economic interest divided the provinces. The vague definition of colonial boundaries in the colonial charters was the source of many conflicts. Maryland, Pennsylvania and Virginia, and Massachusetts and New York, engaged in drawn-out boundary disputes which grew especially acri-

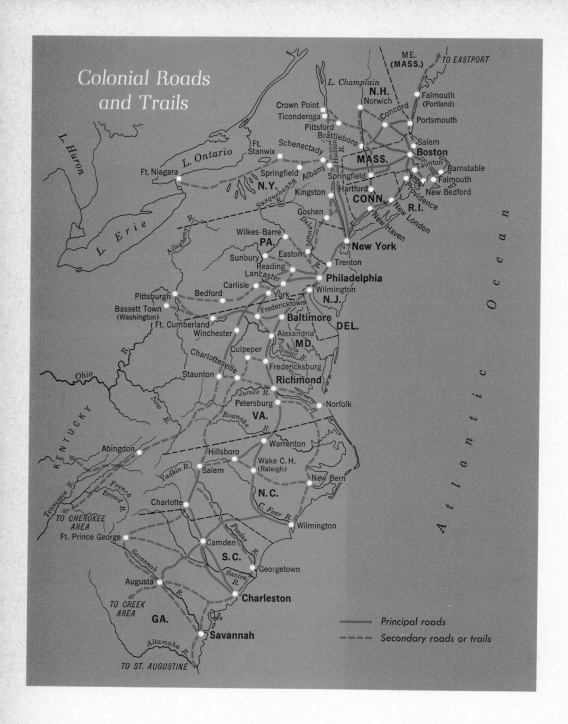

Colonial Roads and Trails

TO EASTPORT

ME. (MASS.)

L. Champlain

N.H.
Norwich

Falmouth (Portland)

Concord

Portsmouth

Crown Point
Ticonderoga
Pittsford
Brattleboro
Schenectady

Ft. Stanwix

Salem

Boston

L. Huron

L. Ontario

Ft. Niagara

Springfield   Albany

MASS.

Springfield

Taunton

Barnstable
Falmouth
New Bedford

N.Y.

Kingston

Hartford

Susquehanna R.

Goshen

CONN.

Providence

R.I.

New London

L. Erie

Allegheny R.

Wilkes-Barre

PA.

Sunbury   Easton
Reading
Lancaster

Delaware R.

New Haven

New York

Trenton

Pittsburgh
Bassett Town (Washington)

Bedford

Carlisle

York

Philadelphia

Wilmington

N.J.

Ft. Cumberland
Winchester

Fredericktown

Baltimore

DEL.

Alexandria

Ohio R.

Charlottesville

Culpeper

Potomac R.

MD.

New R.

Staunton

Fredericksburg

Richmond

KENTUCKY

James R.
Petersburg

Norfolk

Roanoke R.

VA.

Tennessee R.

Abingdon

Warrenton

Hillsboro

French Broad R.

Yadkin R.

Salem

Wake C.H. (Raleigh)

New Bern

TO CHEROKEE AREA

Charlotte

N.C.

C. Fear R.

Ft. Prince George

Camden

Peedee R.

Wilmington

S.C.

Santee R.

Georgetown

TO CREEK AREA

Augusta

Savannah R.

Charleston

GA.

Savannah

Altamaha R.

TO ST. AUGUSTINE

Atlantic Ocean

—————— Principal roads

- - - - - - Secondary roads or trails

monious in the middle of the eighteenth century when great land speculators from the different colonies staked out overlapping claims. These disputes eventually turned colony against colony in feuds that later helped drag out the Revolutionary War and postponed the establishment of a permanent federal government once independence had been declared. The movement of speculators and settlers westward also stirred the Indians to stronger resistance, and the colonies again fell out among themselves in trying to meet the recurrent challenges. Other issues involving the exchange of currency, piracy and smuggling, religion and politics, further complicated colonial relationships—to such a degree, indeed, that to many at home and abroad it seemed that only the stabilizing control of the mother country prevented colonial anarchy.

And yet, unifying influences also were at work. The insularity and provincialism that undoubtedly existed throughout colonial America was frequently noted by American and foreign travelers. But long before the Revolution, many intellectual barriers were being broken down, especially among the leaders in the different settlements who, despite their differences, shared many interests, beliefs, experiences, and aspirations. Waterways and roads brought the businessmen of New York, Philadelphia, Boston, and Charleston into a vital economic network. Itinerant peddlers, printers, and artists passed from colony to colony. Invalids took long journeys to improve their health, and vacationers to broaden their horizons. Well-to-do families paid visits to distant kin; Quakers and Jews sought out their scattered co-religionists. The colleges at Princeton, New Haven, and Cambridge attracted students from the South and the West Indies as well as from neighboring colonies. John Bartram of Philadelphia, one of many naturalists, botanized across the countryside and entertained fellow enthusiasts who came from afar to see his celebrated gardens. Fraternal societies, which were organized in the principal cities as early as the 1730's, welcomed members from other colonies; Washington, Franklin, and other colonial leaders were Masons even before their revolutionary activities brought them closer together. Finally, colonists read one another's newspapers, circular letters, sermons, pamphlets, and almanacs. The literate colonial had at his disposal a variety of information on matters outside his immediate sphere of interest—political, cultural, and economic—that linked him with the destiny of his continent. When the time came, colonial spokesmen were able to appeal to a set of widely shared beliefs and experiences, especially among a few thousand leading families, a few hundred in each colony, whose remarkable gains in

wealth and power underlay their more subtle claims to primacy.

THE SEAT
OF POLITICAL POWER

Nowhere was the emergence of the colonial elite more evident than in the structure and tendency of colonial politics. In each of the colonies in the mid-eighteenth century, the governor nominally was at the head of the government. Only in Connecticut and Rhode Island was he elected by the legislature. In Maryland and Pennsylvania he continued to be appointed by the absentee proprietor in England. In all the other colonies, including Georgia after 1752, he was appointed by the king. The governor himself appointed his council, which formed the upper house of the legislature. The lower house, usually called the assembly, represented those qualified electors who bothered to exercise their franchise. Local government differed from colony to colony; but even in Virginia, where the governor, like the king at home, appointed the justices of the peace, the most important local officers, the justices themselves firmly resisted interference once they had gained their commissions.

The governor's main strength lay in his right to veto provincial legislation. If he was a man of acumen and ability, he could of course influence the legislators to act in conformity with the king's policy; he could temper or constrain assembly actions before abrasive vetoes became necessary. But success in managing the elected representatives depended on mutual confidence between them and the governor, and confidence dwindled in the eighteenth century.

The assembly's main strength lay in its control of appropriations, including those for the governor's salary and for carrying out relevant parliamentary measures. In the eighteenth century, most of the colonial assemblies, like Parliament in England, used their control of the purse to control the entire government. The leading families, in turn, used their wealth and standing to control the assemblies for generations.

Two conditions helped perpetuate oligarchic power. One was the limitation of the franchise in practically all the colonies to those with considerable property, preferably in land. In some colonies, to be sure, such as Massachusetts and Pennsylvania, property qualifications were low enough and land ownership common enough to insure a substantial electorate, more or less representative of the whole adult population. But even in the North, as in New York and Connecticut, for example, many could not meet the property qualifications; in the South, the requirements usually were higher than in the North, and eligible voters relatively fewer. Certain colonies also had religious qualifications for voting, but with the exception of the almost universal disfranchisement of Catholics and Jews, these qualifications tended to be questioned less and less frequently where property qualifications could be met. So-called plural voting also was common. In Virginia and elsewhere, those who met the specific property qualification in each of two or more counties could vote two or more times; to make it easier for the gentry to exercise this privilege where they held land, election dates often were staggered. Property qualifications for office-holding, in turn were usually much higher than for the franchise itself. A member of the South Carolina assembly, for example, had to own at least 500 acres of land, 10 slaves, or other property worth at least £ 1,000.

The second objective condition tending to perpetuate oligarchic control was the under-representation of new inland settlements in the assemblies. The assemblies themselves often refused to establish new counties and towns in distant regions and to reapportion seats in the legislature in accord with changing population density. Inland regions sometimes were happy to be left without responsibility for paying for county or town government or for representation in the assembly and often did not complain of neglect until crises involving Indians or taxation aroused them. In South Carolina throughout the colonial period the inland settlements had no representatives whatever, and no local courts; and the planters in Charleston heard about this often enough.

These objective characteristics of colonial politics may have made it more difficult to overthrow the oligarchs in times of stress; but their rule tended to be sustained by the even stronger sanctions arising from the popular recognition of merit based on family and fortune. Locke's conception of property, on which the defense of oligarchic pretensions rested, went beyond the crassness of mere ownership, exploitation, and accumulation. Property was the foundation of moral independence, morality the foundation of welfare. Property carried obligation as well as power; great property incurred the obligation of great power employed for the common good.

Colonial history is well marked with local rebellions against the ruling oligarchs. One of the most persistent issues between them and the general population was the supply of money. The primary need for currency among the small-farmer population was for taxes, which, in their judgment (and usually they were right), were both too high and unfairly apportioned. Usually the population had the same relationship to speculators and importing merchants as the planters and northern gentry had to merchants abroad—in short, they were in debt for land, supplies, and other commodities they could not make themselves. Like debtors everywhere, they clamored for a plentiful supply of currency—that is, paper money. Often enough their demands were heeded; but since paper money had a tendency to be overissued and thus to decline in value, easy-money policies usually were reversed at what appeared to be the most inconvenient times. At such times, taxes, interest, rent, and due loans would go unpaid, and often enough collectors might be tarred and feathered and chased from the debtors' vicinity at gun point.

The classic battle over the currency supply occurred in Massachusetts in 1741, when the debtor farmers tried to establish a land bank against the will of the conservative Governor Belcher. A thousand farmers, "grown so brassy and hardy," said the angry governor, "as to be now combining in a body to raise a rebellion," prepared to march on Boston on election day and join their allies among the town laborers. Belcher jailed the leaders and election day passed quietly. But when the election results showed a heavy majority in favor of the land bank, Parliament came to the rescue of the defeated creditors by declaring land banks illegal. This decision, though popular among the moneyed gentry, increased the hostility between rich and poor.

Ten years later, largely owing to the scandalous depreciation of paper currency in Rhode Island, Parliament passed the Currency Act of 1751. New land banks were prohibited in New England, old issues of currency were to be called in at the date of their retirement, and new issues had to be guaranteed by taxes and retired after a limited period. These regulations widened the split between Parliament and rural New Englanders, whose violent response a few years later bore out Franklin's warning to London in 1764: "I wish some good Angel would forever whisper in the Ears of your great Men that Dominion is founded in Opinion."

Conflicts over the money supply, taxation, and debt were not necessarily sectional ones, although they became most acute where the "back parts" felt the weight of tidewater and town leaders. Other political conflicts were specifically sectional in origin. One of the most persistent of them arose over the complaints of new settlers on the moving frontier against the failure of the provincial governments to protect them from the Indians, the French, and the Spanish. The failure of the provincial governments to provide passable roads to markets was a second source of sectional conflict. A third was the failure of such governments to set up courts in the back

country and thus save the farmers the heavy cost of several days' travel and neglect of crops to have even minor controversies settled. A fourth was the collection of tithes for the established churches, which had few ministers and few communicants in the wilderness. The failure to extend representation and the suffrage to back country residents grew into a major issue itself largely because of the gentry's reluctance to correct the back country's other grievances.

Yet the rank and file rarely challenged the claims of the aristocracy to political place and power. Probably a fourth of the white population of the colonies was illiterate; probably a fifth of those who could read and write knew little or no English. Many others used it awkwardly. Most rustics, moreover, illiterate or not, could think of no more unnerving experience than having to address constituents in public meetings or to take effective places in legislative bodies. City artisans, shopkeepers, and laborers no doubt shared the misgivings of their country cousins. The common run of voters were still proud to be represented by the great men of their neighborhood or of the colony as a whole. Thus they returned to office generation after generation of Byrds, Carters, Harrisons, and Washingtons in Virginia; of Van Rensselaers, Schuylers, and Livingstons in New York; of Logans, Norrises, Pembertons, and Dickinsons in Pennsylvania. Even in Massachusetts, where the suffrage qualifications were light and educational levels and literacy higher than elsewhere in America, Hutchinsons, Hancocks, Olivers, Bowdoins, and Brattles all were repeatedly returned to rule. A popular political genius like Sam Adams in Massachusetts, the first great rabble-rouser in the colonies, developed a "machine" of his own, known at the outset of the Revolution as the "Caucus Club." But even an Adams made little progress against the oligarchs until they wanted his support to meet the British challenge.

VI. *The World Wars of the Eighteenth Century*

In the eighteenth century, the territory between the Appalachians and the Mississippi was as much a battlefield as a "wilderness." The Indians of this overwhelming forest warred among themselves for lands to insure their supply of game and fish and grain, or for territory rich in the furs that the white man was so eager to buy, or for control of the watercourses and woodland paths over which pelts and skins were hauled to the white man's posts. The invaders, in turn, clashed among themselves, first over control of the hunting and trading tribes, then over the lands in the great drainage basins, and ultimately over the whole of North America. Few understood the terms of the enduring warfare better than the civilized Indian tribes—above all, the five Iroquois Nations of New York (Mohawk, Oneida, Onondaga, Cayuga, and Seneca) whose empire it was that all contended for.

Almost from the start of the fur trade early in the seventeenth century, the Iroquois, the friends of the Dutch, had terrorized the surrounding Algonquians, the friends of the French, and eventually had driven them from the trapping grounds eastward to the sea, where they became the scourge of New England's struggling fishing villages and inland settlements. When the French then turned westward to establish relations with the Hurons, who served the hunting Indians north and west of them as middlemen with white seaboard traders, the Dutch urged their Iroquois allies to "muscle in" on the Huron monopoly. In 1649 the Five Nations launched a brutal invasion of the Huron peninsula, destroyed the high Huron civilization, and sent most of the hunting tribes of the upper Mississippi flying across the prairie to pile up against the borders of the inhospitable Sioux, the fierce horse Indians of the plains.

By the 1660's the French had established new Indian connections in the Northwest and when the Iroquois resumed their policy of harassment, Louis XIV, in 1666, sent a crack military force to Canada to quell the Five Nations. This force struck with such stunning impact that forever after the Iroquois retained a healthy respect for French arms. The setback also caused them to place a higher value on their connections with the English, who had supplanted the Dutch at Albany and New Amsterdam, and to look southward to satisfy their own imperial ambitions.

At its peak in the eighteenth century, the Iroquois empire spread some 800 miles between the Appalachians and the Mississippi, southwesterly from the home valley in central New York all the way to the Creek confederacy on the borders of Spanish Florida. Iroquois warriors probably never numbered more than 10,000, and the task of subduing and holding tributary the hunting and trapping tribes in this vast domain strained the Five Nations to the utmost. Yet until past the middle of the century the Iroquois League managed to dissuade even their British allies from settling permanently in its immensely rich fur empire. And the French, compelled to range exhausting distances for furs north and west of their capital at Quebec, were never permitted to forget the menace of the League at their rear.

THE ANCIEN RÉGIME IN CANADA

For a hundred years after the decimation of the Hurons the fur trade north of the Ohio could as accurately be described as "the fur war." Senseless raids and bloody reprisals kept the wilderness and the settlements that bordered on it in constant turmoil and their denizens, red and white alike, watchful, suspicious, on edge. Armed conflict was supplemented by rival missionary activity, espionage, secret pacts, and frequent treachery.

But the war had its constructive side: the brutal competition for fur provided an overpowering impulse to discovery and exploration. One of the heaviest costs of the fur trade was transportation; and one of the traders' most urgent quests, aside from new beaver lands themselves, was for new waterways to carry the pelts to Atlantic ports. More than geography was involved. As the Jesuit, Albanel, observed in the 1670's, "It is no new thing for the Savages to be extremely cautious in granting strangers a passage, by way of their rivers, to distant Nations. The rivers are to them . . . their sole source of subsistence—whether in the form of fish or game, or in that of traffic." The dynamics of the fur trade drew rival European explorers on an endless search for territory until they spanned the continent; diplomacy, intimidation, and conquest opened up the strategic waterways by which the continent's wealth was realized.

France, it is often said, had many advantages over Britain in the contest for North America, while Spain is supposed to have lain dormant. In fact, the Spanish North American empire grew at France's expense during the half-century and more preceding the expulsion of the French in 1763, and survived another half-century after the French had gone. France's alleged advantages over Britain include: (1) the absolute power of the governor-general of Canada, especially in emergencies, in contrast to the multiplicity of authorities in the British colonies; (2) the professionalism of the permanent military forces in Canada, in contrast to the improvised citizen militias of the British provinces; and (3) the success of French missionaries in converting the natives, and of French lay administrators and traders in holding their affections and allegiance, in contrast to the hatred with which the red man viewed the permanent British settlers who were depriving them of their ancient lands.

But on analysis these alleged French advantages appear dubious. The governor, as we have seen (p. 24), shared power with the intendant and the resident bishop; and since each depended for his authority on rivals for authority at home, New France was always riven by petty jealousies and selfish cliques. "Canada," cried the frustrated Antoine de La Mothe-Cadillac in 1699, "is a country of cabals and intrigues, and it is impossible to reconcile so many different interests." The good relations of the French with the Indians, moreover, were preserved at the cost of erecting solid and self-sufficient communities in the New World upon which their professional military forces might depend.

One of the fundamental failures of the regime was the seigniorial system of landholding. Early in the history of New France, the best river-front lands had been granted under feudal tenure to army officers and other *gentilshommes* who made little effort to bring them under cultivation. Eventually some of the fiefs fell into the possession of thrifty merchants and unusually gifted *habitants,* or peasants, who by scrimping and saving over the years somehow managed to accumulate enough capital to buy out cash-hungry noblemen at bargain prices. Such self-made *seigneurs* often made farming pay. Yet for generations the domestic food supply of New France remained poorer even than that of the Indians before the white man came. As a consequence, the vaunted professional soldiers of New France were always dependent on the home country and on neighboring New England for sustenance.

Canadian industry was even more backward than its agriculture, which meant that the regime had to rely on ocean-going vessels to bring in munitions, trading goods, and other hardware. But the only navigable entry to French warehouses in Montreal and Quebec was by way of the St. Lawrence, which was either frozen or clogged with ice floes half the year. This inadequate supply line from the sea made it easy in times of crisis for the British navy and British and Yankee privateers to offset the nominal military superiority of the enemy.

Besides its internal problems, the French

regime in Quebec faced other difficulties. Compared, for example, with the lush sugar islands of the West Indies, Canada ranked low in the French scheme of overseas empire. This empire itself, moreover, ranked far below the commitments and ambitions of the Bourbon dynasty in Europe. Louis XIV and his successors considered Canada an arctic waste, little better than a place of exile for aristocratic busybodies and other nuisances. All the more astonishing, then, are the successes these outcasts and a handful of devoted empire-builders achieved in the distant reaches of North America.

THE FRENCH BARRIER

The most intrepid and imaginative of the empire-builders of New France was the veteran *coureur de bois,* Robert Cavalier, Sieur de La Salle. La Salle's successful descent of the Mississippi to its mouth in April, 1682 (see p. 24), was a mere preliminary to his breathtaking scheme for a comprehensive commercial system in North America, which involved the subjugation of the British and the Spanish as well. In this scheme, the Mississippi had many attractions besides its grandeur. Control of its whole length would confine the incorrigible Iroquois to the eastern valley and in addition would frustrate plans to link up the Iroquois empire with the British satrapy at Hudson Bay (see p. 24). At the same time it would split the Spanish empire to the south and open the vast American plains to French exploitation. Above all, perhaps, the Mississippi offered an all-weather outlet to the sea for the furs of the virgin lands it dominated.

By December, 1682, La Salle and his company, on their journey upstream from the mouth of the Mississippi, found themselves at the confluence of the great river and the Illinois. At this point, La Salle ordered the construction of an armed post, Fort St. Louis, to serve at once as a beacon to friendly braves eager for trade and a bastion against the Iroquois who, ever since Joliet's voyage (see p. 24), had conducted raids on all interlopers, red and white, and had sworn La Salle's death. Trade flourished during the first spring at Fort St. Louis; but the fickle government of Louis XIV now replaced La Salle's friend, Governor Louis Count de Frontenac, with a new governor, Le Febvre de la Barre, who grew jealous of La Salle's fur monopoly and was unwilling to assist in its defense. Desperate to conclude this phase of his work, La Salle left subordinates in charge at St. Louis and took ship for France to try to obtain additional backing for the construction of another post at the very mouth of the Mississippi to protect Louisiana from the Spanish and provide a port from which the furs of the whole vast valley could be exported to the world. During his absence St. Louis became untenable, and La Salle's own excursion cost him his life. Having found backing in Paris in 1684, he was on his triumphant way back to the future site of New Orleans with four strong ships, when the weather turned stormy, the crews rebellious, and navigation blind. Failing to find the Mississippi, the company piled up hundreds of miles away at Spanish Matagorda Bay. Here the imperious commander was unceremoniously murdered by his men, who in turn were massacred by Comanche warriors.

La Salle's difficulties with the Iroquois—it was they who had delayed the start of his Mississippi enterprise from 1675 to 1682—served as an inspiration to another Frontenac favorite, the *coureur,* Daniel Greysolon, Sieur Du Lhut (anglicized as Duluth). In 1678 Du Lhut proposed to divert the pelts of the virgin West, both from the British at Hudson Bay and their Iroquois allies in the Mississippi country, by resuming the quest for a northwest passage to the Pacific.

Between 1678 and 1681, Du Lhut and his rangers explored the northern reaches of the Mississippi River almost to its distant source and claimed much of the country beyond it for France. But in place of the Iroquois they soon encountered the ferocious Sioux who convinced them that it would be best to go around their territory. The only way around the Sioux open to the French was through the frigid Saskatchewan Valley and the forbidding country still farther north—country that other Frenchmen were to penetrate and explore before the end of the eighteenth century. Du Lhut returned to Quebec in 1681 to answer Jesuit charges that he was setting up a private fur empire and undermining the central administration. The charges did not stick, but Du Lhut never strayed so far again.

Failures like La Salle's and Du Lhut's convinced Canadian officials that they would have to resort to military terror if the Iroquois and other enemy tribes were to be controlled and if the British and the Spanish were to be ousted from the French empire. The Jesuits fought the military policy even more pertinaciously than they opposed the *coureurs;* and the aging Louis XIV, increasingly concerned over his eternal soul, supported the churchmen. Frontenac, however, who had returned as governor in 1689, took his own militant course. Before his death in 1698 the French had built or started forts along the entire length of the Mississippi, across the Great Lakes country, and on the Gulf of Mexico. The northern anchor of this system was Fort Detroit, which Cadillac, after bitter controversies with the Jesuits, managed to finish in 1699. The same year saw completion of the fort at Biloxi. Another was built at Mobile in 1711. In 1718, the fort was completed at New Orleans, the southernmost citadel of the French North American empire.

EUROPE'S WARS
AND AMERICAN EMPIRE

Virtually from the beginning of settlement in North America, the Protestant British and the Catholic Spanish and French, each with their tentative Indian allies, had been warring on one another. The central issue in the enduring conflict was nothing less than the role and purpose of the New World in the European scheme of things. The Spanish, and to a greater degree the French, saw their empires as little more than sources of great enrichment for aristocrats, Church, and Crown at home. The Indians and the land existed merely for rapid exploitation. The British,

and those of other nationalities who settled in the British colonies, had a different view. The New World offered an escape, a haven, from the old, especially for those oppressed by aristocrats, Church, and Crown. The land existed for homesteading as well as for exploitation. The Indians, especially as they fell in with the French and the Spanish to harass the British settlements, were most urgently to be removed from the land. These different attitudes, of course, were not universally held in the different countries nor in America. Many British aristocrats, clergymen, and kings shared Spanish and French ideas, as did certain rising American aristocrats themselves. Many Spanish and French spokesmen, in turn, tried to promote the emigration of their countrymen to permanent settlements. But such exceptions only lent interest to the conflict and did not control its course.

The series of world wars that ultimately settled the future of North America in favor of the British and the Americans began in Europe itself in 1689, when William III became king of England with a strong personal motive for warring against Louis XIV of France (see p. 70). When Louis threatened to overrun William's homeland in the Netherlands in 1689, William led a "grand alliance" against him. Known in Europe as the War of the League of Augsburg, and in America as King William's War, the struggle dragged on until 1697. William's League got none the worst of the fighting on the Continent, but the French had all the best of it in America, where their forces captured York Factory on Hudson Bay, collaborated with the Indians in ferocious raids against British settlements at Schenectady, New York, and on the Maine and New Hampshire frontiers, and harassed the Massachusetts fishing fleet. Governor Frontenac himself turned back a vigorous assault on Quebec led by a worthy antagonist, tough William Phips, Governor of Massachusetts.

While this war was in progress, other parties to the future universal conflict strengthened their New World positions. The Iroquois, alarmed by the new show of French strength under Frontenac, pledged themselves once more to the British; it was on this pledge that British claims to the Ohio and Mississippi valleys were henceforth to rest. As part of the agreement, the Five Nations promised to end their bedevilment of the American settlements verging on their domains. Americans in the Carolinas, meanwhile, pushed their own hunting and trading activities to the very shores of the Mississippi below St. Louis. To check them and the French in Louisiana, Spain enlarged the meager occupation of Texas, New Mexico, and West Florida, and in 1696 established a base at Pensacola, Florida.

The peace of 1697 came to a violent end in 1702. Two years before, the Spanish king had died without an heir, and Louis XIV had grasped the opportunity to extend Bourbon influence to the Iberian Peninsula by installing his grandson on the throne. William III, backing a candidate of his own, allied himself with other continental powers to expel Louis' protégé. With an eye to the balance of power in the New World, moreover, they agreed among themselves, as one of their treaties said, "especially . . . that the French shall never come into possession of the Spanish Indies nor be permitted . . . to navigate there for the purpose of carrying on trade."

William III died in 1702. His successor, Queen Anne, persisting in his policies, fought France and Spain for eleven bitter years in the conflict known in Europe as the War of the Spanish Succession, in America as Queen Anne's War. In the New World the struggle ranged from the Atlantic to the Mississippi, from the Gulf of Mexico to Hudson Bay. In this war, the French and their Spanish allies eventually were defeated everywhere and Spain henceforth declined as a world power. The Peace of Utrecht of 1713 confirmed the Bourbons' occupation of the Spanish throne, which remained in their family until 1931. But in the New World, France surrendered the rich island of St. Christopher in the West Indies to her Protestant enemy, confirmed British supremacy over Hudson Bay, and yielded Acadia as well. Above all, the French recognized the Iroquois as British subjects and the Iroquois empire as a British domain. Britain also won commercial concessions from both France and Spain that boosted her own as well as American trade with the Spanish Main and Spanish Caribbean islands.

The British took such gluttonous advantage of Spain's commercial concessions that the Spanish organized a special Caribbean coast guard, manned by the roughest pirates they could enlist. In 1739 a British officer named Captain Jenkins was haled before Parliament by the "war party" that was growing in opposition to Spanish manhandling of British seamen. In a little box he carried a carefully preserved human ear, which he claimed a Spanish officer had cut from his head as a bloody warning to the British. This dramatic tableau created a sensation, and Britain promptly embarked on "The War of Jenkins' Ear." Disaster followed disaster as the British staged a series of unsuccessful attacks on the Atlantic and Pacific coasts of Spanish America. No final decision was reached until a new general European war broke out in 1745, this time over the Austrian succession.

One of the places Britain had failed to take from the French in 1713 was Cape Breton Island, just to the north of Acadia, which commanded the entrance to the Gulf of St. Lawrence. Here the French had hastened to construct the mighty fortress of Louisbourg, the "Gibraltar of the New World." In the third of the great international conflicts, the War of the Austrian Succession, or King George's War (1745-1748), Massachusetts forces assaulted Louisbourg and, to everyone's surprise, including their own, they managed to capture it. Colonial love for the mother country was hardly warmed by British restoration of Louisbourg to the French in the Peace of Aix-la-Chapelle, which ended this latest struggle. In return, Britain received Madras in India.

The Treaty of Aix-la-Chapelle was more a truce than a permanent settlement. Even before it was signed, both the French and the British had begun preparations for a final showdown. In 1747, with the formation of the Ohio Company of Virginia, Britain had embarked on a shrewd program of encouraging colonial land speculators to stake out huge tracts in the Ohio Valley, "inasmuch as nothing can more effectively tend to defeat the dangerous designs of the French." In 1749, the governor of Canada sent his own representatives, Jean Baptiste Le Moyne, Sieur de Bienville, to occupy the valley. During the next few years other Frenchmen followed to work out a system of military defenses. Governor Dinwiddie of Virginia, an investor in the Ohio Company, caught wind of French activity in 1753 and ordered young George Washington to travel west with a protest. When this mission failed, Washington was sent out the next year with a small force and orders to halt the French. This mission ran up against the newly erected French Fort Duquesne at the forks of the Ohio, the site of modern Pittsburgh. Washington proceeded to build his own Fort Necessity at nearby Great Meadows, but in July was forced to capitulate to a French attack upon it. Although the formal declaration of war between the French and the English did not come until 1756, actual fighting had already begun, appropriately enough, in the New World.

The extension of French fort-building in the West caused the Privy Council in England to look to its own strength in America. This rested heavily on the Iroquois; but the British now sensed the growing discontent of their native allies in the face of such policies that prompted the creation of the Ohio Company itself. American land hunger and frequent confrontations between red men and white on the moving frontier further strengthened Indian suspicions of the sanctity of their preserves. In an attempt to restore Iroquois confidence, the Privy Council called for a meeting at Albany, New York, in June, 1754, at which

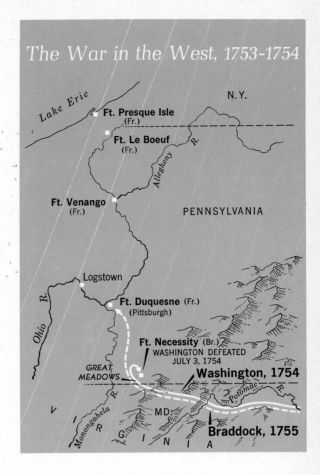

The War in the West, 1753-1754

delegates from all the northern colonies were to meet with Iroquois and other Indian leaders. At the Albany Congress the Iroquois accepted the lavish British gifts but made no promises of their own. To their suspicions of the British were added their growing respect and fear of the military activities of the French.

One objective of the Albany Congress was the formation of an intercolonial union to bring some consistency into colonial Indian policies. Under Benjamin Franklin's leadership a Plan of Union was presented and accepted by the delegates. It called for a "General Government . . . under which Government each Colony may retain its present constitution" except for certain particulars. The super-government would consist of a grand council made up of representatives drawn from each colony on the basis of population and wealth. A president-general (to be appointed by the king) and a treasurer would comprise the executive branch, advised by the grand council but with final authority in matters of peace and war. The grand council would handle Indian affairs, administer the disposal of western lands, govern the frontier territories beyond the precincts of the colonies until the Crown took over, and levy taxes to maintain a colonial army.

Neither the British government nor the individual colonial governments would even consider this enlightened proposal. "The Assemblies," Franklin wrote, ". . . thought there was too much *prerogative* in it, and in England it was judged to have too much of the *democratic*." Land speculators, who were particularly strong in the Virginia government, had no intention of entrusting the distribution of the Ohio lands to an intercolonial congress, and every colonial assembly was jealous of its own control of taxation. The colonies were not ready for union in 1754, and the war against the French was conducted inefficiently and with constant bickering among the colonies themselves and between the colonies and the mother country.

In an effort to nip the impending war in America while Europe itself was in turmoil, the British, in April, 1755, sent General Edward Braddock and 1,400 regulars to America to level Fort Duquesne. He was to be assisted by 450 colonials under Lieutenant Colonel Washington. This entire ex-

pedition, in July, was ambushed and savagely mauled by a force of French and Indians on the Monongahela River about eight miles below the fort. Braddock was mortally wounded. His defeat was an eye-opener to the colonials whose regard for British redcoats declined swiftly. When the survivors were saved by the timely work of Washington and his militia, the Colonel's estimation of their own prowess rose. Braddock's defeat also weakened the waning prestige of the British among the Indians. The French and Indian victory now exposed the western settlements of Pennsylvania, Maryland, and Virginia to a series of French and Indian raids. Other British operations that year were also largely unsuccessful. General William Johnson, with 2,000 British troops and 250 Mohawks, rebuffed a strong French assault on Lake George. Elsewhere, however, the British failed to take Fort Niagara, the key to French control of the West, or Crown Point on Lake Champlain.

In the meantime, the struggle for America had once more become a phase of a world war raging on the Continent, in the Mediterranean, the Indian Ocean, the West Indies, and finally even the Philippines. In a new shift of alliances, France, Austria, Russia, Sweden, many of the German states, and later Spain, were arrayed against Britain, Portugal, and Prussia. Until 1758 the contest went dismally for Britain and her allies. Then the brilliant organizer and strategist, William Pitt, became Secretary of State, and British fortunes picked up. Perceiving the central importance of seapower and of the North American theater of action, Pitt subsidized Frederick the Great of Prussia to carry the burden of war in Europe, used the British fleet to bottle up French ships in French ports, and brought greater energy to bear in the New World. For Pitt the central strategic objective was the conquest of Canada and the capture of the American interior. To this end he used British superiority at sea to strike hardest at the two focal points of French power—Louisbourg and Quebec.

In 1758 the British recaptured Louis-

Campaigns in the North
1755-1760

■ Captured by British

CANADA

Wolfe 1759

Louisbourg

Quebec

Montreal

St. Lawrence R.

L. Champlain

Crown Point

Ft. Ticonderoga

L. Ontario

Ft. Niagara

L. Erie

Boston

British 1755

Ft. Duquesne

NOVA SCOTIA

Atlantic Ocean

bourg, the key to the St. Lawrence River and the Atlantic fisheries, and a standing threat to New England. The event was celebrated with great bonfires in London, Philadelphia, Boston, and New York. In the same year George Washington, now on the staff of Brigadier John Forbes, had the satisfaction at last of taking part in the capture of Fort Duquesne, now known as Pittsburgh. Frederick, meanwhile, turned the tide on the Continent, and Clive began to tame the French in India. The climax among the victories of the following year came when a brilliant young brigadier general, James Wolfe, after bringing a large army up the St. Lawrence from Louisbourg, stormed the Heights of Abraham outside Quebec and took the city from a smaller force under General Montcalm, thus gaining strategic control of the St. Lawrence. Both generals were killed in the battle, but Wolfe lived long enough to know that he had won Canada for the empire. Since the British were also winning on the sea, in the West Indies, in India, and in the American West, the crisis in the war had passed. "Some time ago," said Pitt in the midst of all these triumphs, "I would have been content to bring France to her knees, now I will not rest till I have laid her on her back." Thus the war dragged on until 1763.

By the Treaty of Paris, concluded in February, 1763, Britain won from France all of Canada and all the great interior east of the Mississippi except for the port of New Orleans. France (to the dismay of Pitt, who had been dismissed by George III) retained fishing rights on the Newfoundland banks and two small islands as fishing bases there. Britain also returned to her the captured West Indies islands of Martinique and Guadeloupe. Spain gave up East and West Florida to the British in return for the restoration of Cuba, which had been overrun the preceding year. By a treaty contracted in 1762, France, which had induced Spain to enter the war, compensated her ally by yielding to her all the French territories west of the Mississippi, together with the Isle of Orleans.

Even before the negotiations leading to

the Treaty of Paris, British statesmen realized that they could not have both Guadeloupe and Canada—that if they demanded both, the French would continue the fight. Perhaps most influential in the decision to keep Canada and renounce Guadeloupe was

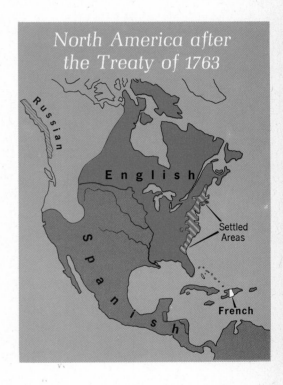

North America after the Treaty of 1763

the pressure exerted by plantation owners in the British West Indies, who feared the competition they would encounter from Guadeloupe's sugar if that island were brought into the empire. But more general considerations also had their effect. Most important among these was the rise in importance of Britain's mainland colonies, especially the rapidly growing Middle colonies and New England, as markets for British goods. Heretofore, the American empire had been valued mainly as a source of raw materials—tobacco and rice in the mainland South, sugar in the West Indies; in 1698, seven-eighths of Britain's American trade had been with these staple producing regions. By the 1760's, two-thirds of Britain's American exports were going to areas north of Maryland. Removing France in Canada from this area, even at the cost of another sugar island, seemed sound policy.

During the argument over the treaty, it was asked whether Canada would not some day revolt and announce its independence of Britain. It was also said that if the French were expelled from Canada, the American colonists themselves would no longer feel so dependent on the mother country for protection. Benjamin Franklin, then in London as a colonial agent, wrote a pamphlet on the subject in which he argued for retaining Canada as part of an American agricultural empire that would offer a vast and rapidly expanding market for British manufactures. The idea of independence Franklin brushed lightly aside. If the North American colonists had been incapable of uniting against the French and Indians, he asked, was there any likelihood that they would unite against "their own nation" which "they love much more than they love one another?" A union among the colonies, he went on, "is not merely improbable, it is impossible."

But here Franklin added an explanation which, though he did not mean it as a warning, might well have been taken as such: "When I say such a union is impossible, I mean without the most grievous tyranny and oppression." There was no assurance, of course, that Englishmen and Americans would agree on precisely what constituted grievous tyranny. When Franklin published his essay in 1760, he could hardly have imagined that 16 years later he would put his signature to a Declaration of Independence and negotiate for loans with Britain's enemies.

Readings

Asterisk indicates that book is available in paperback.

The fascinating story of emigration from the Old World to the New is told in M. L. Hansen, *The Atlantic Migration, 1607-1860* * (1940), and Carl Wittke, *We Who Built America: The Saga of the Immigrant* * (1939). A. E. Smith, *Colonists In Bondage* (1947), is outstanding on white servant immigration. The early history of the Negro in the mainland colonies is recounted in the early chapters of J. H. Franklin, *From Slavery to Freedom* (1956). A. B. Faust, *The German Element in the United States* (2 vols., 1909), is still the standard work. H. A. Pochmann, *German Culture in America: Philosophical and Literary Influences* (1957), is particularly good on the colonial period. For the Scotch-Irish and the Scotch see H. J. Ford, *The Scotch-Irish in America* (1915), and I. C. G. Graham, *Colonists from Scotland, Emigration to North America 1707-1783* (1956).

Three books, among others by T. J. Wertenbaker, cover the social background of the colonial period under the general title, *The Founding of American Civilization*. These are *The Old South* (1942), *The Middle Colonies* (1938), and *The Puritan Oligarchy* * (1947). Carl Bridenbaugh, *Myths and Realities: Societies of the Colonial South* * (1952), is short, iconoclastic, and stimulating. Much insight into Chesapeake society in the eighteenth century is afforded in the first two volumes of the life of Washington by D. S. Freeman under the title, *The Young Washington* (2 vols., 1948). A. H. Hirsch, *The Huguenots of South Carolina* (1928), is suggestive on Charleston society. Volume I of L. C. Gray, *History of Agriculture in the Southern United States to 1860* (2 vols., 1933), offers the standard account. V. W. Crane, *The Southern Frontier 1670-1732* * (1929), is an excellent introduction to life in the interior. A. W. Lauber, *Indian Slavery in Colonial Times* (1913), is a good study of a neglected subject.

Particularly valuable on the cultural, social, and political life of colonial Pennsylvania are: Carl and Jessica Bridenbaugh, *Rebels and Gentlemen: Philadelphia in the Age of Franklin* * (1942); F. B. Tolles, *Meeting House and Counting House: the Quaker Mer-*

chants of Colonial Philadelphia * (1948); and Tolles' *Quakers and The Atlantic Culture* (1960). Michael Kraus, *The Atlantic Civilization: Eighteenth Century Origins* (1949), discusses cultural ties with England in particular. Urban life in the colonial period is authoritatively dealt with in two books by Carl Bridenbaugh: *Cities in the Wilderness . . . 1625-1742* * (1938), and *Cities in Revolt . . . 1743-1776* * (1955). Bridenbaugh, ed., *Gentleman's Progress* (1948), is the account, by Dr. Alexander Hamilton, of his trip from Maryland to New England in 1744.

New England society is adequately if not impartially covered in J. T. Adams, *Revolutionary New England 1691-1776* (1923). To correct Adam's anti-Puritan bias, the reader should consult S. E. Morison, *Intellectual Life of Colonial New England* * (1956); the pro-Puritan biography of an important Massachusetts leader, K. B. Murdock, *Increase Mather, the Foremost American Puritan* (1925); and Perry Miller, *The New England Mind: From Colony to Province* * (1953). C. K. Shipton, *New England Life in the 18th Century, Representative Biographies from Sibley's Harvard Graduates* (1963), affords a vivid panorama of elite activities. W. B. Weeden, *Economic and Social History of New England 1620-1789* (2 vols., 1890), remains the best survey of this subject. This may be profitably supplemented for the later colonial period by J. B. Hedges, *The Browns of Providence Plantations, Colonial Years* (1952), and W. T. Baxter, *The House of Hancock, Business in Boston 1724-1775* (1945). More specialized studies include Bernard and Lotte Bailyn, *Massachusetts Shipping 1697-1714* (1959), a path-breaking statistical study, and G. A. Billias, *The Massachusetts Land Bankers of 1740* (1959). Information on the New England back country can be found in L. K. Mathews, *The Expansion of New England* (1909), and the early chapters of L. N. Newcomer, *The Embattled Farmers: A Massachusetts Countryside in the American Revolution* (1953).

Leonard Labaree, *Royal Government in America, A Study of the British Colonial System before 1783* (1930), affords a comprehensive survey of administration and legislation. Among more specialized works of importance we may note J. P. Greene, *The Quest for Power, The Lower Houses of the Assembly in the Southern Royal Colonies 1689-1776* (1963), and J. A. Schutz, *William Shirley, King's Governor of Massachusetts* (1961). The colonial franchise and representation has been thoroughly restudied in recent years, in such works as R. E. Brown, *Middle-Class Democracy and the Revolution in Massachusetts 1691-1780* (1955); Theodore Thayer, *Pennsylvania Politics and the Growth of Democracy 1740-1776* (1953); and R. P. McCormick, *The History of Voting in New Jersey* (1953). Their general conclusions about the liberality of the franchise and the democratic character of representation are strongly challenged in such works as C. S. Grant, *Democracy in the Connecticut Frontier Town of Kent* (1961), and C. S. Sydnor, *Gentlemen Freeholders, Political Practices in Washington's Virginia* * (1952). The early chapters of Chilton Williamson, *American Suffrage, From Property to Democracy 1760-1860* (1960), afford a scholarly survey of colonial practice.

The eight volumes of Francis Parkman's classic, *France and England in North America*, first published between 1851 and 1892, have been successfully abridged in the far from fragmentary one-volume edition, *The Parkman Reader* * (1955), edited by S. E. Morison. J. B. Brebner, *The Explorers of North America 1492-1806* * (1933), is a splendid account of the discovery and exploration of the interior of the continent. G. M. Wrong, *The Rise and Fall of New France* (2 vols., 1928), is a standard work, which may be supplemented from other points of view by Donald Creighton, *A History of Canada* (1958 ed.), and W. T. Easterbrook and H. G. J. Aitken, *Canadian Economic History* (1956). G. T. Hunt, *The Wars of the Iroquois, A Study of Intertribal Trade Relations* * (1940), and A. W. Trelease, *Indian Affairs in Colonial New York, The Seventeenth Century* (1960), are outstanding on the northern Indians and the fur trade. H. H. Peckham, *The Colonial Wars 1689-1762* * (1964), offers a short, authoritative account of the conflict for empire.

CHAPTER FOUR

The epithets "colonial" and "provincial" carry a connotation of narrowness, rusticity, isolation from the main stream of thought and action in the world. And it is true that in many parts of eighteenth-century America the intellectual baggage brought over by the early settlers had become obsolete and threadbare—if, indeed, it had not been altogether cast off in the wilderness. Few people could find time for philosophy or even for contemplation; when work was set aside for the day, the old forms of religion continued to serve most of those who had not entirely abandoned activities of the mind and nourishment of the spirit.

The Mature
Colonial Mind

Yet the "new world" was in fact new; and even in the realm of traditional religious observance important changes were apparent. By the beginning of the eighteenth century the traditional churches, the Anglicans, Presbyterians, and New England Congregationalists, were losing ground in a number of ways. In one quarter, the once hot fires of sectarian commitment seemed to have been banked. With the passing of the generations, the comfortable, often wealthy members of seaboard congregations relaxed in the severity of their religious views and chose to listen to preachers who made smaller emotional demands on them,

preachers who themselves were often intellectually broadened by new currents of thought. Some of the more advanced divines, like their advanced parishioners, were even beginning to flirt with the "religion of reason," and this tendency grew stronger as the century wore on.

In another quarter, traditional churches were afflicted by a quite different kind of loss. Preachers who had surrendered the old orthodoxies and yet had no stomach for the new modes of thought became simply cold and ineffectual and left their congregations dissatisfied. Members of these congregations gradually turned with growing favor to the revivalist preachers of the Great Awakening of the 1730's and 1740's. Such preachers aroused great waves of religious "enthusiasm," as it was called. They also stirred up new conflicts that permanently split established congregations and denominations. By the end of the colonial period one thus found in America an extraordinarily wide range of religious views, running from austere rationalism to obscure pietism.

Although Europeans, and Englishmen in particular, moreover, might continue to scorn the "colonials" as bumpkins and barbarians, certain leaders of thought had begun to give a distinctive American cast to secular as well as religious ideas. Benjamin Franklin, in particular, honored and respected in the great world of learning, could have sprouted nowhere but in the mainland colonies. By the eighteenth century American prosperity permitted a cultivated minority, at least, to engage in non-utilitarian pursuits and to keep up with the latest intellectual developments on the Continent. This minority created a staunch little world of its own where American savants could talk and speculate and experiment. The Enlightenment became the intellectual hallmark of the eighteenth century; and Americans not only shared in the new universe it opened to the mind, but actually broadened its perspectives and its scope.

I. *The Religious Mind*

PURITANS UNDER STRESS

The sapping of orthodoxy in religion was particularly striking in New England, where the demands of the old divines had been most rigorous and hence contrasted most markedly with the growing wealth and cosmopolitanism of the townspeople. The social changes also affected many of the clergy and cost the church its former internal solidarity and outward high prestige.

Puritan orthodoxy suffered its first serious blow in the "Half-Way Covenant" of 1662 (see p. 56), which permitted church members who had no religious experiences to confess in public to remain in the church and to have their children baptized. A series of dramatic setbacks followed this first one. Under the short administration of Governor Andros (1686-89), the legal foundations of Puritanism were undermined in the Bay Colony and Anglicanism was introduced. Massachusetts' revised charter of 1691 then substituted property for religious tests as a qualification for voting. The excesses of the Salem witchcraft hysteria that followed immediately in 1692 further weakened ministerial authority.

This episode began when two Salem girls accused some townspeople of bewitching them, and soon a perfect epidemic of witch-hunting infected the community. Before the scare had died down, 20 victims had been executed and more than a hundred others were awaiting trial. The ministers and the magistrates who conducted the witch trials soon came to their senses when the most eminent and respected citizens were branded as the Devil's emissaries. Both Increase and Cotton Mather had inadvertently encouraged the outbreak by publishing books proving the existence of witches—this at a time when William Penn dismissed a case against a woman charged with riding on a broomstick by saying "that there was no law in Pennsylvania against riding on broomsticks." During the trials, the Mathers had cautioned the court not to accept as evidence the reports of persons allegedly afflicted by witchcraft. Since neither the Mathers nor the other ministers actively opposed the trials, however, they were subsequently blamed for the abuses and their reputations suffered.

JONATHAN EDWARDS:
YANKEE REVIVALIST

The theological luminary of the next generation in New England was the great revivalist, Jonathan Edwards (1703-58).

A devoted Congregationalist, Edwards was nevertheless strongly attracted to new modes of religious contemplation. In his concern for truths that lay beyond concrete experience, in his rapturous and at the same time astute analysis of religious feeling, evil, and grace, Edwards demonstrated a characteristically American spirit as diverse and contradictory as the country itself: visionary and down-to-earth, deeply radical and solidly conservative, coldly prudent and unexpectedly wild.

Edwards had succeeded his grandfather, the eminent Solomon Stoddard, in the Northampton, Massachusetts, pastorate where he served for 21 years before his congregation dismissed him. The significance—and the tragedy—of Edwards' career was his unsuccessful attempt to restore the sense of God's omnipotence to a people for whom religion had become a conventional routine. Because his own religious experience was so intense, he sought to awaken in his congregation a similar emotion. Ever since his days at Yale, Edwards had been a reader of Newton and John Locke; the science and philosophy of the Enlightenment interested him enormously. But his mystical and poetic disposition prevented him from becoming a rationalist like Charles Chauncy of Boston, Edwards' chief theological opponent. Locke taught Edwards that men's hearts could be touched only by making the abstract come alive. A later generation was to abuse him for his apparent pleasure in threatening his listeners with hell-fire. Actually, most of his sermons dealt with God's mercy, but by occasionally playing on the nerves of his auditors, by reducing hell to something vividly physical, he awakened slumbering hearts. His horrendous picture of evil sprang from a dazzling vision of its opposite; evil was the antithesis of that perfect harmony and virtue and Being, which is God.

Between 1733 and 1735, Northampton underwent an intense religious revival. Edwards attacked the widely held doctrine that salvation depended on reputability and good works, that man possessed the power to save himself. In place of the humanized

Deity, genial and benevolent, who made salvation easy (the God of Franklin), he resurrected the omnipotent and splendid God of Calvin. His revival efforts were followed a few years later by the American tour of the electrifying English evangelist, George Whitefield, one of the precursors of American Methodism, itself an outgrowth of the "Great Awakening" which followed in Whitefield's wake.

THE GREAT AWAKENING

In the early decades of the eighteenth century religion had fallen ever further in esteem outside of New England. Many back-country settlers, particularly in

Jonathan Edwards, engraving by Sartain after a painting by Charles Wilson Peale.

the South, rarely saw a minister. In some areas, no provisions at all had been made for religious instruction. It was during this time of religious apathy that a great religious revival began in the 1730's. Known as the Great Awakening, it was one of the most significant intercolonial experiences before 1776.

The Great Awakening was actually part of a world-wide evangelical movement that had put down its roots in Germany and England. Its leading spirits in the colonies, in addition to the native Jonathan Edwards, and the Englishman, Whitefield, were Theodore Frelinghuysen, a Dutch-Reformed minister living in New Jersey, and William Tennent and his sons, Pennsylvania Presbyterians. The start of the Great Awakening was marked by Whitefield's arrival in 1739, when he promptly spoke to enormous crowds in New England, New York, Philadelphia, Charleston, and Savannah. Many of his listeners traveled for miles to hear him. He preached theatrically, using human-interest stories and appealing to the emotions of his audience rather than emphasizing doctrinal distinctions. Although Whitefield did not mix politics with religion, some of his enthusiastic co-workers offended the conservatives by their extravagance and upset the social order by rejecting forms and creeds. Too often they mistook weeping and screaming and bodily gyrations for the spirit of God.

Enemies of the revival questioned these grotesque manifestations and were shocked by ministers who enacted the sufferings of Christ on the pulpit. Ministers who passed from place to place censuring the local clergy for their lack of piety were themselves most severely censured. In his *Seasonable Thoughts on the State of Religion in New England* (1743), Charles Chauncy referred to these itinerant preachers as "Men who, though they have *no Learning,* and but *small Capacities,* yet imagine they are able, and without Study too, to speak to the *spiritual Profit* of such as are willing to hear them." Chauncy stoutly opposed the contention of some of the revivalists that the conviction of sin with all the motions

that sometimes accompanied it—"bitter *Shriekings* and *Screaming; Convulsion-like Tremblings* and *Agitations, Struggling* and *Tumblings*"—signified conversion.

Between arch-conservatives like Chauncy and uncompromising revival enthusiasts like Tennent, stood a third group—moderates typified by Edwards and Benjamin Colman in Boston. They did not condone the excesses of the Great Awakening, but they welcomed it, at least in the beginning, as a mighty manifestation of God's spirit moving over the land. It is easy to play up the extravagance of the Great Awakening, the foamings and frothings and trances, but it cannot be dismissed as a mere emotional orgy. The consequences of such a far-reaching movement cannot, of course, be precisely measured; they might be summarized as follows:

1. *Religious consequences.* The Great Awakening split the old denominations into two main groups, one espousing the traditional conservative doctrines or forms, the other adopting the "New Divinity." The latter was a religion of personal experience as against a religion of custom or habit. The "New Light" or "New Side" wing, as the revivalists were called, demanded a universal priesthood of believers, a kind of spiritual democracy. The great revival increased the membership of the small dissenting sects at the expense of the established denominations. Presbyterians and Baptists, for example, made impressive gains, and in the backwoods a new group, later to be known as the Methodists, gathered strength. Large numbers of the unchurched were converted. In New England alone, some 40,000 to 50,000 joined churches. Although a distaste for "enthusiasm" drove many of the anti-revivalists into the Anglican fold, the establishment was shaken.

2. *Political consequences.* Some historians believe that the weakening of the established Anglican Church helped to loosen British authority in the colonies, particularly in Virginia where the Baptists and Methodists led the fight against the Anglicans. Elsewhere, too, it has been argued, the Great Awakening served as a leveling move-

ment to prepare the way for the separation of church and state. It required no great stretch of the imagination to extend the liberties of conscience to economic and political liberties.

3. *Social consequences.* The huge crowds who came to hear Whitefield and the other preachers were starved for social contact. In the vast outdoor meetings that were to become a common feature of subsequent revivals, they found release for social and spiritual emotions long repressed. Despite the excesses accompanying the Great Awakening and the backsliding that followed, morals and manners improved as a result of it. Especially among the Baptists, the Methodists, and the Presbyterians, righteous conduct was the test of grace.

Although a good many of the revivalists were suspicious of an educated clergy who (in James Davenport's words) were "leading their People blindfold to Hell," the Great Awakening spawned a number of educational institutions. William Tennent's famous "Log College" at Neshaminy, Pennsylvania, founded in 1736, fathered similar schools for the preparaton of Presbyterian ministers. The Baptists lagged behind the Presbyterians, but they established their own schools—Hopewell Academy, and later the College of Rhode Island (Brown) in 1764. Princeton (Presbyterian), Rutgers (Dutch-Reformed), and Dartmouth (Congregational) were all founded under the impetus of the revival movement. The new colleges hardly represented the spirit of the Enlightenment, for their main purpose was to prepare ministers in an atmosphere uncontaminated by the doctrines of rival denominations or by secular infidelities. In time, however, the narrow sectarian objectives of these new colleges were less emphasized and some grew into great universities.

The Great Awakening, furthermore, quickened the humanitarian spirit of the eighteenth century by forcing men to pay attention to their social as well as their spiritual condition. When Jonathan Edwards defined virtue as "love of Being in general," he was suggesting that there was a divine element in everyone that ought to

be recognized out of love for God. Orphans, Negroes, Indians, and paupers shared in this Being and became the objects of Christian concern.

Well-known Quakers like Anthony Benezet and John Woolman intensified the humanitarianism that had long been a part of the Quaker tradition. Woolman, whose simple, unpretentious journal—the record of a pure and beautiful life—has become an American classic, spoke for the Negro, the Indian, the cruelly exploited everywhere. "To labor hard," he wrote in his homely way, "or cause others to do so, that we may live conformably to customs which our redeemer discountenanced by his example, and which are contrary to divine order, is to manure a soil for propagating an evil seed on earth." Woolman never resorted to harsh abuse, but his journal (as the Quaker poet, John Greenleaf Whittier, later wrote) was a life-long testimony against wrong, and one of the finest expressions of eighteenth-century benevolence.

THE CHURCHES

At the end of the colonial period, there was approximately one church for every 900 people. Despite the Great Awakening, the majority of the colonial population had no church affiliation. Established churches (those that were officially supported by the state) existed in some colonies —Anglican in the South and Congregational in New England. But almost from the beginning many colonies had been battlegrounds for competing sects. When Quakers, Anglicans, Presbyterians, Dutch-Reformed, Catholics, and Jews lived in the same province, as they did in Pennsylvania, an established church became inadvisable if not impossible. The dissenting spirit of Protestantism did not fade away in America. Rather, it took on a new energy as denominations splintered and new sects sprang up. The very multiplicity of religions insured a practical tolerance and the ac-

"The Peaceable Kingdom of the Branch," by the Quaker painter, Edward Hicks (1780-1849).

ceptance of what finally came to be the American principle of the separation of church and state.

Despite the variety of sects and the ethnic and geographical divisions among the denominations, the following generalizations about colonial religion in the 1750's seem valid:

First, colonial religion was overwhelmingly Protestant. Although the colonies provided a refuge for the persecuted of all the Old-World religions, only about 25,000 Catholics and 2,000 Jews were living in America on the eve of the Revolution. The colonists were in a real sense the children of the Reformation, differing radically among themselves in creed and doctrine yet joined in common opposition to Rome. Catholics were not physically molested in eighteenth-century America, but they were the victims of anti-Catholic propaganda spread by Protestant ministers, educators, editors, and publishers of the popular almanacs. England's wars with Catholic France

partly explain this anti-Catholic feeling, but the hostility went far deeper. Particularly in New England, but elsewhere as well, the inhabitants passed on their inherited prejudices against Catholic practices.

Second, the doctrine and organization of American churches reflected the social background of the members. The most powerful and influential denominations in the New World were the New England Congregationalists, the Presbyterians, and the Anglicans. These churches numbered among their adherents many plain folk, in addition to most of the established mercantile and landed middle-class families; but a higher proportion of persons of modest means was found in the Baptist churches, among the Methodists who emerged in the late 1760's, and in various small sects.

Making frankly evangelical appeals, the dissenting churches aroused the fear and disgust of the established denominations. But they reached elements in the colonial

110

population that had hitherto been neglected by the older churches, and they often joined the fight for religious and political liberty. Poor and despised at the beginning, their frugality, perseverance, and industry—the practical morality characteristic of the sects—brought them prosperity, and with prosperity came acceptance and respectability. This cycle was repeated again and again throughout American religious history.

Third, the churches of the non-English-speaking settlers in eighteenth-century America had little influence on the main currents of colonial religion, but they served as vital social organizations. It took some time for European immigrants to accommodate themselves to American ways. Speaking a variety of tongues and forming ethnic centers of their own, these settlers looked to their respective churches for guidance. The ministers delivered their sermons in the language of their congregations and kept alive Old-World traditions and attitudes during the period of transition. By the middle of the eighteenth century, the German immigrant churches, in particular, had to answer the question that was ultimately faced by all foreign-language groups: Should English be substituted for their native tongue? Only by insisting on racial and cultural distinctiveness could the religious leaders prevent their compatriots from being absorbed by the aggressive and competitive American sects. Having lost the official sanction that some of these churches had enjoyed in their European homeland, they had to become more sectarian in order to survive.

Fourth, the tendency throughout the eighteenth century was toward greater religious freedom and the separation of church and state. America had been settled by men eager to "shake off the dust of Babylon." To the sectarian-minded worshiper of the seventeenth century, tolerance or "poly-piety" was the greatest impiety. But no state-enforced religion could survive where dissenters continued to dissent and where men of diverse backgrounds and religions lived side by side. Even in orthodox New

England the persecution of Quakers and Baptists had ceased by 1700, and a robust minister like John Wise of Ipswich could almost singlehandedly foil the attempt of an organized clique of ministers to centralize church government and destroy the autonomy of the independent congregation. In defending the congregational principle and church democracy (in *The Churches' Quarrel Espoused,* 1710, and *The Vindication of the Government of the New England Churches,* 1717), Wise introduced arguments that were later adopted by the Revolutionary patriots in defense of political democracy. All men are born free, he said, and "Democracy is Christ's government in Church and State."

Most influential in the war against an official church were the dissenting sects (Quakers, Baptists, and Presbyterians, in particular) whose protests against discrimination grew more persistent during the eighteenth century. With the breakdown of Puritan control in New England after 1691, all the Protestant sects could ally themselves against the Anglican Church, which was regarded by many colonists as the tool of British absolutism. In 1763, the possibility that an Anglican bishop might be appointed for New England aroused as much heat as the Stamp Act was to generate two years later. Dissenters everywhere saw in the proposition to establish a resident bishop in America a horrible threat to liberty: "We should soon be obliged," read one manifesto, "to bid farewell to that religious Liberty, in which CHRIST hath set us free." Even southern Anglicans agreed with northern dissenters in opposing the appointment of an American bishop.

By 1776, the atmosphere in the colonies made wide religious toleration inevitable. Colonial proprietors found that toleration was good for business, for it attracted foreign settlers. The experience of colonies like Rhode Island and Pennsylvania, which had prospered without an established church, and the opposition of the unchurched and dissenters also contributed to religious liberty.

BETWEEN FAITH AND REASON

As eighteenth-century Americans tended to become humanitarian, secular, and liberal, turning their attention away from God toward man, their God also grew more tractable and kindly, less capricious, more concerned about the happiness of His Children. The domestication of Calvin's God, the fierce and magnificent Autocrat who had worked mysteriously for His own glory, did not occur suddenly, but in 1755 John Adams could speak of "the frigid John Calvin," and rational ministers preaching from influential pulpits were already discarding Calvin's conclusions as sterile.

The drift toward liberalism was expressed in many ways—through sermons, letters, diaries, even in graveyards. The headstones of early Puritans were marked with the skull and crossbones, grim symbols of an austere faith. By the eighteenth century, the skulls on the headstones had begun to sprout wings (emblems of resurrection), and before the century was over cherubs and finally the urn and the cypress (secular symbols of pagan origin) had supplanted the seventeenth-century death's-head.

The change in outlook becomes clear when we contrast two documents published in 1682 and 1720 respectively. The first is the narrative of Mrs. Mary Rowlandson, captured in 1675 by the braves of King Philip. Not only did she survive the horrors of an Indian massacre and the rigors of captivity; she even emerged from her ordeal with her spirit strengthened. At the end of her exciting story, she affirmed that God had exposed her to the terrors of death to show her the "vanity of these outward things." And she concluded: *"It is good for me that I have been afflicted."* Writing 38 years later, a Boston merchant, far from the hazards of frontier life, expressed his belief in a more genial God who relished the comforts of His children. "Solomon tells us," he declared, "that there is nothing better under the sun than for a man to eat and drink, and enjoy the good of his labour. So that I believe we ought not to be sordidly covetous, and deny ourselves the comfort of what we work for, but eat and drink as our circumstances will afford, as not to abuse the favor of heaven to voluptuousness."

The new way of looking at the world comes through strongly in the personalities and ideas of three men who flourished on the eve of the Enlightenment.

Samuel Sewall (1652-1730) was the incarnation of the Yankee, the public-spirited and down-to-earth "booster" who was to become a familiar type in American life. Boston-born and bred, Sewall shared in the new secular attitude, but he still bore the stamp of his Puritan predecessors. As one of the "Stewards" of the province, a conservative man of affairs and a bulwark of the church, he necessarily spoke in the accents of piety. His wonderful *Diary,* a record of his activities between 1674 and 1677 and from 1685 to 1729, contains reports of sermons, funerals, weddings, of visits to graveyards ("an awful yet pleasing treat"), and humorlessly amusing accounts of his courtships. But hard as Sewall tried to present himself as a pious and other-worldly man ("The Lord add or take away from this our corporeal weight," he heavily comments on his very durable 193 pounds, "so as shall be most advantageous for our spiritual growth"), we are always aware of the fleshly Sewall, the curious busy-body, the humanitarian who opposed the selling of Negroes, the chronicler of succulent dinners. His religious sense and training told him that life on earth was transient; every accident, from losing a tooth to breaking a glass, became for him a lesson of mortality. Yet Sewall lived in a world of tangible things. This side of him emerges in the diary entry: "Six swallows together flying and chippering very rapturously."

Sewall typified Boston's merchant class in the age of transition, and William Byrd II (1674-1744) represented the Virginia planter aristocracy of the same period. Byrd grew up in a society in which hunting and horse-racing, politics, military pursuits, and social affairs preoccupied the gentry, but it was by no means an irreligious or free-thinking society. One of the great Virginia planters, Robert Carter, constantly turned to religious matters in his letters and strove to attain what he called a "Practical god-liness." Byrd himself, educated in London and displaying the manners and sometimes the looseness of Restoration courtiers, had his serious side. His graphic and candid diary shows him to have been a scholar who read a chapter of Hebrew every morning, several pages of the Greek version of Jose-phus, and perhaps a bit of Bishop Tillotson, the liberal English Anglican churchman. His library of 3,600 volumes was equaled in North America only by Cotton Math-er's. Like Sewall, Byrd despised the slave trade, and his religious credo, rational and benevolent, evokes the spirit of the new secularism:

I believe that God made man . . . and in-spired him with a reasonable soul to distinguish between good and evil; that the law of nature taught him to follow the good and avoid the evil because the good tends manifestly to his happiness and preservation, but the evil to his misery and destruction.

Cotton Mather (1663-1728), the last great figure of a great New England dynasty, re-flected the transition from faith to reason in a more interesting way than his contempo-raries, Sewall or Byrd. Cotton was the grandson of Richard Mather, one of the original Massachusetts "Saints," a "very hard student" and an eminent minister who lived and died an inflexible Puritan. When asked on his deathbed how he felt, Richard Mather replied, "Far from well, yet far better than mine iniquities deserve." His famous son, Increase, the father of Cotton, "swam quietly in a stream of impiety and carnal security for many years together," as he phrased it, but he was converted in 1654. Educated at Harvard and at Trinity College, Dublin, he served as colonial agent

for Massachusetts and preached in a lead-ing Boston church. From 1685 to 1701, he was President of Harvard College, and his learning was almost as prodigious as his son's.

Cotton Mather wrote of himself: "I be-gan to pray, even when I began to speak." At the same time he began to study. An understanding of Nature, he found, was the best antidote to atheism, and his religious zeal in no way interfered with his lively in-terest in medicine, agriculture, and other rational means of human betterment. In fact, his curiosity about every aspect of the natural world, his loving attention to the humblest practical problem—which drew from him the characteristic observation, "The very wheelbarrow is to be with respect looked upon"—sprang directly from his Christian piety. Implicit in early Puri-tanism was the conviction that scriptural truths might be discerned by "right rea-son," and although God might set aside natural laws when He chose to do so, He created a rational universe whose order any rational man might detect. Peter Ramus, a French Protestant much in vogue among New England thinkers, sanctioned this view, and Cotton Mather (without aban-doning his faith in God's miraculous ways) saw God's hand in the visible order of the universe.

It may seem a far cry from the kind of rationalism espoused by Puritan thinkers like the Mathers to the rationalism of the later Deists. And yet what both types of men firmly believed was that the Almighty had given them a thoroughly rational physical universe and rational faculties with which to understand it. Puritans might use these faculties more for the glory of God, Deists more for their own pleasure.

Deism posited a mechanical universe run by a Heavenly Engineer who had no need to resort to miracles to demonstrate His glory. It dismissed the Trinity, the divinity of Christ, and the Biblical account of the creation of man as superstitions, and maintained that the moral truths of Christianity were better defended by science than by revelation. In marked contrast to Calvinism, Deism emphasized the ethics of Jesus, attacked sectarian dogma, and encouraged humanitarianism. The Deists were not atheists (although they were so labeled by their enemies); but mysticism and superstition they scorned. Nor did they condone "enthusiasm," defined in Dr. Samuel Johnson's famous dictionary as "a vain belief in private revelation, a vain confidence of divine favour or communication." As rational men, the truest was for them the clearest, the most logical, and the most easily explained; and scientific laws were the architecture of religion. Deism, a philosophy of life rather than a religion, reflected the emerging secular view of the world and also promoted it.

II. *The Secular Mind*

THE ENLIGHTENMENT

When Nicholas Copernicus, a Polish-born mathematician and astronomer, published his *Concerning the Revolution of Heavenly Bodies* in 1543, he dismissed the traditional conception of the universe, which pictured the earth at the center with the planets revolving around it, and replaced it with the conception of a sun-centered universe. In so doing, he cast suspicion on man's kinship with the angels and suggested that the whole universe was governed by unchanging natural laws. Subsequently, a growing number of scholars, philosophers, and scientists began to look at man and his environment more objectively, to make orderly experiments and investigations. Their discoveries in astronomy, physics, anatomy, geology, and chemistry weakened the old religious dogmas even more, and by the eighteenth century the learned world accepted the idea of the universe as it appeared in the treatises of the great English mathematician, Sir Isaac Newton (1642-1727). On this idea the Enlightenment in philosophy rested.

According to Newton, the physical world was governed neither by chance nor miracle. It operated mechanically under fixed mathematical laws. Moreover, under these laws it operated perfectly. The men of the Enlightenment proceeded to extend Newton's idea of the physical universe to the moral universe as well. By means of objective investigation and reason, men would discover the mechanism of society and the fixed laws of its operations. Once discovered, all archaic growths and evil obstructions could be removed. Bad environment, rather than original sin, was responsible for social evils. By means of science and reason, an ideal environment could be created in which the natural man might flower. The philosophers of the Enlightenment carried their optimism even further. Working from the dictates of reason, they derived new rules of writing and revised old systems of aesthetics; the qualities that were most highly valued in the study of physics and political economy—reasonableness, clarity, balance—became the criteria of eighteenth-century art and literary expression as well.

BENJAMIN FRANKLIN

The exemplar of the American Enlightenment and one of the greatest men of his age was the renegade Bostonian and adopted Philadelphian, Benjamin Franklin (1706-90). He was himself a living proof of the Enlightenment, an illustration of what might be accomplished by reason, measure, and clarity:

Printer, postmaster, almanac maker, essayist, chemist, orator, tinker, professor of housewifery, ambassador, projector, maxim-monger, herb-doctor, wit:—Jack of all trades, master of each and mastered by none—the type and genius of the land.

So Herman Melville, the great nineteenth-century American novelist, later described Franklin, observing at the same time that he was "everything but a poet." Melville was right. Franklin abhorred mysteries and found metaphysical reasoning disgusting. Incapable of feeling deep religious emotions, he developed a bland and complacent practical faith of his own while remaining completely tolerant of the beliefs of others. In his own eyes, he never "sinned"; rather, he "erred." And in that distinction we can measure the gulf between the piety of his seventeenth-century forebears and the easier morality of the eighteenth century.

Franklin's admirable utilitarianism was neither greedy nor materialistic. He respected tools and the people who used them, and his close attention to the humblest occupations as well as to the loftier ones grew out of his desire to produce "something for the common benefit of mankind." When he had acquired enough money to support himself (by the conscientious application of the principles he described in his celebrated *Autobiography*), he gave up business and devoted his energies to science, public affairs, and writing. He wanted people, he once confessed, to say after his death that "He lived usefully" rather than that "He died rich."

And so Franklin improved the printing press, tinkered successfully with smoky chimneys, suggested changes in the shape and rigging of ships, plotted cyclonic storms, introduced various new plants into the new world, drained swampy land, improved carriage wheels, founded the first American club for mutual improvement, invented the bifocal lens, designed an effective iron stove, recommended a more practical watering trough for horses, showed navigators how to shorten the crossing to Europe by following the Gulf Stream, demonstrated a way of heating public buildings, and constructed a fan for his chair to keep off the flies. This is only a partial list of his accomplishments, which included pioneer work in the science of electricity, studies in American population growth, and a fantastically successful public career. He asked for no rewards and took out no patents on his inventions, because "as we enjoy great advantages from the inventions of others, we should be glad of an opportunity to serve others by any invention of ours." His entire life was a fulfillment of one of his deepest beliefs: "Serving God is doing good to men."

It is this very many-sidedness of Franklin and his zeal for the practical that make it hard to think of him as a philosopher and a man of letters. Yet he took to writing as he took to politics, religion, ethics, science, agriculture, and mechanics—easily and engagingly. Through his writings he expressed the values of thousands of his fellow Americans, the common citizens whose virtues he so uncommonly represented. Their materialistic aspirations he caught in his capitalistic homily, "The Way to Wealth." But his shrewd, cynical,

Benjamin Franklin by David Martin.

and humorous maxims went beyond vulgar pragmatism and embodied the folk-wisdom of the American people:

Fish and visitors stink in three days. Write with the learned, pronounce with the vulgar. Eat to please thyself but dress to please others. Neither a fortress nor a maid will hold out long after they begin to parley. Let thy maidservant be faithful, strong, and homely. Keep your eyes wide open before marriage, half shut afterwards. Where there's marriage without love there will be love without marriage. The most exquisite folly is made of wisdom spun too fine.

Even Franklin's scientific papers, which won him world-wide acclaim during and after his lifetime, were couched in terms that could be readily understood. As Franklin's younger contemporary, the chemist Sir Humphry Davy, expressed it in his fine tribute to the American:

A singular felicity of induction guided all Franklin's researches, and by very small means he established very grand truths. The style and manner of his publications on electricity are almost as worthy of admiration as the doctrine it contains. He has endeavored to remove all mystery and obscurity from the subject. He has written equally for the uninitiated and for the philosopher; and he has rendered his details amusing as well as perspicuous, elegant as well as simple. Science appears in his language in a dress wonderfully decorous, the best adapted to display her native loveliness. He has in no instance exhibited that false dignity, by which philosophy is kept aloof from common applications; and he has sought to make her a useful inmate and servant in the common habitations of man, than to preserve her merely as an object of admiration in temples and palaces.

In his hostility to the restraints of authority, in his humanitarianism, in his faith in progress or "the power of man over matter," Franklin epitomized the Enlightenment. But he retained, perhaps as a Puritan legacy, a certain distrust for uninstructed human nature and a canny insight into human frailty.

SCIENCE IN THE COLONIES
The brilliance of Franklin's career and his exalted reputation abroad have obscured the attainments of his lesser contemporaries whose investigations he encouraged and assisted. They shared his faith in the Enlightenment and like him believed not only that natural philosophy demonstrated the immutable ways of God, but also that it could be put to practical use. "Science," Francis Bacon had written, "must be known by its works. It is by the witness of works rather than by logic or even observation that truth is revealed and established. It follows from this that the improvement of man's lot and the improvement of man's mind are one and the same thing." The American scientists who shared the Baconian attitude were not mere utilitarians, but like scientists in Europe were motivated by disinterested curiosity and a desire for scholarly recognition. Living in a society without wealth, without patronage, and without a learned class, they naturally looked to Europe for sustenance.

Fortunately for the physicians, the teachers, the self-taught botanists, and the amateur mathematicians and astronomers who made up the scientific community in North America, the European savants were keenly interested in the New World. They encouraged the Americans to report their findings on flora and fauna, Indian ethnology, medical lore, earthquakes. By collecting unknown plants, for example, the Americans could help such famed botanists as the Swedish scholar, Carl Linnaeus, to complete his biological classifications. By the middle of the eighteenth century, European scientists had developed a system of communication which kept them informed about one another's findings, and they made the Americans a link in this intellectual chain. Thanks to the efforts of Peter Collinson, a Quaker merchant of London and an influential member of the Royal Society, the reports of the Americans were transmitted to interested Europeans. Through Collinson, isolated Americans also were kept informed of the activities of colleagues in other colonies.

New England from the outset had assumed the leadership in scientific investigation. Many of her leaders and professional men had been trained in English universities, and Harvard teachers and graduates had been elected to the Royal Society before 1700. John Winthrop, Jr., of Connecticut, a charter member of the Society, donated a telescope to Harvard in 1672, and it was this telescope that enabled Thomas Brattle to observe the comet of 1676. Newton used Brattle's observations in his *Principia Mathematica* to illustrate how the orbits of comets are fixed by gravitational force. No less important were the 82 letters that the formidable Cotton Mather sent to the Royal Society's *Transactions* between 1712 and 1724; among them were reports on the hybridization of plants and inoculation against smallpox.

But New England soon lost its pre-eminence to Philadelphia, which by 1750 had become the center of colonial science. Commercial prosperity was partly responsible for the willingness of Philadelphians to support scientific enterprises (see p. 84). Equally important was the Quaker connection of certain Philadelphians with intellectuals abroad. It was the English merchant, Collinson, again, who put the self-taught naturalist, John Bartram, in touch with Linnaeus. When Peter Kalm, a pupil of Linnaeus, visited America in 1748, he came straight to Philadelphia to see Bartram. Their discussions, according to Kalm, ranged from silk-culture, vineyards, stalactites, and truffles to Indian pottery, humming birds, and cures for snake bite. Bartram had a genius for collecting specimens and a knack of communicating his enthusiasm to others.

Half-mystic, half-rationalist, this independent Quaker saw "God in his glory" through the telescope.

Bartram received aid and encouragement from another notable Philadelphia Quaker, James Logan, a rich and highly intelligent merchant who conducted important experiments on the role of pollen in the fertilization of plants. Logan also befriended Thomas Godfrey (who invented an improved quadrant) and Cadwallader Colden (a plant collector highly honored in Europe and author of one of the earliest scholarly treatises on the Indians).

In 1743 Franklin and Bartram tried to set up a scientific society that would correlate the work of experimenters throughout the colonies. The attempt seemed promising at first but it had to be abandoned. Twenty-five years later (1768), it was revived as the American Philosophical Society. The 1771 *Transactions* of the Society carried reports by a number of colonial scientists on a transit of Venus across the sun that had taken place in 1769. In Philadelphia, where the observation took on the proportions of a community enterprise, David Rittenhouse, an ingenious clock-maker and builder of the celebrated orrery (a mechanical planetarium), was the principal contributor. European scientists hailed the Society's *Transactions* as evidence that American science had attained maturity.

III. *Cultural Progress*

EDUCATION

The educational system of the colonies was largely English in origin. The idea of the public grammar school was already a century old before its introduction to North America in 1642, and English universities served as the models for the first colleges in the New World. English pedagogy and textbooks, and English schoolmasters and scholars, enjoyed great prestige.

In the seventeenth century education had been closely tied to religion and the church. But in the eighteenth century the introduction of secular subjects modified the religious emphasis. Social usefulness became an educational goal essential to the eighteenth-century ideal—the public spirited man. The social importance of education was suggested by a well-known Massachusetts clergyman in 1716:

That *Good Order in Families and schools* for the well Educating of Children, are unspeakably useful and needful for a Peoples welfare. Every Child that grows up, will be a useful or hurtful Member of the body Politick and persons thus growing up, are most like to prove *useful* or *hurtful,* according to the good or bad Methods taken in their Education. Those well *instructed, Governed,* Imployed in their Youth; are most likely to be harmless and serviceable in their Generation. Those brought up in *Ignorance* & *Idleness, Pride,* and *Luxory;* are likely to prove Vicious themselves, and be *Poysonous Infexious Plagues* to the Publick. A little Leaven, Leavens the whole lump; what will one *scabby sheep* do?

Education reflected the social cleavages that existed not only in the South, where class lines were very sharply drawn, but also in the Middle and New England colonies. Rich children received a different kind of education from that received by poor children, who, if they were educated at all, were prepared solely for their limited stations in life. Even liberal-minded men in the mid-eighteenth century—revolutionists in the making—accepted these social distinctions as natural and proper. Jonathan Mayhew, a liberal minister of Boston, the epitome of the Revolutionary preacher and the counselor of rebels, bluntly distinguished between the abilities of the base-born and the well-born. "That which principally distinguishes some men from the beasts of the field," he said, "is the different formation of their bodies. Their bodies are *human,* but they are in a manner *brute* all beside. . . . Those of the lower class can go but a little ways in their inquiries into the natural and moral constitution of the world." The Revolutionary decades saw a weakening of this two-class system, but traditional attitudes lingered on into the national period that followed.

The kind and quality of education in eighteenth-century America depended also on the section, the national origin of the settlers, their religion, and their closeness to settled areas. Education in the South, for example, where it was difficult to establish any kind of organized educational system for the scattered plantations, lagged behind that in the North. Pauper schools gave rudimentary instruction to orphans and the children of the poor, but in general only the children of the rich were educated. Standards were higher in the Middle colonies, where the dissenting Protestant denominations emphasized Bible-reading, but the amount and quality of education that most children received was limited to what their parents could afford.

Only in Massachusetts and Connecticut did education become a public responsibility. The Massachusetts school laws of 1642 and 1647 (see p. 56) meant, in effect, that all children must be taught to read. These standards—unique in the English-speaking world at the time—deteriorated as New England society became more decentralized and as educational control passed to the local authorities. By 1700, education was at a low ebb in New England, and illiteracy was prevalent on the frontier. But conditions rapidly improved. During the 40-year period from 1720 to 1760, a number of excellent semi-private academies were established, and New Englanders once again could proudly assert that they were the best-educated people in all North America.

In the cities, several interesting educational experiments were carried on in the eighteenth century. Philadelphia, Boston, and New York, besides having the best private academies, also had a number of private evening schools that featured practical courses ignored by the classical academies. Such subjects as geography, navigation, bookkeeping, mathematics, and surveying had a high practical value in a commercial society. All classes attended evening schools, but the majority of students, of both sexes, came from middle-class homes.

A relatively small number of well-to-do students attended the seven colonial colleges that had been established by 1764. These and the private academies retained the European curriculum (Latin, Greek, Hebrew, and Science) and fostered aristocratic, conservative ideals. Religious training remained ostensibly the chief function of the colleges, but the liberal and rational influences of the age began to be felt as the century waned. The students of the second-oldest college in America, William and Mary, began to debate the philosophy of politics and natural rights. Such eminently practical leaders as Thomas Jefferson and James Monroe were trained here. Harvard became a center of science; the College of Philadelphia became an advocate of *"every thing* that is useful, and *every thing* that is ornamental."* King's College (later Columbia) advertised that while the teaching of religion was its principal objective, "it is further the Design of this College, to instruct and perfect the Youth in . . . The Arts of *Numbering* and *Measuring,* of *Surveying* and *Navigation,* of *Geography* and *History,* of Husbandry, Commerce and Government." The colonial colleges did not ignore classical learning, but their graduates began to embody more and more the American ideal of the useful citizen equipped to meet practical realities.

Naturally enough, the colleges had become the centers of the new science by the first quarter of the eighteenth century. True, no college professor ever matched the self-taught Benjamin Franklin or John Bartram in originality. But America's ablest astronomer, John Winthrop, taught at Harvard College, and David Rittenhouse, astronomer and mathematician, lectured at the College of Philadelphia, as did Dr. Benjamin Rush, the first professor of chemistry in America.

JOURNALISM AND LETTERS

Literacy, by European standards, was high in the colonies, but only a few Americans kept up with the new learning. A somewhat larger number read colonial newspapers. By 1765, twenty-five weekly newspapers were being published in eleven colonies. Most of the columns were filled with excerpts from English papers, but after the famous trial of John Peter Zenger in New York in 1735 greater opportunities opened up for independent reporting.

Zenger was charged with criminal libel for printing an unfavorable report about a crown official. He was defended by the eminent Philadelphia lawyer, Andrew Hamil-

Peter Zenger on "The Liberty of the Press," from the second number of his New-York Weekly Journal.

ton, who appealed to the jury to define libel in a way contrary to the current English theory. For the judges, the question was merely whether Zenger had published the offending articles; for Hamilton, the question was whether the contents of the articles were true. The jury accepted Hamilton's version of libel and held that since the articles were true, Zenger was not guilty as charged. Fifty years passed before the finding in this case became formal law, but the decision did encourage other journalists to become more outspoken.

A more popular medium than newspapers for spreading scientific and political information, especially to rural Americans, was the almanac, an old English institution.

The first colonial almanac appeared in New England in 1639; by 1731, almanacs were being read in all the colonies. Pocket-sized and paper-bound, they served as calendars, astrological guides, recipe books, and children's primers. Sandwiched in between bits of practical information were jokes, poems, and maxims. The better almanacs (published by Nathaniel Ames and Benjamin Franklin) punctured superstition, provided simplified summaries of the new science, and presented tasteful selections from the best British authors. Franklin's *Poor Richard's Almanac,* published in 1732, soon sold 10,000 copies a year.

Literature received more attention in the eighteenth century than it had in the seventeenth, though the Puritan suspicion of the secular imagination had not entirely relaxed. A commercially and politically minded population, however, had little interest in *belles lettres.*

By the 1740's, Philadelphia had become the literary center of the colonies and the first city in which a literary self-consciousness was manifested. There a coterie of young men gathered around the educator and magazine editor, William Smith. But these young writers were even more fettered by English literary conventions than their predecessors had been. Not one of them measured up to the gifted Puritan poet, Edward Taylor, whose verse blended homely details of New England life with magnificent visions of God. None wrote with the urbanity, robustness, and wit of William Byrd II, or with the charm and lucidity of Franklin.

Until the appearance of Philip Freneau's earliest poems in the 1770's, American writing remained derivative and provincial, and yet the American experience was preparing the ground for a fresher and more original kind of expression. Literally as well as metaphorically, Americans had begun to speak a different language from the English. In the seventeenth and eighteenth centuries, English lexicographers and scholars like Dr. Samuel Johnson had pruned and refined Elizabethan English, but many of the barbarisms they eliminated continued to be good usage in the colonies. Surviving archaisms like *I guess, chump, flap-jack, home-spun, to hustle,* and many others came to be regarded as Americanisms. American speech also absorbed words from the Dutch, French, German, and Spanish. New plants, animals, and birds tested the wit of the colonists, as did the peculiar American geography. *Poke-weed, bottom-land, rolling-country, back-woods, land office,* and *crazy-quilt* were all colonial words that described new scenery, new objects, and new situations.

POLITICAL IDEAS

The most important colonial writing in the eighteenth century and the most widely read was not the work of literary men but of theologians, scientists, and political theorists. Among the political writers were some of the ablest and most highly cultivated minds in the New World.

The political philosophy of most thinking Americans before the Revolution derived partly from colonial experience and partly from English and continental sources. Even during the seventeenth century, when faith, revelation, and authority carried more weight than reason, the foreshadowings of democracy were dimly visible. Puritanism, as well as the Enlightenment, nourished ideas of liberty, success, and self-fulfillment. As rationalism gradually undermined old dogmas and as democratic tendencies grew more noticeable, Americans became receptive to ideas from abroad congenial to their own experiences.

Chief among these ideas was the doctrine of natural rights, which received its classic formulation in John Locke's *Two Treatises of Civil Government.* Published in 1690, Locke's essays helped to explode the divine-right theory of kingship which brought the prestige of religion to the support of absolute political authority.

The divine-right theory, as we have seen (p. 38), was attacked long before Locke's time. Locke's distinction was that he restated English constitutional ideas in their most persuasive and popular form: that government (by which he meant the king, the

Parliament, or any other political agency) is responsible to the people, to the community it governs, that its power is limited both by constitutional traditions and conventions and by the moral law that can be deduced from the law of nature.

But what, precisely, were the natural laws that governed the political activities of man? It was one thing for Newton to demonstrate the laws governing the heavenly spheres but quite another thing to demonstrate the existence of a natural order in society. The early theorists of natural law tackled the problem by trying to identify man's elemental needs and faculties. How would man behave, they asked, if he acted solely in accordance with his nature, without social restraints of any sort? Of one thing they were sure: in a natural state men would never consent to live under any form of government that did not protect their life, liberty, and property. Hence, when men accepted government, they entered into a "social contract" with their rulers; in return for security and protection, they accepted the ruler's authority. But if the rulers violated their part of the bargain, the people were no longer bound by the contract. Then they had the right to overthrow the government and establish a new one. These Lockeian ideas were easily digested by practical people. In business, contractual relationships were becoming more and more common, and society was familiar with the Puritan idea of a "covenant" between God and man.

Locke's treatises were widely regarded as the best justification of the Glorious Revolution of 1688. Originally, his sallies were directed against kingly government and were meant to justify the supremacy of Parliament. But Locke's criticisms were phrased in such general terms that the colonists found it easy to convert them into a challenge to Parliament itself. His natural rights philosophy was strengthened by other beliefs that were widely entertained in the colonies. The common-law rights of freeborn Englishmen, for example, were closely identified with the natural rights of men. And these legal rights were sustained by

two English authorities who were immensely influential in America: Sir William Blackstone, known through his *Commentaries on the Laws of England* (1765-69), and Sir Edward Coke, the eminent seventeenth-century English lawyer. From Blackstone the colonists quoted that man's first allegiance was to a God whose will was the universal law of nature, and that human laws were clearly invalid when they conflicted with natural law. The colonial pamphleteers cherished particularly this pronouncement by Coke:

The law of nature is that which God at the time of creation of the nature of man infused into his heart, for his preservation and direction; and this is *Lex aeterna,* the moral law, called also the law of Nature. And by this law, written with the finger of God in the heart of man, were the people of God a long time governed before the law was written by Moses who was the first reporter or writer of law in the world.

Ideas about natural rights were in the air, then, long before the Declaration of Independence was written. They seemed especially appropriate to a people who had in fact created government while still living in a state of nature. When these ideas were challenged in the developing conflict with Britain, colonial pamphleteers increasingly used American experiences to defend them. John Wise based his support of the incipient rebels on the congregational principle. When Jonathan Mayhew composed his famous "Discourse Concerning Unlimited Submission and Non-Resistance to the Higher Powers" (1750), he provided political ammunition for the later Revolutionary pamphleteers. Mayhew admitted that civil authority required obedience, that disobedience was morally as well as politically sinful. But, he added, when rulers pillage the public instead of protecting it, they stop being emissaries of God and become "common pirates and highwaymen." To support a tyrant was to abet him in promoting misery. For Mayhew, the doctrine of the divine right of kings (with its corollary of non-resistance) was "altogether as fabulous and chimerical as transubstantiation; or any reveries of ancient or modern visionaries." The form that a government took was less important than the need for it to have popular support. If government derived from God, as the absolutists said, it was because God moved the people to organize it.

Here was a reasonable and religious basis for popular assemblies that made sense to the learned and the unlearned alike. A century and a half of colonial history, as a conservative Swedish observer noted in 1775, had created a new kind of political animal peculiar to North America:

The chief trait in the character of an American is an immoderate love of liberty, or rather license. . . . And this enthusiasm rules in the breasts of all from the highest to the lowest. Education, manner of life, religion, and government—all contribute to it. Parents exercise no authority over children, beyond letting them for the most part do what pleases them. Everyone can maintain himself without trouble, for here there is room enough, and wages are high. No one, therefore, knows oppression or dependence. All are equally good; birth, office and merits do not make much distinction. Freedom of conscience is unlimited, without the least control by secular law, and church discipline means nothing. The English method of government is in itself quite mild, and is all the less able, in this remote part of the empire, to exercise a reasonable strictness. The reins of government lie so slack that they seldom are noticed, and the hand that guides is never seen. The result of all this is that the people neither know nor will know of any control, and everyone regards himself as an independent Prince.

Readings
Asterisk indicates that book is available in paperback.

Merle Curti, *The Growth of American Thought* (1943), a comprehensive work, affords an excellent introduction to the mature colonial mind. Volume I of V. L. Parrington, *Main Currents in American Thought* * (3 vols., 1927), is a stimulating study from the "rationalist" point of view. Michael Kraus, *The Atlantic Civilization* (1949), is especially good on overseas intellectual connections. Max Savelle, *Seeds of Liberty* (1948), and Clinton Rossiter, *Seedtime of the Republic* (1953), are outstanding intellectual histories with emphasis on political ideas. Rossiter, *The First American Revolution* * (1953), is a useful reprint of part I of his larger work.

An excellent introduction to the religious history of the period is S. E. Mead, *The Lively Experiment: The Shaping of Christianity in America* (1963). T. C. Hall, *The Religious Background of American Culture* (1930), covers the origins of the dissenting tradition in England and its spread in America. L. J. Trinterud, *The Forming of an American Tradition* (1949), is outstanding in Presbyterianism. The liberal reaction and its opponents is well presented in Conrad Wright, *The Beginnings of Unitarianism in America* (1955). W. W. Sweet, *Religion in Colonial America* (1942), is a useful survey of church history. Perry Miller, *The New England Mind: From Colony to Province* * (1953), has an excellent discussion of the Salem witchcraft hysteria. M. L. Starkey, *The Devil in Massachusetts* * (1949) offers a more extended account.

Perry Miller, *Jonathan Edwards* * (1949), and O. E. Winslow, *Jonathan Edwards 1703-1758* (1940), are the leading biographies of the New England divine. S. C. Henry, *George Whitfield, Wayfaring Witness* (1957), is excellent on the revivalist. On the Great Awakening itself, see E. S. Gaustad, *The Great Awakening in New England* (1957); C. H. Maxson, *The Great Awakening in the Middle Colonies* (1920); and W. M. Gewehr, *The Great Awakening in Virginia, 1740-1790* (1930). E. B. Greene, *Religion and the State, the Making and Testing of an American Tradition* (1941), is a good, short study of the separation of church and state. R. B. Perry, *Puritanism and Democracy* * (1944), is a penetrating investigation of the relations of religion and politics. On deism, see G. A. Koch, *Republican Religion: The American Revolution and the Cult of Reason* (1933).

The impact of the Enlightenment is well presented in the general works cited at the head of these *Readings*. Numerous works by and on Benjamin Franklin elaborate this subject: A. O. Aldridge, *Benjamin Franklin: Philosopher and Man* (1965); Carl Van Doren, *Benjamin Franklin* * (1938); I. B. Cohen, *Franklin and Newton* (1956); Franklin's *Autobiography* * (first published 1868); and two well-edited anthologies: I. B. Cohen, *Benjamin Franklin* (1953); and F. L. Mott and C. E. Jorgenson, *Benjamin Franklin* (1936). For a very critical estimate see the essay on Franklin in D. H. Lawrence, *Studies in Classic American Literature* * (1953). A sardonic portrait of Franklin appears in Herman Melville's novel, *Israel Potter* * (1855). The Enlightenment in Philadelphia may be pursued further in F. B. Tolles, *James Logan and the Culture of Provincial America* (1957). Brooke Hindle, *The Pursuit of Science in Revolutionary America, 1735-1789* (1956), is a scholarly monograph. John Duffy, *Epidemics in Colonial America* (1953), is excellent on aspects of medicine. Maurice Cranston, *John Locke* (1957) is a readable modern biography. John Locke, *Two Treatises of Civil Government* * (1690), lays the foundation for political thought in the Enlightenment. Caroline Robbins, *The Eighteenth-Century Commonwealthman* (1959), is an indispensable study, as its subtitle says, "in the Transmission, Development and Circumstance of English Liberal Thought from the Restoration of Charles II until the War with the Thirteen Colonies." The *Readings* for Chapter 5 supply further references on this subject and its relation to the American Revolution. Adrienne Koch, ed., *The American Enlightenment: The Shaping of the American Experiment and a Free Society* (1965), is an outstanding anthology, relevant to this and later chapters.

Paul Monroe, *The Founding of the American Public School System: A History of Education in the United States from the Early Settlements to the Close of the Civil War Period* (2 vols., 1940), is a standard source. Robert Middlekauff, *Ancients and Axioms, Secondary Education in Eighteenth-Century New England* (1963), is excellent on an important region. On higher education, see Frederick Rudolph, *The American College and University* (1962); Richard Hofstadter, *Academic Freedom in the Age of the College* * (1955); and the masterly work by S. E. Morison, *Harvard College in the Seventeenth Century* (1936).

On popular culture, see Sidney Kobre, *The Development of the Colonial Newspaper* (1944), and volume I of F. L. Mott, *A History of American Magazines* (3 vols., 1930-1957). Oliver Larkin, *Art and Life in America* (1949) is a good introduction to American painting. On colonial literature see the work of V. L. Parrington, above, and Moses Coit Tyler, *A History of American Literature, 1607-1765* * (1949). Worth reading for quick surveys are the first chapter of Marcus Cunliffe, *The Literature of the United States* * (1954), and an excellent essay on colonial writing in H. M. Jones, *Ideas in America* (1944). Chapters I and II of Robert Spiller, *et al., Literary History of the United States* (3 vols., 1948), contain up-to-date and scholarly treatments by specialists in colonial literature.

CHAPTER FIVE

In 1763, when the French and Indian War ended, France seemed ruined. Although she was not beyond recovery, as William Pitt warned with characteristic insight, even few Frenchmen expected that she would soon be able to resume the imperial wars.

Britain, by contrast, seemed at the peak of her imperial glory; yet her North American mainland colonies were to rebel against her "tyranny" much earlier than the French themselves would turn on the Bourbons, and indeed would win their independence with French assistance. How did this swift change of fortune come about?

On the eve of the American Revolution

American Independence

half a million white inhabitants of the thirteen rebellious colonies—about one-fourth of their total white population—were not even of English extraction. They included Germans, Scots, Dutch, and Irish and lesser numbers of Spanish and Portuguese Jews, French Huguenots, and a mixture of Scandinavians, predominantly Swedes. These people probably never felt any deep attachment to the so-called mother country. Another half a million Americans were Negroes from Africa or of African descent, most of them submerged in slavery. Even those Americans who were English-born or of English forebears included religious dissenters, or descendants of religious dissenters, who had been harried from their homes, and convicts, or descendants of convicts, who had been forcibly shipped to the New World. Poor materials from which to fashion dutiful subjects to begin with, in America they had strengthened their independence of spirit. Their own political institutions and economic practices reflected the freedom they had learned to cherish.

Even so, very few Americans could have harbored any intention of rebelling against king and Parliament until the cumulative measures of both forced leaders in the New

World to take increasingly drastic steps of their own. John Adams, who acknowledged that Americans, for all the variety of their origins and all their chafing under the imperial system, "had been educated in an habitual affection for England," also wrote many years after the Revolution had been fought and American independence had been won: "What do we mean by the Revolution? The War? That was no part of the Revolution. It was only an Effect and Consequence of it. The Revolution was in the minds of the people, and this was effected, from 1760 to 1775, in the course of fifteen years before a drop of blood was drawn at Lexington."

I. *The Course of British Mismanagement*

GIVING OFFENSE
TO THE MERCHANTS

Rumblings of serious trouble in America had been heard even before the end of the French and Indian War. From the start of that war, colonial merchants, with characteristic disregard for *British* policy, had been supplying the enemy on the mainland and carrying on business as usual with enemy islands in the West Indies. In 1760 Pitt's ministry had ordered colonial governors to make a more determined effort to stop what amounted to American smuggling. To carry out the governor's orders in Massachusetts, the principal center of enemy trade, royal customs collectors applied to the Superior Court of the colony for documents known as writs of assistance. These writs had been in common use for a long time, both in Britain and in America (see p. 71). Authorized by acts of Parliament, they had to be renewed each time a new sovereign came to the throne. Thus when George II died in 1760, new writs had to be authorized in the name of George III. The merchants of Massachusetts seized on this opportunity to denounce the whole practice. As counsel they engaged the young Boston lawyer, James Otis, an "eagle-eyed politician," as a contemporary said, who had personal scores to settle with Chief-Justice Thomas Hutchinson, under whose name the writs were to be issued.

Early in 1761, when Otis appeared in court to protest against some writs that Hutchinson had drafted, he delivered one of the most momentous speeches ever heard in America. "Otis was a flame of fire!" said John Adams. "American independence was then and there born."

Otis rested his case not on legal technicalities but on broad principles. In arguing that an act of Parliament contrary to natural law should be regarded by the courts as void, he laid down the grounds of opposition to Parliament to which the colonists were to return again and again. Parliament had no legal right, he said, to break natural law either in Britain or in America. Fundamental human rights could not be infringed by legislation.

Although the legality of the writs was upheld in this instance and the writs themselves were issued, other colonies soon joined in the protest against them, and judges frequently refused to issue them in spite of heavy pressure from imperial customs commissioners.

MISHANDLING THE WEST

British wartime interference with colonial commerce angered Americans, especially in New England, New York, and Pennsylvania. Britain's taking Canada from France at the end of the war gave the colonists greater freedom and more frequent occasions to vent their anger. So long as the French owned Canada, the colonists had been drawn toward the mother country by the menace of an alien neighbor. The expulsion of the French removed this old danger, but British administration of Canadian affairs quickly presented the colonists with unexpected new ones.

After the French and Indian War, the task of coping with American problems fell first upon the ministry of George Grenville, which lasted from 1763 to 1765. This ministry's first problem was what to do about the Indians on the western frontier, many of whom had been allies of the French and some of whom, especially in the newly acquired provinces of Canada, remained restive after the peace settlement.

Probably no one could have satisfied all the clashing interests on the frontier. The established fur traders in the colonies as well as in Canada wanted the West permanently reserved for the Indian hunters and for the animals that bore the precious pelts. The newly influential land-speculators, on the other hand, were urging settlers to go west, and wanted the frontier made safe for them. Both sides had powerful friends in British politics. Colonial land speculators were particularly active in Pennsylvania and Virginia, and their claims often conflicted with one another's as well as with those of rivals in Britain itself. Benjamin Franklin represented a group of wealthy Pennsylvanians interested in lands along the Ohio. One of the Virginia enterprises was promoted by George Washington, whose Mississippi Company, formed as recently as 1763 as a successor to the old Ohio Company (see p. 99), had its eye on thousands of acres at the junction of the Ohio and Mississippi rivers.

While the British government was struggling to piece together a western policy, the Indians decided to look after themselves. Especially with the French power gone they felt they had to assert themselves more fiercely against the British traders who were cheating them without remorse. Still more menacing was the flood of settlement that would sweep over their lands if the speculators had their way.

Goaded by friendly Gallic traders who talked persuasively of the return of French power to North America, the red men, under the able Ottawa chief, Pontiac (hence the name, "Pontiac's Conspiracy)" went into action in May, 1763. Pontiac had planned a concerted attack on British forts with the objective of sweeping the entire white population into the sea. By the end of June the Indians had destroyed seven of the nine

British garrisons west of Niagara. So desperate had the British become by July, 1763, that they employed infected blankets to "send the *Small Pox*" among the "disaffected tribes." Thousands of braves soon died, and by September, 1764, most of the West had been pacified by this and more conventional means.

One notorious instance of conventional "pacification" occurred in December, 1763, when the "Paxton Boys" of Paxton and Donegal townships in Lancaster County, Pennsylvania, in retaliation for Indian raids on their frontier homes, fell upon the peaceful and innocent Conestoga braves near the town of Lancaster, murdered six of them and then stormed the workhouse where fourteen others had found refuge and "put old and young to the hatchet." Encouraged by the townspeople, the "Paxton Boys" soon grew into a mob of hundreds and moved toward Philadelphia. Ten miles from the

"His Most Sacred Majesty," George III.

city, Franklin and four others met them. "The fighting face we put on," wrote Franklin, "and the reasonings we used with the insurgents . . . turned them back." But the "Christian White Savages," as Franklin called them, nursed an even fiercer hate of the eastern grandees.

News of Pontiac's Conspiracy reached London in August, 1763, and in October the government there issued the Proclamation of 1763, intended as a temporary measure to give Britain time to work out a permanent western policy. The Proclamation set boundaries for three new crown colonies: Quebec, East Florida, and West Florida. Virtually all other western territory stretching from the Alleghenies to the Mississippi, and from Florida to 50° north latitude, was reserved for the time being for the red men alone. Fur traders and land speculators alike were excluded.

But no proclamation issued thousands of miles away could keep speculators out. Many of the colonials must have agreed with George Washington when he urged in effect that the Proclamation of 1763 be disobeyed: "I can never look upon that proclamation in any other light . . . than as a temporary expedient to quiet the minds of Indians. . . . Any person, therefore, who neglects the present opportunity of hunting out good lands . . . will never regain it." Washington promptly staked out his claims in the Ohio Valley. So many others followed his example that the British government itself soon made treaties with the Indians to give the speculators more room. One such treaty was made with the Choctaws and Chickasaws in 1765 to set the boundary of the Floridas. Three more followed in 1768: one with the Creeks at Pensacola affected the borders of South Carolina and Georgia; one with the Cherokees at their village of Hard Labor affected the boundary of western Virginia; and one with the Iroquois at Fort Stanwix in New York defined and in some places extended the colony's northern boundary. By the treaty of Lochaber in 1770, the Cherokees, for a price, accepted a line even farther west than that set at Hard Labor.

Every extension of the boundary line deeper into the continent touched off new bursts of speculation. In 1768 the first actual settlers beyond the Blue Ridge barrier occupied the Watauga Valley of North Carolina. In 1769, having made his first trip west two years before, Daniel Boone traversed the future "Wilderness Road" from the Holston River, through the Cumberland Gap, into Kentucky (see map, p. 130). Here he spent two years exploring the river valleys north to the Ohio, and in 1775, spurred on by Richard Henderson's land enterprises, he guided the first group of permanent settlers to the blue grass region. Unfortunately for the British, the deeper the Americans moved into the West and away from the old centers of power the more determined on self-government did they become.

THE PLANTERS' DISENCHANTMENT

Britain's restrictive western policy was especially hard on the planters of the South. By concentrating on their one money-making crop, the Virginia tobacco planters in particular had depleted the soil of both tidewater and piedmont. Cheap lands farther west seemed their only salvation. "The greatest estates we have in the colony," Washington wrote in 1767, were established "by taking up . . . at very low rates the rich back lands which were thought nothing of in those days but are now the most valuable lands we possess." Washington and others had already begun to shift from tobacco to wheat-growing in anticipation of moving inland.

Land policy was only one source of planter discontent with British rule. British merchants served as middlemen, at exorbitant commission fees, for everything the southerners bought abroad as well as for everything they sold. In addition, British shipowners charged high rates for carrying the planters' produce and purchases across the ocean. As their returns from the depleted lands dwindled, the southerners' debts mounted. Jefferson once estimated that Virginia planters owed at least £2 million to British merchants, and observed that these debts "had become hereditary from father to son, for many generations, so that the planters were a species of property annexed to certain mercantile houses in London." When the planters tried to pay their debts in American paper currency, such a howl of protest arose from the British merchants that Parliament passed the Currency Act of 1764 forbidding this practice and warning that a burdensome penalty would be laid on any colonial

governor who signed a paper-money bill.

The Virginians' discontent became a broad colonial issue as a result of the "Parson's Cause" of 1763. This dispute over how the clergy of the established church were to be paid first brought Patrick Henry to notice. Traditionally, the Virginia

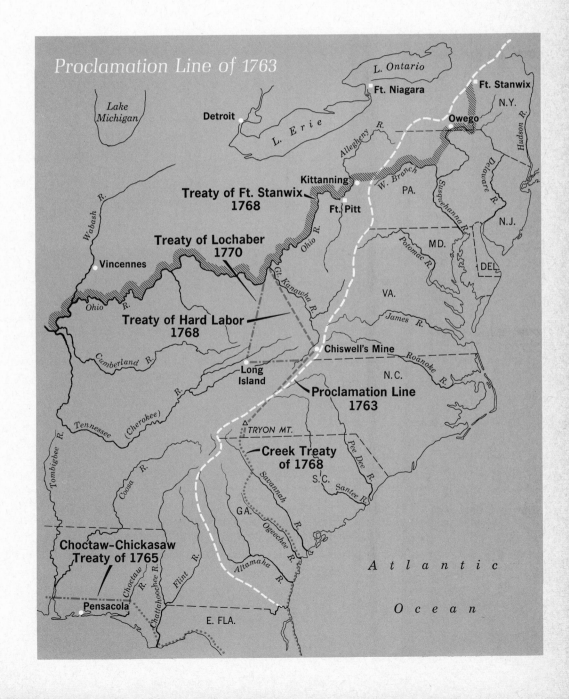

Proclamation Line of 1763

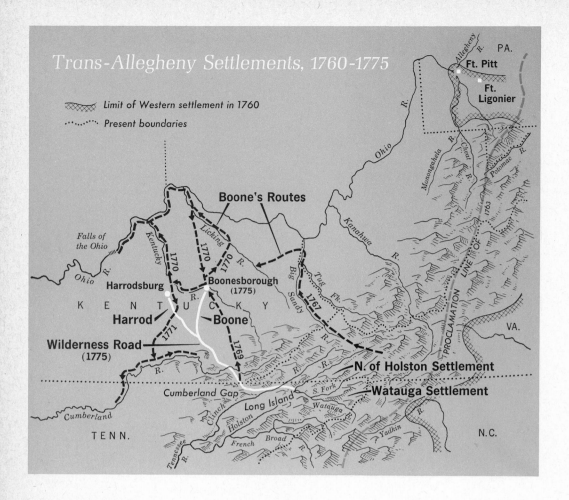

Limit of Western settlement in 1760
Present boundaries

PA.
Ft. Pitt
Ft. Ligonier

Allegheny R.

Ohio R.

Monongahela R.
Cheat R.
Potomac R.

LINE OF 1763

PROCLAMATION LINE OF 1763

VA.

Boone's Routes

Kanahwa R.

Licking R.

1770

1770

Falls of the Ohio

Kentucky R.

Ohio R.

1770

Harrodsburg

Boonesborough (1775)

Big Sandy R.

Tug Fk.

1767

K E N T U C K Y

Harrod

Boone

1771

1769

Wilderness Road (1775)

N. of Holston Settlement

Watauga Settlement

Cumberland Gap

Cumberland R.

Clinch R.

Holston R.

Long Island

S. Fork

Watauga R.

Yadkin R.

N.C.

TENN.

Tennessee R.

French Broad R.

clergy's salary was stated in pounds of tobacco; but when a tobacco shortage in 1758 drove prices far above their usual level, the assembly passed the Twopenny Act which allowed taxpayers to meet their obligation to the clergy at the rate of 2 cents for each pound of tobacco due, even though tobacco had soared to 5½ cents a pound. On complaint of the clergy to the Episcopal Bishop of London, the King in 1759 disallowed the Twopenny Act. Not content with this victory, several Virginia clergymen sued for a year's back pay. In one of these suits, which came to court in 1763, young Henry represented the Virginia tax-collectors. In an inflammatory speech to the jury, he cried that the King, by disallowing the Virginia law of 1758, had "degenerated into a tyrant, and forfeits all rights to his subjects' obedience." The opposing attorney called this "treason," but Henry knew his strong language was safe in a country made up largely of dissenters. The jury awarded only one penny in damages to the churchman who had brought the case, and Henry's victory made him famous.

In 1764 the frontier region in which Patrick Henry lived voted him into the House of Burgesses. From then on he was an effective spokesman for Virginia religious dissenters and the common people generally. Since Virginia herself was so predominant a power in the South, her hurts and her heroes furthered her neighbors' as well as her own preparation for cooperating with rebellious colonists to the north.

II. *The Passion for Self-government*

TAXATION THE GREAT ISSUE

The most divisive problem raised by the French and Indian War was taxation. Britain's long, costly struggles for empire had boosted tax rates to such staggering heights that British landowners by 1763 were turning over about a third of their income to the government. Now the British had to face the cost of garrisoning their expanded possessions. In North America alone, it was calculated that 10,000 troops were needed; and Parliament felt that the colonies should share the cost, which after all went largely to pay for their protection. The British government felt especially justified in its stand by the manifest good thing the northern colonists in particular had made of the war. "You cannot well imagine," a visitor wrote from Boston in 1760, "what a land of health, plenty and contentment this is among all the ranks, vastly improved within these ten years. The war on this continent has been equally a blessing to the English subjects and a Calamity to the French."

The colonists, however, for all their affection for the mother country and their avowed loyalty to the Crown, had long since learned to manage their home finances without British interference and now began to demand that the British solve their financial crisis without troubling America. For one thing, the colonists had worked up a domestic war debt of £2,500,000 which they would have to pay and service themselves. In addition, by Pitt's own estimate, British merchants, under the mercantilist tendency of trade, made a profit of no less than £2,000,000 a year on colonial commerce, and such profits seemed to Americans to be "tax" enough. The very prosperity that made the colonists seem fair game to the British, moreover, had given them, in the words of Governor Hutchinson of Massachusetts, "a higher sense" of their own "grandeur and importance," and stiffened their stand against Parliament's financial innovations and in support of their own novel ideas.

THE SUGAR ACT

In April, 1764, the Grenville ministry took its first financial plunge by imposing on the American colonies what became known as the Sugar Act. By this measure Grenville hoped to raise £45,000 a year. Instead he raised the spirit of revolt.

A duty of six cents a gallon on the importation of foreign molasses essential to the distilling of Yankee rum had been imposed on the colonies in 1733 but was never enforced. The new act halved the duty but made it clear that it would be collected to the penny. The duty on many other essential imports was raised. To insure collection, suits over the payment of the new duties and charges of smuggling on other grounds as well were removed from the regular colonial courts, where Americans usually were let off by friendly juries, to the hated admiralty courts, where there were no juries at all. This provision excited American merchants even more than the ruin they saw in store for them because of the Sugar Act's direct interference with the whole spectrum of colonial commerce.

But what aroused Americans most of all were the ominous implications of the official title of the act—the Revenue Act—and the preamble which elaborated its purpose to tax the colonists directly. Heretofore the charges placed upon the colonists had been explained and excused as a legitimate part of imperial administration. The Sugar Act was the first law ever passed by Parliament with the avowed objective of raising money in the colonies.

The Currency Act, passed in the same month as the Sugar Act (see p. 131), worsened the situation. Faced with one measure designed to draw money from America and another to forbid expansion of American currency, many now groaned under the heavy hand of empire. They were quick to protest, too. The town of Boston, preparing instructions for its representatives in the general assembly, asked an ominous question: "If taxes are laid upon us in any shape without ever having a legal representation where they are laid, are we not reduced from the character of free subjects to the miserable state of tributary slaves?" James Otis wrote a thundering pamphlet in which he declared: "No parts of his Majesty's dominions can be taxed without their consent." The Massachusetts House of Representatives authorized a committee of correspondence to write to other provinces about the issue. In Boston, New York, and elsewhere merchants and mechanics pledged themselves not to buy or use certain British goods. The Sugar Act spawned the idea of non-importation, which soon became so effective as a revolutionary weapon.

THE STAMP ACT

When Grenville announced the Sugar Act, he served notice that another revenue measure was being prepared. This was the Stamp Act, passed by Parliament in March, 1765. Grenville had even higher hopes for this act than for the Sugar Act, for he expected it to bring in £60,000 a year. Every time a colonist required a legal document, or purchased a license, newspaper, pamphlet, almanac, playing cards, or dice, this act required that he purchase a stamp for it ranging in value from a half-penny to £10.

One section of the Stamp Act may have especially alarmed many, and it certainly alarmed the dissenting clergy, who were to become among the most influential of the rebels. This was the section that required stamps on "every skin or piece of vellum or parchment, or sheet or piece of paper,"

as the act said, issuing from any court, including courts "exercising ecclesiastical jurisdiction within the said colonies." There were, as yet, no such courts; but there was a justifiable fear, growing since 1763, that the Church of England might gain the authority to set them up under the bishop it was urging for the whole of America. When the Stamp Act seemed to assume that these courts, and this centralized religious authority, would be imposed, it galvanized the resistance of colonists whose whole tradition was based on congregational self-determination (see p. 111). The Stamp Act provided further that all violators were to be tried in the same hated juryless admiralty courts in which smugglers were brought to account, and heavily fined if found guilty. The Sugar Act had struck mainly at merchants. The Stamp Act hit every articulate and influential person in the colonies—lawyers, printers, editors, tavern-owners, and dissenting preachers.

At the same time as the Stamp Act, Parliament passed a new Quartering Act which to many appeared even worse. This act provided that where barracks were insufficient for housing the new British garrisons in America, public inns and even private barns might be used. Furthermore, soldiers were to be supplied at the colonies' expense with certain materials that had previously been furnished by the army. This made the Quartering Act seem but one more direct levy, in addition to its other obnoxious terms.

In opposing the Stamp Act, the colonists did not confine themselves to words. Agitators quickly set up an intercolonial organization known as the Sons of Liberty, which soon gained notoriety for violent measures against those seemingly insufficiently rebellious. In Boston, Philadelphia, Newport, New York, and Charleston, mobs organized by merchants themselves pillaged the houses of Stamp Act defenders and intimidated the King's officials. In August, 1765, a Boston mob burned the records of the admiralty court, ransacked the home of the comptroller of the customs, and then entered, looted, and wrecked the elegant Hutchinson mansion, stealing or destroying everything down to the last shirt. Even before November 1, when the Stamp Act was supposed to go into effect, every stamp agent in the colonies had been badgered into resigning or promising not to execute his commission.

In October, 1765, nine colonies sent delegates to New York City to a Stamp Act Congress called by the General Court of Massachusetts. Of the four absent colonies, three (Virginia, Georgia, and North Carolina) failed to send delegates only because their royal governors would permit none to be selected. The Stamp Act Congress issued a moderate "Declaration of Rights and Grievances," in which it claimed for the colonists all the rights of Englishmen, and asserted that among these rights was freedom from taxation except "with their own consent, given personally, or by their representatives." The Declaration denounced the recent regulations on trade and the expanded jurisdiction of the admiralty courts, and petitioned for repeal of the Stamp Act. The Stamp Act Congress never threatened rebellion nor urged independence.

The Stamp Act Congress was followed by signed agreements among merchants in the major ports not to buy British goods until the hated law and other objectionable trade regulations had been repealed. When the Stamp Act went into effect on November 1, colonists almost everywhere suspended business in protest. When they resumed business, they did so without using stamps, and not a single one was ever sold in America.

By then, Grenville had fallen from power, to be replaced by the Marquis of Rockingham. The new ministry was confronted not only with opposition in America but with pressure from British merchants at home, who were feeling the pinch of the American boycott. In January, 1766, Pitt added fuel to the fire with a devastating speech in Parliament in which he demanded that "the Stamp Act be repealed absolutely, totally, and immediately."

Pitt and the merchants had their way. The hated act was repealed on March 17, 1766. Few British leaders, however, were willing to admit that it had been repealed because, as Pitt put it, "it was founded on an erroneous principle." To make it clear that repeal was not a renunciation of revenue-raising powers, Parliament passed, along with the repeal, the Declaratory Act, which asserted that Parliament had the full right to make laws "to bind the colonies and people of America . . . in all cases whatsoever." Amid the general rejoicing in America over repeal, this ominous proviso was ignored for the time being.

THE TOWNSHEND ACTS

About four months after the repeal of the Stamp Act the Rockingham ministry fell and Pitt was called upon to form a cabinet. But Pitt, now Earl of Chatham, soon became so ill that he was forced to retire temporarily. Control then fell to the clever Chancellor of the Exchequer, Charles Townshend, whose fiscal measures turned the Americans from resistance to revolution, a turn Pitt himself might have averted.

Townshend had been led by American statements in 1765 and 1766 to believe that the colonists might accept revenue-raising measures if they were presented as "external" taxes on trade. Accordingly, in June, 1767, Parliament passed the Townshend Acts to raise money by new import duties on glass, lead, paints, paper, and tea. But once again attempts to collect the new duties caused trouble. The Townshend Acts reasserted the power of the courts to issue writs of assistance, thus reviving one old colonial grievance. By once again giving admiralty courts the right to try violators of the new customs regulations, the acts rubbed another old sore. Resentment was heightened by the creation under these acts of a new Board of Customs Commissioners whose job it was to spy out every petty violation, and even to invent violations under technicalities the more surely to harass the colonists. The crowning insult was the provision that the salaries of the King's new appointees were to be paid out of the fines and judgments levied against violators convicted in the admiralty courts. The final section of the Townshend Acts hit specifically at New York, which had refused to comply with the Quartering Act of 1766. After October 1, 1767, all legislative functions of the New York Assembly were to be suspended until the members knuckled under.

By now the colonists had become adept at agitation. Non-importation agreements were revived. In November, 1767, John Dickinson of Pennsylvania published a widely read pamphlet, *Letters from a Farmer in Pennsylvania to the Inhabitants of the British Colonies,* in which he assailed the Townshend Acts as unconstitutional. He also denounced Parliament's treatment of the New York Assembly as a threat to the liberties of all the colonies. On behalf of the Massachusetts legislature, Samuel Adams now drew up a circular letter to be sent to the other colonies restating Dickinson's points. Adams' work drew from the newly created office of Secretary of State for America an arrogant reply castigating the circular letter as "a flagitious attempt to disturb the public peace," and instructing all colonial governors to treat the colonial legislatures with "the contempt" they deserved. Governor Bernard in Boston was commanded, in particular, to dissolve the Massachusetts legislature for its refusal to rescind Adams' circular letter. Bernard carried out this order on July 1, 1768, and by the end of September, two regiments of British troops, which the customs officials had requested for protection, reached Boston.

Many colonies now passed "resolves" expressing their support of Massachusetts. The "Virginia Resolves," adopted in May, 1769, were introduced in the legislature by George Washington. They endorsed the colonists' right to be taxed only by their own legislatures, and denounced the British handling of colonial protests. Mainly because of the non-importation movement America's trade with the mother country in 1769 fell by a third.

Lord North, who became prime minister early in 1770, could not help but realize that the Townshend Acts were costing more than they were bringing in. In March, 1770, therefore, he called on Parliament to repeal all the duties except the one on tea, which was to be kept simply to maintain the principle of Parliamentary supremacy. Americans, on learning of this conciliatory step, let non-importation drop.

THE CLARIFICATION OF IDEAS
After repeal of the Townshend Acts, tension abated, but in the next two years agitators like Samuel Adams sought out occasions to keep American rebelliousness warm. One such occasion was the "Boston Massacre" of March 5, 1770, when British soldiers, goaded by a mob, lost their heads and killed five Bostonians and wounded others. John Adams, though an ardent patriot and a future Revolutionary leader, detested mobs. He defended the soldiers in court and managed to get them acquitted of murder charges. Two of the soldiers, found guilty of manslaughter, were released after minor punishment. But the "massacre" itself was picked up as a favorite theme for oratory. Here is how one Bostonian used it:

Has the grim savage rushed again from the wilderness? Or does some fiend, fierce from the depths of hell, with all the rancorous malice which the apostate damned can feel, twang her deadly arrows at our breast? No: none of these . . . it is the hand of Britain that inflicts the wound.

A second incident occurred in June, 1772. The unfortunate *Gaspee,* a British revenue cutter engaged in apprehending colonial smugglers, ran onto the beach near Providence, Rhode Island. A group of colonists promptly overpowered the crew, burned the vessel, and celebrated their "victory."

Sam Adams knew how to exploit such events. His most useful instrument was the committee of correspondence he formed in Boston in 1772 to keep in touch with similar committees whose organization he urged in other towns to spread the news of each new outrage and to exchange revolutionary ideas. Influential Virginians were among the first to pick up Adams' idea, and soon a network of seditious organizations spread over the country.

Americans were driven to take an increasingly daring stand in their resistance not only by the course of events but also by the logic of their arguments. The British themselves could sympathize with colonial resentment against being taxed by a body in which they were not represented. But even at home, the British said, the people of Manchester and Birmingham, for example, sent no members to the Commons. Yet these Englishmen, they argued, were "virtually represented" by members chosen by their countrymen. But this did not impress Americans. To them, 3,000 miles distant from Parliament, "virtual representation" was no representation at all. The Stamp Act Congress had said that the colonists "are not, and from their local circumstances cannot be, represented in the House of Commons in Great Britain." They had their own legislatures which alone might tax them.

In both England and America the constitutional argument was based for a time on the distinction between "external" and "internal" taxes, the one permitting the collection of "an incidental revenue" arising out of the legitimate regulation of trade, the second imposing direct taxes "for the single purpose of revenue." Americans had long accepted "external taxes," especially since they were so easily evaded; but when Townshend tried to impose the second dressed up in the guise of the first, the Americans saw through the ruse and learned to distrust the distinction.

Mulling over this question, Franklin confessed in 1768 that it was

difficult to draw lines between duties for regulation and those for revenue; and if the Parliament is to be the judge, it seems to me that establishing such a principle of distinction will amount to little. The more I have thought and read on the subject, the more I find myself confirmed in opinion, that no middle ground can be well maintained. . . . Something might be made of either of the extremes: that Parliament has a power to make *all laws* for us, or that it has a power to make *no laws* for us; and I think the arguments for the latter more numerous and weighty, than those for the former. Supposing that doctrine established, the colonies would then be so many separate states, only subject to the same king, as England and Scotland were before the union.

These last bold words laid bare the direction the colonial argument was taking—that the colonists should become completely independent of Parliament and united to Britain only by their loyalty to the Crown. Such distinguished American lawyers as James Wilson of Pennsylvania, John Adams, and Thomas Jefferson shared this view. In short, what the American's had come up with was the idea of dominion status, the sort of position Canada was to achieve much later. But this solution was far in advance of its time. The British found it unthinkable. Their leaders flatly rejected it, and in so doing they hurried the Americans along the road toward independence.

TO THE BREAKING POINT

Perhaps the revolutionary tendency became irreversible in 1773, when Parliament passed the incredibly provocative East India, or Tea Act.

No ordinary commercial organization, the East India Company was a gigantic monopoly to which Parliament had entrusted even the government of India. Like the British government itself, the company now was shot through with corruption and mismanagement. Trembling on the brink of bankruptcy, it demanded that Parliament bail it out. The warehouses of the East India Company in England were bulging with 17 million pounds of tea. The Tea Act of May, 1773, granted the company the right to ship this tea to America and to sell it there through its own agents. Cheap tea for colonial consumers was one thing. Cheap tea at the expense of colonial importers was another. Moreover, these importers asked their sympathetic fellow Americans: if Parliament could now bestow a tea monopoly on the East India Company, what was to stop it from granting similar monopolies over other commodities?

By December, 1773, East India Company tea had reached Boston, where it sat under the protection of British troops. To rid themselves of it, patriots under Sam Adams' direction hit on the device of disguising themselves as Indians, boarding the tea ships, and throwing the tea into the harbor. This feat was performed on December 16, 1773.

The North ministry could not ignore so defiant an act, nor could friends of the colonies in Parliament condone it. To punish the Americans, Parliament passed a series of acts early in 1774, called in the colonies Coercive, or "Intolerable," Acts, which killed whatever hope of reconciliation remained: (1) The Port of Boston was to be closed until the East India Company and the British customs had been reimbursed for their losses. (2) Any British official indicted by Massachusetts courts for capital offenses committed while enforcing British laws could be tried at home, away from hostile colonials. (3) In Massachusetts, the King or his governor was given power to fill by appointment many offices heretofore elective; and no town meeting could be held without the governor's permission, and then only on business he approved. (4) A new quartering act was imposed on all the colonies.

With characteristically poor timing, Parliament also picked May, 1774, to pass the Quebec Act which, by recognizing certain features of French law, gratified the former Canadian subjects of France. But these features included trials without juries, and political equality for Catholics—two items which especially alarmed the wary Protestants of neighboring Massachusetts. More objectionable still, to the rest of the colonists, the act enlarged the Province of Quebec to include the territory north of the Ohio and east of the Mississippi where Massachusetts, Connecticut, and Virginia all had claims which the Quebec Act ignored. No longer did the radicals in America have to exaggerate the danger to traditional liberties; the danger had been plainly revealed for all to see. And they had good reason to believe, as Edmund Burke advised the New York Assembly from London, that the purpose of the Quebec Act had been to hem in the old English colonies and to cut off their growth.

The Massachusetts House of Representatives replied to these measures by asking all the colonies to send delegates to Philadelphia in September, 1774, to voice their opposition. The result was the First Continental Congress, in which only Georgia, of the thirteen colonies, was unrepresented. The delegates to this Congress had been named by extra-legal conventions called to elect them and to perform other revolutionary acts unthinkable for regular legislatures and governors.

Work began in Philadelphia with the proposal of the conservative Joseph Galloway of Pennsylvania that a grand colonial council be set up to share power with Parliament on colonial matters. But, spurred on perhaps by false rumors that General Thomas Gage (recently appointed governor of Massachusetts) had bombarded Boston and that New England had taken up arms, the Congress rejected Galloway's scheme by a single vote and resolved on more drastic action.

A meeting of delegates from Massachusetts towns had just adopted the "Suffolk Resolves," which advocated two bold measures: (1) that the colonies raise their own troops; and (2) that they suspend all trade with Britain, Ireland, and the British West Indies. The Congress endorsed these proposals. Companies of "minutemen" soon began to drill on the village greens. To insure that the boycott of British trade be complete, Congress organized a "Continental Association" and authorized the selection of committees "in every County, City, and Town" to enforce the "Non-Importation, Non-Consumption, and Non-Exportation" policy. These committees were also to "encourage Frugality, Economy, and Industry, and . . . discountenance and discourage every species of extravagance and dissipation, especially horseracing, and all kinds of gaming, cock fighting, exhibitions of plays, shews and other expensive diversions and entertainments." They were empowered, moreover, to publish the names of all violators as "enemies of *American* liberty," the better to expose them to public attack. These committees became virtual local governments. Few dared attract their enmity and the Association proved a great success.

The First Continental Congress may rightly be described as the first national government in America. "By assuming the powers of legislation," wrote a Tory critic of the association and other congressional acts, "the Congress have not only superseded our provincial legislatures, but have excluded every idea of monarchy; and not content with the havoc already made in our constitution, in the plentitude of their power have appointed another Congress to be held in May."

Before adjourning on October 26, 1774, the First Continental Congress did in fact agree, unless their grievances had been fully met, to reconvene on May 10, 1775. The date proved to be none too early. Unnerved by the gathering of minutemen around Boston, General Gage, on April 19, 1775, sent 700 troops to destroy the large amount of munitions and supplies that the colonists appeared to be collecting

in Concord, about twenty miles north. Paul Revere, William Dawes, and Dr. Samuel Prescott were sent by Boston patriots to arouse the minutemen along the way, and at Lexington green, five miles short of Concord, the redcoats encountered a line of armed farmers and townsmen. Eight minutemen fell here, and the British moved on. Revere and Dawes were halted by the British before reaching Concord, but Dr. Prescott got through in time to warn the minutemen there to get their supplies away, which they did. Frustrated at Concord, Gage's men turned back toward Boston; but by then, thousands of minutemen lined the road and shot down the redcoats as they passed. By the time they reached Boston the British counted

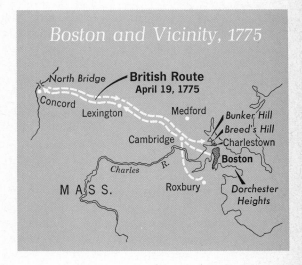

Boston and Vicinity, 1775

273 casualties. Ninety-three Americans had been killed or wounded.

There remained many men on both sides who tried, still, to avert war. But the battle of pamphlets and protest clearly had yielded to a battle of rifles and cannon, and as the news of the start of actual fighting spread, Americans looked anxiously to the Philadelphia meeting for leadership.

III. *Patriots and Loyalists*

When the Second Continental Congress convened hastily in Philadelphia in May, 1775 (all thirteen colonies were to be represented, but distant Georgians did not arrive until September), few of the delegates could have imagined that they were to remain in session almost continuously for fourteen years. They were a divided if distinguished group, but one of their earliest actions, a nearly unanimous one, helped to smooth over many differences. This was the selection of George Washington of Virginia as commander-in-chief of the new Continental Army of nearly 10,000 men that was gathering near Boston. Washington inspired confidence. His courage, honesty, and dignity, his willingness to sacrifice his personal fortune to the cause, all proved in the long run more vital than military genius to rebel success. It was quite in character for Washington even to refuse the pay that Congress voted him and to serve through the war without compensation.

Many in the Second Continental Congress still hoped that Washington, as general, would find little to do. On July 6, 1775, Congress adopted a "Declaration of the Causes and Necessity of Taking up Arms": "Our cause is just," they confidently declared. "Our union is perfect." Then came an open threat: "Our internal resources are great, and, if necessary, foreign assistance is undoubtedly attainable. . . . The arms we have been compelled by our enemies to assume, we will . . . employ for the preservation of our liberties, being with one mind resolved to die free men rather than live slaves." But there was also a note of hope: "We have not raised armies with ambitious designs of separating from Great Britain, and establishing independent States."

At this time Congress also adopted the "Olive Branch Petition," the work of its most cautious members, which begged the King to keep Parliament from further tyrannical measures so that a plan of reconciliation could be worked out. On receiving this petition in August, however, the incautious King himself brushed it aside and issued a proclamation of his own. Americans were rebels, he said, and he warned all loyal persons to refrain from assisting them.

Still, there were conciliators in Britain too. In March, 1775, Edmund Burke, in one of his great speeches, urged Parliament to meet American demands and surrender the right to tax. "An Englishman," he cried, "is the unfittest person on earth to argue another Englishman into slavery." Burke went largely unheeded, but Lord North himself persuaded Parliament to offer last ditch concessions that might have helped in 1765 but in 1775 were too late.

By the time the North plan of conciliation reached Philadelphia, the Battle of Bunker Hill, the bloodiest engagement of the entire war, had been fought. The battle actually took place on Breed's Hill, overlooking Boston, where hundreds of American militiamen had gathered soon after the surviving redcoats had returned from Concord (see map, p. 137). On June 17, 1775, General Gage, strengthened by fresh troops, decided that he would drive the patriots off. He did manage to dislodge them, but at a frightful cost. The Americans lost almost 400 men, but Gage lost more than 1,000—over 40 per cent of those he had moved into battle. Two weeks later, General Washington arrived at Cambridge, outside Boston, to take command.

By this time, too, fighting had begun farther north. Early in May, 1775, in an effort to gain control of Canada, Ethan Allen, from future Vermont, captured the British posts at Crown Point and Ticonderoga in New York. On May 29, the Congress approved an address to their "fellow-sufferers" in Canada, inviting them to join the rebellion; but Canadian "sufferings" had been assuaged by the Quebec Act of 1774 (see p. 136), and their loyalty was not to be shaken. When the British organized a force in Canada to invade New York themselves, Washington decided to try to forestall them. In September, 1775, Benedict Arnold set out for Quebec from Cambridge with about 1,000 men, and early in December was joined below the town by a smaller contingent under Richard Montgomery, which had already taken Montreal. On New Year's Eve, 1775, Arnold and Montgomery made their assault, and it ended in Montgomery's death and Arnold's defeat. Arnold's force kept Quebec isolated through the bitter winter; but with the arrival of British reinforcements in the spring, he was forced to retire to Ticonderoga. The venture only sharpened British concern for Canada's safety, and coming as it did just after Congress had rejected Lord North's last effort at conciliation, it also prompted George III to build up his forces there for the fight to the finish against the rebels to the south.

THE DECLARATION OF INDEPENDENCE

The average Englishman had no heart for the fight against the colonials, and the mother country was obliged to hire foreign mercenaries. Almost 30,000 "Hessians," as they came to be called since so many of them came from the German principalities of Hesse-Kassel and Hesse-Hanau, ultimately served with the British army in America.

Colonial propagandists and America's sympathizers in Parliament were quick to exploit this move, which stiffened the will of those Americans who had already declared for separation. The number of such Americans was raised early in 1776 by a pamphlet called *Common Sense* that appeared in Philadelphia from the hand of Thomas Paine. More than 120,000 copies were quickly sold. "There is something very absurd," Paine said, "in supposing a Continent to be perpetually governed by an island." And he added: "Freedom hath been hunted round the globe. . . . England hath given her warning to depart. O re-

ceive the fugitive, and prepare in time an asylum for mankind."

Such preparation was indeed under way. On April 6, 1776, the Congress had opened American ports to the commerce of all nations except Britain. This, in itself, placed America independent of Britain, as many in Congress realized when they debated the step. A month later Congress advised such colonies as had not already done so to form new state governments (see p. 156). Then on July 2, 1776, after nine hours of debate the day before had helped bring certain reluctant delegates around, Congress adopted Richard Henry Lee's "Resolution of Independence":

RESOLVED, That these United Colonies are, and of right ought to be, free and independent States, that they are absolved from all allegiance to the British Crown, and that all political connection between them and the State of Great Britain is, and ought to be, totally dissolved.

The adoption of this resolution was the great step, but in order to help enlist the support of foreign powers one more step seemed desirable. As Jefferson put it, "a decent respect to the opinions of mankind requires that they should declare the causes which impel them to the separation." On July 4, having made numerous changes in Jefferson's draft of this declaration of causes, Congress finally ordered it "authenticated and printed," and "proclaimed in each of the united states & at the head of the army."

One of Congress's great goals was unanimity before the world; but not until July 19 was it possible to give the declaration its lasting title: "The Unanimous Declaration of the Thirteen United States of America." In order that unanimity be attained, what John Adams called Jefferson's "vehement philippic against negro slavery" had to be struck out, "in complaisance," as Jefferson noted at the time, "to South Carolina and Georgia. . . . Our northern

First page of Jefferson's rough draft of the Declaration of Independence, showing corrections made by Jefferson, John Adams, and Benjamin Franklin.

brethren," he added, "also I believe felt a little tender under these censures; for tho' their people have very few slaves themselves, yet they have been pretty considerable carriers of them to others." There was no difficulty, however, about the ringing opening phrases of the Declaration, "these truths" we hold "to be self-evident." Many years later, John Adams was to belittle Jefferson's achievement, holding that the Declaration merely repeated what men had been saying all along. But Jefferson replied that this was exactly what he had intended to do. The Declaration, Jefferson said, was "to be an expression of the American mind. . . . All its authority rests on the harmonizing sentiments of the day."

Although most of their quarrels had been with acts of Parliament, the list of grievances the Congress subscribed to in the Declaration was directed at "the present King of Great Britain." This was done deliberately. If the delegates had made their case against Parliament, they would have implied that they might still be persuaded to remain loyal subjects of the King. By attacking George himself, they served notice that they accepted no British authority whatever, that they were cutting every tie with the mother country.

The "self-evident" truths in the preamble to the list of grievances were meant to justify this revolutionary step in terms of the doctrine of natural rights, including the right of revolution. John Locke had given the doctrine of natural rights its classic formulation in defending the Glorious Revolution of 1688 in England (see p. 69). By 1776 his ideas had become virtually axiomatic in America. What they meant was that all men share equally in certain basic *political* rights, which government must not invade. "Governments long established," the Declaration acknowledged, "should not be changed for light and transient causes." But in America, Britain's "invasion" involved "a long train of abuses and usurpations" which showed an intention to place the colonists "under absolute Despotism." This a free people had more than a right to oppose; they had a duty to rebel against such tyranny.

The Declaration of Independence, when it stated that "all men are created equal," may not have seemed to Congress to venture beyond the conventional political equality of free citizens. But even before the Declaration was made there were those deeply troubled by the discrepancy between the institution of slavery and the rebels' bold avowals about liberty as their goal. The Association of 1774 (see p. 137),

140

and other non-intercourse proposals of the time, explicitly named the slave trade as one to be boycotted to make unmistakable the aversion to it. When in May of the following year, the question of using slaves as soldiers came up in Massachusetts, it was decided that their enlistment would be "inconsistent with the principles that are to be supported," and they were rejected. When the British, that November, began to make overtures to the slaves to enlist against their masters, however, Americans recognized the danger and altered their stand. In all about 5,000 Negroes, most of them slaves from northern states, served with the American revolutionary army, and most of them were freed on enlistment. In his attack upon slavery in the early drafts of the Declaration, moreover, Jefferson included bondmen among those whose "sacred rights of life and liberty" had been violated by King George.

Like all great political documents, the Declaration of Independence instantly took on a life of its own, consistent with the hopes and aspirations of all men under fetters, not merely white men in the America of 1776. Manumission in the South, abolition in the North, during and after the Revolutionary War itself, gained momentum from the Declaration's self-evident truths (see p. 140). In 1789, when the French rebelled against Bourbon absolutism, the Declaration helped light the way for their leaders. In our own time, among colonial peoples abroad and the repressed at home, the Declaration continues to serve the cause of social as well as political equality.

THE LOYALISTS

While Congress, as a revolutionary body, might easily be won around to the ringing phrases of the Declaration, and while other Americans might even extend the meaning of these phrases to suit their own more advanced thought, a good many colonists, often after agonizing indecision, concluded that they must remain loyal to the Crown. These Loyalists—scornfully called Tories by the patriots—often were

rich merchants, landholders, and lawyers closely tied to British power. Anglican clergymen of the Established Church were also numbered among those horrified at separation. There were, in addition, many ordinary citizens who resented being harried into rebellion and war. "Damn the Rebels," shouted a vehement farmer in Massachusetts. "I wish they were all scalped: damn Congress to hell."

Some ordinary Americans, indeed, embraced the Crown with new fervor rather than support the hated *colonial* aristocrats often found among the rebels. In North Carolina, the Regulators, as such back-country Tories were called, even took up arms against the seaboard patriots. Others remained Tories simply because they felt the colonials could not win the war. Growing patriot intolerance swayed still others toward loyalty to the king, who at least had the sanction of royalty for his impositions.

While Loyalists awaited British authority to smite the upstarts in America, the Whigs, as the patriots called themselves, organized "Tory committees" which imprisoned many of them and drove others out of their homes and communities. Patriots refused to trade with Loyalists or work for them. Loyalist estates and personal property often were confiscated. Few loyalists, however, lost their lives. American Whigs who lived long enough to learn of the horrors of the French Revolutionary terror sometimes remarked on the relative mildness of their own earlier behavior toward the counter-revolutionaries. Clearly, some kind of repression was in order. As Washington asked in 1775, "Why should persons, who are preying on the vitals of the country, be suffered to stalk at large, whilst we know that they will do us every mischief in their power?"

Many Loyalists fled behind the British lines and enjoyed the comfort of British protection, especially in New York City and Philadelphia, where they flourished again once the war was over. Thousands moved for good to Britain or Canada. Others stayed where they were and rendered valuable service to the King's forces. These as well as the refugees were later compensated by the British for their losses to the tune of £3 million.

IV. *The War of Independence*

Loyalist warnings that Britain possessed enormous military advantages in the looming war were well founded. A disorganized population of about 2.5 million, with no army or navy and no true central government, was ranged against a great imperial power of 10 million persons, the mistress of the seas, with thousands of experienced troops at her command.

Yet Britain suffered many strategic disadvantages to which the United States was to grow accustomed in the twentieth century. She had to wage the war across 3,000 miles of ocean, on unfamiliar terrain, much of it trackless forest. As one of her officers put it, the difficulty of moving supplies into the interior "absolutely prevented us this whole war from going fifteen miles from a navigable river." In contrast, the Americans were swift and mobile, adept at swooping down for short skirmishes, pecking away at the enemy's supply lines, and taking cover in the woods.

This sort of "guerrilla warfare," a term to be applied to other colonial conflicts later on, left British officers bewildered. In Lord George Germain, the Colonial Secretary, they had an intelligent and meticulous organizer who fully appreciated the difficulties "of opposing an enemy that avoids facing you in the open field." Germain gave his American commanders wide latitude in planning their maneuvers under the new conditions. As time proved, however, he was too optimistic about Loyalist assistance and trusted too much in officers who lacked energy and imagination. One of their failings was contempt for the American "yokels" (less widespread at the war's end than at the beginning), an attitude that led to careless and extravagant behavior. Even at Yorktown many of them were to surrender gracelessly, preferring to bow before the trim French forces instead of the ragged Yanks. The morale of the British troops was further weakened by faltering support on the home front. British civilians as a rule were almost as confused as their troops. Many were not even sure of what they were trying to accomplish. Hence their support of the war was lukewarm at best.

On their part, most Americans tended to underestimate their own difficulties. The same stubborn individualism, the same jealous attachment to their liberties that had made the Americans quick to resist the assaults of Parliament, now made them slow to accept the tight organization and the onerous discipline that were needed to carry on a war. Raising an army was hard enough; whipping it into a disciplined force was harder; and keeping it active in the field was all but impossible. Although some 300,000 persons may have taken up arms in the rebel cause, the largest army Washington ever pieced together at one time amounted to a little over 20,000 men. Usually he had hardly as many as 5,000, most of them state militia accustomed to marching under friendly officers elected by themselves and resentful of outside commanders. Most soldiers, concerned with families and farms back home, were reluctant to sign up for more than a few winter months, and few were ready to reenlist. Southerners resented being sent to New England to fight, and New Englanders returned the compliment. With the Continental army sadly in need of professionals, the Americans were glad to welcome such foreign volunteers and sympathizers as Baron Friedrich W. A. von Steuben of Prussia, Count Casimir Pulaski of Poland, and the Marquis de Lafayette, a

20-year-old volunteer from France. Von Steuben in particular was the kind of drill-master raw troops most needed.

As long as the war lasted, Washington plagued Congress with requests for fighting men. The delegates were powerless to do anything more than pass his demands on to the states. No one was satisfied with the results. Yet Congress' record was not as poor as it is often painted. The new nation, which had previously looked to the mother country for its manufactures, was always hard put to feed, clothe, arm, and pay the relatively few soldiers it could put in the field at any time. Washington's army often was desperately small. And yet the country could not have supported a much larger one than Congress did supply.

The story of the war-time economy is similar. Congress lacked not only the power to tax, but also—given the origins of the Revolution—the inclination to do so. Moreover, much of the taxable specie in the country—English guineas, Spanish pieces of eight, Dutch florins, and, for that matter, household silver—had gone with the Loyalists. Specie loans, foreign and domestic, were slow in coming, and they were used up with disheartening swiftness. Thus the war was financed mainly with paper money (especially the Continental currency, which had no observable resources behind it) and a whole Pandora's box of I.O.U.'s, the variety of which reflects credit only on Congress' ingenuity. The paper money eventually became valueless and the I.O.U.'s depreciated greatly.

The riot of speculation that accompanied the rise of commodity prices, expressed in terms of the depreciated currency, angered Washington more deeply than almost any other problem of the Revolution. At the same time, rising prices served to induce legitimate producers among farmers, miners, and manufacturers to increase their output greatly. Profits soared; but so did the quantity of goods available to the Continental army. Robert Morris expressed the philosophy of the wartime entrepreneurs, a philosophy that did not cost them the good opinion of their

friends: "It seems to me that the present oppert'y of improving our fortunes ought not to be lost, especially as the very means of doing it will contribute to the service of our country." It is doubtful if any greater economic effort could have been elicited had the Congress' money been as sound as that of the Bank of England and its credit buttressed (as it later was) by a bank of its own.

FROM LONG ISLAND
TO SARATOGA

On being dislodged from Breed's Hill in June, 1775, patriot forces successfully occupied Dorchester Heights overlooking Boston. There, Washington armed

"General Washington at Princeton," by Charles Peale Polk (1767-1822).

his men with cannon laboriously hauled down from Fort Ticonderoga early in 1776. Confronted by this force, the British General, Sir William Howe, who had supplanted General Gage, decided, in March, 1776, to evacuate Boston for Halifax, Nova Scotia. From there he would assault New York City, which, with its heavy Loyalist population and fine harbor, he hoped to make his headquarters. Washington expected this move, and in April he rallied as many soldiers as he could and marched them off to protect the city. But here he soon found himself confronted with Howe's army of 32,000 men on Staten Island. Sensing that it would be risky to concentrate his troops in the city itself, Washington fortified Brooklyn Heights on Long Island, hoping thereby to gain control of Manhattan as Dorchester Heights had given him control of Boston. On August 27, however, Howe defeated the rebels on Long Island. Two days later Washing-

ton entered Manhattan itself, where he was chased up the island to White Plains. Here he was beaten again, and fled to Hackensack, New Jersey, where he reformed his ranks.

By now Washington had his strategy firmly in mind. "We should on all occasions avoid a general action," he told Congress, "or put anything to the risque, unless compelled by a necessity, into which we ought never to be drawn." These tactics were made all the easier by General Howe's own lethargy on the attack.

In December, 1776, nevertheless, Howe did chase Washington from Hackensack to Trenton, New Jersey, and then across the Delaware River into Pennsylvania. Washington wrote to Congress that he must have more troops, or "I think the game will be pretty much up." But he did not wait for Congress' help before acting. Realizing, that Howe's troops must be spread thin, Washington counterattacked brilliantly. On

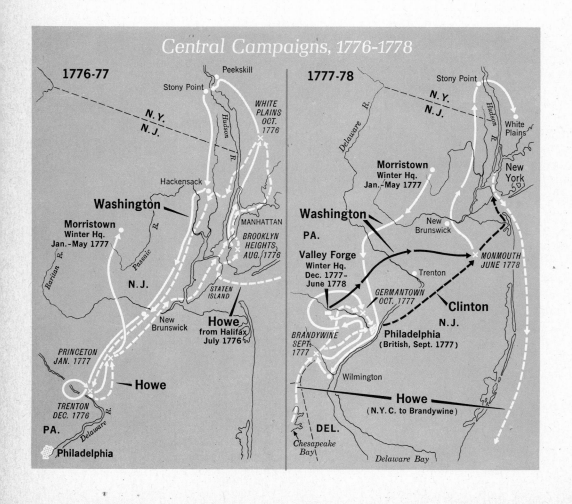

Central Campaigns, 1776-1778

1776-77

Peekskill
Stony Point
N. Y.
N. J.
WHITE PLAINS OCT. 1776
Hudson R.
Hackensack
Washington
MANHATTAN
Morristown Winter Hq. Jan.-May 1777
BROOKLYN HEIGHTS AUG. 1776
Passaic R.
N. J.
STATEN ISLAND
Raritan R.
New Brunswick
Howe from Halifax July 1776
PRINCETON JAN. 1777
Howe
TRENTON DEC. 1776
Delaware R.
PA.
Philadelphia

1777-78

Delaware R.
Stony Point
N. Y.
N. J.
Hudson R.
White Plains
Morristown Winter Hq. Jan.-May 1777
New York
Washington
PA.
New Brunswick
Valley Forge Winter Hq. Dec. 1777- June 1778
Trenton
MONMOUTH JUNE 1778
GERMANTOWN OCT. 1777
Clinton
N. J.
BRANDYWINE SEPT. 1777
Philadelphia (British, Sept. 1777)
Wilmington
Howe (N.Y.C. to Brandywine)
DEL.
Chesapeake Bay
Delaware Bay

the stormy Christmas night of 1776 he re-crossed the Delaware, surprised the sleepy Hessians at Trenton, killed their commander, and took almost 2,000 of them prisoners. Washington followed up this victory with another near Princeton, January 3, 1777. Before retiring for the winter near Morristown, New Jersey, he had cleared the British out of the state and once again dared hope for ultimate success.

These hopes soared with the defeat of "Gentleman Johnny" Burgoyne at Saratoga, New York, in October, 1777. General Burgoyne had worked out an elaborate plan to divide and conquer the rebels. With a large force from Canada he himself would push southward along Lake Champlain. At the same time, a smaller force under Colonel Barry St. Leger would march eastward through the Mohawk Valley from Fort Oswego on Lake Ontario. Still a third force, under General Howe, was to move northward up the Hudson Valley from New York City. Converging on Albany, the three armies would crush any American opposition, proceed to control New York and cut New England off from the south. Then the independent rebel states could be picked off, one by one.

Burgoyne's strategy was sounder than his communications. With Germain's permission, Howe undertook to nail down Philadelphia, the rebel capital, before moving north. On September 11 he overcame the defenders at Brandywine Creek, but not until September 26 could he enter the city itself. On October 3, at nearby Germantown, Howe repelled Washington's attempt to dislodge him. When Franklin, in Paris (see p. 146), heard that Howe had captured Philadelphia, he dissented. "No," he said, "Philadelphia has captured Howe." And so it was. Deserting Burgoyne, the pleasure-loving Howe lolled in the lap of Philadelphia's grateful Loyalist society.

Although tempted by fewer attractions than Howe, St. Leger was also lost to Burgoyne. On August 22, after Benedict Arnold's clever ruse at Fort Stanwix deprived him of his Indian contingents, St. Leger, battered in earlier engagements on

the way, decided to return to Fort Oswego.

Of the three British armies essential to Burgoyne's campaign, only one remained to him—his own. Blissfully unaware of his predicament, "Gentleman Johnny" started southward from Canada on June 17, with his wine, his fine clothes, his camp-following women, and almost 8,000 redcoats.

Misfortune dogged Burgoyne at almost every step, and of a kind that he and his men most detested. Impromptu bands of "country yokels," materializing suddenly, riddled his proper formations and as suddenly dissolved. On August 11, at Bennington, a group of Green Mountain Boys led by John Stark fell fiercely upon a force of 700 men whom Burgoyne had sent out to forage, and destroyed them entirely. A few days before, Burgoyne had received the dismal news of Howe's Philadelphia enterprise. "I little foresaw," Burgoyne wrote to Germain, "that I was to be left to pursue my way through such a tract of country,

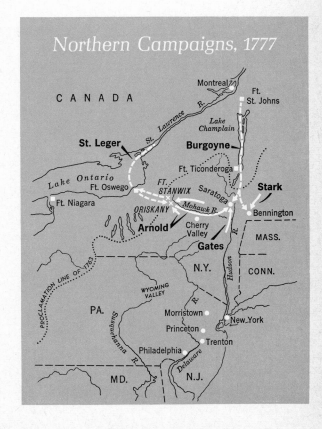

Northern Campaigns, 1777

and hosts of foes, without any co-operation from New York." But he pushed on to the vicinity of Saratoga, where on September 19 he was checked at the battle of Freeman's Farm. At last, his defeated force overwhelmingly outnumbered, he was met by Gates and Arnold at Bemis Heights. While Gates was arguing in his quarters with a captured British officer about the merits of the Revolutionary cause, Arnold led a magnificent assault. On October 17, 1777, Burgoyne surrendered his battered army.

Arnold's victory was an eye-opener to the redcoats. As one British officer captured at Saratoga wrote:

The courage and obstinacy with which the Americans fought were the astonishment of every one, and we now become fully convinced, they are not that contemptible enemy we had hitherto imagined them, incapable of standing a regular engagement, and that they would only fight behind strong and powerful works.

Burgoyne's dramatic defeat in turn electrified all Europe.

THE FORCE
OF THE FRENCH ALLIANCE
From the start of the Revolution, European governments had looked with mixed pleasure and concern at Britain's plight. On the one hand they yearned to see the island kingdom humbled and the balance of power restored; on the other, they feared the example of American success among their own people, at home as well as in their overseas possessions.

As early as November, 1775, Congress began to play upon Europe's hopes and fears by sending Silas Deane to France. Deane was successful in gaining secret assistance in the war both from France and from her ally, Spain. After the Declaration of Independence, Congress lifted its sights and dispatched Arthur Lee, then serving secretly in London, and the renowned and engaging Franklin, to assist Deane in Paris in negotiating a formal alliance. Franklin charmed the French, but they did not ca-

pitulate until they had learned of Burgoyne's surrender at Saratoga. In order to short-circuit Franco-American negotiations, Lord North's government, following Burgoyne's defeat, offered to suspend all laws passed in relation to America since 1763, and also appointed a peace commission to seek to end the war on these terms. In order to short-circuit Anglo-American negotiations which might restore British strength in America, France was ready to jump into the war on the rebel's side.

Congress rebuffed Lord North's offer. Nothing short of recognition of independence would do, and this the British could not grant. Congress also, on March 4, 1778, ratified the treaty with France which Franklin and Deane had concluded on February 6: "The essential and direct end" of the alliance cemented by the treaty was "to maintain . . . the liberty, sovereignty, and independence absolute and unlimited, of the United States." In case war broke out between Britain and France (Britain did declare war in June, 1778), the United States and France agreed "to make it a common cause," and neither party was to make peace without consulting the other. The French generously consented not to interfere if the Americans could conquer Canada and Bermuda; and, not to be outdone in generosity at Britain's expense, the Americans gave the French *carte blanche* in the British West Indies. In a separate commercial treaty negotiated at the same time, the two nations also granted one another favorable trade terms.

Before the French alliance American privateers did plenty of damage to British commerce, but American efforts to build a navy had come to little, partly because the privateersmen themselves outbid Congress for good men and ships. John Paul Jones and other commissioned sea captains, sometimes using French bases, harrassed British coastal towns, but there and elsewhere, simply "to Surprise and spread Alarm," as Jones said, they operated individually or in small, uncooperative squadrons, not as an effective fleet. With the French alliance, the rebels acquired naval support ready made, even though for some years it took the form of independent French actions against the common enemy.

One exception to this policy was French cooperation with John Paul Jones in September, 1779, in the battle of which the famous engagement between *Bonhomme Richard* and the British warship, *Serapis,* was a part. Although *Bonhomme Richard* was sunk in the meeting, Jones and his men successfuly boarded *Serapis* and took her to port in France. It was during this engagement, when invited to surrender by the heavier British vessel, that Jones is said to have replied, "I have not yet begun to fight." Fight he did, as he never had before even during his own extraordinarily violent career, but the outcome had no military effect on the progress of the cause.

The French alliance transformed the American war for independence into a renewal of the European struggle for power. Spain, Holland, and Russia soon joined the fray to nibble at British trade and feast on British shipping. The British held their own against these rivals, and their own privateers continued to improve their showing against rebel shipping itself. At the same time, foreign pressure on her control of the seas forced the British henceforth to wage a defensive war in America and eventually to capitulate. The Americans' success was delayed in part because, so divided were the states, so poor the people, they could not long sustain the buoyant spirit of Saratoga and the French alliance; and in part because the French themselves, belatedly concerned for the safety of their own West Indian possessions, were slow in making their critical naval contributions to America's final victory.

THE NADIR OF THE CAUSE

After his defeat at Germantown (p. 145), Washington had taken his battered bitter-enders to nearby Valley Forge where they endured their well known winter ordeal. Howe's pleasures in Philadelphia at the same time were wearing thin and he asked to be relieved of "this very painful service." His failure to disperse Washing-

ton's ragged, starving army prompted Germain to accede to his request, and in May, 1778, Howe was supplanted at the head of the British forces by General Henry Clinton. Clinton's orders were to evacuate Philadelphia and to prosecute a vigorous new campaign in New York.

When Clinton began his move from Philadelphia on June 18, Washington emerged from Valley Forge to intercept him. On June 28, the two armies met at Monmouth Courthouse in New Jersey, in an action that was a credit to neither side. General Charles Lee, at the head of Washington's advance force, behaved in a way that soon led to his court-martial and suspension from duty. When Clinton, however, tried to take advantage of Lee's mistakes, other Americans checked him. Clinton was allowed to steal away under cover of night to Sandy Hook, where his troops embarked on waiting transports for Manhattan.

Except for an expedition to South Carolina in December, 1779 (see p. 148), Clinton remained in New York until the end of the war. Washington himself followed Clinton to New York and again encamped at White Plains to keep an eye on the enemy. In the meantime, Loyalist and Indian bands terrorized frontier settlements in the Wyoming Valley in Pennsylvania's eastern interior and in Cherry Valley in central New York.

While the principal armies thus were playing their waiting game in the East, Virginia's own forces under George Rogers Clark undertook to destroy the Indians assisting the British in the West (see map, p. 149). In May, 1778, with 175 riflemen, Clark floated down the Ohio almost to the Mississippi and proceeded to take the undefended old French towns of Kaskaskia, Cahokia, and Vincennes. Colonel Henry Hamilton, the hated English commandant at Detroit, known as the "Hair Buyer" for paying his Indian auxiliaries for American scalps, counterattacked and recaptured

Vincennes. Clark then performed one of the most remarkable feats of the war. With an "army" of 127 men, half of them French, he marched 180 miles from Kaskaskia to Vincennes—triumphing over cold, floods, and hunger—and forced Hamilton to surrender on February 24, 1779. Clark never reached Detroit, as he hoped, nor did his victories clinch the lower Ohio and Illinois country for the Americans. But he lifted the Indian pressure from the settlements in Kentucky and West Virginia.

In accordance with his orders as he understood them, Clinton, beginning in May, 1779, began making sporadic forays against rebel forts in upstate New York, which Washington's contingents, especially the one under General Anthony Wayne, repulsed. Other rebel forces, in turn, took the offensive against the marauding Loyalist and Indian bands in New York and by August, 1779, had destroyed 40 Seneca and Cayuga villages. These actions neutralized the Iroquois menace in the East as Clark's had quieted the other tribes in the West.

Success against Britain's Indian allies in the interior, however, could not offset the deterioration in numbers and morale of Washington's main army in New York. Unpaid, ill-clothed, miserably fed, this army grew ever more restive as it saw, on the one hand, Congress's inability to stem the inflation that forced up the cost of war supplies, and on the other the high life of civilian profiteers. Late in 1779, Washington took this army to winter quarters in Morristown, New Jersey, where its sufferings outdid those at Valley Forge, and where hope for improvement vanished. Desertions soared, and before camp was broken in the spring of 1780, Washington had to quell an armed mutiny of Connecticut regiments.

The British tried to make capital of the rebels' plight by offering handsome bribes to alienated officers. Their best catch was the brilliant Benedict Arnold, already conscious of real and imagined snubs, who began sending Clinton information on American troop movements as early as May, 1779. Arnold was soon found out, but escaped with reprimands. The next year, his plot to gain command at West Point and to turn the fortress over to the British collapsed when the enemy agent, Major John André, was caught behind the American lines with incriminating evidence and hanged as a spy. On learning of André's fate, Arnold, on September 25, 1780, fled to a British warship on the Hudson. The British soon made him a general and enriched him besides, and he fought the rest of the war on their side.

Back in 1778, in the so-called "Conway Cabal," a group in Congress had given serious consideration to supplanting Washington with a more manageable commander. Under the changed circumstances of 1780, a new congressional delegation set out for Morristown in April empowered, as they said, to offer him "a kind of dictatorial power, in order to afford satisfaction to the army." As Washington ignored the Conways, so he rejected the desperate alternative. The delegation was warmly received by General Nathanael Greene and other officers who had similar plans of their own, but Greene sensibly steered them away from his chief. "He has strange notions about the cause," Greene said, "and the obligation there is for people to sacrifice fortune and reputation in support thereof." Washington never forgot that he was engaged in a war on tyranny as well as on tyrants, and his patience with the people soon had its reward.

TO YORKTOWN

The final battles of the war were fought in the South. Although Henry Clinton, along with Lord Cornwallis and Admiral Sir Peter Parker, had failed to take Charleston, South Carolina, in a combined sea and land attack back in June, 1776, Clinton believed that Loyalist support was heavy in the South and could be more fully exploited. Soon after he had taken over from Howe in 1778, Clinton planned an attack on Savannah, Georgia, which was successfully carried out in December that year. From Savannah, Georgia was overrun. One year later, Clinton personally led the new expedition against Charleston from New York, and on May 12, 1780, the town fell and with it over 5,000 men, 300 cannon, and four ships. Clinton then returned to New York, leaving Cornwallis in charge. Cornwallis followed up with a smashing victory over General Gates at Camden, South Carolina, on August 16, 1780.

With Georgia and South Carolina firmly held (despite the partisan warfare of South Carolina guerrillas like the daring "Swamp Fox," Francis Marion), the British commanders now turned to North Carolina, but here the tables were rudely turned. At King's Mountain, on October 7, 1780, an army of 1,100 Tories was shot up by backcountry patriots. Then, General Daniel Morgan's victory at Cowpens on January 16, 1781, and a severe engagement at Guilford Courthouse in March, at last persuaded Cornwallis to abandon the state

and move on to Virginia. General Nathanael Greene, who after Gates' disheartening defeat at Camden had taken over the command of the Continental army in the South, then cleared the British out of most of South Carolina in 1781. Not until December, 1782, however, did the British defense of Charleston itself collapse.

When Cornwallis, after raiding villages and farms, took up his position at Yorktown, Virginia, on August 1, 1781, he believed that British naval superiority would assure the evacuation of his troops, if such a move became necessary. In two months it did, but the evacuation was foiled by France's greatest contribution to rebel success.

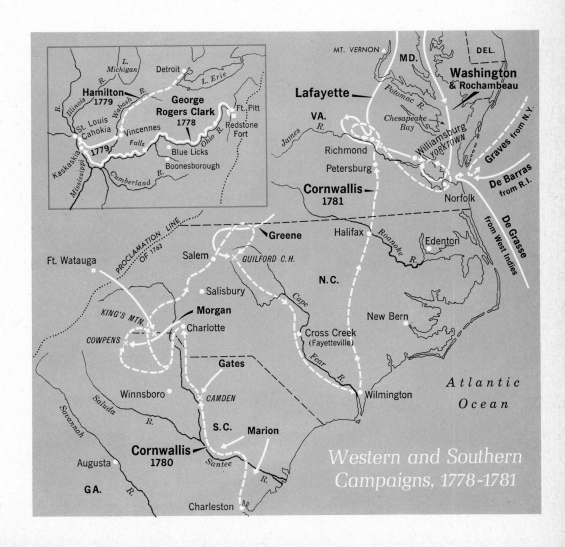

Western and Southern Campaigns, 1778-1781

In 1778, and again in 1780, French fleets had arrived in America, the first soon to leave again for the West Indies, the second to find itself bottled up by the British in Newport, Rhode Island, after landing the Comte de Rochambeau and 5,000 men. In May, 1781, Washington, still eyeing Clinton in New York, learned of the approach of a third French fleet of twenty warships under Admiral de Grasse. He tried to get Rochambeau to use this fleet to help get Clinton out of New York; but de Grasse himself was headed south and Washington promptly decamped and marched his men to meet him. British naval units around New York also sailed south; but on discovering the French strength, they sailed right back again and Cornwallis was finished. Pinned down between the French fleet and a combined Franco-American force of 16,000 men, Cornwallis had to yield As his defeated troops, numbering about

7,000, stacked their arms, American bands played a march called "The World Turned Upside Down."

The British surrender at Yorktown on October 19, 1781, virtually ended hostilities. Lord North, on learning the news, cried out again and again, "Oh God! it is all over!" In March, 1782, he resigned in favor of the Marquis of Rockingham, and his long and disastrous ministry came to an end.

The British, however, showed signs of fight even after Yorktown. The final peace was not worked out until almost two years later, and during that time Admiral Rodney defeated a French fleet at the Battle of the Saints in the West Indies in April, 1782. This belated victory went far toward redressing the balance of power at sea. The following autumn, the British turned back with heavy enemy losses a well prepared French and Spanish attack on the fortress of

United States in 1783

Gibraltar. These successes did not alter the fact that Britain had lost the war, but they did enable her to hold out for less costly peace terms.

THE TREATY OF PARIS

The American peace commissioners, Benjamin Franklin, John Jay, and John Adams, who were sent by Congress to Paris in 1782, had to proceed very delicately in their negotiations. Congress had instructed them to consult with France on matters of diplomacy, but the commissioners knew that Spain had never approved of American independence and that she opposed the Mississippi River boundary the envoys were seeking. Since it seemed likely that France would support Spain, the three Americans ignored their instructions and reached a preliminary independent agreement with the British delegation that gave America the territory she coveted up to the Mississippi shore. In return, America renounced all claims to Canada. Vergennes, the French minister, was chagrined by these behind-the-scenes deals, but the adroit Franklin managed to soothe him and even to extract another fat loan for the United States.

The treaty between the United States of America and Great Britain was signed in Paris on September 3, 1783, and ratified in Philadelphia on January 14, 1784. Known as the Treaty of Paris, it included the following provisions: (1) Britain recognized American independence. (2) America obtained all the territory bounded by the Mississippi River on the west, the 31st parallel on the south (the line agreed upon if Britain ceded Florida to Spain, which she did), and the Great Lakes on the north. (3) Britain acknowledged America's right to the Newfoundland fisheries, but (4) retained the privilege with America of navigating the Mississippi. The United States agreed (5) to impose "no lawful impedi-

ment" to the recovery by British creditors of private debts due them but (6) consented only to "recommend" that the states restore Loyalist property.

The American negotiators had done well. Although the treaty left many important issues unresolved, many commercial agreements uncertain, and some boundaries dangerously inexact, American independence was a recognized fact, and a vast area from the Alleghenies to the Mississippi lay open to settlement. An epoch had begun, a New Jersey congressman observed. "It opens a new scene to Mankind, and is big with inconceivable Effects in the political and I hope in the moral world." Washington, for all his disappointments and disgusts, agreed. Back in 1778, he cried out in anguish: "The States separately, have very inadequate ideas of the present danger. . . . Party disputes and personal quarrels are the great business of the day, whilst the momentous concerns of empire . . . are but secondary considerations." But in 1783, the opportunity for empire, and for the "self-evident truths" that would make empire in America different from empire abroad, seemed much brighter. In that year, the war at an end, victory attained, Washington said:

The citizens of America, placed in the most enviable condition, as the sole lords and proprietors of a vast tract of continent, comprehending all the various soils and climates of the world, and abounding with all the necessaries and conveniences of life, are now, by the late satisfactory pacification, acknowledged to be possessed of absolute freedom and independency. They are, from this period, to be considered as the actors on a most conspicuous theatre, which seems to be peculiarly designated by Providence for the display of human greatness and felicity.

Readings

Asterisk indicates that book is available in paperback.

L. H. Gipson, *The Coming of the Revolution, 1763-1775** (1954), and J. R. Alden, *The American Revolution 1775-1783** (1954) are up-to-date summaries of the events leading to the Revolution and of the war itself. See also C. L. Becker, *The Eve of the Revolution* (1918); C. M. Andrews, *The Colonial Background of the American Revolution** (1924); J. C. Miller, *Origins of the American Revolution* (1943), and Bernhard Knollenberg, *Origin of the American Revolution** (1960). J. C. Wahlke has assembled a number of differing points of view in *The Causes of the American Revolution** (1950). E. S. Morgan, *The Birth of the Republic: 1763-89** (1956), is an authoritative summary. E. B. Greene, *The Revolutionary Generation, 1763-1790* (1943), is a social history of the period.

Modern scholarship on British politics is represented in three books by Sir Lewis Namier: *The Structure of Politics at the Accession of George III** (2nd ed., 1957); *England in the Age of the American Revolution* (1930); *Personalities and Powers** (1955). Namier and John Brooke, *Charles Townshend* (1964), goes beyond biography to study the policies of the controversial chief minister. O. A. Sherrard, *Lord Chatham and America* (1958), volume 3 of Sherrard's outstanding life of William Pitt, is excellent on America's great champion. Richard Pares, *King George III and the Politicians* (1953), is in the Namier tradition. A dissenting voice is offered in Herbert Butterfield, *George III and the Historians* (1957). Eric Robson, *The American Revolution, 1763-1783* (1955) is a succinct discussion of the Revolution as a problem of British policy by an English scholar.

Bernard Bailyn, ed., *Pamphlets of the American Revolution,* vol. I, 1750-1765 (1965), is a useful anthology with a penetrating introduction on the colonial response to British measures and the gathering revolutionary struggle. British documents are combined with American ones in Max Beloff, ed., *The Debate on the American Revolution, 1761-1783* (1949). This theme is further developed in A. M. Schlesinger, *Prelude to Independence: The Newspaper War on Britain 1764-1776* (1958); Philip Davidson, *Propaganda and the American Revolution* (1941); B. I. Granger, *Political Satire in the American Revolution, 1760-1783* (1960); and A. M. Baldwin, *The New England Clergy and the American Revolution* (1928). The thrust of American ideas of liberty and empire is illuminated in Clinton Rossiter, *Seedtime of the Republic* (1953), and a shorter version, *Six Characters in Search of a Republic** (1953); and in Max Savelle, *Seeds of Liberty* (1948); V. L. Parrington, *The Colonial Mind, 1620-1800,** volume I of *Main Currents of American Thought* (3 vols., 1927); Gerald Stourzh, *Benjamin Franklin and American Foreign Policy* (1954); C. D. Bowen, *John Adams and the American Revolution** (1950); and Carl Bridenbaugh, *Mitre and Sceptre: Transatlantic Faiths, Ideas, Personalities and Politics, 1689-1775* (1962).

C. L. Becker, *The Declaration of Independence** (1922), is the outstanding study of that document. The background for it and many other related subjects is fully revealed in J. P. Boyd, ed., *The Papers of Thomas Jefferson,* volume I, 1760-1776 (1950). See also Adrienne Koch, *The Philosophy of Thomas Jefferson** (1943).

Special studies of British action and colonial reaction include also A. M. Schlesinger, *Colonial Merchants and the American Revolution 1763-1776* (1918); E. S. and H. M. Morgan, *The Stamp Act Crisis: Prologue to Revolution** (1953); and three excellent books on the West: Clarence Alvord, *The Mississippi Valley in British Politics* (2 vols., 1916); J. M. Sosin, *Whitehall and Wilderness: The Middle West in British Colonial Policy, 1760-1775* (1961); and T. P. Abernethy, *Western Lands and the American Revo-*

lution (1937). J. R. Alden, *The South in the Revolution, 1763-1789* (1957), ably covers that section's participation. G. M. Wrong, *Canada and the American Revolution* (1935), is an authoritative study. R. B. Morris, ed., *The Era of the American Revolution* (1935), is an exceptionally valuable collection of essays.

In addition to certain biographically oriented works cited above, the following lives of leading figures are of value: D. S. Freeman, *George Washington: A Biography* (6 vols., 1948-1954), completed by J. A. Carroll and M. W. Ashworth (vol. 7, 1957); Marcus Cunliffe, *George Washington, Man and Monument* * (1959); Carl Van Doren, *Benjamin Franklin* * (1938); V. W. Crane, *Benjamin Franklin and a Rising People* * (1954); Page Smith, *John Adams* (2 vols., 1962); Gilbert Chinard, *Honest John Adams* * (1933); Chinard, *Thomas Jefferson, The Apostle of Americanism* * (1929); Dumas Malone, *Jefferson and His Time* (3 vols., 1948-1962); J. C. Miller, *Sam Adams: Pioneer in Propaganda* (1936); M. D. Conway, *The Life of Thomas Paine* (2 vols., 1892); R. D. Meade, *Patrick Henry* (vol. I, 1957); Esther Forbes, *Paul Revere and the World He Lived In* * (1942).

H. S. Commager and R. B. Morris, eds., *The Spirit of "Seventy-Six"* (2 vols., 1958), is a superb anthology of participant accounts covering the war on the battlefronts and in civilian life. S. E. Morrison, *John Paul Jones, A Sailor's Biography* * (1959), offers an admirable introduction to the war at sea. Especially useful on the military phases of the war viewed from the American side are W. M. Wallace, *Appeal to Arms* * (1951); and Christopher Ward, *The War of the Revolution* (2 vols., 1952). Piers Mackesy, *The War for America 1775-1783* (1965), is outstanding on British strategy. See also G. S. Brown, *The American Secretary: The Colonial Policy of Lord George Germain, 1775-1778* (1963), is illuminating on the British conduct of the war.

S. F. Bemis, *The Diplomacy of the American Revolution* * (1935), is a scholarly account of its subject. American relations with France are presented in E. S. Corwin, *French Policy and the American Alliance* (1916). R. B. Morris, *The Peacemakers: The Great Powers and American Independence* (1965), is the indispensable study of the Peace of Paris. On the effects of the Revolution in Great Britain, see R. Coupland, *The American Revolution and the British Empire* (1930).

The financing of the Revolution is ably dealt with in Clarence Ver Steeg, *Robert Morris* (1954); and E. J. Ferguson, *The Powers of the Purse: A History of American Public Finance, 1776-1790* (1961). On the Continental Congress, see Lynn Montross, *The Reluctant Rebels* (1950), and E. C. Burnett, *The Continental Congress* * (1941). On the Loyalists, see Lewis Einstein, *Divided Loyalties* (1933), and C. H. Van Tyne, *The Loyalists in the American Revolution* (1902).

CHAPTER SIX

In December, 1776, Tom Paine published the first number of *The American Crisis,* which opened with the famous words: "These are the times that try men's souls." During the war Paine published about a dozen more *Crisis* essays on current issues —how to treat Tories, what to do with Loyalist and western lands, the need for *federal* taxation—issues that seriously divided the "united colonies." The last *Crisis* appeared on April 19, 1783, the eighth anniversary of Lexington and Concord, when America's triumph had been all but formally signed and sealed. " 'The times that tried men's souls,' are over—," Paine began

A More

Perfect Union

his valedictory, "and the greatest and completest revolution the world ever knew, gloriously and happily accomplished. . . . So far as my endeavours could go," the pamphleteer reminded his public, "they have all been directed to conciliate the affections, unite the interests, and draw and keep the mind of the country together." Then he underscored his transcendent theme:

We have no other national sovereignty than as United States. . . . Individuals, or individual states, may call themselves what they please; but the world, and especially the world of enemies, is not to be held in awe by the whistling of a name. Sovereignty must have power to protect all the parts that compose and constitute it; and as UNITED STATES we are equal to the importance of the title, but otherwise we are not. Our Union, well and wisely regulated and cemented, is the cheapest way of being great—the easiest way of being powerful, and the happiest invention in government which the circumstances of America can admit of.—Because it collects from each state, that which, by being inadequate, can be of no use to it, and forms an aggregate that serves for all.

Paine's words fell sweetly on the ears of many patriots. Yet there were perhaps even more Americans who wondered whether union was desirable now that independence had been won. Their experience with the mother country made them only the more suspicious of any new centralizing agency that might interfere in their local affairs, and indeed of local government itself and its nosing into their private lives. So far as these Americans were concerned, government meant snooping tax-collectors, mortgage-foreclosing courts, hamstringing regulations, and little else—and the less of it the better.

Some of the men who drew up the new state constitutions that followed the Declaration of Independence understood this attitude, and the weak Articles of Confederation of 1777 is a monument to it. By 1787, however, even many of the localists had grown disillusioned with their deteriorating central administration and had come around to Paine's high view of a sovereign state. Opposition was far from dissipated, but in that year these men and the unionists of old at last wrote a new Constitution forming the "more perfect union" that the American people still enjoy today.

I. *The First State Constitutions*

THE FUNDAMENTAL LAW

Although the American colonies, of course, were older than the American nation, the independent *states* that eventually formed the Union were themselves set up following the advice or actions of the revolutionary central government known as the Second Continental Congress.

Even before the Declaration of Independence, this Congress had advised four provinces troubled by the "convuls'd state" of their affairs under makeshift revolutionary administrations, to draw up permanent constitutions that "shall best conduce to the happiness and safety of their constituents in particular, and America in general." With the adoption of the Declaration of Independence by the Congress in July, 1776, the legal basis on which most of the colonies had been governed—their royal charters—was swept away, and the remaining provinces had to follow the lead of the first four. Rhode Island and Connecticut, simply by deleting all reference to the king, were able to go along under their old corporate charters. By 1780, all the other states had written new instruments of government.

In most of the states, the revolutionary provincial congresses, self-conscious tribunes of the people, drew up and adopted the new constitutions without troubling to consult the voters. Massachusetts, however, set an example that was later followed by the others when they came to rewrite their basic law, and by the Republic itself when the Great Convention of 1787 wrote the fundamental law of the land.

In Massachusetts, when the provincial congress asked the people for power to draw up the new state constitution, the majority conferred it, but the people of the town of Concord objected. As much as they cherished liberty under government, they cherished even more the principle of individual liberty *against* government. In resolutions published in October, 1776, the Concord town meeting declared: "We Conceive that a Constitution . . . intends a System of Principles established to Secure the Subject in the Possession & enjoyment of their Rights and Privileges, against any Encroachments of the Governing Part." If the provincial congress makes the constitution, argued the Concord meeting, what is to prevent it from unmaking it? If the fundamental law has no sanction superior to that of ordinary legislation, what will protect our liberties? Concord demanded that a special "Convention . . . be immediately Chosen, to form & establish a Constitution," and for no other purpose.

The Massachusetts provincial government ignored Concord's novel proposal and drafted a new constitution. But the Concord notion spread, and when the provincial congress presented its work to the people in 1778 they rejected it by a 5-to-1

156

majority. Recognizing that the principal objection to the constitution was indeed its authorship, the provincial congress voted in June, 1779, to embrace the Concord idea. By March, 1780, under the leadership of John Adams, a specially elected convention completed a new framework of government that has lasted—with amendments, of course—for almost two centuries. By June, the voters had approved.

John Adams, when he was vice-president.

Even the state constitutions written and adopted by the provincial congresses themselves, moreover, after declaring their independence of any authority except that of the people, set forth at the outset the "bill" or "declaration" of "unalienable" or "natural" or "inherent" rights, of which the "Governing Part," as the Virginia Constitution said, "cannot by any compact deprive or divest their posterity."

These rights included: "acquiring, possessing, and protecting property"; freedom of worship, speech, and assembly; moderate bail, prompt hearings, trial by jury, and punishments to fit the crime; protection from general search warrants and from liability to serve in or support standing armies; exemption from maintaining any special class of men by "exclusive or separate emoluments or privileges from the community, but in consideration of publick services." Above all, "when any government shall be found inadequate or contrary to [the people's wishes] . . . a majority of the community hath an indubitable, unalienable and indefeasible right to reform, alter or abolish it." To reduce the likelihood of revolutions, elections must be "free, . . . frequent, certain, and regular." And in such elections, all "men having sufficient evidence to permanent common interest with, and attachment to the community, have the right of suffrage."

Conservatives found it easy enough to live with these gaudy generalizations. An equal right to acquire property was scarcely an open sesame for social climbers. Freedom to worship as one pleased seemed not necessarily inconsistent with the continuation of compulsory tithes for established churches. Moderate bail and humane penalties were after all, elastic injunctions. "Free, frequent, certain, and regular" elections could, with good conscience, be limited to the popular lower house of the legislature. "Sufficient evidence to permanent common interest with, and attachment to the community," gave oligarchs wrapped in deep esteem for their own social values ample latitude for sharp restrictions on the privilege to vote. Nor did the constitutional requirements undo in the least such old dodges as under-representing western counties, setting election days at inconvenient seasons, naming polling places at inaccessible sites.

And yet the "Bills of Rights" gave the populace, in the language of the times, "a standing law to live by." Without the promise of such a Bill of Rights they almost certainly would have rejected the new federal constitution of 1787 (see p. 178). Reformers, moreover, eventually used the leverage afforded by the liberal language of these bills to open the land on easy terms, abolish imprisonment for debt, provide free schools, prohibit the use of public funds for favored religious sects, promote free expression in the press, reform the courts, improve the jails, liberalize the qualifications for office holding, and broaden the franchise. They turned the principle of liberty against the "governing part" into the pursuit of equality with the governing parties, employing government itself to remove the barriers to liberty defined as opportunity (see Chapter 10).

Such reforms were often slow in coming, and sometimes disappointing in their practical consequences. Among the earliest reforms based explicitly on the Bills of Rights in the constitution-making period itself were the gradual abolition of slavery north of Delaware and (at least for the time being) the removal of many restrictions on manumission, especially in Virginia.

The Bill of Rights of the first Vermont constitution of 1777 (see p. 167), straightforwardly abolished slavery, and when Vermont after entering the Union in 1791 drew up a new constitution two years later, the abolition provision was carried over. In Massachusetts, a court decision in 1783 used the Bill of Rights to justify fining a slaveholder on the charge of assaulting and shackling a runaway. Thereafter slaves began to leave their masters, and in the census of 1790 Massachusetts was the only state to report no slaves. New Hampshire soon was in the same position. Between 1780 and 1804, all the states from Rhode Island to New Jersey put abolition in process by legislation freeing children of slave mothers once they had reached a certain age, ranging from 18 to 28.

In the northern states the slave population was relatively small and the number of free Negroes grew only slowly. In Virginia, after private manumission was eased in 1782, the number of free Negroes jumped from 2,000 to almost 13,000 in 1790, and to 30,500 in 1810. In Maryland, the legislature rejected easing bills, but the restrictions there had been comparatively mild. In 1790 more than 8,000 free Negroes lived in Maryland, and thereafter their number multiplied as rapidly as in Virginia. Farther south, although abolition and manumission were often mentioned in connection with the struggle for liberty, progress was slight.

The leaders of the revolutionary generation had profound faith in the concrete definition of rights and duties. "The blessings of society," John Adams in 1776 advised the states then framing their new basic laws, "depend entirely on the constitutions of government." Yet the Negro freed by abolition or manumission, by legislation or by courts, north or south, hardly entered the free world the law prescribed. Adams himself, in 1795, told how slavery really ended in his state:

Argument might have [had] some weight in the abolition of slavery in Massachusetts, but the real cause was the multiplication of labouring white people, who would no longer suffer the rich to employ these sable rivals so much to their injury. . . . If the gentlemen had been permitted by law to hold slaves, the common white people would have put the negroes to death, and their masters, too, perhaps. . . . The common white people, or rather the labouring people, were the cause of rendering negroes unprofitable servants. Their scoffs and insults, their continual insinuations, filled the negroes with discontent, made them lazy, idle, proud, vicious, and at length wholly useless to their masters, to such a degree that the abolition of slavery became a measure of economy.

158

In the North as well as in the South, as the numbers of free Negroes grew, their social fetters multiplied. As a result, they seemed to become incorrigible public problems and costly public charges. Sometimes the very laws designed to open up the world of opportunity for the whites explicitly closed that world to the blacks and hardened their pariah status (see p. 264).

THE FRAMEWORK
OF GOVERNMENT

Soon after the new state constitutions were written, Congress had them collected and printed for general distribution, and numerous editions were required to meet the demand at home and abroad. The bills of rights, setting forth the "higher law" of nature from which the supreme law itself derived its validity, aroused the greatest interest. This interest has survived the test of time. The bills of rights have been the most enduring parts of the constitutions, and along with the Bill of Rights of the federal Constitution have figured most prominently in constitutional issues since raised and resolved.

The actual framework of government worked out in many of the new state constitutions also raised issues at the time. On the whole, the designers followed colonial precedents. Such deviations as there were reflected the antipathy to administrative control born in the empire, nourished in the rebellion, and often stubbornly clung to after the framework of government was strengthened to combat it.

Generally speaking, where the old colonial charters had been conservative in nature—as in Maryland and New York—the early state constitutions also were conservative. Where the colonial charters had been more democratic—as in Pennsylvania and Georgia—the constitutions tended in the same direction. Where the colonial charters had been moderately liberal—as in Virginia and Massachusetts—the new constitutions also reflected the past.

These terms—conservative, democratic, moderate—refer basically to two areas: qualifications for the franchise, and qualifications for office-holding. In conservative New York, for example, no one could vote for members of the upper house of the legislature who did not own land worth £ 100; in conservative Maryland, no one could *sit* in the upper house who did not own property worth £ 1,000. In democratic Georgia, all white male inhabitants who paid taxes (whether they owned property or not) could vote for all state legislators; in democratic Pennsylvania, *membership* in the legislature was open to all taxpaying freemen. In moderate Virginia, all landowners could vote for members of both houses; in moderate Massachusetts, a freehold of £ 300 or personal property worth £ 600 was required for *membership* in the upper house.

But there were other phases of government to which these characterizations also apply. In conservative Maryland, for example, while the membership of the lower house of the legislature was renewed each year, the upper house was elected for a solid five years. Democratic Pennsylvania, on the other hand, having resisted for decades all efforts of the colonial governors' council to share in legislation, now dispensed with an upper house altogether and concentrated power in a unicameral legislature elected annually by the people. Moderate Virginia, while providing a four-year term for members of its upper chamber (as against a one-year term for the lower house), also stipulated that one-fourth of this chamber must retire annually.

"The oftener power Returns into the hands of the people the Better," the manifesto of a Massachusetts town meeting declared in 1778. As the terms of legislators in many of the new states indicate, "rotation in office" had already become one of the political shibboleths of the age. In ten states the lower house was elected for twelve months; in Connecticut and Rhode Island for but six; only in South Carolina did representatives serve as long as two years.

A second shibboleth, deriving from Montesquieu's attack on "despotism" in his *The Spirit of Laws* (first published in France in 1748 and widely read in the colonies), was the "separation" and "balance" of powers. Article XXX of "Part the First" of the Massachusetts constitution of 1780 was most explicit on this point:

In the government of this commonwealth, the legislative department shall never exercise the executive and judicial powers, or either of them: the executive shall never exercise the legislative and judicial powers, or either of them: the judicial shall never exercise the legislative and executive powers, or either of them: to the end it may be a government of laws and not of men.

Almost two hundred years of independent political practice in America (not to speak of an even longer history in England, and in America under English rule) have failed to clarify in any absolute way where legislative, executive, and judicial power begins and ends. Separated in theory, these departments of government have always been dependent on and usually at war with one another. "Balance," indeed, seems to imply interference just where "separation" suggests independence.

Under the old colonial regime, interference was most successfully practiced by the assemblies. Colonial governers, as we have seen (p. 91), could veto legislation, control the speakership of the house, summon or adjourn the assembly, make key political appointments with the advice of their hand-picked councils, and otherwise enjoy the privileges of patronage. But the assemblies by their control over money and by other means, had gradually sucked the strength from the governor's position and had made him, for all the verbal force of his functions, often little more than a functionary. At the same time, the assemblies had asserted control over local judiciaries and had shown contempt for royal tribunals like the admiralty courts.

When the time came to write the new state constitutions, the power of the purse was universally retained in the legislature, and in three states—Virginia, South Carolina, and New Jersey—it was assigned exclusively to the lower house. But the constitution-making congresses and conventions were hardly satisfied to insure legislative control over the executive simply by keeping the money power in legislative hands. Conservatives, democrats, and moderates alike, all explicitly stripped the executive of the absolute veto power, and in all but two states—Massachusetts and New York—of any veto power whatever. Only in New York did the governor retain a certain limited control over the date and duration of legislative sessions; elsewhere the constitutions specifically set forth when the legislature should convene, and left the houses themselves free to make their own rules and elect their own officers. Almost everywhere the governor retained the right of appointment, with the advice of the upper house; but now the upper house, like the lower, was an elected body far more jealous of legislative prerogatives than the old colonial councils had been.

The degradation of the executive was capped by the mode of his election and the nature of his tenure. In New England and New York the voters elected the governor; but from New Jersey southward—in eight states—he was elected by the legislature itself. In New York, Pennsylvania (where he was simply the "president" of an executive council), and Delaware, his term ran three years; in South Carolina, two. But in the remaining nine states, the governor was elected for only twelve months. Most states, moreover, applied the policy of rotation in office with peculiar severity to the governorship. In New England, New York, and New Jersey the same man was eligible to run for two or more consecutive terms. Elsewhere—in seven states—his eligibility was circumscribed by provisions like that of conservative Maryland, where he could serve his one-year term only three years in any seven; or like that of moderate South Carolina, where he was ineligible for a second two-year term until four years had elapsed since his first.

160

The courts no more than the executive escaped the pervasive power of the legislatures. Every state constitution provided that the legislature "have full power and authority to erect and constitute judicatures," to use the words of the Massachusetts document. In Connecticut, Rhode Island, and South Carolina the legislature alone named the judges; and in no state was the legislature without some voice in their appointment and removal.

In 1787, while addressing the Great Convention in Philadelphia, James Madison said: "Experience in all the States has evinced a powerful tendency in the legislature to absorb all power into its vortex. This was the real source of danger to the American Constitutions; and suggested the necessity of giving every defensive authority

to the other departments that was consistent with republican principles." In later years, constitutional conventions in all the states—either by proposing amendments or by rewriting the entire fundamental law—undertook to rectify this gross imbalance among the "separated" departments. The principal changes enlarged the governor's freedom of action; but not until regular political parties developed and the governor became the head of his party in the state was he able to assert executive leadership and overcome the fruitless factionalism of what even Jefferson denounced as "legislative tyranny."

II.   The "Firm League of Friendship"

THE FIRST
FEDERAL CONSTITUTION
In July, 1775, ten months before the revolutionary instructions to form permanent governments went out to the states, Benjamin Franklin disclosed to certain members of the Second Continental Congress a draft of "Articles of Confederation and Perpetual Union" under which a permanent national government might also be set up. Franklin's friends found that too many delegates "were revolted" by the idea of creating a permanent government while some lingering hope of conciliation with Britain remained, and the trial balloon was laid aside until the next year. In June, 1776, Congress named a committee to work over Franklin's plan; but no less than a year and a half passed before its own draft was sufficiently advanced to be submitted to the states. John Dickinson of Pennsylvania was the principal author of the new document, which undertook to establish a firm national government without weakening the self-determination of the individual commonwealths. This, of course, was difficult to accomplish. Dickinson's own name for his government, "a

firm league of friendship," strongly suggests that where there might be conflict of authority, the states, not the new government, would triumph.

Congress was only too aware of the defects of its offspring. In its letter to the states in November, 1777, asking formal approval, it apologized for the "uncommon embarrassment and delay" in framing the Articles and solicited the most generous consideration of their form, "as that alone which affords any tolerable prospect of general ratification." Franklin's draft offered membership in "our Association" to "any and every Colony from Great Britain upon the Continent of North America," including the islands of the West Indies. He even opened the door to Ireland. Congress' aspirations were more sober. It ordered the Articles translated into French so that "the inhabitants of Canada, &c." might subscribe.

Under the Articles of Confederation, each state elected and paid the salaries of its own delegates and reserved the right to recall them. Voting in the single-chamber legislature was by state, and each state had only one vote, no matter how many delegates it sent. Important legislation required a two-thirds majority of the states, a margin made more difficult to attain by the provision nullifying a state's vote if its delegation were evenly split. The administration of such laws as could be passed was hamstrung by the provision making the only executive a "committee of the states" consisting of one delegate from each state. Nor could the Articles be amended except by the unanimous consent of the states.

The Articles gave the new government considerable powers: Congress might (1) make war or peace and fix state quotas of men and money for the national army; (2) make treaties and alliances; (3) decide interstate disputes, limit state boundaries, and admit new states; (4) borrow money and regulate standards of coinage and weights and measures; and (5) establish post offices. But such basic perquisites of sovereignty as levying taxes, raising its own troops, and regulating commerce were denied it.

The framers of the Articles, having made every concession they could to the states' own freedom of action, expected quick approval by the state governments. One last concession to Virginia, however, aroused the suspicion of Maryland and other "landless" states and delayed ratification for almost four more years. This concession stated that, "no state should be deprived of territory for the benefit of the United States."

Seven "landed" states—Virginia, New York, the two Carolinas, Georgia, Massachusetts and Connecticut—on the basis of their original charters or on other grounds, laid claim to territory extending either to the Mississippi or all the way to the Pacific. By the Quebec Act of 1774 (see p. 136), the British had overridden these claims; and Maryland now argued that since the war against Britain was a common effort, the western territories claimed by the "landed" states should be "considered as common property, subject to be parceled by Congress into free, convenient, and independent governments." New Jersey and Delaware soon aligned themselves with Maryland. As

the costs of the war mounted, these "landless" states became increasingly alarmed at the high taxes they would be forced to levy, whereas the "landed" states would be able to pay their shares out of land sales. The "landless" states were also troubled by the likely growth in population and power of the others; they feared that their own people would be lured by low taxes to the western territories of the "landed" states, which would make these states predominant in any central government. Speculators in certain "landless" states added their influential voices to those of their representatives. Before the Revolution, such speculators had purchased millions of acres from the Indians in areas claimed especially by Virginia. If Virginia's claims were now allowed to stand, their own claims surely would be invalidated in favor of Virginia speculators.

The deadlock over ratification of the Articles held until early in 1780. In February, that year, finding, because of the weight of taxes, "a violent inclination in most of the States to appropriate all the western Lands to the use of the United States," New York proposed, "especially to accelerate the federal alliance," to tender its lands to Congress. Connecticut soon followed suit. When Virginia at last yielded in January, 1781, Maryland withdrew its objections to the Articles. In February, Congress named March 1 as the day to proclaim the start of the new government. The Second Continental Congress then became the formal ruling body of "The United States of America," the "Stile," as the Articles said, "of this confederacy."

WEAKNESS IN FOREIGN AFFAIRS

"As to the future grandeur of America," wrote the influential Englishman, Josiah Tucker, Dean of Gloucester, at the close of the Revolution, "and its being a rising empire under one head, whether republican or monarchical, it is one of the idlest and most visionary notions that ever was conceived even by writers of romance. . . . A disunited people till the end of time, suspicious and distrustful of each other, . . . [the Americans] will be divided and subdivided into little commonwealths or principalities . . . [with] no centre of union and no common interest."

As early as 1781 nationalists like Gouverneur Morris of New York who feared the realism of Tucker's observation, were suggesting that peace be indefinitely postponed until "that great friend to sovereign authority, a foreign war," might speed the day when the American "government would acquire force." After 1783, Congress itself may have looked forward to the foreign problems arising from the peace treaty and from independence to strengthen its hand at home. If it did, it was once more proved wrong, the far-seeing Tucker right. It had, in fact, been all but impossible to get enough delegates together even to ratify the treaty of peace. When this step at last could be taken, on January 14, 1784, it seemed almost a signal for the formal abdication of the American government. January 14-16, 1784, were the only three days in a period of four months on which as many as nine states were represented in Congress. Sometimes the number fell as low as three.

Only because a fanatical little group "were unwilling to familiarize the idea of a dissolution of the federal government," did efforts to build a "peace establishment" proceed. The results were discouraging. American spokesmen were especially concerned over the figure a headless government cut in "a world of enemies." "Whatever little politicians may think," wrote Charles Thomson, the "perpetual secretary" of Congress, in September, 1784, ". . . a government without a visible head must appear a strange phenomenon to European politicians and will I fear lead them to form no very favourable opinion of our stability, wisdom or Union."

According to the treaty of peace, the British were to give up their military and fur-trading posts in the Northwest "with all convenient speed." But the British continued to hold the posts in order to protect the rich Canadian fur trade until, as they hoped, the new nation would col-

lapse. To speed up this collapse they egged on the Indians against American settlers whom Congress was powerless to keep off Indian lands. They went so far as to use force, moreover, to deny Americans use of the Great Lakes.

Indian problems also arose in the Southwest, an area that Spain was determined to keep free of American settlers. During the Revolution, Spain had offered to mediate between the colonists and Britain if they would cede to her the territory between the Ohio River and the Gulf of Mexico and between the Appalachians and the Mississippi. Congress had refused this offer, but Spain had entered the war anyway in support of France, and in a separate treaty in 1783 had received East and West Florida from Britain. Here she established forts of her own, and in 1784 entered into treaties with the local Indians obliging them to join in the harassment of American frontiersmen.

British (and for that matter, Spanish) recalcitrance over the West was hardened by American weakness in other areas. Although the treaty of peace had declared that no legal impediments should hinder creditors on either side from collecting old debts, actually the great bulk of the debts were owed by the ex-colonials. And although Congress urged the new states themselves to honor the treaty provision, it had no power to prevent their passing legislation to frustrate the British instead. Not until 1802 did the United States settle private debts incurred by Americans before the war by agreeing to pay the sum of £600,000 to British creditors.

In accordance with the terms of the peace treaty, Congress also made "earnest recommendation" to the states to restore confiscated Loyalist property to its former owners. But most states chose to ignore this recommendation, and even after the war patriots continued to confiscate Loyalist lands without being punished by the courts. The treaty also permitted Loyalists to return for 12 months to try to recoup their losses, but many who came back received only tar and feathers for their pains. Years later, Britain herself awarded £ 3,300,000 to about 5,000 Loyalists for property lost in America during the Revolution.

In the treaty of peace, Britain had agreed that Americans were to enjoy the right to navigate the Mississippi and use the port of New Orleans as a place to deposit their export goods. But now Spain insisted that these rights had not been Britain's to grant, and Congress had no means of forcing her to accept Britain's terms.

Westerners were especially outraged with Congress over this failure, and Spain lost little time in trying to capitalize on their discontent by suggesting that they secede from the United States and become part of the Spanish empire. Congress' efforts in 1785 to negotiate a commercial treaty with Spain only aggravated western feelings. Congress' agent in these negotiations was John Jay, now Secretary for Foreign Affairs. Jay, the urbane New Yorker, believed that the development of the West would only "fill the wilderness with white savages . . . more formidable to us than the tawny ones which now inhabit it." With this prejudice in mind, he concluded long negotiations with Don Diego de Gardoqui, the first Spanish minister to the United States, as a result of which the United States was to surrender her claims to the use of the Mississippi for 25 years, in exchange for favorable treatment of American ships in Spanish ports elsewhere. Seven states, most of them in the commercial North, supported Jay's agreement in Congress against the opposititon of the southern states, which had ambitions of their own in the Southwest. Seven states were not enough to approve the agreement and it fell through. The fact that Jay had negotiated this treaty, however, made him —and the commercial interests generally— suspect in the West and in the South for decades. The failure of the treaty also cost Congress the support of the commercial interests of the East. Congress' growing weak-

ness at home, in turn, only worsened its standing abroad.

FINANCIAL DEBILITY AT HOME

Besides international problems arising from the peace treaty, Congress was confronted after 1783 by domestic problems growing out of independence. Bereft of the power to lay and collect taxes, it had to face its predicament without the sinews of sound finance. Worse, with no money to pay the Continental troops, Congress was physically menaced by its own army, which, sharing the almost universal lack of confidence in the government, refused to disband without first receiving its due compensation. In June, 1783, apprised that the Philadelphia militia would not raise a single musket against mutinous Pennsylvania regiments, and having no force of their own with which to "hazard the authority of government," the few delegates in attendance hied themselves to the hamlet of Princeton, New Jersey. "The great Sanhedrin of the Nation," jeered the unpaid Pennsylvania officer, Major John Armstrong, "with all their solemnity and emptiness, have . . . left a state, where their wisdom has long been question'd, their virtue suspected, and their dignity a jest."

Many other claims arising from the war poured in upon Congress. Above all there was the back interest to be paid on the public debt, not to speak of the principal itself. Robert Morris, named Secretary of Finance in 1781, urged Congress to establish a national tariff so that it would no longer have to beg the states for funds; he also proposed a land tax, a poll tax, an excise on distilled liquors. But none of these measures would the state delegates enact. When Congress in 1782 then requested $10 million from the states for the next year, it received less than $1.5 million.

In January, 1783, his patience exhausted, Morris decided to quit. When no successor could be found he was prevailed upon to remain until the army had been paid. In June, Washington got the troops to go home, even though they were not to be paid for some months to come, and even then not in cash but in warrants to western lands from which the Indians were determined to bar white settlers. A loan from Holland enabled the government to limp along for a time; but when Morris finally left in September, 1784, the treasury was empty as usual.

Morris' efforts, however, were not wholly in vain. In 1781 he proposed to Congress the creation of a commercial bank, the first of its kind in America, and that same year Congress chartered the Bank of North America with a paid-in capital of $400,-000, to be located in Philadelphia. This bank eventually lent millions to the government and saw it through some of its most critical situations, but most of the bank's business was with private entrepreneurs. Like other American institutions under the Confederation, this bank—and others modeled after it in New York and Massachusetts in 1784—performed strongly even though the government itself continued to weaken.

CONGRESS AND
THE PRIVATE ECONOMY

Historians still disagree about how dark or how bright general economic conditions actually were during the Confederation years from 1783 to 1787. But it is certain that specific areas were hurt by a postwar depression.

American shipowners were especially hard hit by the loss of their favored position in the trade with Britain and the British West Indies. When Congressional envoys tried to get Britain to reopen the West Indian trade in particular to American goods and American ships, they were laughed out of court. The loss of British trade was only in part offset by West Indian smuggling, by the new trade opened up with China in 1784, and by increased trade following upon commercial treaties with Baltic nations, France, and other continental countries.

Immediately after the war, the pent-up American hunger for British finery and other goods had given American importers a taste of prosperity. But once the splurge was over, importers joined the chorus of protest against Congress. Blaming their plight

on the shortage of domestic currency and the insecurity of domestic credit, they demanded financial reforms. American manufacturers, in turn, who had practically monopolized the American market during the conflict, demanded protection against the influx of British goods and sought subsidies to support their own programs of industrial expansion—neither of which Congress was in a position to provide.

Fortunately, most Americans, especially the inarticulate farmers who made up 90 per cent of the population, did not depend on Congress for their well-being. Even those who did, often seemed to get along better than their petitions to Congress suggested. Public creditors, in particular, though angry over the government's continuing failure even to keep up interest payments, apparently had enough reserve capital to sponsor new business ventures; and the years immediately following the war saw unprecedented activity in road and canal construction, bridge building, house building, insurance, land sales, and banking. Not all the new ventures were successes, of course. For all its potential wealth, the United States was still a poor country. Settlement had to precede intensive development; subsistence had to be gained before capital for long-term investment could be spared.

In Pennsylvania in the 1780's, Oliver Evans perfected a much-needed machine to make wool "cards"—the toothed instruments used for combing out strands of wool—but he found few takers. Evans anticipated modern assembly-line techniques by developing a "straight-line" method which, without the intervention of manual labor, allowed raw grain to be put through all the steps needed to transform it into flour ready for shipment. But the conservative farmers resisted his innovations. Evans' greatest achievement, though he never found backing for it, was the development of plans for a "steam carriage," the forerunner of the railroad locomotive.

The Charles River bridge, 1789.

Evans' contemporaries, James Rumsey in Virginia and John Fitch in Pennsylvania, were also working on steam boilers and steam boats. These men were not unknown. Rumsey had worked for Washington himself. Neither capitalists nor potential users, however, would back them. Evans lived long enough to become moderately successful in the early decades of the nineteenth century; Rumsey and Fitch both died in the 1790's, broken in spirit and without funds.

Even so, a new business spirit was abroad in America after the Revolution—a spirit that Congress might dampen but could not destroy. In Pennsylvania in 1784 Washington found a "spirit of enterprise [which] may achieve almost anything." In New York he noted a "temper, genius, and policy" directed single-mindedly toward capturing trade. Washington advised Virginia to adopt the commercial spirit. Otherwise, she "must submit to the evils" of commercial competition "without receiving its benefits."

Perhaps the most significant signs of economic progress during the period of

political crisis were the resumption of immigration to America, the rapid growth in the number and size of families, and the settlement of new lands on the frontiers in the North and West. What order there was in these developments was introduced mainly by individual land-speculators—evidence of the weaknesses of Congress. But the developments themselves gave evidence of the vigor of the native-born and immigrants and of the country at large.

CONGRESS AND THE FRONTIER

In writings about American history, the term "frontier" is always used to describe the West in an early phase of its development, and the "moving frontier" is taken to be the line marking the latest advance of permanent western settlement. This is as it should be; the history of the frontier is essentially the history of the westward movement of population. But this use of the term tends to obscure the opening of the "northern frontier" of Vermont, New Hampshire, and Maine. Great areas in each of these New England states remained wilder than much of Kentucky or Tennessee, Ohio or Michigan, throughout the early decades of the nineteenth century; through most of the eighteenth century, they remained as virgin and primitive as in Champlain's time.

Vermont, unlike Maine and New Hampshire, was a wholly landlocked territory, and the last part of the northern frontier to be penetrated by white settlers. Both New York and New Hampshire claimed the territory, but not until 1769 did migrants from either state venture into it to build permanent homes. After Ethan Allen's victory for the rebel states at Fort Ticonderoga in 1775 (see p. 138), he and his brother Levi tried to get the Governor of Canada to guarantee Vermont's independence in exchange for their future neutrality in the war. Failing here, the Allens, in 1777, when about 30,000 persons had settled in Vermont, set up an independent government. After the war, when the population had reached about 80,000 and many wanted to join the Union, Ethan and Levi swore "at all risks, . . . that Congress shall not have the parcelling of [Vermont] lands to their avaricious Minions." Congress did nothing for the unionists and not until 1791 did Vermont become the fourteenth state.

Far to the southwest, meanwhile, other individualists were also staking out territory for independent settlements. During the 1770's, James Robertson and John Sevier, two Virginia speculators, took settlers into the region of the Watauga and Holston rivers. In 1784, when North Carolina finally ceded her old claims in this region to Congress, the Wataugans, now 10,000 strong and aware that Congress could do nothing for them that they could not do better themselves, set up the independent state of Franklin, with Sevier as governor. In 1788, North Carolina rescinded her cession and reclaimed Franklin, but the next year she returned the territory to Congress. Ultimately the Watauga country became part of Tennessee.

Another private state was staked out in the vicinity of Nashville in the Cumberland Valley by James Robertson, and still an-

other in future Kentucky by Judge Richard Henderson's Transylvania Company. Robertson's government lasted but two years. During the Confederation period, Henderson's satrapy was torn by strife between settlers who wanted to join forces with Spain in order to win commercial privileges on the Mississippi, and those who wanted to retain their status in the United States. During these years, ten conventions were held in Kentucky by settlers seeking statehood, and on three occasions Virginia herself supported their demands. Once again, Congress did no more than it had about Vermont; but, like Vermont, future Kentucky continued to burgeon despite official neglect.

The organization of the southwestern frontier thus was haphazard and disorderly, so much so that Washington, after a visit to the region in 1784, warned Congress "that scarce a valuable spot within a tolerable distance of [the Ohio River] is left without a claimant." He urged Congress, in developing the land above the Ohio, to follow the Yankee tradition of orderly survey and purchase. Once the cessions of the landed states were complete and the Indian title "quieted," Congress followed Washington's advice. The first effective measure for developing the Northwest Territory was the Land Ordinance, written by a committee headed by Jefferson and enacted by Congress in 1785.

The Land Ordinance reserved no less than one-seventh of the Northwest Territory "for the use of the continental army." It also reserved four lots in each township for the United States, and one lot "for the maintenance of public schools." Except for a small sector retained by Connecticut as its "Western Reserve," the rest of the Northwest Territory was to be surveyed into townships of 36 sections, each section 640 acres, or 1 square mile, in area. The minimum purchase, at auctions to be held at convenient locations, was to be one section;

the minimum price, $1 per acre in cash. Congress hoped that good land would command a better price. But sales were disappointing even at the minimum. The requirement of $640 in cash shut out most of the small settlers and $1 an acre discouraged speculators.

After the first seven ranges of townships surveyed had failed to produce the revenue for which Congress longed, the delegates yielded to the proposals of speculators who offered 9 cents an acre for some 1.5 million acres beyond these ranges. Having made their huge purchase, these speculators, organized as the Ohio Company, prodded Congress to get the government of the new territory in order so that settlement could proceed. Congress responded by adopting

the Northwest Ordinance of 1787, probably its most important piece of legislation.

By the terms of this Ordinance, the Northwest Territory was to be set up as a single unit with a governor to be appointed by Congress. When 5,000 free male inhabitants had settled in the Territory those who owned at least 50 acres apiece were to elect a territorial legislature whose acts would be subject only to the governor's veto. The voters would also send a non-voting delegate to Congress. No less than three and no more than five states were to be carved out of the Territory, and the boundaries of three future states were tentatively laid out. When a potential state had 60,000 free inhabitants, it was to be admitted to the Union on an equal footing

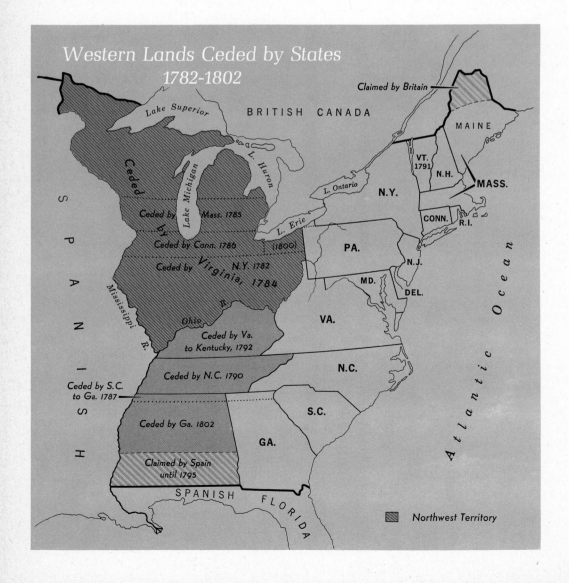

Western Lands Ceded by States
1782-1802

Claimed by Britain

Lake Superior

BRITISH CANADA

MAINE

L. Huron

VT.
1791

N.H.

Lake Michigan

L. Ontario

MASS.

Ceded by Mass. 1785

N.Y.

CONN.

Ceded by Conn. 1786

(1800)

R.I.

Ceded
by

L. Erie

PA.

Ceded by Virginia, 1784

N.Y. 1782

N.J.

MD.

DEL.

Mississippi R.

Ohio R.

VA.

Ceded by Va.
to Kentucky, 1792

S
P
A
N
I
S
H

N.C.

Ceded by N.C. 1790

Ceded by S.C.
to Ga. 1787

S.C.

Ceded by Ga. 1802

GA.

Atlantic Ocean

Claimed by Spain
until 1795

SPANISH FLORIDA

Northwest Territory

with the original states. The Northwest Ordinance required, in addition that "the people and states" in the Territory, adopt "articles of compact" with the "original states" which shall "forever remain unalterable, unless by common consent." These articles in effect set forth the first *federal* bill of rights, similar to those in the first state constitutions (see p. 157), and with the momentous provision prohibiting slavery in the Territory and in all the states to be carved from it.

Organized settlement followed hard upon this enactment. The Ohio Company sent out a small group of pioneers in December, 1787, and in the spring of the next year they established the village of Marietta at the junction of the Ohio and Muskingum rivers. A second group, sent out by the New Jersey speculator, John Cleves Symmes, to settle a tract he also had purchased from Congress, laid the foundations of Cincinnati in 1788. Eight years later Moses Cleaveland led a band of pioneers to Connecticut's Western Reserve, where they built the town of Cleveland on Lake Erie.

THE FINAL SHOCKS

The Northwest Ordinance and the beginning of settlement in the Northwest Territory were great achievements. Otherwise, Congress had little to point to with pride during the postwar years. American ships were harassed on the high seas, their cargoes barred from foreign ports. When Congress' envoys abroad attempted to improve commercial relations with foreign countries, they were insulted. At home, American manufacturers suffered from foreign competition that Congress was at a loss to regulate by tariffs or other means. Even on the frontier, the new settlers were left almost entirely to their own resources in combating the Indians, the British, and the Spanish. Frontier violence and threats of violence stifled the demand for land and caused speculators to grumble as their holdings failed to appreciate in value.

Only the established small farmer in the older sections of the country remained secure—he was exposed neither abroad nor

at home, neither on the sea nor on the land. So long as British, French, and Continental forces remained mobilized in America and needed his stores and supplies, his market for cash crops remained lively. Where he was essentially a subsistence farmer, conditions got even better when cheap British imports started to come in after the war. By 1785, however, the foreign troops had been withdrawn, the American army had been disbanded, and the farmer's market had shrunk. War-time creditors began to press the farmers for back interest. To make matters worse, the state legislatures began to raise taxes and to demand that they be paid in specie, so that the states themselves could pay the back interest on their Revolutionary debts. Stunned by this bitter reversal of fortune, the farmers, and the small retailers who depended on them, cried out for relief. As in colonial times, they agitated for the states to issue paper money that would serve as legal tender in the payment of all debts, public and private; and they demanded that the states enact stay laws that would postpone the foreclosure of farms on which mortgage payments were in arrears.

In most of the states, the farmers did win certain concessions. Seven states issued some form of paper money, often with good effect. But in states like Massachusetts, the creditors and the conservatives in the legislature successfully resisted the farmers' demands, and the seaboard commercial towns managed to shift a disproportionate part of the tax burden onto the inland farmers. It has been estimated that after 1780 the average Massachusetts farmer had to surrender a third of his income in taxes.

Even in Rhode Island, where the debtors were particularly influential, the farmers suffered sharply from the market slump. They pressured the legislature into issuing paper money in 1786, but the value of the money that was issued depreciated rapidly. So worthless did it become that merchants refused to accept it, and even began to avoid their debtors for fear that they might be paid. The legislature responded by passing a law that made refusal to accept the paper money a crime punishable by fines, without even the ceremony of a jury trial. One Rhode Island butcher, John Weeden, appealed his conviction under this law to the state supreme court. In the famous case of *Trevett* v. *Weeden* (1786), the court dismissed Weeden's complaint on the ground that it had no jurisdiction over the case. It went further, announcing its opinion that the law was repugnant to the provisions of the Rhode Island charter and was therefore unconstitutional.

In New Hampshire, the militia had to be called out in 1786 to disperse a mob that had surrounded the legislative meeting house in an effort to coerce the members to issue paper money. It was in Massachusetts, however, that conservatives experienced the greatest shock. Here the legislature, its upper house dominated by merchants, failed to heed the farmers' demands for relief, and actually levied higher taxes that had to be paid in specie. On July 31, 1786, to evade the farmers' protests, the legislature adjourned until the following January 31. This cowardly act precipitated the violent uprising known as Shays' Rebellion.

Shays, thirty-nine years old at the time, was typical of the thousand men who eventually participated in the Rebellion. He had been born into poverty in Middlesex County in eastern Massachusetts, but before the Revolution had moved to the western part of the state where he found work as a farm laborer. The events of Lexington and Concord aroused his militancy and he enlisted in time to see action at Bunker Hill. "A brave and good soldier," a subordinate described him after the war; but bitterness had begun to enter his soul during the four years he had to wait for a promised commission as a captain. After a year in this exalted position, he was mustered out in 1780 and returned to his home in Pelham in Hampshire County to await payment, like thousands of other disappointed officers, for his long service to his country. His farming went badly, his army compensation was delayed, and his debts and obligations accumulated until "the specter of debtors' jail always hovered close by."

An articulate rebel, Captain Shays became a spokesman for his neighbors when the western counties became increasingly agitated over their worsening economic straits. Some of these counties were too poor to pay the cost of sending delegates to the legislature in far-off Boston; and in some of the towns no men were to be found who could meet the property qualifications to sit in the General Court. In effect, the farmers, most of them veterans of the Revolution, were deprived of any voice in the state government, a weakness the rich men of Boston and other port towns were quick to take advantage of. To make their protests heard, the farmers resorted to the time-honored device of county conventions. Here men from neighboring towns would gather at county seats on a basis of personal equality and give voice to their political feelings by means of published resolutions and petitions to the legislature. After the legislature adjourned in July, 1786, having ignored the petitions of the disfranchised and having done nothing to relieve their distress, more and more county conventions were called in all parts of the state.

Under the leadership of ex-officers like Shays—plain depressed citizens, none of them brilliant agitators or commanders—the members were warned to "abstain from all mobs and unlawful assemblies until a constitutional method of redress can be obtained." But popular discontent soon overrode these cautions and hotheads took advantage of the seething situation to organize riotous mobs. Their targets were the civil courts where foreclosure proceedings by the hundreds were scheduled. After forcing the suspension of many of these courts, the mobs attacked the criminal courts to prevent the trial of rioters. Finally, when federal arsenals were menaced, the government no longer could postpone action.

By October, 1786, the fires of rebellion

had been fanned by numerous Massachusetts merchants and other businessmen eager to prove the impossibility of democratic government. At the same time, moderate leaders were forced to put themselves at the head of the mobs if only to restrain them from greater violence. Somehow Shays had risen to the leadership of the whole movement and the troops who rallied to him became the targets of state forces hastily gathered by General Benjamin Lincoln at the behest of Governor James Bowdoin. Fighting between Shays' forces and Lincoln's continued from mid-January to the end of February, 1787, when the Rebellion finally was crushed and Shays fled to Vermont. A number of his straggling followers, captured during the fighting, were freed by the legislature in June. The bitterness that followed in the wake of this uprising emerged in the subsequent elections, when the aging John Hancock defeated Governor Bowdoin. No reprisals of an enduring kind, however, were imposed on Shays or his followers, and the Massachusetts legislature itself held off harsher taxes that were on its agenda and passed

laws exempting household goods and workmen's tools from confiscation for debt.

Shays' Rebellion shocked conservatives throughout the nation. They now felt more acutely than before the necessity of preventing attacks on courts of law and physical intimidation of legislatures. To protect their interests, they sought to prevent legislatures from impairing the obligations of private contracts and from establishing depreciated currencies as legal tender for the payment of debts. Many of them also joined the movement for a stronger central government which would reduce the power of the states as well as protect them from mob pressures. Washington, embittered by the spectacle of the faltering Congress, referred to it as "a half-starved, limping government, always moving upon crutches and tottering at every step." Others voiced even lower opinions. But the immediate "crisis" was soon to be over and the nation more soundly launched.

III. *Toward a More Perfect Union*

THE STRENGTH
OF LEADERSHIP

In the early 1780's few American leaders failed to realize that the new nation was going through a "critical period." Some had grown so discouraged about the entire experiment that they advocated the deliberate breaking up of the Union. "Some of our more enlightened men," wrote Benjamin Rush in 1786, "have secretly proposed an Eastern, Middle, and Southern Confederacy, to be united by an alliance, offensive and defensive." Those, on the other hand, who still hoped to preserve the Union—"even respectable characters," as Washington said—"speak of a monarchical form of government without horror," with Washington himself as monarch. "What a triumph for our enemies," exclaimed the General, "to verify their predictions! What

a triumph for the advocates of despotism to find we are incapable of governing ourselves, and that systems founded on the basis of equal liberty are merely fallacious!" Washington, steadfast in his republicanism, would tolerate none of this. Even before the Articles of Confederation had been ratified, he and some others were already advocating their improvement to strengthen the Union, not to destroy it; to prove the possibility of republicanism, not to discredit it. They carried the day, but not without revolutionary steps of their own.

As early as 1780, Alexander Hamilton had asked for a new and more energetic government to press the war forward. In 1782 the New York Legislature and in 1785 the Massachusetts Legislature passed resolutions calling for conventions to supplant the Articles, but nothing came of them.

James Madison (1751-1836).

Alexander Hamilton (1755-1804).

Early in 1785 delegates from Maryland and Virginia met at Mount Vernon, Washington's home, where a discussion of bi-state trade was enlarged to include a more general discussion of American issues with delegates from neighboring Delaware and Pennsylvania. This group recommended to the Virginia Legislature that it call a meeting of all the states at Annapolis, Maryland, in September, 1786. Only five states sent delegates to Annapolis. But one of them was New York—and among New York's delegates was the far-seeing and indefatigable Hamilton. The Annapolis Convention was supposed to deal only with matters of commerce, but the opportunity to do more was too good to miss.

The convention adjourned promptly. Its report, written by Hamilton, spoke of the numerous and important defects of the Articles of Confederation, not merely those relating to commerce. It ended with a call for a great new convention to meet in Philadelphia the following May to amend the Articles. The state legislatures listened to Hamilton's proposal more seriously than they had to the Virginia legislature's call to Annapolis, and all the states save Rhode Island sent delegates to the Philadelphia Convention of 1787. John Adams, John Jay, and Jefferson were absent on other duties; Sam Adams was not named a delegate; Patrick Henry, appointed by Virginia, refused to attend. Otherwise the cream of the country was there, led by Franklin and James Wilson of Pennsylvania; James Madison, Edmund Randolph, and Washington from Virginia; and Hamilton from New York, who left early and whose influence waned as the meeting progressed.

Of the 74 men named to attend, only 55 ever appeared. Many of them had been young officers in the Revolution, and 27 belonged to the Society of the Cincinnati, an organization formed to look after the interests of such officers. Only eight had signed the Declaration of Independence. Lawyers predominated. Most of the others were practical young businessmen.

Not until May 25 did delegates from a majority of the states reach Philadelphia.

Foreshadowing their ready agreement later, the 29 delegates in attendance that day unanimously elected Washington as presiding officer. Next they decided to protect themselves from the pressures of the populace and the press by keeping their sessions secret. There was then debate about their purpose in coming together, with some maintaining that they must adhere to the instructions from their states, which empowered them only to amend the Articles. But those who were determined to supplant the Articles had their way. On May 30, only five days after the opening session, Edmund Randolph disclosed something of the revolutionary temper of the leaders by offering these resolutions:

1. That a union of the states merely federal will not accomplish the objects proposed by the Articles of Confederation—namely common defense, security of liberty, and general welfare.
2. That no treaty or treaties among the whole or part of the states, as individual sovereignties, would be sufficient.
3. That a *national* government ought to be established, consisting of a *supreme* legislative, executive, and judiciary.

Congress promptly agreed to put off debate on propositions 1 and 2; but sitting as the *"Committee of the Whole"* on the state of the Union"—not, on the state of the Articles—it directly applied itself to the summer-long task of shaping an instrument of government conforming to proposition 3.

AGREEMENT
IN THE CONVENTION
Although the Constitutional Convention spent a good bit of time settling differences among the delegates, in their general philosophy of "balanced government" and on a great number of specific objectives the majority were in substantial agreement. They understood the force and value of ambition; yet they also realized that if any single interest in society—the slave-owning interest, the commercial interest, the rising manufacturing interest, and the like—or any particular arm of government went on indefinitely adding to its power, it would certainly become tyran-

nical. Therefore, they felt they had to find ways of harnessing the selfish impulses in men, and of offsetting one with another.

The delegates generally acknowledged that the people must have a voice in government. But they felt they knew from the record of ancient republics and Italian city-states, as well as from their own recent experience, that the people could be stampeded into following demagogues, tyrants, and plunderers of the rich. Hence, the people's role must be limited. Although the delegates were themselves largely men of property who distrusted democracy, they harbored no illusions about the benevolence of the rich, who they felt would plunder the poor if they could. Thus they sought a legislative system that would give "the people" and the well-to-do a distinct voice in the government, and an executive strong enough to limit both.

Naturally, the delegates did not agree unanimously, even on the application of these general principles. Some delegates from New York and Maryland were so concerned lest state power be eclipsed that they could not enter sympathetically into the proceedings; others, like George Mason of Virginia, were so sure that the establishment of a national sovereignty would swallow up traditional personal liberties that they earned reputations merely as obstructionists.

Alexander Hamilton stood on the extreme conservative side of the Convention. An admirer of the British system and candidly disdainful of popular judgment and democratic procedures, Hamilton once said, "the people seldom judge or determine right," and he would have reduced their role in government almost to nothing. He favored a centralization of power so drastic that the delegates, for all his valuable services to the movement for the Constitution, hardly gave him a serious hearing. "The gentleman from New York," it was said, "has been praised by everybody, he has been supported by none." Although he worked hard in the movement for the Constitution and indeed for its ratification, Hamilton, by 1802, had come to think of it as "a frail and worthless fabric."

Most of the delegates were able to negotiate between these extremes in fulfilling their main purpose of clothing the new government with concrete powers while at the same time checking what Madison called "the mutability of the laws of the states." In economic matters in particular they were almost unanimous in deciding what the powers of the national government should be: (1) The new Congress should have what Congress under the Articles so sadly lacked—the power to levy and collect taxes, tariffs, and excises. (2) It should be able to coin and borrow money. (3) It should be able to pay all debts contracted by the United States before the adoption of the Constitution. (4) It should be able to raise and maintain an army and a navy. (5) It should be able regulate interstate and foreign commerce. The states, in turn, should be forbidden to coin money, to make anything but gold and silver legal tender for the payment of debts, to make laws impairing the obligation of contracts, to levy duties on imports or exports.

COMPROMISE
IN THE CONVENTION

Issues nevertheless did arise in the convention that almost wrecked it and could only be settled by give and take. One of these had to do with the relative power of large and small states.

Once the delegates had agreed to give up the idea of amending the Articles they took up Edmund Randolph's so-called "Virginia Plan" for a new government embodying proposals that were attractive chiefly to the large states. Randolph proposed a two-house "National Legislature" with membership in both houses allotted among the states in proportion to their free population. Members of the upper house were to be elected by the members of the lower, who were themselves to be elected by the people. The whole "National Legislature"

was then to elect the "National Executive" and the "National Judiciary."

This plan violated the prevailing theory of the separation of the executive, legislative, and judicial powers, and aroused general disapproval on that account. The most vigorous objections came from the small-state delegates. They feared that their states would be overwhelmed in the popularly elected house by the heavily populated states, and that some states might get no representatives at all in the second house. To protect themselves the small states offered a plan of their own, presented to the Convention by William Paterson of New Jersey and known since as the "New Jersey Plan." According to this plan Congress was to remain, as under the Articles, in a single house, and all the states, large and small alike, would continue to have only one vote apiece. The delegates quickly rejected this futile proposal and used the Virginia Plan as the preliminary model from which to construct the final document.

The issue between the large and small states that caused the most difficulty was how to determine their relative strength in the new Congress. The debate on this issue grew long and sharp in the hot Philadelphia summer. At one point the small states were on the verge of leaving and disrupting the entire Convention, but cooler heads averted catastrophe. A special committee, headed by Elbridge Gerry of Massachusetts, was named to restudy the whole issue of representation, and after tempers cooled this committee presented to the Convention a compromise scheme devised largely by Franklin: There would be a two-house legislature, with membership in the lower house apportioned according to population, thus satisfying the large states, and with membership in the upper house equal for all states, thus satisfying the small ones. This arrangement, adopted only after much argument, provided the basis for the "Great Compromise" of the Constitution and determined the general character of the two bodies that soon came to be called the House of Representatives and the Senate.

The two-house plan enabled the delegates to incorporate another element of balance into government under the Constitution, the establishment of the lower house as the people's branch. The members of this house were to be elected by all voters in each state who were eligible to vote for "the most numerous branch of the State Legislature." This opened the choice of representatives to a broad electorate, and was considered adequate to protect "the people." The upper house, whose senators were to be chosen, more restrictively, by the state legislatures, was expected to have members who would be more congenial to propertied interests and more conservative.

A second issue arose over the "direct taxes" the new government had power to levy. Such taxes were to be apportioned among the states according to population, just as representation was to be apportioned in the lower house. But the slave states wanted their Negroes, if they were counted at all in apportioning taxes, to be given less weight than free men. The North wanted Negroes to be given less weight only in apportioning congressional representation. The upshot was a second compromise, the "three-fifths compromise," which specified that for *both* direct taxes and representation, five Negroes were to be counted as equivalent to three whites.

Delegates from the commercial North urged that the new government be granted full power to regulate interstate and foreign commerce and to make treaties which the states must obey. The Convention readily agreed on these points. But the South, fearful of being outvoted in the new Congress, demanded that commercial regulations and all treaties require the consent of a two-thirds majority of the Senate rather than a simple majority. The southerners were particularly concerned about taxes on exports, for they were heavily dependent on selling tobacco and other staples in competitive world markets. They were also worried lest the slave trade be tampered with.

To allay these fears, the Convention negotiated a third compromise. To satisfy the South, the Constitution prohibited all taxes on exports; it also guaranteed that for at least 20 years there would be no ban on "the migration or importation of such persons as any of the states now existing shall think proper to admit;" and that any "person held to service or labor in one State, . . . escaping into another, . . . shall be delivered up on the claim of the party to whom such service or labor may be due." By these provisions the prohibition of the slave trade was delayed and fugitives' quest for freedom frustrated, even though most delegates abhorred slavery sufficiently even to avoid using the word. "The thing," as Lincoln said later, "is hid away in the Constitution, just as an afflicted man hides away a wen or cancer which he dares not cut out at once, lest he bleed to death." Finally, the South won the provision requiring a two-thirds vote in the Senate for the ratification of all treaties. In exchange for these concessions, the northerners won their point on a simple congressional majority for acts regulating commerce.

TOWARD SOVEREIGN POWER

Government under the Confederation had two fatal flaws. Congress had neither the power of the purse nor the power of the sword. The delegates in Philadelphia saw to it that the new Constitution remedied these weaknesses. They gave the new Congress power to tax the people, to raise and maintain an army and navy, to declare war, suppress insurrections, regulate commerce, coin money, and—very broadly—to provide for the "general welfare of the United States." To insure that sovereignty would not be impaired by technicalities, the framers added the famous "elastic clause," enabling Congress "to make all laws which shall be necessary and proper for carrying into execution the foregoing powers."

A third flaw in the Confederation had been the absence of a responsible executive. To remedy this defect, the Constitution created a president—a single responsible executive—elected independently of Congress. After many arguments—especially between the centralists, who wanted the president elected directly by the people, and the state sovereignty men, who wanted him chosen by the state legislatures—the Convention devised the elaborate electoral-college plan. This left the method of choosing electors up to the legislature of each state, and thereby mollified the state sovereignty men. The centralists were consoled by the virtual apportionment of the electors by population. Each state was to have as many electors as it had representatives and senators.

The president was empowered, with the consent of the Senate, to appoint his own administrators. (The power of removing these appointees, though not specifically mentioned, was later held to be included.) The president was to be commander-in-chief of the army and navy. He could make treaties with the consent of two-thirds of the Senate. He could call Congress into extraordinary session, and he could veto acts of Congress—although his veto could be overridden by a two-thirds vote in both houses. In the future, of course, the effectiveness of presidential leadership grew even beyond the expectations of the framers, partly because of the dynamic qualities of certain individual leaders, but also because of the development of the American party system and presidential patronage.

A fourth weakness of the Confederation was its lack of a judiciary independent of state courts. This fault the Constitution remedied by setting up a national judicial system. At the head of the system was the Supreme Court of the United States. It could decide cases on appeal from lower federal courts which Congress was empowered to establish, and from the state courts in cases involving the Constitution, the laws of the United States, or treaties with other nations.

The Constitution made no specific provision for "judicial review" of federal legislation—that is, the power of the federal Courts to declare acts of Congress unconstitutional and void—but the Supreme Court itself under Chief Justice John Mar-

shall later clarified this issue (see p. 202). Article VI, Section 2, of the Constitution did make it plain that any state acts or laws that encroached on the supreme powers of Congress must be found unconstitutional by the federal Courts.

Thus, the Philadelphia Convention erected a government that could act with speed, strength, and dignity. By the Tenth Amendment (in force after 1791) the states were permitted to retain all powers not specifically delegated by the Constitution to the new federal government. But in the exercise of the powers it received, the new government was supreme.

BUILDING
FOR THE AGES

If the framers sought primarily to substitute a strong central government for the weak Articles, they also hoped to create a government, as Madison put it, "for the ages." Their success in this respect rests in part on certain features they introduced and on others unforeseen by them, that proved at least as important.

From the framers' point of view, the Constitution's built-in checks and balances were its best safeguards and the best safeguards of the Republic. Constrained by them, no chief executive could become a man on a white horse. And no transient surge of popular feeling, reflected in the legislature, even in its "democratical branch," could lawfully unseat the president or overturn the courts.

A second source of the Constitution's lasting strength is the amending process. The futility of trying to amend the Articles by the required unanimous consent of the states had hastened their demise. The easier amending process in the Constitution was at first sparingly used—but only after the promised first ten amendments constituting the much desired federal Bill of Rights had been adopted. Patrick Henry had opposed the movement for the Constitution and would fight its ratification in Virginia. Once he had lost this fight, the amending process alone reconciled him to the new system. "I will be a peaceable citizen," he said. "My head, my hand, and my heart shall be at liberty to retrieve the loss of liberty, and remove the defects of that system in a constitutional way."

A third somewhat less tangible source of the Constitution's long life lies in the general terms in which the document is written —no accident, but a result of the framers' classical training and universal way of thinking. Statesmanship required that they leave important powers to the jealous states. Having done this, they wrote down the prerogatives of the sovereign national government so broadly that essential powers could be retrieved when changes in national life made it imperative that they be exercised on the national level.

Among the non-constitutional sources of the Constitution's long life we may note the two-party political system that developed early in the United States and tended to sponge up a host of divisive issues; the enlargement of the role of the Cabinet and the strength it added to the administrative powers of the executive; the committee system in the House and Senate, which, though often obstructive, nevertheless gave order and insight to legislation; and the bureaucratic civil service, which preserved professional continuity (sometimes, indeed, against the public wish, if not the public interest) in spite of the frequency of elections and changes of political chiefs.

The Constitutional Convention, for all its conservatism, set up what was surely by world-wide standards a radical government, a democratic nation among aristocratic ones, a republic among oppressive monarchies. Under the Constitution, said John Marshall, who rose as a new leader during the ratification controversy in Virginia, "It is the people that give power, and can take it back. What shall restrain them? They are the masters who give it, and of whom their servants hold it."

For all its stress on private property, which, in the eighteenth century was thought to be the best foundation for public responsibility, the Constitution stipulated no property qualification for office, not even that of president. It also required

"a compensation—to be ascertained by law, and paid out of the Treasury of the United States" for all elective posts, so that the poor as well as the rich might hold them. In the instrument itself, before the Bill of Rights was appended, the Constitution forbade religious tests for any federal position. It provided that "for any speech or debate in either House," senators and representatives "shall not be questioned in any other place," thereby assuring their fullest freedom of expression. It also guaranteed trial by jury for all crimes, "except in cases of impeachment"; and forbade suspension of "the privilege of the writ of habeas corpus" except in times of invasion or rebellion.

RATIFICATION

The Constitutional Convention was in session from May 25 to September 16, 1787. Of the 55 delegates who took some part in the deliberations, 42 stayed to the end, and 39 signed the document. The other three, Gerry of Massachusetts, and Randolph and Mason of Virginia, refused to go along, their reasons accumulating as the sessions drew out. These refusals gave warning of the storm ahead when the Constitution would be offered to "we the people" for approval. But the signers were not to be diverted from their course by fear. The day after the Convention itself adopted the Constitution, a copy was sent to Congress, largely out of courtesy, and with a letter that did not mince words. "In all our deliberations on this subject," said the signers, "we kept steadily in our view that which appeared to us the greatest interest of every true American—the consolidation of the Union—in which is involved our prosperity, felicity, safety, perhaps our national existence." They petitioned Congress for no vote. Nor would they apply to the state legislatures for confirmation. In keeping with their revulsion from existing governments, in the Constitution itself they asked only the assent

REDEUNT SATURNIA REGNA.

On the erection of the Eleventh PILLAR of the great National DOME, we beg leave most sincerely to felicitate " OUR DEAR COUNTRY."

Rise it will.

The foundation good—it may yet be SAVED.

The FEDERAL EDIFICE.

ELEVEN STARS, in quick succession rise—
ELEVEN COLUMNS strike our wond'ring eyes,
Soon o'er the *whole*, shall swell the beauteous DOME,
COLUMBIA's boast—and FREEDOM's hallow'd home.
    Here shall the ARTS in glorious splendour shine!
And AGRICULTURE give her stores divine!
COMMERCE refin'd, dispense us more than gold,
And this new world, teach WISDOM to the old—
RELIGION here shall fix her blest abode,
Array'd in *mildness*, like its parent GOD!
JUSTICE and LAW, shall endless PEACE maintain,
And *the* " SATURNIAN AGE," *return again.*

A salute to "Our Dear Country" showing the 11 states that ratified the Constitution before it went into effect. From the Massachusetts Centinel, *August 2, 1788.*

of nine special conventions like their own.

While the election of delegates to these conventions was in progress, the Constitution began to be discussed and debated throughout the country. Rufus King, a member of the Massachusetts ratifying convention, summed up the feelings of the opposition, though he did not share them, when he wrote to James Madison in January, 1788: "An apprehension that the liberties of the people are in danger, and a distrust of men of property and education have a more powerful effect upon the minds of our opponents than any specific objections against the Constitution."

But the Constitution's critics, named "Antifederalists" by the Constitution's friends, did offer plenty of specific objections: There was no bill of rights; state sovereignty would be destroyed; the president might become king; the standing army would be everywhere; only the rich and well-born could afford to hold office; tax collectors would swarm over the countryside; the people could not bear to be taxed by

both state and national governments; commercial treaties would sell out the West and the South; debtors would no longer be able to defend themselves through recourse to state paper money and state stay laws. In March, 1787, George Washington had remarked that "A thirst for power [has] taken fast hold of the states individually; . . . the many whose personal consequence in the control of state politics will be annihilated [by a national government] will form a strong phalanx against it." But it was not merely the local lions who felt themselves menaced by the proposal. Many honest citizens shrank from so drastic an innovation.

At the beginning, however, ratification went along smoothly. Between December 7, 1787, and January 9, 1788, five states ratified, and the conventions of three (Delaware, New Jersey, Georgia) did so without a single opposing vote. A fourth state, Connecticut, ratified by 128 to 40. In Pennsylvania alone among the first five was controversy heated. By staying away, opponents of the Constitution tried to prevent the legislature from forming the quorum it needed before it could vote to call a ratifying convention. The Federalists then resorted to strong-arm tactics, seizing some of their opponents and forcibly dragging them into the chamber to make up a quorum. But in the Pennsylvania ratifying convention itself the Federalists won handily, 46 to 23.

In Massachusetts, the sixth state to ratify, the contest was close. Its convention debated from early January to early February, but Federalist leaders maneuvered ingeniously to win over such popular opponents as John Hancock and Sam Adams, and placated many opponents by promising to support amendments guaranteeing popular liberties. Finally, Massachusetts voted for the Constitution, 187 to 168.

In Maryland and South Carolina ratification went smoothly and won easily. In New Hampshire, the opposition was powerful, and after a first convention failed to reach a vote, a second convention ratified on June 21, 1788, by the narrow margin of 57 to 46. Technically speaking, the new government could now go into effect, for nine states had accepted it. But no one believed that it could function without Virginia and New York, and in these two states the outcome was very doubtful.

In Virginia, an extraordinarily thorough and brilliant review of the issue took place, with the opposition led by the scholarly George Mason and the inflammatory Patrick Henry. Washington's influence and the knowledge that he would consent to serve as first president was responsible for the unexpected conversion of Edmund Randolph, who had refused to sign the Constitution; and the promised addition of a bill of rights softened the opposition and helped to swing the convention. Four days after New Hampshire had ratified, Virginia fell in line, 89 to 79. By arrangement between Madison and Hamilton, couriers were quickly dispatched with the good news to New York, where a very close struggle was in process.

In New York, Hamilton led the Federalist fight in support of ratification, Governor Clinton the opposition. Well aware of Clinton's strength, Hamilton, assisted on a

few occasions by John Jay and more elaborately by Madison, began to write articles in the press supporting the Constitution. Later published as *The Federalist,* these articles provide the best commentary on the Constitution by its contemporary advocates. But they did not create a landslide for the Constitution in New York. More important in the vote here was the news of Federalist success in New Hampshire and Virginia, for it changed the issue from helping to form a new union to joining one that seemed almost certain to be established. Once again, the promise of amendments constituting a bill of rights also overcame some opposition. Having agreed to support such amendments, the Federalists finally won on July 26 by 30 to 27.

Rhode Island and North Carolina were so hostile to the Constitution that they did not join the Union until after the new government was in operation. North Caro-

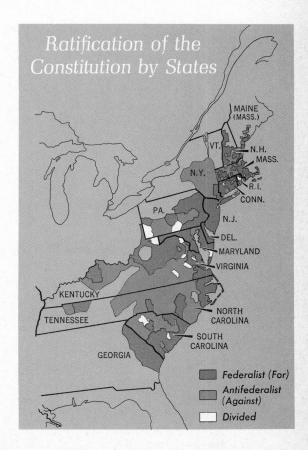

Ratification of the Constitution by States

MAINE (MASS.)
VT.
N.H.
MASS.
N.Y.
R.I.
CONN.
PA.
N.J.
DEL.
MARYLAND
VIRGINIA
KENTUCKY
TENNESSEE
NORTH CAROLINA
SOUTH CAROLINA
GEORGIA

Federalist (For)
Antifederalist (Against)
Divided

lina, by a wide margin, decided to join in November, 1789. Rhode Island held out until May, 1790, when Congress had in view a bill placing her on the footing of a foreign nation. Even then Rhode Island decided to enter only by the narrowest of margins.

Over 50 years ago, the distinguished historian, Charles A. Beard, tried to show that the vote for and against the ratification of the Constitution took place along class and sectional lines. Speculators, men with large holdings in public securities, and other investors favored the proposal, Beard wrote, while the frontiersmen, small farmers, and debtors opposed it. The bitter struggle that raged over the Constitution, he argued, was won by the Federalists against the wishes of the majority largely because so many of the opponents were disfranchised and because the Federalists were better organized, better educated, and more aware of their interests.

This materialistic view shocked many in Beard's day, and ever since it has arrayed historians themselves in contesting camps. Few subjects have so aroused students of American politics; and the subject refuses to die because of its great interest on the one hand, and the elusiveness of the data on the other.

Beard's own most significant contribution to the discussion of the adoption of the Constitution was his pursuit of new sources in support of his hypothesis. Since he used these sources carelessly, his conclusions have been subjected to more abuse than his materialism alone might have stirred up. In more recent times, historians and political scientists, less concerned with Beard's materialism, have themselves come to the problem with new ideas and have pursued new data in support of them. The structure of politics and the behavior of voters and leaders has interested them more than the structure of the economy and the behavior of businessmen of different sorts.

The Beardian literature, pro and con, is enormous, intricate, and available. On the basis of it, but on the basis of politically oriented research as well, we may present another picture which, in any case, tallies more closely with what the Founding Fathers themselves appear to have thought they were undertaking. That is, that the Constitution was conceived, drawn up, and promoted by an extraordinary generation of political leaders who had no false modesty about their own abilities, as few leaders did in their day; that, for all the controversy their work stirred up, these leaders had persuaded the politically active public to make a drastic change in the structure of their government without violence, without bloodshed, without coercion; and finally that these leaders were given an ample opportunity to show that the Constitution which had been won on paper could now be made to work in actuality.

Readings
Asterisk indicates that book is available in paperback.

The most substantial account of state politics during the "Critical Period" is Allan Nevins, *The American States During and After the Revolution, 1775-1789* (1924). Equally thorough on the national government of the period is E. C. Burnett, *The Continental Congress** (1941). E. P. Douglass, *Rebels and Democrats* (1955), is best described by its subtitle, "The Struggle for Equal Political Rights and Majority Rule during the American Revolution." R. A. Rutland, *The Birth of the Bill of Rights 1776-1791** (1955), covers the subject in the states, the Constitutional Convention, and the ratifying process. Informative but perhaps exaggerated accounts of the social impact of the Revolution include J. F. Jameson, *The American Revolution Considered as a Social Movement** (1926), and E. B. Greene, *The Revolutionary Generation, 1763-1790* (1943).

On constitution-making in the states, see R. J. Taylor, ed., *Massachusetts, Colony to Commonwealth, Documents on the Formation of Its Constitution** (1961); Richard McCormick, *Experiment in Independence: New Jersey in the Critical Period 1781-1789* (1950); E. W. Spaulding, *New York in the Critical Period* (1932); and Dumas Malone, *Jefferson the Virginian* (1948). Other biographies of the Founding Fathers that deal with the "Critical Period" and the Constitution are Irving Brant, *James Madison* (6 vols., 1941-1961), and Broadus Mitchell, *Alexander Hamilton* (2 vols., 1957-1962).

The old but exceedingly influential work by John Fiske, *The Critical Period of American History, 1783-1789* (1888), still merits serious consideration. Merrill Jensen, *The New Nation: A History of the United States During the Confederation, 1781-1789** (1950), is a comprehensive study of American politics and society. Jensen develops the idea that conditions in this period were not as bad as proponents of the new Constitution claimed. His work derives from C. A. Beard's outstanding scholarly monograph, *An Economic Interpretation of the Constitution of the United States** (1913). Beard's principal critics include, R. E. Brown in *Charles Beard and the Constitution** (1956), and Forrest McDonald, *We the People: The Economic Origins of the Constitution** (1958). Criticisms of the critics, with illuminating observations of their own, include Lee Benson, *Turner and Beard: American Historical Writing Reconsidered** (1960), and J. T. Main, *The Anti-Federalists, Critics of the Constitution, 1781-1788** (1961). R. A. East, *Business Enterprise in the American Revolutionary Era* (1938), and E. J. Ferguson, *The Power of the Purse, A History of American Public Finance, 1776-1790* (1961), are comprehensive studies of important subjects. On the development and administration of the land, see P. J. Treat, *The National Land System, 1785-1820* (1910). M. L. Starkey, *A Little Rebellion* (1955), is excellent on Shays' revolt. A good shorter account is R. B. Morris, "Insurrection in Massachusetts," in Daniel Aaron, ed., *America in Crisis* (1952).

The best text of the Constitution, with an analysis of each clause and summaries of Supreme Court interpretations, is E. S. Corwin, *The Constitution of the United States of America: Analysis and Interpretation* (1953). The classic commentary on the Constitution is *The Federalist,** written in 1787-1788 by Hamilton, Madison, and Jay, and since reprinted in many editions. The spirit of the Constitution and its makers is best indicated in *Records of the Federal Convention,* Max Farrand, ed. (4 vols., 1911-1937). Its reception by the ratifying conventions is revealed in *The Debates in the Several State Conventions on the Adoption of the Federal Constitution,* Jonathan Elliot, ed. (5 vols., 1836-1845). A helpful work, which rearranges the Convention debates by subject matter, is A. T. Prescott, ed., *Drafting the Federal Constitution* (1941). Perhaps the best brief book on the making of the Constitution is R. L. Schuyler, *The Constitution of the United States* (1923). A more recent treatment is Clinton Rossiter, *1787—The Grand Convention* (1966). Good biographies of opponents of the Constitution (the framers are dealt with above) include E. W. Spaulding, *His Excellency, George Clinton, Critic of the Constitution* (1938), and Helen Hill, *George Mason* (1938).

On judicial review, R. K. Carr, *The Supreme Court and Judicial Review* (1942), is brief and clear. Other leading studies include C. G. Haines, *The American Doctrine of Judicial Supremacy* (1932); E. S. Corwin, *The Doctrine of Judicial Review* (1914); and C. A. Beard, *The Supreme Court and the Constitution* * (1912).

For light on ratification in the states see F. G. Bates, *Rhode Island and the Formation of the Union* (1898); R. L. Brunhouse, *The Counter-Revolution in Pennsylvania, 1776-1790* (1942); L. I. Trenholme, *The Ratification of the Federal Constitution in North Carolina* (1932); S. B. Harding, *The Contest over Ratification of the Federal Constitution in the State of Massachusetts* (1896); and for Virginia, volume I of A. J. Beveridge, *The Life of John Marshall* (4 vols., 1916-1919).

CHAPTER SEVEN

March 4, 1789, was the date set for the assembling of the new Congress in New York City. At dawn, the guns at the Battery on the southern tip of Manhattan saluted the great day, and the city's church bells rang out. But it was an empty gesture. As late as March 30, a quorum of neither representatives nor senators had completed the rough journey to the capital. New York's old City Hall, remodeled under the supervision of the French architect, L'Enfant and renamed Federal Hall, stood ready for the lawmakers. Its elegance, one historian has said, "was enough to disturb the republican souls of members from the rural

Federalists
and Jeffersonians

districts and the small towns." It was the emptiness of Federal Hall, however, that disturbed the Federalist leaders already in New York awaiting their tardy colleagues. "The people will forget the new government before it is born," moaned Fisher Ames of Boston, the conservative who had defeated Sam Adams for Congress.

By April 1 the House of Representatives was ready to convene, and by April 6 the Senate had its quorum and could join the House in examining the ballots of the presidential electors. Washington, with 69 votes, was chosen president, and John Adams, second in the balloting with 34 votes, was named vice-president. After a triumphal journey from Mount Vernon, Washington arrived in New York on April 23, 1789. On April 30, with the sun shining on the gaily decorated streets, he was inaugurated.

The choice of New York as the first national capital gave a fillip to the already dashing social life of the country's second largest city. Madison's unhappiness over the "scanty proportion" of representatives "who will share in the drudgery of the business" was scarcely dispelled by the round of dinners, dances, and balls that quickly caught up his colleagues. The sun shone on the American economy as brightly as it had

Triumphal Arch at Trenton, on Washington's route to New York, April 21, 1789.

on the inauguration, and new fortunes were reflected in the boisterousness and ostentation of the capital's entertainments.

Congress, nevertheless, got on with its business. The leaders of the first Congress were determined to make good—and to make a good impression. John Adams, for example, as President of the Senate, a body which Gouveneur Morris hoped would "show us the might of aristocracy," was so insistent upon dignified titles and procedure that the Antifederalists soon dubbed him "His Rotundity." This preoccupation with decorum made Congress seem almost ridiculous at first, but the need for getting down to more serious business soon sobered it up. The Constitution offered few suggestions on procedure, though it was clear enough on objectives, and the times were making their own persistent demands.

New York was the capital of what was still a weak nation—a nation beset by foreign and domestic debts, surrounded by enemies, harassed on its borders by hostile Indians, on the sea by bold pirates, and in foreign ports and foreign waters by unfriendly navies. Nor was there to be unity at home.

I. *The New National Government*

FIRST FEDERALIST MEASURES

"Few who are not philosophical spectators," President Washington wrote at the outset of his administration,

. . . can realize the difficult and delicate part, which a man in my situation has to act. . . . my station is new, and, if I may use the expression, I walk on untrodden ground. There is scarcely an action, the motive of which may not be subject to a double interpretation. There is scarcely any part of my conduct which may not hereafter be drawn into precedent.

Much has been made of the "furious pace" with which Alexander Hamilton in particular worked to get the new government off the ground. One reason for Hamilton's administrative zeal may well have been that Washington had allowed a precious five months to elapse before commissioning the new Secretary of the Treasury on September 11, 1789. In taking other steps the President acted with similar deliberation, and Congress followed his example.

The Constitution placed on Congress the responsibility of raising money for government activities; now the delicate business of designing and collecting taxes had to be

184

faced. The Constitution created a National Judiciary made up of a Supreme Court and "such inferior courts as Congress may from time to time ordain and establish"; now the machinery for federal law enforcement had to be built. The Constitution created a potentially strong Executive; now the Executive departments had to be organized and manned. Congress, for all its dilatoriness in getting under way, dealt successfully with each of these constitutional tasks in its opening session. One of its first substantive steps was to enact and submit to the states the first ten amendments, constituting the promised Bill of Rights (see p. 179). These amendments were ratified by December, 1791.

The government's most urgent need was for money to cover its day-to-day expenses, and Madison hoped to raise the necessary funds by means of a modest tariff bill, which he submitted to the House of Representatives even before Washington was inaugurated. Debate, however, delayed its passage until July 4, 1789. In its final form, the act placed a tax of about 8½ per cent on the value of certain listed imports. But of course no revenue could be obtained until inspectors, weighers, collectors, port surveyors, and other personnel had been appointed. The new tariff was designed to benefit American carriers as well as to bring money to the federal treasury. Goods imported in American ships were taxed at a rate 10 per cent lower than goods arriving in foreign ships. A second act passed later in the year put tonnage duties of 6 cents per ton on American ships entering American ports and 50 cents per ton on foreign ships.

While the House was occupied with debate on the tariff, the Senate began to work on what was to become the Judiciary Act of September 24, 1789. This act helped cement the federal system by spelling out the procedure by which federal courts could review and, if necessary, declare void, state laws and state court decisions involving powers and duties delegated by the Constitution to the federal government. It also specified that the Supreme Court be manned by a

chief justice and five associate justices. The system of federal courts was to be completed by three circuit courts and thirteen district courts. Attached to each district court were to be United States attorneys and their deputies to serve as federal prosecutors, and United States marshals and their deputies to serve as federal police. One of the duties of these marshals and deputies, with numerous special assistants, was to take the

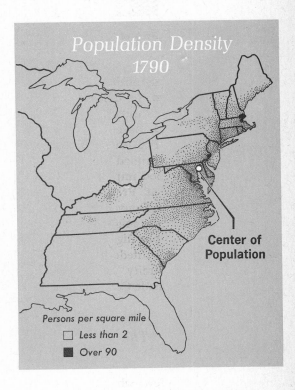

Population Density 1790

Center of Population

Persons per square mile
☐ Less than 2
■ Over 90

first census in 1790, as provided in Article I, Section 2 of the Constitution.

The executive had been one of the weakest links in the old Confederation. Yet the three executive departments created under the Confederation in 1781—Foreign Affairs, Treasury, and War—continued for a time to function unchanged under the new government. Not until July, 1789, did Congress create the new Department of State to manage foreign relations. The new War Department was set up soon after; the Treasury Department not until September.

While the House and the Senate busied themselves with such basic measures, the President considered appointments to the positions he knew must be created. Washington wanted to surround himself with the best men available, but he preferred not to appoint an opponent of the Constitution even to a lesser office when a sympathizer could be found. Washington also considered it politically expedient to spread his appointments among the states. Thus General Henry Knox of Massachusetts, one of the army's most outspoken opponents of the old Congress, became Washington's Secretary of War. To Edmund Randolph of Virginia went the Attorney-Generalship. To the Treasury, Washington named Alexander Hamilton of New York. John Jay of New York, in charge of foreign affairs for the old Congress, continued to direct them until 1790, when Thomas Jefferson of Virginia took over. Jay himself became the first Chief Justice of the Supreme Court.

THE FUNDING PROGRAM

Near the end of the first session of Congress, Hamilton was asked to prepare fiscal reports for the session to begin in December, 1789. His first report, on the public credit, was ready on January 9, 1790. This one was followed the next December by his report on a national bank, and in 1791 he reported to the Second Congress on the mint and manufactures. Hamilton looked to the moneyed class for America's natural leaders. If he could bind the capitalists to the new government, he reasoned, the whole nation would be firmly united. This objective inspired his fight to supplant the old Articles, and it continued to influence his program under the new Constitution.

In his report on the public credit, Hamilton made three major recommendations: (1) that the foreign debt, of about $12 million, including arrears of interest, be repaid by means of a new bond issue; (2) that the domestic debt, made up of many kinds of Revolutionary securities valued in 1789 at about 25 cents on the dollar, be exchanged at its face value, plus back interest, for additional new bonds amounting to $40 million; (3) that the remaining state debts, totaling about $20 million, be assumed by the federal government and refunded on a similar basis.

Congress enacted Hamilton's proposal for refunding the foreign debt with very little debate. His program for the domestic debt had much tougher going. The plan had become known to certain of his friends before he made his report, and by the time the House took up the bill to implement it, speculators in and out of Congress began surreptitiously buying up old bonds. Included in the issues to be refunded were the certificates with which the Revolutionary veterans had been paid. Large amounts of these certificates, along with other issues, were scattered throughout the hinterland. Eastern speculators loaded with cash dispatched fast boats to southern ports and fast stages to the back-country, and there bought up cheaply securities that were soon to go up in value. The Antifederalists, led by Madison, cried corruption; but they could offer only a cumbersome, hastily prepared bill as an alternative to Hamilton's plan. Their efforts were wasted. Their bill was defeated, and Hamilton's plan won.

The opposition to this refunding measure was led by the South, where money for speculation in securities was scarce. The South was even more hostile to Hamilton's proposal that the federal government should assume responsibility for paying the state debts. Georgia, which had few debts, and Virginia, which had paid its debts through paper-money issues, led the objectors. To these states, Hamilton's proposal meant that their citizens would be taxed again to pay off the debts of the northern states. When "assumption" came up for a vote in April, therefore, Congress defeated it. After many subsequent failures, Hamilton got Jefferson's support for the measure by offering to locate the new national capital in the South. "Assumption," to the tune of $21,500,000 was approved by Congress in July, 1790. As part of Hamilton's deal, Philadelphia would be the seat of the capital for ten years, starting in 1790. A new site on the Potomac was to be ready in 1800.

HAMILTON'S BANK

It is "a fundamental maxim, in the system of public credit of the United States," said Hamilton, "that the creation of debt should always be accompanied with the means of its extinguishment." But in practice Hamilton undertook to supply only the means for paying the interest, not the principal of the debt. He did not want to eliminate the bonds which were both a source of income for the moneyed classes and collateral for loans for further speculation. The annual interest on all the new bonds averaged about $2 million yearly for the period 1791-1795, and came to nearly half the government's total expenditures for these years. The government could not raise even this small amount from the tariff of 1789, which was its main source of revenue. Thus, besides successfully urging an increase in the tariff, Hamilton made two more proposals. Both were adopted, but not without further factional strife.

The first of these proposals called for a national bank with a capital of $10 million, one-fifth to be subscribed by the government, the rest by private capitalists. The Federalists, opposed on principle to government paper money, planned to have the Treasury issue only minted gold and silver. Consequently, Hamilton argued that a bank was needed to supply notes that would serve as currency in business transactions. This bank would also assist the government in its short-term borrowing and would serve as a depository for government funds. Finally, by making personal loans, the bank would make it easier for individuals to pay their taxes.

"This plan for a national bank," objected Representative James Jackson of Georgia, "is calculated to benefit a small part of the United States, the mercantilist interests only; the farmers, the yeomanry, will derive no advantage from it." But Hamilton's bill passed the House, 39 to 20. Thirty-six of the favoring votes came from the commer-

cial North, 19 of the opposing votes from the South. In February, 1791, the Bank of the United States was chartered for 20 years with headquarters in Philadelphia, and in December it opened. Ultimately, eight branches were established in port cities from Boston to New Orleans.

In the debate on this bill in the House, Madison argued that a national bank would be unconstitutional. The Constitutional Convention, he insisted, had expressly rejected the proposition that the federal government be empowered to charter companies. When the bill was sent to Washington for his signature, he asked Jefferson and Hamilton for their opinions on its constitutionality. Jefferson supported Madison. But Hamilton argued that since the government had been delegated the power to regulate currency, it had the "implied power" to establish a bank to issue that currency. Washington rejected the Virginians' "strict interpretation" of the Constitution in favor of Hamilton's "broad interpretation."

THE CRISIS ON THE FRONTIER

Hamilton's second proposal for raising money, excise taxes on various commodities including distilled liquors, was enacted quietly enough in March, 1791, but the storm it raised on the frontier soon cost the Federalist party dearly.

Opposition to the excises was strong in the South, where whiskey was held essential to men working in the hot climate. The most violent resistance to Hamilton's measure, however, occurred in western Pennsylvania where government efforts to collect the excise were often resisted with gunfire. Here, as on other frontiers, to save transportation costs on bulky grain, farmers often converted it into whiskey, which indeed became a medium of exchange. A tax on whiskey thus was viewed as a tax on money itself. There were also deeper reasons for resentment. Hamilton himself had acknowledged in the *Federalist* (see p. 179) that "the genius of the people will ill brook the inquisitive and peremptory spirit of excise laws." How right he was became clear as early as September, 1791, when opponents of the excise, meeting in Pittsburgh, resolved that "it is insulting to the feelings of the people to have their vessels marked, houses . . . ransacked, to be subject to informers," and so forth.

One of the most objectionable features of the excise was the provision requiring those prosecuted for infractions to stand trial in federal courts, the nearest one to the Pittsburgh district, for example, being 350 miles away in Philadelphia. Besides obliging farmers to halt all work to attend court, the cost of the trip itself was equivalent to a heavy fine. In June, 1794, Congress attempted to mitigate this "great popular grievance" by permitting state courts to exercise jurisdiction in excise cases which arose more than 50 miles from the nearest federal court. Far from being received as a concession, however, this act was looked upon as inflammatory, for its application was specifically withheld from "distillers who had previously to its enactment incurred a penalty." To make matters worse, in May, 1794, the federal court in Philadelphia had issued writs against 75 western Pennsylvania distillers returnable in that court, but had delayed until July to serve them. When federal marshals came west with the writs, they were attacked by a mob shouting, "The Federal Sheriff is taking away men to Philadelphia!"

Hamilton interpreted the uprising that followed against all federal collectors in the disaffected area as a rebellion against the United States and prevailed upon Washington early in August, 1794, to order the mobilization of 13,000 militiamen to crush the farmers. Hamilton, naturally, rode west with the troops, whom Washington himself journeyed out to inspect at Carlisle. Although they found no organized opposition, the militia rounded up about a hundred men. Two of them were later convicted of treason and sentenced to death, but Washington eventually stepped in and pardoned them.

In the year of the so-called "Whiskey Insurrection," receipts from the excise on distilled liquors fell lower than ever and the cost of collection, including the cost of the military display, naturally skyrocketed. But Hamilton, having already devised excises on additional essentials like salt and coal, and boots and shoes, to eke out the interest on the government debt, persisted in the "experiment" of collection to prove to the skeptical capitalists of the world that a republic could coerce its citizens where financial responsibility was at issue.

If the excise venture advanced the standing of the administration abroad, it only aggravated opposition on the frontier already aroused by other grievances.

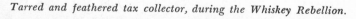
Tarred and feathered tax collector, during the Whiskey Rebellion.

On the southwestern frontier Spain put pressure on Washington's administration by continuing to contest the Florida border as defined in the Treaty of Paris (see p. 151), and by keeping the Mississippi at New Orleans closed to American shipping. In the Northwest, Britain persisted in using military power to help Canadian fur trappers against American entrepreneurs. Neither Spain nor Britain tried to restrain the Indians in their territories from systematically molesting American frontiersmen. Coupled with the failure of Washington's own efforts to deal with the Indians on American territory, this situation was doubly depressing to settlers on the borders who had looked to a strong central government for protection against repeated Indian raids.

Not until 1794, in the Battle of Fallen Timbers, did General "Mad Anthony"

Wayne subdue the northwestern tribes, and not until 1795, by the Treaty of Fort Greenville, did these tribes yield most of their Ohio land to the United States. At about the same time, private action by John Sevier and James Robertson in the Kentucky region quieted the southwestern tribes. But the Treaty of Fort Greenville came too late for the Federalists to retrieve the political support that earlier failures on the northwestern frontier had cost them. And for the accomplishments of Sevier and Robertson in the Southwest the Federalists won no credit at all. The awareness that a substantial opposition party was beginning to form only served to intensify a sense of crisis in Federalist ranks.

II. *The Origins and Issues of Party Politics*

CONSOLIDATING
THE REPUBLICAN OPPOSITION

Hamilton's ambition for America was greater than that of most of his followers, and his vision far exceeded theirs. His blueprint for converting the United States into a powerful industrial nation was his celebrated Report on Manufactures, sent to Congress in December, 1791. In it he urged the value of industry to the community, and the need for protective tariffs, subsidies, and other aids while industry was in its infancy. Congress gave this report a cold reception. The merchants, moreover, in whose hands the money of the country was concentrated were to remain cool to industrial enterprise, and hence to tariffs and subsidies, for another quarter of a century.

Hamilton's agrarian opponents outstripped him in both ambition and vision. Hamilton had no respect for the men who were opening up the vast reaches of the new country. He despised farmers, and he hated westerners as troublemakers. In his plan to unify the nation, he assigned to both groups inferior roles. In less than a

decade after the start of the new government, however, the majority who lived on the land were to show that they counted for more than the minority in the cities, and that votes counted for more than wealth. The rise of the agrarian Republican party insured that Hamilton's program and that of the Federalists would not enjoy a long life. Without Washington's support, the party would not have ruled as long as it did.

We cannot assign specific dates to the beginnings of political parties in America. During the colonial period so-called "factions" came and went, with as little continuity as Washington hoped the "factions" of his own time would have. The issue of the Constitution again divided the country into what became known as "Antifederalists" and "Federalists." The latter, as the victors in this confrontation, while trying to strengthen the opinions and mobilize the votes of their followers, succeeded rather in consolidating the opposition.

In the looming contest between these two camps the Federalists at first enjoyed great advantages. Above all, they had a strong, clear program and, in Hamilton, a resourceful, energetic, and uncompromising leader. Most of the well-educated, wealthy men in the country were Federalists; so were most of the newspaper editors, clergymen, and other makers of opinion. Hamilton showed, too, that the Federalists controlled the army, and were quite willing to make use of it. A readymade network of chambers of commerce, units of the Society of Cincinnati, and other going organizations worked for Federalism on the local level, and the party quickly developed a grassroots patronage system to give sinecures to local party workers. Even in the First Congress, Federalist leaders caucused and corresponded on platforms, candidates, and campaigns as though they were members of an organized machine.

The men who opposed the Federalists showed a preference for the prerogative of the states and the privacy of the people as against the national government as conducted under the Constitution by Hamilton and his friends. In the contest for national power this preference seemed to be a weakness that the Federalists quickly exploited —to their own undoing.

Far from uniting the states and the people, Hamilton's program only magnified existing antagonisms. Every Hamiltonian measure was essentially a northeastern measure: funding, assumption, the national bank, the excise, protective tariffs—all served to divide the South from the North, the West from the East. Every Hamiltonian measure was a capitalist's measure that alienated debtors from creditors, even in the Northeast. Every Hamiltonian attitude was an aristocratic attitude that pleased the "gentlemen of principle and property" and offended the "people of no particular importance."

Jefferson, as much as Hamilton, sought stability and dignity for the new government, but he believed that men "habituated to think for themselves"—American yeomen, in short—were much easier to govern than men (usually city-dwellers, he thought) who were "debased by ignorance, indigence,

and oppression." By 1791, Jefferson was convinced that Hamilton and his "corrupt squadron" menaced the country, and he wrote Washington to say so. By then, Jefferson, with Madison's support, had worked out a plan to save the United States in his own way. Essential to his program was getting the people to use their great privilege of the franchise.

To no other people, said a traveler about Americans at this time, were the "smiles and frowns of political government" of so little consequence. How right he was is shown by the vote: Hardly one-fourth of those eligible had voted for delegates to the state conventions to ratify the Constitution; the percentage voting for representatives to the First Congress was still smaller. Jefferson's approach to getting out the vote was to explain what, indeed, individuals could do for themselves if each flexed his political muscle.

"If left to me to decide whether we should have a government without newspapers, or newspapers without a government," Jefferson once wrote, "I should not hesitate for a moment to prefer the latter." He had disapproved of the secrecy of the Constitutional Convention, and his first step in the looming party battle was to enlist the best man available to keep the public informed of what he believed to be the plot of the victors at the Convention. This man proved to be the poet, Philip Freneau, who had been Madison's classmate at Princeton. In October, 1791, Freneau issued the first number of the *National Gazette,* a new Antifederalist paper published in Philadelphia, for the time being the national capital. Freneau so quickly took the play away from John Fenno, the editor of the Hamiltonian *United States Gazette,* that Hamilton felt obliged to enter the newspaper battle himself.

If Jefferson was the philosopher of agrarian politics, Madison, strategically situated in Congress where issues were argued and supporters mobilized, soon emerged as "the great man of the *party*." Serious party work began as early as the winter of 1791-92, when Madison wrote a number of articles for the *National Gazette* in which he gradually developed the position of "the Republican party, as it may be termed." Thereafter, influential allies, local lieutenants, grass-roots clubs, and candidates who could afford the time and money to campaign and hold office were all arranged for. In addition to Jefferson and Madison, those enlisted under the new banner included Governor Clinton of New York, who, in opposition to General Schuyler, Hamilton's rich father-in-law, controlled the upstate vote; and Aaron Burr of New York City (Clinton had recently helped Burr defeat Schuyler for the Senate), whose followers in the Society of Tammany, a drinking club and benevolent association, already were hungering for patronage. The leaders in Virginia and New York were soon joined by the brilliant young Swiss, Albert Gallatin, who had settled on the frontier in western Pennsylvania. In all the other states, intellectual, professional, and literary luminaries helped fill out the Republican officers' corps.

The Republican party was too young to run a presidential candidate in 1792, and in any event its leaders preferred Washington to any other man. The Federalists, in turn, were far from ready to risk going on without him. Once more the reluctant General was elected unanimously; the Republicans, however, had the satisfaction of throwing a scare into the Vice-president, John Adams. Their candidate, Governor Clinton, carried the great states of Virginia and New York, together with North Carolina and Georgia. All told, Clinton polled 50 electoral votes to Adams' 77.

REPUBLICANISM
ABROAD AND AT HOME

During Washington's first administration, party lines had been clearly drawn over financial issues and difficulties on the frontier. In his second administration, problems of foreign policy, as Colonel Higginson of Massachusetts said, "not merely divided parties, but moulded them; gave them their demarcations, their watchwords, and their bitterness." Some of these problems were carry-overs from the war with

Britain. But the French Revolution, which began just a few weeks after Washington first took office in 1789, was the source of most of the trouble.

At first, most Americans welcomed the French Revolution. In 1790, when Lafayette sent the key to the Bastille to Washington, the President acknowledged it as a "token of victory gained by liberty over despotism." A year later, the Hamiltonians had aligned themselves with Edmund Burke's condemnatory *Reflections on the Revolution in France,* and the Jeffersonians championed Tom Paine's libertarian response, *The Rights of Man.* The execution of Louis XVI in January, 1793, disgusted most American conservatives, and the Jacobin "reign of terror" that followed confirmed their deepest misgivings about excessive democracy. In the meantime, the French wars against the continental monarchs, who had combined to end the threat of republicanism, had begun in 1792, and early in 1793 they spread to Britain and Spain.

For weeks, westerly gales kept news of the executions and the wars from reaching America. When all the news flooded in at once, in April, 1793, it strengthened the Hamiltonians in their stand against France. The Jeffersonians, on the other hand, held to their hatred of monarchs and monarchy and voiced their confidence in the people of France against the autocrats of Britain.

News of the French war with England heightened the conflict in American opinion. More important, it created a dispute over foreign policy. The French treaty of 1778 (see p. 146) provided that the United States must defend the French West Indies in case of an attack on France herself, and also that American ports must receive prizes captured at sea by French privateers and men-of-war. The Girondists, who ruled revolutionary France in 1792, assumed that this treaty remained in force, as indeed it did, and they sent "Citizen" Edmond Genêt as envoy to America to see that it was carried out. Genêt had other instructions as well. He was to organize expeditions from America to detach Louisiana and Florida from Spain, and to outfit American privateers to prey upon British shipping. These enterprises were to be financed with American funds made available by a speed-up in American payments on the old French loan.

Genêt, an attractive and enterprising young man, landed in Charleston, South Carolina, a pro-French stronghold, on April 8, 1793, and, after a warm welcome, went right to work without bothering to present his credentials to the government in Philadelphia. By the time he arrived at Philadelphia, Washington, after consulting Jefferson and Hamilton, had issued his Neutrality Proclamation of April 22, making it clear that the United States would not participate in the French wars. Jefferson had argued that the treaty of 1778 was with the French nation, whatever its government might be, and this interpretation was strictly true in international law. He also urged that since only Congress could declare war, only Congress could proclaim neutrality. Thus a presidential proclamation of neutrality was unconstitutional. He felt, too, that if such a proclamation were actually issued, Britain should be forced to make certain commercial concessions in return. Hamilton, on the contrary, held that the French treaty had died with the French king, and that neutrality in any case was the only feasible American policy. Jefferson, having made the arguments that supported his position, did not persist in opposing the practical step, and Washington's proclamation followed.

By this time, Genêt had already commissioned enthusiastic Charleston ship captains as French privateers to prey on British shipping; he had also organized a South Carolina military adventure against Spain in Florida, and had induced George Rogers Clark and other Kentuckians to float down the Mississippi and dislodge the Spanish from New Orleans, a mission dear to Kentuckian hearts. The warmth of Genêt's reception had convinced him that the people were with him, whatever the government

might do. Thus when Washington received Genêt with forbidding coldness and gave him to understand that the government would no longer tolerate his operations, let alone abet them under the old treaty, Genêt decided to ignore the President and proceed with his revolutionary work on his own.

Even Jefferson was put out by this persistence, and when Genêt, contrary to Washington's express warnings, allowed *Little Democrat,* a prize ship converted into an armed vessel, to sail as a privateer, Jefferson voted with the President and the rest of the Cabinet to ask for Genêt's recall. By then, Genêt's group had fallen out of favor at home and, fearing for his life, the young envoy decided to remain in America. He married Governor Clinton's daughter and retired to a country estate on the Hudson. The new French administration then sent over a less amateurish representative.

THE PROFITS AND
PROBLEMS OF NEUTRALITY
The war in Europe greatly increased the belligerents' need for food and other materials, and at the same time tied up the commercial ships that might have brought in the needed supplies. This situation opened the way for a boom in the carrying trade of neutrals; as a leading maritime nation, the United States was among the greatest gainers. Since the French, particularly, had only a small fleet, painfully vulnerable to British attack, they desperately needed neutral assistance. Early in the war, France at last surrendered her monopoly of the French West Indian trade and opened the islands' ports to American ships and American produce—a turn of events that gave great impetus to American commerce.

The British, determined to monopolize world shipping and especially to keep the late rebels down, retaliated quickly. Trade, according to them, was simply an arm of war. They resurrected the "rule of the War of 1756," which held that trade barred to a nation in peacetime could not with impunity be opened to it during hostilities. This applied with special force to the French West Indian trade. In November,

1793, they decreed that all shipping to or from the French colonies would be subject to British seizure. The Americans had by then swarmed into the Caribbean to serve the French islands, and the British seized about 300 American vessels, abused their passengers, and forced many of their sailors into the British navy.

Even so, American trade continued to flourish. Many ships were captured, but many more slipped through with profits that more than compensated for the great risks involved. Ship losses served as an additional stimulus to the ship-building industry. By 1794, however, the British had become so brazen that even the Federalists expected war. The United States insisted that neutral ships made neutral goods, but the British enforced the right to search for enemy supplies anywhere in any ship. The United States insisted that a blockade, to be effective, must be enforced by actual patrols of the closed ports. But the British simply announced "paper blockades" and undertook to enforce them on the oceans wherever they found a vessel presumably bound for a forbidden harbor. Food, the United States insisted most firmly, could not be classified as contraband. But the British were more realistic and did not hesitate to capture as prizes ships sailing with food for France and her allies.

Painful as these British measures were to Federalist shippers, it was the Republicans who made the most of them by labeling them monarchist affronts to the American flag. Recalling how effective commercial retaliation had been against the British in the great days of the Revolution, the Republicans now demanded an embargo to keep British ships out of American ports and American ships off the seas, where they were subject to British seizure.

As if to keep American memories fresh, the British in Canada chose this time to incite the Indians to raid the Ohio country, where thousands of farmers were settling. The British also made it clear that they had no intention of relinquishing their armed posts on American territory, which were giving assistance and encouragement to the

Indians. Public opinion, aroused over the hot issues of trade and territory, forced the Republicans' embargo through Congress early in 1794. It was to remain in effect for one month, but at the expiration of that period it was extended for two months more.

JAY'S TREATY

The embargo hurt Federalist merchants' own trade as much as it did British commerce, and when the British, in March, 1794, revoked the harshest of their rules for neutrals, the Federalists decided to try to gain additional concessions through diplomacy. On April 16, 1794, Washington named John Jay, now Chief Justice, to go to England and settle the main differences between the two countries. Jay was instructed (1) to get the British to surrender their military posts in the Northwest, (2) to pay for American ships that had been captured illegally, and, (3) to accept and respect the American position on the rights and privileges of neutrals. Jay was also to negotiate the best commercial treaty he could. Failing to get the British to agree on all these points, Jay was to try to get the northern countries of Europe to agree jointly to enforce the rights of neutrals.

Jay had a good case, and the British needed American friendship. But Hamilton nullified these advantages. For years, while serving as Washington's closest adviser, Hamilton had also served as a secret consultant—"No. 7" in the British cipher—with British secret agents in the United States. Once the French Revolution began and democracy seemed to be making headway in the world, his own commitment to monarchical Britain became ever stronger. As early as October, 1789, Hamilton told Major George Beckwith, his secret contact reporting on American affairs: "I have always preferred a connexion with you, to that of any other country, *we think in English,* and have a similarity of prejudices and predilections." Thereafter, Hamilton let nothing pass to Britain's disadvantage. In 1794, while Jay was still at sea on his voyage to England, Washington received a proposal from Sweden and Denmark, two of the northern neutrals Jay was to consult if he failed to gain British concessions. They suggested to the United States just what Jay was instructed to suggest to them —that all three nations unite in combating British assaults on neutral shipping. Washington naturally inclined toward adopting a proposal so similar to his own. In this he had the support of Edmund Randolph, Jefferson's successor as Secretary of State. Nevertheless Hamilton managed to dissuade him, arguing that far from strengthening Jay's hand in his negotiations, such action would only make the British all the more difficult to deal with. Hamilton, moreover, promptly told George Hammond, the British minister in New York, of Washington's decision; and Hammond lost no time in conveying this information to the British negotiators. Jay's bargaining power thus was short-circuited. The result was an uphill fight for the American envoy and a very unsatisfactory agreement.

By the Treaty of London (completed on November 19, 1794, and henceforth known in America as Jay's Treaty), the British agreed once more to evacuate their posts in the Northwest, and by 1796 had done so. But Jay had to barter away a great deal in return. The British could still carry on the fur trade on the American side of the Canadian border and they could still trade with the Indians, who were hostile to advancing American settlement. These concessions almost nullified the surrender of the posts and hardly pleased the westerners, who had remained suspicious of Jay ever since his negotiations with Gardoqui (see p. 164). As for the British paying for captured ships, settlement of this issue was left to a future joint commission which would determine what, if anything, was owed. On the rights of neutrals, Jay failed altogether. The Treaty of London said nothing that would keep the British from continuing to stop and search all ships on the seas and to impress their crews at will. The treaty also left the British the privilege of defining contraband goods as best suited their purposes.

Jay's efforts to get commercial concessions were equally abortive. The treaty did assert the so-called "most-favored-nation" principle, by which American goods entering British home ports and British goods entering American ports were to be treated on the same terms as the goods of the nation having the most favorable commercial agreement with each. But the jewel of the British empire, so far as American merchants were concerned, was the British West Indies, and here Jay made his most objectionable arrangement. For the privilege of visiting Indies ports (a privilege limited to small American ships of no more

A Federalist view of Congressman Albert Gallatin in 1796 when he was arguing that the House could, by withholding appropriations, effectively veto a treaty made by the President and the Senate, and thereby "stop the wheels of government." The guillotine signifies the Federalists' resentment of Gallatin's French-speaking noble ancestry.

than 70 tons), American cargoes of molasses, coffee, cocoa, sugar, and cotton—the only worth-while British West Indian commodities—had to be carried directly to American ports. World trade in these commodities was denied to American merchants, but the

British could continue to carry them anywhere, including American ports. The Senate forced the removal of this provision before it would ratify the treaty.

Jay's whole agreement was so unsatisfactory that Washington hesitated a long time before he even sent it to the Senate. The Senate, in turn, made every effort to keep the terms from the people lest the call for war against Britain become too strong to withstand. The terms did leak out before the treaty was ratified in the Senate on June 25, 1795, by the slenderest possible two-thirds majority. The public response was as violent as expected. In the months following, "Sir John Jay" was hanged in effigy throughout the country and damned to eternity.

In the Congress that met in December, 1795, the question was asked whether the House of Representatives, by failing to vote appropriations required under the agreement, could in effect reject the treaty even though the Senate had accepted it. The House voted 57 to 35 that it had the constitutional right to reject the treaty, but it went on to approve the appropriations in April, 1796, by a vote of 51 to 48.

PINCKNEY'S TREATY

In June, 1795, while the Senate was considering Jay's Treaty with Britain, Spain withdrew from the British coalition against France and made peace with the revolutionary government there. This step

made her fearful of British reprisals which might take the form of attacks on her empire in America. She also feared attacks from American frontiersmen. When Britain and America concluded Jay's Treaty, however unsatisfactory its terms for the United States, Spain's fears for her empire grew, and she decided to try to win American friendship to offset Britain's enmity. After several proposals failed to lure Thomas Pinckney, the American minister who had gone to Madrid on Spain's invitation in 1794, Pinckney was able to write home in August, 1795, that the King of Spain was now prepared "to sacrifice something of what he considered as his right, to testify to his good will to us."

Pinckney proceeded to negotiate the Treaty of San Lorenzo, usually called Pinckney's Treaty, which the Spanish signed in October, 1785, and the United States Senate unanimously approved in March, 1796. This agreement settled the northern boundary of Florida at the latitude of 31 degrees. Much more important, Spain consented to open the Mississippi "in its whole length from its source to the ocean" to American traffic and to allow Americans the free use of the port of New Orleans for three years, after which time the arrangement could be renewed.

III. *John Adams' Administration*

THE ELECTION OF 1796

Washington had been so serious about not running again in 1792 that he had asked Madison and others to draw up ideas for a "valedictory address" to the nation. Early in 1796 he resurrected these papers and turned them over to Hamilton (who had resigned from the Cabinet in 1795) with a request for a new draft. Nothing could deter Washington now from leaving his high office. He looked with deepest dismay, he said, on the "baneful effects of

the spirit of party," but at the same time he took keen satisfaction in many of his accomplishments.

Washington did not deliver his Farewell Address in person; he simply published it in the newspapers on September 17, 1796, a date so close to the presidential elections that it stirred the keenest resentment among the opposition leaders, who felt that his delay in announcing his decision handicapped them in mounting an effective campaign. They felt, also, that his strictures on party spirit were attacks on them and not equally on the governing party.

Washington noted as a "matter of serious concern that any ground should have been furnished for characterizing parties by *geographical* discriminations—*Northern* and *Southern, Atlantic* and *Western*." In much of his address he urged upon the country the need for preserving "the unity of government which constitutes you one people." Only toward the end did he discuss foreign affairs; nowhere was there an admonition against all "entangling alliances." Washington actually said:

> The great rule of conduct for us in regard to foreign nations is, in extending our commercial relations to have with them as little *political* connection as possible. . . . It is our true policy to steer clear of permanent alliances with any portion of the foreign world. . . . Taking care always to keep ourselves . . . on a respectable defensive posture, we may safely trust to temporary alliances for extraordinary emergencies.

The party strife that Washington deplored was nearing its peak when he retired. Debate in the House over Jay's Treaty had continued well into 1796, and Washington's own decision intensified the conflict by opening up the highest office to the rising political machines. The Federalists had considered Jay as a candidate, but the furor over the treaty killed his chances. Widespread satisfaction with the Treaty of San Lorenzo, on the other hand, made Thomas Pinckney a plausible choice. In the end, the Federalists brought out a ticket of John Adams of New England and Pinckney of South Carolina. The Republicans named Jefferson as their standard-bearer, and Aaron Burr of New York for vice-president.

Hamilton and Adams had long since grown cool toward each other, and Hamilton maneuvered to get Pinckney elected president. But his elaborate scheme backfired. Not only did Adams, with 71 votes, win the presidency, but Jefferson, with 68 votes, was second in the balloting and defeated Pinckney for the vice-presidency.

Americans now take the transition from one presidential administration to another as a matter of course. In 1796 the public was experiencing the first transfer of presidential power from one man to another, and its anxiety was deepened by the fact that a leader of Washington's stature was about to retire. The President, writes Leonard D. White, in his history of Federalist administration, "had already determined to demonstrate to the world the supreme achievement of democratic government— the peaceful and orderly change of the head of the state in accordance with the voice of the people." John Adams himself was moved by the historic event; reporting his inauguration to his wife he said, "All agree that, taken together, it was the sublimest thing ever exhibited in America."

JOHN ADAMS' FOREIGN POLICY

No one in the United States had written more than John Adams about the nature of man. But, as Jefferson shrewdly observed, in practice Adams was "a bad calculator" of the "motives of men." He made the mistake of retaining in his Cabinet such second-rate Hamiltonians as Secretary of State Timothy Pickering and Secretary of the Treasury Oliver Wolcott, who had surrounded Washington toward the end when even the great General himself could not induce able administrators any longer to forego private business for the public service. Worse, by being absent from his post more often, perhaps, than any president in history, Adams inadvertently gave these Hamiltonians free rein.

In later years, after his retirement, Adams counted as one of his major achievements that he, like Washington, had kept the United States at peace with France. Hamilton's anti-French friends in Adams' virtually autonomous Cabinet, however, carried the administration to the brink of all-out hostilities despite the President.

The French had taken less kindly than the Spanish to Jay's Treaty; interpreting it as a British diplomatic victory, they intensified their attacks on American ships bound for British ports. By the time of Adams' inauguration in March, 1797, the French had captured about 300 American vessels and had manhandled their crews. In the meantime, Washington had recalled the francophile minister, James Monroe, for having told the French first that Jay's Treaty would never be ratified, and then that it would never become operative because Washington would be defeated in the forthcoming election. Washington sent Charles C. Pinckney to replace Monroe, but after he had been in France the two months allowed to foreigners, the French police notified him that unless he got a permit to remain they would arrest him. Pinckney fled to Amsterdam in a rage. By the time news of Pinckney's treatment reached Philadelphia, Adams had become president and the Federalists were clamoring for war with the brutal French.

Adams withstood their demands, but without querying the French government, he decided as one of his first presidential measures to send a three-man mission to Paris to persuade the French to stop their raids on American shipping. Pinckney, ordered back to France, was joined in Paris by the Federalist, John Marshall, and the Republican, Elbridge Gerry. When Talleyrand, then foreign minister of France, refused to negotiate until the Americans had given a bribe of $250,000 to three subordinates, Gerry's Federalist colleagues left Paris in a huff. Gerry stayed on to parley with Talleyrand, and came home only when Adams demanded that he cease dallying with the revolutionists.

In their reports home the American envoys had referred to Talleyrand's three subordinates as X, Y, and Z. When the reports became public, an uproar broke out among the partisans of both parties over the so-called "X.Y.Z. Dispatches," during which someone is said to have cried, "Millions for defense, but not one cent for tribute." Congress did vote millions for the expansion of the army and navy in 1798 and 1799; it also created a separate Navy Department and repealed all treaties with France.

To the chagrin of Hamilton, who was aching to lead it into battle, the new army materialized very slowly. Adams himself saw little use for it in fighting for the free-

dom of the seas and was most reluctant to burden the country with mounting military costs. The new Navy Department, on the other hand, promptly pushed to completion three well-armed frigates that had been under construction, produced 20 other ships of war, and unleashed hundreds of American privateers to prey upon the French. In 1798 and 1799, an "undeclared naval war" raged with France in which American ships, operating mainly in the Caribbean, took almost a hundred French vessels, and suffered losses themselves.

Hamilton's friends in the Cabinet and Congress, meanwhile, were pushing the expansion of the army with such zeal that many suspected a plan to use it against domestic as well as foreign enemies. Their suspicions were confirmed in February, 1799, when troops were sent once more to western Pennsylvania to put down a rebellion led by John Fries against the collection of new taxes just levied to pay for the army itself. The Hamiltonians even induced Washington, only a few months before his death, to take nominal command of the army once more, a step that helped persuade Adams, much against his inclination, to name Hamilton as next in command and effectively in charge. But Adams would go no further. To the consternation of Hamilton and his friends, the President refused to make any use of the army against foreign enemies or to ask Congress to make the war with France official.

News that France was relenting in her attitude in the face of Adams' naval policy confirmed the President in his hopes for peace. The same news only drove the Hamiltonians to desperation and the Federalist party to defeat and to the verge of destruction. When, early in 1799, Adams named a new three-man commission to reopen negotiations with Talleyrand, the Hamiltonians berated him fiercely, and Hamilton's friend, Timothy Pickering, still Secretary of State, went so far as to delay the sailing of two of the three commissioners not already in Europe. When the three Americans finally assembled in France early in 1800, they found that the best they could get from her negotiators was confirmation of the principle that "neutral ships make neutral goods." An indemnity for losses already suffered on the high seas in violation of this principle proved to be out of the question.

When the Hamiltonians learned in September that the American envoys had agreed to peace on these meager terms, they launched their fiercest attack yet on John Adams. Hamilton himself gave the signal in a "fatal tirade" against the President early in October, in which he referred to Adams' "extreme egotism," "terrible jealousy," and "violent rage," and proceeded to question even "the solidity of his understanding." This attack so shattered the Federalist party that, as one former leader said to another, "We have no rallying-point; and no mortal can divine where and when we shall again collect our strength. . . . Shadows, clouds, and darkness rest on our future prospects."

THE ALIEN
AND SEDITION ACTS

At the time of Adams' election, Madison had written to Jefferson: "You know the temper of Mr. A. better than I do, but I have always conceived it to be rather a ticklish one." One thing Adams quickly became "ticklish" about was the Republican taunt that he was "President by three votes." Other partisan attacks on him and his administration aroused him, early in the summer of 1798, to strike out at his detractors. Adams felt especially imposed upon by the Swiss, Albert Gallatin, who on Madison's retirement from Congress in 1797 had become Republican leader of the House; by the English radical, Thomas Cooper, who had come to America in 1794 and soon proved himself a vigorous Republican pamphleteer; and by a number of recently arrived French intellectuals, including the chemist, Pierre A. Adet, the botanist, André Michaux, and Victor Du

Pont, all of whom Adams suspected of engaging in espionage. Many undistinguished but noisy French Jacobins who had fled the repression of the Directory after 1795 also set up a clamor against Adams. Most offensive of all, perhaps, to anglophile Federalists, were the defeated fighters for Irish freedom, who chose this time to carry their insatiable hatred of Britain to the United States.

Nor did Adams forget American-born Republican journalists. Outstanding among them was Franklin's grandson, Benjamin Bache, known as "Lightning-rod Junior," whose Philadelphia *Aurora* had supplanted Freneau's *National Gazette* in 1793 as the leading Republican paper.

Adams might easily have overcome his pique had not the most violent men of his party in June and July, 1798, pushed through Congress a series of measures known as the Alien and Sedition Acts. Angered as he was, the President grasped the weapons so gratuitously presented. The first of these measures was a Naturalization Act which raised the residence requirement for American citizenship from five to fourteen years and would have meant permanent disfranchisement for many. The second, the Alien Act, empowered the president in peacetime to order any alien from the country, and to jail for not more than three years those who refused to go. The third, the Alien Enemies Act, permitted the president in wartime to jail enemy aliens at his pleasure. No arrests were made under either alien act, but they did scare hundreds of foreigners from the country.

The fourth measure was the Sedition Act. Its key clause provided severe fines and jail penalties for anyone speaking, writing, or publishing "with intent to defame . . . or bring into contempt or disrepute" the president or other members of the government. Its intent to gag the Republican opposition until after the next presidential election is evident in the provision continuing the act, "in force until March 3, 1801, and no longer."

Matthew Lyon, an outspoken Irish-born Republican congressman from Vermont, while campaigning for re-election against a "government" man, was the first to be jailed under the Sedition Act. Jefferson protested that Lyon was treated the same as the vilest criminals of the day. "I know not which mortifies me most," he remarked on learning of Lyon's fate, "that I should fear to write what I think, or my country should bear such a state of things." Lyon's constituents backed him to the hilt. During his four-month jail term they re-elected him to Congress.

Many others, most of them Republican editors, followed Lyons to jail and Republican papers had to shut down. With few exceptions the trials were travesties of justice dominated by judges who saw treason behind every expression of Republican sentiments. Grand juries for bringing in the indictments and trial juries for rendering the monotonous verdict of guilty were hand-picked by Federalist United States marshals in defiance of statutes prescribing orderly procedure. The presiding judges often ridiculed the defendants' lawyers and interrupted their presentations so outrageously that many threw up their hands and their cases, leaving the accused to the mercy of the courts. The courts, at the same time, fell sharply in the estimation of the people. In January, 1798, the states had ratified the eleventh amendment to the Constitution excluding "the judicial power of the United States" from countenancing any suit "against one of the United States by citizens of another State, or by citizens of any foreign state." This amendment had grown out of a Supreme Court verdict against the state of Georgia in *Chisholm* v. *Georgia* in 1794, in a case in which the state had been sued by a British creditor. The amendment was a blow to the federal court system which stirred John Marshall a few years later to heroic efforts to restore the standing of the judiciary (see p. 202). His task was made all the harder by the conduct of the courts in Sedition Act cases, which left Marshall, himself a solid Federalist, mortified.

Madison called the Sedition Act "a monster that must forever disgrace its parents."

He and Jefferson both recognized it as the start of the Federalist campaign for the elections of 1800, and they quickly set in motion a broad-gauged attack on the whole Federalist philosophy. Their offensive took the form of a series of resolutions for which their allies won the approval of the legislatures of Kentucky and Virginia in November and December, 1798. The resolutions were then circulated among the rest of the states.

Jefferson wrote the Kentucky Resolutions, Madison those adopted in Virginia. Both sets attacked the Hamiltonian "broad interpretation" of the Constitution and developed the state rights position later used to justify nullification and secession. In Jefferson's words, "the several states composing the United States of America, are not united on the principle of unlimited submission to their general government"; that government, in Madison's terms, is but a "compact to which the states are parties." The Kentucky Resolutions held that, as parties to the "compact," the states had the right to declare what measures went beyond their agreement and were "unauthoritative, void, and of no force," and to decide what remedies were appropriate. Madison, in the Virginia Resolutions, said that the states together might "interpose" to check the exercise of unauthorized powers. Jefferson, in his Kentucky Resolutions, went further: he held that the legislature *of each individual state* had this right.

No interpretation of the intent, purpose, or action of the Great Convention of 1787 could have been more far-fetched than that expressed in these Resolutions (see p. 173). But Madison and Jefferson at least had a liberalizing goal absent from later state rights movements in pressing their argument this far. As Jefferson put it in the Kentucky Resolutions, the Alien and Sedition Acts, by employing the loosest construction of the Constitution to impose the tightest tyranny, soured "the mild spirit of our country and its laws."

THE ELECTION OF 1800

While the "X.Y.Z." affair (p. 197) and other affronts by France had cost the francophile Republicans some strength in the country, their prospects for the presidential campaign of 1800 were brightened by the sharp split in Federalist ranks between the Adams men and the Hamiltonians.

For the campaign of 1800 the Republican caucus named Jefferson and Burr. The Federalists were so divided that no caucus of their leaders was possible. By devices difficult to disentangle, the ticket of Adams and C. C. Pinckney finally was made public; but once again, as in 1796, the central drama revolved around Hamilton's determination to defeat Adams by means of his own running mate. No one was willing to go along with Hamilton's strategy, however, and what was worse, the Republicans, as many Federalists expected, polled enough votes to make the maneuver meaningless. The electoral college voted 65 for Adams and 64 for Pinckney; Jefferson and Burr each received 73 votes.

The Republicans triumphed in a campaign that one writer describes as "a havoc of virulence." But worse was to come. Burr had no pretensions to the presidency at this time; but many Federalists, especially those from commercial New England and New York, saw in his tie vote with Jefferson an opportunity to raise to the presidency, "a friend of the Constitution . . . a friend of the commercial interests . . . the firm and decided friend of the *navy*." The *Washington Federalist,* which carried these words in January, 1801, went on to say: "The *Eastern* States have had a President and Vice President; So have the *Southern.* It is proper that the *middle* states should also be respected. . . . Mr. Burr can be raised to the Presidency without any *insult* to the feelings of the Federalists, the friends of Government."

According to the Constitution, the House would have to decide between the two Re-publicans. There the voting was to be by states, not individual representatives, and nine states (out of 16) were needed to win. The first ballot in the House was taken on February 11, with the results that Jefferson had forseen: he carried eight states, Burr six, and two were undecided. And so it went for a feverish week during which 35 ballots were taken.

While the deadlock persisted, Federalist strategists, whose party still retained a majority in Congress, began to think in terms of having the Senate "appoint a Presidt. till another election is made," as Monroe reported to Jefferson. Jefferson replied on February 15: "We thought best to declare openly and firmly, one & all, that the day such an act passed, the Middle States would arm, & that no such usurpation, even for a single day, should be submitted to."

The deadlock finally was broken on February 17 on the 36th ballot. *This was done,* Jefferson wrote, in italics, *"without a single vote coming over."* He went on to explain the intricacies of the strategy by which, by voting blanks, certain Federalists took their states out of Burr's camp. "Their vote [none whatever having been cast directly for the Republicans] showed," Jefferson added, "what they had decided on, and is considered a declaration of perpetual war."

The next Congress put an end to this kind of problem by sending the Twelfth Amendment to the states, which ratified it by September, 1804. This amendment provided that, henceforth, "The electors . . . shall name in their ballots the person voted for as President, and in distinct ballots the person voted for as Vice-President."

The transfer of power from the Federalists to the Republicans had been much more foreboding than the transfer of the presidency from Washington to Adams in 1796. Yet it had been accomplished peacefully after all, and henceforth an organized opposition was to be allowed its own free voice and aspirations to power without any taint of treason or disloyalty.

Although the Republicans in 1800 captured the presidency and control of both the House and the Senate, nevertheless the country's first great shift in political power was not quite complete. Just before adjourning, in March, 1801, the retiring Federalist Congress gave Adams a new judiciary act which relieved Supreme Court and district court justices from riding to the circuit courts, created a whole new group of circuit court judges, and increased the number of district court judges. Adams filled these

life-time jobs and other new judicial posts with Federalist sympathizers. Most important, he named John Marshall as Chief Justice of the Supreme Court, a position he was to hold during more than 30 years of Republican political control.

IV. *Jefferson as President*

THE REPUBLICANS
TAKE OFFICE

Jefferson took the Republican victory in 1800 much more seriously than some historians have taken it since. "The Federalists," he wrote later in life from a perspective of many years, "wished for everything which would approach our new government to a monarchy; the Republicans, to preserve it essentially republican." This preservation, he held, had been assured by his triumph. "The revolution of 1800 was as real a revolution in the principles of government as that of 1776 was in its form."

At the time of the Republican success at the polls, Jefferson could hardly deny that the Federalist leaders had put up a hard fight and that their followers had been numerous. But the desperate maneuvers during the struggle with Burr in the House, he held, foreshadowed the Federalist party's early extinction. "Our information from all quarters," he wrote to a fellow Virginian soon after his victory, "is that the whole body of federalists" in the country had been alienated from the Federalist leadership, "and I verily believe they will remain embodied with us, so that this conduct of the minority [in Congress] has done in one week what very probably could hardly have been effected by years of mild and impartial administration."

Jefferson's inaugural address is often described as a bid for conciliation after the bruising election struggle: "Let us, then, fellow-citizens, unite with one heart and one mind. . . . Every difference of opinion is not a difference in principle. . . . We are all Republicans, we are all Federalists. If there be any among us who would wish to dissolve this Union or to change its republican form, let them stand undisturbed as monuments of the safety with which error of opinion may be tolerated where reason is left free to combat it."

And yet Jefferson's tolerance of minority rights did not delay for a moment his joining battle with Federalist irreconcilables. "Possessing a chosen country, with room enough for our descendants to the thousandth and thousandth generation," the people, Jefferson thought, required neither the elaborate contrivances of John Adams' "divine science of politics" to guard them from their baser selves, nor Hamilton's rod of iron to curb their unseemly aspirations. All that was needed "to close the circle of our felicities" was "a wise and frugal Government, which shall restrain men from injuring one another, shall leave them otherwise free to regulate their own pursuits of industry and improvement."

In naming his cabinet, Jefferson could hardly be expected to choose any Federalists—if, indeed, any of the "Anglican monarchical aristocratical party," as the Republican press described the opposition, could be found to serve his administration. Of the five cabinet positions, nevertheless, Jefferson gave two to New England, where Federalism was most intransigent. A New Englander also got the Postmaster-Generalship, which had not yet attained cabinet rank. The two most important cabinet posts went to the two most important Republicans after Jefferson: James Madison became Secretary of State, and Albert Gallatin became Secretary of the Treasury. In filling the hundreds of other federal jobs, Jefferson fired few Federalists, but he hired even fewer.

By refusing, also, to recognize many of Adams' "midnight appointments" to judicial positions, Jefferson set the stage for the famous case of *Marbury* v. *Madison* and his own subsequent war on the judiciary.

President Adams had signed William Marbury's commission as justice of the peace in the District of Columbia so late that it could not even be delivered to him before Jefferson took office. Madison (the Secretary of State in those days was charged with certain domestic duties as well as the conduct of foreign affairs) now refused to deliver Marbury's commission. Marbury in turn asked the Supreme Court to issue a writ ordering Madison to hand it over. The Court, by the Judiciary Act of 1789 (see p. 185), had the power to do as Marbury asked. But John Marshall, in his decision in *Marbury* v. *Madison* (1803) refused to exercise it. He held, indeed, that Marbury, despite the Judiciary Act, had no case at all.

The Constitution, Marshall argued, stated explicitly in what actions the Supreme Court had original jurisdiction, and Marbury's complaint was not among them. Only an amendment to the Constitution could extend the Court's jurisdiction to it. That being so, Marshall continued, the provision in the Judiciary Act of 1789 that granted the Supreme Court the authority to issue such writs as Marbury sought was unconstitutional.

In 1792, without arousing any significant discussion, a United States circuit court in Pennsylvania had declared a federal statute unconstitutional, so Marshall's decision did not set a precedent. What made the decision memorable was Marshall's firmness in confronting Jefferson and the theory of the Kentucky Resolutions (see p. 199) with grand *ex cathedra* proclamations of his own which have stood the test of time. Marshall's commitment later on to the broadest interpretation of the Constitution and the widest legislative latitude (see p. 235) has obscured the point that in *Marbury* v. *Madison* he forced himself to use a case involving the strictest interpretation of the Constitution, and especially of the powers of the legislature, in order to make his larger case on the nature of judicial review and on the role of the Supreme Court.

The Constitution, said Marshall, was law, to be enforced by *courts;* it was, moreover, the *supreme law* to which even federal legislation must conform to be valid; and in conflicts over the meaning of the Constitution as law, or over the validity of legislation under it, "it is emphatically the province and duty of the judicial department"—and not of the states or the popularly elected legislature—"to say what the law is."

That the power of judicial review should be placed uniquely in the Supreme Court, by an irremovable Federalist so early in the first Republican administration, and, gallingly, in a case in which the administration was nominally the victor, taunted Jefferson into taking up his war on the "despotic branch." For if Federalist judges, the Republicans reasoned, could check legislation simply by declaring it unconstitutional, the legislature must have some means to counteract them. Congress, the Republican legislators now held, had these means in the power of impeachment.

The most conspicuous victim of the impeachment policy was the vulnerable Supreme Court Justice Samuel Chase, who had a habit of entertaining juries with anti-Republican harangues. The House impeached him for misconduct in 1805, but he escaped conviction in the Senate. The Republicans did not try this maneuver again. Instead, they looked to the growing popular approval of their program to bring the courts into closer harmony with the election returns.

REPUBLICANISM IN SPIRIT AND SUBSTANCE

It is fitting that Jefferson should have been the first president to begin his term in the rude capital on the Potomac. He himself had suggested the layout of Pennsylvania Avenue, and on many other details had advised the French engineer, Pierre Charles L'Enfant, who planned the city of Washington. An Irishman, James Hoban, designed the White House, and an Englishman, B. H. Latrobe (with the American, William Thornton), designed the Capitol.

Adams' Alien Act offered poor hospitality to such men. Jefferson, once he had named his advisers and manned his administration, began by allowing this "libel on legislation" to lapse, and distinguished foreigners were welcomed to the country once more. Next he freed all who had been jailed under the Sedition Act, and recommended to Congress the return of all fines collected under it. He also recommended the restoration of a five-year residence requirement (instead of the Naturalization Act's 14-year requirement) for foreigners who wanted to become American citizens. Congress acted favorably on both suggestions.

Having thus righted matters of the spirit, Jefferson turned to matters of the purse. He admonished Secretary of the Treasury Gallatin to keep the finances so simple "that every member of the Congress and every man of any mind in the Union should be able to comprehend them." In his first "state of the Union" message, which he sent to Congress in December, 1801, instead of delivering it "from the throne," as Washington and Adams had done, he recommended that the legislature forestall waste by appropriating funds only for specific purposes, rather than in lump sums for the various departments as had been the practice. He also advised Congress to require annual accountings from the Secretary of the Treasury, something Hamilton would have taken as a personal affront. By such good management, Jefferson thought, Congress could save enough to make it possible to repeal the hated excise immediately and still speed up payments on the public debt and save millions in interest.

Jefferson himself undertook to restore true republican simplicity to the executive

arm of government. He halted the expansion of the navy and reduced the size of the army. He dismembered the diplomatic corps, eliminated many tax-collectors, and cut out costly presidential social affairs.

Another Jeffersonian economy move was entirely unlooked for in New England and must have surprised everyone who thought the President a poor custodian of national honor. This was Jefferson's "Barbary War."

Jefferson's economies in the naval and military establishments were prompted in part by the theory, a favorite of his, that every foreign nation felt such a vital interest in American trade and the use of American ships and harbors, that none would dare risk war. But this blanket proposition failed to cover such outlaw nations as Morocco, Algiers, Tunis, and Tripoli, whose rulers were in league with the Barbary pirates who preyed on Atlantic and Mediterranean shipping, and at the same time demanded tribute from European powers. Britain, who paid tribute herself, often connived with the pirates to keep other nations from encroaching on her trade. When the United States became an independent nation, American shipping proved a particularly attractive target. During their administrations, Washington and Adams had sweetened pirate treasuries with $2 million, but valuable ships, cargoes, and men were still being lost. When Tripoli, in May, 1801, suddenly demanded an increase in American payments, Jefferson decided it might be cheaper to check the extortion by taking the offensive himself.

In May, 1801, Jefferson ordered a navy squadron to sew up the pirates in their home ports. For a navy "supported" by an economy-minded administration, however, such action was more easily ordered than achieved. The war against Tripoli in particular dragged on until 1805, when the Pasha, threatened with the loss of his throne from other quarters, sued for peace. The treaty, in the words of Commodore Edward

"The United States Capitol in 1800," watercolor by Thomas Birch. Below, "Thomas Jefferson," by Rembrandt Peale, 1800.

Preble, the American naval commander during most of the fighting, put American relations with Tripoli "on more honorable terms than any other nation has ever been able to command." The United States continued to pay tribute to Barbary nations until 1816, but at a lower rate.

JEFFERSON AND THE WEST

Late in 1801 Jefferson wrote: "The increase of [our] numbers during the last ten years we contemplate not with a view to the injuries it may enable us to do others, . . . but to the settlement of the extensive country still remaining vacant within our limits."

To encourage settlement of the public lands, Congress, in 1796 and 1800, had lowered both the minimum acreage a pioneer had to buy and the actual cash he had to put down. In 1804 Jefferson got Congress to reduce requirements to the point where, for a down payment of only $80, a man could get title to a quarter section of 160 acres.

These measures speeded up the settlement

of the Northwest Territory, out of which Ohio (admitted to the Union in 1803) was the first state to be formed. Under the Land Ordinance of 1785 (see p. 167), each state created out of the Northwest Territory was to receive from Congress one section of land (640 acres) in every township, the proceeds from the sale of which were to be used to support education in the state. In the act admitting Ohio, Congress specifically made this grant, the first of its kind.

Jefferson also tried to promote settlement in the Southwest, where conflicting claims to huge tracts of land near the Yazoo River in present-day Mississippi presented a major obstacle. In 1789, the state of Georgia, which then owned this territory, sold about 25 million acres of it to speculators. When the buyers failed in their operation, Georgia, in 1795, re-sold much of the same land to other companies at the extraordinarily favorable price of 1½ cents an acre. All but one of the members of the Georgia legislature were in on the second deal. Responding to a charge of fraud, a new legislature the next year rescinded the sale. But in the meantime the companies had sold stock widely, and the owners of the stock demanded delivery of the land.

When Georgia finally ceded her western lands to the federal government in 1802, the Yazoo stockholders carried their demands along to President Jefferson. He set up a commission which in 1803 recommended that the Yazoo claimants be reimbursed through the sale of 5 million acres of Yazoo land. The commission also recommended that the United States quiet the Indian claim to territory within the boundaries of Georgia, and that the rest of the land ceded by Georgia should itself become a state when its population reached 60,000.

Georgia and the federal government accepted these recommendations. In the House of Representatives, however, John Randolph led the fight against compensating the Yazoo claimants, insisting that the precious rights of the soverign state of Georgia had been forfeited, with Jefferson's connivance, for the benefit of corrupt speculators. On these grounds he successfully op-

posed payment for more than ten years, and split the Republican party in the process. Randolph was supported by the die-hard state-rights Republicans whose philosophy Jefferson himself had buttressed with the Kentucky Resolutions of 1798. Jefferson, however, was to prove no stickler for state rights or for a narrow interpretation of the Constitution where America's expansion was concerned, and the majority of the Republican party clung to his leadership.

In 1810, John Marshall added his resounding voice to the Yazoo argument. In the case of *Fletcher* v. *Peck,* the Chief Justice declared the Georgia sale of 1795 a legitimate contract which the next legislature had no power to break without the consent of the other party to it. This decision strengthened the position of the Yazoo stockholders and finally, in 1814, with Randolph out of Congress for the time being, Congress awarded them $5 million. Within five years, Alabama and Mississippi, both made up of territory ceded by Georgia, were admitted as states.

Jefferson, meanwhile, had developed far larger plans for the West, looking, as he said, "to distant times, when our rapid multiplication will expand itself" to "cover the whole northern, if not the southern, continent, with a people speaking the same language" and "governed . . . by similar laws." To further his plans Jefferson, early in 1803, got Congress to appropriate money to be used to send Meriwether Lewis and William Clark on an expedition to the Pacific ostensibly for scientific purposes, but also to seek new sources and outlets for American fur-trappers and traders. The appropriation was secret, for the explorers were to traverse foreign territory. By the time they completed their mission in 1806, Lewis and Clark had crossed the Rockies at the Continental Divide and traced the Columbia River to its mouth, thereby establishing an American claim to Oregon. By then, also, much of the country they crossed had become part of the United States through the Louisiana Purchase.

THE LOUISIANA PURCHASE

Spain, with Jefferson's blessing, held Louisiana—or New Orleans, as the whole western country was often called—from 1762 to 1800. "Till our population can be sufficiently advanced [in numbers] to gain it from them piece by piece," Jefferson thought, it could not "be in better hands." It is not hard, therefore, to imagine the President's anxiety on learning early in 1802 from Rufus King, the American minister in London, that by a secret treaty in October, 1800, the insatiable Napoleon, compensating Spain with territory elsewhere, had retrieved Louisiana for France.

Napoleon intended to develop Louisiana into a source of food for the French West Indies, thus ending their dependence on the United States. But he could not proceed with this plan until he had secured his position in Europe. In Santo Domingo, moreover, a stubborn slave insurrection led by the Negro General Toussaint L'Ouverture, threatened to spread to the rest of the French West Indies and ruin Napoleon's whole vision of a new American empire. Once Napoleon had quieted Europe with the Peace of Amiens in 1802, he sent 20,000 men to crush Toussaint and then occupy the port of New Orleans. But this campaign failed.

When Jefferson first learned of the treaty by which Napoleon had reacquired Louisiana, he warned the French that their action might "completely reverse all the political relations of the United States" and drive us into the arms of England. "There is on the globe one single spot," he added, "the possessor of which is our natural and

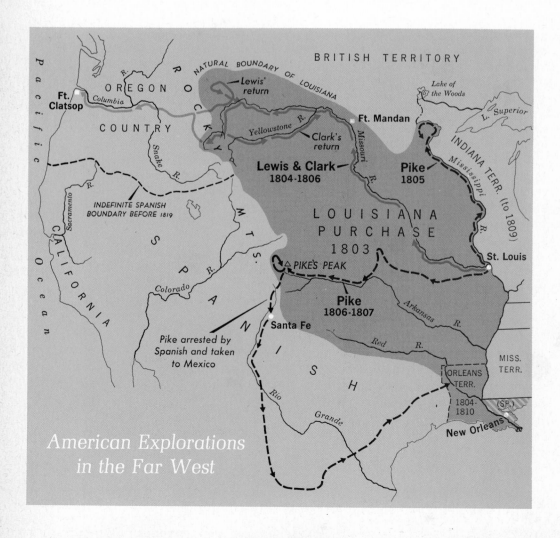

American Explorations
in the Far West

habitual enemy. It is New Orleans, through which the produce of three-eighths of our territory must pass to market, and from its fertility it will ere long yield more than half of our whole produce and contain more than half of our inhabitants." In May, 1802, Jefferson had instructed Robert Livingston in Paris to try to get France to put a price on New Orleans (and on the Floridas, which Jefferson mistakenly assumed had also passed into French possession). Before Livingston could make much progress, Jefferson learned that in October, 1802, the Spanish *intendant* still in charge at New Orleans had been instructed by France to suspend the American right, under Pinckney's Treaty (see p. 195), to deposit cargoes there. Nothing could more strongly have confirmed French enmity. "The agitation of the public mind" over this step, Jefferson wrote in January, 1803, "is extreme." He continued with an analysis of American opinion:

In the western country [the agitation] is natural, and grounded on honest motives; in the seaports it proceeds from a desire for war, which increases the mercantile lottery; in the Federalists generally, and especially those of Congress, the object is to force us into war if possible, in order to derange our finances; or if this cannot be done, to attach the western country to them as their best friends, and thus get again into power.

Jefferson was determined that "nothing but dire necessity, should force us from the path of peace." To quiet the agitation for war, he asked the Senate, in January, 1803, to confirm his nomination of James Monroe as minister extraordinary to assist Livingston in Paris. The Senate complied and, with the House, appropriated $2 million for Monroe's use. Monroe sailed in March with instructions to offer up to $10 million for New Orleans and the Floridas. If France refused to sell and persisted in keeping New Orleans shut to American commerce, Monroe and Livingston were to suggest to Britain that she join the United States in the event of a new war with Napoleon. By the time Monroe arrived in Paris, he found his

elaborate instructions obsolete. A staggering offer of the whole Louisiana Territory had been made to Livingston, and on April 30, 1803, the two Americans closed the deal.

The American envoys were not quite sure what they had bought; the terms said simply that they were to receive Louisiana with the boundaries "that it now has in the hands of Spain." If this seemed vague, said Talleyrand, Napoleon's negotiator, "I suppose you will make the most of it." The final price was $15 million, a fourth of which was to be used to settle the claims of American shippers and shipowners against the French government. The purchase treaty also specified that the inhabitants of Louisiana, most of them Catholic, were to become American citizens and be protected in the practice of their religion.

To negotiate such a treaty was one thing; to get the money for such a "noble bargain," as Talleyrand called it, was quite another. To begin with, there were many irregularities about the sale. France had never actually taken over the territory from Spain; the French Constitution, moreover, prohibited the disposal of territory without a legislative vote. And the American Constitution did not delegate the power to purchase territory. Jefferson was so troubled on this point that he suggested an amendment to make the treaty legitimate. But, warned that delay might cause Napoleon to renege, Jefferson swallowed his scruples and pushed the treaty through. In November, 1803, the Senate ratified it 26 to 5, and the House appropriated the needed money, 90 to 25. On December 20th, the United States formally took possession. The next year, two territories were made of the Purchase, to be administered as under the Northwest Ordinance of 1787. Under these terms, Louisiana, with its present-day boundaries, became a state in 1812.

Florida had not been included in the deal, since Spain had never actually yielded it to France. But Jefferson was far from discouraged. "If we push them strongly with one hand, holding out a price in the other," he said, "we shall certainly obtain the Floridas, and all in good time."

The method if not the results of the Louisiana Purchase troubled the Randolph Republicans in the South. But the strongest reaction came from Federalists in New England who expected their influence in the nation to be utterly destroyed by the acquisition of this enormous new territory. So distraught were some of the northerners that they proposed to leave the Union; desperately, they turned for help to Aaron Burr, Jefferson's alienated Vice-President, who was then running for governor of New York. If victorious, Burr was to take his state into a new northern confederation with New England, and thereby escape from the "Virginia dynasty." Hamilton helped defeat Burr, and the projected confederation collapsed. Embittered by this and other offenses, real and imaginary, Burr challenged Hamilton to a duel in which Hamilton was killed, on July 11, 1804. Burr himself fled west where he further discredited himself by plotting futilely with Britain and Spain to detach Louisiana and older American territory.

TRIALS OF A NEUTRAL

The schemes of Burr's Yankee conspirators so weakened the already battered Federalist party even in New England that in the presidential election of 1804 Jefferson carried every state but Connecticut and Delaware. The new vice-president was George Clinton, to whom, instead of Burr, Jefferson had entrusted the distribution of Republican patronage in New York.

Jefferson's first administration had coincided more or less with the first years of peace in Europe since the French Revolution, and had been marked by domestic achievements capped by the Louisiana Purchase. His second administration had hardly begun when the country was plunged once more into the maelstrom of the Napoleonic Wars and Jefferson was obliged to defer his domestic plans.

By 1805 Napoleon's military victory at Austerlitz had given France control of much of the European continent, and Nelson's naval victory at Trafalgar had given Britain control of the seas. This apparent stalemate led only to a relentless war of attrition, with disastrous results for neutral carriers, especially those of the United States.

The first new blow was the decision of a British court in the case of the ship *Essex* in 1805. In 1800, a British court had ruled that American ships could carry goods from the French West Indies to France provided the goods were first landed on American shores, duty-free. This decision had given a great impetus to the so-called "re-export" trade which, by 1805, accounted for more than half of America's booming neutral commerce. In the case of the *Essex,* however, the British court revoked the earlier decision and now held that French colonial goods could be sent to France only if a duty had been paid on them in America and only if other evidence proved that the goods had not been meant for France in the first place. Any ships that could not produce this evidence to Britain's satisfaction were vulnerable to British capture.

Britain also stepped up her attacks on other American commerce, and the impending termination of the 12-year commercial agreement made at the time of Jay's Treaty in 1794 threatened to leave American shipping more vulnerable than ever. To remedy the situation, Jefferson in 1806 got Congress to pass a non-importation act prohibiting the landing in the United States of any British goods that could be purchased elsewhere or manufactured at home. With this as a club (the act was not enforced until later), he sent William Pinkney to join Monroe, who was now the regular minister in London, in an effort to make a new commercial treaty and otherwise put an end to British attacks.

As a result of new victories on land, Napoleon soon lifted the pace of his own activities on the sea. In November, 1806, he issued his Berlin Decrees nominally closing the entire European Continent to Britain, her goods, and her friends, and blockading the British Isles. When Pinkney and Monroe negotiated a treaty in London, the British stipulated as a condition of enforcement that the United States must resist these Berlin Decrees. But Jefferson would have nothing to do with such dictation, and he did not even submit the treaty to the Senate. In 1807, Napoleon added the Milan Decrees to the Berlin Decrees, ordering the confiscation of all ships, especially neutral ships, that had visited any British port or might be bound for one. Britain responded with a series of "orders-in-council." The major orders, in January and November, 1807, stated that "all ports and places of France and her allies or of any country at war with His Majesty," were blockaded, and that neutral ships that sailed toward them did so at their peril.

IMPRESSMENT
AND EMBARGO

Between 1804 and 1807, the United States lost hundreds of ships to the British alone. She also lost many men to the British practice of stopping ships on the high seas to search for and take off alleged deserters from the British navy, the practice known as impressment.

The British navy, a harsh institution which had been enormously expanded to fight Napoleon, was characteristically short of men. This shortage was intensified by competition from American ship-owners and the United States government, who offered higher wages and better working conditions than the British and lured thousands of British sailors who happened to be in American ports to sign on American vessels. To the beleaguered British, who believed that "Once an Englishman, always an Englishman," this was intolerable.

In June, 1807, one affront led to violence and talk of war. The new American frigate, *Chesapeake,* suspected by the British of having a certain deserter on board, was sailing off Norfolk, Virginia, outside the three-mile limit, when the British warship *Leopard* intercepted her and demanded the right of search. *Chesapeake's* captain refused, and a few minutes later *Leopard* opened fire. *Chesapeake,* her new guns ill-mounted, and her decks cluttered with as yet undistributed gear, suffered 21 casualties before being boarded by *Leopard's* officers. They found the deserter they were after and along with him took three Americans who had served in the British navy.

To almost everyone but Jefferson, it seemed, this attack meant war. But Jefferson had a policy of his own. He called a special session of Congress in October, which voted an appropriation of $850,000 to strengthen the navy. Only in the regular session in December did he show his true hand. Under a policy that he called "peaceful coercion," he decided to keep American vessels off the seas in order to save ships and men from capture, and to save the country from incendiary insults. Thus deprived of American goods and American carriers, he reasoned, the warring powers would be forced to recognize American neutral rights. On December 22, 1807, Congress gave Jefferson the Embargo Act, which ruled that no ships could leave United States ports and no goods could be exported, even overland.

The Embargo Act meant ruin, not to Britain and Europe, but to American commerce and American ports. In spite of the losses caused by the European wars, between 1803 and 1807 American exports had grown from $55 million to $108 million. By 1808, they had dwindled to the little that could be smuggled out of the country. In New York, as one traveler reported, "the grass had begun to grow upon the wharves." Industries associated with commerce, such as shipbuilding and sail-making, were also at a standstill, their artisans unemployed.

Fourteen months of embargo were enough even for many of the Republicans, and on March 1, 1809, three days before Jefferson's retirement, he was forced to sign an act repealing the measure. He also approved a strong substitute—a Non-Intercourse Act proscribing trade with England and France, but opening it to all other countries. If either England or France, however, would cancel its orders or decrees against American shipping, then the ban would apply only to the other.

JEFFERSON'S RETIREMENT

Jefferson, like Washington, wanted to keep America free of European entanglements; his embargo illustrates how far he would go to accomplish this end. He was even more determined to expel Europe from America, as the Louisiana Purchase, his thirst for Florida, and his desire for South America and Canada all testify. In spite of all his efforts, however, the United States became increasingly involved in Europe's affairs and Europe in ours, and by 1806 Jefferson was "panting for retirement."

As early as 1805, Jefferson had written: "George Washington set the example of voluntary retirement after eight years. I shall follow it. And a few more precedents will oppose the obstacle of habit to anyone after a while who shall endeavor to extend his term. Perhaps," he added, anticipating what actually occurred in 1951, "it may beget a disposition to establish it by an amendment of the Constitution."

By the time of the presidental election of 1808, the Republican party had already broken into factions, and Jefferson's withdrawal as a candidate, as in the case of Washington in 1796, only heightened the ambitions of the different leaders. The Republican congressional caucus reflected the disunity in the party, while leaders outside the caucus strained the party fabric further by endorsing independent candidates of their own, such as Monroe and Clinton. Jefferson remained influential enough, however, to keep the nomination in the power of the caucus and to win that body over to his favorite, James Madison. Since the embargo fiasco had helped resurrect the Federalist party, Madison faced a real fight for the presidency.

In 1807 every New England state but Connecticut had a Republican governor. By the summer of 1808, after six months of embargo, every New England governor had been turned out in favor of a Federalist. Federalist representation in the House, moreover, was to double between 1807 and 1809. For the presidential campaign of 1808, without the formality of a caucus, the revived party made a demonstration of its national, not merely New England, character by renaming its ticket of 1804— Charles C. Pinckney of South Carolina for the presidency, and Rufus King of New York as his running-mate. This ticket carried Maryland, North Carolina, and Delaware as well as all New England but Vermont. All told, Pinckney and King each garnered 47 electoral votes. Madison won with 122, while Clinton won the vice-presidency with 113.

Jefferson's successor had been established. Far from retiring from political affairs, however, the aging political philosopher held political court at his home, Monticello. For the next 17 years younger Republicans beat a much-used path to his door.

Readings

Asterisk indicates that book is available in paperback.

A good brief introduction to the problems of getting the new government under way is H. J. Ford, *Washington and His Colleagues* (1921). This book may be supplemented by J. C. Miller, *The Federalist Era* * (1960); and L. D. White, *The Federalists* (1948), and *The Jeffersonians* (1951). C. G. Bowers, *Jefferson and Hamilton* (1925), is a colorful account with a strong Antifederalist bias. Equally good reading on the Federalist side are volumes II and III of A. J. Beveridge, *The Life of John Marshall* (4 vols., 1916-1919). The biographies of the Founding Fathers cited in the *Readings* for Chapters 5 and 6 are relevant to this chapter. E. S. Maclay, ed., *The Journal of William Maclay* (1928) provides lively comment on the First Congess by an Antifederalist senator. His views may be compared with those of an arch-Federalist from Massachusetts, in Seth Ames, ed., *Works of Fisher Ames* (2 vols., Boston, 1854). Joseph Charles, *The Origins of the American Party System* * (1961), is a penetrating short account.

Outside of biographies, Hamilton's policies are sympathetically presented in Bray Hammond, *Banks and Politics in America: From the Revolution to the Civil War* (1957); and in Clinton Rossiter, *Alexander Hamilton and the Constitution* (1964). A severe indictment of Hamilton's role in relations with Britain is J. P. Boyd, *Number 7, Alexander Hamilton's Secret Attempts to Control American Foreign Policy* (1964). The classic earlier account is S. F. Bemis, *Jay's Treaty* * (1923). Bemis' *Pinckney's Treaty* * (1926) is the standard work. On other aspects of foreign policy in the Federalist period, of value are Felix Gilbert, *To the Farewell Address, Ideas of Early American Foreign Policy* (1961); Alexander DeConde, *Entangling Alliance* (1958); L. M. Sears, *George Washington and the French Revolution* (1960); and A. P. Whitaker, *The Spanish-American Frontier, 1783-1795* (1927), and *The Mississippi Question, 1795-1803* (1934). L. D. Baldwin, *Whiskey Rebels: The Story of a Frontier Uprising* (1939), is a readable account of that episode. F. S. Philbrick, *The Rise of the West, 1754-1830* (1965), covers the Federalist and Jeffersonian periods thoroughly.

On Adams' administration, authoritative and up-to-date works are M. J. Dauer, *The Adams Federalists* (1953); and S. G. Kurtz, *The Presidency of John Adams: The Collapse of Federalism, 1795-1800* * (1958). Adams was one of the most cogent thinkers of his day. A fascinating work made up of his marginal comments on books by his contemporary philosophers is Zoltán Haraszti, *John Adams and the Prophets of Progress* * (1952). A more conventional anthology is Adrienne Koch and William Peden, eds., *The Selected Writings of John and John Quincy Adams* (1946). Useful are J. C. Miller, *Crises in Freedom: The Alien and Sedition Acts* * (1951), and J. M. Smith, *Freedom's Fetters* (1956). L. W. Levy, *Legacy of Suppression: Freedom of Speech and Press in Early American History* * (1960), is especially useful for background on issues raised by the Sedition Act.

C. A. Beard, *The Economic Origins of Jeffersonian Democracy* (1915), may be supplemented by two books by N. E. Cunningham, Jr., *The Jeffersonian Republicans: The Formation of Party Organization 1789-1801* (1957), and *The Jeffersonian Republicans in Power: Party Operations 1801-1809* (1963). Two excellent one-volume editions of Jefferson's writings are Bernard Mayo, ed., *Jefferson Himself* (1942); and Adrienne Koch and William Peden, eds., *The Life and Selected Writings of Thomas Jefferson* (1944). L. J. Cappon, ed., *The Adams-Jefferson Letters* (2 vols., 1959) is invaluable.

One of the classics of American history is Henry Adams, *History of the United States During the Administrations of Jefferson and Madison* (9 vols., 1889-1891). Abridged versions are available in paperback. Edward Channing, *The Jeffersonian System* (1906), is short and useful. On "The Federalist Party in the Era of Jeffersonian Democracy," to quote the subtitle, see D. H. Fischer, *The Revolution of American Conservatism* (1965).

On the war with the judiciary, besides volume III of Beveridge's life of Marshall, see C. G. Haines, *The Role of the Supreme Court in American Government and Politics, 1789-1835* (1944); and E. S. Corwin, *John Marshall and the Constitution* (1919).

The main strands of foreign relations in Jefferson's administration are dealt with in the following works: Bradford Perkins, *First Rapprochement: England and the United States, 1795-1805* (1955); G. W. Allen, *Our Navy and the Barbary Corsairs* (1905); E. W. Lyon, *Louisiana in French Diplomacy 1759-1804* (1934); J. K. Hosmer, *History of the Louisiana Purchase* (1902); J. F. Zimmerman, *Impressment of American Seamen* (1925); and L. M. Sears, *Jefferson and the Embargo* (1927). J. E. Bakeless, *Lewis and Clark, Partners in Discovery* (1947), is good on the two explorers. The most scholarly account of Burr's western maneuvers is T. P. Abernethy, *The Burr Conspiracy* (1954).

CHAPTER EIGHT

"Our lawyers and priests," Jefferson once wrote, "suppose that the preceding generations held the earth more freely than we do; had a right to impose laws on us, unalterable by ourselves." Jefferson supposed quite the contrary. He believed that "the earth belongs to the living not to the dead," that each generation must make its own laws. When, in 1809, he turned over to his friend and protégé, James Madison, all the problems his embargo had failed to solve, he saw an exciting new generation on the threshold of power in the United States and optimistically awaited the future that lay in its hands.

The

National Focus

Benjamin Franklin, John Hancock, Washington, and Patrick Henry had died in the 1790's. Between 1803 and 1806, Sam Adams, Hamilton, and Robert Morris had followed them to the grave. Ready to take their places were men like Henry Clay, the idol of the West; John C. Calhoun, the idol of the South; and Daniel Webster, the idol of New England, all youthful enough never to have been British subjects, all eager to build a great American empire of their own. The oldest of the new group, at 42, was Andrew Jackson, North Carolina-born, who, one fine day in his early twenties, it is said, loomed on the Tennessee frontier astride a grand horse, and equipped with dueling pistols and fox hounds, all picked up during a spree in Charleston financed by a legacy from an Irish relative. "Knowing little about jurisprudence but a great deal about making his own way," Jackson promptly set up as a lawyer to seek his fortune among the influential and well-to-do.

The earlier generation of statesmen had won independence and established a nation. It was the role of the new generation to overcome, if they could, the persistent problems of sectionalism at home and contempt abroad, to infuse the people with a national spirit, and foreign nations with respect.

I. *Opportunities for Smart Young Men*

In the first decade of the nineteenth century, while Europe was bled and impoverished by war, the United States blossomed with opportunities for smart young men. The Louisiana Purchase, by doubling American territory, seemed to have insured the future indefinitely. To the east of the Purchase, tens of thousands of new settlers each year were clearing the forests and bringing new land under cultivation. By 1810, more than a million persons lived between the Appalachians and the Mississippi, most of them in a great triangle with its apex at St. Louis, a thousand miles from the Atlantic coast. Outside this triangle to the north Indiana had already become a territory and Illinois was soon to seek admission to the Union. In the South, Alabama, Mississippi, and Louisiana were on the verge of statehood.

In all of these new areas, speculators were doing a land-office business, and the litigation that grew out of conflicting claims enriched lawyers as well. Some on the frontier did settle down to produce goods for market, and by 1810 thousands of flat boats were floating down the western rivers each year, themselves to be broken up into saleable lumber at the end of the journey and added to the cargo supplied by farmers, woodsmen, and trappers. Hardy sailors sometimes poled small shipments of provisions, clothing, and tools up-river in keel boats. Where there were no navigable streams or where the current was too strong to oppose, road construction had begun. Men talked again of canals and, wonder of wonders, the steamboat, which Robert Fulton in 1807 proved could be propelled even against the current of the mighty Hudson.

In 1808, John Jacob Astor in New York organized the American Fur Company (see p. 244) to extend the fur-trading frontier overland to the Pacific, thereby showing the continental sweep of American enterprise. Yankee, Yorker, and Quaker ship captains, meanwhile, were capturing much of the world's carrying trade from the beleaguered British. Driven by the embargo to give their home ports a wide berth, many of them sailed all the seas serving Russian, Chinese, Japanese, Asia Minor, and South American traders. In South America they often turned a pretty Spanish dollar buying and selling cargo on their own account. Some of them married Spanish girls, raised families, and took active parts in the revolts against Spain, which early in the nineteenth century established the independence of the Latin-American nations, hopefully on the model of the United States (see p. 231).

Enterprising southerners, in the meantime, finding their tobacco shut out of European markets by the French wars, were taking up new lands easily adaptable to cotton-growing (see p. 247). By 1810, South Carolina and Georgia were producing enough cotton to account for almost one-fourth of all American exports and also to supply the new cotton-spinning industry that had arisen in New England. Innovations in wool production kept up with improvements in cotton. Spanish sheep of the extraordinarily fine merino strain were introduced into the United States in 1802. By 1810, some 20,000 merinos, along with millions of ordinary sheep raised in Pennsylvania, New York, and New England, were supplying raw wool to a number of new factories and to thousands of spinners and weavers working at home.

Cut off from vital supplies by the European wars and Jefferson's embargo, the United States became nearly self-sufficient in many manufactures besides cottons and woolens. By 1810, the value of such manufactures (most of them produced as yet in homes, not factories) was placed at almost $200 million annually. To help move such products, as well as the raw materials of farm, forest, sea, almost 200 turnpike companies had been chartered in New England by 1810, almost 100 in New York, and about

40 in Pennsylvania, while hundreds of miles of good free roads had been built across the face of the land.

Some critics had predicted that capital would flee the country under a "dangerous" president like Jefferson. Actually it multiplied as never before—sometimes hindered, but more often prodded, by war abroad. Rapidly rising business activity called for expanding credit. To meet the need, 58 new state banks were opened between 1800 and 1811, more than doubling the country's total. Private banks added to the sources of domestic credit, and foreign bankers, notably the English Barings, extended liberal credit to American merchants.

II. *The War of 1812*

THE FAILURE OF DIPLOMACY

James Madison was 58 when he was sworn in as fourth president of the United States on March 4, 1809. Although older by many years than the enterprising new generation, he showed his sympathy with their ideas by appearing at his inauguration dressed in a full suit of cloth of American manufacture. In his inaugural address he spoke warmly of the need to promote American industry and external as well as internal commerce. Albert Gallatin, Madison's Secretary of the Treasury and strong right arm throughout his first administration, shared the views of his chief. "I cannot be content," Gallatin wrote in 1809, "to act the part of a mere financier, to become a contriver of taxes, a dealer of loans." In his Report on Roads and Canals in 1808, and in his more famous Report on American Manufactures in 1810, Gallatin laid out an ambitious program of federal aid to American industry, independent of European raw materials, markets, or wars. This program foreshadowed Henry Clay's "American System" of later years (see p. 265). Before it could be realized, however, the nation itself had first to be preserved.

Unfortunately, James Madison was not quite the man for the crises he inherited from Jefferson. Along with other presidents in American history, Madison mistakenly believed he had only to issue an order or confer a responsibility to fulfill his obligations as chief executive or commander-in-chief. But orders often were ignored or countermanded by subordinates whose divided political loyalties inside the Republican party made them uncertain whether their main allegiance was to their country, their superior, or themselves. The lack of unity in the administration was aggravated by the sectional controversies carried over from Jefferson's time. A few New Englanders, frightened by the Louisiana Purchase and outraged by the embargo, still talked of rejoining the British Empire. Many southerners, in turn, viewed the closing of American ports to British ships by the Non-Intercourse Act (see p. 209) as a surrender of the southern export economy to New England shipping interests. These southerners might have been glad to see the Yankees withdraw. Under Madison the sectional controversies grew so acrimonious that even a foreign war failed to unite the country. This war itself probably was postponed until 1812 only because Britain was too occupied with her own internal and international problems to exploit American sectionalism.

When Madison took office in 1809, many nostalgic Englishmen still had not forgiven their American cousins for the Revolution and lived for the day when the American flag would be wiped off the seas. Their policy was to keep at a high level the pressure of impressments and captures that had forced Jefferson so to offend New England. Wiser English heads looked ahead to Britain's progress in the Industrial Revolution and realized that her future lay in manufacturing more than in the carrying trade. They were willing to tolerate commercial rivalry if it helped preserve American markets for British industrial goods and if it kept the United States and Britain at peace. Foreign Minister George Canning, though himself a leader of the anti-American die-hards, nevertheless saw the merit in the tolerant position of the other camp. Rule of the seas was his preferred policy, but the fact that Napoleon's Continental System (see p. 208) had left the United States as Britain's only sizable customer for manufactures led Canning to accept the policy of conciliation that the British industrialists demanded. At least he seemed to accept it.

Canning had come into office in 1807. In one of his first steps, taken probably for home consumption, he sent George Rose to America in 1808 to try to settle the differences with the United States. Since Rose was empowered to make no concessions and actually made some new demands, he got nowhere, as Canning probably intended. Just after Madison's inauguration in 1809, the British minister in Washington, David Erskine, who had married an American woman and who showed a fondness for American society, was instructed by Canning to try where Rose had failed. Erskine offered to withdraw the British orders-in-council (see p. 209) if, among other things, the United States would end non-intercourse with Britain while retaining it with France. The offer was sweetened in other ways, and Madison grasped it. Scores of American ships, loaded with goods, now hovered around British ports awaiting the resumption of trade, while hundreds of other American vessels set sail. Commerce boomed; but the situation proved too good to last.

Actually, Erskine had never been granted the power to rescind the orders-in-council. And in his eagerness to befriend America he had failed to insist on explicit acceptance of certain more onerous terms of his instructions. When Canning learned of the settlement, he immediately disavowed it and recalled Erskine. In Erskine's place, he sent Francis J. Jackson, an implacable anti-American who spent a year exasperating everyone he met. On Jackson's recall, no replacement was named. Madison, in the meantime, had been obliged to restore non-intercourse with Britain and to continue it with France.

Talk of war grew louder when Congress reconvened in December, 1809, and added inflammatory debate to ill-conceived legislation. One unfortunate measure, effective May 1, 1810, was the so-called "Macon's Bill Number 2," named for the chairman of the House Committee on Foreign Affairs. This act put an end to non-intercourse, but provided for its revival against France if Britain rescinded her orders-in-council, and its revival against Britain if France agreed to rescind her Berlin and Milan decrees (see p. 208). With little to lose, Napoleon instructed his foreign minister to let the Americans know that the French decrees were revoked as of November 1, 1810. To the consternation of New England, Madison took the bait and restored non-intercourse against the British, a step Congress confirmed with a new Non-Intercourse Act in March, 1811. Napoleon, as many had foreseen, failed to abide by his announced revocation, and French attacks on American commerce continued. At the same time, William Pinkney, the American minister in London, discovered that the revocation of non-intercourse with France had failed to coerce Canning to withdraw the British orders. Soon after, Pinkney returned home. There was now little chance of improvement in American-British relations, for there was no British minister in Washington and no American representative in London.

THE URGE TO WAR

Popular disgust with the stalemate in foreign affairs was recorded in the elections of 1810 and 1811, in which the voters unseated many members of the Eleventh Congress. Conspicuous among the replacements who arrived in Washington in November, 1811, were bristling young men from the southern, western, and northern frontiers. Unconcerned with foreign attacks on American ships, except as affronts to the American flag, these newcomers were determined to extend American territory at the expense of embattled Europe.

On the southern frontier, Spain still held the Floridas, which had become a haven for runaway slaves and marauding pirates and a home for hostile Indians. By 1810, however, most of the settlers on the rich lands of West Florida were Americans, who, bemoaning Spain's inability to protect them, revolted and asked to be annexed by the United States. Madison, as eager as Jefferson to acquire new territory, had connived in this uprising. He proclaimed the annexation of West Florida in October, 1810, and early in 1812 an armed American expedition set out to take weakly defended East Florida as well. Spain's threat to de-

clare war, and New England's threat to revolt if war came, obliged Madison to recall the troops. This action appeased Spain and New England, but is was deemed treachery by the expansionists of the Southwest.

North of the Floridas, on American territory, an Indian war was imminent. All along the frontier, the Indian tribes had been tricked into making grant after grant of land by treaties they ill understood. Between 1801 and 1810, one hundred ten million acres in the Ohio Valley had been taken from them. Having formally ceded this territory, the Indians nevertheless were

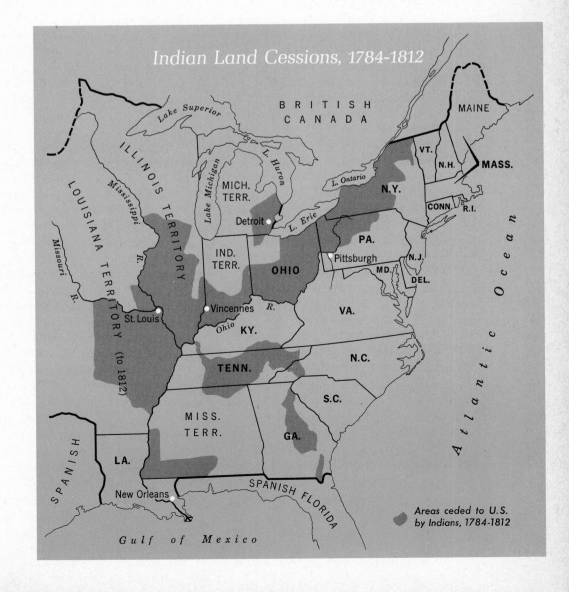

Indian Land Cessions, 1784-1812

Areas ceded to U.S. by Indians, 1784-1812

slow in moving out, and sporadic violence between red men and whites increased. By force of arms the white settlers gradually made American title to the land effective while the dislodged aborigines of the Valley—Creeks, Cherokees, Kaskaskias, Shawnees, and others—were forced ever closer to the Mississippi and on to lands of the aggressive Sioux and Chippewas, who gave them only the fiercest kind of welcome. In 1811 the great Shawnee chief, Tecumseh, decided that a stand against the frontiersmen must be made. He insisted that the land belonged to all Indians and that no individual tribe had the right to trade away a single acre; further attempts at settlement, he said, would be resisted by a united force.

In July, 1811, Tecumseh warned Governor William Henry Harrison of Indiana Territory that he intended to enlist southern tribes for a general defense. This announcement, meant to intimidate Harrison, only inspired him, once Tecumseh had left Prophetstown, the central Indian village on the Wabash, for the South, to launch a sudden attack on the leaderless tribes. On November 6, 1811, with a thousand soldiers, Harrison arrived at Tippecanoe Creek adjacent to Prophetstown. Learning of his presence, the Shawnee braves themselves attacked at dawn on November 7. Harrison's men repulsed them, though suffering heavy losses, and proceeded to burn Prophetstown to the ground. Finding the charred ruins of the village on his return, Tecumseh mobilized the survivors and swore them to eternal war against the white man. By the spring of 1812, many families of would-be settlers were fleeing for their lives to more protected areas.

Frontiersmen had long believed that the British in Canada were supplying Tecumseh with arms and egging him on against the settlers. Hence they acclaimed the victory at Tippecanoe as a triumph over the British as well as over the Indians. Tecumseh's retaliatory assaults after the battle they saw as part of a British plot, so the cry on the frontiers grew louder for the conquest of all Canada (for how else could

the British be eliminated from "Our Continent"?) and for the conquest of all Florida, lest Spain be used as a cat's-paw for Britain's re-entry.

The handful of frontiersmen who carried this cry to the halls of Congress in November, 1811, were promptly branded by the easterners as "War Hawks." Among them were Calhoun, from upland South Carolina, whose grandmother had been scalped by Cherokees, and Felix Grundy, of Tennessee, who had lost three brothers in Indian raids. Their leader was "Harry of the West," Henry Clay of Kentucky.

Taking advantage of the political rivalry among the older members of the decaying Republican party, Clay's friends quickly elected him Speaker of the House; he then used the Speaker's prerogative to name them chairmen of the major committees. Soon Clay and his backers placed before the House bills for enlisting a large army, recruiting a modest navy, and letting the world know, as Clay said, that "we could fight France too, if necessary, in a good cause—the cause of honor and independence."

Congressional opinion on these bills was sharply divided, but events played into the hands of the war party. Early in May, 1811, for example, the British became unusually active in impressment raids off New York harbor, and the American frigate, *President,* a formidable 44-gun man-of-war, was ordered to patrol these waters to protect American ships. The Britisher, *Guerrière* (38 guns), had been an especially successful raider, and when the captain of *President* thought he had spotted her off Sandy Hook, he immediately gave chase. When his prey refused to identify herself, the captain ordered her bombarded. Nine British were killed and 23 wounded. *President* suffered no casualties, for the good reason that the British ship was not *Guerrière* at all, but the little 20-gun corvette, *Little Belt,* which could offer small resistance. The American government tried to settle British claims amicably in exchange for revocation of the orders-in-council. The British refused to be pressured in this manner, and the American public was just as glad. The pounding of *Little Belt* was hailed as a great triumph in the United States and helped dissolve any lingering fears of "the mistress of the seas."

A few months after the *Little Belt* affair, disclosure of the notorious "Henry Letters" further inflamed America's warlike ardor. These letters included reports of a Canadian secret agent, John Henry, on the extent of disunion sentiment in New England at this time. British interest in this subject enraged many Americans and brought irresistible pressure on Madison to declare war.

On June 1, 1812, the President reluctantly sent a war message to the House. On the 18th he announced that both the Senate and the House had declared for war on Britain. "I verily believe that the militia of Kentucky are alone competent to place Montreal and Upper Canada at your feet," boasted Henry Clay during the congressional debates. Congress must have believed him, for when it adjourned on July 6 it had voted no new taxes and only a few new men to carry on the war it had declared.

In his war message, Madison had said nothing about Canada and Florida, territories dear to the War Hawks' hearts, and little about the allegedly British-inspired Indian troubles on the frontier. Instead, he stressed the accumulation of intolerable offenses against American citizens, American ports, American ships, and American commerce. Impressment topped his list of war issues, and he attacked most bitterly the hovering of British men-of-war around American harbors, the "pretended blockades," and the "sweeping system" of orders-in-council.

The maritime areas in the Middle States as well as in New England had voted against the war mainly because they knew that their ships would bear the brunt of the fighting and their commerce the brunt of the cost. The South, which had lost its European tobacco market because of Napoleon's Continental System, and which was losing cotton sales because the British could no longer sell their manufactured

cotton textiles across the Channel, supported the war. Except in upper New York State and part of upper Vermont, where relations with Canada were close and where trade across the border was profitable, the war had the vociferous support of the exposed frontier. Some doubted, however, that western deeds would prove as brave as western words. "When a man rises in this House," said Representative Stow of New York in January, 1812, "you may almost tell how ardent he will be, by knowing how far distant he lives from the sea."

Two days before Congress declared war, Castlereagh, Canning's successor as British foreign minister, had announced the repeal of the orders-in-council. A few days later, Monroe, now Secretary of State, instructed Jonathan Russell, the American *chargé* in Paris who was filling in at London, to arrange an armistice "if the orders-in-council are repealed, and no illegal blockades are substituted for them, and orders are given to discontinue the impressment of seamen from our vessels, and to restore those already impressed." Castlereagh's repeal and Monroe's letter crossed at sea, but neither could have prevented war. Monroe demanded too much; on learning of his armistice offer from Russell, Castlereagh exclaimed, "No administration could expect to remain in power that should consent to renounce the right of impressment, or to suspend the practice." Castlereagh, in turn, offered too little. That strictly maritime concessions would scarcely have been enough to swing the frontier to peace is indicated in a letter that Andrew Jackson had written the previous March:

We are going to fight for the reestablishment of our national character, . . . for the protection of our maritime citizens impressed on board British ships of war, . . . to vindicate our right to a free trade, and open market for the productions of our soil now perishing on our hands because the *mistress of the ocean* has forbid us to carry them to any foreign nation; in fine, to seek some indemnity for past injuries, some security against future aggression, by the conquest of all the British dominions upon the continent of North America.

Jackson's spirit had not carried over into measures required to make the grand war a success. Early in 1811, the war party in Congress had allowed the Bank of the United States to die at the expiration of its 20-year charter—an action that deprived the government of one of its main fiscal agencies just when it was needed most. Despite the urging of Secretary Gallatin, Congress put off consideration of war taxes until 1813. In the meantime, with no bank to lend assistance, only half of an authorized bond issue of $11 million could be sold. Throughout the war, new taxes were reluctantly voted and expertly evaded; new loans were optimistically authorized and niggardly subscribed.

Madison said the war was to be fought for freedom of the seas. Jackson said it was to be fought against the "mistress of the ocean." Yet not until six months after war had been declared did Congress appropriate money to enlarge the meager American navy. The army faced a similar plight. "Such is the structure of our society," wrote Henry Clay in 1812, "that I doubt whether many men can be engaged for a longer term than six months." Yet Clay and other War Hawks had voted for an addition of 25,000 men to the regular army (making a total of 35,000), all to be enlisted for five years. Kentucky, Clay's state, had panted for war more hotly than any other; yet in the first two months of the war only 400 Kentuckians enlisted. To augment the regular army, early in 1812 the President was authorized to accept 50,000 volunteers for a year's service. But scarcely 5,000 signed up in the following six months. A little later, the President was authorized to call out 100,000 state militia, but few of those who took up arms would follow their officers across the borders of their own states. At the outset of the war, the free population of the United States was about twelve times the population of Canada; yet, according to Henry Adams, two months after the declaration of war "the Canadian outnumbered the American forces at every point of danger on the frontier."

The American army was no worse than its generals deserved. "The old officers," observed the rising Winfield Scott at the outset of hostilities, "had very generally slunk into either sloth, ignorance, or habits of intemperate drinking." The newer ones, mainly political appointees, included a few good men, Scott acknowledged. But most were "coarse and ignorant"; or, if educated, were "swaggerers, dependents, decayed gentlemen, and others unfit for anything else." Admittedly it would have been difficult for anyone to uncover talent in the army as it was then constituted. But Madison magnified the difficulty by permitting "the advisory Branch of the appointing Department," as he called the Senate, to dictate to, overrule, and intimidate the executive department.

Confusion in American minds over the objectives of the war muddied strategy from the outset. Canada, it was agreed, was the only "tangible" place to engage Great Britain, but New England, the logical base for an invasion of Canada, opposed the whole war (see p. 225). The South proved to be no more enthusiastic, fearing that the acquisition of Canada "as an object of the war," would, if successful, put slaveholders at a great disadvantage in the government in the future. The West agreed with Jefferson that "the cession of Canada . . . must be a *sine qua non* at a treaty of peace." But for all its hunger for Canada, the West in turn would not tolerate the withdrawal of troops to the north from the garrisons guarding the western frontier against the Indians.

To conquer Canada, Montreal, the main port of entry for British assistance, had first to be taken and held. But checked by such antipathy at home from making a quick and concerted push on Montreal, the

220

United States, at the opening of the war, tried three timid and uncoordinated forays against Canada, scattered over almost a thousand miles of border. The first of these, in July, 1812, found General William Hull not only failing to penetrate Canada from Detroit but being forced to yield Detroit to the brilliant Canadian, General Isaac Brock, who had infiltrated his rear from Niagara. In 1814, Hull was sentenced to death by a court-martial for cowardice and neglect of duty, but he was allowed to escape the penalty because of his record in the Revolution.

The second American foray took place early in October and cost the Canadians General Brock's life. Captain John Wool

graceful. Here militia under General Henry Dearborn marched north 20 miles, decided that was far enough from home, and marched back again.

Before 1812 was over, a new American force under the vigorous direction of General William Henry Harrison stood poised to recapture Detroit. When the Canadians routed a large detachment of Harrison's troops under General James Winchester at Frenchtown on the Raisin River, January 22, 1813, Harrison postponed further action, but he was to be heard from later on.

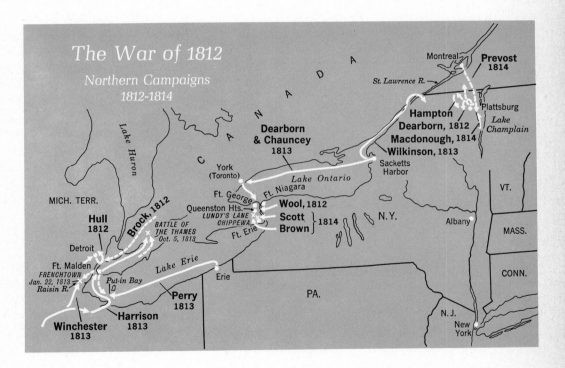

The War of 1812
Northern Campaigns
1812-1814

led an American detachment across the Niagara River and took Queenston Heights, where New York militia were to join him and push on. But New York's militiamen refused to cross their state line and stood by while Canadian reinforcements mowed down Wool's men. The third foray in November, this one directed at last against Montreal itself from Plattsburg on Lake Champlain in New York, was no less dis-

Canada clearly was not as "tangible" as had been supposed. Far from occupying it (it "will be a mere matter of marching," Jefferson had said), after six months of fighting the Americans found their own frontier pushed back to Ohio.

At sea, a more satisfactory story was unfolding. Statistically the American navy was no match for the enemy, yet in the opening months of hostilities American ships recorded startling victories over British men-of-war in single-ship engagements. The winter of 1812-1813 found most of the American navy back in harbor, where the British, intensifying their blockade of American ports south of New London, Connecticut (they left friendly Rhode Island and Massachusetts ports alone), succeeded in bottling it up for the rest of the war. But they could not discourage American privateers, who, all told, captured more than 800 British merchantmen, most of them after 1813.

WITHSTANDING
THE BRITISH REGULARS

A week after the American declaration of war, the Czar of Russia joined Britain in the struggle against Napoleon. One of his first moves was to sound out the American minister in St. Petersburg, John Quincy Adams, on the chances of peace between his new ally and her old colonies in order to free Britain for the greater struggle on the Continent. No one wanted peace more than Madison, especially with the presidential elections of 1812 coming up. As soon as he learned of the Czar's thinking, he sent Gallatin and the former Federalist Senator, James A. Bayard, to join Adams in Russia. The British, however, spurned both the Czar's approaches and the American envoys, and the war sputtered on.

In the election, De Witt Clinton of New York was nominated by the "peace party" among the Republicans. Clinton also had substantial support from Federalist maritime interests in every state north of Maryland. Supporting the maritime interests were thousands who had become discouraged with military prospects after the failures of recent months. Thousands more who detested fighting on the same side as the despot Napoleon turned against Madison. The President himself hated to run as the candidate of the "war party." With Federalist aid, Clinton carried every northern state except Pennsylvania and Vermont. Madison, however, added to the votes of those two states the solid Republican support of the South and West, and won.

Perhaps it was the "war party's" political victory which inspired more aggressive efforts in the field. The first step seemed to be to regain Detroit, and General Harrison and others agreed that control of Lake Erie was essential to success here. The task of clearing the British from the lake was given to young Captain Oliver Hazard Perry. By August, 1813, Perry's laboriously constructed lake fleet was ready, and on September 10, he caught the British lake squadron in Put-in-Bay at the western end of the water and defeated it in a bloody but decisive engagement. Since Perry's ships penned the British in, the fight was more like a land action, with both sides firing away at each other. At the end of the engagement Perry reported to Harrison, "We have met the enemy and they are ours."

Harrison followed up Perry's victory by setting out after the Canadian General Henry Proctor, who had abandoned Detroit when he lost his naval support. Proctor marched east toward Lake Ontario, where another British naval squadron was in control, but Harrison's forces caught and defeated him on the way, at the battle of Thames River, October 5. Tecumseh, who had earlier gone over to the British, was killed in this engagement and his Indian forces ceased to be a factor in the war.

Encouraged by Perry's success on Lake Erie, Captain Isaac Chauncey of the United States navy collected a few vessels on Lake Ontario and, in collaboration with General Dearborn, attacked York (present-day Toronto), the capital of Upper Canada. The town was taken by Dearborn's men, but not before a powder magazine near the town exploded, killing 300 American soldiers and giving the survivors an excuse to burn the capital's parliament houses. Since Chauncey could not establish American naval supremacy on Lake Ontario, Dearborn's hold on York remained tenuous and the United States forces soon abandoned it. Still farther east, Generals Wilkinson and Wade Hampton planned a new march on Montreal, but, characteristically,

Contemporary British version of "the taking of the city of Washington" under Major General Ross, 1814.

turned back after brief skirmishes near the Canadian border.

In April, 1814, Napoleon abdicated and Britain was eager for peace. But peace could wait until she had put the upstart Americans in their place. First, in May, 1814, the British extended their blockade to northern New England ports and strengthened it elsewhere, steps that permitted the harassment of American seaboard cities all the way to Maine, and the incitement of slave insurrections in and around southern ports. On one such adventure, emanating from Chesapeake Bay, a force of British regulars supported by a British fleet began a march on Washington. The hastily mobilized defenders, led by the incompetent General William H. Winder,

were routed at Bladensburg, leaving Washington open to the invaders. On August 24, in retaliation for the exploit at York, the British set fire to the Capitol and the White House. The failure of an assault the next month against Baltimore and Fort McHenry prompted the British to withdraw from the area on October 14.

The burning of the government buildings was of little military importance, but, as Leonard D. White writes, it marked "probably the lowest point ever attained in the prestige of the presidency." Before the burning, Secretary of War Armstrong had rejected Madison's warnings that a British attack was imminent and had taken no measures to prepare for it. When Madison took the city's defense on his own

223

shoulders, Armstrong washed his hands of the capital and rode off to Maryland. Unfortunately for Madison, his tactics were disastrous. After the debacle, the President wrote to Armstrong that "threats of personal violence had . . . been thrown out against us both." He warned the absent Secretary to stay away from the troops, and explained by saying that "I had within a

Southwest Campaigns, 1813-1815

few hours received a message from the commanding general of the Militia informing me that every officer would tear off his epaulets if Gen'l Armstrong was to have anything to do with them."

Only after further delay did Madison demand Armstrong's resignation; and only after still more procrastination did he appoint Monroe, virtually on the latter's demand, as Secretary of War.

Of greater military significance than the burning of Washington was a three-pronged attack that the British directed successively

against Niagara, Lake Champlain, and New Orleans, starting in the summer of 1814. All phases of this attack failed. At Niagara, in July, new vigorous American commanders, General Jacob Brown and his subordinate, Winfield Scott, fought the British to a standstill. A month later, 10,000 veterans of Wellington's Napoleonic campaigns under Sir George Prevost arrived at Montreal ready to march south toward Lake Champlain. Their objective might have been to detach northern New York and New England and restore them to the British empire. Whatever their purpose, they were foiled in the battle of Plattsburg Bay (see map p. 221).

Although the Americans at Plattsburg were heavily outnumbered by the British, they had two advantages: First, they were installed in fortifications erected by the new army engineers, the first experienced graduates of West Point, which had been established in 1802. Second, they were protected by Captain Thomas Macdonough's flotilla on Lake Champlain. Early in September, Prevost moved his fine army toward Plattsburg in coordination with a British flotilla on the lake. Macdonough's men and ships were battered in the ensuing battle of Plattsburg Bay; yet their victory was so complete that Prevost, rather than try a match of arms on land, turned back.

Plattsburg Bay was the last battle before the Treaty of Ghent officially ended hostilities (see p. 226). But it was not the last battle of the war. In the Southwest, Andrew Jackson had been campaigning more or less on his own against the Indians, and after routing the Creeks at the battle of Horseshoe Bend in Alabama in March, 1814 (see map), he compelled them to yield by treaty many thousands of acres of excellent land. The vigor of Jackson's actions brought him full command in the southwestern theater and the responsibility for checking the British attack in that sector—the third prong of their comprehensive assault. Aware that the British might use Pensacola in Spanish Florida as a base, Jackson invaded the area and burned the town. Then he marched to New Orleans and was ready for the British when they arrived.

The battle between General Sir Edward Pakenham's 8,000 veterans of the Napoleonic campaigns and a ragtail collection of militiamen, sailors, and pirates under Jackson, took place on January 8, 1815. The British lost more than 2,000 men in this useless encounter. American casualties numbered 21. Jackson himself went on from this triumph to become the country's most popular hero since Washington.

THE HARTFORD CONVENTION

If Prevost, before Plattsburg Bay, had hoped to detach New England from the United States and restore it to Britain, many New Englanders, men already soured by the whole tendency of Republican diplomacy, would have wished him luck. Besides Republican diplomacy, Republican expansionism, especially in the West, had also stirred the deepest misgivings in Yankee hearts. As early as January 4, 1811, during the opening stages of the debate over the admission of Louisiana as a state, the Massachusetts congressman, Josiah Quincy, told the House of Representatives that favorable action would make it "the duty of some to prepare definitely for a separation—amicably if they can, violently if they must." Once "Mr. Madison's War" began, New England decided to have as little to do with it as possible, except insofar as it feathered her nest.

The British blockade of the American coast below New London, Connecticut, at the outset of the war (see p. 222) had left the rest of the nation at the mercy of Massachusetts and Rhode Island for imports, and Yankee merchants in these states made the hated administration pay dearly for wartime goods. New England's commercial prosperity was matched by that of her manufactures. New England produced many critical commodities, but the boom was especially marked in cotton textiles. Between 1810 and 1814 the number of cotton spindles in the region increased from 80,000 to 500,000 and looms to weave cotton cloth multiplied proportionately.

Yankee industrialists, like Yankee merchants, put a high price on their products and not least on those most needed by the government in the war effort.

Their control of commerce and manufactures, in turn, gave Yankee capitalists control of the nation's money supply. For critical domestic goods as well as for those imported they demanded hard cash, thereby draining the rest of the country of its specie. Between 1811 and 1814 the banks of Massachusetts alone quadrupled their hoards of Spanish milled dollars and the other hard currency of the country. Yet of $40 million in long-term bonds floated by the federal government in this period, New Englanders subscribed less than $3 million.

New England was as niggardly with men as with money. She suffered for this after May, 1814, when the British, as we have seen, extended the coastal blockade all the way to Maine and began raiding Yankee towns as they had earlier those to the south. New England's persistent refusal to place her militiamen under federal orders left the government in Washington helpless to defend her in her new emergency. The fact that she was herself largely to blame for her distress did not make her any more tolerant of the administration. Quite the contrary. The new pressures of the war on New England only made certain of her more extreme spokesmen the more insistent upon abandoning the Union altogether for British protection. Ironically enough, the widespread expectation that British success in New Orleans might then bring about the final separation of the West from the rest of the country only strengthened the resolve of many Yankees to flee the dissolving Union.

New England's intransigence came to a head in the dark days of October, 1814, when the Massachusetts legislature voted to call upon her sister states to send delegates to a convention to meet at Hartford, Connecticut, in December. Having gone this far with the zealots, the legislature issued a moderate statement of purposes: to consider their "public grievances and concerns," to strengthen their "defence against the enemy," and "to take measures, if they shall think proper, for producing a convention of delegates from all the United States, in order to revise the Constitution thereof." The legislature also placed at the head of the Massachusetts delegation the moderate George Cabot, who came out of retirement, as he said, "to keep the young hot-heads from getting into mischief."

When the convention did assemble in secret session on December 15, it was found that only Massachusetts, Rhode Island and Connecticut had sent state delegations. These were accompanied by representatives from a few counties in Vermont and New Hampshire. The moderates, moreover, took command from the start and smothered the secessionist tendency.

At the conclusion of the Convention in January, 1815, a "Report" was issued vigorously condemning the administrations of Jefferson and Madison in state-rights terms reminiscent of their own Virginia and Kentucky Resolutions of 1798. The Report also proposed the adoption of amendments to the Constitution for protecting New England, within the Union, from the rising majority in other sections. One amendment would have eliminated the "three-fifths" clause of the Constitution (see p. 175), thereby depriving the South of that part of its representation based on slaves. Another would have limited the presidency to one term and prohibited the election of successive presidents from the same state, i.e., Virginia. A series of additional amendments would have required a two-thirds majority in each house for the admission of new states, the "interdiction of commercial intercourse" with foreign nations, and declarations of war.

The Convention named a committee of three, headed by Harrison Gray Otis, a moderate of Massachusetts, to carry its Report to Washington and to present it to Congress. Promising to reconvene for more drastic action if Congress rejected its demands, the Convention closed just when the war itself was coming to an end.

A few days before the Hartford emissaries reached Washington early in February, the news of Jackson's victory at New Orleans and of the signing of the treaty of peace at Ghent (see below) had arrived in the capital. Talk of sectional or state rights, let alone of secession, was out of the question at the moment of national celebration. The Hartford men stole away from the scenes of triumph, and New England leaders showed the good sense thereafter to forego the promised new meeting.

III. *"Our Continent" Diplomacy*

THE TREATY OF GHENT

The British, having dealt Napoleon his final blow, as they thought, in April, 1814, launched their military offensive in America that summer (see p. 224), partly to gain a better position from which to dictate terms to the United States once they had settled accounts with her. When the peace commissioners of the two nations met formally for the first time in the Belgian town of Ghent in August, 1814, the British were confidently awaiting reports of new victories in America and they confronted Madison's negotiators with the most exacting demands. Besides Gallatin, Bayard, and John Quincy Adams, who had been in Europe for more than a year (see p. 222), the American group included Henry Clay and his unstable satellite, Jonathan Russell. Although the British got nowhere in the end, their terms were well calculated to set the Americans at one another, especially Clay the westerner and Adams the Yankee whose temperamental differences only sharpened their sectional ones.

The British "team" told the Americans at the start that they proposed to move the boundaries of Canada southward to give that province access to the Mississippi. They would also retain those parts of Maine that were still held by British troops. To keep American fur-traders and settlers out of the Northwest, moreover, the British suggested that an Indian buffer state be established in the fur-trapping region. At the same time, the British negotiators were to concede nothing on impressment or any other maritime issue, including the right of New Englanders—granted in 1783 but withdrawn at the outbreak of the War of 1812—to fish in Newfoundland and Labrador waters and to dry their catch on nearby uninhabited shores.

Britain's extravagant claims to the American West angered Clay, but not nearly so much as Adams' willingness to concede them if necessary in order to recover New England's fishing privileges. These privileges Clay, in turn, was ready to trade away for territorial demands of his own, consistent with the War Hawks' grand war aims. Although Gallatin succeeded in keeping the negotiations from foundering on the Americans' fierce antagonism toward one another, neither he nor his colleagues could force the British to back down on anything.

The British in London were also at odds among themselves, especially on the issue of continuing the war if need be to gain their territorial goals. But the Duke of Wellington impatiently warned them that the cost of a more conclusive victory in America would be greater than the people would bear. News of the British reversals at Niagara and Plattsburg Bay seemed to confirm his opinion, and the British expansionists finally gave ground. Britain at this time had begun to fall out with her recent allies at the Congress of Vienna where Napoleon's fate and that of his erstwhile empire were being decided. Her difficulties here made it all the more urgent for her to make peace if she could with the United States and perhaps eventually to seek her support in a new balance of power.

The British retreat at Ghent reminded the American negotiators that their own principal purpose was simply to make peace.

On Christmas Eve, 1814, the two powers at last agreed to the treaty which the Senate promptly ratified when it reached that body the following February. This treaty left most issues precisely where they had been at the war's start, but it also provided for commissions to meet later to settle questions of boundaries, fisheries, and the terms of commercial intercourse.

John Quincy Adams characterized the Treaty of Ghent as "an unlimited armistice [rather] than a peace, . . . hardly less difficult to preserve than . . . to obtain." Congress agreed, and though devoid of funds, voted in March, 1815, to set up a standing army of 10,000 men, to enlarge appropriations for West Point, and to spend $8 million for new warships.

Adams felt constrained to add to his earlier statement on the Treaty: "We have abandoned no essential right, and if we have left everything open for future controversy, we have at least secured our Country the power at her option to extinguish the war." In later months, Adams, Clay, and Gallatin were all to enlarge upon the salutary gains in national spirit earned by the successful confrontation of the greatest power in the world. In January, 1816, for example, Clay challenged the House of Representatives:

Let any man look at the degraded condition of this country before the war—the scorn of the universe, the contempt of ourselves—and tell me, if we have gained nothing by the war. What is our present situation? Respectability and character abroad; security and confidence at home; . . . our Constitution placed on a solid basis, never to be shaken. . . . Is there a man who could not desire participation in the national glory acquired by the war?

Like Adams, Clay spoke plainly of the uses to which this new spirit must be put. In the same speech in the House, he said:

That man must be blind to the indications of the future, who can not see that we are destined to have war after war with Great Britain, until, if one of the two nations be not crushed, all grounds of collision shall have ceased between us.

New wars, as it turned out, were evaded, but many "grounds of collision" kept the threat of renewed hostilities alive.

COLLISION AND CONCILIATION IN ANGLO-AMERICAN RELATIONS

About the events at sea leading to the war of 1812, Clay had observed at the time: "The real cause of British aggression was not to distress an enemy, but to destroy a rival." When the war ended, Americans rushed to replenish their supplies of European—mainly British—finery and other goods. Imports soared to record levels, and British manufacturers deliberately dumped goods in American markets at bargain prices. "It was well worth while," Henry Brougham told Parliament in defending this policy, "to incur a loss on the first exportation in order, by the glut, to stifle in the cradle those rising manufactures in the United States which the war has forced into existence, contrary to the natural course of things." As petitions rolled into Congress demanding that such British aggression be checked, Clay led the fight for the first avowedly protective tariff in American history, which Congress passed and Madison signed in April, 1816.

This tariff had the solid support of the country; even 16 congressmen from the South, which had few factories of its own and which preferred to look abroad for manufactured goods, voted for the measure, although 35 southern congressmen opposed it. When the act failed to protect the new American manufactures, Clay said it was not because of the defects of the measure, which were many, nor because of smuggling, "which has something bold, daring, and enterprising in it," but because of Britain's "mean, barefaced, cheating, by fraudulent invoices and false denominations."

While the British thus forced themselves into American markets, they also kept Americans out of theirs. In July, 1815, for example, a commercial treaty was at long last worked out between the two nations removing discriminations against the commerce of either party in the ports of the other. The stone in the shoe, however, was Britain's insistence that the precious West Indian trade be kept closed to Yankee ships. And closed it remained until Jackson forced it open in October, 1830 (see p. 277).

The "armistice" of Ghent, meanwhile, soon spawned those "future controversies" that Adams had foretold. Article I of the treaty, for example, required that "any slaves or other private property . . . taken by either party from the other during the war, . . . shall be restored without delay." Americans claimed that as many as 3,600 slaves taken by the British in raids in the Chesapeake region and around New Orleans were on ships of the Royal Navy at the time of the ratification of the Treaty. These, they said, must be paid for. The British demurred; they said the Treaty did not apply to slaves already aboard their ships. Eventually the Czar of Russia was asked to arbitrate. In 1826 he decided in favor of the Americans, and the British paid $1,200,000 to settle the claims.

The silence of the Treaty on impressment was certain to lead to new incidents, especially since the British continued after the war to search American vessels for British deserters on the Great Lakes themselves. On this issue, at last, controversy led to conciliation. When Madison learned that the British were building new frigates in Canada for lake service, he proposed to Foreign Secretary Lord Castlereagh that the building be abandoned and that both nations agree to keep naval ships off these waters. Castlereagh, eager as the President to avoid a costly arms race, welcomed Madison's suggestion. In April, 1817, Charles Bagot, the British representative in Washington, and Richard Rush, Madison's acting Secretary of State, worked out their famous agreement under the terms of which neither country would maintain more than four small armed vessels on the Great Lakes. Except for certain technical changes, the Rush-Bagot settlement was still in force 150 years later.

The successful demilitarization of the

Great Lakes was a good omen for the settlement of the other boundary issues left to commissions by the Treaty. By 1818 four separate commissions had worked out the permanent boundary between the United States and Canada as far west as the "Great Stony [Rocky] Mountains." The peaceful settlement of the line this far was exceedingly gratifying to those concerned with America's "continental destiny." Knowledge of geography beyond the mountains was still vague, and Britain and the United States agreed to occupy the "Oregon Country" jointly. When settlement was extended to this region in the 1840's, America's "continental destiny" had become an obsession with many, and joint occupation became intolerable enough to inspire new talk of war (see Chapter 12). The Maine boundary also remained an irritant for decades (see p. 316); while the issue of the fisheries continued to aggravate all other Canadian-American disputes until 1910.

WEAKENING THE GRASP
OF THE SPANISH AND THE INDIANS

The apparent improvement in Anglo-American relations arising from the peaceful negotiations over the Canadian boundary was endangered by events on the Spanish and Indian frontiers even before these negotiations were concluded. Trouble first occurred in the "badlands" situated between American West Florida and Spanish East Florida, the haunt of hostile Seminoles, discontented Creeks and runaway slaves.

When violence in this wild region seemed to endanger settlers moving into Georgia after the war, the state asked the federal government to wipe out the disturbing elements. Early in 1817, General Jackson got the nod, or so he believed, to perform

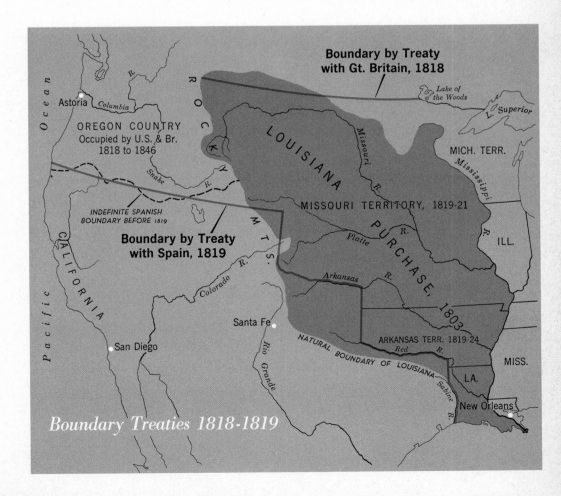

Boundary Treaties 1818-1819

this service; and in his usual manner he performed it thoroughly, burning Indian villages and hanging Indian chiefs. Jackson also arrested, courtmartialed and executed two Britishers, an old Scottish trader, Alexander Arbuthnot, and a young adventurer, Robert Ambrister, who, he believed, had stirred up Indian discontent. He then marched on the Spanish in Pensacola where the Seminoles had found a haven, ejected the governor, installed his own garrisons, and claimed the territory for the United States, as he had promised he would "in sixty days."

Many Britishers demanded war over the execution of Ambrister and Arbuthnot,

Acquisition of Florida
1810-1819

to no purpose, while Spaniards, outraged over the invasion of their territory, made blustering gestures of their own. Congress, meanwhile, where Jackson had powerful enemies, stormed over the uncontrollable general's arbitrary aggressions. The envious Clay and the self-righteous Secretary of War, Calhoun, both of whom saw in Jackson a threat to their presidential ambitions, urged that apologies be made to Britain and Spain. But Secretary of State John Quincy Adams held that Spain had got what she deserved for failing to keep order on American borders. Far from apologizing, Adams demanded that Spain pay the costs of Jackson's excursion. He also issued a virtual ultimatum to the Spanish minister in Washington, Luis de Onís, demanding that his country govern East Florida with a stronger hand or cede it to the United States.

The Spanish government, harassed by unrest at home and rebellion in Latin America (see p. 231), recognized the handwriting on the wall. Spain could not strengthen her hold in Florida or anywhere else in America; before the United States simply took what she wanted, Spain would negotiate. In the Adams-Onís Treaty of February, 1819, she surrendered her remaining claims to West Florida, and ceded East Florida. In exchange, the United States agreed to assume, up to $5 million, the claims of American merchants who had lost ships and cargoes to Spain during the Napoleonic wars.

The Adams-Onís Treaty went beyond the Floridas to establish the boundary between the United States and Mexico all the way to the Pacific (see map, p. 229). Adams was disappointed in not getting Texas in the bargain; but the American interest here was only just awakening, and the Secretary of State, finding little support, did not press the issue. Revolution in Spain itself delayed approval of the treaty there until 1820; the United States Senate approved in February, 1821.

For the time being, at least, the land-hunger of the Republicans was satisfied by the agreements with Britain and Spain on the northern and southern boundaries and by the acquisition of Florida from Spain. But before the land within these generous borders could be settled, the Indians who still occupied it would have to be either subjugated or expelled. Tecumseh's death (p. 222) had deprived the northern tribes of their leader, and Britain's retirement from the Great Lakes area had deprived them of their only remaining friend. The Indians' plight encouraged the United States to embark on an ambitious building program in this region. By 1822, older outposts like Fort Wayne and Fort Harrison in Indiana had been restored, and a string of new forts had been built along the Mississippi in Illinois and Wisconsin. If this show of American force further cowed the Indians, in an effort to keep them from seeking any new allegiance with Canada, the government added a string of trading centers at which the braves could buy goods below cost. This stick and carrot policy gradually made the Indians in the Northwest Territory more tractable, and they at last agreed, in a series of new treaties, to move beyond the Mississippi.

In the Southwest, the redmen had been overawed by Jackson's wartime victories and his ruthless subsequent assaults. Now the government offered them (in what was regarded as a humane move) the choice of taking up agriculture on the lands where they lived, or of moving west. To the chagrin of the whites, most of the Indians preferred farming to abandoning their homes, and not until Jackson became president in 1829 were the "Civilized Tribes" of the Southwest forcibly ejected from their lands (see p. 272).

THE MONROE DOCTRINE

In 1800, although she had yielded her exclusive claim to the Oregon country to Britain and Russia, and her vast territory of Louisiana to France, Spain still owned an immense New World empire ranging through nearly 100 degrees of latitude from Upper California to Cape Horn. Portugal, in turn, owned in Brazil a land that would soon encompass half of South America. Twenty-five years later, Spain's New World empire had been reduced to Cuba and Puerto Rico; Portugal's to nothing.

The immediate cause of this shattering collapse was Napoleon's successful invasion of Portugal in 1807 and of Spain in 1808. The Portuguese king and his family fled to Brazil and ruled there until called home in 1821, when the king's son was left behind to continue the monarchy in their New World land. Independence under the Portuguese heir was established in Brazil by 1823. The Spanish Hapsburgs suffered a less happy fate after Napoleon had placed his brother, Joseph, on their throne in 1808. The Spanish empire was the personal possession of the Hapsburgs, and when the emperor fell, the colonies refused allegiance to the usurper. Revolts against the new administration began in Spanish America

about 1810 and 1811, and the independence of the last of the new separate states was completed in 1824, when the Spanish viceroy of Peru capitulated.

The earliest uprisings in Spanish America had gained the blessing of President Madison who, like Jefferson and others, ached for the establishment of the American "system," preferably under United States control, throughout the western hemisphere. After Napoleon's downfall in 1814 and the restoration of the Hapsburgs, Spain made a serious effort to regain her New World lands. But she was successfully defied by such Latin-American patriots as José de San Martín, the founder of Argentina; Simón Bolívar, the founder of Venezuela; and Bernardo O'Higgins, the dictator of Chile.

When these new countries first sought formal recognition, the United States was negotiating for the purchase of Florida, and the new Monroe administration (see p. 233) was wary about affronting Spain. Clay, in Congress, took a bolder stand. He demanded as a point of honor that the Republic embrace the new rebels against hateful monarchy. And more than honor was involved. Britain, from the first, had lent money to the Latin-American revolutionaries and was using their friendly disposition toward her to get in on the ground floor for trade and investment. It was high time, Clay thought, for the United States to combat the advantages already gained by the most hateful monarchy of all. Congress thought otherwise, however, and adopted a neutrality act in 1818. During the next few years, with the Florida treaty concluded and the Spanish-American revolutions farther advanced along the path of seemingly stable government, the United States did extend diplomatic recognition to some of the new nations.

The restoration of the Bourbons in Spain in 1814, besides heightening the revolutionary spirit in Spanish America, soon led to repression and revolution at home. By 1822 the "Holy Alliance," set up by the Congress of Vienna especially to combat the republican spirit in Europe, was ready to suppress the Spanish revolt. When, in 1823, France, the instrument of the Holy Alliance, did in fact invade Spain, Britain and the United States both believed that the invasion might easily reach across the Atlantic to suppress the revolutions in Spanish lands here. That spring, Canning, who had supplanted Castlereagh as British Foreign Secretary after the latter's suicide in 1822, "unofficially and confidentially" suggested to Richard Rush, now American minister in London, that their two countries declare to the world, for the benefit of France, that "we conceive the recovery of the [American] colonies by Spain to be hopeless." Canning innocently suggested further that they state that "we could not see any portion of them transferred to any other Power with indifference."

Canning's proposal was forwarded to Washington, where it arrived in October, 1823, and immediately became the subject of debate in the Cabinet and of profound consideration by the retired Republican patriarchs, Jefferson and Madison. Jefferson, acknowledging that "Great Britain is the nation which can do us the most harm of any one," advised that "with her on our side we need not fear the whole world." He recommended accepting Canning's proposal. Madison concurred—and went even further. He proposed that the joint statement be extended to oppose French intervention in Spain and to support the current revolt of the Greeks against Turkey, a revolt that had won American sympathy.

Secretary of State John Quincy Adams was not so easily lulled. He feared that Canning was trying to lure the United States into a statement that would seem to be a pledge against future American acquisition of any territory still held by Spain—particularly Cuba. He urged that the United States, having freed herself from Britain in 1776 and made good her independent stature in 1815, should act in the Western Hemisphere alone. President Monroe yielded to Adams'

arguments, and in his annual address to Congress on December 2, 1823, he used the words that have since been described as his "doctrine":

The political system of the allied powers [of Europe] is essentially different . . . from that of America. . . . We owe it, therefore, to candor and to the amicable relations existing between the United States and those powers to declare that we should consider any attempt on their part to extend their system to any portion of this hemisphere as dangerous to our peace and safety. . . . With the governments who have declared their independence and maintained it, and whose independence we have . . . acknowledged, we could not view any interposition . . . by any European power in any other light than as the manifestation of an unfriendly disposition toward the United States.

Latin America was not the only area of the Western Hemisphere in which European aggression worried Monroe's government. The Russians had been in Alaska for decades. In 1821, the ambitious Alexander I issued a decree declaring that "the pursuits of commerce, whaling, and fishery, and of all other industry on all islands, posts, and gulfs, including the whole of the northwest coast of America, beginning from Behring Straits to the 51° of northern latitude . . . is exclusively granted to Russian subjects." Nothing could have aroused Secretary Adams more; and he immediately advised the American minister in Russia that "the United States can admit no part of these claims."

To deter the Russians, Monroe added "as a principle," in his message to Congress, that the American continents ". . . are henceforth not to be considered as subjects for future colonization by any European powers." The following April the American minister in Russia was able to advise his government that the Czar had agreed on 54°40' as his southern boundary in North America.

Once Monroe had made his remarks (they were not known as the "Monroe Doctrine" until many years later), interested Latin Americans queried Secretary Adams on how the United States would implement the new policy in case of real need. For all his chauvinism, Adams had to admit that his government would fall back upon the British Navy, still mistress of the seas. Yet, if Monroe's message did little to buttress Latin America's security, it served to re-

mind European reactionaries that the time had come to recognize the United States as a new force in world politics.

IV. *The Test of National Unity*

THE ELECTION
OF MONROE

James Monroe had been elected President of the United States in 1816 after gaining the nomination in the Republican caucus. The Randolph state-rights Republicans in the caucus had pressed the candidacy of William H. Crawford of Georgia, but Crawford himself did not oppose Monroe's nomination, and with Madison's support, Monroe became the Republican standard-bearer. His Federalist opponent was Rufus King of New York whose selection was dictated by the desire of those New Englanders who still dominated the Federalist party to make its appeal less sectional in character than it was. Monroe found the election easier to win than the nomination. He received 183 electoral votes to 34 for King, the last Federalist candidate in history, who carried only Massachusetts, Connecticut, and Delaware.

Born in 1758, Monroe had early in life become an admirer and follower of Jefferson. Later on he fancied himself a worthy competitor of Madison's. Lacking both the imagination of the "Sage of Monticello" and the intellectual energy of the scholar of "Montpelier," he was slower than either in divesting himself of his narrow localism. Yet, by refusing to join the die-hard state-rights men he kept himself available for regular Republican preferment. Monroe twice served as Governor of Virginia; on the national scene his major activity was in the field of diplomacy, which he capped by becoming Madison's Secretary of State in 1811. In 1814 he also served as Secretary of War, and his vigorous performance in this position brought him the popular ac-

claim that helped raise him to the office of Commander-in-Chief.

Monroe had suffered many defeats during his long political career, some of them humiliating. Yet these setbacks failed to dampen his ambition or lower his estimate of his own abilities. Unlike many men jealous of power, he felt strong enough to surround himself with able associates. Indeed, his Cabinet was probably the strongest since that of Washington's first administration. Monroe's most inspired stroke was the naming of the New Englander, John Quincy Adams, as Secretary of State—a selection, as we have seen (pp. 226, 230), that put the conduct of foreign affairs in the hands of an able diplomat and appeased Yankee feelings.

Shortly before his inauguration in March, 1817, Monroe had been invited to visit New England by the editor of the *North American Review,* a journal that had been so determinedly Federalist during the war that it was often referred to as the "North Unamerican," but which was now ready to bury the hatchet. Monroe accepted the invitation and made a triumphal journey through the northeastern states. His visit was topped by a cordial reception in Boston, where, soon after, the *Columbian Sentinel* published the article entitled "Era of Good Feelings," in which it noted with pleasure "all the circumstances . . . during the late Presidential Jubilee." By 1817, the Republicans had indeed shown so much concern for manufactures and the tariff, for an army and a navy, even for the chartering of a national bank (see p. 234), that the old issues seemed no longer to stand in the way of sectional reconciliation. Virginia and Massachusetts appeared to have made peace at last; and indeed Monroe was re-elected in 1820 with but one electoral vote (from New Hampshire) cast against him.

THE BOOM, THE BANK, AND THE BUST

The apparent conversion of the Republican agrarians to policies favorable to American commercial, industrial, and financial growth had been effected by the War of 1812. In 1813 Jefferson himself acknowledged that "manufactures are as necessary to our independence as to our comforts." To further the efforts of the bright young men who were seeking to promote manufactures and related activities, Jefferson favored subsidies, bounties, and patent laws as well as protective tariffs. Others, of course, took the same bent, with the same end in view. Their efforts seemed successful for a time; but once the War of 1812 ended, most of the "war babies" among American factories succumbed to British competition.

Britain's own postwar boom, however, soon sparked a non-industrial boom in the United States. The spurt in British textile manufacturing, for example, reflected in her massive exports to the United States, brought with it an enormous demand for southern cotton to feed her tireless machines. The end of the war also reopened European markets for southern tobacco. Poor European harvests in 1816 and 1817 added to the demand for American grain. These agricultural exports helped Americans pay for their record postwar imports of manufactures.

The boom in agriculture soon brought a boom in land speculation, especially in the West and Southwest, where population soared. By 1820, Ohio had become more populous than Massachusetts; and the entire West, with about 2,200,000 settlers, had more people than New England. Land, naturally, was in great demand, and helping speculators sell it and settlers buy it were the 300 or more state and "private" banks that had been established after the First Bank of the United States went out of existence in 1811. By 1817, these new banks

had issued $100 million in paper money, much of it unnegotiable even in neighboring communities.

By 1817, the Second Bank of the United States entered the picture. Back in 1814, financiers who had lent large sums to the government for wartime needs had begun promoting a new national bank to help mobilize the country's financial resources. In 1815, Congress adopted a measure conforming to their plan but Madison vetoed it. Once the war was over and imports began pouring in, more and more specie was drained from the country to supplement the agricultural exports used to pay for them. Much of the hard money that remained soon became tied up in land speculation, and by 1816 the government found itself hard pressed to meet its daily needs. Early in 1816, therefore, Secretary of the Treasury Alexander Dallas wrote a new bank bill tailored to the President's requirements. In April, this bill was passed over the opposition of New England, whose own banking system was the strongest in the land, and approved by Madison.

Like the first national bank, the Second Bank of the United States was chartered for 20 years as the sole depository for government funds. Its capital was placed at $35 million, three and a half times that of the earlier bank. Of this sum, the government was to subscribe one-fifth, or $7 million. Of the remainder, $7 million was to be subscribed in specie and $21 million in the form of securities of the United States. Five of the Bank's 25 directors were to be appointed by the president of the United States; the rest by American stockholders. Foreign stockholders, who became numerous, were to have no voice in the Bank's affairs. The Second Bank had the right to establish branches in different parts of the country. Foreseeing competition, however, influential local bankers had persuaded some states to write into their constitutions provisions against "foreign banks" doing business within their borders.

Ill-managed from the first, the new Bank of the United States proceeded to justify local fears by outdoing even the state banks in the lavishness of its loans. These were extended in the form of notes that were more acceptable than the notes issued by the local banks and thus tended to drive notes of local issue out of circulation. In retaliation, the injured bankers induced their state legislatures to try to tax out of existence both the branches and the notes of "the monster." In the summer of 1818, the Bank of the United States was at last ready with deflationary measures to control the boom. But these measures only made it as unpopular with the people as it remained with the local bankers. The sudden contraction of credit kept many debtors from making the payments due on their loans, and before 1819 ended, the boom collapsed.

Actually, the economic collapse was worldwide. The revival of European agriculture after the Napoleonic wars and the weakening of the postwar textile boom combined to create a glut both of wheat and cotton in world markets. But the depression was most severe in the United States and was most devastating in the West.

The crisis prompted a number of states to abolish the useless and degrading practice of punishing debtors with imprisonment and to pass liberal bankruptcy laws and laws easing the settlement of contracts. Congress also came to the aid of the West with a new land act in 1820, which permitted a settler to buy an 80-acre homestead for $100 in cash. The next year Congress added a relief act to assist those people whom earlier credit provisions had got into trouble.

THE NATIONALISM
OF JOHN MARSHALL

Against this background of local self-assertion, business depression, and heightened conflict between debtors and creditors, John Marshall issued a series of historic Supreme Court decisions. We have already observed how, following his appointment in 1801, he had laid the basis in *Marbury* v. *Madison* (1803) for the Court's power to declare acts of Congress unconstitutional (see p. 202), and how, in *Fletcher* v. *Peck* (1810), he had upheld the

obligation of contracts against unilateral state interference (see p. 205).

In 1819 and succeeding years, Marshall had welcome opportunities to enlarge on his earlier opinions. Of sweeping importance was his decision in 1819 in *Dartmouth College* v. *Woodward,* which raised the question of whether a charter granted to the College in 1769 by George III and later acknowledged by the New Hampshire legislature could subsequently be changed by the legislature alone. Marshall decided that the charter was a contract and that certain action taken by the legislature without consulting the College had been taken unconstitutionally. The College was gratified by its victory, but far more important was the security Marshall's decision gave to business corporations; for it now appeared that their charters, defined as contracts, were substantially unchangeable, except with the consent of both parties.

A second decision in 1819, in *Sturges* v. *Crowninshield,* dealt with a New York State bankruptcy law. Marshall found that even though Congress was empowered to pass bankruptcy laws, the states could also enact them if Congress failed to exercise its powers. But insofar as the New York law sought to relieve a debtor of the obligation to pay his debt, Marshall found it in violation of the clause of the Constitution forbidding legislation that would impair contractual obligations. Marshall stuck to his guns eight years later in the case of *Ogden* v. *Saunders* (1827); but for the first and only time on the contract issue he failed to carry the Court with him. By a 4 to 3 vote, the Court upheld a New York bankruptcy law which relieved debtors of the obligation to pay up fully on debts contracted after the passage of the law, when its terms were known to debtors and creditors alike.

In confirming the supremacy of the federal government and the Supreme Court over state *legislation* on constitutional issues, Marshall's regime was a spectacular

John Marshall (1755-1835).

success. During his 34 years as Chief Justice, the Court acted no less than 13 times to set aside state laws as contrary to the Constitution. In *Martin* v. *Hunter's Lessee* (1816), the Court, speaking through Justice Joseph Story, asserted its supremacy over state *courts* as well in interpreting the Constitution. Five years later, in *Cohens* v. *Virginia* (1821), Marshall went out of his way to state this principle in the broadest possible terms.

Two other decisions in 1819 and 1824 clarified and broadened the powers of Congress over matters of decisive economic importance. In *McCulloch* v. *Maryland* (1819), the constitutionality of the national bank was questioned; this case grew out of an attempt by the state of Maryland to tax the Baltimore branch of the Bank of the United States out of existence. In broad language, Marshall found that the act by which the Bank had been created was constitutional: "Let the end be legitimate, let it be within the scope of the Constitution,

and all means which are appropriate, which are plainly adapted to that end, which are not prohibited, but consist with the letter and spirit of the Constitution, are constitutional." This, one of the most famous sentences in American constitutional law, underpinned the broad interpretation of implied powers of Congress, for which Hamilton, among the Founding Fathers, had worked the hardest. As for the Maryland law taxing the Bank, Marshall found it unconstitutional. "The power to tax," he said, "involves the power to destroy." If states were permitted to nullify acts of Congress by attacking its agencies, they could "defeat and render useless the power to create." Hence states do not have the power to "retard, impede, burden, or in any manner control" the operation of constitutional laws passed by Congress to execute powers granted to the federal government.

Finally, in the case of *Gibbons* v. *Ogden* (1824), Marshall spoke out on the power of Congress to regulate commerce. New York had granted Robert Fulton and Robert R. Livingston a monopoly of steam navigation in state waters, and Aaron Ogden had bought from them the right to operate a ferry between New York and New Jersey. When Thomas Gibbons set up a competing ferry under a federal coasting license, Ogden tried to invoke the state-sanctioned monopoly to restrain him from running it. The original grant by New York encroached upon the exclusive right of Congress to regulate interstate commerce, but Marshall did not rest content simply with throwing out the New York monopoly. He went on to construe the term "commerce" so broadly as to include in it navigation within a state. And he excluded the states from acting on "commerce" when their acts came "into collision with an act of Congress."

It is frequently stated that Marshall, while the Republicans dominated the legislature and the executive, handed down Federalist law from the fortress he held for 34 years in the Supreme Court. But it is closer to the truth to say that, once his war with Jefferson had ended (see p. 202), Marshall gave all his energies to extending national power, just as Jefferson gave his to extending the national domain. Both were expansionists; the work of one complemented that of the other. Together they gave Americans of the oncoming Jacksonian era the limitless space and legal spaciousness within which to seek their destinies unencumbered by local monopolists.

THE MISSOURI COMPROMISE

The expansiveness of the postwar era was to be checked by the reopening of the slavery issue. Many Americans had feared such a happening for generations; yet as they had hidden the subject in the Constitution, so they had hidden it in their consciousness. When it was brought into the open once more in the controversy over Missouri in 1820, Jefferson himself wrote that, "like a fire bell in the night," the "momentous question . . . awakened and filled me with terror." And well it might.

Before the War of 1812, most western settlers had been southerners who moved through the mountain passes of Virginia to Kentucky and Tennessee and beyond. Often they carried slaves along with them. After the war, large numbers of Yankees also went west and "made" farms with their own hands. Many of them hated slavery with religious zeal. The planners of Jefferson's generation had forbidden slavery in the Northwest Territory. And so it was that the first momentous clash over the extension of the "peculiar institution" took place just beyond, in the so-called Upper Louisiana Territory, whose settlers in 1818 applied for admission as a state under the name of Missouri.

The "enabling act" to grant Missouri statehood raised no problems in Congress until Representative James Tallmadge of New York, on February 13, 1819, shocked the South by offering an amendment to prohibit the introduction of any additional slaves into the new state. He proposed, further, that all children born of slaves in that region be freed when they reached the age of 25. The Tallmadge Amendment passed the House promptly by a narrow margin, reflecting the predominance of northern strength in that chamber, which itself reflected the greater population of the free states. The story in the Senate was different. Even though the free states outnumbered the slave states 11 to 10 at the time, a number of northern senators who had been born and brought up in the South voted with the large minority of southern senators and helped defeat the Tallmadge Amendment, 22 to 16.

The deadlock between House and Senate carried over to the next session, which got under way in December, 1819. By then the situation had changed significantly. For one thing, the country had debated and divided on the issue. In October, 1819, Madison received a letter from a fellow-Virginian which expressed the rising tension: "Union must snap short at last," wrote this correspondent, "where Liberty ends, and Slavery begins. The Missouri Question is bringing on the Crisis." A second change was Alabama's application for statehood. There was no question about admitting Alabama as a slave state, and she was accepted as such on December 14, 1819. Alabama became the twenty-second state and established the balance between slave and free states at 11 each. Missouri, as a slave state, would thereby give the South a virtual veto in the Senate of all legislation enacted by the preponderantly northern House.

The northern majority in the House insisted on keeping Missouri closed to slavery. When the northeastern part of Massachusetts applied for admission to the Union as the independent state of Maine, however, many members of Congress, led by Henry Clay, grasped the chance to break the deadlock. Many in Maine did not relish their role. In a letter which, according to the historian Edward Channing, expressed a sentiment that was widespread in the North, one Maine inhabitant objected to his state being "a mere *pack-horse* to transport the odious, anti-republican principle of slavery into the new State of Missouri,

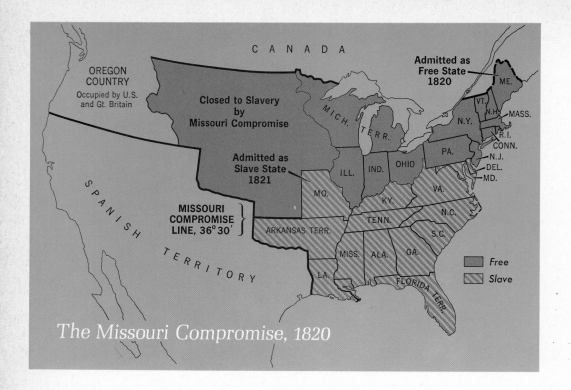

The Missouri Compromise, 1820

against reason and the . . . great fabric of American liberty."

But the compromisers were not to be diverted by such objections. In a series of measures known as the "Missouri Compromise," they arranged for the temporary preservation of the balance of power in the Senate by admitting Missouri as a slave state and Maine as a free one. The most significant provision of the Compromise permitted slavery in Missouri, but prohibited it "forever . . . in all territory ceded by France to the United States . . . which lies north of 36°30' . . . not included within the limits of [that] state." President Monroe hesitated to sign the compromise measures on the ground that the Constitution nowhere gave Congress the power to exclude slavery from a territory. But the unanimous urging of his Cabinet overcame his scruples and he signed the Missouri Compromise on March 6, 1820.

When Congress took up the matter of approving Missouri's new state constitution, as required by the admitting process, new trouble arose. This constitution provided that the state should never emancipate slaves without the consent of their owners; worse, it contravened the equal privileges and immunities clause of the federal Constitution by absolutely prohibiting the entry of free Negroes into the state. Through the efforts of Henry Clay, Congress finally accepted the state constitution, but not before the so-called "Second Missouri Compromise" had been hammered out. This new compromise required the state legislature to guarantee that it would never deny any of the privileges and immunities of citizens of the United States inside the borders of Missouri. There the slavery issue rested for a generation, but the Missouri controversy intensified sectionalism and gradually submerged the focus on nationalism that the war generation had labored so hard to bring about.

Sectional Strains
in Economic Growth

Spain forced to recede upon her troubled self, the United States became freer to pursue her own destiny, to organize her energies for the unwavering pursuit of wealth and welfare that was to become her hallmark in the virtual world she called her own.

Although hostile Britain still reigned in Canada, hostile Spain in the south and southwest, and hostile aborigines in the open spaces between them, and although haughty monarchs overseas continued to view the United States as a pawn in their own power game, the American preoccupation with foreign affairs gradually yielded to domestic issues. Among these, sectionalism overshadowed all others. Many issues, open or covert, obvious or obscure, lent their weight to pulling the country apart. Heaviest of all, perhaps, were those arising from the spectacular surge in economic growth, once the people turned to the discovery and development of their vast endowment in natural resources. Economic growth and its instrumentalities surely added to the strength of union too. But the Civil War disclosed the greater force of the sectional strains that began to rend the young nation once she embarked on her own way.

I. *Enterprise and Empire*

In 1815, and indeed for several decades thereafter, the majority of free Americans in the South as well as in the North still lived on family farms, with all but a few of their needs supplied by the husbandry of men and boys, the spinning, stitching, baking, and brewing of women and girls. These people, or their forebears, had come to America in search of personal freedom based on economic independence. Although by their mere zealous occupation of the land they were the true emissaries of empire, they remained relatively unconcerned about economic enterprise or growth. Innovations in crops, tools, agricultural methods, and marketing techniques left most of them scornful and skeptical. They traded little and traveled less. Cultivating the land was to them a complete and gratifying way of life, which left them isolated from the ups and downs of the world and worldly affairs.

The fish of the sea supplied another great natural resource from which many Americans eked out a fiercely independent existence long after the Revolution. In 1821, Timothy Dwight, reporting on his travels through New England, said of the fishing ports south of Boston: "The whole region wears remarkably the appearance of stillness and retirement; and the inhabitants seem to be separated in a great measure, from all active intercourse with their country." Fishermen in these ports went out, typically, like farmers, only for the day. Each had his own boat and brought back his catch for his family, though he might sometimes barter a surplus for grain, clothing, or equipment. At more active fishing centers like Newburyport and Beverly, and on Cape Cod, fishermen showed greater enterprise. Their voyages were longer and better organized. But here too the rule was that each man supplied his own gear and provisions in return for a share of the catch.

The fisherman always preferred going out "on his own hook," a phrase that originated with these Yankees.

One specialized fishing occupation—whaling—ranked very high in value of product until kerosene supplanted whale oil as an illuminant after the Civil War. Until the War of 1812, just about every New England port had its whaling fleet, but after the war, Nantucket and New Bedford, Massachusetts, almost monopolized the industry. After 1820, New Bedford became the whaling center of the world, with perhaps a third of the international fleet. "New Bedford is not nearer to the whales than New London or Portland," wrote Emerson, "yet they have all the equipments for a whaler ready, and they hug an oil-cask like a brother."

The concentration of whaling activities in New Bedford added to the efficiency of operations; otherwise, whaling remained a conservative industry in which the only significant changes since colonial times were that voyages grew longer, captains crueler, and crews—paid, like fishermen, a share of the catch—more ruthlessly exploited. After 1820 no self-respecting American seaman would ship on a whaler. Innocent farm boys sometimes were lured on board by false and fancy promises, but many of them either mutinied or deserted at the first opportunity. Less rebellious hands often found themselves abandoned on some foreign shore by the captain, who thus avoided paying them their shares. On return voyages, crews were made up of men from every primitive island and backwater of civilization. Even Fiji islanders, and Polynesians like the harpooner Queequeg in Melville's *Moby Dick,* could be seen parading through the streets of New Bedford after a whaler had put in.

In lumbering, as in farming, fishing, and whaling, few innovations were made in the first third of the nineteenth century. The industry grew, of course. Wood remained the great staple for commercial and domestic construction, cooking, heating and furniture, and for power where streams were lacking. But until the railroads added their own huge demand for wood for fuel, ties, and rolling stock, and helped to settle the prairies and the plains where there were no trees, lumbering remained the occupation of uncompromisingly individualistic loggers, who supplied timber to widely scattered and independently owned saw mills.

The Indians had taught the first settlers how to grow corn, harpoon whales, and girdle and kill trees before felling them. For more than two centuries, these basic techniques of farming, fishing, and lumbering spread unchanged as the country gradually expanded. Enterprises that specialized in making such other commodities as flour, leather goods, and iron ware usually were organized locally and conducted according to time-tested methods by generation after generation in the same family. Such enterprises offered a living and a way of life; they were marked by stability rather than speculation, tradition rather than innovation. Until vast new markets were opened up by improved transportation, such enterprises continued to characterize the American economy, even if they did not portend its future.

THE FUR TRADE
AND THE CHINA TRADE

Early in the nineteenth century, no one in America was more isolated than the fur-trapper and trader. The fur-trader, Robert Glass Cleland writes, "started from frontiers at which more cautious pioneers were glad to stop . . . and wandered through the reaches of the outer West with all the freedom of the lonely wind." But, unlike the other primary occupations in America, the fur trade gave a new direction to American life, a new method to American business, and a new spirit to the American economy.

Fur—mink, otter, lynx, fox, and the ubiquitous beaver, as well as the coarser bear, wolf, deer, rabbit, muskrat, "coon," and "possum"—had been one of the first

staples exported by the colonies. The finer pelts were used in hats, cloaks, and robes; the coarser ones in blankets for man and beast. The Indians, who did most of the actual trapping, traded their valuable furs for tinsel, shoddy, and drink. Consequently, from the start, profits had been large and competition keen. As early as 1700, over-trapping had depleted the fur-bearing animals in some areas, and in the next 50 years French traders from Canada and Spanish traders from Mexico, as well as the English colonists, had forced their way a thousand miles inland, far in advance of settlement.

Two thousand miles beyond even the farthest inland fur-trading post in the Mississippi Valley were the sea-otter waters off the Oregon coast. Sea captains from New England and New York, turning to the China trade immediately after the Revolution, discovered an eager market for the strikingly beautiful sea-otter skins (as well as for other domestic furs) among the wealthy mandarins of North China, where tastes were elegant, winters frigid, and dwellings unheated.

New Englanders, especially, were attracted to the sea-otter because it gave them a commodity to export in exchange for the tea, silk, spices, and cheap cottons ("nankeens") of the Orient, which were in such demand at home. By the early 1800's the sea-otter was nearing extinction. Profits from Chinese imports, however, had proved even greater than those from the sale of furs in China, and when the sea-otter supply failed, approximately at the outbreak of the War of 1812, the ship captains began to carry Hawaiian sandalwood to the Orient where it was used for incense in the joss houses. They also began to smuggle opium from the Dutch East Indies and neighboring islands into China to pay for tea. The leading New Englander in the China trade was Thomas Handasyd Perkins, who clung to it until the 1830's. The most active New Yorker in the trade was John Jacob Astor, who as early as 1800 had become the leading fur merchant in New York City.

The fur market in China had attracted land trappers and traders as well as sea captains, and following the return of Lewis and Clark from their trail-blazing expedition across the continent in 1806, mountain men in quest of pelts and sins began to exploit the upper Missouri, the Yellowstone, the Green and other northwestern rivers, and the Colorado and the Gila in the southwestern desert. The farther trappers and traders reached out from their Mississippi base at St. Louis, however, the greater difficulty they found in carrying on their business. One reason for this was the hostility of the Plains Indians, with whom, it seemed, only large and well-armed expeditions could safely deal. Of more lasting importance was the fact that time and distance cost money; only well-financed organizations were able to send trappers and traders into distant fur-producing areas for a year or more at a time.

In 1809, a number of experienced St. Louis traders grasped the situation and pooled their funds in the Missouri Fur Company, a partnership. Other traders deeper in the West followed their lead; but it soon became evident that all of them suffered from undercapitalization and other evidences of inexperience in big business, and they quickly failed. Speeding their demise was Astor's American Fur Company, a corporation chartered by New York State in 1808 for 25 years and capitalized at $1 million.

In applying for the charter, Astor had stressed the patriotic aspects of his venture. His aim, he said, was to build a string of company posts along the route of Lewis and Clark to the Pacific, thereby saving the United States government the expense of maintaining its own posts in this wild territory, and hastening the day when it would be opened to settlement. Astor set up his enterprise as a corporation to give weight to this great national objective, which, as he suggested, could hardly be won by a single individual. But as Astor's friend, Washington Irving, wrote, the entire "cap-ital was furnished by [Astor] himself—he, in fact, constituted the company." He had simply played up the "sagacious and effective" idea that a group of responsible capitalists was behind the venture to justify his demand for a monopoly of the western fur trade.

Although New York refused to grant Astor the monopoly he hoped for, the state did give him a corporate charter, on the basis of which he went ahead. In September, 1810, he sent an expedition by sea to set up a trading post at the mouth of the Columbia River in Oregon, and in October he sent an overland expedition west from St. Louis. By the time the cross-country party arrived in Oregon early in 1812, the sea contingent had already landed and begun to build the settlement of Astoria.

Canadian fur-traders eyed Astor's maneuvers with growing hostility, and on the outbreak of the War of 1812 they decided to put an end to the American company. News of the war reached Astoria in January, 1813, along with information that a British warship was headed toward the settlement. Since resistance would have been futile, Astor's men made the best deal they could by selling out to the North West Company, a Canadian firm, for $58,000. For a generation thereafter, the Canadians succeeded in barring Americans from Oregon and held a monopoly of the region's fur.

But they did not succeed in stopping Astor. Once the War of 1812 was over, his American Fur Company, by means of efficient business methods and political maneuvers, set out to capture the fur trade east of Oregon. In 1816, at Astor's urging, Congress passed a law forbidding foreigners (i.e., Britishers) from engaging in the fur trade of the United States, except when licensed as employees of American traders. Subsequently, he got Governor Lewis Cass of Michigan Territory to issue licenses almost exclusively to his men. As Astor's agent wrote to him in 1817: "The Canadian Boatmen . . . are indispensable to the successful prosecution of the trade, their places cannot be supplied by Americans, who are far . . . too independent to submit quietly to a proper controul . . . and although the body of the Yankee can resist as much hardship as any Man, tis only in the Canadian we find that temper of mind to render him patient and docile and preserving. . . . It is of course your object," concluded this wide awake agent, "to exclude every foreigner except those for whom you obtain licenses."

By such means Astor's American Fur Company managed to average about $500,-000 a year in profits until the 1830's. Then styles in Europe suddenly changed. "It appears that they make hats of silk in place of beaver," Astor observed during a European trip in 1834. By then, the fur reserves of the entire continent had almost become exhausted. They were the first natural resource to be exploited by the new business methods, and the first to go.

The fur trade trampled and estranged the Indian, taught him to drink "firewater," and armed him with guns and ammunition. But it also opened the path of civilization "to that ocean," as Lewis and Clark said of the Pacific in 1805, "the object of all our labours, the reward of all our anxieties."

The fur trade also nurtured the China trade, which led in turn to the start of continuous American settlement in Hawaii. The China trade also promoted the development of capitalism in New England and New York. It made Astor the first American millionaire, and his American Fur Company the first integrated corporation, rich in capital, strong in management, aggressive in competition, and active in politics.

THE SANTA FE TRAIL

Less dramatic than the fur trade, and involving far fewer men and far less

capital, was the trade across the Santa Fe Trail. Spain had established the isolated outpost of Santa Fe in the desert of New Mexico early in the seventeenth century, and had supplied it most laboriously from Vera Cruz, 1,500 miles away. The early efforts of Americans to trade at Santa Fe were frustrated by Spain's rigid colonial policy, which sternly excluded foreigners. Soon after Mexico won freedom from Spain in 1821, however, she opened the settlement to her northern neighbors, a step she later regretted and reversed (see chapter 12). The Santa Fe Trail, which ran westward from Independence, Missouri, through Kansas Territory, was surveyed by the American army in 1825. For the next 20 years, caravans of American farm wagons trekked across it, hauling all sorts of goods from the East and from Europe to be exchanged at fabulous profits for Spanish gold and silver.

The arrival of the caravan each year was a great event in the Spanish town. Gradually, some of the Americans settled in Santa Fe, and others, attracted by the fertile land bordering the eastern stretches of the trail, staked out farms along the way. When in 1844 Santa Anna, the Mexican leader, closed the trail, Americans viewed his act as interference with their rights and "destiny." The Santa Fe trade never engaged more than a couple of hundred persons a year. But, like the fur trade, it opened a new path across the continent, lured American businessmen into new country, and led to a political and territorial claim that eventually would be made good by the Mexican War.

II. *The Rise of the Middle West*

THE EARLY SETTLERS

Well to the east of the fur-trappers and traders, but traveling over the trails they had marked through the wilderness,

moved frontier families like that of Abraham Lincoln. Thomas Lincoln, the president's father, was the typical frontier settler of the early nineteenth century, part backwoodsman, part farmer, part handyman-carpenter. Thomas had been born in the western Virginia hills in 1778. Four years later found the Lincolns in Kentucky, where Thomas grew up "a wandering laboring boy," altogether without schooling. In 1806, he married the illiterate Nancy Hanks, who bore their son Abe in 1809. The Lincolns and the Hankses rarely stayed put for long, and by 1816 the whole tribe had reached Indiana, where they "squatted" the first year. For the whole of that time they occupied that "Darne Little

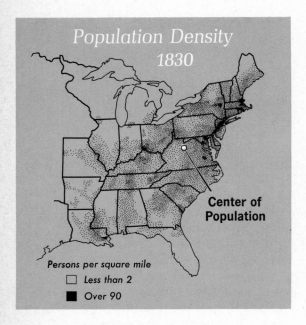

Population Density 1830

Center of Population

Persons per square mile
☐ Less than 2
■ Over 90

half face camp," a three-sided wickiup before which a fire was kept burning around the clock. "We lived the same as the Indians," one of the Hankses said years later, " 'ceptin' we took an interest in politics and religion." After a year, they managed to build a typical log cabin, without floor, door, or window. A roof stuffed with mud and dry grass afforded their only protection from the rain. This remained their home for a decade before they pushed on to Illinois.

By 1816, more than a million people had trampled over the Lincolns' trail to set up households in the West. Most of them traveled on foot, their possessions on their backs or in wheelbarrows, or saddled to a few scrawny cows that had been transformed into beasts of burden. Travelers from abroad noted the characteristic bluish complexion of these settlers, many of whom suffered from forest fever, milk sickness, and especially the swamp-bred ague (malaria). The land was cheap and fertile, but life was hard. "The rugged road, the dirty hovels, the fire in the woods to sleep by, the pathless ways through the wilderness, the dangerous crossings of the rivers"—why, asked the Englishman, William Cobbett, in 1817, did the settlers put up with all this? "To boil their pot in gipsy-fashion, to have a mere board to eat on, to drink whiskey or pure water, to sit and sleep under a shed far inferior to English cowpens, to have a mill at twenty miles' distance, an apothecary's shop at a hundred, and a doctor nowhere." Englishmen, confessed Cobbett, could never have survived such conditions. But Americans, as Jefferson said, found it "cheaper to clear a new acre than to manure an old one." So on into the West they moved.

Congressman Peter B. Porter of Buffalo, New York, described the western country and the plight of the pioneers in 1810:

There is no better place where the great staple articles for the use of civilized life can be produced in greater abundance or with greater ease, yet as respects most of the luxuries and many of the conveniences of life the people are poor. . . . The single circumstance of want of a market is already beginning to produce the most disastrous effect, not only on the industry, but on the morals of the inhabitants. Such is the fertility of their land that one-half of their time spent in labor is sufficient to produce every article which their farms are capable of yielding, in sufficient quantities for their own consumption, and there is nothing to incite them to produce more. They are therefore naturally led to spend the other part of their time in idleness and dissipation.

On the few occasions when these people might see a bit of money—from the chance sale of a hog or a horse to a newcomer who still had coin in his jeans—it would go east to buy salt for curing meat and fish, iron for muskets, lead for bullets, powder for the charge. Usually, though, they had a bundle of skins with which to pay for such necessities. Everything else the settlers needed, they either made themselves or did without. They used up their capital instead of augmenting it, and even their boys, adept from childhood with rifle and rod, "lit out for the tall timber" on their own.

"KING COTTON"
AND THE WEST

After 1815 the prospects of the West improved rapidly. The subjugation of the Indians, the departure of the British from their military posts and the Great Lakes, the disintegration of Spanish rule on the Gulf Coast all opened up new lands to permanent settlers. The government aided the pioneers by liberalizing its land-sale policies, and by showing more tolerance of "squatters." Two epochal developments then opened a growing market for western produce and supplied the means for reaching that market cheaply. The first was the phenomenal rise of King Cotton in the neighboring South (and large-scale sugar growing in Louisiana). The second was the introduction of the steamboat on western waters.

Before 1793, only fragile long-staple cotton, grown in a few selected areas, could be cleansed of its oily seeds at a reasonable cost. Thereafter Eli Whitney's gin, invented that year, made it practical to clean the green seeds from the hardier short-staple boll, which could be grown on almost any soil if the warm season were long enough. By 1816, 60 per cent of the nation's cotton crop was produced in South Carolina and Georgia, most of it in the piedmont region. By 1820, however, the land was used up as tidewater land had been earlier. The piedmont, said a traveler at this time, presented a scene of "dreary and uncultivated wastes . . . half-clothed negroes, lean and hungry stock, houses falling to decay, and fences wind-shaken and dilapidated." Turning their backs on this disheartening scene, cotton planters pushed west into Alabama and Mississippi. By 1830, their combined population exceeded 400,000, even though

247

The original cotton gin, 1793.

the large planters had been steadily buying up many small farms in the best cotton-producing areas. Sections of Tennessee, Arkansas, and Florida suitable for cotton-planting also became heavily settled, as did the Louisiana sugar country.

The rapid growth of the new regions is reflected in the rising traffic at New Orleans. In 1816 only 37,000 bales of cotton were shipped from this Mississippi port. By 1822, the figure was 161,000 bales, and by 1830, 428,000. Most of this cotton found its way to English textile factories, although some went to the Continent and increasing amounts to New England mills.

Until the beginning of the nineteenth century, South Carolina had exported considerable quantities of wheat and corn as well as cotton; and other southern states had exported horses, mules, and swine. Such diversity then disappeared. An English visitor observed in 1826:

There is not a finer grazing country in the world than South Carolina; and were attention paid to the raising of cattle, sheep, goats, hogs, horses, mules, etc., this state might supply itself as well as the West India islands with these useful animals; but every other object gives place to cotton.

A year later, a traveler wrote of his visit to Louisiana:

Corn, sweet potatoes, melons and all northern fruit, with the exception of apples, flourish here; though the planters find the great staples, cotton and sugar, so much more profitable than other kinds of cultivation that many of them calculate to supply themselves with provisions almost entirely from the upper country.

The Cotton Kingdom's growing need for food and work-animals gave the slack westerners the impulse they needed to lay down their rods and guns and to think seriously about farming. As markets and prices improved, many farmers began to thirst for more land and to go into debt to acquire it and the seed, and tools, and other items needed to bring it into production. Soon speculation in land became widespread and debt mounted, forcing the farmers to concentrate almost as singlemindedly as the planter on cash crops. Southern specialization in cotton spurred western specialization in grain and meat and mules. The marvelous Mississippi River system conveniently tied the two sections together, and the steamboat tightened the knot.

III. *The Growth of Intersectional Commerce*

TRANSPORTATION PROBLEMS

In colonial America the ocean had afforded the easiest means of communication and trade. As farms and plantations were developed along the eastern rivers, they also began to carry their share of people and goods. The progress of settlement in the West brought the Mississippi River system into the transportation network, and the steamboat made it the foremost inland carrier of all. The first steamboat on the western waters was *New Orleans,* built in 1811 by Robert Fulton, four years after his success with *Clermont* on the Hudson. As he had in New York, Fulton promptly won a monopoly of the carrying trade of the West. In 1824, however, John Marshall, in his momentous decision in *Gibbons* v. *Ogden* (see p. 236), dealt a death blow to all monopolies on interstate waters. Fulton's associates (Fulton himself died in 1815) had been faced with illicit competition even before this ruling was handed down, but now everyone seemed to rush into the steamboat business. By 1830, nearly 200 steamboats were plying western rivers.

Keel-boat rates between Louisville and New Orleans had been about $5 per hundred pounds of freight. By 1820, steamboat rates for this trip were $2 per hundred pounds, and by 1842 competition had driven them down to 25 cents, still a profitable price, since technological improvements had so greatly increased the carrying capacity and operating efficiency of the vessels. Western staples now were sped down to the levees of New Orleans for shipment

Mississippi River System about 1830

overseas or for distribution by coastal vessels to the rest of the South and Southwest and even to the East. Commodities from abroad or from the East also were funneled into the booming port for transshipment inland.

The Mississippi system, however, was less hospitable than it seemed. The river itself and most of its tributaries were full of snags, hidden banks, floating trees, whirlpools, and eddies, and the entire system was infested with pirates. Seasonal floods often swept with boat and boatmen to destruction, and severe droughts pinched the river channels into narrow ribbons, leaving boats stranded in shallow water. So pernicious, indeed, was this hazard that most Mississippi traffic came to be bunched on the floodtides of spring and fall. This tactic eased the problems of navigation, but it intensified the problems of marketing. During the floodtide seasons, the New Orleans market was glutted with produce, and prices fell sharply. It was costly to store the crops until prices rose again, and in any case grain spoiled so quickly in the humid air of the Mississippi Basin that shippers could not hold their produce off the market for long.

The difficulties of road transport were, if anything, greater than those on the rivers. From the earliest times, many Americans chose to settle far from neighbors on land several miles from water routes. And yet somehow they had to travel to the grist mills, tobacco warehouses, cotton gins, forges, country stores, county courts—and to the rivers themselves. As time went on, a crude network of roads spread across the sparsely settled countryside, often following old Indian trails and the paths of trappers and traders. Only a few of these roads were wide enough for wagon or cart. They ran through dense, dank forests, and usually bristled with tree stumps. In spring and fall, they were transformed into muddy quagmires; in winter, they were frozen into malevolent ruts.

The greatest road-building enterprise of the early years of the republic was the "National Highway," chartered by Congress in

1806 and built with federal funds. In 1811, the first crews began to cut the road westward from Cumberland, Maryland, and by 1818 it had been pushed as far as Wheeling, Virginia, on the Ohio River. The failure of Congress to provide funds checked construction here, but work was resumed in 1825 and by mid-century the road had reached Vandalia, Illinois, its westernmost point.

The "National Highway" was an efficient carrier. Other useful roads included the privately financed Lancaster Turnpike and others modeled on it. The Lancaster "Pike" had been built in 1794 at a cost of $465,000 across the 62-mile stretch from Philadelphia to Lancaster, Pennsylvania. Tolls were collected along the way and the enterprise proved moderately profitable. In the next 30 years, private companies, mostly in New England and the Middle states, built more than 10,000 miles of turnpikes. The best roads cost from $5,000 to $10,000 per mile. State and local governments often gave the turnpike companies a helping hand by buying their stock and by contributing the proceeds from the sale of government bonds.

Most of the turnpike companies, however, were modest enterprises, and their short stretches of road did little to improve the sorry network of country paths. Moreover, the pikes were rarely used for the transportation of heavy agricultural produce, for the high tolls discouraged shippers, who were always hardpressed for coin. By the 1830's, the management and maintenance of the privately operated turnpikes had become so costly, and the returns so scanty, that thousands of miles of turnpike were either abandoned or turned over to the states.

THE CANAL BOOM

Turnpikes, clearly, were not the way for New York, Philadelphia, Boston, and the other eastern seaports to compete with New Orleans for the growing trade of

A view of the Erie Canal, 1829. Watercolor drawing by John William Hill.

the West. These cities turned instead to canals to link up the great waterways with which nature had endowed the American continent. But Canals were even harder and more expensive to build than turnpikes. They cost, not $5,000, but $25,000 a mile; some cost as much as $60,000 and $80,000 a mile. They took not a year or two to build, but seven to ten years. Thus they presented new problems of finance and labor supply, and new problems of engineering and management.

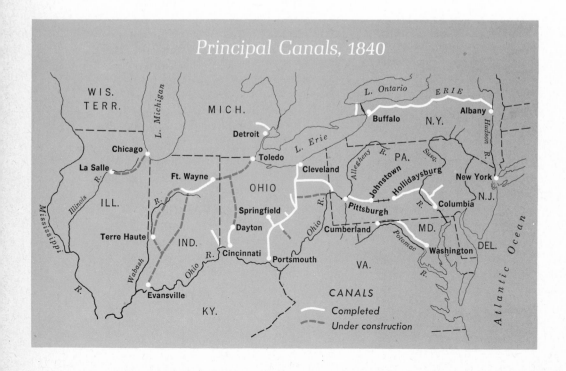

Principal Canals, 1840

CANALS
— Completed
--- Under construction

In 1816 only three American canals were more than two miles long, none ran as far as 30 miles. All told, the country boasted 100 miles of these artificial waterways. As early as 1810, the New York State legislature had appointed a committee to investigate the feasibility of digging a canal to the West, and in 1816 De Witt Clinton again raised the issue. So convincing were his arguments that even his political opponents voted for his project—a canal to connect the Hudson River with Lake Erie, 363 miles away. Clinton's canal was to have 83 locks, and was to cost over $7 million in state funds. Construction of the Erie Canal began in 1817, and by 1823 a 280-mile stretch was in operation from Albany to Rochester. The tolls that came pouring in from the traffic on this part of the canal were used to help finance the final leg to Buffalo, which was completed in 1825. In 1823, New York had also opened the Champlain Canal, connecting the Hudson River and Lake Champlain to the north. In 1825, returns from both projects exceeded $500,000, and over the next nine years the Erie paid back its total original cost of $7 million. Two figures tell the story of the Erie's success: It reduced freight rates between Buffalo and Albany from $100 to $15 a ton, and it reduced travel time from 20 to 8 days.

Spurred to action by New York's dramatic success, Boston, in 1825 induced the Massachusetts legislature to consider building a canal of its own into the interior. The difficult Massachusetts terrain disheartened the promoters, and when Boston did gain her entry to the West in 1842, it was by way of three railroads strung across Massachusetts to the eastern end of the Erie Canal. In 1826, Philadelphia got state approval for yet another scheme to tap the West, an undertaking that was even more ambitious than the one Boston had abandoned. This system which included a main canal and railroad tracking, was completed to Pittsburgh in 1834, at a cost of more than $10 million, all of it supplied by the state.

In 1827, Baltimore joined in the race for western business by announcing plans for the Chesapeake and Ohio Canal. The Mary-

land legislature thought the project visionary from the start, but work got underway with private and federal funds. The legislators turned out to be right, for construction on the canal was brought to a halt by the broad southern mountains. In 1828, a private corporation began to lay track for the Baltimore and Ohio Railroad, the first successful line in America. But it was to be many years before the Baltimore & Ohio reached the Ohio River in the 1850's.

Westerners were as energetic as easterners in seeking ways to promote east-west trade, for they soon discovered that their rich soil could produce more wheat and corn, and that their corn could fatten more hogs, than the southern market could absorb. Moreover, the westerners were weary of trying to cope with the hazards of river transportation. In the 1820's they turned a sympathetic ear to Henry Clay's program for high tariffs and "internal improvements," the first to promote the growth of eastern factory towns, the second to provide the means for opening these towns to western produce. "Internal improvements" would also mean that manufactured goods could be shipped more cheaply from the east.

Clay's program never was enacted into law (see p. 265). Without federal aid, Ohio and other western states soon embarked on their own ambitious canal and railroad programs. By 1837 Ohio boasted no less than 750 miles of canals, its most important one connecting Portsmouth on the Ohio River with Cleveland on Lake Erie, and, by way of "Clinton's Big Ditch" and the Hudson River, with New York City. Indiana began building her canal system in 1827, and in the 1830's Illinois, Michigan, and Wisconsin all projected ambitious works which, though interrupted by the Panic of 1837 (see p. 282), eventually were carried to completion.

By 1840, some 3,326 miles of canals, most of them in the North and West, had been constructed in the United States at a cost of $125 million. Private American investors were able to supply only a small fraction of this sum; federal and state subscriptions to the securities of private canal companies accounted for part of the balance; and more than half the total was provided directly by the states out of revenues or through the sale of state bonds abroad, mainly in England. The impact of the canals on the economy of the West was as great as expected. The South continued to be a valuable customer of the West, and the Ohio and Mississippi river systems continued to be heavily used. But the West's connection with the North and East became ever stronger as the canal system developed.

Travel over canals was much cheaper than over turnpikes, but for four months of the year the northern canal routes were frozen solid. Railroads finally freed shippers from the uncertainties of weather and from the medieval pace of oxen and tow horses. By 1840, there were 3,328 miles of railroad in the United States, almost exactly equal to the canal mileage. But only about 200 of these railroad miles could be found in the West. For some time after 1840, rivers, canals, and turnpikes continued to be the main channels of inland commerce.

THE SPECTACULAR RISE OF NEW YORK CITY

In the competition for western trade, then, the East gradually outstripped the South. And in the East itself, New York City gradually pulled far ahead of the rival cities of Boston, Philadelphia, and Baltimore. Nature was partly responsible for this success, for New York had a far greater hinterland market than Boston; the Hudson and Mohawk rivers gave her a far more serviceable water route to western markets than either Philadelphia or Baltimore enjoyed; and she was ideally situated for the coastal trade, since Boston was far to the north, and Philadelphia and Baltimore were too far upstream for easy access. All these advantages in domestic commerce combined to make New York the best warehousing site for transatlantic trade as well. Competition, however, remained keen for a long time, and New York won its eventual supremacy through the enterprise shown by her businessmen in capitalizing on the advantages bestowed by nature.

The construction of the Erie Canal was the most rewarding accomplishment of the New Yorkers; but even before the canal was begun they had made other innovations. One was a modified auction system for disposing of imports—a scheme that assured merchants of a rapid turnover of goods for cash. Although auctions were held in many American ports, the common practice was to offer goods and then to withdraw them if the bids were unsatisfactory. But in New York City, after 1817, purchasers were assured that the highest bid would be accepted and that their purchases would be delivered as promised.

Another New York innovation was the development of regular schedules for transatlantic packets. The vessels of New York's Black Ball Line were the first in the world, starting in January, 1818, to operate on this basis, "full or not full." This so-called "Atlantic Shuttle" grew steadily after 1820, when the American West began to feed industrial Europe as well as America, and the United States began to offer an expanding market for Old-World manufactures. By 1828, New York's share of the American merchant marine was almost equal to the combined shares of Philadelphia, Boston, and Baltimore.

Dependable auctions and dependable sailings brought businessmen and goods flooding *into* New York. But the city's merchants still needed an adequate export staple to balance their trade. Western produce pouring into the city over the Erie Canal helped some, but in the 1820's New York's ambitious shippers began to sail right into New Orleans, Mobile, and other southern ports to pick up cotton to carry to Britain and the Continent. There they exchanged the cotton for manufactures and other goods, which they brought back to New York for distribution in the city and in the interior. Eventually they brought imports directly to the cotton ports themselves.

So successful were the New York merchants in this new trade that by 1830 it was estimated that 40 cents of every dollar paid for cotton went north—almost exclusively to New York—to cover the cost of freight tolls, insurance, commissions, and interest. In 1837, a convention in the South that had been called to promote the revival of direct trade with Europe said to southern merchants, "You hold the element from which [the New York merchant] draws his

strength. You have but to speak the word, and his empire is transferred to your own soil." But the word was not spoken. Two years later a similar convention declared that "the importing merchants of the South [had become] an almost extinct race, and her direct trade, once so great, flourishing, and rich, [had] dwindled down to insignificance."

IV. *The Industrial Revolution*

DIFFICULT BEGINNINGS

The spread of commercial agriculture in the West, the rapid growth of western population, and the growing accessibility of western markets, all gave a strong impetus to the development of eastern industry. The concentration on cotton-planting in the South also made that section a market for textiles and other manufactures that it might otherwise have produced itself. Until western and southern markets were opened, however, factory industry had a hard time getting started.

In 1791, the same year in which he sent his Report on Manufactures to Congress (see p. 186), Hamilton himself helped organize the Society for Establishing Useful Manufactures, a corporation chartered by New Jersey and capitalized at $1 million. In the next few years, this corporation founded the city of Paterson, New Jersey, erected numerous buildings to house its works, smuggled in skilled British mechanics, and began manufacturing yarn, cloth, hats, and other commodities. By 1796, however, both the works and the town were moribund. A few similar undertakings suffered a similar fate.

The first full-time factory in America to survive for more than a few years was the cotton-spinning plant of Almy & Brown, Providence merchants. Under the direction of an experienced Englishman, Samuel Slater, this factory began operations at Pawtucket in 1791. Nine children, working for wages of 12 to 25 cents a day, tended its 72 spindles under full-time supervision. Slater's, of course, was a tiny affair, and only Almy & Brown's well-established market connections kept the company afloat. After the outbreak of the Napoleonic Wars in Europe in 1799, Americans found it increasingly difficult to get British manufactures. To supply their needs, Slater's mill expanded, and many imitators, as we have seen (p. 214), moved in to enjoy a share of the market. Few of these enterprises were capitalized at more than $10,000; since their managers were inexperienced in keeping accounts, handling money and men, and exploiting markets, conservative banks would simply have nothing to do with them. They drew their labor from the poorest farm families in the area, often employing both the parents and their small children. The thread they spun was given out to home weavers to make into cloth. But Almy & Brown complained in 1809 that "a hundred looms in families will not weave so much cloth as ten . . . under the immediate inspection of a workman." Once the long war was over, most of the wartime mills shut down. The shining exception became one of the most profitable of all American enterprises and laid the foundations for the industrial revolution in the United States.

THE ENTRY
OF BIG CAPITAL

This exception was the Boston Manufacturing Company of Waltham, Massachusetts, organized in 1813 by Francis Cabot Lowell, Patrick Tracy Jackson, and Nathan Appleton, great New England merchants. The Boston Manufacturing Company was as distinct a step forward in its day as Slater's mill had been 22 years before. The organizers, who had already demonstrated their abiilty to manage hazardous, large-scale enterprises, invested liberally in the new company. They poured $600,000 cash into it in the first six years, and held as much or more in reserve for operating and emergency expenses. They built the first wholly integrated cotton-manufacturing plant in the world; all operations were under one roof, from the unbaling of the raw cotton to the dyeing and printing of the finished cloth. They even established their own selling agencies, instead of depending on local jobbers as earlier companies had done.

The scale on which it operated, and its carefully integrated production, enabled the Boston Manufacturing Company to eliminate middlemen and unsupervised domestic workers, and to reduce the time spent in carrying goods from place to place for successive processing steps. The managers made their system even more economical by introducing power looms and power spindles and by giving constant attention to other improvements in technology, from the design of water wheels and power-transmission systems to the fastness of dyes.

In another innovation, these New England merchants devised an original scheme for attracting and holding workers. Instead of hiring children and parents from the im-

Cut-away view showing probable layout of Old Slater Mill.

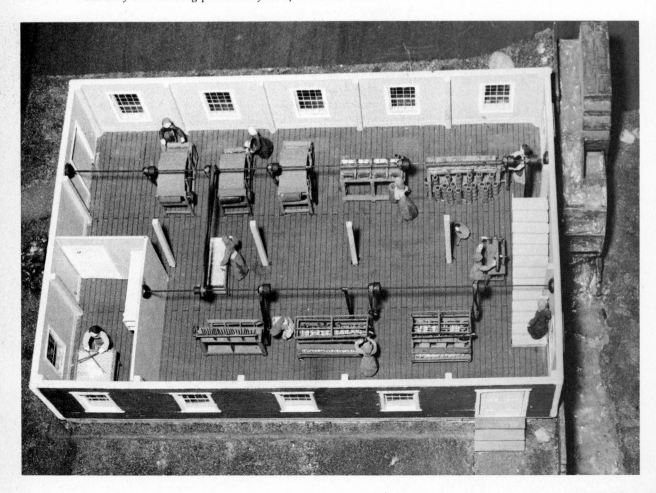

mediate neighborhood, the Boston Manufacturing Company took on young women ranging in age from 18 to 22, and sheltered and fed them in newly constructed houses that made up a company town. Here, under the sharp eyes of the organizers, religion was cultivated, educational opportunities were made available in leisure hours, and cleanliness and hygiene were insisted upon. All these devices were calculated to attract a sturdy, ambitious, hard-working group of young women from respectable farm families. And they succeeded in doing just that. Absenteeism was low and industrial discipline was easily imposed. The Boston Manufacturing Company did not begin operations until 1816 when the flood of British imports sank many struggling American mills. It proved an immediate and lasting success. In 1817, it earned a dividend of 12.5 per cent for its stockholders; thereafter, despite the Panic of 1819 (see p. 235), annual dividends were even higher. By 1822, dividends totaling 104.5 per cent had been paid to the original investors.

THE CORPORATION
AND INDUSTRIAL PROGRESS

Around 1823 Harrison Gray Otis of Boston wrote: "There has been a curious 'revival' in the spirit of men . . . which is quite remarkable. Two years ago our sun had sunk never to rise again. . . . All is now reversed and [manufacturing] stocks as well as spirits have risen inordinately. . . . It is amazing to see what is done by the puff on one hand and the panic on the other." The opening up of the West and the expansion of the Cotton Kingdom in the South spurred the general business upturn. The revolutions against Spain in South America (see p. 231) opened up the first foreign markets for American manufactured goods. After 1826, more and more such goods were also sent to China to help pay for the tea that was being consumed in ever greater quantities in the United States.

All these changes were reflected in the expansion of the firms that had survived the depression and in the large numbers of new textile corporations that set up in business

during the 1820's and 1830's. Some of these new companies were organized and chartered by the same group that had started the Boston Manufacturing Company. Between 1821 and 1835, these men, often referred to as the "Boston Associates," opened nine new companies in Massachusetts and southern New Hampshire, each specializing in a particular textile product on a large scale. More important, during and after the depression these men founded insurance companies and banks to maintain and concentrate their supply of capital, real-estate companies to take over the best factory sites, and water-power companies to control dams and dam sites and to harness the power of the great rivers. After 1823, Lowell on the Merrimack supplanted Waltham on the Charles as their main operating center.

The corporation had first been used as a legal device for securing a monopoly by means of a special charter. Astor employed it next as a symbol of prestige. The turnpike and bridge companies used the corporate form mainly as a means of accumulating capital through the sale of inexpensive shares to numerous subscribers. By the time the canal and railroad companies were being formed, the idea of limited liability had become well established in law and finance. Limited liability meant that the owners of corporation stock were liable for the obligations of the company only to the extent of their own investment, regardless of how great their personal fortunes might be. This protection helped to attract the great supplies of capital required for costly, long-term projects.

The "Boston Associates" used the corporate form for all these purposes, and for certain new purposes of their own. In their hands, the corporation became a device by which a few able men, through the ownership of only a fraction of the total stock, could direct the activities of many and varied businesses. The corporate form also

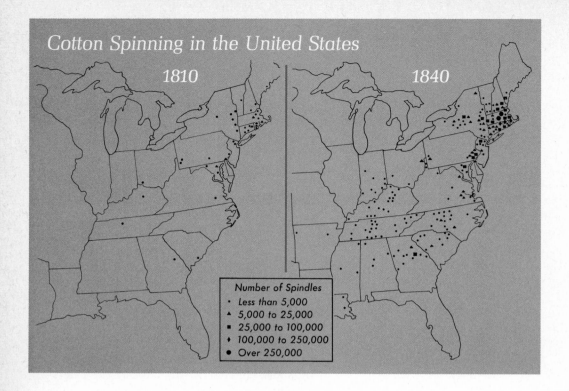

Cotton Spinning in the United States

1810   1840

Number of Spindles
· Less than 5,000
▲ 5,000 to 25,000
■ 25,000 to 100,000
♦ 100,000 to 250,000
● Over 250,000

made it possible for them to reside in Boston while actual operations were conducted in distant mill towns under the supervision of hired professional managers. Since corporate securities could be more easily disposed of than investments in partnerships or single-owner businesses, corporate enterprises could look forward to a long life, uninterrupted by the death or withdrawal of investors. Finally, stocks could easily be transferred without seriously affecting the financial structure of a business.

The cotton textile industry was the proving ground for these new techniques. It was the first mature American industry that was geared not to the individual craftsman but to the machine, that was financed not by the owner alone or by his bank, but by the accumulated private savings of numbers of people, and that was managed by hired professionals accountable to capitalists living in the great financial centers.

THE EARLY
LABOR MOVEMENT

The corporation gave a tremendous impetus to American economic and social progress, but almost from the outset it re-

vealed a seemingly inherent tendency toward harshness in human relations. Before Samuel Slater set up his first mechanized spinning plant in 1791, America had had many "spinning houses" and "spinning schools," the first of which appeared in Jamestown, Virginia, as early as 1646. These schools were set up to provide useful employment for the children of the poor. Slater's factory was modeled on these public institutions, and the children who worked for him were not abused. Many of Slater's imitators, however, were less charitable, especially when the heat of competition prompted the less efficient firms to make extravagant demands on their workers in a bid for survival. By 1810, few of the little spinning corporations scattered through southern New England retained any aspects of philanthropy.

A more striking deterioration in working and living conditions blighted the factories and factory towns of the Boston Associates and *their* imitators, especially after scrupulous founders turned direct management over to outsiders whose efficiency was checked in Boston through the medium of financial reports. Here is the way an observer in Lowell described the factory routine in that city in 1846:

The operatives work thirteen hours a day in the summer time, and from daylight to darkness in the winter. At half past four in the morning the factory bell rings, and at five girls must be in the mills. A clerk placed as a watch, observes those who are a few minutes behind the time, and effectual means are taken to stimulate punctuality. This is the morning commencement of the industrial discipline (should we not rather say industrial tyranny?) which is established in these Associations of this moral and Christian community. At seven the girls are allowed thirty minutes for breakfast, and at noon thirty minutes more for dinner, except during the first quarter of the year, when the time is extended to forty-five minutes.

Some years earlier, in 1840, the reformer, Orestes Brownson, described the plight of Lowell girls who presumably had gone to work just long enough to accumulate a dowry or to add to the family income until they married:

The great mass wear out their health, spirits, and morals without becoming one whit better off than when they commenced labor. The bills of mortality in these factory villages are not striking, we admit, for the poor girls when they can toil no longer go home to die.

These conditions were particularly prevalent after the Panic of 1837 (see p. 282), when corporate managements cracked down on factory superintendents whose accounts showed too much red ink. But even before that panic, conditions had become so bad in some of the cotton factories that the girls were driven to strike. In February, 1834, a thousand or more Lowell girls walked out in protest against a 15 per cent wage cut, "determined to 'have their way, if they died for it.'" Actually, the girls went back to work in a few days at the reduced wages— all but the leaders, who were discharged. Other such pathetic rebellions in the 1830's almost always ended in quick failure.

One of the weapons the corporations used against strikers was the law itself, which held all strikers to be subject to prosecution for criminal conspiracy under the common law. The pretext for such

prosecution lay in the idea that all labor combinations were organized to *injure* some person or persons. Judge Roberts made this point perfectly clear in a famous decision in a Pittsburgh labor trial in 1815:

In many cases of conspiracy the means employed . . . are frequently such as would be lawful in an individual. For instance, you have a right to have your boots, your coat, or your hat made by whom you please. You may decline employing any particular shoemaker, tailor, or hatter. . . . But should you combine and confederate with others, to ruin any particular shoemaker, tailor, hatter, or other mechanic, or tradesman by preventing persons from employing him, this would be unlawful and indictable.

In Judge Roberts' terms labor organizations were illegal conspiracies *per se;* their mere existence menaced both employers and workers who did not join up. This was the prevailing attitude until Chief Justice Shaw of the Massachusetts Supreme Court decided in 1842, in *Commonwealth* v. *Hunt,* that the objective of labor unions, even though they "may have a tendency to impoverish another, that is, to diminish his gains and profits," might nevertheless "be highly meritorious and public spirited." But even Justice Shaw left a wide loophole for employers by declaring that if the objective of labor unions "be carried into effect . . . by falsehood or force, . . . it may be stamped with the character of conspiracy." He at least permitted the supposition, however, that labor unions as such may be "to say the least, innocent"; and thus granted them legal standing for the first time.

Yet this improvement in the legal climate served chiefly to demonstrate that economic and social conditions, not the law, really underlay the workers' weak position. For a long time, the factory labor force simply remained too small in numbers to make much headway in an agrarian society.

Little progress was made in organizing American industrial workers until the 1930's. The first successful labor unions were those in the *skilled crafts*. These crafts originally were manned by the so-called "mechanics" of the eighteenth century and earlier, independent artisans—shoemakers, tailors, blacksmiths, bricklayers—who bought their own raw materials, fabricated them for their own customers in their own shops, and set their own prices. They sometimes employed journeymen who actually traveled from farm to farm to make shoes, repair houses and barns, and do other jobs beyond the capacity of the farm family. Below the journeymen ranked young apprentices, whose families contracted them out to artisans for as long as 20 years.

By the beginning of the nineteenth century, improvements in transportation had opened wider markets to the artisans, some of whom gave up hand work to become "merchant capitalists"—that is, businessmen who gathered up larger orders than one artisan and a few helpers could fill, and who employed artisans and journeymen to work for them. Others who had never been artisans also entered the different crafts as merchant capitalists. By the 1820's, competition among them had become so keen that they were forced to cut the wages of their craftsmen. The artisans themselves were further embittered by the loss of their independent status. Another complaint was that their specialized skills were being broken up into simpler tasks which were then given to less well-trained workers who further depressed wage rates.

It was in protest against these conditions that the first unions were formed in America. The Philadelphia shoemakers had organized as early as 1792, but it was not until the middle 1820's that other craftsmen, in defiance of the conspiracy law, turned to united action. In New York, Philadelphia, and other large centers, the craft unions combined in citywide organizations; and in 1834 six of these combinations joined forces in a "National Trades' Union." In the next three years the membership of the craft unions scattered throughout the country soared from 26,000 to 300,000, and the unions conducted at least 175 strikes, many of them called to win improvements in working conditions, not merely to keep them from growing worse. In 1828, the Philadelphia unions created the American Working Men's party to seek, by political means, such improvements as the 10-hour day for themselves and free public education for their children.

The business collapse of 1837 crushed the early craft-union movement. Some of the crafts, especially those in construction or in specialized fields like printing, managed to maintain a semblance of organization even in the worst years. The crafts that were subject to rising competition from factory production, however, tended to disappear, along with their unions and merchant capitalists. Workers who made cotton or woolen clothing, carpets, boots and shoes, and iron machinery and other hardware by hand simply could not survive in an environment marked by large-scale operations and mechanized techniques.

True, the United States was still many years away from becoming a mature industrial country unified by railroads, telegraph, telephone, automobiles, and TV. But by 1830 migration to the cities had begun to compete seriously with migration to the West, and it was becoming clear that the Jeffersonian ideal of a society made up of independent and individualistic farmers spread over the whole continent, if not over the whole hemisphere, would never be realized.

Readings

Asterisk indicates that book is available in paperback.

Roger Burlingame, *The March of Iron Men** (1938), is a penetrating social history of American technology before the Civil War and provides an excellent introduction to the subject of this chapter. More conventional, but scholarly and comprehensive, is G. R. Taylor, *The Transportation Revolution 1815-1860* (1951). A brief presentation will be found in the early chapters of T. C. Cochran and William Miller, *The Age of Enterprise** (1942). D. C. North, *The Economic Growth of the United States 1790-1860* (1961), is a careful appraisal of causes, which should be compared with Stuart Bruchey, *The Roots of American Economic Growth 1607-1861* (1965). W. P. Strassman, *Risk and Technological Innovation* (1959), and H. J. Habakkuk, *American and British Technology in the 19th Century* (1962), examine the machine process in relation to profits and labor productivity. Useful material on American agriculture in the early national period is available in L. B. Schmidt and E. D. Ross, eds., *Readings in Economic History of American Agriculture* (1925), especially Part II. For contemporary material on other aspects of the economy, see G. S. Callender, ed., *Selections from The Economic History of the United States 1765-1860* (1909).

Herman Melville, *Moby Dick** (1851), is a great American novel that provides much fascinating and authentic whaling lore. E. O. Steckpole, *The Sea-Hunters* (1953), is authoritative on this subject, as are the chapters in S. E. Morison, *The Maritime History of Massachusetts, 1783-1860** (1921). A valuable biography of the main figure in the fur trade is K. W. Porter, *John Jacob Astor* (2 vols., 1931).

L. D. Baldwin, *The Keelboat Age on Western Waters* (1941), is a good introduction to river transportation before the age of steam. J. T. Flexner, *Steamboats Come True* (1944), is a popular account of the development of new carriers. Unmatched on its subject is L. C. Hunter, *Steamboats on the Western Rivers* (1949). J. A. Durrenberger, *Turnpikes* (1931), is a scholarly work on the toll roads. Carter Goodrich, *Government Promotion of American Canals and Railroads 1800-1890* (1960), is outstanding; on the Erie Canal and related subjects, an excellent work is Nathan Miller, *The Enterprise of a Free People: Aspects of Economic Development in New York State During the Canal Period 1792-1838* (1962). Three other works are illuminating on the relations and the state and business enterprise in this period: Louis Hartz, *Economic Policy and Democratic Thought, Pennsylvania 1776-1860* (1948); Oscar and M. F. Handlin, *Commonwealth, A Study of the Role of Government in the American Economy, Massachusetts 1774-1861* (1947); and J. N. Primm, *Economic Policy in the Development of a Western State: Missouri 1820-1860* (1954). Volume II of Joseph Dorfman, *The Economic Mind in American Civilization* (5 vols., 1946-1959) is valuable for the thought behind the policies. Seymour Dunbar, *A History of American Travel* (4 vols., 1915), is an absorbing work lavishly illustrated. Excellent on ocean shipping, in addition to Morison, cited above, is R. G. Albion, *Square Riggers on Schedule* (1938). The same author's *The Rise of New York Port 1815-1860* (1939) is superb on New York's rise to greatness. Milton Reizenstein, *The Economic History of the Baltimore and Ohio Railroad 1827-1853* (1897), is a valuable study of the first railroad. For other works on railroad history, see Chapter 14.

Jeanette Mirsky and Allan Nevins, *The World of Eli Whitney** (1952), is a first-rate study of the emergence of the industrial spirit. C. F. Ware, *The Early New England Cotton Manufacture* (1931), presents all phases of America's first modern industry in scholarly fashion. An illuminating special study is Vera Shlakman, *Economic History of a Factory Town* (1935). Of special interest on the history of the corporation are E. M. Dodd, *American Business Corporations until 1860* (1954), and J. W. Cadman, Jr., *The Corporation in New Jersey 1791-1875* (1949). Volume I of V. S. Clark, *History of Manufactures in the United States* (3 vols., 1928), is very informative on the rise of industry. Much the best account of the early labor movement is to be found in volume I of J. R. Commons and others, *History of Labor in the United States* (4 vols., 1918-1935).

CHAPTER TEN

When James Monroe left the White House in 1825, the age of the Founding Fathers had clearly ended. The new nation at last had won that standing and respect abroad which gave her the security she needed to direct the energies of her people toward the immeasurable opportunities beckoning at home. These opportunities were grasped with a will in all sections of the country (see Chapter 9), and their rewards had already fostered that great leveling tendency which was to culminate in widespread democratic reforms at the same time that they enlarged imperial hemispheric ambitions.

The Jeffersonians, the levelers and ex-

General Jackson
and His Times

pansionists of the early national period, built their power by urging "the people," especially the people who had won a stake in the land, to vote. The philosophy that goes by the name of Jeffersonian Democracy assumed that nature had endowed the common man, the yeoman farmer, with enough good sense to vote for those among his betters who manifestly had his best interests in view. In the new age, governed by the philosophy called Jacksonian Democracy, one's "betters" seemed to have retreated to the backwaters of power or else to have been swallowed up in the strong surge toward equality, which open oppor-

tunity had favored. The Jacksonians, so-called, urged the people to seek office as well as to vote; careers in politics, as in business and the professions as well as on the land, were now open to talent no matter how coarse the garb it might be clothed in.

Few men were more coarsely clothed than "Old Hickory" himself. When friends hinted to the General early in the 1820's that he was "by no means safe from the presidency in 1824," he replied with his usual downrightness: "No, sir, I know what I am fit for. I can command a body of men in a rough way; but I am not fit to be

President." But after the people had twice elected him to the highest office, in 1828 and 1832, he acknowledged their superior authority. "Never for a moment," he said then, "believe that the great body of citizens of any State can deliberately intend to do wrong." If, by accident, they or their duly elected representatives, nevertheless, in his opinion, did wrong, as president of all the people, he knew he was the man to set things right again.

Jackson's heroic past was irresistible to the new breed of career politicians, who, as one of them put it in 1823, "always bow to a 'rising sun,' and stand prepared to dance round the 'golden calf.'"

Once in office, moreover, Jackson's high and mighty posture only embellished his reputation with the people. Congress, the Supreme Court, the National Bank; the Indians, the English, and the French; the "interests" of the North, the "nullifiers" of the South, the "internal improvements" men of the West—all were to feel the sting of his wrath. With self-righteous zeal, Jackson slew imaginary dragons of inequality. Even on such a technical issue as the removal of the government's deposits from Biddle's Bank (see p. 280), and in such a formal missive as a communiqué to his Cabinet, he felt obliged to over-extend his guardian hand:

The president repeats, that he begs the cabinet to consider the proposed measure as his own. . . . Its responsibility has been assumed, after the most mature deliberation and reflection, as necessary to preserve the morals of the people, the freedom of the press, and the purity of the election franchise.

"The morals of the people!" cried Henry Clay, when he learned of Jackson's statement. "What part of the Constitution has given to the president any power over 'the morals of the people?' None." And the same for "the freedom of the press" and the "purity of the franchise."

Jackson's zeal in searching out enemies of the people and his rhetoric in demolishing them enabled the politicians of his party to keep their idol in the public eye. Unfortunately for them, the politicians of Clay's own party borrowed Jacksonian methods to defeat Jackson's handpicked heir. In the election of 1840, when the Whigs mobilized Jackson's opponents in all sections behind another old hero, General William Henry Harrison, the full strength of "Jacksonian Democracy" for the first time really showed itself at the polls. By broadening the scope of the office, Jackson helped give a new and lasting focus to democratic politics. By further refining the tactics of such politics, Jackson's opponents ultimately unseated his partisans.

I. *The Rise of the Common Man*

THE DEMOCRATIC IMPULSE

On July 4, 1826, the fiftieth anniversary of the Declaration of Independence, the Jacksonian historian-to-be, young George Bancroft, said in a commemorative address:

We hold it best that the laws should favor the diffusion of property and its acquisition, not the concentration of it in the hands of the few to the impoverishment of the many. We give the power to the many in the hope and to the end, that they may use it for their own benefit.

At the time Bancroft spoke, a greater proportion of American citizens than ever before had acquired the power to vote, and to vote for candidates named by themselves. Between 1816 and 1821, six new states (all in the West or Southwest but Maine) entered the Union with constitutions that required no property qualifications for voting. But it was the older states, not those on the moving frontier, that had set the precedent and offered the example. As early as 1801, George Cabot of Massachusetts declared: "The spirit of our country is doubtless more democratic than the *form* of our government." According to the great Philadelphia architect, Benjamin H. Latrobe, writing in 1806, the "form" was already in the process of being made consistent with the spirit. "After the adoption of the Federal Constitution," wrote Latrobe, "the extension of the right of suffrage in the States to a majority of all the adult male citizens, planted a germ which had gradually evolved and has spread actual and practical democracy and political equality over the whole union."

Andrew Jackson (1767-1845).

The Vermont constitution of 1777, although containing other restrictive conditions, was the first explicitly to free the right to vote from property-holding or tax-paying qualifications, and this constitution was continued when Vermont was admitted to the Union in 1791. Kentucky in 1799, New Jersey in 1807, Maryland in 1810, Connecticut in 1818, then successively liberalized the franchise. Connecticut became a model for such northern states as Maine (one of the six new states), Massachusetts, and New York. As the New York *National Advocate* said in August, 1821, "In Connecticut they disarmed the poorer classes by taking them into the body politic." New York followed suit that year (with further

liberalizing constitutional amendments in 1826), after Maine and Massachusetts had acted in 1819 and 1820 respectively.

The South, generally, lagged behind the North and the West, and Virginia, despite the Jeffersonian tradition, lagged behind the rest of the South, becoming in 1852 the last state in the Union to surrender the property test. Only a few years earlier, Louisiana altered her heavy taxpaying qualification, so that the franchise was significantly broadened. Elsewhere in the slave states, prompted in large part by the argument of Senator Morgan of Virginia, the more liberal example of Maryland already had been followed. "We ought," said Senator Morgan in 1829, "to spread wide the foundation of our government, that all white men have a direct interest in its protection." What he meant specifically was protection against Negro slave revolts.

Besides Virginia and Louisiana, the only state in the Union that did not achieve virtual white male suffrage by 1840 was Rhode Island. Here, the state government still functioned under the colonial charter of 1663 according to which freeholders alone, now making up less than half of the adult males in the state, could vote. In 1841, the state administration rejected a proposed new "People's Constitution" with liberal franchise qualifications that had been drafted in orderly fashion and ratified by a large number of citizens. The determined reformers responded in 1842 by electing their own governor, Thomas W. Dorr, thereby creating a second government in Rhode Island. Now the official regime declared the Dorr party in rebellion, imposed martial law, and called out the militia. When both sides appealed to President Tyler (see p. 285), he felt obliged under the United States Constitution (Art. IV, Sec. 4) to promise "protection" to the regular government "against domestic violence." After a Dorrite assault on the state arsenal failed (the extent of the "Dorr War"), Dorr surrendered. In 1844 he was tried and sentenced to life imprisonment, but the next year the sentence was withdrawn. In 1843, meanwhile, the official regime saw the light and accepted a new constitution liberalizing the franchise qualification.

The democratic spirit of the country failed to carry over to one significant class of the population—the free Negroes. As late as 1820, free Negroes were permitted by law to vote equally with whites in northern New England, in New York and Pennsylvania, and even in such southern states as Tennessee and North Carolina. This right, however, usually had arisen only from omissions in the law and was subject to every abuse until the law itself was tightened. As a delegate to the Pennsylvania constitutional convention of 1837 said on his way to the assemblage that would disfranchise the free Negro, "the people of this state are for continuing this commonwealth, what it always has been, a political community of white persons." By then, the free Negro's right to vote survived only in New England north of Connecticut. In the other states where they once enjoyed the franchise they had been deprived of it (or, where past Negro voters could continue to vote, as in Connecticut after 1818, newly freed ones had been disfranchised), usually by the very same article which for the first time provided virtually full manhood suffrage for whites. No state entering the Union after 1819 permitted the free Negro to vote before the Civil War.

Loss of the franchise, moreover, was only one of the lengthening list of free Negro disabilities in the free as in the slave states. Consigned to miserable alley slums, confined by curfews, beyond the pale of the judicial and educational systems, barred from all but the most menial urban occupations and from the land as well, he was "cast upon the world," as an Oregonian said even of his own distant commonwealth in the 1850's, "with no defense; his life, liberty, his property, his all, are dependent on the caprice, the passion, and the inveterate prejudices of not only the community at large but of every felon who may happen to cover an inhuman heart with a white face." By then, many western states would not even allow free Negroes in.

For the "political community of white persons," on the other hand, even more significant perhaps than the legal extension of the suffrage was the heightened interest of the common man in exercising that right. While proportions running up to 70 per cent of the electorate had voted earlier in hot local contests, presidential elections until 1828 seemed to have left most voters cold. Even in 1824, when Jackson himself first was a candidate (see p. 265), only 355,000 votes were counted, compared with 1,155,000 in 1828. In the following twenty years the number going to the polls soared 250 per cent.

One reason for the voters' new interest was the gradual restoration of the two-party system after 1824 and sharper party differences on issues. Another was the voters' enlarged participation in actually naming the candidates. The old system of nominating presidential candidates by a "caucus," or meeting, of congressmen kept the inner-party clique in power. Rising politicians hated "king caucus," while to the public it seemed a symbol of aristocratic rule. The first break in the system came in 1824 when growing sectional differences made it difficult for the Republican party to agree on a candidate and independent groups named men of their own. The credit for developing the modern method of nominating candidates by means of national conventions made up of delegates "fresh from the people," went to a short-lived minor party, the Anti-Masons, who held the first convention in 1830. The major parties also adopted the innovation in time for the election of 1832 (see p. 278).

Still another institution gave way before the demand to bring government closer to the people. This was the old system under which, in most states, presidential electors had been chosen by the state legislatures. By 1828, all the states except Delaware and South Carolina had substituted for this system the popular election of members of the electoral college. Jackson, as he often reminded his opponents, thus became in fact the first president who could claim to have been elected directly by the voters. Governors also began to be popularly elected, and property qualifications for that office and others were swept away. Finally, in the 1840's state judges were being elected rather than appointed—an innovation that would have startled even the more democratic of the Founding Fathers.

THE ELECTION OF 1824

If Jackson thought little of himself as presidential timber in 1824, the rising new politicians, party not public leaders, who saw in their power to control the popular vote a surer path to wealth and influence than office-holding, were eager to tie their fortunes to the General's coat tails. One of them was William L. Marcy of New York, who coined the slogan, "To the victors belong the spoils." Others were Amos Kendall of Kentucky and William B. Lewis of Tennessee, who, with Marcy, later became part of Jackson's "Kitchen Cabinet." In 1824 they entered "Old Hickory" in the presidential sweepstakes. Jackson's opponents in 1824 were William H. Crawford of Georgia, the caucus candidate, who suffered a stroke during the campaign and was not a serious contender; John Quincy Adams, of Massachusetts, and Henry Clay, now Speaker of the House.

Clay and Adams, although far apart in origins and temperament, both subscribed to Clay's celebrated "American System." Clay pictured an industrial East providing a growing home market for southern cotton and western grain and meat and an agricultural West and South providing an expanding market for eastern manufacturing enterprise. For the East he would supply protective tariffs; for the West and South "internal improvements" such as canals and railroads to lower transportation costs. Transactions between the sections would be facilitated by a stable credit system underwritten by a national bank. This plan, said Clay, would "place the confederacy upon the most solid of all foundations, [that] of common interest."

Just what Jackson stood for was less clear, even to himself. When pressed he said he was for a "judicious" tariff, which only caused Henry Clay to explode, "Well, by—, I am in favor of an injudicious tariff!" Jackson's stands were likely to be strongly personal. The biographer, James Parton, long ago successfully appraised Jackson's character:

. . . honest, yet capable of dissimulation; often angry, but most prudent when most furious; endowed by nature with the gift of extracting from every affair and every relation all the strife it can be made to yield; at home and among dependents, all tenderness and generosity; to opponents, violent, ungenerous, prone to believe the very worst of them . . . not taking kindly to culture, but able to achieve wonderful things without it.

Once he had overcome his humble North Carolina origins and made his mark as a lawyer in Tennessee, Jackson had never shown himself a "Jacksonian" democrat. His party affiliation was Jeffersonian; but

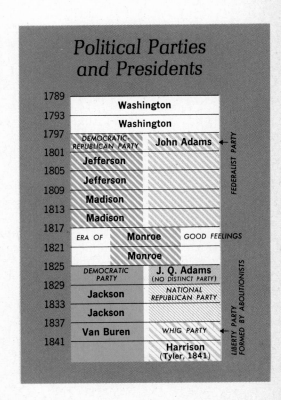

Political Parties and Presidents

Year	Party	President	
1789		Washington	
1793		Washington	
1797	DEMOCRATIC-REPUBLICAN PARTY	John Adams	FEDERALIST PARTY
1801		Jefferson	
1805		Jefferson	
1809		Madison	
1813		Madison	
1817	ERA OF	Monroe	GOOD FEELINGS
1821		Monroe	
1825	DEMOCRATIC PARTY	J. Q. Adams (NO DISTINCT PARTY)	
1829		Jackson	NATIONAL REPUBLICAN PARTY
1833		Jackson	
1837		Van Buren	WHIG PARTY
1841		Harrison (Tyler, 1841)	

LIBERTY PARTY FORMED BY ABOLITIONISTS

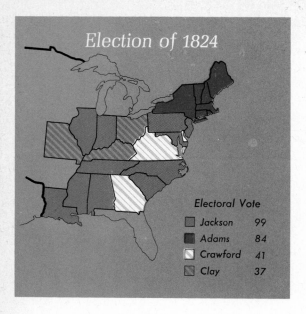

Election of 1824

Electoral Vote

☐	Jackson	99
■	Adams	84
▨	Crawford	41
▨	Clay	37

his narrow state-rights views made it easy for him to mingle with the powerful in the states, and not the common man. His practice placed him on the side of the "land barons" or "nabobs," and against the "leather shirts." He favored creditors over debtors, absentee landlords over squatters. Jackson shared with other westerners the willingness to judge men by their attainments, not by their social backgrounds. If this helped his backers to present him as the champion of the common man, so much the better for them all, even though the attainments of his friends were uncommon.

The Hero of New Orleans did not disappoint the politicians. In the election of 1824 he won 153,000 popular votes to Adams' 108,000, Crawford's 46,000 and Clay's 47,000. In the electoral college, however, his 99 votes fell considerably short of the required majority, and the contest was thrown into the House of Representatives. Here Clay, with the lowest electoral total, was eliminated. At the same time he was so placed as to be able to decide between Jackson and Adams by swinging his strong House following behind either man. Clay had no love for Jackson. "I cannot believe," he said, that killing 2500 Englishmen at New Orleans qualifies [him] for the various difficult and complicated duties of the Chief Magistracy." After a private talk with Adams, who sympathized with Clay's ideas on

foreign policy as well as with his "American System," Clay swung his supporters to the Yankee. Thanks largely to Clay's influence, Adams was elected in the House, where the vital support of New York went to him by a single vote.

One of Adams' first presidential acts was to name Clay Secretary of State, and thereby, in the opinion of the age, as his successor. The Jackson men lost no time in charging that a "corrupt bargain" had been made at the Clay-Adams talk. Even had a bargain been made, there need have been nothing corrupt about it between men so sympathetic to one another's program. But "bargain and corruption" became the Jacksonians' slogan for the campaign of 1828, which they opened once they learned of their defeat in 1824. For four years they successfully manipulated public suspicion, and Adams' administration began, and ended, under this cloud.

JOHN QUINCY ADAMS IN OFFICE

The alleged "deal" was not the only issue that haunted Adams in the White House. A sensitive and high-minded man, he regretted having to accept the presidency with, as he said, "perhaps two-thirds of the whole people adverse to the actual result." Adams, nevertheless, was not to be deterred by popular symptoms from launching a program he considered right for the country. In his first annual message to Congress he displayed both his stubborn courage and his political ineptitude by making a sweeping argument for a strong national government vigorous in the use of its powers for national improvements directed from the top. Warned by Henry Clay and all but one of the rest of his Cabinet that, at a time when state-rights feelings were rising and sectional jealousies were strong, it was all but suicidal for a president—and a minority president at that—to launch upon such a course, Adams at least conceded that his program was a "perilous experiment."

Congress under the Constitution, Adams argued in his message, had the power to "provide for the common defense and general welfare." This power would justify "laws promoting the improvement of agriculture, commerce, and manufactures, the cultivation and encouragement of the mechanic and of the elegant arts, the advancement of literature, and the progress of the sciences, ornamental and profound." To refrain from exercising this power in the grand manner would be "treachery to the most sacred of trusts." Accordingly he called for the establishment of a national university, the financing of scientific expeditions, the building of astronomical observatories ("light-houses of the skies"), the promulgation of a uniform standard of weights and measures, the reform of the patent laws, the creation of a Department of the Interior, and the development of a large-scale program of internal improvements.

To suggest, as Adams thoughtlessly did, that the monarchical governments of Europe were doing something superior to democratic America in maintaining observatories only offered proof to his enemies that Adams was a monarchist at heart, one hardened in his attitudes by his long experience abroad. Adams' further suggestion that it would be shameful for Congress to be "palsied by the will of our constituents," was simply to seal the doom of his experiment from the outset.

A dozen years later, Adams explained that "the great effort of my administration" was to apply "all the superfluous revenue of the Union into internal improvement," and thereby provide employment for thousands while enriching the nation.

With this system in ten years from this day the surface of the whole Union would have been checkered over with railroads and canals. It may still be done half a century later and with the limping gait of State legislature and private adventure. I would have done it in the administration of the affairs of the nation.

Adams continued this explanation with an analysis of the defeat of his program:

When I came to the Presidency this principle of internal improvement was swelling the tide of public prosperity, till the Sable Genius of the South saw the signs of his own inevitable

downfall in the unparalleled progress of the general welfare in the North, and fell to cursing the tariff and internal improvement, and raised the standard of free trade, nullification, and state rights.

In fact, many in the Middle States and the Middle West joined with the South in rejecting Adams' proposals. At the same time, many self-made men (Clay first coined this term to describe the rising manufacturers of Kentucky) were ranged on Adams' side. It is sometimes said that the President's paternalism dampened the spirit of such men; but Adams correctly identified his principle enemies and their's as the state-rights men, the focus of that "mass of local jealousies," as one historian puts it, in the South as elsewhere.

Adams' own misguided morality must also bear part of the blame. Having made his too grandiose proposals to a lukewarm Congress in offensive rhetoric, he refused to use the power of the presidency to push them through. He especially resisted the employment of presidential patronage to gain votes even for a program to which he was profoundly committed. During his entire term he removed but 12 civil servants from office and then only for fraud or malfeasance. No wonder he and his supporters were shocked later by Jackson's theory and practice of the "spoils system" (see p. 270).

Adams' comprehensive program for centralized economic development, and his failure to push it through, encouraged his state-rights opponents everywhere to mobilize their own machines behind the pleasingly vague and perfectly popular Jackson. His additional setbacks in Indian and foreign relations made their task all the easier. Adams' efforts to preserve the lands of the Creek Indians in Georgia, against the violent resistance of the state, its speculators, and its potential frontier settlers, proved most humiliating in their outcome. This confrontation led up to the case of *Worcester* v. *Georgia*, which itself was to provide the occasion for Jackson's major victory over the Supreme Court (see p. 272).

Adams was no more successful in diplomacy. The United States had been invited to attend a congress of Latin-American republics in Panama in 1826 called by Simon Bolívar, the great South American liberator, to discuss common problems. Clay was particularly eager to have the United States represented, and Adams thought the congress might provide a first step toward the acquisition of Cuba. Adams tactlessly agreed to send delegates without first consulting the Senate. His enemies there, led by Martin Van Buren and John Randolph, held up appropriations for the delegates' expenses; they attacked one of the appointees as "an acknowledged abolitionist" and described the Latin-Americans as "an ignorant and vicious people." When the Panama conference came to end, no representative from the United States had made an appearance.

A more discouraging blow to national prestige resulted from Adams' clumsy and ill-timed negotiations with the British Foreign Secretary, George Canning. Adams had brought pressure on the British government to permit American ships to engage in direct trade with the British West Indies. But Canning was unyielding, and, in fact, imposed even more drastic restraints on American commerce. Adams' opponents added this failure to their already impressive list of campaign issues.

THE ELECTION OF JACKSON

By the time of the congressional elections of 1826 Adams' program had gained the name of National Republicans for his followers, while his opponents became known as the Democratic Republicans. In those elections, for the first time in the history of the country, as Adams himself ruefully acknowledged, a president lost his majority in Congress after his first two years in office. When the new Congress convened in December, 1827, under Jacksonian leadership, its only purpose was to further Jackson's presidential prospects in 1828. When the Jackson men, led by the rising

Van Buren of New York, placed their hand-picked candidate in the Speakership of the House, Senator John Tyler commented that "the opposition party constitutes the *administration*. Upon it rests the responsibility of all legislative measures." Even Adams' Vice-president, Calhoun, although still a nationalist, went over to the Jacksonians and agreed to become their vice-presidential candidate. Very likely, Calhoun expected the 61-year-old Jackson not to run for a second term and to leave the succession to him.

The Jacksonian strategy was to woo support in all key or questionable states by means of legislative largesse. Beyond that, Van Buren and his aides undertook so to blacken Adams' name that this austere Yankee intellectual, because of his long experience abroad, was made to seem "a very compost of European vices," and unfit for high office.

The campaign of 1828 marked a new high in electioneering activity and a new low in political dignity. Jackson's supporters introduced a rough-and-tumble carnival spirit into the presidential contest that persisted in later years. They paraded with hickory sticks to symbolize the toughness of "Old Hickory," and brandished hickory brooms to suggest the need for sweeping the rascals out. Feeling among the Jacksonians ran extraordinarily high. "Adams, Clay and Company—" ran a toast that was drunk in South Carolina, "Would to God they were like Jonah in the whale's belly; the whale to the devil; the devil in hell; and the door locked, key lost, and not a son of Vulcan within a million miles to make another." To top off their personal attacks on Adams, they accused the President of having purveyed an innocent American girl to the lust of Czar Alexander I while serving as United States minister to Russia years before.

Adams condemned the resort to abusive smears, but he had backers who outdid the Jackson men in scurrility. They went so far as to brand Jackson an adulterer on a trivial technicality over his wife's divorce from her former husband almost forty years earlier. Jackson's wife suffered intensely from such publicity and died shortly after the election. Jackson never forgave "those vile wretches who have slandered her" and, in his opinion, killed her.

The vile tactics of his advisers did Adams no good whatever. Jackson's efforts to deal with issues, in turn, probably cost him votes. The principal issue was the protective tariff. By a tariff act in 1824, Congress had raised the duties on key manufactures. This act had won the support of the industrial Middle states and the Old Northwest, which continued to look eastward for markets for its agricultural surplus. New England, with big manufacturers of her own, yet still heavily committed to commerce, had split on the measure. The cotton South, in turn, which had surrendered its hopes for manufacturing, overwhelmingly opposed it. Here was an alignment out of which Jackson's lieutenants, already heavily engaged in deals of all sorts, notably in granting federal public lands to politically doubtful states, might make more political hay. Their means was the tariff of 1828, whose object, as John Randolph said, was to encourage "manufactures of no sort but the manufacture of a President of the United States."

Because it raised the general level of the duties, southerners branded the tariff of 1828, "the tariff of abominations." But because it failed to protect woolens manufacturers while at the same time it raised duties on raw wool and other raw materials, the tariff of 1828 also distressed certain northern industrialists. By embracing the princi-

Election of 1828

Electoral Vote

☐ Jackson   178
■ Adams   83
▨ Divided

ple of protection, Jacksonians may have sought support among manufacturers in the forthcoming elections; but by writing a bill which manufacturers might help defeat, they may also have hoped for southern backing. If such was their plan it failed, for the bill passed, abominations and all.

Jackson survived the backfiring of the tariff scheme. As the hero of New Orleans, the champion of the common man, the most visible old soldier in the country for four solid years, he polled 647,000 votes. The surprise, if any, was that Adams, with 508,000 votes, was far from routed. In the electoral college Jackson won, 178 to 83. Despite the tariff catastrophe he carried the entire South. Only New England, and Delaware and New Jersey, ran against him.

II. "Old Hickory" in the White House

THE HEAD
OF THE GOVERNMENT

Jackson's inauguration attracted to Washington an immense crowd which seemed to think, as Daniel Webster said, that "the country is rescued from some dreadful danger." The people surged through the still unpaved streets and pressed into the White House as if to make themselves equally at home as their hero.

In the White House itself the new chief was busily engaged with his personal friends in naming the official functionaries of his administration. Martin Van Buren emerged as Secretary of State, John McLean of Ohio, Adams' Jacksonian Postmaster-General was retained in his post and the post itself soon was raised to Cabinet level. One disappointed big fish said of the rest of the Cabinet that it reflected "The Millennium of the Minnows," and he was not far wrong. But it did not matter too much because Jackson's principal advisers, besides Van Buren, were in his private not his public Cabinet. In addition to Kendall and Lewis, these advisers included the young nephew of Jackson's wife, Andrew Jackson Donelson, whom the President himself had raised, and such trusted western newspaper editors as Duff Green and Francis Preston Blair. Whatever these men or Jackson himself may have thought about the urgent new issues in national politics—the tariff, internal improvements, the bank, land and Indian policy—they all shared "Old Hickory's" feeling about the presidency itself. Jackson's worst enemies wondered whether the arbitrary old General would turn out to be a tyrant, whether republican government was safe in his hands. These enemies eventually came together as Whigs (see p. 283) in defiance of "King Andrew I." Jackson did not, in fact, become a tyrant. But the first principle of his two administrations was the congenial one of executive supremacy. The president alone was elected by all the people and was the chief instrument of their will, as interpreted by himself.

Jackson's policy in relation to the executive civil service was consistent with his independent view of his high office. The President shocked the Adams men by discharging about 900 jobholders from among the 10,000 he found on the payroll. Actually, his party chieftains, having made many commitments in two campaigns, wanted more heads to roll, more places to fill; but Jackson restrained them. The Adams press made a great noise about the new "reign of terror," and the grim "purge" that was bloodying Washington's streets; but in the long run it was the President's gratuitous defense of the "spoils system," rather than the particular replacements themselves, that so firmly associated his name with it. Earlier presidents had removed opposition partisans from office without raising many eyebrows. Jackson was the first to make the "spoils system" seem a social and moral as well as a political "reform."

The political aspect Jackson covered in his inaugural address, conveniently closing his eyes to the deals made by his own promoters, and noting as "inscribed" by the recent election, "in characters too legible to be overlooked, the task of *reform,* which will require particularly the correction of those abuses that have brought the patronage of the Federal Government into conflict with the freedom of elections."

The social aspect Jackson dealt with in his first annual message to Congress in December, 1829. In this message he proposed "a general extension of the law which limits appointments to four years," thereby furthering "that rotation which constitutes a leading principle in the republican creed, giving healthful action to the system." Such a law, he continued, in a style that was to become characteristic of his presidential pronouncements, would nullify the prevailing idea that "office is . . . a species of property, and government . . . a means of promoting individual interests, . . . an engine for the support of the few at the expense of the many." Jackson was ready to exclude judges, cabinet officers, and diplomats "of the highest rank" from this egalitarian rule. Otherwise, "the duties of public offices" are "plain and simple," and plain and simple men could best perform them in the people's interest.

The moral aspect Jackson dealt with in his "Outline of Principles," according to which his heads of departments were to examine the "moral habits" of incumbents and to fire those lax in "private or public relations."

The four-year law Jackson suggested was not enacted; but he and his successors did so well without it in finding just rewards for party workers hungry for "the loaves and fishes" that the reform of Jackson's "reforms" eventually became the leading issue in American politics (see Chapter 20).

"THE LEGITIMATE SPHERE
OF STATE SOVEREIGNTIES"

In his relations with Congress and the courts the new Chief Executive proved no less aggressive than in his attitude toward the "unfaithful" office holders he inherited.

Earlier presidents had been largely content to administer the laws passed by Congress. But Jackson grasped the constitutional power given the executive to participate in making (or better, unmaking) the law as well as executing it. In his two terms Jackson vetoed more legislation than all former presidents together. This would appear a remarkable record for one so openly attached to popular government; but Jackson, especially after his experiences in the election of 1824 (see p. 266), had come to regard Congress, in his usual vein, as the home of "aristocratical establishments" like the national bank, and his own office as the only popular bulwark against such "interests" as the new industrialists. In his inaugural address he promised that, "in administering the laws of Congress, I shall keep steadily in view the limitations as well as the extent of the Executive power." He did not necessarily mean the limitations of his own power, only the limitations on Congress in requiring the Executive to do what he did not wish to do. Jackson's vetoes usually were based on the specific constitutional point of unwarranted congressional invasions of state rights.

One of Jackson's most famous vetoes killed the so-called Maysville Bill of 1830, which would have required the federal government to subscribe to the stock of a private corporation promoted to build an "internal improvement" in Clay's state of Kentucky. Because the Maysville road would lie wholly within a single state, Jackson's stand was easier to take. He knew it would also find strong support in such states as New York and Pennsylvania which had been so important in his election victory and which, having developed transportation systems at their own expense, were determined to keep the federal government from helping to construct competing systems farther west. He could also expect support from the South Atlantic states, increasingly committed to slavery and hence to the principle of state rights, the strongest constitutional bastion of slavery. These states were also increasingly opposed to protective tariffs on essential manufactures, which supplied the federal funds available for internal improvements.

Jackson, in his two administrations, approved unprecedented appropriations for river and harbor improvement bills and similar pork-barrel legislation sponsored by worthy Democrats in compensation for local election support. On the basis of this record a case has been made for the old General's genuine sympathy for federal aid to internal improvements of a national character, and hence for the exceptional nature of the Maysville veto, influenced, it is said, by strategic party considerations. But Jackson was eternally at pains to disavow any such interpretation and to make it clear that he believed federal aid to internal improvements of any sort an unconstitutional invasion of state prerogatives.

In his first annual message, Jackson told Congress that "the mode . . . hitherto adopted" for the "improvement of inland navigation and the construction of highways . . . has been deprecated as an infraction of the Constitution." He went on to propose, "that the most safe, just, and federal disposition which could be made of the surplus revenue would be its apportionment among the several states." He then proceeded to draw the general moral:

The great mass of legislation relating to our internal affairs was intended to be left where the Federal Convention found it—in the State governments. Nothing is clearer, in my view, than that we are chiefly indebted for the success of the Constitution under which we are now acting to the watchful and auxiliary operation of the State authorities. This is not the reflection of a day, but belongs to the most deeply rooted convictions of my mind. I can not, therefore, too strongly or too earnestly, for my own sense of its importance, warn you against all encroachments upon the legitimate sphere of State sovereignties.

In his Maysville veto message, he reminded Congress that "the act which I am called upon to consider has, therefore, been passed with a knowledge of my views on this question." Such disrespect was intolerable to "Old Hickory," and the veto stuck. The more firmly to underscore the principle, Jackson, while he could not avoid approving additional funds for the extension of the National Road (see p. 249), as his predecessors since Jefferson all had done, destroyed the national character of the great project by turning over completed sections to the states in which they lay.

In asserting his independence of the Supreme Court also, Jackson put state rights first. His most famous stand against the Court came in 1832, following John Marshall's decision in *Worcester* v. *Georgia,* concerning Georgia's claims to sovereignty over Cherokee lands.

In 1802, as we have seen (p. 205), when Georgia ceded her western lands to the United States, the federal government agreed to quiet Creek and Cherokee title to the region. Federal action, however, was slow; and as cotton-growing spread in the state, the planters' patience ran out. The planters had the full sympathy of Georgia's militant Governor, George M. Troup, who, in 1826, ordered a state survey of Creek lands with an eye to their prompt sale and settlement. When President Adams threatened to halt the survey with federal forces, Governor Troup said he would resist force with force. Civil war was averted only by the Creeks' own capitulation to the inevitable and their decision to move beyond the Mississippi.

The Cherokees, like the Creeks, had embraced the white man's ways, set up farms and factories, erected schools, and published a newspaper. In 1827, they decided to form an independent state on the American model. They also adopted a constitution under which this state would be governed. Georgia responded by nullifying all federal Indian laws and ordering the forcible seizure of Cherokee lands. When her courts next tried and convicted a Cherokee of murder, the Supreme Court of the United States ordered the conviction set aside; but Governor Troup and the state

legislature ignored the federal government's "interference" and executed the prisoner. By then, Jackson had become President; and it was well-known in Georgia, as elsewhere, that his concern for the redmen was as cold as his sympathy for the planters was warm.

Unlike Adams, Jackson did nothing to assert federal authority over Georgia in Indian affairs. The Cherokees, however, did have friends who sought an injunction in the Supreme Court forbidding the extension of Georgia law over Indian residents and Georgia's seizure of Indian lands. In 1831, John Marshall, in the case of *Cherokee Nation* v. *Georgia,* denied the long-standing rule that the Indians were tantamount to "foreign nations" with whom the United States made treaties which federal courts were empowered to enforce. The Indians, he said, were "domestic dependent nations," who could not sue in United States courts. He denied the injunction, but he asserted, nevertheless, that the United States alone, and no single state, had sovereignty over the redmen and over the disposition of their lands. In 1832, Marshall had an opportunity to strengthen this opinion in the case of *Worcester* v. *Georgia.* One Samuel Worcester had been convicted by Georgia for occupying Cherokee land without having first obtained a state license to do so. Marshall reversed the conviction, and went on to say that the Cherokee nation was a legitimate political community, with clearly defined territories, where "the laws of Georgia can have no force, and which the citizens of Georgia have no right to enter" without Cherokee consent by law or treaty. Georgia herself boycotted the Court's proceedings. It was after this case that Jackson is reported to have exclaimed, "John Marshall has made his decision, now let him enforce it."

Unfortunately for the Cherokees, the Jacksonian House of Representatives tabled the enforcement order introduced to restrain Georgia from evicting the Indians. This meant that no federal troops were made available to support Marshall's decision, and the spoliation of the Indian lands continued. By 1835, only a remnant of Indians still retained their lands, and after the subjugation of the Florida Seminoles (1835-42) millions of fertile acres were thrown open to white occupation. The Indians meanwhile made their trek westward over what became known as the "trail of tears," and rightly so. A fourth or more died on the journey; officials overseeing them robbed them of their funds; what they had left went for burial rites. Of the Cherokee removal in particular, Emerson cried out that, "such a dereliction of all faith and virtue, such a denial of justice, and such deafness to screams for mercy were never heard of in time of peace . . . since the earth was made."

THE WEBSTER-HAYNE DEBATE

While the head of the government in the White House was asserting his leadership of the whole nation and of all the people, the "heads of the sections" in Congress were clarifying their differences and sharpening their defenses. Many issues divided the slave from the free states, and the free West from the free East. And if compromises like the Missouri Compromise of 1820 from time to time cemented over sectional breaches, new developments in the rapidly expanding country broke them open again. Two of the most disruptive issues were public lands and protective tariffs, and the Webster-Hayne debate in the winter of 1830 plumbed the sectional depths of both.

From the 1820's on, the West had campaigned for cheap public lands (once the Indian title had been bought off and the aborigines themselves removed), and for protection for the "squatter" who claimed government land before it had officially been opened to settlement. The squatter who had improved his land during his illegal tenure, demanded the right to buy it at the minimum rate when it was finally placed on the open market. But even the minimum rate of $1.25 an acre seemed excessive to many for whom Senator Thomas Hart Benton of Missouri became the spokesman. As early as 1824, Benton had proposed that the price of unsold government land

be gradually reduced to 75 cents an acre and then to 50 cents. If no takers appeared even then, the land should be given away free. This proposal came to be known as "graduation," and it was the first formally to place a higher value to the nation as a whole on the work of the pioneer in opening up the country than on land-sale receipts to the Treasury.

Easterners regarded Benton's plan as one more scheme to tap their labor supply and force wage costs up; they also saw the quickening of the development of the West as a further threat to their political strength in the nation. On the other hand they were forced to recognize that if land sales were continued at the established prices they would bring into the Treasury money enough to invalidate one of their principal arguments for high tariffs—the need for additional revenue to pay off the national debt and support government services. Easterners like John Quincy Adams had hoped that the chaotic growth of the American economy could be brought under the discipline of a central plan administered from the top; more particularly, they wanted the price of land kept up, and the proceeds distributed among the states to help them improve public education. When nothing came of this, they resorted to the rather desperate proposal that the West be closed to settlement altogether. In December, 1829, Senator Samuel A. Foot of Connecticut offered a resolution to this effect, urging specifically that public-land surveys be stopped for a time and that future sales be limited to lands already on the market.

Senator Benton, speaking for the West, angrily denounced Foot's resolution as a manufacturer's plot. Spokesmen for the slave South, in turn, supported Benton in the hope that they could thereby aggravate the growing differences between the free East and the free West. The South's purpose was to lure the West away from the protective tariff phase of the "American System," so much desired by eastern manufacturers.

Senator Robert Y. Hayne of South Carolina presented the South's case, but his most divisive remarks were derived from an anti-tariff essay published anonymously by Vice-president Calhoun in 1828 under the title of *The Exposition and Protest*. According to Calhoun, the tariff of 1828 (see p. 269) reduced the South to serfdom to northern industrialists. They forced her to pay exorbitantly for their manufactures or for manufactured imports from Europe. At the same time, they goaded Europe into retaliating against American tariffs by raising their own against southern rice and cotton. "The tariff is unconstitutional and must be repealed," Calhoun wrote. "The rights of the South have been destroyed, and must be restored, . . . the Union is in danger, and must be saved." No free government, Calhoun argued, would permit the transfer of "power and property from one class or section to another." The tyranny of the majority could be met by the constitutional right of each state to nullify an unconstitutional act of Congress.

It was Hayne's introduction of Calhoun's nullification theory into his argument against Foot's resolution that moved Daniel Webster to reply to the South Carolinian in January, 1830. The debate was prolonged, but Webster, stirred to make an especially noble effort by Hayne's references to the New England Federalists' disloyalty to the Union during the War of 1812, had the last word.

When Webster made his final reply, beginning on January 26, the Senate realized that the debate had moved from the merely troublesome issue of public-land policy to the truly dangerous one of the underlying nature of the Union. The Union, said the "God-like Daniel," was not a mere compact among state legislatures; it was "the creature of the people." They had erected it; they alone were sovereign in it; their government, in its own right, was every bit as sanctified as the governments of the states. It was for the Supreme Court, not for the states, to decide whether laws passed by Congress were in keeping with the Constitution. If a single state had that right, the Union was dissolved and liberty itself was menaced. Webster closed his speech with what Senator Benton called "a fine piece of rhetoric misplaced," a vision of two Americas. One was of a land "rent with civil feuds, or drenched . . . in fratricidal blood," the other of a republic "now known and honored throughout the earth, still full high advanced, its arms and trophies streaming in their original lustre." He ended with the famous words: "Liberty *and* Union, now and forever, one and inseparable."

Senator Foot's resolution was lost sight of in the hubbub over the greater issues his proposal had brought more clearly into the open. Once the debate was over, the first question everyone asked was, where does Jackson stand? Hayne was his close personal friend, a constant visitor to the White House, the companion of his family. As early as January 28, publisher Duff Green, of the Kitchen Cabinet, appeared to have let the cat out of the bag, when he declared in his *United States Telegraph:* "The doctrine contended for by General HAYNE is too well understood and too firmly established . . . to be shaken." This opinion surely did no violence to Jackson's views as we have presented them up to this point of his administration. But still he kept his peace. A month passed before Webster and Hayne would release their polished-up speeches to the hungry press and people. Thereafter the pressure for a presidential statement mounted. Many Jacksonians accused Webster of hazardous demagoguery in attacking so fiercely the straw man of disunion. But once again, the man in the White House would go his own way. When he did make up his mind to talk, he would confront not Hayne the spokesman, but Calhoun, the philosopher behind the spokesman.

NULLIFICATION

The doctrine of nullification was a curious lure for the South to choose to capture the heart of the West. Beyond the coastal tier of the thirteen original commonwealths, each of which had asserted its own independence of Britain, all the new states were themselves created by the national government of the United States. They had never known independence; they had grown and flourished in and with the Union. Where they stood on the issue of nullification finally became clear enough to Jackson himself. And where the Union was involved he was with them. He was for state rights; about that there was to be no mistake. But he was for state rights *within* the Union of which he never forgot that he was president. There was to be no mistake about that either.

In April, 1830, when the leading Democrats were gathered at a Jefferson birthday dinner, "Old Hickory" looked Calhoun in the eye and proposed this toast: "Our Union—it must be preserved!" Before news of the toast was released, Hayne prevailed upon Jackson to soften the blow by inserting the word, "Federal" before "Union." But "Federal" or not, Calhoun was to be unrepentant. To Jackson's words, he rose to reply: "The Union—next to our liberty, the most dear." In the following months, old personal grudges and new personal conflicts, produced a clean break between Jackson and Calhoun which profoundly influenced the developing sectional fight.

In the spring of 1830, through some of his advisers who disliked Calhoun, Jackson discovered that in 1818, when Calhoun was Secretary of War, he had favored punishing Jackson for his conduct during the Seminole War (see p. 230). Nervously Calhoun tried to explain himself in an embarrassed letter, but he only convinced the President of his lack of candor. "Understanding you now," wrote the unforgiving Jackson to his vice-president, "no further communication with you on this subject is necessary." When Calhoun next attributed his misfortunes to Van Buren's machinations, the President viewed this as a blow at his trusted friend. His break with Calhoun became final, and the position of Calhoun's supporters in the Cabinet untenable.

The split in the Cabinet was now intensified by a social dispute that rocked Washington. In 1829, Jackson's Secretary

of War, John H. Eaton, had married Margaret O'Neale Timberlake, an ex-barmaid and the daughter of a tavern-keeper whose first husband had died while serving in the navy. Eaton's name had been scandalously linked with hers before their marriage. When Mrs. Calhoun, followed by the wives of other Cabinet members, refused to receive Mrs. Eaton, Jackson did not hesitate to defend her, no doubt remembering the attacks on his own wife. Van Buren, a widower, took advantage of the situation to ingratiate himself all the more deeply with Jackson by acting cordially to the unconventional but charming wife of his colleague Eaton.

Realizing that the social atmosphere of the Cabinet would be a liability to the administration, however, Van Buren offered his resignation in the hope that it would force Jackson to reorganize the whole Cabinet. This shrewd move relieved him from the charge that he was manipulating the administration in his own interests and further convinced other Jackson men of Van Buren's unselfish devotion. Eaton had also submitted his resignation, and Jackson now called for similar action by the remaining members. In appointing their successors, Jackson passed over the Calhoun men and chose a well-knit group of loyal backers. Van Buren was soon nominated as minister to Great Britain, and Eaton was appointed governor of Florida Territory.

It was obvious now that Jackson regarded Van Buren and not Vice-president Calhoun as his successor. More important, the Cabinet shake-up confirmed the ascendancy over Virginia and South Carolina in the Jacksonian party of a coalition comprising the newer states of the West and Southwest and the large Democratic states of Pennsylvania and New York.

Calhoun, nevertheless, still had a few volleys of his own to fire. As President of the Senate he was able to cast the tie-breaking vote by which Van Buren's nomination as minister to Britain was rejected, 24-23. He also found a more significant occasion to press not only his defiance but his doctrine. Unfortunately for him, Jackson chose the same occasion to show who was boss. The South went largely with Calhoun; the free West and the free East clung to each other and to "Old Hickory."

The tariff, once more, provided the decisive issue. Receipts from the existing duties were so high that by 1830 the national debt had been almost entirely paid off. Jackson believed protective (as against revenue) tariffs to be as unconstitutional as appropriations for internal improvements, and in his message of December 6, 1831, he urged Congress to revise the Tariff of 1828 downward. If he hoped to appease the discontented South by this proposal, he also sufficiently modified the requested reductions so as not to antagonize the industrial Northeast. On July 14, 1832, Congress passed a tariff bill that met Jackson's specifications. It hardly satisfied Calhoun, however, and the vice-president rushed home from Washington to mobilize southern opposition.

The doctrine of nullification was reasserted. This time, moreover, in a series of dramatic steps, South Carolina moved to put Calhoun's theories into effect. A legislature overwhelmingly favorable to nullification was elected. This legislature then ordered the election of delegates to a special state convention. On November 19, 1832, this convention assembled and soon adopted by a vote of 136-26 an ordinance of nullification which declared the tariffs of 1828 and 1832 void. The convention also (1) ordered the legislature to prohibit the collection of the duties in state ports after February 1, 1833; and (2) asserted that the use of armed federal forces to collect the duties would be followed by secession.

Jackson, more assertive than ever after his recent smashing success in the election of 1832 (see p. 280), replied on December 10 with his ringing Nullification Proclamation, which made his position plain:

I consider . . . the power to annul a law of the United States, assumed by one State, incompatible with the existence of the Union,

contradicted expressly by the letter of the Constitution, unauthorized by its spirit, inconsistent with every principle on which it was founded, and destructive of the great object for which it was formed.

Jackson warned that the laws of the United States compelled him to meet treason with force.

In February, 1833, the Senate passed a "Force Bill" empowering the president to use the army and navy if rebellious South Carolina resisted federal customs officials. While the Force Bill was being debated, Henry Clay offered a new tariff bill calling for a gradual reduction of the 1832 duties. South Carolina leaders now waited to see what would happen to these two measures. They had already learned that other southern states had repudiated nullification and that a vigorous Unionist faction inside their own borders would continue to fight it.

On the day (March 2) that the Force Act became law, Jackson also signed Clay's tariff of 1833. This tariff provided for a gradual reduction of duties until, by July 1, 1842, none would be higher than 20 per cent. It also lengthened the list of commodities that could be imported duty free. Even Calhoun, who had resigned as vice-president in order to be named by the Carolina legislature for the Senate so that he could speak for his state there, voted for this bill. After its enactment, South Carolina showed her satisfaction by withdrawing her nullification ordinance. But she saved face by passing a new ordinance nullifying Jackson's Force Act. Since that act was now no longer needed, Jackson wisely ignored this empty formal defiance.

"SHIRT-SLEEVE" DIPLOMACY

"Old Hickory" was as vigorous in asserting American rights in foreign relations as he was in projecting the rights of the chief executive at home. He appointed his diplomats, moreover, on the same basis as he appointed domestic spoilsmen, and their "shirt sleeve" methods, at a time when diplomatic protocol was most strict, caused many a shock abroad.

It was Jackson's own handling of two

long-standing issues, however, that brought the most satisfying results. By using the velvet glove approach, he at last persuaded Britain to open the British West Indian trade to American ships on the same basis that American ports would be opened to British ships engaged in the West Indian trade. This matter was settled in October, 1830. By using the iron fist approach the following year, he also persuaded the French to agree to pay up American claims against them for ships and cargoes lost during the Napoleonic wars. When the French delayed making the actual payments, Jackson recommended to Congress that it vote reprisals on available French property. This recommendation was accompanied by such harsh words that the French demanded a

formal apology. But Jackson retorted: "The honor of my country shall never be stained by an apology from me for the statement of truth and the performance of duty." The British at last undertook to mediate the dispute and the French eventually paid up in full.

Jackson was less vigorous and less provocative in his relations with Mexico over the issue of Texas independence, even though he personally favored both the initial independence of the Lone Star State and her eventual annexation by the United States (see p. 320).

III. *The Bank War*

PARTY PREPARATIONS FOR 1832

With the defection of Calhoun and the intransigent state-rights men from the Jacksonian ranks, a new anti-Jackson coalition began to take form. The strength of this coalition was eventually to be found in the Whig party, largely Adamsite in its attitudes, but ready to unite for campaign purposes with all others opposed to Jackson's "presidential tyranny." As the elections of 1832 neared, this essentially conservative group was anxious to find some way of tapping the rising democratic sentiment of the country to which Jackson had so successfully appealed. Allegiance with an odd new political party—the Anti-Masonic party—seemed to offer the leaders of the anti-Jackson camp their opportunity.

Masonry had been widely condemned for its secrecy (a "horrid, oath binding system"), which seemed to confirm its allegedly anti-democratic character. The fact that such a large proportion of established political leaders and judges were Masons suggested that Masonry constituted a kind of office-holding clique and a gigantic conspiracy against the common man. Moreover, Masonry was associated with free thought, and many found in it a threat to Christi-

anity; others, excited by the rumor that alcohol was used with abandon in Masonic ceremonies, embraced Anti-Masonry almost as a temperance crusade.

All of these anti-Masonic attitudes were brought into focus between 1826 and 1827 by the disappearance of a certain William Morgan, a stonemason and homespun intellectual of Batavia, New York. A Mason himself, Morgan had become embroiled in disputes with fellow members and threatened to write a book exposing the secrets of the society. One day in 1826 he was abducted by a group of unidentified men, and was never again seen. A year later, the body of a drowned man was washed ashore from Lake Ontario, and was rather uncertainly identified as Morgan's. The latent suspicion that he had been murdered by a group of Masons now quickened into life, and an Anti-Masonic party soon was formed to make political capital of the new "enthusiasm." In the New York state elections in the fall of 1827, the new party carried several western counties and sent 15 members to the state assembly. The movement spread to other states and soon attracted anti-Jackson politicians on the make. Best of all, Jackson himself was a Mason.

Among those most determined to use anti-Masonic sentiment against Jackson was the hard-boiled Rochester editor, Thurlow Weed, who hoped to put Henry Clay into the White House in 1832. Embarrassingly enough, Clay too was a Mason. Moreover, he had as little use for Weed as for Jackson. Weed and his henchmen, Clay said in 1830, were "in pursuit of power . . . without regard to the means of acquiring it." The Anti-Masons at last found a candidate in the aged William Wirt of Maryland, and at their national convention in Baltimore in September, 1831—the first such convention in history, as we have said (p. 264)—named him their standard bearer. Wirt also was a Mason and he accepted this early nomination mainly with the hope of using it to strengthen his chances for being named by the National Republicans as well. But the latter, in their first national convention in Baltimore in December, 1831, stuck with Clay. The Anti-Masons had adopted the convention system since they had no body of office holders to form a caucus; they made the most of this situation by stressing the democratic nature of the convention system as against the authoritarianism of Jackson. Not to be outdone, the Democrats, as the Jacksonians now formally called themselves, also held a nominating convention in Baltimore, in May, 1832, where they named "Old Hickory" and "Little Van" by acclamation.

At the National Republican convention in Baltimore, Jackson was taken to task for his stand on internal improvements, Indian removal, and the tariff. But the principal target was his administration's unfriendly attitude toward the Second Bank of the United States. As it turned out, the Bank question overshadowed all other issues in the 1832 campaign.

PRESIDENT JACKSON
V. PRESIDENT BIDDLE

For ten years prior to the election of 1832, the Second Bank had been managed by the able Philadelphian, Nicholas Biddle, a reformed Federalist who had first been appointed a director by President Monroe in 1819, and who in 1824 and 1828 had voted for Jackson himself. On becoming President of the Bank in 1823, Biddle had intensified the deflationary policies that his predecessor had introduced during the Panic of 1819 (see p. 235). Not only was Biddle cautious about issuing notes of his own Bank, but also by refusing to accept at face value the notes of state and local banks that had issued more paper than their specie reserves warranted, he forced upon such banks an element of caution that they and their clients came to resent. Resentment was deepest in the West, which was growing faster than the rest of the country and felt its financial needs stunted by Biddle's watchdog policies.

The Bank, moreover, was an enormous institution, and its large capitalization, its far-reaching powers over the economy, and its privileged custodianship of the Treasury's deposits made it possible for its critics to denounce it as a monopoly. No one embraced this view more thoroughly than Jackson's supporter, Senator Benton of Missouri. In February, 1831, Benton introduced a resolution against rechartering the Bank and declaimed for several hours on the threat it represented to democracy: It was "the sole authority . . . to which the Federal Government, the State Governments, the great cities, corporate bodies, merchants, traders, and every private citizen, must, of necessity, apply, for every loan which their exigencies may demand." Skillfully Benton exploited the egalitarian feelings against the Bank: "It tends to aggravate the inequality of fortunes; to make the rich richer and the poor poorer; to multiply nabobs and paupers; and to deepen and widen the gulf which separates Dives from Lazarus." Benton's resolution was not adopted, but he had given a strong impetus to anti-Bank sentiment.

Benton's fear that the Bank was "too great and powerful to be tolerated in a government of free and equal laws" reflected a widespread conviction that this great agency, aside from its economic force, was corrupting political life. Its critics were aware, for example, that many congressmen had received low-interest loans and special services from the Bank. As a Bank lawyer, Webster was paid a substantial retainer which he was at pains to collect. News editors also received Bank favors, and their papers made considerable profit in circulating propaganda paid for by Biddle. In the Bank's defense it could be argued that most of the loans made to politicians and editors were sound enough, and that it would have been suicidal to refuse to do business with such influential men.

In addition to those who were troubled by the Bank's credit policies and possibly corrupt practices were those of the old Republican school who had never accepted its constitutionality. Among these Jackson himself ranked high. "You know my opinion as to the banks," he wrote William Lewis in 1820, "that the Constitution of our State, as well as the Constitution of the United States, prohibited the establishment of banks in any state." Thereafter Jackson seemed so often to have changed his mind that he became an enigma to Biddle who desperately needed to understand him. In November, 1829, Biddle had an interview with the old soldier in which Jackson set forth his old philosophy. Jackson handsomely acknowledged the Bank's services to the government, but he added:

I think it right to be perfectly frank with you—I do not think that the power of Congress extends to charter a Bank out of the ten mile square [District of Columbia]. I do not dislike your Bank any more than all banks. But ever since I read the history of the South Sea Bubble I have been afraid of banks.

Jackson added: "I have read the opinion of John Marshall [on the Bank's constitutionality in *McCulloch* v. *Maryland,* 1819], . . . and could not agree with him."

Jackson's first annual message to Congress was under consideration among his advisers at the time of the Biddle interview. They urged him not to rock the boat, to say nothing about the Bank. But Jackson could not restrain himself. "My friend," he told one of them, "I am pledged against the bank." When the time came to submit this message in December, Jackson remained silent on the Bank almost to the

end. Then he said it was not too soon for the issue of rechartering the Bank in 1836 to be submitted "to the deliberate consideration of the Legislature and the people." To assist them in their deliberations, he added: "Both the constitutionality and the expediency of the law creating this bank are well questioned by a large portion of our fellow-citizens." Two years later, in his message to Congress in December, 1831, the President reaffirmed his views of the Bank "as at present organized."

Jackson himself, underestimating popular support for his position, would have preferred to keep the Bank out of the 1832 campaign, and his Secretary of State and Secretary of the Treasury were busy talking to Biddle's friends about certain renewal after the election if application were put off. But Webster and Clay, grossly overestimating public support for the Bank, urged Biddle to take the offensive against the President and petition Congress for a new Bank charter now. Biddle, increasingly confused in the political maelstrom, at last yielded to such seemingly authoritative advice, and on July 3, 1832, as forecast, the recharter bill passed both houses. Jackson, now bedridden, grimly observed to his heir-apparent: "The Bank, Mr. Van Buren, is trying to kill me, *but I will kill it.*"

When the old soldier's decision to veto this recharter bill was seen to be final, his most intimate White House advisers "prayed, begged, and entreated" him to make his veto "soft," so that the three million people included in the census of 1830 but as yet unrepresented in Congress might have a chance to ballot on the issue in the impending election. But Jackson dissented. For all his urging "deliberate consideration" upon them, Jackson felt he did not need the vote to know the people's mind. He would crush the "Monster" once and for all.

In his veto message of July 10, Jackson did not fail to note at the start that the recharter bill had come to him on the Fourth of July, and that he had considered it, "with that solemn regard to the principles of the Constitution which the day was calculated to inspire." Such consideration confirmed his old belief that, "some of the powers and privileges possessed by the existing bank are unauthorized by the Constitution, subversive of the rights of the States, and dangerous to the liberties of the people." If the Supreme Court, virtually to everyone else's satisfaction, disagreed, "the opinion of the judges has no more authority over Congress than the opinion of Congress has over the judges, and on that point the President is independent of both." Jackson went on to denounce the Bank as a monopoly operating to the advantage of the privileged few and open to the danger of control by foreign owners of its stock, a negligible possibility. His closing remarks were well suited to the coming election:

Distinctions in society will always exist under every just government. Equality of talents, of education, or of wealth cannot be produced by human institutions. In the full enjoyment of the gifts of Heaven and the fruits of superior industry, economy, and virtue, every man is equally entitled to protection by law; but when the laws undertake to add to these natural and just advantages artificial distinctions, to grant titles, gratuities, and exclusive privileges, to make the rich richer, and the potent more powerful, the humble members of the society—the farmers, mechanics, and laborers—who have neither the time nor the means of securing like favors to themselves, have a right to complain of the injustice of their Government.

Biddle thought so little of Jackson's "manifesto of anarchy" that he had it circulated as pro-Bank propaganda. But Jackson swept the election with 687,000 votes to Clay's 530,000. In the electoral college it was Jackson by 219 to 49. Jackson, moreover, interpreted his triumph as a mandate to press his war against Biddle's "Hydra of corruption."

In this war Jackson had the often-wavering support of various groups in the country. In the early stages, he held the allegiance of old Bank enemies, substantial state bankers who had fought Biddle's unwelcome com-

petition. More lasting in their support were the so-called "wild-cat bankers" of the West and the Southwest whose land-speculator clients were always demanding bigger and longer-term loans. A third group came to be represented by the "Locofocos" of New York, who got their name from the "locofoco" matches they used when party "regulars" shut off the lights after losing control of a Democratic meeting to these "radicals." The Locofocos were hard-money business and professional men who opposed the Bank as they opposed all monopolies that seemed to block business opportunity.

As the war on the Bank grew warmer, the country's business leaders in all sections rallied to Biddle, while the ranks of the Jacksonians became strained. Jackson triumphed. But his victory was to prove very costly to the country as a whole.

TO THE PANIC OF 1837

Jackson's opening shot in the renewed battle with Biddle was to order the removal of government deposits from the Bank's branches on the grounds that Biddle's policies no longer insured the safety of the public's funds. He then ordered that these deposits and all new government revenue be placed in selected state institutions that became known as Jackson's "pet banks." These orders were more easily issued than carried out. The Secretary of the Treasury alone had the power to withdraw government deposits, and Jackson's Secretary was a friend of the Bank. Such obstacles did not long deter "Old Hickory." He fired two secretaries of the Treasury until he found in Roger B. Taney of Maryland the man who would do his bidding. Late in 1833 Taney began the removal of the deposits, and by the end of the year 23 state banks had been named to receive federal funds.

Even though his bid for a new charter had been beaten, Biddle did not take this new assault on his Bank with complacency. If the Bank was to be forced to close, it must begin to call in its loans and restrict its new business. Soon after the federal deposits had been removed, therefore, Bid-

280

dle embarked on this policy with zeal. His object was to create a business panic so widespread that public opinion would force Jackson to reverse his stand on the charter. For some months in 1833 and 1834, a panic indeed seemed imminent. But once again Biddle miscalculated the political effects. To petitioners who began to press Jackson for help, the President insistently replied, "Go to Nicholas Biddle." In time, even segments of the business community appealed to Biddle to relent, and finally he gave in.

Relief over Biddle's capitulation promptly turned the near panic into a soaring boom, especially in the South and West where land was most in demand. The boom was fostered by the inflationary practices of the state banks which depended on federal deposits as reserves for heavy speculative loans. By throwing millions of acres of public land on the market at this time, the administration further stimulated speculation.

The land boom caused an immediate demand for internal improvements, accompanied by reckless investments in turnpikes, canals, and railroads. Many of these projects were financed in part by foreign capitalists who would not risk their money in private American corporations but were willing to purchase state bonds, backed by state revenues, which many states now issued to support internal improvement schemes. The optimistic state programs were spurred on in the summer of 1836 when it became clear that the federal government was about to distribute to the states some of the $35 million Treasury surplus that had accumulated from tariff revenues and the sale of public lands. A measure sponsored by Henry Clay, and passed in June, 1836, provided

"The Downfall of Mother Bank" shows the effect of Jackson's removal of the government deposits. "Nick" Biddle (with horns) and his newspaper hirelings scurry for their lives. Jack Downing, symbolizing the people, hurrahs.

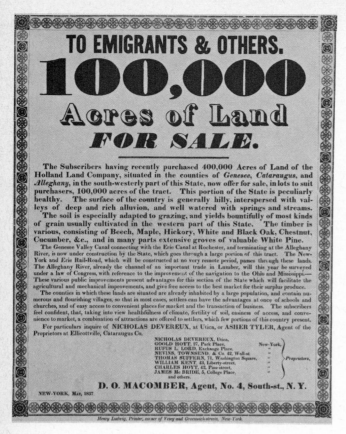

Broadside, 1837.

TO EMIGRANTS & OTHERS.

100,000
Acres of Land
FOR SALE.

The Subscribers having recently purchased 400,000 Acres of Land of the Holland Land Company, situated in the counties of *Genesee, Cataraugus,* and *Alleghany,* in the south-westerly part of this State, now offer for sale, in lots to suit purchasers, 100,000 acres of the tract. This portion of the State is peculiarly healthy. The surface of the country is generally hilly, interspersed with valleys of deep and rich alluvion, and well watered with springs and streams.

The soil is especially adapted to grazing, and yields bountifully of most kinds of grain usually cultivated in the western part of this State. The timber is various, consisting of Beech, Maple, Hickory, White and Black Oak, Chestnut, Cucumber, &c., and in many parts extensive groves of valuable White Pine.

The Genesee Valley Canal connecting with the Erie Canal at Rochester, and terminating at the Alleghany River, is now under construction by the State, which goes through a large portion of this tract. The New-York and Erie Rail-Road, which will be constructed at no very remote period, passes through these lands. The Alleghany River, already the channel of an important trade in Lumber, will this year be surveyed under a law of Congress, with reference to the improvement of the navigation to the Ohio and Mississippi.— These various public improvements present advantages for this section of the State which will facilitate the agricultural and mechanical improvements, and give free access to the best market for their surplus produce.

The counties in which these lands are situated are already inhabited by a large population, and contain numerous and flourishing villages, so that in most cases, settlers can have the advantages at once of schools and churches, and of easy access to convenient places for market and the transaction of business. The subscribers feel confident, that, taking into view healthfulness of climate, fertility of soil, easiness of access, and convenience to market, a combination of attractions are offered to settlers, which few portions of this country present.

For particulars inquire of NICHOLAS DEVEREUX, at Utica, or ASHER TYLER, Agent of the Proprietors at Ellicottville, Cataraugus Co.

NICHOLAS DEVEREUX, Utica,
GOULD HOYT, 27, Park Place, New-York,
RUFUS L. LORD, Exchange Place,
NEVINS, TOWNSEND, & Co. 42, Wall-st.
THOMAS SUFFERN, 71, Washington Square, *Proprietors,*
WILLIAM KENT, 43, Liberty-street,
CHARLES HOYT, 42, Pine-street,
JAMES McBRIDE, 5, College Place,
and others.

D. O. MACOMBER, Agent, No. 4, South-st., N. Y.

NEW-YORK, MAY, 1837.

Henry Ludwig, Printer, corner of Vesey and Greenwich-streets, New-York.

---

ment measure, Jackson's "Specie Circular."

Like many of his supporters, Jackson himself was a hard-money man, greatly in favor of economic expansion yet fearful of speculation and debt. With speculation and debt rampant, on July 11, 1836, he issued his famous "Circular," which required that all land purchased from the federal government after August 15 be paid for in silver or gold. Settlers, as distinguished from speculators, were permitted to use bank notes for an additional four months, provided their purchases were less than 320 acres.

This drastic reversal of policy abruptly checked land sales and sent prices plunging. In the spring of 1837 stock and commodity prices also broke, and soon the Panic of 1837 was on in earnest. Like other panics, that of 1837 was worldwide and had worldwide as well as American causes and effects. Especially hard hit were British investors in American securities and British banks engaged in financing American trade, mainly trade in cotton. Their calls on American merchants forced many to the wall.

The failure of Biddle's bank, which had been operating since 1836 under a Pennsylvania charter, helped deepen the depression. After suspending activities twice, beginning in the fall of 1839, the bank was finally turned over to trustees for liquidation in 1841. Biddle was charged with fraud but subsequently acquitted. In 1844, at the age of 58, he died a broken man, the victim not merely of his own arrogance, but of the bitterness of American politics and the curious state of American financial thought.

---

that all money in excess of $5 million in the Treasury on January 1, 1837, was to be apportioned during the year among the states in accordance with population. The measure passed in time to sustain the boom, but the surplus disappeared before payments could be completed. What dissipated the surplus was the collapse of the boom itself. This was speeded by another govern-

IV. *Jackson's Legacy*

THE ELECTION OF VAN BUREN

When the voters went to the polls in 1836 to choose Jackson's successor, the boom was still in full swing, and the surface prosperity helped sustain "Old Hickory's" popularity. He had checked nullification, had adopted a democratic and popular position in the Bank war, and had conducted foreign policy with notable success. The principal complaint against him was that

of "executive usurpation," as his enemies called it. The fact that the Democratic candidate in 1836 was Jackson's handpicked heir, "Little Van," made the charge of autocracy the more telling.

No less an authority on the Constitution and the office of the Chief Executive than E. S. Corwin remarks that Jackson's presidency was "no mere revival of the office—it was a remaking of it." In his own day,

Henry Clay most bitterly attacked the "revolution, hitherto bloodless," as he told the Senate in December, 1833, "but rapidly tending toward . . . the concentration of all power in the hands of one man." Clay and his friends were most deeply mortified by Jackson's manipulation of the power of appointment, in arrogant disregard of the Senate's rightful role. He had far exceeded presidential prerogatives, in their eyes, by requiring a Secretary of the Treasury to remove the government's deposits from Biddle's Bank to the "pet banks."

In 1834, at Clay's instigation, the Senate gave Jackson a taste of his own medicine by adopting, 26 to 20, the following unprecedented resolution:

Resolved, That the President, in the late Executive proceedings in relation to the public revenue, has assumed upon himself authority and power not conferred by the Constitution and laws, but in derogation of both.

Jackson responded promptly with an eloquent "Protest," which the Senate refused to enter in the journal of its proceedings. On their part, Jackson's supporters in the Senate waged a ceaseless battle for almost three years to have the censure resolution expunged from the record, and at last, in January, 1837, they had their way. But in the process of the debate, Clay expressed the resentment of many of his fellow senators over what they regarded as Jackson's aggrandizement of his rights.

The Senate has no army, no navy, no patronage, no lucrative offices, nor glittering honors to bestow. Around us there is no swarm of greedy expectants, rendering us homage, anticipating our wishes, and ready to execute our commands. How is it with the President? Is he powerless? He is felt from one extremity to the other of this republic. By means of principles which he has introduced, and innovations which he has made in our institutions, alas! but too much countenanced by Congress and a confiding people, he exercises uncontrolled the power of the state. In one hand he holds the purse and in the other brandishes the sword of the country! Myriads of dependents and partisans scattered over the land are ever ready to sing hosannahs to him and to laud to the

skies whatever he does. He has swept over the government like a tropical tornado.

Clay's theme became the keynote of the new Whig party, inheritors of National Republicanism, in the campaign against Van Buren. Consistent with this theme was the makeup of the Whig coalition— Jackson-haters from all sections of the country. The Whig party attracted old Adams men in New England, Clay men in the West, Anti-Masons in the Middle States, and disgruntled Democrats of Calhoun's stamp in the South. The party had money, brains, a lively press, and popular leaders. Its presidential strategy for 1836, however, was dictated by its apparent weakness in its first campaign, the congressional elections of 1834, when the Democrats captured 145 seats in the House to the Whigs' 98.

Realizing that they could not beat Jackson's chosen successor in 1836 if they entered into the usual two-sided contest, the Whigs decided to run a number of strong candidates who would appeal to different sections of the country: Webster to New England, William Henry Harrison of Ohio to the Middle States and the West; Judge Hugh L. White to Tennessee. South Carolina, where the presidential electors were still chosen by the state legislature, named the anti-Jacksonite, Willie P. Mangum. The Whigs hoped to duplicate the situation of 1824, when the electoral votes were so divided that the election had been thrown into the House of Representatives. But Van Buren won out by a narrow margin. He received 762,000 votes to a total of 735,000 for all his opponents combined. In the electoral college, Van Buren got 170 votes, Harrison 73, and the rest trailed. Harrison had shown enough popular appeal to make him a likely candidate for 1840.

DEPRESSION PANACEAS

The problems facing Van Buren when he took office in March, 1837, quickly

Currier print of General Harrison at Tippecanoe, published at the time of his campaign for the presidency, 1840. His men are trying in vain to restrain him from riding up to the point of attack.

became formidable. Financial panic was in full swing by May. Banks closed, prices of food and other necessities soared, factories shut down, and severe unemployment with all its attendant miseries gripped the Northeast. Merchants and business leaders besieged the President with petitions to relieve the distress by withdrawing Jackson's Specie Circular, which, they claimed, "had produced a wider desolation" than the cholera epidemic "which depopulated our streets." Conditions were just as bad in the South, where land and slaves fell sharply in value. Eventually the West again became the worst sufferer of all.

Van Buren was given plenty of conflicting advice on how to end the economic crisis. Biddle, for example, hinted that now was the time to restore the Bank of the United States. The conservative wing among the Democrats urged the President

to recall the Specie Circular but to continue the state-bank system. The Locofocos proposed that the government go even farther than the "Circular" in its hard-money crusade. They also demanded that it remove public funds from all banks, so that United States fiscal operations might no longer be "embarrassed by the doings of speculators."

Van Buren favored the Locofoco approach to banks and throughout his administration sought to create an "Independent Treasury" system under which government specie and other funds would be placed in sub-treasuries around the country and used to pay obligations in cash. The first Independent Treasury bill was presented to Congress in September, 1837, where it got a cool reception not only from Whigs but from Democrats sympathetic to state-banking interests. Van Buren persisted until, in 1840, significant shifts having been made in the Democratic alignment, an Independent Treasury Act squeaked through. The administration margin was supplied by Calhoun and his southern followers who had returned to the Democratic fold from the Whig party to which Calhoun's feud with Jackson had driven them. This "divorce of bank and state" marked the peak of Locofoco influence in the Democratic party.

TIPPECANOE AND TYLER TOO

Although such luminaries as Webster and Clay still were available for the Whig nomination in 1840, the nod went to the old Indian fighter, William Henry Harrison, who had run so well in 1836. Thurlow Weed, now Whig boss, balanced the ticket with John Tyler of Virginia.

Much was made during the campaign of Harrison's "victory" over Tecumseh at Tippecanoe, Indiana, all of thirty years earlier. The Whigs also derided "Little Van's" vanity, the "Regal Splendor of the President's Palace," the "Turkish divan" on which he reposed. When a Baltimore newspaper taunted the Whigs by saying that Harrison would be perfectly satisfied with a log cabin and a good supply of cider, his managers capitalized on the slur and made the log cabin an effective party symbol. "It tells of virtues," Thurlow Weed declared, "that dwell in obscurity, of the privations of the poor, of toil and danger." The log cabin, this "emblem of simplicity," was far removed from Harrison's gentlemanly origins and habits but helped elect him by a popular majority of 145,000 votes. In the electoral college, Harrison won, 234 to 60.

More significant than Harrison's edge, or even his election, in 1840, was the size of the vote—40 per cent (far higher than the rate of population growth) above that in Jackson's day. Tens of thousands of new voters had become eligible under liberalized franchise laws; but more important was the extraordinary 78 per cent of the eligible voters that had turned out, compared to a maximum of 56 per cent in "Old Hickory's" campaigns. The persistence of the depression had presented a clear issue on which rival groups now arrayed under Democratic or Whig banners could rally their partisans. The new methods of campaigning (see p. 268) helped bring party appeals to the hearts and minds of the electorate.

Unfortunately for the Whigs, Harrison died after but one month in office. During that month he had humbly accepted the guidance of Webster and Clay. Of Clay, a New York newspaper correspondent had this to say at the time: "He predominates over the Whig Party with despotic sway. Old Hickory himself never lorded it over his followers with authority more undisputed, or more supreme." No doubt Clay hoped that John Tyler, on becoming President, would be as pliable as Harrison had promised to be, and that the real power of the administration would rest safe in his own hands. But Tyler, with the example of Jackson before him, was to be no cipher.

Tyler was a Whig only because he had followed Calhoun out of the Democratic party after the break with Jackson. A veteran of the Virginia legislature and of both houses of Congress, he had had many opportunities in the past to disclose his strong anti-tariff views, his antagonism to Biddle's bank, his distaste for federal aid to internal improvements. Beyond these issues, he sided with Calhoun on nullifica-

tion. The Whigs had named him for the vice-presidency in order to attract southern anti-Jackson support; they paid dearly when this state-rights enthusiast became President under their banner.

On one matter Clay and Tyler were able to agree: Congress passed and the President signed in 1841 a measure repealing Van Buren's Independent Treasury Act. But when Clay pushed farther, he and his colleagues were unceremoniously rebuffed. In August, 1841, Congress actually passed a bill creating a new national bank. When Tyler returned it with a firm veto, the Whigs, in September, adopted a new bank bill designed to satisfy Tyler's constitutional scruples. When Tyler vetoed this bill too, about 50 Whig congressmen met in caucus and read Tyler out of the party. Moreover, with the exception of Secretary of State Webster, who was busy with the negotiations that eventually led to the Webster-Ashburton Treaty (see p. 317), all the Cabinet members resigned. Tyler promptly named a new Cabinet which, with two exceptions, was entirely southern. Webster himself resigned in 1843 when his diplomatic work was done, and after a brief interval was replaced by Calhoun—evidence of the South Carolinian's unquestioned re-

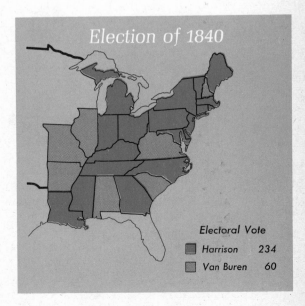

Election of 1840

Electoral Vote

■ Harrison   234
■ Van Buren   60

turn to the Democratic party and confirmation of the party's becoming the standard-bearer of the slaveocracy.

PRE-EMPTION: A FRONTIER TRIUMPH

Just before the Cabinet resigned, Tyler put his signature to a measure that marked a great victory for the West in the field of public-land policy. This was the Pre-emption Act of September, 1841, adopted with bi-partisan support.

Pre-emption meant that a settler who took up government land without authorization should have first chance to buy his land at the minimum price. Otherwise he would have to bid for his "own" land at competitive prices or be evicted from it when it was bought by others. During the 1830's pre-emption had been voted for short periods of time. Now it was enacted for an unlimited period. The principal provision of the Act of 1841 permitted any head of a family or single male adult to preempt 160 acres of public land and then pay the minimum price—$1.25 an acre—when the land was officially opened to settlement. Other provisions stated that 500,000 acres be given to each new state for the construction of internal improvements; that 10 per cent of the revenues obtained from selling federal land were to be returned to the state in whose boundaries the land lay; that the rest be distributed among the states in proportion to their representation in Congress. Another provision was included to meet the demands of southerners who feared that depletion of the Treasury would provide a good argument for the supporters of a high tariff: If the tariff schedules should exceed 20 per cent, the apportionment of land revenues would be inoperative. In August, 1842, a tariff was enacted which exceeded that level and explicitly repealed the distribution part of the Act. But preemption survived, the major triumph for the frontier until the Homestead Act of 1862 (see p. 434).

Readings
* Asterisk indicates that book is available in paperback.

The spread of democratic political practices is best traced in volume II of M. Ostrogorski, *Democracy and the Organization of Political Parties* (2 vols., 1902). Chilton Williamson, *American Suffrage, from Property to Democracy 1760-1860* (1960), provides a reliable analysis. See also Kirk Porter, *A History of Suffrage in the United States* (1918). Useful state studies include A. B. Darling, *Political Changes in Massachusetts 1824-1848* (1925); D. R. Fox, *The Decline of Aristocracy in the Politics of New York* * (1919); and R. P. McCormick, *The History of Voting in New Jersey: A Study of the Development of Election Machinery 1664-1911* (1953). L. D. White, *The Jacksonians: A Study in Administrative History 1829-1861* (1954) is outstanding on the "spoils system" and its effects. P. P. Van Riper, *History of the United States Civil Service* (1958), is a good general account. On the types of men appointed to high office in the early republic, see S. H. Aronson, *Status and Kinship in the Higher Civil Service* (1964).

W. E. Binkley, *American Political Parties: Their Natural History* (1943), affords a good general introduction. R. P. McCormick, *The Second American Party System, Party Formation in the Jacksonian Era* (1966), clarifies a complicated subject. On particular parties other than Jackson's, the following are recommended: Charles McCarthy, *The Anti-Masonic Party* (1902); E. M. Carroll, *Origins of the Whig Party* (1925); and A. C. Cole, *The Whig Party in the South* (1913). C. S. Sydnor, *The Development of Southern Sectionalism 1819-1848* (1948) is excellent on nullification and other issues.

George Dangerfield, *The Era of Good Feelings* * (1952), and *The Awakening of American Nationalism 1815-1828* * (1965), afford well-written analyses of American politics leading up to the election of Jackson. Shaw Livermore, Jr., *The Twilight of Federalism:*

The Disintegration of the Federalist Party 1815-1830 (1962), stresses the survival of Federalist ideas and alignments despite the "disintegration." S. F. Bemis, *John Quincy Adams and the Union* (1956), is the standard work on the administration of the sixth president. A scholarly introduction to the organization of the Jacksonian party in the early 1820's is H. R. Stevens, *The Early Jackson Party in Ohio* (1957). R. V. Remini, *Martin Van Buren and the Making of the Democratic Party* (1959), is illuminating on New York's role. Remini's *The Election of Andrew Jackson* * (1963), is the standard work.

G. G. Van Deusen, *The Jacksonian Era 1828-1848* * (1959), is a modern survey. The following offer varied points of view on Jacksonian Democracy: E. C. Rozwenc, ed., *Meaning of Jacksonian Democracy* (1963); Arthur Schlesinger, Jr. *The Age of Jackson* * (1945); Joseph Dorfman, *The Economic Mind in American Civilization 1606-1865* (2 vols., 1946); Richard Hofstadter, *The American Political Tradition* * (1948); J. W. Ward, *Andrew Jackson, Symbol for an Age* * (1955); Marvin Meyers, *The Jacksonian Persuasion: Politics and Belief* * (1957); and Lee Benson, *The Concept of Jacksonian Democracy, New York as a Test Case* * (1961). In an older but hardly irrelevant tradition are F. J. Turner, *Rise of the New West 1819-1829* * (1906); and T. P. Abernethy, *From Frontier to Plantation in Tennessee* (1932).

Marquis James, *The Life of Andrew Jackson* * (1938), is excellent reading. See also, J. S. Bassett, *The Life of Andrew Jackson* (2 vols., 1925). Most useful on Van Buren besides Remini, above, is Holmes Alexander, *The American Talleyrand* (1935). J. C. Fitzpatrick, ed., *The Autobiography of Martin Van Buren* (1920), tells what Van Buren wished to be told. Clement Eaton, *Henry Clay and the Art of American Politics* * (1957) is sound and short. Carl Schurz, *Life of Henry Clay* (2 vols., 1887), remains valuable. C. M. Fuess, *Daniel Webster* (2 vols., 1930) is standard. The short biography, R. N. Current, *Daniel Webster and the Rise of National Conservatism* * (1955) may also be recommended. C. M. Wiltse, *John C. Calhoun, Nullifier 1829-1839* (1949), is best on its subject. This work may be supplemented by A. O. Spain, *The Political Theory of John C. Calhoun* (1951); Frederic Bancroft, *Calhoun and the South Carolina Nullification Movement* (1928); and D. F. Houston, *A Critical Study of Nullification* (1896). T. H. Benton, *Thirty Years' View* (2 vols., 1854-1856), offers an illuminating inside account. W. N. Chambers, *Old Bullion Benton, Senator from the New West* (1956), is a substantial biography. O. P. Chitwood, *John Tyler: Champion of the Old South* (1939); and Robert Seager II, *And Tyler Too* (1963), are best on this President.

On land and Indian policy, see R. G. Wellington, *The Political and National Influence of the Public Lands 1826-1842* (1914); Grant Foreman, *Indian Removal, The Emigration of the Five Civilized Tribes of Indians* (1932); Angie Debo, *The Road to Disappearance* (1941); and F. P. Prucha, *American Indian Policy in the Formative Years: The Indian Trade and Intercourse Acts 1790-1834* (1962).

A good short introduction to the Bank War (which is also treated in virtually all the Jacksonian books cited above), is G. R. Taylor, ed., *Jackson versus Biddle* * (1949). Bray Hammond, *Banks and Politics in America: From the Revolution to the Civil War* (1957) is the most elaborate study. Volume 1 of Fritz Redlich, *The Molding of American Banking, Men and Ideas* (2 vols., 1947, 1951) is full of insight. T. P. Govan, *Nicholas Biddle, Nationalist and Public Banker 1786-1844* (1959), and R. C. McGrane, ed., *The Correspondence of Nicholas Biddle Dealing with National Affairs 1807-1844* (1919), give Biddle's side. On the Bank itself see R. C. H. Catterall, *The Second Bank of the United States* (1903), and W. B. Smith, *Economic Aspects of the Second Bank of the United States* (1953). R. C. McGrane, *The Panic of 1837* (1924), and W. B. Smith and A. H. Cole, *Fluctuations in American Business 1790-1860* (1935), are illuminating on the end of the boom.

CHAPTER ELEVEN

In his brilliant essay on "Fenimore Cooper's
White Novels," in his book, *Studies in
Classic American Literature,* the English
writer, D. H. Lawrence, asked the telltale
question, "Can you make a land virgin by
killing off its aborigines?" Toward the close
of the nineteenth century, Americans were
to grow less and less certain of the answer
to this question; but the generation that
came to manhood in the Age of Jackson
had few if any doubts. Its greatest spokesmen salved the national conscience. Ours,
said Emerson, "is a country of beginnings,
of projects, of vast designs and expectations. It has no past; all has an onward and

America

in Ferment

prospective look." "We," said Melville, "are the pioneers of the world; the advance guard sent on through the wilderness of untried things, to break a new path in the New World that is ours. In our youth is our strength; in our inexperience our wisdom."

Americans in this self-conscious age took ever greater pride in distinguishing their "system," as they came to call it—open, expansive, an Eden for the world's oppressed—from the closed system of declining Europe. And even before they had fulfilled what they long believed to be their rightful "destiny" to occupy the whole cointinental range from ocean to ocean, (see Chapter 12), their pretensions worked on Europe's fears. As early as 1824, following the bold assertions of the Monroe Doctrine (p. 232), no less a personage than Prince Metternich of Austria, the reigning head of the Holy Alliance formed to repress Europe's own republican tendencies, pointed the finger at the formidable new foe:

These United States of America, which we have seen arise and grow, and which during their too short youth already meditated projects which they dared not then avow, have suddenly left a sphere too narrow for their ambition. . . . In their indecent declarations they have cast blame and scorn on the institutions of Europe most worthy of respect. . . . In fostering revolutions wherever they show themselves, in regretting those which have failed, in extending a helping hand to those which seem to prosper, they lend new strength to the apostles of sedition and reanimate the courage of every conspirator.

And yet questions beyond that posed by D. H. Lawrence remained to prod an ambitious people. Granted the virginity of the land and the rightness of their possession of it, what would Americans make of their wealth? And what would they make of their power? Would they succeed, as Horace Mann put it in 1842, in "converting material wealth into spiritual well-being?" The question of the character and quality of the civilization which was to encompass the globe, if Americans had their way, kept the nation, and not merely its intellectuals, artists and reformers, in continuous ferment.

I. *The American Temperament*

A RESTLESS SOCIETY

All observers agreed that Americans worked harder, ate faster, moved around more, and relaxed less than Europeans. In America, Tocqueville wrote in 1835,

. . . a man builds a house in which to spend his old age, and he sells it before the roof is on, . . . he brings a field into tillage, and leaves other men to gather the crops, he embraces a profession and gives it up, he settles in a place, which he soon afterwards leaves, to carry his changeable longings elsewhere.

Nothing seemed finished in America. "Improvement," both personal and collective, was a national preoccupation. People were on the move, in transit, going from somewhere to somewhere. The symbol of the young republic might have been the locomotive that never ceased its labors, or the steamboat that moved up and down the rivers—and frequently blew up.

A COMMERCIAL SOCIETY

American society was primarily a business society.

It will require but little reflection to satisfy us [wrote a spokesman for the mercantile and banking interests in 1848] that the resources of this country are controlled chiefly by the class which, in our own peculiar phraseology, we term "the business community"—embracing all those who are engaged in the great occupations of buying, selling, exchanging, importing and exporting merchandise, and including the banker, the broker, and under-writer.

Every American, declared the editor of a well-known commercial periodical, was in some sense a trader. The physician traded his "benevolent care," the lawyer his "ingenious tongue," the clergyman "his prayers."

But even America's severest critics usually agreed that there was nothing mean-spirited or sordid, indeed that there was something large and even heroic, in this pursuit of wealth. Never was there to be greater opportunity for self-made men in America; and those who prospered often assumed the responsibilities that went with success. Public opinion regarded money as an "engine" of benevolence as well as a good in itself. Many of the merchants, like the public-spirited Abbott Lawrence of Boston, shared this view and supported humanitarian and cultural enterprises.

AN IDEALISTIC SOCIETY

In spite of their insistence on the practical and the useful, even those Americans most triumphant in business competition felt the spiritual leavening of their conquests. In February, 1853, his fortune having soared to $11 million, Cornelius Vanderbilt wrote to his friend, Hamilton Fish: "I have a little pride as an American to sail over the waters of England and France, up the Baltic and through the Mediterranean, without a reflection of any kind that it is a voyage for gain." When, later that year, "old Cornele" set out in his magnificent steamer, *North Star*, especially constructed in the most extravagant manner so "as to be a credit to our *Yankee Land*," his fellow tycoon, James Gordon Bennett of the New York *Herald*, hailed the expedition. "Although it is solely a personal matter," Bennett said, "it partakes somewhat of a national character," one calculated to display "the refinement of those whose enterprise, industry and genius have placed them at the head of the social scale" solely by their own efforts.

Lesser Americans, with the world still to conquer, were themselves susceptible to every sort of evangelical appeal. This was preeminently the age of "Causes" to hasten on the new world acoming—of Hungarian Independence, missionary crusades to Pacific islands and Africa and Asia, dietary panaceas, abolitionism, new religions and cults, pseudo-science, seances and exhibitions. Tocqueville found a "fanatical and almost wild spiritualism" rampant in America, and surmised that religious enthusiasm was probably natural in a society "exclusively bent upon the pursuit of material objects." A people who made so great a virtue of common sense, Tocqueville believed were most prone to "burst the bonds of matter by which they are restrained" and "soar impetuously towards Heaven."

DEMOCRACY AND EQUALITY

In our government [declared an orator in 1840], we recognize only individuals, at least among whites; and in social life, the constant effort to do away with the castes produced by difference of fortune, education, and taste. The motto upon the flag of America should be "Every man for himself." Such is the spirit of our land, as seen in our institutions, in our literature, in our religious condition, in our political contests.

Democracy meant (to many, if not to all) social as well as political equality. To paraphrase Tocqueville again, men pounced "upon equality as booty" and clung to it "as some precious treasure." Most egalitarian of all, perhaps, were freedom-hungry immigrants drawn, as was said as early as 1828, by "a moral influence," from "the old and worn out governments of Europe and hurrying . . . across the Atlantic to participate in the renovated youth of the new republic of the West; an influence which, like that of nature, is universal and without pause or relaxation."

It was not that American society was

Commodore Vanderbilt's steam-yacht, The North Star.

without distinctions of class, and indeed that such distinctions might actually have been sharpened by the growing wealth of some. Distinctions there were. Although it is impossible to chart the fine gradations of rank and repute, successful planters, business leaders, bankers and lawyers occupied the top rungs of society. Clergymen, physicians, and teachers, too, if they were patronized by the influential, might claim similar high standing. Below this privileged group ranged the rest of the white citizenry, with subtle distinctions among themselves.

Yet no fixed and artificial barriers prevented the mechanic or the clerk or the farmer—referred to in the press as the "bone and sinew" of the Republic—from rising rapidly. All citizens, moreover, remained equal before the law, no class demanded special respect from another, and men of different degrees mingled indiscriminately in business and travel. Almost everyone had some stake in society, and despite the fears of conservatives the American people embarked on no wildly revolutionary course. Wrapped up in his daily affairs, and schooled to accept the ideas and prejudices of the majority, the citizen usually abided by the "empty phantom of public opinion," which was "strong enough to chill innovators and to keep them silent and at a respectful distance."

INDIVIDUALISM AND COOPERATION

Much has been made, and correctly, of the pre-Civil War era as the heyday of individualism, of the self-propelled hero. But this was also a time of cooperation, of voluntary, not coercive "association." The achievements of the single man have come to overshadow the accomplishments of the group in American folk-lore, but when Tocqueville visited America he was immensely impressed by the fact that "the most democratic country on the face of the earth . . . carried to the highest perfection the art of pursuing in common the object of their common desires."

For the American to pool resources, both material and intellectual, and to throw in his lot with the community in which he worked and lived, simply seemed the most sensible thing to do at the time. A society of "lone wolves" would not have survived. Businessmen who joined together in companies in all the major lines of enterprise, very often to protect themselves against the competition of foreign merchants, well understood this. In other walks of life, citizens hungry for culture set up libraries and mutual improvement clubs, and immigrants formed societies with their fellow countrymen. Charitable, reform, fraternal, and benefit organizations sprang up naturally in a democracy where there was no ruling class with a tradition of social responsibility to supervise civic undertakings. "Many can accomplish what one cannot," said one organizer, defending his trespassing on individualism. But he was quick to add this qualification: "We mean to receive as much as we give, and we ask others to join us on that principle."

SECTARIAN RIVALRY

But if Americans poured their energies into countless societies, often pulling in many directions at once, what was it, if anything, that held their society together? Many observers during the 1830's and 1840's were disturbed by the diffuseness of American activity, by the "lack of a common skeleton." Emerson, in 1847, noted America's "immense resources," but he was also struck by America's "village littleness." America, he concluded, "is great strength on a basis of weakness."

A major weakness in a country of churches was sectarian rivalry. Americans seemed to be the most religious of peoples and yet the one most afflicted by denominational discord. The United States had always provided a fertile soil for new sects, but in the 1830's and 1840's the splintering of dissenting churches, with each group claiming possession of the authentic faith, reached a peak of frequency and ferocity. The Baptists and Methodists, the fastest-growing denominations of the day, were most susceptible to schisms, but new cults sprang up everywhere and the competition for the souls of immigrants pouring into

292

the Mississippi Valley was frequently un-christian. Doctrinal differences created a good deal of friction. Some denominations, moreover, considered themselves socially superior to others, even in the sight of God, and such false pride only broadened religious differences. Presbyterians, Congregationalists, Episcopalians, and Unitarians differed in theology and in church organization, but they all drew their membership from the well-to-do. Baptists, Methodists, Campbellites, and Universalists were socially a cut below, and the immigrant and Free Negro churches were at the bottom.

Most Protestants, though they squabbled among themselves, shared a common hatred of the Roman Catholic Church. Even to sophisticated ministers like Lyman Beecher, the father of Harriet Beecher Stowe and president of Lane Seminary in Cincinnati, Catholicism still smacked of the sinister rites of the Inquisition and of political autocracy. The gullible readily swallowed crude fictions about Catholic atrocities and sensational "exposés" of Catholic depravity. Sometimes Catholics were insulted and attacked, their churches burned.

Anti-Catholic prejudice deepened after 1830 when immigration began to rise. Between 1830 and 1850, 2.5 million newcomers arrived, many of them Catholics from Ireland and Germany. In 1830, there were 500 Catholic priests in the United States and

about 500,000 communicants. By 1850 there were 1,500 priests serving 1,750,000 of their faith. In addition, the Church had established seminaries, schools, colleges, monasteries, convents, hospitals, and other parochial institutions. A Catholic press, starting with the *United States Catholic Miscellany,* in 1822, also had come into being, along with a Catholic Tract Society, founded in Philadelphia in 1827 to combat Protestantism and to promote the Church.

Yet despite America's social differences and institutional rivalry an inner unity—built on the general acceptance of democracy, private property, and Christian faith—bound the country together. True, the idea of the Union was to prove too weak to triumph over the passions aroused by slavery, but the social fabric seemed tough enough to withstand every other strain. Between 1825 and 1850, almost every institution was questioned. Conservatives trembled for the future. But no heads fell and no property was expropriated. Reform could never get out of hand among a people who regarded "temporal prosperity" as the "chief end of existence" and who pursued their material welfare with an intensity that amounted to a spiritual commitment.

II. *Writers and Society*

PRECURSORS OF A NATIONAL LITERATURE

"Men of genius," according to a Boston critic in 1820, were "outlaws" because, "for the most part, they want that getting-along faculty which is naturally enough made the measure of man's mind in a young country, where every one has his future to make." And yet during the next three decades the United States experienced an intellectual flowering scarcely equaled by any other generation in American history. In 1802, when Washington Irving began to write, America had no literature and hardly

a reading public. When he died, a year before the Civil War began, Emerson, Thoreau, Hawthorne, Poe, Melville and Whitman had already struck off their masterpieces.

The achievements of these writers seem all the more remarkable when we consider the unpromising environment from which they sprang. Besides the prevailing hostility to genius in general there was the specific hostility to literature, and more particularly to American literature. After the Revolution, patriots had called for a national literature that would reflect the dawning greatness of the new nation, but such American poets as Timothy Dwight and Joel Barlow, who planned mighty and unreadable epics, turned out only pale imitations of English literary forms and deferred to English standards of taste. Among the would-be writers of this period, only the poet Philip Freneau (1752-1832), and the imaginative Philadelphia novelist, Charles Brockden Brown (1761-1810), possessed more than a minor talent. For some time thereafter, the few Americans with literary interests preferred the easily obtainable works of popular British authors. Sir Walter Scott, Byron, Bulwer-Lytton, Mrs. Felicia Hemans, and Charles Dickens crowded American writers out.

American authors understood their neglect. America, they said, had no ancient traditions, no peasants, knights or kings, no ivy-covered castles, no Gothic churches, no legendary mist to stimulate their imagination. Washington Irving was only one of a long line of American writers who felt the charm of Europe, where the necessary romantic background was available.

I longed [Irving said] to wander over the scenes of renowned achievement,—to tread, as it were, in the footsteps of antiquity,—to loiter about the ruined castle,—to meditate on the falling tower,—to escape, in short, from the commonplace realities of the present, and lose myself among the shadowy grandeurs of the past.

American writers also had to reckon with the religiously inspired distrust of literature as Satan's snare. Fiction, it was said, "pampers and bloats the intellect with unwholesome food, and enfeebles and demoralizes all future exertions of the mind."

Yet the better-known American writers overcame or ignored these cultural handicaps and managed to attract a following of their own. Irving (1783-1859), an urbane New Yorker, was the first professional man of letters to win great poularity at home and applause abroad. Irving lived much in Europe and wrote his best books about it. When still in his twenties, however, he wrote and published in America his *History of New York* (1809), a rousing burlesque of the early Dutch and later backwoods democrats, that had the whole country laughing. Irving's *History* ranks second in popularity among his works only to *The Sketch Book* (1819-20), an instantaneous success in Britain as in the United States, in which he made Rip Van Winkle and Ichabod Crane luminous American characters in the rural and village setting of his native state. In *A Tour on the Prairies* (1835) Irving evoked the charm of the landscape on the moving frontier.

Irving's friend and contemporary, William Cullen Bryant (1794-1878), grew up in the Berkshire Hills of Massachusetts, but he made his career in New York City as poet, newspaper man, and reformer. No lisping imitator of British sentiment, Bryant wrote of his native habitat in a way that won Emerson himself. It was Bryant, Emerson noted, who "subsidized every solitary grove and monument-mountain in Berkshire or the Katskills . . . every water fowl and woodbird . . . so that there is no feature of day or night in the country which does not, to the contemplative mind, recall the name of Bryant."

An even more illustrious member of the New York group was the novelist, James Fenimore Cooper (1789-1851). In Europe, where he lived and wrote for a number of years, Cooper truculently defended the government and institutions of his native land. In America, he berated his countrymen for bad manners, chauvinism, contempt for privacy, their slavish submission to public opinion. Cooper's upbringing among the landed gentry of New York did not block his early sympathy for Jackson and Jacksonian America. If his "democracy" soured in the last years of his life, his thoughtful depiction of republican government, *The American Democrat* (1838), is still one of the best political essays ever written by an American.

What first brought Cooper fame both in Europe and at home were his early "white novels," especially *The Pilot* (1823), a forerunner of many masterly tales of the sea. Of deeper interest today is the celebrated "Leatherstocking" series: *The Pioneers*

(1823), *The Last of the Mohicans* (1826), *The Prairie* (1827), *The Pathfinder* (1840), and *The Deerslayer* (1841)—the romance of the white hunter, Natty Bumppo, among the Indians of the woods, the lakes, and the open country. These novels, "a *decrescendo* of reality, and a crescendo of beauty," D. H. Lawrence says of them, are alive with the problems of white men befriending redmen and redmen befriending whites on the proving ground of the wilderness. Mark Twain, in 1895, called attention to "Fenimore Cooper's Literary Offences," which shine all the more brightly now, like dead fish. But they do not betray the clear American character of the stories, the unique beauty of their settings, their grasp of the issues in the clashes of men of different colors on American soil.

A surer gauge of American taste in this early period of American literature is the phenomenal success of the New England poet, Henry Wadsworth Longfellow (1807-1882), a milder writer than Cooper.

Born in Portland, Maine, and educated at Bowdoin College, Longfellow, like Irving and Cooper, had spent several years in Europe. He went there to prepare himself to become a professor of modern languages, first at Bowdoin and later (1836) at Harvard College. Sitting in his Cambridge study, Longfellow composed volume after volume of mellifluous verse that soon made him famous throughout the world. *Hyperion* (1839), *Evangeline* (1847), *Hiawatha* (1855), and *The Courtship of Miles Standish* (1858) delighted the largest audience, perhaps, that any American poet ever commanded. His sentimentality, his didacticism, his optimism, and his antiquarianism satisfied popular taste. If his Hiawatha smacked more of Cambridge, Massachusetts, than of the shores of Gitchie Gumee, and if the brawny "Village Blacksmith" was a Whig dream of a docile and respectful workingman, poems like "A Psalm of Life" expressed without irony the aspirations of middle-class America.

> Let us, then, be up and doing,
> With a heart for any fate;

> Still achieving, still pursuing,
> Learn to labor and to wait.

Longfellow and his Boston and Cambridge associates belonged to the coterie of writers who contributed to what Van Wyck Brooks called, following the self-satisfied Yankees' own estimate of themselves, "The Flowering of New England." The emphasis placed by historians on this regional renaissance has partially obscured the intellectual and artistic activity of other sections. Yet, New England's "golden day" was real enough. No other area contained such a hive of industrious writers. Much of their culture was thin and bookish, and the great reputations once enjoyed by James Russell Lowell, Oliver Wendell Holmes, and John Greenleaf Whittier have deservedly shrunk. But the cumulative output of New England between 1830 and 1850 remains impressive, and the great names live on: Francis Parkman and William H. Prescott, historians; Ralph Waldo Emerson, and Henry David Thoreau, essayists and poets; Nathaniel Hawthorne, writer of romances and tales.

EDGAR ALLAN POE

One Bostonian who did not relish Boston's appreciation of itself was Edgar Allan Poe (1809-1849). Although born in the "hub of the universe," a city he sarcastically referred to in later life as "Frogpond," Poe regarded himself as a Virginian. After the death of his actor parents while he was an infant, he grew up in Richmond where his foster-father, John Allan, was a substantial merchant. He attended the University of Virginia until Allan's stinginess and Poe's own gambling debts forced him to leave. His subsequent career included a two-year hitch in the army, a West Point commission, and a court-martial in 1831. In between, he managed to publish two volumes of verse (*Tamerlane,* 1827, and *Al Aaraaf,* 1829), and after the West Point fiasco he became a professional man of letters.

Nothing could seduce Poe from this "most noble profession," as he once referred to it, but he spent the rest of his short life in the American Grub Street, writing and editing brilliantly for inferior men, and publishing poems, stories, and critical essays that brought him little. In his most productive year, 1843, Poe earned $300. The shabby and unrewarding years that he spent with the literary Bohemia of Philadelphia, Baltimore, and New York aggravated his natural instability. In 1836 he had married his 13-year-old cousin, Virginia Clemm. "I became insane," he wrote after her death ten years later, "with long intervals of horrible sanity." In 1849, Poe was found lying unconscious in a Baltimore street, and died in delirium at the age of 40.

Poe was no apostle of progress. Democracy displeased him, and he had no taste for middle-class truths. As a literary critic he performed a tremendous service by attacking American provincialism in cruel reviews of bad books. His own poetry and fiction contained most of the weaknesses he detected in the writings of his inferiors: theatricality, bombast, and sentimentality. But in stories like "The Fall of the House of Usher," "The Imp of the Perverse," "The Black Cat," "The Man in the Crowd," and "The Premature Burial"—tales of murderers, neurotics, the near-insane—his vulgarity was redeemed by an extraordinary intelligence and intensity. The owner of the black cat who sorrowfully cuts out the eyes of his pet, the brother who entombs his sister alive, the lover who pulls out the teeth of his mistress while she sleeps in a cataleptic trance, all live in a tormented world far removed from Emerson's optimistic America. Yet Poe's very exoticism proved a tonic for the democratic culture he rejected.

Ralph Waldo Emerson (1803-1882).

EMERSON AND TRANSCENDENTALISM

The most universal literary figure of his generation was Ralph Waldo Emerson (1803-1882). Boston-born and Harvard-educated, he entered the ministry as his father and grandfather had done before him, but he resigned his pastorate in 1832 because church forms had become meaningless for him. Thereafter, he devoted himself to writing and lecturing. *Nature* (1836), which contained in condensed form most of the themes he was to treat in his later works, was followed by two volumes of essays (1841, 1844), *Poems* (1847), *Representative Men* (1850), *English Traits* (1856), and *The Conduct of Life* (1860).

Half Yankee and half yogi, Emerson contained within himself and confronted all others with the warring tendencies of his age. Part of him belonged to the practical American world of banks and railroads, and no one commended more enthusiastically than he (see his essays on "Wealth," "Power," and "Napoleon") the deeds of powerful individualists. At the same time, Emerson was a mystic and an idealist who looked upon the external world as a passing show and detected an unchanging reality behind it. This shrewd and canny man declared himself to be "part and particle" of God and rejoiced in the unsettling effect his theories had on his countrymen.

Emerson, like many other Boston intellectuals of his day, had rebelled against the coldness and formality of the Unitarian faith which repudiated the harsh Calvinist doctrine of human depravity and a vengeful God but in the process became passionless. Emerson wanted to revive the old Puritan fervor without the rigidities of Puritan theology. Quakerism, with its doctrine of the inner light, its gentleness, and its humanitarianism, moved him deeply, and he was drawn to any philosophy that broke down the barriers between mind and matter. In Emerson's youth, the philosophy of the English materialist, John Locke, was still much in vogue. Locke had held that ideas did not arise spontaneously in the mind, but that they were implanted there by the impressions of the external world acting through the senses. This meant that spirit was subordinate to matter. Emerson's own disposition told him otherwise, and he found support for his idealism in the works of certain continental and Scottish philosophers, oriental poets and sages, and in English romantic poetry.

Transcendentalism, the philosophy associated with Emerson and his sympathizers, was not a systematic faith; it had no creed and it could not be easily defined. To some, the word "transcendentalist" covered "all those who contend for perfect freedom, who look for progress in philosophy and theology, and who sympathize with each other in the hope that the future will not always be as the past." To the journalist and critic, Orestes Brownson, the only common bond shared by the transcendentalists was their opposition "to the old school":

They do not swear by Locke, and they recognize no authority in matters of opinion but the human mind, whether termed the reason with some of them, or the soul with others. They have all felt that our old catechisms need revision, and that our old systems of philosophy do not do justice to all the elements of human nature, and that these systems can by no means furnish a solid basis for a belief in God, much

less in Christianity. Some of them . . . *ignore* all philosophy, plant themselves in their instincts and wait for the huge world to come round to them. . . . Some of them reason . . . others merely dream.

Although vague in its outlines, transcendental doctrine was nobly formulated in Emerson's essays and lectures, in which he announced to his fellow Americans that they, too, could speak to God directly without the assistance of churches and creeds. He urged them to be self-reliant and to get their experience at first hand. Every object in the physical world had a spiritual meaning, and those who were capable of seeing that material things were the symbols of spiritual truths might understand nature's purpose. The ability to communicate with God, or the "Over Soul," was given to everyone, but only a small number of poets, scholars, and philosophers (Emerson called them men of "Reason") had developed this inborn capacity. From them, other men could learn that only the idea is real, that evil is negative (the mere absence of good), and that a kindly destiny awaited them.

These ideas Emerson expressed in fresh and audacious language. Even in his most abstract utterances, he used simple concrete words and homely illustrations:

The world of any moment is the merest appearance. Some great decorum, some fetish of a government, some ephemeral trade, or war, or man, is cried up by half mankind and cried down by the other half, as if all depended on this particular up or down. The odds are that the whole question is not worth the poorest thought which the scholar has lost in listening to the controversy. Let him not quit his belief that a popgun is a popgun, though the ancient and honorable of the earth affirm it to be the crack of doom.

To an audience absorbed in material concerns, Emerson argued against the tyranny of *things* over the *spirit,* and he seemed to speak intimately to any person who read or

Portrait of Walt Whitman in 1887, by Thomas Eakins.

heard him, encouraging every man to stand up against public opinion and be an individual:

What I must do is all that concerns me, not what the people think. This rule, equally arduous in actual and in intellectual life, may serve for the whole distinction between greatness and meanness. It is harder because you will always find those who think they know what is your duty better than you know it. It is easy in the world to live after the world's opinion, it is easy in solitude to live after our own; but the great man is he who in the midst of the crowd keeps with perfect sweetness the independence of solitude.

A number of Emerson's contemporaries tried to live according to his precepts: Henry David Thoreau as the transcendental adventurer of Walden Pond, Walt Whitman as the democratic poet, Theodore Parker as the minister-reformer, and many others.

298

Henry David Thoreau (1817-1862), like Emerson, his friend and mentor, was a graduate of Harvard College and a resident of Concord, Massachusetts. "He declined," Emerson later wrote of him, "to give up his large ambition of knowledge and action for any narrow craft or profession, aiming at a much more comprehensive calling, the art of living well." Throughout his life, Thoreau gave himself over to self-cultivation and self-exploration. His literary medium was the diary-like record of his intellectual experiences.

In *A Week on the Concord and Merrimack Rivers* (1849), *Civil Disobedience* (1849), and especially *Walden; or, Life in the Woods* (1854), Thoreau expressed his tart and unconventional opinions about literature, religion, government, and social relations. Many of the reformers were his friends, but he was never a "joiner"; he distrusted reform movements and tried to keep himself free from what he called "greasy familiarity." Good fellowship he once described as "the virtue of pigs in a litter, which lie close together to keep each other warm." "Not satisfied with defiling one another in this world," he wrote, "we would all go to heaven together. . . ."

Like most transcendentalists, Thoreau was an unblushing egoist, but he wrote about himself, he said, because he did not know anyone else so well. Moreover, his own accounts of how he discovered the miraculous in the common were also suggestions for those men who led "lives of quiet desperation." He asked a generation geared to practicalities, what do the practicalities of life amount to? The immediate things to be done, he said, are trivial and can wait; the wealth of the world is less significant than one true vision.

The ways by which you may get money almost without exception lead downward. To have done anything by which you earned money *merely* is to have been truly idle or worse. . . . There is no more fatal blunderer than he who consumes the great part of his life getting his living . . . you must get your living by loving. . . . It is not enough to tell me that you worked hard to get your gold. So does the Devil work hard. . . . I believe that the mind can be permanently profaned by the habit of attending to trivial things, so that all our thoughts shall be tinged with triviality.

Thoreau advised his countrymen to simplify their private lives and to simplify their government, too, for he was a supreme individualist who regarded the organized state as a threat to true independence. Abolitionist, naturalist, poet, and rebel, and a down-to-earth but subtle writer—he attracted no great notice while he lived. In our day, *Walden* is justly considered a literary masterpiece, and its author—who discovered a universe in Concord—is regarded as one of the most original and challenging minds of the New England renaissance.

WALT WHITMAN

The poet whose arrival Emerson had predicted in his essay, "The Transcendentalist" (1842), was soon to appear. Emerson had written,

We have yet had no genius in America, with tyrannous eye, which knew the value of our incomparable materials, and saw, in the barbarism and materialism of the times, another carnival of the same gods whose picture he so admires in Homer. . . . Banks and tariffs, the newspaper and the caucus, Methodism and Unitarianism, are flat and dull to dull people, but rest on the same foundations of wonder as the town of Troy and the temple of Delphi, and are as swiftly passing away. Our log-rolling, our stumps and their politics, our fisheries, our Negroes and Indians . . . the northern trade, the southern planting, the western clearing, Oregon and Texas, are yet unsung. Yet America is a poem in our eyes; its ample geography dazzles the imagination, and it will not wait long for metres.

The "genius" Emerson demanded was Walt Whitman (1818-1892), born on Long Island and a life-long New Yorker. During his formative years, Whitman was a schoolteacher, printer, carpenter, journalist, publisher, and editor. When *Leaves of Grass,* his first volume of poems, appeared in 1855, its undisguised references to the body and sex caused Whitman to be denounced as the "dirtiest beast of his age." The most friendly review described his verse as "a

sort of excited compound of New England transcendentalism and New York rowdy." Emerson was the only eminent writer who immediately discerned Whitman's freshness and found (as he wrote to the poet) "incomparable things, said incomparably well." Whitman continued to revise and add to the *Leaves* until 1892, in addition to publishing other volumes of prose and verse, but the recognition he deserved came only after his death.

Whitman's poems, like Emerson's essays, embody the idea of progress, celebrate the innate goodness of man, and idealize nature; they insist on the spiritual reality underlying the material world. But Whitman was more passionately democratic than the New Englander, and he looked to the people rather than his own soul for his inspiration. Other poets, he said,

. . . have adhered to the principle, and shown it, that the poet and the savant form classes by themselves, above the people, and more refined than the people, I show that they are just as great when of the people, partaking of the common idioms, manners, the earth, the rude visage of animals and trees, and what is vulgar.

This belief prompted him to write poems about Negroes and Indians, carpenters, coach-drivers, sailors, and trappers, felons and prostitutes. In his poems he used the common words ordinarily excluded from polite verse ("I reckon," "gallivant," "duds," 'folks," 'blab," "loaf"). This living language, and the free and unconventional verse forms he developed for it, give his writing its peculiar breeziness and special touching quality as well:

The carpenter dresses his plank, the tongue of his fore-plane whistles its wild ascending lisp. . . .

* * *

Of the turbid pool that lies in the autumn forest,
Of the moon that descends the steeps of the soughing twilight,
Toss, sparkles of day and dusk—toss on the black stems that decay in the muck,

Toss to the moaning gibberish of the dry
limbs.

* * *

I depart as air, I shake my white locks at the
runaway sun,
I effuse my flesh in eddies, and drift it in
lacy jags.

In his poems, Whitman wrote of the love
of comrades, of man for man, but this was
to be only the prelude to a larger human
brotherhood. He imagined ranks, races, and
civilizations commingling, and it was to be
America's mission to promote this final fellowship of peoples. He saw much in his
generation to displease him. His optimism
was severely tested by the Civil War, and
his faith in America severely shaken by
events after 1865 (see *Democratic Vistas,*
1871), but he did not despair, and he died
believing that in the people there existed
"a miraculous wealth of latent power and
capacity."

THE NAY-SAYERS

Emerson made many trenchant
criticisms of American society, but his optimism never flagged. Others were not so sure.
Nathaniel Hawthorne (1804-1864) was one
who could not slough off the pessimistic doctrines of his Puritan forefathers on the irretrievable fall of man. The son of a Salem
shipmaster, Hawthorne attended Bowdoin
College with the more sanguine Longfellow
and grew up to be a robust, masculine person who held government jobs and enjoyed
human contacts. He was not the recluse he
has sometimes been painted, but his ideas
went against the grain of his age. In his
tales and sketches, and in his novels—*The
Scarlet Letter* (1850), for example—Hawthorne painted a somber moral landscape
where men and women were devoured by
vices they were constrained to keep secret,

but which he exposed. These terrible facts
of life mocked the claims of progress, and
in his works reformers, scientists, and secret
probers are changed into monstrous villains
thwarted in their search for perfection (see
The Blithedale Romance, "Ethan Brand,"
and "Rappaccini's Daughter").

Hawthorne's New York friend, Herman
Melville (1819-1891), also clung to the idea
of original sin. After his father's bankruptcy, Melville endured the humiliations
of genteel poverty which were only deepened by teaching school. In 1841 he quit
city life and sailed on a whaling ship to the
South Seas. Three years of adventuring in
the Pacific provided materials for his two
best-selling books, *Typee* (1846) and *Omoo*
(1847). His reputation declined, however,
when he stopped writing light-hearted
sketches of Polynesian life and turned to
his private conflicts.

In rejecting transcendental optimism,
Melville reacted even more strongly than
Hawthorne against Emerson's blandness.
Evil, for Melville, resided not merely in the
tainted heart, that "foul cavern," as Hawthorne called it; evil hung over the world
like a curtain. In *Moby Dick* (1851), his
finest novel, Melville struck through the
"pasteboard mask" of life to confront this
eternal menace. Ahab, a Yankee whaling
captain, the lost hero of the novel, spends
himself in pursuit of Moby Dick, the
gigantic white whale that symbolized the
beauty, the wickedness, and the mystery of
nature. The pursuit fails; Ahab dies. If man
were half-divine, as the transcendentalists
insisted, according to Melville he nonetheless faced a tragic destiny. He was incapable
of solving the ambiguities of the world.
God remained unknowable, progress an
illusion, the seeker one only led on and deceived by what he saw and thought.

III.   *The Plastic and the Popular Arts*

PAINTERS AND SCULPTORS

The would-be painter and sculptor
in America was even worse off than the
writer. The fine arts seemed particularly

aristocratic to many sturdy democrats. *The
North American Review* in 1825 described
them as the products of "corrupt and despotic courts, the flatterers of tyranny, the

300

panders of vice." In addition, the Bible forbade the making of images and likenesses that praised man rather than God.

In an environment in which no utility could be found for the "meager productions of the pencil, the brush or the chisel," it is not surprising that many American artists began their careers in the more practical roles of artisans and mechanics. One such was the sculptor, Hiram Powers (1805-1873), who worked in a Cincinnati organ factory and made wax statues before turning to art as a career. Powers' "Greek Slave" won him international fame but reveals only his pandering to popular notions of ideal form devoid of the fruits of his practical past.

Powers' work pleased the critics of the 1830's who only praised art that raised "the mind above the sordid interest of a merely material life." American artists were invited to contemplate native forests, rivers, and sunsets, which "inspired the soul of man with visions of the ideal, the beautiful, the immortal." The painter, Thomas Cole (1801-1848), became famous in this period for his romantic renditions of the Hudson River and Catskill Mountain regions. Asher Durand (1796-1886) and Thomas Doughty (1793-1856), contemporaries of Cole, also painted America's scenic wonders. By 1860, a stronger school of landscape painters had emerged who caught the character of the horse Indians and early settlers on the Great Plains. Among the best of them were George Catlin (1796-1872) and Alfred Jacob Miller (1810-1874).

A few iconoclasts tried to break down the unhappy distinction between the beautiful and the useful. Emerson argued that an object was beautiful if it had nothing superfluous about it and if it served the use for which it was made. Whitman celebrated the splendor of locomotives. Thoreau defended the functional house, and Horatio Greenough, the architect, wrote at length about the beauty of sailing ships, bridges, and machinery:

The men who have reduced locomotion to its simplest elements, in the trotting wagon and the yacht *America*, are nearer to Athens at this moment than they who would bend the Greek temple to every use. I contend for Greek principles, not Greek things. If a flat sail goes nearest the wind, a bellying sail, though picturesque, must be given up. The slender harness, and tall gaunt wheels, are not only effective, they are beautiful for they respect the beauty of a horse, and do not uselessly tax him.

But views like these were not popular. A few people really interested in artistic and intellectual matters supported the arts out of a sense of duty. A few art societies made promising starts in the larger cities, but they soon languished. Since only six art schools had been founded before 1860, American artists either got their training

"Kindred Spirits," by Asher B. Durand. The figure on the left is the poet, William Cullen Bryant. His companion is the landscape painter, Thomas Cole, celebrated for his romantic scenes of the Hudson River Valley.

as apprentices or went to the Continent to study. Once trained, they found it hard to reach the apathetic public, and many grew resentful.

DRAMA AND MUSIC

If moralists had serious reservations about literature and the fine arts, they felt even more strongly about the theater. Dramatic productions, as one of them declared, "lead the minds of youth from serious reflection, or if they reflect at all, their thoughts are employed on things which never had any existence but in the vain imagination of some distempered fancy like their own." Lay-preachers assailed the "vagabond profession" and the indecency of "the displays of half-clad females." The most damning criticism of the theater was that it unfitted "mankind . . . for the common concerns of life."

But the theater seemed more vital than the fine arts and despite these objections it flourished. Audiences heard and applauded everything from Shakespeare to the broadest farce. New York remained the dramatic center, but cities in every section supported theaters. Famous stars like Edwin Forrest, James K. Hackett, and Fanny Kemble had national reputations. At a time when the leading statesmen performed in a highly theatrical manner in the public arena, serious drama never made much headway on the stage. Burlesque and popular opera ruled. Minstrel shows like E. P. Christy's, and toe-dancers like the ravishing Fanny Elssler, performed before huge audiences.

Foreigners might comment on the "barbarity" of American music, but between 1820 and 1860 instrumental and choral performances improved. Visiting artists from abroad successfully toured the country, and local musical societies in New York, Boston, and elsewhere offered orchestral and choral programs to appreciative if uncritical audiences. The ingratiating ballads of Stephen Foster (1826-1864), one of the first of a long line of northerners to romanticize the "sunny South," were sung across the land; and opera, introduced about 1825, had some success in a few of the larger cities. Hymn-writers like Boston's Lowell Mason (1792-1872), composer of "Nearer My God to Thee" and "From Greenland's Icy Mountains," evoked a more genuine response and grew rich from the sales of their edifying songs.

NEWSPAPERS AND MAGAZINES

"The influence and circulation of newspapers," wrote an astonished visitor to the United States about 1830, "is great beyond anything known in Europe. . . . Every village, nay, almost every hamlet, has its press." From 1801 to 1833, the number of newspapers rose from 200 to 1,200; only 65 were dailies; most of the rest, weeklies. Competition in the larger cities was ferocious. In 1830, New York City alone had 47 papers, only one daily among them claiming as many as 4,000 subscribers. Enterprising editors reduced the price of their papers to a penny and sought to lure readers by featuring "robberies, thefts, murders, awful catastrophes and wonderful escapes."

Benjamin Day's New York *Sun* pioneered in the new sensationalism, but Day's rival, James Gordon Bennett of the *Herald,* soon surpassed him. Bennett played up the news value of New York society (he headlined his own marriage), and developed circulation techniques that were eagerly picked up throughout the country. New printing presses and improved delivery methods helped meet the rising demand.

Yet the newspapers did more than pander to low tastes. "A newspaper", Tocqueville wrote, "is an adviser who does not require to be sought, but who comes of his own accord, and talks to you briefly every day of the Common weal." Each paper usually appealed to the prejudices and needs of particular groups. Mercantile interests, religious denominations, and political parties sponsored their own papers, and each editor rode his private hobby-horse. The best editors explained and interpreted pertinent issues, sometimes making demands upon readers that few modern editors would attempt.

Magazines also sprang up by the dozens in the middle decades, but few survived.

Delinquent subscribers were probably most responsible for the high mortality of periodicals, but the penny press and cheap imprints of pirated English books also reduced their audience. Almost every hamlet bravely launched a literary monthly or quarterly review, but only a few managed to carry on. *The North American Review* (Boston), *The Knickerbocker Magazine* (New York), *Graham's Magazine* (Philadelphia), and *The Southern Literary Messenger* (Richmond) achieved a national circulation. They printed pieces by Cooper, Poe, Bryant, Hawthorne, Holmes, and Longfellow, and by lesser figures, but they provided only a meager outlet for American talent.

The "female" audience had its choice of *The Ladies Magazine,* edited by Sarah Josepha Hale, and *Godey's Lady's Book,* with which the former merged in 1836. *Godey's* did more than dictate fashions and

rule over morals and manners. Miss Hale, literary editor of the magazine for many years, is best known as the author of "Mary's Lamb," but she published and reviewed intelligently the productions of leading American writers, paid for poems and articles (a significant innovation), and between 1837 and 1849 increased her magazine's circulation from 10,000 to 40,000. The success of *Godey's* and its imitators indicated that American women—the principal consumers of books and magazines—would soon dominate the cultural life of the nation. Their interest was indispensable, but it meant that women were able to impose a kind of petticoat tyranny over American letters and narrowly define the limits of propriety.

IV.   *Education: Formal and Informal*

SCHOOLS

The religious spirit that had such a powerful effect on literature and the arts in America was felt even more strongly in education. One of the goals of organized religion had always been to create a Christian citizenry. Intellect without virtue, as the saying went, "makes a splendid villain"; what American leaders wanted was a "baptized intelligence." In many respects, education was a secular kind of religious training. Most Americans favored Bible-teaching in the schools because, as the famous Presbyterian minister, Lyman Beecher, expressed it, the Bible gave no sanction "to civil broils, or resistance to lawful authority, but commands all men to follow peace, and to obey magistrates that are set over them, whatever the form of government may be." The Bible would show European immigrants, "extensively infected with infidelity and Rationalism," that a "land of liberty is not a place to indulge in irreligion and license."

But despite the lip-service paid to Christian, democratic, and practical education, crusaders for public schools faced an apathetic and often hostile public. Men who could afford to educate their children in private academies saw no reason why they should be taxed to educate the children of the poor. The administrators of the private and parochial schools, farmers, and non-English-speaking groups joined the conservatives in fighting the free-school movement. It was attacked as a threat to individual liberty, as a radical innovation, as impractical nonsense. But the defenders of free public schools had strong arguments of their own: the extension of education would reduce poverty and crime, increase productivity, rectify social injustice, and preserve democratic institutions. Every class would benefit, according to one free-school advocate in 1832:

The man who is poor must see that this is the only way he can secure education for his children. The man in moderate circumstances . . . will have his children taught for a less sum than he pays at present. The rich man, who

"The Country School," by Winslow Homer.

will be heavily taxed, must see that his course secures to the rising generation the only means of perpetuating our institutions, and the only guarantee that his children will be protected.

The leaders of the free-school movement—men like Horace Mann in Massachusetts, Henry Barnard in Connecticut, and Calvin Stowe in Ohio—hammered away with these arguments in reports and articles based on thorough investigations, and finally won their battle. By 1860, most northern states had installed a tax-supported school program.

The free-school movement broke down one more vestige of caste in democratic America, but it did not work miracles. Education on all levels, in fact, continued to suffer from low salaries, poor physical equipment, primitive pedagogy, unmanageably large classes, and a short school term.

Throughout the period, educational reformers, classicists and anti-classicists, utilitarians and liberals, suggested a variety of schemes to raise the educational level. One focus of controversy was the Swiss educator, Johann Heinrich Pestalozzi, who held that all education should proceed from the known to the unknown and the abstract. There was more point, his disciples argued, in teaching a child something about local geography than in making him memorize the rivers of Mesopotamia. Although Pestalozzi's ideas found some followers in America, rote memory drills prevailed.

Attempts by American schoolmasters to make education more interesting met stiff opposition. In defense of the critics, it must be acknowledged that many quacks flourished in the profession, and "painless" methods for acquiring a quick education were in vogue. Nevertheless, the quality of education improved enough for foreigners to comment on the exceptional literacy of the American public. The graded school with orderly upward progress made higher standards easier to impose; and improved teaching made the high standards easier to achieve.

Formal teacher-training came about largely through the work of Horace Mann, who established the first so-called "normal schools" for the preparation of teachers, and Henry Barnard, one of the founders of the American Association for the Advancement of Education (1855) and editor of the influential *American Journal of Education.* Teachers' societies sprang up throughout the country, and educational periodicals disseminated advanced pedagogical methods.

Private academies were providing elementary and secondary education for girls by the 1840's. In 1833, Oberlin became the first co-educational college; in 1858, the University of Iowa, the first co-educational state university. For the most part, girls' seminaries concentrated on the ornamental accomplishments. The learned woman, or "blue-stocking," was considered a monstrosity, "an unsexed" creature who "does not fill her true place in the world." Yet schools like Mount Holyoke and Miss Emma Willard's Troy Female Seminary and Catharine Beecher's Hartford Female Seminary did attempt to provide a more substantial intellectual diet for their students.

There were few public high schools until 1840, but during the next two decades the number increased substantially, especially in Massachusetts, New York, and Ohio. Such schools offered a more practical kind of education than private schools.

COLLEGES

The number of so-called American "colleges" increased from 16 in 1799 to 182 in 1860. During these years 412 others started and died. Colleges, said a prominent educator in 1848,

. . . rise up like mushrooms on our luxuriant soil. They are duly lauded and puffed for a day; and then they sink to be heard of no more. . . . Our people, at first, oppose all distinctions whatever as odious and aristocratical; and then, presently, seek with avidity such as remain accessible. At first they denounce colleges, and then choose to have a college in every district or county, or for every sect and party—and to boast of a college education, and to sport with high sounding literary titles—as if these imparted sense or wisdom or knowledge.

The multiplication of colleges resulted in part from the difficulties and expenses of travel, but sectarian rivalry and local pride were probably the principal causes. Religious control of institutions of higher

learning was even more marked than on the elementary-school level. Each important denomination and many minor ones supported one or more colleges that helped to rekindle the spirit of piety. Most of these colleges, which students might enter at 14 or 15, were hardly more than dressed-up academies. The so-called "universities" were hardly more than large colleges. Sometimes they included a theological or law department, but most professional schools in this period, law and medicine schools in particular, were separate institutions.

The curriculum in colleges and universities varied little throughout the country. Latin, Greek, mathematics, science, political economy, and moral philosophy offered a solid enough program, but teaching by rote was as common as in lower schools. Professors rarely were paid more than $1,000 a year. Long hours and poor libraries, moreover, encouraged neither research nor publication. In 1839, only 18 college libraries held as many as 10,000 books, led by Harvard's 50,000 and Yale's 27,000.

SELF-HELP

Philosophers of democracy like Franklin and Jefferson had insisted that only an educated electorate could sustain a republican government. Many, too busy or too old to go to school, continued to believe them. One institution designed to meet their needs, especially in the towns and cities, was the mutual improvement, or benefit, society. Just as men voluntarily joined up in business, social, and political associations, it was believed that they could educate themselves by organizing cooperatives for study. During the 1830's and 1840's, many mutual-improvement societies, some with literary facilities, were formed.

An even more popular informal educational institution was the lyceum, which grew out of the proposals of the Englishman, Lord Henry Brougham, leader of the English Whigs, and founder of the Useful

Knowledge Society. In his *Political Observations Upon the Education of the People* (1825), which went through more than 30 editions in five years, Brougham called for a system of public lectures on the arts and sciences, the formation of discussion societies, the establishment of libraries for workingmen, and the publication of cheap books. His admirers in America, spurred on by a New Englander, Joseph Holbrook, soon put his recommendations into practice.

By 1835, Lyceums could be found in 15 states, their activities coordinated by a national lyceum organization. By 1860, no less than 3,000 lyceums had been set up, mainly in New England, New York, and the upper Mississippi Valley, where public school sentiment was strong. The lyceums sponsored talks on every conceivable topic, with scientific and practical subjects arousing the greatest interest. Eminent men like Emerson addressed lyceum audiences on such themes as "Wealth" and "Power," and others of stature discoursed on the issues of the day.

The lyceums had their faults. They often "confounded knowledge of useful things with useful knowledge." The education they offered was likely to remain superficial and was often remote from the very classes for which it was theoretically designed. Yet lyceums helped to bridge the gulf between the learned minority and the community and spread the ideal of popular culture in a predominantly commercial society.

v. The Reformers

TEMPERANCE AND HUMANITARIANISM

The spirit of reform of which the free-school and lyceum movements were only two reflections pervaded America during the middle period. It derived in part from the general optimism and also from faith in the power of cooperation to solve all problems and hurry progress on. Most reformers were religious people, motivated by an evangelical zeal to promote pet projects. Some were freakish and wild, insisting that salvation lay in the universal acceptance of reform in dress or diet, or in the abandonment of money. Some believed that the "social destiny of man" lay in new forms of communal society. But reform had its less visionary side as well. During the 1830's and 1840's, a number of men and women devoted their lives to stamping out specific social evils or to supporting particular causes: temperance, the treatment of the insane and the criminal, the education of the deaf, dumb, and blind, equality for women, and world peace.

Until abolitionism aroused the country after 1830, the movement for "temperance" in the use of alcoholic beverages was the most intense reform activity of all. What caused the increasing consumption of liquor is hard to say, but the social scapegoats most frequently pointed to in this period were the excessive mobility of the American population, the attendant break-up of families and disruption of community life, the loneliness and fatigue of the farmer, and the long hours of the industrial worker newly arrived in the impersonal city from the country or from another country. In 1820, census-takers would not list distilling as a separate industry since almost everyone in rural areas engaged in it. In the cities, saloons were numbered in the thousands.

The agitation against drinking had been given a strong impetus by the publication in 1805 of Dr. Benjamin Rush's *Inquiry into the Effect of Ardent Spirits upon the Human Mind and Body*. But whereas Rush attacked drinking as bad for the health, the temperance reformers stressed its moral viciousness. This approach was promoted after 1810 by Lyman Beecher and his fellow evangelical preachers who, with the support of Bible and Tract societies and missionary boards, soon induced millions to take the pledge as "teetotalers." In 1826 the American Temperance Society was organized in Boston to coordinate the activities of hundreds of local groups. In 1833, when more than 2,000 such groups were functioning, a stronger national organization was set up in Philadelphia as the United States Temperance Union. Three years later, with the affiliation of Canadian societies, its name was changed to the American Temperance Union.

One surviving example of teetotaling propaganda is Timothy Shay Arthur's *Ten Nights in a Bar-Room*. But the temperance crusaders went beyond persuasion to legislation. The first Prohibition law was enacted in Maine in 1846, and within five years 12 other states, all in the North, had adopted some kind of liquor control law. Many who supported such legislation were opposed to total prohibition and their quarrels with the teetotalers eventually weakened the movement. Yet the campaign against "demon rum" probably reduced the consumption of alcohol. It also offered a training ground for supporters of other reform movements.

One of the most salutary of these was the crusade for humane and effective treatment of the insane and feeble-minded, led by Dorothea Lynde Dix (1802-1887). In her *Memorial to the Legislature of Massachusetts* (1834), the result of painstaking investigation, Miss Dix depicted conditions in asylums throughout the state that were medieval in their barbarity. In the popular mind, insanity was a hideous moral regression into animality, and Miss Dix found that its victims were whipped and caged and neglected as if they were indeed dangerous beasts. In her fact-strewn and quietly effective summary, she omitted nothing: "The condition of human beings, reduced to the extremest states of degradation and misery, cannot be exhibited in softened language or adorn a polished page."

During the next 15 years, her influence extended into every section of the country. Eleven states established hospitals for the insane partly as a result of her work. Before she died in 1887 she played an important part in the founding of 21 others.

THE COMMUNITARIANS

In the early stages of the industrial revolution in America as in Britain and France, the condition of the workers often seemed so oppressive that leading industrialists themselves thought there must be some alternative to the barbarism around them, and substitutes for private capitalism won respectable and even conservative consideration. Cooperatives, and indeed, whole new cooperative communities were proposed by the most forward looking, who, filled with the utopian spirit of the times, lectured to audiences and conducted short-lived community experiments until their bored, disillusioned, or offended disciples deserted them.

It is now fashionable to debunk the early nineteenth-century communitarians as escapists and nitwits, even as the precursors of twentieth-century totalitarianism. But in pointing out the obvious limitations of the utopian mentality, one need not throw out the baby with the bathwater. Early American communities, both religious and secular, were efforts to improve society, not escape it. Unlike the doctrinaire socialist, the communitarian believed in social harmony rather than in class warfare, in voluntary action rather than in compulsion.

The two most controversial community experiments during this period were inspired by Robert Owen, a successful manufacturer and industrial reformer from New Lanark, Scotland, and Charles Fourier, a French socialist.

Robert Owen came to America in 1825 to found a community at New Harmony, Indiana, on a site that he had purchased from a group of German communitarians known as the Rappites. Owen believed that man was the product of his environment and that for a society to be happy and moral, its members must enjoy material equality. A number of gifted European scholars came to Owen's utopia, and for a time the community offered the best educational instruction in the country, but the rank and file had more than their share of human frailties. According to Timothy Flint, a missionary and novelist, New Harmony attracted

> . . . the indolent, the unprincipled, men of desperate fortunes, moon-worshippers, romantic young men . . . those who had dreamed about earthly Elysiums, a great many honest aspirants after a better order of things, poor men simply desiring an education for their children.

A good many people wondered even in 1825 whether Owen's ideas could "keep alive that spirit of liberty and self-respect for one's own opinion, that so peculiarly belongs to the American people," and Owen's experiment did indeed fail after two years. But a large share of the failure of New Harmony can be attributed to the carelessness and imprecision of its founder. Owen's anti-religious views provoked more abhorrence than his fluctuating economic opinions, which Owen always regarded as secondary to his main purpose: the establishment of a rational system of society. Apparently the collapse of his experiment did not weaken the influence of his basic communitarian idea which in the 1830's inspired many new ventures.

Owenism had suggested radical workingman's parties, free-thought, and free-love to middle-class Americans. The doctrines of Fourier seemed less dangerous, and during the 1840's were espoused by a talented and respectable nucleus: Albert Brisbane, Fourier's chief propagandist; Parke Godwin, reformer and critic; Margaret Fuller, feminist, famed conversationalist, critic, and one-time editor of *The Dial,* the organ of the transcendentalists; George Ripley, founder of Brook Farm; and many others. Most of them eventually gave up their early radicalism, but for some years they spread Fourier's theories across the country.

The Fourierists (or "Fury-ites," as their enemies called them) regarded private capitalism as wasteful and degrading. If men would only abandon the competitive way and gather in *phalanxes,* or associated groups, they could transform the world of work into a paradise. What particularly appealed to the Fourierists, many of whom were New England transcendentalists, was the emphasis that Fourier put on practical idealism and the dignity of the worker.

Between 1840 and 1850, Fourier's followers organized more than 40 phalanxes in the United States. None was successful, but one at least became a lasting legend, the subject of Hawthorne's *The Blithedale Romance.* This was Brook Farm, organized by a group of transcendentalist intellectuals in 1841 and expressly converted to Fourierism in 1843-1844. More interested at first in the Over-Soul than in their bank accounts, they decided to demonstrate the possibility of combining the life of the mind with manual labor. ("After breakfast," Hawthorne noted in his diary, "Mr. Ripley put a four-pronged instrument into my hands, which he gave me to understand was called a pitch-fork; and he and Mr. Farley being armed with similar weapons, we all commenced a gallant attack upon a heap of manure.") The community, which never numbered more than 100, attracted about 4,000 visitors a year. But its practical side proved less successful. In 1847 a fire ruined the already insolvent enterprise and it was abandoned.

Secular communities like Brook Farm failed because the volunteers had neither the knowledge nor the temperament to sustain them. But the communal settlements of the German sectarians—who brought with them a tradition of village cooperation, and who were skillful farmers held together by strong religious ties—showed time and again that the communitarian idea could be made to work. Yet Americans as a rule were too individualistic to sink their private ambitions in such projects.

ABOLITION

From the 1830's on, one reform issue grew larger and more portentous until it overshadowed all the others: the anti-slavery cause, or abolition. Its origins reached back to the late seventeenth century, when humanitarian Puritans like Samuel Sewall and Roger Williams spoke out against the ownership of human chattels. The Quakers had long fought the buying and selling of slaves, and in the Revolutionary and post-Revolutionary eras liberals in every section had deplored slavery as a mortal disease. It was this conviction that inspired the American Colonization Society, founded in 1817 with private, state, and federal support, to establish Liberia in 1822 as a colony for ex-slaves. Unfortunately for the proponents of colonization, hardly more than a thousand free Negroes were transported to Africa between 1822 and 1830, and the others showed little desire to emigrate. By 1860 no more than 15,000 Negroes had been settled outside the country. The failure of the colonization plan and the apparent ineffectiveness of those who believed in gradual emancipation encouraged the radical abolitionists to start their campaign for immediate emancipation.

In 1831, William Lloyd Garrison began publishing the *Liberator,* the first outright abolitionist periodical. Its appearance marked the beginning of the great anti-slavery offensive. Garrison was a Massachusetts journalist, neurotic and wayward yet gentle and humorous, tolerant on occasion yet uncompromising in his cherished beliefs. As with many of his followers, abolition was only one of Garrison's causes. He was an ardent worker for women's rights and international peace, a fervent opponent of capital punishment and imprisonment for debt. But after 1830 slavery absorbed him. He denounced slavery not because it was inefficient or undemocratic or unjust, but because it was sinful. The Constitution, which guaranteed slavery, he described as "a covenant with death and an agreement with hell," and he publicly burned copies.

Garrison's vituperative attacks against the "Southern oppressors" did much to intensify anti-abolition sentiment in the South, while his fanaticism frightened moderate anti-slavery people everywhere, and his refusal to resort to political action minimized his effectiveness. More useful work was done by Theodore Dwight Weld of Ohio, who organized and directed the activities of the

abolitionist societies in the Northwest. Weld preferred patient organization to flamboyant pronouncements. and his devoted followers, well versed in the techniques of revival meetings, converted thousands to the abolitionist cause. Before 1850, almost 2,000 societies had been formed with a membership close to 200,000, and the talent and conscience of the North had rallied to the anti-slavery standard. John Greenleaf Whittier of Massachusetts became the bard of abolition, and Emerson, Thoreau, Whitman, Longfellow, and Melville also condemned slavery. Boston's eloquent Wendell Phillips thundered against it, as did famous ministers like Theodore Parker and William Ellery Channing. Southerners like James G. Birney and the Grimké sisters renounced their slave property and joined the anti-slavery cause.

The strength of the abolitionists lay in their unselfish dedication and their appeal to Christian principles. Their weakness lay in their refusal to reckon sufficiently with the social barriers to be overcome by the Negroes once they might be declared free and even equal to whites. Since the abolitionists saw in slavery not so much a social evil as a sin, they concentrated upon arousing the conscience of the country, trusting to a newly awakened righteousness not only to break the slave's shackles but to welcome him to the open society. In his discussions of slavery, Theodore Weld once said, he had "always presented it as preeminently a moral question, arresting the conscience of the nation. . . . As a question of politics and national economy, I have passed it with scarce a look or a word." "To be without a plan," cried one of Garrison's followers, "is the true genius and glory of the Anti-Slavery enterprise!"

Such pronouncements reflected the abolitionist's conviction that the appeal to conscience must not be allowed to fail. If it failed, all would be lost. Violent revolution by the slaves was abhorrent to practically all abolitionists, a fact not often understood in the South, nor did they envisage a civil war over slavery. Once the war started most of them preferred to let the South go in peace in the hope that slavery would wither sooner there if the section were isolated from the rest of the world. As the war progressed, they gradually altered their stand and were in the forefront of those who helped convert the war into a struggle for emancipation (see p. 435). When emancipation finally did come, the abolitionists themselves had worked out a constructive program for weaning the ex-slave to full citizenship.

But all that was in the future. In the middle 'thirties, public opinion stigmatized the abolitionists as a band of misguided bigots whose activities would destroy the Union if they were left unchecked. They were heckled, stoned, tarred and feathered, and lynched. New York, Boston, Philadelphia, Charleston, Richmond, Cincinnati—towns and cities in every section— were swept by anti-Garrison riots and mobbings, in defiance, or with the connivance, of the local authorities. Garrison was dragged through the streets of Boston by an angry mob; George Thompson, an English abolitionist, was howled down and threatened; Elijah Lovejoy, an anti-slavery editor in Alton, Illinois, was murdered by a mob in 1837.

Despite the stern repression of the abolitionists in the North, and the constant assurances given to southern leaders that the majority of people in the free states detested the ideas of the *Liberator,* the South grew ever more uneasy (see Chapter 13). It demanded penal laws against anti-slavery terrorists and threatened economic reprisals if they were not silenced. Southern postmasters confiscated suspected abolitionist literature. Southern fears of slave insurrection and resentment against atrocity stories in abolitionist propaganda made the South magnify the strength of the anti-slavery movement in the North. The intemperate response of the southerners, in turn, only increased northern anti-slavery sentiment. As the sectional conflict deepened, the dream of the millennium that had stirred the hearts of the reformers in the 1830's and 1840's faded away.

Readings
Asterisk indicates that book is available in paperback.

Alexis de Tocqueville, *Democracy in America* * (1835), is a profound analysis of the period covered in this chapter. Useful and readable general accounts are A. F. Tyler, *Freedom's Ferment: Phases of American Social History to 1860* * (1944); R. E. Riegel, *Young America, 1830-1840* (1949); Meade Minnigerode, *The Fabulous Forties, 1840-1850* (1924); and E. D. Branch, *The Sentimental Years, 1836-1860* * (1934). V. L. Parrington, *The Romantic Revolution in America, 1800-1860* * (1927), should be consulted.

On individual writers, see R. L. Rusk, *The Life of Ralph Waldo Emerson* (1949); J. W. Krutch, *Henry David Thoreau* (1948); A. H. Quinn, *Edgar Allan Poe* (1941); Mark Van Doren, *Nathaniel Hawthorne* * (1949); Newton Arvin, *Herman Melville* * (1950); and G. W. Allen, *The Solitary Singer: A Critical Biography of Walt Whitman* * (1955). D. H. Lawrence, *Studies in Classic American Literature* * (1923), is also available in full, with other penetrating literary studies in the superb anthology, Edmund Wilson, ed., *The Shock of Recognition: the Development Literature in the United States Recorded by the Men who Made It* * (1943). F. O. Matthiessen, *American Renaissance* (1941), is a brilliant interpretation of America's literary flowering. Lewis Mumford, *The Golden Day* * (1926), is also revealing. R. W. B. Lewis, *The American Adam* * (1955), treats the theme of innocence in American literature. Leo Marx, *The Machine in the Garden* (1964), is concerned with innocence under pressure. On this theme see also, Perry Miller, ed., *Margaret Fuller, American Romantic* (1963).

O. W. Larkin, *Art and Life in America* (1949), covers the history of painting and sculpture. Horatio Greenough's essays are conveniently collected in H. A. Small, ed., *Form and Function* (1957). On drama and popular entertainment see, A. H. Quint, *A History of the American Drama from the Beginning to the Civil War* (1923); O. S. Coad and Edwin Mims, Jr., *The American Stage* (1929); and J. T. Howard, *Our American Music, Three Hundred Years of It* (1946). C. M. Rourke, *American Humor* * (1931) is full of insight. F. L. Mott, *American Journalism: A History of Newspapers in the United States* (1950 ed.), is standard, as is Mott's *A History of American Magazines* (4 vols., 1930-1957).

The literature on education is more extensive than exhilarating. Relevant for this chapter are S. L. Jackson, *America's Struggle for Free Schools: Social Tension and Education in New England and New York, 1827-42* (1941), and Paul Monroe, *Founding of the American Public School System* (1940). Merle Curti, *The Social Ideas of American Educators* * (1935) contains some excellent chapters. L. H. Tharp, *Until Victory: Horace Mann and Mary Peabody* (1953), is a readable biography of the leading education reformer. The history of colleges is well presented in Frederick Rudolph, *The American College and University* * (1962). There are informative chapters in Richard Hofstadter and W. P. Metzger, *The Development of Academic Freedom in the United States* * (1955). The best account of the lyceum movement is in Carl Bode, *The American Lyceum, Town Meeting of the Mind* (1956).

Leading books on special aspects of the reform movement include J. A. Krout, *The Origins of Prohibition* (1925); H. E. Marshall, *Dorothea Dix, Forgotten Samaritan* (1937); Albert Deutsch, *The Mentally Ill in America* (1937); Charles Nordhoff, *The Communistic Societies of the United States* (1875); Lindsay Swift, *Brook Farm* * (1899); and A. E. Bestor, *Backwoods Utopias: The Sectarian and Owenite Phase of Communitarian Socialism in America, 1663-1829* * (1950). Religion and reform are treated in T. L. Smith, *Revivalism and Social Reform in Mid-Nineteenth Century America* (1957).

P. J. Staudenraus, *The African Colonization Movement, 1816-1865* (1961), is a scholarly monograph on efforts to settle the American Negro abroad. Of the many books on abolitionism we may recommend Louis Filler, *The Crusade Against Slavery, 1830-1860* * (1960); G. H. Barnes, *The Anti-Slavery Impulse, 1830-1844* * (1933); Allan Nevins, *Ordeal of the Union* (2 vols., 1947); A. B. Hart, *Slavery and Abolition* (1900); Jesse Macy, *The Abolition Crusade* (1919); and Laurence Lader, *The Bold Brahmins* (1961). J. L. Thomas, ed., *Slavery Attacked: The Abolitionist Crusade* * (1965), is a useful anthology of abolitionist writings. S. M. Elkins, *Slavery* * (1959), contains a critique of the abolitionist approach. Biographical studies of such abolitionist leaders as Charles Sumner, James G. Birney, William Lloyd Garrison, Theodore Parker, Wendell Phillips, Gerrit Smith, and Theodore Dwight Weld are rewarding.

CHAPTER TWELVE

The struggle for power among the older sections of the country during the reign of "Old Hickory" did not obscure the beckoning opportunities in regions still to be encompassed in America's "empire for liberty."

Throughout the 1820's and 1830's, Americans were very much on the move not only into new states in the Louisiana Purchase but also deep into foreign territory beyond, all the way to the Pacific Coast and even to Pacific islands. Within little more than a quarter of a century thereafter, the unbroken expanse of the United States had been extended to its present limits, the an-

Manifest Destiny

nexation of Hawaii had been proposed, and the purchase of Alaska completed. Canada to the north and Cuba to the south, meanwhile, fed a craving for full hemispheric sovereignty that was curbed only with increasing difficulty once the slogan, "Manifest Destiny," seemed to give the impetus of inevitability to America's explosive course.

The phrase, "Manifest Destiny," became identified with expansionism only after 1845, but the idea of celestial design it embodied was much older. According to this idea, the "Father of the Universe," or "the Great Architect," had set aside the Ameri-

can continents and their island environs "for the free development of our yearly multiplying millions." No physical barrier, no foreign force, least of all the sinister absolutism of the European system, could thwart the providential mission of the American people to extend *their* system across this hallowed land.

This vision of a mighty people on the march swelled an already inflated national rhetoric in the 1840's and 1850's and inspired often ridiculous oratorical displays couched in the current, racist, imperialist, and mercenary idiom. But the rhetorical excesses of the "Manifest Destiny" school

313

also derived in part from the prevalent optimistic idealism. New lands wrested from Indians and Mexicans, not to say Spaniards and Britons (as expansionists like Walt Whitman anticipated), by providing asylum and opportunity for the oppressed of Europe, would undermine world despotism, and by providing endless space for the full flowering of the American spirit, could only strengthen world democracy.

In this vein, Lewis Cass of Michigan told his fellow senators in February, 1847:

> In Europe . . . men are brought too much and kept too much in contact. There is not room for expansion. Minds of the highest order are pressed down by adverse circumstances, without the power of free exertion. . . . I trust we are far removed from all this; but to remove us further yet, we want almost unlimited power of expansion. That is our safety valve. The mightiest intellects which when compressed in thronged cities, and hopeless of their future, are ready to break the barriers around them the moment they enter the new world of the West, feel their freedom, and turn their energies to contend with the works of creation; converting the woods and the forest into towns, and villages, and cultivated fields, and extending the dominion of civilization and improvement over the domain of nature.

Practical politicians in charge of America's day-to-day diplomatic and military policies in the 1840's promoted more tangible objectives than the propagandists. They had their eyes fixed on domination of northern Pacific waters and of the trade with the Orient, which they saw (and later generations continued to see) as the legitimate extension of the American West itself. The whole grand stretch of the Pacific Coast of North America afforded but three good locations for the necessary port facilities: the Strait of Juan de Fuca, leading into Puget Sound and then to disputed Oregon country; breathtaking San Francisco Bay inside Mexico's Californian Golden Gate; and the Bay of San Diego farther south, "as fine a bay for vessels under three hundred tons," said an American captain in the 1820's, "as was ever formed by Nature in her most friendly mood to mariners." American spokesmen from all sections of the country were in agreement on grasping these few fine anchorages and thereby keeping out rival powers, especially the rival who too proudly called herself Mistress of the Seas.

Much has been made in recent years of the force of these tangible objectives in effecting America's unparalleled expansion in this period, as against the vague vaporings of the "Manifest Destiny" enthusiasts. But it is safe to say that these tangible objectives themselves gained in realism, as they gained in grandeur, for being promoted in the heady atmosphere of divine purpose which America's European rivals did not yet breathe (see Chapter 23).

I. *Confrontations on the Canadian Border*

THE SEEDS OF SUSPICION

The westward surge of the American people and their star-spangled prognostications that their flag would soon wave from Patagonia to the North Pole only strengthened official British opinion (along with that of the rest of monarchical Europe) that the Yankees were a nation of bullies and braggarts who must be carefully watched and closely constrained.

Among the watchers in the 1830's and 1840's were the swarms of British travelers who made quick tours of the upstart land and reported it as dirty and swaggering and shamelessly dollar-conscious as they thought it before they left home. These tours culminated in the visit of the famous "Boz," the still youthful Charles Dickens, in 1842, and the publication two years later of his novel, *Martin Chuzzlewit*.

Dickens' discontent with the United States was aggravated by his personal resentment against American publishers who pirated his own enormously popular works with no profit to himself. Deeper down was the revulsion he shared with his countrymen against the American states which had repudiated their debts to British creditors after the Panic of 1837 (see p. 284). Major Pawkins, Dickens writes in *Chuzzlewit,* "was a great politician; and the one article of his creed in reference to all public obligations involving the good faith and integrity of his country was, 'run a moist pen slick through everything, and start fresh.' This made him a patriot."

The soaring (Dickens said, "spurious") spirit of American democracy—"we are a model of wisdom, and an example to the world, and the perfection of human reason, and a great deal more to the same purpose, which you may hear any hour in the day"—also angered many John Bulls especially after Britain's First Reform Act of 1832 showed the force of Brother Jonathan's spirit abroad. The American defense of slavery and assaults on abolitionists, after Britain had led the world in emancipating the Negroes in her colonies in 1833, only deepened the disenchantment with the American brand of liberty.

If Americans were to be watched and vilified within their very gates, they were to be constrained at the nearest vantage point outside, which was their Canadian border. The British, if possible, thought even less of their Canadian subjects than they did of the restless old rebels to the south, and for Canada itself as a paying colony they had learned to entertain the meagerest expectations. Yet Canada had her uses, "above all," wrote the future Colonial Secretary, E. G. Stanley, in 1824, "in case of [a third] war with the United States (no improbable future contingency)." In such an event, Stanley added, Canada "furnishes ample assistance in men, timber and harbours for carrying on the war, and that on the enemy's frontier." How seriously the British took the American menace is evidenced, beginning late in the 1820's, by their expenditure of millions of pounds (after the Canadians themselves refused to be taxed for the purpose) in constructing the inland Rideau Canal as an alternative to the St. Lawrence waterway in case control of the latter ever fell to American invaders. The British spent millions more rebuilding strategic citadel of Quebec.

THE CAROLINE AFFAIR

Late in the 1830's and early in the 1840's three confrontations gave John Bull and Brother Jonathan welcome cause for honing up the weapons to be used beyond the war of words, if words failed. The first of these is known as "the *Caroline* affair."

In November and December, 1837, inspired to a degree by the advance of the "great experiment" below the border, successive insurrections flared up in lower and upper Canada against the Crown. Loyal forces quickly suppressed these uprisings, but not before certain Americans had rallied to the rebels' cause. On the night of December 29, 1837, *Caroline,* a small American steamer engaged in ferrying supplies to the insurgents, lay moored on the New York side of the Niagara River. A party of loyal Canadian volunteers rowed across, routed *Caroline's* crew, set her afire, towed her out, and watched her sink. During the scuffle one American was killed.

The United States promptly demanded an apology for the British "invasion" of American territory. But the British replied that *Caroline,* by abetting the criminal conspiracy in Canada, had become fair game. They were on less tenable ground for having taken direct action without first formally protesting to American officials and giving them a chance to discipline their own citizens—an oversight which reflected the British Foreign Secretary, Lord Palmerston's, lifelong contempt for American claims to nationhood. Further to rub it in, Queen Victoria knighted the Canadian officer who had led the boarding party.

Many Americans soon showed as little concern for protocol as Palmerston. While the stalemate over *Caroline* held, tens of thousands of backwoodsmen all along the border from Vermont to Michigan, many of them made jobless by the current business depression, joined together during the summer of 1838 in "Hunter's Lodges," well-armed secret organizations which nevertheless openly proclaimed their purpose, "to emancipate the British Colonies from British Thraldom." Each "Hunter" also swore an oath to "help destroy . . . every power, or authority of Royal origin, upon this continent, . . . So help me God!" Certain bands of "Hunters" soon crossed into Canada and engaged in futile skirmishes. But they misjudged the eagerness of most Canadians to throw off their yoke as Texans had recently thrown off that of Mexico, and were soon induced by General Winfield Scott, President Van Buren's persuasive emissary, to disband.

The *Caroline* affair might also have been allowed to die had not one of the alleged participants in the vessel's destruction, Alexander McLeod, been arrested by New York State authorities in November, 1840, and charged with murder and arson. Palmerston now acknowledged that the raid had been officially planned to forestall American aid to the insurrectionists and demanded McLeod's release on the ground that any actions he may have committed were done under orders. McLeod's execution, Palmerston warned, would mean war.

New York's Governor Seward insisted that McLeod face trial in the state courts, though he promised Secretary of State Daniel Webster that if convicted McLeod would be pardoned. Fortunately, McLeod was acquitted. Lest similar incidents occur, Webster, with presidential support, drafted a measure establishing federal jurisdiction in all cases involving aliens accused of committing acts under the direction of a foreign government. Congress passed this measure in August, 1842.

THE "AROOSTOOK WAR"

The Rideau Canal (see p. 315), was not the only military-inspired transportation project of the British in Canada during these troubled times. The freezing of the St. Lawrence had hampered the movement of troops in putting down the Canadian insurrections of 1837, and the next year the British decided on the construction of an overland road from St. John on the Bay of Fundy in New Brunswick to Mont-

real and Quebec. In February, 1839, work began on the proposed route in the rich Aroostook River valley where the conflicting claims of the State of Maine and the province of New Brunswick grew ever more roundly assertive as the value of the timber in the valley soared. When the "foreign" lumberjacks now once more entered the disputed area and began felling trees for the road project, the hastily mobilized Maine militia chased them out.

The "Aroostook War" was a bloodless affray, but in this second Anglo-American confrontation on the Canadian border war fever in Washington had grown even warmer than during the *Caroline* incident. Congress confirmed the gravity of the situation by appropriating $10 million for war purposes and authorizing President Van Buren to enlist 50,000 volunteers.

As it turned out, neither money nor men were needed, for in March, 1839, General Winfield Scott again succeeded in smoothing things over at the scene. Scott, however, could not eliminate the source of the trouble, which lay in the rankling vagueness of the frontier line. The scene of the "Aroostook War" had been in dispute since the end of the Revolution and soured Anglo-American relations until the Webster-Ashburton treaty of 1842 (see p. 317).

THE CREOLE CASE

The third Anglo-American confrontation of this period, the *Creole* case of 1841, is related to the Canadian border only because it so strained Anglo-American relations on another touchy subject that it made the formidable border issues more difficult to settle. This confrontation arose out of an encounter on the high seas involving the slave trade.

In her attempts to destroy the slave traffic, especially after the emancipation of 1833, Britain had made treaties with many nations giving her navy even in peacetime the right to stop and search suspected merchantmen under all flags. Palmerston boasted that Britain had enlisted in the fight against the slave trade, "every state in Christendom which has a flag that sails on the ocean, with the single exception of the United States of North America." This was not entirely true; France, like the United States, had resisted Britain's assumption of holier-than-thou authority. But it suited Palmerston to point the accusing finger, and with some justice, for many slave ships escaped search and seizure simply by running up the Stars and Stripes in time.

Hard feeling aroused by Britain's affronts to the flag in the slave trade heightened American indignation in the *Creole* case. While carrying about 130 slaves from Virginia to New Orleans, the American vessel, *Creole,* was taken over by the Negroes in a successful mutiny during which one white passenger was killed. The Negroes then sailed her to the British port of Nassau, in the Bahamas, and went ashore. Those not held for the killing were permitted to live in the Bahamas as free men, despite the protests of *Creole's* owners to local authorities and the efforts of American officials to reclaim them.

Daniel Webster (1782-1852).

THE WEBSTER-ASHBURTON TREATY

Behind each confrontation between Britain and her mettlesome former colonies throughout the nineteenth century lay the growing commercial and industrial rivalry of the two nations. This rivalry inspired

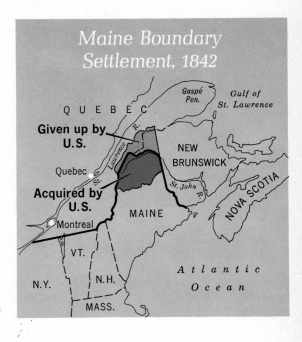

Palmerston, the curmudgeon, to prick every Yankee pretension, and Americans to reply in kind. Palmerston's unremitting insults and attacks finally sickened even his own people and his colleagues in the Cabinet. When he fell with the Melbourne ministry in 1841, both nations breathed sighs of relief. Soon after, Lord Aberdeen, as the new Foreign Secretary, and Webster, the American Secretary of State, arranged to meet in an attempt to improve Anglo-American relations. Aberdeen showed his goodwill by accepting Washington as the scene of negotiations and by appointing as his special envoy Lord Ashburton, the husband of an American heiress.

The principal subject of the Webster-

Ashburton talks was the Canadian-American border. Webster ultimately compromised on the Maine boundary issue and reached an agreement that gave the United States approximately 7,000 of the 12,000 square miles in question. The 5,000 square miles granted to Britain were sufficient to protect the communications she so strongly desired between Quebec and New Brunswick. In return, she accepted the inaccurately surveyed boundary line running along the northern frontier of Vermont and New York and extending westward to Minnesota and Ontario. Agreement here eliminated the likelihood of conflict as settlement moved outward on the frontier. The line decided on, moreover, left the United States with the Mesabi iron ore deposits in northern Minnesota, unknown then, but of immense value later.

Webster enlarged the discussions by raising the question of the *Creole* incident, but Ashburton merely promised that henceforth British colonial authorities would not interfere with American vessels "driven by accident or violence" into British ports. The Americans, on their part, agreed to assist the British in patrolling the African coast and suppressing the slave-runners. Ashburton also refused to eat humble pie over the *Caroline* affair. He merely "regretted" that "some explanation and apology for this occurrence was not immediately made," and Webster had to make the best of the word "apology."

Extremists in Britain and America protested that their respective countries had suffered a diplomatic defeat in these negotiations, but the Webster-Ashburton Treaty, signed on August 9, 1842, was a model of compromise that paved the way for other peaceful settlements during the next two decades. Anglo-American relations were further improved in 1846 when Sir Robert Peel's government repealed the British Corn Laws and Polk's administration (see p. 325) pushed the Walker Tariff through Congress. The British measure opened her ports more freely to American wheat; the low duties in the Walker Tariff opened American markets more freely to British manufactures.

Canadian sentiment for annexation to the United States, however, continued strong, as did American sentiment (except in the South) for satisfying the Canadian feeling. The repeal of the Corn Laws particularly, by ending the favorable position enjoyed by Canadian wheat in Britain, fed the hopes of annexationists in Canada and in the United States, for Canadian growers now longed for free entry into the American market by means of the union of the two lands.

II. *The Lone Star State*

LIMITATIONS
ON SOUTHERN EXPANSION

The manifest destiny of Texas, and of the even more inviting empire beyond, had become far closer to realization by the time of the Webster-Ashburton Treaty than the destiny still reserved in optimistic American minds and hearts for the vast expanse of Canada. Texas' speedier progress toward fulfillment in American terms stemmed largely from the unsatisfied, and as yet insatiable, land hunger of the South.

In the North, after the removal of the Sauk and Fox tribes in 1833, emigrants from Illinois, Indiana, Ohio, and Kentucky had begun to spill into the newly opened Iowa and Wisconsin country. By 1840, some 75,000 settlers had established themselves on the rich farmlands here, and smaller numbers, including lumbermen and trappers, were pushing into Minnesota. The small southern farmer, as well as the planter, had no such vast tracts at his disposal. By 1840, most of the best land on the southern Gulf plains was occupied by big planters and was being worked by slave gangs. After the admission of Arkansas in 1836, the only remaining prospective slave state under the provisions of the Missouri Compromise was the territory of Florida.

Immediately to the west of the last southern settlements lay the "permanent Indian frontier," established in the 1820's in much of present-day Oklahoma and Kansas to hold forever, it was said, the displaced woods Indians of the East as well as the numerous hostile tribes native to the region. As late as the 1860's this Indian reserve was known as "the Great American Desert" and had no appeal and offered no solution to slaveholders whose "peculiar institution," in any case, was barred by law if not by nature from its northerly portion.

South and west of the Indian range stretched Texas, recently become precariously independent of shaky Mexican regimes. Beyond Texas lay Mexico's vague and vaguely held California empire whose charms had so long and so lavishly been reported by far-ranging mountain men and mariners. Both Texas and California had ultimately to be fought for, but their fall seemed destined none the less.

Senator Robert J. Walker of Mississippi, Polk's promoter for the presidency in 1844 on an aggressively expansionist platform (see p. 324), and then the power behind the throne, caught the spirit of the times in a letter to Democratic leaders across the country in January of the election year:

If the Creator had separated Texas from the Union by mountain barriers, . . . there might be plausible objections; but he has planed down the whole [Mississippi] valley, including Texas, and united every atom of the soil and every drop of the waters, . . . and marked . . . the whole for the dominion of one government and the residence of one people; and it is impious in man to attempt to dissolve the great and glorious union. . . . Who will desire to check the young eagle of America, now refixing her gaze upon our former limits, and repluming her pinions for the returning flight?

THE LONE STAR REPUBLIC

In 1819, when she obtained Florida from Spain, the United States had surrendered her dubious claim, based upon the carefree geography of the Louisiana Purchase treaty, to the Mexican province of

Texas in the state of Coahuila—much to the disgust of later frontier politicians like Senator Walker, who kept harping on "our former limits." American traders and military adventurers nevertheless continued the

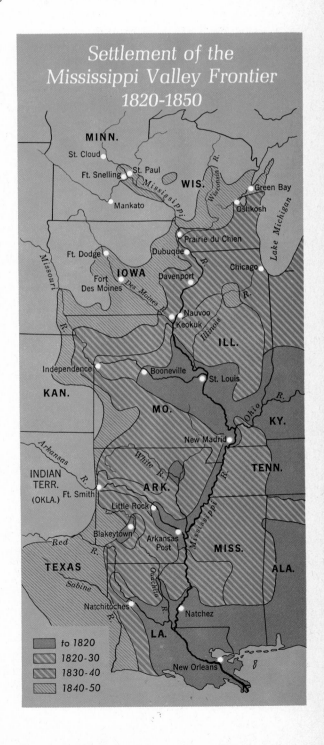

Settlement of the Mississippi Valley Frontier 1820-1850

illicit commercial relations they had already established with the Mexicans against Spain's strong wishes. When Mexico, with the assistance of such traders and fighters, won her independence from Spain in 1821, she promptly put American commerce on a legitimate footing and invited additional Americans to settle in Texas and develop the resources of the land.

Connecticut-born Moses Austin, who obtained a land grant from the Mexican government in 1820 after the Panic of 1819 had got him into serious financial difficulties in neighboring Missouri, pioneered the American colonization of Texas. Moses Austin died in 1821 and could not develop his tract, but in 1823 Mexico validated the

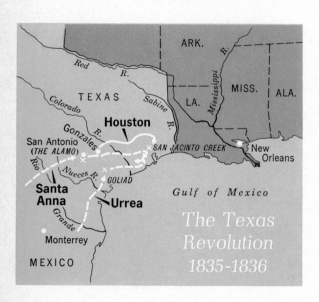

The Texas Revolution 1835-1836

grant for his son, Stephen, who carried through the first colonization program. Other American promoters, or *empresarios,* received concessions similar to the Austins'.

Mexican officials had hoped that the settlement of Texas by white Americans would protect their country from Indian raids and from possible aggression by the United States. But they soon realized they had miscalculated. Between 1820 and 1830, about 20,000 Americans with approximately 2,000 slaves had crossed into Texas, largely from the lower Mississippi frontier. Most of them were law-abiding people, but rougher ele-

ments, particularly in eastern Texas, soon made the Mexicans subscribe to John Jay's old complaint that white frontiersmen were more troublesome than red Indians. The Texans, on their part, soon began to champ at their lack of self-government. As part of the state of Coahuila, Texas province was under the thumb of the Mexican-dominated state legislature. As early as 1826, after an *empresario* named Haden Edwards quarreled with the authorities over land titles, his brother, Benjamin, proclaimed the Republic of Fredonia and staged a rebellion that the Mexicans easily put down.

Offers by the United States to purchase Texas in 1827 only served to deepen Mexico's anxiety over Yankee expansionism. Mexico had complaints about Yankee independence as well. American settlers in Mexico had failed to become Catholics, as they were required to do by the terms of their invitation. They had ignored a Mexican prohibition against the slave trade by substituting a thinly disguised "indenture" system. Some, moreover, had spilled over into territory reserved by law for Mexicans.

In 1830 the Mexican government sent troops to occupy Texas, called a halt to further American immigration, and passed other restrictive measures, including the abolition of slavery itself. This change in policy angered the American Texans already aroused by the government's refusal to separate Texas from the state of Coahuila. In 1832 General A. L. de Santa Anna emerged as Mexico's strong man, instituted a centralist program, and three years later abolished all local rights. Early in 1836 he led an army of 6,000 into Texas to bring the rebellious Americans to book. Confronted with Santa Anna's threat to exterminate them, Americans in Texas declared their independence on March 2, 1836, set up a provisional government under a constitution that sanctioned slavery, and appointed Sam Houston Commander-in-Chief of the few hundred men mobilized at Gonzales. Santa Anna already had the Alamo mission in San Antonio under siege and when it fell on March 6 he massacred the 187 defenders including the commander, William B. Travis, and such legendary figures as Davy Crockett and Jim Bowie. Three weeks later more than 300 were massacred at Goliad on surrendering to the Mexican General, José Urrea.

Such brutal attacks prompted Houston to beat a steady retreat eastward until he reached the vicinity of San Jacinto creek. Here, on April 21, 1836, he suddenly turned on his unprepared pursuers. Fired up by the cry, "Remember the Alamo," Houston's force routed that under Santa Anna and took the dictator himself captive. On May 14, Santa Anna signed a treaty pledging Texan independence and fixing a vague boundary between Texas and Mexico. Although the Mexican Congress promptly repudiated the treaty, it could do nothing to reverse it.

ANNEXATION EFFECTED

Sympathy for the Texas insurrectionists had been strong in the South and also in the Northwest, where their cause was identified with the struggles of the underprivileged. As one Ohio supporter declared in 1835:

The Texans are mostly composed of the poorer classes of society: men whom misfortunes have driven from our country; men who have gone there at the instance of the invitation of the Mexican Government, on the full assurance of the protection of that government; in the hope and expectation of being able to retrieve their shattered fortunes, and procure bread for their suffering families.

Behind the boasts of the time about "the generous anglo-saxon blood" triumphing over the "blood thirsty barbarians of Mexico," was the widespread feeling that the Texans had fought the war of humanity and democracy.

Support for the Texans' cause, however, was less enthusiastic in the Northeast, especially among members of the Whig party, who viewed the Texans' request to enter the Union after they defeated Santa Anna as a slave-owners' plot. From five to seven states, it was pointed out, might be carved out of the huge Texas domain, thus insuring southern control of Congress. Opponents of

annexation protested so vehemently that President Jackson held off even recognizing the Lone Star Republic until just before he left office in 1837. Van Buren also withstood growing annexationist pressure, a policy that was to cost him dearly during Tyler's administration when his enemies in the South sought to unseat him as the titular head of the Democratic party, and thereby improve Calhoun's chances for the White House. In this strategy southern expansionists received enthusiastic support from western political leaders.

Denied admission to the United States and menaced by unforgiving Mexico, the Lone Star Republic sought protection elsewhere. Britain liked the idea of an independent Texas that would export cotton and import British manufactured goods on a free-trade basis. Britain also opposed slavery. In December, 1843, the British Foreign Secretary, Lord Aberdeen, was at pains formally to notify the United States that "it must be well known" to her "and to the whole world, that Great Britain desires, and is constantly exerting herself to procure the general abolition of slavery throughout the world," and "with regard to Texas, we avow that we wish to see slavery abolished there, as elsewhere." But slavery in Texas did not keep Britain from seeking permanent relations with her.

That Texas might link herself with Britain was a frightening prospect to northern businessmen, but it was even more frightening to slave-owners who felt that the abolition of slavery in Texas as a result of British pressure would invite violent insurrection in the slave states themselves.

Sam Houston, now President of Texas, cleverly played upon American fears until the annexationists were ready to do almost anything to bring Texas into the Union before Britain succeeded in keeping her permanently out. President Tyler himself worked tirelessly to gain credit for annexation before his successor took office.

In April, 1844, Tyler submitted a Texas statehood treaty to the Senate drawn up by Calhoun, whom he had just appointed Secretary of State. It was only on taking office that Calhoun first learned of Lord Aberdeen's dispatch of the previous December and unfortunately for him he attached to the treaty proposal a letter he had just written in reply. In this letter, Calhoun defended southern slavery as a humane institution. He declared, furthermore, that Britain's abolitionist policy compelled the United States to absorb Texas out of self-protection.

Calhoun's little disquisition on the beauties of slavery delighted his disciples, but it insured the repudiation of the annexation treaty in the Senate by a vote of 36 to 16. Men who had been on the fence about Texas began to interpret annexation as a barefaced grab for slave territory. Tyler was chagrined by the Senate vote, but in February, 1845, after expansionism had seemingly triumphed in the 1844 election (see p. 324), he succeeded in persuading both houses of Congress to pass a joint resolution favoring annexation. This resolution squeaked through the Senate 27 to 25 and made unnecessary the two-thirds vote required for treaty ratification. Texas now was offered statehood if she would agree to submit a proper constitution, assume her debts, and agree to the possible subdivision of her territory into not more than four states. In return, she would be permitted to keep her public lands and to retain slavery under the terms of the Missouri Compromise. Texas accepted this offer in October, 1845, and on December 29 that year became the 28th state in the Union. Mexico, at the same time, recalled her minister in Washington.

III. *"Manifest Destiny" in the Far West*

THE FUTURE OF OREGON

The future of Oregon as well as the future of Texas had reached a critical point as Americans rallied to their party standards for the campaign of 1844.

Distant though it was from the mainstream of European and American politics and business, the Oregon country since the eighteenth century had been the scene and subject of competition among France, Spain, and Russia, as well as Britain and the United States. Early in the nineteenth century France and Spain both had surrendered their claims to the region; and in 1824, the Russians, expanding southward from Alaska, had agreed to fix their own southern boundary at 54° 40′. This left Britain and the United States free to settle ownership of the remainder of Oregon between themselves.

After John Jacob Astor's Pacific Fur Company was forced out of Oregon by the British North West Company in 1812 (see Chap. 9), Americans lost interest in Oregon for a generation. The British, on their part, feeling wholly secure in the region, made no effort to keep out those few adventurers from the United States who might find their way there. By the 1830s, however, American expansionists began to feel cramped even in their own vast territories and interest in Oregon revived. In 1832 and again in 1834, Nathaniel J. Wyeth, a merchant of Cambridge, Massachusetts, sent several expeditions to the region. These were financial failures, but they served to call attention once again to the feasibility of the overland route to the Northwest that had first been explored almost three decades earlier by Lewis and Clark.

Accompanying Wyeth to Oregon in 1834 was the first band of Methodist missionaries led by Jason Lee. The fertility of the soil in Oregon's Willamette Valley so captivated these men that its cultivation quickly took precedence over conversion of the Indians. By 1844, the home church in the East washed its hands of the enterprise, but the settlement in Oregon flourished. In the meantime, other denominations had followed the Methodists' lead. Marcus Whitman founded a Presbyterian mission near

The Mormon Migration 1846-1848

of mythology and prophecy which recalled an ancient legend that the Indians were descendants of the lost tribes of Israel and which enjoined Smith's followers to convert them from their heathenish ways.

On the basis of his revelation, Smith in 1830 founded the Church of Jesus Christ of the Latter-Day Saints and published his book. Along with other Messianic movements of the times, Mormonism spread into the Western Reserve in Ohio, and there, at Kirtland, the distinctive pattern of Mormon community living—markedly similar to the seventeenth-century New England settlements centered on the church—first took shape.

Thereafter trouble dogged the Mormons. Following the Panic of 1837 financial difficulties in Ohio drove them to the frontier in Missouri; but within a year, scorned as a sect of thieving Yankee abolitionists and heretics, they were harried back across the Mississippi to Nauvoo, Illinois. Here they found peace until, following Joseph Smith's own example, the practice of plural marriages spread. Whether these marriages were "sealed for a time," that is, consummated in this life, or "sealed for eternity," that is, to be consummated in Heaven, or both, this practice alienated the monogamists of the sect and infuriated the non-Mormon inhabitants.

When the anti-Smith faction among the Mormons attacked him in their newly established newspaper in 1843, Smith and his friends smashed their press. For this offense, the civil authorities threw him and his brother Hyram into jail. Soon freed, they were jailed again on a related charge and in 1844 were shot dead in their cell by members of an aroused mob. Joseph Smith's murder almost killed the Mormon movement. On the other hand, it also supplied the Mormon church with a martyr in whose name a new leader might rally its forces. Such a leader appeared in the person of Brigham Young, a loyal follower of Joseph Smith, who became the new "Lion of the Lord."

In 1842, Smith had envisaged a Mormon homeland "in the midst of the Rocky Mountains" and had even dispatched some of his followers to "investigate the locations of California and Oregon, and hunt out a good location, where we can . . . build a city in a day, and have a government of our own." Forced out of Illinois after the Prophet's assassination, the Mormon host began their tortuous exodus westward, led by Young, in the winter of 1846. On June 24, 1847, the first wave of Mormons entered the Salt Lake Valley—a Zion isolated on a barren Mexican plateau remote from the lands of the gentiles where (to quote a Mormon historian) the Saints had been "eternally mobbed, harassed, hunted, our best men murdered and every good man's life continually in danger." Here, encircled by mountain and desert, the Mormon leaders created a theocracy superbly organized for survival.

The Salt Lake community was cooperative rather than competitive. Since its very existence depended on controlling the limited water supply brought in by the mountain streams, Young devised an irrigation system that distributed water equitably to the whole community. He and his advisers parceled out land in a manner reminiscent of the seventeenth-century New England town-planners. Between 1847 and 1857, they laid out 95 communities in which they closely regulated commerce and

tives, the last four (1835-1839) as Speaker. As President, Polk remained the solid Democrat he had always been. He opposed protection, and in 1846 signed the Walker Tariff which put the country back on low duties for revenue only. He opposed a national debt and meant to keep it low enough to be serviced (and reduced when possible) by the revenues available. He opposed banks and restored Van Buren's Independent Treasury System for handling federal funds. He gave nullifiers no comfort. Above all, he was as expansionist and isolationist as Jefferson himself.

In his inaugural address in March, 1845, Polk asserted "the right of the United States to that portion of our territory which lies beyond the Rocky Mountains. Our title to the country of the Oregon," he said, "is 'clear and unquestionable,' and already are our people preparing to perfect that title by occupying it with their wives and children." Moreover, in his first annual message to Congress in December, 1845, Polk stretched the Monroe Doctrine by making two assertions that are often called the Polk Doctrine: (1) "The people of *this continent* alone have the right to decide their own destiny"; (2) The United States cannot allow European states to prevent an independent state from entering the Union.

War with Britain over Oregon would have been foolhardy while war with Mexico over Texas still threatened. Polk was responsible enough to realize this and found a way to back down after the election was over and the 50° 40' slogan had served its purpose. Polk had been reliably advised that Oregon above the 49th parallel was clearly ill-suited to agriculture. Below the 49th parallel, he said, "the entrance of the Straits of Fuca, Admiralty Inlet, and Puget's Sound, with their fine harbors and rich surrounding soils." A concession to Britain on the boundary, moreover, might speed America's effort to secure the even more valuable California ports.

Three times before, Britain had offered to divide Oregon at the 49th parallel, which in fact was a direct extension of the northern border of the United States westward from the Rockies. Britain herself now had reasons to try again. She was finding it increasingly difficult to keep unruly American elements out of Oregon. At the same time, the depletion of the supply of fur-bearing animals along the Columbia River gave her justification for getting out herself. British hostility to the United States and her aspirations, furthermore, had decreased with the reduction of American tariffs on British manufactures in 1846. Negotiations, therefore, were resumed in a conciliatory atmosphere, and on June 15, 1846, a treaty was signed that proved advantageous to both countries. The line drawn along the 49th parallel to Puget Sound and from there to the Pacific through the Straits of Juan de Fuca was simply an extension of the Canadian-American boundary that had been fixed in 1818 as far as the Rockies. The territory north of the Columbia, though it was clearly British by right of settlement, fell into the American sphere. Britain retained Vancouver Island and navigation rights on the Columbia River.

THE MORMONS IN UTAH

While thousands of Americans from the North and the South were moving west to "perfect," as Polk said, American title to North America, one group moved west to escape the thralldom of American government. This group was the Mormons. In 1823, Joseph Smith, a visionary in Vermont, claimed to have been led by angels to a place where "there was a book deposited, written upon gold plates," and "two stones in silver bows . . . deposited with the plates." The "possession and use of these stones," Smith wrote, "were what constituted Seers in ancient or former times; and . . . God had prepared them for the purpose of translating the book." As God's helper, Smith used the stones in revealing the Book of Mormon, a composite

View of Salt Lake City (1853).

industry, and experimented in social planning. The Mormon state of Deseret (Congress later changed the name to Utah) was probably the most successful communitarian project in American history.

Remote as the "Saints" were, they soon found that they could not escape the American environment. In two years the American war with Mexico (see p. 329) brought Young's community once more under United States jurisdiction. Furthermore, the Mormon state lay athwart one of the routes to California and inevitably became involved in the American push to the Pacific. The Mormons were not the only people in the country who were governed by heavenly dictates. All Americans, it seemed, had the responsibility "to redeem from unhallowed hands a *land* above all others favored of heaven, and hold it for the use of a people who know how to obey heaven's behests."

ON TO CALIFORNIA

California had been loosely held by Spain since the middle of the eighteenth century, when she opened a number of Franciscan missions, protected by small garrisons, for the double purpose of converting the Indians and preventing British and Russian penetration down the California coast. In theory, these missions were temporary establishments set up to teach the Indians agriculture and the household arts, and the Franciscans did succeed in Christianizing and training thousands of redmen. After completing this task, the Franciscans were expected to move on to new fields and allow the regular clergy to take over. The mission lands would then be broken up and distributed to private owners. But who was to decide when each move was to be made? Anticlericals hungered for the lands from the start; and when Mexico won her independence from Spain early in the 1820's, officials and land-speculators pressed for distribution of mission property. By 1834 half the mission lands had passed into private hands, and the other half was soon lost to landsharks. At the outbreak of the Mexican War in 1846, the Indians had hopelessly degenerated and few signs of the missions remained.

During the preceding 25 years, American whalers from Nantucket and New Bedford had stopped at the California ports of Monterey and San Francisco, and New England traders had sailed there and farther south to exchange everything from Chinese fireworks to English cart-wheels for hides and tallow. These visitors year by year left behind them deserters and adventurers who, along with emigrants from the Oregon and Mississippi frontiers, began to acquire large tracts of California land and to monopolize commerce and industry.

Richard Henry Dana, Jr, whose classic *Two Years Before the Mast* (1840), contains the best account of California life in the 1830's, succumbed to the elegance and pride of the Mexicans encountered by these Yankee mariners, but he also saw the sources of their defenselessness against the interlopers. He found the Mexicans "an idle people" incapable of making anything, bad bargainers, and suspicious of foreigners. "Indeed," he wrote, "as far as my observation goes, there are no people to whom the newly invented Yankee word of 'loafer' is more applicable than to the Spanish Americans." For the interlopers themselves, the most helpful and knowledgeable figure on the coast was Thomas O. Larkin, who settled in Monterey in 1832 and later became a confidential agent of the American government. His counterpart in the interior was Captain John A. Sutter, who built a fort in the Sacramento Valley in 1839 and set up a small trading empire of his own. (See map p. 323).

Although California had not been an issue in the 1844 campaign, it soon became identified in the popular mind with Oregon. No one was more eloquent in its praises than the witty Larkin, who described the pleasures of "hunting wild Deer and dancing with tame Dear." By the summer of 1845, talk about a mighty nation extending from sea to sea had become common, and expansionists warned Polk to take over California before the British stepped in. Polk himself aired plans for a transcontinental railroad to link the Golden Gate with the Mississippi Valley. San Francisco, all agreed, was the great prize, twenty times more valuable, thought Daniel Webster, than the whole of Texas. California's San Diego harbor, in turn, according to many observers, would prove far more important to American interests than any part of Oregon.

The United States, alas, had no claims to California except desire. During Jackson's and Tyler's administrations, the American government had tried to buy California, but these moves only deepened Mexican suspicions. In 1842 Daniel Webster sought British help in forcing Mexico to sell California in return for concessions to Britain in the Anglo-American dispute over Oregon, but he was rebuffed. In the same year, an American naval officer, Commodore Thomas ap Catesby Jones, who had been mistakenly informed in Peru that the United States and Mexico were at war and that the British were planning to seize California, sailed into Monterey and captured the city. When he discovered his mistake, he promptly apologized to the Mexicans, but the significance of this hostile gesture was plain enough.

In 1845, on learning that the government of General Herrera was in such desperate straits that it might be persuaded at last to sell California, President Polk hurriedly sent a representative, John Slidell, to Mexico City with another offer to buy, and with instructions to pay as much as $40 million for California and New Mexico if necessary. By then, however, United States and Mexican forces had already begun to make military passes at each other over Texas, and the recently installed Mexican regime would not even receive Slidell. The envoy wrote to Polk that nothing could be done with the Mexicans "until they shall have been chastised."

Autonomous action in California itself was still possible, especially since the canny Larkin had a plan all ready by which the United States would encourage a "spontaneous" rebellion of Spanish-speaking Californians favorably disposed to annexation. Nothing came of Larkin's scheme, but its feasibility was indicated by a spontaneous revolt of other Americans in California north of San Francisco Bay where, on July 5, 1846, they set up an independent state with its own bear flag. On learning of the formal outbreak of war between the United States and Mexico, these rebels disestablished the "Bear Flag Republic" and joined the American forces.

iv. *The Mexican War and Its Legacy*

A SHORT AND FRUITFUL WAR

With Texas wrenched from her and California obviously slipping away, Mexico, if only to save face, had to take a stand against her neighbor to the north. Her opportunity came early in 1846, when, on hearing from Slidell about the failure of his mission, Polk ordered General Zachary Taylor to occupy disputed territory on the southern boundary of Texas. Taylor had carried out his orders by the end of March. Such a show of force, thought Polk, might cause the Mexicans to reconsider their refusal to negotiate, but, failing that, it might cause an incident that would serve as an excuse for a declaration of war.

Mexico responded to Polk's strategy by sending up troops of her own and on April 25, 1846, they clashed with Taylor's men. Polk had already prepared a war message and on May 11 he sent it to Congress. The shedding of American blood on what the United States claimed to be its own soil put Congress in a mood to act without lengthy debate. On May 13 Congress declared war by a vote of 40 to 2 in the Senate and 174 to 14 in the House.

New England anti-slavery spokesmen, James Russell Lowell, Theodore Parker, Ralph Waldo Emerson, and others, vigorously denounced the war. Polk, nevertheless, had hoped for formal bipartisan support, which he failed to win. His refusal openly to declare his war aims (the seizure of New Mexico and California) encouraged the Whigs in both sections to attack his entire Mexican policy. To some northern Whigs, Polk, by forcing an unwilling people into war, was simply "attempting to consummate a scheme for the extension and strengthening of slavery and the Slave Power." Some southern Whigs themselves feared that the acquisition of the new terri-

tories would intensify old sectional controversies and destroy their party. But if the Whigs publicly castigated Polk, they did not obstruct the war effort and indeed began to make all the political capital they could out of the triumphs of two Whig generals, Zachary Taylor and Winfield Scott.

Within the Democratic party itself two strong factions fought Polk's policies from the beginning: the Van Burenites and the Calhounites. The Van Buren men, who had opposed Texas annexation, supported the war only under pressure of patriotism. They deplored its political consequences and saw only party suicide in the advancement it afforded for the presidential aspirations of victorious Whig generals. Calhoun and his followers agreed. And they were even more concerned with the effect of the war on the government's tariff policy. Would not the debts piled up by the war encourage the protectionists to demand higher tariffs on manufactures?

The moral and political dissatisfaction with the war was most in evidence in the Northeast, the most populous part of the country, which supplied only 7,930 recruits. Some 20,000 southerners and 40,000 westerners enlisted, however, and the war was quickly won.

Taylor captured Monterrey, Mexico, on September 24, 1846, and defeated a Mexican force of 15,000 men under General Santa Anna at Buena Vista on February 23, 1847. Lest one Whig general gain too much acclaim, Polk appointed another, General Scott, to lead an expedition against Mexico City, the enemy capital. Scott overcame tough resistance on landing at Vera Cruz and went on to take Mexico City on September 14, 1847. Farther west, an army under Colonel Stephen W. Kearny, starting from its base at Fort Leavenworth, Missouri, captured Santa Fe and pushed through to California. Commodore Robert F. Stockton and a battalion of troops under General John C. Frémont had already proclaimed the annexation of California in August, 1846, but the Mexican rebels who had been fighting among themselves settled their differences and in September drove the Americans from southern California. When Kearny arrived at San Diego in December, he joined with American naval units under Stockton and with Frémont's men, to re-establish American rule. By January 13, 1847, all the Mexican forces in California had surrendered.

When news of the victories at Buena Vista and Vera Cruz reached Washington, Polk decided to try to arrange a peace with the Mexican leaders. For this mission he chose the State Department's Spanish-speaking chief clerk, Nicholas P. Trist. Trist was instructed to demand the Rio Grande boundary and the cession of New Mexico and California, and was authorized to offer to pay American claims against Mexico and an additional sum of $15 million. The last provision was presumably meant to salve the American conscience by giving the annexations the character of a purchase.

Almost immediately after Trist arrived at Vera Cruz, he quarreled with General Scott, who resented the appearance of a State Department clerk whose authority exceeded his own. The two men soon became fast friends, however, to the alarm of the President, who had come to regard Scott as a serious political rival. When Trist's negotiations with Santa Anna broke down and the temporary armistice ended in August, 1847, Polk ordered his emissary back to Washington. The President and his Cabinet now began to consider a prolonged occupation of Mexico, the annexation of New

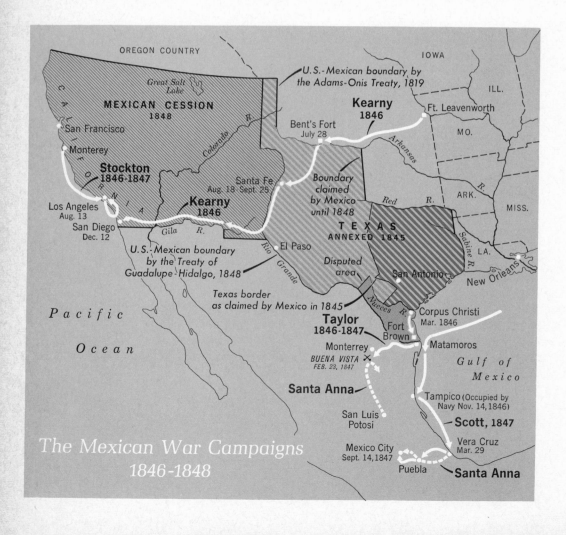

The Mexican War Campaigns 1846-1848

View of the battle of "the Angostura," fought near Buena Vista. From a sketch made on the spot by Major Eaton, aide-de-camp to General Taylor.

Mexico and California without payment, and a levy on the people of Mexico to pay the costs of occupation. There even was serious talk of a permanent annexation of all Mexico, an objective, strangely enough, opposed by southerners of both major parties. Anti-slavery men, they felt, would insist on keeping the annexed country free. Some, like Calhoun, also feared that the American government would become more centralized than ever in the effort to administer a conquered empire. Trist himself sympathized with these objections.

The rise to power of a moderate party in Mexico prompted Trist to ignore his instructions to return, and without authorization he pressed on with his negotiations. On February 2, 1848, he signed the Treaty of Guadalupe Hidalgo. In it he secured the Rio Grande boundary, Upper California, including the much-desired port of San Diego, and New Mexico. He agreed that

the United States would assume Mexican obligations to Americans up to $3.25 million and would pay Mexico $15 million.

Astonishing as Trist's independent behavior was (Polk called him "an impudent and unqualified scoundrel"), the President nevertheless accepted the treaty and sent it to the Senate for approval. After all, it conformed to Trist's original instructions. Moreover, prolonged negotiations would surely excite violent criticism in Congress, especially in the House, where the Whigs held a majority. The Senate on March 10, 1848, approved Trist's work by a vote of 38 to 14, most of the opposition coming from those who wanted all Mexico. The Treaty of Guadalupe Hidalgo added a magnificent 500,000 square miles to the continental domain of the United States. Although Trist failed to acquire a strategic 54,000 square miles along the southern New Mexico border, a strip of land that offered the best route for a southern Pacific railroad, this oversight was corrected by the "Gadsden Purchase" of 1853 for $10 million.

THE "FREE SOIL" ELECTION

As American soldiers stormed into Mexico, Ralph Waldo Emerson wrote in his journal: "The United States will conquer Mexico, but it will be as the man who swallows the arsenic, which brings him down in turn. Mexico will poison us."

The symptoms of this poisoning were swift to appear. As early as August, 1846, David Wilmot, a free-soil Democrat from Pennsylvania, offered an amendment to an appropriation bill in the House, proposing that, "neither slavery nor involuntary servitude shall ever exist in any part" of the territory that might be acquired from Mexico. The House adopted the amendment; the Senate defeated it. But that was far from the end of the matter. The "Wilmot Proviso" was persistently added to bill after bill in Congress and was hotly debated there and in the country generally. At the same time, the admission of Iowa and Wisconsin to the Union was pending; Minnesota was soon to apply for statehood; and even Oregon Territory was readying its petition. For all these inevitably free states to enter the Union while the South at the same time was to be deprived of slave states in the new territory won largely by her sons was an intolerable prospect to many southern spokesmen. But growing numbers of northerners saw in slavery an unmitigated evil that at least must be contained where it was.

Did Congress, indeed, have authority, to determine whether or not slavery might exist in territory obtained by the United States? Southerners who first raised this question replied that since the Constitution recognized and protected property in slaves, owners of such property could not lawfully be discriminated against by being prohibited to carry such property wherever they went, even across the Missouri Compromise line. But anti-slavery northerners replied that ever since 1789, when it confirmed the clause in the Northwest Ordinance of 1787 that excluded slavery from the Northwest Territory, and especially in adopting the Missouri Compromise in 1820, Congress had exercised its prerogatives over property and territory as the Constitution (Art. IV, Sec. 3) plainly said it could.

A third position on the issue of extending slavery to the territories now appeared. This was "squatter sovereignty," or "popular sovereignty," a doctrine hopefully set forth by Lewis Cass of Michigan and Stephen A. Douglas of Illinois. They argued that there was a long-established precedent in America for communities to act as the best judges of their own interests. Let the new territories be set up with the question of slavery left open, and then permit the people to decide for themselves. Plausible enough, this doctrine nevertheless left disastrously vague precisely when a territory should decide this momentous question—after slaves had already been brought in or before, if free settlers had come before slave-owners? By leaving resolution of the question open to zealots of both camps, popular sovereignty also left it open to violence, which in fact broke out a few years later in Kansas (see Chapter 15).

By 1848 the issue of the extension of slavery to new territories had become so poisonous that both major parties, in preparing for the presidential campaign, shunned it. The "regular" Democrats, at their convention in Baltimore, nominated Lewis Cass who ran on a platform that ignored slavery altogether. The "regular" Whigs, at their convention in Philadelphia, hoped to silence talk of all issues by nominating the "Hero of Buena Vista," General Zachary Taylor.

The watchword of the "regulars" in both parties was "party harmony." But they reckoned without the determined antislavery northern Democrats—in New York and New England they became known as "Barnburners", because they were said to be willing to "burn down" the Democratic "barn" in order to get rid of the pro-slavery "rats." The "regulars" also reckoned without the "conscience," as against the "cotton," Whigs. In August, 1848, the anti-slavery Democrats and Whigs, who had bolted from the regular party conventions, met in Buffalo with other anti-slavery leaders and formed the Free Soil Party, with the slogan, "Free soil, Free speech, Free labor, and Free men." They named as their standard-bearer Martin Van Buren, who had won their sympathy as he had lost that of the Democratic regulars, by his clear stand against the annexation of Texas.

The 1848 election itself aroused little popular enthusiasm. Neither Taylor nor Cass appealed particularly to his respective party, and Van Buren—despite his forthright repudiation of slavery—could not live down his reputation as a slippery fox. Horace Greeley dismissed Cass as a "pot-bellied, mutton-headed cucumber," but he supported Van Buren only as a lesser evil. Webster, after some hesitation, gave Taylor a cold endorsement. In the balloting, Taylor won 1,360,000 votes to Cass' 1,220,000. The Free-Soilers polled only 291,000 votes, but they absorbed enough Democratic support in New York to give that state's electoral vote to Taylor, and enough Whig support in Ohio and Indiana to give those states to Cass. The Free Soil party also elected thirteen congressmen to a divided House where they might hold the balance of power. Most important of all, the Free-Soilers had demonstrated the potential strength and disruptive power of a purely sectional party. Henceforth, there could be no slurring over of the slavery issue. Southern extremists now had fresh grounds on which to convince the moderates and Unionists in their states that a southern party must be formed to combat northern aggression against the "peculiar institution."

THE COMPROMISE OF 1850

Sectional tensions relaxed for a moment when the news of gold in California spread across the nation early in 1848. Americans of every class and occupation dropped whatever they were doing and headed for the Pacific Coast. Men from all over the world joined them. Some risked the perilous voyage around the Horn or the portage across Panama (see p. 373). Others took the overland route through Salt Lake City, thereby enriching the Mormons who sold supplies to the miners at fabulous prices. To Henry Thoreau, already launched on his own pilgrimage in Concord, the rush to California was a shocking reflection of American materialism: The "world's raffle," he called it.

What a comment, what a satire on our institutions! . . . And have all the precepts in all the Bibles taught men only this? . . . Is this the ground on which Orientals and Occidentals meet? Did God direct us to get our living, digging where we never planted,—and He would, perchance, reward us with lumps of gold?

By 1849, California had a wild and violent population of over 100,000, and an inadequate military government to cope with it. Polk had retired before a deeply divided Congress could decide California's future. Taylor, the new president, blunt, well-intentioned, but politically inept, recommended, on appeals from California leaders, that California, and New Mexico and Utah as well, draw up constitutions and decide without congressional direction whether or not slavery should be excluded. Congress, however, was in no mood to let the new president run things. This was especially true of pro-slavery spokesmen whose fears over anti-slavery decisions in the Far West were soon confirmed by the action of all three territories in writing constitutions which forbade slavery. These spokesmen, amidst talk of the certainty of secession, now prepared to take an uncompromising stand in Congress on all sectional issues. Should slave depots be banned in the District of Columbia? Should the Fugitive Slave Law be tightened? Must Texas, a slave state, yield part of its western land to the proposed territory of New Mexico? Southern unity in defense of slavery had never been so strong.

Contemporary lithograph showing the San Francisco Post Office, corner of Pike and Clay Streets, in 1849.

President Taylor's reaction to the heightening crisis was simply to ask Congress, in December, 1849, to avoid "exciting topics of sectional character." At a time when senators and representatives carried Bowie knives and Colt revolvers, and Washington newspapermen seriously discussed the possibility of bloody violence in the House, Taylor's request was tantamount to abdication. Clearly the South had no intention of allowing California to enter the Union as a free state unless it received important concessions. The South would secede rather than accept the Wilmot Proviso.

Fortunately there remained more realistic leaders than the President, yet men who put the Union first and the section second. Their leader was Henry Clay, 73 years old now, but still a powerful and persuasive speaker who understood the truly desperate mood of the South. On January 29, 1850,

Clay offered the following resolutions in the Senate: (1) that California be admitted as a free state; (2) that the territorial governments set up in Utah and New Mexico decide for themselves whether slavery should be permitted or abolished; (3) that the western boundary of Texas be fixed so as to exclude "any portion of New Mexico"; (4) that in return for this concession, the United States would assume that portion of the public debt of Texas contracted before annexation; (5) that slavery within the District of Columbia would not be abolished without the consent of Maryland and the residents in the District, and "without just compensation to the owners of slaves within the District"; (6) that slave-trading be prohibited in the District of Columbia; (7) that a stricter fugitive slave law be adopted; and (8) that "Congress has no power to promote or obstruct the trade in slaves between the slave-holding States."

The battle for the Compromise of 1850 was one of the most bitterly contested in congressional history. Arrayed against Clay were: (1) The angry and suspicious President Taylor, firm in his conviction that California must be admitted to the Union without any reservations, and prepared to treat even moderate and Union-loving southerners as traitors if they protested. (2) Fiery secessionists like Jefferson Davis (Mississippi), Robert Barnwell Rhett (South Carolina), and Louis T. Wigfall (Texas)—contemptuous of compromise and certain that Clay's plan was simply a disguise for the ambitions of a brutal North. (3) Extreme anti-slavery men and radical free-soilers like William H. Seward (New York), Salmon P. Chase and Joshua Giddings (Ohio), and Charles Sumner (Massachusetts), who stood pat on the Wilmot Proviso and placed the law of Congress, and the Constitution, below the "Higher Law"— the law of God—under which slavery could never be justified.

But Clay's resolutions were broad and conciliatory enough to win over reasonable men, North and South, and devout Union-

ists in every section. Among the staunchest of the Unionists was Daniel Webster, who, in a moving speech in the Senate on March 7, 1850, brooked the wrath of his fellow Yankees by supporting even Clay's proposal for stricter enforcement of the fugitive slave law. Massachusetts humanitarians accused Webster of making another bid for the presidency and never forgave him. They talked of him as a fallen and tarnished hero who with other "deformed, mediocre, sniveling, unreliable, false-hearted men . . . insulted and betrayed" their country.

Webster himself had underestimated northern revulsion against returning fugitive slaves and free-soil hatred of the whole plantation system. But for the moment at least, his efforts strengthened the Unionists' position to which other eloquent men rallied. Outstanding among them was Stephen A. Douglas, who brought many in Congress around to the view that the Southwest was unsuitable for slave labor. After the aged Clay had been forced to retire from the fray exhausted, Douglas whipped the Ken-

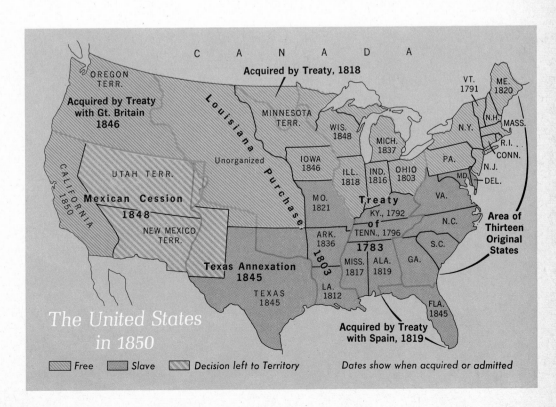

The United States in 1850

Free   Slave   Decision left to Territory   Dates show when acquired or admitted

tuckian's resolutions through. Five separate measures made up the Compromise of 1850. Their adoption became certain when President Taylor, unyielding in his opposition, died suddenly early in July, 1850, and was succeeded by the moderate Vice-president, Millard Fillmore, a free-soiler who nevertheless favored the Compromise.

Under the provisions of the Compromise of 1850, California entered the Union as a free state, and the western boundary of Texas was fixed where it is today, at the 103rd meridian. Texas received $10 million for giving up her claims to New Mexico. Two new territories, New Mexico and Utah, were created, with the proviso that the question of slavery be left for the people to decide in their constitutions at the time of their becoming states. Slave-trading, but not slavery, was prohibited in the District of Columbia. Finally, a severe fugitive slave law was passed, with many northern congressmen abstaining from voting.

Several northern states, beginning with Vermont in 1850, virtually nullified the fugitive slave law by enacting new "personal liberty laws" enabling alleged fugitives to have legal counsel, jury trials, and other means of defending their freedom. Northern Negroes themselves also took up the defense of fugitives. Negroes, they said, had for too long been characterized as meek and yielding. "This reproach must be wiped out," declared the free Negro leader, Frederick Douglass, "and nothing short of resistance on the part of the colored man, can wipe it out. Every slavehunter who meets a bloody death in his infernal business, is an argument in favor of the manhood of our race."

THE ELECTION OF 1852

The nation as a whole, nevertheless, exulted when news of the compromise became known, and in the first presidential election after the compromise the national yearning for sectional tranquility and moderation seemed to persist. In this election, in 1852, Franklin Pierce, the Democratic candidate, easily defeated General Scott, now the Whig candidate, running up a popular plurality of 214,000 votes and a margin of 254 to 42 in the electoral college. The Free Soil candidate, John P. Hale, won only half as many votes as Van Buren in 1848, as northern Democrats in particular returned to the fold.

But in the long run the issue of slavery and its extension could not be compromised, and civil war loomed as the manifest destiny of the nation all the more certainly as the manifest destiny of continentalism was pursued. An ominous sign of trouble ahead was the breaking up of the Whig party following the deaths of such staunch unionists as Webster and Clay in 1852. The Democrats still stood as a great national party, to which, indeed, many southern Whigs were now drawn. The rest of the Whigs would soon form the backbone of a new *northern* party to be called the Republican party (see p. 397). Politics, moreover, was not the only realm of sectional division. The slave South had become profoundly conscious of its differences from the burgeoning North and West in all phases of life. These sections, in turn, developed a sense of their own individuality which grew clearer and stronger as the South felt impelled to stress its distinctive culture.

Readings
Asterisk indicates that book is available in paperback.

General accounts of continentalism are available in the diplomatic histories cited in our general bibliography. On British and Canadian relations, see H. C. Allen, *Great Britain and the United States* (1955); Donald Creighton, *A History of Canada* (1958); H. T. Manning, *The Revolt of French Canada, 1800-1835* (1962), and A. B. Corey, *The Crisis of 1830-1842 in Canadian-American Relations* (1941). An excellent review of the expansionist period may be found in R. A. Billington, *The Far Western Frontier, 1830-1860* * (1956), and more generally in the same author's *Westward Expansion* (1949). Albert Weinberg, *Manifest Destiny* * (1935), is comprehensive on the expansionist spirit. H. N. Smith, *Virgin Land* * (1950), is an imaginative study of Americans' conception of the West and its place in their destiny. N. A. Graebner, *Empire on the Pacific* (1955), stresses the commercial side of expansionism. Bernard De Voto, *The Year of Decision* * (1943), is a fine popular history of the events of 1846.

E. C. Barker, *Mexico and Texas, 1821-1835* (1928), offers a good account of the beginnings of American interest; W. C. Binkley, *The Texas Revolution* (1952), carries the narrative further along. R. N. Richardson, *Texas, the Lone Star State* (1943); Stanley Siegel, *A Political History of the Texas Republic, 1836-1845* * (1956); and E. D. Adams, *British Interests in Texas* (1910), are informative on special subjects. More comprehensive older works include J. S. Reeves, *American Diplomacy Under Tyler and Polk* (1907); G. L. Rives, *The United States and Mexico, 1821-1848* (2 vols., 1913); and two books by J. H. Smith, *The Annexation of Texas* (1911), and *The War with Mexico* (2 vols., 1919). A good shorter history of the war is A. H. Bill, *Rehearsal for Conflict: The War With Mexico, 1846-1848* (1947).

C. J. Brosnan, *Jason Lee: Prophet of the New Oregon* (1932), and C. M. Drury, *Marcus Whitman, Pioneer and Martyr* (1937), supply the missionary background. Francis Parkman's classic, *The California and Oregon Trail* (1849), is better known in modern editions simply called *The Oregon Trail.** A well-written modern work is David Lavender, *Westward Vision: The Story of the Oregon Trail* (1963). D. O. Johansen and C. M. Gates, *Empire of the Pacific: A History of the Pacific Northwest* (1957), is among the best general accounts. R. G. Cleland, *Early Sentiment for the Annexation of California* (1915), may be supplemented by Cleland's *From Wilderness to Empire: A History of California, 1542-1900* (1944), and J. W. Caughey, *California,* 2nd ed. (1953). On the gold rush and mining, see the Readings for Chapter 18. Nels Anderson, *Desert Saints: The Mormon Frontier in Utah* (1942), is outstanding. L. J. Arrington, *Great Basin Kingdom: An Economic History of the Latter-day Saints, 1830-1900* (1958), is best on the material side of Mormon history. T. F. O'Dea, *The Mormons* * (1957), is a detached and informative discussion of Mormon history and doctrine. Excellent biographies of the Mormon leaders are Fawn Brodie, *No Man Knows My History: The Life of Joseph Smith* (1945), and Preston Nibley, *Brigham Young, the Man and His Work* (1936).

Allan Nevins, *Ordeal of the Union* (2 vols., 1947), offers a scholarly survey of the politics of this period. It may be supplemented by two older works, W. E. Dodd, *Expansion and Conflict* (1915), and volumes V and VI of Edward Channing, *A History of the United States* (6 vols., 1905-1925). T. C. Smith, *The Liberty and Free-Soil Parties in the Northwest* (1897), is still valuable. J. T. Carpenter, *The South as a Conscious Minority* (1930), and A. O. Craven, *The Growth of Southern Nationalism, 1848-1861* (1953), are good on the slave section's position. Holman Hamilton, *The Compromise of 1850* (1964), offers a scholarly analysis.

Numerous biographies also supply invaluable background: C. G. Sellers, Jr., *James K. Polk: Jacksonian, 1795-1843* (1957); E. I. McCormac, *James K. Polk* (1922); Allan Nevins, ed., *Polk: The Diary of a President, 1845-1849* (1952); Holman Hamilton, *Zachary Taylor* (2 vols., 1941, 1951); R. J. Rayback, *Millard Fillmore: Biography of a President* (1959); F. B. Woodford, *Lewis Cass, The Last Jeffersonian* (1950); G. F. Milton, *Eve of Conflict: Stephen A. Douglas and the Needless War* (1934); G. M. Capers, *Stephen A. Douglas, Defender of the Union* (1959); C. B. Going, *David Wilmot, Free-Soiler* (1924); A. J. Beveridge, *Abraham Lincoln* (2 vols., 1928); U. B. Phillips, *The Life of Robert Toombs* (1913); and the lives of Clay, Calhoun, and Webster cited in Chapter 8.

CHAPTER THIRTEEN

The challenge of the South, the persistent discrepancies between its values and its condition, its longings and its impotence, is older than the Union (see p. 81). These discrepancies grew especially harsh starting perhaps a century and a half ago when industrialism under a regime of free labor captured the spirit of the country and the western world while the South with its slaves clung only the more compulsively to plantation and subsistence agriculture.

For a time, while the open land lasted in the South and industrialism elsewhere often was convulsed by its own growing pains, southern spokesmen successfully deluded

The

Southern Nation

themselves with dreams of grandeur sweetly nourished by the elevation slavery gave even to the crudest planter's ego and by the immense role of King Cotton in the industrial revolution itself. The growing differences, and the growing rivalry, between the slave states and the rest of the country in this period evoked enough interest to multiply the number of inquisitive visitors to the South, and her leaders remained confident enough to let them in. Many of them learned, indeed from troubled southerners themselves, that nineteenth-century cotton, like eighteenth-century tobacco, was in fact keeping the South a colony, not a kingdom, one characteristically producing raw materials for the enrichment of distant carriers and processors. They found, also, that slavery was making the section a pariah in a democratic age, one shunned by most newcomers to the country. The increasingly hostile reports of these visitors, their savage exposure of the dream of white excellence built upon black thraldom, caused the South as early as the 1830's to turn ever more self-consciously inward, to ravel up the many and varied strands of her own culture, and with fierce intransigence to see to the defenses of her "peculiar institution" and its fruits.

Richard Hildreth, the New England historian, visited the South late in the 1830's and in 1840 published his book, *Despotism in America; or An Inquiry into the Nature and Results of the Slave-Holding System in the United States*. Within the "great social experiment of Democracy" in America, he found in the South, "another experiment, less talked about, less celebrated, but not the less real or important, to wit, the *experiment of Despotism*. . . . The Southern States," he wrote, "are Aristocracies; and aristocracies of the sternest and most odious kind." Hildreth anticipated modern scholars who have found the slave systems of Brazil and Spanish America more humane than that in the United States. After examining these systems and others, he concluded that slavery in the South, "is a far more deadly and disastrous thing, more fatal to all the hopes, the sentiments, the rights of humanity, than almost any other system of servitude which has existed in any other community."

Hildreth saw only two classes in the southern aristocracies, the privileged planters and all lesser whites who aspired to planter status on the one hand, and their "hereditary subjects, servants and bondsmen" on the other. "Extremes meet," he added. "Ferocity of temper, idleness, improvidence, drunkenness, gambling—these are vices for which the masters are distinguished, and these same vices are conspicuous traits in the character and conduct of slaves."

This was the image of Dixie that was also spread in the abolitionist tracts of the day. Some in the South undertook to expose the excessive simplicity of the image and thereby discredit and destroy it. The section's most aggressive defenders, however, following the lead of Calhoun himself, preferred an equal simplicity and meeting of extremes the better to convey an alternative image of their own. In January, 1838, Calhoun told Congress:

This agitation [against the slave system] has produced one happy effect at least; it has compelled us to the South to look into the nature and character of this great institution, and to correct many false impressions that even we had entertained in relation to it. Many in the South once believed that it was a moral and political evil; that folly and delusion are gone; we see it now in its true light, and regard it as the most safe and stable basis for free institutions in the world.

Calhoun continued:

It is impossible with us that the conflict can take place between labor and capital, which makes it so difficult to establish and maintain free institutions in all wealthy and highly civilized nations where such institutions as ours do not exist. The Southern States are an aggregate, in fact, of communities, not of individuals. Every plantation is a little community, with the master at its head, who concentrates in himself the united interests of capital and labor. . . . These small communities aggregated make the State [in which] labor and capital [are] equally represented and perfectly harmonized. The blessing of this state of things extends beyond the limits of the South. It makes that section the balance of the system; the great conservative power, which prevents other portions, less fortunately constituted, from rushing into conflict. . . . Such are the institutions which these deluded madmen are stirring heaven and earth to destroy, and which we are called on to defend by the highest and most solemn obligations that can be imposed on us as men and patriots.

Recent historians have returned to the view that the structure of southern society before the Civil War was in fact more complex than Hildreth's hell or Calhoun's heaven. All authorities now concede that aristocratic planters were few and that many Negroes enjoyed adequate creature comforts. They add that the "poor white trash," who once were lumped indiscriminately with all non-slaveholding whites, were but a small minority reduced by disease to what subsistence they could scratch from otherwise unwanted land, eked out by fish and game; and that the statistically "average" southerner was an independent "yeoman" farmer who worked his own quarter-section, more or less, with the help of his family, all perhaps laboring side by side with their one or two Negro "hands." This independent yeoman is especially celebrated in the work of Frank L. Owsley, whose influential studies of *Plain Folk of the Old South* are devoted to making the slave section seem in fact an agrarian utopia. Other historians have rediscovered the Creoles of Louisiana and neighboring states, the mountaineers of Appalachia and the Ozarks, the "crackers" of the piney woods. Still others recall that the South had its professional class, doctors, lawyers, editors, teachers, and its urban and even its industrial centers. These were dominated, of course, by the cotton trade, but were also active in the manufacture of sugar and tobacco products and of the textiles and iron ware that were to serve the section so surprisingly well during the Civil War.

And yet, as that war forcibly reminds us, the simpler picture probably remains the more valid and more realistic one. Creoles, crackers, and mountaineers, commercial and industrial workers, trained professionals, were but marginal groups in the Old South. The average yeoman, moreover, decided neither his own fate nor the fate of his section. It was the planter, in an increasingly unfriendly universe, and his "niggers" bereft of their manhood, who set off

the South from the rest of the country and from more and more of the world. The old Virginians knew this and regretted it. As the hateful system spread itself, the romantic fiction of Old Dominion cavaliers helped cloak the crude violence of frontier life. The "Great Revival" in religion, from which abolitionism itself took fire (see p. 357), also burned through the South and Southwest and spawned many lasting reforms, especially against whiskey drinking and its attendant degradation. To many northerners newly admitted to the "mighty Baptism of the Holy Spirit," no greater sin could be found in Christendom than pride of pigment, property in men, the enslavement of one Christian brother by another. To many southerners, the word of the Lord placed the black sons of Ham in everlasting bondage. Fundamentalism in religion reinforced the slave foundations of southern life.

I. *The White People of the South*

DIXIE LAND

No one knew of the South as "Dixie" until Dan Emmett, a blackface minstrel out of Mount Vernon, Ohio, sang the new song of that name in a New York City theater in 1859. Two years later the band played "Dixie" at Jefferson Davis's inauguration as first President of the Confederacy, and it then became the unofficial anthem of the southern republic. No one knows just where the term "Dixie" came from. One of the more dubious derivations is one of the most suggestive—that is, that it was a corruption of the name of Jeremiah Dixon who surveyed the Mason-Dixon line. The Mason-Dixon line helped settle the boundary between Pennsylvania and Maryland in the 1760's. Its extension westward, roughly along the Ohio River, also helped settle the northern boundary of Dixie. Above that

boundary slavery had been put well on the way to extinction around the turn of the nineteenth century (see p. 158). Below that boundary slavery existed in all the sixteen states and neighboring territories. Dixie was the land of slavery. It was also, as the song says, "the land of cotton."

There are many parts of the South where the growing season is too short for cotton, where the weather is too cold for rice, where it snows every winter and even beasts need sheltering barns. Yet the characteristic and distinguishing feature of the southern climate is the prevailing heat—*90° In The Shade* Clarence Cason titled his moving book on the South published in 1935, one of the early works of our time to expose the fiction and frailties of the utopian legend. A slightly later (1941) and more penetrating book is W.J. Cash's history of *The Mind of the South,* in which the weather also evokes the moving prose: "If the dominant mood is one of sultry reverie," writes Cash,

the land is capable of other and more sombre moods. . . . There are days when the booming of the wind in the pines is like the audible rushing of time—when the sad knowledge of the grave stirs in the subconsciousness and bends the spirit to melancholy. . . . And there are other days . . . when the nerves wilt under the terrific impact of sun and humidity, and even the soundest grow a bit neurotic. . . . There are other days, too, when . . . hurricanes break forth with semi-tropical fury; days when this land which, in its dominant mood, wraps its children in soft illusion, strips them naked before terror.

If the weather drew the characteristic southerner outdoors, the terrain and what it held helped keep him there. All across the Cotton Kingdom were the densest forests in the world; as late as 1860 a large part of the slave's labor was given to clearing new land to let in the sunshine as well as to prepare fields for cultivation. The forests rewarded the hunter with ample and varied game. The Kingdom was also exceedingly well endowed with navigable streams to carry cotton and other staples to export centers, and with thousands of smaller brooks and creeks and rivulets, lakes and ponds, to feed the marshes and water the earth. These waterways rewarded the fisherman with ample and varied fare. "His leisure," writes Cash,

left the Southerner free to brood as well as to dream—to exaggerate his fears as well as his hopes. And if for practical purposes it is true that he was likely to be complacently content with his lot, and even though it was the lot of white-trash, it is not yet perfectly true. Vaguely the loneliness of the country, the ennui of long burning empty days, a hundred half-perceived miseries, ate into him and filled him with nebulous discontent and obscure longing. Like all men everywhere, he hungered after a better and a happier world.

A more concrete ambition also stirred the southerner's soul, like that of enterprising businessmen everywhere in America. The Cotton Kingdom was not extended in a single generation from South Carolina to Texas by men content to brood and dream at home. No better cotton land existed anywhere than in the Red River Valley of northern Louisiana and Texas. A typical Red River planter, accosted one day on a steamboat by a representative of the Education Society selling a "Bible Defence of Slavery," shouted: "Now you go to hell! I've told you three times I didn't want your book. If you bring it here again, I'll throw it overboard. I own niggers; and I calculate to own more of 'em, if I can get 'em, but I don't want any damn'd preachin' about it."

Yet southern society was more homogeneous than northern, more settled and conservative in its ways, and less exposed to social and intellectual ferment. To the novelist John De Forest, who lived with the "Southrons" immediately after the Civil War, they seemed as different from the people in New England as the Spartans were from the Athenians. "They are more simple than us," he wrote, "more provincial, more antique, more picturesque; they have fewer of the virtues of modern society, and more of the primitive, the natural virtues." The violence of southern life has no doubt been exaggerated, but the "Arkansas toothpick" (as the Bowie knife was sometimes called) was one of the principal instruments for settling differences in the rougher sections, and even in the older and more settled regions the code of honor prevailed.

The history of the Tillmans, a South Carolina family, is a saga of violence. Benjamin Ryan Tillman, the first, was an industrious but lawless planter who gambled as hard as he worked, killed a man in 1847, and died of typhoid fever two years later, aged 46. His wife, Sophia, a commanding, efficient woman, bore him three daughters and seven sons. Thomas, the oldest son, was killed in the Mexican War. The second, George Dionysius Tillman, might have served as the hero of a Faulkner novel. (Faulkner speaks of the "glamorous fatality" of southern names.) This erratic and intelligent young man spent a year at Harvard, read law, and served in the state legislature. On two separate occasions, he fought and wounded his opponent; shortly after, he killed a third man during a card game. George fled the country, filibustered in Cuba, and returned in 1858, repentant, to spend two luxurious years in the local jail. Another son, handsome and ill-tempered, was killed by two brothers whose family he had insulted, and still another son was slain over some domestic quarrel.

Despite such endemic violence, travelers found the people hospitable and friendly until the virus of suspicion spread.

THE SOUTHERN CASTES

In 1850, about 6,185,000 white people lived in the South, of whom only 350,000 were slave-owners. With their families, this group probably made up less than a third of southern whites. Most of them owned but one or two Negroes, only a small number as many as ten. A mere 8,000 planters owned 50 or more slaves, 254 owned 200 or more, and only 11 in the entire South owned 500 or more. The cotton kings,

whose vast holdings and splendid mansions figure so prominently in southern romances, never amounted to more than 1 per cent of the white population.

No doubt a conspicuous number of the large-planter caste lived the high life of saber-rattling, fire-breathing "cavaliers." But they were likely to be more worrisome than wonderful even to their own families. When they were young, sons of the well-to-do often were sent West with the hope that they might settle down under the cares of plantations of their own. Many did; but many more only found broader scope for recklessness and violence to match the rough and somber environment. Those who, like our Red River planter, were determined to develop their priceless natural endowment, spent many years in crude surroundings. The saw mill itself came late to Alabama, Mississippi and Louisiana, and

Southern mansion, typical of those built by the Southern aristocracy before the Civil War, at Sumter, South Carolina.

even in the 1840's and 1850's wealthy planters continued to live in the typical "two pen" log house, with crevices between the unhewn logs to let in the only light as well as the rain and the wind.

In the older South many of the gentry lived well, and some extravagantly. But most of them also bore the cares that went with ownership of property and had little time to enjoy anything more than the simple pleasures of rustic society. Hunting, horse-racing, card-playing, visiting, and perhaps an annual summer pilgrimage to the mountains or the sea to escape the heat, pretty well exhausted their recreations.

What one southern writer, John Pendleton Kennedy, referred to as "the mellow, bland, and sunny luxuriance" of old-time Virginia society is delineated in the pages of his own *Swallow Barn, or a Sojourn in the Old Dominion* (1832), and in Susan Dabney Smedes' charming account of her father, Thomas S. G. Dabney of Virginia and Mississippi, the *beau ideal* of the southern planter. Humane, upright, generous, and courteous, such hard-working and practical gentlemen as Dabney were most deeply involved with sick slaves, the price of cotton, and unreliable overseers, subjects too unliterary for southern romancers, but making up the meat of plantation diaries and account books, with their records of hazards, anxieties, and disappointments. "Managing a plantation," as Mrs. Smedes observed, "was something like managing a kingdom. The ruler had need of great store, not only of wisdom, but of tact and patience as well." Nor was the planter's wife exempt from irksome domestic duties.

If one added to the two-thirds of the southern white families who owned no slaves at all those who worked their small holdings side by side with a Negro helper or two, the proportion of "plain folk" in the ante-bellum South would be considerably higher still. The farms of these "average" yeomen might be found tucked away among the large plantations in the cotton and tobacco country, but they were most numerous in the upland South—in eastern Tennessee, western North Carolina, northern Georgia, Alabama, and Mississippi. Here, while some produced the southern staples, most of the plain folk grew subsistence crops—grains and cereals, sweet potatoes, sorghum cane—or raised livestock. The plain folk also included the storekeepers, the mechanics, and other artisans in southern villages and towns.

Seen through the candid but critical eyes of Frederick Law Olmsted, who traveled through the southern hinterlands in the early 1850's, the living standards of the yeoman whites seemed distinctly low when compared with those of northern farmers. And yet, though Olmsted complained of wretched cookery, vermin-filled beds, and rude manners, he also noted that the white farmers in general presented a picture of a sturdy, proud, and friendly people. "If you want to fare well in this country," he was told in northern Alabama, "you stop to poor folks' housen; they try to enjoy what they've got while they ken, but these yer big planters they don' care for nothing but to save." Riding through an area of thin sandy soil, Olmsted reported that it was

. . . thickly populated by poor farmers. Negroes are rare, but occasionally neat, new houses, with other improvements, show the increasing prosperity of the district. The majority of dwellings are small log cabins of one room, with another separate cabin for a kitchen; each house has a well, and a garden enclosed with palings. Cows, goats, mules and swine, fowls and doves are abundant. The people are more social than those of the lower country, falling readily into friendly conversation. . . . They are very ignorant; the agriculture is wretched and the work hard. I have seen three white women hoeing field crops to-day. A spinning-wheel is heard in every house . . . every one wears home-spun. The negroes have much more individual freedom than in the rich cotton country, and are not infrequently heard singing or whistling at their work.

Among such farmers, as one who grew up among them in Mississippi reported, "people who lived miles apart, counted themselves as neighbors, . . . and in case of sorrow or sickness, or need of any kind, there was no limit to the ready service" they rendered one another. Such social activities as might bring them together centered around the church, the county court, the market towns and the village taverns.

The "bottom sill" of southern white society was the so-called "poor white trash." Perhaps even more than the Negro himself, the "poor whites" were the victims of slavery. Their illiteracy, their disdain for manual labor, and their prejudices were in large measure the result of slavery. This was the conclusion of one bitter southerner, Hinton Rowan Helper, whose sensational and propagandistic book, *The Impending Crisis of the South: How to Meet It* (1857), made slavery "the root of all the shame, poverty, ignorance, tyranny and imbecility

of the South." Although Helper's widely publicized analysis distorted the southern picture, it contained some uncomfortable truths that were hardly answered by calling its author a "miserable renegade."

Of the "poor whites," the discerning Olmsted wrote:

They are said to "corrupt" the negroes, and to encourage them to steal, or to work for them at night and on Sundays, and to pay them with liquor, and to constantly associate licentiously with them. They seem, nevertheless, more than any other portion of the community, to hate and despise the negroes.

II. *The Life of the Southern Negro*

THE NEGRO POPULATION

Slavery took root in the South because African Negroes provided a cheap and available labor force to cultivate the staple crops. By the time Congress closed the slave trade in 1808, about 1,160,000 slaves were owned in the southern states. Others were subsequently smuggled in (one estimate places the number at about 270,000 between 1808 and 1860), but most of the slaves who were transported to the newly opened lands in the Southwest came from slave populations of the older states. Between 1830 and 1860, Virginia alone, in what had become a profitable business, exported close to 300,000 Negroes, South Carolina about 170,000. On the eve of the Civil War there were about 3.8 million slaves in Dixie, and about 200,000 free Negroes.

The slave population in the ante-bellum South was far from evenly distributed (see map, p. 349). In southern Appalachia and the Ozarks where the land was unsuited for staple crops, slaves were a rarity. But they were numerous in areas better suited to the plantation method of production: in the tobacco regions of the Chesapeake, in the rice flats along the coastal sections of South Carolina and Georgia, in the sugar fields of Louisiana and Texas, and in the Cotton Kingdom of the middle and lower South. In some counties and parishes in each of these areas slaves made up as much as two-thirds of the total population. The 1850 census estimated that out of the 2,500,000 Negro slaves engaged in agriculture in the South, no less than 1,815,000 were employed in growing cotton. Tobacco occupied 350,-000; sugar 150,000; rice 125,000; and hemp 60,000.

The heaviest concentration of slaves and cotton could be found in the prize lands of the South: in the "Black Belt" that stretched across central Alabama into northwest Mississippi; in the flood plains of the Mississippi River; and in parts of southern Texas that drained into the Gulf of Mexico. By 1850, the Black Belt had become the greatest cotton-growing region in the world. And here it was that the slave system could be studied in its most mature form. Labor on plantations of from 1,000 to 2,000 acres (the most efficient size) was reduced to a series of routine operations with the slaves divided into plow and hoe gangs under the direction of "drivers" and "overseers." Relations between master and slave were of necessity more impersonal on the large plantations than on the smaller ones, and discipline was more strict. The well-run plantation "factories," which often became self-sufficient units producing corn, peanuts, and livestock in addition to cotton, were serviced by slave carpenters, masons, and weavers, as well as field hands.

Few free Negroes lived in the South's agricultural regions, but among them were some who themselves had become great planters and slaveowners. Such Negro "kings" were especially conspicuous on the frontier in Mississippi, Alabama, and Louisiana before the period of "ultraism" in white supremacy following upon the onset of the abolitionist crusade; and they were treated as gentlemen among gentlemen. In the cities, too, slaves belonged to free Negro businessmen who hired them out for all sorts of urban tasks.

In the first quarter of the nineteenth century, slaves made up at least 20 per cent of the urban population of the South; in places like New Orleans and Richmond they were more numerous; and in Charleston, South Carolina, they outnumbered the whites. Thereafter, however, the slave population of southern cities declined. By 1848 it was said that "slavery exists in Louisville and St. Louis only in name." Two reasons were offered for the falling off in urban slaves: "The first is a dense population, . . . the next is the intelligence of slaves." Among Negroes, as among whites, cities presented a stimulating environment far different from the isolation of plantations. To be remunerative, city slaves had to be hired out singly or in small numbers, not in gangs under overseers. Thus, flight or mere disappearance could be more easily effected, and with his skills learned as a slave a Negro could make a living as a free man.

Even so, at the outbreak of the Civil War, approximately 500,000 slaves were living in southern cities and towns as servants or artisans or were engaged in such non-agricultural pursuits as cutting wood for steamboats, lumbering, mining, iron-manufacturing, or construction.

THE SLAVE'S WORLD

One of the attractions and advantages of the slave system was the uniformity that could be imposed upon huge masses of labor engaged in routine and repetitive work. Yet the lot of the bondsman in the ante-bellum South depended upon many factors: age and sex and the nature of his employment, the region in which he worked, the size of the farm or plantation or town in which he lived, the character and disposition of his master, and his own temper and personality. Undoubtedly the conditions on some of the rice plantations, situated in malarial districts and managed by overseers for absentee owners, were inhumane. In general, the slaves on the cotton and sugar plantations in the lower South were more harshly treated than their fellows farther north. Even some of the anti-slavery men, however, acknowledged that ordinarily the slaves were adequately housed, clothed, and fed. The slave's diet of pork, corn-meal, molasses, and greens was coarse and monotonous, and the slave quarters were unhygienic by modern standards. But many white farmers lived no better. Slaves worked no longer than many northern agricultural and industrial laborers and, in areas where the "task" system was employed, a slave might complete his assigned chores by early afternoon and spend the rest of the day as he chose. Progressive planters made incentive payments and encouraged their slaves to cultivate truck gardens and to raise pigs and chickens for their own use or for sale. Holidays, and entertainments alleviated the drudgery on some plantations, and where the work became too exacting the slaves developed their own slow-down techniques. House-servants found life much easier than field hands, and some gifted slaves were rewarded with positions of trust and responsibility. It seems true enough that many white southerners treated their slaves affectionately and that slaves responded to such treatment with loyalty and devotion.

Yet all slave-owners were bound by the system under which black men, and women, were their chattels, in an environment of violence and mutual fear and dread. Since it required the nicest judgment to maintain a balance between laxness and severity in the management of slaves, the best of masters had to apply methods of discipline that might be offensive to his own inclinations. Given the plantation system, he had to rely on the assistance of overseers, who often could produce a profitable crop only by driving the slaves and ignoring the owner's admonitions. The kindliest slaveholder, either as a buyer or seller, was sometimes forced to break up Negro families which themselves had no standing under law.

Abolitionists sometimes exaggerated the brutalities of slavery, but they did not have to invent stories of whippings, brandings, mutilations, and murder. The custom of flogging recalcitrant Negroes was widespread. Some planters set their dogs on runaway slaves, and hundreds of authentic records testify to the brutal punishment of Negroes who struck white men or who committed misdemeanors. Some were burned alive; others were starved, shot, or hanged. Slave-owners who killed their slaves often escaped punishment, for Negro witnesses were not permitted to testify against a white man in the courts.

The claim that Negro slaves were contented, that their happy-go-lucky temperament enabled them to adjust to their menial position, and that they did not respond to slavery as white men would have done is contradicted by documented evidence. Many tried to buy their freedom, and a few succeeded. Failing this, they often ran away from their masters, even those who treated them kindly. Slaves often feigned sickness, mutilated themselves, simply loafed, and sometimes openly rebelled to escape forced labor. The fear of slave revolts in the antebellum period kept the South increasingly uneasy. One serious conspiracy of slaves—organized by a free Negro, Denmark Vesey, in Charleston, South Carolina—was crushed in 1822. In 1831, a Negro preacher named Nat Turner, believing himself to be di-

vinely appointed, led an abortive but bloody slave insurrection in Southampton County, Virginia, in which 57 whites and about a hundred Negroes were killed. This was the last organized slave revolt, but insurrection panics occurred a number of times between 1831 and 1860, and "reports of Negro plots" provided sensational material for jittery southern newspaper editors. Riding night patrols was one task even irresponsible planters took seriously, whiskey often bucking them up against the terrors of darkness. In the towns and cities, police costs "for the purpose of 'keeping down the niggers'," as one traveler reported made up the largest municipal budget item. Olmsted wrote that in nearly every southern city he visited, " . . . you come to police machinery such as you never find in towns under free governments: citadels, sentries, passports, grape-shotted cannon, and daily public whippings . . . for accidental infractions of police ceremonies."

Of all the institutions of slavery, the slave market was perhaps the worst, for white and black alike. Lincoln, in 1854, reminded the South that "the great majority" there as in the North, "have human sympathies, of which they can no more divest themselves than they can of their sensibility to physical pain." The one who tried those sympathies to the utmost was "a sneaking individual, of the class of native tyrants, known as the 'SLAVE-DEALER.' " Lincoln went on:

He watches your necessities, and crawls up to buy your slave, at a speculating price. If you cannot help it, you sell to him; but if you can help it, you drive him from your door. You despise him utterly. . . . Your children must not play with his; they may rollick freely with the little negroes, but not with the "slave dealer's" children. . . . It is common with you to join hands with the men you meet; but with the slave dealer you avoid the ceremony—instinctively shrinking from the snaky contact. Now why is this? You do not so treat the man who deals in corn, cattle or tobacco.

A slave auction—from an original sketch by Theodore R. Davis.

III. *The Plantation System*

MINOR SOUTHERN STAPLES

The southern economy lagged behind that of the North for some reasons that had nothing to do with slavery. The North had a more invigorating climate, more varied natural resources, better harbors. But it was the single crop system, the gang-labor system, the slave system, that kept the South from making the most of its own natural endowment.

The first southern agricultural staple was tobacco, and the first slave-labor plantations were devoted to growing the leaf in tidewater Virginia and Maryland. After 1800 tobacco culture spread westward across the upper South, and by mid-century this newer area was raising more tobacco than the old. In the 1850's, however, Virginia, North Carolina, and Maryland made such

a spectacular comeback in tobacco production that seven of the ten leading tobacco counties in the entire country were in those three states. The source of their new prosperity was the discovery in 1839 by a slave, Stephen, a Negro overseer and blacksmith on a North Carolina plantation, of a way of curing a type of tobacco, the "Bright Yellow Tobacco," that grew better on the poor sandy soil of the Roanoke Valley and inland Maryland than on the worn out soil of the tidewater. Great plantations again became the rule in the Old Dominion and her neighbors, and the distasteful business of breeding slaves for the West declined. But compared to cotton, tobacco remained a minor southern crop, and the tobacco revival did not bring general prosperity even to the three leading states. In

1860, only 36 per cent of Virginia land and 27 per cent of land in North Carolina was "improved," compared to 68 and 61 per cent for New York and Pennsylvania.

Although the chief beneficiaries of the tobacco boom were great slaveholders, tobacco was grown by a large number of small farmers. Small farmers were the main producers of another minor crop, hemp, which became a staple in Kentucky and Missouri. Only rich planters, on the other hand, could embark on the production of rice and sugar, the South's two other important minor staples. In 1860, indeed, not even the Gulf states of the Cotton Kingdom could match the rice regions of South Carolina and Georgia in the relative density of their slave populations and the scale of their plantations. The only estate of more than 1,000 slaves in the whole South was in the South Carolina rice country. Besides South Carolina and Georgia, rice was produced in lowland regions in Louisiana, Texas and Arkansas. Because rice plantations were usually situated in hot marshy districts, their owners normally spent the spring and summer in more salubrious spots to escape malaria. Under hard-driving overseers, their

slaves fared badly. Cholera and yellow fever, as well as malaria, thinned their ranks.

Cane-sugar planting gained a great impetus after 1822 when steam-engines were introduced to crush the cane. The cost of machinery for a sugar plantation might run as high as $14,000, and the harvesting of cane called for intensive periods of the hardest labor by gangs of slaves. Only owners of the large plantations in the rich delta lands of Louisiana and the alluvial soils regions of southeastern Texas and coastal Georgia could afford the cost of sugar-milling equipment. They were able to compete with the more favorable situated West Indian producers only because of the high tariff on imported sugar.

THE COTTON KINGDOM

As early as 1820, the South's cotton crop had become more valuable than all its other crops combined. By 1835, as we have seen (p. 247), the Cotton Kingdom had spread more than a thousand miles from

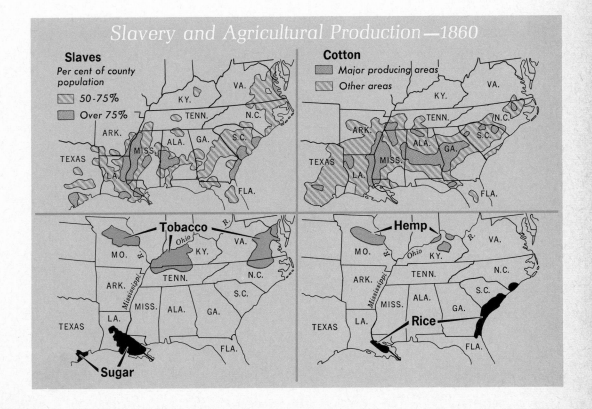

Slavery and Agricultural Production—1860

South Carolina to Texas and ranged some six or seven hundred miles up the Mississippi Valley. By 1850, the states bordering the Gulf of Mexico had become the greatest cotton-growing region in the world. In 1859, the United States produced a record crop of 5,387,000 bales, two-thirds of it in the Gulf states. At that time, cotton accounted for two-thirds of the *nation's* exports.

With a little capital, a small acreage, and a few slaves, a cotton farmer could still make a profit. Cotton could survive rough handling when it was shipped to market, and it did not spoil—important considerations where roads were bad and transportation facilities lacking. Much of the American cotton crop, even on the frontier, was in fact grown by small farmers; yet cotton, with its huge market and great adaptability to slave-gang labor, was the ideal staple for the slave owning planters who spread over the virgin lands of the Southwest. By 1860, slave-owning cotton growers produced more than 93 per cent of the Mississippi crop.

Where land was plentiful and cheap and labor dear, the essence of good plantation management was high production per slave, not per acre. Under effective overseers and gang bosses, the more slaves a planter had, the greater his margin of success was likely to be. It was this circumstance that helped put such great pressure on overseers and on the slaves themselves. Good overseers were hard to find and to keep; the most successful planters were those who kept a close eye on all their affairs and even dispensed with overseers when they could. Large-scale operations gave big planters other advantages as well. Necessities that they could not grow or make on the plantation they could purchase in large quantities at wholesale rates. They could also market their crops more efficiently. Wealthier planters, moreover, were more likely to be interested in conserving the soil, more willing to experiment with new agricultural techniques.

PROFITS AND PENALTIES
OF THE PLANTATION SYSTEM

Those who argue, as many did in the South as well as the North before 1860,

and as many continue to argue today, that slave labor was more costly in cotton-growing than free labor would have been, and that slavery would have disappeared eventually if left alone, have tended to make a mere bookkeeping problem of a profound social issue. It is true that only exceptional cotton plantations earned large profits, even on the rich virgin soil of the Gulf area. It is also true that such profits as were earned were menaced by high slave mortality, and the cost of maintaining aged slaves and slave children. Despite efforts to quicken their incentive, moreover, slaves proved to be a reluctant labor force, and solicitude for their welfare was not enough to prevent them from working carelessly and damaging equipment. They were "a troublesome property," as one historian has said. To make matters worse, the cost of prime male field hands jumped in the 1840's and 1850's from $1,000 to $1,200 or more. The planter necessarily found that a heavy proportion of his capital was tied up in slaves. But he was no more motivated on that account to abandon slavery than Queen Victoria was motivated to abandon monarchy because of the rising cost of soldiers.

If slavery was in fact an economic disadvantage to the cotton South, it need not bear all the responsibility for southern economic backwardness. Even in ante-bellum days men like Edmund Ruffin of Virginia argued that southern soil exhaustion, for example, was only indirectly connected with the unchanging routines of slave gangs. Soil exhaustion, they said, was primarily the result of short-sightedness, itself encouraged by the easy availability of new land; and of ignorance, promoted by widespread illiteracy and indifference to technology. But even these men acknowledged that the plantation system itself discouraged widespread education even in agricultural processes, and that slavery induced an indifference to technological innovation.

Would slavery have persisted after the lands suitable for staple crops had been used up? Many southerners and northerners believed that nature had confined slavery to a restricted area and that the institution on that account would not outlast the century. Lincoln and many others in the North who fought so bitterly in the political arena against the extension of slavery to new territories (see Chapters 12 and 15), obviously did not believe this argument. Those in the South who as bitterly opposed restrictions on free expansion presumably did not believe it either. It has been argued, moreover, by Lewis C. Gray, the leading historian of ante-bellum agriculture in the South, that the expansion of the railroads would have brought fresh lands into easy reach of the migrating planter, and that industry might well have absorbed the surplus slave population. Although slaves, as we have seen (p. 346), did in fact work in southern industries and in other urban occupations, however, the growing need to defend the slave system and the plantation system from attack by the industrial north drained such incentive as there might have been among the great planters really to develop a dynamic industrial regime in their own area. The need to justify the slave system and the plantation system in its own terms, indeed, helped dissipate the profits that were made on the land and turned the proud Cotton Kingdom into a disenchanted colony of industrial and commercial Britain and the North.

THE COLONIAL STATUS
OF THE KINGDOM

Southerners were perfectly familiar with the invidious contrasts drawn by their own representatives between the busy, contented North—enterprising, public-spirited, prosperous—and the indolent, poverty-stricken southern country. Many of them nevertheless feared the effects of introducing factories into an agrarian slave society. Some felt (though there was evidence in some southern factories to the contrary) that a Negro working in a factory was already half-free; others believed that Negroes were not capable of mastering machinery. Many, moreover, harbored the old distrust of cities that Jefferson had expressed so vividly in his *Notes on Virginia*.

In spite of all these doubts and apprehen-

sions, a favorable attitude toward manufacturing developed during the 1820's and 1830's when tariff controversies made the South acutely conscious of its dependence on northern industry. Georgians and Virginians petitioned their legislators to encourage planters to build their own factories to employ the hitherto unproductive poor whites, and thereby to restore the glory of the South by keeping her wealth at home.

Not until the 1840's, however, did the arguments for building up southern manufactures begin to take hold. This decade was a time of falling cotton prices and economic stagnation in the South Atlantic states, and the people were in the mood to listen to a thoughtful Charleston businessman, William Gregg. His *Essays on Domestic Industry* (1845)—written after a tour of the New England mills—pointed the way to an economic and moral rehabilitation of the poor whites through industrial employment. Gregg's proposals, embodied in his own model factories run along the lines of the Lowell plan (see p. 254), contained nothing offensive to southern prejudices. Gregg did not advocate the use of slave labor for manufacturing. Nor did he demand tariff protection, for the coarse variety of cotton cloth produced in the South did not compete with foreign textiles. His program was applauded by the growing number of southern nationalists (already looking ahead to southern independence) who wanted a strongly industrialized South when the great day came. Another influential group backed the industrial program for precisely opposite reasons: They hoped that factories would make the South prosperous and that prosperity would remove the chief cause of animosity between the sections.

Yet little came of Gregg's work. Between 1850 and 1860, the number of industrial workers in the South rose only from 165,000 to 190,000. On the eve of the Civil War, the South was producing less than 10 per cent of the nation's manufactured goods. In 1860, the Lowell mills alone operated more spindles than all the cotton-spinning factories of the South combined.

The South showed an even greater aversion to commerce than to manufacturing, with even stiffer penalties for producers of staple crops that had to be marketed abroad and carried to their purchasers. The planter relied on commission merchants, or "factors," to sell his crops. These factors, who resided in port cities or in interior market towns, shipped the produce northward or directly to Europe for a commission. They also sold supplies to the planter, advised him when to sell his crop, bought slaves for him, and performed personal services. Frequently, the planter fell so deeply in debt to his factors that they could dictate the kind of crop they wanted consigned to them for payment. The factor system therefore increased the concentration on cotton, since this was the safest cash crop, and restricted the most lucrative commercial activity to the seaboard cities and to a few river towns like Memphis.

Many factors were New Englanders, backed by New York capital. They were often criticized by planters for charging high brokerage fees—up to 2½ per cent for selling a crop and from 2½ to 10 per cent for buying supplies. A more valid reason for the planters' constant indebtedness was the business organization that permitted New York commercial interests to tap the profits from southern exports (see p. 252). By the 1850's about 40,000 American seamen were employed in the cotton-carrying trade, but few of them were southerners on southern ships. At the numerous commercial conventions held in the South between 1830 and 1860, the southern imagination was fired with rhetorical visions of teeming cities, happy artisans, and bustling marts, all the rewards of recapturing the cotton-carrying trade. But the steamship lines that were to provide direct communication with Europe, the railroads that were to tap the western markets, the trade that was to spring up with South America, and the cotton factories that were to turn New England into a desert, rarely passed beyond the planning stage.

THE ROOTS OF SOUTHERN LOYALTY

Profitable as slavery may have been to a few thousand planter families at most, it was socially disastrous for the South. "It may seem a paradox, and yet it is true," declared a North Carolinian in 1853, "that a community of planters may grow rich while they are impoverishing and depopulating their country." Slavery discouraged diversity in agriculture, accelerated the flow of southern yeomanry to the free-soil states, and created an illusory prosperity based on the ownership of land declining in fertility and of slaves rising in cost.

For the Negro, the physical and psychic injuries that resulted from his enforced servitude were obviously immense and lasting. The penalties that slavery imposed upon many slave-owners were almost as disastrous, though less obvious and less physically trying. The possession of such complete authority over human chattels brought out the worst in many slave-owners, not merely among the perverse and the depraved but in many well-meaning men and women as well. The barbarism of the institution affected even the most well-intentioned of the planters, and tempted them into practices that left a legacy of guilt. The very zeal with which they volunteered unconvincing justifications for black servitude suggests that they were frequently far from easy in their minds, and privately they often confessed as much. A few slave-owners publicly acknowledged their spiritual discomfort, as the following extract from the will of a North Carolinian who emancipated his slaves makes clear. He gave four reasons for his action:

Reason the first. Agreeably to the rights of man, every human being, be his or her colour what it may, is entitled to freedom. . . . Reason the second. My conscience, the great criterion, condemns me for keeping them in slavery. Reason the third. The golden rule directs us to do unto every human creature, as we would wish to be done unto. . . . Reason the fourth and last. I wish to die with a clear conscience, that I may not be ashamed to appear before my master in a future World.

And yet the allegiance of the vast majority of southerners to the slave system and the plantation system after 1830 only deepened. Their attachment to the "peculiar institution," of course, varied according to class, region, and occupation, but the following considerations help to explain why slavery received such overwhelming support in the decades preceding the Civil War:

1. *Fear of becoming a white minority.* The heavy concentration of Negro slaves in much of the South created a serious problem in race relations. Anti-slavery northerners, southern spokesmen declared, living in states where Negroes comprised only a tiny fraction of the population, had no inkling of what it was like to live in South Carolina or Mississippi where Negroes outnumbered whites. The total Negro population of the 16 free states in 1850 was under 200,000. In 1860, each of five southern states had twice that number of Negroes.

2. *The Negro unfit for freedom.* It was widely held in the South that the Negro would only be harmed by abolition. And this conclusion was strengthened by reports about the condition of free Negroes in the North. Everywhere in the free-soil states, even in the centers of abolition, as we have seen (p. 264), Negroes were abused and discriminated against politically, economically, and socially, and then blamed for their low condition as though the reasons were congenital. In the South, free Negroes were often worse off, especially after the growing fear of slave revolts made them objects of suspicion.

3. *The anti-Negro sentiments of white laborers.* White workers in southern cities, like most northern workingmen, did not want to see slavery abolished. Negro competition, whether slave or free, threatened their security, and they often refused to work with Negroes, who underbid them or who demeaned their social position by the mere fact of competing against them. Race prejudice was particularly strong among immigrant groups, like the Irish, who performed menial jobs too dangerous for high-priced slaves.

4. *The social ambitions of the small planter.* Small planters, linked to the gentry either by kinship or common interest, felt that their chances of rising in the world would be jeopardized by abolition. They, and many yeoman farmers too poor to own any slaves, looked forward to the time when they would be masters of larger plantations. Hence, anti-abolition sentiment was strong in many areas where the slave population was small.

5. *The "poor white" committed to racial inequality.* Finally, the impoverished southern whites, disease-ridden and shiftless, fanatically supported slavery as a way of preserving what little status they had. When the time came, they fought for slave property and for a class that looked upon them with contempt.

IV. *The Mind of the South*

LIMITATIONS ON THE REFORM SPIRIT

The ante-bellum South produced some admirable types, but opinions have differed widely over the range and depth of its culture. Measured by conventional standards—illiteracy rates, public schools, museums, the fine arts, and publishing—the South lagged behind the North. To the Bostonian, Henry Adams, the southerners he met at Harvard between 1854 and 1858 seemed incredibly archaic, sunk in a simplicity beyond the comprehension of the most unsophisticated New England student. "Strictly, the Southerner had no mind; he had temperament," Adams wrote later in his celebrated *Education*. "He was not a scholar; he had no intellectual training; he could not analyze an idea, and he could not even conceive of admitting two."

Adams' sweeping generalization was provincial enough. Calhoun, a brilliant though somewhat doctrinaire analyst, more ingenious than profound, was one of a number of acute thinkers in the South who reasoned only too well. But the claim of impassioned pro-slavery men that the South had erected a superior culture on a slave base was no less mistaken. Intellectual novelties were not welcomed in the South, and the arts got little encouragement; old ways and old ideas retained their hold longer in this agrarian society, and intellectual pursuits were largely confined to an upper-class minority. There was no counterpart, for example, of the educated New England rustic or the self-taught Yankee artisan. An agricultural people was more likely to produce soldiers, orators, and politicians than artists and poets.

Although the South had no industrial revolution, no literary renaissance, it did pass through a period of social and political ferment between 1820 and 1860. Again, reform movements did not explode violently in a society that was still instinctively conservative, and "isms" did not flourish in the southern atmosphere. The fundamentalist temper of the old South discouraged liberal and transcendental religious speculation as well as the yeasty fads and visionary doctrines that flourished in the North. So-called "Northern fanaticism," much exaggerated by fiery southern patriots, could not take root in a society where both clergy and press remained constantly alert to "socialism, or to social equality, nihilism, communism, or to infidelity in any of its shapes or shades." Because few European immigrants settled in the South, alien ideas usually came by way of the North. In the southern mind, all "isms" became tinged with abolitionism—feminism, transcendentalism, Fourierism, and the rest, a tinge that was sound enough, since northern abolitionists like Garrison, Theodore Parker, Theodore Weld, and Horace Greeley *were* interested in the whole range of reform programs. But the South spurned extrava-gant reforms for other reasons as well. Feminism outraged the southern ideal of womanhood. Experiments like Frances Wright's plantation in Nashoba, Tennessee, where Negroes and whites were to live happily together, failed completely. Some southern mavericks—notably the aristocratic Grimké sisters, Angelina and Sarah, of Charleston—turned abolitionist or succumbed to other enthusiasms, but they were among the exceptions.

Yet the repudiation of Yankee intellectual notions and panaceas did not mean that the South was wholly immune to the humanitarian influences that touched most Americans in the 1830's and 1840's. The rise of evangelical religion was accompanied by a concerted effort to check frontier brutality and to discipline breaches of moral conduct. In the South, as elsewhere, criminal codes were humanized, prison reforms were introduced, and improvements were made in the treatment of the insane. Dorothea L. Dix was one Yankee reformer whom the South loved and cherished. Her visit to Tennessee and North Carolina in 1847-48 brought immediate action, and the asylum that was opened in Raleigh, North Carolina, in 1853 bore her name. During the same period, schools for the deaf and dumb patterned after northern models were established in a number of southern states. Perhaps the most enthusiastically supported reform movement in the prewar South was the temperance cause. Backed by religious and political leaders, temperance societies sprang up everywhere to the accompaniment of parades and petitions and the publicized testimony of reformed drunkards.

ANTI-SLAVERY SENTIMENT

Until the anti-slavery crusade in the North gathered momentum in the early 1830's, a number of southerners criticized slavery or apologized for it, and looked forward to its ultimate extinction. Many years before slavery aroused the humanitarian zeal of the North, southern men and women who knew slavery at first hand had listed its baneful effects on the whites. In the eighteenth century, William Byrd II complained that slaves by their very presence "blow up the pride and ruin the industry of the white people, who seeing a rank of poor creatures below them, detest work for fear it should then make them look like slaves." During the Revolutionary period, southern leaders like Washington, Jefferson, Madison, and Patrick Henry were well aware of the incongruity of slavery in a Republic dedicated to the principles of the Declaration of Independence. The declining value of tobacco lands and the surplus of Negroes in the upper South probably heightened the readiness of these men to consider abandoning the whole "peculiar institution."

As late as 1817, southerners dominated the American Colonization Society, which was headed by George Washington's nephew. In Virginia, abolition was seriously argued in 1829, when a new state constitution was being drafted, and again in the legislature of 1831-32. The second debate followed on the heels of Nat Turner's insurrection. The anti-slavery group not only played up the constant threat of slave revolts but also raised many of the arguments against slavery that northern abolitionists were later to use: that slavery was wedded to the destructive one-crop system so injurious to the land, that the presence of slaves discouraged immigration to the South, that slavery kept the South poor. "Wherefore, then, object to slavery?" asked one of the delegates in 1832. "Because it is ruinous to the whites, retards improvements, roots out an industrious population—banishes the yeomanry of the country—deprives the spinner, the weaver, the smith, the shoemaker, the carpenter, of employment and support."

The change in southern attitudes had begun as early as 1793 when Whitney's cotton gin gave the South a strong new reason for expanding the plantation and the slave systems (see p. 247). The abolitionist crusade in the North and the awareness of strong anti-slavery opinion in Europe also made the South increasingly sensitive to criticism and more eager to provide slavery with an ideological defense.

THE DEFENSE OF SLAVERY

During the 1830's, the pro-slavery forces in the South launched their counterattack first against the southerners opposed to slavery and then against the northern emancipationists. In order to combat abolitionist exaggerations and present slavery as an idyllic and humane institution, they felt obliged to demonstrate that slavery was sanctioned by religion, political economy, science, and culture. Southern professors, ministers, jurists, scientists, and journalists had to justify slavery constitutionally and show that it fostered a genuine and classical form of democracy distinct from the "mongrelized" industrial democracy of the North.

A spate of books and pamphlets was written to prove that the Bible authorized slavery, that the Negro belonged to a degraded race, that he was physiologically as well as morally inferior to whites, that men were not born free and equal, and that talk about inalienable rights was so much nonsense. George Fitzhugh's *Sociology for the South; or, The Failure of Free Society* (1854) and *Cannibals All! or, Slaves Without Masters* (1857) managed to include most of the familiar arguments of the day.

The slave system, as it appeared in Fitzhugh's artful descriptions, was a kind of benevolent socialism. In the South, he claimed, capital and labor were not divorced, thus following Calhoun's prized lead. The fierce exploitation of one class by another, which characterized the cruel and cannibalistic laissez-faire economy of the North, was blessedly absent. He contrasted the hideous conditions in northern and British industrial cities and the miseries of the white slave or "hireling" with the blissful life of the plantation Negro, nurtured and guarded from cradle to grave. Northern capitalism, he declared, led to the impoverishment of the masses and to revolution. No such danger threatened the South. Fitzhugh even called on northern conservatives to accept slavery as a fact, to join the planters in maintaining a stratified society, and to repress the social upheavals in the free states that Fitzhugh attributed directly to unregulated capitalism.

Fitzhugh's extreme views were presented in his exuberant style and made an impression in the North that only fostered misunderstanding. Everyone's attention focused on slavery, some seeing it as a curse and some as a blessing, but other problems that were just as important in understanding the ills and promise of the South were obscured. It was convenient for the northerner to ascribe soil exhaustion, illiteracy, and economic instability to slavery alone, just as it was convenient for the southerner to attribute the social and economic backwardness of his region to greedy northern middlemen and to high tariffs.

EDUCATION

The extension of the suffrage just before the abolitionist campaign got under way went further in the North than in the South, but even in the slave section it raised the threat of an "ignorant and debased" electorate. Public education in the slave states was almost nonexistent, and its advocates faced even greater obstacles than did northern educational reformers. Even a Horace Mann could not have made much headway in the thinly populated rural areas of the South where rich planters resisted taxation for public schools while those who would have benefited from them felt they bore the stigma of charity. Until the 1840's, private rural elementary schools and academies sufficed for those with the interest and income to attend. There were some 2,700 academies in the South by 1850, over two and a half times the number in New England and 600 more than in the Middle states. But the quality of education in these preparatory schools fell below the standards of northern schools, and only a minority attended them. The rate of illiteracy tells the story. The 1850 census showed that 20 per cent of southern whites were illiterate as against 3 per cent in the Middle states and 1 per cent in New England.

Southern higher education compared more favorably with that in the North, but even after abolitionism had soured them on northern ideas southern families who could afford it continued to send their sons to Princeton, Harvard, Yale, and the University of Pennsylvania rather than to their own state universities and denominational colleges. At the same time, a greater percentage of young southerners than northerners were receiving college training. In 1860, for example, when the northern population was two and a half times that of the white population of the South, each section counted about 26,000 college students. Most southern colleges, to be sure, were less richly endowed with funds or facilities than those in the North. But the University of Virginia, South Carolina College, and briefly, Transylvania, measured up to the standards of the best above the Mason-Dixon line.

As anti-northern sentiment intensified in the 1840's and 1850's, southern leaders made strenuous efforts to throw off the intellectual yoke of the Yankees. Conventions passed resolutions urging that southern youth be educated at home by native teachers, and that textbooks coincide with "the educational wants and the social condition of these States, and the encouragement and support of inventions and discoveries in the arts and sciences, by their citizens." It was particularly galling for southern students to be given biased northern texts. One book, for example, spoke of the upper-class southerner's addiction to drinking and gambling. Another described slavery as "that stain on the human race, which corrupts the master as much as it debases the slave." Agitation against importing poisonous alien doctrines, however, apparently did not halt the sale of northern books in the South nor keep significantly larger numbers of southern students from Northern schools.

RELIGION IN THE SOUTH

The political and religious liberalism so marked in the Jeffersonian South (see p. 355) declined after 1825 when the skeptical spirit fostered by the Enlightenment among the aristocracy gave way to the fundamentalism of the common man. The great religious revivals in the early 1800's converted thousands to the Methodist and Baptist faiths, and ministers of the evangelical denominations now assumed a powerful influence over the raw democracy. From southern pulpits came denunciations against infidelity and abolitionism. The atheist, the Deist, the Unitarian (all often lumped together) were regarded by the fundamentalists as subversive. In 1835, a North Carolina constitutional convention voted to exclude Jews, atheists, and skeptics from public office. Six years later, a Georgia court held the testimony of Universalists (who did not believe in hell-fire) invalid.

Such evidences of intolerance were by no means confined to the South. Heresy hunts and anti-infidel crusades occurred in the North and West at the time, but in the South the skeptical minority had to keep silent. During Jefferson's lifetime, Deist and Unitarian opinion found expression in the southern disciples of the English scientist, Joseph Priestley, and of the revolutionary political philosopher, Thomas Paine. Jefferson himself had tried to obtain a professorship at the University of Virginia for the free-thinking Dr. Thomas Cooper. He failed, but Cooper was president of South Carolina College between 1821 and 1834. His political views endeared him to the South Carolinians, for he vigorously upheld the southern position on slavery, state rights, and the tariff. But his attacks against the clergy and against Biblical literalism became too extreme to be condoned. His successor, J. H. Thornwell, not only stoutly championed slavery as ordained by God but also struck mighty blows against infidelity. Conservative Presbyterians captured lost ground in Kentucky when they ousted the liberal Unitarian, Horace Holley, from the presidency of Transylvania University in 1827. Unitarianism soon practically disappeared from the South. The Episcopal and Presbyterian churches appealed to the gentility of the tidewater, but elsewhere, those whom the frontier preacher described as "profane sinners, downright skeptics, and God-defying wretches" were either converted or silenced.

LITERATURE

No literary flowering occurred in the South that was in any way comparable to New England's, during the ante-bellum period, even though a number of talented writers published fiction, poetry, and essays of high quality. Edgar Allan Poe, born in Boston, as we have seen (p. 296), has long been regarded as one of America's greatest writers and regarded himself as a Virginian, but his "southernism" is usually ignored or denied. Poe's South Carolina contemporary, William Gilmore Simms, is now hardly known, nor are such interesting figures as the eccentric poet, Thomas Holley Chivers, or William Elliott, author of the southern classic, *Carolina Sports by Land and Water* (1846).

Southern writers were exposed to the same romantic currents that stimulated the literary renaissance in the North. They too had to combat the national indifference to literature and contempt for the writer. But the problems of the southern authors were magnified by conditions peculiar to their section.

So long as the older and better-educated families dominated southern culture, the literary tastes and standards that prevailed were those of cultivated amateurs who believed that professional writing was not a suitable occupation for a gentleman. They enjoyed biography and history and shared the national enthusiasm for British authors, but they gave little practical encouragement to their own writers. The "highbrows" of Charleston, according to the poet, Paul Hamilton Hayne, who grew up among them, were great devotees of the classics but read little else. They might admire their distinguished townsman, Simms, but they did not buy enough of his books to please him. "The South," Simms wrote to a friend in 1847, "don't care a d—n for literature or art. Your best neighbor & kindred never think to buy books. They will borrow from you & beg, but the same man who will always have wine, has no idea of a library. You will write for & defend their institutions in vain. They will not pay the expense of printing your essays."

Northern writers, to be sure, faced similar difficulties but not to the same degree. Southern college graduates were often well-informed and intelligent, but politics, agriculture, and the sports of the field absorbed their attention. When, for patriotic reasons, southern writers published in the South, their books sold poorly. Well-written magazines like the *Southern Literary Messenger* might praise their works, but only the approval of the more numerous and better-printed northern periodicals had cash value. Southern writers resented their dependence on northern publishers, periodicals, and critics. They felt discriminated against and accused northern reviewers of puffing Yankee mediocrities and ignoring southern genius. Without northern publishers and a northern audience, however, such popular writers as Poe and Simms would not have fared as well as they did. Simms' conclusion about his countrymen seems just: "We are not, in fact, a reading people. We are probably, at best, only the pioneers for those, who will atone to letters and the arts hereafter, for our grievous neglect." The brilliant renaissance of southern letters in our own century has borne out the prophecy.

As sectional animosities grew more bitter, southern writers found themselves in a dilemma. According to the Charleston poet, Henry Timrod, any truthful account of the South antagonized northern readers, and southern readers were quick to detect any lapse in local pride. Writers were expected to fight with their pens to uphold the southern gospel against such intellectual incendiaries as Emerson.

His name [declared a critic in the *Southern Literary Messenger*] is like a rag-picker's basket full of all manner of trash. His books are valuable, however, for the very reason they are no earthly account. They illustrate the utter worthlessness of the philosophy of free society. Egoism, or rather Manism (if we may coin a word,) propounded in short scraps, tags, and shreds of sentences may do well for a people who have not settled opinions in politics, religion or morals, and have lived for forty years on pure fanaticisms. We of the South require something better than this no-system. Your fragmentary philosopher, of the *Emerson* stamp, who disturbs the beliefs of common folk . . . is a curse to society.

In the light of these peculiar circumstances, what can be said of the literary achievements of the Old South? Taken as a whole, southern writers did not depict the agrarian society as accurately or as fully as they might have. Nowhere is slavery or the Negro treated meaningfully. Simms, the section's most prolific novelist, contributed his full share of wooden heroes, whose lips curl and whose eyes flash, and of doll-like ladies who speak in stilted phrases. But at least his low-life characters, his traders, tavern-keepers, and poor whites, are real. He was the only southern novelist before the war who depicted the yeomanry and the riff-raff believably. His novels, loosely and carelessly written though they are, capture the violence and gustiness of the southern frontier, and his fondness for brutal detail makes him seem at times a precursor of the twentieth-century school of southern naturalists.

The plain people of the South are also graphically portrayed in the sketches of the southern humorists—journalists, doctors, sportsmen, lawyers. They wrote of "frolics," quilting parties, horse-swaps, gander-pullings, camp-meetings, and fights, and their "tall tales" provide a vivid panorama of the frontier South. Augustus Baldwin Longstreet's colorful descriptions of rural Georgia were justly praised by Poe as masterpieces of reporting. Johnson Jones Hooper invented a fabulous rascal, Simon Suggs, whose motto, "It's good to be shifty in a new country," summed up the spirit of the raw Alabama hinterlands. The Cumberland Mountain country inspired another frontier humorist, George Washington Harris.

The South's greatest writer, Edgar Allan Poe, was the least obviously southern. His literary domain was the landscape of the mind; the romantic southern scene with its plantations, cavaliers, and magnolias did

358

not interest him, nor did the southern past. And yet the distinguished modern Virginia novelist, Ellen Glasgow, felt that Poe was a "distillation of the Southern":

The formalism of his tone, the classical element in his poetry and in many of his stories, the drift toward rhetoric, the aloof and elusive intensity,—all these qualities are Southern. And in his more serious faults of over-writing, sentimental exaggeration, and lapses now and then, into a pompous or florid style, he belongs to his epoch and even more to his South.

A "CONSCIOUS MINORITY"

After 1831, abolitionist assaults against slavery heightened the southerners' sense of isolation and drove their public men and their intellectuals into truculent defense of southern institutions. Against such biting attacks as Theodore Weld's *American Slavery as It Is* (1839), and its fictional counterpart, Harriet Beecher Stowe's *Uncle Tom's Cabin* (1852), the South replied with pro-slavery arguments, fiery proclamations in defense of state rights, and a rallying of public opinion against anyone in Dixie whose loyalty to southern ideals was suspect. "Unreliable" professors were removed from southern colleges; free discussion of slavery was quashed; newspapers kept silent on the dangerous subject. Before 1860, the South had succeeded in insulating itself against antislavery thought.

The man whose career symptomized the southern shift from nationalism to sectionalism was John C. Calhoun. Starting as an ardent defender of positive government, a constitutional "loose constructionist," he ended as the apostle of nullification after becoming convinced that northern industrial interests were enslaving the agrarian South.

Calhoun loved the Union too much to advocate secession, and yet he grew convinced that existing constitutional safeguards could not protect a minority from a rapacious majority capable of taxing it out of existence. In his posthumous reflections, *A Disquisition on Government* (1851) and *Discourse on the Constitution and Gov-*

John C. Calhoun (1782-1850).

ernment of the United States (1851), Calhoun proposed his theory of "concurrent majorities," which would grant any interest group (in effect, a section like the South) the right to veto an act passed by the majority (in effect, Congress). Calhoun's solution, in other words, was nothing less than a rationale for minority veto of a majority act. It was a device whereby a section that was out of power could protect its property against a section that was in power "by dividing and distributing the powers of government."

Like his northern opponents, Calhoun was often misinformed, unrealistic, and parochial in his thinking, but his clearly reasoned speculations pointed up the threat of majority tyranny in a democracy. Unfortunately, he spoke in behalf of slaveowners and did not carry over his defense of political minorities to intellectual minor-

359

ities. He shared a large part of the responsibility for the throttling of independent opinion in the ante-bellum South. His appeal to southern honor, his inflammatory speeches on southern wrongs, kept the South constantly agitated, and after his death in 1850 his devoted followers kept the emotional fires burning.

Readings
Asterisk indicates that book is available in paperback.

F. B. Simkins, *A History of the South* (1956), and W. B. Hesseltine, *The South in American History* (1960), are two useful surveys of southern life. Clement Eaton, *A History of the Old South* (1949), offers a more detailed survey up to the Civil War. Eaton's *The Growth of Southern Civilization 1790-1860* * (1961), deals more comprehensively with the period of this chapter. W. E. Dodd, *The Cotton Kingdom* (1919), and R. S. Cotterill, *The Old South* (1939), are stimulating short analyses. Politically oriented but valuable for all aspects of southern life in this period are, C. S. Sydnor, *The Development of Southern Sectionalism, 1819-1848* (1948), and A. O. Craven, *The Growth of Southern Nationalism, 1848-1861* (1953). Allen Nevins, *Ordeal of the Union* (2 vols., 1947), contains richly documented analyses of many aspects of southern life.

L. C. Gray, *History of Agriculture in the Southern United States to 1860* (2 vols., 1933), is an outstanding study of broad scope. It should be supplemented with the chapters on the South in P. W. Gates, *The Farmer's Age: Agriculture, 1815-1860* (1960). J. C. Sitterson, *Sugar Country, The Cane Sugar Industry in the South, 1753-1950* (1953), and J. C. Robert, *The Story of Tobacco in America* (1952), afford illuminating surveys of other southern staples besides cotton. J. H. Moore, *Agriculture in Ante-Bellum Mississippi* (1958), is useful for frontier husbandry. A. O. Craven, *Edmund Ruffin, Southerner* (1932), is an account of a southern pioneer in scientific agriculture. Other aspects of economic life in the South are covered in Broadus Mitchell, *William Gregg, Factory Master of the Old South* (1928); L. E. Atherton, *The Southern Country Store 1800-1860* (1949); R. E. Russel, *Economic Aspects of Southern Sectionalism 1840-1861* (1924); and U. B. Phillips, *A History of Transportation in the Eastern Cotton Belt* (1908).

The Cotton Kingdom, of course, is treated in detail in many of the books cited above. Indispensable and extraordinarily interesting on this basic subject are F. L. Olmsted's records of his travels in the South, presented in the excellent modern edition by A. M. Schlesinger as *The Cotton Kingdom* (1953). Volume II of W. S. Tryon, ed., *A Mirror for Americans, Life and Manners in the United States 1790-1870* (3 vols., 1952), presents the reports of numerous other American travelers in the Cotton Kingdom. H. R. Floan, *The South in Northern Eyes, 1831-1861* * (1958), is a useful monograph. Other revealing glimpses of southern life may be found in J. P. Kennedy's idealistic picture of plantation society in *Swallow Barn, or a Sojourn in the Old Dominion* (1832); Susan D. Smedes, *Memorials of a Southern Planter* (1887); F. B. Simkins, *Pitchfork Ben Tillman* (1944); R. W. Shugg, *Origins of the Class Struggle in Louisiana 1840-1875* (1939); and J. H. Franklin, *The Militant South 1800-1861* * (1956). Everett Dick, *The Dixie Frontier* * (1948), is excellent on life in the raw Southwest. F. L. Owsley, *Plain Folk of the Old South* * (1949), has been most influential in emphasizing the yeoman and the agrarian as against the plantation tradition. A penetrating examination of the lasting costs of this emphasis is made in W. H. Nicholls, *Southern Tradition and Regional Progress* (1959).

J. H. Franklin, *From Slavery to Freedom: A History of American Negroes* (1956), is the standard account, starting with African origins. Two older works by U. B. Phillips, *Life and Labor in the Old South* * (1929), and *American Negro Slavery* (1918), should be read in conjunction with K. M. Stampp, *The Peculiar Institution: Slavery in the Ante-Bellum*

South * (1956), a revisionist study. R. B. Flanders, *Plantation Slavery in Georgia* (1933), and C. S. Sydnor, *Slavery in Mississippi* (1933), are outstanding state studies. An introduction to the statistical analysis of the slave system of labor will be found in A. H. Conrad and J. R. Meyer, *The Economics of Slavery, and Other Studies in Econometric History* (1964). H. D. Woodman, "The Profitability of Slavery: A Historical Perennial," an essay in *Journal of Southern History*, XXIX, No. 3 (August, 1963), pp. 303-325, affords a thoroughly documented survey of studies of this subject from the 1840's to the 1960's. R. C. Wade, *Slavery in the Cities, The South 1820-1860* (1964), is a scholarly monograph on a neglected subject. Frank Tannenbaum, *Slave and Citizen, The Negro in the Americas* * (1947); and S. M. Elkins, *Slavery, A Problem in American Institutional and Intellectual Life* * (1959), afford comparisons of southern slavery with the institution in other American lands. Herbert Aptheker, *American Negro Slave Revolts* * (1943), is standard on its subject. The slave and the free Negro had few opportunities to record their own experiences and attitudes. Aptheker, ed., *A Documentary History of the Negro People in the United States* * (1951), is a painstaking and illuminating anthology of the Negro's own words from colonial times to 1910.

W. J. Cash, *The Mind of the South* * (1941), is a penetrating study of illusion and reality in southern life and literature, exceptionally well written. W. R. Taylor, *Cavalier and Yankee: The Old South and American National Character* * (1961), probes the conflict of attitudes that helped bring about the Civil War. F. P. Gaines, *The Southern Plantation: A Study in the Development and Accuracy of a Tradition* (1924), confronts southern romanticism with certain aspects of realism. Other challenges to southern thinking are examined in R. G. Osterweis, *Romanticism and Nationalism in the Old South* (1949), and J. T. Carpenter, *The South as a Conscious Minority* (1930). Clement Eaton, *Freedom of Thought in the Old South* * (1940), is a broader commentary on southern culture than its title suggests. D. R. Fox, *Ideas in Motion* (1935), contains an illuminating essay, "Cultural Nationalism in the Old South." E. L. McKitrick, ed., *Slavery Defended: The Views of the Old South* * (1963), is a valuable anthology of the writings of the pro-slavery apologists. This subject is dealt with in W. J. Jenkins, *Pro-Slavery Thought in the Old South* (1935), and Harvey Wish, *George Fitzhugh: Propagandist of the Old South* (1943). J. B. Hubbell, *The South in American Literature 1607-1900* (1954), is a comprehensive history. Edmund Wilson, *Patriotic Gore, Studies in the Literature of the American Civil War* (1962), is a masterly analysis of the most influential literature in both sections. The collected *Letters* of William Gilmore Simms (1952-1955), are full of interesting material on the life of the southern writer. V. W. Brooks, *The World of Washington Irving* (1944), contains several provocative chapters on the South.

CHAPTER FOURTEEN

At the end of 1854, after a decade of unprecedented expansion, a brief depression
befell the American economy. The stock
market crashed, tens of thousands of factory
workers were thrown out of work, prices of
western produce tumbled, and land values
collapsed. The depression was short-lived,
but the recovery that began in 1855 raised
the speculative fever to such a pitch that a
new and more resounding crash occurred
in 1857. All sections of the country suffered
except the South, and all sectors of the
economy were depressed except the culture
of cotton. "The wealth of the South" announced that section's leading economist,

The

Expansive North

J. D. B. DeBow of New Orleans, "is permanent and real, that of the North fugitive and fictitious."

Never was thinking more wishful or more wrong. The South's economy, though prosperous, lacked the vitality and variety of the North's; and the ups and downs in northern production reflected the dynamism of industry that would soon make the United States the richest country in the world. Perhaps we should speak of industrial*ism* rather than of industry alone, for it was the spirit of machine production that was at work—a spirit that was to pervade commercial agriculture and steamboating and railroading as well as the factories.

I. *Peopling the "Middle Border"*

Mechanized agriculture first became widespread in the United States on the free family farms of the northern prairies and the eastern edges of the unforested Great Plains. This fertile country, Hamlin Garland's "Middle Border," stretched from upper Indiana and Illinois northward to central Wisconsin and Minnesota, and westward through Iowa and upper Missouri to the eastern townships of Kansas and Nebraska. Even more than the southern coastal plains themselves, this level, lush terrain invited the large-scale corporate type of farming that characterizes much of the area in the twentieth century. At the outset, however, most of its settlers were independent small farmers from the neighboring states to the east or immigrants from the British Isles and the continent of Europe.

Driven by debt during the world-wide depression of the early 1840's, tens of thousands of farm families in the Ohio Valley and the country bordering Lake Erie and Lake Michigan sold their cleared and cultivated homesteads to newcomers with capital. Drawn by the government's liberalized land policy (see p. 286) to try again on the distant frontier, they settled in such numbers that Iowa became a state in 1846, and Wisconsin in 1848. By 1860, hundreds of thousands of other farm families, including "shoals" of Yankee abolitionists, had helped to treble the population of these

new states. Minnesota had grown large enough for statehood by 1858, and the admission of Kansas was delayed until 1861 for political reasons, not for lack of population. Nebraska and even the Dakotas to the north were also becoming inhabited.

During this period, economic distress, accompanied by political repression and religious persecution, had spread across Europe. Among the worst sufferers were the Irish Catholics, who were especially hard hit by the potato crop failure and the famine that followed in 1845 and 1846. In the decade that ended with the business panic of 1854, about 1,300,000 Irish had fled the Emerald Isle for the United States. For all their attachment to the "old sod," they were usually too poor even to move inland from the coastal cities in which they landed. Some of them did travel west as laborers with canal and railroad-building crews, and of these a few eventually were drawn back to the soil. Second in numbers to the Irish were the 940,000 Germans who arrived during this decade, followed by about 375,000 Englishmen, Welshmen, and Scots. A few thousand Scandinavians also came, the heralds of a large migration later in the nineteenth century, along with small contingents of Dutch, Swiss, Belgians, French, and Czechs.

All told, between 1844 and 1854 almost 3 million immigrants braved the Atlantic crossing to America. The hazards of the voyage in filthy steerage quarters were such that on some immigrant ships 10 per cent of the passengers died mainly from diseases contracted during the journey. Most of the newcomers shunned the land of cotton, although some of the thousands who were crowded into cotton ships on the return voyages from English ports remained in New Orleans where they were landed. Others transferred their few belongings to Mississippi River steamboats (under conditions hardly better than those encountered on the ocean) and proceeded north to non-slave country.

A majority of the immigrants were young, unmarried adults, who, as industrial and construction workers, farmers, farm-labor-

Settlement of the
Middle Border, 1820-1860

■ to 1820 ▨ 1820-30 ◪ 1830-40
▨ 1840-50 ▨ 1850-60

MINN.

MICHIGAN

Ft. Snelling   St. Paul

Wisconsin R.

Oshkosh

WIS.

Lake Michigan

Ft. Dodge

IOWA

Mississippi R.

Des Moines R.

Galena
Chicago

NEB.

Missouri R.

Nauvoo

Keokuk

Illinois R.

Wabash R.

IND.

ILL.

Terre
Haute

R.

Independence

St. Louis

KAN.

MO.

Ohio R.

KY.

ers, or domestic servants, immediately swelled the working force of the free section. Others came in family groups, among them independent, outspoken middle-class businessmen, lawyers, doctors, scientists, and journalists, who brought new skills, new learning, and new leadership to western cities like Cincinnati and St. Louis, and to aspiring frontier towns like Chicago and Des Moines. More numerous than these urban settlers were rural "reading families," who were readily identified by their bookish preparation for life in the New World. Such families were devoted to the Bible and often were led to America by their old-country pastors. By 1860 they made up 30 per cent of the population of Wisconsin and Minnesota and were almost as numerous in the other states that comprised the Middle Border.

So determined were these religious newcomers to preserve their old way of life in the wilderness that they sometimes segregated themselves in a "New Germany," a "New Norway," or a 'New Bohemia." But many caught the vision of a brighter future, and their commitment to the homeland and to the past grew dimmer with the passing

years. "The prairies," said the son of one of the English immigrants of the 1850's, "possessed a charm created by beauty instead of awe." The Illinois landscape, he recalled, "was an inspiration," and the land of Iowa and Kansas "sloped upward to the West, giving to the mind an ever-increasing sense of hope and power."

So long as the cotton planters kept their labor system to themselves, away from the Lord's free soil, these western pioneers as a rule were against meddling with the institution of slavery. Their own labor supply came from their large families; they kept their sons and daughters on the land, and invested in machines to multiply their productivity. The religious mysticism and pseudo-science of the times fed the belief that iron poisoned the earth, and some of these settlers were as wary of iron and steel implements and machines as of abolition itself. But they could not long withstand the competitive force of innovation and the sweeping tide of progress.

II. *The Agricultural Revolution*

BREAKING THE SOD

For most of the decade and a half before the Civil War, the settlement of the free West ran well ahead of the railroads. Pioneer families traveled on foot, in wagons, and in boats on the rivers and the Great Lakes. Groups of families sometimes settled a particular region, but even here the whole territory was so vast that farms were often a day's travel or more apart. One reason for choosing isolated sites was the settlers' habitual suspicion of intruders. More important was his hope of adding more land to the quarter-section with which he usually started.

Having prayerfully picked his land and registered it at the nearest land office, a farmer would build a one-room log cabin or, in treeless country, a hut constructed of

slabs of sod, and a barn of the same material. Meanwhile, he would turn his few sheep, cows, and oxen out to graze on the wild buffalo grass and fence them off as best he could from the kitchen vegetable garden—the care of which was one of the many responsibilities of his wife. Once he had fenced in his main fields, at a cash outlay of $1 or $1.25 an acre, he would begin the laborious round of cultivation. At this point the pioneer would discover that the plow he had carried with him from the East, though it took two men to handle and four oxen to pull, would hardly scratch the heavily matted, grass-rooted virgin soil. So at a further cost of $1.75 to $2.50 an acre, he would have to hire professional "breakers," teams of men with massive plows drawn by 8 to 12 oxen, who would cut the first shallow furrows on the prairies and the plains. In these furrows, in holes dug deeper with axes, the farmer would plant his Indian corn, and some pumpkins and beans to eke out the produce of the kitchen garden. In subsequent seasons, the farmer and his family would be able themselves to plow and plant the land broken by the professional teams.

An acre or an acre and a half a day—perhaps 40 acres of a 160-acre quarter-section—was the most the pioneer could hope to put under cultivation with his available ox-power and equipment. But men who had moved their families to the prairies and the plains with the idea simply of re-establishing an independent way of life based on self-help and Christian charity were quite satisfied to do as well as this. In the belief, dearly cherished in the United States, that the tiller of the soil was of all creatures closest to God—a belief that gave a Christian base to the Jeffersonian ideal of a democracy of farmers—they tended to resist rapid changes that promised nothing more than greater material reward for their labors.

And yet the sheer fertility of the Border's soil, superficially cultivated though it was by backward methods and outmoded tools, soon inundated the pioneers with surplus crops. Many of them welcomed an opportunity to market their produce for cash. And even the more idealistic always needed money to pay old debts, to purchase bare necessities like salt, ammunition, harness, and boots, and to maintain their wagons and equipment. Every farmer, or at least every farmer's wife, aspired to move on from the crude log cabin or musty sod hut to a neat frame dwelling with proper furniture and a touch of color in a table covering, a window curtain, or a picture on the wall. Money was needed for such "improvements," and until the crash of 1857 money was crying to be made. The crash, indeed, reminded many of how deeply they had sunk into the sin of covetousness, and in 1858 a new sweep of revivalism in the West recalled backsliders—for a time at least—to religion and church.

EXPANDING MARKETS

For all the Christian traditionalism of the "New Germanys" and the "New Norways," and the terrifying isolation of the American settlements, the prairie farmers in this Age of Progress were in fact the vanguard and support of a world-wide business surge. In Europe, industrialism was spreading, the last serfs were being freed from their ties to the land, cities were growing rapidly, tariffs on agricultural imports were coming down, the exchange of currencies was being simplified. Accompanying these social changes were the revolutions, famines, and wars that cast so many immigrant families onto American shores in search of asylum and a fresh start. These circumstances taken together created a lively demand for foodstuffs which the virgin American West, manned so largely by the immigrants themselves, could quickly supply.

Nor was the business ferment restricted to Europe. After 1844, American ships and the vessels of other nations enjoyed new rights in the treaty ports of China; in 1854, Commodore Matthew Perry, with a fine show of American naval power, opened up the "Hermit Kingdom" of Japan to American trade; in 1856, Siam broadened the privileges accorded 20 years before to American exporters; and all this stirring in the Pacific warmed our interest in salubrious Hawaii. The Orient never became a market for the produce of American farms, but Oriental trade in other goods helped transform the American merchant marine into the largest fleet in the world and its home ports into booming metropolises. In these ports, as in the great cities of Europe, landless multitudes were clamoring to be fed.

In the West itself the farmers were also finding growing markets at government frontier forts, among the loggers who had recently opened up the north woods of Wisconsin and Minnesota, and among the lead miners who, after the 1830's, extended their operations from Galena, Illinois, into neighboring Wisconsin and Iowa. Gold-mining camps farther west even than the organized frontier settlements had also begun to look to the nearest farmers for flour and meal.

From the beginning of the westward movement, corn was always the first marketable crop of the frontier settler. Easily converted into fattened hogs (which were commonly turned loose in the corn fields to "hog down" the ripened ears), corn could be made to walk to market when other transportation was lacking. Corn was also suitable winter feed for beef cattle, which could be walked even farther than hogs. For human consumption, corn was distilled into a potable and packageable "likker," or was eaten off the cob, baked into bread, and prepared in many other ways. In the famine years of the late 1840's, even the hungry Irish brought themselves to eat American corn; but they and other Europeans never developed a taste for it, and corn failed to become a stable or significant export. In the United States, on the other hand, corn bread and corn-fed pork made up the bulk of the national diet.

As late as 1849, Tennessee and Kentucky had led in the production of corn-fed hogs. Ten years later these states had fallen behind Indiana and Illinois. In the production of corn itself, Illinois by then had risen to first place; Missouri had passed Tennessee and Kentucky; and Iowa, Kansas, and Nebraska were making noticeable inroads on the market. American corn production reached 838 million bushels in 1859, an increase of 40 per cent in ten years, and most of the gain was supplied by the Middle Border states.

Wheat was far more selective than corn in soil and climate, and even in suitable latitudes it grew best on land that had already produced a corn crop. In 1849, Pennsylvania, Ohio, and New York were the leading wheat states. By 1859, though the country's total wheat production had soared 75 per cent to a record 173 million bushels, each of these three states produced less wheat than it had a decade earlier. Illinois, Indiana, and Wisconsin had moved to the head of the wheat states; and in succeeding decades, reflecting the momentum of the westward surge of wheat-growing, first Iowa, then Minnesota, then Kansas, and then the Dakotas entered the ranks of the leaders.

Acre for acre, wheat paid better than

The first landing of Americans in Japan, under Commodore Matthew C. Perry, on July 14, 1853.

corn, over which it had advantages both in marketing and production. Unlike corn, wheat was eaten all over the world. Less bulky than corn in relation to value, it could bear high transportation costs more easily, and it also withstood shipment more successfully. Finally, on the open prairies and plains, where land was plentiful and hired labor scarce, wheat production responded magnificently to improved tools and labor-saving machinery.

MECHANIZED FARMING

The western farmer's first need in the way of equipment was a new plow. Back in 1837, John Deere, an Illinois blacksmith, had produced the first American steel plow, and by 1858, after making many improvements on his original design, he was manufacturing 13,000 a year. Light enough for a strong man to sling over his shoulder, the Deere plow nevertheless was the first to cut deep, clean furrows in the prairie sod. Nor did it take bovine strength to draw it, and the weaker but faster-moving horse began to supplant the ox on western farms. So great was interest in plow improvement that by the time of the Civil War 150 varieties of plows were on the market, and experimenters were working on steam-powered "plowing engines" that could cut as many as six furrows at once.

Even more striking improvements were being made in machines especially designed for wheat-growing. Cyrus Hall McCormick of Virginia (in 1834) and Obed Hussey of Ohio (in 1833) had patented practical steel-toothed reapers in the early days of the

westward movement. With McCormick's horse-drawn machine a single man could do the work of five men equipped with scythes. Sales lagged, however, until in 1848 McCormick (while Hussey languished in the East) moved his plant to Chicago and hurried his demonstrators off to the western frontier. Ten years later, by means of the "American System," as admiring Europeans had begun to call the assembly of interchangeable parts, McCormick was manufacturing 500 reapers a month and was still failing to keep up with the demand.

At first, entire neighborhoods had to be mobilized to harvest the vast quantities of wheat the new reapers could cut down. But in the 1850's progress was being made in the design of mechanical wheat-binders, which in the next decade would eliminate much of the harvesting army. In the 1850's, mechanical threshers were already in use, and, according to the census report of 1860, they were 60 per cent more efficient than "the old flail mode."

In 1800, the average American farmer had spent about $15 to $20 for his tools, and the equipment the emigrants toted west in the 1840's was worth little more. By 1857, *Scientific American* was recommending that every farmer with 100 acres of land should have machinery worth about $600. Although many wheat farmers got along with less, the expansion of wheat production could not have occurred had not most of the farmers sloughed off their traditional methods and adopted mechanized techniques. By the time of the Civil War, about $250 million was invested in

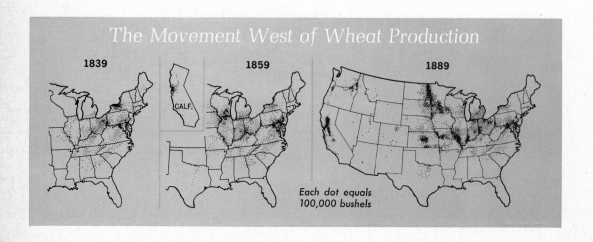

The Movement West of Wheat Production

1839   1859   1889

CALF.

Each dot equals 100,000 bushels

Thresher of the 1850's was powered by horses on treadmill.

farm implements and machines, an average of about $120 for each farm in the country. On the wheat farms of the prairies and the plains, the average investment was much higher.

FARMING AS A BUSINESS

Once the western farmer had committed himself to machinery, he found his life greatly altered. The most disturbing change came from his discovery that he was suddenly in the grip of forces over which he had less and less control. His key machines, for example, such as reapers and threshers, could speed the production of wheat but they could be used for little else when the wheat market fell off, as it did in 1854. The fact that these machines were usually purchased on credit and that the debt had to be paid in cash further narrowed the farmer's range of choice, for wheat, the specialty of the new machines, was also the cash crop *par excellence.* When wheat prices fell the wheat farmer was simply forced to grow more wheat than ever in order, at lower prices, to get as great an *aggregate* cash return as before. But increasing his wheat production often meant breaking or buying new land, either of which would plunge him still more

deeply into debt. Then he would need still larger wheat crops in order to acquire the cash to maintain the payments on his larger obligations.

The continuous round of specialization, mechanization, and expansion in the free West gave a momentum to wheat production that was a priceless boon to the world. Other aspects of wheat-growing on the prairies and the plains, however, were hardly boons to the farmer. In some years, frost, hail, and other visitations far more severe than in the East destroyed much of the crop before it could be harvested. Even in the best growing seasons, moreover, the servicing of broad new markets seemed to involve an endless spiral of new charges. The steps between the wheat-grower and the ultimate urban consumer, for example, seemed to multiply disastrously with distance. All along the line, weighers, graders, storage-elevator operators, rail and water carriers, warehouses, local haulers, insurers, money-lenders, and speculators—the whole urban apparatus of finance and distribution—mysteriously placed a hand on the farmer's fate, and worse, in the farmer's pocket.

The world-wide collapse of prices in 1857 staggered the wheat farmer. His debts went unpaid, the threat of foreclosure and

369

indeed foreclosure itself soured his prospects, and his mind turned once more to the free frontier. In 1858, western wheat farmers began attending meetings other than religious revivals, and from these meetings arose broad denunciations of conspiratorial "trading combinations," monopolistic elevator and railroad operators, and grasping moneylenders. The farmer's special place in God's plan was given renewed publicity, and the farmers were urged to "assert not only their independence but their supremacy" in society. Vague proposals also began to be made for farm cooperatives and for state and federal control of railroads and other big businesses.

Out of it all, before the Civil War, came a stronger demand than ever for two specific programs. One was for agricultural colleges to educate farm youths in the science of agriculture and to afford them broader educational opportunities as well. These colleges were to be set up by the federal government and financed by federal land grants. The second demand was for free homesteads—free of payment and free of slaves—on the remainder of the public domain. Over southern opposition, Congress enacted a land-grant college bill in 1859, only to have President Buchanan veto it. In June, 1860, he vetoed a homestead bill that would have made western lands available at 25 cents an acre. In the elections later that year, the farmers of the West, crying the slogan "Vote Yourself a Farm," helped carry the country for Lincoln, even though they were aware that his policy of no extension of slavery to the territories could carry the nation to war.

THE AGRICULTURAL REVOLUTION IN THE EAST

Right up to the outbreak of the Civil War southern planters remained active customers of the western farmers, but the great bulk of western grain and meat flowed to the Northeast. So great did this volume become that the agricultural revolution in the West forced upon the East an agricultural revolution of its own.

Let the West "supply our cities with grain," William Buckminster of Massachusetts had said in 1838:

We will manufacture their cloth and their shoes. [Our farms] shall find employment in furnishing what cannot so well be transported from a distance. Fresh meats, butter, hay, and the small market vegetables must be supplied by the farmers of N. England.

What Buckminster had foreseen developed with a rush in the following 20 years —not only in New England but also on the more friendly soil of other eastern states. Two items that Buckminster failed to enumerate became the most profitable of all—milk and fruits.

Dairying, once a routine chore in most households, had become big business by 1850. In that year, the Harlem Railroad brought about 25 million quarts of milk into New York City. Every other sizable city in the East had developed its own "milk shed," a nearby expanse of pasture land where carefully bred and carefully tended herds of cows were reared especially for milk production.

Fruit orchards were as common as pastures in the East. But after 1840, the growing of apples and peaches was expanded and brought under scientific care. Strawberries, blackberries, and many varieties of melons added interest and nourishment to the urban American's diet. The tin canister, or the "tin can," an English invention for packaging perishables, which became widely used in America in the late 1840's, enlarged the market for such products and even extended it to men at sea.

A revival of scientific farming in the East furthered the agricultural revolution in that section. An earlier scientific farming movement, which had been restricted to gentlemen farmers, had died in the 1830's. But after 1845, when success or failure hinged increasingly on special knowledge and up-to-date processes, eastern dirt and dairy farmers took a keen interest in information about climate, soils, fertilizers, methods of cultivation, and the idiosyncrasies of different crops. Agricultural associations, fairs, magazines, books, courses, and schools all multiplied in the East in the 1840's and 1850's.

Railroad and water routes between the East and the West encouraged each section to produce specialties of its own. Railroads and water routes *in* the East and especially in New England so covered the land that farmers in this section could specialize in perishables with the assurance that their produce would be speeded to city markets.

III. *A Modern Transportation Service*

THE REVIVAL
OF FOREIGN TRADE

When the Civil War began, the railroad had become the dominating factor in the economy of the free North and a powerful influence on the welfare of the entire nation. But the railroad had to fight for ascendancy, and during the period of its rise other avenues of exchange and other forms of transport were helping to build up the country.

One of the most important commercial developments of the 1840's and 1850's was the revitalization of America's foreign trade. During the depression that followed the crash of 1837, foreign trade had fallen to a point well below the level even of the early years of the Republic. In 1843, combined imports and exports were only $125,250,000, a trough never touched in the preceding 30 years. Then began an almost continuous rise to a record $687,200,000 in 1860. In almost every year during this period, imports exceeded exports. Eighty per cent of the half-billion dollars in gold taken from the California mines before 1857 was sent abroad to make up the difference. The rapidly increasing export of western wheat and flour helped keep the imbalance within reasonable limits.

The revival of foreign trade had a tremendous effect on immigration. Without the vast fleets of merchantmen that plied the Atlantic between Europe and America, the millions of newcomers to the United States in the late 1840's and in the 1850's could never have found passage to the New World. Seventy-five per cent of American commerce, and an even greater proportion of the immigrant traffic, was carried in American sailing ships.

The average westward crossing by sail from Liverpool, England, to New York took about 33 days. Steamships, which had been used in ocean commerce since 1838, could make this crossing in the 1850's in 10 to 15 days. But they were unreliable and excessively costly to operate. As late as 1899, all ocean steamships carried sails for auxiliary or emergency power. By 1860, only a tiny fraction of the world's ocean commerce had been captured by steamships, most of which were British.

THE SURGE
OF DOMESTIC COMMERCE

In the fifteen years before the Civil War, American domestic commerce far surpassed even the record foreign trade both in volume and rate of growth. The vitality of foreign trade itself contributed significantly to this development, for the mere collection at American ports of commodities for export created a great deal of business for home carriers. Similarly, the need to distribute to the interior the increasingly voluminous imports landed at a few great coastal cities added steadily to the demand for domestic transportation.

But domestic commerce was far more than an adjunct of foreign trade. As the American population grew—and it grew with phenomenal rapidity in the free North in the 1840's and 1850's—the home market naturally expanded. As different regions began to specialize in particular commodities, the need for exchange among them increased. Exchange itself was made easier by the gold being mined in California and by the improved credit facilities of the expanding banking system. Between 1851 and 1860, money in circulation in the

The clipper ship, Flying Cloud.

United States, including specie and bank-notes, rose 9 per cent per capita. But the importance of this increase to trade was even greater than this figure indicates, for the telegraph and the railroads were now speeding up business transactions and accelerating the collection of bills. This meant that the actual money in circulation could be used many more times in a single year than heretofore; and, since the amount of money itself was rising rapidly, the whole pace of domestic commerce quickened. Between 1843 and 1860, while American foreign trade grew five and a half times, domestic trade grew ten times. By 1860, domestic carriers were hauling goods worth at least 15 times the combined value of exports and imports, or about $10 billion worth a year.

THE CLIPPER SHIP ERA

Before the railroad boom of the 1850's, domestic commerce was almost monopolized by water carriers; and of these carriers the oldest and for a long time the most successful were the coastal sailing ships. In 1852, the value of goods carried by American coastal vessels (the coastal trade was closed by law to foreign ships) was three times the value of goods hauled by the railroads and canals combined.

The most glamorous period of coastal commerce was the era of the clipper ship,

the boldest commercial sailing vessel ever built. The designers of the clippers, among whom Donald McKay in East Boston, Massachusetts, was the unchallenged master, drew out the ordinary three-masted packet ships to extraordinary lengths and then reduced the ratio of beam to length so drastically that traditional shipbuilders were dazed. The result was the most graceful hull that ever took to the sea. The hulls were topped with the tallest masts available and the largest spread of canvas ever to challenge a captain's courage. The captains themselves were selected from among the most relentless "drivers" of the day. Probably the most famous of the clipper ships was McKay's aptly named *Flying Cloud.* Launched in the summer of 1851, she made a day's run of 374 miles during her maiden voyage—"the fastest day's run," writes the historian Robert G. Albion, "yet made by a ship—nearly forty miles better than any steamship travelled in a single day up to the Civil War."

The first genuine clippers were built early in the 1840's in an attempt to shorten the seemingly endless voyage to the Orient, where trade, as we have seen, had taken a promising turn. But the clippers came into their own with the growth of California gold mining after 1850. Since the clippers' designers had sacrificed cargo space for speed, their owners had to charge higher rates for their limited cargoes than most shippers could afford. To the California adventurers, however, money was no obstacle and speed was all-important. Conventional sailing ships arriving at San Francisco in the summer of 1850 from Boston and New York had averaged 159 days for the journey around the Horn. The next summer, *Flying Cloud* arrived from New York after a voyage of 89 days, 21 hours, a record that stood until she herself reduced it by 13 hours three years later. It was for this "coastal" trade that most of the great clipper ships were built and in it that they enjoyed their golden era.

Unfortunately for the clippers, they were beaten at their own game just about the time they seemed to have perfected it.

Even before the gold rush to California, New York steamship operators had organized an alternate route by which the trip to the West Coast could be completed in five weeks or less, as against the clippers' best time of three months. This route involved sailing to Panama, a portage across the Isthmus, and then sailing north again in another steamship to American ports. At first this route was intended to serve the settlers of Oregon, but by the time the initial voyage was made, in January, 1849, news of the California gold discoveries had swept through the country, and San Francisco supplanted Oregon as the main destination.

The difficulty with this short cut to the West Coast was the Panama portage, a nuisance that discouraged many travelers and made the handling of heavy freight impossible. Even so, enough profit was made by the New York entrepreneurs to attract Cornelius Vanderbilt, the richest man in the country, who had made his fortune as a ship operator. In 1851, Vanderbilt launched a competing line to the West Coast, using a Nicaragua portage instead of the one across Panama. In 1855, Vanderbilt, in turn, was challenged by still other New Yorkers bold enough to try to dislodge him from Nicaragua by supporting William Walker in his successful efforts to take over the government of that country. Vanderbilt promptly retaliated by hiring agents to raise a force among neighboring Central American states with which to overwhelm Walker's government. The conflict between the two camps effectively ended the Nicaraguan episode.

Events in Panama, meanwhile, greatly improved the competitive position of the original steamship operators. There, in 1855, after many engineering difficulties had been overcome, an efficient railroad was opened across the Isthmus. This railroad and its affiliated steamships virtually monopolized traffic to the West Coast until 1869, when the first transcontinental railroad was opened across the United States (see p. 518). Long before that, many of the surviving clippers, their magnificence

quite tarnished, had sunk to the status of tramps sailing random routes with random cargoes under alien flags.

Sea-going commerce to California by sail or steam effectively tied the East and West coasts to each other and made a single, throbbing organism of the free states. It also sharpened the interest of northern businessmen in faster east-west carriers of heavy freight.

In response to this interest Congress, in 1853, instructed the army to survey potential routes for a trans-continental railroad. This decision stirred a hornet's nest of sectional controversy over the location of the first cross-country line, and not until the South left the Union in 1861 were the first transcontinentals chartered. By 1853, however, many lesser railroads and highways as well as the western river systems had begun to meet the expanding needs of inland commerce. They proved so successful that the coastal carrying trade, inescapably rigid and roundabout in its routes, suffered a precipitous decline.

THE STEAMBOAT CRISIS

The early success of coastal shipping can be attributed in large part to the great volume of goods brought down to Atlantic and Gulf ports over the navigable rivers with which the United States was so lavishly endowed. Most of the river traffic moved through the Ohio and Mississippi river systems (see p. 249), which profited both from the expansion of the free Northwest and the extension of cotton culture into the Southwest. All told, about 750 steamboats plied the western rivers in the 1850's, and the traffic they carried climbed to its historic peak in that decade. The boom probably was most spectacular on the upper Mississippi, where sleepy St. Paul became transformed into a bustling port by settlers sending first furs, then lumber, and then wheat, downstream. The bulk of river commerce was increased by an immense traffic in passengers, many of them immigrants heading west, but most of them native Americans characteristically on the go.

If the coastal trade suffered from having to traverse great distances over roundabout routes, the river trade suffered from the inflexibility of the main streams. Rivers could not be relocated to accommodate the inland settlers. River commerce reached its peak about 1851; but even then, so great had the total of domestic commerce become that the rivers carried but one-twentieth of it. By 1851, the upstart canals and the rising railroads each carried goods worth three times those transported on all the rivers of the country. The relative share of rivers in the commerce of the West, where other means of transportation were less developed than in the East, was no doubt much greater; but the fight to maintain this share proved less successful each year.

In order to compete with the railroads and canals, river men began cutting their rates to the bone. That was bad enough. but as they engaged in fierce competition among themselves for a worthy share of the traffic saved by rate-cutting, they also saddled themselves with suicidal rising costs. Never was western steamboat travel so speedy, so luxurious, so gilded with gaudy inducements at is was in the middle 1850's. But the river men themselves grew only more and more depressed. In days gone by, races between the river boats had been one of the joys of competition and had lent sparkle and spirit to river life. But now the grim competitors sought literally to knock one another out, and collisions, explosions, and fires took a sharply rising toll of property and lives.

COMPLETING THE CANALS

When canals between the East and the West were first built, the river men hoped that the new artificial waterways would serve as feeders to hungry river craft, just as the natural rivers fed the coastal carriers. And in many eastern states the canals actually did perform this function. None, of course, performed it better than the Erie Canal, which poured a flood of western commodities into boats standing ready at Albany to carry them down the Hudson to New York harbor.

And yet in the long run the Erie, in concert with the Ohio canals and others completed in the West before 1837, took trade away from the western rivers. By 1838, Buffalo, at the Erie's western end, was receiving more grain and flour annually than New Orleans itself. And once western canal construction had begun in the 1840's (there was little more canal building in the East after 1837), virtually every project was aimed at swinging more and more of the western trade away from the Mississippi system toward the North and the East.

Much of the canal-boat traffic originated right in the vigorous market towns that sprang up along the canal routes. By reversing the direction of southbound traffic on the Ohio, the Illinois, and the northern Mississippi, the canals transformed these once-proud rivers into humble feeder streams. By supplying commodities for the canal boats, the carriers on these rivers managed to compensate somewhat for the sharp decline in volume of their downstream runs.

In the 15 years before the Civil War, a struggle for control of western commerce occurred between the Mississippi River system and the Great Lakes—a struggle that paralleled the rivalry of the free states and the slave for control of the West itself. By the 1850's, the canals had swung the victory irrevocably to the Lakes. Two canals, one of which was foreign-built and neither of which was in any way associated with the great north-south river system, added to the Lakes' supremacy. The first was the Welland Canal, which circumvented Niagara Falls. Built by the Canadian government, this canal joined Lake Erie with Lake Ontario, and thence by way of the St. Lawrence River connected the Northwest with the East at Quebec. In the late 1850's, vessels laden with western goods were beginning the voyage from Chicago all the way to Liverpool, England, over this route.

The second Great Lakes canal was the Sault-Ste. Marie, popularly known as the

374

Soo Canal. This one was needed to by-pass the turbulent St. Mary's Falls, which blocked the passage of ships between Lake Superior and Lake Huron. After two years of incredible construction feats under the guidance of engineer Charles T. Harvey, the Soo was opened in April, 1855, just in time to catch the massive flow of iron ore from the Marquette range of northern Michigan to the mills of Pittsburgh, Cleveland, and Chicago. Northern wheat also found a convenient outlet through the Soo.

The value of goods carried by Great Lakes vessels, which was set at $150 million in 1851, quadrupled in the next five years. This increase reflected the growth of the canals that were diverting traffic away from the South, but it also reflected the rise of the western Great Lakes country itself as a power and a prize.

THE TRIUMPH OF THE RAILROAD

The striking extension of the canal system in the late 1840's and the 1850's serves to remind us that the railroad was not so obvious an improvement over other means of inland transportation as we might suppose. Practical steam locomotives had been invented in England and the United States years before 1829, when their commercial feasibility was first established. But as late as 1848 the directors of the Pennsylvania Railroad declared that "railroads must be used exclusively for light freight." They were wrong, of course. By 1860 Americans had built a railroad network 30,000 miles long—one of the marvels of the world. In that year, American passenger trains sped along at more than 20 miles an hour, though only at mortal peril to travelers, and freight trains carrying light and heavy freight alike averaged about 11 miles an hour.

Of the 3,328 miles of railroad track in the United States in 1840, a meager 200 miles lay rusting in the West, mute testimony to the debts and disappointed hopes of Michigan, Indiana, and Illinois (see p. 251). The rest of the mileage was shared almost equally by the Northeast and the

old South. No railroad linked the two sections, and neither section had succeeded in thrusting a line across the Appalachians to the Ohio or Mississippi valley. In 1840, Pennsylvania, with about one-third of all the northern mileage, was the nation's leading railroad state. But most of Pennsylvania's track had been laid in the northeastern part of the state, where small lines, privately built, had begun to haul anthracite to barges on nearby rivers and canals. The state government was determined to protect its canal system to the West—so determined, in fact, that even when the legislature did grant a charter in 1846 to the privately financed Pennsylvania Railroad Company, permitting it to build a line from Harrisburg west to Pittsburgh, the new company was required to pay the state's canal administration 3 cents for each ton-mile of freight hauled.

Second to Pennsylvania in railroad mileage in 1840 was New York State, most of whose lines were located in the Albany-Troy-Schenectady region at the eastern end of the Erie Canal, or west of that region roughly parallel to the canal itself. Until 1851 New York, as eager as Pennsylvania to protect its canal investment, forbade the railroads to carry any freight except when the Erie Canal was frozen over or otherwise closed to navigation. In 1840, New York City had only one tiny railroad, the New York and Harlem, which connected the metropolis with the independent town of Harlem seven miles to the north.

Boston's thriving capitalists, on the lookout for new investment opportunities (see p. 254), did not allow Massachusetts to lag for long in railroad construction. By 1850 almost every town in the state with 2,000 persons or more was served by trains. Boston became the hub of the whole New England railroad network, and, more important, rail connections with the Welland and Erie canals now made her a vigorous competitor for western trade. To further this trade, in

The DeWitt Clinton, *first railroad in Albany.*

the late 1840's Boston capitalists under the leadership of John Murray Forbes began investing heavily in railroads in distant western cities.

Baltimore was as free as Boston from the prior claims of a state canal system to western traffic. In 1842 the promoters of the Baltimore and Ohio Railroad began gathering new capital with an eye to pushing their road over the mountains to Wheeling, Virginia, on the Ohio River. The B.&O. actually reached Wheeling in 1853.

The enterprise of Boston and Baltimore in extending their railroads toward the West jolted Pennsylvania and New York out of their complacent confidence in canals. The Pennsylvania Railroad was opened from Philadelphia to Pittsburgh in December, 1852, months before the B.&O. itself reached Wheeling. Five years later, the Pennsylvania bought out the state canal system and the short railroad lines the state had built to feed the canals with traffic.

Henceforth, the Pennsylvania Railroad was to dominate the transportation structure of the commonwealth.

New York City gained its first western rail connection in 1851 when the Hudson River Railroad was opened all the way to the Erie Canal at East Albany. Two years later, under the direction of Erastus Corning, an iron manufacturer and former Mayor of Albany, seven independent railroads strung out from Albany to Buffalo were consolidated into the New York Central Railroad. In conjunction with the Hudson River Railroad, the Central could offer a continuous water-level route from New York to the West. A few years later, a second New York railroad, the Erie, was opened all the way from Jersey City to Buffalo, thereby becoming the fourth great eastern road in competition for east-west traffic.

By March, 1852, some 10,800 miles of railroad (about three times the mileage of

a decade earlier) had been completed in the United States, and an additional 10,900 miles were under construction. Most of the completed roads were either in the Northeast or else connected that section with waterways beyond the Appalachians. With few exceptions these railroads originated in the great cities and ran through hundreds of miles of rich and populous territory; clearly they promised to return ready profits to investors. Although most of the roads were assisted by state and local governments, they could be and were financed largely by the sale of corporation stock to private investors.

Most of the railroads built during the 1850's were in the West—in Ohio, Indiana, Illinois, Missouri, Michigan, Iowa, and Wisconsin. By 1860, these states, with 11,000 miles of track, had more railroads than the Middle states and New England combined. The western roads faced entirely different conditions from those in the East, for private investment capital was scarce beyond the mountains, population was sparse, and corporation stock difficult to market.

Before 1850, the federal government had given about 7 million acres of the national domain to road and canal companies to assist them in building transportation facilities in thinly settled areas. The recipients of these land grants could sell or mortgage the property in return for the cash they needed for construction and for operational expenses in the first few years. Congress made the first land grant for railroad construction in 1850, for the benefit of a system of railroads to run north and south from Chicago to Mobile, Alabama. Congressman Stephen A. Douglas of Illinois whipped this legislation through with the help of southern votes attracted by the Mobile terminal. Actually, Congress granted the land to the states that would be crossed by the railroads (except Tennessee and Kentucky, where the federal government owned no land), with the understanding that the states in turn would give the land to the companies that were chartered to build and operate the lines. All told, the first grant ran to 3,736,000 acres, 2,500,000 of them in Illinois, the only state to complete its part of the new system.

In the legislation authorizing this land grant, Congress had provided for a 200-foot-wide right-of-way, and had also relinquished the even-numbered sections (640 acres) of land to a depth of six miles on either side of the line. The government retained the intervening odd-numbered sections for sale at a later date. This grant served as the model for most subsequent grants of western lands, though some railroads were to receive their lands directly, instead of by way of the state governments. By 1860, Congress had granted 18 million acres in 10 states for the benefit of 45 different railroads.

In 1851, the Illinois state legislature was the scene of a heated contest among the financial interests struggling for possession of the land grant and for the privilege of constructing the new railroad. The victors were a group of New York capitalists allied with the Bostonian, John Murray Forbes, who called their company the Illinois Cen-

tral. Construction soon got underway and by 1858 Chicago at last was linked by rail with the Mississippi at Galena to the west and Cairo to the south. Forbes had interests in other western railroads, among them the Michigan Central, which linked Detroit with Chicago. Two years later, Chicago was also reached by the Lake Shore and Michigan Southern, which paralleled the Michigan Central across the state.

The next step in western railroad expansion was to push the rails across the Mississippi. By 1856 Forbes and his associates had integrated and constructed various lines to form the Chicago, Burlington & Quincy Railroad, the first to penetrate the state of Iowa from the east. By tying this line to the Michigan Central, and by making arrangements between the Michigan Central and Corning's New York Central, Forbes by 1856 was able to offer service all the way from New York City to Burlington, Iowa. Not to be entirely outdone, the Michigan Southern promoters soon tied their line with the Erie and other railroads to complete a system running from Jersey City in the east, through Chicago to Rock Island, Illinois, on the east bank of the Mississippi just across from Davenport, Iowa.

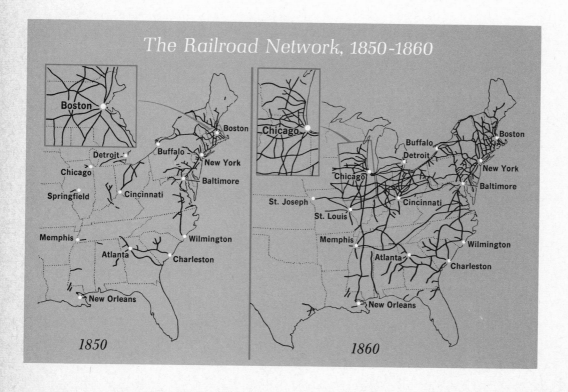

The Railroad Network, 1850-1860

1850

1860

In 1851 Chicago did not have a single railroad connection with another city. By 1856, it had become the nation's largest railroad center. Almost 2,500 miles of track radiated out from the city into the East, the South, and the West, tapping the traffic of 150,000 square miles. By 1860, a total of 5,000 miles of track extended Chicago's connections from the Atlantic all the way to the Missouri River at St. Joseph, Missouri. The Mississippi River had been bridged in twelve places, nine of them served by roads connecting with Chicago, a mere three with St. Louis.

All over the West the railroad knocked out the canal systems and decimated river traffic. Railroad trains were faster than canal barges or steamboats. Moreover, railroad spurs could be laid directly to factory doors and warehouses. The competitive practices of railroad managers hastened their triumph. Where they encountered water rivals, the railroads cut their rates even below cost to capture the available traffic. They recouped the losses on such runs by charging all the traffic would bear at non-competitive terminals.

And yet two waterways survived the inroads of the railroads. One was the Great Lakes route, over which heavy freight like wheat and iron ore could still be carried more efficiently than it could by freight cars. The other was the Erie Canal. The continued use of these two waterways reflected the massive volume of the east-west trade, which needed every carrier available to meet the demands of the rising population of the western farms and the eastern cities. As for the east-west railroads themselves, the census of 1860 reported, "So great are their benefits that, if the entire cost of railroads between the Atlantic and the western States had been levied on the farmers of the central west, their proprietors could have paid it and been immensely the gainers."

IV. *The Advance of Northern Industry*

INDUSTRY AND THE UNION

"Could the Union endure?—that," writes Allan Nevins, "was the anxious, all pervading question that faced the politicians" of the 1850's. "Could a truly national utilization of the country's resources be achieved?—that was the major question confronting business leaders." The steamboat and clipper-ship operators, and the canal- and the railroad-builders, had done everything they could to further this "truly national utilization." But by drawing the East and the West closer together, they seemed only to broaden the chasm between the free states and the slave. The spread of manufacturing in the free states, and the southern states' continued concentration on cotton-growing, made still clearer the profound differences in their ways of life.

In the 1850's southern businessmen—merchants, land-speculators, manufacturers, and railroad promoters—sometimes saw that their section's future lay in joining the "truly national" development of the country. Some of the richest planters themselves were investing their fluid capital in northern lands, northern mines, and northern railroads. But these southerners, who were among the last to yield to their section's secessionist agitators, remained but a corporal's guard in an overwhelmingly agrarian society. The southern leaders decried the fact that as cotton-planting flourished, their section's entire economy grew more and more dependent on northern textile factories for markets, on northern ships to carry cotton to factories abroad, and on northern bankers and brokers to finance cotton transactions. At the same time, they made a virtue of southern character, which, they said, saved men from the demeaning industrial and commercial pursuits.

Northern businessmen, in turn, often valued their southern business connections.

Almost without exception they deplored the abolitionist campaign in their own section, and were among the last to yield to the cry for war once the South had left the Union. Yet few northern businessmen, uncoerced, would restore to embittered New Orleans or St. Louis the commerce that New York and Chicago had captured by enterprise and energy. Fewer still would grant the slaveocracy the first transcontinental railroad or the western lands it would traverse. Southerners might take part in the country's development, and welcome. But they could not be allowed to forestall it or fence it in.

In the 1850's, the North was almost unanimous in the belief that the country's growth would proceed apace even if the South should desert the Union. In the North in the 1850's, writes Nevins, "the underlying forces of the industrial revolution were simply irresistible." Among them he notes the country's natural resources, the movement of immigrants into the labor force, the energy and inventiveness of the people, the flow of capital from California gold mines and from abroad, government friendliness to industrial objectives as shown in tariff policies and low taxes, and government subsidization of transportation. All these, he writes, "combined like a chain of bellows to make the forge roar."

INDUSTRY AND FARMING

And yet even in the North the roar of industry had only begun to be heard. As late as 1860, the richest northerners were, with few exceptions, merchants rather than industrialists. Among them were H. B. Claflin, who had built up a great wholesale drygoods business on the modern principle of mass sales at low unit profits; A. T. Stewart, one of the creators of the American department store, whose retail emporium later became John Wanamaker's in New York; and Charles L. Tiffany, who made his fortune selling jewelry and silverware to other rich merchants. China traders like John Murray Forbes and importers like George Griswold, Jonathan Sturges, and Morris Ketchum,

not industrialists, also supplied much of the early railroad enterprise and capital in the United States.

The stock-in-trade of all these men had been manufactured goods not from American factories or handicrafters but almost exclusively from abroad. The limits of industrial progress in the United States before 1860 are indicated by the urgent missions the North itself had to send to Europe at the outbreak of the Civil War to purchase arms and woolen cloth for uniforms. These purchases, like the imports brought in before the war, were paid for largely by the export of our vast agricultural surpluses, whose value even during the years of "irresistible" industrial progress was increasing at a faster rate than the value of manufactured goods.

The first fairly accurate census of American manufactures was taken in 1850. The results were doubly dramatic, for they showed (1) that the annual output of American industry had just passed $1 billion in value, and (2) that this figure was a few million dollars more than the value of all agricultural products, including cotton. In the next ten years, as the Census of 1860 showed, American manufacturers had pushed their production almost to $2 billion. (The exact figure was $1,885,862,000.) Yet by 1860, agriculture seems to have regained the lead it had lost ten years earlier, for agricultural commodities were now valued at $1,910,000,000.

The growth of manufacturing and the growth of agriculture, of course, reinforced each other. As the industrial cities grew, their landless populations provided expanding markets for farm products; and as the number of farms increased, farm families provided an expanding market for domestic manufactures. Yet it is remarkable how closely related to agriculture large segments of American manufacturing still remained. One of the great industries of 1860 was the making of lumber from the virgin forests that still covered much of the nation's land. Lumber production that year was evaluated by the census at $105 million, about equal to the value of cotton-textile production itself. Far higher than either in value were the flour and meal produced by the milling industry, whose output in 1860 was placed by the census at nearly $250 million—more than one-eighth of the nation's entire industrial production. The distilling of spirits, the brewing of beer, the tanning of leather, and the packing of meat also were growing rapidly.

All these industries were represented in the cities of the East, but it was the factories of the West that produced the greatest volume. The scale of their operations, however, was not the only modern characteristic of these factories. By the 1850's, many lumber mills had begun to *specialize* in the production of barrel staves or shingles or railroad ties, and employed single-purpose machines for the work. Specialization and mechanization characterized other industries as well, particularly meat-packing, which, in addition, developed to a high degree the modern principle of utilizing by-products. The hams and shoulders of hogs were packed as meat. Then the rest of the flesh was rendered into oil, which was in demand as a lubricant and shortening; the bristles were used for brushes; the blood for chemicals; the hooves for glue. What remained of the animals was then ground into fertilizer.

Another modern feature of meat-packing was the use of inclined tables down which each carcass would slide past a stationary worker who was responsible for removing a particular part. This "continuous-flow" method remains one of the main principles of the modern assembly-line technique. In the milling of flour, mechanical conveyor belts were achieving the same "continuous-flow" economies. One of the great industries of the West was the manufacture of agricultural machinery, in which mass production based on the assembly of interchangeable metal parts was perhaps more advanced than in any other industry in the United States.

PROGRESS IN INVENTION

At the 1851 "world's fair" held at the Crystal Palace in London, few exhibits won greater admiration than the display of American farm devices. Everything from road-scrapers and sausage-stuffers to curry-combs and hayrakes "bore off the palm" for their "ingenuity, utility, and cheapness." Few of these inventions were ever patented, and we know hardly any of the inventors' names.

Non-agricultural inventions still were far less numerous than agricultural ones, but they helped swell the number of patents issued by the United States Patent Office each year after it was opened in 1790. In 1835, a record number of patents, 752, were issued; in 1860, 4,700 were granted. Most, no doubt, went to the actual inventors of the devices, but some went to those who only promoted their ideas.

One of the great inventions of the nineteenth century was the electric telegraph, for which Samuel F. B. Morse, a painter, received the first American patent in 1840. But Morse's contribution to the telegraph, which was perfected for commercial use in the United States in 1844, had more to do with promotion than with mechanics. Back in 1831, Joseph Henry, one of America's most brilliant scientists, and later the first director of the Smithsonian Institution in Washington, rang a bell with an electric impulse transmitted over a mile of wire. This accomplishment was based on knowledge about electricity that had taken a century to accumulate—knowledge with which Morse had scarcely a nodding acquaintance. In 1837, Henry made his idea available to an English inventor, Charles Wheatstone, who proceeded to furnish his homeland with practical telegraph service. The principal American contribution to telegraph operation was the "Morse Code," but Morse himself designed neither the apparatus nor the alphabet, for which much of the credit belongs to his partner, Alfred Vail.

It was Morse, however, who prodded Congress into contributing financially to the telegraph's development in 1843. With government money, Morse staged the famous tableau on May 24, 1844, in the Supreme Court Chambers in Washington, when he sent the message, "What hath God wrought?" to Vail in Baltimore, who then returned it. This demonstration aroused great public interest in the telegraph, and companies began bidding for the rights to use it. By 1860, there were 50,000 miles of telegraph wire strung about the United States, and the next year a transcontinental service was opened.

In England, the telegraph was first used in controlling railroad traffic, an application that came later in the United States. The first use to which the American telegraph was put was to transmit business messages and public information. Its effect on the newspaper business was enormous. The "penny press" already dominated American journalism, and printing machinery had been developed that could produce 1,000 newspapers an hour. But with the coming of the telegraph, the demand for newspapers leaped so sharply that there was a demand for presses which could turn out at least 10,000 an hour. This resounding figure was achieved in 1847 with the cylindrical press developed by Richard March Hoe. Steady improvement thereafter in presses and other printing equipment enabled publishers to keep pace with the people's growing appetite for "hot news," advertising, and printed entertainment.

Two industrial patents merit special notice: (1) the vulcanization of rubber, and (2) the sewing machine. "India" rubber (most of which came from South America, though the East Indies supplied some) had a unique imperviousness to rain, snow, and mud, but when it was exposed to heat it melted, grew sticky, and collapsed. Finally, after years of effort, Charles Goodyear, a stubborn, sick, impoverished Yankee, hit on just the right mixture of raw rubber, chemicals, and heat that would yield a stable product at all ordinary temperatures. This process, called "vulcanization," was patented by Goodyear in 1844. A profitable rubber-goods industry quickly arose,

licensed under Goodyear's patent. Goodyear himself died in 1860, leaving debts of $200,000.

Before the automobile, most rubber was used in the boot and shoe industry—an industry that received another boost with the patenting of Elias Howe's sewing machine in 1846. This invention aroused little interest in America until 1851, when Isaac Merritt Singer entered the picture. Singer was a clever inventor in his own right, and he made many improvements on Howe's original machine. But his main contribution was the invention of installment selling, an idea he sold through mass advertising. Having worked up an impressive market demand, he proceeded to mass-produce the machines by means of assembly-line methods. By 1860, a total of 110,000 sewing machines had been manufactured, largely for home use but for factories as well. Almost all boots and shoes were now factory-sewn, and the ready-made-clothing industry now made its appearance.

Before the Civil War, the announcement of new inventions often led to the development of entirely new industries—some for the manufacture of the new devices, and others for their employment. This tendency attests to the genuine creativity of American society, but it also suggests that our industrial community was still a long way from maturity. The only genuinely advanced industry in the United States was the manufacture of cotton and woolen goods, and here spectacular new inventions were no longer to be looked for. Even so, a continuous round of invention greatly speeded up production and turnover.

The acceleration of the industrial pace was more marked in the cotton-goods industry than in woolens. But in both, new machines like the Crompton loom, which permitted the weaving of patterns, and new applications of chemistry, which led to improved dyes of many colors, added to the variety of factory-made cloth. Middle-class consumers now had a wide range of styles and qualities to choose from at prices importers no longer could match. Women became increasingly conscious of fashion, and began to feel that they had to follow the annual shifts in style if they were to keep up with the Joneses. By 1860, the cotton-goods industry ranked second only to milling in value of product. This category, of course, included the value of the raw materials. In "value *added by manufacture*," the cotton-textile industry was the nation's leader.

THE IRON INDUSTRY

The whole cycle of invention from the simple steel plow to the Hoe press and the sewing machine gave a great boost to the American iron industry. New reapers and threshers, rakes and seed drills, were fabricated from iron and steel parts. By 1860, about 3,500 steamboats had been built for the western rivers alone, and all of them required boilers made of iron sheets —as well as boilers to replace those that blew up. The hulls of the clipper ships were themselves reinforced with iron forms. The telegraph was strung entirely with iron wire until copper began to replace it in the 1860's. By 1846, John A. Roebling, the future builder of the Brooklyn Bridge, had begun to use wire rope in bridge suspension. Four years later, James Bogardus, an imaginative New Yorker, erected the world's first completely cast-iron building. Cast iron buckled under strain; but when wrought-iron beams began to be rolled for building construction, the invention of the skyscraper was in the offing. The first wrought-iron building was New York's Cooper Union, erected in 1854. Machinery for the manufacture of textiles and for other industries also required growing amounts of iron. And for machines that made machines, iron was indispensable.

By far the biggest single user of iron in the 1850's was the railroad—for rails, locomotives, wheels, axles, and hundreds of other parts of the railroad's stationary equipment and rolling stock. The railroads, moreover, had by far the most extensive machine shops in the country, which not only made parts and repairs but also turned out their own iron and steel tools and machinery.

In the refining of iron ore and the manufacture of iron products, as in so many other industrial processes, heat is the key element. One of the fundamental changes in iron manufacture after 1840 was the rapid shift in fuel from wood and charcoal (half-burned wood) to anthracite and coke (half-burned soft coal). Far greater temperatures could be attained with these new combustibles, and the rate of production was boosted to still higher levels. A second great change was the widespread use of rolling mills, in place of the hand forge, for shaping iron forms. Improvements in iron-making were reflected in a four-fold increase in the production of pig iron in the two decades between 1842 and 1860, when its annual volume stood at 920,000 tons.

Dramatic as all these developments seem, the American iron industry in the 1850's developed very slowly in comparison with progress abroad. In 1860, the United States was mining less iron ore and manufacturing less pig iron than Britain had been 20 years earlier. Britain's coal production in 1860 was five times the output of United States mines, and even little Belgium mined 60 per cent as much coal as Americans did. In 1856, Abram Hewitt, America's leading iron manufacturer, observed: "The consumption of iron is a social barometer by which to estimate the relative height of civilization among nations." But America's consumption of iron merely suggested that the country had a long way to go to catch up with the other industrial nations of the day.

Certain scattered incidents underline the immaturity of our industrial spirit. In 1829, drillers had brought in an oil gusher in Kentucky; but it only terrified and angered the workmen, who had been looking for salt. Two years later, Joseph Henry had worked out the essentials of the electric dynamo; but many decades were to pass before his "philosophical toy," as he called his electromagnetic machine, found practical employment. In 1847, William Kelly, a Kentucky ironmaster, had discovered the essential process for the mass production of steel; but scarcely anyone was apprised of his discovery until an Englishman, Henry Bessemer, sought American patents in 1856 for a similar process and the machinery for its use. Even so, it was another 15 years before Bessemer steel was being produced in large commercial quantities in the United States.

v. *Industry and Society*

By 1860, invention and industry had begun to transform the face of America and the character of its people. But the majority of farmers and the commercial elements in the cities misjudged—and with good reason—both the force and the imminence of the revolution that was taking place. Three years before, in 1857, the country had suffered a severe economic decline. But there had been panics in the past, notably in 1819 and 1837, so there was nothing particularly remarkable in the occurrence of yet another one.

Still there were certain peculiar features in the crash of 1857 that might have given a hint of the extraordinary changes America had undergone in the preceding 20 years. For one thing, the unemployment that followed the crash was far more severe than anything the country had yet experienced. By 1857, factory employment had risen to 1,300,000, and together with construction laborers made up an industrial working force of almost 2 million persons. Even when they were employed and received regular wages, the members of this new urban proletariat suffered from the worst working and living conditions that had yet been found in America. Factories had become the centers of petty tyrannies ruled by foremen who themselves were under unremitting executive pressure to keep the hands busy and the rebellious away from the plants. Back-breaking tasks and long hours helped to quench the spark of leadership in the ranks, and efforts to form unions and gain reforms were pitiful. Organization and strikes were also deterred because living conditions in the segregated slums of large industrial cities had grown so miserable that many workers preferred to put in long hours in the factories, sheltered and among friends, rather than spend their time at home. Under these circumstances, the

Run on a New York bank during the Panic of 1857.

crash of 1857, which threw hundreds of thousands out of work, was necessarily more brutal than earlier ones.

Earlier panics had been precipitated largely by the absorption of capital in land-speculation at prices far in advance of any reasonable expectation of return. By 1857, overinvestment in productive facilities was very important in bringing about the stringency of funds. By then more than a billion dollars had been invested in manufacturing and another billion in railroads, two-thirds of it in the seven years just preceding the crash.

The source of funds for these investments introduced another new element, which was still to grow in importance—speculation in corporate stocks and bonds. Securities often were bought with mere token down payments eked out with high-interest loans from New York banks. These banks, in turn, often paid interest to depositors, among whom were included so many other banks that in the late 1850's, 70 per cent of the entire country's bank reserves were on deposit in New York. In times of financial emergency, country banks sought to withdraw some of their funds from the metropolis. To satisfy their country bank depositors the New York banks would have to call in the loans made with the country deposits. Such action was almost certain to distress city security speculators and push many of them into bankruptcy. Their failures, in turn, left their creditor-banks insolvent or nearly so.

On August 24, 1857, the New York branch of the Ohio Life Insurance and Trust Company, Ohio's leading bank, was forced to close its doors after discovering that its treasurer had embezzled most of its funds. The parent bank in Ohio soon failed, causing runs on many New York banks. By October 13 all but one of them had closed down, as had most of the banks in the country.

This crash confirmed conservatives in their belief that American finance had changed very little since 1837. There had been huge land-speculations in the 1850's, the number of banks in the country had expanded rapidly, and their loans had grown faster than their numbers. But American industrial overexpansion lay at the bottom of the trouble. From the crash, fortunately, industrialists and financiers learned valuable lessons.

In the 1850's most leading businessmen were still merchants, many of whom hoped, like the diarist Philip Hone, to earn enough by 40 to retire to the good things of life. But the representative businessmen with the future on their side already were industrial corporation executives, often administrators for absentee owners or scattered stockholders, confronted with the high daily toll of overhead costs, alert to rapid changes in technology, markets, and sources of raw materials, sensitive to the nuances and rumors of the money markets. Such men no longer looked for profits in the lucky voyage or the fortunate speculation or the simple soundness and progress of the country. Profits would come henceforth from strict attention to management, from cautious financing, careful bookkeeping, enhancement of labor productivity, adaptability to changing markets. Profits promised to grow enormously beyond the dreams of speculative avarice; but they were likely to be made up of mountains of pennies and fractions of pennies, which were just as likely to disappear unless constant attention was given to such insignificant sums.

The lure of speculation did not die; unsettled conditions during the Civil War, and the expansion of the country after the war ended, created a speculator's paradise. But American industrialists had learned something of the industrial discipline; and the North, and ultimately the nation, were the stronger for it.

Readings

* Asterisk indicates that book is available in paperback.

Of the books suggested for Chapter 9, many are also important for this chapter, especially those by Roger Burlingame, S. E. Morison, G. R. Taylor, T. C. Cochran and William Miller, L. C. Hunter, Seymour Dunbar, R. G. Albion, C. F. Ware, V. S. Clark, and J. R. Commons. These may be supplemented with D. C. North, *The Economic Growth of the United States, 1790-1860* (1961); Stuart Bruchey, *The Roots of American Economic Growth, 1607-1861* (1965); Allan Nevins, *Ordeal of the Union* (2 vols., 1947), especially volume II, chapters I and V-VIII; and E. W. Martin, *The Standard of Living in 1860* (1942).

The writings of Hamlin Garland on the Middle Border are full of interest. The reader might start with *A Son of the Middle Border* (1917). A moving account of pioneer life in Illinois is Francis Grierson, *The Valley of Shadows* (1948). For the immigrants, M. L. Hansen, *The Atlantic Migration, 1607-1860* * (1940), is indispensable. Somewhat less formal is the same author's *The Immigrant in American History* * (1940). A more general account is Carl Wittke, *We Who Built America* * (1939). On the relation of the farmer to God and the soil, see H. N. Smith, *Virgin Land* * (1950). P. W. Gates, *The Farmer's Age: Agriculture 1815-1860* (1960), is the standard work.

On American trade the best general survey is E. R. Johnson, and others, *History of Domestic and Foreign Commerce of the United States* (2 vols., 1915). A thorough compendium of shipbuilding and shipping is J. G. B. Hutchins, *The American Maritime Industries and Public Policy 1789-1914* (1941). The leading works on the clipper ships are A. H. Clark, *The Clipper Ship Era, 1843-1869* (1910), and C. C. Cutler, *Greyhounds of the Sea* (1930). One of the best business biographies, and relevant to shipping as well as railroads, is W. J. Lane, *Commodore Vanderbilt* (1942). An excellent study of another New Yorker is I. D. Neu, *Erastus Corning, Merchant and Financier, 1794-1872* (1960). Most valuable on the canals is Carter Goodrich, *Government Promotion of American Canals and Railroads 1800-1890* (1960).

An excellent introduction to railroad history is F. A. Cleveland and F. W. Powell, *Railroad Promotion and Capitalization in the United States* (1909). More analytical from a modern "econometric" approach, is R. W. Fogel, *Railroads and American Economic Growth: Essays in Econometric History* (1964). A. D. Chandler, Jr., *Henry Varnum Poor: Business Editor, Analyst, and Reformer* (1956), stresses the role of management in railroad development. Exceedingly thorough on the theme indicated by their titles are L. H. Haney's *A Congressional History of Railways in the United States to 1850* (1908), and the same author's *A Congressional History of Railways in the United States, 1850-1887* (1910). The major work on New England railroads is E. C. Kirkland, *Men, Cities and Transportation 1820-1900* (2 vols., 1948). Useful railroad histories include F. W. Stevens, *The Beginnings of the New York Central Railroad* (1926); G. H. Burgess and M. C. Kennedy, *The Pennsylvania Railroad Company 1846-1946* (1949); and two books by Edward Hungerford, *The Story of the Baltimore and Ohio Railroad 1827-1927* (2 vols., 1928), and *Men of Erie* (1946). Two first-rate books on railroads and western lands are P. W. Gates, *The Illinois Central Railroad and Its Colonization Work* (1934); and R. C. Overton, *Burlington West* (1941). T. C. Cochran, *Railroad Leaders, 1845-1890: The Business Mind in Action* (1953), fulfills the promise of its subtitle.

Besides the volumes by Burlingame and others suggested at the head of this list, illuminating works on American industry and invention in this period include the imaginative *Made in America* * by J. A. Kouwenhoven (1948); the more analytical W. P. Strassmann, *Risk and Technological Innovation* (1959); and D. H. Calhoun, *The American Civil Engineer* (1960). On the iron industry, see Allan Nevins, *Abram S. Hewitt,* *with Some Account of Peter Cooper* (1935). Waldemar Kaempffert, ed., *A Popular History of American Invention* (2 vols., 1924), is very informative. An important book on a badly neglected figure is Thomas Coulson, *Joseph Henry, His Life and Work* (1950). On the conditions of labor, a basic account is Norman Ware, *The Industrial Worker, 1840-1860* * (1924). Worth reading too is C. M. Green, *Holyoke, Massachusetts, A Case History of the Industrial Revolution in America* (1939). On banking and the money market, see M. G. Myers, *The New York Money Market* (1931); L. H. Jenks, *The Migration of British Capital to 1875* (1927); and *Henry Varnum Poor* by A. D. Chandler, Jr., referred to above. Much the best account of the ups and downs of economic life is W. B. Smith and A. H. Cole, *Fluctuations in American Business, 1790-1860* (1935). G. W. Van Vleck, *The Panic of 1857* (1943), offers a readable analysis.

CHAPTER FIFTEEN

At the beginning of the 1850's the North
and the South, like two bellicose nations,
warily eyed each other. Responsible statesmen, of whom there were too few in either
section, tried desperately to find ways of
reconciling sectional differences, but powerful forces seemed to defeat their every effort.

The most divisive force, of course, was
slavery. Northern abolitionists, and growing
numbers of others in the North, looked
upon slavery as a sin, one all the worse for
its menace to the Union. To southerners,
slavery had become the linchpin of their
civilization, the agency of their material
well-being. If all the world was right about

A Decade
of Failure

slavery and had put it on the road to extinction, all the more tenaciously would the South, and a few outlying centers of the institution like Cuba and Brazil, defend it.

While abolitionists in the North and fire-eaters in the South heated the atmosphere, businessmen and promoters and indeed plain settlers in both sections continued to follow the main chance—to speculate, to settle the land, to seek profits from services and supplies to one another—overlooking sectional differences or sectional aims when they could. Moral issues often seemed secondary to them, but they could not go far along their own paths without encountering the moral combatants. In the promotion of railroads, the organization of territories, the settlement of disputed areas such as Kansas, businessmen plunged ahead. But those in the North and the South, full of the sense of their own righteousness and often heedless of the slave himself, also held their own fatal course.

In the past, political leaders had been able to mediate between the sections whenever the slavery issue threatened to upset the sectional balance. The Federal Convention of 1787, for example, had devised the "three-fifths compromise," and had put off for twenty years Congress's power to prohibit further slave importations. The next generation had negotiated the Missouri Compromise. Most recently, the great leaders who were just passing from the scene had exerted themselves to the utmost to bring about the Compromise of 1850. In the next decade compromise after compromise was attempted, even as late as 1861. But the bonds of the Union had become too frayed by sectional friction, the opposition of North and South too sharply honed by argument, and all compromise efforts failed.

1. *The Slave Issue Confronts Pierce*

HUNTING FUGITIVES

Franklin Pierce of New Hampshire took office as the fourteenth President of the United States on March 4, 1853. A "vain, showy, and pliant man," as a contemporary commentator said, Pierce quickly showed those qualities which made his administration quail before the contesting forces, free and slave, that sought to dominate the country.

Most Americans in 1853, including the President, still hoped that the Compromise of 1850 would stifle the agitation over slavery once and for all. But extremists did their best to keep the issue burning. The North had gagged particularly on the provision in the Compromise of 1850 requiring the return of fugitive slaves to the owners, and many northern states deliberately hampered the recovery of runaways. Actually, the number of slaves who managed to escape was infinitesimal, but the South regarded the northerners' cooperation with the fugitives as one more proof of the free section's conspiracy against southern institutions. Even those northerners, on the other hand, who disliked Negroes as much as they respected property, now began to condemn slavery as a stench to the whole nation and to look forward to the time, as Lincoln put it later, when "the hateful institution, like a reptile poisoning itself, will perish by its own infamy."

The person who singlehandedly did more than any other American to deepen hatred of slavery was the novelist, Harriet Beecher Stowe. A New Englander who had lived close to slavery in the border city of Cincinnati, Ohio, Mrs. Stowe wrote *Uncle Tom's Cabin* (1852) in the belief that once the South recognized the sinfulness of the "peculiar institution," the Negroes would be freed. She felt no malice toward the slave-owners. The villain of her novel, Simon Legree, was a Yankee. Her most eloquent spokesman against slavery was a humane southern planter. The sensational incident, humor, and pathos of *Uncle Tom's Cabin* appealed to a vast audience in the North, especially women, who responded with tears to the episodes of Negro mothers forcibly separated from their children. Southern matrons also wept at those passages.

Mrs. Stowe's novel sold 300,000 copies in its first year, and its stage version became a smash hit. One young southerner, after reading the novel in 1853, observed that it

A poster advertising Uncle Tom's Cabin.

390

... greatly tended ... to inflame one-half of the nation against the other, to produce disunion and to stir up a civil war. ... Can any *friend* of the human race, or any *friend* of the Negro desire such an issue?

Northern resistance to the Fugitive Slave Law was quickened by *Uncle Tom's Cabin,* and slave-owners pursuing runaways into free states often were glad to get home safely even without their quarry. In Chicago, Detroit, Boston, and elsewhere, federal officers trying to reclaim fugitive slaves were menaced by mobs.

THE OSTEND MANIFESTO

The South considered the incitement of runaways and the breakdown of the Fugitive Slave Law as clear violations of its constitutional property rights and sought counter-measures. A vociferous minority demanded the reopening of the African slave trade. A more influential group, supported by Pierce himself, sought the acquisition of Cuba, the slave-packed "pearl of the Antilles."

Cuba, like the rest of the Western Hemisphere, had been eyed by American expansionists for decades. In 1848 President Polk had offered Spain $100 million for the island, but was haughtily turned down. Three years later, although alarmed by two filibustering expeditions from the American mainland, launched by Cuban rebels against Cuba, Spain again rejected offers of purchase. In 1854, a naval incident at Havana in which, on a mere technicality, Spanish officials seized an American merchant vessel, gave Pierce an excuse to press the question once again, even though it was plain that a war with Spain over Cuba—given the excited state of popular feeling in the United States—would split the country and the Democratic party.

Before sitting down with Spanish representatives, Secretary of State William L. Marcy asked Pierre Soulé, the American minister in Madrid, to discuss the problem of Cuba with James Buchanan, the American minister in England, and John Y. Mason, the American minister in France. The three diplomats met at Ostend in Belgium,

and on October 15, 1854, sent a confidential dispatch to Marcy recommending that the United States offer $120 million for Cuba. If the offer was rejected, they added, "by every law, human and divine," the United States "shall be justified in wresting [the island] from Spain," on the ground that Spain's control of it gravely endangered "our internal peace and the existence of our cherished Union."

The diplomats were merely advising Marcy to do what he already contemplated; what he had hoped for from them was not this incendiary avowal of his own plans, but an estimate of how the European powers would react to them. When Pierce's enemies in the House of Representatives insisted on the publication of the confidential dispatch, what became known as "The Ostend Manifesto" was out of the pot. Free-soilers denounced it vigorously—the New York *Tribune* called it a "Manifesto of Brigands" —and Marcy had to repudiate its proposals.

Quite possibly enough public support could have been mustered by the Pierce administration to annex Cuba had not Congress, some months before the Ostend Manifesto, passed a momentous measure which, in the words of a New York paper, "has forever rendered annexation impossible." This was the Kansas-Nebraska Act, which, by reopening the question of slavery in the western territories, heightened northern determination to check the spread of slavery anywhere.

THE KANSAS-NEBRASKA ACT

Nebraska country, a veritable empire in itself ranging west of the 95th meridian all the way to Oregon Territory and north to the Canadian border, stood athwart the aspirations of the contending older sections of the country for two reasons: (1) Its southern part bordered the slave state of Missouri, but slaveholders were forbidden to extend their peculiar institution there by the Missouri Compromise of 1820; (2) this segment and the area north of it, all the way to the Great Bend of the Missouri River which now forms the eastern boundary of the State of Nebraska, also lay just beyond the "Permanent Indian Frontier" (see p. 319). Here, in the words of Stephen A. Douglas, and the italics are his, the Indians, by treaty, had been guaranteed "perpetual occupancy, *with an express condition that* [the land] *should never be incorporated within the limits of a territory or state of the Union.*" This "barbarian wall," Douglas continued, "was to have been a colossal monument to the God terminus saying to christianity, civilization and Democracy, 'thus far mayest thou go, and *no* farther.' "

As early as the congressional session of 1843-1844, "with a direct view of arresting the further progress of this savage barrier to the extension of our institutions," Douglas, then a freshman member of the House of Representatives from Illinois, had introduced the first bill to break the Indian treaties and organize the Territory of Nebraska. "From that day to this," Douglas wrote in December, 1853, when he had risen to the chairmanship of the Committee on Territories in the Senate, "I have taken care always to have a bill pending when Indians were about to be located in that quarter." Others, meanwhile, led by Senator David R. Atchison of Missouri, who vowed he would see Nebraska "sink in hell" before allowing it to be organized as a free territory, also had bills at hand to forestall any measure to keep slavery out.

Much else had risen besides Douglas himself by 1853, including his own aspirations for the presidency and the fever of the sectional conflict. The sectional conflict itself was intensified by the growing rivalry between North and South for the first transcontinental railroad.

By 1853, Douglas had become the leading spokesman for the construction of the first transcontinental over a northern route that would link the Pacific coast with his beloved Chicago, where he owned much real estate. But he was not selfish about that. "Continuous lines of settlement," he said then,

with civil, political and religious institutions all under the protection of law, are imperiously demanded by the highest national considerations. These are essential, but they are not sufficient. No man can keep up with the spirit of this age who travels on anything slower than the locomotive, and fails to receive intelligence by lightning. We must therefore have Rail Roads and Telegraphs from the Atlantic to the Pacific, through our own territory. Not one line only, but many lines. . . . The removal of the Indian barrier and the extension of the laws of the United States in the form of Territorial governments are the first steps toward the accomplishment of each and all of those objects.

For these purposes, Douglas reported his fourth and fateful Nebraska bill to the Senate on January 4, 1854.

Douglas' report was deliberately vague and crafty. He specifically undertook to apply in Nebraska, part of the Louisiana Purchase north of 36° 30′, the "popular sovereignty" provisions applied in the Mexican cessions of Utah and New Mexico by the Compromise of 1850 of which he was so proud (see p. 336). He would not, however, expressly repeal the Missouri Compromise, which specifically forbade slavery in Nebraska but not in Utah and New Mexico. Some "eminent statesmen," Douglas' report said, thought the Missouri Compromise was unconstitutional. But the Committee on Territories was "not now prepared" to make recommendations "as to the legal points involved." If they never came up, so much the better. On one unfortunate provision of the Compromise of 1850, nevertheless, the committee was prepared to make a recommendation: that in Nebraska, as in all other territories and states, the Fugitive Slave Law must be enforced.

Douglas' tactic has been called "astute." If, as his committee said, it hoped by this means to hasten the progress of the Great West while avoiding a repetition of "the fearful struggle of 1850," no doubt it was a supportable gambit and possibly the only one that offered any prospect of success. But its evasions also offered too attractive an invitation to the committed spokesmen of the contending sections to make the "legal points" Douglas so conspicuously passed up.

They lost little time in doing so, and in an especially incendiary manner because of the committee's shilly-shallying on freedom while standing firm on the return of fugitive slaves.

Douglas' report of January 4 ordinarily would have been only a routine step by which to place his Nebraska bill before the Senate in preparation for a full-dress debate at some future date. This date, as it happened, was to be January 24, but it was not until January 30 that formal debate began. By then, the bill had already been bitterly argued in and out of Congress and had been so fatally altered under sectional pressure that Douglas himself is said to have predicted that in its latest form it would raise "the hell of a storm."

Three critical alterations were made in the bill, two of them outright victories for the slave section, and the third, one which the South hoped to turn to advantage.

As orginally written it seemed that the bill did not necessarily deprive Congress of its constitutional power to "make all needful Rules and Regulations respecting the Territory . . . belonging to the United States," including those respecting slavery. If, as the bill said, the constitution of a new state in the territory itself permitted slavery, Congress appeared still to have the power to accept or reject this constitution during the admission procedure. Under unyielding pressure from Senator Atchison and his southern colleagues, who perceived this loophole, Douglas was forced to correct what he lamely called this "clerical error" in the bill, explicitly taking the power over slavery from Congress and giving it, "in the Territories and in the new States to be formed therefrom, . . . to the people residing therein, through their appropriate representatives." This change left Nebraska open to slaveholders, regardless of Congress or of the Missouri Compromise.

Once he had thus enlarged the area of application of the principle of "popular sovereignty," whose ambiguities had already become anathema to many in the North (see p. 332), Douglas was next forced specifically to concede, in the bill, that the

Missouri Compromise was henceforth to be "inoperative and void." It was "inconsistent," as the bill now read, "with the principle of non-intervention by Congress with slavery in the States and Territories, as recognized by the legislation of 1850 commonly called the Compromise Measures."

Douglas' third concession revolved around the railroad issue. It was clear to all that Congress at this time would help build no more than one transcontinental line. A government sponsored survey in 1853 had shown that a southern route along the Mexican border offered the fewest physical obstacles for the construction of such a line. The Gadsden Purchase from Mexico, in fact, had been made explicitly for possible railroad use (see p. 332). Atchison's pro-southern group in Missouri, at the same time, advocated a central route originating in St. Louis. They would not even consider supporting any transcontinental, including their own, which passed through territory forever closed to slavery. Fearful of their strength, and fearful that the southern part of Nebraska bordering Missouri would indeed fall to slavery, a group of Iowa congressmen urged Douglas to divide Nebraska into two territories to insure the passage of the transcontinental through the free valley of the Platte in the more northerly part. Douglas had said of the whole of Nebraska, "in that climate . . . it is worse than folly to think of its being a slaveholding country." Although skeptical of their fears, he felt constrained to concede the Iowans' request as he had conceded those of their enemies. His bill was altered to divide Nebraska into two territories, Nebraska and Kansas. And Kansas was immediately marked for slavery by the South.

These three alterations in fact make up the substance of the Kansas-Nebraska Act as finally passed on May 30, 1854. The first transcontinental was itself to remain a will-o'-the-wisp for ten more years. But the law was readied for the belated extension

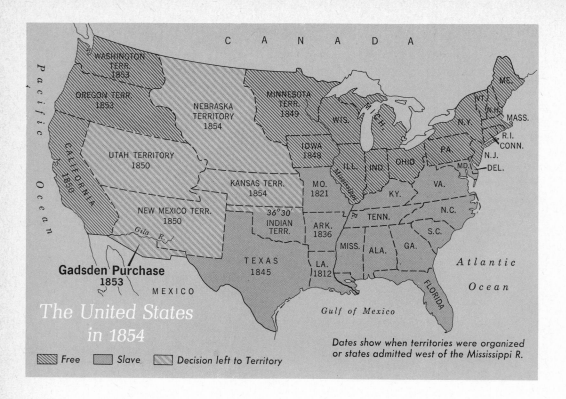

C A N A D A

WASHINGTON TERR. 1853

OREGON TERR. 1853

CALIFORNIA 1850

Pacific Ocean

NEBRASKA TERRITORY 1854

UTAH TERRITORY 1850

NEW MEXICO TERR. 1850

Gila R.

Gadsden Purchase 1853

MEXICO

TEXAS 1845

MINNESOTA TERR. 1849

WIS

IOWA 1848

KANSAS TERR. 1854

36°30'

INDIAN TERR.

ARK. 1836

LA. 1812

MICH.

ILL.   IND.   OHIO

MO. 1821

Mississippi R.

KY.

TENN.

MISS.   ALA.   GA.

ME.

VT.   N.H.

MASS.

N.Y.

R.I.

CONN.

PA.

N.J.

MD.   DEL.

VA.

N.C.

S.C.

FLORIDA

Atlantic Ocean

Gulf of Mexico

The United States in 1854

Dates show when territories were organized or states admitted west of the Mississippi R.

▨ Free   ▨ Slave   ▨ Decision left to Territory

of slavery into new country and for another dislodgment of the aborigines from it.

In the Senate, which was less subject than the House to political storms, the Kansas-Nebraska Act passed, 37 to 14. In the House, which in 1854 was up for election, the bill had much harder going before it squeaked through, 113 to 100. Every one of the 45 northern Whigs in the House voted against the bill. This group received the support of almost half the northern Democrats, thereby fracturing the principal *national* party, on whose unity Douglas himself had staked his own future as well as that of the Union. A solid bloc of southern Democrats and half the northern Democrats, on the other hand, together with the majority of the *southern* Whigs, had put the measure across. Thus the Whig Party was split as well.

It took southerners outside of Congress a little time to grasp the value of their coup. One paper declared that the Kansas-Nebraska Act was "barren of practical benefit." Others gradually came to see it as "a measure . . . just in regards to the rights of the South, . . . and reasonable in its operation and effect." In Missouri it was said that

Kansas must be a slave state because "it is suited and adapted only to slave labor," and because "we have both the numerical and moral strength to make it so." Howell Cobb of Georgia, sending Douglas his congratulations on the measure, declared that "he who dallies [in support of it] is a dastard and he who doubts is damned."

One reason for the South's growing truculence was the "mad ferocity" with which many in the North had begun to assault the measure from the start. The repeal of the Missouri Compromise, in particular, sent a thrill of excitement through the people. Lincoln himself wrote in his third-person autobiographical sketch that by 1854, "his profession had almost superseded the thought of politics in his mind, when the repeal of the Missouri Compromise aroused him as he had never been before." Perhaps the most influential attack, written while Douglas' draft was still undergoing alteration, but not widely published until after the act's adoption, was the "Appeal of the Independent Democrats in Congress to the People of the United States," the work mainly of Senators Salmon P. Chase of Ohio and Charles Sumner of Massachusetts, but also signed by other members. The "Appeal," one of the first stimulants for the formation of the Republican Party (see p. 397) branded the Kansas-Nebraska Act as a

(see p. 397)

> . . . criminal betrayal of precious rights; as part and parcel of an atrocious plot to exclude from a vast unoccupied region immigrants from the Old World and free laborers from our own States, and convert it into a dreary region of despotism, inhabited by masters and slaves.

That they were not to let this "betrayal" pass is clear from their other statements. "They celebrate a present victory," said Chase when the act passed the Senate, "but the echoes they awake will never rest till slavery itself shall die." Sumner added: The act was "at once the worst and the best which Congress ever enacted. It is the worst bill, inasmuch as it is a present victory of Slavery. . . . It is the best bill, . . . for it annuls all past compromises with Slavery, and makes all future compromises impossible. Thus it puts Freedom and Slavery face to face, and bids them grapple. Who can doubt the result?"

When Douglas himself attempted to speak in defense of his act, even in his home base in Chicago, he was hooted off the platform by members of his own party and menaced by mobs in the streets.

"BLEEDING KANSAS"

The Kansas-Nebraska Act failed its first test in the new territory of Kansas itself. Under the theory of "popular sovereignty," did a new territory have the power to prohibit or legalize slavery before framing its constitution and before seeking statehood? According to Douglas, it did. According to southern spokesmen, it did not. No territory could decide this question, southerners said, until it became a state. So long as it was still a territory it could not keep slaves out. As settlers moved into Kansas, the issue passed beyond debate.

Most of those who settled in Kansas after the organization of the territory were slaveless farmers from adjacent states. Along with them, as in all other frontier settle-

ments, came the characteristic body of rovers and opportunists bent on bleeding the newcomers. These men were indifferent to slavery, and indifferent to politics except as it offered patronage and prey. As a cover for their unsavory activities, they were no doubt callous enough to keep the controversy over slavery boiling.

Others, however, also helped turn Kansas into a battleground. To "beard oppression in its very den," as they said, the New England Emigrant Aid Company and similar associations organized in the North between 1854 and 1855 financed the migration of more than a thousand right-thinking Yankees to Kansas to see that the new settlers voted correctly when the issue of free soil or slavery came up, and to participate in the vote themselves. To support their mission, boxes of "Beecher's Bibles" were sent them. Henry Ward Beecher, a vigorous antislavery clergyman, had preached that rifles might have stronger effect than the Bible on the pro-slavery camp, and he was taken at his word. Missourians, led by the ubiquitous Senator Atchison, viewed this activity as part of an abolitionist plot to use Kansas as a launching pad for an assault on slavery in the entire Southwest. To forestall these Yankee "serfs," "paupers," and "cut-throats," as they called them, hotheaded Missourians—"bar-room rowdies," "blacklegs," and "border ruffians," said the Yankees, returning the compliments—as well as hundreds from Alabama, Georgia and South Carolina, also poured into Kansas, determined to pack the first Kansas territorial legislature with pro-slavery men.

On election day, March 30, 1855, slightly more than 2,000 Kansans were registered to vote, but over 6,000 ballots were cast, most of them by Missourians who had come into Kansas for this day only. Andrew H. Reeder, a Pennsylvania Democrat who had been appointed governor of the Kansas Territory by Pierce, tried to disqualify eight of the thirty-one members who had been elected irregularly, but Pierce himself refused to back his governor. Over Reeder's vetoes, the new legislature passed a series of savagely repressive laws that, among other punishments, prescribed the death penalty for aiding a fugitive slave. Simply to question the legality of slavery in Kansas carried a sentence of two years at hard labor.

But the free-soilers in Kansas were not intimidated. When Pierce eventually sent William Shannon to replace the uncooperative Reeder, the free-soilers sent Reeder to Congress as their territorial delegate. In the fall of 1855 they met in Topeka and drew up their own constitution. In January 1856, they elected their own legislature and Charles Robinson as governor.

With two rival administrations, Kansas was ripe for war. And in May, 1856, while Pierce hesitated, war came. At that time a force of pro-slavery men led by a United States marshal raided the Kansas town of Lawrence in search of some free-soil leaders who had been indicted for treason by the pro-slavery legislature. Fortified by alcohol, the raiders burned down the hotel, destroyed homes, and smashed free-soil printing presses.

This celebrated "sack of Lawrence," blown up to horrendous proportions by northern newspapers, took two lives and spawned a bloodier sequel. John Brown, of Osawatomie, Kansas, a fanatical abolitionist who was soon to become better known, gathered six followers, rode into the pro-slavery settlement at Pottawatomie Creek, and wantonly hacked five men to death. He acted, so he said, under God's authority. But his sacred vendetta started a guerrilla war in which over 200 persons were killed.

Violence over Kansas, moreover, had already spread from the territory to the very halls of Congress. On May 19, 1856, shortly after the "sack of Lawrence," but before news of the incident reached Washington, Charles Sumner of Massachusetts rose to speak in the Senate in favor of the free-soil constitution of Kansas. His speech lasting all of two days flailed away at the "harlot slavery," and especially at the "murderous robbers" of Missouri, "hirelings picked from the drunken spew and vomit of an uneasy civilization." But Sumner aimed his choicest epithets at Senator Andrew P. Butler, of South Carolina, and drove Butler's nephew, Preston Brooks, congressman from South Carolina, to avenge his uncle, his state, and his section. Two days after his speech, as Sumner sat at his desk in the Senate chamber, Brooks beat him repeatedly over the head with a cane and injured him so severely that Sumner remained an invalid for the next three and a half years. The assault on Sumner by "Bully" Brooks, together with the news from Kansas, came unfortunately just when preparations were being made for the presidential campaign in 1856.

A NEW PARTY ALIGNMENT

The decline of the Whig party had set in even before the election of 1852 (see p. 336), and the party's defeat in the presidential election that year speeded its breakup. Events during Pierce's administration, in turn, so aggravated sectional strife that the foundations of his own party, the Democrats, also crumbled. Their old allegiances broken, politicians and their followers looked anxiously for new homes.

The first of the new parties, the short-lived American party, raised its standard in 1852. *"Americans must rule America,"* said its leaders. The party took its name from its fundamentalist opposition to the growing foreign immigration of the period, especially of the Irish Catholics. In its first published platform in 1856, it urged "a change in the laws of naturalization, making a continued residence of twenty-one years, . . . an indispensable requisite for citizenship," and hence for the franchise. "Whether of native or foreign birth," it added, "no person should be selected for political station who recognizes any . . . obligation of any description to any foreign prince, potentate, or power."

The American party was itself so fearful of its own biases that it placed its members under strict regulations requiring them to pretend to "know nothing" when pressed for information. Thus they soon became known as the "Know Nothings." Plain snobbery and the spell of cabalistic hand-clasps and mystifying passwords no doubt added to the party's ranks. But the Know Nothings also made a more rational appeal to so broad a spectrum of the population that they saw themselves supplanting the Democrats as the great national party while the opposition shriveled up as the sectional party of the South.

The old Whigs in the cities, North and South, formed the foundation of American party ranks. But many Democrats, sick of the corruption of their own party machines under leaders who virtually owned the immigrant vote, also welcomed the chance to shift their allegiance. Native-born laborers, fearful of immigrant pressure on their wages; Protestants, alarmed by the increase of adherents of the Papacy; temperance reformers who associated Catholics with grog shops—all seemed eager to join up.

Nor were country contingents lacking, especially in the South. In upland North Carolina, for example, the old Whigs, who hated the Democratic slaveowners, became Know Nothings almost to a man. And even Democratic aristocrats found solid value in the movement. "Foreignism," said Congressman William Smith of Virginia,

brings 500,000 who settle annually in the free states with instincts against slavery, making fifty representatives in ten years to swell the opposition to the South. . . . The effect of Know Nothingism is to turn back the tide of immigration and our highest duty to the South is to discourage immigration.

But the new party won stanch enemies as well, among them the aroused Abraham Lincoln who was slower than most to disown his long Whig allegiance. Lincoln wrote in 1855:

I am not a Know-Nothing. That is certain. How could I be? How can anyone who abhors the oppression of negroes be in favor of degrading classes of white people? Our progress in degeneracy appears to me to be pretty rapid. As a nation, we began by declaring that 'all men are created equal.' We now practically

read it 'all men are created equal *except negroes.*' When the Know-Nothings get control, it will read 'all men are created equal except negroes *and foreigners and Catholics.*'

Like the two major parties, the American party could not avoid a split over the inescapable issue of slavery and when, in 1854, its national convention voted to support the Kansas-Nebraska Act, most of its following returned to the Democrats or joined the new Republican party.

One firm principle brought the Republicans together in 1854—the conviction that

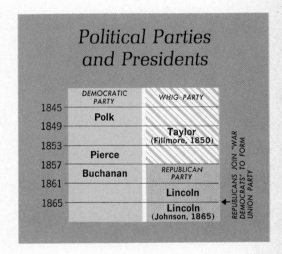

Political Parties and Presidents

	DEMOCRATIC PARTY	WHIG PARTY
1845	Polk	
1849		Taylor (Fillmore, 1850)
1853	Pierce	
1857	Buchanan	REPUBLICAN PARTY
1861		Lincoln
1865		Lincoln (Johnson, 1865)

REPUBLICANS JOIN "WAR DEMOCRATS" TO FORM UNION PARTY

Congress had the power to keep slavery out of the territories. Free-soilers, of course, flocked to Republican ranks. So did "conscience Whigs" and Anti-Nebraska Democrats, who rejected further compromise with the South. Even outright abolitionists joined up. Along with the nativist Know-Nothings, probitionists also came in. Oddly enough, German immigrants, their hatred of nativism and temperance proving weaker than their detestation of slavery, added a sizable contingent. Few Republicans seem to have had any special concern for the well-being or the future of the Negro. What they most wanted free was the land.

II. *Buchanan's Ordeal*

Franklin Pierce actively sought renomination for the presidency in 1856, and to improve his chances as the conventions approached he made militant gestures in Kansas as well as in foreign affairs. But the Democrats had had enough of his incompetence. At the same time they dared not nominate Douglas, whose successes, as in the adoption of the Kansas-Nebraska Act, were even worse than Pierce's failures. Instead they named a veteran of forty inconsequential years in politics, the conservative Pennsylvanian, James Buchanan, who as minister to Britain, had been out of the country and distant from the party squabbles of Pierce's administration.

"Old Buck" was soon to be despised as a "Dough-face," a northern man with southern principles. Temperamentally unsuited for leadership in a time of crisis, he was nevertheless an honest man and a lover of the Union. The efficient Democratic machine, moreover, brought him home ahead of his Republican opponent, the glamorous soldier-explorer, John C. Frémont. The expiring American party's candidate, ex-President Millard Fillmore, finished a poor third.

Although Buchanan won 174 votes in the electoral college, to Frémont's 114 and Fillmore's 8, his popular vote was only 45 per cent of the ballots cast. Nor did the sectional character of the vote augur well for the country. New England, stung by the Kansas-Nebraska Act and increasingly hostile to slavery, voted overwhelmingly (61.7 per cent) for Frémont. Frémont also won New York. Had he captured Pennsylvania and Illinois, the Republicans would actually have taken the election. Hence what solace the South found in the Democratic victory hardly compensated for the extraordinary Republican show of strength.

THE CASE OF DRED SCOTT

Buchanan was in office only a few days when the first great crisis of his administration confronted him. The trouble arose over the Supreme Court decision in the case of *Dred Scott* v. *Sandford,* which confirmed the southern contention that Congress had no right under the Constitution to exclude slavery from the territories.

Dred Scott, a slave, had been taken by his master in 1834 from Missouri to the free state of Illinois, and from there to the Wisconsin Territory where he stayed until his return to Missouri several years later. The anti-slavery group who backed his suit for freedom hoped to prove that Dred Scott's sojourn in free Illinois and in a territory where slavery was illegal under the Missouri Compromise had made him a free man. Scott lost his suit in the Missouri Supreme Court. His ownership, meanwhile, had passed into the hands of a New York citizen named Sandford, against whom Scott brought suit for his freedom in the United States Circuit Court. The case had been taken out of the Missouri courts and into the federal courts on the constitutional ground that it was an action between citizens of different states.

The Dred Scott case finally reached the Supreme Court in May, 1856, and was decided March 6, 1857. The justices might simply have dismissed it on the grounds that Scott was not a citizen of Missouri or of the United States and hence was not entitled to sue in the federal court. Or, falling back on an earlier Supreme Court decision (*Strader* v. *Graham,* 1850), they might have ruled that Scott's residence in a free state only suspended his slave status temporarily. But the Court knew that Buchanan was expecting it to resolve the thorny issue of the status of slavery in the territories, with which neither the executive nor legislative departments had had any success. Buchanan had even gone so far as to indicate his expectation to Justices Catron and Grier while the case was pending; and on receiving their agreement, he had stated in his inaugural address two days before the decision: The issue of slavery in Kansas "is a judicial decision which legitimately belongs to the Supreme Court of the United States before whom it is now pending, and will, it is understood, be speedily and finally settled."

No fewer than eight of the nine justices on the Supreme Court wrote separate opinions on different aspects of the *Dred Scott* case. In speaking for the Court for more than two hours, Chief Justice Taney spent half his time arguing that since Negroes had been viewed as inferior at the time the Constitution was adopted, its framers did not intend to include them within the meaning of the term "citizens." Therefore, the right of citizens of different states to sue in the federal courts could *never* apply to a former slave or descendant of a slave. Only two justices would concur in Taney's rank racial concepts and *ex parte* perversions of history. These two, and four others, however, joined Taney in finding that Scott, even had he become free, had reverted to slavery on his return to the slave state of Missouri under whose laws his status was determined. By those laws he was a slave; because he was a slave and not a citizen, he had no right to sue in a federal court.

Five justices joined the Chief Justice in plunging further. The slave, they said, is property, pure and simple. According to the Fifth Amendment to the Constitution, "No person shall be . . . deprived of life, liberty, or property without due process of law." The prohibition against taking slave property into the territories they found to be a violation of this clause. "No word can be found in the Constitution," Taney observed, "which gives Congress a greater power over slave property, or which entitles property of that kind to less protection than property of any other description." Thus Congress had no right under the Constitution to exclude slavery from the territories and the Missouri Compromise was, and always had been, unconstitutional.

The Kansas-Nebraska Act, as we have seen (p. 393), had already declared the Missouri Compromise "inoperative and void." If, as the Court now held, the attempt of the Compromise to legislate slavery out of the territories, was also unconstitutional, then the fundamental objective for which the Republican party itself had been organized was unconstitutional. Even the Douglas Democrats, moreover, were troubled about the decision, for if Congress did not have the power to exclude slavery from the territories, then neither did any territorial legislature which existed by congressional authorization, and "popular sovereignty" in the territories was dead.

Buchanan had been so confident of this agreeable settlement that he had gone on to say of the Court in his inaugural: "To their decision, in common with all good citizens, I shall cheerfully submit." But the New York *Tribune* accurately reflected northern opinion in its response to the President: "You may 'cheerfully submit,' of course, you will . . . But no man who really desires the triumph of Freedom over Slavery in the Territories will do so. . . . Happily this is a country in which the People make both laws and Judges, and they will try their strength on the issue here presented."

In June, 1857, as part of his continuing campaign against Douglas' "popular sovereignty" position, Lincoln said of the *Dred Scott* decision:

If this important decision had been made by the unanimous concurrence of the judges, and without any partisan bias, and . . . had been in no part, based on assumed historical facts which are not really true; or, if . . . it had been before the court more than once, and had there been affirmed and re-affirmed through a course of years, it then might be, perhaps would be, factious, nay, even revolutionary, to not acquiesce in it as a precedent.

But when, as it is true, we find it wanting in all these claims to the public confidence, it is not resistance, it is not factious, it is not even disrespectful, to treat it as not having yet quite established a settled doctrine for the country.

THE SECTIONAL ISSUE
HEIGHTENED

The burning issue of slavery in the territories was most comprehensively examined during the contest for senator from Illinois in 1858 after the rising Republican candidate, Abraham Lincoln, in July that year, challenged his Democratic opponent, "the little giant," Stephen A. Douglas, to a series of joint debates. Before the Lincoln-Douglas debates began, however, two events in 1857 and 1858 soured the hopes of the South as much as the Dred Scott decision had sweetened them.

The first of these events was the business panic of August, 1857 (see p. 384). The sudden collapse of the free enconomy did allow southern spokesmen to point with pride to the relative stability and success of the slave system. But the depression following the actual panic aligned all the more strongly with the anti-slavery Republican party (1) free businessmen (and the workers they employed), who favored the Republican plank for high tariffs to stimulate free industry and industrial employment; and (2) free farmers, who endorsed the Republican plank for free homesteads. The slaveocracy had a mortal fear of both high tariffs and free land and thus grew all the more determined to preserve for the southern political camp all the western territories not yet lost to slavery.

The second event was the state constitutional convention at Lecompton, Kansas, in October, 1857. Here, pro-slavery delegates named in a rigged election not only wrote a constitution explicitly guaranteeing slavery, but wisely, from their point of view, refused to permit the electorate as a whole to vote on it. Under severe pressure they did offer the electorate a proposition which restricted the entry of new slaves but which protected slave property already in the state. The dominant anti-slavery voters abstained from balloting on this proposition and the pro-slavery party thereby carried it.

Governor Robert J. Walker, a Buchanan appointee, confronted the President himself with his demand that all Kansas be allowed in an honest election to vote on the Lecompton Constitution. But Buchanan, leaning heavily in the direction of southern Democratic strength, decided that the vote on the slavery proposition was a valid vote on the constitution itself. He therefore presented the constitution to Congress as the document on which admission of Kansas as a state should be determined. Walker immediately resigned. Senator Douglas valiantly fought the entry of Kansas on these terms, but the bill accepting the Lecompton Constitution won in the Senate. In the House, however, "Douglas Democrats" in favor of honest "popular sovereignty" joined with Republican congressmen to defeat it.

The stalemate was broken in May, 1858, when Congress passed the English Bill that would grant Kansas immediate statehood together with a federal land grant if her voters decided to accept the Lecompton Constitution, or that would continue territorial status if they decided to reject it. Given the chance, Kansans overwhelmingly voted down the Lecompton Constitution, 11,812 to 1,926. Here the matter rested until 1861, when Kansas entered the Union as a free state.

THE LINCOLN-DOUGLAS DEBATES

The Illinois state Republican convention that was to nominate Lincoln as its senatorial candidate to run against Douglas met in Springfield on June 16, 1858. Here is how Lincoln described himself about this time: "It may be said I am, in height, six feet four inches, nearly; lean in flesh, weighing on average one hundred and eighty pounds; dark complexion, with coarse black hair and gray eyes. No other marks or brands recollected." Lincoln was cleanshaven during this period. His lank frame, careless dress, and rugged yet sensitive face were not so well known as they soon would be, but in Illinois he was already a popular figure, a prosperous lawyer and Whig leader who had served a term in the United States House of Representatives. In his speech accepting the senatorial nomination, he observed that the slavery issue had grown worse each year. "In my opinion," he said, "it will not cease until a crisis shall have been reached and passed. 'A house divided against itself cannot stand.' "

This address, subsequently known as the

"House Divided" speech, was carefully studied by Senator Douglas and furnished the basis for his attacks against Lincoln. The seven Lincoln-Douglas debates that followed went beyond local issues and touched on questions affecting Americans everywhere. Douglas, who admired Lincoln personally, stigmatized him as a sectionalist whose "house-divided" philosophy would end in "a war of extermination." Why, Douglas asked, did the Republicans say that slavery and freedom could not peaceably co-exist? Lincoln replied that his party did not propose to interfere with slavery where it already existed, nor did he wish to enforce social equality between Negro and white, as Douglas alleged. But, in keeping with the Republican program, he flatly opposed the further extension of slavery. At Freeport, Illinois, Lincoln then asked Douglas a momentous question: "Can the people of a United States territory, in any lawful way, against the wish of any citizen of the United States, exclude slavery from its limits prior to the formation of a State constitution?" To answer this question, Douglas either had to abandon his popular sovereignty concept or defy the Dred Scott decision. If the people could not exclude slavery, popular sovereignty meant little. If they could exclude it, popular sovereignty was as much in conflict with the Dred Scott decision as the Republican principle of congressional exclusion.

Douglas answered that the people of a territory could take this step, in spite of the Dred·Scott decision. Slavery could not exist for a day, he explained, if the local legislature did not pass the necessary laws to protect and police slave property. Therefore, merely by failing to arrange for slavery, a territorial legislature, without formally barring it, could make its existence impossible. His realistic answer kindled further opposition to him in the South, and widened the split in the Democratic party, as Lincoln had expected. Douglas won the senatorial election in the state legislature despite Lincoln's popular plurality, since inequalities in apportionment permitted Douglas men to dominate. But the war be-

tween Douglas and Buchanan's administration left the Democratic party more divided than ever before.

JOHN BROWN'S RAID

The most portentous event in the sectional struggle was John Brown's raid on the federal arsenal at Harpers Ferry, Virginia, October 16, 1859. Brown and his men actually captured the arsenal, but the next day a company of United States Marines under Colonel Robert E. Lee assaulted the group, killed 10 and took Brown prisoner.

Brown's wild scheme was believed to be nothing less than an attempt to foment a slave revolt by distributing the captured military stores to the Negroes. Eminent northern reformers had known about the plan, and although they did not incite Brown to violence, they did provide him with money and weapons ostensibly intended for anti-slavery partisans in Kansas.

Brown's exploit might have been passed off in normal times as the act of an unbalanced mind, but coming when it did, it brought a furious reaction. Throughout the South, vigilante groups beat up and banished anyone who was suspected of anti-slavery sympathies, and dangerous books were publicly burned. Governor Wise of Virginia did nothing to calm the excitement. Huge meetings in New York, Boston, and elsewhere, meanwhile, organized by northern conservatives, attacked Brown and his methods. Seward, Lincoln, Douglas— men of all parties—joined in the condemnation. But when Wise rejected the plea of Brown's relatives and friends that Brown was insane and ordered him hanged, he insured Brown's martyrdom. The bravery and dignity of Brown on the scaffold touched millions of people who had abhorred his deeds.

Now, if it is deemed necessary that I should forfeit my life for the furtherance of the ends of justice, and mingle my blood further with the blood of my children and with the blood

"John Brown Going to His Hanging," by Horace Pippin.

of millions in this slave country whose rights are disregarded by wicked, cruel, and unjust enactments, I say, let it be done.

So spoke John Brown. His demeanor prompted one conservative New Yorker to confide in his journal: "One's faith in anything is terribly shaken by anybody who is ready to go to the gallows condemning and denouncing it." The deification of John Brown that followed was partly the work of American writers like Emerson and Thoreau, who converted a brave monomaniac into an "angel of light." After the execution, as Thoreau observed, John Brown became "more alive than ever he was."

By convincing many in the South that the entire North was implacably hostile to slavery, the John Brown episode weakened further the frayed ties that held North and South together. "I have always been a fervid Union man," wrote a North Carolinian shortly after Brown was hanged, "but I confess the endorsement of the Harpers Ferry outrage . . . has shaken my fidelity and . . . I am willing to take the chances of every probable evil that may arise from disunion, sooner than submit any longer to Northern insolence and Northern outrage."

III. *No Compromise*

LINCOLN'S ELECTION

In April, 1860, the Democratic national convention assembled at Charleston, South Carolina, the very heartland of secession sentiment. Southern extremists had resolved to insist on a plank in the party platform declaring that neither Congress nor a territorial government could abolish slavery or impair the right to own slaves. Northern Democrats, hoping to nominate

Douglas, were no less firm for popular sovereignty. When it became evident that the plank advocating federal protection of slavery in the territories could not be adopted, most of the representatives from eight southern states withdrew. Their departure made it impossible for Douglas to get the two-thirds of the ballots needed to win the nomination, and the convention adjourned.

On June 18 the Democrats reconvened in Baltimore. When the southern delegates bolted once more, this convention went ahead to nominate Douglas on a popular-sovereignty platform. The southerners then met independently on June 28 in Baltimore and chose John C. Breckinridge of Kentucky, himself a moderate, to represent their position on slavery in the territories. With two Democrats in the field, the last unionist bond—a great political party with large followings in both North and South—had broken.

The Republicans, buoyed up by the Democratic fiasco at Charleston, met in Chicago on May 16. Their most impressive leader was William H. Seward of New York. But Seward had a perhaps undeserved reputation as an extremist because he once had spoken of the "irrepressible conflict" between North and South. The unsavory reputation of his backer, the political boss Thurlow Weed, and the rowdy actions of Weed's henchmen at the convention, also handicapped him. Two other possibilities were Salmon P. Chase of Ohio and Edward Bates of Missouri. The former's reputation for radicalism exceeded even Seward's; the latter's flirtation with the "Know Nothings" had alienated the German vote. But it was Abraham Lincoln, strongly supported by the powerful Illinois and Indiana delegations and acceptable to both East and West, who won the nomination on May 18. Lincoln had written to a friend six weeks before the convention: "My name is new in the field; and I suppose I am not the *first* choice of a very great many. Our policy, then is to give no offence to others—leave them in a mood to come to us, if they shall be impelled to give up their first love." This strategy paid off when the Pennsyl-

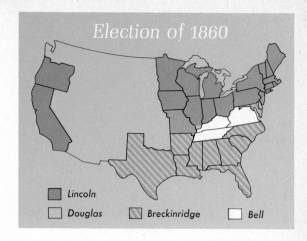

Election of 1860

Lincoln — Douglas — Breckinridge — Bell

vania and Ohio delegations threw their strength to Lincoln instead of Seward.

The Republican platform made a shrewd appeal to powerful economic interests and at the same time sounded a high moral tone. It included planks for a protective tariff, free homesteads, a Pacific railroad, and the rights of immigrants. It denounced southern disunionism and expressly denied "the authority of Congress, of a territorial legislature, or of any individuals to give legal existence to Slavery in any Territory of the United States." Practical politicians knew that to win the election, Pennsylvania and either Illinois or Indiana would have to go Republican. The tariff was a bid to the iron interests in Pennsylvania; Lincoln was the lure to Indiana and Illinois.

A fourth group, calling itself the Constitutional Union party, assembled in Baltimore on May 9 and chose John Bell of Tennessee for the presidency. Basing its hopes on such unionist sentiment as might be found in all sections, this party vainly, and vaguely, called on the people "to recognize no political principle other than the Constitution of the country, the Union of the states, and the enforcement of the laws."

The 1860 election presented the remarkable picture of a divided nation simultaneously carrying out two separate contests for a single office: one between Breckinridge and Bell in the South, the other between Lincoln and Douglas in the North. Ten southern states did not even place Lincoln's name on the ballot. Of his 1,866,000 popular votes, Lincoln won a meager 26,000 in the entire South. Douglas, although acknowledged as a candidate, also ran poorly there. In the North, at the same time, Breckinridge, the other Democrat, and Bell, the Constitutional Unionist, made no headway. Only in Missouri, California, and Oregon could the election be described as a contest between more than two of the four parties. In Missouri, where Douglas won by a bare 140 ballots, all four candidates ran pretty evenly. Douglas and Breckinridge also made good showings in the Pacific states. Lincoln carried California by 643 and Oregon by 264 out of 119,000 and 13,000 votes respectively.

Although sectional loyalties proved decisive in the 1860 election, the significance of the unionist vote in the South must not be overlooked. Bell won Kentucky, Tennessee, and Virginia; he barely lost Maryland and Missouri. Breckinridge had a clear majority in only seven southern states and in his sole campaign speech flatly denied that he was a disunionist or had any disunionist connections. Nevertheless, although Lincoln had a decisive majority in the electoral college, he carried less than 40 per cent of the popular vote, and none could deny that a sectional candidate had become president of the United States.

THE DEEP SOUTH MOVES OUT

Southern leaders had repeatedly warned after Lincoln's nomination that a Republican victory would be followed by secession—for, as the governor of South Carolina put it, the election of a sectional northern candidate would . . . "inevitably destroy our equality in the Union, and ultimately reduce the Southern states to mere provinces of a consolidated despotism, to be governed by a fixed majority in Congress hostile to our institutions and fatally bent upon our ruin."

These expectations perhaps supply the best answer to the question, Why did the South move out? During the 1850's, three free states, California, Minnesota and Oregon had been added to the Union, but no slave state had come in. The North, growing visibly and rapidly in wealth and population, had also linked itself firmly with the West by railroad connections. It was winning the new territory. Would it not ultimately become strong enough to act directly against slavery and destroy the civilization of the Old South.

An informed southerner could hardly have imagined that the election of Lincoln would lead to immediate abolition in states where slavery had always been legal. Lincoln denied any such intention. His party, moreover, controlled neither the Senate nor the Supreme Court, which was still composed, as in the days of the *Dred Scott* case, of five southern and four northern justices. Many southerners, of course, were not well informed, and looked upon Lincoln as nothing but, "the daring and reckless leader of Abolitionists." To understand secession, it is also important to understand that, aside from its more profound motivations, few men in the South anticipated its melancholy aftermath. It was by no means certain that the North would go to war to keep a reluctant South in an unhappy Union. And if war came, why should not the South win, and quickly? Many southerners imagined that the will to fight in the crass commercial civilization of the North would be weak. For success they also looked to the sympathy of foreign aristocrats, the commercial power of "King Cotton," and to pro-southerners in the North who would sap its spirit.

Secession also had positive lures. No longer would the South be drained of its resources by paying taxes and tariffs that chiefly benefited the North. No longer would it pay tribute to northern banking and shipping interests. Perhaps the slave trade would be reopened and more cheap labor brought in. Cuba, Santa Domingo, Mexico, even territories in Central America, beckoned enterprising planters.

On December 20, 1860, South Carolina at last took the initiative to bring such thinking to fruition. A convention formally repealed the state's ratification of the Constitution and withdrew from the Union. By February 1, 1861, six other commonwealths—Mississippi, Florida, Alabama, Georgia, Louisiana and Texas—had reluctantly followed her example. In almost every case, even in the deep South, the momentous step was taken over articulate opposition ready to give Lincoln a chance to show whether he would really enforce the Fugitive Slave Act and meet other southern demands.

Perhaps the most important debate took place in Georgia, whose wealth, geographical position, western connections, and railroad communications made her allegiance essential to the secessionist cause. In men like Herschel V. Johnson, Benjamin H. Hill, and Alexander H. Stephens, the Georgia moderates had able spokesmen; and in the northern hill country and pine-barren areas, inhabited by small farmers and stockraisers, unionist sentiment was strong. But the rich cotton-planters in the Savannah River valley and the urban Georgians led by such extremists as Senator Robert Toombs, Governor Joseph E. Brown, and Howell Cobb carried the day. Secessionist delegates at the state convention defeated by a vote of 164 to 133 the proposal to postpone action until a convention of slaveholding states had presented southern demands to the North. Fatalistically accepting defeat, a number of moderates then voted

with the disunionists to take Georgia out of the Union, January 19, 1861.

As in Georgia, cooperationist sentiment in Alabama centered in the relatively slaveless sections in the northern counties. Secessionists in the state convention outnumbered the unionists 54 to 46, thus assuring secession on January 11, 1861, but 33 of the delegates refused to sign the secession ordinance without a state plebiscite and blamed the extremists for refusing to consult with other southern states before voting.

Unionism had strong advocates in both Louisiana and Texas, but here, too, the disunionists cleverly circumvented the opposition. In Texas, Governor Sam Houston—an uncompromising unionist—blocked secession efforts for a while by refusing to call the legislature into session. "You may," he warned a Galveston crowd, "after the sacrifice of countless thousands of treasure and hundreds of thousands of precious lives, as a bare possibility, win Southern independence, if God be not against you; but I doubt it." This was a brave stand, but

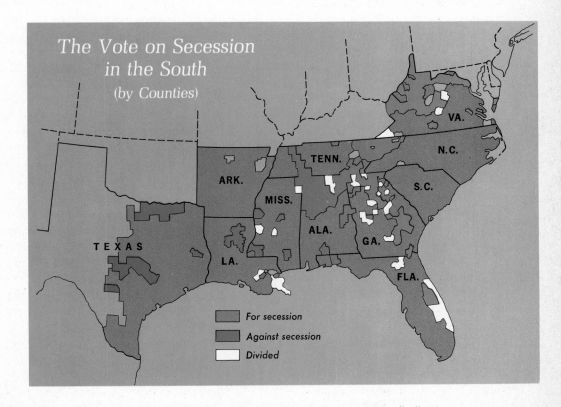

The Vote on Secession in the South (by Counties)

For secession
Against secession
Divided

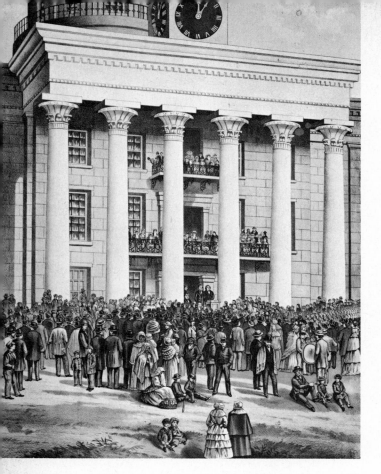

The inauguration of Jefferson Davis, February 18, 1861. Copy of a photograph taken in front of the State Capitol, Montgomery, Alabama.

the disunionists nevertheless forced Houston to call a state convention which voted to submit the secession ordinance to a plebiscite, the only one held in the lower South. In this dramatic test the secessionists won by a majority of more than 3 to 1.

Pockets of unionism persisted in the lower South. Yet by the spring of 1861 the majority of southerners of all classes were ready to secede. Older men naturally were more cautious about making the break. "It was disgusting to me," wrote an Alabama father to his secessionist son, "to think that I had Raised a child that would Cecede from under the government that he was born and raised under. . . . Tha have got you puft up with Cecessionism as tight as a tode I dont See what you nede to Care for you hant got no Slaves." His son replied as most young firebrands would: "Henry Bell Is my Name

406

and fite I will before I will submit to black republican princiles lose my life I will first."

On February 4, 1861, with seven states having seceded, but with Texas absent, delegates from six states met at Montgomery, Alabama, to form a new government, which they called the Confederate States of America, to adopt a new flag, the "Stars and Bars," and to write a new constitution.

A FEDERAL VACUUM

Secession, which had begun promptly with Lincoln's victory, took place while Buchanan was still in the White House. Thus, at the moment of greatest urgency, the country had a "lame-duck" president, one without the will or the power to make commitments. Although Buchanan declared that secession was unconstitutional, he also argued that Congress had no power under the Constitution to prevent it!

While Buchanan talked of conciliation others sought to do something about it. Significantly, the two main compromise efforts came from the border states, where men knew that if secession were followed by war their land would become a battleground.

The most seriously considered of the compromise proposals was the Crittenden Plan, drawn up on December 18, 1860, two days before South Carolina's formal departure from the Union. This plan, put forward by Senator John J. Crittenden of Kentucky, offered these constitutional amendments: (1) Slavery was to be barred in the territories north of the line 36° 30'. (2) But it was to be established and maintained under federal protection south of that line. (3) Future states were to come in as they wished, slave or free. (4) The Fugitive Slave Law was to be enforced, and compensation paid by the federal government when enforcement failed because of the action of northerners. (5) The Constitution was never to be amended so as to authorize Congress to interfere with slavery in any state or the District of Columbia.

This comprehensive program failed to win either northern or southern support.

Southern leaders would not accept it unless it was endorsed by the Republican party. Lincoln himself, though he favored enforcement of the Fugitive Slave Law and would accept an amendment protecting slavery where it then existed, was wholly opposed to any compromise on the exclusion of slavery from the territories.

The second compromise effort was made by Virginia. On the very day the Confederacy was being organized in Montgomery, Alabama—February 4, 1861—a peace convention called by Virginia assembled in Washington itself. Twenty-one states, free and slave, dutifully sent representatives, but the best they could offer were the discredited Crittenden proposals, and these got nowhere.

iv. *The Final Failure*

LINCOLN'S INAUGURAL

When, on March 4, 1861, Abraham Lincoln stood up to take the oath of office, secession was an accomplished fact, a Southern Confederacy had been formed, and important federal properties had fallen into the hands of rebel states. Yet a far greater territory than the then existing Confederacy was still very much at issue. The upper South—Virginia, Maryland, North Carolina, even Delaware—was riven by conflict as individuals, families, neighborhoods, and entire regions wrestled with their awful alternatives. Farther west, in the more authentic "border states" of Tennessee, Kentucky, Arkansas, and Missouri, genuine battles were fought before allegiance to the North or the South could be established. In all these states the President's inaugural address had been almost too long awaited, and his words when received were pounced upon like Nevada nuggets and minutely assayed for their true value.

Early in his oration Lincoln stressed the perpetuity of "the more perfect Union" established by the Constitution, and then followed his sharpest words to the rebels:

No State upon its own mere motion can lawfully get out of the Union; . . . resolves and ordinances to that effect are legally void; and . . . acts of violence, within any State or States, against the authority of the United States, are insurrectionary or revolutionary, according to circumstance.

"The mails, unless repelled," Lincoln declared, "will continue to be furnished in all parts of the Union. So far as possible, the people everywhere shall have that sense of perfect security which is most favorable to calm thought and reflection."

The President was as conciliatory as his office and his nature allowed. As chief executive, he was bound to enforce federal regulations, including those requiring the return of fugitive slaves. He even went so far as to say that he had no objections to a proposed constitutional amendment guaranteeing that "the Federal Government shall never interfere with the domestic institutions of the States"—meaning slavery. Other constitutional obligations required that he "hold, occupy, and possess the property and places belonging to the Government, and to collect the duties and imposts" in every American port. But in performing these acts, "there needs be no bloodshed or violence; and there shall be none, unless it be forced upon the national authority."

In your hands, my dissatisfied fellow-countrymen, and not in mine [Lincoln reminded the intransigents near the end of his address], is the momentous issue of civil war. The government will not assail you. You can have no conflict, without being yourselves the aggressors. You have no oath registered in Heaven to destroy the government, while I shall have the most solemn one to "preserve, protect, and defend" it.

But Lincoln could not stop on a note of iron, and added this eloquent paragraph:

I am loath to close. We are not enemies, but friends. We must not be enemies. Though passion may have strained, it must not break, our bonds of affection. The mystic chords of memory, stretching from every battlefield and patriot grave to every living heart and hearthstone all over this broad land, will yet swell the chorus of the Union when again touched, as surely they will be, by the better angels of our nature.

Few if any inaugural orations in our history bore the burden of Lincoln's first. Few if any played so deliberately for time. In the terrible economic crisis of 1933, Franklin D. Roosevelt caught the public mood when he declared in *his* inaugural address, "In their need [the people] have registered a mandate that they want direct, vigorous action." But Lincoln, though pressed by zealots of every political creed, electrified the nation by putting action off:

My countrymen, one and all, think calmly and well upon this whole subject. Nothing valuable can be lost by taking time. If there be an object to hurry any of you in hot haste to a step which you would never take deliberately, that object will be frustrated by taking time; but no good object can be frustrated by it.

SUMTER FALLS

And yet there was action, precipitate action, required of Lincoln himself. With no reprisal from Buchanan, the Confederacy early in 1861 had seized federal forts, post offices, and custom houses throughout the

Scale model of Fort Sumter, South Carolina.

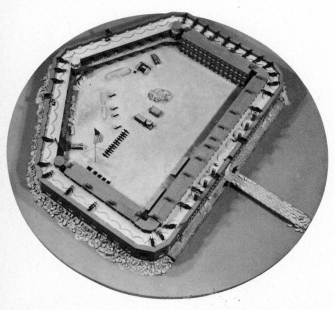

South. Only Fort Sumter in Charleston harbor, and three forts off the coast of Florida, now remained in federal hands. On March 5, the day after his inauguration, Lincoln was given a letter from Major Robert Anderson, in charge at Sumter, reporting that the fort could be held only with the immediate aid of 20,000 men, a large naval force, and ample provisions.

Anderson, in effect, recommended evacuation. But if Lincoln retreated, as his advisers suggested, he would have taken the first step toward recognizing the power if not the legality of the Confederacy. If, on the other hand, he attempted by force to strengthen Sumter, he would be made to appear the aggressor. Lincoln moved in a way that involved neither of these alternatives. He would attempt to provision Sumter peacefully. "If such attempt be not resisted," he wrote Governor Pickens, "no effort to throw in men, arms, or ammunition will be made."

Lincoln's decision shifted the burden to Confederate authorities. If they permitted Sumter to be provisioned, the fort would stand indefinitely in the mouth of one of their few good harbors, a threat to their prestige throughout the world. If they attacked a peaceful expedition bringing food, *they* would have fired the first shot.

When requested by the southern general, Pierre G. T. Beauregard, to surrender Sumter before the supply ships arrived, Anderson promised to evacuate by April 15, unless he was relieved or ordered to remain. But the Confederates dared not risk so long a delay. They gave Anderson until 4 A.M. April 12 to capitulate. At 4:30 A.M. the batteries from the Charleston shore began their 34-hour bombardment. Lincoln's provisioning flotilla lay in the vicinity of the fight, but without the support of *Powhatan*, the navy's most powerful warship, which had failed to escort the supply vessels as a result of official bungling, no provisions could be landed. When Anderson at last ran down the flag on the afternoon of April 13, Sumter was virtually consumed in flames and her ammunition gone. Only then did the federal ships approach, with Confederate permission, to take off the defenders. Remarkably, not a man had been hit on either side during the engagement. But a war that was to overshadow even Napoleon's campaigns in casualties had begun.

Before Sumter, northern opinion had divided sharply on the proper response to secession. Radical abolitionists like Garrison, Phillips, and the poet, John Greenleaf Whittier, thought that it would be futile to enforce union "where one section is pinned to the residue by bayonets." For once, the business community, still suffering the effects of the Panic of 1857 and concerned over collecting southern debts and holding southern markets, agreed wholeheartedly with their policy to let the "erring sisters go in peace." Bellicose northerners, on the other hand, spoke early and often. "If South Carolina is determined upon secession," warned the *New York Times,* "she should take the plunge with her eyes open. She must face the consequences—and among them all, the most unquestionable is war . . . there is no possibility of escaping it." Detestation of disunion was especially widespread in the Northwest, where freedom was the very watchword of the Lord, and the free use of the Mississippi from its source in Minnesota to its mouth below New Orleans the foundation of economic life. No section uttered "Amen" more appreciatively to Lincoln's March 4 dictum, "Physically speaking, we cannot separate."

After Sumter, peace partisans still were heard here and there in the North. But with the Confederacy branded before the world as the aggressor, it became easier than before to portray hostilities as a *defense* of the Union. Lincoln's call on April 15 for 75,000 three-month volunteers met with overwhelming response everywhere. Walt Whitman in Manhattan, whose *Drum Taps* establish him as the Union poet of the war, caught the new surge of spirit:

Forty years had I in my city seen soldiers parading,
Forty years as a pageant, till unawares the lady of this teeming turbulent city,
Sleepless amid her ships, her houses, her incalculable wealth,

With her million children around her, suddenly,
At dead of night, at news from the south,
Incens'd struck with clinch'd hand the pavement.
A shock electric, the night sustain'd it,
Till with ominous hum our hive at daybreak pour'd out its myriads.

From the houses then and the workshops, and through all the doorways
Leapt they tumultuous, and lo! Manhattan arming.

THE UPPER SOUTH
AND THE BORDER DECIDE

It is sometimes said that South Carolinians, aware that a Confederacy without Virginia would be a tragic sham, hastened the bombardment of Sumter to force the Old Dominion's hand in taking up arms to defend the South against the expected retaliation from the North. But as late as April 13, three months after it was called together, Virginia's "secession convention" still refused to vote for disunion, despite constant urging from hotheads farther south. Then, on April 14, Lincoln framed the fateful proclamation calling forth "the militia of the several States of the Union . . . in order to suppress" a "combination too powerful to be suppressed" by available means. On April 15 this proclamation was received with hosannas throughout the North. Throughout the upper South and the border states it came like the toll of death. Should Virginia and the rest answer the President's call and yield their militia to the Union cause? Should they stand by while the deep South was invaded by southern men and arms?

More than Lincoln's election, more than his inaugural, more even than the attempt to provision Sumter itself, Lincoln's proclamation of April 15 sealed the issue of war and peace. On April 17 the Virginia convention at last passed its ordinance of secession 88 to 55. One week later it leagued the Old Dominion with the Confederacy and put its armed forces at the service of the Stars and Bars. On May 21 the provisional Confederate government named Richmond its permanent capital and prepared to move from Montgomery in June. On May 23 a referendum in Virginia sanctioned all these steps. And only then did the President acknowledge all hope gone: "The people of Virginia have thus allowed this giant insurrection to make its nest within her borders; and this government has no choice left but to deal with it where it finds it." * Only then were the federal mails cut off from Confederate routes. Secession was now complete in Virginia, even to the point where the western counties themselves were organizing to secede from the new Confederate state.

Virginia ranks among the Confederacy's greatest conquests, one enhanced by the satellites and stragglers that now quickly took the same path. In North Carolina on May 20 a convention called by the legislature voted unanimously to secede. In Tennessee, the governor and legislature

---

* On April 19 Lincoln supplemented his proclamation calling out the militia with an order to the navy to blockade the ports of the first seven Confederate states. On April 27 he extended the blockade to Virginia and North Carolina. The Supreme Court was later to rule that the war legally began with these blockade orders, which officially recognized that a state of "belligerency" existed between two powers. Lincoln himself never accepted this idea; he never recognized the Confederacy as a nation, nor secession as anything but "insurrection."

took the state into the Confederacy even before the people ratified this decision on June 8 by a vote of 104,913 to 47,238. Arkansas sharply repudiated Lincoln's request for troops and vowed, in their governor's words, to defend "to the last extremity, their honor, lives, and property, against Northern mendacity and usurpation." The Arkansas convention, after rejecting secession in March, voted for it on May 6.

Nevertheless, unionist regions could still be found in the upper South and on the border. Like the western Virginians, the yeomen of eastern Tennessee would probably have rejoined the Union had Confederate troops not prevented them. Four indecisive slave states, moreover—Kentucky, Missouri, Maryland, and Delaware—were retained by the Union. Maryland's strategic position forced Lincoln to take strong unconstitutional measures against pro-southern agitators there, and with the show of federal force the secessionist spirit in Maryland subsided. Rich and populous Kentucky maintained a precarious neutrality until September, 1861, when the legislature voted to remain loyal to the Union. Kentucky volunteers for the Confederates numbered about 35,000, and approximately 75,000 fought with the Federals. In Missouri the division between pro-southern and pro-northern supporters flared up into a small civil war, but only 20,000 Missourians fought with the South as against 100,000 who joined the Union armies.

Readings

* Asterisk indicates that book is available in paperback.

The most comprehensive survey of this fateful decade, and excellent reading, is to be found in Allan Nevins, volume II, *Ordeal of the Union* (2 vols., 1947), and *The Emergence of Lincoln* (2 vols., 1950). A. O. Craven, *The Coming of the Civil War* (1942); R. F. Nichols, *The Disruption of American Democracy* * (1948); H. H. Simms, *A Decade of Sectional Controversy* (1942); and Bruce Catton, *The Coming Fury* (1961), offer differing explanations of the sectional schism. A short and incisive study is D. L. Dumond, *Anti-Slavery Origins of the Civil War* * (1939). Two general books on the Civil War also discuss events that led up to it: J. G. Randall and David Donald, *The Civil War and Reconstruction* (1961 ed.); and Clement Eaton, *A History of the Southern Confederacy* * (1954).

American expansionism in the 1850's is thoroughly analyzed in Nevins, *Ordeal* (cited above). Douglas and his ideas are well presented in R. W. Johannsen, ed., *The Letters of Stephen A. Douglas* (1961); and G. M. Capers, *Stephen A. Douglas, Defender of the Union* (1959). Also valuable is Basil Rauch, *American Interest in Cuba, 1848-1855* (1948). To Nevins' summary of the Kansas issue should be added two books by J. C. Malin: *John Brown and the Legend of Fifty-Six* (1942), and *The Nebraska Question, 1852-1854* (1953). Also important are P. W. Gates, *Fifty Million Acres: Conflicts over Kansas Land Policy, 1854-1890* (1954), and C. V. Woodward's essay on John Brown in Daniel Aaron, ed., *America in Crisis* (1952). Edward Stone, ed., *Incident at Harpers Ferry* * (1956), is an excellent collection of contemporary material on John Brown's last act.

For parties and politics, the general works cited above are sufficiently detailed, but the following are also recommended: R. F. Nichols, *Franklin Pierce* (1931); for the Buchanan administration, P. G. Auchampaugh, *James Buchanan and His Cabinet on the Eve of Secession* (1926); for the Know-Nothing movement, R. A. Billington, *The Protestant Crusade, 1800-1860* * (1938), and W. D. Overdyke, *The Know-Nothing Party in the South* (1950); for the background and origins of the Republican party, A. W. Crandall, *The Early History of the Republican Party, 1854-1856* (1930), J. A. Isely, *Horace Greeley and the Republican Party, 1853-1861* (1947), and M. B. Duberman, *Charles Francis Adams* (1961). David Donald, *Charles Sumner and the Coming of the Civil War* (1960), is an outstanding modern biography. C. B. Swisher, *Roger B. Taney* (1935), is excellent on Dred Scott, as is Nevin's analysis in *Ordeal* (cited above). See also Vincent Hopkins, *Dred Scott's Case* (1951). Valuable background material will be found in Charles Warren, volume II, *The Supreme Court in United States History* (2 vols., 1922). G. W. Van Vleck, *The Panic of 1857: An Analytical Study* (1943), is good on that crisis.

The story of Lincoln's emergence is well presented in short compass in D. E. Fehrenbacher, *Prelude to Greatness, Lincoln in the 1850's* * (1962). See also B. P. Thomas, *Abraham Lincoln* (1952). A. J. Beveridge, *Abraham Lincoln, 1809-1858* (2 vols., 1928), and Carl Sandburg, *Abraham Lincoln, the Prairie Years* * (1-vol. ed., 1929), are classic studies. A. C. Cole, *The Era of the Civil War* (1919), contains interesting information. The Lincoln-Douglas debates are presented in full in P. M. Angle, ed., *Created Equal* (1958). A stimulating analysis is H. V. Jaffa, *Crisis of the House Divided* (1959). R. H. Luthin, *The First Lincoln Campaign* (1944), is authoritative.

The secession movement is admirably chronicled in A. O. Craven, *The Growth of Southern Nationalism, 1848-1861* (1953). Craven's *Civil War in the Making 1815-1860* (1959), is a short summary of this author's later views. Ollinger Crenshaw, *The Slave States in the Presidential Election of 1860* (1945), adds an important link to the story. Secession itself is the theme of D. L. Dumond, *The Secession Movement, 1860-1861* (1931); U. B. Phillips, **The Course of the South to Secession** * (1939); and **R. A. Wooster,** *The Secession Conventions of the South* (1962). For Lincoln's role, see David Potter, *Lincoln and His Party in the Secession Crisis, 1860-1861* * (1942). K. M. Stampp, *And the War Came: The North and the Secession Crisis, 1860-1861* * (1950), analyzes the northern position in general; and P. S. Foner, *Business and Slavery: The New York Merchants and the Irrepressible Conflict* (1941), describes the attitude of businessmen in the North toward slavery and secession. For a private view of the crisis, *The Diary of George Templeton Strong* (4 vols., 1952), splendidly edited by Allan Nevins and M. H. Thomas, is strongly recommended.

CHAPTER SIXTEEN

Beat! beat! drums!—blow! bugles! blow!
  Make no parley—stop for no expostulation,
  Mind not the timid—mind not the weeper or
    prayer,
  Mind not the old man beseeching the young
    man,
  Let not the child's voice be heard, nor the
    mother's entreaties,
  Make even the trestles to shake the dead
    where they lie awaiting the hearses,
  So strong you thump O terrible drums—so
    loud you bugles blow.
  (Walt Whitman, "Beat! Beat! Drums!" 1861)

A Confederate general, writing when the
Civil War was over, said: "Aggrieved by the
action and tendencies of the Federal Gov-

Civil War

ernment, and apprehending worse in the future, a majority of the people of the South approved secession as the only remedy suggested by their leaders. So travelers enter railway carriages, and are dragged up grades and through tunnels with utter loss of volition, the motive power, generated by fierce heat, being far in advance and beyond their control."

Secession, whether or not a majority in the South did in fact approve it, led directly to the war. It was not to be so easy to sever the Union as southern leaders might suppose—to tear away a third of its occupied land, to set artificial barriers against the course of its rivers, to defy its sovereign laws, to thwart at one stroke its grand continental aspirations and its great experiment in republican government. The South was not to be allowed to depart in peace. "Beat! beat! drums!—blow! bugles! blow!"

And yet, from the start of the war a pall seemed to lie on both combatants. The Civil War became the longest and deadliest war ever fought on this continent. Even some of its earlier engagements were marked by a shockingly high toll in lives. Nevertheless, the war was amazingly slow in gaining direction, agonizingly slow to those on both sides whose most fervent wish was that, once begun, it might soon be over.

And when it was over, little indeed seemed to have been secured by the slaughter. Not that, in the judgment of history, nor even in the judgment of the times, it was in vain. Lincoln made that clear in the Gettysburg Address: "from these honored dead we take increased devotion to that cause for which they gave the last full measure of devotion—that . . . this nation, under God, shall have a new birth of freedom—and that government of the people, by the people, for the people, shall not perish from the earth." The war pointed the way "for us the living," as Lincoln said, to dedicate themselves to "the unfinished work which they who fought here have thus far so nobly advanced." And yet "the living" were to stride but a very short distance forward, and then only to turn back; and their heirs for a century would leave the "unfinished work" untouched.

The war was not soon forgotten in the North; the Republican party itself was to live for generations on Lincoln's and Grant's success. But with the Union forcibly restored, with the land made free not slave, the people of the North resumed all the more passionately for the four hateful years of delay, the development of the resources of the land which the war had so rudely interrupted. The pursuit, and eventually the problems, of the immense private wealth the land would yield, engrossed their attention, along with the heady progress of their country among the imperial powers of the world.

The people of the South, although checked momentarily by the zeal of Radical Reconstruction, thereby were left freer themselves to retrieve and restore the scattered fragments of their lives. "The Lost Cause" became an inspiration, an eternal light. Surrender need not mean submission. Their own glorious dead might be redeemed. "The Past!" cried Tom Watson of Georgia, a leader of the postwar generation, "There lies our brightest and purest hopes, our best endeavors, our loved and lost. . . . Come back to us once more, Oh dream of the old time South!"

I. *Enemies Face to Face*

THE QUESTION OF MANPOWER

In April, 1861, about 22 million persons lived in loyal states and territories. Nine million (5.5 million whites and 3.5 million Negroes) lived in "Secesh" country. But Union superiority in manpower was not so great as the gross figures suggest.

Half a million persons, scattered from Dakota to California, could make no substantial contribution to Union strength. On the contrary, every year during the Civil War, Union regiments were sucked into the Wild West to wage a desperate war against the Indians (see Chapter 18).

Hundreds of thousands of Americans in loyal border states and millions more in southern Ohio, Indiana, and Illinois, moreover, favored the Confederacy and worked or fought for southern independence. Even such hotbeds of abolitionism as Massachusetts, Vermont, Michigan, and Wisconsin—

and indeed every northern state—furnished men for the southern cause. Many southerners, of course, clung to the old flag and the Union. "Old Fuss and Feathers," General Winfield Scott, the ancient head of the armed forces of the United States at the outbreak of hostilities, was one Virginian who had no need to search his soul, as did Robert E. Lee, to decide where his allegiance lay. He "had fought fifty years under the flag," Scott told Senator Douglas, "and would fight for it, and under it, till death." But there is little doubt that more Federals than Confederates "crossed over."

Certain other considerations, when it was seen that the North really meant to fight, may also have tempered southern discouragement in the face of apparently overwhelming Union numbers. One was superior officer personnel. For twenty years before Lincoln's inauguration a southern clique

414

headed by General Scott himself ruled the army. Under this regime, many northern West Pointers, including Sherman and Grant, found little opportunity for advancement and resigned their commissions early in life for civilian careers. Virtually all the young officers pushed up the ladder by Scott were southerners, and most of them, unlike Scott, embraced the Confederate cause.

A second comfort to the South was its confidence in cotton, largely produced by slaves. Secession leaders expected to exchange their famous staple for all the foreign manufactures they needed without sacrificing fighting men to factory work. A third consideration reinforced the second. The South's vaunted military tradition, which meant, practically speaking, that white men of all classes were trained from childhood to the horse, the hunt, and the use of firearms, had left southern women with the drudgery of running small farms and even some large plantations. When the men went off to "hev a squint at the fighting," the women redoubled their efforts in raising dirt crops, cattle, and swine.

A fourth, and the most important, consideration was strategic. Throughout the fighting, the men in gray defended short "interior" lines against invaders who were forced to traverse and protect long avenues of communication and to attack on a broad periphery. The Confederacy, moreover, had no need to divert "effectives" to such tasks as garrisoning captured cities and holding subjugated territory. "Owing to the character of the conflict," concludes the historian Edward Channing, "instead of two or three Northern soldiers for every Southern one, there should have been five or six.

By the end of the war, from its 1.5 million white men of fighting age, the South had enlisted about 900,000. Thousands of slaves performed fatigue duty and other tasks for the services, but no Negroes except such as might pass for whites were armed. Rebel forces probably reached their numerical peak at the start of 1864, when some 480,000 were in uniform.

From its 4 million white men of fighting age, the Union enrolled approximately 2 million, nearly half of them toward the end

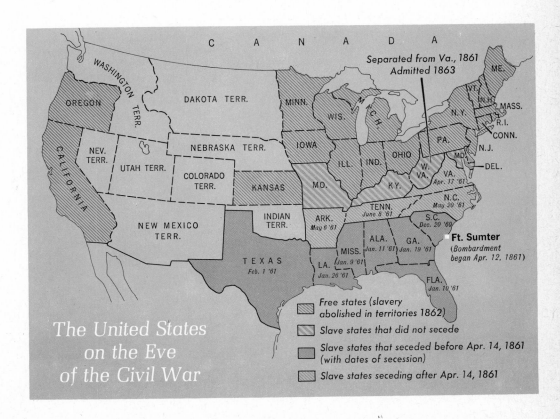

The United States on the Eve of the Civil War

- Free states (slavery abolished in territories 1862)
- Slave states that did not secede
- Slave states that seceded before Apr. 14, 1861 (with dates of secession)
- Slave states seceding after Apr. 14, 1861

Separated from Va., 1861 Admitted 1863

Ft. Sumter (Bombardment began Apr. 12, 1861)

of the war. In addition, after 1862, about 200,000 Negroes, most of them former slaves from border states or occupied Confederate territory, were enlisted in the Union army (and to a small extent in the Union navy), many of them forcibly and under discriminatory conditions in pay and quarters. Congregated in their own regiments, mainly under white officers who resented such assignments, they nevertheless performed hearteningly well in the opinion of those who had their capacity for freedom in mind.

In a short war northern numerical superiority would have availed little. As the war drew itself out, and as generals were found with the will to take advantage of the disparities in their favor, northern numerical strength became a psychological as well as a physical weapon. During the closing years of the struggle, Union armies suffered terrible casualties but seemed to grow stronger with every setback. At the same time, Confederate losses sapped the southern will to fight.

THE QUESTION OF MACHINES

The fact that the Civil War stretched over years instead of months magnified every other material advantage of the North—in money and credit, factories, food production, transport. It took precious time to redirect the free economy of the North to the requirements of the battlefield, especially as these requirements were persistently underestimated because of wishful thinking about the likely duration of the war. But the South, with its intense concentration on cotton-growing even at the expense of foodstuffs, found it even more difficult than the North to convert to a war footing. Abominable roads and poorly built railroads which bypassed many strategic centers magnified every difficulty. Texas and Arkansas, the Confederacy's leading food-

growing states, had no train connections whatever with the rest of the South.

As the war lengthened, southern troops suffered miserably from short rations and ragged clothing. Yet the Confederacy was never so lacking in basic materials of war—small arms, artillery, ammunition, and horses—that it could not carry out whatever actions its strategy or its predicament required. Every rural home in the South had its weapons, and some estimates place as high as 5 million the number of such private arms available for the cause. Large quantities of munitions also were garnered from captured federal forts and federal positions. To these were added imports run through the blockade (see p. 410). Under the brilliant administration of its chief of ordnance, Josiah Gorgas, a Pennsylvanian who had long since adopted the sentiments of his Alabama wife, the Confederacy also developed its own munitions plants to supplement the output of the giant Tredegar Iron Works in Richmond.

General Beauregard put the South's situation most clearly:

No people ever warred for independence with more relative advantages than the Confederates; and if, as a military question, they must have failed, then no country must aim at freedom by means of war. . . . The South, with its great material resources, its defensive means of mountains, rivers, railroads, and the telegraph, with the immense advantage of the interior lines of war, would be open to discredit as a people if its failure could not be explained otherwise than by mere material contrast.

Beauregard placed most of the blame for the South's defeat on the failure of President Davis and the civilian command to follow up strategic victories in the field with bold and comprehensive campaigns. Lee's official wartime correspondence strongly confirms Beauregard's conclusion.

II. *The Civilian Commands*

THE CONFEDERATE CONSTITUTION

When the delegates from the first seceding states met at Montgomery, Ala-

bama, in February, 1861, to draft a frame of government for the new southern republic (see p. 406), they had hoped, by not departing too greatly from the familiar federal document, to attract their as yet uncommitted neighbors in the upper South and on the "border." In squelching democratic extremists, they also had their eye on the good opinion of the conservative states of Europe. Because so many in the South remained more firmly opposed than ever to surrendering state rights to a central government, certain weaknesses so successfully fought in 1787 nevertheless crept into the Confederate version.

Nothing was said in the new constitution of the right of secession, which, in southern opinion, was sufficiently sanctioned in the older document. The very preamble of the new constitution, however, declared that it was established, not by "We, the people," the clarion cry of the Union, but by "the people of the Confederate states, each state acting in its sovereign and independent character." While the new Congress was granted the power "to . . . provide for the common defense," no mention was made of promoting the "general welfare." Tariffs "to promote or foster any branch of industry," and appropriations "for any internal improvement intended to facilitate commerce," were forbidden, in true agrarian style. "The judicial power of the Confederate States" was placed in a supreme court and certain lower tribunals. But no supreme court ever was set up. The old federal district courts, indeed, continued to sit in the Confederacy, often under their old judges who applied the old rules and precedents, each as he saw fit. The president's term, optimistically, was extended to six years; but whatever advantage in stability was sought by this change was vitiated by the provision barring his re-election. The Confederate president soon became a lame-duck with little political leverage or allegiance. A more salutary innovation permitted the Congress to grant Cabinet members seats on the floor of either house with the privilege of discussing measures relating to their departments.

The new constitution contained provisions designed to make it a weapon as well as a vehicle of government. Of course, it "recognized and protected . . . the right of property in negro slaves." Yet it explicitly prohibited "the importation of negroes . . . from any foreign country." As a sop to Virginia and other slave-breeding states not yet in the Confederacy, it excluded the slaveholding states of the United States from this prohibition. But as a manifest threat to such states, it empowered the Confederate Congress, when it wished, to include in the ban "any State not a member of . . . this Confederacy."

JEFFERSON DAVIS' ADMINISTRATION

The Montgomery Constitutional Convention named Jefferson Davis of Mississippi provisional president, and Alexander H. Stephens of Georgia provisional vice-president. Neither man sought nor wanted his job, but in the first Confederate elections in November, 1861, the voters confirmed the convention's choices.

Like so many Mississippians, Jeff Davis was born out of the state, in Kentucky. A West Pointer of the class of 1828, at heart he was a soldier hungry for honor in the field. In 1846, he had resigned his seat as a Democratic congressman to lead his regiment of "Mississippi Rifles" in one grand stand at Buena Vista. This exploit convinced him perhaps more than it did the Mexicans that he was born to generalship, an opinion that was to be of no help to Confederate officers. From 1847 to 1851, and again from 1857 to 1861, Davis served in the Senate, and during the whole of Pierce's administration was Secretary of War. In the Senate, his ardent expansionism was tempered somewhat by his vision of a united nation dominated by the South. Much as he wanted new territories, he became one of the bitter-enders, one of a mere ten, against the admission of California as a free state under the Compromise of 1850. His strong southern chauvinism soon linked him with the anti-Douglas wing of the Democratic party. But he was no fire-eater, and while sympathetic to secession, he had hoped that the South could take the plunge united and not be harried into the fatal step piecemeal by headstrong individual commonwealths like South Carolina.

Ill health may have accounted for Davis's testiness as president. But his constant quarrels with subordinates also arose from the inadequate and even hostile civil personnel he commanded. Vice-president Stephens, especially, although he stayed home in Georgia most of the time, was a thorn to his harassed commander-in-chief. Stephens was a wizened little scholar wracked by rheumatism and neuralgia, who yearned only for the solitude of the study. The convention named him mainly to appease his state for refraining from pushing the vainglorious Howell Cobb and for withdrawing Robert Toombs, her hard-drinking favorite son. As a stickler for state rights, Stephens complained on every exercise of presidential power that Davis was becoming a despot with Bonapartist ideas of grandeur. Saddest of all, Stephens had been certain from the start that not even a Bonaparte could establish a free Confederacy, and his pessimism became contagious.

Davis' Cabinet scarcely made up in strength for the Vice-president's weakness. Either because Davis would not appoint them or because they would not serve one so careless of state rights, great planters were conspicuous by their absence. Many of them, of course, preferred to serve in the field. Fourteen different men filled the six Confederate Cabinet posts during the life of the southern republic. Such turnover alone would have forced the President to lean increasingly on the few familiar figures about him; and of these Judah P. Benjamin, a brilliant New Orleans lawyer who served through the whole ill-fated administration, first as Attorney-General, then as Secretary of War, and finally as Secretary of State, was by far the ablest. Benjamin's task was made none the lighter by the ceaseless slander of his character by newspapers and legislators from 1862 on. His determination to make the Confederacy face up to the grim reality of its financial, economic, and diplomatic predicament earned him the appellation, "the hated Jew."

The Confederate Congress, more stable in personnel than the Cabinet, was no more responsible. Three distinct congresses held office during the life of the Confederacy. Many men served in all three, and as conditions worsened they came to grate so on one another's nerves that the more truculent brandished guns and bowie knives, in addition to the traditional horsewhips and canes, to cut short distasteful harangues. As federal forces occupied "Secesh" territory, irresponsibility increased, for many legislators found themselves representing lost constituencies which could not vote them out. The South's military genius was paraded daily in congressional halls, where Davis' strategy came under ever harsher scrutiny. Military setbacks, in turn, only heightened opposition to Davis' program for mobilizing the South's men and resources.

LINCOLN AS PRESIDENT

By temperament and character Lincoln was better fitted than Davis for presidential responsibility. Patient as a possum, tolerant, flexible, and crafty, Lincoln had a genius for giving men enough rope to hang themselves. If they escaped the noose, so much the better.

Throughout his term, the President was savagely handled by most newspapers and abused by politicians of his own and other parties. Nor was he popular with the electorate. But Lincoln took the verbal abuse, it seemed, with a kind of wry satisfaction in his critics' scratching for barbs. Even to men who knew him longest he remained something of a mystery, enlivening meetings with the earthiest kind of stories and yet remaining melancholy and aloof.

According to Republican Senator John Sherman of Ohio, Lincoln peppered his Cabinet with men intensely jealous of one another, "as by that means he would control rather than be controlled by it." In any case, a coalition of many interests had made Lincoln's election possible, and, like it or not, he could not ignore their claims on high office. The President himself seldom acted until he felt that the groundswell of public opinion would sustain him, a point he reached by a process of divination to which his associates contributed much by their discussions, but how much and in what way precisely they could not tell.

Nor was he always right, especially in simply taking time. Lincoln's lapses encouraged the ambitious egotists around him—Secretary of State Seward, for example, and Secretary of the Treasury Chase—each to strive to assume "a sort of dictatorship for the national defense" in order to fill the vacuum they found in presidential power. But all learned sooner or later, as Seward acknowledged after an early brush with the rail-splitter's own ego, that "the President is the best of us. There is only one vote in the Cabinet and it belongs to him. Executive ability and vigor are rare qualities, but he has them both."

In 1861 the federal government was honeycombed with secessionists. No president, not even Jackson, cleaned house so indiscriminately as "Honest Abe." Few, on the other hand, chose replacements with such care. Lincoln labored so painstakingly in selecting loyal Republicans that idealistic critics accused him of frittering away his time with low politics while the nation was splitting apart. His justification was that patronage was the cement of the Republican party, which alone held the North together.

DISUNITY WITHIN THE UNION

In reality, throughout the war the North remained as bitterly divided as the South.

Extremes sometimes met in opposition to the administration. Many dedicated abolitionists, for example, were also dedicated pacifists. In addition, they had preached "disunion" as vigorously as Calhoun. Their argument, that by sloughing off the slave section the Union itself would be purified (a goal somewhat different from their most widely advertised one), fed on the fond hope that in an isolated South slavery would wither away. Now these abolitionists demanded that the rebels be allowed to depart

in peace, slaves and all. "Peace" was also the goal of many Democrats, often called "Copperheads," who spared Lincoln no abuse but who saved their heaviest fire for the abolitionists themselves.

As the war proceeded and congressional support for emancipation grew, partly indeed as a result of continued abolitionist agitation, most abolitionists eventually embraced the fight to the finish. Many, indeed, came to fear an early end to the conflict lest it lead to a compromise peace, with the "peculiar institution" still intact in the South. As the Confederacy's chances declined, on the other hand, the "Copperheads" grew shriller in their demands for compromise and more active in retarding

Woodcut of Abraham Lincoln by Albert Hunt, March 27, 1865.

Union enlistments, while encouraging northerners to fight for the slave power.

Copperhead sentiment was strongest in southern Ohio, Indiana, and Illinois, Ohio supplying, in ex-congressman Clement L. Vallandigham, the acknowledged leader of the faction in this region. Arrested early in May, 1863, on a charge of declaring sympathy for the enemy, Vallandigham was summarily tried by a military commission, found guilty, and jailed. While his friends sought a reversal of the verdict in more formal courts, Lincoln, mingling mercy with humor, had Vallandigham released and banished to the Confederacy. From there he fled to Canada by ship and soon showed up again in Ohio where, with no further official notice, he resumed his earlier course. In the closing years of the war, rumors were rife of traitorous plots by secret Copperhead societies, but these groups, largely made up of the ill-educated and untrained, never constituted an effective "fifth column."

As abolitionists gradually came around to conceding the rightness of the fighting, they also threw their support to the faction within the Republican party most in sympathy with emancipation as the objective of the war. This faction became known as the "Radicals." The "Regulars," or "Conservatives," sought only to suppress the "insurrection" and to restore the Union for the white man regardless of the freedom and progress of the black. The split between the Radicals and Conservatives widened as the war proceeded and had far deeper consequences than that between the Republican party as such and the dissidents outside.

Lincoln who never ceased to fear offending the slaveholders of the loyal border states, likewise never disavowed his Conservative leanings. But he also kept in touch with the Radicals to whom he harkened at least as patiently as to others. The Radicals, who fought not only to free the slaves but to impose the "permanent dominion" of free institutions on the slaveocracy, were less patient with him. By their cannonading criticism of Lincoln's "sickly policy of an inoffensive war" they early earned the epithet "Vindictives," which was not unacceptable to them.

The Radicals boasted a formidable array in both houses of Congress, led in the Senate by Sumner of Massachusetts, Wade of Ohio, and Chandler of Michigan, and in the House by the most vindictive Radical of all, Thaddeus Stevens of Pennsylvania, chairman of the regal Ways and Means Committee. Born and bred on the Vermont frontier, Stevens had made his career in Pennsylvania, where he owned extensive iron works. There, in 1837, he refused to sign the new constitution, to the writing of which he had contributed a great deal, because the convention had rejected his demand that Negroes as well as whites be given the suffrage. He had seen much of slavery in those parts of Maryland that adjoined his Pennsylvania haunts and he early denounced it as "a curse, a shame, and a crime." A lawyer as well as a businessman, Stevens defended fugitive slaves without a fee and usually secured their freedom. The Civil War crowned a political career notable for its ups and downs. After the war Stevens's determination that the slaveocracy should never rise again made him for a time the most powerful figure in the country (see Chapter 17).

LINCOLN'S "DICTATORSHIP"

Lincoln allowed nearly a whole year to pass after the first shocking act of secession before he would acknowledge, and even then not fully, that the awful chasm between the two sections could be closed only by the dead of both. He hated bloodshed. Determined to get the war over as expeditiously as possible, he nevertheless was reluctant even to begin the fighting. As late as December 3, 1861, he told Congress: "I have been anxious and careful that the inevitable conflict . . . shall not degenerate into a violent and remorseless revolutionary struggle."

Lincoln nevertheless lost no time in readying the Union for survival. Between April and July 1861, with Congress cooling its heels at home (against the wishes of many members who wanted their special session to begin in March when Lincoln

420

was inaugurated, and not in July, as he had designated), Lincoln earned the epithets, "despot," "tyrant," "dictator," more justly than any other president.

On May 3, without presidential precedent or legislative authority, Lincoln issued a call for 40 regiments of three-year *United States* volunteers to supplement the *state* militia he had called out in April (see p. 409). On no firmer constitutional grounds, he ordered a rapid expansion of the fleet for blockade service. The Constitution states: "No money shall be drawn from the Treasury, but in Consequence of Appropriations made by Law." Without any law, Lincoln ordered Chase to scratch for funds to pay for the new army and navy, and Chase obliged.

More widely opposed than these military and monetary stratagems were Lincoln's trampling of traditional safeguards of personal rights. Neither private letters nor telegrams were safe from federal prying eyes, and holders of passports questionable in any respect were subject to detainment and inquisitions at major ports. Military commanders in particular were empowered to make summary arrests without warrants and "in the extremest necessity," in Lincoln's words, to suspend the writ of *habeas corpus*. Under this edict and even harsher later ones, at least 15,000 Americans were jailed, and despite Lincoln's characteristic clemency, many remained in jail until the war's end and without ever having been faced with their accusers or informed of the charges against them.

But even these high-handed measures were mild compared with Lincoln's militancy in Maryland, Kentucky, and Missouri, whence the most anguished cries of dictatorship arose. These border states (along with Delaware) had refused to follow Virginia into the Confederacy (see p. 410). But (unlike Delaware) they denied the federal government the use of their state militias, as called for on April 15, and instead declared their individual *"armed neutrality."* Each of these states had immense strategic importance. Maryland virtually surrounded Washington and, with Virginia gone, could make the national capital the captive of the Confederacy. Baltimore, Maryland's leading port and railroad center, was also Washington's main link with the outside world. Kentucky, in turn, controlled the use of the Ohio River. Missouri, with Kentucky, controlled the use of the Mississippi. "An arming of these states . . . under the guise of neutrality," Lincoln said, "recognized no fidelity to the Constitution, no obligation to maintain the Union."

Maryland, because of its proximity to Washington, was the first of the "neutrals" to feel Lincoln's heel. After a riot in Baltimore on April 15, 1861, between Massachusetts troops bound for Washington and secessionist-minded citizens, Lincoln sent a force into Maryland under Brigadier-General Benjamin F. Butler with orders to take all necessary measures to forestall the state authorities from arming the people against the Union, "even, if necessary, to the bombardment of their cities." Butler, a notorious "problem on two legs," soon roughly rounded up and jailed the mayor of Baltimore, 19 members of the state legislature, and other citizens. Butler engaged in so much other inflammatory activity that Lincoln felt obliged to recall him. But Lincoln did not undo the General's work; and Maryland, especially the secessionist eastern sector, was held to the Union side throughout the war chiefly by uninvited Union forces.

"I hope I have God on my side," Lincoln said, "but I must have Kentucky." By the time Kentucky formally declared her neutrality on May 24, 1861, Simon Bolivar Buckner, the commander, had molded the state militia into an effective army of 61 companies. Buckner's Confederate sympathies had already aroused suspicion, and another Kentuckian, a former naval lieutenant, William Nelson, went to Lincoln for permission to organize and arm a countervailing loyal force. Nelson's mission was successful and, under cover of night, he soon had 10,000 "Lincoln rifles" distributed among his "home guard." By June, 1861,

Union sentiment in the Kentucky legislature was so strong that funds requested by Buckner were voted for Nelson instead. By then, too, Lincoln had ordered the establishment at Danville, Kentucky, of a Union recruiting camp to offset camps the Confederates were conducting on Kentucky's border in Tennessee.

The delicate balance held in Kentucky until September 4, 1861, when General Leonidas Polk, unnerved by the growing unionism Lincoln had patiently nourished, ordered his rebel forces to occupy the strategic town of Columbus on the Mississippi. When Polk's men moved in, the recently commissioned Ulysses S. Grant swung over from Cairo, Illinois, to occupy Paducah, Kentucky, on the Ohio (see map, p. 427). Davis tried to recall Polk's forces and retrieve his hasty step. But it was too late. Kentucky declared her allegiance to the Union (although a separate convention of Confederate volunteers voted in November to join Kentucky to the South), and was held thereafter, but only at great cost.

Unlike Maryland, which had a Unionist governor, and Kentucky, which had a Unionist legislature, Missouri's government was wholly Confederate in temper. Here Lincoln went so far as to sanction the establishment of a revolutionary Union government which, throughout the great war, carried on a local civil war with the secessionist regime it had unseated. Thousands were killed in Missouri even before the first battle of Bull Run in July, 1861.

In still a fourth area, western Virginia, traversed by the Baltimore and Ohio Railroad, Washington's principal link with the West, Lincoln early took advantage of Union sentiment to create a Union bulwark. His agent here was General George Brinton McClellan, who, in June, 1861, drove Virginia state forces from the western mountain passes and restored service on the B. & O. which these forces had disrupted. Local civil war persisted in Virginia until 1865; but the western counties—and after 1863, the new state of West Virginia as such—remained a firm part of the Union-held border stretching from the Atlantic to the Mississippi.

McClellan reported his successes in western Virginia in such resounding language that he became the first Civil War soldier to win official citation by Congress. After the Union rout at Bull Run it was to this officer, largely on his literary performance, that the country turned three times for safety—each time to suffer twinges of regret.

III. *"Forward to Richmond!"*

THE FIRST BATTLE OF BULL RUN

Lincoln's principal military adviser in the early months of the war was the General in Chief of the United States Army, Winfield Scott—"magnificent as a monument and nearly as useless," as an ungenerous critic described him in 1861. Born in 1786, Scott was a year older than the Constitution. But difficult as he sometimes found it to keep his eyes open, he was one of the few who had been wide awake to the fact that the Union must prepare for a long struggle. Scott, moreover, was perfectly clear-headed about the uses to which he would put the many months he wanted. Clamp a vise of steel on the border states, he said; master the whole course of the Mississippi; screw down the blockade on every rebel port on the Atlantic and the Gulf. Then, when the enemy had begun to writhe under pressure, speed his inevitable end by marching in the overpowering armies for whose preparation all earlier steps would have gained the necessary time.

Lincoln's early success in thwarting the neutrality of the border states provided a favorable start in carrying through Scott's plan on the land. The early success of Secretary of the Navy, Gideon Welles, in making Lincoln's "paper blockade" of April 19 (see p. 410) effective, further-improved prospects on the water. In a few months all but a few rebel seaports were closed in, and the

South's foreign trade had been cut at least 80 per cent.

Jefferson Davis, as revolted as Lincoln by the likelihood of bloodshed and reluctant to surrender the fantasy that the South would be permitted peacefully to sever the Union, had a war plan of his own that played right into Scott's hands.

The South, Davis said, had seceded to get away from, not to conquer, the North. He saw a perfect "natural frontier" stretching along the Mason and Dixon Line onward to the Black Hills of the Dakotas. Plant along this sweeping border, within which the Confederacy would have ample room for growth, a forest of impregnable forts. Then look to the naval power of Britain and France—hungry as these countries must quickly become for the cotton that was King of the Universe—to unlock southern ports, free southern trade, and protect independent southern commerce. As early as March 16, 1861, almost a month before Beauregard's bombardment of Fort Sumter, Davis, in one of his first steps as President, had sent three commissioners to Europe to carry out this "cotton diplomacy." Their initial goal was to arrange for massive munitions and supplies needed immediately by the Confederacy. How Lincoln's own commissioners foiled this mission, except in one significant respect (see p. 433), may have been a straw in the wind. Far more than cotton, with which she had filled her warehouses in anticipation of the war, Britain in particular in 1861 needed wheat. Wheat could be purchased elsewhere but the Union's ability to pay with massive wheat exports for the munitions and supplies her own envoys ordered in large quantities in the early years of the war made it difficult for Davis' agents to close any deals.

In the end, the Civil War was to be fought out as the confrontation of Davis' defensive plan, full of holes from the start though it was, and Scott's aggressive "anaconda," painfully slow though it proved to mount.

But both strategies had their enemies from the outset. Many Confederate leaders, General Beauregard among them, urged a relentless Confederate offensive without delay. This camp banked on the supposed superior valor of southern troops and on the less satisfying realization that if the South did not win quickly she was not likely to win at all.

The most popular Union plan seemed to count on just such rebel strategy as Beauregard proposed. In June, 1861, the main rebel army under Beauregard himself was stationed at Manassas Junction in Virginia, a critical railroad crossing between Washington and Richmond. Wipe out this army, sweep triumphantly down to the rebel capital, and crush the insurrection in one stroke—that was the siren plan to which Lincoln himself, nursing his own fantasy of a "ninety-day war," remained for some time trustingly drawn.

Each morning during the week preceding the return of Lincoln's Congress to Washington for its special session, Horace Greeley flaunted on the editorial page of his nationally read New York *Tribune,* "Forward to Richmond!" Then, on July 4, the day Congress opened, the *Tribune* cried: "Forward to Richmond! Forward to Richmond! The Rebel Congress must not be allowed to meet there on the 20th of July. By that date the place must be held by the National Army."

Thereafter, Radical demands mounted for "action—crushing, irresistible, overwhelming." The President may have done wonders; indeed, in some respects, too much. But the essential thing remained undone: to engage the enemy and destroy him. A touch of hysteria magnified the pressure. The Confederacy, everyone said, was gathering a rebel host for its own assault on Washington. "Why don't they come?" was the anxious question on every tongue. At last, on July 16, with the "three-months men" nearing the end of their service, General Scott, on Lincoln's authorization, ordered General Irvin McDowell to move.

McDowell's 30,000 were green as saplings,

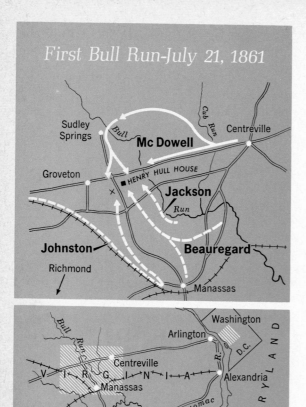

First Bull Run—July 21, 1861

out with the Federals to see the rebels crushed, were engulfed in the retreat as it became a headlong scramble of innocent youth homeward. Some of McDowell's men, their three-months service over, kept going all the way to New York, New Hampshire and Maine, where they first had volunteered.

In the presence of a congressional delegation in the White House after the battle, General Scott told the President: "Sir, I am the greatest coward in America. I deserve removal because I did not stand up, when the army was not in condition for fighting, and resist it to the last." "Your conversation seems to imply," Lincoln remarked, "that I forced you to fight this battle." Scott replied, "I have never served a President who has been kinder to me than you have been."

Recriminations also were rife in the South. "Give me 10,000 fresh troops, and I will be in Washington tomorrow," "Stonewall" Jackson is reported to have stated after Bull Run. But President Davis clung to his defensive plan and Washington, if indeed it was in mortal danger, was saved.

"ALL QUIET ON THE POTOMAC"

In his opening message to the new Congress on July 4, 1861, Lincoln had reviewed the record of his autonomous four months. "Of all that which a President might constitutionally and justifiably do in such a case," he said, "everything was forborne without which it was believed possible to keep the government on foot." When three days later, however, a joint resolution was introduced seeking to validate the President's extra-legal acts in Congress's absence, the majority laid the resolution aside. Even those members who sympathized with Lincoln's conduct refused to sanction, *post facto,* an invasion of their powers when they themselves deliberately had been left out in the cold. Congress would not even vote Lincoln the men and money he requested, "the legal means for making this contest a short and decisive one," until after the debacle of Bull Run. Only on August 5, the day before the session closed, and then merely as a rider to an army pay bill, would both houses vindicate

but Beauregard's force, estimated at 24,000, was no more mature. As McDowell marched southward, Beauregard probed northward to meet him on suitable terrain. By July 20 he had settled in on the southern side of the little stream of Bull Run, and there, the next morning, the Federals found him. By noon a Union triumph seemed certain. Then General Thomas J. Jackson's "stonewall" stand in one sector, followed by a succession of counter-attacks, their fury embellished by the "rebel yell," first heard here, halted the Union offensive.

In the afternoon, Confederate reinforcements under General Joseph E. Johnston arrived from the Shenandoah Valley where the rebels were to maintain a force for most of the war like a gun at Washington's back. McDowell, disappointed at not receiving reinforcements of his own, soon deemed it the better part of valor to retire. Fashionable ladies and congressmen and correspondents who, in a holiday mood, had set

Lincoln's military steps. His suspension of *habeas corpus* never was approved.

On August 6 the Radicals pushed through Congress a portentous measure of their own which Lincoln, fearful of driving the South to vengeful retaliation, said he "had some difficulty in consenting to approve." This was the so-called first Confiscation Act (a second was to be passed in July, 1862; see p. 436), making it the duty of the President to seize all property used in aiding the insurrection. Hateful as it was to the Radicals to identify Negroes as property, the act nevertheless included as subject to forfeit all slaves employed in building fortifications and in other military and naval work. Lincoln did sign the measure. "This government will be preserved," cried Congressman Hickman of Pennsylvania in approval, "and the gallows will eventually perform its service."

But the rebels had to be caught before they could be hanged. Immediately after Bull Run, Lincoln relieved McDowell, created a new Division of the Potomac, and placed McClellan, then a cocky 34 years of age, at its head. "All tell me that I am held responsible for the fate of the nation," the new commander wrote to his wife. A few days later, with his characteristic flourish, he added the telltale plan: "I shall carry this thing *en grande* and crush the rebels in one campaign." Under the paralyzing pull of Richmond, on the one hand, and the paralyzing fear for Washington's safety on the other, the "anaconda" policy was on its way toward official oblivion. By November 1, Scott himself had been outgeneraled in the struggle for power in the capital and was retired. McClellan, who had his hand in everything, including the overthrow of his old chief, was elevated to Scott's place. At the same time, this General's officious buzzing about in nonmilitary affairs, against the background of the prolonged inactivity of the army he was readying, caused confidence in him, and indeed in Lincoln on his account, to curdle.

McClellan's task on taking charge of the Division of the Potomac was unenviable. The remnants of McDowell's force—"it could not properly be called an army," said McClellan—were much the worse for having tasted the demoralization of defeat. The large new levies voted by Congress, in turn, were slow in gathering and wholly raw. Washington, moreover, lay ominously open to the enemy, its lack of a protective shield of forts perhaps justifying McClellan in his unwillingness to depart. If the young commander needed still another reason for not lunging hastily at the rebels, he found it in the nightmare of a second Bull Run, one all the more perturbing in view of the huge Confederate armies he himself conjured up on Washington's threshold.

McClellan's orders were, in the vicinity of the anxious capital, to forge the Army of the Potomac into a mighty sword and with it to bring the rebels to their knees. He was, in fact, a masterly organizer and conditioner. His failing was his pride in smart execution of the drill, his exasperating reluctance to risk his beauties in battle. By the time Congress reconvened for its regular session on December 2, 1861, McClellan was still grandly housed in Washington, still marching his men, and beginning to tax even the patience of Lincoln. Although the rebels were making restless forays nearby, and in one of them, at Ball's Bluff in October, had trapped and slaughtered a federal force sent by McClellan to see what was up, "Forward to Richmond!" was forgotten by the press and the people. Although rebel batteries also were making the Potomac River untenable for commercial vessels, "All Quiet on the Potomac" had become the derisive Union slogan of the day.

Little more than two weeks after Congress reconvened, the Radicals, their ranks augmented in the legislature by the apparent indolence of the executive, succeeded in establishing a Joint Committee on the Conduct of the War, with wide powers of investigation. Conservatives decried this "attempt on the part of the legislative branch to direct or supervise the military movements of the administration." The Radicals denounced them as "the diluted spawn of pink-eyed patriots." It was the "bounden duty" of Congress, they said, to scrutinize "executive agents," including generals who made a practice of returning fugitive slaves and were otherwise retrograde on "the Negro question." McClellan, well-known for his "softness" on slavery, soon became the Committee's pet target and hence doubly Lincoln's concern. Radical suspicions grew that he was in fact more unwilling than unready to fight the rebels, a view the President, although still dreading the onset of a war to the finish, dared not allow to be confirmed.

At last, on January 27, 1862, his patience spent, Lincoln issued General Order No. 1, naming Washington's Birthday, February 22, as "the day for a general movement of the land and naval forces of the United States against the insurgent forces." But even this unmistakable command went unheeded by McClellan. "In ten days I shall be in Richmond," he boasted on February 13. But not until April would he move.

COMING TO GRIPS IN THE WEST

While Washington remained preoccupied with the long quiet on the Potomac, the war was far from quiet in the West, where subordinate Union officers had taken things more or less into their own hands. One such officer was the rough Republican firebrand, Nathaniel Lyon, who earlier had forced the removal of his chief in St. Louis for his southern sympathies.

Lyon's efforts to rid divided Missouri of rebel troops were checked on August 10, 1861, when, outnumbered two to one, he lost a bitterly fought engagement at Wilson's Creek in the southwestern corner of the state. Lyon was killed in this battle, and his new chief, the flamboyant John C. Frémont, for failing to support him with men and supplies, was blamed for his death as well as his defeat. In November, Frémont was replaced in command of the Department of the West by General Henry W. Halleck, "Old Brains" to his cronies, but characterized by McClellan as "the most

hopelessly stupid [man] I have encountered in high position."

Regular Confederate forces held on in southwestern Missouri until March, 1862, when General Samuel R. Curtis, serving under Halleck, chased them into Arkansas and on March 8 defeated them at Pea Ridge. In southeastern Missouri, General John Pope drove the rebels from New Madrid on March 13, and from heavily fortified "Island No. 10" in the Mississippi on April 7, thereby opening the great river all the way to Memphis.

In neighboring Kentucky, Confederate General Albert Sidney Johnston, having seized Bowling Green in mid-September, 1861, and made it his headquarters, labored all fall to firm up a line across the southern range of the state from the Mississippi almost to Virginia. If he could not advance farther into Kentucky, Johnston, if he were lucky, planned at least to protect Tennessee and the heartland of the deep South she guarded.

The western anchor of Johnston's line was Columbus, Kentucky, where Polk had established his rebel camp on September 4. Bowling Green held down the center. The eastern end lay in the vicinity of the Cumberland Gap. Johnston could not establish his line without some successful skirmishing with federal parties, but the first real fighting of the war in Kentucky was bad news for him. On January 19, 1862, having earlier unnerved his superior, General Don Carlos Buell, with experimental advances toward Tennessee, General George H. Thomas caught one of Johnston's outlying contingents just above Mill Springs on the Cumberland River. The rebels tried to shoot their way out, but Thomas quickly gained the initiative and sent them flying while his own men gathered up abandoned Confederate munitions, horses, and mules.

Mill Springs undid Johnston's line in the east. It was followed up on February 6 (after a month of hard petitioning for Halleck's approval) by the triumph of Commodore Andrew H. Foote, directing a flotilla of gunboats under Grant's command, at Fort Henry on the Tennessee River. On

February 16 (with no authorization from Halleck at all) Grant's and Foote's combined operation took nearby Fort Donelson on the Cumberland. The loss of Fort Henry cut Johnston's communications between Bowling Green and Columbus and prompted him to quit his Kentucky line. The loss of Fort Donelson prevented him from taking a stand even in Tennessee. It was at Donelson that Grant made the demand on Johnston's subordinate, Simon Bolivar Buckner, which caught the fancy of the North: "No terms but immediate and unconditional surrender." The rebels had suffered a terrible setback, and the Federals had found a fighter able to make them look for more of the same. Yet all the worst fighting lay ahead for both sides.

In his *Personal Memoirs* Grant wrote, "immediately after the fall of Fort Donelson the way was opened to the National forces all over the Southwest without much resistance." The way was closed because no "one general who would have taken the responsibility had been in command." Grant himself was relieved of duty by the confused Halleck on March 4, and while his army was broken up for tactical operations here and there (including those of Pope in southeastern Missouri), "the enemy," Grant added, gained time "to collect armies and fortify his new positions."

During the month following Donelson, Albert Sidney Johnston was left free to lead his men across the whole of Tennessee to the strategic railroad center of Corinth, Mississippi. Trailing along behind, Buell mopped up in Tennessee. When Grant resumed command on March 17, he found most of his force at Pittsburg Landing on the Tennessee River, just above Tennessee's southern boundary opposite Corinth. Before pushing south once more against Johnston, Grant decided to await Buell's arrival. But Johnston took the offensive himself before Buell showed up.

On April 6, Johnston led the attack on Grant's exposed encampment at Shiloh, southwest of Pittsburg Landing, and with the advantage of surprise pushed the Federals back to the Tennessee River. There

Buell's vanguard appeared and helped stiffen Union resistance. Johnston himself was killed the first day, and on the next, the combined armies of Grant and Buell drove off the shaken rebels, now led by General Beauregard. Halleck soon appeared to take personal command of pressing the Union counter-offensive into Corinth. But he procrastinated for weeks as usual, and while his strength persuaded Beauregard, at the end of May, to abandon Corinth, the rebels got away again with their army intact.

Neither side could take much satisfaction from the bloody Shiloh engagement (the Federals lost 13,000 of 60,000 men; the Confederates almost 11,000 of 40,000), yet it gave each a healthier respect for the other. When Grant saw that the rebels here "not only attempted to hold a line farther south, . . . but assumed the offensive and made such a gallant effort to regain what had

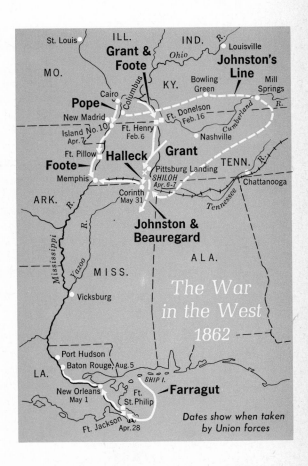

Dates show when taken by Union forces

The naval engagement between Virginia, *equipped with four-inch armor and iron ram at the bow; and the ironclad "cheese-box on a raft,"* Monitor. *Drawn on the spot, at Hampton Roads on the 9th of March, 1862.*

been lost, then, indeed," he wrote in his *Memoirs*, "I gave up all idea of saving the Union except by complete conquest." Robert E. Lee, in turn, still cooling his heels in Richmond as a presidential adviser, warned Davis that unless he outdid himself to hold the lower Mississippi and keep the Confederacy from being split, Grant's "complete conquest" would not be far off.

Lee's warning was underscored soon after Shiloh by more decisive Union operations farther west. At the end of April a Union fleet led by Captain David G. Farragut smashed through Confederate fortifications below New Orleans and forced that great Mississippi port to surrender. Baton Rouge fell soon after to a force under General Butler. In the meantime, Foote's formidable flotilla had come pushing down the Mississippi to Memphis where it destroyed a Confederate fleet. Between Memphis and New Orleans only Vicksburg, Mississippi, and Port Hudson, Louisiana, now blocked Union control of the mighty river, the outermost border of the "anaconda" plan.

THE PENINSULAR CAMPAIGN

Union operations in the West early in 1862 received only the barest notice in Washington, where protection of the capital and preparation of the *"en grande"* as-

sault on Richmond were the main concerns.

Lincoln, who had taken to studying books on military strategy to compensate for the manifest inadequacy of his advisers, had formed very definite opinions about how Richmond might be taken. In short, he was for a new direct frontal attack, which would have had the advantage of keeping the Army of the Potomac between the Confederates and Washington itself. Largely because he had not been consulted about it, McClellan opposed Lincoln's plan. The Confederate capital, the General argued, should be approached by way of the peninsula formed by the York River (on the north) and the James River (on the south). The peninsular plan involved a hazardous combined sea-and-land operation dangerously distant from Washington. To the normal difficulties of such an operation were added in this instance Confederate control of the Norfolk navy yard at the mouth of the James.

In March, 1862, just as they had tried to close the gap in Davis' perimeter in Kentucky, the Confederates had in Norfolk tried to break the Union's blockade on the Atlantic. For this purpose, Confederate engineers had transformed the wreck of the old United States frigate, *Merrimac,* found in Norfolk Harbor, into a freakish man-of-war—an iron-plated fortress which they re-named *Virginia,* a vessel too unseaworthy to venture into open water but capable of floating safely in the calm off Hampton Roads. Anchored there were five wooden Union warships on blockade duty. On March 8, 1862, *Virginia* floated down to attack them. Impervious to the heavy fire from the Union ships, *Virginia* destroyed or damaged three of the largest before engine trouble forced her to withdraw.

The Confederacy was jubilant over the victory. In Washington, in turn, the pro-clivity to panic was never more apparent. Both reactions, however, proved premature. When *Virginia,* her running gear patched up, returned the next day to finish off the last of the wooden Union ships, she found herself confronted by an even more fantastic craft than herself. This was the famous *Monitor,* the "cheese-box on a raft," de-signed by the imaginative Swedish-born in-ventor, John Ericsson. On March 9, *Monitor* met the much larger *Virginia* off Hamp-ton Roads. Neither ironclad could sink the other and in the end *Virginia* retreated

upstream. She had failed to open a perma-nent breech in the Union blockade, but on the James she still remained a menace to any Union advance.

Could McClellan rely on Union naval support while *Virginia* menaced Chesa-peake Bay? Lincoln thought not. Thankful, however, that McClellan at last proposed to move, Lincoln let him have his way. But Lincoln insisted that McClellan surrender to the President himself his supreme com-mand, retaining command only of his new Army of the Potomac, and that he leave behind under other generals a part even of this army to guard the capital.

The first contingents of McClellan's force—all told, 110,000 strong—were landed successfully on the peninsula on April 4, 1862. Yorktown, the first Confederate stronghold on the way to Richmond, might have been overrun in a day. McClellan, still fearful of a new Bull Run, took a

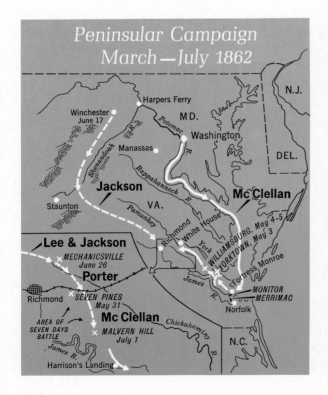

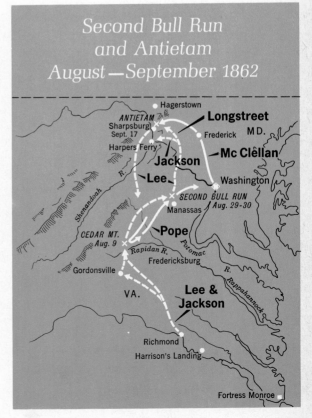

month to level and enter the town. Almost another month was lost while the General, vainly awaiting expected reinforcements, was led slowly up the peninsula by wily "Joe" Johnston who had a rendezvous with reinforcements of his own. What kept McClellan's reinforcements away was "Stonewall" Jackson's brilliant foray up the Shenandoah Valley, where, as Lincoln had anticipated, he menaced Washington from the rear (see map, p. 429). Jackson's masterly campaign won grudging admiration even from the northern press. The New York *Mercury* described him as "no mortal man," and remarked that his "abstemiousness enables him to live for a fortnight on two crackers and a barrel of whisky." Having unnerved the Union capital sufficiently to force Lincoln to keep even a stronger army there than he had planned, Jackson himself dashed back to the main front to lend his strength to Johnston.

Before Jackson arrived, McClellan had been drawn to within five miles of Richmond where, on May 31, he narrowly averted disaster at Seven Pines. "Joe" Johnston was badly wounded in this battle, and McClellan might have taken advantage of the Confederates' ill-luck to press on. Instead, he left 25,000 men under General Fitz-John Porter in the vicinity of Richmond and returned with the rest to his base at White House, some 20 miles to the east. Here he waited once again, in expectation of the still more men he had requested to oppose the vast host that he imagined stood before the Confederate capital. While McClellan waited, on June 1 Lee at last was returned to the field as the wounded Johnston's replacement. On taking charge, he gave his troops the name, "The Army of Northern Virginia," his only command until Davis, in February, 1865, named him General in Chief of all the forces of what had become "The Lost Cause."

Lee possessed the capacities as well as the appearance of a hero. His many admirers regarded him as the greatest military genius of the war—as an inspired commander who performed miracles with under-manned and poorly equipped armies. His soldiers themselves came to look upon him as a man "above his race" who "communed with the angels of Heaven." Some military historians have argued that Lee was so concerned with defending his native state that he never developed a coordinated over-all strategy. But Virginia's front for too long was all he was vouchsafed and he used it, with his forays into the North itself (see pp. 431, 439), as the most effective means of relieving Union pressure elsewhere. Other writers point to Lee's failure to provide adequate supplies for his armies, which kept him from exploiting his victories; his habit of giving too much independence to his generals in the field; and his practice of taking on staggering burdens of staff work that he should have delegated to others. So long as he could draw on brilliant corps commanders, however, Lee's confidence was rarely misplaced. In the later stages of the war—particularly after the loss of "Stonewall" Jackson, at Chancellorsville in May, 1863 (see p. 439)—the caliber of his junior officers declined.

Soon after he had taken the field, Lee learned of how McClellan had split his army and immediately formed a plan to send a small force "looking numerous and aggressive" to intimidate the susceptible General, while he himself moved in overpowering strength to crush Porter. This accomplished, Lee hoped to outflank McClellan and cut his own force to pieces.

Unfortunately for Lee, Porter and McClellan were prepared. Lee's "eye" in spying out McClellan's position was his dashing cavalry chief, "Jeb" Stuart. It was Stuart's nature to improve any opportunity for showmanship. In a marvelous manifestation of contempt for the enemy—and of foolish disregard of the risk for his own cause—for three days (June 12-15, 1862) he drove his worthies completely around the idling Federals and, unscathed, brought Lee the wanted information. His exploit also alerted the Union invaders. McClellan regrouped his forces and surprised the Confederates with his mobilized strength. Having done so, however, he returned once more to the strategy of retreat. In the Seven Days' Battle, between June 26 and July 1, McClellan inflicted very heavy losses on Lee's advancing troops, but his own sorry objective was Harrison's Landing on the James River where the Union Navy, if necessary, could evacuate his men.

BLOODY ANTIETAM

Lincoln visited McClellan at Harrison's Landing on July 9. When McClellan proposed that he renew the assault on Richmond, Lincoln vetoed the suggestion. In fact, under Radical pressure, he called off the whole Peninsular Campaign and decided to bring back McClellan's army. He also placed this army and all the Union forces under a military leader once more. That he appointed Halleck as the new chief is often considered a serious blunder, but there is no evidence that anyone else who seemed eligible would have been better.

Lee, relieved of pressure from McClellan's large force, now left a small group to watch over the Federals' withdrawal and took his own army on a new advance northward. To meet him Halleck assigned the rash and boastful Pope who had been fighting Jackson in the Shenandoah Valley. As Pope moved slowly southward from the vicinity of Bull Run toward the strategic town of Gordonsville, he was intercepted by Jackson and defeated, August 9, at Cedar Mountain. Lee and Jackson then gradually maneuvered him northward once more and forced him to take a stand again near Manassas. On August 29-30 the two armies clashed in their full might in the momentous Second Battle of Bull Run, and Pope, completely outgeneraled, was routed with the loss of 16,000 out of 75,000 troops. Lee lost 9,000 of his 48,000. Halleck must bear some of the onus for this stunning new disaster. When reinforcements for Pope might have averted defeat, Halleck had refused to issue the orders that would have given Pope the unified command of a larger force than he had.

This fresh setback left the Union bitter and discouraged. In June, 1862, McClellan had been on Richmond's threshold, three strong Union armies appeared to have control of the Shenandoah Valley, and western Virginia was in Union hands. Now, at the

end of August, as Douglas S. Freeman says, "the only Federals closer than 100 miles to Richmond were prisoners . . . and men . . . preparing to retreat." In desperation, Lincoln turned again to McClellan to take temporary command of the disorganized army in the east. "If he can't fight," Lincoln said, "he excels in making others ready to fight."

Lee, meanwhile, characteristically pressed the attack, hoping for the first time to penetrate the North itself. Across his path lay the refurbished federal arsenal at Harpers Ferry, Virginia, with 10,000 men, and munitions and supplies much needed by his own ragged and hungry troops. If he could take the arsenal and move from there into Maryland, he might win new recruits in this and other border states with which to move on to Pennsylvania. France and Britain then might recognize the southern republic and actively intervene on its behalf. McClellan at the same time would be forced into defensive activity with a still demoralized force backed by a disheartened citizenry.

On September 9 Lee boldly ordered the division of his army, one part under Jackson to move on Harpers Ferry, the rest, under General James Longstreet, to push toward Hagerstown, Maryland. Harpers Ferry, to Lee's discomfort, held out until September 15; by then it was clear, as well, that Maryland would not rally to the southern invaders. In the meantime, an unlucky accident, on September 13, helped make certain the frustration of Lee's project. On that day a Union officer picked up on the road a dispatch (wrapped around three cigars) from Lee to one of his generals disclosing how Lee had split up his force. Here was McClellan's chance to crush the enemy before he could regroup. McClellan's 70,000 men at Frederick, Maryland, outnumbered Lee's entire force by almost two to one. His natural hesitancy, however, and Halleck's fear of a trap, held him back until September 17, and by then the triumphant Jackson had rejoined Lee. At last, the Federals stormed across Antietam Creek, near Sharpsburg, Maryland, and nearly engulfed the Confederate lines, but then McClellan faltered. He lacked, according to one of his Confederate opponents, "that divine spark which impels a commander, at the accepted moment, to throw every man on the enemy and grasp complete victory." Instead, he permitted the exhausted enemy to slip back across the Potomac. In the one-day battle 25,000 men, divided almost equally between the two rivals, were lost.

Antietam has been called, "a defeat for both armies." But the Union, at least, had repulsed an invasion on which the South had spent perhaps too much. "Our maximum strength has been mobilized," Jefferson Davis told his Secretary of War after the battle, "while the enemy is just beginning to put forth his might."

IV. *The Civilian Response*

CONFEDERATE WAYS AND MEANS

The brutal, inconclusive engagement at Antietam was an appropriate symbol of the course of the whole war. Under the stress of political demands or military expediency, both sides seemed long since to have forgotten their high hopes and grand strategies, and the conflict had devolved into a series of separate engagements, one more violent than another. In the North, Scott's anaconda plan was scarcely more than a memory to most of those charged with the responsibility of restoring the Union. Richmond had become the prime target, and Richmond remained more distant than ever in a military sense. Davis' defensive and diplomatic tactics, on the other hand, had brought the Confederacy little but frustration, Lee's belated offensives little but death. Naturally the civilian fronts bent under the pressure of the aimless slaughter.

One manifestation of civilian discontent was the mounting criticism of the conduct of the war. To check it in the Confederacy, Davis, on February 27, 1862, prevailed upon his Congress to enact the first Confederate law granting the executive power to suspend the writ of *habeas corpus* and to impose martial law. But so intense had state-rights sentiment become in the South, that no sooner were Davis' critics locked up under Confederate authority than state authorities released them. Southern editors were frequent victims of the regime. Yet criticism would not be stilled.

The military stalemate was even more acutely felt by those charged with maintaining the resources and manpower of the fighting forces. As early as April, 1862, the Confederate Congress was obliged to enact the first conscription act in American history, calling up for three years' service all white men 18 to 35. Later acts raised the age limit to 50. But anyone could escape the draft by paying for a substitute, and occupational exemptions were numerous. Evasion, moreover, had the support of certain state-rights governors who ran their states like private satrapies dissociated from the capital.

The poor showing reflected in southern draft statistics veils the true serviceability of the conscription acts. "Conscript" became such a brand of opprobrium that many youths hastened to volunteer before their age group was called, and they more than the conscripts themselves maintained Confederate military manpower. On the other hand, the draft acts' official sanction of the purchase of substitutes seemed to confirm the disheartening slogan, "a rich man's war and a poor man's fight." Desertions soared to well over 100,000—only a third, perhaps, of Union desertions, but much more keenly felt. As the Confederate economy foundered, and as disheartening letters to the front revealed the plight of the home folks, many of the men saw no disgrace in leaving the lost cause to succor their suffering families. If not they, who would? Surely not the rising race of speculators—the "little whipper-snapper blear-eyed . . . wretches," in the lexicon of a Richmond editor, "who would bottle the universal air and sell it at so much a bottle."

Symptoms of economic difficulties could be detected in the South even during the first year of the war. Loans in specie were virtually impossible to make in a country where wealth was traditionally tied up in land and slaves. By 1862 the Confederacy was trying "produce loans" by which planters were expected to pay in cotton and other commodities for Confederate bonds. But these loans had two drawbacks. Many planters would not surrender their commodities for government paper; and when they did, the government found it as hard as its citizens to transform commodities into cash.

The Confederacy had little better luck with taxes, and like other governments frustrated in the quest for gold, it began to print paper money in 1861. Before the end of the war a billion dollars' worth of these notes had been issued by Davis' government, and another billion by southern states and cities. By 1864 a dollar in Confederate paper was worth, on average, a cent and a half in specie. Prices naturally soared, thus encouraging speculation and hoarding. Food was especially hard hit; and widespread famine, made more difficult to fight by the growing breakdown of transportation, hurt Confederate morale even more than setbacks in the field.

THE FAILURE
OF SOUTHERN DIPLOMACY
Confederate difficulties at home were aggravated by the collapse of southern diplomacy abroad, after some early successes.

The ruling classes in Europe had no love for slavery, but as aristocrats they feared popular government as practiced in the United States and would have been pleased with the failure of the "American experiment." Britain and France in particular had hastened early in 1861 to recognize the Confederacy's independent status as a belligerent power if not as a sovereign government. Britain, moreover, made warlike

gestures at Lincoln's administration in November, 1861, after a Union cruiser stopped the British mail steamer, *Trent,* on the high seas and removed two Confederate diplomats on their way to London and Paris. War was averted when Secretary of State Seward heeded British representations and released the two rebels.

The Confederates had the last laugh over the *Trent* episode. They were especially encouraged when Britain followed up its representations by transporting 8,000 troops to Canada. The check Confederate forces received a year later at Antietam, however, destroyed hopes for European intervention. When Lincoln, moreover, took this occasion to announce an emancipation proclamation (see p. 437), the surge of Union sentiment among foreign middle- and working-class elements made it most unlikely that foreign rulers would risk discontent at home by again backing the wrong horse in America. Early in November, 1862, the British government firmly rejected the last French approach to intervene in the war and henceforth resisted all Confederate pleadings as well.

The effects of one phase of British interventionism persisted, however. This was British willingness to build Confederate sea-raiders. International law permitted neutrals to build non-naval craft for belligerents, but it forbade them to be "equipped, fitted out, or armed" for fighting purposes. British shipbuilders evaded this restriction by permitting apparently inoffensive hulls to "escape" to obscure and unpoliced ports, there to take on guns and munitions. All told, 18 of these "brigands of the sea" (*Alabama* was the most successful of them) preyed on northern shipping.

In July, 1862, Charles Francis Adams, the Union minister in Britain, protested in vain against the "escape" of *Alabama*. By 1863, however, Union threats to loose a "flood of privateers" against Britain's nominally neutral trade had the desired effect.

No new Confederate raiders were launched; but the American merchant marine did not recover until World War I from the blows of those already at sea, and American claims against the British for the raiders' wartime damages became a hot political issue after 1865.

By 1863 an air of caution had taken hold in France as well, where Napoleon III had dreams of reinstating a monarchy in Mexico, to which the Confederates might look for help. Maximilian of Austria, a puppet of Napoleon's, actually was placed at the head of Mexico's government soon after French army units had taken over Mexico City in June, 1863. But thereafter he received scant French support, and when Maximilian was captured and executed by Mexican rebels in June, 1867, the French acquiesced quietly in his extinction.

THE NORTH IN WARTIME

The conduct of the war, of course, was the overwhelming civil as well as military responsibility of Lincoln's government. Yet the Republican party had also made many civil commitments that had nothing to do with the war, and many in the party's leadership were eager to meet these commitments while the South was out of the Union and unable any longer to obstruct federal fostering of industrial growth.

Thus the Republican congress soon enacted the following measures: (1) In 1861 it passed the Morrill Tariff, which raised duties to their 1846 levels. The protective tariff was steadily raised throughout the war, and once the war was over duties continued to soar. Payment of the war debt was to become one of the sacred arguments for postwar protectionism (see Chapter 20). (2) In 1862 the Republican congress voted to build the long-debated transcontinental railroad over a central route and to help finance it with lavish grants of public lands and generous cash loans (see p. 518). (3) In 1863, with revisions in 1864, Congress created a national banking system that was congenial to northern capitalists.

Nor did Republican leaders neglect their strong free-soil supporters. The Homestead Act passed in 1862 made available to adult citizens and to those who declared their intention of becoming citizens, 160 acres of the public domain. The land itself was free of charge, but there were stipulations requiring prompt improvement and settlement (see p. 506). Only men who had borne arms against the United States were excluded. Farmers also benefited from the Morrill Land Grant Act of 1862, the result of a long campaign led by Jonathan B. Turner, an Illinois educational and agricultural reformer. This act donated public lands to the states and territories to provide colleges for agriculture, the mechanical arts, and military science.

The impact of these legislative measures was to be felt far into the future. During the war itself, after a year-long depression caused by the loss of $300 million in uncollectible southern debts and uncertainty about the war's duration, financing, and success, the North enjoyed a substantial boom. Historians have questioned the role of the war in stimulating general economic growth in the North; but it cannot be denied that the splurge of government war buying in particular gave a great impetus to the expansion and mechanization of agriculture, the production of shoes and other apparel, the manufacture of munitions. "Shoddy" millionaires made fortunes foisting off on the government much useless material. Other millionaires of the future, Rockefeller, Carnegie, Mellon, Morgan, all laid the foundations for their great wealth in wartime business activity. Even if industrial growth was spotty, the accumulation of capital for future business expansion was great. The war prosperity had its harsh side, of course. Industrial wages, for example, rose far more slowly than living costs, causing much hardship in cities where food speculators flourished. Families living on fixed incomes were especially hurt by the wartime inflation. Yet few northerners suffered the privations that became all but universal in the Confederacy.

Despite the boom, Lincoln's government had a difficult time financing the war, partly because it failed to realize how long the war would be. There were other obstacles in the form of monetary doctrines. Treasury-Secretary Chase, for example, distrusted bankers and paper money, but when heavy excise taxes and even an income tax enacted in 1861 failed to provide anything like the revenue needed, he found he had to rely on both. The bankers, unfortunately, became less and less enthusiastic about bond issues as the military situation worsened. Chase next tried to sell bonds directly to the public, but failed until, in 1862, a private banker named Jay Cooke was put in charge of the program. That year, with high-pressure publicity, Cooke sold $400 million worth of bonds to individuals. But that figure marked the peak of his success.

The administration's most criticized fiscal step was its printing between 1862 and 1863 of $450 million in Treasury certificates known as "greenbacks." Unsupported by gold, these certificates were nevertheless made legal tender for domestic debts. By the summer of 1864, when Union armies were still in straits, the greenbacks had fallen in value to their low of 39 cents on the gold dollar. Thereafter Union bonds began to sell well again, no more paper money was issued, and the greenbacks' value rose. The question of the continued circulation of the greenbacks became a heated political question after the war.

Despite the sizable emigration from Europe to the North during the war, shortages of manpower hurt the Union military effort at certain junctures almost as much as they hurt the Confederacy. By March, 1863, conscription could no longer be put off, and on the 3rd of that month, almost a full year after the Confederacy's measure, Congress imposed the first Union draft. Far from helping the manpower situation, the wording of the act was like a torch to inflammable social discontent. One of its provisions permitted a man to escape military service simply by paying a fee of $300 to the authorities, leaving them with the responsibility of finding substitutes ready to serve for a bounty. In July, 1863, a New York City mob gave sinister expression to widespread resentment against the act by setting

fire to buildings and attacking free Negroes. Soldiers had to be drawn from the battlefield to suppress the violence. As in the South, however, the draft prompted tens of thousands of recruits to enlist to avoid the brand of "conscript."

THE PROGRESS OF EMANCIPATION

If Lee, before Antietam, and again before Gettysburg (see p. 438), yearned to end the war's hateful slaughter by breaking the North's morale through invasion, Lincoln, as the dreary reports from the battlefields indicated no release from the dreadful stalemate, yearned to end it through political action. That, no doubt, is what he meant when he said that "military necessity" required the Emancipation Proclamation of January 1, 1863. "Military necessity" was a phrase that the pertinacity of the abolitionists themselves first made popular and palatable as the proper ground for emancipation. It also offered, in Lincoln's eyes, perhaps the only constitutional justification for the Proclamation. But he used the phrase for more than merely expedient or technical reasons.

From the day he took office Lincoln had "struggled," as he said, against every kind of pressure, religious, journalistic, political, personal, to declare the slaves free without compensating their owners and without undertaking to "colonize" freed Negroes outside the country. Even had he sympathized with such demands, he felt too keenly the sensitivity of the border states within the Union, where slavery still persisted, not to speak of northern sentiment in general, to yield to them. During the early months of the war such bold anti-slavery generals as Benjamin F. Butler, John C. Frémont, and David Hunter, in pursuing their duties as they understood them, had threatened, and in certain cases had effected, the emancipation of slaves in the areas of their commands. They had even enlisted freed Negroes in the fighting forces. Lincoln countermanded their actions and rebuked them for their precipitancy. "On the news of General Frémont having actually issued deeds of manumission" in Missouri in August, 1861, Lincoln declared, "a whole company of our volunteers threw down their arms and disbanded." He added that "the Kentucky legislature would not budge [in the direction of loyalty] till that proclamation was modified."

As the fighting spread in the border states and in the South itself, and increasing numbers of Negroes sought the security of Union lines, the generals in the field were left more or less to their own discretion in dealing with them until in March, 1862, Congress adopted "an additional article of war" forbidding officers, on pain of dismissal from the service, from using any of their forces to return fugitive slaves to their owners. In August, 1862, the War Department issued the first specific authorization for the recruitment of fugitive slaves as soldiers. This authorization, although of very limited application, was accompanied by the request that it "must never see daylight because it is so much in advance of public opinion." In itself, however, it reflected a further liberalization of feeling which led, after January, 1863, to the enrollment of Negro regiments.

Following the "first confiscation act" of August, 1861 (see p. 425), Congress added more steps to the ladder of freedom. In April, 1862, it passed and Lincoln signed a measure abolishing slavery in the District of Columbia. Under this act, former owners were to be paid, on the average, $300 per slave. In June that year Congress, with Lincoln's consent, also abolished slavery in United States territories, with no compensation granted. In July, Congress adopted the so-called "second confiscation act," providing for the conviction for treason of all persons engaged in rebellion, "or who shall in any way give aid . . . thereto," and including as among its penalties the stipulation that "all slaves" of such persons "shall be forever free of their servitude." Lincoln prepared a veto message explicitly rejecting this bill on the grounds of the un-

constitutionality of the word "forever." According to the Constitution, he pointed out, "no attainder of treason shall work corruption of blood, or forfeiture, except during the life of the person attainted." This was a technicality under the circumstances, and when Congress, equally technical, formally acknowledged that "forfeiture" was not meant to extend beyond the life of the guilty, Lincoln withheld his veto and signed the act. His proposed veto message, nevertheless, revealed the progress of his own thinking. In it he had observed:

It is startling to say that congress can free a slave within a state; and yet if it were said the ownership of the slave had first been transferred to the nation, and that congress had then liberated him, the difficulty would at once vanish. . . . I perceive no objection to Congress deciding in advance that they shall be free.

Union generals had dealt with slavery mainly with emergency measures. Congress had dealt with it under the whip of Radical opinion. When he signed the "second confiscation act" on July 17, 1862, Lincoln had already failed in his own first effort to use emancipation as an instrument to end the war and restore the Union. This effort was made in March, 1862, when he proposed to Congress that both houses adopt a joint resolution offering to "any state which may adopt gradual abolishment of slavery, . . . pecuniary aid . . . to compensate" it for the "change of system." His object was to wean the border states from their attachment to the "institution." In his message to Congress, Lincoln explained his thinking:

The leaders of the existing insurrection entertain the hope that this government will ultimately be forced to acknowledge the independence of some part of the disaffected region, and that all the slave States north of such part will then say, "the Union for which we have struggled being already gone, we now choose to go with the Southern section." To deprive them of this hope substantially ends the rebellion, and the initiation of emancipation completely deprives them of it as to all the States initiating it.

In Congress, border state votes helped reject Lincoln's proposal. On July 12 Lincoln invited border state representatives to the White House in an effort to change their minds. "If you had voted for the resolution," he told them, "the war would now be substantially ended." He urged them to reconsider, in preparation for the next Congress. But in 48 hours their spokesmen returned and told Lincoln the majority among them felt that his plan would not "lessen the pressure for 'unconstitutional' emancipation by proclamation of the remaining three million slaves in the seceded states, which [they] were unwilling to approve."

Having lost his appeal to the border states to free their slaves and save the Union, Lincoln, as a last peaceful recourse, now decided to admonish the slave states to return to the Union or see their slaves freed. For this purpose he immediately began work on his so-called preliminary emancipation proclamation which he was prevailed upon to hold from the public at least until word from the battlefield improved. He was unwilling to wait beyond Antietam, which, on September 17, 1862, saw the frustration of Lee's war-ending effort (see p. 431). Thus, on September 22, 1862, Lincoln proclaimed his emancipation plan, which the newspapers printed the next day.

In it, Lincoln said that at the next meeting of Congress in December he would recommend the enactment "of a practical measure" offering to *all* slave states not then in rebellion against the United States and having "voluntarily adopt[ed] immediate, or gradual abolishment of slavery within their limits," the same type of "pecuniary aid" as he had offered the border states in March. He also promised to continue his efforts to "colonize persons of African descent, with their consent." On January 1, 1863, this proclamation continued, he would designate which states still were in rebellion, and in them, "all persons held as slaves . . . shall be then, thenceforward, and forever free," with no compensation whatever. Moreover, "the military and naval authority" of the United States would make no effort to suppress any efforts slaves may then make to

effect their freedom; on the contrary, this authority would do whatever necessary to maintain it.

In his second annual message to Congress on December 1, 1862, Lincoln accordingly urged the adoption of an amendment to the Constitution providing that each slave state which abolished slavery "any time before the 1st day of January, 1900, shall receive compensation from the United States"; but only those not in rebellion against the United States on January 1, 1863, might participate in this offer.

Conservatives in the North, sick of the military stalemate and fearful that any tampering with slavery would only prolong the South's resistance, registered their disapproval of the preliminary emancipation proclamation in the fall elections of 1862, when the Democrats cut deeply into the Republican majority in the House and won the governorship in New York. The Radicals, on the other hand, deplored Lincoln's tortuous and tolerant maneuverings and demanded that he get on with the "revolutionary struggle" he abhorred. In mid-December, 1862, following the elections and the Union military disaster at Fredericksburg (see p. 438), Senator Sumner led a congressional delegation to the White House demanding that Secretary of State Seward, McClellan's friend, be dropped, and a further shuffling of the Cabinet. Lincoln's friend, Senator Browning, advised the President that the goal was to transform his Cabinet into a thoroughly Radical body which would run the war from the Executive Department the way the Committee on the Conduct of the War, in Congress, wanted it run. Lincoln turned the tables on the visitors, got Chase's resignation instead of Seward's, and cried, "Now I can ride!"

On January 1, 1863, his "full period of one hundred days" of grace gone by with no takers among the rebellious commonwealths (they, in fact, viewed the proclamation as little short of an invitation to slave revolts and a servile war) Lincoln issued his final proclamation, identifying those "States and parts of States, wherein the people thereof" remained "in rebellion against the United States," and restating his memorable words: in these areas, "all persons held as slaves . . . are, and henceforward shall be free."

No slaves, in fact, were freed by the proclamation. No more than Lincoln's other political efforts, moreover, did it end or shorten the war. Nevertheless it insured the death, beyond resurrection, of the hateful institution when the war would be won. In his message to Congress in December, 1862, Lincoln said, "in *giving* freedom to the *slave,* we *assure* freedom to the *free.*" The last months of 1862, politically trying to Lincoln's administration, were to be tragic for the Union armies. But the South and the world knew there could no longer be any surrender to slavery.

v. *Gettysburg, Vicksburg, and Atlanta*

THE LONG ROAD TO GETTYSBURG

After Antietam, McClellan had Lee at his mercy but withstood every demand that he move until Lincoln, in utter disgust, removed him in November. As before,

Fredericksburg to Gettysburg 1863

his replacement at the head of the still formidable Army of the Potomac, General Ambrose E. Burnside, proved worse.

Burnside guilelessly tried to steal a march on Lee while mounting still another frontal assault on Richmond. As might have been expected, Lee turned the tables on his opponent. Their brutal meeting took place at Fredericksburg, Virginia, on December 13, after Lee with 70,000 men had been given a month to set up impregnable defenses on the surrounding heights. Six times Burnside ordered the full force of his 125,000 men against this barrier. Six times his gallant lines were cut to pieces. Burnside was eager to keep up the dreadful assault; but his more merciful subordinates persuaded him to withdraw after he had lost more than 12,000 of his best men.

In January, 1863, Lincoln relieved Burnside and turned the eastern command over to "Fighting Joe" Hooker, an intriguer and blusterer who once had declared that the country needed a dictator in the President's place. "What I now ask of you is military success," Lincoln told Hooker, "and I will risk the dictatorship." By springtime, the Army of the Potomac was up to 130,000 men and again in splendid trim. "My plans are perfect," Hooker boasted, "and when I start to carry them out, may God have mercy on General Lee, for I will have none."

Hooker recognized that Lee's army of 60,000, still safe in its Fredericksburg entrenchments, remained too formidable to be taken by frontal assault. He decided to feign such an assault, repeating Burnside's disastrous maneuver, while actually bringing his main force around to strike at Lee's undefended rear. On April 27, the Federals carried out the first part of the plan to perfection. Drawn from their Fredericksburg entrenchments by the new Union activity, Lee's heavily outnumbered forces encountered Hooker at Chancellorsville, a small cross-roads settlement to the west. Seizing the initiative, Lee split up his troops, dispatching "Stonewall" Jackson to roll up Hooker's vulnerable right flank while Lee himself attacked the Union front. On May 2, Jackson descended on the unprepared Federals and completely demoralized them. He also demoralized Hooker who might have counterattacked successfully and destroyed the divided Confederates but who instead, against the entreaties of his corps commanders, decided to run away. On May 5, having lost more than 17,000 men, Hooker recrossed the Rappahannock northward toward Washington. "My God, my God," Lincoln is reported to have cried out on learning the news, "What will the country say! What will the country say!"

Chancellorsville, following Fredericksburg, marked the peak of Confederate success in the eastern theater. Military historians call it "Lee's masterpiece," but it was to prove a monstrous victory. The battle cost Lee 12,000 men. Worse, it had taken the life of his flaming field commander, "Stonewall" Jackson. Worse still, even with Jackson gone, it opened up to Lee what he saw as the opportunity—the very last such opportunity—to win the war with one blow: to surge northward once more, to bring bloodshed and destruction to Pennsylvania and Ohio, to dissolve the last shreds of Union morale and Union resistance. For this purpose he demanded of Davis every possible man of the quarter-million or more the Confederacy had fully under arms at the time. Davis would allow him no more than those he had in his Virginia command. Davis was not without justification. Simultaneously with the ever more vicious engagements in the East, the pace of the war was rising in the West (see

p. 441). Men were needed there too. Lee had come to believe the West irrelevant to final success. He ignored his setback at the President's hand. Move he would, and move he did. "General Lee," one of his lieutenants said at this time, "believed that the Army of Northern Virginia, as it then existed, could accomplish anything." He was wrong.

Lee began his fateful march toward Harrisburg, Pennsylvania, on the strategic Susquehanna River, on June 3, 1863. Up ahead he sent his Second Corps under General Richard S. Ewell, who had fallen heir to most of Jackson's men. Then came the First Corps under Longstreet, and finally the Third Corps under A. P. Hill, the last to abandon the Rappahannock entrenchments. Ordered to cover the whole long thin line of march was the consolidated cavalry under unpredictable "Jeb" Stuart. Hooker, unchastened, thought he detected in Lee's departure yet one more, one more chance to move on Richmond. But Lincoln, grown wiser with the years, undertook to set him straight: "Lee's army, not Richmond, is your true objective point. If he comes toward the upper Potomac, follow on his flank and on his inside track, shortening your lines while he lengthens his."

Lee's army moved steadily up the familiar Shenandoah Valley, past already historic Harpers Ferry, across the Potomac into Maryland. Hooker's army beat a roughly parallel path between the Valley and Washington. Here and there, as they marched through Maryland, the enemies made contact, the cavalry of each, the "eyes" of the army, engaging in numerous indecisive skirmishes as they tried to keep the "feel" of one another. At Brandy Station, Virginia, on June 9, Hooker's Pleasanton and Lee's Stuart engaged in the biggest cavalry fight in American history before each proceeded once more on his way. By June 23, Ewell's advance Corps had reached Chambersburg, Pennsylvania, and was soon to push on to within ten miles of Harrisburg—the deepest penetration of the war. Stuart, that same day, boldly sallied to within four miles of Washington, where he cut off a wagon train with supplies the Confederates much needed. Disastrously for him, on June 25, Hooker got between Stuart and Lee, and Lee's "eyes" were lost. Two days later, Lee's whole army was in Pennsylvania, with Chambersburg as its base, but Lee no longer knew where Hooker was. Worried about his communications, Lee called Ewell nearer "home," abandoned the Harrisburg objective, and prepared for the showdown.

As it happened, even had he had his "eyes," Lee would not have been able to find "Fighting Joe." With battle impending, Hooker managed to get into an altercation with Halleck, still, unaccountably, at the head of the Union armies, and on June 28 was replaced by "the old snapping turtle," George Gordon Meade.

On June 30, while Lee and Meade were seeking contact at some favorable point, a group of A. P. Hill's men entered the crossroads town of Gettysburg, Pennsylvania, looking for shoes and other supplies. There to greet them was Union cavalry under John Buford, Meade's most northerly watch. Heavily outnumbered, Buford sent word for help and then fought for all he was worth. Word of the encounter quickly reached Lee and Meade, and on July 1 the Battle of Gettysburg began in earnest.

Pouring into Gettysburg from the north, Ewell and Hill swept through the town, slaughtering the hastily mobilized Federals under Winfield Scott Hancock. But Hancock rallied his regiments quickly, led them to the lee of Cemetery Ridge just below Gettysburg, and there holed in while lookouts anxiously watched "the masses of blue coats toiling forward." At the end of the day Meade's men reached Cemetery Ridge in force. Parallel to Cemetery Ridge, to the west, across a mile-wide valley where "the fields were yellow with the golden harvest," lay Seminary Ridge, which the Confederates hastened to make their own.

The setting was almost perfect for a fight to the death. Cemetery Ridge had a peculiar shape, often compared to a fish hook. Longstreet, whose every instinct rebelled against assailing this redoubtable escarpment, urged Lee to outflank it on the south, interpose his army between Meade and Washington, and force the Federals to attack him. This may have been more easily advised than accomplished; in any case, Lee knew that he and his men had come this far to advance farther and not to retreat or maneuver, and on July 2 he ordered the assault to begin.

The fighting on July 2 did not start until very late in the afternoon. Then it was fierce but indecisive. The next day Lee renewed the attack. Once more, on the morning of July 3, Ewell's men breasted the slopes of Culp's Hill on the northeasterly end of Cemetery Ridge, fought valorously, yet were repulsed. Still farther east, and unknown to most of the soldiers on the Ridge, Stuart's cavalry was making its own fierce effort to break into the Union rear and prepare a path for encirclement. But Stuart, too, was repulsed. Would Lee dare drive up the middle? Meade thought he would and decided to wait. At one o'clock a terrific artillery barrage began to rake the Union positions, and through the smoke Union men saw the Confederate preparations for Pickett's suicidal charge. The artillery had done little damage. When General George E. Pickett and his Virginians—supported by Pettigrew, Wilcox, and Trimble —15,000 troops in all, at last sallied forth across the valley heading for the center of Cemetery Ridge, the big Union guns opened fire. Many fell, but more came on. Gradually Pickett's flanks dissolved; then his main body came into infantry range and was picked to pieces; some dauntless men even scaled the heights of the Ridge, but there they were surrounded and subdued.

The greatest battle of the war was ended, but the war itself would go on. Union casualties at Gettysburg are estimated at 23,000; Confederate casualties at 28,000. "Call no council of war. . . . Do not let the enemy escape," Halleck, at Lincoln's instructions, wired the victorious Meade. But Meade called a council of war while Lee made good his retreat. "Our army held the war in the hollow of its hand," Lincoln said later, "and would not close it." In a restrained but bitter letter to Meade (which he decided not to send), Lincoln wrote:

You stood and let the river run down, bridges be built, and the enemy move away at his leisure without attacking him. Again, my dear General, I do not believe you appreciate the magnitude of the disaster involved in Lee's escape.

Many months after the memorable battle, the bodies of thousands who there "gave their lives" still lay unburied. The degrading sight led to a call for a national cemetery in their honor. It was at the dedication ceremonies for this cemetery, on November 19, 1863, that Lincoln delivered the Gettysburg Address, promising "that these dead shall not have died in vain."

GRANT IN THE WEST

On July 4, 1863, on the heels of the victory at Gettysburg, came the thrilling report of as great a Union triumph in the West. Grant had taken Vicksburg, "The Gibraltar of the Mississippi."

Operations to crack Vicksburg had begun in May, 1862, but all efforts to take it from the north had failed. In 1863, Grant decided to strike from the more vulnerable southern and western approaches. He transported his troops across the Mississippi above Vicksburg, marched them down the western shore to a point south of the city, and there transport ships that had run through the batteries of the fortress ferried them across to the eastern shore. Abandoning their supply trains, Grant's troops sped ahead, living off the country. Once he had eliminated the Confederate concentration at his rear in Jackson (May 14), Grant turned back toward Vicksburg, which, after a harrowing siege, capitulated July 4. On July 8, Port Hudson, the last Confederate stronghold on the Mississippi, also surrendered. Then it was that Lincoln wrote his memorable words: "The Father of Waters again goes unvexed to the sea."

After Vicksburg, one Confederate army

and part of the Confederacy itself were isolated west of the Mississippi, but another Confederate army under General Braxton Bragg was still operating in central Tennessee. Late in June, 1863, after months of shelly-shallying, General William Rosecrans had begun his pursuit of Bragg southeasterly from Murfreesboro and by July 4 had forced him all the way across the Tennessee River into the strategic rail center of Chattanooga. A month of additional delay followed before Rosecrans crossed the river himself southeast of the city and after further maneuvering on both sides, finally confronted Bragg, on September 19 at Chickamauga Creek. Here, only the deadly defensive action of General George H. Thomas averted a complete Union rout, and Rosecrans was now himself bottled up in Chattanooga, which had become useless to both sides. Grant, who in October had been put in command of the Union armies operating between the Alleghenies and the Mississippi, ordered Thomas to take over from Rosecrans and moved swiftly to raise the siege. Two corps from the Army of the Potomac under Hooker sped westward by rail to Nashville, where they hastened back toward Chattanooga, while General William T. Sherman marched his army eastward from the Mississippi. Grant himself arrived late in October to take personal charge. On November 25, with Thomas' troops, 18,000 strong, scaling Missionary Ridge, the seemingly impregnable anchor of Bragg's position, the Confederate center was broken in spectacular fashion, and Bragg was forced to retire. Sherman moved on to relieve the Union army penned up at Knoxville, and succeeded in liberating all pro-Union Tennessee. The Confederacy now was split north and south as well as east and west, and lay open to Sherman's march to the sea.

LINCOLN'S GENERAL

Grant's performance as supreme commander in the West could not have

"*Pursuit of the Army Marching in the Rain, near Emmitsburg, Maryland, 1863,*" by E. Devin Forbes.

been in more striking contrast to the dreary plodders who had so far made a brutal shambles of the war elsewhere. No longer would Lincoln, yearning for a leader, have to review the same disheartening circle—the McDowells, McClellans, Frémonts, Burnsides, Hallecks, Hookers, and Meades. On February 26, 1864, Congress revived the highest office in the army, that of lieutenant-general. On March 1, Lincoln named Grant to the post, and on the 2nd the Senate confirmed the nomination. By March 9 Grant had arrived in Washington for the first time for his initial meeting with Lincoln.

Grant possessed none of the glamor that surrounded so many of the colorful Confederate and Union prima donnas. A stubby, nondescript man, carelessly dressed, taciturn, shy, he seemed the very antithesis of the splendid soldier. One of Grant's devoted officers, General Horace Porter, wrote of him that "he never carried his body erect, and having no ear for music or rhythm, he never kept step to the airs played by the bands, no matter how vigorously the bass

drums emphasized the accent." In battle, Grant moved swiftly, nevertheless, and in the words of one of his Confederate opponents, he had the "disagreeable habit of not retreating before irresistible veterans." His own "art of war" best sums up his military theory: "The art of war is simple enough. Find out where your enemy is. Get him as soon as you can. Strike at him as hard as you can and keep moving on."

His commission as supreme commander of all Union forces received, Grant got right down to work on the victory program. In the West his forces held all important communication centers and could lay waste the interior of the Confederacy from Mississippi to Virginia. In the East, back in the vicinity of Fredericksburg, Lee had rebuilt the army he had been allowed to salvage at Gettysburg into a formidable force, once again capable of menacing Washington. Grant's plan was for the Army of the Potomac, itself rebuilt and now directly under himself and Meade, so to occupy Lee's army that it could not link up with any other

rebel force—and to bleed it daily in the bargain. While the Army of the Potomac thus was to cling to the Confederacy's leg, as it were, Sherman's army was to push eastward from Tennessee into Georgia and take Atlanta, skinning the Confederacy's body as it went. Franz Sigel, at the same time, was to operate in the Shenandoah Valley and protect Washington from that direction; while still another army, under "Ben" Butler at Fortress Monroe, was to repeat McClellan's peninsular maneuver and strike at Richmond, from the defense of which Lee was to be kept.

The first reports of Grant's campaign were disheartening. As the Army of the Potomac, on May 4, 1864, marched south across the Rapidan from Culpeper, Virginia, where it had been encamped since its return from Gettysburg, it was met,

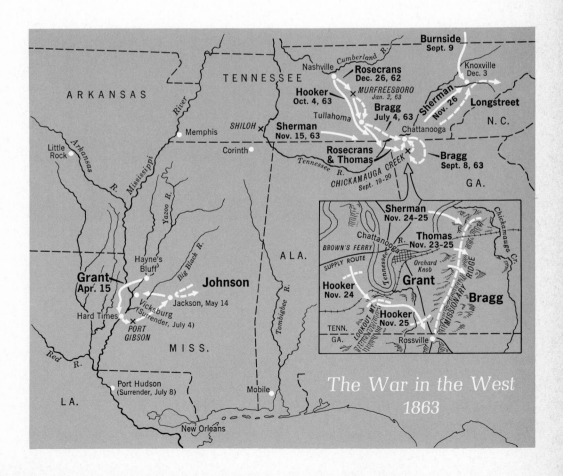

The War in the West
1863

Robert E. Lee (1807-1870).

rather earlier than Grant had planned, by Lee's heavily outnumbered force on the grim terrain of the "Wilderness." So thick was the forest, the fighters on either side could only be detected by the smoke of rifles. The woods quickly caught fire and wounded men were trapped in the flames and burned to death. After two days of gruesome fighting, neither army had gained an advantage, and cynical Union veterans expected they would now retreat. Instead, Grant advanced inexorably, forcing Lee southward toward Spotsylvania in fierce hand-to-hand fighting. There, on May 10, Union and Confederate troops struggled blindly at "the Bloody Angle," a bend in Lee's line, where there occurred (to quote one of the participants), "the most terrible twenty-four hours of our service in the war."

Grant (leaning over bench) in council of war at Bethesda Church, June 2, 1864. Photograph taken by Timothy H. O'Sullivan, June 1864.

By midnight the rebel lines had been cracked, but at the cost of 7,000 Union casualties. Despite the shocking losses, Grant kept advancing, and this fact alone had a tonic effect on the morale of his army. According to Charles Francis Adams, Jr., who served with Meade during the Wilderness campaign, "this Army [is] now just on its second wind, and more formidable than it ever was before." As events turned out, it needed to be.

By the end of May, Grant had re-established contact with Lee's army at Cold Harbor, Virginia, and on June 1 and 3 he ordered suicidal assaults against the entrenched Confederates. After a momentary success, the attack was savagely repulsed. "Our men have, in many instances, been foolishly and wantonly sacrificed," a Union staff officer wrote home. "Assault after assault has been ordered upon the enemy's entrenchments when they knew nothing about the strength or position of the enemy."

The enormous federal casualties in the Wilderness and at Cold Harbor—Grant is said to have lost a colossal 55,000 men in this first month of his campaign—aroused strong resentment in the North, and newspapers began to speak of Grant as "the butcher." Lincoln stood by his General: "I have just read your dispatch," he wrote to Grant after Cold Harbor. "I begin to see it. You will succeed. God bless you all." Grant himself, however, had begun to have second thoughts. On June 12, he decided to disengage his army from Lee's, to swing down to the peninsula, and with Butler's assistance to get at Richmond once more from the South. Butler botched his orders sufficiently for the rebels to block Grant at Petersburg, 20 miles below Richmond, long enough for Lee to move his own forces to this front. Nine months later, in March, 1865, Grant's siege of Petersburg still was on.

In July, 1864, to help lift this siege, Lee sought to re-enact "Stonewall" Jackson's old diversion of 1862: to menace Washington by way of the Shenandoah Valley. By July 11, under General Jubal Early, the rebels, after being checked at Monocacy for 24 hours by a raw force under General

Lew Wallace two days earlier, actually entered the District of Columbia. On July 13, on learning that Grant had at last released a sizable contingent to protect the capital, Early decided to return to the Valley and create more havoc there. Early's success led to the replacement of Sigel with Grant's top cavalryman, General Philip Sheridan, who took command in the Valley on August 7. Grant's orders to Sheridan said, "nothing should be left to invite the enemy to return. . . . If the war is to last another year we want the Shenandoah Valley to remain a barren waste." By March, 1865, Sheridan had carried out these orders with the thoroughness of a Sherman. "A crow would

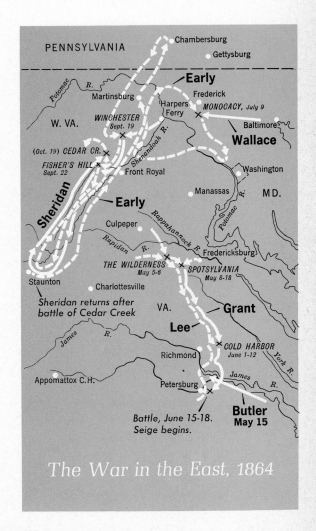

The War in the East, 1864

have had to carry its rations," he said, "if it had flown across the valley." Sheridan then joined Grant for the Richmond campaign.

Since May, 1864, Sherman himself, with three veteran armies in the West, had been slowly forcing the redoubtable Joseph E. Johnston toward Atlanta. On September 3, Sherman wired Washington, "So Atlanta is ours, and fairly won." On November 16, having left Atlanta, as he said, "smouldering and in ruins," Sherman and his "bummers" began their "picnic" march to the sea (see map, p. 447). "To realize what war is," Sherman said, "one should follow in our tracks."

VI. *To Appomattox*

THE ELECTION OF 1864

Sherman's victory at Atlanta in September, 1864, had more than military significance. Early in the year the politicians had begun to prepare for the presidential elections in November and Lincoln, for the good of the Republican party, had been urged not to seek renomination. By the time of the party convention at Baltimore in June, however, his Radical opponents had failed to agree among themselves on a candidate and his loyal backers put him across. To bolster the ticket they named the "War Democrat," Andrew Johnson of Tennessee for vice-president. In fact Lincoln and Johnson ran under a "Union party" label.

When the Democrats met at Chicago in August, a hodgepodge (to quote Gideon Welles) of "Whigs, Democrats, Know-Nothings, Conservatives, War men and Peace men, with a crowd of Secessionists and traitors to stimulate action," promptly chose McClellan for president after the bid of Governor Seymour of New York fizzled out. The "war failure" plank in the Democratic platform, drafted by Vallandigham, declared that four years of war had not restored the Union, that hostilities should cease, and that the "Federal Union of the States" should be re-established on the old basis. This was nothing less than an armistice offer. McClellan, after serious soul-searching, decided to reject this plank and to commit himself to continuing the war until the southerners agreed to rejoin the Union. At the same time, some of Lincoln's advisers had begun to press him to make peaceful overtures to Richmond.

Sherman's victory at Atlanta did a great deal to check peace talk in the North, and the rising confidence in the administration was shown in many local elections in October, when most Democrats went down to defeat. Lincoln's own renewal of confidence was rewarded by his winning 55 per cent of the popular vote in November. His electoral vote was 212 against McClellan's 21. The Republicans also won control of Congress and most of the state governments. Victory, not negotiated peace, now became the military theme as well.

THE END IN SIGHT

While Sherman and his men were gouging their way through Georgia, George Thomas and his subordinate, John Schofield, had been left to clean up in the West. Their objective was the Confederate Army commanded by General John Bell Hood, who had replaced "Joe" Johnston just in time to yield Atlanta to Sherman. Having saved his army then, Hood lost little time turning back to try to regain Tennessee, but on December 15 Thomas annihilated Hood at Nashville in one of the most crushing defeats of the war. Five days later Savannah fell to Sherman in Georgia. By his own estimate, Sherman had lost Georgia some $100 million in military resources, $80 million of it "simple waste and destruction."

From Savannah, in February, 1865, Sherman headed north toward the "hellhole of secession," South Carolina, where, as he said, "the devil himself could not restrain his men." By February 17, the "pitiless march" had brought him to Columbia, South Carolina's capital, and soon, whether by accident or design, one of the most beautiful cities in the country was being consumed in flames. Charleston, outflanked by Sherman, was occupied the next day by Union forces blockading the harbor after the defending rebels had fled. Sherman, meanwhile, pounded on into North Carolina, where, on February 22, Wilmington, the very last of the Atlantic ports of the blockade-runners, was evacuated, like Charleston, by the rebel defenders and taken by Union harbor contingents.

On March 19, Sherman's progress was checked at Bentonville, North Carolina, by a considerable force commanded, once again, by Joseph E. Johnston, whom Lee had restored to service. Johnston yielded Bentonville to Sherman's larger army after a fight, but the contact with the Confederates convinced Sherman that it would be best to leave Richmond and Lee to Grant and Sheridan while he kept the capable Johnston away.

Gettysburg, Vicksburg, Atlanta, the humiliating failure of cotton diplomacy, the

bruising wall of the blockade—none of these had quite managed to dissipate the Confederacy's material capacity for war. But before Sherman's devastation the southern spirit drooped. As early as September, 1864, Davis acknowledged that "two thirds of our men are absent . . . most of them absent without leave." Soon after, he began negotiations for a peace conference on terms capable of "firing the Southern heart." But no such terms remained. On February 3, 1865, on a Union steamer in Hampton Roads, occurred the extraordinary conference between Lincoln—ready always for peace *and* union—and Vice-president Stephens, carrying Davis' terms of peace and independence. There was no chance that they could agree. "Davis," Lincoln said, "cannot voluntarily reaccept the Union; we cannot voluntarily yield it." The conference came to naught.

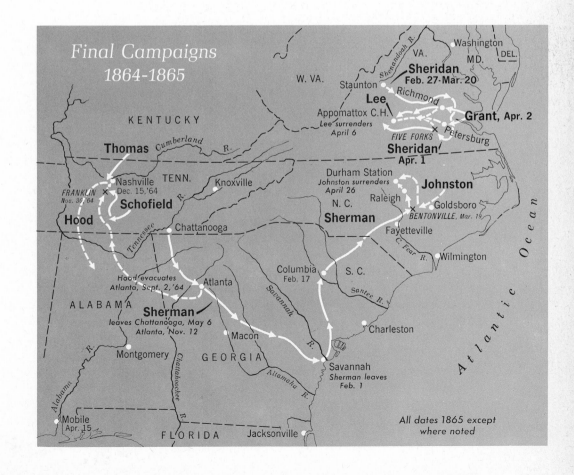

Sgt. Major William Jackson, 12th New York Infantry. Private Albert Hall, 1st Reg. Georgia Volunteers.

On February 9, 1865, in what was to be his last public address, Secretary of State Benjamin reviewed the desperate straits into which Lee's proud forces had sunk and proposed to retrieve the situation by enrolling all slaves "who might volunteer to fight for their freedom." The next day a measure for Negro enlistments was introduced into the Confederate Congress; but six stormy weeks were spent eviscerating it. To arm slaves was to propose terror enough; to encourage enlistment with the promise of emancipation was unthinkable. The measure as finally passed offered the Negro nothing, and came far too late to lift Lee's sinking heart.

By the end of March, 1865, Lee and Grant had been facing each other before the railroad junction of Petersburg for nine cruel months. Opportunity after opportunity had

been lost by the Federals to crack the Confederate defenses and crash into Richmond; yet Grant had been making progress nonetheless. As he gradually extended his lines to cut off Petersburg's communications with the rest of the Confederacy, he forced Lee to attenuate his own lines in order to guard his flanks. This was a tactic that Lee's depleted army could only carry out for so long before becoming attenuated to death. By the end of March the once nearly even opponents numbered 115,000 Federals to 54,000 "rebs." The time had come for Lee to pull out of his hateful trenches while he still had so formidable a force, try to join up with Johnston in North Carolina, and carry on the war from there.

Under cover of darkness on April 2, the Confederate exodus began. On April 3, while Davis and his government fled from their capital, exposed at last by the evacuation of the Petersburg front, contingents of Grant's army poured into Richmond. Grant and Sheridan themselves pursued Lee. On April 7, his path to North Carolina irretrievably sealed off, Lee asked for terms. On April 9, impeccable in a new uniform, he met the mud-spattered Grant in the McClean farmhouse at Appomattox Court House, a village some 95 miles west of Richmond. "Give them the most liberal terms," Lincoln had ordered Grant and Sherman.

Let them have their horses to plow with, and, if you like, their guns to shoot crows with. I want no one punished; treat them liberally all round. We want those people to return to their allegiance to the Union and submit to the laws. Again I say, give them the most liberal and honorable terms.

Grant complied. On April 26 "Joe" Johnston surrendered his army to Sherman at Durham Station, North Carolina. On May 10, the fleeing Davis was caught in Georgia, imprisoned for two years, released, and permitted to retire.

LINCOLN'S DEATH

When news of Richmond's fall reached Washington on April 3, the city exploded with joy, and for the next 11 days the holiday mood continued. Then, on

April 14, Good Friday, Lincoln was shot by the mentally unbalanced John Wilkes Booth as the President sat in his box at Ford's Theatre in Washington watching a performance of *Our American Cousin*. At 7:20 the next morning he died.

Lincoln had charged the nation to act "with malice towards none; with charity for all." He had acknowledged the guilt of the North as well as the South for "the bondsman's two hundred and fifty years of unrequited toil." At first Robert E. Lee would not credit the news of Lincoln's death. Then, on that Sunday, he told a visitor that he had "surrendered as much to [Lincoln's] goodness as to Grant's artillery." Now Lincoln and "goodness" were removed, with what consequences Herman Melville foretold when he wrote in "The Martyr":

> He lieth in his blood—
>   The father in his face;
> They have killed him, the Forgiver—
>   The Avenger takes his place. . . .
>
> There is sobbing of the strong,
>   And a pall upon the land;
> But the People in their weeping
>   Bare the iron hand:
> Beware the People weeping
>   When they bare the iron hand.

Readings

Asterisk indicates that book is available in paperback.

The best modern study of all phases of the Civil War era is that in progress by Allan Nevins. The two volumes so far published under the general title *The War for the Union* are, *The Improvised War 1861-1862* (1959) and *War Becomes Revolution 1862-1863* (1960). A shorter scholarly survey is J. G. Randall and David Donald, *The Civil War and Reconstruction* (rev. ed., 1961). A. C. Cole, *The Irrepressible Conflict 1850-1865* (1934), stresses social history. The strong national feeling in the North is well-documented in G. M. Frederickson, *The Inner Civil War: Northern Intellectuals and the Crisis of the Union* (1965).

Northern industrial potential is measured in E. D. Fite, *Social and Industrial Conditions in the North during the Civil War* (1910). Lincoln's interest in industry is the subject of R. V. Bruce, *Lincoln and the Tools of War* (1956). Unusually interesting on industry in the Confederacy is F. E. Vandiver, *Ploughshares into Swords: Josiah*

Gorgas and Confederate Ordnance * (1952). More general is J. C. Schwab, *The Confederate States of America* (1901), which emphasizes financial and industrial matters. Thomas Weber, *The Northern Railroads in the Civil War 1861-1865* (1952), and R. C. Black, III, *The Railroads of the Confederacy* (1952), are scholarly accounts. Ralph Andreano, ed., *The Economic Impact of the American Civil War* * (1962), and D. T. Gilchrist and W. D. Lewis, eds., *Economic Change in the Civil War Era* (1965), present stimulating essays on how the war promoted or repressed industrial growth. E. P. Oberholtzer, *Jay Cooke, Financier of the Civil War* (2 vols., 1907), is good on bond sales. W. C. Mitchell, *A History of the Greenbacks* (1903), is the classic account.

Clement Eaton, *A History of the Southern Confederacy* * (1954), is the best general survey. Also of value are N. W. Stephenson, *Day of the Confederacy: A Chronicle of the Embattled South* (1919); E. M. Coulter, *The Confederate State of America 1861-1865* (1950); and C. P. Roland, *The Confederacy* * (1960). A. D. Kirwan, *The Confederacy* * (1959), is an illuminating "social and political history in documents." A. H. Stephens, *Recollections* (1910) offers a remarkable inside view by the Confederate Vice-president. On the Confederate President and his administration see, Hudson Strode, *Jefferson Davis, American Patriot* (1955), and *Jefferson Davis: Confederate President* (1959); R. W. Patrick, *Jefferson Davis and His Cabinet* (1944), and B. J. Hendrick, *Statesmen of the Lost Cause: Jefferson Davis and His Cabinet* (1939). F. L. Owsley, *State Rights in the Confederacy* (1925), is a valuable monograph.

Of the many books on Lincoln as president, Carl Sandburg, *Abraham Lincoln: The War Years* * (4 vols., 1939), remains preeminent. The following also are recommended: J. G. Randall, *Lincoln, the President: Springfield to Gettysburg* (4 vols., 1945-1955)— the last volume was completed by R. N. Current after Randall's death; and B. P. Thomas, *Abraham Lincoln* (1952), the most up-to-date one-volume life. R. P. Basler, ed., *The Collected Works of Abraham Lincoln* (9 vols., 1953-1955), is a manageable set that makes excellent reading. Original and illuminating is David Donald, *Lincoln Reconsidered* * (1956). More information on Lincoln and his Cabinet may be found in *The Diary of Gideon Welles* (3 vols., 1911); David Donald, ed., *Inside Lincoln's Cabinet: The Civil War Diaries of Salmon P. Chase* (1954); and B. P. Thomas and H. B. Hyman, *Stanton: The Life and Times of Lincoln's Secretary of War* (1962). Lincoln's troubled relations with his party are discussed in D. M. Potter, *Lincoln and His Party in the Secession Crisis* * (1942); T. H. Williams, *Lincoln and the Radicals* * (1941); H. J. Carman and R. H. Luthin, *Lincoln and the Patronage* (1943); and H. B. Hesseltine, *Lincoln and the War Governors* (1948). Copperheadism is described in Wood Gray, *The Hidden Civil War* * (1942), and F. L. Klement, *The Copperheads in the Middle West* (1960). J. G. Randall, *Constitutional Problems under Lincoln* * (1926), offers a rigorous examination. The role of the abolitionists during the war is presented in J. M. McPherson, *The Struggle for Equality, Abolitionists and the Negro in the Civil War and Reconstruction* (1964). F. M. Brodie, *Thaddeus Stevens* (1959), and David Donald, *Charles Sumner* (1961), are outstanding on the leading Radicals. J. H. Franklin, *The Emancipation Proclamation* * (1963), is the leading monograph on that document.

A vast literature exists on the military aspects of the Civil War. Moving and authoritative accounts of the Union army in the East may be found in four books by Bruce Catton: *Mr. Lincoln's Army* * (1951); *Glory Road* * (1952); *A Stillness at Appomattox* * (1954); and *This Hallowed Ground* * (1956). Also recommended is Catton's *Centennial History of the War* (3 vols., 1961-1965). A handy summary is Fletcher Pratt, *A Short History of the Civil War* * (1935). T. H. Williams, *Lincoln and His Generals* (1952), treats an interesting phase of the war, as does K. P. Williams, *Lincoln Finds a General: A Military History of the Civil War* (4 vols., 1949-1956). A classic account of the campaigns is *The Personal Memoirs of U. S. Grant* * (2 vols., 1885-1886). See also, Lloyd Lewis, *Captain Sam Grant* (1950), and its sequel by Bruce Catton, *Grant Moves South* (1960). Another classic contemporary record is W. T. Sherman, *Memoirs* (2 vols., 1886) which may be supplemented by Lloyd Lewis, *Sherman, Fighting Prophet* (1932). McClellan's apologia, *McClellan's Own Story* (1887), does not compare with Grant's or Sherman's memoirs. A sympathetic study in W. W. Hassler, Jr., *General George B. McClellan, Shield of the Union* (1958). Union naval history is covered in R. S. West, Jr., *Mr. Lincoln's Navy* (1957).

The southern side of the war is reported as richly as the northern. Classic works are D. S. Freeman, *R. E. Lee, A Biography* (4 vols., 1934-1935), and *Lee's Lieutenants* (3 vols., 1942-1944). An outstanding one-volume life is Clifford Dowdey, *Lee* (1965). Dowdey and L. H. Manarin, eds., *The Wartime Papers of R. E. Lee* (1961), is a rich collection. G. R. F. Henderson, *Stonewall Jackson and the American Civil War* * (2 vols., 1898); and Burke Davis, *Jeb Stuart* (1957), are also valuable. Readers will find many biographies of the other celebrated generals on both sides. For the ordinary man's role in the war, see the excellent anthology, H. S. Commager, ed., *The Blue and the Gray: The Story of the Civil War as Told by Participants* (2 vols., 1950); B. I. Wiley, *The Life of Johnny Reb* * (1943), and *The Life of Billy Yank* * (1952); and J. M. McPherson, *The Negro's Civil War* (1965). Important phases of the war are treated in A. B. Moore, *Conscription and Conflict in the Confederacy* (1924); F. A. Shannon, *The Organization and Administration of the Union Army, 1861-1865* (2 vols., 1928). Benjamin Quarles, *The Negro in the Civil War* (1953); D. T. Cornish, *The Sable Arm: Negro Troops in the Union Army, 1861-1865* (1958); and B. I. Wiley, *Southern Negroes 1861-1865* * (1938), are revealing. W. L. Rose, *Rehearsal for Reconstruction* (1964) is an able account of "The Port Royal Experiment" in Negro freedom in 1861-1862. Also worth reading is W. B. Hesseltine, *Civil War Prisons: A Study in War Psychology* (1930). T. W. Higginson, *Army Life in a Black Regiment* * (1870) is a fascinating account of the Negro Union soldier.

The diplomatic aspects of the war are covered in the general histories previously cited, but F. L. Owsley, *King Cotton Diplomacy* (1931), and M. B. Duberman, *Charles Francis Adams* (1961), on the Union minister in London, should not be overlooked.

Wartime Washington is colorfully described in Margaret Leech, *Reveille in Washington, 1860-1865* * (1941); southern civilian life is presented in B. I. Wiley, *The Plain People of the Confederacy* * (1943). Mary B. Chesnut, *A Diary from Dixie* * (1905), records the wartime experiences of a perceptive southern matron. The reader should not miss Whitman's *Drum-Taps* (1865) and *Specimen Days* * (1875), and Melville's *Battle-Pieces and Other Aspects of the War* (1866). John De Forest, *Miss Ravenal's Conversion* * (1867), is the first realistic depiction of Civil War battles in fiction and incorporates the author's own experiences. De Forest's Civil War letters and articles have been collected in *A Volunteer's Adventures* (1946). Stephen Crane, *The Red Badge of Courage* * (1895), is a vivid account of battle by an author who got his material second-hand. S. V. Benet, *John Brown's Body* (1928), is a long narrative poem about the Civil War and an impressive interpretation of it.

CHAPTER SEVENTEEN

Most of the wars of the nineteenth century, once the great Napoleonic struggle had ended, were waged for limited objectives, by professional forces, between nations that rarely questioned one another's sovereignty. The wars between the United States and Mexico (see Chapter 12) and the United States and Spain (see Chapter 23) were such wars. The American Civil War also began as a war for limited objectives, but with the question of sovereignty at its very heart. And it soon engaged an entire people in a struggle for survival. Confederate Vice-president Alexander H. Stephens made this clear when he said in

The

Reconstructed South

1863: "A large majority in both sides are tired of the war; want peace. . . . But we do not want peace without independence, so they do not want peace without union." For the Confederacy to succeed, the Union had to be destroyed. For the Union to survive, the Confederacy had to be obliterated. The Union survived. The men in blue, said one disillusioned southerner late in 1865, "destroyed everything which the most infernal Yankee ingenuity could devise means to destroy; hands, heart, fire, gunpowder. and behind everything the spirit of hell, were the agencies which they used."

Two days after Appomattox, three days before his assassination, Lincoln, on April 11, 1865, said of the South:

Unlike the case of a war between independent nations, there is no organized organ for us to treat with. No one man has authority to give up the rebellion for any other man. We must simply begin with, and mould from, disorganized and discordant elements.

Lincoln's view of the realities of the southern situation was consistent with and congenial to his whole theory of secession, rebellion, and reconstruction. As we have seen (p. 407), Lincoln held from the outset that the Union was indestructible and that states could not break away from it even though their people might rebel. Rebellious citizens could be restored to citizenship by presidential pardon and then could set about manning new governments in states which themselves had never been defunct. This view became the foundation of Lincoln's program for reconstruction by the *Executive* department. At his very last Cabinet meeting before his assassination, according to his Navy Secretary, Gideon Welles, Lincoln had called it "providential" that "the rebellion was crushed just as Congress had adjourned. . . . If we were wise and discreet," he added, "we should reanimate the States and get . . . the Union reestablished before Congress came together in December."

What Lincoln calculatingly closed his eyes to in his program was that along with all the other destruction in the South during the war, the great fact was that the slave foundations of southern society had been washed away. The Radicals, he knew, not only had their eyes open to this event but had made its accomplishment their own central objective in the war. After the war, they aimed to rebuild southern society around the equality of freedman and white, come what may. Lincoln's Radical Secretary of the Treasury, Salmon P. Chase, stated it clearly to the President: "This way is recommended by its simplicity, facility, & above all, justice. It will be, hereafter, counted equally a crime & a folly if the colored loyalists of the rebel states shall be left to the control of restored rebels, not likely, in that case, to be either wise or just, until taught both wisdom and justice by new calamities." According to Radicals in Congress, the rebel states had forfeited all connection with the Union and were reduced to the status of territories. In seeking statehood once again, they came under the jurisdiction, not of the Executive but of the *Legislative* department in whose hands territorial affairs lay.

Lincoln, an ex-Whig, had not forgotten the strength this nationalist party had found among business leaders and professional men in the Old South. By his policy of "malice toward none; charity for all," as he said in his second inaugural in March, 1865, he hoped to wean surviving southern Whigs to the Republican standard, which would only be strengthened in the North itself by his leaving the Negro's fate to the South. If he could swing his old project of Negro colonization overseas, a project he never surrendered (see p. 460), so much the better. The Radicals, on the other hand, saw the Negro vote in the South as the only means of gaining that section for the Republicans and insuring their party's national character and strength. To protect the freedman from southern pressure, the Radicals also tried to develop an educational program to nourish his mental independence and a land program to support his economic liberty.

The issue between the conservative Executive and the Radical legislators, clearly joined during the war, reached its climax in the impeachment proceedings against President Andrew Johnson in 1868. Thereafter, for almost a decade, the Radicals ruled in the South and the nation, gradually fatiguing themselves and the people with what seemed more and more a thankless and degrading task. Even among the Radicals and their sympathizers, many failed to recognize the depth of the problem they had undertaken quickly to resolve. Color was one overweening obstacle. Race, in so far as it was distinguishable from color in this case (as it was in the case of the deep prejudice against the Irish) was another. The vogue of "Social Darwinism," with its emphasis on direct biological competition and the "survival of the fittest" (see p. 515), was a third—an especially significant one for those Radicals who were determined to overcome their racial and color prejudices but saw no reason to go against the best scientific theory of the day. "Now, we totally deny the assumption," said the liberal *Nation,* "that the distribution of other people's land to the negroes is necessary to complete the work of emancipation." Once free, it was held, the Negro's economic status must be determined by his own enterprise.

The failure of Radical Reconstruction is not to be taken to mean that Lincoln's alternative was preferable. The evidence is overwhelming that the South's attitude toward the ex-slave was as unregenerate just after the war as it was after Radical Reconstruction was formally abandoned in 1877. A Virginia judge reported the observation of a friend of his in 1866: "Sooner than see the colored people raised to a legal and political equality, the Southern people would prefer their total annihilation." The

judge added, "I regarded him [the friend] as well informed and almost as candid a man as we have." Radical Reconstruction postponed the legal and political annihilation of the freedman for a decade, and it laid the legal and political foundation for his regeneration when the Negro found his own leaders in the twentieth century.

1. *The Conquered Section*

The Civil War ravaged the fighting families of the North as well as the South; and it was difficult even for the most conciliatory Unionists to forget for long "the patriot hosts that had fallen on fearful battlefields." Yet the North, as Whitman stated it, had its great compensation:

> The ship is anchor'd safe and sound, its
> voyage closed and done,
> From fearful trip the victor ship comes in
> with object won;
> Exult O shores, and ring O bells!

The North had more mundane compensations as well on which to build a mighty future. Its $4 billion in direct wartime expenditures gave a fillip to business enterprise, an impetus to industry. The prosperity did not extend to all lines of business. The cotton textile industry, for example, broke down; the merchant marine and the shipbuilding industry suffered losses from which they did not recover until World War I; railroad-building was sharply retarded. Yet, as John Sherman wrote to his brother, General William T. Sherman, in 1865, wartime expenditures by the federal government lifted the hopes of businessmen in the North. "The close of the war," he said, "with our resources unimpaired gives an elevation, a scope to the ideas of leading capitalists, far higher than anything ever undertaken in this country before. They talk of millions as confidently as formerly of thousands."

Direct Confederate expenditures for the war exceeded $2 billion, and expenditures by the individual southern states added many millions more to the total cost. But in the South, by contrast, these outlays were an utter loss in an utterly losing cause. Only a few southerners had managed to accumulate capital during the war. Some of them had succeeded in running cotton through the northern blockade. Some had preyed very profitably on Yankee shipping. Others had been canny enough to demand gold or goods from their neighbors instead of Confederate paper money in payment for food, clothing, and farm supplies. But most of the South was impoverished. The section's $2.5 billion investment in slaves in 1860 had vanished. Its $1.5 billion investment in land was evaluated as late as 1870 at only $750 million, a reduction of 50 per cent. Its $1 billion in banking capital had been wiped out; and worse, the credit system on which the staple planters had been dependent for all essential purchases was paralyzed. At the end of the war, each of the boys in blue went home at government expense with about $235 in his pocket and with every hope of returning to the fruitful land, to business, or to school. The boys in gray turned homeward with their pockets empty, their prospects grim. Some of Lee's soldiers, writes Dixon Wecter, "had to ask for handouts on the road home, with nothing to exchange for bread save the unwelcome news of Appomattox."

Fighting had occurred in only a relatively few sections in the South, but in these areas the destruction was likely to be complete. Writing of Columbia, South Carolina, believed by many to have been the most beautiful city in North America, one traveler said in September, 1865, that it was "a wilderness of ruins. . . . Not a store, office, or shop escaped [the burning]; and for a distance of three-fourths of a mile on each of twelve streets there was not a building left."

Nor had rural areas escaped. Five years after the war an English traveler described the Tennessee Valley country:

> The trail of war is visible throughout the valley in burnt-up gin-houses, ruined bridges, mills, and factories . . . and in large tracts of once cultivated land stripped of every vestige of fencing. The roads, long neglected, are in disorder, and . . . in many places . . . impassable.

Southern river ports and coastal harbors were put out of commission. Levees were destroyed or neglected, and floods washed out miles of farm land.

But the South lost even more in nonmilitary damage.

> Weak their hearts from too much sorrow,
> Weak their frames from want and toil . . .

So ran the lament of southern women left with responsibility for land, buildings, tools, and machinery when even the boys ran off to fight. Every third horse and mule had died, wandered off, or been taken by Union or Confederate foragers, so that after the war men and women often harnessed themselves to the old plows in order to prepare their fields for planting. Southern factories, in turn, frequently had to be forsaken for want of the materials to make even simple repairs; gradually they fell into irretrievable decay.

In the disorganization of southern life, few suffered more than the ex-slaves. The problem of free and footloose Negroes had been forced upon the Union armies and the Union government at the very outset of the war, as Negro families in both the border states and the Confederacy fled to the shelter of the Union lines. Land-hunger probably gave the greatest impulse to the Negro's wandering. As early as 1862, in debates over the Confiscation Acts (see p. 436), Radicals in Congress had talked seriously of colonizing freed Negroes on land captured by Union forces; subsequently, various Union generals had taken over conquered territory and made it available to ex-slaves on easy terms. Since many of the new farmers did well, others were eager for a chance to gain land of their own, but nothing ever came of such hopes. Eventually, thousands of Negroes were corralled in Union "contraband camps" so flimsy, filthy, and crowded that death from epidemics, exposure, and crime soon claimed as many as 25 per cent of the inmates. Private philanthropy, first organized in the North in 1862, supplemented these early official measures with somewhat happier results.

When the Emancipation Proclamation of January 1, 1863, sharply focused attention on the plight of free Negroes, Congress began to consider bills to establish a bureau for their care. Not until March 3, 1865, however, did Congress create, as part of the War Department, the Bureau of Refugees, Freedmen, and Abandoned Lands—or, simply, the Freedmen's Bureau. This agency, which was to operate for only one year after the end of the war, was authorized to issue "provisions, clothing and fuel . . . for . . . destitute and suffering refugees and freedmen." The commissioner at its head was empowered to set aside land within the Confederacy which "shall have been abandoned" or confiscated, and to assign at a fair rent "to every male citizen, whether refugee or freedman . . . not more than forty acres of such land."

At first, the Freedmen's Bureau did nobly. But once the full flush of liberty struck the Negro, the rate of migration soared and the Bureau became so hard-pressed merely to sustain life that the land program languished. In the summer of 1865, more than 20,000 ex-slaves flocked into Washington. Greater numbers congregated in Charleston, New Orleans, Memphis, and other southern cities. Without resources

Freed Negroes joining the lines of the Union forces at New Bern, North Carolina. From a wood engraving in Harper's Weekly, 1863.

themselves, these cities could do nothing but increase the number and size of their already overtaxed "contraband camps." Death and disease rates soared; during the first two postwar years in some camps a third of the ex-slaves died.

White farmers and planters often fared little better than the Negroes. Famine struck many parts of the South as early as 1862, and the disruption of the transportation system prevented people in the more fortunate areas from sending food to their starving neighbors. By 1865, the statewide systems of relief set up during the war years in all the Confederate commonwealths had collapsed in the general ruin. Moreover, the 1865 harvest was extremely lean, so that, as one official of the Freedmen's Bureau reported, it was "a common sight, an every-day sight . . . , that of women and children, most of whom were formerly in

good circumstances, begging for bread from door to door." In the first four years after the war the Freedmen's Bureau alone issued almost 21 million rations, 6 million of them to impoverished whites.

Perhaps the heaviest blow to the South was the moral cost of war and defeat. The losses in youth and talent hurt beyond measure. Among the survivors, purpose, morale, and aspiration drooped. In Georgia, in 1865, one reporter noted that "aimless young men in gray, ragged and filthy, seemed, with the downfall of the rebellion . . . to have lost their object in life." Mississippi alone, it was estimated, had 10,000 orphans. As late as 1879, a journalist remarked that the migrants who were leaving the Old South for Texas had "no progress in them, no love for adventure, no ambition." Those who stayed behind, though often the most stable persons in the com-

457

munity, were often the most discouraged. "These faces, these faces," cried a northern observer in 1873 on a visit to New Orleans: "One sees them everywhere; on the street, at the theater, in the salon, in the cars; and pauses for a moment struck with the expression of entire despair."

The war crippled all social agencies in the South. Church buildings were demolished, their congregations scattered. Schools and colleges simply ceased to exist. Policemen, sheriffs, courts, judges—the instruments of law enforcement—could scarcely be found. Heartless bands led by ex-Confederate guerillas like Jesse and Frank James roamed the countryside, refusing to give up the war against the victors and their society. "Our principal danger," said one observer, "was from lawless bands of marauders. . . . Our country was full of highwaymen . . . tne off-scourings of the two armies and of the suddenly freed negro population."

It was not until 1877 that the South produced a cotton crop as large as that of 1860, not until 1879 that cotton exports to England reached the level of 1859. Much is sometimes made of postwar southern industrialism in smoothing the "road to reunion." Yet as late as 1900, the so-called industrialized New South actually produced a smaller proportion of American manufactures than did the Old South in 1860.

II. *Presidential Reconstruction*

LINCOLN'S COMMITMENT

Many of those who, like Lincoln, closed their eyes to the inescapable challenge of the slaveless South were encouraged to do so by the official Union objective in the war, to which Lincoln himself adhered to the end of his life. This objective was set forth as follows in the Crittenden Resolution adopted by the House on July 22, 1861, with but two dissenting votes:

This war is not waged . . . for any purpose of . . . overthrowing or interfering with the rights or established institutions of . . . the Southern States, but to defend and maintain the supremacy of the Constitution and to preserve the Union, with all the dignity, equality, and rights of the several States unimpaired; and . . . as soon as these objects are accomplished the war ought to cease.

Three days after the House acted, the Senate, with but five dissenting votes, adopted the virtually identical Johnson Resolutions.

True to the Crittenden criteria, Lincoln in 1862, when much of Tennessee, Louisiana, and North Carolina had fallen to Union arms, hastened to appoint military governors to shepherd these states back to the shelter of the Constitution. These governors were simply to pave the way for the re-establishment in their states of "such a republican form of State government, as will entitle the State . . . to be protected . . . by the United States against invasion and domestic violence," as the United States Constitution (Art. IV, Sec. 4) prescribed, and nothing more.

One of Lincoln's shining virtues was his flexibility; and many of those who mourn his passing at the very moment when the reconstruction of the South had to be undertaken in earnest see in his loss the cause of subsequent extremism in the North and South alike. Lincoln showed his flexibility in December, 1863, when Arkansas and certain other rebel states seemed on the verge of capitulation and a more general reconstruction program was required. On December 8 he issued his "Proclamation of Amnesty and Reconstruction." which became known as Lincoln's "ten per cent plan." By then, under mounting Radical pressure, Congress had passed the Second Confiscation Act and other anti-slavery measures (see p. 436), and Lincoln himself had issued the Emancipation Proclamation (p. 437). Lincoln adapted the terms of his new proclamation to these *political* realities.

The "ten per cent plan" excluded from participation in southern politics all high military and civil officers of the Confederacy or its states and any others who had attempted to return Negro prisoners of war to slavery. To all other Confederates who would take an oath of loyalty to the Constitution and "solemnly swear" to "abide by all acts of Congress passed during the existing rebellion with reference to slaves, . . . and faithfully support all proclamations of the President . . . having reference to slaves," a general amnesty would be granted by the President and any confiscated property other than slaves would be restored. As soon as 10 per cent of a state's *1860 electorate* had taken the oath and sworn allegiance to the Union, that state, having thereby gained Executive recognition, could proceed to write a new constitution, elect new state officers, and send members to the United States Congress. The House and Senate, of course, were to retain their constitutional privilege of seating or rejecting such members.

Other provisions of this proclamation, at the same time, disclose how *in*flexible Lincoln was to remain on the *social* realities of the emancipation measures. The "ten per cent" Proclamation, for example, assured the states to which it applied, "that any provision" they may make "in relation to the freed people of such State, . . . which may yet be consistent with their present condition as a laboring, landless, and homeless class, will not be objected to by the national Executive." The Proclamation backed down still further: "It is suggested as not improper," Lincoln said, that "subject only to modifications made necessary" by emancipation, "in constructing a loyal State government, . . . the general code of laws, as before the rebellion be maintained." This was nothing short of an invitation to the reconstructed states to adopt such notorious "Black Codes" as in fact they did adopt in 1865 and 1866 (see p. 463).

Two further observations on Lincoln's Proclamation are in order: (1) He was at pains in it to reassure all states that had remained loyal to the Union that the congressional anti-slavery measures and the Emancipation Proclamation did not yet apply to them. (2) He was also at pains to notify these and the rebel states that Congress could repeal or modify its anti-slavery measures, and that the Supreme Court could nullify them and the Emancipation Proclamation.

To make congressional repeal more difficult, Supreme Court nullification impossible, and emancipation itself more general, two Radical congressmen, only a few days after Lincoln's "ten per cent" proclamation, introduced in the House a proposal for an amendment to the Constitution which would forever abolish slavery throughout the United States. A few months later, the Senate joined the House in considering a joint resolution to submit such an amendment to the states. The resolution passed the Senate in April, 1864, by 38 to 6. In June, the House voted for it, 93 to 65, with 23 abstentions. Lacking the two-thirds majority needed, the House resolution failed.

This action by a Congress in which the South was wholly unrepresented only confirmed Lincoln's skepticism about northern concern for the Negro's welfare. The amendment promptly became a leading issue in the presidential campaign of 1864, the Republican platform declaring that "slavery . . . must be, always and everywhere, hostile to the principles of Republican Government," and committing the party to "such an amendment as shall terminate and forever prohibit [its] existence . . . within the limits of the jurisdiction of the United States." Yet in August, 1864, during the campaign, Lincoln told a conservative critic, "If Jefferson Davis wishes to know what I would do if he were to offer peace and reunion, saying nothing about slavery, let him try me."

Lincoln intetrpreted his reelection by a large majority in November, 1864 (see p. 446), as a demand for the amendment, and in the lame-duck Congress that met in December his effective log-rolling among House Democrats won over enough votes to the Radical side to squeeze out the bare two-thirds margin by which that chamber approved the proposal on January 31, 1865, and allowed it to be sent to the states, the Senate's earlier approval having carried over. Yet a mere three days later, Lincoln, according to his old Whig friend, Alexander H. Stephens, told a peace delegation headed by the Confederate Vice-president, that in his opinion the Emancipation Proclamation freeing the slaves of the South "was a war measure, and . . . as soon as the war ceased, it would be inoperative for the future. It would be held to apply only to such slaves as had come under its operation while it was in active exercise." At that time, at least 3,000,000 slaves still were in bondage in the Confederacy.

The Thirteenth Amendment was ratified in December, 1865, by the required 27 states, including 8 formerly of the Confederacy, which Congress, for other purposes, did not even recognize as states (see p. 465). The leading Radical in the Senate, Charles Sumner of Massachusetts, believed that the unprecedented second section of the Thirteenth Amendment—"Congress shall have power to enforce this article by appropriate legislation"—meant that Congress could enfranchise the ex-slave if, in its judgment, the Negro required the right to vote in order to preserve his freedom. Not many, as yet, even among the Radicals, went along with the Senator. In his last public address on April 11, 1865, Lincoln dallied with the idea " . . . that the elective franchise" might be "now conferred on the very intelligent" among the colored men, "and on those who serve our cause as soldiers." But for "the great mass of Negroes," as Kenneth M. Stampp writes, ". . . he never abandoned his hope that they could be persuaded to leave the country." One of Lincoln's last efforts at overseas colonization was one of the most disastrous. This occurred early in 1864 when he won the reluctant approval of the government of Haiti to allow certain northern promoters to settle hundreds of freedmen on an island off the Haitian coast. A virtual return to slave conditions under the most ruthless exploitive methods killed half the victims before the rest were brought home.

THE CONGRESSIONAL RESPONSE

Very early in the war, Senator Sumner observed that, "Mr. Lincoln's administration acted in superfluous good faith with the Rebels." As the war proceeded, Sumner found few reasons to change his mind; and as the end neared, he meant to see to it that Lincoln's policy did not cost the Union the fruits of victory. Sumner was one of the five Senators who had refused to vote for the Johnson Resolutions in July, 1861 (see p. 458). His alter ego in the House, Thad Stevens of Pennsylvania, had cast one of the two votes against the Crittenden Resolution. To these determined men, the war had been fought to free and elevate the slaves. They were not opposed to the "constitutional" reconstruction of the Union, but they had further terms which they would not surrender even if reconstruction itself were sacrificed.

Stevens had championed the Negro all his life (see p. 420), and was determined that his ideas of social equality, though advanced even for the North, be forced upon the proud planters.

The whole fabric of southern society [he declared] *must* be changed. . . . The Southern states have been despotisms, not governments of the people. It is impossible that any practical equality of rights can exist where a few thousand men monopolize the whole landed property. . . . If the South is ever to be made a safe republic let her lands be cultivated by the toil of the owners or the free labor of intelligent citizens. This must be done even though it drive her nobility into exile. If they go, all the better.

Surely the crimes of the South, said Stevens, "are sufficient to justify the exercise of the extreme rights of war—'to execute, to imprison, to confiscate.'" And Sumner added his insistent voice: "If all whites vote, then must all blacks. . . . Without them the old enemy will reappear, and . . . in alliance with the Northern democracy, put us all in peril again."

If Lincoln had a reconstruction plan for restoring the southern states but none for elevating the southern Negro, Sumner and Stevens had a plan for the Negro, but none that they openly championed at first for the southern states. Their principal early goal was to slow down political reconstruction so that southern congressmen would not soon reappear in Washington and exert political influence. In this objective they had the support of many conservative Republicans who were fearful that northern and southern Democrats would close ranks as before the war and overturn Republican economic legislation.

The Radical leadership did not offer an alternative to Lincoln's ten per cent plan of December, 1863, until July 4, 1864, when Congress, on the last day of the session, adopted the Wade-Davis bill. This bill would have made reconstruction of the South by southerners impossible. It required a *majority* of citizens, not just ten per cent, to swear loyalty to the Union before an acceptable state government could be established in a seceding state. This majority, moreover, had to swear not only that it would be loyal in the future but that it had been consistently and continuously loyal in the past. The bill also prescribed that new state constitutions in the South must abolish slavery, repudiate state debts, and disfranchise ex-Confederate leaders. Sumner tried to get the Senate to write into the bill a provision requiring the extension of the franchise to all male citizens regardless of color, but he gave up the idea when he saw that it would cost votes needed to insure the bill's passage.

The Radical strategists hoped by this bill to commit the Republican party to the Radical reconstruction program in the 1864 presidential elections. Lincoln attempted to forestall them by permitting the Wade-Davis bill to die by a pocket veto and issuing a proclamation justifying his action. Lincoln said rebel states might follow Wade-Davis provisions if they wished, but he refused to make them mandatory. The Radicals replied with the Wade-Davis Manifesto of August, 1864. "The President," it declared, "by preventing this bill from becoming a law, holds the electoral votes of the Rebel States at the dictation of his personal ambition. . . . A more studied outrage on the legislative authority of the people has never been perpetrated."

Most of the Radical leaders supported Lincoln in the 1864 campaign because they did not want to smash the Republican party machinery which they hoped soon to control. Once the election was over, they again resumed their own bent. In January, 1865, as we have seen, they adopted the Thirteenth Amendment (p. 460). In February, Congress refused to admit members from Louisiana which Lincoln had declared "reconstructed" under his ten per cent plan. On March 3, it created the Freedmen's Bureau with, among other things, its power over abandoned or confiscated land (see p. 456). The next day, Congress went home, with the Radicals determined to keep up the steam in their boilers and blow their whistles every day. "There's ample public opinion to sustain your course," Wendell Phillips, the abolitionist, admonished Sumner; "it only needs a reputable leader to make this *evident* . . . We have six months to work in . . . & if you'll begin an agitation—we will see that it reaches the Senate room."

ANDREW JOHNSON CARRIES ON

When Lincoln died on April 15, 1865, Andrew Johnson, 56 years old, became President of the United States. Born, like Lincoln, into the direst poverty, Johnson never succeeded in outgrowing his self-pity. Early in his political career this attitude had taken the form of aggressive dislike for the nobby cotton planters, and a good deal of Johnson's almost unbroken success at the polls in non-slaveholding eastern Tennessee may be attributed to his ability as a stump speaker in rousing the poor farmers against the plantation class.

Johnson won his first elective office—as alderman of Greenville, Tennessee—at the age of 20. Thereafter, he served successively as mayor, member of the state House and Senate, United States congressman, governor of Tennessee, and United States senator. Of all the southern senators in 1861,

Johnson alone had refused to abandon his seat. While still a senator, in March, 1862, he was appointed by Lincoln as military governor of Tennessee and succeeded in restoring civil government to that state before the threat of Confederate re-entry was ended. Under his regime, Tennessee became a kind of laboratory for Lincoln's reconstruction policy and Johnson's success there earned him the nomination of the Republican (Union) party for the vice-presidency in 1864, even though he had been a dedicated Jacksonian Democrat all his life.

During the 1864 campaign, Johnson made himself attractive to many Radicals by his characteristic denunciations of the rebel leaders. They have "ceased to be citizens," he cried. They have become "traitors." Traitors, he went on, must not only be punished; they "must be impoverished." Within ten day of Lincoln's death, Senator Chandler of Michigan declared that Johnson "is as radical as I am and as fully up to the mark." In May, Carl Schurz himself reported that, "The objects he aims at are all the most progressive friends of human liberty can desire." "Johnson, we have faith in you," exclaimed the jubilant Ben Wade of Ohio. "By the gods, there will be no trouble now in running this government."

Others, however, suspicious of Johnson's southern background and political past, held back. Congressman George W. Julian of Indiana, an old abolitionist, recalled that early in the war, Johnson had been as energetic a Negro colonizer as Lincoln. Julian acknowledged Johnson's hatred of the planters; but he recognized that as one of the yeoman class he was also "as decided a hater of the negro . . . as the rebels from whom he separated." Julian also feared the state-rights bent of Johnson's Jacksonian philosophy.

Julian and others, nevertheless, were willing to give Johnson a chance. If he failed them, they would know how to deal with him. Johnson had no claims on Republican party allegiance. What small hold he may have had on the people, he sacrificed by the disaster of his inauguration as Vice-president. Exhausted and ill, Johnson had

agreed to attend the ceremonies only on Lincoln's urging. On the morning of the inauguration he unfortunately tried to buck himself up for the great occasion by taking a little too much to drink. His inauguration speech grew more and more garbled until, at last, nearby officials cut in, administered the oath of office and led him compassionately away. Once president on his own, moreover, Johnson, foolishly perhaps, took over Lincoln's Cabinet with its strong Radical contingent led by Secretary of War Stanton intact.

Thus armed, the Radicals confronted the future optimistically. But Johnson moved more swiftly and independently than they anticipated. Early in May, 1865, he recognized Lincoln's ten per cent governments in Louisiana, Tennessee, Arkansas, and Virginia. He next appointed military governors in the seven states that had not yet complied with Lincoln's ten per cent plan. On May 29, he offered executive amnesty to citizens of these states except high Confederate military and civil officers, and citizens worth more than $20,000. These people had to make personal application for amnesty to the President. The "whitewashed" electorate—that is, those who benefited by the amnesty offer—were then to elect members to a constitutional convention in each state, which would abolish slavery, rescind the state's secession ordinance, adopt the Thirteenth Amendment, repudiate the state war debt, and call an election for a new state government. The suffrage for this election was to be determined by each state rather than by Congress. The Negro, clearly, would not get the ballot in the South any more than in most states in the North.

By the winter of 1865, all the seceding states but Texas had complied with Johnson's terms, and their sincerity was confirmed by the reports of investigators Johnson had sent to find out if the South actually did accept the judgment of arms. One investigator, however, Carl Schurz, found that "there is as yet among the southern people an *utter absence of national feeling* [Schurz's emphasis] . . . and a desire to preserve slavery in its original form as much and as long as possible." Johnson received this report with "great coldness," and only at Sumner's urging did Schurz decide to make it public. Few deny today that of all Johnson's emissaries, Schurz was the one who was right, and that southern extremism was plainly evident even before Radical Reconstruction itself began (see p. 464).

For all his yeoman animosity to the southern Old Guard, Johnson no doubt also had a sneaking admiration for them. His personal grants of amnesty exceeded all bounds. The whitewashed electorate, in turn, proceeded to elect ex-Confederate generals as governors, ex-Confederate solons as United States senators, ex-Confederate war heroes as local legislators. Other candidates, as a correspondent from Alabama informed Johnson, were cried down as "traitors to the South" and were routed at the polls. In some states, moreover, the secession ordinances were merely repealed, not repudiated. In others a reluctance to renounce the rebel debt was accompanied by a determination to resist taxation for redemption of the Union debt. The Georgia constitutional convention was not alone, again, in pressing claims for compensation as its price for "acquiescence" in a "war measure" like the Emancipation Proclamation. In ratifying the Thirteenth Amendment the reconstructed states were no less stiff-necked. Almost as a unit they warned Congress to keep hands off "the political status of former slaves, or their civil relations," to quote the South Carolina legislature. In the "Black Codes" adopted in 1865 and 1866 by all the reconstructed states but Tennessee, the freedman's "political status" was nullified simply by being ignored.

Some sort of code to meet the new social conditions of the South, as Lincoln had suggested, was of course essential. But the spirit in which the Black Codes were adopted would have given any fair-minded person pause. The Black Code of Mississippi, harsh though it was, was not the harshest. Adopted November 20, 1865, it opened as follows, with italics in the original:

Under the pressure of federal bayonets, urged on by the misdirected sympathies of the world

in behalf of the enslaved African, the people of Mississippi have abolished the institution of slavery. . . . We must now meet the question as it is, and not as we would like to have it. . . . The negro is free, whether we like it or not. . . . *To be free, however, does not make him a citizen, or entitle him to social or political equality with the white man.* But the constitution and justice do entitle him to protection and security in his person and property, both real and personal.

The Black Codes usually granted Negroes the right to sue, to give evidence in court, to go to school, to have marriages sanctified, and to have apprenticed children protected by the state. But nowhere could Negroes hold office, vote, serve on juries, or bear arms. In some states, the codes permitted Negroes to own property, to work at any jobs they could hold down, and to quit a job freely. But in most states, Negroes were prohibited from working as artisans, mechanics, and in other capacities where they competed with white labor, and they could not leave their jobs except under stated conditions. At the same time, as the Mississippi code put it, the law ". . . shall not be construed as to allow any freedman, free negro or mulatto to rent or lease any lands or tenements." The vagrancy laws were the most oppressive provisions of the codes. In Georgia, for example, the law said that "all persons wandering or strolling about in idleness, who are able to work and who have no property to support them," might be picked up and tried. If convicted, they could be set to work on state chain gangs or contracted out to planters and other employers who would pay their fines and upkeep for a stated period.

The Black Codes, said the Radical Schurz, are "a striking embodiment of the idea that although the former owner has lost his individual right of property in the former slave, 'the blacks at large belong to the whites at large.'" The conservative Gideon Welles at the same time recorded in his diary: "The entire South seem to be stupid and vindictive, know not their friends, and are pursuing just the course which their opponents, the Radicals, desire. I fear a terrible ordeal awaits them in the future."

III. *Congress and the South*

THE STORM BREAKS

When Congress met in December, 1865, it was faced with Johnson's executive coup and the South's execrable response to it. Stevens improved the opportunity thus offered when he said, "Let all who approve of our [principles] tarry with us. Let all others go with copperheads and rebels. Those will be the opposing parties."

As their first move, the Radicals set up the Joint Committee of Fifteen—six senators and nine representatives—to scan the qualifications of the men elected in the southern states and to review the whole presidential reconstruction plan that had brought such "traitors" to the very threshold of Congress. These men were never permitted to take their seats. Without them, Congress proceeded early in 1866 to enact a bill continuing the Freedmen's Bureau, which was gradually becoming an instrument of Radical policy. Johnson, believing that the future care of the Negroes had better be left to the state legislatures, vetoed the bill. The Radicals overrode the veto in the House, but failed in the Senate.

In March, 1866, Johnson vetoed a civil rights bill which forbade states to discriminate among their citizens on the basis of color or race, as they had in the Black Codes. But by now a sufficient number of conservative senators were ready to join the Radicals in defense of congressional prerogatives, if not of Radical principles, and both houses overrode the President. A few months later, in July, 1866, the Radicals pushed through a second Freedmen's Bureau bill over Johnson's veto.

The Radicals were showing their parliamentary mettle as well as their political policy. The real test developed over the Fourteenth Amendment, perhaps the most far-reaching one ever added to the Constitution. When the Republicans introduced this amendment in June, 1866, they were concerned over the constitutionality of coercing the states under the Civil Rights Act and the danger that another Congress might repeal this act. A civil-rights amendment would set the constitutionality issue at rest and would also make repeal more difficult.

The amendment's opening section for the first time defined citizenship in the United States as distinct from citizenship in a state. By identifying as citizens "all persons born or naturalized in the United States," it automatically extended citizenship to American-born Negroes. (Some years later, the courts held that the amendment also extended United States citizenship to such "legal persons" as business corporations; see Chapter 20). The amendment forbade any state from abridging "the privileges and immunities" of United States citizens, and further impinged on state power by declaring that no state shall "deprive any person of life, liberty or property, without due process of law," nor "deny to any person within its jurisdiction the equal protection of the laws."

The second section of the amendment did not give Negroes the vote, but it penalized a state for withholding it by reducing its representation in Congress in the same proportion that those deprived of the vote bore to the "whole number of male citizens twenty-one years of age in such State." Northern as well as southern states, of course, were subject to the penalty, but in no northern state was the colored population large enough to bring about a reduction in representation in case Negro suffrage continued to be withheld. By 1866, only six northern states had enfranchised the Negro.

Third, the amendment disqualified from office, unless Congress specifically lifted the disqualification by a two-thirds vote, all Confederates who before the war had taken a federal oath of office. Finally, the amendment guaranteed the Union debt and outlawed the Confederate debt and any claims for compensation for loss of slaves.

At the time the Fourteenth Amendment was proposed many in the South as well as in the North hoped that it would provide "the final condition of restoration," as a Boston paper put it; that it would in effect be a lasting "treaty of peace" re-establishing the Union. The leading Radicals, however, thought it too full of compromises and hoped to stiffen its provisions later on. No one backed Negro suffrage more fervently than Stevens. Yet in speaking in favor of the amendment in Congress, Stevens said:

In my judgement we shall not approach a measure of justice until we have given every adult freedman a homestead on the land where he was born and toiled and suffered. Forty acres of land and a hut would be more valuable to him than the immediate right to vote. Unless we give them this we shall receive the censure of mankind and the curse of Heaven.

But Stevens himself acknowledged even of the indirect suffrage provisions of the Fourteenth Amendment, let alone its failure to insure the freedman's economic independence: "I believe it is all that can be obtained in the present state of public opinion."

The Radicals demanded that the southern states ratify the amendment before they could be represented in Congress. Johnson advised the states not to ratify, and by mid-February, 1867, all but Tennessee—that is, 10 of the 11 ex-Confederate states—had followed his advice. Legally, the amendment was dead. At the time of the adoption of the Thirteenth Amendment, Congress had agreed that the 11 as yet unreconstructed states should be counted as part of the Union for purposes of ratification, making 37 states in all. The same 37 were to vote on the Fourteenth Amendment, which could thus be defeated (according to the constitutional provision requiring approval by three-fourths of the states) by 10 commonwealths. For good measure, Delaware and Kentucky, in addition to the 10 ex-Confederate states, had also rejected the amendment by this time, making 12 rejections in all. When the last of the southern rejections

had arrived, James A. Garfield of Ohio declared: "The last one of the sinful ten has at last with contempt and scorn flung back into our teeth the magnanimous offer of a generous nation. It is now our turn to act."

THE RADICAL SURGE

The Fourteenth Amendment had been rejected in most of the ex-Confederate states while the congressional elections of 1866, the first national elections since the close of the war, were taking place. The amendment had drawn the issue clearly between the President and Congress. Between August 28 and September 15, Johnson made his unfortunate "swing around the circle," visiting key cities on behalf of congressional candidates who favored his policy. Many people considered such campaigning unseemly for a president, and all the more so in Johnson's case, since he was often indiscreet as an impromptu political speaker. The more he talked, the more the Radicals made fun of him. Fodder for the Radicals' own campaign was supplied by violence in the South, which reached its peak during a riot in New Orleans on July 30 over Radical efforts to force Negro suffrage on the state of Louisiana. Negroes and whites clashed and 41 men were killed.

The Radicals used such incidents to pound home the intransigence of the Confederates. As if to underscore the need for vigilance, Union veterans completed the organization of the Grand Army of the Republic just before the elections, and in November, 1866, the G.A.R. held its first national encampment in Indianapolis. The Radicals made a big play for the soldier vote. They also reminded businessmen what a threat to high tariffs, hard money, and the national debt the South's return to national power would be. Stung by the South's rejection of the Fourteenth Amendment, the Radicals worked hard for a sweeping victory that they might interpret as a mandate for even severer measures. Indeed, they sought to win enough seats to give them two-thirds majorities in both houses so as to insure the enactment of their bills over presidential vetoes. Nor were they disappointed. They carried the Senate with 42 Republican seats to 11 for the Democrats, and the House 143 to 49.

So convincing was the Radicals' victory that even before the new Congress met they were able to marshal all the votes they needed to proceed with a virtual revolution in the government. Ordinarily, the new Congress would not have convened until December, 1867, unless called into special session by the president. One of the first acts of the old Congress on January 22, 1867, was to take it upon itself to call the new Congress into session on March 4, the day the old Congress was required by law to adjourn. Having insured Congress' uninterrupted presence in Washington the Radicals moved to concentrate all power in congressional hands.

Their initial and most comprehensive measure was the so-called First Reconstruction Act, which was passed over Johnson's veto on March 2, 1867 (supplementary Second, Third, and Fourth Reconstruction Acts elaborated its language and filled out its enforcement machinery). By the terms of this act, all existing southern state governments except that of Tennessee, which had been accepted back into the Union in 1866, were declared illegal. The South was organized into five military districts, each under a general to be named by the president. Each general was to have an armed force at his command to help him maintain martial law if necessary. The general's main task was to call a new constitutional convention in each state, the delegates to be elected by universal adult male suffrage, Negro and white. Although the Fourteenth Amendment had been dead for nearly a month, the act explicitly cited its provisions to indicate those in the "said rebel states" who were to be excluded from serving as or voting for delegates.

Once manned, the new conventions would proceed to establish state governments in which Negroes could vote and hold office. Once in operation, these governments were to ratify the arbitrarily revived Fourteenth Amendment as a condition for their return to the Union and the acceptance of their representatives by Congress.

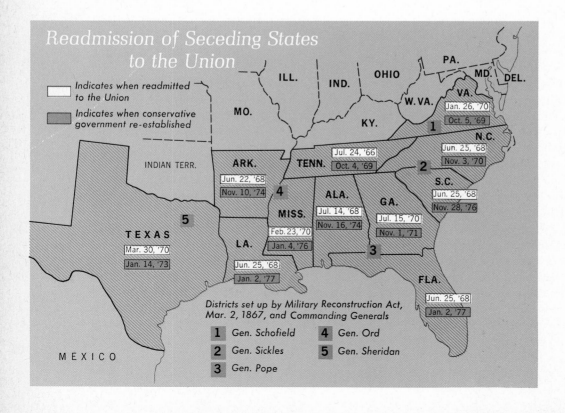

Readmission of Seceding States to the Union

Indicates when readmitted to the Union
Indicates when conservative government re-established

Districts set up by Military Reconstruction Act, Mar. 2, 1867, and Commanding Generals

1 Gen. Schofield   4 Gen. Ord
2 Gen. Sickles   5 Gen. Sheridan
3 Gen. Pope

By June, 1868, all but three states—Mississippi, Texas, and Virginia—had been "reconstructed" by Congress in time to participate in the presidential elections that year, though in some of them armed forces remained to protect Republican rule for as long as ten years more. In July, 1868, Secretary Seward announced the completion of ratification of the Fourteenth Amendment, but only after Congress a week earlier by a joint resolution wholly unsanctioned by the supreme law had declared the amendment part of the Constitution. The three recalcitrant states were re-admitted in 1870. In that year, Georgia, whose reconstruction had been suspended because of the expulsion of Negro members from her legislature, was also re-admitted for the second time.

The Radicals' next step was to protect their program from the Supreme Court. In the case of *ex parte Milligan* (1866), which arose over Lincoln's suspension of *habeas corpus* in Indiana during the war, the Supreme Court had held that if military rule "is continued *after* the courts are reinstated, it is a gross usurpation of power." When the First Reconstruction Act was passed, southern courts were open, and the act deliberately defied this decision. When, in *ex parte McCardle,* the constitutionality of this act was challenged, the Radicals attached a rider to a minor bill, withdrawing appellate jurisdiction from the Court in *habeas corpus* matters. Johnson vetoed the whole bill, but the withdrawal provision was then passed over his veto, in March, 1868. The Court had already put *ex parte McCardle* on its schedule but, against the judgment of two justices, the majority yielded to the Radicals, allowed the case to be quashed, and the First Reconstruction Act survived.

Having successfuly defied the Supreme Court, the Radicals next set about eliminating the Executive. Two measures had been passed at the same time as the First Reconstruction Act, in March, 1867, with this end in view. The first, the Tenure of Office Act, declared that the president could not remove federal officers who had been ap-

pointed with the consent of the Senate without first getting the Senate's consent to their removal. The second, the Command of the Army Act, forbade the president to issue orders to the army except through the General of the Army, General Grant. These measures left the president at the mercy of Radical office-holders and divested him of his constitutional role as commander-in-chief. But the Radicals were not satisfied.

After almost a full year of investigation in 1867, the House Judiciary Committee, in November, though failing to draw up any list of Johnson's "high crimes and misdemeanors," had voted by a bare 5-to-4 majority to recommend to the whole chamber that the President be impeached and haled before the Senate for trial. The committee's grounds were simply that the President's offenses were all referable "to the one great overshadowing purpose of reconstructing the . . . rebel States in accordance with his own will, in the interests of the great criminals who carried them into rebellion." This charge proved too vague for the whole House to swallow, and in December, 1867, it rejected the committee's recommendation 57 to 108. By attempting to remove Secretary of War Stanton, the remaining Radical in his Cabinet, and thereby also to test the validity of the Tenure of Office Act, Johnson soon gave his congressional enemies a second chance. On Febraury 21, 1868, Stanton was formally removed. Three days later, a new impeachment resolution came before the House, this one reported out not by the Judiciary Committee, but by the Committee on Reconstruction, of which Stevens was chairman. Once more no bill of particulars was leveled at the Chief Executive; yet the House now voted for impeachment, 126 to 47, and only then promised the Senate in due time "to exhibit particular articles of impeachment . . . and make good the same." By March 2, eleven "particular articles" had been drawn up, all but one of them referring to the Tenure of

Office Act. The exception was the notorious "Butler article," number 10, which charged Johnson with "inflammatory, and scandalous harangues" calculated to bring Congress into disgrace, but which mentioned no law that had thereby been violated.

On March 5, Chief Justice Chase solemnly organized the Senate as "a court of impeachment for the trial of the President of the United States," but proceedings did not seriously get underway until March 13. That bad penny, Ben Butler, took the lead for the prosecution and promptly turned the affair into "a solemn theatrical fiasco," to use the words of James Schouler. An effort was even made to implicate Johnson in Lincoln's assassination; and while most of the other charges had no better foundation, Johnson escaped conviction only by the barest margin. The trial drew out for more than two months. But when, on May 16 and again on May 25, seven Republicans showed their determination to desert the Radical leadership, the Radicals' game was up. These 7, together with 12 Democrats, made 19 against Johnson's removal. Thirty-five voted for it, one short of the two-thirds needed to carry.

THE ELECTION OF 1868

In the presidential election of 1868, the Radicals succeeded in getting General Grant nominated by the Republicans. Grant had no known political principles, nor for that matter any known political ambitions. But on his war record he appeared a certain winner, and that was enough for Johnson's enemies. Johnson sought the Democratic nomination, but the party turned instead to an untainted if unenthusiastic northerner, former governor Horatio Seymour of New York.

The Democrats tried to make a campaign issue of cheap money. In 1866 Congress had passed a measure providing for the gradual retirement of the wartime greenbacks (see p. 435), and in the next two years almost $100 million worth had been withdrawn from circulation. Although the greenbacks had fluctuated widely in value, they always held below the value of gold and hence were popular with long-term debtors like farmers who wanted cheap money with which to pay their fixed mortgage obligations. To curry favor with the farmers of the West, the Democrats now adopted a platform plank advocating the reissuance of the retired greenbacks to redeem war bonds which did not specifically require redemption in gold. Since the author of this plank was George H. Pendleton of Ohio, the party's vice-presidential candidate in 1864 and an early aspirant for the presidential nomination in 1868, this "soft money" proposal became known as the "Ohio Idea."

The Republicans scotched the Ohio Idea in the strongly Union-minded West by reminding the farmers, in difficulties though they were because of the falling off of the wartime demand for foodstuffs and fibers, that redemption of war bonds in anything but gold smacked of rebel repudiation of a sacred debt that had been contracted to preserve the Union. At the same time, the Republicans promised businessmen that they would extend redemption "over a fair period" so as not to disturb the business credit structure, and that when the time came, all bondholders would be paid in gold. Having thus dealt with the complex problem of money, the Radicals proceeded to keep before the public the main political issue—Radical Reconstruction.

In the elections of 1866, the Republicans had had great success "waving the bloody shirt," a tactic by which they reviled the Democratic party as the standard-bearer of rebellion, Negro repression, and financial repudiation. "In short," cried Oliver Morton, the Radical governor of Indiana, in a typical "bloody shirt" foray, "the Democratic party may be described as a common sewer and loathsome receptacle, into which is emptied every element of treason North and South, and every element of inhumanity and barbarism which has dishonored the age." In 1868, and in subsequent elections, such tirades served as the staple of Republican oratory. Practical Republican electioneering was handled by the Union League clubs which had been organized in the North in 1862 to spread Union propaganda. Gradually they extended their wartime activity to captured southern territory. By 1867, more than 80 chapters of the League were operating in South Carolina alone, where most Negroes were enrolled as members.

Yet the Republican campaign did not overwhelm the opposition. In 1868, against a weak opponent, Grant was elected with a popular plurality of a mere 310,000. Had the Union League not helped deliver the votes of about 700,000 Negroes in the seven hastily reconstructed southern states, Grant might have had no plurality at all.

The fact that Negroes in certain states such as Louisiana and Georgia had been prevented from casting what might have been much-needed Republican votes led Radicals to attempt to strengthen the Fourteenth Amendment's protection of the Negro franchise. When Congress convened early in 1869, it promptly passed the Fifteenth Amendment, which provided that: "The right of citizens of the United States to vote shall not be denied or abridged by the United States or by any State on account of

race, color, or previous condition of servitude." This amendment was sent to the states in February, 1869, and was declared ratified in March, 1870.

"The agitation against slavery," declared the *Nation,* "has reached an appropriate and triumphant conclusion." But many retained doubts about the *Nation's* own conclusion. During the debate on the measure in the Senate, the Indiana Radical, Oliver P. Morton, accurately forecast the future:

This amendment leaves the whole power in the States just as it exists now except that colored men shall not be disfranchised for the three reasons of race, color, or previous condition of slavery. . . . Sir, if the power should pass into the hands of the Conservative or Democratic population of those [southern] States, if they could not debar the colored people of the right of suffrage in any other way they would do it by an educational or property qualification . . . and thus this amendment would be practically defeated in all those States where the great body of colored people live [see page 484].

IV. *The Day of the Carpetbagger*

REVISIONS
IN THE RADICAL CAMP

When Grant accepted the nomination of the Republican convention in May, 1868, he wrote, "Let us have peace." Many men, recalling his magnanimous surrender terms to Lee, thought that the severity of Radical Reconstruction might now be softened. The death of Stevens in August, 1868, the defeat of Ben Wade for the Senate later that year, and Sumner's decline soon after (see p. 474) gave substance to this hope.

But Grant's administration was easily dominated by such surviving Radicals as Senators Zachariah Chandler of Michigan, Simon Cameron of Pennsylvania, and Roscoe Conkling of New York. These men were untinged by the abolitionist idealism that had marked the Stevens-Sumner leadership,

but they had ample partisan reasons— chief among them the wish to protect wartime tariff, railroad, and banking legislation from attack by returning southerners —for keeping ex-Confederates disfranchised and the Negro voters safe in the Republican camp. In pursuing their aims in the South they had the help of Radical carpetbaggers who had begun to go South right after the war to show what northern "brains and sinew" could accomplish. The number of carpetbaggers soared after the adoption of the First Reconstruction Act, when, under the protection of the military, they virtually took charge of politics. In the seven states reconstructed in 1868, 10 of 14 United States senators, 20 of 35 congressmen, and 4 governors were carpetbaggers. The others, with few exceptions, were "scalawags"— southerners who rode to office on Radical coattails but eventually broke with the carpetbaggers on the race issue. The few exceptions were Negroes.

CARPETBAGGERS AS REFORMERS

Many carpetbaggers, especially the early ones, were genuine reformers who tried to help the freedmen become useful citizens, economically independent and politically and legally the equal of whites. Often enough the objectives of the reformers were not in conflict with those of the self-seekers who came later, and under carpetbag rule political and social advances were made in the South which benefited both races.

Many of these gains grew out of the provisions of the new southern state constitutions written by the "black and tan" conventions, as southerners branded the assemblages called by the Radical generals. These constitutions, unlike most of those in the North itself, gave the Negro the right to vote and hold office before the Fifteenth Amendment had been ratified. They also eliminated property qualifications for voting and office-holding. Representation in state legislatures and in Congress was more fairly apportioned. These constitutions also abolished imprisonment for debt and other archaic social legislation. For the first time in many southern states, they provided for public schools—for whites and Negroes.

Next to giving the vote to Negroes, nothing offended the South more than Radical efforts to give them schooling. The slogan, "Schooling ruins the Negro," expressed the general belief. As early as July, 1865, Carl Schurz had noted instances of Negro schools being burned and of teachers and students being threatened. Yet by 1877, 600,000 Negroes were enrolled in southern elementary and secondary schools; and several colleges and universities, including Fisk and Howard, had been established by the Freedmen's Bureau and northern church and philanthropic agencies. Night schools for adults also flourished. "The great ambition of the older people," said Booker T. Washington, "was to try to learn to read the Bible before they died."

The ballot, though at first misused, was a notable step forward for the freedman. Office-holding, though also abused, was another significant advance, but it was not so widely shared as the term "black reconstruction" might imply. Only in South Carolina, in 1868, did Negro legislators outnumber whites, 88 to 67, but the sessions were not controlled by Negroes. In other state legislatures, Negroes made up sizable minorities, but the white politicians always dominated the proceedings. One mulatto, P. B. S. Pinchback, became lieutenant-governor of Louisiana. Several Negroes became congressmen and two became United States senators. Others gained administrative posts, in which they did well.

CORRUPTION AND REACTION

Many southern leaders actually found little fault with the Radicals' tariff, railroad, and money policies, and felt that the Republicans could trust the South sufficiently to give its spokesmen a voice in national affairs once again. Southern whites also felt that by 1868 they had made every concession that a vanquished nation (as they thought of themselves) ought to have been asked to make by the victors in the late war. The South had disbanded the remnants of its army, repudiated the Confederate debt, renounced secession as a constitutional device, and accepted the Thirteenth Amendment abolishing slavery. None of these concessions had been made gracefully, but they had been made. When the Radicals began to court the Negro vote to insure protection for their national legislative program, southerners balked at what they called "barbarization of the South," and prepared, if not to resume the war, at least to promote violence and terror to thwart the Radicals' plan.

The mere existence of the carpetbag governments within their borders seemed insulting and shameful to many southerners. Carpetbag corruption made the affront even harder to bear, even though it was not as bad as it has been painted. Between 1868 and 1874, the bonded debt of the 11 Confederate states grew by over $100 million.

But this enormous sum was not itself evidence of crime. To raise money, the southern states had to sell bonds in the North, where southern credit was so poor that investors often demanded a 75 per cent discount from the bond's face value. Thus for every $100 worth of bonds sold, a southern state might actually receive only $25. Many of the social and humanitarian reforms of the Reconstruction legislatures, moreover, were expensive, as was the relief that had to be extended to the starving and homeless of both races.

Nevertheless, much of the debt was corruptly incurred, though not necessarily by carpetbaggers. A large part of it was piled up through the sale of state bonds to back southern-sponsored railroad enterprises that never built a mile of track, or to aid companies that merely distributed as profit the money they received. Carpetbaggers were more likely to busy themselves with more traditional forms of graft. A considerable portion of the debt was created, for example, by politicians who won large contracts for construction or printing, and then supplied little of the services or goods that the contracts called for. Public funds also were spent for personal furniture, homes, carriages, jewelry, liquor, leather goods, and other amenities. But such conspicuous corruption probably cost the least.

Taxes to pay for carpetbag government expenditures and to service the rapidly growing debt fell most heavily on the oppressed planters, who before the war had been able to pass taxes on to other groups in the South. Business firms escaped with small levies, and personal taxes were low and could be easily evaded.

The growing public debt and the unequal taxation aroused the ire of the former leaders of the South. But the majority of the people complained most bitterly about the gross conduct, the bizarre legislative sessions, the flamboyant or slovenly dress, and the posturing of the new political leaders, Negro and white. Negro militia roamed the southern countryside and sometimes shot up city streets. Negro legislatures were something new on the face of the earth, and

travelers came from Europe and the North to watch them in action. What the visitors expected to find in a society so recently upended is not clear, but their reactions often matched the horror of the southerners themselves. Rubbed into the unhealed sores of the war, this kind of "reconstruction" completed the moral rout of the South. Sidney Lanier, the poet, said during this period in a letter north, "Perhaps you know that with us of the young generation in the South, since the war pretty much the whole of life has been merely not dying."

To combat carpetbag rule and the Negro vote on which it rested, thousands, even from the most respectable elements in the South, banded together in the Ku Klux Klan, the Knights of the White Camelia, and other secret groups. Between 1867 and 1869, hooded or otherwise incognito, they roamed the land, shot, flogged, and terrorized Negroes and their supporters, burned homes and public buildings, attacked Reconstruction officials, and, under the guise of keeping order (which, indeed, sometimes needed keeping), perpetrated other acts of violence dedicated to the maintenance of white supremacy. After 1869, some of these white organizations engaged in such random pillage and murder that the respectable elements abandoned them in horror. But the organizations themselves persisted.

RADICAL REPRISALS
AND RETREATS

The Radical leadership in Congress did not permit the activities of the violent white organizations to go unchallenged. In May, 1870, they passed a "Force Act" designed to strengthen the protection of Negro voting rights by imposing heavy fines and jail sentences for offenses under the Fourteenth and Fifteenth amendments. This act also gave federal courts controlled by carpetbaggers, rather than southern state courts, original jurisdiction in all cases arising under these amendments.

In spite of the Force Act, the Democrats made substantial gains in the congressional elections of 1870, and by the following year southern whites had recaptured the state governments of Tennessee, Virginia, North Carolina, and Georgia. Attributing these successes to violence, the Radicals next forced through Congress the Ku Klux Klan Act of 1871. This act gave federal courts original jurisdiction in all cases arising out of conspiracies or terrorism against freedmen. It also empowered the president to suspend *habeas corpus* in any terrorized community, to declare martial law, and to send in troops to maintain order.

Within a short time, about 7,000 southerners were indicted under these two acts, and although few were convicted or even tried, the personal harassment served to smother white political activity. In October, 1871, to convince remaining skeptics that the Radicals still meant business, Grant declared nine counties of South Carolina, where the Klan was especially active, to be again in rebellion and placed them under martial law. An investigation by a congressional committee presently placed its seal of approval on the President's militancy.

The South Carolina episode marked the peak of forceful repression of southern whites. Upon many in the North, Radical excesses in their own section (see p. 474) had already begun to pall. Testimony offered at the few trials of persons indicted in South Carolina and elsewhere, and evidence inadvertently publicized by the congressional investigating committee's report, disclosed the severe political and social disabilities which the Radicals had fastened upon the southern states and which were retarding their recovery. Under mounting pressure, Congress passed a liberal amnesty act in May, 1872, which restored voting and office-holding privileges to all southern whites with the exception of a few hundred of the highest surviving Confederate dignitaries. In the same year the Freedmen's Bureau, the protector of the Negro's rights, was permitted to go out of existence.

The fact that 1872 was a presidential election year no doubt prompted the Radicals to make these concessions. One feature of the 1872 presidential campaign was the "Liberal Republican" movement, which had begun in Missouri where a faction led by Carl Schurz and B. Gratz Brown had overthrown the Radical regime in 1870 and elected Brown to the governorship and Schurz to the Senate. Years earlier, Schurz, as we have seen (p. 462), had favored imposing a vindictive reconstruction program on the defeated South. But by 1870, he had come to realize that the Radical carpetbaggers in Missouri were mainly corruptionists who used the Negro vote only to maintain their tyranny over the local whites. He had also been alienated by the coarseness of Grant's associates, the plotting of his closest advisers, and the special-interest legislation promoted by his cronies in Congress. By 1872 Schurz had taken the lead in transforming his Missouri movement into a national party whose principal aim was to unseat the tarnished General. By concessions to the South, the Radicals hoped to preserve Grantism in Washington.

v. *Radical Republicanism in the North*

GRANTISM

On observing the Washington scene early in 1869, young Henry Adams, grandson and great-grandson of early presidents, remarked that "the progress of evolution from President Washington to President Grant was alone evidence enough to upset Darwin." An organism as simple as U. S. Grant, thought Adams, "had no right to exist. He should have been extinct for ages."

In fact, however, Grant, as President, was no throwback but very much a product of his time. A failure in business himself, he became infatuated with business success. He wanted to make A. T. Stewart, the department store king and a lavish contributor to his campaign fund, Secretary of the Treasury; but it was discovered that a law of

1789 forbade persons engaged in commerce to hold that post. The Senate stubbornly refused a request by Grant that Stewart be excepted from the law, and Stewart's name had to be withdrawn. In Washington, Grant was frequently entertained by Henry Cooke, whose business it was to report to his financier brother, Jay, what he could learn at the nation's capital. Fond of the horse-racing at Saratoga Springs, New York, Grant, in the summer of 1869, accepted the use of Commodore Vanderbilt's private car to travel there. He once described Jim Fisk as "destitute of moral character"; yet, as President, he saw nothing wrong in using Fisk's sumptuous boats, dining publicly with Fisk and Gould, and otherwise enjoying the hospitality of the Erie looters while making them privy to the country's financial affairs.

Grant's political appointments were hardly likely to keep the President's businessman associates from using the information they collected. In making his appointments, the President, of course, turned first to his old army friends, most of whom were as innocent of the ways of politics as their chief. Grant's White House staff, it was said, had "nothing but uniforms." General Horace Porter became Grant's private secretary. The assistant secretary, in the key position of making up Grant's daily visitor list and controlling access to the President, was his former military aide, the foppish Colonel Orville E. Babcock. These men dominated Grant's "Kitchen Cabinet." With three exceptions, his regular Cabinet was made up of men who frightened people by their very obscurity. The three exceptions were Secretary of State Hamilton Fish, who served through Grant's two administrations; and Secretary of the Interior Jacob D. Cox, and Attorney-General Ebenezer Rockwood Hoar, both of whom were supplanted in a little over a year by more pliant souls.

The Kitchen Cabinet made most of the decisions on the appointment of federal job-holders, among whom Grant's relatives and neighbors, and retainers of the Kitchen Cabinet itself, were numerous. Federal patronage had grown enormously with the growth of government activity during and after the war, and in dispensing it men like Babcock (on the example of the President himself) often ignored the tradition of consulting the party's senators from the various states. This practice angered senatorial leaders and quickly cost Grant any chance he had for the support of such senators as Sumner and Schurz, and Lyman Trumbull of Illinois, an old favorite of Lincoln's. Alienated also were some of the less-principled patronage-mongers in Republican states like New York and Pennsylvania, who resented being shortchanged on political jobs in favor of Babcock's Radical Republican cronies, men as dishonest as themselves. Schurz and Trumbull were among the leaders of the movement for federal civil-service reform, which the enormous war-time rise in patronage had inspired. It was their aim to place federal job-holding on a merit basis, with candidates selected by objective examinations. But the patronage-mongers found it easy to mobilize congressional opposition whenever civil-service legislation loomed.

Even worse than Grant's handling of major appointments and patronage in the ranks was the way he allowed himself and his great office to be used by the corruptionists who surrounded him.

One of the most unsavory incidents occurred only a few months after Grant's inauguration. This was "Black Friday," September 24, 1869, when Grant's long overdue action in releasing $4 million in government gold to New York banks broke a gold corner that Jim Fisk and Jay Gould had planned by earlier persuading the financially innocent President not to release any government gold that fall. Fisk and Gould were foiled, but not before many speculators and others who needed gold in their business transactions had been ruined.

"Black Friday" occurred in the midst of negotiations over the annexation of Santo Domingo (now the Dominican Republic), for which other of Grant's cronies had won his pledge "privately to use all his influence." An island exceedingly rich in minerals, timber, and fruit, Santo Domingo had won its independence from Spain in 1865. Among those who now hungrily eyed Santo Domingo were a couple of discreditable Massachusetts promoters who, like so many of the kind, got Orville Babcock's ear. On visiting the island late in 1869, Babcock was able to negotiate a treaty of annexation. When Attorney-General Hoar denounced Babcock's treaty-making as illegal, Grant removed Hoar from office. When Charles Sumner, Chairman of the Senate Foreign Relations Committee, then denounced the entire "deal," the Senate defeated Babcock's treaty in 1870. Grant's senatorial friends retaliated the next year by stripping Sumner of his committee post and practically reading him out of the Republican party.

LOBBIES AND LEGISLATION

Grant, no doubt, was personally innocent of corruption. As a victorious general he had become accustomed to receiving the lavish patronage of the rich. Before his candidacy for the presidency, a group of millionaires headed by A. T. Stewart had presented him with a fully furnished mansion in Philadelphia. Another group, including Hamilton Fish, had helped pay off the $100,000 mortgage on Grant's Washington home. Many of these men had made fortunes on war contracts, but in Grant's eyes they had also contributed handsomely to winning the war. Now they were sustaining the postwar boom (see Chapter 19). Suppose their accomplishments did require forcing special-interest legislation through Congress? No one in the postwar epoch could be pure and progressive at the same time.

To those who would point a finger, moreover, Grant could reply that he had inherited a government already far gone in corruption. The competition for war contracts and the fight for other wartime legislation covering protective tariffs, land grants, and the money system, had made lobbying a full-time occupation. Men like John Lord Hayes, who represented the woolen manufacturers, and James M. Swank, who spoke for the iron and steel interests, spent almost all their time cultivating legislators in wartime Washington and actually prowled the floor of the House to keep their congressmen in line. Just before concluding four years in Congress in 1873, Job Stevenson of Ohio told his colleagues that "the House of Representatives was like an auction room where more valuable considerations were disposed of under the speaker's hammer than in any other place on earth."

Few political plums were more valuable than the tariff, which by 1870, had become "a conglomeration of special favors." The situation is indicated in this comment by General Robert C. Schenck, representative from Ohio from 1863 to 1871: "Sitting here as a friend of protective tariffs for eight years, I have voted aye or nay as those who got up the tariff bills have told me."

The railroads also shared in congressional handouts. The last federal land grant for railroad-building was made in 1871, by which time the total distributed to the roads directly or through the states came to 160 million acres, valued conservatively at $335 million. The roads also had received lavish government loans. After the Union Pacific and Central Pacific railroads had received their loans, Congress annually considered legislation that would have provided for their eventual repayment. The transcontinentals fought this legislation stubbornly and successfully. It was on one such occasion, in the session of 1867-68, that Congressman Oakes Ames distributed shares in the Crédit Mobilier (see p. 518) among senators and representatives "where they will do the most good to us." The revelation of Oakes' action on the eve of the presidential election of 1872 simply added one more scandal to the Republican record under Grant.

Nor were northern financiers left out of the "Great Barbecue," as Grant's regime has been called. In March, 1869, in fulfillment of Republican promises, both houses of Congress adopted a resolution pledging

474

the government to redeem the entire war debt in gold or in new gold bonds. This pledge, and the laws soon passed to carry it out, sent the value of war bonds soaring and brought substantial profits to speculators. These laws, it should be said, proved salutary as far as the government's credit was concerned. Forced during the war to offer interest as high as 6 per cent, the victorious national government was soon able to borrow for as little as 2½ per cent. Yet the new laws permitted the Secretary of the Treasury to issue new bonds more or less at his pleasure, and rumors, hot tips, and cloakroom gossip about Treasury activities flowed between Washington and New York and other financial centers. Such news often caused mad flurries in the money markets, disastrous, as some said, to "legitimate business," but remarkably lucrative to those in the know.

THE ELECTION OF 1872

Since much of the corruption in Grant's first administration was not revealed to the public until after the election of 1872, Schurz and his friends could not use it in their efforts to withhold the regular Republican nomination from the General and name a reform candidate. On May 1, 1872, therefore, the reformers assembled in Cincinnati, organized a new national party, the Liberal Republican party, and wrote a platform with special emphasis on civil-service reform. Old-line Republicans like Senators Sumner and Trumbull, ex-ambassador Charles Francis Adams, and ex-cabinet members Cox and Hoar rallied to the new standard. They were joined by such newly influential independent journalists as Godkin of *The Nation* and George W. Curtis of *Harper's Weekly,* and, in the Middle West, Horace White of the Chicago *Tribune* and Murat Halstead of the Cincinnati *Commercial.* All were Republicans who felt that the party of free soil and free men had clearly become the party of adventurers. Unfortunately for them, Liberal Republican ranks were promptly infiltrated by many other less dedicated angry men: businessmen who had been victimized by

Thomas Nast cartoon lampooning the 1872 Liberal Republican convention. "A (Mud) Mountain was once greatly agitated. . . . After long expectation . . . out popped a Mouse!" The mouse, B. Gratz Brown, the vice-presidential nominee, is being examined by Horace Greeley at left and Carl Schurz at right.

Radical grafters, and political hacks who had lost out in contests for patronage and simply sought a vehicle for revenge. Many northern Democrats also joined the movement, hoping thereby to cast off the treasonous label of their own party and win their way back to positions of power.

At the Cincinnati convention the irreconcilable differences in this motley array became apparent from the start and the leaders were forced to choose a compromise candidate, Horace Greeley, with B. Gratz Brown as his running mate. Greeley was a strange choice. As befitted a man who had long been an abolitionist, Greeley remained an outspoken Radical. Worse, he was a stanch high-tariff man, an enemy not only of free trade, but of foreign relations of any kind. Worse still, as editor for more than 30 years of the New York *Tribune* he had supported so many contradictory political positions that he had become universally known as a crackpot.

If Greeley's nomination was a misfortune for the Liberal Republicans, it was a tragedy for the Democratic party. Its only chance to gain national power was to support Grant's opponents. Yet Grant's opponents had nominated the man who in 1866 in the *Tribune* had publicly branded the Democrats as ". . . the traitorous section of Northern politics." The Democrats eventually swallowed their pride and at their convention in Baltimore in July named Greeley as their own standard-bearer. This move made the election fight very easy for Grant, who had been nominaed without opposition at the regular Republican convention in Philadelphia in June. The General was reelected by a majority of 763,000 and carried all but six states. His share of the popular vote, 55.6 per cent, made his the most decisive victory since Andrew Jackson's in 1828.

GRANT'S SECOND TERM

During Grant's campaign in 1872, Roscoe Conkling told a receptive New York audience: "If the name and the character of the administration of Ulysses S. Grant have been of value to the nation, no one knows it so well as the men who represent the property, the credits, the public securities and the enterprise of the country." These men truly were in debt to the Republican party, and as a group were to become its strongest backers over the years. Yet even many of them had begun to grow restless over the ceaseless exactions of the Radical Republicans who controlled the party, Conkling himself being a particularly nasty thorn in their flesh.

The outright scandals of the administration, in turn, soon soured many more Republicans and fostered the Democratic revival. The first major Grant scandal, the Crédit Mobilier affair (see p. 474), broke while the 1872 campaign still was in prog-

ress. After the Panic of 1873 (see p. 529), each new revelation struck with added force, and once the Democrats captured the House in 1874, revelations and prosecutions snowballed.

Two affairs hit close to Grant himself. One was the uncovering of the "Whiskey Ring" in St. Louis, which had defrauded the government of millions of dollars in internal revenue charges. Deeply involved in this, as in other frauds, was Grant's ubiquitous assistant secretary Orville Babcock, whom the President saved from imprisonment only by incessantly interfering in his trial. The second affair led to the impeachment of Grant's third Secretary of War, W. W. Belknap, who, since his appointment in 1870, had been "kept" by traders in Indian Territory under his jurisdiction. When his impeachment appeared imminent, Belknap had taken the precaution to offer his resignation to the President, which Grant, with characteristic loyalty to his betrayers, accepted "with great regret." The House proceeded with Belknap's impeachment despite his resignation; but the Senate, more a stickler for forms, allowed his friends to forestall conviction on the grounds that that body no longer had jurisdiction.

The ultimate outrage to both the reformers and the public was the "Salary Grab Act" of 1873 by which congressmen raised their own salaries 50 per cent from $5,000 to $7,500 and made the raise retroactive for two years, thereby voting themselves a virtual gift of $5,000. The act also raised the salaries of the president, the Cabinet, and Supreme Court justices.

While his cronies were undermining Republican strength in the North, Grant, by persisting in the forbearance evident before the election of 1872 (see p. 472), was helping to enhance Democratic strength in the South. In particular, he refused any longer to call upon the army for additional support for troubled Republican regimes. Encouraged by Grant's turnabout, southern leaders in states still under carpetbag rule became more determined than ever to "redeem" their states through their own efforts.

In communities where Negroes were a majority or nearly so, these efforts centered around the so-called Mississippi Plan which operated openly with full white support and thus proved more effective than the secret covert Klan. The aim of the Mississippi Plan was to force all whites into the Democratic party while at the same time forcing Negroes to desist from political action. Where persuasion failed, violence was used against both groups by such well-armed, semi-military enforcement agencies as Rifle Clubs, White Leagues, and Red Shirts. Whites who resisted were virtually driven from their homes and from their communities. Recalcitrant Negro share-croppers, in turn (see p. 481), were denied credit by southern merchants, evicted from their land, denied other employment, and assaulted and murdered. Many Negroes themselves had had their fill of northern domination and proved willing to cooperate with their new masters. "Redemption" was also accelerated by the growing inability of the carpetbaggers to make their scalawag collaborators get along with Negro officials. Quarrels with Negroes led more and more scalawags to cast their lot with the "white supremacy" advocates. After the Panic of 1873, northern capitalists looking south for investment opportunities also aided the white "redeemers."

As the election of 1876 neared, the administration began to have second thoughts about revived Democratic strength. To counteract it, the House, in February, 1875, passed a new Force bill. During the debate on the measure, it was said that the 138 "electoral votes of the reconstructed States rightfully belong to the Republican party," and "if the bill now pending . . . becomes a law it will secure these votes to that party, and otherwise they will be lost." The Senate was not impressed by this threat and rejected the bill. At the same time, it joined the House in adopting a new Civil Rights Act which Grant signed on March 1. This act recognized "the equality of all men before the law," and imposed stiff penalties for denying any citizen "full and equal enjoyment of . . . inns, public conveyances,

. . . theaters, and other places of public amusement." Penalties were also placed on the denial of equal rights to serve on juries.

Eight years later, in the momentous *Civil Rights Cases* of 1883, the Supreme Court declared much of the Civil Rights Act unconstitutional, ruling that the federal government had no jurisdiction over discrimination practiced by private persons or organizations. Later on it sanctioned state segregation laws requiring separate public facilities for the different races. In *Plessy* v. *Ferguson* in 1896, the Court decided the Negro's equal rights under the Fourteenth Amendment were not abrogated if the separate facilities on railroads were themselves equal. In *Cumming* v. *County Board of Education* in 1899, the Court extended the philosophy of "separate but equal" to schools. These decisions ruled until the desegregation decisions of the 1950's and 1960's (see Chapter 30).

Wood engraving, after Thomas Nast, depicting the plight of the Southern Negro at the hands of the white "redeemers."

VI. *The Extension of White Supremacy*

With the approach of the national nominating conventions in 1876, the Grand Old Party, as the Republicans had taken to calling themselves, was split more deeply than ever over the growing issue of corruption. The "Stalwarts," the hard-core political professionals closest to Grant, wanted the General to run for still a third term in order to insure the wherewithal for party machines and party workers. These men put politics first; if business wanted favors, it would have to continue to come to them and pay up. The "Halfbreeds," the name given in contempt by the Stalwarts to those Republican reformers who had *not* deserted to the Liberal Republicans in 1872, lined up behind their acknowledged leader, the "Plumed Knight," Congressman James G. Blaine, of Maine.

As Stalwart luck would have it, it was the reformer, Blaine, whose candidacy was undermined by the dramatic disclosure early in 1876 of his shady relations with the Union Pacific while serving as Speaker of the House during the preceding five years. Blaine might still have won the nomination. Although he labored under the handicap of having no war record, his well-publicized hostility to Britain made him attractive to Irish voters and his astuteness as a campaigner was admitted by all. He made the mistake, however, of denouncing the Stalwarts as "all desperate bad men, bent on loot and booty," thus incurring the hatred of the formidable Conkling. When the Republican convention met in Cincinnati in June, Conkling and the old guard exacted the penalty. Balked in their attempts to renominate Grant, they threw their support to Rutherford B. Hayes, the reform Governor of Ohio.

Eastern, western, and southern Democrats differed on many important issues such as money policy, the tariff, and federal subsidies for internal improvements. But hunger for the spoils of the presidency, long denied them, led them to close ranks at their June convention in St. Louis behind Samuel J. Tilden, a rich corporation lawyer and hard-money man who had won a national reputation as a reform governor of New York. Tilden's strongest claim on the nomination was his success, in 1872, in sending "Boss" Tweed, the notorious head of Tammany Hall, the leading Democratic club in New York City, to the penitentiary. During the preceding three years, the Tweed Ring had looted the city government of no less than $100 million.

Republican scandals, the hard times following the crash of 1873 (see p. 529), and the rising demand for reform all seemed to work to the Democrats advantage, so much so that Hayes himself privately forecast his own defeat. No one was certain, however, how the "redeemed" white South would vote. Many of the new southern leaders were former Whigs to whom Lincoln had looked so optimistically. They had never been comfortable in the Democratic party, into which secession and the war had forced them. As harbingers of a new industrialized and business-minded South, they often found the Republican economic policies more attractive than Democratic economic programs, and they especially resented the failure of northern Democrats to support land grants and other federal subsidies to southern railroads.

The attitudes of the Whiggish southern Democrats were not lost on Hayes' political managers who were eager to create a southern Republican wing to offset the losses the party had suffered through corruption in the North and repression of the Negro in the South. One group in particular caught their eyes, a group made up of southerners who, along with powerful northern railroad interests led by Tom Scott of the Pennsylvania, were seeking federal subsidies for a new transcontinental line to link Texas with the Pacific. No political bargains were struck between Hayes' managers and the railroad cabal, but it was understood that if Hayes won the presidency, the government might look kindly on supporting "internal improvements of a national character."

First reports of the election results seemed definite enough. The Democratic candidate, Tilden, had a plurality of 250,000 votes, and the press proclaimed him the new president. But Republican strategists suddenly awoke to the fact that the returns from Louisiana, Florida, and South Carolina, the three states where carpetbagger control was still supported by military contingents, had not yet come in because of election irregularities. These states, together with Oregon (one of whose three electoral votes was claimed by the Democrats on a technicality), held a total of 20 disputed electoral votes. Tilden needed only one of them to win; Hayes needed all to gain the 185 electoral votes required for election. Although both parties had resorted to the most bare-faced skullduggery, evidence now indicates that Tilden deserved Florida's four electoral votes and Hayes the others. In 1876, however, Congress had to decide which of the double sets of returns from the three states should be accepted, the Democratic count or the Republican.

Amidst renewed talk of insurrection, the two parties agreed to decide the election by turning the problem over to a commission of five representatives, five senators, and five Supreme Court justices. One of the justices, David Davis, presumably was independent in politics; the remaining fourteen members of the commission were equally divided between Democrats and Republicans. Unfortunately for Tilden, Davis quit the commission before it met and was replaced by a Republican justice. The Republican majority of eight then voted unanimously for Hayes.

One step that helped placate the South was a Republican pledge to grant subsidies to southern railroads. In exchange, southern leaders, Democrats though they nominally were, and Democratic though the new House of Representatives was to be, agreed to vote for the Republican, James A. Garfield, as Speaker.

THE "SOLID SOUTH"

Very soon after Hayes' inauguration it became clear to the South that the new administration would fail to fulfill its promise of railroad subsidies. Unfortunately, one reason for the Republican defection on this score was the failure of the southern leaders in the House to deliver enough Democratic votes to give the promised speakership to Garfield. Thus the compromise by which a new return to armed conflict was averted broke down almost at its very first test. The North immediately

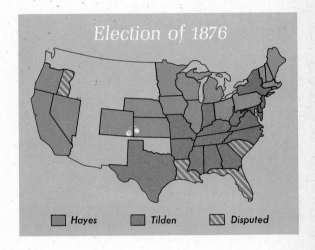

Election of 1876

☐ Hayes   ☐ Tilden   ▨ Disputed

reverted to the thesis that the South had not been reconstructed. At the time the agreements leading to Hayes' victory had been made, northern Republican newspapers had written warmly of the South's return to statesmanship and nationalism. By 1877, they had reverted to the old theme that "the spirit of rebellion still lives and is liable at any moment to be again entrenched in arms." At the same time, Republican politicians once more brought out the tattered bloody shirt that had carried them to so many electoral victories in the recent past.

Hayes, however, was not to be stampeded by northern Stalwarts nor southern sectionalists. He showed his mettle against the

Stalwarts by giving control of the distribution of party patronage to Liberal Republican leaders who were promoting civil-service reform. At the same time, he helped fight off all southern Democratic efforts in Congress to repeal the Force Act of 1870, even though the Supreme Court in *United States* v. *Reese,* in 1876, had already deprived the act of much of its power to protect the Negro's right to vote. By the end of April, 1877, nevertheless, Hayes had fulfilled his campaign pledge to remove the last federal troops from the South. When he did so, the last Radical state governments collapsed.

The Radicals had hoped to sustain their program for the nation and for the South by making the South solid for the Republican Party. But they succeeded only in making the South solidly Democratic. For the next seventy-five years, with the sole exception of the election of 1928, the "Solid South" was to deliver the section's electoral vote to the Democratic presidential candidate.

THE ECONOMIC UNDERTOW

While the Radicals tried to reconstruct the Union by extending to the conquered section the familiar political privileges of freedom, their failure to buttress political with economic gains had given southerners themselves a better opportunity to reconstruct their *section* by restoring the familiar economic disabilities of slavery. The Radicals' failure, in particular, to distribute land to the freedmen left the national government with no instrument but force to protect the political rights of its charges; but force was a wearing and costly instrument, wearing as much on those who had to pay for it and to bear the responsibility of its abuse as on those constrained and abused by it. When the policy of force was given up, the bitter fruits of the freedmen's economic dependency were harvested. The economic plight of the South and its people, colored and white, was worsened by many other federal policies, although a few were ameliorative.

One of the first economic needs of the South after the war was the restoration of markets and transportation, and here the federal government lent a helping hand. By July, 1865, all restrictions on the exchange of commodities between the former enemies were withdrawn and the blockade of Confederate ports was terminated, thus allowing goods to move north and south and across the sea. Soon after, the federal government returned southern railroads it had taken over—many of them in better condition than before the war. River transport was at least as important to the South as railroads, but twenty years of Republican rule were to pass before the South got a fair share of river and harbor improvement funds, and many navigable streams long remained unusable for commerce. As for wagon roads, the South was left to its own devices, with the characteristic result that roads were rebuilt more with an eye to horse racing than to hauling.

The South's need for capital was as urgent as that for markets and transport. Many planters had hoped to raise the money with which to restore land, buildings, and equipment to their former productivity by selling at the incredibly high prices of 1865 the stores of cotton they had built up during the war, presumably for export. But these hopes were quickly dashed. Ordered, at the end of hostilities, to confiscate all Confederate *government* assets, federal Treasury agents indiscriminately raided private as well as public warehouses and kept much of their loot. The Treasury eventually paid some 40,000 southerners $30 million for their losses, but this was only a fraction of what was taken and in any case came too late to help in the first postwar years. Confiscatory federal taxes further depleted southern capital. In three years following the war, a so-called revenue tax on cotton alone took $68 million from the South—far more than the total amount spent on relief and reconstruction by all northern agencies.

Before the war, most of the great southern plantations had been heavily mortgaged. After the war, creditors, hard pressed themselves, began demanding payments of interest and principal. The fear of imminent foreclosure stirred some planters to an unwonted show of activity, but the federal confiscation and confiscatory taxes checked them. Some southern planters fended off the day of judgment by selling off part of their land in order to finance cultivation of the rest. Others leased out acreage for money rent. But obviously there was not money enough available to sustain these expedients for long. The upshot was the re-enactment of the familiar routine of the prewar South, by which planters paid no wages for labor while their workers paid no rent for land. Instead, each was to share in the *forthcoming* crop. That was the rub.

In order to get this crop into the ground both parties to the arrangement had to borrow. Since they had no other security, they had to give a first lien on what they hoped to produce. Only against this *forthcoming* collateral would the supply merchant advance the required seed, fertilizer, and equipment, as well as food and clothing. For his own stock-in-trade, the local merchant had to seek credit from northern suppliers. Risks in the South were so great that these suppliers demanded high prices for the goods they sold directly and high interest for the credit they extended. In addition, oppressive fees were charged for transportation, insurance, and other commercial services. All these charges the merchant passed on to the landlords and croppers whose liens he held. The merchant also added his own profit and perhaps a generous tithe to reward himself for his literacy at the expense of borrowers who could not read his books. Under this regime, the South became more firmly chained to northern creditors than ever, while the cropper was enslaved to the merchant.

The South drifted the more deeply into the sharecropping and crop-lien systems because they offered a solution to the problem of labor as well as capital. Immediately after the war, many planters tried to hold on to their newly freed workers by offering them keep and cash. To protect the Negroes from being packed off as soon as the crops were in, the Freedmen's Bureau insisted,

often over the objections of the suspicious freedmen themselves, that the working arrangements be confirmed by written contracts. In the hope that the Negroes would stay at least until the harvest was over, the planter usually was willing to sign. The Black Codes, in turn (see p. 463), made it dangerous for the ex-slave to wander. A typical contract stipulated that the planter pay wages of $10 to $12 a month, less the cost, determined by the planter, of "quarters, fuel, healthy and substantial rations." In exchange, the freedman agreed "to labor . . . faithfully . . . six days during the week, in a manner customary on a plantation."

The wage system failed on the plantations largely because, as before, there was too little money. For what money there was, moreover, the planter usually found good prior uses. "The freedmen have universally been treated with bad faith," wrote General W. E. Strong from Texas in 1866, "and very few have received any compensation for work performed." The Negro himself often did not help matters. Emancipated, he quickly learned to resent working "in a manner customary on a plantation."

Sharecropping gradually stabilized labor relations in the cash-poor South. It also helped preserve the plantation system. Under sharecropping, the land was divided into many small "holdings" which gave the illusion of small independent farms, and indeed did represent a significant upward step for the freedman relieved of the gang labor of the slave system. But many small holdings together actually formed parts of single plantations, which, through foreclosures, gradually fell to the supply merchants or their own creditors. These businessmen helped liquidate the survivors of the old planter caste, but they themselves gained much gratification from becoming great landowners. Besides strengthening the tendency toward land monopolization, the credit system also furthered the concentration on cotton, the great cash crop. Lest the crop fail, moreover, the businessman-planter assumed a degree of supervision over the life of the cropper and his family that old-time overseers would hardly have felt worthwhile.

During the late 1860's and early 1870's, the cotton crop never reached the prewar levels of 3.5 to 4 million bales and prices held at 15 cents a pound or more. Under the sharecropping system, overproduction soon became the rule and cotton prices tumbled. By 1890, the South was growing 8.5 million bales, and the price had fallen to 8½ cents. In 1894, production reached a record high of 10 million bales, and the price sank to a record low of 4½ cents. Falling prices and mounting debts sapped whatever spirit of enterprise had survived the social conflicts and legalized abuses of the time.

THE PLIGHT
OF THE WHITE FARMER

At the outbreak of the Civil War, eight times as many Negroes as whites had been employed in growing cotton, most of them concentrated on the newer plantations of the rich Gulf plain and the Mississippi Valley. After the war, many of these Negroes had become sharecroppers and continued to work these once excellent lands. Many of them found it easier than the old slaveless yeoman farmers to adjust to the inertia of the new system. Their lingering servility, in turn, recommended them to the landowner and the merchant. White croppers were likely to be "ornery." They also tended to look down upon the new businessman "planters" as worse by far than their Damyankee models, as parvenus, usurpers, betrayers of the Lost Cause. This attitude only sharpened the parvenu's hunger for black "help" to authenticate the new plantation life. "White labor," said an Alabama planter in 1888, "is totally unsuited to our methods, our manners, and our accomodations." Another in Mississippi said, "Give me the nigger every time. . . . We can boss him, and that is what we southern folk like."

The devastation of the war, however, also soon caught up with the white farmer, as it had with the great planter. It was not long before he too needed credit from the local merchants to get his land back into production and his home and barns repaired. And, as in the case of the croppers, the merchants dictated that the white farmers also grow nothing but cotton. At first, the white farmers gave the merchant a lien on their forthcoming crops. As debts mounted, the merchant demanded a mortgage on the farmer's land as well; and as the cotton market deteriorated, the merchant ultimately foreclosed. Some white farmers managed to beat the trend and became large landowners and even merchants. But most of them went under.

The independent white farmers had learned early to look on sharecropping as a Negro institution. When they lost their land, they tried working as tenants on rented land, but lack of cash eventually forced them into sharecropping—"like victims of some horrid nightmare," said the imaginative Tom Watson of Georgia, "powerless—oppressed—shackled." Those who refused to give up their independence were relegated to the poorest land, from which their offspring began drifting to the towns. By the 1880's, many white farmers had lost virtually everything but their pride of race. It was to restore employment and ambition to white farm youth that the idea of the "New South" was born—a South in which the Negro "hands" would "keep their place" growing cotton and tobacco in the hot sun while the whites found remunerative work in textile and tobacco factories, iron and steel mills, and other industrial enterprises.

The movement to save the South through industrialism took on the guise of a crusade. After 1880, white doctors, preachers, lawyers, professors, and a veritable army of old generals and colonels gave their names and reputations, their energy, and their capital, to the mission. The textile industry, which had already revived, continued to grow fastest, but during the depression of the mid-1880's, southern iron began to compete successfully with Pittsburgh's, the North

Carolina tobacco manufacturing industry responded optimistically to the new fad of cigarette smoking, and a bit later the cottonseed oil manufacturing industry spurted upward. Another and more important goal of the crusade was to draw northern capital southward. It was to this goal that Henry Grady, publisher of the powerful *Atlanta Constitution,* gave most attention. Invading the North to recruit capital, management, and men, Grady told the barons of the New England Club in New York: "We have wiped out the place where Mason and Dixon's line used to be. . . . We are ready to lay odds on the Georgia Yankee as he manufactures relics of the battle-field in a one-story shanty and squeezes pure olive oil out of his cotton-seed, against any down easterner that ever swapped wooden nutmegs for flannel sausages in the valleys of Vermont."

In the 1880's northern capital had good reason for looking hopefully to the South. "The South," Chauncey M. Depew, the railroad lawyer and politician, told the Yale alumni, "is the Bonanza of the future. We have developed all the great and sudden opportunities for wealth . . . in the Northwest States and on the Pacific Slope." In the South lay "vast forests untouched; with enormous veins of coal and iron. . . . Go South, Young Man." There were still other inducements. "Long hours of labor and moderate wages will continue to be the rule here for many years to come," promised the *Southern Manufacturers' Record.* An Alabama publicist in 1886 offered this additional security: "The white laboring classes here are separated from the Negroes . . . by an innate consciousness of race superiority. This sentiment dignifies the character of white labor. It excites a sentiment of sympathy and equality on their part with the classes above them, and in this way becomes a wholesome social leaven."

Unfortunately for the promoters of the New South, as late as 1900 fewer than 4 per cent of the people in the important textile state of South Carolina were as yet engaged in manufacturing, while 70 per

cent remained in agriculture. The ratios in the rest of the South were little different. And what did the white industrial family gain? "Their power," writes a critic of the factory owners, "was peculiarly Southern. Unconsciously copying the planters, they established their workers in villages which resembled the slave quarters of old." In return for this "benevolence" they received a "feudal obedience."

And as for the agrarian south? In 1888, young Tom Watson wrote in his journal: "Mr. Grady thinks that 'Plenty rides on the springing harvests!' It rides on Grady's springing imagination. . . . In Grady's farm life there are no poor cows . . . lands all 'Rich—Richer—Richest.' Snowy Cotton, rustling corn. In reality—barren wastes, gullied slopes—ruined lowlands. . . . Gin houses on crutches. Diving down in the grass for cotton." In notes for a speech which Grady's *Constitution* would not print, Watson jotted: " 'New South' idea. If it means apology, abject submission—sycophancy to success—perish the thought. . . . Shame to Southern men who go to Northern Banquets and Glory in our defeat. . . . Unpaternal, patricidal."

THE CLOSED SOCIETY

While the Supreme Court's decision in the *Civil Rights Cases* of 1883 opened the way for social segregation under the law in the South (see p. 477), and the "separate but equal" decisions extended the legality of such segregation to educational institutions (see p. 477), Negro voting in many parts of the South survived the end of Radical Reconstruction in 1877 and the violence of the white supremacists (see p. 477). One reason for this was the heavy concentration of Negroes in the old plantation districts; another was that, in many localities where they did not actually make up a majority of the electorate, they were sufficiently numerous to hold the balance of power when white voters split, as they often did on important local issues. When these splits occurred, even though their own interests might be closer to those of the small white farmers, the Negroes usually were courted with success by the ruling conservatives, or Bourbons. Perhaps the successors to the old masters indeed knew how to manage their colored hands. In any case, their tactics, when they wanted the Negro vote, also included economic intimidation in the form of threats of loss of land, credit, or jobs; and economic and other inducements such as bribes and fiery libations. When intimidation and inducement failed, open resort was had to crude election frauds. All these expedients came to be used against vulnerable whites as well.

In the late 1880's and early 1890's, when agricultural depression caused discontented farmers across the land to organize in the Populist Movement (see Chapter 20) and to pit their strength against conservative business and political leaders, it seemed possible in the South that poor white and Negro farmers might join together politically to unseat the Bourbons. Populist leaders like Tom Watson now began to preach cooperation among poor croppers regardless of race. Only in North Carolina, however, were the Populists able, by joining with the Republicans still to be found there, to defeat the Bourbon Democrats. In 1894 the Populists won control of the state legislature, captured a majority of the state's congressional seats, and elected both United States senators. In 1896 they retained control of the state legislature and also won the governorship. Most colored voters supported them in these elections and they rewarded hundreds of Negroes with jobs.

North Carolina promptly became the target of the entire South which rallied to the support of the Democratic party in the state and helped it violently to dislodge the biracial Populists in the election of 1898. Elsewhere in the South, Negro support of the hated Bourbons, even at the peak of Populism's highly emotional appeal, only intensified the small farmers' antipathy toward the Negro himself, and their racism and resentment of Bourbonism both ran amuck.

In order to restore some stability to white unity after they had thwarted the Populist challenge, the Bourbons displayed a growing willingness to sacrifice what remained of those Negro prerogatives which had served themselves so well. They were the more strongly motivated to do this by their own profound revulsion from the corruption and violence and even the sheer high cost of bribery that increasingly marred southern elections as differences among white voters widened. By appealing, at the same time, to the small farmers' deepened commitment to white supremacy, the Bourbons hoped to induce them to sacrifice some of their own prerogatives for the cause, and thereby offset Bourbon losses in Negro voting strength.

The small farmers proved very reluctant to be induced; yet, after making some genuine concessions, sometimes simply by legislation, sometimes by constitutional amendments, but most frequently by wholly new constitutions, the Bourbons carried the day after all. Their concessions included such Populist demands as railroad regulatory commissions, and paid public appraisers of corporation property so that it might more rewardingly be taxed. But the stormiest issue was the central one of the suffrage, and the broadest concessions were made here. These took such forms as the notorious "understanding" tests, "grandfather" clauses, "veterans" privileges, and "good character" provisos, all to be administered by Democratic registration boards and similarly "discreet" election officials. As the Chairman of the Judiciary Committee of the Louisiana Constitutional Convention of 1898, Thomas J. Semmes, said of the grandfather clause adopted there, by this means ". . . every white man . . . although he may not be able to read and write, although he does not possess the property qualifications, may, notwithstanding, if he register himself pursuant to this ordinance of the Constitution, be thereafter entitled to vote."

Such were the sieves—and there were others, such as long residence requirements and disqualifications for the pettiest of crimes, that were especially effective against peripatetic and sufficiently provoked Negroes—that were to trap the Negro aspirant but let the white man through. Because they "did not on their face discriminate between the races," as they were forbidden to do by the Fifteenth Amendment, but rather "swept the circle of expedients" remaining, the Supreme Court itself, in the case of *Williams* v. *Mississippi*, April 25, 1898, held them to be "within the field of permissible action under the limitations imposed by the Federal Constitution."

Nevertheless, there were catches for the whites as well. One of them was the time limit often placed on the escape provisions. As Semmes said of the white man's grandfather clause, "If he doesn't choose to register between now and the 1st of September next, he loses the privilege conferred upon him, and therafter he can only vote provided he possesses the qualifications which I have just mentioned—the property or education. That is the temporary clause." The property qualifications, in turn, were uniformly high, while the education clauses could be enforced stringently enough to discourage respectable illiterates from exposing their limitations in schooling to their neighbors. Another effective catch was the poll tax usually imposed by the new regulations. This tax was cumulative from year to year. Since little effort would be made to collect it, it often mounted up. The only penalty for non-payment might be the loss of the right to vote, a loss the more stoically borne as the amount soared.

The small farmers had been so certain that any means of disfranchising the Negro under the Fourteenth and Fifteenth amendments would necessarily disfranchise themselves that they vigorously fought even the calling of the new constitutional conventions. So certain were the Bourbons, in turn, that the escape clauses for the whites would prove unsatisfactory to these farmers that, except in Alabama, they declared the new fundamental laws adopted without submitting them to referendums. Both groups were proved right. In state after state, following Mississippi's example of 1890, as the new suffrage laws were adopted, Negro vot-

ing virtually ceased, white voting also fell off, and small Democratic oligarchies gained control of political machinery. Such control insured Bourbon domination of most social institutions in the South and kept them lily white.

THE SOUTH AND THE NATION

By returning their friends to Congress year after year, the Bourbon Democrats of the South gained extraordinary power in major congressional committees, where seniority ruled. This was especially true during Democratic administrations which they themselves helped elect by delivering the "Solid South" to the party.

In *Origins of the New South*, C. Vann Woodward compares the South's position in the Union before the Civil War with her status in the reconstructed Union to 1912. "For almost fifty of the seventy-two years between the inauguration of Washington and that of Lincoln," he writes, "Southern men held the presidency, and for sixty of those years a Southern chief justice presided over the Supreme Court." Between 1861 and 1912, on the other hand, "no Southerner, except Andrew Johnson, served as President or Vice-President, nor did one achieve so much as the nomination of a major party for either office. Of the 133 cabinet members appointed during that period, only 14 were from the South, and of the 31 justices of the Supreme Court, only 7."

While the South thus remained a section in much more than a geographical sense alone, the rest of the nation drew farther and farther away from it. The movement of textile factories from New England to South Carolina and other southern states late in the nineteenth century did tend to break down economic barriers; the discovery of oil in Texas with the coming in of the great gusher at Spindletop in 1901 marked an even more important milestone in the weakening of the South's pervasive agricultural tradition; but not until World War II and the immense prosperity that followed it, was the South as a whole brought firmly into the orbit of industrialism and national business enterprise. The wartime demand for manpower, and the demand for industrial labor during the prosperous postwar years were among the most important factors that helped to open opportunities for southern Negroes. One of the major consequences of the South's own prosperity was the weakening of segregation in many areas and its own contribution, on that account, to eroding one of the most unfortunate anomalies of American life in both the North and the South. The difficulties in the way of making desegregation general were to become painfully clear after the Supreme Court decision of 1954 on equality of educational opportunities. But the greater difficulties of resisting the Supreme Court edict promised to broaden the Negro's participation in the privileges, as well as the obligations, of citizenship (see Chapter 30).

Readings

Asterisk indicates that book is available in paperback.

The best introduction to the Reconstruction period is K. M. Stampp, *The Era of Reconstruction 1865-1877* (1965). J. H. Franklin, *Reconstruction After the Civil War* * (1961), is an able survey. See also Franklin's standard history of American Negroes, *From Slavery to Freedom* (1956). J. G. Randall and David Donald, *The Civil War and Reconstruction* (2nd ed., 1961), is a comprehensive study, with special emphasis on constitutional matters. Other general works from various points of view include, W. A. Dunning, *Reconstruction, Political and Economic, 1865-1877* * (1907), and *Essays on the Civil War and Reconstruction* * (1904); E. M. Coulter, *The South During Reconstruction 1865-1877* (1947); W. L. Fleming, *The Sequel of Appomattox* (1919); and W. E. B. Du Bois, *Black Reconstruction in America 1860-1880* * (1935). W. J. Cash, *The Mind of the South* * (1941), is as stimulating on this period as on others. P. H. Buck, *The Road to Reunion, 1865-1900* * (1937), is a unique study of the influences tending, with too little success, to reunite the sections. W. L. Fleming, *Documentary History of Reconstruction* (2 vols., 1906), is a comprehensive collection. Much illuminating material appears in Herbert Aptheker, *A Documentary History of the Negro People in the United States* * (1951). Two shorter useful anthologies are R. N. Current, *Reconstruction, 1865-1877* * (1965); and J. P. Shenton, *The Reconstruction, A Documentary History: 1865-1877* * (1963). Outstanding works on the national setting of the Reconstruction period include Allan Nevins, *The Emergence of Modern America, 1865-1878* (1927); Matthew Josephson, *The Politicos, 1865-1896* * (1938); and J. F. Rhodes, *History of the United States, 1850-1877* (7 vols., 1906).

The following may be suggested from a long list on the postwar devastation of the South: Whitelaw Reid, *After the War, A Tour of the Southern States, 1865-1866* * (1965 ed.); Sidney Andrews, *The South since the War* (1866); and J. T. Trowbridge, *The South* (1866). Travelers accounts later in the Reconstruction period include Robert Somers, *The Southern States since the War, 1870-1871* (1871), and Edward King, *The Southern States* (1875). J. W. DeForest, *A Union Officer in the Reconstruction* (1948), is a revealing account.

Reconstruction of the South really began with the movement southward of northern troops. The Lincoln biographies cited in the Readings for Chapter 16 cover much of his program. Early reconstruction efforts are examined in W. L. Rose, *Rehearsal for Reconstruction, The Port Royal Experiment* (1964), and Joel Williamson, *After Slavery, The Negro in South Carolina during Reconstruction, 1861-1877* (1965). E. L. McKitrick, *Andrew Johnson and Reconstruction* * (1960), a critical modern account, may be supplemented by such older works as G. F. Milton, *The Age of Hate: Andrew Johnson and the*

Radicals (1930); and H. K. Beale, *The Critical Year: A Study of Andrew Johnson and Reconstruction* (1930). LaWanda and J. H. Cox, *Politics, Principle and Prejudice, 1865-66* (1963), emphasizes Johnson's role in efforts to restore the Democratic party in the North.

T. H. Williams, *Lincoln and the Radicals* * (1941), offers a starting point for the study of Stevens, Sumner and company. F. M. Brodie, *Thaddeus Stevens, Scourge of the South* (1959), is the leading biography. Moorfield Storey, *Charles Sumner* (1900), will serve until David Donald brings his modern life of the Senator to the Reconstruction period. J. M. McPherson, *The Struggle for Equality, Abolitionists and the Negro in the Civil War and Reconstruction* (1964), is an outstanding monograph on certain sources of Radical thinking. B. B. Kendrick, ed., *The Journal of the Joint Committee of Fifteen on Reconstruction* (1914), elaborates this theme. Illuminating monographs on the Fourteenth Amendment include J. B. James, *The Framing of the Fourteenth Amendment* (1956), and Jacobus tenBroek, *The Antislavery Origins of the Fourteenth Amendment* * (1951). On the Fifteenth Amendment, see William Gillette, *The Right to Vote, Politics and the Passage of the Fifteenth Amendment* (1965). Paul Lewinson, *Race, Class and Party, A History of Negro Suffrage and White Politics in the South* * (1932), is an able study of its subject from 1860 to 1930. S. D. Smith, *The Negro in Congress, 1870-1901* (1940), is a scholarly account. G. R. Bentley, *A History of the Freedmen's Bureau* (1955), is best on that agency. V. L. Wharton, *The Negro in Mississippi, 1865-1890* * (1947) is a model study; among other such special accounts the following may be noted: A. A. Taylor, *The Negro in Tennessee, 1865-1880* (1941); and G. B. Tindall, *South Carolina Negroes, 1877-1900* (1952).

Allan Nevins, *Hamilton Fish: The Inner History of the Grant Administration* (1936), is the definitive account. See also Josephson, *The Politicos,* * already cited, and the Readings for Chapter 20. Horace Greeley, *Recollections of a Busy Life* (1868), supplies first-hand background on the Liberal Republican campaign. See also E. D. Ross, *The Liberal Republican Movement* (1919); C. M. Fuess, *Carl Schurz, Reformer* (1932); and Glyndon Van Deusen, *Horace Greeley: Nineteenth-Century Crusader* * (1953).

Four outstanding works by C. V. Woodward offer the best introductions to the demise of the Reconstruction spirit: *Reunion and Reaction: The Compromise of 1877 and the End of Reconstruction* * (1951); *Origins of the New South, 1877-1913* (1951); *Tom Watson, Agrarian Rebel* * (1938); and *The Strange Career of Jim Crow* * (1966 ed.). On sharecropping and related subjects, see the relevant chapters in F. A. Shannon, *The Farmer's Last Frontier: Agriculture 1860-1897* (1945). Theodore Saloutos, *Farmer Movements in The South 1865-1933* * (1960), is excellent on organized protest and self-help. R. B. Nixon, *Henry W. Grady: Spokesman of the New South* (1943), is a useful introduction to the industrial spirit. Broadus Mitchell, *The Rise of Cotton Mills in the South* (1921), shows the community character of the movement. R. W. Logan, *The Negro in American Life and Thought, The Nadir 1877-1901* * (1954), is a detailed study of the abandonment of Radical goals, north and south. R. F. Durden, *James Shepherd Pike, Republicanism and the American Negro, 1850-1882* (1957); and V. P. De Santis, *Republicans Face the Southern Question—The New Departure Years, 1877-1897* (1959), illuminate the role and method of the dominant national party. A. W. Tourgée. *A Fool's Errand* (1879); L. H. Blair, *A Southern Prophecy, The Prosperity of the South Dependent upon the Elevation of the Negro* * (1889; modern ed., 1964), and Arlin Turner, ed., *The Negro Question, A Selection of the Writings on Civil Rights in the South by George W. Cable* (1958 ed.), foreshadow some modern ideas.

CHAPTER EIGHTEEN

Only about half of the United States, geographically speaking, had been seriously engaged in the sectional conflicts of the 1850's, in the Civil War, and in the issues of Reconstruction. As late as 1860, except for Texas, not a single state had been set up on the vast plains beyond the Mississippi Valley, roughly between the 95th and 104th parallels. Farther west, in the forbidding mountain country of the Rockies and the Sierras, and in the Great Basin between these ranges, political organization by the white population had hardly begun. News of the great events of the Civil War often failed to reach the men who roamed this distant wilderness—and even those who

Taming
the West

heard the news were not always interested in it. Yet such men were the vanguard of the millions from the Middle West, the East, and the old countries of Europe who would soon follow across the paths the pioneers made. They would populate the land, develop its resources and in general, within the framework of the big business system that soon tamed the West, promote the advance of the newly reunited nation.

I.   *The Conquest of the Plains*

THE LAND AND THE PEOPLE

In the 1540's the Spaniard, Coronado, had described the enormous western plains as "uninhabited deserts," a description that persisted for more than three centuries. When, in 1820, following the western boundary settlements with Britain (see p. 228), Major Stephen H. Long returned from his explorations of the region, he called the plains worthless for an agricultural people. His own report used the term, "Great American Desert," which henceforth appeared on all maps of the West. As late as 1856, the *North American Review*, refer-

489

ring to the elaborate surveys that had been made for transcontinental railroads, said "We may as well admit that . . . whatever route is selected, . . . it must wind the greater part of its length through a country destined to remain forever an uninhabited waste." Horace Greeley's judgment three years later was hardly more sanguine. After his overland journey from New York to San Francisco in 1859, he said, "The desert is steadily enlarging its borders and at the same time intensifying its barrenness."

The uncharted vast expanse of the plains, which extended well into Mexico and Canada, was as boundless and unbroken as the ocean and offered hardly a hollow for cover. Even more discouraging was the almost complete lack of trees for fuel, houses, fences, or shade. Only the lightest rains fell here, but violent hail storms and crushing falls of snow as dry as sand periodically afflicted the region, driven by winds that often surged to gale velocity. Sucked dry in their passage over the snow-crowned western mountains, these winds brought extremes of heat and cold to the plains, and the few rivers on their surface were alternately parched and frozen.

Most of the people who journeyed to the woodlands and watercourses of Oregon and California before the first transcontinental railroad was opened in 1869 completely avoided the "desert." Many traveled by clipper ship around the Horn. Others used the Panama route. Their wisdom was confirmed by the experiences of the relatively few who undertook to cross the "desert" by wagon train. So strewn were the plains with the wrecks of conveyances, the carcasses of cows and oxen, and the earthly remains of loved ones that Mark Twain once exclaimed, "The desert was one prodigious graveyard."

Yet the arid, treeless plains, like the high mountain ridges and the clear mountain streams that the western trappers plied so successfully, teemed with life. Hundreds of millions of jack rabbits and "prairie dogs" (really rodents) fed on the prevalent grass; tens of millions of wolves and coyotes fed on the rabbits and the "dogs." Most significant and most picturesque were the immense herds of buffalo. "Of all the quadrupeds that have lived upon the earth," wrote W. T. Hornaday, an expert nineteenth-century naturalist, "probably no other species has ever marshalled such innumerable hosts as those of the American bison. It would have been as easy to count or to estimate the number of leaves in a forest as to calculate the number of buffaloes living at any given time during the history of the species previous to 1870." The American buffalo herd in the 1850's and 1860's has been estimated at 12 million head. The Plains Indians lived off the buffalo. His flesh provided their food, his skin their clothing, his hide the sheltering cover of their tepees. Their daily life revolved around the buffalo hunt, and their ritual and worship were dedicated to its success.

For centuries, the Plains Indians had hunted the buffalo on foot, and the herds multiplied. In the sixteenth century, the Spaniards brought the horse to the American continent, and during the next 200 years hundreds of thousands of horses wandered northward from Mexico. By the time Americans began crossing the plains in the nineteenth century, the Indians had long since made the wild horses their own. George Catlin, who spent almost all his mature life painting pictures of the Plains Indians, said of the Comanche tribe:

I am ready, without hesitation, to pronounce the Comanches the most extraordinary horsemen that I have seen yet in all my travels, and I doubt very much whether any people in the world can surpass them. . . . Comanches . . . in their movements . . . are heavy and ungraceful; and on their feet, one of the most unattractive and slovenly-looking races of Indians that I have ever seen; but the moment they mount their horses, they seem at once metamorphosed, and surprise the spectator with the ease and elegance of their movements. A Comanche on his feet is out of his element, and comparatively almost as awkward as a monkey on the ground . . . ; but the moment he lays his hand upon his horse, his *face* even becomes handsome, and he gracefully flies away like a different being.

"*Buffalo Hunt Under the Wolf-skin Mask,*" *by George Catlin.*

Other riders of the plains—the Sioux, Cheyenne, Pawnee, Blackfeet, and Crow—were nearly as proficient horsemen as the Comanches. A little to the south, the rather less nomadic but equally fearsome Osage, Kiowa, Iowa, Omaha, and related tribes also took well to the horse and the hunt. In the Southwest, on the more authentic desert of Arizona and New Mexico, rode the formidable Navajos and Apaches.

A mounted Indian was a much more effective hunter than one on foot. As the buffalo herds diminished, the horse carried hungry tribes of Plains Indians to lands traditionally claimed by others and intensified tribal conflict. As time passed, wars among the Indians for possession of the precious beast became more frequent and bloody. To survive, the Indians grew steadily more nomadic, more violent, and more hostile to trespassers of any kind or color. The Plains Indians gradually developed a short bow, no more than two and a half or three feet across and superbly adapted to shooting from horseback. They also carried a long spear, and (in warfare) a circular shield fashioned from the hide of buffalo neck. These shields were so carefully smoke-cured and hardened they could even deflect bullets that struck at an angle.

More important than his fighting equipment was the Indian himself. "We were surprised, incredulous, almost offended," said visitors to Kansas in 1854, "when a young officer . . . deliberately asserted that our mounted men, though armed with revolvers, were in general not a match in close combat, for the mounted Indians, with their bows and arrows." Riding outside (not atop) his horse, with both hands free, one to feed and the other to release his bow, and shooting under the neck or belly of his mount while remaining virtually invisible himself, the Indian would circle madly, frighten ill-trained army horses with his curdling yells, and thus render "any certain aim with the revolver impossible, while his arrows [were] discharged at horse and man more rapidly than even a revolver [could] be fired."

Not all the Indians of the distant West were as violent and efficient as the fighting tribes of the plains. In the poor but protected areas of the Colorado Plateau and the southern Great Basin, for example, agricultural and essentially peaceful tribes, such as the highly civilized Hopi and Zuñi, built their pueblos into the Basin's cliffs and cultivated fields sometimes as far as 20 miles from their homes. To the north and west, in the upper regions of the Great Basin and on the Columbia Plateau, lived such primitive tribes as the Utes, Shoshones, Bannocks, and Snakes, who never took up agriculture but eked out a thin diet of occasional bear and elk by eating reptiles, rodents, vermin, grasshoppers, and, as Mark Twain said, "anything they can bite." Still farther west lived the despised "Digger Indians" of California, who subsisted on roots, tubers, and seeds that they literally dug out of the earth. Mark Twain found them "the wretchedest type of mankind I have ever seen." Completing the Indian population were the sad remnants of the Five Civilized Tribes of the East who had been forcibly removed to Oklahoma country, and other "woods Indians" who had been pushed west. Both groups soon fell prey not only to government neglect but also to the "horse" tribes.

In 1860, about 225,000 Indians shared the "desert" and the mountain country with the buffalo, the wild horse, the jack rabbit, and the coyote. But the white man could not be excluded altogether. In the future Dakotas, Montana, Idaho, Wyoming, Colorado, New Mexico, Arizona, Utah, and Nevada, were about 175,000 whites—probably 90 per cent of them male. Their numbers soon were increased by Civil War deserters from the North and the South. Except for the 25,000 Mormons settled in Utah, these whites, like the Indians themselves, kept on the move. They prospected for precious metals, hunted buffalo, trapped martens and beavers, drove cattle and sheep, guided and sometimes misguided emigrant trains bound for California and Oregon, scouted for the army, hauled overland freight and mail, gambled, drank, and wenched when occasion offered, and traded and fought with the Indians. Some of them,

like Kit Carson and Jim Bridger, were as free on a horse and as sharp on a trail as any red man.

While inhabitants of older sections of the country were making the United States a powerful newcomer among the great nations, and were keeping abreast of developments in science, philosophy, literature, and the arts, the Wild West was living an extraordinary life of its own—a life that has entered profoundly into the American spirit and mythology. Even before the Civil War was over, the pattern of cowboys, rustlers, and roundups, of six-shooters and branding irons, warpath and council fire, wide-open mining towns and posses and sheriffs, had imposed itself on the Great American Desert. After the war, it became so firmly implanted in the American consciousness that it remains a TV staple.

Yet the Wild West had but a short life. By 1890, only Utah, Arizona, New Mexico, and Oklahoma had yet to become states. The older culture of the East had fully asserted itself over the West; railroads had long since spanned the continent and opened connecting lines in the new mining, cattle, and farming areas of the "desert." Mining, cattle-raising, and even farming had come conspicuously under the control of great corporations financed by eastern and foreign capital. By 1890, the Indian wars were over; the army had been withdrawn from the western forts; the frontier itself was officially declared closed.

REMOVING THE INDIANS

Commenting years later on the disease that had wiped out the Wampanoags and other tribes in Massachusetts within a decade after the arrival of the *Mayflower,* Cotton Mather said: "The woods were almost cleared of those pernicious creatures, to make room for a better growth." From the very beginning of white settlement in North America, the paganism of the natives served to justify Christian violence.

The white migration to Oregon in the late 1840's, the surveys for transcontinental railroads starting in 1853, the organization and settlement of the Kansas-Nebraska region in 1854, and the Colorado Gold Rush of 1859 convinced the Indians of "the fatal tendency of their new environment." If further evidence was needed, it was furnished by the attitude of the United States government. Demands from traders, travelers, and explorers for protection against the Indians prompted the army in the 1840's and 1850's to establish a line of forts on the plains. In 1851, the policy of maintaining "one big reservation" on the whole expanse of the "desert" ended, and treaties were made with the Plains Indians forcing them onto reservations that (1) deprived them of their traditional hunting grounds, and (2) crowded them onto the lands of other tribes who resented their presence.

In the meantime, the administration of Indian affairs, which had previously been a function of the army, was given in part to the new Bureau of the Interior, created in 1849. The discontent among the Indians caused by the new reservation policy was fanned into rebellion by the maladministration of this new department. From the first, many of its officials were extremely corrupt; they made large fortunes by supplying the reservation Indians with shoddy of all sorts, by cheating them of their lands, and by selling them forbidden liquor. Many westerners took part in the Bureau's dealings with the Indians and naturally supported it. But the army was reluctant to yield its power to civilian politicos. Moreover, since army garrisons brought a great deal of money and business into the West, many western merchants wanted the troops to stay. Between corrupt administrators and touchy soldiers, the Indian was either starved on the reservations or killed in the open country. In the 1850's, one western settler wrote:

It was customary to speak of the Indian man as a Buck; of the woman as a squaw. . . . By a very natural and easy transition, from being spoken of as brutes, they came to be thought of as game to be shot, or as vermin to be destroyed.

The treaties of 1851 and after curtailed Indian lands and permitted the government to build roads and railroads across Indian preserves. As always, these treaties were made only with nominal Indian leaders and rump groups. Most of the Indians were never consulted; if they raised their voices in protest, they were ignored. But it was one thing to set aside Indian reservations, and another to force the Indians onto them and to keep them there under the guns of the army. Trouble was constantly brewing. In 1862, when regular army units were recalled from the plains for Civil War service and were replaced by inexperienced recruits, the earliest of the Indian wars on the plains broke out.

That year a small band of irresponsible Sioux youths murdered five whites near a reservation in the vicinity of New Ulm, Minnesota. To forestall retaliation, the Sioux, under Little Crow, took to the warpath, killed hundreds of settlers, and burned their farmhouses. The militia finally overwhelmed them and 38 braves were hanged in a ghoulish public ceremony. Running conflict between the eastern Sioux and the army continued until late in 1863, when Little Crow fell in battle. The Sioux lands in Minnesota were confiscated, and the remnants of the tribe moved elsewhere.

Two years later, in an attempt to satisfy the miners' demands for better access to supplies and civilization, the government tried to build a sound wagon road along the Bozeman Trail from Fort Laramie, Wyoming, north to isolated Bozeman and Helena, Montana. This road would have cut across the choicest hunting grounds of the western Sioux. Red Cloud, chief of the western tribes, led his warriors in unremitting harassment of the work. "Every straggler was cut down, every wagon train bringing in supplies raided, every wood-cutting party attacked." To protect the project the army started three forts along the Trail and in December, 1866, a wood train approaching one of them was set upon by the Indians. To see the caravan through and to relieve the unfinished fort, a small force under Captain W. J. Fetterman was ordered to the scene. Red Cloud's braves dissolved into the wilderness and Fetterman foolishly led his men after them. The Indians quickly ambushed Fetterman's force and massacred all 82 of them, including the rash Captain. Inflamed by their success, the Sioux increased the frequency and violence of their assaults, and in the next few months forced the abandonment of the whole Bozeman Trail project. They also forced a disconcerted country to rethink its approach to the red men. "Our whole Indian policy," cried the *Nation* after the "Fetterman massacre," "is a system of mismanagement, and in many parts one of gigantic abuse."

To the south, meanwhile, warfare with the Cheyenne and Arapaho tribes had been raging since 1861, when miners claimed their Colorado lands. This phase of the Indian wars came to a climax in 1864, when a force under Colonel John M. Chivington butchered about 450 men, women, and children in a Cheyenne encampment at Sand Creek. The Indians, under their chief,

Black Kettle, had tried every means to surrender peacefully, first by raising an American flag and then the traditional white flag. But Chivington's native lust had been set aflame by a telegram from his superior, General S. R. Curtis, United States army commander in the West: "I want no peace till the Indians suffer more." And suffer they did. A white trader, witness to the slaughter, reported that the Cheyenne "were scalped, their brains knocked out; the men used their knives, ripped open women, clubbed littled children, knocked them in the head with their guns, beat their brains out, mutilated their bodies in every sense of the word." Such savagery fed upon itself, and Indian-army warfare in the Southwest grew more and more brutal until 1868. In that year, at Washita, in Oklahoma, an army contingent under Colonel George A. Custer (he had lost his title of Major-General when the volunteer army was disbanded following Appomattox) defeated a band of Cheyenne and Arapaho

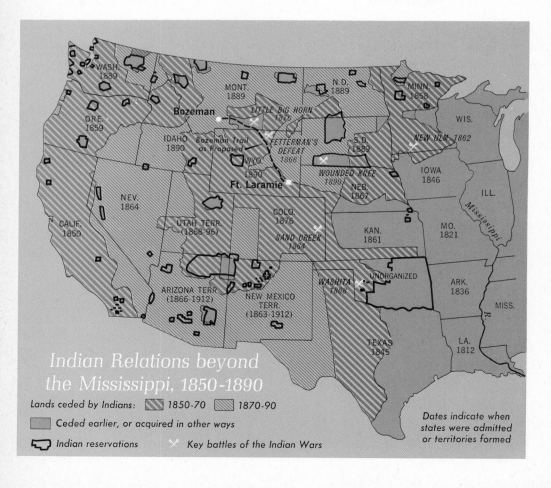

Indian Relations beyond the Mississippi, 1850-1890

Lands ceded by Indians: ▨ 1850-70 ▧ 1870-90

▦ Ceded earlier, or acquired in other ways

⬠ Indian reservations   ✕ Key battles of the Indian Wars

Dates indicate when states were admitted or territories formed warriors. Black Kettle was killed in the engagement and his braves thus the more easily subdued.

Scores of other battles took place between the army and the Indians and between Indians and marauding white civilians. But the Sioux and Cheyenne wars convinced a parsimonious Congress that the cost of subduing the Indians was too great and that the rate of subjugation was too slow. Thus, in 1867, peace commissioners were sent westward to convince the tribes to move to selected reservations, one in the Black Hills of Dakota, the other in present-day Oklahoma. By 1868, treaties to this effect were forced upon the war-weary Indians. General Sherman wrote:

We have now . . . provided reservations for all, off the great roads. All who cling to their old hunting grounds are hostile and will remain so till killed off. We will have a sort of predatory war for years—every now and then be shocked by the indiscriminate murder of travelers and settlers, but the country is so large, and the advantage of the Indians so great, that we cannot make a single war end it. From the nature of things we must take chances and clean out Indians as we encounter them.

As Sherman predicted, between 1869 and 1875 over 200 pitched battles were waged between the army and the Indians. The nature of these conflicts may be deduced from a statement of General Francis A. Walker, Commissioner of Indian Affairs, in 1871: "When dealing with savage men, as with savage beasts, no question of national honor can arise. Whether to fight, to run away, or to employ a ruse, is solely a question of expediency." On the reservations, meanwhile, a new civilian Board of Indian Commissioners, created in 1869, tried to convert the Plains Indians to agriculture on inadequate land. By ekeing out the pitiful crops with bonuses, annuities, and other doles, these commissioners made the Indians increasingly dependent, and pauperization completed their moral undoing.

In the 1870's, violence continued to flare as the Indians were kept on the new reservations only with great difficulty, and as the whites, with equal difficulty, were kept off them. Moldy flour, spoiled beef, and moth-

eaten blankets made up the typical fare supplied to the reservation Indians by the commissioners. The Sioux in Dakota were further enraged by the encroachment on their reservation of Northern Pacific railroad crews, and by the influx of prospectors when gold was discovered in the Dakota Black Hills in 1874. In 1876, war broke out again. It was during this conflict that Colonel Custer made his famous "last stand" against Crazy Horse and Sitting Bull in the Battle of the Little Big Horn on June 25, 1876. The Sioux annihilated Custer, but shortages of ammunition and food forced them to scatter. An ill-timed attack on a wagon train gave away the location of the largest group of Indians, and their capture in October, 1876, ended the war. Sitting Bull fled to Canada but, facing starvation, returned in 1881.

In Oregon, the Nez Percé tribe, whose religious leaders urged them to drive out the whites, took to the warpath against encroaching miners in 1877. Until they succumbed to starvation and disease, the Nez Percé, under Chief Joseph, led 5,000 government troops on a wild chase over Oregon and Montana. In the 1880's, the Apaches in New Mexico went on a prolonged rampage until their chief, Geronimo, was captured in 1886.

What finally destroyed the Indians was the extermination of the buffalo herd. The building of the Union Pacific in the late 1860's cut the herd in two and left the southern bisons at the mercy of every railroad worker, miner, adventurer, and traveler. Since a stampeding herd was capable of overturning a train, buffalo-hunting became a regular feature of railroad-building. "Buffalo Bill" Cody got his reputation by killing some 4,000 buffalo in 18 months as a hunter for the Kansas Pacific Railroad. As railroads continued to open, buffalo-hunting became a popular and devastating western "sport." In 1871, the fate of the buffalo was sealed when the sport changed

The mass slaughter of the buffalo on the western plains in the early 1880's.

into a business. In that year, a Pennsylvania tannery discovered that it could process buffalo hides into commercial leather; the hides, which had hardly been worth retrieving before, suddenly became worth $1 to $3 apiece. Between 1872 and 1874, the annual carnage of buffalo averaged 3 million, and by 1878 the southern herd had vanished. In 1886, when the National Museum wanted to mount some buffalo, it found only about 600 of the northern herd left, deep in the Canadian woods.

When Columbus discovered America, probably a million aborigines lived on the continent to the north of Mexico. These natives were grouped in more than 600 distinct tribes, few of which numbered more than 2,000 persons. With the coming of the horse, small groups of Plains Indians began to break off from the western tribes to hunt independently, and only once a year, in the summer, did they reunite for tribal ceremonies which grew into a decadent agglomeration of activities known, inaccurately, as the Sun Dance. This ritual, which lasted for four days, centered around offerings to the buffalo. In 1884, the Sun Dance and other Indian religious practices were prohibited by the government, but in 1890 the Sioux went ahead with the dance on their reservation. When troops appeared, the Indians fled. The troops followed, and in the "battle" of Wounded Knee massacred the half-starved remnants of the once fierce tribe. By then, hardly 200,000 Indians remained in the United States.

Three years before Wounded Knee, in 1887, Congress had passed the Dawes Act, which defined the government's basic Indian policy until 1934. This act broke up tribal autonomy even on the reservations. It divided up reservation land and gave each family head 160 acres to cultivate. After a probation period of 25 years, he was granted full rights of ownership and full citizenship in the United States. In 1924, the United States granted full citizenship to all the Indians in the country.

The Dawes Act, a dramatic reversal of former Indian policy, was the result of widespread humanitarian opposition to the extermination policy that had been conducted by the army and the Interior Department. A highlight of the humanitarian campaign was the publication in 1881 of *A Century of Dishonor,* and in 1884, of the novel *Ramona,* both by the prolific Massachusetts versifier and writer of children's books, Helen Hunt Jackson. The first, a scorching indictment of traditional governmental policy toward the red men, is no longer read except by scholars. *Ramona,* a kind of *Uncle Tom's Cabin* of the Wild West, has survived as a popular romance about the last days of Spanish rule in California, and has been the subject of a Technicolor movie and a popular song hit.

Despite Mrs. Jackson and Mr. Dawes, the reversal of the traditional Indian policy by the Dawes Act did the Indian little but harm. In dividing the land as the act provided, the poorest territory was usually

496

given to the Indians, and the best was sold to white settlers. Even where he gained good land, inexperience with ownership and with legal matters left the individual Indian vulnerable to the same kind of sharp practice that had marked the making of tribal treaties. Again and again, the red men were tricked into selling their best holdings. More disastrous still, they had neither the tradition nor the incentive to cultivate the land they retained. Great numbers of them became paupers, though there were a few exceptions—like the handful of Indians who held onto their oil-rich Oklahoma lands and became millionaires.

The Indian Reorganization Act of 1934 again reversed Indian policy. Under men like John Collier, who had lived much of his life among the Navajos, the Office of Indian Affairs succeeded in restoring tribal land-holding and tribal incentive on a wide scale. Collier's administration turned the "vanishing Americans" into one of the fastest-growing groups in the population of the United States. By 1966 their number approached 600,000.

II. *The Last Frontiers*

MINING COUNTRY

The plains and mountains of the West, as we have seen, were far from being desert wastes; they pulsated with plant, animal, and human life. The 30 years after the Civil War were to reveal that this country was also rich in agricultural and mineral wealth, the enormous extent of which has even yet to be appraised accurately. The most productive of the earth's wheat lands, once the secret of cultivating them had been discovered, stretched across the Dakotas and eastern Montana. In the most westerly parts of these states, in large areas of Wyoming, Colorado, and Texas, and even in sections of Nevada, Utah, and Arizona, seemingly boundless grazing lands lay ready to feed the cattle and sheep that would supply most of America's and the world's beef, mutton, hides, and wool. Other parts of the plains and the mountains held some of the world's largest and purest veins of copper and iron ore, some of the world's most extensive deposits of lead and zinc, and valuable seams of coal. Beneath the earth in Texas (and elsewhere in the West, as time proved), were incredible reserves of crude petroleum and natural gas.

For centuries, nature had developed and stored these riches. But for generations the forest-oriented nation had even less use for them than did the Indians who roamed the western lands. Americans had plenty of land elsewhere; their need for coal as a fuel and for iron in construction remained small, since the older settled areas were still well supplied with wood. Copper was almost wasted on a people with little use, as yet, for electric wire. The supply of Pennsylvania petroleum, which was burned almost exclusively as an illuminant rather than a fuel, was more than adequate for a nation still awaiting the automobile. In the mid-nineteenth century, traditional channels of investment continued to reward American capital well enough, and men of means were content to leave to prospectors with little standing and less credit the job of searching out new wealth. And the prospectors cared little about the future requirements of organized society; they followed, unflaggingly, only the most ancient of lures —the precious metals, gold and silver.

The early prospectors for gold in California had a fine code and fine camaraderie. "Honesty was the ruling passion of '48," one of them wrote. "If an *hombre* got broke, he asked the first one he met to lend him such amount as he wanted until he could 'dig her out.' The loans were always made and always paid according to promise." A year later, however, the California crowds had thickened:

Hordes of pickpockets, robbers, thieves, and swindlers were mixed with men who had come with honest intentions. . . . Murders, thefts, and heavy robberies soon became the order of the day. A panic seized that portion of the diggers who had never before been out of sight of 'marm's chimbly.' . . . Most of them presented the appearance of traveling armories; yet it was evident they wouldn't shoot. But men were to be found who had ridden the elephant of this world all their lives and well knew the course we had to pursue under the change of affairs. Whipping on the bare back, cutting off ears, and hanging soon became matters of as frequent occurrence as those of robbery, theft and murder.

Conditions grew steadily worse in California during the 1850's as the fabulous discoveries at Sutter's Fort and elsewhere in the San Joaquin and Sacramento valleys were thoroughly staked out and some of the best locations began to run thin. In a single decade, miners extracted hundreds of millions of dollars in gold from these hills and streams, much of it by the crudest placer-mining methods. All a man needed was a shovel to throw "pay dirt" into a washing pan, a little water in which the swirl the dirt so that the mud and gravel were

separated from the grains of gold, and some kind of tool to scrape the grains from the bottom of the pan. The "cradle" was an improvement over the crude washing pan, for it had cleats to catch the gold, and it could be rocked with one hand while dirt and water were fed in with the other. The "sluice box" offered a still more efficient method. A long wooden box, called a "long Tom," with openings at one end and cleats at the other, was placed so that the flow of a fast-moving stream could be diverted through it. The miner then shoveled dirt into the box, let the water carry it away, and collected the gold that was caught.

With these methods a man could take $50 a day from a rich lode. By the end of the 50's, the pickings in California had become slim; plenty of gold remained, but it was buried under enormous deposits in hills that had to be blasted away, or was locked in tough veins of quartz that had to be tunneled and worked with costly equipment and teams of men.

Blasting and quartz-mining required more capital and business ability than most of the prospectors had. Those who managed to strike it rich usually gambled away their "dust" or squandered it in other ways. When the surface gold ran out, a few took up more stable occupations; some became miners for the mining corporations, and others even became farmers. Tens of thousands made "prospectin' " a way of life. The call of gold became too strong to resist, and ears were tuned to every murmur of new strikes. Distance and inaccessibility meant nothing: Australians, South Americans, Africans, and Europeans—all had come to California. Soon they were taking Californians back with them to prospect in their home countries. Gold-fever was a disease from which thousands suffered all over the world. Few ever got over it, and fewer still got rich. But taken together, the prospectors gave a great impetus to the wealth of nations and the flow of trade.

The most persistent rumors in the late 1850's murmured of gold and silver in Colorado and Nevada. Even on the way to California in 1848 a pair of adventurers, Cap-

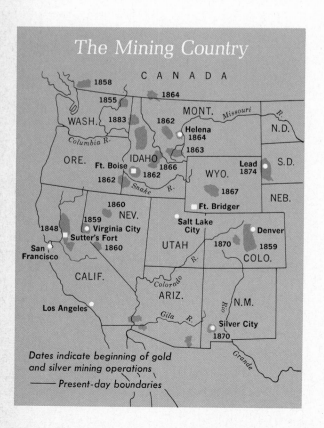

The Mining Country

Dates indicate beginning of gold and silver mining operations
—— Present-day boundaries

tain John Beck of Oklahoma country and W. Green Russell of Georgia, had seen signs of gold around the South Platte River in northeastern Colorado. In 1858, having sold out in California, they decided to look further into Colorado's possibilities and in July, 1858, staked out the first claim in the Pike's Peak region near present-day Denver. Soon eastern newspapers were full of news of other Colorado strikes, and by the end of 1858 the cry, "Pike's Peak or Bust," echoed through the land. By June, 1859, over 100,000 "yonder-siders" from California and "greenhorns" from Kansas and points east had made the trek to Colorado. Tall stories kept the gold bugs coming, but the truth soon became known: there was gold around Pike's Peak, but very little of it. When the trek homeward began, the wagons carried the slogan, "Pike's Peak and Busted." Some of the prospectors, as in California, stayed on to try their hand at farming and grazing and to lay the foundations for Colorado's future economy.

In May, 1859, John H. Gregory made a

new Colorado strike in an area west of Denver that became known as Gregory Gulch. By June, the 5,000 people there in new Central City were much more richly rewarded than those at Pike's Peak. One of them was George Pullman, the future builder of Pullman cars, who is said to have got the idea for his sleepers from the miners' double-decked bunks. The mines around Boulder to the north were opened soon after those at Central City. In the early 1870's, rich beds of silver were successfully prospected near Leadville, and a bit later gold was found in the region of Cripple Creek. These discoveries, coupled with the growth of Denver as a commercial center, spurred the campaign for statehood, and in 1876 Colorado was honored with admission to the Union as the "Centennial State."

Rumors of precious metals in Nevada had persisted throughout the 1850's. After

"Sunday Morning in the Mines," painted by Charles C. Nahl, 1872.

the 1859 failure in Colorado, the Nevada rumors became magnified into a sure thing, and the mob poured in. In the spring of 1859 the fabulous Comstock Lode on Davidson Mountain was struck, and by summer 20,000 men—with their horses and mules, their picks, shovels, and pans, their whiskey, cards, and camp-following women—swarmed into the wild country and established never-to-be-forgotten Virginia City. In the next four years, about $15 million, more of it silver than gold, was taken from the Comstock Lode alone, but this was only "placer" pickings. By ancient Mexican "reducing" methods, still universally used in the early 1860's, it cost $50 to get $200 in silver from a ton even of high-grade ore, and even then the yield was but 65 per cent. In the decade after 1868, new methods cut costs to $10 per ton and raised the yield to 85 per cent. Four men made the most of the new methods: John W. Mackay and his partners, James G. Fair, James C. Flood, and William S. O'Brien. All told, they took $150 million from the Comstock Lode.

A Prussion immigrant, Adolph Sutro, also saw new business possibilities in Davidson Mountain. With capital collected largely in Europe, in 1869 he began construction of the famous Sutro Tunnel to supply drainage, ventilation, and transport for the deep Comstock mines. Sutro was a train engineer, and his tunnel, on its completion in 1877, proved a milestone in engineering history. It was too late, however, to reward Sutro. By 1877, Comstock miners had gone deeper than the tunnel, and in any case had taken the cream off the Lode, no less than $306 million.

The discovery of the Comstock Lode in 1859 set others looking for deposits nearby, and by 1861 Nevada had several settlements and a population larger perhaps than it has ever been since. Organized as a territory in that year, Nevada become a state in 1864.

In 1860, the cry of "Gold!" on the reservation of the Nez Percé Indians in present-day Idaho brought 15,000 miners into that country. By 1863, the Territory of Idaho, with Boise as its center and with Montana and much of Wyoming included in it, was carved from old Washington territory. The Boise district alone claimed as many as 25,000 hopefuls—a number that soon fell off sharply. The census of 1870 reported only 15,000 in all of Idaho Territory, which by then had been somewhat reduced in area. Not until 1890 did Idaho become a state.

In 1864, gold was discovered in Last Chance Gulch, present-day Helena, Montana, and within six years more than $100 million in gold was taken from the mines. A typical mining town, Last Chance Gulch was described as follows by a resident after three months of its existence:

This human hive, numbering at least ten thousand people, was the product of ninety days. Into it were crowded all the elements of a rough and active civilization. Thousands of cabins and tents and brush wikiups . . . were seen on every hand. Every foot of the gulch . . . was undergoing displacement, and it was already disfigured by huge heaps of gravel, which had been passed through the sluices and rifled of their glittering contents. . . . Gold was abundant, and every possible device was employed by the gamblers, the traders, the vile men and women that had come in with the miners . . . to obtain it. Nearly every third cabin in the town was a saloon where vile whiskey was peddled out for fifty cents a drink in gold dust. Many of these places were filled with gambling tables and gamblers. . . . Not a day or night passed which did not yield its full fruition of fights, quarrels, wounds, or murders. . . . Sunday was always a gala day. The stores were all open. . . . Horse-racing was among the most favored amusements. Prize rings were formed, and brawny men engaged in fisticuffs until their sight was lost and their bodies pommelled to a jelly. . . . Pistols flashed, bowie knives flourished, and braggart oaths filled the air, as often as men's passions triumphed over their reason. . . . All classes of society were represented at this general exhibition. Judges, lawyers, doctors, even clergymen, could not claim exemption.

In the Southwest, where the Spanish had lived for centuries, deposits of precious metals had long been known, but not until 1862 did prospectors turn their serious attention to the gold and silver of Arizona and New Mexico. By 1863, Arizona had grown populous enough to become a territory. The lasting monument to its placer-mining history is the reputation, which persists to this day, of Tombstone, one of the most violent towns of the epoch.

The era of the prospectors' West was drawing to a close when, in 1874, the presence of gold was at last firmly established on the Sioux reservation in the sacred Black Hills of South Dakota. These somber black mountains, their pine-clad slopes rising to great rounded domes above the desolate northern plains, loomed as a heartening reminder to white men that the earth was not everywhere a flat, inhospitable, shelterless expanse. Yet the Black Hills had long been made unapproachable by the ferocious Sioux. The United States army also was as determined to keep the wild braves incarcerated in their reservations here as it was adamant about keeping white intruders out. Prospectors themselves were happy to give the region a wide berth so long as the mountain country farther west afforded them opportunities. Yet stories of Indians with bags of nuggets, of army officers concealing their knowledge of outcroppings lest their troops desert, and of a few desperate men who worked a stake and ran, kept the lure of the Hills alive.

> An old trail, a bold trail,
>   The old French trappers knew,
> A far trail and a war trail
>   Through the land of the fighting Sioux;
> A rough trail, once a tough trail,
>   Where oft the war-whoop thrills,
> The gold trail is a bold trail
>   As it bears to the far Black Hills.

By October, 1876, the army despaired any longer of keeping the irrepressible prospectors out, and the Sioux reservation was opened to all who cared to chance the Indians' vengeance. Fifteen thousand prospectors poured in almost at once, and the Army under Colonel Custer did its best to protect them (see p. 495). In the winter of 1876, the richest veins were discovered around Deadwood Gulch, and Deadwood, South Dakota, soon outdistanced Tombstone as the toughest of the "badman" towns. All told, the Black Hills mines yielded $287,500,000.

Henceforth big business came increasingly to dominate the development of the

Wild West. In 1881 the first far western copper seam was discovered in "the richest 'hell' on earth," conventionally known as Butte, Montana. By the end of the decade—sparked by the booming demand for copper wire, a far more efficient carrier of electric power than iron or steel—annual copper production had passed that of gold in value; by 1900, it neared that of gold and silver combined. The production of another mundane metal, lead, also grew rapidly with the growing use of electric storage batteries. Missouri remained the main source of lead, but after 1880 sizable quantities were coming from the Leadville district of Colorado and the Coeur d'Alene district of Idaho. In 1901, in time for the commercialization of the automobile, "Black Gold" roared onto the western scene from the fabulous gushers of the Spindletop fields in Texas. Like the silver of Davidson Mountain, these new metals and minerals required heavy capital investment in plant and machinery for their exploitation; and it was not long before financiers like Henry H. Rogers and the Rockfellers of New York, the Guggenheims of Philadelphia, and the Mellons of Pittsburgh were controlling the economy of the "desert."

Although the mining country was wide open and offered a haven to every kind of refugee from society, it early developed its own legal code. This code applied not only to personal crimes, but also to such matters as claims, assays, and water rights. Enforcement was difficult, however, and in the fifties and early sixties Congress was pressed to extend federal justice to the West. In 1866 it simply declared that the mining country was free to all, "subject to local customs or rules of miners in the several mining districts." This attitude put a premium on vigilantism. But the settlement of the West eventually brought about the establishment of more formal government agencies, which were strengthened by improved communication facilities.

And yet it was these very facilities that offered the last opportunity to western desperadoes. Before the railroad penetrated the Wild West, freight was hauled to the mining camps and other settlements by trains of "prairie schooners" run by express companies like Russell, Majors, and Waddell, and Wells, Fargo. The overland mail was also carried by these companies and, in the short but exciting period of 1860-1861, by the Pony Express, a project of William H. Russell, who was determined to show that mail could be carried profitably to the West Coast without a government subsidy. By April, 1860, Russell had set up 190 stations about ten miles apart between St. Joseph, Missouri, and San Francisco. At these stations 500 of the strongest and fastest horses available stood ready. At each stop the mail pouches were switched to a fresh pony and whisked away. The Pony Express kept 80 riders in the saddle, 40 racing west and 40 returning, all of them light-weight lads specially clothed to reduce wind resistance to a minimum. Until they were supplanted by the transcontinental telegraph in October, 1861, the Pony Express riders made the 2,500-mile run between St. Joseph, Missouri, and San Francisco in the incredible time of ten days.

Before the completion of the transcontinental railroads, express and mail holdups were daily affairs in the West. Thereafter, the headline "Great Train Robbery" became a regular feature of western news. But in 1881, even this phase of wild western life was brought under control. In that year, the railway and express companies joined the Governor of Missouri in placing such a high price on the heads of Jesse and Frank James that one of their own men shot Jesse in the back for the reward. In Oklahoma country in the 1890's, the notorious Dalton brothers re-enacted some of the bloodiest of the Jameses' exploits, but by then the West had generally become a safer if not a saintlier place.

THE CATTLE KINGDOM

The violence of the mining camps and mining towns kept the more staid and settled members of American society out of the western country for a long time. And the violence of the trail, the range, and the cow town kept them off the Great Plains. In the cattle kingdom as in the mining country, the population was almost wholly male, but the monotony was relieved in the towns by the usual coveys of obliging women. Tombstone and Deadwood had nothing on Dodge City, Kansas, the "Cowboy's Capital," where 25 men are said to have been killed during the town's first year.

Ranching and cowpunching came into American life with the annexation of Texas in 1845. Long before, Mexicans had designed the bit, bridle, saddle, and spurs, the lariat, chaps, and five-gallon hat of the traditional cowboy; for centuries they had broken broncos, grazed calves, roped steers. But they were too careless to use the branding iron. When Americans from Missouri, Mississippi, Alabama, and Tennessee began to trickle into Texas in the 1820's, many of them simply put their brands on what they deemed to be wild herds and set themselves up as cattle kings. Other Americans, meanwhile, were grasping horses and cattle that had broken away from the Mexican herds to wander northward. In this way the range cattle industry in Kansas and Nebraska began. These ranchers supplied beef and fresh horses to emigrants going farther west, and to mining camps and railroad crews. Compared with the herds of Texas, however, these northern herds were tiny.

In the 1850's, some of the more enterprising Texas ranchers undertook to drive their cattle westward to the Colorado and California markets, or northward to Illinois. But these drives proved uneconomical. The herds and the herders were easy prey to the Indians, and many of the steers that reached their destination were maimed and lame. Almost all of them, moreover had become too thin and tough to command a price that would cover the cost of the venture. While the cattlemen awaited the opening of more accessible markets, their herds multiplied. By the time of the Civil War, nearly 5 million longhorns, all of them owned but most of them unbranded "mavericks," were crowding even the almost limitless Texas range.

As soon as the war was over, Texas ranchers began looking with renewed interest for markets. When they learned that steers, which sold for no more than $3 or $4 a head in Texas, would command as much as $40 a head in the northern markets, they decided to try the drive north. By this time a new factor had come into play: the railroad. In 1865, the Missouri Pacific was opened from Kansas City to Sedalia, Missouri. Before 1865, the ranchers had driven their cattle directly to the abattoirs. In the spring of 1866, they were ready for the first of the "long drives" to a railroad town, from which the railroad would haul the cattle to city markets. Before fall, some 260,000 steers had hit the trail for Sedalia.

As a business venture, this first drive was a failure. The trail to Sedalia wound through unfamiliar forests, which made the longhorns of the open range stampede. The trail also crossed over new Missouri farm land, where protesting "nesters," as the cowboys called the settlers, came rushing out with their guns. Moreover, most of the horse Indians, though nominally on their reservations, still roamed the plains. In the end, only a few of the Texas steers ever got to Sedalia. But those that did brought $35 a head, a price that encouraged many ranchers to try again the next year.

By that time, an enterprising Illinois meat-dealer, Joseph G. McCoy, realized that he could make a fortune if he could establish a convenient meeting point for northern buyers and Texas and western breeders. After scouting around, McCoy chose Abilene, Kansas, on the Kansas Pacific route, which, with the Hannibal and St. Jo railroad and other lines, connected Abilene with Chicago. At Abilene McCloy built a hotel, and barns, stables, pens, and loading chutes. In 1868, Abilene received 75,000 head of cattle, and the figure soared to 700,000 in 1871.

As the Kansas Pacific was extended westward across Kansas, new cow towns nearer the cattle range were used. Ellsworth,

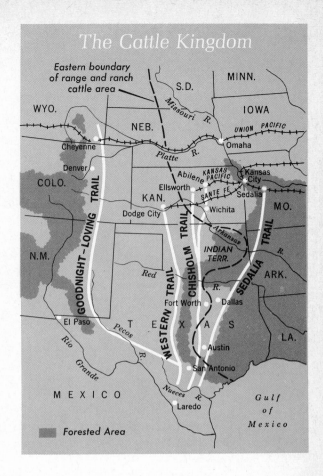

The Cattle Kingdom

Kansas, which succeeded Abilene, received over a million head between 1872 and 1875. Next came the fabulous Dodge City, to which another million head were driven between 1876 and 1879. On the Union Pacific route, first Cheyenne and then Laramie became important cattle railheads.

The "long drive" has become a romantic chapter in the history of the West, but there was little glamor in it. The cowboys went out in groups of six, working for $24 to $40 a month. Equipped only with cow ponies, lassos, and six-shooters, they tried to keep safe and under control a thousand head of hungry, thirsty, touchy steers for two months of grueling travel. P.A. Rollins, one of the veterans of the drive, wrote: "It was tiresome grimy business for the attendant punchers, who travelled ever in a cloud of dust, and heard little but the constant chorus from the crackling of hoofs and of ankle joints, from the bellows, lows, and bleats of the trudging animals."

Of the men's daily round Rollins wrote in his book, *The Cowboy:*

The caravan started forth each morning at "sun-up," crawled on till late afternoon. . . . Only the kindliest of routes permitted a day's march to exceed ten miles. . . . The animals throughout their day-long march, nipped at the grass that they passed; but at the evening halt they set themselves to a solid meal. . . . Two hours after dark the cattle one by one sank down to sleep, to rise again at midnight and to browse until that depressing time of night, two o'clock, when all vitality ebbs and the Death Angel frequently calls dying men. . . .

All through the darkness men of the "night herd," working in shifts from two to four hours, rode about the animals; and as the men rode they constantly serenaded the beasts by crooning to them. . . . This . . . was done partly to hold the cattle under the compelling spell of the human voice, and partly to disabuse from the mind of any fearsome member of the herd suspicion that either a puncher's silhouette against the sky-line or else the noise of his moving pony might represent a snooping dragon. The rider, when "singing to the cattle," as his vocal efforts were styled, disgorged all the words he knew set to all the tunes he could remember or invent, but omitted any sound or inflection which might startle. Sacred airs were usual . . . but the words set to these churchly airs well might have surprised the clergy. The proper words, accounts of horse-races, unflattering opinions of the cattle, strings of profanity, the voluminous text on the labels of coffee or condensed milk-cans, mere humming sounds . . . were poured on many a night into the appreciative ears of an audience of cloven hoofs. . . . But man and horse were ready to wake like a shot and to act the instant that a steer started to "roll his tail," an infallible sign of confident expectation to disregard both distance and time.

Since even the drive to the nearest railhead did grown steers little good, it became the practice in the 1870's to drive young Texas steers out to graze on the northern range in western Kansas and Nebraska, and

"*Herding Cattle in New Mexico,*" *drawn by Captain Russell for* Frank Leslie's Illustrated Newspaper, *1874.*

in Colorado, Wyoming, Montana, and the Dakotas—the area where the buffalo herds were being obliterated. With the buffalo went the Indians' food supply, and with the food supply went the Indians themselves. Now the northern "feeders" could buy longhorns and other breeds, and fatten them free on the lush grass of the public lands until they were ready for market at four to five years of age. As time went on, the best cows and bulls were culled from the herds, and the breeds were constantly improved. The open-range cattle industry came into its own after 1878, when the distressing Panic of 1873 had run its course and beef prices revived. For the next seven or eight years, it was one of the most profitable industries in the country.

Like the isolated mining centers, the range too had to make its own laws. Here the need for water was vital, and "range rights" along a stream became the most precious part of cattleman's ranch. Local regulations had the force of law in determining the extent of each man's or company's "range rights," but claims often had to be backed up with the six-shooter. Even where the ranchers respected one another's territory, the cattle did not. Here again rules had to be established for recording brands and for disposing of "mavericks." Since the ranches covered as many as 30 or 40 square miles, they could not be policed efficiently and rustling became common.

The enforcement of rude justice was one of the main objectives of the numerous stock-growers' associations that were organized on the plains in the 1870's. Eventually, these groups developed a hidden government in the territories that were being cut from the range. One of their more important business objectives was to forestall competition by making it difficult for newcomers to become members, and by making it dangerous for them to operate without joining up. This objective grew out of an awareness of the speed with which the range, endless though it seemed, could become disastrously overstocked.

In spite of all the stock-growers' efforts, news soon leaked out about how five-dollar

steers could be transformed into property worth $45 to $60 a head, with only the investment of four years of free grazing. New ranchers flocked to the range like prospectors to the mines, and when the anticipated profits materialized, large investors set up corporations further to enlarge activities. Returns of 40 or 50 per cent became common in the early 1880's, but by 1885 the range finally grew overcrowded, and the disastrous winter of 1885-86, followed by a blistering summer, destroyed most of the feed and cattle. The steers that did find their way to market were of such poor quality that beef prices crashed, despite the intense shortage. It was at this time that the sheep herders began to cross the range in large numbers. Their flocks, which tainted the water and made the atmosphere noxious to cows and cowboys alike, ate not only the grass but the roots themselves, leaving in their wake wide swaths of barren range. To add to the stockgrowers' misery, farmers began homesteading the plains and fencing in the open range. Many farmers kept herds of their own on fenced fields where they could control breeding more carefully and regulate the feed. The beef they produced was superior to any grown on the open range. In 1882, range beef commanded $9.35 a hundred pounds in Chicago, by 1887, the price had fallen to $1.90. By then, the cowboys were singing mournfully:

> I little dreamed what would happen
>   Some twenty summers hence
> When the nester came with his wife
>   and kids,
>   His dogs and his barbed-wire fence.

The West had indeed changed. One open-range cowboy working on a fenced-in ranch had this to say in the late 1880's:

I remember when we sat around the fire the winter through and didn't do a lick of work for five or six months of the year, except to chop a little wood to build a fire to keep warm by Now we go on the general roundup, then the calf roundup, then comes haying—something that the old-time cowboy never dreamed of—then the beef roundup and the fall calf roundup and gathering bulls and weak cows,

and after all this a winter of feeding hay. I tell you times have changed.

The end of the open range brought an end to the last frontier.

III. *The Farmer on the Plains*

SETTLING THE LAND

"These fellows from Ohio, Indiana, and other northern and western states," an old trail-driver complained in the '70's, "—the 'bone and sinew of the country,' as politicians call them—have made farms, enclosed pastures, and fenced in water holes until you can't rest; and I say D—n such bone and sinew!" Although the cattlemen were just on the verge of their greatest boom, revolutionary agricultural developments were to make that boom their last. Perhaps the most important of these changes was the development of barbed-wire fencing, first patented by three different inventors in 1874. One cattleman expressed the feelings of all when he wished that the "man who invented barbed wire had it all around him in a ball and the ball rolled into hell."

Although the Homestead Act of 1862 (see p. 434) opened the West to free settlement under liberal conditions, much of the best land was appropriated before the homesteaders could get to it. Certain other circumstances, having to do with both the law and the land itself, further restricted the act's usefulness. For example, the quarter-section (160 acres) offered by the act, though suitable for the Mississippi Valley, and lavish for New England (the two areas from which most of the proponents of the measure came), was either too large or too small for the arid, treeless plains. For the small settler, the cost of breaking enough of the 160 acres to get a paying crop, plus the cost of irrigation, buildings, equipment, taxes, and hired help, were prohibitive; in 1871, the Department of Agriculture estimated that wood fencing alone for such a farm would cost $1,000. For the large farmer or farming corporation, on the other hand, willing to use the costly new machinery so well fitted to the broad expanse of the plains, a mere quarter-section hardly justified the investment.

Belated recognition of these problems prompted the passage of the Timber Culture Act of 1873. On the theory that trees brought rain, this act offered an additional quarter-section to the settler who would put at least 40 acres of it into timber. Far too few settlers complied with the provisions of the act, and it was repealed in 1891.

Two other measures, passed ostensibly to stimulate settlement of the West by farmers, actually worked to keep them out. One was the Desert Land Act of 1877. This act allowed a settler to occupy 640 acres on payment of 25 cents an acre; the holder could win clear title to the land in three years for an additional payment of $1 an acre, provided he could prove he had irrigated the plot. Thousands of farmers agreed to try to irrigate the land, but the job proved too difficult and most of them gave up long before the three years had expired. The Desert Land Act was really a ruse used by the cattlemen to win private title to the once open grazing range. They registered thousands of acres in cowboys' names and then, to prove that they had irrigated the land, they got the cowboys to testify that they "had seen water on the claim."

The second measure was the Timber and Stone Act of 1878, an attempt by the lumbermen to wrest public lands for themselves. This act offered a maximum of 160 acres of rich timber land—land "unfit for cultivation"—in California, Nevada, Oregon, and Washington, at $2.50 an acre, "about the price of one good log," as R. A. Billington has commented. Since even aliens who had done no more than file their first citizenship papers were eligible for these grants, a land-office business was set up right in the waterfront courthouses. In return for on-the-spot bonuses ranging from $10 to $50, thousands of alien seamen were induced to register claims and then to sign them over to lumber-company agents.

All told, between 1862 and 1900, 80 million acres were registered under the Homestead Act, and this figure includes many dummy registrations used by speculators in accumulating large holdings. During the same period, railroads, land companies, and states receiving grants of federal land under the Morrill Act of 1862 (see p. 434) sold at least five or six times as much land. These sellers charged from $2 to $10 an acre, a fair enough range for the best sites near transportation and markets. Companies eager to sell often gave purchasers credit for equipment as well as for land.

By 1868, when the Union Pacific was nearly ready for passengers, Kansas and other states on the edge of the frontier were being placarded with railroad advertisements calling their lands "Better than a Homestead." Henceforth every land-grant railroad had both its Land Department and its Bureau of Immigration. In the 1870's, the Union Pacific and the Burlington railroads each spent over $1 million in advertising their lands abroad, often in spectacular fashion. Other railroads and land companies also advertised, and most of them had London offices and agents scouring the Continent for settlers. Their efforts were supplemented by bureaus of immigration set up by western states with land to sell, and by steamship companies engaged in carrying immigrants to the New World.

These land-sales campaigns were remarkably successful. According to the 1880 census, 73 per cent of Wisconsin's population was of foreign parentage, 71 per cent of Minnesota's, 66 per cent of the Dakotas', and 44 per cent of Nebraska's. In the following two years, "American fever" rose to epidemic proportions in western and central Europe. In 1882 alone, the record nineteenth century year, almost 650,000 foreigners debarked in American ports. Large

numbers of these immigrants remained in the teeming coastal cities, and many others got no farther west than the mills of Pittsburgh and Cleveland. But hundreds of thousands of them found their way to the farmlands of the plains. Between 1860 and 1900, the land held by American farmers more than doubled, from 407 to 841 million acres, and the proportion of land under cultivation rose from 40 to almost 50 per cent.

PLAINS FARMING

Before the new settlers of the plains could transform the country into farmland, they had to overcome many obstacles. Not even rude log cabins could be built on the treeless plains; the first shelters were dank and dark sod huts. The lack of wood also made it difficult to heat dwellings in a region that covered some of the coldest parts of the United States. The first settlers burned dried buffalo dung. Hay next became a common fuel, in special stoves designed to burn it slowly. But nothing proved satisfactory until the railroads brought coal to the plains.

The aridity of the region, which increased as one moved westward, offered even greater difficulties, espcially to families at a distance from the infrequent rivers. By 1880 mechanical well-digging equipment was in use but even when wells could be dug the necessary 200 or 300 feet, there remained the problem of getting the water to the surface. Windmills that harnessed the power of the strong prevailing breezes promised to provide an answer, but before windmills became cheap enough for the average farmer he had solved the problem of water in other ways. One solution, still widely used though undependable and costly, was "dry farming." With this system, a field is harrowed after each precious rainfall in order to retard evaporation. The turned-over mud itself forms a mulch to store water upon which roots continue to feed long after the rain has ended.

The Rawding family and their sod house, north of Sargent, Nebraska, 1880.

Scarcity of water was only one of many problems in cultivating the virgin land. The tough sod of the plains, as we have seen, resisted the old-fashioned plow. John Deere's steel plow was a great improvement, but only for those who could afford its high prices. In 1868, James Oliver of Indiana began making innovations in the chilled-iron plow which by 1877 had become a cheap, versatile, and efficient tool. Plowshares soon were being mounted on sulkies, and as time passed their number was increased so that several furrows could be cut at once. The next step was to mechanize the sulky and further increase the number of plowshares mechanical power could pull. Other innovations accompanied those in the plow. By 1874, grain drills has been designed to mechanize planting. In a region battered by hail storms, wind storms, and sudden frosts, a farmer's production was most sharply limited not by how much he could plant but how much he could harvest. The "cord binder," perfected about 1880, greatly speeded up the harvesting process. This device permitted two men and a team of horses to harvest 20 acres of wheat a day.

Old-time eastern farmers dared not plant more than eight acres of wheat a season; by 1890 one plains farmer with a cord binder could count on harvesting 135 acres.

But there had to be a revolution in the grain industry before such a wheat harvest became worth while. Eastern wheat farmers grew soft-kernel winter wheat, which was traditionally milled by grinding the husks between two millstones. Easterners usually planted their crop in September or October, let it grow during the winter, and harvested it in June or July. The first farmers in Wisconsin and Minnesota found that the early winters there killed the tender seed before it could sprout. On the open plains, the winters proved even more severe. Moreover, the moisture needed for the soft winter wheats was lacking here.

Spring wheat, planted in May and harvested before the first frosts, had been known to farmers before 1860. But the known varieties lacked hardiness and, worse, their tough husks could not be milled economically. In the 1860's, after a long journey from Poland via Scotland and Canada, a new type of hard spring wheat

508

appeared on the plains, and by the end of the decade a new process for milling the hard grain had been brought over from Hungary. This process employed a series of revolving rollers instead of the old millstones. In 1872 or 1873, settlers from the Crimea introduced into Kansas a hard *winter* wheat known as "Turkey Red." This too became commercially manageable through the new milling process which itself was steadily improved.

Both hard wheats became profitable and popular among millers and bakers, and plains farming forged ahead. In 1879, Illinois, the leading wheat state for 20 years, was still in first place; by 1899 it had fallen out of the first ten, which were dominated by the hard-wheat states of Minnesota, the Dakotas, Kansas, California, and Nebraska. Oklahoma and northern Texas also were growing ever larger wheat crops.

During the 1870's, plains farmers became more and more insistent that the ranchers fence in their cattle; the ranchers, in turn, either urged the "nesters" to move away or else demanded that they bear the high cost of fences to keep the cattle out. The sharp hostility between the two groups often led to open gun battles, but cheap fencing, not guns, eventually won the plains for the farmers.

Joseph F. Glidden, one of three independent holders of the patent on barbed wire, set up the first barbed-wire factory in DeKalb, Illinois, in November, 1874. By 1876, barbed wire was in mass production. That year, 3 million pounds of barbed wire were sold at about $20 per hundred pounds; four years later sales had zoomed to 80 million pounds, and the price had been cut to $10 per hundred. By 1890, the price was down to $4, and much of the arable land of the plains had been fenced in, most of it for wheat-growing.

Once a disastrous series of grasshopper invasions of the plains ended in the early 1870's, everything conspired to make the new wheat country the El Dorado that the advertisements pictured. After 1875, Europe suffered one famine after another. The widespread hardship was deepened by the Russo-Turkish War of 1877-78, which closed Russia's ports and left the rest of the Continent increasingly dependent on American grain. All the great improvements in American farm technology coincided with the growth of the European market—a market that was to continue to

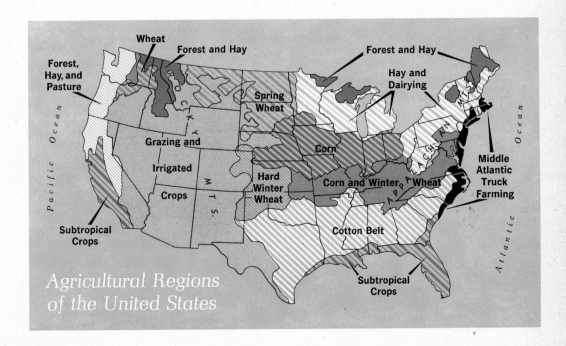

Agricultural Regions of the United States

expand as western Europe turned from farming toward industry, with populous manufacturing cities that had to be fed. The future of wheat-growing on the plains appeared all the rosier because for eight consecutive years after 1877 the region enjoyed such plentiful rainfall that many believed its characteristic aridity had passed.

While American agricultural production soared, the seemingly limitless demand kept prices high. From 1866 to 1875, the average annual price of a bushel of wheat was $1.24. In the next decade the average price was still 92 cents. Such prices encouraged expansion, mainly by farmers mortgaging

their land to the limit in order to acquire more land before the next fellow got it. This practice was encouraged by the banks and their optimistic managers.

Wise heads knew that the West was riding for a fall; over-production in the United States by the mid-1880's, the entry of India and Australia into the world wheat market, the revival of Russian wheat production, the rise of tariff barriers in Europe, all were ill omens. Yet just as buffalo had drawn the Indians to the virgin West, as gold had drawn the prospector, and grass the rancher, so wheat had drawn the farmer. He alone had come to stay.

Readings
* Asterisk indicates that book is available in paperback.

R. A. Billington, *Westward Expansion* * (1967), has informative and admirably organized sections on each of the themes discussed in this chapter. Useful also are T. D. Clark, *Frontier America: The Story of the Westward Movement* * (1959); F. L. Paxson, *The Last American Frontier* (1910); and Allan Nevins, *Emergence of Modern America, 1865-1878* (1927). W. P. Webb, *The Great Plains* * (1931), J. C. Malin, *The Grassland of North America* (1948), and Isaiah Bowman, *The Frontier Fringe* (1931), are extraordinarily imaginative studies that add greatly to our understanding of the relationship between the natural environment and social life. Thurman Wilkins, *Clarence King* (1958); W. C. Darrah, *Powell of the Colorado* (1951); and Wallace Stegner, *Beyond the Hundredth Meridian: John Wesley Powell and the Second Opening of the West* * (1954), are unusually interesting biographies of men who first assayed the natural resources of the Far West. Good regional studies include O. O. Winther, *The Great Northwest* (1950); R. N. Richardson and C. C. Rister, *The Great Southwest* (1934); J. C. Caughey, *History of the Pacific Coast* (1933); and H. E. Briggs, *Frontiers of the Northwest: A History of the Upper Missouri Valley* (1940). Robert Taft, *Artists and Illustrators of the Old West 1850-1900* (1953), is well illustrated and contains much useful information.

A moving modern account of Indian life is found in J. C. Collier, *Indians of the Americas* * (1947). See also the general accounts in the Readings for Chapter 1. F. G. Roe, *The Indian and the Horse* (1955), is outstanding. Harold McCracken, *George Catlin and the Old Frontier* (1959), is scholarly and superbly illustrated. Wayne Gard, *The Great Buffalo Hunt* (1959), does justice to its subject. J. P. Dunn, *Massacres of the Mountains* (1886), is a comprehensive contemporary account of the Indian wars. R. G. Athearn, *William Tecumseh Sherman and the Settlement of the West* (1956), offers a modern introduction to this subject. Angie Debo, *And Still the Waters Run* (1940), is excellent on the later phases of Indian removal. H. H. Jackson, *A Century of Dishonor* * (1881), is a passionate indictment of Indian policy to that date. L. G. Priest, *Uncle Sam's Stepchildren: The Reformation of United States Indian Policy 1865-1887* (1942), is a scholarly modern examination of this subject.

The standard study of the mining country is T. A. Rickard, *A History of American Mining* (1932). More detailed on special subjects is Rickard's *Man and Metals* (2 vols., 1932). An outstanding more recent survey is R. W. Paul, *Mining Frontiers of the Far West*

1848-1880 * (1963). Useful also is W. J. Trimble, *The Mining Advance into the Inland Empire* (1914). More colorful are G. C. Quiett, *Pay Dirt, a Panorama of American Gold Rushes* (1936), and C. H. Shinn, *The Story of the Mine* (1896), mainly the story of the Comstock Lode. Shinn's *Mining Camps: A Study in American Frontier Government* * (1885) is solid. R. E. and M. F. Stewart, *Adolph Sutro* (1962), tells the story of the tunnel and its maker. Mark Twain, *Roughing It* (2 vols., 1872), is the great writer's stirring account of Nevada days. J. V. Frederick, *Ben Holladay, the Stagecoach King* (1940), is informative on transportation before the coming of the railroad, as are Arthur Chapman, *The Pony Express* (1932), and L. R. Hafen, *The Overland Mail, 1849-1869* (1926).

Three sound general works on the cattle kingdom are E. S. Osgood, *The Day of the Cattleman* * (1929); E. E. Dale, *The Range Cattle Industry* (1930); and Louis Pelzer, *The Cattleman's Frontier* (1936). More specialized are O. B. Peake, *The Colorado Range Cattle Industry* (1937); M. G. Burlingame, *The Montana Frontier* (1942); and Charles Lindsay, *The Big Horn Basin* (1932). On the cowboy himself, Andy Adams, *Log of a Cowboy* * (1903), and P. A. Rollins, *The Cowboy* (1922), are well worth reading. J. B. Frantz and J. E. Choate, *The American Cowboy: The Myth and the Reality* (1955), offers a modern appraisal. Enlightening on the badmen and the coming of law and order to the West is Wayne Gard, *Frontier Justice* (1949).

F. A. Shannon, *The Farmer's Last Frontier: Agriculture, 1860-1897* (1945), is a scholarly analysis of the settlement of the West and the transition from ranching to farming. On the distribution and sale of the western domain, useful accounts may be found in R. M. Robbins, *Our Landed Heritage* * (1942); B. H. Hibbard, *A History of the Public Land Policies* (1924); and A. M. Sakolski, *The Great American Land Bubble* (1932). A scholarly study of land policy in the twentieth century is E. L. Peffer, *Closing of the Public Domain: Disposal and Reservation Policies, 1900-1950* (1951). H. R. Lamar, *Dakota Territory 1861-1889: A Study of Frontier Politics* (1956), is a good introduction to statehood preliminaries. Farm technology is discussed in volume II of Waldemar Kaempffert, *A Popular History of American Invention* (2 vols., 1924). More specialized and detailed is W. T. Hutchinson, *Cyrus Hall McCormick* (2 vols., 1935). On pioneer farm life, Everett Dick, *The Sod-House Frontier, 1854-1890* (1937), and Mari Sandoz, *Old Jules* * (1935), present detailed and dramatic stories. Very revealing also are the novels of Ole Rölvaag, especially *Giants in the Earth* * (1929), and Willa Cather's *O Pioneers!* * (1913), and *My Antonia* * (1918).

CHAPTER NINETEEN

In the year 1890, the Superintendent of the United States census made one of the most unnerving announcements in American history:

Up to and including 1880 the country had a frontier of settlement, but at present the unsettled area has been so broken into . . . that there can hardly be said to be a frontier line. In the discussion of its extent and its westward movement, etc., it can not, therefore, any longer have a place in the census reports.

For almost three hundred years the open spaces of the North American continent had stood as evidence to the world of free oppor-

The Thrust
of Business Enterprise

tunity in American society. Now civilization had cut through the forests, traversed the prairies and the plains, scaled the formidable crests of the western mountains, and altogether encompassed the primeval wilderness of the stone-age braves. An epoch in American life had ended, one that, as Frederick Jackson Turner, the most influential historian of the frontier, insisted, had made the strongest impact on the American character and tradition and one that helped most clearly to distinguish the American from the European way of life (see p. 600).

To many Americans, the announcement by the Superintendent of the census was

hardly news. As early as 1881, the New York *Tribune* printed a letter from a correspondent who wrote that America's resources had all been claimed, and who advised: "The nation has reached a point in its growth where its policy should be to preserve its heritage for coming generations, not to donate it to all the strangers we can induce to come among us." The following year, in response to organized agitation in many parts of the country, Congress took its first tentative steps toward sealing the ports of the United States against foreign settlers. The business community itself had begun to consolidate as well as to expand its enterprises, to nurse as well as to nourish its creative urge.

Yet the United States was to survive the closing of the land frontier. By breaching the new frontiers of science, technology, and business management, moreover, the American people were to make the resources of the country yield wealth and riches far beyond the dreams even of the most optimistic prospectors and promoters of the past. The old frontier, once the aborigines had been removed, pitted men against raw nature, and its extension west-

ward brought more casualties than Americans care to count. The new frontiers more often pitted man against man, more often demanded the leadership of the few and the discipline of the many. The casualties on the new frontiers usually were counted in business defeats and financial failures rather than in deaths, but these casualties often were as harrowing as those that had marked the breaching of the frontiers of old. The conquests on the new frontiers helped push the United States to world industrial supremacy.

I. *The Vogue of Materialism*

In January, 1840, from his job with the bankers, E. W. Clark & Co. in Philadelphia, young Jay Cooke wrote home to his brother Pitt in Ohio: "Among our customers are men of every age and of every position in society. . . . Through all the grades I see the same all-pervading, all engrossing anxiety to grow rich. . . . This is the only thing for which men live here." A few years later, Abbott Lawrence, a leader among the creative Yankee cotton manufacturers and an early promoter of steam railroads, told a competitor, "If you are troubled with the belief that I am growing *too rich,* there is one thing that you may as well understand: I know how to make money, and you cannot prevent it."

During the Civil War, inducements to enterprise became greater than ever and the materialist frame of mind grew more pronounced. "Such opportunities for making money," wrote Judge Thomas Mellon of Pittsburgh in 1863, "had never existed before in all my former experience." That year his oldest son James, then a young lawyer in Milwaukee, had written home asking for permission to enlist. The Judge ordered, "Don't do it. It is only greenhorns who enlist. Those who are able to pay for substitutes do so, and no discredit attaches." And he added:

It is not so much the danger as disease and idleness and vicious habits. . . . I had hoped my

boy was going to make a smart, intelligent business man and was not such a goose as to be seduced from his duty by the declamations of buncombed speeches.

The Judge carried the day, and indeed he himself soon resigned from the bench to go into business again.

The end of the war, with the North triumphant, found many of its spokesmen advancing their victory as proof of the superiority of their industrial civilization. During the spectacular postwar boom, the vogue of the English philosopher, Herbert Spencer, helped make the triumph of materialism complete. Spencer had been raised in the tradition of English nonconformism with its radical resistance to the authority of the state. Such formal education as he had, at the same time, introduced him to the world of science. His nonconformist background prepared him for a ready acceptance of laissez-faire economics. His scientific education led him to give such economics, which had been ethical and humanitarian in orientation, a natural and hence a deterministic bent. "Morality," Spencer wrote as early as 1851, "is essentially one with physical truth." When, eight years later, Charles Darwin published his epochal work—*On the Origin of Species by Means of Natural Selection or the Preservation of Favored Races in the Struggle for Life,* to give it its full title—Spencer and his followers had ready at hand all the

514

"physical truth" they needed to make laissez-faire economics seem both inevitable and sacrosanct. Where Darwin went to fauna and flora, pigeons and parasites for evidence, the Spencerians or "Social Darwinists," as they came to be called (see Chapter 22), went to them for analogies. The Darwinian "struggle for existence" was readily transformed into the system of unregulated business competition; the inevitable "survival of the fittest" was manifested in the way such creations as John D. Rockefeller's Standard Oil "trust" swallowed up many smaller, weaker creatures (see p. 525). The progress of society demanded that these complex industrial organisms be left entirely to their "natural" proclivities. Just as nature worked untrammeled in "selecting" her elite, so that society moved most rapidly toward perfection which allowed its elite free play. "The American Beauty rose," Rockefeller once assured his Sunday-school students,

can be produced in the splendor and fragrance which bring cheer to its beholder only by sacrificing the early buds which grow up around it. This is not an evil tendency in business. It is merely the working-out of a law of nature and a law of God.

The leading American Social Darwinist was the Yale professor, William Graham Sumner, who said early in the 1880's:

The millionaires are a product of natural selection, acting on the whole body of men to pick out those who can meet the requirements of certain work to be done. . . . They get high wages and live in luxury, but the bargain is a good one for society. There is the intensest competition for their place and occupation. This assures us that all who are competent for this function will be employed in it, so that the cost of it will be reduced to the lowest terms.

A few years earlier, when unregulated competition had helped cast the whole economy into the severe depression of the 1870's (see p. 529), Sumner admonished those economists "frightened at liberty especially under the forms of competition":

They think it bears harshly on the weak [he wrote]. They do not perceive that here "the strong" and "the weak" are terms which admit of no definition unless they are made equivalent to the industrious and the idle, the frugal and the extravagant. They do not perceive, furthermore, that if we do not like the survival of the fittest, we have only one possible alternative, and that is the survival of the unfittest. The former is the law of civilization; the latter is the law of anti-civilization.

When Andrew Carnegie first read Spencer, he recalled in his *Autobiography,* "Light came as in a flood and all was clear." Earlier, Carnegie had noted for his own guidance:

Man must have an idol—the amassing of wealth is one of the worst species of idolatry— no idol more debasing than the worship of money. . . . To continue much longer overwhelmed by business cares and with most of my thoughts wholly on the way to make more money in the shortest time, must degrade me beyond the hope of permanent recovery.

But reading Spencer helped resolve Carnegie's doubts. "Not only had I got rid of theology and the supernatural, but I had found the truth of evolution. 'All is well since all grows better' became my motto, my true source of comfort." Others were not to be so fortunate.

II. *Completing the Railroad Network*

COMPETITION
AND CONSOLIDATION

After the Civil War, as earlier, Americans moving westward often ran

ahead of the railroads, which continued to be built largely in populous areas that promised the most traffic. Even the completion of the transcontinentals in the late

Cornelius Vanderbilt on the pediment of his downtown freight depot in New York City, 1869.

1880's (see p. 521) left hundreds of settlements distant from transportation and communication facilities until the coming of the automobile a generation later.

In 1865 there were approximately 35,000 miles of railroad track in the country. By the time of the business crash of 1873 (see p. 529), this figure had been doubled. About 5,000 miles of new track had been laid in the South; most of the remainder was built in the East and the Old Northwest where trunk lines were being extended to the Mississippi Valley and a network of feeder lines opened up. Virtually all of this construction was privately financed through security issues sold mainly on the New York Stock Exchange. None of it enjoyed land-grant benefits, and little of it received any other kind of government assistance.

As important as railroad-building in the older areas was the consolidation of independent lines into large companies that offered coordinated service over wide areas. One of the great railroad consolidators and operators of the postwar period was the steamship magnate, Commodore Vanderbilt, who was prompted by the decline in sea-borne commerce during the Civil War to begin investing in railroads in 1862. By 1869, through a series of stock manipulations, Vanderbilt had bought control of the New York Central and the two more or less parallel lines that connected it with New York City—the Hudson River Railroad, and the Harlem Railroad. This maneuver gave Vanderbilt a through route from New York City to Buffalo.

In the midst of his New York Central negotiations, Vanderbilt had tried to capture the Erie Railroad, which loomed as a competitor to his new combination. He was foiled by the agility of the Erie management, led by the unscrupulous Daniel Drew and his wily lieutenants, Jay Gould and Jim Fisk. The "Erie War," one of the *causes célèbres* of the postwar decade, started in 1866 when Vanderbilt quietly began buying Erie stock in Wall Street. Aware of his intention, the Erie management printed more and more Erie securities

516

and released them on the stock exchange, where the Commodore unwittingly gobbled them up. At last Vanderbilt and his agents realized what was happening. For more than a year the opposing sides battled for the road in the securities market, in the courts, where each sought injunctions obstructing the operations of the other, and in the state legislature, where each side sought to saddle investigating committees with cooperative politicians. The unconcealed corruption to which the contestants resorted helped open the eyes of the public to the political malignancy of the new business forces.

In 1868, a settlement finally was worked out in which Vanderbilt retired from the fray, but his price for withdrawing was so high that it emptied the Erie treasury. Drew also retired from the Erie at this time, bequeathing the well-milked road to Gould and Fisk. By employing methods similar to those they had perfected during the Erie War, the two survivors were able to make their first millions out of the road, bankrupt though it remained.

His falure to acquire the Erie may have soured the aging Vanderbilt on further expanding his railroad holdings; but prodded by his son, William H., he turned next to the Lake Shore and Michigan Southern, which he acquired in 1870. This link gave the New York Central system a magnificent, wholly owned through route to Chicago by way of Cleveland and Toledo. In 1870, the Vanderbilts entered into working agreements with other roads that extended their operations all the way to Omaha, Nebraska, and by 1877, the year the Commodore died, they had also gained entry to Detroit and Toronto over the Michigan Central and its connections.

The Vanderbilts were more than just railroad-builders. They were also among the ablest railroad managers of their time. Under their direction, the Central's lines were double-tracked with heavy, sturdy rails, while road beds, bridges, and embankments were rebuilt to provide greater safety, even with the speedier engines the Central used. In 1871 the Commodore

opened the first Grand Central Terminal in New York City, from which passenger trains made the 965-mile run to Chicago in the then incredible time of 24 hours. Two years earlier he had built a downtown freight depot which may have supplied the occasion for the coining of the "Robber Baron" legend. During its construction, a huge bronze pediment was set in place atop the structure on which in sculptural low relief were strewn cogwheels, anchors, and other symbols of Vanderbilt's career, "with a colossal Cornelius looming up in the midst of the chaos." This event prompted E. L. Godkin to comment in the *Nation:*

There in the glory of brass, are portrayed in a fashion quite good enough, the trophies of a lineal successor of the medieval baron that we read about, who may have been illiterate indeed; and who was not humanitarian; and not finished in his morals; and not, for his manners, the delight of the refined society of his neighborhood; nor yet beloved by his dependents.

In the 1870's the Pennsylvania Railroad, guided by its masterful vice-president, Thomas A. Scott, also built and bought up numerous lines to gain wholly owned through routes from Philadelphia to Chicago and St. Louis. In 1871 the Pennsylvania at last gained access to New York City by acquiring most of the railroads that ran across New Jersey. The B. & O., meanwhile, although it had extended its track from Baltimore to Cincinnati, failed to make a New York City connection and fell far behind the Pennsylvania, the New York Central, and even the Erie in the cutthroat trunk-line competition of the postwar decades. In this competition cities like Chicago, Cleveland, and New York, which had rival railroads, were courted royally with low rates and fine service. Cities like Pittsburgh, on the other hand, where the Pennsylvania had a monopoly of the traffic, were treated, as Allan Nevins says, "with outrageous insolence."

Much more spectacular than the railroad-building in the older sections was the construction of the transcontinentals that had been chartered during the Civil War. In 1862, after a decade of surveys, debates, discussions, and sectional threats, Congress chartered the Union Pacific to build across the continent westward from Omaha. At the same time it gave the Central Pacific, a California corporation chartered in 1861, the right to build eastward from Sacramento. To both companies Congress made unprecedentedly large land grants. In addition, the companies were to receive loans for each mile of track laid, amounting to $16,000 per mile on level ground, $48,000 in mountain country, and $32,000 in intermediate territory. In return, these roads, like others that received government assistance, were required to carry the mail at low rates and to be on call for the movement of troops.

Despite all the fanfare over the charters and the land grants, both companies experienced difficulty in raising money with which to begin the actual construction that would make them eligible for the government loans. Having failed to dispose of more than a few shares of stock in all San Francisco, Charles Crocker of the Central Pacific, early in 1863, went to Virginia City, Nevada, the mining El Dorado (see p. 500). This is what he reported:

> They wanted to know what I expected the road would earn. I said I did not know. . . . "Well," they said, "do you think it will make 2 per cent a month?" "No," said I, "I do not." "Well," they answered, "we can get 2 per cent a month for our money here," and they would not think of going into a speculation that would not promise that at once.

The Union Pacific, promoted mainly by eastern capitalists, had little better luck in New York, Boston, or elsewhere, and by the end of 1863 the whole enterprise was on the verge of collapse. The next year, while the railroads' agents were spending at least half a million dollars in Washington trying to get the government to relax its terms,

Congress agreed to double the land grant for each road. More important, it agreed that its loans should be secured only by a second mortgage, and that the roads themselves could issue first mortgage bonds up to the amount of the government's bonds, backed by completed 20-mile sections of track. These provisions doubled the amount of bonds available to the roads; but not even the new well-secured first-mortgage bonds could find a market except when sold at an average discount of 12.5 per cent.

The actual building of the Union Pacific was carried through not by the corporation chartered by Congress but by a separate construction company which enjoyed the imaginative and ambiguous name, Crédit Mobilier. Among its leaders was Congressman Oakes Ames of Massachusetts, a member of the Pacific Railroad Committee in the House. A similar construction company had been organized by the California "Big Four"—Crocker, Leland Stanford, Collis P. Huntington, and Mark Hopkins—to build the Central Pacific.

Construction companies had been used earlier in the nineteenth century in the building of canals, but the stakes this time were much higher and the procedure more vulnerable. A congressional investigation of the construction of the transcontinental railroads later reported that, by means of companies like these, "the persons who under the guise of a corporation that was to take the contract to build the road held complete control of the corporation for which the road was to be built." This investigation disclosed that the Crédit Mobilier ultimately was paid $93 million in Union Pacific securities on which it realized $73 million in cash for an estimated $50 million worth of work completed. The difference of $23 million went to the men who acted as directors of *both* of the companies. The "Big Four's" construction agency returned a similar rate of profit.

The chance to make such fortunes, shady though they were, was what impelled the promoters to push the construction of the transcontinentals across largely uninhabited terrain. Union Pacific construction crews, made up mainly of Civil War veterans and Irish immigrants, located, laid, and equipped 568 miles of road in a single year. All told, the Union Pacific laid 1,086 miles of track. The Central Pacific, its construction crews manned largely by Chinese coolies, laid 689 miles. In the spring of 1869, the two lines approached one another, and on May 10 they were joined by golden spikes at Promontory Point, near Ogden, Utah. The engineering problems had been at least as trying as the financial ones, and, though both roads had to be almost completely rebuilt some years later, the feat of crossing the broad plains and the forbidding mountain ranges remains one of the great engineering accomplishments in history.

THE CONTEST FOR THE GREAT WEST

Before the business crash of 1873, three other transcontinentals were chartered and enriched by the federal government— the Northern Pacific in 1864, the Atlantic and Pacific in 1866, and the Texas and Pacific in 1871. Of the three, only the Northern Pacific was ever completed to the coast, and its arrival was long delayed. By 1872, the other two, along with their land grants, had fallen under the control of the Central

Pacific's "Big Four." In an effort to dominate all California railroading, this group also acquired the Southern Pacific Railroad, a company that had been chartered in California in 1865 to connect San Francisco and San Diego. After 1876, they began pushing the Southern Pacific eastward through the two best mountain passes, at Needles in California and Yuma in Arizona, thereby controlling the access routes to California as well as the lines within the state. In planning their monopoly, however, they reckoned without the ubiquitous Jay Gould and others as unscrupulous as themselves.

After selling out his Erie securities (see p. 517) for millions in cash on the eve of the Panic of 1873, Gould soon began buying up the depressed securities of the Union Pacific. Having won virtual control of this great transcontinental by 1878, he proceeded to buy up other western roads, including the shaky Kansas Pacific, which paralleled the Union Pacific from Denver east to Kansas City. By threatening to extend the Kansas Pacific west from Denver to Salt

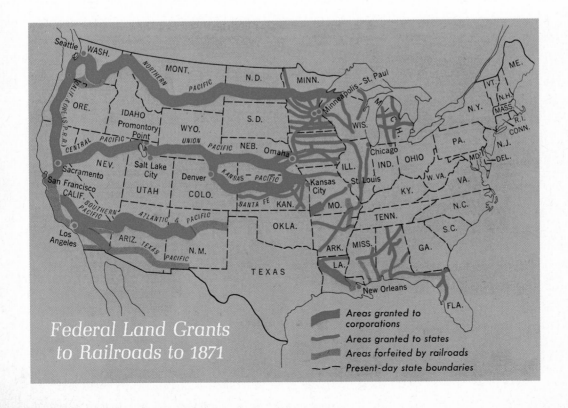

Federal Land Grants to Railroads to 1871

Areas granted to corporations
Areas granted to states
Areas forfeited by railroads
- - - Present-day state boundaries

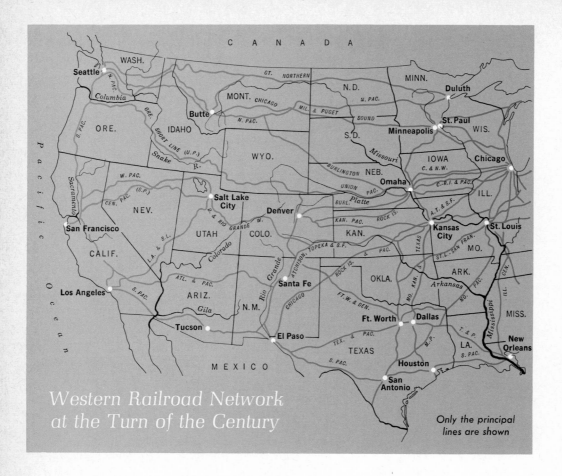

Western Railroad Network
at the Turn of the Century

Only the principal
lines are shown

Lake City, where it would find the Central Pacific ready to carry its cars all the way to California, Gould early in 1880 forced the directors of the Union Pacific to buy the Kansas Pacific from him. He had bought into the Kansas Pacific at under $10 a share; he sold out at over $90. Gould also foisted on the Union Pacific many of his other western roads.

While he was milking the Union Pacific, Gould began quietly selling off his own stock in the company at the high prices that prevailed until the true state of the road's finances became known. Before ridding himself of his last U.P. shares in 1883, he had the company build a number of new branches which were paid for by the issuance of $10 million in new stock. A goodly portion of the proceeds from these issues found its way to Gould's pocket through a quarter-interest he held in the construction company that built one of the new branches that, in fact, ran nowhere.

Gould's toying with the Union Pacific engaged only his left hand. With his right, he pushed his way into Huntington's Southern Pacific. His weapon was a pasted-up system of southwestern roads, the key parts of which were the Missouri Pacific, which tied Kansas City to St. Louis, where it met the Pennsylvania and other trunk lines running to the Atlantic; the Missouri, Kansas and Texas (well-known as the "Katy" line), which ran from near Kansas City to Dallas; and the last of the land-grant transcontinentals, the Texas and Pacific, which since 1877 had been building west from Dallas toward El Paso. By 1881, El Paso had become the Southern Pacific's eastern terminal. Faced with the threat that the Texas and Pacific might cut off his path through Texas, Huntington hastened to make a traffic-sharing and rate-fixing agreement with Gould in 1881. Thereafter Gould himself played an increasingly important role in the develop-

520

ment of the Southern Pacific's power in California.

Gould's own system, meanwhile, dominated the Southwest east of California. Most of the roads that made up this system had been poorly constructed, and throughout the 1880's Gould added many miles to them that were of no better quality. In fact, they had been laid mainly to provide Wall Street with signs of activity and progress. By 1890, Gould was in control of about 9,000 miles of railroad in the Southwest, nearly half the total mileage of the section, and he held the shippers of his domain in bondage.

The other major system in the Southwest was the Atchison, Topeka, and Santa Fe, which had been chartered by Kansas in 1859 with the modest aim of connecting Atchison, Kansas, with the state capital at Topeka. The Santa Fe's promoters gradually acquired transcontinental ambitions, however, and it was to shut them out of California that the Southern Pacific had grasped the two best southern passes through the Sierras. In 1885, the Santa Fe worked out a route of its own to San Diego; but its freedom was short-lived, for the following year its charter fell to Huntington and Gould. Under their aegis, the road was quickly consolidated with others, and by 1888 it had made connections with far-off Chicago. By then, the Santa Fe had grown into a 7,000-mile system. More striking was the fact that 2,000 of these miles had been built between 1886 and 1888, not to meet any transportation needs but simply to saturate strategic railroad territory and to kill off the competition of the roads already there.

Huntington and Gould had come to consider the entire West Coast, if not indeed the entire West, as their private railroad domain. Far to the north, however, they were confronted with vast transcontinental enterprises they could not quite control. One of these was the Northern Pacific, which in 1864 received the most lavish of all federal land grants, running to some 40 million acres. Even so, its promoters failed to attract construction capital until, in 1869, the buoyant Jay Cooke took up the

charter. The Panic of 1873 soon crushed the House of Cooke and all its works, and not until Henry Villard captured the Northern Pacific in 1881 was it pushed onward to Portland, Oregon, and then, by 1883, to Tacoma, Washington.

Villard, an educated German who had come to America in the 1850's and found his way into finance through promotional journalism, had grandiose ideas for the development of the Northwest which tested his finances to the utmost. The New York bankers, Drexel, Morgan and Company, at one point backed Villard's rivals in Oregon. Huntington and Gould also became his enemies. In the background, moreover, sat James J. Hill, who had his own ideas about the Pacific Northwest and how to build and run railroads.

Hill had come to St. Paul from Canada as a young man in 1856, and at the end of 20 years had risen no higher than a transportation agent handling the transshipment of Mississippi River cargo between the United States and Canada. He had also become something of a town character—"that Hill," as he was called—with all his talk about the future of the Northwest. Hill's chance came after the crash of 1873 had left the grandiosely named St. Paul and Pacific Railroad—it ran only about 200 miles west from St. Paul—in bad shape. After biding his time, Hill with his tall talk won the help of Canadian financiers in acquiring the road in 1878. In 1889, it took the name of Great Northern. By then, with little government assistance, Hill and his backers had pushed construction 2,775 miles west through Minnesota, North Dakota, and Montana, and up to Winnipeg in Canada. In 1893, the Great Northern, on a route north of Villard's line, reached Puget Sound.

In 1883, when Villard reached the West Coast, Hill had written: "I think the time is at hand when railway property generally will be tested by its capacity to pay net earnings. . . . I think the Northern Pacific will have its greatest trial when . . . its finances are no longer sustained by sales of bonds, but all payments must be made from earnings." Hill was right. From the very start, Hill had insisted on constructing the Great Northern track and roadbed with the best materials available. He had also chosen to build around mountains rather than over them. Not only did this approach greatly reduce the cost of construction, an objective abhorred by the construction-company type of promoter whose purpose was to spend as much as possible, but it also reduced operating costs once a road was built. The Great Northern's long trains and heavy trainloads, which neither the track nor the mountainous routes of other western roads could carry, became the wonder of the railroad world. The proof of Hill's policies came in 1893 when the Great Northern alone of all the transcontinentals survived the crash.

In the next decade, the Great Northern not only acquired the Northern Pacific—which had been reorganized with the aid of J. P. Morgan in 1898—but, with Morgan's collaboration, Hill in 1901 also gained control of the strategic Chicago, Burlington & Quincy, the best entry to Chicago from the west. The Burlington acquisition touched off a bitter fight between Hill and Edward H. Harriman, as thorough a railroad man as Hill himself.

As a young man, Harriman had worked his way up in Wall Street and was thoroughly attuned to its operations. In the 1880's, he had gained control of the Illinois Central, and in 1895, with Illinois Central support, he had won control of the Union Pacific. In 1900, at Collis Huntington's death (Gould had died eight years earlier), Harriman acquired 45 per cent of the stock of the Southern Pacific. Harriman's backers were the bankers, Kuhn, Loeb and Company, who themselves enjoyed the financial confidence of the Rockefeller Standard Oil crowd, which had long been looking for likely outlets for its millions. Thus the stage was set and the parts assigned—Kuhn, Loeb; Rockefeller; Harriman; and the National City Bank, versus Morgan, Hill, and the First National Bank—for one of the great financial contests of the twentieth century, with control of the western, and indeed the national, railroad network as the prize.

After a titanic Wall Street battle that ruined many unoffending investors but settled nothing, the antagonists, in November, 1901, finally decided to merge their interests. For this purpose they formed the Northern Securities Company. But in 1904 the Northern Securities Company was broken up by a Supreme Court decision that was one of the highlights of "Teddy" Roosevelt's regime (see p. 654), and the contestants had to make less formal arrangements to keep from killing one another off. By then, the American railroad grid of about 200,000 miles had been virtually completed. There was nothing like it anywhere else in the world, but to say that Americans took satisfaction in it and its management would be grossly to misrepresent the case.

THE RAILROADS AND THE PUBLIC

While Hill was giving the railroad men of the Far West lessons in railroad construction, management, and responsibility—lessons they were reluctant to learn —some of the roads in the older sections, as we have seen, had begun to mend their lines and their ways. The most far-reaching of the great improvements in service before the crash of 1893 stemmed from the introduction of the steel rail. As late as 1880, only 30 per cent of American rails were made of steel. By 1890, the proportion had climbed to 80 per cent; by 1900, virtually to 100 per cent. Steel rails could bear ten or fifteen times the weight of iron rails and still last twenty times as long. They made possible the use of stronger locomotives, larger freight cars, and shorter schedules, and assured safer and more reliable service. A related development was the double-tracking and quadruple-tracking of thousands of miles of busy routes in the West as well as in the East. Many roads in all sections of the country also laid much new track in order to extend their service to an ever-widening list of cities and towns that were growing busy enough to warrant railroad interest. By 1887 about 33,000 American communities had gained regular train service; but one of the great issues of railroad regulation grew out of the fact that all but 2,700 of these communities as yet were served by but a single line, and that line was likely to take advantage of its monopoly position to charge what the traffic would bear. After 1875, moreover, "through service" between large metropolises at last began to take on the smoothness and coordination that had merely been promised earlier. In addition, clean and often elegant dining cars were added to many long-distance passenger trains and sleepers were continuously improved. Terminals and stations, once open sheds or mere platforms, were becoming carefully planned architectural façades on the model of Vanderbilt's terminal in New York City for roads that had begun to take pride in their names and emblems.

Yet none of these improvements seems to have muffled the cry for railroad regulation and reform which swept across the country especially after the Panic of 1873, and which gathered new intensity after 1884 when another panic forced many speculative roads to the wall. It is usually believed that the farmers of the West, who

were so dependent on the railroads to get their produce to market and to get it there in season, led the demand for railroad regulation. And so they may have. Yet the railroads themselves had helped to create a national market for many non-agricultural commodities either imported from abroad or manufactured in American cities, and the distributors of these commodities were far from backward in making their complaints against railroad rate practices heard. Many other railroad practices also came under attack (see Chapter 20). The railroads fought the growing agitation by spending large sums making political friends and employing the best legal talent. "War," said the English commentator, James Bryce, in the 1880's, "is the natural state of an American railway towards all other authorities." In this war, as the reformers complained, the railroads enlisted "the ablest [attorneys] in the United States, all of them paid out of the people's money. . . ." This open flouting of the people's government, this open corruption of all the channels of political practice, would have been enough in itself to raise the protest against the railroads to irresistible levels.

III. *Enterprise in Industry*

THE SPIRIT OF THE AGE

Railroad expansion and railroad improvement, of course, had a great deal to do with the surge of northern industry after the war. Actual railroad construction expanded the market for all kinds of goods ranging from steel for rails to meat and blankets for construction crews. Railroad financing, in turn, so familiarized the public with investment procedures that industrial corporations as well as railroads found ready takers for the securities they were offering for sale in the rising money markets of the country. Railroad financing also drew large amounts of foreign capital to America. Foreign capital not only helped build the

railroads, but also made it possible for industrialists like Carnegie, Armour, and Rockefeller to use their profits to expand their enterprises and to exploit profitable by-products, fully confident that others would supply the wherewithal for transporting raw materials to their factories and carrying their commodities to market.

But railroad development itself only confirmed the spirit of optimism and enterprise that dominated the victorious North after the war. "Everybody and everything's goin' places," observed an Indiana farmer in the late 1860's. In 1869, David A. Wells, the Special Commissioner of Revenue in the federal government, reported:

Within the last five years, more cotton spindles have been put in operation, more iron furnaces erected, . . . more steel made, more coal and copper mined, more lumber sawed . . . , more houses and shops constructed, more manufactories . . . started, and more petroleum collected, refined, and exported than during any equal period in the history of the country.

And the country was still only midway through the industrial boom that would see even the fabulous accomplishments of the late 1860's overshadowed before the Panic of 1873 called but a temporary halt to northern progress.

THE STANDARD OIL NEXUS

Nowhere was the spirit of enterprise more evident than in the newest industry of all, the production and refining of petroleum. In the 1850's whale oil, then the world's chief commercial illuminant, had become so scarce that its price edged toward $5 a gallon. Surface petroleum had been detected in many parts of the world for centuries and as kerosene had recently been used to give light. But no one knew how to find enough of it to meet the rising demand. Then, in 1857, a group of pioneers sent "Colonel" E. L. Drake to the neighborhood of Titusville, Pennsylvania, to make the first deliberate attempt to drill for oil. In August 1859, "Drake's Folly" gushed in. Twentieth century drillers sometimes go down two miles and more for oil. Drake most laboriously got down to 69½ feet, and his first well yielded 20 barrels of crude oil a day. By 1864, wildcatters, as oil prospectors were called, had covered the district about Titusville with so many oil derricks that annual production exceeded 2 million barrels. By 1872, the oil fields covered 2,000 square miles in Pennsylvania, West Virginia, and Ohio, and total production had soared to 40 million barrels. Of this massive total, John D. Rockefeller's Standard Oil Company was already refining no less than one-fifth.

Rockefeller was born in 1839 in Richford, New York. Aged 26 in 1865, he had already accumulated a wartime fortune of $50,000 in a grain and meat partnership in Cleveland. Two years earlier Rockefeller had invested in a small Cleveland oil refinery to which he was now ready to devote all his time. He dissolved the old partnership and set up a new one with Samuel Andrews, a man experienced in oil-refining.

Rockefeller saw early that an efficient refinery could be built for as little as $50,000, and that an industry into which entry was so cheap and easy must be intensely competitive. In order to outdo all rivals, he and

Cover of one of the Alger books, which were popular with rural youth in the 1870's and 1880's.

Andrews started with $200,000. Moreover, they located their first plant away from the raw materials in the oil fields—where skilled labor and bank credit were scarce and markets distant. They chose the rising city of Cleveland. In 1867, they added Henry M. Flagler as a partner, and won additional backing from Stephen V. Harkness, a rich Ohio brewer and distiller. In 1870, these men, and John's brother, William Rocke-

524

feller, organized the Standard Oil Company with a capital of $1 million. These funds supplied the wherewithal for a triple attack on the competition, which was located mainly in the oil regions and in Cleveland, Pittsburgh, and New York.

First, Rockefeller spent heavily to make his plants the most efficient in the country so that he could undersell all competitors and still make sizable profits. Often enough, he would sell his products well below cost in selected markets in order to ruin a competitor—the practice known as "cut-throat competition." To recoup his losses he would then charge more than ever before once he had the market to himself. *Second,* with his volume of business steadily rising, Rockefeller demanded that the railroads grant him lower freight rates than any of his competitors. Railroad rates nominally were public and equal, but Rockefeller sought his advantage by requesting secret rebates from the regular charges. Since railroad competition in Cleveland was so intense, the railroads complied to hold his business.

Having by these means eliminated almost all competition in Cleveland, Rockefeller, in 1872, took the *third* step to bring the industry elsewhere to book. This step involved him in the notorious South Improvement Company, which Tom Scott of the Pennsylvania Railroad had chartered in 1870 with the grandiose idea of eliminating cut-throat competition among the railroads by bringing as many rival lines as possible under one management, his own. Scott had done little with his scheme before 1872, by which time Rockefeller had developd similar "pooling" ideas to eliminate the cut-throat competition that continued to plague the oil industry. Many of the refineries in Pittsburgh, New York, and other centers had already been shaken by Rockefeller's competitive tactics. What Rockefeller needed was a club to brandish at the holdouts. No better bludgeon could have been invented than discriminatory freight rates on oil shipments, which a railroad pool such as the one Scott had in mind could enforce.

The South Improvement scheme was finally worked out in January, 1872, among the Erie, the New York Central, and the Pennsylvania and their affiliates on the one hand, and the Standard Oil Company leaders on the other. It involved a series of steps: (1) The South Improvement Company was reorganized as an oil company headed by Standard Oil chiefs; (2) the railroads were to be permitted to double their charges for hauling crude oil and oil products; (3) the South Improvement Company alone was not to be charged the increase; (4) more than that, the South Improvement Company and not the railroads was to receive—as "drawbacks"—most of the increase paid by Standard's competitors; (5) the railroads were to report daily to the South Improvement Company on all shipments made by competitors, informing the company of the amount, quality, price, and destination of the oil involved; (6) to keeps tabs on these reports, the South Improvement Company was to have access to all the railroads' books. In exchange, the railroads received a small part of the rate increases and the promise that the South Improvement Company would distribute its patronage as evenly as practicable over the heretofore ruinously competitive railroad lines.

When word of this bold scheme leaked out the Standard publicly abandoned it, but Rockefeller got his rebates and drawbacks from some of the more vulnerable lines after all. By 1879, he held about 95 per cent of the refining capacity of the country and had captured almost the entire world market for his products. Rockefeller himself said a bit later:

This movement [toward monopoly] was the origin of the whole system of modern economic administration. It has revolutionized the way of doing business all over the world. The time was ripe for it. It had to come, though all we saw at the moment was the need to save ourselves from wasteful conditions. . . . The day of combination is here to stay. Individualism has gone, never to return.

Rockefeller was not the only one in the oil industry to employ sharp tactics. Samuel Downer, a leader in refining before Rockefeller so outdistanced the field, once said to Henry Flagler: "Flagler, I am opposed to the whole scheme of rebates and drawbacks—without I'm in it!" Most of the refiners who could exert enough pressure on the railroads had been "in it."

By 1879, the oil pipeline was well on the way to supplanting the railroad tank car as the great oil carrier, and before long the Standard had used its enormous power to gain a virtual monopoly of pipe-line transportation from the Pennsylvania and neighboring oil fields. A more daring and original move made late in the 1880's protected and extended the company's position. Petroleum production in Pennsylvania and neighboring oil regions had hit an all-time peak in 1882, but the Pennsylvania oil fields were not bottomless, and thereafter oil men began to worry that the entire industry would dry up. So alarmed were they that within a few years John D. Archbold, Rockefeller's own closest and most trusted associate, quietly began to sell off his Standard Oil stock at 75 cents on the dollar. In 1885, a great new oil field was discovered near the town of Lima in western Ohio, and soon a second field was opened just across the Indiana border. The difficulty, however, was that the oil produced here, though richer than Pennsylvania's in some respects, was contaminated with excessive sulphur, an odoriferous ingredient that earned it the name "pole cat oil," or "skunk juice."

By 1887, Lima-Indiana oil had become a drug on the market. But Rockefeller decided that a way could surely be found to remove its stench. By threatening to go it alone if need be, he forced the Standard Oil directors to organize the Ohio Oil Company in 1887 with the purpose of monopolizing production in this new oil region, and then hired a team of chemists to make its products marketable. In a short

time they succeeded, and Standard Oil was in a position to keep newcomers from the new source of supply, and from new markets in the Mississippi Valley and beyond.

BESSEMER AND OPEN-HEARTH STEEL

Before the Civil War, steel had been a rare and costly metal which could be produced only in quantities of 25 to 50 pounds by processes that took weeks to complete. As early as 1847, William Kelly of Kentucky had discovered a simple method by which tons of excellent steel could be made in a matter of minutes; but nothing much was heard of his discovery until ten years later, when Kelly contested the application of an Englishman, Henry Bessemer, for an American patent on a process similar to his own and on an efficient "converter." Patent controversies soon were straightened out, yet as late as 1867 only 2,600 tons of what has since become known as Bessemer steel were produced in the United States.

In 1872, fresh from his long experience in railroading and the building of steel railroad bridges, Andrew Carnegie entered the steel manufacturing industry, but he put off adopting the Bessemer process. "Pioneering doesn't pay a new concern," he said: "we must wait until the process develops." A trip to England the next year convinced Carnegie of the practicality of the new process, and on his return he could talk of nothing else.

In 1873, Carnegie organized a new firm, Carnegie, McCandless & Company, and built the biggest steel mill in the world, the J. Edgar Thomson Steel Works, near Pittsburgh, shrewdly named after the president of the Pennsylvania Railroad. On intimate terms with Thomson, Tom Scott, and other railroad kings, Carnegie ignored the depression of the succeeding years and "went out," as he said, "and persuaded them to give us orders" for steel rails. By 1879, American steel production had risen to 930,000 tons, three-fourths of it in the form of steel rails, almost all of them manufactured by the Carnegie company.

By 1890, American steel production had taken another spectacular leap to an annual figure of over 4 million tons. By then, three other giant steel enterprises had arisen or were on the verge of completing their consolidation out of numerous smaller companies: the Tennessee Coal and Iron Company in the South, the Illinois Steel Company in the Middle West, and the Colorado Fuel and Iron Company in the mountain region. The "Pittsburgh district," however, continued to dominate steel production, and Carnegie was acknowledged to have "almost absolute control" of the steel business there.

Carnegie's success sprang in part from his own abilities as a salesman. But he also had a vision of big business that far outstripped the thinking of any of his competitors, and he had the energy and discipline to bring his vision to fruition. Other steel men (like the wildcatters in oil) often lived off their profits in the grand style, but Carnegie, like Rockefeller, constantly plowed back his own and his company's earnings into the expansion, integration, and modernization of the enterprise. Before he sold his company and retired in 1901, Carnegie had acquired immense holdings in the fabulous Mesabi ore lands of Minnesota, from which as much as 85 per cent of America's entire iron ore needs in the first half of the twentieth century were to come. He also bought up Pennsylvania coal fields and scattered limestone quarries, and the coke business of Henry Clay Frick, taking Frick himself, an excellent manager, into partnership.

Ore, coal, limestone, and coke are the basic raw materials for the manufacture of steel; to insure their regular delivery to his plants, Carnegie also invested heavily in ore ships and railroad cars. Beyond all this, Carnegie was one of the first industrialists to employ a full-time scientifically trained chemist to study and control the tricky metallurgy of steel in order to produce a more uniform and satisfactory product. He introduced sound cost-accounting and developed a successful incentive pay system for executives and workers alike.

At about the same time that Kelly and Bessemer had discovered the Bessemer steel-making process, other inventors were developing the open-hearth method, which had two important advantages over Bessemer production. The open-hearth furnace could attain a higher temperature than the Bessemer converter; yet it was easier to draw samples from it for testing during actual production. The greater heat broke down the elements of iron more thoroughly than a Bessemer converter could, and the easy testing gave the worker greater control in recombining them or mixing them with alloying metals.

As experience with steel grew, and as metallurgy furnished more precise explanations for faults and accidents, the quality of steel improved. Bessemer steel was especially satisfactory for steel rails. But when steel came into greater demand for other uses—in skyscraper construction, in high-speed factory machinery, in the manufacture of automobiles—the finer open-hearth steels became more popular. By 1910, United States steel production exceeded 26 million tons, two-thirds of it open-hearth.

ADVANCES IN THE USE OF ELECTRICITY

Small businesses, especially in relatively unmechanized industries, continue to this day to outnumber the large combinations in the United States and even to employ more people. In the later nineteenth century, the new big firms grew faster than the old and encountered many new management problems. Among these were sheer mechanical problems of communication between boards of directors in large cities and their many scattered plants.

Among new mechanical devices helping to speed business communication were the typewriter, which first appeared in 1867, and the adding machine, which became practical in 1888. Both set in motion the mechanization of the office that was to make such huge strides when electronic equipment became common after World War II. More fundamental were the expansion of the electric telegraph and the development of the telephone. By 1878, Western Union owned 195,000 miles of telegraph routes and controlled 80 per cent of the telegraph business. In 1881, at a cost of nearly $25 million, the company proceeded to buy out its two rising competitors, the American Union Company and the Atlantic and Pacific. This accomplished, President Norvin Green of Western Union declared to his stockholders:

> Successful competition with your Company is improbable if not actually impossible. . . . Competition may be a popular demand, and it may be good policy on the part of your Company to indulge competing lines between the principal points. This would not materially interfere with remunerative dividends.

But secure as Western Union seemed in 1881, two years later a strong new rival loomed. This was the Commercial Cable Company, partly owned by John W. Mackay, the Comstock Lode millionaire. A disastrous rate war with Western Union began in 1886, and the following year both companies were ready to call it quits. They did not merge, but they did agree to end all competition in rates.

In 1876, Alexander Graham Bell patented the telephone he had invented the year before. In 1877, Western Union, which first scorned Bell's invention as an "electrical toy," decided it had better enter the field. Backing a rival patent by Elisha Gray, it organized the American Speaking Telephone Company and proceeded to use all its political influence to block the Bell Company from winning franchises from local communities. The Bell Company, under the direction of Theodore N. Vail, was not awed by its great rival and proceeded to sue Western Union for infringement of patents. Bell's case was so good that Western Union settled out of court in 1879. By then, Western Union had hastily set up some 56,000 telephones in 55 cities, and Bell paid handsomely for this equipment and the accompanying franchises.

During the 1880's, the Bell Company was beset by competitors, all of whom it ultimately bought out at a total cost of $225 million. In this and later decades, constant improvement was made in the telephone instrument and in the wires, and new patents kept the Bell Company invulnerable to competition. One of the major innovations was the development of long-distance telephone service, beginning in 1884. To expand this business, the Bell directors set up a new corporation, the American Telephone and Telegraph Company. In 1900, A.T. & T. became the over-all holding company of the entire Bell system, with a capitalization of $250 million. In that year, 1,350,000 Bell telephones were in use in the United States. Service still cost New Yorkers $240 a year for a private phone. At such rates, A.T. & T.'s profits became the envy of industry.

While Bell and others were experimenting with the telephone, Thomas A. Edison was experimenting with electric lighting. The earliest commercial use of electricity had been in communication, and until the 1880's its use was still restricted to telegraphy and the telephone. Then, in 1879, Edison perfected a reasonably priced incandescent bulb. In 1882, he succeeded in building the first central electric power station, the Pearl Street station in New York City, from which he soon distributed *direct* current to 85 buildings wired to receive it. Direct current, which Edison believed the only current commercially feasible, could be transmitted great distances only at great cost. With the use of transformers, *alternating* current could take direct current from a power plant, cheaply step up the voltage a hundred times for distant transmission, and then step it down again for practical use.

In collaboration with William Stanley, George Westinghouse, the inventor of the railroad air brake and other devices, developed the first generators and transformers to make alternating current practical. Before it could be used for mechanical power, however, a suitable motor had to be devised. Such a motor was perfected in 1888 by Nikola Tesla, a Serbian immigrant. Soon after he bought up Tesla's patent, Westinghouse made alternating current famous by using it to light up Chicago's World Fair in 1893. By 1895, Westinghouse had succeeded in harnessing the water power of Niagara Falls and carrying the current generated there 20 miles, then considered an incredible feat.

Electric power revolutionized American business and American life even more than cheap steel did; but the great era of electricity was to be the twentieth century. In the nineteenth century, the United States as well as the rest of the world still looked to water and steam for power.

SCIENCE, CYCLES, AND CONSOLIDATION

Increasingly, in the later nineteenth century, science was becoming the servant of industry in the manufacture of other commodities besides petroleum products and steel. Labor shortages during the Civil War had driven many manufacturers to invest in the newest, most efficient labor-saving machinery almost regardless of its initial high cost; and the demand for goods during the first postwar boom seemed to justify continued investment in the new and often revolutionary equipment that science was making possible.

Periodic over-expansion of industry and over-investment in plant and machinery were to remain basic characteristics of rapid growth in America's free-market economy. They were also to contribute heavily to the dramatic ups and downs in the business cycle in the face of which management had to discipline itself. Some managers learned their lessons early and well; others, incurably infected with the prospector psychology of American expansion, never learned them.

The first great downswing in American postwar economic activity was touched off by the Panic of 1873. Signs of trouble became apparent as early as 1871, when the number of business failures reached 3,000. By 1872 more than 4,000 additional firms had collapsed. A clue to their difficulties

may be found in the fact that during the boom period from 1868 to 1873 the volume of American bank loans had grown seven times as fast as bank deposits. The entire economy was being strained to sustain the boom. Two accidental tragedies made the strain almost unbearable. One was the spectacular Chicago fire of 1871, which cost insurance companies $200 million. The second was a great fire in Boston in 1872, which cost such companies $73 million.

The crash began on September 8, 1873, when the New York Warehouse and Securities Company went into bankruptcy. The greatest shock came ten days later with the failure of Jay Cooke and Company, the most famous banking house in the country. "Whatever may be the result of the crisis in Wall Street," observed the New York *Tribune,* "we shall regard the disaster to Jay Cooke and Company as nothing less than a public calamity." The New York Stock Exchange, "to save [Wall] Street from utter ruin," suspended all trading for ten days on September 20. Shock gradually gave way to profound depression as railroads halted construction and defaulted on their bonds, and as mills closed down and threw half the factory population out of work. As late as 1876-77, over 18,000 business firms failed.

To many people the crash of 1873 was utter tragedy. Unemployment reached levels never before approached in American history, and business and professional men in the thousands, like millions of the unskilled, were obliged to seek public charity in order to survive. To businessmen like Rockefeller and Carnegie, who understood both the normal rhythm of capitalist ups and downs and the basic soundness of the country, the crash simply spelled opportunity for renewed investment and expansion. "The man who has money during a panic is a wise and valuable citizen," said Carnegie. After the crash, many of those who had bought stock in his early iron and steel enterprises became desperately short of cash.

"So many of my friends needed money," Carnegie explained later about the years 1874-78, "that they begged me to repay them. I did so and bought out five or six of them. That was what gave me my leading interest in this steel business."

Once the depression of the 1870's had run its course, it was followed by such a resurgence of industrial production that the prices of most commodities fell steadily. This state of affairs put a premium on the use of the most efficient machinery to keep production costs down, and it also stimulated manufacturers to rethink the processes by which many commodities were being produced. Engineering, which had been largely limited to problems of transportation such as bridge construction and railroad surveys, was now brought into the manufacturing plant. We have already read about the prewar use of interchangeable parts in the fire-arms and farm-machinery industries, and the use of assembly-line methods in meat-packing. In the 1870's and after, both the manufacture of interchangeable parts and their assembly along a continuous line became common techniques in many new industries. Their highest refinement was to come in the making of automobiles which could hardly have developed into a mass-market business without such mass-production methods (see Chapter 26).

By furthering the rapid mechanization of factories and the specialization of workers' jobs, science made it possible for businessmen to reduce the cost of production greatly. Yet there was a catch. So high was the initial investment now required to build and equip modern plants in many industries that economies of production were realized only when plants were operated at or near capacity. If plants produced fewer items than they were geared for, the cost of each item rose remarkably. On the other hand, if they produced at capacity, their volume was so great that the market would be flooded and the price of their output would fall. Every source of hope for new markets in the postwar era—the opening of a new railroad line, a boom in immigration, a burst of exports, a rise in the tariff—promoted expansion and mechanization. But each new development soon ran its course and left behind idle plants and equipment —usually purchased with borrowed money on which interest had to be paid.

This situation became a constant hazard of American business life in the 1880's. As the *Bulletin* of the American Iron and Steel Association said in 1884, "Indeed it might almost be rated the exception for half the works in condition to make iron to be in operation simultaneously." The National Association of Stove Manufacturers reported in 1888: "It is a chronic case of too many stoves and not enough people to buy them." As a result, many independent plants in heavily mechanized industries were forced to close down. In 1880, for example, the country had almost 2,000 woolen mills; by 1890, there were only 1,300. The 1,900 manufacturers of agricultural implements in 1880 had been reduced to 900 a decade later. During the same ten years, three-fourths of the manufacturers of leather goods went out of business. A second and equally fateful consequence was the movement toward industrial pools and trusts. The objective in each case was for one or a few firms to control the output, prices, and market areas of entire industries so that a satisfactory level of profits could be assured to the survivors.

Pools, which had long been known to industry as well as to railroads, were essentially agreements among competitors to restrict output, maintain prices, and divide markets. They usually were created in emergencies, and they usually collapsed when the emergency passed. Pools enabled independent entrepreneurs to retain a semblance of individuality and to express it if need be. When the pools failed, they were usually supplanted by trusts, of which the first in this epoch was the one organized by Rockefeller in 1879 and reorganized in 1882. "Its success," said a New York legislative committee that investigated it in 1888, "has been the incentive to the formation of all other trusts or combinations."

In forming a trust, the stock of many competing companies is turned over to a group of trustees agreed upon by the combining companies; in exchange for such stock, trustee certificates are issued. Ownership of the stock remains in the original hands, but management of the enterprises represented by it is concentrated in the hands of a single board of trustees. In the decade after the founding of the Standard Oil Trust, there appeared the Cottonseed Oil Trust, the Salt Trust, the Whiskey Trust, the Sugar Trust, the Leather Trust, the Cordage Trust, and others. Not all were strictly "trust" arrangements, but the tag was pinned to any large combination whose objective was to restrain cut-throat competition. An example was the so-called "Sugar Trust," of which Judge Barrett of the New York Supreme Court said:

It can close every refinery at will, close some and open others, limit the purchases of raw material, artificially limit the production of refined sugar, enhance the price to enrich themselves and their associates at the public expense, and depress the price when necessary to crush out and impoverish a foolhardy rival.

Pools and "trusts" seemed to be the answer to problems of brutal competition abroad as well as in the United States. In Germany in particular, the cartel, which was essentially a large pooling arrangement with more or less severe penalties for backsliders, became the characteristic method of controlling production, marketing, and prices. In Europe, such arrangements usually had the overt sanction of the state. In the United States, where free competition had become the accepted path to progress, the government for a long time was forced to give tacit sanction to consolidations of every sort while at the same time seeming to impose restraints on monopolistic tendencies. The Sherman Anti-Trust Act of 1890 (see p. 557), the first restrictive federal measure, reflected the growing public opposition to the "artificially" raised prices and "artificially" closed opportunities that the trusts brought about. Competition, however, grew more intense than ever after the passage of the Sherman Act, and especially after the new Panic of 1893, when, again, thousands

of industrial firms were forced into bankruptcy, banks shut down, and one railroad of every six went into receivership.

The panic began in February, 1893, when the Philadelphia & Reading Railroad, with negotiable assets of a mere $100,000 and short-term debts of $18,000,000, was forced into bankruptcy, carrying many of its creditors with it. As the business collapse snowballed and unemployment forced millions to seek public assistance, the federal government for the first time was bombarded with demands for direct relief. Pressure on government grew the more intense because of the prophets of doom even among the most conservative leaders of the nation. No earlier panic had elicited such fears of revolution. In 1894, Francis Lynde Stetson, perhaps the leading corporation lawyer in the country and J.P. Morgan's personal attorney, warned President Cleveland, "We are on the eve of a very dark night, unless a return of commercial prosperity relieves popular discontent."

At the same time, just as the Panic of 1873 had given Carnegie and Rockefeller great opportunities for expansion at bargain rates, so the Panic of 1893 gave Morgan and a few other investment bankers their opportunity to consolidate economic control in their own hands. Their first objective was to bring order out of the chaos wrought by the panic in railroad finance. By 1904, on the eve of the Northern Securities case, 1,040 separate American railroad lines had been consolidated into six huge combinations, each of which, in turn, was allied either to the Morgan or Kuhn, Loeb interests, these giants between them controlling in railroads alone $10 billion of American capital.

Success in railroad consolidation turned these giant interests to industry and to the rising public utilities. The return of prosperity in 1898 made it all the easier for them to market the securities of new combines, many of which were formed, indeed, merely to help bankers profit from the flotation of new securities. By 1893, after the previous great merger movement following the Panic of 1873, only twelve great industrial companies with an aggregate capital of less than a billion dollars had emerged. In the new movement, one corporation alone, Morgan's creation, the United States Steel Corporation, formed in 1901, had almost $1.5 billion in capital. In 1904, John Moody, in his classic study, *The Truth About the Trusts,* listed no less than 318 new industrial combinations with an aggregate capital of $7,250,000,000. They controlled 5,288 separate plants. Moody also listed 111 public utility combinations, all but fourteen of them organized after 1893. They controlled 1,336 plants with an aggregate capital of $3,700,000,000.

There was still more to the story. The power of the House of Morgan, and that of its competitors in the investment banking business, arose from their ability to supply the wherewithal for growing and groping companies. Once they had raised money for such companies from investors who acted largely on their confidence in the bankers themselves, the bankers felt the necessity to place their own men on the companies' boards of directors and thereby take a direct hand in management. In this way, the bankers' economic power, and Morgan's especially, spread far from the financial community to the heart of the big business system.

A second salient feature of the Morgan method became the banker's control of, or close alliance with, not only American users of capital but the growing American institutional sources of it. These institutions included commercial banks, the trust companies that administered large estates and other properties, and the immense life insurance companies whose premium collections from millions of small policy holders mushroomed during Morgan's heyday. Thus the bankers' influence spread far from the big business community itself, virtually over the entire population.

IV. *The Conditions of Labor*

THE FACTORY WORLD

By 1860, $1 billion had been invested in American industry, and the factories and shops that made up our industrial community produced goods that year valued at about $1.8 billion. By 1890, the capitalization of industry had soared to $6.5 billion, and the annual value of industrial production approached $10 billion. These are simply crude indices of the transformation of the United States in a short 30 years from an essentially agrarian nation to one of the leading industrial nations of the world. This transformation opened up unprecedented opportunities to the poor in America and to those in other parts of the world who were drawn to America in the period of intense industrialization. It also brought undreamed-of wealth to the country at large and to hundreds of individuals who made the concept of the millionaire the hallmark of American progress. On the other hand, it wiped out thousands of individual, independent businesses; and although their owners often started new enterprises, these were likely to be less rewarding in terms of profit and personal satisfaction. Many other former owners were forced to become employees of national corporations, where some found wider scope for their talents while the rest languished in their new and unaccustomed bureaucratic environment.

Accompanying the transformation of American business life in the period from 1860 to 1890 was a 300 per cent rise in nonagricultural employment, compared with a rise of but 50 per cent in the number engaged in agriculture. By 1890, more than 4,600,000 persons worked in American factories, and another 3 million were divided equally between construction industries and transportation. In the last two decades of this 30-year period, the fierceness of business competition, as we have seen, kept the prices of essential commodities falling. At the same time, the wages paid unskilled non-agricultural workers remained virtually fixed at $1.25 to $1.50 a day. Skilled workers were paid twice that and more. Since such fixed money wages could buy more and more goods at progressively falling prices, it would appear that industrial labor was constantly improving its situation. In fact, industrial workers, skilled and unskilled, often were harder hit than the expropriated independent businessmen.

One of the major factors that forced industrial concerns into pools, trusts, and consolidated giant corporations was their inability to keep their expensive machinery going all the time. Translated into the worker's terms, this meant that although his daily rate of pay remained unchanged, the number of days he worked in any year was likely to fluctuate violently. Except for skeleton staffs of highly skilled labor, few industrial workers had job security. After trusts or giant corporations had come into control in many industries, moreover, and had shut down the less efficient plants, they made no provision for the workers who were thereby displaced. Under such conditions, some areas became blighted by more or less permanent unemployment, or by the exodus of workers who could pay the cost of moving to more likely places.

One of the conditions making periodic unemployment a certainty in some industries was the tendency to keep factories in operation for excessively long hours when demand was high. Work-weeks ranging from 60 to over 80 hours were common; and the seven-day week was the rule in steel and paper mills, oil refineries, and other highly mechanized plants. Advances in technology, in turn, accelerated the pace of industrial production, and where this occurred the human worker was expected to keep up. Rapidly operating machines greatly increased the physical danger of factory work, while long hours and fatigue ran up the toll in accidents, injuries, and deaths.

Another consequence of advancing technology was that the machines themselves did more and more of the skilled work. Skilled labor remained in demand in un-

mechanized crafts, in complex machine processes, and in the setting up and maintenance of machines. But in general the old skills gradually were broken down, work tended to become little more than an endless series of identical and monotonous movements devoid of personal satisfaction, and skilled craftsmen were leveled to the status and the pay of the unskilled.

Outside the factory the worker's life was likely to be no happier. Many worked for organizations like the Pullman Company in Chicago or the textile mills of the South, which owned their own towns, required their employees to live in them, and supplied town services at exorbitant rates. The big cities themselves rarely made any provision for the industrial workers that the new factories brought swarming in. Housing, sewerage, water supply, schools, police and fire protection all broke down, and disease, crime, and illiteracy spread steadily (see Chapter 21). Underscoring the brutality of the workers' new environment was the fact that many of them had so recently come from the farms, where sunlight and fresh air were taken for granted, and where fresh fish, meat, and fruit were often to be had simply for the taking.

WORKING ON THE RAILROAD

Work in railroad transportation was freer than work in the factories, but it had its own overpowering hazards. To ameliorate the consequences of these hazards, the skilled workers on the railroads organized the first railroad labor organizations, starting in the 1860's. These were in no sense militant unions, and indeed often were to oppose militancy and unions both.

The principal hazard in railroad work was the demand for speed, which constantly outran the capacity of the roadbeds, the bridges, the rolling stock, and the railroad workers themselves. The result was such a heavy toll in accidents that sound insurance companies rejected railroad workers outright as bad risks. It was principally to establish some means of self-protection and protection for their families that the railroad workers set up their early organizations. Significantly, the constitutions of these "Brotherhoods" and "Orders," as the "Big Four" of organized railroad workers are still called, omitted all reference to collective bargaining. Their members, moreover, paid "premiums," not dues.

The first of the railroad workers' organizations was the Brotherhood of the Footboard—later changed to the Grand International Brotherhood of Locomotive Engineers—founded in Detroit in 1863. Four years later, to enhance their "post-mortem security," the members created their own Mutual Life Insurance Association. In 1868, a handful of Illinois Central men, meeting in Chicago, formed the Order of Railway Conductors to furnish "material aid . . . to disabled members . . . and their widows, children and heirs." In 1873, the day after one of their colleagues had been killed in a boiler explosion on the Erie, eleven "furnace feeders" met at Port Jervis, New York. The first order of business was to collect some money for the dead man's widow; the second, to establish the Brotherhood of Locomotive Firemen to receive and administer compulsory contributions to an insurance fund. The last of the "Big Four," the Brotherhood of Railroad Brakemen of the Western Hemisphere—later, the Brotherhood of Railroad Trainmen—was organized in a caboose on a Delaware and Hudson siding in 1883. Soon it had set up the most elaborate insurance business of all.

Besides loss of life and limbs, railroad workers in train service had other grievances that heightened the hazards of their occupation. As in the factory, these may be grouped under the speed-up and the stretchout, made possible by such technological advances as steel rails, steel-plate boilers, and faster engines, and such managerial advances as consolidations of lines. For the men on the roads these changes simply added up to the necessity of carrying heavier and heavier loads at faster and faster clips over greater and greater dis-

tances. Engineers might be forced to remain at the throttle for 20 to 40 hours of uninterrupted service, with firemen keeping up steam and brakemen staying constantly on the alert. "Our railroads are barbarizing our Trainmen as rapidly as possible," wrote Robert Harris, President of the Burlington, in 1877, "by keeping them unceasingly at work." The sheer physical exhaustion of railroad toil, moreover, was in no way relieved by rising pay. On the contrary, since labor costs made up nearly 65 per cent of railroad operating costs, and since railroad competition was often cutthroat, pay scales were likely to be slashed as the work itself became most taxing and most dangerous. Striking gains in productivity were made by the railroads throughout the post-Civil War period, but where the financial benefits did not go to support the extravagant capital structures of the corporations they were dissipated in extravagant rate wars.

THE GREAT RAILROAD STRIKE OF 1877

Working conditions on the railroads grew so bad during the depression of the 1870's that in 1877 violent strikes spread spontaneously across the country. The stage had been set by local railroad strikes earlier in the depression and by strikes in other industries, notably the famous "Long Strike" among the anthracite coal workers of Pennsylvania, which lasted from January to June, 1875, when hunger forced the miners to capitulate and accept a 20 per cent wage cut.

By 1875, many of the anthracite coal deposits had come under the control of the Philadelphia & Reading Railroad, most of whose traffic involved carrying coal to the factories and homes of Philadelphia and to coaling ships in Philadelphia port. The Philadelphia & Reading had shown the way in breaking the coal strike with Pinkerton detectives; it was also responsible for working up its violent sequel.

For some years before the strike of 1875, the coal regions had been plagued by murders, beatings, and other savagery, widely

534

attributed to the "Molly Maguires," a faction, reputedly, of the Ancient Order of Hibernians, which had been incorporated in Pennsylvania in 1871 as a "humane, charitable, and benevolent" association. A few months after the coal strike, 24 men, most of them members of the broken miners' union, were picked up by the police in the anthracite region, charged with the "Molly Maguire" atrocities, held until tried early in 1876, and then uniformly convicted as charged. Ten of the 24 were summarily hanged, the rest jailed. The evidence that convicted them had been supplied by one of the Reading road's Pinkertons, James McParlan, and supported by other men criminally involved themselves but granted immunity in exchange for their testimony. The evidence remains inconclusive to this day. The purpose behind the arrests and the trials, however, was to smear labor generally with accusations of "riot, sabotage, arson, pillage, assault, robbery, and murder"; and this purpose seemed to have been achieved. Early in 1877, the *Commercial and Financial Chronicle* boasted that "Labor is under control for the first time since the war."

As the impending railroad strikes would soon show, however, the *Chronicle* underestimated both the popular hatred of Vanderbilt, Gould, and company and the depression-fed discontent of the men who moved their trains. At the same time, the strikes revealed how the "Molly Maguire" accusations may well have undermined popular patience with labor violence.

One of the railroad workers' major complaints by mid-1877 was the corporations' practice of blacklisting all who dared join even the timid brotherhoods and orders. Yet the three such associations in existence at the time of the outbreaks kept their hands strictly off the strike. Another complaint was the railroads' aggravation of the speed-up and stretch-out by ordering greater numbers of "doubleheaders"—that is, trains of approximately twice the normal number of cars without added trainmen. The revolt itself, however, was triggered by the announcement late in the spring of 1877 of

further wage cuts. The unled uprising began on July 16, when the firemen on the B. & O. quit work. On July 22, the Baltimore *Sun* said in an editorial:

There is no disguising the fact that the strikers in all their lawful acts have the fullest sympathy of the community. The 10 per cent reduction after two previous reductions was ill advised. . . . The singular part of the disturbance is in the very active part taken by the women, who are the wives and mothers of the firemen. They look famished and wild, and declare for starvation rather than have their people work for reduced wages. Better to starve outright, say they, than to die by slow starvation.

By July 19, the strike had spread to Pittsburgh, where the local militia actually fraternized with the men of the hated Pennsylvania Railroad and fought on their side against federal troops. From the Pennsylvania the strike spread along the Erie and New York Central. Coal miners, stevedores, farmers, small businessmen, and thousands of unemployed—all overflowing with antipathy to the "James boys in frock coats"—joined in demonstrations sympathetic to the workers' cause. Less desirable friends also pitched in, and soon the looting, burning, murder, and mayhem that the respectable elements foresaw became general. The strike disintegrated into a wild, nation-wide melee that quickly turned public-opinion away in horror even from the just cause of the original strikers.

By August 2, after hundreds of strikers and others had been killed and thousands injured, railroad service was forcibly restored on all lines, but not the *status quo ante*. According to one authority, the railway strikes of 1877 "involved the largest number of persons of any labor conflict in the nineteenth century." To a contemporary who survived it, "it seemed as if the whole social and political structure was on the very brink of ruin." To preserve themselves, and by that token to preserve the country, the railroad leaders now demanded that national guardsmen in the states be trained specifically to combat "labor violence" with greater discipline and dispatch. To further such training, many states did in fact appropriate large sums for the expansion of their guards and the construction and equipment of new armories. The railroads, in turn, and many other corporations as well, looked more actively than before to the use of Pinkerton detectives in private armies of their own. The roads also employed the Pinkertons to ferret out all union members, who were promptly fired, and forced new employees to sign "yellow-dog" contracts obliging them to shun union activity.

At the same time, railroad workers themselves grew more militant, and certain factions forsook the brotherhoods to join the broadly based Knights of Labor (see p. 536). When the engineers' Brotherhood did strike vigorously against the Burlington Road in 1888, members of the Knights' faction signed on as strikebreakers in retaliation for Brotherhood scab activity against them during a conflict with the Reading shortly before. Such intramural hostility frustrated those who saw their best chance in united effort. By the time of the Burlington strike the men in the railroad shops and yards had organized craft unions of their own and some steps were taken to coordinate their activities with those of the train service brotherhoods. But railroad labor was to remain torn even during the great Pullman strike of 1894 (see p. 537), while the antagonism of the white-collar public to strikes and violence hardened. Labor had patrician and middle-class allies who sought through legislation and other means to bring about reforms like the eight-hour day, workman's compensation for industrial accidents, mandatory safety measures, and recognition of labor's right to engage in collective bargaining. Yet many decades elapsed before such gains were realized.

UNIONIZATION
AND INDUSTRIAL WARFARE

We have already described how the panics of 1837 and 1857 brought about the collapse of the *national* labor organizations of their day. After the Civil War, a number of new efforts were made to organize labor nationally, of which two (before the advent of the A.F.L. in 1886) are worth noting. The first was the National Labor Union formed in Baltimore in 1866 by delegates from local labor organizations and reform groups. In 1872, this union grew ambitious enough to form a Labor Reform party and to run a presidential candidate. Most of its other efforts were as impractical as this one, however, and although at one time it claimed a membership of nearly 650,000 it failed to survive the crash of 1873.

As miscellaneous in its membership and as unfocused in its aims was the Noble Order of the Knights of Labor, organized in 1869 by Uriah S. Stephens, a Philadelphia tailor. The Knights' principal aim was to unite the whole country—except for liquor dealers, lawyers, gamblers ,and bankers—into one big union to engage in the production and distribution of goods on a cooperative rather than a capitalistic basis. The Noble Order made little headway until Terence V. Powderly, a Scranton, Pennsylvania, machinist, became "Grand Master" in 1878. An energetic organizer, Powderly traveled all over the country recruiting enthusiasts for the cooperative idea and established more than 30 cooperative enterprises under the Knights' auspices. Although Powderly opposed strikes and violence, a successful strike of certain unions affiliated with the Knights against Jay Gould's Missouri Pacific Railroad in 1885 forced Gould to rescind a wage cut and rehire hundreds of union men he had fired. This victory so raised the Knights' standing that within a year membership grew from 100,000 to more than 700,000.

Powderly soon had reason to believe that nonviolence was the best policy after all. On "May Day," 1886, Knights of Labor unions and other groups sponsored a massive demonstration to promote the eight-hour day. In Chicago, where a strike against the McCormick Harvester Company was in progress, the demonstration was followed by outdoor meetings addressed by anarchists. At a meeting in Haymarket Square on May 3, a bomb thrown at the police killed an officer. Seven more policemen and four civilians were killed in a riot that followed. The bomb-thrower never was found, but seven anarchists were sentenced to death for murder after a farcical trial and four were executed. One committed suicide. The sentence of the other two soon was changed to life imprisonment, and six years later, accusing the sentencing judge of "malicious ferocity," Illinois Governor John P. Altgeld unconditionally pardoned them.

The Haymarket riot outraged the general public, and although the Knights of Labor had had nothing to do with it, skilled workers within the organization began to desert in large numbers. The organization suffered also from growing internal dissension, and in a few years it shrank almost to extinction.

The American Federation of Labor was an entirely different kind of national labor organization. Its members were not workers as such, but national craft unions affiliated together. The A.F.L. imposed certain standards on its members. It insisted on their collecting regular dues to provide themselves and the federation (which took a share) with strike funds in advance of need. It required members to hire full-time organizers. It undertook to settle all issues of jurisdiction that arose when two or more member unions tried to organize workers in similar fields, and it sought to protect its members from raids by non-affiliated rivals.

The A.F.L., under the leadership of Samuel Gompers, had no political aspirations and little faith in reform legislation. Its dominating aim was to force business to engage in collective bargaining with member unions on such everyday issues as wages, hours, and working conditions. An essential goal was the establishment of the "closed shop"—that is, a shop that would agree to employ only members of A.F.L. affiliates. Gradually, initiation fees were pushed up in order to give the A.F.L. complete control over certain crafts by virtually closing entry to them. But this was a later development. At first, the federation aimed to expand rather than restrict its membership.

Between 1886 and 1892, the A.F.L.

gained the affiliation of unions with some 250,000 members. Progress in making collective-bargaining agreements also was satisfactory. One of the feathers in Gompers' cap was a contract negotiated with the Carnegie Steel Company in 1890. In 1892 and 1894, however, the A.F.L. became involved in two violent and losing strikes which retarded union progress.

The first of these strikes was incited by the Carnegie Steel Company itself when, with Carnegie in Europe, President Henry Clay Frick tried to cut wages. The Amalgamated Association of Iron and Steel Workers, an A.F.L. member, refused to accede to Frick's proposal, and on July 1, 1892, Frick anticipated a walkout by closing down the great Homestead plant and hiring 300 Pinkerton detectives to protect it. When the Pinkertons arrived by barge on July 6, they were overwhelmed by an army of angry workers. Frick then requested the governor of Pennsylvania to call out the state militia to preserve order. Only after five months did the workers begin to go back to their jobs on company terms. But by then they had lost more than the strike. Public sympathy had been with them at first; but when an anarchist, who had nothing to do with the strike tried to assassinate Frick, unionist sentiment declined.

The second strike began two years later at the Pullman Company town near Chicago but soon spread to most of the western railroads. With the onset of the depression in 1893, the Pullman Company began discharging workers and cutting the pay of those kept on by as much as 25 per cent. In May, 1894, the workers asked for some reduction in company rents and store prices. They were refused and their negotiators were summarily fired. The workers then walked out and appealed for help to the American Railway Union, which many of them had joined. This was the union of all levels of railroad workers that Eugene V. Debs had begun to organize in August,

1893, when he found the individual railroad craft unions inadequate to fight the roads. Debs' union was fresh from a victory over Jim Hill and the Great Northern and was eager to tackle the Pullman Company. On Pullman's refusal to arbitrate with Debs late in June, 1894, 120,000 railroad workers joined the Pullman strikers and the western roads were paralyzed. On July 1, Debs thought he had won the strike. The railroads' "immediate resources were exhausted," he wrote, "and they were unable to operate their trains." All this was accomplished with "no sign of violence or disorder."

The very next day, however, the outlook changed. The General Managers Association, an employer organization representing all the railroads terminating in Chicago, had earlier appealed to Attorney-General Richard Olney for federal troops to get the trains running. Olney, a former railroad lawyer himself, was more than willing to oblige. When restrained for the time being by President Cleveland, he proceeded, on July 2 and 3, to get a series of "blanket" injunctions in federal courts in states affected by the strike enjoining the union and "all other persons whomsoever" to desist from virtually every kind of activity impeding railroad operation, even "persuasion" of workers to quit their jobs. With the federal injunctions issued, Olney, by July 3, had gathered the first of thousands of federal marshals in the Chicago area to see that the injunctions were obeyed. Their presence soon provoked a crowd to the first violence in the strike. An exaggerated report of this affair moved Cleveland to send in federal troops, beginning on July 4. Mobs of workers responded by burning railroad cars and cargoes. Incensed by federal troops in his state without invitation from the governor, as the Constitution required, Governor Altgeld now poured in his own militia and by July 10 there were 14,000 soldiers in Chicago and on the railroads' right of way. In twenty states the national guard had been mobilized, and many American Railway Union members were arrested.

On July 10, moreover, Debs himself and three other union officers were indicted for conspiracy in restraint of trade under the Sherman Anti-Trust Act (see p. 557) and on other grounds; were arrested; and then were released on bail. A week later they were picked up once more, this time on charges of contempt of court for disobeying the original federal injunctions. The harassment of the union leaders soon disorganized the strikers and their boycott of the railroads collapsed. The American Railway Union itself disintegrated, and such Pullman workers as the company would rehire straggled back to work under the old conditions in August and September. In December, the United States Circuit Court convicted Debs of the contempt charge and sentenced him to six months in jail. This sentence was upheld in May, 1895 by the Supreme Court in the case of *In re Debs*.

The decision in this case had momentous consequences for organized labor. Heretofore, many injunctions had been issued and sustained in labor cases, but only on the grounds of strikes being *criminal* conspiracies against the public under the common law. These grounds were wholly unsatisfactory to employers who were forced to proceed through long and uncertain jury trials to make the criminal charges stick. By then, strike damage probably was complete and the strike over. In *In re Debs,* the Supreme Court placed labor injunctions under equity, not criminal, proceedings, thereby permitting civil courts in the future to issue them in order to *forestall* a public nuisance or *prevent* damage to property. This new doctrine gave employers a remedy against strikes and boycotts at their very outset. Even if an equity injunction were indefensible or merely temporary, it usually was enough to kill organized labor action before labor leaders could get the injunction set aside or quashed. On the other hand, if they chose to ignore such injunctions they became immediately vulnerable to the full penalties for contempt of court regardless of the legality or illegality of any strike activity. Henceforth, blanket injunctions became the most widely used and effective weapons against strikes and other militant union activity until outlawed by the Norris-LaGuardia anti-injunction act of 1932.

The Homestead strike and the Pullman strike disclosed the chasm that was opening up between big corporate business on the one hand and the mass of workers on the other. Yet for all the prominence given to labor warfare and labor organization, the vast majority of workers in the factories remained unorganized and docile. By 1898, their number had soared to more than 17 million. Yet of this vast number, a mere 500,000 were members of labor unions.

One of the most vigorous early efforts to enlarge the ranks of organized labor was the formation in Chicago in 1905 of the Industrial Workers of the World—the menacing "Wobblies"—under the leadership of "Big Bill" Hayward of the Western Federation of Miners. Like the A.F.L., the "Wobblies" believed in direct economic action to improve the workers' condition. Unlike that of the A.F.L., its direct action was of the revolutionary "syndicalist" brand. Like the old Knights of Labor, the I.W.W. wanted to abolish the wage system; unlike the Knights with their cooperatives, the "Wobblies" meant to gain their economic ends by the violent abolition of the state and the creation of a nationwide industrial syndicate directed by the workers themselves. Most of their recruits were unskilled migratory workers in the West, engaged in lumbering, mining, fruit-growing, dock labor, and similar rough occupations. But the "Wobblies" also moved east, especially into the oppressive textile industry where, in 1912, they won one of the bloodiest strikes in labor annals, in Lawrence, Massachusetts. This success marked the peak of "Wobbly" influence. In 1913 they had a hand in the strikes of textile workers in Paterson, New Jersey, and of rubber workers in Akron, Ohio; but both strikes ended in utter failure. Under the growing pressure of patriotism and conformity after the entry of the United States into World War I, the I.W.W. came increasingly under vigilante attack and federal prosecution and waned as a force in the labor movement.

THE INDUSTRIAL IMMIGRANT

In the decades after the Civil War, with the new industrial giants like Rockefeller and Carnegie as their models, American farm boys swarmed into the cities with the expectation of working just a few years in the factories before scaling the heights of enterprise on their own. In Europe a similar movement from rural to urban life was under way, of which the migration of millions to the cities of the United States was but a part (see Chapter 21).

The belief in individual opportunity no doubt accounted for much of the indifference of American workers to the attempts of unions to recruit them into their ranks. Another cause of indifference was the farm boys' complete ignorance of such ideas as organization and institutional discipline. A third factor was that opportunity of a kind usually did exist: a sweeper or shoveler, if he behaved himself, might rise to be a machine operator, an operator to be a foreman, a foreman to be a section superintendent. Another major factor was the steady introduction of foreigners into factory work.

European immigration to the United States reached its nineteenth-century peak in 1882, when almost 640,000 newcomers were admitted (see p. 571). Swelling the tide that year were the all-time record arrivals of Germans (250,600) and Scandinavians (105,300), and a total from Great Britain (103,000) that was exceeded in only two other years and then by just a few thousand. Immigration was not resumed on a rising scale until after the turn of the twentieth century, and in the decade that ended with the outbreak of World War I in 1914 it broke all previous records. But by that time, it was made up largely of people from areas that had sent very few emigrants to the United States during the nineteenth century (see Chapter 21). The year 1882 is a kind of watershed between the "old immigration" from Britain, Germany, and western Europe, and the "new immigration" from central and southeastern Europe.

The old immigration had had its quota of illiterates and had supplied much of the unskilled labor for American industry and for mining and construction crews; but it had also included millions of farmers and large numbers of skilled artisans, businessmen, and professional men, who tended to travel on to the rising cities of America's "inland empire." The new immigration was made up of poorer people, less well educated, who were often coralled in Europe by tricky American agents of industry, land-grant railroads, and steamship companies, and then victimized after they had landed in the incredible, bewildering world of the United States. By 1910, such immigrants, plus Negroes migrating from the South, made up two-thirds of the workers in 21 major branches of American industry.

Each new influx—first the Irish and the Germans, and later the Italians, Poles, Hungarians, and others—tended to start at the bottom only to be pushed upward by less experienced newcomers. Gradually native American workers monopolized the top of the "blue shirt" hierarchy and found it distasteful to unite with the immigrants in common action against common grievances. Most immigrants themselves shrank from the comradeship of unions and clung to their own communities and churches.

The conditions of the immigrants' life often made them hostile to the American institutions around them, which seemed to offer no protection and no way out. This hostility, in turn, was gradually reciprocated by the Americans over whom the irresistible tide of immigration soon swept. Many circumstances fed the agitation for immigrant exclusion (see Chapter 26), to which organized labor and organized industry contributed heavily. Organized labor was determined that American jobs be held for American workers; whatever the unorganized optimists in the labor force might think of American opportunity, the organized firmly believed in holding on to what they had. In 1885 the Knights of Labor had succeeded in getting Congress to forbid the importation of contract laborers after Hungarians and Italians had been brought in under contract the previous year to be used as strike-breakers. Businessmen joined the agitation for immigration restriction after measuring the gains of having an unrestricted supply of new workers against the costs of such "foreign ideas" as socialism and anarchism, which seemed to be spreading in the depression years of the 1890's and with which all immigrants were supposed to be infected.

The agitation for immigration restriction took many forms but it was not until well into the twentieth century that general restriction was successfully imposed by Congress. Until that time, the United States seemed to have prospered as no other nation in history under the policy of free entry that had been hers since the Revolution and that had settled the colonies long before independence had been won.

Readings

Asterisk indicates that book is available in paperback.

E. C. Kirkland, *Industry Comes of Age, Business, Labor and Public Policy, 1860-1897* (1961), offers an expert, comprehensive examination of the American economy of the period. Other general accounts of value include I. M. Tarbell, *The Nationalizing of Business 1878-1898* (1936); and T. C. Cochran and William Miller, *The Age of Enterprise* * (1942). D. A. Wells, *Recent Economic Changes* (1890), is a most illuminating contemporary account. Sigmund Diamond, ed., *The Nation Transformed: The Creation of Industrial Society* (1963), is a rewarding anthology of contemporary material. Roger Burlingame, *Engines of Democracy* (1940), stresses invention and technology. Matthew Josephson, *The Robber Barons* * (1934), reflecting more of the spirit of the 1930's than the 1880's, nevertheless is useful. See also S. H. Holbrook, *The Age of the Moguls* (1953).

Ray Ginger, *Age of Excess, American Life from the End of Reconstruction to World War I* (1965), ably places the thrust of business enterprise in its social context.

Richard Hofstadter, *Social Darwinism in American Thought* * (rev. ed., 1955), is a comprehensive introduction. Sidney Fine, *Laissez Faire and the General-Welfare State, A Study of Conflict in American Thought, 1865-1901* * (1956), examines conservative thought and action. E. C. Kirkland, ed., *The Gospel of Wealth and Other Timely Essays by Andrew Carnegie* * (1962), affords a good selection of Carnegie's writings. A more elaborate anthology is Moses Rischin, ed., *The American Gospel of Success, Individualism and Beyond* (1965). Thorstein Veblen, *Absentee Ownership* (1923), is an excellent introduction to Veblen's work. E. C. Kirkland, *Dream and Thought in the Business Community, 1860-1900* * (1956) is an interesting complement to the third volume of Joseph Dorfman, *The Economic Mind in American Civilization* (1949).

The best biography of Cornelius Vanderbilt is W. J. Lane, *Commodore Vanderbilt* (1942). Julius Grodinsky, *Jay Gould: His Business Career, 1867-1892* (1957), supplies much illuminating information. On the transcontinentals, see R. R. Riegel, *The Story of the Western Railroads* * (1926); Oscar Lewis, *The Big Four* (1951); Stuart Daggett, *Chapters on the History of the Southern Pacific* (1922); and R. W. Fogel, *The Union Pacific Railroad, A Case in Premature Enterprise* (1960). For the details of railroad manipulation and consolidation see Stuart Daggett, *Railroad Reorganization* (1908), and E. G. Campbell, *The Reorganization of the American Railroad System, 1893-1900* (1938). Two books by W. Z. Ripley merit special study: *Railroads: Rates and Regulation* (1912), and *Railroads: Finance and Organization* (1915). T. C. Cochran, *Railroad Leaders 1845-1890: The Business Mind in Action* (1953), admirably fulfills its subtitle. A. D. Chandler, Jr., *The Railroads* * (1965), is an illuminating anthology of primary sources.

H. F. Williamson and others, *The American Petroleum Industry 1859-1899: The Age of Illumination* (1959), and *The American Petroleum Industry 1899-1959: The Age of Energy* (1963), are the best accounts of the oil industry. Allan Nevins, *John D. Rockefeller* (2 vols., 1954 ed.) is authoritative. I. M. Tarbell, *The History of the Standard Oil Company* (one-vol. ed., 1950) is excellent on the spirit of the early oilmen. Three books, none wholly satisfactory, tell the story of Andrew Carnegie: his *Autobiography* (1920); J. H. Bridge, *The Inside History of the Carnegie Steel Company* (1903); and the official biography, B. J. Hendrick, *The Life of Andrew Carnegie* (2 vols., 1932). Herbert Casson, *The Romance of Steel* (1907), is useful. Matthew Josephson, *Edison* * (1959), is the best biography. See also A. A. Bright, Jr., *The Electric-Lamp Industry* (1949), and H. C. Passer, *The Electrical Manufacturers, 1875-1900* (1953).

Rendigs Fels, *American Business Cycles, 1865-1897* (1959), is an outstanding analysis. On Morgan and the other bankers see Lewis Corey, *The House of Morgan* (1930); G. W. Edwards, *The Evolution of Finance Capitalism* (1938), and F. L. Allen, *The Great Pierpont Morgan* (1949). John Moody, *The Truth about the Trusts* (1904), is indispensable.

The standard work on labor history is J. R. Commons and others, *History of Labor in the United States* (4 vols., 1918-35). A first-rate survey is J. G. Rayback, *A History of American Labor* (1959). N. J. Ware, *The Labor Movement in the United States, 1860-1895* * (1929), deals largely with the Knights of Labor. T. V. Powderly, *Thirty Years of Labor* (1889) and *The Path I Trod* (1940), are autobiographical accounts by the "Grand Master" of the Knights. On the formation of the A.F.L. see Samuel Gompers, *Seventy Years of Life and Labor* (2 vols., 1925). A useful biography of Eugene V. Debs is Ray Ginger, *The Bending Cross* * (1949). W. G. Broehl, Jr., *The Molly Maguires* (1964), is excellent. On the great railroad strike, see R. V. Bruce, *1877: Year of Violence* (1959). Henry David, *History of the Haymarket Affair* * (1936), is justifiably the standard account. On the Homestead Strike, see Leon Wolff, *Lockout: The Story of the Homestead Strike of 1892* (1965). See Readings for Chapter 21 for the industrial immigrant.

CHAPTER TWENTY

In his famous *Education,* Henry Adams
wrote of the politics of the Gilded Age:
"One might search the whole list of Congress, judiciary, and executive during the
twenty-five years 1870 to 1896 and find
little but damaged reputations. The period
was poor in purpose and barren in results."

The verdict of history, however, may be
less harsh or at least less one-sided than
this contemporary assessment. Callous and
corrupt, politics was also critical and creative. Henry Adams' 25 years were the
heyday of the political machine, the spoils
system, the protective tariff lobby. But they
were also the period of the Granger and
Populist movements, of the beginnings of

Stalwarts
under Stress

civil-service reform and public regulation of big business. In these years, as President Garfield's Attorney-General, Wayne Mac-Veagh said, in attempting to explain the voters' apathy in 1884, "the average American citizen care[d] very little about politics . . . because the government . . . touch[ed] his life very rarely, and only at points of very little importance to him." Yet Mac-Veagh himself was one of the many Americans who long since had turned with anger and action against the advantage taken of public apathy by the Stalwart party machines. In the next generation there were to be enough insurgents like him to topple the Stalwarts from power.

I. *Regulars and Reformers*

THE BEDROCK OF PARTY LOYALTY

The poverty of political issues following the Reconstruction settlement of the mid-1870's is suggested by the success of the Republican party in living for decades off the issues of the fading past. Fully exploiting the advantages of being the party of Lincoln, of the Civil War victory, and of

543

the Union, the Republican managers continued to wave the bloody shirt, to keep the wounds of the rebellion open, and to belabor the Democrats as the party of treason. Through such appeals the Republicans were able to hold the allegiance of many citizens outside the South, not least the many veterans of the Union armies organized in the G.A.R. (see p. 465). As the party of high tariffs, liberal aid to railroads, and, for the greater part, sound money, the Republicans had the support of substantial numbers of industrialists. The eastern and western wings of the party occasionally clashed over economic issues, and the party was riven by the feud between the Stalwart regulars and less cynical Halfbreeds (see p. 478). But it usually managed to compromise its differences and act in a reasonably well-disciplined manner.

The Democrats, despite the treason label plastered on them by their rivals, offered strong opposition. After the collapse of the carpetbag governments, they dominated the South. They also developed powerful machines in the great cities of the North where Irish bosses in particular proved able organizers of the swarming immigrant population. The Democrats had less support from industry than the Republicans, but they attracted other segments of business, especially merchants and commercial bankers who most keenly felt the constraints on trade of tariff and railroad abuses. The so-called "Bourbon," or conservative, Democrats of the South and Midwest joined with these eastern conservatives to hold down for the most part the more radical sections of the party in the more distant West.

The Democrats lost control of the presidency when Lincoln was elected in 1860 and did not regain it until the election of Cleveland in 1884. Yet the two parties retained almost equal strength throughout the last three decades of the nineteenth century. In no election from 1876 to 1896 was the winning side's share of the popular vote greater than 50.8 per cent. In two elections, 1876 and 1888, the Republican candidate won with fewer popular votes than his Democratic rival. In the thirteen Congresses elected between 1870 and 1894, moreover, the Democrats controlled the House nine times. Such balanced voting put the politicians on their mettle.

High-minded persons were unhappy with the political parties of the Gilded Age because they seemed to be little more than unprincipled machines clawing each other for the spoils of victory—jobs for loyal party workers and graft from business supplicants for political favors. "The cohesive force" in American political parties, James Bryce observed in 1888, "is the desire for office and for office as a means of gain." "It is like a fight of wolves over a carcass," wrote Secretary of the Navy, John D. Long, ten years later. "Shameful and disgraceful picture: that a Senator of the United States should be running his legs off, wasting his time, when great questions are at stake, about this carrion of patronage."

Nevertheless, by then "great questions" had been at issue for some time—questions of economic development, the proper role of government, the force of plutocracy, the future of democracy. It may be true that for a generation after the Civil War and Reconstruction the American public, still acutely aware of the disastrous confrontation of stiffly principled men and strongly principled parties, was content to hear little about "great questions." Yet politics was not wholly devoid of stirring controversies over money, tariffs, trusts, railroads, and reform of the party system itself. For some time such controversies remained sharper inside party organizations than between them; and since conservatives in both parties usually emerged victorious, they presented to the public an undifferentiated front. For this reason campaign debates, especially in national presidential contests where sectional and local issues were smothered, awakened little interest. Yet there were soon to be determined sectional and local party revolts.

THE DIVIDED COUNSELS
OF REFORM

Conservatives could more readily dominate the parties because their opponents so often were divided. Advocates of such special panaceas as Henry George's "single tax" (see p. 594) aroused wide intellectual interest in the cities but had little political impact even there. Monetary reformers who sought the cure-all for rural economic ills in currency inflation won larger political followings, but only in isolated sections of the country. The Grangers (see p. 553), who advocated more varied solutions to the farmers' problems, actually gained some political victories, but again these were regional, notably in a few midwestern states, and short-lived. Much of their strength, moreover, was sapped by internal controversies over political versus direct action, as in the establishment of cooperatives, and over relations with such other reform groups as labor unions. The unions, in turn, were riven by their own internal differences (see p. 537). All such reformers together, moreover, were confronted by the prevailing doctrines of Social Darwinism and laissez faire, which offered powerful intellectual deterrents to political interference with the individual and his social institutions. Yet the economy had become a national unit with political assistance in such critical areas as railroad building and protective tariffs, and reformers complained most bitterly of the abuse of political power by its business beneficiaries.

In the Gilded Age these demands were most effectively voiced by those called "Mugwumps" by their enemies, and the fragmentation in reform ranks was only heightened by Mugwump fears that all other reformers were "radicals."

Mugwumps got their name from an Indian word meaning "chief," used derisively by Republican regulars to designate overly independent party members too fastidious for Stalwart tastes. Mugwump spokesmen

included E. L. Godkin, editor of *The Nation;* George W. Curtis, editor of *Harper's Weekly;* and Henry and Brooks Adams, scions of two presidents who felt shut out of their rightful heritage of power by vulgarians.

In many respects the Mugwumps were more conservative than the regulars, devout reformers though they were. They especially despised the aggressive new plutocrats and the masses of immigrants who worked for them. In politics, the bosses who did these plutocrats' business, and the patronage system that kept the bosses in power, came under their severest attack. The Mugwumps tried to sustain older ideals of political morality and of the sacredness of the public trust. But they were so stuffy about it that although they drew a following among solid citizens, they had slight appeal for the mass of American voters. Their fastidiousness, in turn, diluted what little native talent they may have had for political organization. Dorman B. Eaton, a well-meaning and well-known Mugwump reformer, expressed an attitude common in his group when he wrote, concerning New York City machine politics: "There are whole election districts in the city so degraded that hardly a Republican will reside there. [It is] the very worst—the very nadir of civilization—where the highest party principles and the spoils system—the machine and the gin-shops . . . are much the same." And yet the Mugwump types soon did help to improve the tone of party politics and to constrain and eventually to overturn the Stalwarts.

II. *The Republican Presidential Years*

HAYES IN OFFICE

By the time of the presidential election of 1876, as we have seen (p. 478), the Republican party had been so blackened by the scandals of Grant's adminis-

tration on the national level and the Democratic party by such scandals as those of Boss Tweed in New York on the local level that each already felt obliged to name a proven reformer as its candidate. Rutherford B. Hayes, the victor over the Democrat, Tilden, had run on a campaign promise of "thorough, radical, and complete" political housecleaning. True to his character as an honest man and as a political square-shooter, he tried to fulfill his promise on taking office in March, 1877. Hayes did the best he could. But the times, and the intransigence of the Stalwarts, whom the times protected, thwarted him. The frauds surrounding his own election (see p. 479), were to make him so vulnerable that his Republican as well as his Democratic enemies called him "Rutherfraud," and "His Fraudulency."

In choosing his Cabinet, Hayes boldly ignored the old gang of patronage dispensers and appointed honest and capable men. In his inaugural address he was outspoken about the need for a permanent federal civil service beyond the reach of thieves and grafters and hungry party hacks. To show that he meant business, he courageously named the Liberal-Republican civil-service reformer, Carl Schurz, as his Secretary of the Interior. The principal center of the spoils system was the New York Customs House, its major domo that Stalwart of Stalwarts, Roscoe Conkling, who had been New York's "favorite son" at the convention that nominated Hayes. With the aid of his able new Secretary of the Treasury, the Republican Halfbreed, John Sherman, Hayes succeeded in dislodging Conkling's minions, but not for long. It was a simple matter for the New Yorker to rally many good Republicans to defy Hayes' order forbidding federal office-holders to manage political organizations or to collect "assessments for political purposes." Such party men agreed with Conkling's view of reformers: "They forget that parties are not built up by deportment, or by ladies' magazines, or gush!"

The Democrats naturally took full advantage of Republican disunity and especially in Congress worked tirelessly to discredit Hayes and his administration, but with little success. One of Hayes' own most important victories was the forestalling of Democratic efforts to repeal the Force Act of 1870, designed to strengthen the protection of Negro voting rights (see p. 480). When the Democrats attached repeal measures as riders to appropriation bills on seven occasions, Hayes responded with seven vetoes and ultimately compelled Congress to pass the appropriations without riders.

The President's aggressive handling of the railroad strike of 1877 (see p. 534) met with no opposition from Congress. When four state governors begged Hayes for federal troops, he felt it his constitutional duty to oblige. Only once before, during Jackson's administration, had federal forces intervened in a struggle between private industry and its employees, and Hayes took this fateful step with some misgivings. He shared none of the vindictiveness of the anti-labor people who applauded his action, although he had only the simplest notions about the causes of the social unrest that marked the early part of his administration.

Hayes' veto in 1879 of a bill restricting the number of Chinese passengers on ships bound for the United States was also widely interpreted as an anti-labor gesture. Although the President disapproved of the Chinese "labor invasion" that had been stimulated by mining and railroad corporations, he felt that the bill violated the spirit of the Burlingame Treaty of 1868 with China, which gave Chinese unlimited immigration rights. Workingmen's parties in the West condemned him, but Hayes followed the correct diplomatic procedure of negotiating a new treaty with China in 1880 that gave the United States the privilege of regulating or suspending Chinese immigration. In 1882, Congress closed off Chinese immigration for ten years.

THE MANIPULATION
OF MONEY

In currency matters Hayes lived up to his reputation as a hard-money man. From the 1860's onward, a great debate raged, often ferociously, over federal monetary policies. Ranged against the farmers in the South and West, chronic debtors, were the conservative creditors in the industrial East and the gradually industrializing older Middle West. The status of the greenbacks issued by the federal government during the Civil War (see p. 435) heightened the monetary conflict. Of the $450 million in greenbacks issued, by 1868 almost $100 million had been retired (see p. 468) and the rest had risen significantly in value. In 1869, in the case of *Hepburn* v. *Griswold* the Supreme Court decided belatedly that Congress could not simply declare paper money legal tender when it had no gold behind it—as Congress had done in 1862 and 1863 when it first created the greenbacks. This decision sent the value of the greenbacks fluttering downward. Then, in 1871, the Court reversed itself. In the Legal Tender Cases of that year (*Knox* v. *Lee* and *Parker* v. *Davis*), it said Congress *could* declare paper money legal tender.

Congress also manipulated the currency. Early in the depression of the 1870's (see p. 529), when debtors were scrambling for currency with which to fend off their equally hard-pressed creditors, Congress yielded to public pressure with a bill returning enough greenbacks to circulation to bring their face value up to $400 million. But Grant tried to keep the volume of currency stable by vetoing the bill. In 1875, with the emergency over, Congress recovered from its lapse. That year, after a decade of agitation, it passed the Resumption Act under which, for the first time since the war, the government became obliged to resume paying specie on demand for all its paper currency, greenbacks included. This action soon placed the greenbacks on a par with gold-backed paper. The act also required the government to resume withdrawal of greenbacks on January 1, 1879, until the amount in circulation was stabilized at $300 million.

Hayes had strongly backed the Resumption Act of 1875 when he was governor of Ohio. In 1877 his Secretary of the Treasury, John Sherman, began to build up a gold supply to pay for the retirement of the greenbacks beginning in 1879. Returns from the sale of bonds raised the gold reserve, and so did a favorable trade balance made possible by bumper Ameri-

can harvests and European crop failures. Even before 1879, the greenback, which had sunk as low as 38 cents in terms of gold dollars during the war, was worth 100 cents, and on January 1 of that year, with $200 million worth of gold in the Treasury representing a solid bullion backing for the paper currency, no one bothered to redeem his greenbacks.

To the agricultural producers who comprised a majority of the population, the Resumption Act simply meant costlier dollars, even if made of paper, and hence lower prices. Not content with the fact that the actual circulation of greenbacks had not been curtailed, farm groups began to agitate for new issues of them. Their hopes were supported by the nascent Greenback party which reached its high point in the elections of 1878 when, in conjunction with dissident labor groups, it elected 14 congressmen. The revival of trade the next year boosted farm prices and the party declined thereafter.

Another cheap-money panacea had begun to gather strength during Hayes' administration: the movement for the unlimited coinage of silver. In 1834, Congress had fixed the ratio of silver to gold in the dollar at 16 to 1—that is to say, there was 16 times as much silver by weight in the silver dollar as there was gold in the gold dollar. Until 1849, this ratio adequately reflected the value of the two metals, but the flood of gold mined during the gold rush (see p. 498) reduced its value to the point where the 16 to 1 ratio undervalued silver. Owners of silver found it more profitable to sell it on the open market as a metal than to present it to the mint for coinage. So no one protested when Congress adopted a new law in 1873 terminating the minting of silver dollars.

Had the price of silver not fallen sharply after 1873, the demand to restore the coinage of silver might never have arisen. The discovery of new western deposits of silver and new refining methods, however, soon lowered its price. By 1878, the old ratio of 16 to 1 clearly undervalued gold and it became worth while again to offer silver for coinage. On discovering the law against coining silver, the inflationists now charged a sinister group of bankers with engineering the "Crime of '73," as they branded the coinage act of that year. They immediately launched their campaign for the "Crime's" repeal.

The first important test for the silverites came in November, 1877, when Richard ("Silver Dick") Bland of Missouri introduced a bill in the House for the unlimited coinage of silver at 16 to 1. The silver dollar at this time was worth about 89 cents and was dropping in value. Bankers warned Hayes that the passage of the Bland Bill (which would permit the debtor to pay his creditor in depreciated currency) amounted to debt repudiation and that capitalists would never buy government bond issues in gold if silver became legal tender. Hayes agreed, but he knew that if he vetoed the bill Congress would override him. He was rescued from his dilemma when the original Bland Bill was quietly emasculated in the Senate by Iowa's smooth-talking William Allison. The amended Bland-Allison Bill (passed in 1878 over Hayes' veto) substituted "limited" for "unlimited" coinage of silver. It required the Treasury to buy not less than $2 million and not more than $4 million worth of silver every month. These controlled silver purchases neither drove gold out of circulation nor raised prices. And so matters rested for 12 years (see p. 556).

THE ELECTION OF 1880

Hayes had surrendered whatever chance he may have had for domination over the cruder elements in the party when he announced soon after his nomination that he would serve only one term. By 1879 his old enemy, Conkling, had reasserted his authority over party hacks who saw nothing to gain in following a lame duck President. With other Stalwart leaders Conkling began plotting to revive the pliable Grant for a third term. "Blaine from Maine" and John Sherman of Ohio also made themselves available for the Republican candidacy.

Slipshod management at the Republican national convention in Chicago in June, 1880, cost the Stalwarts their chance to put Grant over. At the same time, James A. Garfield, the veteran Ohio congressman, so brilliantly managed the campaign of his fellow Ohioan, Sherman, that he won even the support of the Grant men as the "dark horse" to break the deadlock that had developed between Sherman and Blaine. To appease the Stalwart faction and mortar over the cracks that had widened in party unity before facing the Democrats in the fall, the delegates then rallied behind Chester A. Arthur of New York for the vice-presidency. Arthur, Conkling's leading henchman, had been made Collector of the Port of New York by Grant in 1871 and held the job until 1878 when Hayes threw him out for violating an executive order prohibiting federal administrators from pursuing party work. The candidates chosen, the delegates proceeded to frame a platform boldy declaring for veterans' pensions and Chinese exclusion, but pussyfooting on civil-service reform, the protective tariff, and other meaningful issues.

Three weeks later the Democrats met in Cincinnati and shrewdly named as their standard-bearer one of the heroes of the Battle of Gettysburg, Winfield Scott Hancock of Pennsylvania. Hancock was described as "a good man weighing 250 pounds." Futile politically, he nevertheless came close to winning. Garfield squeaked into office with a plurality of only 9,464 votes out of almost 9 million cast. His large electoral majority—214 to Hancock's 155—was the result of narrow victories in two pivotal states, Indiana and New York, which had been carried by Republican discipline and plenty of hard cash.

After the election, Conkling and his friends expected recognition for their pains, but the new President, who had reached the top after a brilliant Civil War career and an arduous apprenticeship in the House, was a man of some delicacy who

The Bosses of the Senate, a Keppler cartoon, 1889.

had an instinctive dislike for the coarse-grained professionals. He disapproved of Grant, and he broke with Conkling immediately after his inauguration by giving the most lucrative patronage post in the United States, Chester Arthur's old position as the Collector of the Port of New York, to an anti-Conkling Republican, W. H. Robertson. Pressure on behalf of Conkling's prerogatives by other senators did not budge Garfield, and by holding up all other New York appointments he forced a balky Senate to confirm his own man. Conkling and the junior senator from New York, Thomas Platt, then took the extraordinary step of resigning their Senate seats. Their strategy was then to go to Albany to win vindication from the state legislature. But the New York legislators shilly-shallied and finally refused to re-elect them. This startling denouement marked the beginning of the end for the Stalwarts.

James G. Blaine, rewarded with the prestigeful post of Secretary of State, was more than pleased with Garfield's firm conduct and looked forward to an auspicious administration. This hope was dashed in July, 1881, when Garfield was shot down as he entered the Washington railroad depot by a mentally unbalanced Chicago lawyer, Charles Guiteau, who had failed to get a European consulship. Garfield died two months later and Arthur succeeded to the presidency. Although he dutifully filled his Cabinet with Stalwarts, his administration saw the beginning of civil-service reform that eventually sucked out the marrow of Stalwart rule.

THE "CHIEF EVIL"

Civil-service reform was not merely one issue among many. As the Maryland patrician, Charles Bonaparte, said in 1879, the aim of civil-service reform was to correct the "chief evil" of the day, from which all others stemmed—"the alliance between industrialists and a political class which thinks like industrialists." Civil-service reform would unseat such vandals and put in their place "gentlemen . . . who need nothing and want nothing from government except the satisfaction of using their talents," or at least "sober, . . . middle class persons who have taken over . . . the proper standards of conduct."

Even veteran politicos who owed a great deal to machine support had grown thoroughly sick of the "hungry applicants for office . . . lying in wait . . . like vultures for a wounded bison." Until Garfield's martyrdom, however, what Conkling liked to call "snivel-service" reform had languished. The first significant step toward the merit system of appointment to public office was taken with the Pendleton Act of 1883. This act gave three civil-service commissioners, to be named by the president, authority to draw up practical competitive examinations. The act forbade assessing federal employees for campaign funds or firing them for political reasons. It required that within 60 days Treasury and postal employees be classified in civil-service categories and permitted the president to extend the coverage. During Arthur's administration about 12 per cent of the federal employees, compared to 85 per cent in the mid-twentieth century, were classified.

The Pendleton Act, by depriving the parties of funds from public employees, forced party leaders to turn more and more to big business for the wherewithal for campaigns —a consequence not foreseen by the reformers. Shrewd party managers such as "Matt" Quay of Pennsylvania, "Tom" Platt of New York, and "Mark" Hanna of Ohio, thus were soon representing their big-business clients as efficiently as hired lawyers. And so were the candidates they chose. By 1889, as William Allen White put it:

A United States senator . . . represented something more than a state, more even than a region. He represented principalities and powers in business. One senator, for instance, represented the New York Central, still another the insurance interests, . . . Cotton had half a dozen senators. And so it went.

III. *Protection and Regulation*

THE DEMOCRATS RETURN

All in all, Arthur conducted himself creditably during his time in office. His appointments to the Civil Service Commission included strong advocates of reform, who later acknowledged his "constant, firm, and friendly support." He did not draw back from prosecuting Stalwart culprits in post-office frauds, and held off pork-barrel raids on the Treasury. He was never able, however, to throw off the taint of his earlier associations so far as the reformers were concerned, and his independence as president displeased the old guard. Consequently, the Republican convention in 1884 passed him by in favor of the perennial aspirant, James G. Blaine.

Blaine had most of the attributes that make for a successful presidential candidate, including political shrewdness derived from many years in the House. But his House years had also marked him inescapably with the blemishes of the age which deprived him of his highest ambition. E. L. Godkin expressed the reformers' view when he said that Blaine had "wallowed in spoils like a rhinoceros in an African pool."

The old Liberal Republicans, who had opposed Blaine's nomination as staunchly as they would have fought a true Stalwart, found themselves in a quandary. Should they "follow a noble impulse," as Carl Schurz put it, and desert the orthodox wing of the party? Rising young Republicans like Henry Cabot Lodge and Theodore Roosevelt wavered and then rationalized their decision: They would be of more service to the cause of reform inside the party than outside it. The more dedicated reformers, like the university presidents Charles W. Eliot of Harvard and Andrew D. White of Cornell, and the preacher Henry Ward Beecher, decided to follow Schurz out of the party. Having taken this step, these "Mugwumps," as they were henceforth called, came out for the 1884 Democratic nominee, Grover Cleveland.

Blunt and honest, his solid build and bulldog features truly reflecting his character, Cleveland had attracted notice as a reform mayor of Buffalo and as governor of New York. His enthusiasm for hard money and a hard-nosed defense of property rights earned him industrial and banking support. But issues remained secondary in the scurrilous campaign.

The Republicans thought they had their rivals on the run when they dug up and gleefully publicized the fact that the bachelor Cleveland had acknowledged paternity of an illegitimate child. The Democrats, in turn, unearthed new letters proving that Blaine had used his influence while Speaker of the House in favor of certain railroads. These personal reflections on the candidates caused a witty Mugwump to suggest the ideal solution: Since Blaine was delinquent in office, he said, but blameless in his private life, and Cleveland was a model of official integrity but far from blameless in his personal affairs, "we should therefore elect Mr. Cleveland to the public office which he is so well qualified to fill, and remand Mr. Blaine to the private station which he is admirably fitted to adorn."

Shortly before election day, the Democrats capitalized on two episodes that seriously damaged Blaine's candidacy. In pledging support for Blaine, the Reverend Samuel D. Burchard, a spokesman for a New York delegation of clergymen, observed that the Democratic party's "antecedents have been rum, Romanism, and rebellion." Apparently Blaine was not listening when these fatal words were uttered. But a Democratic reporter was, and he quickly informed Irish voters that Blaine had not rebuked the minister for his insulting allusion to their drinking habits and religion. On the same day, Jay Gould and other "money kings" tendered a lavish testimonial dinner to the Republican candidate which was described in the Democratic press as "The Soft Soap Dinner" or "The Royal Feast of Belshazzar Blaine."

In the balloting, Blaine lost New York by 1,149 votes, and New York turned out to be decisive in the electoral college where Cleveland squeaked through, 219 to 182. His popular plurality was only 23,000 out of the 10-million votes cast. Some experts believed that the votes won by the Prohibition candidate, John P. St. John, and by the Greenback nominee, the notorious Benjamin F. Butler, were responsible

for Blaine's defeat. Others credited Cleveland's victory to Mugwump support or to the clergyman Burchard's impolitic words. Whatever the cause, the Democrats had come back to the White House after 24 years. Gratefully they chanted:

The *World* says the Independents Did It;
The *Tribune* says the Stalwarts Did It;
The *Sun* says Burchard Did It;
Blaine says St. John Did It;
Theodore Roosevelt says it was the Soft Soap Dinner;
We say Blaine's character Did It;
But We Don't Care What Did It, It's Done.

Even more than with Republican presidents of the day, Cleveland had to face up to the problem of jobs for his patronage-starved party. His position was complicated by the support he had received from the Mugwumps, whose pet theme was the extension of the merit system. Within a year, Carl Schurz wrote to the President with a bluntness Cleveland knew to be deserved: "Your attempt to please both reformers and spoilsmen has failed." Cleveland, however, did earn one success. The old Tenure of Office Act (see p. 467) permitted Republicans in the Senate to obstruct Cleveland's appointments to positions that required Senate approval by refusing to acknowledge his right to dismiss Republican holdovers. By appealing to the people, Cleveland forced Congress, in June, 1886, to repeal the Tenure of Office Act, thereby restoring to the Chief Executive the power to function through men of his own choosing.

Cleveland's conception of government was almost entirely negative. He especially disliked what he called "paternalism." In the cause of destroying this evil he foiled "pension grabs" by veterans and tariff grabs by industry, and even retrieved 81 million acres of the public domain from railroads that had failed to meet the terms of their land grants. By the same token, Cleveland fought federal regulation of business. But he lost that fight to public pressure.

We have already noted the significant improvements in railroad-building and railroad service that management made during the late 1870's and 1880's (pp. 517, 522). Yet none of these improvements muffled the cry for railroad reform.

One of the principal sources of discontent was railroad rate policy. Naturally, shippers at points where a single railroad had a monopoly suffered in competition with shippers where railroad competition itself forced rates down. The most resentful shippers were situated at monopoly points along roads that terminated at competitive points. Such shippers often had to pay more for short hauls along the small monopolized portion of the road than shippers at the terminals paid for long hauls across the road's entire length. The willingness of the railroads to grant rebates and other favors to powerful shippers such as the Standard Oil Company also brought cries of protest from those discriminated against. When competing railroads combined in pools to maintain profitable rate levels, those whose rates were raised screamed too.

Railroad dividend policies also made few friends. Always eager for capital, the roads sought to maintain liberal dividend payments in order to attract investors. Often they did not earn the dividends paid out. Such payments, if persisted in, could lead only to insolvency. When roads went bankrupt, as they often did, investors cried that they had been cheated. Unsavory railroad lobbying for charters, land grants, tax favors, and other assistance added many more to the roll of enemies.

The first railroad regulatory commission was set up in Massachusetts in 1869. It had no punitive powers but only the right to investigate railroad abuses and make its findings public. Despite fierce railroad opposition, 14 states had set up railroad commissions by 1880, and some had enacted more severe measures. City manufacturers and distributors, and their banker allies, sometimes initiated the fight for railroad regulation, but the most widespread action was that taken by the Patrons of Husbandry, which began organizing farmers into local "Granges" in 1867. A year after the Panic of 1873, the Grangers boasted 1,500,000 members, principally in Iowa, Wisconsin, Minnesota, and Illinois. Here they won legislation that even fixed maximum rates for railroad traffic within particular states, and also for the use of grain elevators, where farmers had to store their staples while awaiting shipment.

Railroad management quickly opposed the "Granger legislation" in the courts. Rate-fixing by public bodies they particularly attacked as legalized confiscation. In 1876, in *Munn* v. *Illinois,* the most important of the "Granger cases" to reach the Supreme Court, a majority of the bench found against the grain elevators and the railroads. Owners of property "in which the public has an interest," said the Court, must "submit to be controlled by the public for the common good."

Nevertheless, the railroads soon made it clear that state regulation was inadequate to solve a problem of interstate dimensions. The problem itself, moreover, was growing more severe. Between 1882 and 1885, the average stock-market quotations for 28 major railroad issues fell about 35 per cent, from 116 to 75. By 1886, 108 roads with 11,000 miles of track, nearly 10 per cent of the whole railroad system, had sunk into receivership. These evidences of railroad weakness prompted plungers like Jay Gould to buy up many of the bargains available and frighten the public further with the specter of a great confederacy of railroads that would bear down upon shippers and the government with consolidated force. Between 1880 and 1888, in fact, 425 railroad companies, nearly a fourth of all American railroad corporations, were brought under the control of other roads.

Two events in 1886 made it virtually impossible for the federal government to postpone action longer. The first was the report, in January, of an investigation into railroad practices conducted by a Senate committee headed by Shelby M. Cullom of Illinois. This committee was anything but a radical group; but its report scorched railroad management in general as "extravagant and wasteful" and urged the creation of an independent national commission to intervene on the public's behalf in railroad matters. "Upon no public question," the committee concluded, "are the people so nearly unanimous as upon the proposition that Congress should undertake in some way the regulation of interstate commerce." The second event, in October, was the Supreme Court decision in the so-called *Wabash* case. This decision sucked much of the strength from *Munn* v. *Illinois* by forbidding any state henceforth to set rates even within its borders on railroad traffic entering from or bound for other states.

The Interstate Commerce Act, reluctantly signed by Cleveland February 4, 1887, derived largely from the findings of the Cullom Committee. The act forbade higher rates for non-competitive short hauls than for competitive long ones and banned rebates to favored shippers. It also prohibited railroad self-regulating practices, such as agreements to pool traffic and maintain high rates. What it did not do was to provide means for enforcing its restraints.

President Cleveland showed his good faith by appointing excellent men to the Interstate Commerce Commission set up to administer the act. But the "cease and desist" orders the commissioners were empowered to issue could be made to stick only by court action which the railroads were very adept at delaying. In the end, moreover, the railroads almost always won. In the first ten years of its existence, 90 per cent of the commission's orders on rate charges were overruled by the judiciary. Of the 16 cases heard by the Supreme Court between 1887 and 1905, moreover, the majority of the highest bench upheld the carrier in 15. In the process it demolished all the commission's pretensions to setting "reasonable and just" rates on its own initiative.

In 1890, the commission noted the continuing "general disregard" of the prohibitions against rebating and began vigorous prosecutions. The roads responded not only with obstructionist tactics, but with a concerted attack on the commission itself. Wiser heads, however, saw a little farther than the railroad spokesmen and advised them, even as early as 1892, along lines that history, at least for a generation, would justify. In that year, the corporation lawyer, Richard S. Olney, soon to become Cleveland's Attorney-General, wrote to a railroad friend:

My impression would be that, looking at the matter from a railroad point of view exclusively, it would not be a wise thing to undertake to abolish the Commission. . . . The Commission, as its functions have now been limited by the Courts, is, or can be made of great use to the railroads. It satisfies the popular clamor for a government supervision of railroads, at the same time that such supervision is almost entirely nominal. Further, the older such a commission gets to be, the more inclined it will be found to take the business and railroad view of things. It thus becomes a sort of . . . protection against

The Farmer and the railroads: the Grange awakening the sleepers. A cartoon of 1873.

hasty and crude legislation hostile to railroad interests. . . . The part of wisdom is not to destroy the Commission, but to utilize it.

Time proved Olney perfectly right. Yet the Interstate Commerce Act was not a complete failure. It clearly affirmed the right of the federal government to regulate private interstate business, and it supplied a foundation upon which a system of increasingly effective regulation could be built in the twentieth century. By mid-century, indeed, effective regulation had been commonplace for so long that many believed that it had sapped the initiative and enterprise of railroad management.

THE GREAT ISSUE
OF "PROTECTION"

Although Cleveland was unimaginative and often shortsighted, his response to Democratic politicians who advised him to soft-pedal the tariff issue is a measure of his superiority to the other presidents of his epoch: "What is the use of being elected or reelected, if you don't stand for something?" Following his own course, in December, 1887, the President devoted his third annual message to Congress entirely to the tariff. "Our present tariff laws," he said, "the vicious, inequitable, and illogical source of unnecessary taxation, ought to be at once revised and amended."

Cleveland had no quarrel with advocates of protection who sought to nurse "infant industries" into "perennial vigor." Beginning with the wartime duties of 1864, however, as Frank W. Taussig, the leading tariff historian, put it, "protection ran riot." By 1887 no fewer than 4,000 separate items were dutiable.

One of the tariff advocates' favorite themes was the patriotism implicit in protection. Reduction of the tariff, they said, meant reduction of revenues and repudiation of the national debt. This argument was most successful, said an Ohioan in 1867, in winning and maintaining "a consistent and solid front" for protection in the West. But Cleveland had an answer. Those who buy imports, the President warned Congress, "pay the duty thereon into the public Treasury." This, he said, must be encouraged by keeping duties below a level that made imports prohibitive.

Cleveland was sophisticated enough to add an even more telling point often overlooked: "The great majority of our citizens, who buy domestic articles of the same class [as dutiable imports] pay a sum at least approximately equal to this duty to the home manufacturer." The latter's price, he said, may sometimes be reduced by domestic competition "below the highest limit allowed by such duty. But it is notorious that this competition is too often strangled by combinations prevalent at this time, frequently called trusts. . . . The people can hardly hope for any consideration in the operation of these selfish schemes."

In response to growing public pressure, President Arthur in 1882 had appointed a bipartisan tariff commission to study the tariff schedules and to recommend simplifying changes. Most of the experts on tariff-making, however, were associated with the protected industries, and Arthur's commission reflected the dilemma that was to face others who would seek expert advice later on. Of all people, John Lord Hayes, the most effective tariff lobbyist of his generation and the spokesman for the woolen interests, was named chairman of Arthur's group. In addition, as Senator Aldrich himself pointed out, "there was a representative of the wool growers on the commission; there was a representative of the iron interests on the commission; there was a representative of the sugar interests on the commission; and those interests were very carefully looked out for."

Actually, this commission did a fair job. The agglomeration of special duties was simplified and the general level of protection was reduced by some 20 per cent. Many of the reductions, however, hardly cut deep enough to invite the importation of competitive goods. Once the commission's proposals reached Congress, moreover, they were disfigured by lobbyists who saw to it that the rates were raised not only above those the commission recommended but above those collected at the time.

554

In response to Cleveland's tariff message of December, 1887, the House early in 1888 was presented with the Mills Bill, a measure reflecting deep study of industry's real needs and recommending the moderate reductions that mild revisionists such as Cleveland demanded. The Mills Bill passed in the House with deceptively few changes. The elections of 1888 were nearing, and an appearance of satisfying the public clamor against industrial greed was more essential to congressmen than to senators with six-year terms. The lobbyists thus let House members soothe the electorate, while looking to the upper chamber with a confidence that was not misplaced.

On receiving the Mills Bill, the Senate responded with the so-called "Allison substitute," which called, as usual, for a general rise in the tariff. "I am satisfied," Joseph Wharton, the Pennsylvania iron and steel king, wrote to Senator Allison in July, 1888, "that your aim is to report a bill . . . which can command the votes of such men as . . . have industrial interests." "We all know," Wharton added meaningfully,

that the legitimate expenses of a general election are heavy, and that failure to provide for them sometimes entails defeat. I am in a position to know that the success of appeals for funds among the steel rail men will be jeopardized if the party they are asked to support proposes a measure that looks to them nearly as fatal as that proposed by the other party.

Other industrial spokesmen reached Allison with urgent reminders of satisfying "the people who have money to give for the success of Republican principles."

The "Allison substitute" was essentially a device to kill the Mills Bill until after the presidential election of 1888; and the Senate thus debated the tariff to election day, when the Mills Bill expired. In the meantime, the election machinery had begun to grind. For the "holy work" of protecting protection, Tom Platt, New York's "Begging Chief," besieged Wall Street. James P. Foster, of the protectionist Republican League, said, "I would put the manufacturers of Pennsylvania under the fire and

fry all the fat out of them." Henceforth the cry for "fat" resounded through all the business houses. "All unnecessary taxation is unjust taxation," said the Democratic platform of 1888. The Republicans, at pains to disavow the use of the word "tax" in connection with tariffs, had this reply. Said the G.O.P. platform:

We are uncompromisingly in favor of the American system of protection. The President and his party . . . serve the interests of Europe; we will support the interests of America. . . . We denounce the Mills Bill as destructive of the general business, the labor, the farming interests of the country . . . we favor the entire repeal of internal taxes, rather than the surrender of any part of the protective system.

This last statement referred to the great surplus that was piling up in the Treasury from tariff revenues and other sources. Protectionists feared that if the surplus were not reduced, reduction of tariff rates for fiscal reasons alone might upset their whole program. The Democratic high-tariff man, Representative Samuel J. Randall of Pennsylvania, urged in defense of the interests of his state that duties be raised altogether out of sight. "No imports, no revenues," cried Randall. This policy, the foes of the tariff protested, might push prices out of sight too. But young Republican Congressman McKinley of Ohio had an answer: "Cheap," he said, "is not a word of hope; it is not a word of inspiration! It is the badge of poverty; it is the signal of distress."

THE STALWARTS IN THE SADDLE

Cleveland was renominated by acclamation at the Democratic convention in St. Louis, in June, 1888. The Republicans, gathering in Chicago two weeks later, found the cupboard bare of possible nominees after Blaine's decision not to run again. Seven ballots were taken before the party put its stamp on Benjamin Harrison, a dreary corporation lawyer from the pivotal state of Indiana. As the grandson of President William Henry Harrison, he was hopefully dubbed "Young Tippecanoe."

Under the astute management of National Party Chairman "Matt" Quay, the Republicans waged a vigorous campaign. They charged that Cleveland's "free-trade" policy (as they insisted on labeling the mild reforms of the Mills Bill) would ruin American manufacturing and betray the American worker to the "pauper labor of Europe." Even the Knights of Labor succumbed to this argument and endorsed Harrison. Where tariff "education" failed to convince, cash often succeeded.

Of great help to the Republicans in the last days of the campaign was a widely publicized letter written by the British minister in Washington to a Republican who had represented himself as an English-born American seeking advice on how to vote in the coming election. Which candidate, the correspondent asked, would be more friendly to England? The minister foolishly replied that Cleveland was to be preferred. Falling in so neatly with the Republican claim that reduced duties would play into the hands of British industrialists, this missive was peculiarly disastrous. It had the further effect of swinging many Irish-American votes, traditionally Democratic, to Harrison. Cleveland's popular vote topped Harrison's by more than 100,000, but Harrison won an electoral majority of 65. A switch of only 6,500 votes in New York would have given Cleveland that state and the election. When Harrison solemnly proclaimed that "Providence has given us the victory," Matt Quay exploded: "Think of the man! He ought to know that Providence hadn't a damn thing to do with it." Quay added that Harrison "would never know how close a number of men were compelled to approach the gates of the penitentiary to make him President."

It was in Harrison's administration that the Senate became known as the "Millionaires Club," for the money the members brought in; and the whole legislature became known as the "billion-dollar Congress," for the money it handed out. To diminish the surplus the billion dollar Congress in 1890 provided pensions for all disabled Union army veterans (whose votes had helped defeat the Democrats) even when their disability had no connection with the war. Pensions were also provided for the widows of veterans. The pension bite on the surplus thereby rose from $98 million in 1889 to $156 million in 1893.

Later the same year Congress took care of the industrial contributors to the campaign with the McKinley Tariff. The highest and broadest thus far in American history, this tariff so effectively shut off imports that the receipts augmenting the surplus soon fell sharply. Understandably, Secretary of State Blaine feared that exporting nations hit by the new duties would refuse to buy American farm surpluses. As a club over such nations, Blaine induced Congress to place a "reciprocity" clause in the new tariff act giving the president authority to remove remaining items from the free list in retaliation against any discriminatory duties on American produce.

The McKinley Tariff raised havoc with Hawaiian sugar-growers by placing competitive sugars as well as their's on the free list and at the same time giving American growers a bounty of 2 cents a pound. Other American farmers were courted by duties on foreign eggs, potatoes, and similar products, of which only the minutest quantities ever were brought into the United States.

In return, further, for western votes on the McKinley Tariff, Congress in 1890 passed the Sherman Silver Purchase Act. This act authorized the Treasury to issue notes redeemable in gold or silver coin in exchange for greater amounts of silver than had been permitted under the Bland-Allison Act of 1878 (see p. 548). Virtually a bounty to the silver-mining companies, the Silver Purchase Act was defended as an agrarian cheap-money measure, but it did not satisfy those inflationists who were pressing for unlimited silver coinage.

One more sop offered to the public was the Sherman Anti-Trust Act, which passed Congress in July, 1890, with scarcely a murmur of dissent about its final form. Earlier, many states had enacted "anti-trust" statutes, which were no more effective against "trusts" chartered in other states than state regulation of interstate railroads had been. After the *Wabash* decision of 1886 cut the ground away from stronger state measures against private corporations (see p. 553), the demand for federal regulation grew.

The Sherman Anti-Trust Act sounded severe. It made combinations in restraint of trade illegal, subjected perpetrators to heavy fines and jail sentences, and ordered that triple damages be paid to persons who could prove injury by such combinations. Few courts, however, sustained any of the actions brought under the measure.

One of the grave defects of the Sherman Act was its failure to protect non-business "combinations" from attack under its terms. Senator James Z. George of Mississippi put this point most clearly when he said,

. . . the farmers and laborers of this country who are sending up their voices to the Congress of the United States, . . . imploring us to take action to put down trusts, . . . will find that they themselves in their most innocent and necessary arrangements, made solely for defensive purposes against the operation of these trusts, will be brought within the punitory provisions of this bill.

The Senator's fears soon were justified. Although Republican and Democratic Attorneys-General alike refused to administer the new law with zeal, four labor unions soon fell afoul of its terms. Business combinations cited were likely to get off scot free. As Finely Peter Dunne, the political humorist, said of the Sherman Act, "What looks like a stone wall to a layman, is a triumphal arch to a corporation lawyer."

The Sherman Act did prompt certain groups of companies to alter their specific "trust" arrangements and to merge into huge monolithic corporations which, without having to act any longer in concert, succeeded in dominating their industries at least as thoroughly as the trusts had. In other industries, the holding company device was employed. The holding company was an independent corporation which owned enough stock in other companies to control their policies effectively. Dodges such as these neutralized the Sherman Act for a short period; but in the twentieth century political administrations and the courts gradually gave substance to the terms of the act. Business consolidation and centralization continued apace; but antitrust legislation did serve as a brake on many combinations deemed adverse to the public interest. According to some mid-century analysts, indeed, it served as too tight a brake on combinations which would have afforded the consuming public in particular many real economies of bigness.

THE ELECTION OF 1892

Blaine warned his crasser colleagues that the McKinley Tariff "will protect the Republican party only into speedy retirement." Despite such sops to the voters as the Anti-Trust and Silver Purchase acts, the congressional elections of 1890 proved Blaine right. In 1890 the Republicans lost control of the House, where the Democrats gained no less than 76 seats. This Democratic surge foreshadowed Harrison's eclipse in the elections of 1892. Out of necessity, his party nominated him once more, though many leaders would have preferred, had it been possible, to lure Blaine out of political retirement. Running against Cleveland again, Harrison, in 1892, polled 5,176,000 votes. But Cleveland won 5,556,000. Narrow though his margin was, it represented the most decisive presidential election victory since 1872. The electoral college count was Harrison 145, Cleveland 277.

Labor unrest, culminating in the Homestead strike against the Carnegie Steel Company in July, 1892 (see p. 537), added to Harrison's burdens. Cleveland hardly dreaming, perhaps, that two years later he would help break the Pullman strike, issued a sardonic statement about "the tender mercy the workingman receives from those made selfish and sordid by unjust governmental favoritism." Republican leaders begged Carnegie and Frick to relent in their labor policies because the Homestead affair would lose votes for the party; but the industrialists were much less frightened by the idea of a Cleveland victory than by a labor-union victory.

The decline of Republican strength in the trans-Mississippi West where the People's party, founded in 1890 and familiarly known as the Populist party, was flourishing (see p. 560), gave the conservatives in both major parties even more to think about. The Populist candidate, General James B. Weaver of Iowa, received over a million votes and captured four states in the 1892 election.

IV. *The Rise and Fall of Populism*

THE FARMERS' PLIGHT

In 1887 Colonel Leonidas L. Polk, a North Carolina farm editor, expressed the views of hundreds of thousands of farmers in all parts of the country when he wrote:

There is something radically wrong in our Industrial system. There is a screw loose. . . . The railroads have never been so prosperous, and yet agriculture languishes. The banks have never done a better . . . business, and yet agriculture languishes. Manufacturing enterprises never made more money, . . . and yet agriculture languishes. Towns and cities flourish and "boom," . . . and yet agriculture languishes.

The cash-crop farmers were not always the best diagnosticians of their own ills, but no historian has doubted that they truly suffered. What is more, they suffered only slightly less in good times than in bad, only slightly more in their mental than in their monetary condition. Broadly speaking, they were faced with four principal difficulties: (1) the high cost of transportation, (2) heavy taxes and tariffs, (3) falling prices, (4) the high cost of credit. Together, these made farming a second-class economic activity, one that held few attractions for rural youths.

(1) Few enterprises had received more enthusiastic civic support than did the railroads of the West, and the farmers, understandably, felt that the railroads in return owed the community moderate freight and passenger rates. But the farmers' expectations came to nothing. Farmers in the many agricultural regions off the main lines suffered most from railroad policies. The farther west one moved, moreover, the worse conditions became even on the main lines. In 1887, for instance, the ton-mile charge on the Pennsylvania Railroad east of Chicago was 95 cents; on the Burlington from Chicago to the Missouri River it was $1.32; on the Burlington west of the Missouri it jumped to $4.80.

Railroad officials held that they had no choice but to charge high rates in sparsely populated regions. They also pointed to gradual rate reductions in some areas. To ship a bushel of wheat from Chicago to New York in 1870 cost 30 cents; in 1875, only 17 cents; by 1900, only 10 cents. But such rate tendencies were irrelevant to farmers on the moving frontier who, as Frank Norris put it in *The Octopus*, likened the railroad to "a gigantic parasite fattening upon the life-blood of an entire commonwealth."

(2) The burden of unfair taxes only made the burden of high railroad rates harder to bear. Before the era of corporations, personal property consisted chiefly of land and livestock, on which it was relatively easy to assess a personal property tax. Railroads and other corporations created new kinds of personal property—stocks and bonds—which proved far easier to conceal from assessors. Since the railroads also pressed the politicians for tax exemptions or low rates on their own huge landholdings and other real property, taxes fell more and more oppressively on the middle-class farmer who could not, in the freely competitive market, pass them along to the consumer, as could many large industrial corporations.

The protective tariff constituted still another kind of discriminatory tax which was the more burdensome since, in the farmers' opinion, the tariff "mothered" the trusts. The trusts, they said, had the power to force down the prices they paid for raw materials produced on the farms, and to force up without fear of foreign competition the prices they charged for farm machinery and other manufactures.

(3) **Falling farm prices,** of course, made heavy taxes seem all the more oppressive. The prices of staples began to sag in the 'eighties. In the depression years of the 'nineties they hit bottom. Wheat, for instance, brought $1.20 a bushel in 1881, and 50 cents in 1895; cotton, 10½ cents a pound in 1881, and 4½ cents in 1894. Of course, prices of non-farm products fell too. But the fall in farm prices hit the grower particularly hard, because he was a debtor with fixed *money* obligations. His intense concern with the currency stemmed from his determination to keep these obligations stable in terms of the *commodities* needed to pay them. Their critics told the farmers that they received low prices because they produced too much. But the only way the individual farmer could think of to make more money when prices were falling was to raise even bigger crops. The price decline, he said, reflected a cold-blooded Wall Street conspiracy to squeeze the farmers.

(4) The high cost of credit seemed only to confirm this view. We have seen how the credit system helped force the landless southern farmer, and eventually the small southern landholder as well, into the vicious circle of share-cropping and the crop lien (p. 481). Tenancy came later in the West, where land was more easily obtained and thus more easily mortgaged. But when mortgage money cost 15 per cent or more a year, as it did in Kansas and states farther west in the 1880's, the day of foreclosure loomed.

THE ORIGINS OF POPULISM

The roots of the People's party, which was organized in 1890, were firmly planted in American history. Comparable farmers' movements went back at least to Shays' Rebellion in 1786, and more recently farmers had organized in the Grange (see p. 552). Populism can be traced to farmer organizations—"Wheels," "Unions," and "Alliances"—that had sprung up in the 1880's to supplant the Grange. By 1890, many of these had consolidated into two regional groups, the Southern Alliance, which claimed over a million members, and the somewhat smaller National Farmers' Alliance in the Northwest.

The Alliances gave an immense stimulus to the social life and the thinking of their members. Like the Granges, they held meetings, picnics, conventions, and rallies to help overcome the isolation and bleakness of farm life. They disseminated agricultural information and tried to foster better business methods among their members. They sponsored economic and political discussions and established circulating libraries which enabled members to read books of social criticism and speculation. They helped circulate farm papers, like the well-edited *National Economist* of Washington, D.C., and magazines of general discussion like the *Arena* of Boston. At one time perhaps as many as a thousand local newspapers were connected with the movement. One Alliance sympathizer wrote about the intellectual ferment that resulted:

People commenced to think who had never thought before, and people talked who had seldom spoken. On mild days they gathered on the street corners, on cold days they congregated in shops and offices. Everyone was talking and everyone was thinking. . . . Little by little they commenced to theorize upon their condition. Despite the poverty of the country, the books of Henry George, Bellamy, and other economic writers were bought as fast as the dealers could supply them. They were bought to be read greedily; and nourished by the fascination of novelty and the zeal of enthusiasm, thoughts and theories sprouted like weeds after a May shower. . . . They discussed income tax and single tax; they talked of government ownership and the abolition of private property;

fiat money, and the unity of labor; . . . and a thousand conflicting theories.

In December, 1889, all the major farm organizations met at St. Louis in separate sessions. The Northern and the Southern Alliances were on hand, and the presence of the Knights of Labor, the Farmers' Mutual Benefit Association, and the Colored Alliance suggested that all the forces of protest might join together. A number of issues, however, kept them apart. For one thing, the Southern Alliance regarded secrecy as a distinct advantage, while many of the northern representatives objected to it. Secondly, the northern representatives resented southern insistence that Negroes be excluded from the consolidated membership, though southern spokesmen were willing to go so far as to leave to each state organization the right to decide on the eligibility of colored persons within its jurisdiction, so long as white persons only were elected to the National Council. In the end, when the southerners lost patience with the northern representatives, the proposal for union failed. The more militant northern state organizations of Kansas and the Dakotas then seceded from the Northern Alliance and joined the Southern Alliance, which soon assumed the leadership of the whole movement.

Despite organizational differences, the programs of the Northern and Southern Alliances proved to be very much alike. The northerners were somewhat more concerned about the railroad issue and about the disposition of the public lands, the southerners more interested in farm finances, farm credit, and the tariff, but these were only differences in emphasis. The most important proposal for solving the credit problem came from Dr. C. W. Macune, organizer of the Texas Alliance and editor of the *National Economist*. Macune suggested that the federal government set up a subtreasury office and warehouse in every county that offered for sale more than $500,000 worth of farm products annually. Farmers who placed non-perishable crops in these warehouses would receive as a loan

Treasury notes in amounts up to 80 per cent of the local market value of their stored crops. This loan was to be repaid when the crop was sold. Macune's plan, later incorporated into the agricultural programs of the 1930's, had the double advantage of allowing the farmer to hold his crop for the best price, and of increasing the money supply.

Eastern conservatives laughed off the subtreasury plan and other Alliance proposals as "hayseed socialism," but they could not laugh off the political stampede behind them. Between 1887 and 1890, Southern Alliance men, working at first through the Democratic party, elected three governors and won control of the legislatures of eight states. Northern Alliance candidates, in the major parties or in local "third parties" in the grain states of the Northwest, if less successful, still made impressive gains. It was in Kansas that the "third party" was first called the People's party, its members becoming known as "populists," the foes of "plutocrats."

THE PEOPLE'S PARTY

By 1890 the radical farmers of the Northwest were eager to start a new national party. Southern Alliance members held back for fear that a split between the voters in the South would threaten white supremacy, but the third-party men nevertheless went ahead with a convention in Cincinnati in May, 1891. To this convention came relics of defunct parties, ambitious politicians, visionaries, and utopians, as well as the inspired Alliance men.

The Cincinnati convention postponed until 1892 the question of whether to start a national party, but the delegates nevertheless drew up a People's party platform calling for unlimited coinage of silver; direct election of senators (who were still elected by state legislatures); nationalizing of banks, railroads, and utilities; prohibition of foreign ownership of land; and an eight-hour day. A year later, in St. Louis, on February 26, 1892, the national People's party, including the Southern Alliance, was formally organized. After adopting the Cincinnati platform, the delegates called for a presidential nominating convention to meet in Omaha in July. At Omaha the party chose James B. Weaver of Iowa for the presidency. The Omaha platform now made additional demands, including the sub-treasury plan.

Populist leaders in the 'nineties bore such wild-sounding names as "Sockless" Jerry Simpson and David H. "Bloody Bridles" Waite, and their orators spoke with a vehemence that shocked many easterners. Yet the campaign of 1892 was far from the "lawless, irresponsible, incendiary" thing the eastern press described it. Allan Nevins, Cleveland's biographer, says the 1892 campaign was "the cleanest, quietest, and most creditable in the memory of the post-war generation." In the balloting, as we have seen (p. 558), Weaver received over a million votes, more than 8 per cent of the total cast. With the exception of the Republicans in 1856, no third party had done nearly so well in its first national effort. Shortly after the election, Weaver confidently announced: "The Republican party is as dead as the Whig party was after the Scott campaign of 1852, and from this time forward will diminish in every State of the Union and cannot make another campaign."

A sober look at the distribution of the Populist vote might have put a brake on Weaver's optimism. True, he had run strong in a few plains and mountain states and in a half-dozen states of the South. But in the entire East and in such older agricultural states as Iowa, Wisconsin, and Illinois, he received less than 5 per cent of the votes cast. The Populists, in short, had shown strength enough in 1892 to worry the major parties, but no more than that. The next year one of the worst depressions in American history began and discontent spread across the entire land, preparing the stage for another campaign in which Populism would alarm every conservative.

CLEVELAND AND THE CRASH

Many Democrats placed the blame for the Panic of 1893 (see p. 531) on Harrison's "billion-dollar Congress." Cleveland

and other conservatives, blamed the Silver Purchase Act, which, they said, destroyed business confidence. Even the withdrawal of foreign capital, they argued, had been prompted by European fears that America was going off the gold standard. This move, indeed, seemed imminent by April, 1893, when the Treasury's gold reserve dropped below $100 million.

Cleveland's first thought was to repeal the Silver Purchase Act, which permitted holders of silver certificates to exchange them for gold. For this purpose he called a special session of Congress in the summer of 1893. "Gold" Democrats and Republicans closed ranks against the inflationists in both parties and enacted the repeal in October. By then, however, a run on the Treasury was gaining momentum, and after the failure of other measures to stop it, Cleveland, in February, 1895, was forced to borrow $62 million in gold from the Morgan and Belmont banking syndicate on terms decidedly unfavorable to the government. The inflationists denounced the President as a tool of Wall Street. But the bankers, by bringing gold from Europe, succeeded in reversing the drain on the Treasury. With confidence restored, the government floated another loan in January, 1896, which ended this crisis.

Cleveland's resolute defense of the gold standard aggravated discontent in the West and South as much as it heartened eastern financiers, and it probably destroyed any hope of getting mass support for the tariff reform he had promised once again. The tariff act Congress did finally pass in August, 1894, the Wilson-Gorman Tariff, Cleveland regarded as a disgrace to the party and it became law without his signature. This act did contain one provision that the Populists wanted, a 2 per cent tax on incomes over $4,000. But in 1895 by a 5-to-4 decision the Supreme Court declared the income tax unconstitutional on the ground that "direct taxes" could only be apportioned among the states on the basis of population, not personal wealth.

As the business depression deepened, the public mood grew ever more sullen. Thousands of unemployed roamed the country, sometimes in large gangs. Since the government offered no relief to the destitute, agitators proposed schemes of their own. In 1894 one of them, General Jacob S. Coxey, of Massillon, Ohio, a rich man himself, convinced frightened property-holders that a revolution had actually begun. Coxey proposed that Congress authorize a half-billion dollar public works program. To dramatize his plan, Coxey planned a march on Washington. Soon "armies" all over the country were heading for the capital, but "Coxey's Army" of about 300 men was the only one to arrive. Police speedily dispersed it after arresting Coxey and a few of his leaders for stepping on the grass. Nevertheless, Coxey's march helped make unemployment a well-aired national issue, one on which the Populists hoped to capitalize in the elections of 1896. The silver issue, however, soon crowded out all others.

THE BATTLE
OF THE STANDARDS
The barrage of propaganda from western silver interests following Cleveland's repeal of the Silver Purchase Act in 1893 told very quickly on the farmers who had been demanding inflation for years and now began to see the "conspiracy" against silver as another example of Wall Street treachery. In 1894, when he published *Coin's Financial School,* William H. Harvey gave the silverites an ideal little handbook that reduced the complex subject of money to terms that individual farmers themselves could readily grasp. It was also a model of Populist rhetoric.

A Virginian by birth, Harvey had experienced all the frustrations of his generation in a series of unsuccessful stabs at ranching, prospecting for silver, and editing. Finally, with *Coin's Financial School,* he found his métier. In his book he portrayed one "Professor Coin" as conducting a school at which the leading bankers, businessmen,

and orthodox economists of the day were taught the undeniable truths of free silver. With great wit and ease, Coin turned aside the conventional arguments of his listeners to the delight of his horde of readers. Profusely illustrated, and distributed in cheap editions, *Coin's Financial School* sold 300,-000 copies the first year. Another 125,000 were given away by silver-mine owners during the presidential campaign of 1896.

Harvey described the country as "distracted" by the hard times, with "tens of thousands . . . out of employment; the jails, penitentiaries, workhouses, and insane asylums . . . full;" and "hungered and half-starved men marching toward Washington." Not always had the country suffered so. Up to 1873, under bimetallism, with gold merely "a companion metal enjoying the same privileges as silver," prosperity and growth had been the rule. Then came the demonitization of '73. This act was

a crime, because it has confiscated millions of dollars worth of property. A crime, because it has made ten thousands of tramps. A crime, because it has made thousands of suicides. A crime, because it has brought tears to strong men's eyes and hunger and pinching want to widows and orphans. A crime, because it is destroying the honest yeomanry of the land, the bulwark of the nation. A crime because it has brought this once great republic to the verge of ruin, where it is now in imminent danger of tottering to its fall.

And this crime had only been compounded by Cleveland's repeal of the Silver Purchase Act—which the Populists were already calling the "Crime of '93." The only solution was the immediate resumption of free and unlimited coinage of silver.

More conservative men than Harvey agreed that it would be good to raise the price of silver and expand the currencies of the world. But they insisted that it would be disastrous for the United States alone to try to buy all the world's silver that would be offered at the higher price, and that the cooperation of Great Britain and others would be essential. The internationalists claimed, cried Harvey, "that we must adopt for our money the metal England selects, and can have no independent choice in the matter." But it would not be American to give up without trying. "If it is true, let us attach England to the United States and blot her name out from among the nations of the earth." He went on:

A war with England would be the most popular ever waged on the face of the earth. . . .

The gold standard will give England the commerce and wealth of the world. The bimetallic standard will make the United States the most prosperous nation on the globe.

Such silverite propaganda no doubt hurt the "Gold Democrats" most and contributed to the 42 per cent rise, in two years, in the Populist vote. In the elections of 1894, when the Republicans won overwhelming control in the House, the Populists elected six senators and seven congressmen. Even more ominous for Democratic prospects, anti-administration Democrats in the South, men like "Ben" Tillman of South Carolina, viciously attacked Cleveland. "When Judas betrayed Christ," Tillman charged, "his heart was not blacker than this scoundrel, Cleveland, in deceiving the Democracy." He promised to take his pitchfork to Washington and prod the "old bag of beef in his old fat ribs."

THE ELECTION OF 1896

Such dissension among the Democrats naturally pleased the Republicans, who now predicted an easy victory in 1896. They failed to realize that many Republicans as well as Democrats were receptive to a third party.

In June, 1896, the Republican convention, meeting in St. Louis, chose William McKinley of Ohio, sponsor of the tariff of 1890 and governor of his state from 1891 to 1895, as its presidential candidate. McKinley owed his nomination to his friendship with Marcus Alonzo Hanna—king of Great Lakes shipping, banker and street-railway magnate—who, as Republican boss, dominated Ohio politics. Months before the convention, Hanna had captured a majority of the delegates by persuasion and money, and McKinley's nomination on the first ballot came as no surprise.

The Republican platform was harder to settle. Hanna wanted McKinley to straddle the money issue in order to keep silverite Republicans from bolting the party. But he yielded on a sound-money plank in return for needed eastern financial support in the campaign. "We are . . . opposed to the free coinage of silver," the Republican declaration read, "except by international agreement . . . and until such agreement can be obtained the existing gold standing must be preserved." On the adoption of this plank, silver Republicans led by Senator Henry M. Teller of Colorado walked out.

The Democratic National Committee, like its Republican counterpart, favored the gold standard, but other Democrats, seeing a windfall in the Republican money plank, sought to draw Populist strength to themselves and win the election after all. At their convention in Chicago, which met shortly after the Republicans, the Democratic silverites routed the "goldbugs." The platform, written largely by John P. Altgeld, whose pardon of the Haymarket rioters in 1893 and handling of the Pullman Strike the next year (see p. 537) had made him anathema to conservatives everywhere, repudiated Cleveland's policies all along the line, and came out flatly for *unlimited* coinage of silver at the ratio of 16 ounces of silver to 1 ounce of gold. A sharp debate preceded the adoption of the silver plank, but the issue was resolved once the 36-year old Nebraskan, William Jennings Bryan, had spoken in its favor. The Democratic nomination was also resolved by this memorable speech, for Bryan's name suddenly was on every one's tongue, and he was named the candidate on the fifth ballot.

Young as he was, Bryan, in 1896, was no Johnny-come-lately. A lawyer in Lincoln, Nebraska, he served in Congress from 1890 to 1894 as a vigorous member of the growing "silver bloc." Defeated for the Senate in 1894, he became editor-in-chief of the influential Omaha *World-Herald,* and soon enhanced the reputation he had made in the House as an orator by embarking on the Chautauqua circuit. When he made his convention speech, his friends were already working quietly for his nomination.

Bryan's speech was modest and dignified, distinguished by the absence of personal bitterness against Cleveland and by a firm confidence that Bryan's cause was that of the people. "We are fighting in the defense of our homes, our families, and posterity," Bryan said. He defended the principle of the income tax and denounced the Supreme Court's recent decision upsetting it; he invoked Benton, Jefferson, and Jackson on the banking question; he challenged those who wanted to protect creditors against inflation by asking why debtors had not been protected against deflation in 1873; he declared firmly that money was by far the most important of the issues. "You come to us and tell us that the great cities are in favor of the gold standard; we reply that the great cities rest upon our broad and fertile prairies. Burn down your cities and leave our farms, and your cities will spring up again as if by magic; but destroy our farms and the grass will grow in the streets of every city in the country." And he closed with the striking image

William Jennings Bryan, who became the perennial Democratic presidential candidate after his "cross of gold" speech in 1896, in a characteristic oratorical pose.

by which his speech has ever since been known:

Having behind us the producing masses of this nation and the world, supported by the commercial interests, the laboring interests, and the toilers everywhere, we will answer their demand for a gold standard by saying to them: You shall not press down upon the brow of labor this crown of thorns, you shall not crucify mankind upon a cross of gold.

Even before the election of 1896, many Populists had been sickened by the emphasis on silver and the neglect of the more radical reforms in the People's party platform. Henry Demarest Lloyd called the free-silver issue "the cowbird of the Reform movement. It waited until the nest had been built by the sacrifices and labour of others, and then it laid its eggs in it, pushing out the others which lie smashed on the ground." When the Populists met at their convention in St. Louis in August they were forced to confront this sad dilemma: to wage a separate Populist campaign would be to split the silver vote and hand the election to the Republicans; to fuse with the Democrats in support of Bryan would mean their party's extinction. Most of the delegates approved of Bryan, but the southern Populists strongly opposed fusion with the Democrats, most of them Bourbon Democrats in their section with whom they had been fighting bitterly for years (see p. 484). The fusionists, however, could point out that the Democratic platform besides demanding the unlimited coinage of silver, did attack Cleveland's deals with the bankers, did recommend stricter railroad regulation, and did support a constitutional amendment to make an income tax possible. Against the wishes of the die-hards, the Populist convention nominated Bryan for president, but they could not stomach the Democratic vice-presidential candidate, Arthur Sewall, a rich Maine banker. In his place, they nominated the fiery Georgian, Thomas E. Watson.

The campaign of 1896 was one of the most dramatic in American history. Bryan, strapped for money and handicapped by two running-mates who detested each other, subordinated all issues to free silver. The redoubtable Hanna, in the meantime, was extracting millions for McKinley from monied interests eager to sink the silver ship. Bryan waged a whirlwind campaign, traveling more than 18,000 miles and delivering over 600 speeches, while McKinley stayed securely put at his old home in Canton, Ohio and simply read carefully drafted statements to the scores of delegations his party brought to his front porch. "Nobody," the New York Republican boss, Thomas C. Platt, had observed on the eve of the campaign, "can look at McKinley's record and read the flabby things he has said without perceiving that he has no fixed opinions, but has been turned and twisted by changing public opinion." During the campaign McKinley was given no chance to twist and turn, and his managers carried the day. McKinley's plurality was over 600,000, the largest of any presidential candidate since Grant defeated Greeley in 1872. He won 271 electoral votes to Bryan's 176. Even such agrarian strongholds in the Northwest as Iowa, Minnesota, and North Dakota went Republican.

No doubt the flood of propaganda, the pressure that employers put on industrial workers, and the identification of Bryanism with anarchy and revolution, had something to do with McKinley's success. But there were more obvious causes. Republicans argued, with much justice, that an inflationary price movement would leave wages behind, and that workmen would be the losers. Urban workers failed to provide the mass support Bryan hoped for. Moreover, every middle-class American with savings invested in stocks, banks, or insurance was, in a small way, a creditor himself, and it was easy for him to see the point of the Republican argument that inflation would reduce the value of his holdings. McKinley won, according to the perceptive Kansas editor, William Allen White, because "he could unite to a political solidarity the American middle class."

REPUBLICAN "GOOD TIMES"

"God's in his Heaven, all's right with the world!" Hanna telegraphed Mc-

Kinley when the returns were in. More revealing was the language of the New York *Tribune*. Bryan, cried the editor,

the wretched, rattle-pated boy, posing in vapid vanity and mouthing his resounding rottenness . . . goes down with the cause. . . . Good riddance to it all . . . to the foul menace of repudiation and Anarchy against the honor and life of the Republic.

It is doubtful that McKinley's election in 1896 restored prosperity, as the Republicans claimed, but Bryan's defeat surely soothed the fears and raised the confidence of those who stood to gain most from protective tariffs and sound currency. The Republican administration quickly adopted the Dingley Tariff of 1897, which raised schedules even above those of the McKinley Tariff of 1890 (see p. 557). Three years later, McKinley signed the Currency Act of 1900 which made the gold dollar the single unit of value and required all paper money to be redeemable in gold.

To the losers, at the same time, the results were profoundly disheartening. It seemed that all the laborious efforts at reform from the days of the Grangers and Greenbackers down through the careful building of the Farmers' Alliances and the hopeful launching of the Populist party had yielded nothing. The Populist party itself was smashed. The espousal of silver had brought the Democrats to a defeat

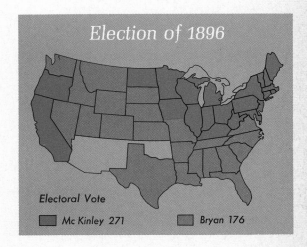

Election of 1896

Electoral Vote

McKinley 271   Bryan 176

more severe than they had experienced for many years, and had left their party divided. Who now would relieve the desperate farmers from the ills they had suffered so long? Hundreds of thousands must have sympathized with the defeated Tom Watson, who doubted that "any soldier of the Southern Confederacy carried away from Appomattox a heavier heart than I took with me into my enforced retirement."

But history takes many strange turns. The glee of the victors may have been justified; the despair of the losers was not. Soon the money supply was augmented by new flows of gold from the Klondike, South Africa, and Australia, and by enlarged United States production due to a new cyanide process for extracting gold from low-grade ores. Ironically, the inflation that the agrarian reformers failed to win through their precious silver came through the detested gold. Good harvests and good prices became the rule and farmers were finding it easier to pay off their creditors. In the election of 1900, McKinley again defeated Bryan, this time even more decisively than in 1896. "Republican prosperity" was the victor's theme; and the Republican slogan, "The Full Dinner Pail," seemed an appropriate one for a resurgent country.

Even so, several of the radical planks in the Populist program that Bryan and the Democrats had neglected for silver in 1896

soon were enacted into law: railroad legislation, the direct election of senators, the income tax, an expanded currency and credit structure, the initiative and referendum, postal savings banks, and certain features of the subtreasury plan. Thus the doctrines of Populism outlived the party. Moreover, the McKinley victory did not long quiet the forces of protest. One of its main targets became the cities of the nation that had grown up without direction or goals in the iron age of industrial growth and agrarian discontent.

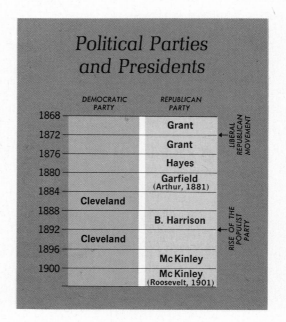

Readings

Asterisk indicates that book is available in paperback.

Matthew Josephson, *The Politicos 1865-1896* * (1938), is the most comprehensive, if contentious, account. Able works of a more recent vintage include Ray Ginger, *Age of Excess, American Life from the End of Reconstruction to World War I* (1965); and H. U. Faulkner, *Politics, Reform, and Expansion* * (1959). E. F. Goldman, *Rendezvous with Destiny: A History of Modern American Reform* * (1952), is a spirited account of the opposition to the prevailing conservatism. The relevant chapters in W. E. Binkley, *American Political Parties: Their Natural History* (1943), are conventional but useful. Outstanding on the administration of the federal government in the Stalwart era is L. D. White, *The Republican Era 1869-1901* (1958). J. G. Blaine, *Twenty Years in Congress* (2 vols., 1884-1886), is something more than an apologia. For first-hand reporting on the Blaine era, see Frances Carpenter, ed., *Carp's Washington* (1960). James Bryce, *The*

American Commonwealth * (2 vols., 1888); and volume II of Moisei Ostrogorski, *Democracy and the Organization of Political Parties* * (2 vols., 1902), are classic analyses.

Useful biographies of the presidents include, Harry Barnard, *Rutherford B. Hayes and His America* (1954); R. G. Caldwell, *James A. Garfield, Party Chieftain* (1931); G. F. Howe, *Chester A. Arthur* (1934); Allan Nevins, *Grover Cleveland* (1932); H. J. Sievers, *Benjamin Harrison* (1959); H. W. Morgan, *William McKinley and His America* (1963); and Margaret Leech, *In the Days of McKinley* (1959). On the lives of others highly placed in politics, see, D. S. Muzzey, *James G. Blaine* (1934); P. W. Glad, *The Trumpet Soundeth: William Jennings Bryan and His Democracy* (1960); P. E. Coletta, *William Jennings Bryan* (1964); Herbert Croly, *Thomas Alonzo Hanna* (1912); and N. W. Stephenson, *Nelson W. Aldrich* (1930). Outstanding biographies of Populist leaders include, C. V. Woodward, *Tom Watson: Agrarian Rebel* * (1938); Martin Ridge, *Ignatius Donnelly* (1962); and F. E. Haynes, *James Baird Weaver* (1919).

On civil service reform, see P. P. Van Riper, *History of the United States Civil Service* (1958); and Ari Hoogenboom, *Fighting the Spoilsmen* * (1961). Relevant to the whole issue of patronage, but of more general interest, is D. J. Rothman, *Politics and Power, The United States Senate 1869-1901* (1966). The legislative background of federal railroad regulation is well presented in L. H. Haney, *A Congressional History of Railways in the United States 1850-1887* (1910). An authoritative analysis is W. Z. Ripley, *Railroads: Rates and Regulation* (1912). Lee Benson, *Merchants—Farmers—and Railroads* (1955), stresses the urban origins of the call for regulation. The most comprehensive study of the Sherman Antitrust Act is H. B. Thorelli, *The Federal Antitrust Policy* (1955).

I. M. Tarbell, *The Tariff in Our Times* (1911), is excellent on the political side of tariff-making. For the acts themselves and their economic consequences, see F. W. Taussig, *The Tariff History of the United States* * (1914), and *Some Aspects of the Tariff Question* (1934). Milton Friedman and A. J. Schwartz, *A Monetary History of the United States 1867-1960* * (1963), is comprehensive. For a brief account see, Richard Hofstadter's introduction to the John Harvard Library edition of *Coin's Financial School* * (1963). Irwin Unger, *The Greenback Era, A Social and Political History of American Finance 1865-1879* (1964), is excellent. On the politics of money, see J. A. Barnes, *John G. Carlisle, Financial Statesman* (1931), and citations below on the farm revolt. On certain other political issues of the day, see M. R. Dearing, *Veterans in Politics, The Story of the G.A.R.* (1952); S. P. Hirshon, *Farewell to the Bloody Shirt* (1962); D. L. McMurry, *Coxey's Army* (1929); and essays in H. W. Morgan, ed., *The Gilded Age* * (1963).

F. A. Shannon, *The Farmer's Last Frontier 1860-1897* (1945), is the best introduction to agricultural problems after the Civil War. S. J. Buck, *The Granger Movement* (1913); and J. D. Hicks, *The Populist Revolt* * (1931), are the standard accounts of farmer unrest and political action. More general accounts will be found in R. B. Nye, *Midwestern Progressive Politics* (1951); and H. S. Merrill, *Bourbon Democracy of the Middle West 1865-1896* (1953). Richard Hofstadter, *The Age of Reform* * (1955), is more analytical. See also, Norman Pollock, *The Populist Response to Industrial America* * (1962); and W. T. K. Nugent, *The Tolerant Populists, Kansas, Populism and Nativism* (1963). Outstanding on the South are C. V. Woodward, *Origins of the New South 1877-1913* (1951); and Theodore Saloutous, *Farmer Movements in the South* * (1960). R. F. Durden, *The Climax of Populism* (1966), is a scholarly study. G. B. Tindall, *A Populist Reader* * (1966), is an ably edited anthology. J. R. Hollingsworth, *The Democracy of Cleveland and Bryan* (1963), emphasizes intraparty conflicts. G. H. Knoles, *The Presidential Campaign and Election of 1892* (1942); and S. L. Jones, *The Presidential Election of 1896* (1964), are exceptional election studies. Valuable also are P. W. Glad, *McKinley, Bryan and the People* * (1964); and Bryan's own account, *The First Battle* (1896).

CHAPTER TWENTY - ONE

In Europe the idea of the "city" has always implied a center of power and learning, of religion and art. The great city—Athens, Rome, Paris, London, Milan, Moscow—traditionally was a place of palaces, kings, and aristocrats, of universities and great churches, of architects, sculptors, painters, poets, philosophers, scholars, doctors. In agrarian America, by contrast, the city was looked upon as a "problem" and little else. "When we get piled upon one another in large cities," Jefferson observed in 1787, "we shall become as corrupt as in Europe, and go to eating one another as they do there." In the 1850's northern moralists were shuddering at the "immense accumu-

The

Urban Challenge

lations of ignorance and error, vice and crime" to be found in the rapidly expanding towns. Even as late as 1895 one commentator wondered over the readiness of farm youth to "leave the country where homes are cheap, the air pure, all men equal, and extreme poverty unknown, and crowd into cities" where they seemed to find "in the noises, the crowds, the excitements, even in the sleepless anxieties of the daily struggle for life, a charm they are powerless to resist." By then the growth of cities had become recognized as an irreversible force—to most Americans a force for evil that had better be contained but in the end could not be.

I. *America's Urban Population*

THE SURGE IN CITY GROWTH

In 1840, only one-twelfth of the American people lived in cities of 8,000 or more. By 1860, the proportion of city-dwellers had grown to one-sixth, and by 1900 to one-third, of the population. In 1900, more than 25 million Americans were living in cities, most of them in the metropolises that had grown so lustily in the preceding 50 years. In 1850, New York City and independent Brooklyn together had a population of 1,200,000. By 1900 (after official consolidation in 1898), their population had soared to over 3 million. In the same period, Philadelphia rose from 560,000 to 1,300,000, and Pittsburgh from 67,000 to 450,000. Most spectacular of all was the development of Chicago. A muddy trading post on the prairie in 1831, with 12 families and a meager garrison as its only inhabitants, Chicago had grown by 1850 to 30,000; by 1880, to 500,000. In the next 20 years, its population reached 1,700,000, placing it far ahead of Philadelphia and second only to New York in size. No other city quite matched the speed of Chicago's rise. But striking in its own right was the sudden thrust forward of places that had scarcely existed in 1860. Denver, a small mining camp on the eve of the Civil War, had 134,000 persons in 1900. In the same period, Minneapolis grew from 2,500 to 200,000; Los Angeles from 5,000 to 100,000. Birmingham, Alabama, was not founded until 1871, but in 1900 it had 38,000 inhabitants.

Two harbingers of the new industrial metropolis had begun to transform the urban American landscape even before 1860: the steam railroad and the stationary steam engine. By the 1850's, the rattle of the railway cars and the whistle of the locomotive had disrupted the solitude of rural towns and villages:

To do things 'railroad fashion' [wrote Thoreau in *Walden*] is now the byword; and it is worth the while to be warned so often and so sincerely by any power to get off its track. There is no stopping to read the riot act, no firing over the heads of the mob, in this case. We have constructed a fate, an *Atropos,* that never turns aside. (Let that be the name of your engine.)

Thoreau's relentless railroad pushed into cities whose economy and way of life had been geared to the river and the canal; it pre-empted the most picturesque sites for freight yards and depots, demolished old landmarks, altered the direction of urban expansion. The wide range of the steam railroad speeded the substitution of more efficient steam power for water power in factories and hastened the expansion of the pre-Civil War mill town to supply manufactures for ever greater and more distant markets. The railroad also brought in the coal from which steam power was generated. The steam railroad and steam power in factories combined to create large new industries which drew thousands of workers into cities and multiplied their problems as well as their wealth.

The rapid growth of American cities after the Civil War was but one reflection of the enormous increase in the scale and the pace of American business enterprise (see Chapter 19). The development of Pittsburgh and Birmingham were attributable directly to the expansion of the iron and steel industries, that of Minneapolis to the rise of the grain trade and flour-milling. Chicago had risen to eminence first as a wheat port, next as a railroad hub, and then as the meat-packing center of the world. Industry and trade so boosted Chicago's business activity that it also became the financial capital of the West. Its credit facilities, moreover, drew a great variety of new industries and new distributing enterprises, such as the Marshall Field store. Philadelphia and New York profited largely from the development of the commercial ties that had been established fairly early in their histories, and also from new industries —such as the manufacture of ready-to-wear clothing, enormously accelerated by the demand for uniforms during the Civil War.

In cities all over the country, moreover, opportunities were opening up in "white-collar" and "service" occupations. Between 1870 and 1910 the number of wholesalers grew approximately 3.5 times, from 16,000 to 58,000; the number of retailers from 376,000 to 1,106,000; the number of salespeople and clerks in stores, from 105,000 to 1,232,000; and the number of commercial travelers from a mere 7,000 to 164,000. Almost equally spectacular in growth was the number of domestics and of persons employed in laundries, restaurants, boarding houses and hotels, barbershops, real estate offices, and banks. All told, in 1910, about

570

7,250,000 persons—not all of them, of course, white-collar workers—were employed in trade and service occupations, a figure almost 4.5 times greater than that for 1870. If the 2,750,000 persons engaged in transportation, urban and interurban, are included in the service category, the 1910 total for trade and service just about equals the totals for agriculture and for manufacturing and mining combined.

THE SOURCES
OF CITY POPULATION

A great part of the American urban population, of course, came from American farms. With such new industrial giants as Rockefeller and Carnegie as their models, farm boys swarmed into the industrial cities with the expectation of working for just a few years before scaling the heights of enterprise on their own.

In Europe, at the same time, a similar movement from rural to urban life was under way, of which the migration of millions to the cities of the United States was but a part. Eventually this migration was to overwhelm the native-born urban families. By 1900, three-fourths of Chicago's population was foreign-born, and the proportion

of foreign-born in New York City was by far the highest in the country. Greater New York's Italian population in the 1890's equaled that of Naples; its German population equaled that of Hamburg. Twice as many Irish lived in New York as in Dublin. The flood of arrivals alarmed many native-born Americans concerned, as one of them confessed in the 1890's, "at the prospect of adding enormously to the burden of the municipal governments in the large cities, already almost breaking down through corruption and inefficiency." And yet the real surge of immigration had hardly begun.

The year 1882, as we have said (p. 540), marked the peak of nineteenth-century immigration to the United States. After 1882, although the aggregate annual figures show ups and downs more or less corresponding with the business cycle, immigration from Europe fell to an 18-year low of 216,400 in 1897, a year in which a mere 22,000 Germans came, compared to 250,000 fifteen years earlier. Had there not been, in the early 1880's, a striking shift in the sources of

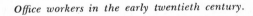

Office workers in the early twentieth century.

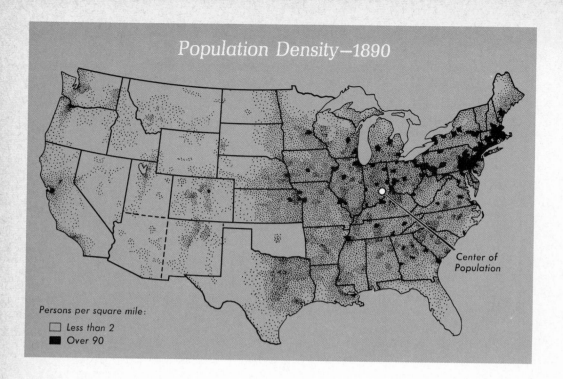

Population Density—1890

Center of
Population

Persons per square mile:
☐ Less than 2
■ Over 90

immigration that had little to do with the business cycle, this fall would have been much sharper; and the recovery—to the blue-sky peak of the early twentieth century—would scarcely have taken place.

Just as the grim famines of the mid-1840's had touched off the massive Irish migrations before the Civil War, and Bismarck's "blood and iron" policies thirty years later had touched off the massive German migrations starting a decade or so after that war's end, so specific calamities and convulsions marked the early surge of the "new" immigration. Beginning in 1881, anti-Semitic pogroms swept Russia and Poland with increasing frequency and virulence, and tens of thousands of Jews (the forerunners of later millions) began to look for avenues of escape. In 1887, an especially severe cholera epidemic ate out the *Meridionales* (southerners) of lower Italy, a visitation that set able-bodied survivors there cascading toward the shore and the ships. At about the same time a blight devastated the province of Pribich, once the richest vineyard of Croatia, and poverty-stricken grape-growers by the hundreds set out for America to earn enough in the factories to replant their lands.

Relations among nations as well as calamities within them added appreciably to the ranks of the uprooted. In the 1880's, international competition in imperialism and navalism took on an intensity that was to make World War I virtually unavoidable (see Chapter 23). As suspicion among countries grew, armaments grew apace. Compulsory military service in southern and eastern Europe was greatly extended, training was tightened up, and delinquents were treated with mounting severity. While young men were thus drawn from the land, as a young Slav put it, "to give three of their best years to the army, where they would be slapped, kicked, and cursed," new taxes to support the growing military establishments crushed those left to work the unrewarding soil. These taxes, in turn, passed down as they were by absentee landlords, pressed most harshly upon the unspoken-for "bottom sill." Flight became the watchword of the peasantry, and the "new" migration to America soared.

Yet calamities and convulsions can no more explain the "new" immigration than the "old," let alone the shift from one to the other. Underlying both in the second half of the nineteenth century was the cruel and complex revolution in factory industry and commercial agriculture—and the same pressure of population growth—that we have already described in the United States itself. In short, peasant agriculture had become too inefficient to meet the growing needs for food and fiber in new industrial cities, and industry itself failed to expand sufficiently to accommodate those cast off the land by agricultural reorganization.

Many in the "new" immigration as in the "old" came to America to replenish the spirit and nourish the substance of liberty; and they should not be lost sight of among the myriads of the unskilled, the "migrant industrials," who, as a commentator on the twentieth-century Italian migration said in 1906, "have to choose between emigration and starvation." Yet it was America's capacity and willingness to absorb these desperate millions into the productive web of a rapidly expanding economy that obviously exercised the strongest pull of all.

According to the Industrial Commission report of 1900, "the principal means" by which this pull was exercised over the millions being pushed out of Europe was the "American letter." T. V. Powderly, the Grand Master of the Knights of Labor, charged that plant superintendents in the United States, especially in times of labor disputes or the sudden expansion of plants in competitive labor areas, "bribed" Hungarian, Greek, Italian, and Slavonian workmen to write to friends and relatives at home, urging them to join the American labor force. But in good times cash wages and the gnawing loneliness for compatriots gave sufficient impulse to immigrant workers to crowd around one who could write—or around the priest, or the editor of his native-language paper—to get him to convey the news of America home.

Well-organized institutions also found the business of supplying American industry with millions of foreign workers lucrative. In Europe, the growth of such great steamship companies as the British Cunard and White Star lines, the North German Lloyd, and the Italian and French lines had recently been stimulated by government

subsidies justified under the naval building programs that accompanied imperialist expansion. By the turn of the century these lines had tied in with new European railroad networks—themselves promoted with a sharp eye to troop movements—to channel the immigrant hordes into the few great British and continental ports that alone could dock the large new liners carrying American grain and machinery eastward and prepared to haul human cargoes on the return trip.

The steamship companies maintained literally tens of thousands of commission agents in southern and eastern Europe to capitalize on the pressures that beset the peasantry and entice them by every form of misrepresentation to purchase steerage tickets. The dark story of this traffic remains buried in the records of the companies themselves; but it is clear from immigrants' own accounts and other reports that the steamship lines spared no means of advertising and publicity to reinforce the message of the "American letter," and no avenues of political pressure to fight immigration control.

On the American side of the business were the rank labor contractors of every sort who flourished like weeds in American ports in the absence of government supervision over the placement of the newcomers. In 1855, Castle Garden at the tip of Manhattan Island became the formal reception center for most of the immigrants reaching the United States. In 1891, Ellis Island in New York Harbor supplanted the old, overcrowded headquarters. Officials at the Garden and the Island, however, did little more than record the immigrant's arrival. Overshadowing them in activity were the swarming Italian bankers, who made a good thing of exchanging home country currency for American dollars; the *padroni*, who organized Italian labor gangs on the spot and contracted them to industry or construction promoters at so much a head to be paid to the *padrone* himself (he, in turn, paid the captive immigrant whatever he saw fit); and Jewish sweat-shop operators, and other brokers and agents who helped see their compatriots through the portals of the City before herding them off to harsh employment. Some immigrants might be met by representatives of immigrant welfare societies or immigrant churches, or by relatives and friends—although it was often difficult for the writers of the "American letters" to get a day off to receive them. Many were left to shift entirely for themselves—except for the assistance of swindlers and crooks of every nationality, including Americans, who had mastered all means of fleecing the masses dumped by the steamship lines.

RECORD NUMBERS
AND "NATIVE" FEARS

One of the most widely discussed questions in the United States early in the twentieth century, when immigration from southern and eastern Europe to American cities made its last and strongest surge, was that "of race suicide, or, as one may choose to call it," in the words of Robert Hunter, "the annihilation of the native American stock." Just where the masses of earlier Catholic immigrants from Ireland or of German immigrants from the Rhineland fitted into "native American stock" was not made clear. But certain inescapable statistics strongly suggest that "native" concern about the later immigration must have arisen as much from honest fears as from hypocrisy.

1. Up to 1880, immigrants from the Austro-Hungarian empire and neighboring satellites in Central Europe never numbered more than 8,800 a year; up to 1900, they never numbered more than 77,000 a year. Between 1900 and 1914, on the other hand, their number never fell below 100,000 annually, and in those 15 years alone, more than 3,100,000 Austro-Hungarians entered the United States.

2. Up to 1880, immigrants from Italy never numbered more than 8,700 a year; up to 1900, they never numbered more than 77,500 a year. Between 1900 and 1914, on the other hand, their number never fell below 100,000 annually, and in those same 15 years, more than 3,000,000 Italians entered the United States.

3. Up to 1880, immigrants from Russia and related Baltic states never numbered more than 8,000 a year; up to 1900, they never numbered more than 81,500 a year. Not until 1902 did their number exceed 100,000, and again not until 1914 did it dip under that figure. In the 15 years, 1900 to 1914, Russia and her Baltic neighbors sent more than 2,500,000 persons to the United States.

4. From the Balkan countries of eastern and southern Europe (and adjacent Asia)—for example, Romania, Bulgaria, Greece, Turkey, and Syria—the aggregate number of immigrants to the United States before 1900 rarely exceeded 10,000 a year. Yet between 1900 and 1914, these countries sent out an annual average of nearly 60,000 and an aggregate for 15 years of nearly 900,000 persons.

Thus, in a *single decade and a half,* at the start of the twentieth century, approximately 9.5 million exotic people (equal, almost to a man, to the 9.5 million who had come from the familiar United Kingdom over a period of a hundred years and more) engulfed the North Atlantic ports of the United States, most of them pouring into the port of New York, which many of them never left. Other peoples, of course, continued to arrive in northern cities in particular, including the advance guard of Negro migrants from the South, but they entered almost unnoticed in the flood of strangers—Magyars, Croats and Ruthenians, Neapolitans and Sicilians, Serbs and Slovaks and near-Orientals, Roman Catholics, Greek Orthodox, Jews, and Mohammedans.

These bringing with them unknown gods and rites,
Those, tiger passions, here to stretch their claws,
In street and alley what strange tongues are loud,
Accents of menace alien to our air,
Voices that once the Tower of Babel knew!

574

"O Liberty," cried the genteel poet, Thomas Bailey Aldrich,

> O Liberty, white Goddess! is it well
> To leave the gates unguarded? . . .

Under pressure from "race-suicide" propagandists and other xenophobes, Congress in the early 1920's adopted a national "quota system" by which immigration henceforth was effectively checked (see Chapter 26). Before this quota system could be enforced, an extraordinary investigation of the "national origins" of the American population at the time had to be carried out. This investigation revealed the remarkable fact that, despite the entry of considerably more than 35 million immigrants since the Revolution (a figure approximately 10 times larger than the American population in 1783), 51 per cent of the American people were descended from colonial families, and only 49 per cent were foreign-born or descended from all the post-Revolutionary newcomers, including those from Great Britain.

Other statistics may be cited to show that the turn-of-the-century alarmists were frightened by a bogey of their own creation. In 1880, for example, long before the massive migrations from eastern and southern Europe had begun, about 12 per cent of the American population was foreign-born. In 1930, soon after the massive immigration had been extinguished, the figure was still 12 per cent. True, between 1890 and 1910, the proportion of foreign-born had risen to 15 per cent of the whole population, but this small and temporary advance was hardly commensurate with the rise in the temperature of the "race-suicide" ranks. Between 1890 and 1930, moreover, while the total number of foreign-born *and* the native-born children of foreign or mixed parentage *nearly* doubled (from 20.7 to 40.2 million), the number of native whites of native parents *more than* doubled (from 34.4 to 70.1 million).

Fear of "the annihilation of the native American stock," whatever was understood by that phrase, proved groundless. Yet certain features of the massive "new" immigration, and not least its suddenly massive dimensions, make the turn-of-the-century alarm among the cities' growing middle and upper classes understandable. "We came not empty-handed here," wrote the immigrant poet, Adam Dan, "But brought a rich inheritance." That, few Americans would deny. The trouble was, this inheritance suddenly had become far too rich for many to assimilate without uneasiness, and the immigrant soon became a more imposing scapegoat than ever for urban ills.

II. *The Slough of City Life*

THE SHAME OF THE CITIES

The full impact of urban growth was not to be felt until the Progressive era (see Chapter 24), during which, in fact, the massive expansion of immigration took place. In earlier decades immigration only aggravated the difficulties of city government which native Americans had long endured. Dominant merchants, lawyers, and bankers put their faith in rising land values and trusted others to look out for themselves. Most city-dwellers took at best only a half-hearted interest in civic projects that did not immediately affect their own pocketbooks or pleasure. City development lay in the hands of real-estate operators who cut up the land into rectangular lots divided by a gridiron of streets. City authorities took no steps to save desirable areas for public use. They permitted land-owners to erect factories, shops, and business offices wherever they pleased. Industrialists polluted rivers and streams and transformed ideal residential sections into ugly slag-heaps. In an age of laissez faire, when planning was out of fashion, the convenience of businessmen determined the city's form and future.

The cities did provide some indispensable public services, however. Municipal gas mains were constructed; water supplies were maintained; police and especially fire protection was made available; garbage was regularly collected; transportation and lighting of a sort were supplied. But facilities for recreation and health were provided only as afterthoughts, if at all. Living quarters for the working population usually lacked adequate space, ventilation, and plumbing. As the century waned, American cities became more deeply scarred with slums and infected with vice and crime. To make matters worse, the very size and impersonality of the sprawling cities discouraged attempts to improve them.

As early as the 1880's, the poor administration of American cities had become, according to the English observer, James Bryce, "the one conspicuous failure in the United States." A prominent educator announced in 1890 that "with few exceptions, the city governments of the United States are the worst in Christendom—the most expensive, the most inefficient, and the most corrupt."

In his celebrated study, *The American Commonwealth* (1888), Bryce discussed some of the causes of city mismanagement that he had extracted from a report drawn up by a New York commission in 1876. He listed them as follows: (1) crooked and incompetent officials, (2) the "introduction of State and national politics into municipal affairs," and (3) the control of local affairs by state legislatures unfamiliar with the processes and needs of city government. Then he added a comment of his own:

In great cities we find an ignorant multitude, largely composed of recent immigrants, untrained in self-government; we find a great proportion of the voters paying no direct taxes, and therefore feeling no interest in moderate taxation and economical administration; we find able citizens absorbed in their private businesses, cultivated citizens unusually sensitive to the vulgarities of practical politics, and both sets therefore specially unwilling to sacrifice their time

and tastes and comfort in the struggle with sordid wire-pullers and noisy demagogues.

Bryce's comments begged some interesting questions; they also contained much truth.

In most American cities, power resided in the mayor, in the single- or double-chambered city council, or in independent boards. These agencies determined how municipal funds should be spent. They granted franchises for street railways, let out contracts for building sewers, bought fire-fighting equipment, and granted monopolies to public utilities. Most of these activities were entrusted to committees drawn from elected aldermen or council members, and unscrupulous political bosses found it easy enough to place their henchmen in key positions where they could mulct the city treasuries.

William M. ("Boss") Tweed's career in New York City in the late 1860's was the prototype for the classic political swindler. In 1868 Tweed and his Tammany cronies installed John M. Hoffman in Albany as Governor. The following year, by spending enormous sums bribing legislators (some Senators were given as much as $40,000), Tweed got the legislature to pass a new charter for New York City which he used to make himself a virtual dictator. He formed the famous "Tweed Ring" in the Board of Appointments, controlled judges as well as legislators, and proceeded to plunder New York of sums which have been estimated as high as $100 million.

Tweed's technique was delightfully simple. Everyone who worked for the city was instructed to pad his bill—at first only by 10%, later 66%, finally 85%. The padding was turned over to Tweed's gang. Thus, when Tweed built his notorious Court House, whose final cost ran to many times the original estimate of $3 million, an item charged to the "repair" of fixtures ran to over $1,149,000 before the building was even completed. Forty chairs and three tables cost $179,000, thermometers $7,500 apiece. The carpenter who got $360,000 was surpassed by "The Prince of Plasterers," as the *Times* called him, who drew over $2,870,000 for nine months' work.

When respectable citizens howled, Tweed insolently challenged them: "What are you going to do about it?" None the less, the volume of criticism mounted, and due particularly to scathing editorials in the *New York Times* and the memorable cartoons by Thomas Nast in that paper and in *Harper's Weekly,* Tweed was ousted in 1871 and in 1876 he died in jail, friendless and penniless. A considerably cleaner Tammany regime followed under "Honest John" Kelly, but in the 1890's, when Tammany was bossed by Richard Croker, the whole cycle of corruption was repeated while lesser thieves plundered other cities.

Reformers hastened to attribute the success of the political bosses and their corrupt machines to what one of them called the "typical immigrant . . . a European peasant, whose horizon has been narrow, whose moral and religious training has been meager and false, and whose ideas of life are low." Native-born businessmen on the make, in quest of tax favors, valuable franchises, pliable legislators, purchasable judges, and sympathetic police probably were as responsible as any group for municipal corruption. Yet it is true that the sheer multitude of newcomers to the cities helped sustain boss rule.

The unassimilated foreigner living in the slums, ignorant of American democratic practices, voted dutifully for the city bosses who speeded up his naturalization proceedings, presented him with gifts at Christmas, found city jobs for him or his sons, encouraged his ethnic customs, and mediated with the law when he or his children got into trouble. Many immigrants had carried with them to America feudal notions of government—especially the idea that aristocrats were bound to be the rulers—and could not think of themselves as active participants in public affairs even after they had become American citizens. The average immigrant was suspicious of reforms to improve the efficiency of city administration, for "efficiency" in government might well mean that he and his relations would be dropped from the city payroll. Fearful of change, the peasant-immigrant disliked the

very sound of "reform"; the reformer, lacking any notion of the immigrant's real needs and desires, further alienated himself by attacking the very men to whom the immigrant felt most loyal—the political bosses. Reformers also had their troubles with the well-educated native voter taken in by politicians who cleverly exploited party loyalties and merged non-political local issues with national political ones. Many honest and respectable men, rather than endanger their national party, chose to support the corrupt city and state machines. Or they tolerated government by the bosses on the grounds that it was good for business; or that, despite its high cost, it worked well; or that it protected the good citizen from the mob.

At the same time, the scandals that made the administration of American cities so notorious had more deep-seated causes whose cure demanded knowledge not yet available. There were no sciences of urban management, no experts on garbage-collecting or sewage disposal, no up-to-date budgeting methods. No wonder that unwise borrowing piled up huge municipal debts and the control of finances was so haphazard.

The so-called "Dark Ages" in American municipal history lasted through the 1880's. In 1894, local reform groups meeting in Philadelphia federated in the National Municipal League which soon offered much new technical information on city management. But even in the Progressive Era, urban problems persisted and sometimes worsened (see Chapter 24).

EARLY

TECHNICAL ADVANCES

The late nineteenth-century American city clearly deserved the condemnation of its many critics. But even in this period some progress was made in solving technical problems arising from sheer growth.

To relieve traffic congestion in great cities

and to carry the millions of urban workers to and from their jobs, a swifter and more reliable vehicle was needed than the horse-car whose maximum speed of about six miles an hour had sufficed for a simpler society. As early as 1867 the steam-driven elevated railroad had been tried out in New York City and came into every day use there during the '70's. Horse-car companies fought the new lines bitterly, and citizens complained of the soot and smoke that poured through their windows and the hot ashes that dropped on pedestrians' heads. As time passed, elevated steam railroads were gradually abandoned, but not because of the discomforts they produced. It simply became too expensive to construct elevated structures capable of supporting heavy locomotives—the only kind powerful enough to draw a long train of cars at satisfactory speeds. A still newer and cheaper method had to be found to transport people who were being forced by urban overcrowding to live farther and farther from their work.

The cable-car, propelled by an underground cable, was used in San Francisco in 1873 and in Chicago ten years later. The most promising innovation, however, was electric traction, developed by Frank Julian Sprague, whose successful system in Richmond in 1887 demonstrated the practicability of the trolley car in large cities. In getting his system into operation, Sprague first had to solve difficult technical problems. He invented the first satisfactory car-motors, trolleys, wires, and cars, and devised a scheme for moving the cars so that traffic jams would not clog the single-and double-track lines.

The men who owned and operated steam railroads in the great cities, having invested a great deal of capital in their enterprises, were extremely reluctant to switch to the new method, but eventually they had to yield. Clearly, electric trolleys surpassed in every way the steaming, stinking, clangorous coal-burning locomotives, nor did they require the old networks of elevated track that cut off air and light. The electric lines needed no heavy locomotives, since each car had its own power. The cars could be run singly or in trains; they could be switched easily; and repair problems were cut to a minimum. Eventually the elevated trains, too, were electrified, and subways (which had been operating in London since 1886) were introduced in Boston in 1897 and in New York in 1904.

Besides providing the energy for transportation, electricity also solved the problem of lighting American cities. Flickering gas lamps gave way to improved arc lamps in 1879, and soon after, electric signs, in anticipation of the "Great White Way" of the modern city, lit up a few streets. Interior lighting by electricity became commercially feasible after Thomas A. Edison's perfection of the incandescent bulb the same year (see p. 528). Gas, however, was by no means driven out as an illuminant. In 1885, an Austrian, Auer von Welsbach, invented a conical gas mantle that produced an intense diffused light, and for many years the gas lamp was more widely used indoors than the electric bulb.

In dealing with such matters as water supply, waste-disposal, and street-cleaning, which had been handled relatively well in the past, American cities grew less and less conscientious. By 1870, the disposal of waste had reached a critical stage in the larger cities, where sanitation methods scarcely differed from those employed in the villages of a century before. Not one American city filtered its water, even though the indiscriminate dumping of sewage and garbage into streams often polluted the supply. The typhoid fever epidemics common in Chicago and Philadelphia in the last decades of the century could be traced to the drinking of contaminated water.

URBAN HOUSING

Until the Civil War, the American city had retained its provincial character, and even with the advent of the industrial age, the vestiges of a simpler agrarian and commercial society had not yet been entirely effaced. Especially in New England and in the cities of the eastern seaboard, pleasant wooden houses set back from elm-

578

lined streets could be found. After 1865, the appearance of the city changed as new styles of architecture were introduced and as machine-made pressed brick displaced wood as the standard building material. Not all the houses built in the next generation were the architectural absurdities some critics have declared them to be; the appearance of many streets and districts in the major American cities was by no means displeasing. Yet the urban landscape, as a whole, became dingier. Even the very rich, who with their armies of servants and their private equipages, escaped many of the trials of the poor, often lived in mansions situated near gasworks and slaughterhouses, and breathed the same sooty air as the slum-dwellers. In middle-class dwellings throughout the country, interiors were dark and crammed with overstuffed furniture peculiarly susceptible to dust. The bulk and clutter of Victorian living suited a generation that overate, whose women attached bustles to their dresses, and who lived what might be described as upholstered lives.

The very poor lived under conditions that were scarcely endurable. As the open sections of big cities became covered over with factories, the native-born middle classes withdrew to sections temporarily free of industry and aliens. Their old houses then were converted into multiple family dwellings, each becoming ever more crowded as rooms as well as entire floors were divided up. Whole families, and sometimes more than one, lived in the airless closets of these houses usually without sanitary facilities, lighting or heat. The practice of leasing rows of abandoned middle class houses for conversion into tenements had begun in New York City even before 1840. After 1865, such tenements spread over metropolitan America like a disease.

The first tenements designed expressly to provide cheap lodging for working-class families were constructed in New York in 1850. Their owners, driven by ever rising land costs, built on every available square inch, leaving no room for grass or trees or air. Soon whole districts were occupied by dingy and unhygienic barracks. Jacob Riis

quotes the following description of the typical tenement in his classic study, *How the Other Half Lives* (1891):

It is generally a brick building from four to six stories high on the street, frequently with a store on the first floor which, when used for the sale of liquor, has a side opening for the benefit of the inmates and to evade the Sunday law; four families occupy each floor, and a set of rooms consists of one or two dark closets, used as bedrooms, with a living room twelve feet by ten. The staircase is too often a dark well in the centre of the house, and no direct through ventilation is possible, each family being separated from the other by partitions. Frequently the rear of the lot is occupied by another building of three stories high with two families on a floor.

Into these noisome rookeries swarmed the immigrant poor, paying extortionate rents yielding profits as high as 30 per cent. Landlords usually refused all pleas to repair or improve their property and evicted occupants who did not pay in advance.

In 1879, the "dumb-bell tenement," so called because of the shape of its floor plan, was introduced as the model housing unit in New York City. This structure provided fire-proof stairways, a toilet for every two families, and an outside window for each room. Nevertheless, the solid rows of five- or six-story "dumb-bell" buildings on 25-foot lots and extending 90 feet to the rear, quickly degenerated into pest-houses as bad as the old tenements and simply postponed thorough-going tenement reform.

Although New York's slums were the worst in the nation, wretched conditions prevailed elsewhere as well. Philadelphia constructed small two-story houses instead of tenements for its working-class population, but overcrowding produced the same hideous conditions. Other cities resorted to the wooden "three-decker" apartment building, first introduced in Boston during the 1840's and 1850's. From there it spread west to Chicago.

The interior of a New York tenement; photograph by Jacob Riis, c. 1910.

III. *Urban Reformers*

THE HUMANITARIANS

One way to deal with city slums was simply to move away from them, and many middle-class families during the '70's and '80's began the continuing escape to the suburbs. By the 1880's improved rail service made it possible for businessmen to commute from suburban homes to city offices, and quiet villages near New York City, Philadelphia, Chicago, and Boston soon fell prey to the fashionable exodus.

Fortunately, though, not everyone took this way out. A number of urban reformers, philanthropists, and churchmen, moved by moral considerations and sometimes by fear of social revolution, worked alone or through humanitarian organizations to make life more livable for the slum-dwellers. A few far-sighted planners tried to bring the country to the city. The vision of the garden city had been caught in 1858 when Calvert Vaux and the great landscape archi-

tect, Frederick Law Olmsted, planned Central Park in New York. Philadelphia's Fairmount Park, opened in 1855, was considerably larger than Central Park, but Olmsted's and Vaux's ingenious and tasteful efforts to accommodate roads, lawns, and buildings to the topography ushered in a new era in landscape design. At first, many people complained that parks were aristocratic, un-American, and un-businesslike, but this prejudice disappeared in later years. Between 1872 and 1895, Olmsted and his disciples laid out parks in Boston, Washington, Buffalo, Detroit, Rochester, and elsewhere. Although the parks could hardly transform an industrial metropolis into an Eden, they at least preserved a vestige of nature in a world of iron and stone.

While landscape architects were beginning to beautify the city, social workers began to investigate the casualties of urban life: the criminal, the cast-off, the sick and the helpless. According to the traditional view, poverty and misfortune were the results of personal weakness, but in the 1870's urban reformers began to realize that the causes of poverty were complex, that material success was not simply a matter of individual superiority. Illness, the death of the bread-winner, unemployment, and low wages, clearly created more paupers and criminals than either alcoholism or laziness. The city poor needed practical aid more than they needed sermons. The first step was poor relief simply to keep thousands alive. By the 1870's, the problem had become so vast that private charities working independently could no longer do the job properly. In 1877, Buffalo became the first city to coordinate its relief organizations. A decade later, 25 associated charities throughout the country had cut out much of the inefficiency of the earlier social agencies.

By swelling the number of those most susceptible to agitation and discontent, the slums, many believed, intensified the danger of social upheaval. Hoping to lessen the gulf between the privileged and the underprivileged, middle-class reformers established settlement houses in the poorer districts which afforded guidance, recreation, and companionship free of charge.

The idea of the settlement house originated in England, where the existence of "two nations [as Disraeli remarked] . . . who are as ignorant of each other's habits, thoughts, and feelings as if they were dwellers in different zones or inhabitants of different planets," had prompted a few dedicated spirits to work with the London poor in the 1870's. The founding of Toynbee Hall in East London in 1884 provided a model for at least four American settlement houses whose founders had visited the new institution soon after it was opened.

Jane Addams (1860-1935) following a two-year sojourn in Europe beginning in 1887, when she visited Toynbee Hall, became the leader of the movement in America. With her friend, Ellen Gates Starr, in 1889, she converted the old Hull mansion on the Chicago West Side into a settlement house called Hull House. Settlement houses,

she knew, solved no basic issues, but they brought some measure of hope to the "potentially useful citizen who simply needed help." Women like Jane Addams, wrote the municipal reformer, Frederic Howe, saw the "city in the light of the home. The vice, the saloon, the schools, the libraries, the water, gas, and transportation questions are to her questions of the family, of the child, questions of comfort, of happiness, of safety." Jane Addams put it differently:

The settlement [she wrote] is an attempt to relieve . . . the overaccumulation at one end of society and the destitution at the other; but it assumes that this overaccumulation and destitution is most sorely felt in the things that pertain to social and educational advantages. It must be grounded in a philosophy . . . which will not waver when the race happens to be represented by a drunken woman or an idiot boy.

In Boston, Cleveland, and Pittsburgh, college men and women soon put Jane Addams' philosophy into practice. They formed clubs for boys and societies for wayward girls, transformed settlement houses into a combination day-nursery, men's club, school, gymnasium, and employment bureau, and campaigned resolutely for improved sanitary regulations, better housing, and penal reform.

The scientific approach to social welfare did not slow down the crusade against intemperance and the saloon (see p. 653). On the contrary, this movement gathered greater momentum than ever after the heavy-drinking years of the Civil War. The women who were in the forefront of the temperance and prohibitionist campaign also were to be found at the head of the campaign for women's suffrage, which was believed to be an essential instrument for the correction by legislation of the growing evils of urban life (see Chapter 24).

THE CHURCHES

The response of the churches to slums and poverty was at first halting and indecisive, for few ministers had any first-hand knowledge of lower class life. Some of them had reported a falling off of working-class attendance in their churches even before the Civil War, a trend that continued in the postwar decades. But they tended to attribute this merely to godlessness. When workingmen's demands for shorter hours and for government regulation of working conditions grew loud, church leaders reminded them: "Whatever you suffer here from injustice of others will turn to your account hereafter. Be quiet. Whatsoever your hands can find to do, do it, and be content with your wages. God will take care of the rest." But such advice could not withstand the exposés of city conditions, and during the 1870's, the churches began to modify their stand.

The Social Gospel movement, which burgeoned during the last two decades of the nineteenth century, was organized by socially conscious ministers from various denominations and rested on the conviction that man is born "in a sinful society, which fact is the cause of deep evil." Christ, the Social Gospelers believed, came to "establish a new environment" as well as "to save rebellious men." Hence all Christians ought to be social reformers.

Some liberal clergymen went no farther than to advocate moderate reforms in wages, housing, and working conditions. The more radical, however, impatient with efforts to preserve the economic status quo, insisted that the nation's business system be reformed from the bottom up. Ministers like Washington Gladden, R. Heber Newton, Henry Codman Potter, and Walter Rauschenbusch boldly defended the demands of trade unions and wrote and preached against laissez faire. Gladden's *Applied Christianity* (1886), and Newton's *The Morals of Trade* (1876), expressed the Social Gospel ideal that Christian solutions existed for all social problems, and that contrary to the Social Darwinists (see p. 591), the remedying of social ills was neither impractical nor impossible. By the 1880's, theological seminaries were offering courses in social Christianity and social ethics.

Yet despite its influence, the Social Gospel movement was confined to a minority of intellectuals and did not touch the majority of American churchgoers. In general, churches like the Baptist and Methodist, whose membership consisted largely of artisans, shopkeepers, and farmers, preferred to keep the old emphasis on individual responsibility for sin. The fact that many of the newly rich were Baptist and Methodist laymen (John D. Rockefeller was a prominent Baptist elder, Daniel Drew a fervent Methodist) may also help to explain why their churches did not quarrel with society as they found it. Indeed, most of the influential American clergymen themselves were orthodox in their economics even when they were unorthodox in their theology.

Henry Ward Beecher, one of the most celebrated ministers of his day, repudiated the hell-fire and damnation doctrines of his famous father, Lyman Beecher, and preached a liberal theology congenial to his wealthy Brooklyn congregation. He also sanctified the cult of business success. Beecher condemned the eight-hour day, insisted that poverty was a sign of sin, and urged that strikers be put down with violence if necessary. Commenting in 1877 apropos of the sharp wage cuts suffered by the railway workers, he observed:

It is said that a dollar a day is not enough for a wife and five or six children. No, not if the man smokes or drinks beer. It is not enough if they are to live as he would be glad to have them live . . . But is not a dollar a day enough to buy bread with? Water costs nothing; and a man who cannot live on bread is not fit to live. What is the use of a civilization that simply makes men incompetent to live under the conditions which exist . . .

These sentiments were so deeply appreciated by Beecher's national following that not even the scandalous stories of his adulterous practices brought out in the Beecher-Tilton divorce trial in 1875 could extinguish the intense loyalty of his following.

Some Protestant ministers who, like Beecher, thought that the workingman could do without beer if not without bread, also thought he could do without God.

That "the classes which are eminently non-intelligent or non-respectable" should be "non-church-goers," said one, might be taken for granted. Others, however, were growing deeply apprehensive about the "un-churched masses," and sought ways to reclaim them. One device was the revival meeting presided over by itinerant evangelists who ignored economic and political issues and preached the "old-time" religion.

Among the most effective of the evangelists was Dwight L. Moody. In 1870, this former shoe salesman from Boston, teamed up with the singer Ira D. Sankey to launch a mighty campaign for saving souls. Moody preached a simple but powerful message, urging his listeners to be brave, cheerful, and enthusiastic, to abandon "the cold formalism that has crept into the Church of God," to persevere for Christ. Sankey chanted the tender old hymns, "Saved by Grace," "Almost Persuaded," and "Safe in the Arms of Jesus," with such compelling sweetness that thousands were melted into grace. From Chicago, where Moody had evangelized successfully in the "Little Hell" on the North Side, Moody and Sankey carried the question "Are You a Christian?" to England. Having silenced the scoffers there, they returned to carry every large city in the United States by storm. The Chicago Bible Institute for Home and Foreign Missions, founded in 1899, was only one of many monuments erected to them.

The evangelist spirit was more tangibly expressed in the Young Men's Christian Association, founded as an American off-shoot of an English society in 1851, and the Young Women's Christian Association, founded in 1858. Both associations were dedicated to "the physical, mental, social, and spiritual benefit" of their members and of men and women everywhere. By 1897, the Y.M.C.A. had 263,298 members in the United States and the Y.W.C.A. about 35,000. Another importation from England was the Salvation Army, organized by a Wesleyan Methodist, "General" William Booth. This army of Christians devoted themselves to feeding and sheltering the city's unfortunates and restoring their souls.

After the first American branch was established in 1880, the Salvation Army's "slum brigades" marched out into the tenement areas and "skid rows." Their methods were hardly scientific, for they ignored the basic causes of urban sickness. Yet the soldiers of General Booth brought much comfort and relief to the neglected poor.

The more well-to-do city-dwellers, owing, it was sometimes suggested, to the hectic pace of urban living, required another sort of spiritual balm. This was provided by a remarkable woman, Mrs. Mary Baker Eddy, whose *Science and Health* (1875) contained the basic doctrines of the Church of Christ, Scientist, a sect that numbered 35,000 by 1900. In brief, Mrs. Eddy taught that "Disease is caused by the mind alone" and that "Science," another name for the wisdom of God, had been revealed to man by His Son, Jesus Christ. Christ showed how the Mind, the equivalent of God, Truth, or Spirit, could overcome sickness and disease. "Mind constructs the body, and with its own materials instead of matter; hence no broken bones or dislocations can occur." Christian Science had obvious connections with older theologies, but no one before Mrs. Eddy had announced the unreality of death, pain and sin as demonstrable science. Her message appealed to many Americans for whom science had come to have magical qualities.

The activities of the Protestant churches hardly touched the Roman Catholic urban proletariat. Catholics in the United States had increased from roughly 6 million in 1880 to 12 million in 1900, largely as the result of heavy immigration from Italy and eastern Europe. Unlike the Protestants, who had not paid much attention to social welfare until the 1880's and who were inclined to attribute personal misfortune to the sins of the sufferer, the Catholic clergy had traditionally addressed themselves to the needs of the urban poor. Isaac T. Hecker, a Catholic convert and a former member of the Brook Farm community, had established the Paulist Fathers among the poverty-stricken New York Irish in 1858. After the Civil War, the Church founded philanthropic institutions and schools and carried on an effective program to Americanize Catholic immigrants.

Roman Catholic success with the urban masses led certain Protestant leaders to suspect that the priests were plotting to take over the country. The Congregationalist Josiah Strong argued that "the strength of Romanism is in the city, and the city is soon to dominate the nation." The influx of Catholic immigrants again brought to the surface all the anti-Catholic fears that had been latent since the days of the Know Nothings (see p. 397). The American Protective Association, a secret society formed in 1887 to exploit the bigotry of the rural Middle West against the influence of Roman Catholicism in labor and politics, capitalized on these fears. The A.P.A. warned that a concealed army of 700,000 papal soldiers was ready to take over the American government, even though at this very time Catholic leaders like Cardinal James Gibbons of Baltimore and Arch-

bishop John Ireland of St. Paul were championing political democracy and accepting the separation of church and state. The A.P.A. quickly spread its activities to the cities, but since it rarely attracted influential citizens it lost its impetus after 1896.

Protestant fears that the Catholic Church might "take possession of the nation" eventually led Protestant clergy to imitate Catholic methods. Indiscriminate almsgiving and individual congregations working in isolation obviously were not sufficient for the gigantic task of spiritual and social renovation. Ministers they said, would have to acquaint themselves "with the movements of the masses" as the Catholic priests had done. "Too long," a Methodist Conference declared, "has Rome been allowed a practical monopoly of the humanitarian agencies of religion." During the post Civil War decades, sectarian isolation gave way to non-denominational mission societies. The "institutional church" made its appearance —replete with club rooms, gymnasiums, youth organizations, and women's societies —in an effort to reach the hitherto neglected poor.

IV. *Editors and Architects*

URBAN JOURNALISM

Even before the Civil War, writers and editors had discovered that crusades against civic corruption or private iniquity not only improved the moral tone of the public but also paid off in sales. In 1858, *Frank Leslie's Illustrated Newspaper* conducted a sensational campaign against New York milk-producers accused of selling milk from diseased herds, and succeeded in arousing such a public clamor that the state legislature in 1861 was forced to prohibit the sale of milk from cows nourished on the waste products of distilleries. A decade later, *Harper's Weekly,* featuring the savage cartoons of Thomas Nast as we have seen (p. 577), led the fight to overthrow Boss Tweed. This crusade trebled the *Weekly's* circulation. Henry and Charles Francis Adams' revelations in the *North American Review*

of Jay Gould's financial piracies, Josiah Strong's denunciation of slums, immigration, and despotic capitalists in his book *Our Country* (1885), and W. T. Stead's lurid reports of Chicago wickedness in *If Christ Came to Chicago!* (1894) were other highly moral testaments that evoked a wide response.

Civic vice gave such a jolt to circulation that newspaper editors began to invent "causes" or to feature crime. Recent arrivals from the farm were particularly responsive to stories that seemed to confirm their suspicions about life in the "wicked city." Reporters who were able to "crash" the lavish entertainments of the rich and to describe them from the inside, or who could draw a tear by writing authentic reports of the sordid experiences of the poor, brought a new individuality and a new glamor to newspaper careers. The new methods helped to enlarge daily newspaper circulation from 2,800,000 in 1870 to 24 million in 1899. Increased revenue from subscriptions and sales, and above all from advertising, helped free editors from political pressure and enabled them to become powerful manipulators of public opinion.

Joseph Pulitzer, owner of the St. Louis *Post-Dispatch* and later of the New York *World,* exemplified the new type of publisher. Combining the crudest sensationalism with effective exposés the *World* lived up to Pulitzer's promise to publish a "journal that is not only cheap but bright, not only bright but large, not only large but truly democratic . . . devoted more to the new than the old world, that will expose all fraud and sham, fight all public evils and abuses." The *World* introduced comics in color and exploited all the inventions that were revolutionizing publishing during this period: improved newsprint made from wood pulp, the Linotype machine (1886), typewriters, telephones, and the telegraph. These improvements, put to sound use, produced startling rises in circulation—from 20,000 to 40,000 within two months after Pulitzer took over in May, 1883; to 100,000 by the fall of 1884, and 250,000 by 1886.

Pulitzer's methods were quickly copied by papers in other large cities and by ruthless competitors in New York. E. W. Scripps' papers in Cleveland, St. Louis, and Cincinnati successfully employed Pulitzer's techniques. William Randolph Hearst, fresh from Harvard and backed by his father's millions, outdid Pulitzer in sensationalism in his New York *Journal.* One result of the fierce newspaper rivalry was "yellow journalism," a name that derived from the yellow ink used in comics but that came to stand for lurid publishing. Conservative editors were quick to criticize "yellow journalism," but the only effective answer was to produce a good newspaper that sold widely without resort to it. Adolph S. Ochs proved that this could be done when he took over the moribund *New York Times* in 1896, cut its price to a penny, in-

troduced new features, and revived its circulation by full and trustworthy coverage of foreign and domestic news.

When Congress, by an act of March 3, 1879, granted low postal rates to magazines, their circulation grew even more spectacularly than that of newspapers. *McCall's* (1870), *Popular Science* (1872), *Woman's Home Companion* (1873), *Cosmopolitan* (1886), *Collier's* (1888), *Vogue* (1892), and *Outdoor Life* (1898) were only a few of the magazines that benefited from the new postal act. By and large, these publications, as well as old-established monthlies like *Harper's, The Atlantic, Scribner's,* and *The Century,* appealed to the literary tastes and the moral code of the middle-class urban reader. In the last decade of the century, magazines became more sensational in their methods and gave more attention to controversial current issues—a tendency that foreshadowed the muckraking magazines of the early 1900's (see p. 649). New techniques in printing and heavier subsidies from advertisers helped publishers lower magazine prices, so that by 1900 with the additional benefit of low mailing costs hundreds of thousands of families could subscribe annually.

Cyrus H. K. Curtis' *Ladies Home Journal,* founded in 1883, became the most spectacular magazine success, reaching a million in circulation by 1900. His brilliant editor, Edward Bok, filled the *Journal* with features designed to draw feminine readers avid for advice on how to bring up their children, decorate their homes, and preserve their health. Bok bought the fiction of the most popular American and English writers, and paid them well for their stories. Soon this "monthly Bible of the American home" had become a national force which, among other accomplishments, influenced American domestic architecture, led a campaign to force municipal authorities to clean up their cities, and pioneered in the crusade against patent medicines.

Much has been made of the ignorance and vulgar display of the "taste-makers" of the Gilded Age. We hear of plutocrats who bought "old masters" especially manufactured for them in Paris studios, or of the millionaire steel baron who, learning of a famous artist named Copley, told his secretary to get in touch with him "to paint the kids." Then there is the caricature of Henry C. Frick seated on his Renaissance throne under a baldacchino and immersed in a copy of the *Saturday Evening Post*. Anecdotes like these reveal the tastelessness of the nouveau riche, but they do not explain the bad architecture and painting of the Gilded Age, or the failure of its genteel critics to appreciate the possibilities of art in an industrial era.

Realistic writers pictured the modern city as a kind of hell. The Chicago heroine of Hamlin Garland's *Rose of Dutcher's Coolly* (1895), for example,

> . . . looked out across a stretch of roofs, heaped and humped into mountainous masses, blurred and blent and made appalling by smoke and plumes of steam. A scene as desolate as a burnt-out volcano—a jumble of hot bricks, jagged cave-spouts, gas-vomiting chimneys, spiked railings, glass skylights, and lofty spires, a hideous and horrible stretch of stone and mortar, cracked and seamed into streets. It had no limits and it palpitated under the hot September sun, boundless and savage. At the bottom of the crevasses men and women speckled the pavement like minute larvae.

Henry James, returning to New York City at the turn of the century after many years abroad, found everything "impudently new." He was struck by the "multitudinous sky-scrapers standing up to view, from the water, like extravagant pins in a cushion already overplanted." Over old Trinity Church a "vast money-making structure" loomed "horribly . . . with an insolent cliff-like sublimity." James clearly preferred the architectural monuments of Europe.

And yet, in spite of all its ugliness, the Gilded Age saw some striking gains in American building. It took a different kind of imagination than James possessed to see the originality and beauty in America's bridges, causeways, railroad stations, grain elevators, viaducts, warehouses, and office buildings. Brooklyn Bridge, conceived by John Roebling in 1869 and built by his son Washington Roebling between 1869 and 1883, performed a practical function. But its unadorned steel structure was also beautiful. Many skyscrapers of the period evoked a similar functional attractiveness. High ground rents had made imperative the maximum use of space in business districts, and the vertical, soaring office building seemed to escape from the city's limited dimensions. Such buildings were made possible by the electric elevator, which was perfected in the 1880's, and by cheap steel, which replaced the customary bulky masonry walls or stone columns of business buildings with a light, strong "cage." James Bogardus, a New York architect, had designed buildings with supporting iron columns in 1847, but it was not until the 1860's that the needs of industrial America compelled even the architectural aesthetes, men trained to regard iron as beneath the dignity of the artist, to work in metal and glass.

Henry Hobson Richardson (1838-1886) borrowed boldly from traditional forms in his railroad stations, warehouses, and office buildings, but he stamped his personality on every structure he designed, and his mature work was never derivative. Richardson would never promise that a finished building would conform to a client's "ideas of beauty and taste," but the huge seven-story granite Wholesale Store that he designed in 1885 for the Chicago merchant Marshall Field had a businesslike beauty of its own. "Four-square and brown, it stands," wrote Richardson's contemporary, the architect Louis Sullivan, "in physical fact a monument to trade, to the organized commercial spirit, to the power and progress of the age, to the strength and resource of individuality and force of character."

Richardson, an audacious experimenter in masonry construction, died before steel-frame construction came into general use. But under his influence a group of archi-

586

tects—men like John W. Root, Daniel Burnham, William L. Jenney, and (in his early designs) Louis Sullivan—who helped to rebuild Chicago after the fire of 1871 perfected the skyscraper and combined the beautiful and the purposeful in an exciting way. The skyscraper eventually turned streets into canyons, shut out the light and air, increased congestion. But at its best it embodied what Horatio Greenough many years before (see p. 301), had called "the principle of unflinching adaptation of forms to function."

THE DREAM CITY

In 1876, a centennial exposition at Philadelphia had convinced the world of America's technological, if not her artistic, maturity. Her chief contribution lay in what William Dean Howells described as "the superior elegance, aptness, and ingenuity" of her machinery. "It is still in these things of iron and steel," Howells wrote, "that the national genius most freely speaks; by and by the inspired marbles, the breathing canvases, the great literature."

The World's Columbian Exposition, held in Chicago from May to October in 1893, did not fulfill Howells' prophecy, but the 21 million Americans who visited it did catch a glimpse of a white city rising miraculously from the shores of Lake Michigan. The Exposition is no longer regarded as the architectural awakening many once thought it. Nevertheless, as one observer noted, it was ". . . the climacteric expression of America's existence." It dramatized the tremendous progress that had been made in American industry, organizational skill, and inventiveness.

The idea of a world's fair to commemorate the discovery of America was conceived by Congress in 1889. Washington, St. Louis, and New York all contested for the privilege of housing the fair, and New York was so certain of success that investors actually bought up unoccupied land north of Central Park to serve as a site. But the Republican-dominated Congress, determined that the Tammany Democratic machine would get no such plum, awarded the

honor to Chicago. Her enterprising business leaders raised the $10 million required by Congress, hired a corps of artists and designers to transform a marshland into a garden, and erected a temporary city of white plaster of Paris. An army of architects, painters, sculptors, and designers worked out plans for housing more than 65,000 foreign and domestic exhibits, and a national commission representing the states joined forces with a local Chicago committee to direct the mammoth proceedings. The total cost of the Exposition came to approximately $60 million.

The landscape designer, Frederick Law Olmsted, and his assistant, Henry Codman, scored a brilliant success in laying out the grounds, but even their skill could not transform the Exposition into an artistic triumph. Two Chicagoans, John W. Root and Daniel H. Burnham, had been named to direct the construction of the buildings. But the sturdy Root, who, in the Richardson tradition, contemplated structures that suggested the purpose for which they were designed, died during the planning stage. A group of eastern classicists, dominated by Richard Morris Hunt and (by this time) the conservative firm of McKim, Mead, and White, took over. They made a specious classicism the motif of the Exposition, and its glittering theatricality appalled sensitive observers. Only Louis Sullivan's Transportation Building broke with the past. The 9,000 paintings hung in the Art Palace, the murals that glorified the arts and sciences, and the monumental sculpture that loomed everywhere showed hardly a trace of originality or a hint of the vital new art flourishing abroad. The classical buildings of the Court of Honor were destined to have a pernicious influence on the untutored American imagination and to produce a dismal progeny of pillared banks, town halls, and railroad stations.

On the positive side, the Exposition illustrated the virtues of planning, of unity, and magnitude, a lesson that was not to be ignored. William Dean Howells rightly noted that the White City's importance lay not in its architectural banalities but in the idea of design it embodied, ". . . the effect of a principle, and not the scraggling and shapeless accretion of incident." Critics might disagree about the artistic merits of the Exposition, but on one further point there was no dissent: The White City was an object lesson in how a well-managed city ought to be administered for the pleasure and convenience of its inhabitants. An electrified railway, and electrically powered boats on the lagoons, efficiently transported the hundreds of thousands of visitors. Sanitation squads cleaned up the day's debris every night, and adequate rest rooms were provided. Polite and considerate "Columbian Guards" suggested how a model police force should conduct itself. In contrast to Chicago proper, a jungle of disorder lying outside the gates of the Exposition, the White City was managed by the ablest and most respected men in Chicago. Inside, one visitor wrote, a man "could feel for once in his life that he was not liable to be snubbed by the police, nor bullied by car-conductors, nor brow-beaten by salesmen."

The Exposition began at the outset of a severe depression and ended as the depression deepened. Even before it closed, the temporary buildings had cracked and the laths had begun to show beneath the plaster. But the ideal of a garden city—livable and harmonious—lived on.

Readings
* Asterisk indicates that book is available in paperback.

A. M. Schlesinger, *The Rise of the City 1878-1898* (1933), provides a useful general survey. Blake McKelvey, *The Urbanization of America* (1962); and C. M. Green, *The Rise of Urban America* (1965), reflect much modern scholarship. A. F. Weber, *The Growth of Cities in the Nineteenth Century* * (1899), affords valuable statistics. Lewis Mumford, *The Culture of Cities* (1938), and *The City in History* (1961); and Max Weber, *The City* * (1958), are penetrating studies.

The literature on individual cities is growing. From a long list, we may suggest B. L. Pierce, *History of Chicago* (3 vols., 1940-1957); P. U. Kellogg, ed., *The Pittsburgh Survey* (6 vols., 1910-1914); Lloyd Morris, *Incredible New York: High Life and Low Life in the Past 100 Years* (1951); two volumes on Washington, D.C., C. M. Green, *Village and Capital 1800-1878* (1962), and *Capital City 1879-1950* (1963); three volumes on Rochester, Blake McKelvey, *The Water Power City 1812-1854* (1945), *The Flower City 1855-1890* (1949), and *The Quest for Quality 1890-1925* (1956); and Bayrd Still, *Milwaukee, The History of a City* (1948).

On the immigrant sources of postwar urban population, see especially Charlotte Erickson, *American Industry and the European Immigrant 1860-1885* (1957); R. T. Berthoff, *British Immigrants in Industrial America 1790-1950* (1953); J. R. Commons, *Races and Immigrants in America* (1920 ed.); M. R. Davie, *World Immigration with Special Reference to the United States* (1949); Oscar Handlin, *The Uprooted* * (1951), and *Immigration as a Factor in American History* * (1959); R. E. Park and H. A. Miller, *Old World Traits Transplanted* (1921); W. C. Smith, *Americans in the Making: The Natural History of the Assimilation of Immigrants* (1939); and Moses Rischin, *The Promised City, New York's Jews 1870-1914* * (1962). The 42-volume report of a federal immigration commission appointed in 1907 is summarized in J. W. Jenks and W. J. Lauck, *The Immigration Problem* (1912). Its assumptions and findings are attacked in I. A. Hourwich, *Immigration and Labor* (1912).

W. I. Thomas and Florian Znaniecki, *The Polish Peasant in Europe and America* (2 vol. ed., 1958); and R. F. Foerster, *The Italian Emigration of Our Times* (1919), are models of scholarship on these components of the "new immigration." See also Jerome Davis, *The Russian Immigrant* (1922); Thomas Capek, *The Czechs in America* (1920); H. P. Fairchild, *Greek Immigration to the United States* (1911); and Samuel Joseph, *Jewish Immigration to the United States from 1881 to 1910* (1914). John Higham, *Strangers in the Land, Patterns of American Nativism 1860-1925* * (1955), is outstanding on immigrant reception and restriction.

James Bryce, *The American Commonwealth* * (2 vols., 1888), offers an outsanding contemporary critique of city government. Lincoln Steffens, *The Shame of the Cities* * (1904), is masterly. Other recommended works include W. B. Munro, *The Government of American Cities* (1913); C. W. Patton, *The Battle for Municipal Reform: Mobilization and Attack 1875-1900* (1940); R. M. Lubove, *The Progressives and the Slums: Tenement House Reform in New York City* (1962); and Arthur Mann, *Yankee Reformers in the Urban Age* (1954). On urban public transportation and other utilities, see H. C. Passer, *The Electrical Manufacturers 1875-1900* (1953); M. D. Hirsch, *William C. Whitney* (1948); and S. B. Warner, Jr., *Streetcar Suburbs* (1962).

R. H. Bremner, *From the Depths: The Discovery of Poverty in the United States* * (1956), is outstanding. A pioneering study of the same subject is Robert Hunter, *Poverty* * (1904). Jacob Riis, *How the Other Half Lives* * 1890), is a famous report of slum conditions, as is his *The Battle with the Slums* (1902). The classic introduction to the settlement house movement is Jane Addams, *Forty Years at Hull House* * (1935).

The church's part in urban reform is well told in A. I. Abell, *The Urban Impact upon American Protestantism, 1865-1900* (1943), and *American Catholicism and Social Action* * (1960); and in Henry May, *Protestant Churches and Industrial America* (1949). The Social Gospel movement is the theme of C. H. Hopkins, *The Rise of the Social Gospel in American Protestantism, 1865-1915* (1940). Beecher's extraordinary career is sardonically chronicled in Paxton Hibben, *Henry Ward Beecher, An American Portrait* (1927), and briefly in C. M. Rourke, *Trumpets of Jubilee* (1927). On the evangelical movement, see W. W. Sweet, *Revivalism in America, Its Origin, Growth, and Decline* (1944); Gamaliel Bradford, *D. L. Moody, A Worker in Souls* (1927); and B. A. Weisberger, *They Gathered at the River* (1958), which has fascinating portraits of leading evangelists. T. L. Smith, *Revivalism and Social Reform in Mid-Nineteenth-Century America* (1957), shows the early penetration of revivalism in the cities. For the Y.M.C.A., see C. H. Hopkins, *A History of the Y.M.C.A. in North America* (1951). The histories of Christian Science are biased pro and con. Favorable and official is Sibyl Wilbur, *The Life of Mary Baker Eddy* (rev. ed., 1913), and critical is E.F. Dakin, *Mrs. Eddy: The Biography of a Virginal Mind* (1929). On the role of the Catholic Church, in addition to Abell, above, see Msgr. J. T. Ellis, *American Catholicism* * (1956). The best treatment of anti-Catholic sentiment is in John Higham, *Strangers in the Land* * (1955).

On the press, see F. L. Mott, *American Journalism* (1941), and *A History of American Magazines 1885-1905* (1957); and W. G. Bleyer, *Main Currents in the History of American Journalism* 1927). Two outstanding publishers and editors are dealt with in J. W. Barrett, *Joseph Pulitzer and His World* (1941); and Edward Bok, *The Americanization of Edward Bok* * (1920). On architecture, illuminating studies include Lewis Mumford, *Sticks and Stones* * (1924), and *The Brown Decades* * (1931); Wayne Andrews, *Architecture, Ambition, and Americans* * (1955); Christopher Tunnard and H. H. Reed, *American Skyline: The Growth and Form of our Cities and Towns* * (1955); and J. E. Burchard and Albert Bush-Brown, *The Architecture of America* (1961). On the Exposition of 1893, see O. W. Larkin, *Art and Life in America* (1949).

CHAPTER TWENTY-TWO

Historians have invented a number of epithets to describe the post-Civil War decades. The most familiar term, the "Gilded Age," was the title of a novel by Mark Twain and Charles Dudley Warner published in 1873. In this exposé of political corruption, the authors caught the cynical spirit of the new plutocracy. But they also reflected the prevailing mood of hope, enterprise and adventure. Vast resources were awaiting development, and thousands of men felt they could do the job if the government would permit the laws of competition to operate unopposed.

The businessman's faith was sanctioned for some time by the makers of public

Minds

in Transition

opinion. Great educators and editors supported laissez faire, popular ministers praised money making as a form of public service, and economists and sociologists extolled the laws of competition. These defenders of economic orthodoxy drew on every realm of faith and knowledge to support their arguments. Even Darwinian ideas, so radical in many of their implications, were at first seized upon by conservatives who adapted them to their purposes. By the beginning of the twentieth century, however, many thinkers had begun to undermine the naive confidence of their predecessors and to carry the scattered protests of earlier rebels to the rim of intellectual life.

1. Conservatism and Dissent

SOCIAL DARWINISM

When Charles Darwin published his momentous book, *The Origin of Species,* in 1859, the age of the earth, the process of its formation, and the origins of its denizens had long been discussed by naturalists and other savants, but none reached such firm conclusions buttressed with such convincing evidence. Darwin argued that the species of life all around us, far from having been created by separate acts of God in seven days, had gradually evolved, over millions of years, out of lower orders of life through the operation of the principle of "natural selection." According to Darwin, all forms of life were engaged in an unceasing "struggle for existence" in a constantly changing natural environment. Although some died, the fittest—those whose physical variations had enabled them to adapt to changing conditions—would survive, and would pass on to their offspring their favorable characteristics. Over long ages of time, such accumulating changes would develop entirely new species.

Darwin's idea frightened and outraged Biblical fundamentalists and offended some leading scientists as well, among them Louis Agassiz of Harvard. More remarkable, however, was the readiness of Americans to embrace the new ideas. Darwin's popularizers in America—men like the Harvard botanist, Asa Gray, and the historian and lecturer, John Fiske—helped out. Such men saw nothing anti-religious in the belief that man was the result of a long evolutionary process. To them it seemed a marvelous proof of Providence. The Darwinian, said Fiske, "sees that in the deadly struggle for existence which has raged through aeons of time, the whole creation has been groaning and travailing together in order to bring forth that last consummate specimen of God's handiwork, the Human Soul."

But it remained for the English philosopher, Herbert Spencer (see p. 514), to reconcile Darwinism with American optimism. His "synthetic philosophy," as he called it, explained the new biology in terms that the ordinary man could understand. Spencer believed that evolution was not merely change but progress. Ultimately, the process would culminate in a state of existence where "evil and immorality must disappear." For God, Spencer substituted the "Unknowable," thus satisfying thousands of Americans who no longer held to a literal interpretation of the Bible yet clung to their faith in a supernatural agency.

Spencer's ideas took the United States by storm. By 1900, about 350,000 copies of his books had been sold in America, a fantastically high figure for sociological and philosophical works. These books must have been read by millions. No saint ever had more devoted disciples than Spencer had in Edward Livingston Youmans and John Fiske. Beginning in the late 1860's, these two apostles spread the gospel of Social Darwinism over the country through magazine articles, popular books, and lectures. Harvard in 1869 and Yale, Johns Hopkins, and other universities in the 1870's, adopted the Spencerian philosophy in teaching religion as well as biological and social sciences.

Even the churches succumbed. In 1867, Henry Ward Beecher of Plymouth Church in Brooklyn (see p. 582) said that he found "arising in the studies in Natural Science a surer foothold for [his evangelical] views than they ever had." Fifteen years later he pronounced himself "a cordial Christian evolutionist," and acknowledged Spencer as his intellectual foster father of many years' standing. "Men have not fallen as a race," Beecher exclaimed. "Men have come up." For evidence he had only to turn to his rich, satisfied parishioners, men more secular perhaps than the Puritans of old but no less certain of their elect status, as evidenced by their possession of the good things of life on earth.

American businessmen in particular appreciated the application of Spencer's evolutionary ideas to social and economic practices (see p. 515). Convinced that the intrusion of the state into economic and social spheres only interrupted the process by which impersonal nature rewarded the strong and eliminated the unfit, Spencer opposed poor relief, housing regulations, public education, and even laws to protect consumers from medical quacks. If society changed at all, Spencer wrote, it must move with millennial slowness. Attempts of reformers to hurry it along were both mischievous and futile.

The most original thinker among the American Darwinians was William Graham Sumner (1840-1910) of Yale (see p. 515),

592

whose brand of Social Darwinism was more rigorous and less optimistic than Spencer's. Sumner, like Darwin and Spencer, accepted the theory of the great English economist T. R. Mathus that population increase outstrips food supply, but unlike Spencer he did not feel that the pressure for food or the struggle for life made for inevitable progress. Reformers, in turn, he saw as meddlers engaged in an absurd effort to make the world over; their victim was the "forgotten man" who worked hard and minded his own business. Unlike many professed Social Darwinists, Sumner was consistent in his individualism, opposing even government hand-outs in the form of high tariffs. Nor had he any sympathy for the racists and imperialists who glorified the Anglo-Saxon as the peak of perfection and who cited Darwin to justify American expansion at the expense of "inferior" peoples (see Chapter 23).

THE DISSENTERS

Unlike the apologists for the standing order, the critics of society bypassed Spencer and went back to Darwin himself to strengthen their case. They accepted *The Origin of Species* but rejected as unscientific and unchristian the Social Darwinist's notion that man's situation was just like the animal's and that natural selection in biology justified laissez faire in economics. They criticized the Spencerians also for neglecting the power of the human mind to shape the environment.

One of the most outspoken antagonists of Spencer and his American school was the largely self-taught sociologist, Lester Ward (1841-1913), who had to struggle for a hearing and did not obtain an academic position until he had reached his sixties. Ward's first major work, *Dynamic Sociology* (1883), sold only about 500 copies in ten years. Ward countered the prevailing theory that "neither physical nor social phenomena are capable of human control" with the assertion "that all the practical benefits of science are the result of man's control of natural forces." Ward pointed out that nature was uneconomical and

wasteful. Its value to mankind depended on its being governed by what he called "telic" forces (forces originating in the human mind) as against blind and directionless "genetic" forces. Man's duty, then, in both the natural and the social sciences, was not to imitate nature but to dominate it. Far from assuring the survival of the fittest, competition often prevented it. Ward emphasized the superiority of selective breeding over natural breeding by pointing out that vegetables and fruit from an artificially cultivated garden were far superior to those that grew untended. Because Ward believed in social planning, he welcomed the intervention of government—"one of these artificial products of man's devising"—in social matters. A democratic government operating in the interests of all would permit a truer individualism by breaking up monopolies that strangled opportunity.

Ward's assault on Social Darwinism was

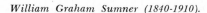

William Graham Sumner (1840-1910).

backed by another group—they might almost be called secular evangelists—whose most popular spokesman was the reformer Henry George (1839-1897). Spencerian philosophy, George said, sinned against the divinity of man by treating him like "a thing, in some respects lower than the animal." This philosophy also failed to explain why it was that some peoples progressed while others did not. George rejected Spencer's talk of the "survival of the fittest" as specious. Progress, he said, depended on the human association and equality that unleashed man's creative powers. When inequality prevailed, association stopped and civilization declined.

What was the cause of inequality? George thought he had found the answer in California, where he went from his native Philadelphia in 1857. The frontier society of California, simple and equalitarian, had been transformed before his eyes into a wealthy and class-stratified society. As George put it, "The tramp comes with the locomotive, and almshouses and prisons are as surely the marks of 'material progress' as are costly dwellings, rich warehouses, and magnificent churches." George felt that progress was accompanied by poverty because of the iniquitous system of private land ownership. The value of land, he thought, was largely a matter of social accident. For example, the high cost of land in metropolitan New York was "not because of what its owners had done." Rather, it was "the presence of the whole great population" that made it worth millions of dollars an acre. If this was true, the land-speculators who bought up land inexpensively and waited for it to rise in value did not deserve to reap a profit that they had not really earned. Since land took on value because of the people who lived on it, George argued, this unearned rent ought to return to the public in the form of a "single tax" on land values. He would leave the husk of ownership in private hands but would socialize the "kernel"—rent. George thought that the single tax on land would make other taxes unnecessary and would promote "the Golden Age of which poets

have sung and high-raised seers have told us in metaphor!"

When George set down his theory in *Progress and Poverty* (1879), his influence spread throughout the world. The book's appeal lay partly in its rhapsodic style and in the skill with which George reduced economic complexities to everyday language, and partly in its central theme that material progress without social justice leads to despotism. George continued to develop his theme in subsequent books. He narrowly missed being elected mayor of New York City in 1886. He ran again in 1897 but died five days before the election.

George's contemporary, Edward Bellamy (1850-1898), also rejected the conservative fatalism of the Social Darwinists, but, unlike George, Bellamy concentrated his attack on the competitive system itself. His radicalism had something in common with the communitarian experiments of Fourier's American disciples (see p. 308) and with the Social Gospel movement (see p. 582). In *Looking Backward,* his Utopian novel published in 1888, Bellamy presented his vision of an ideal society of the year 2000 whose beauty, tranquillity, and efficiency contrasted vividly with the smoky, suffering, and strike-ridden America of the '80's. The Golden Age had dawned after the nationalizing of the great trusts and the "substitution of scientific methods of an organized and unified industrial system for the wasteful struggle of the present competitive plan with its countless warring and mutually destructive undertakings."

The millions of Americans who read Bellamy's charming tale were impressed by his amiable and persuasive tone and delighted by the vision of his immaculate and gadget-filled city of the future. Amazed by the impact of his book, Bellamy concluded that the American people might put his theories into practice. "Nationalism," as he called his system, was not a class movement. It rested on the idea that all people

. . . are victims in mind, body, or soul, in one way or another, of the present barbarous industrial and social arrangements, and that we are all equally interested, if not for ourselves, yet for our children, in breaking the meshes which entangle us, and struggling upward to a higher, nobler, happier plane of existence.

"Nationalist" clubs sprang up throughout the country. "Nationalist" magazines advocating such measures as public ownership of railroads and utilities, civil-service reform, and government aid to education were widely circulated. Before Bellamy's death, "Nationalism" had been absorbed by the agrarian reformers, but he had accomplished his purpose of familiarizing a large audience with Socialist ideas.

Bellamy and his co-workers deliberately avoided the word "socialism," for, as he wrote to Howells,

In the radicalness of the opinions I have expressed I may seem to outsocialize the Socialists, yet the word socialist is one I could never well stomach. In the first place it is a foreign word itself and equally foreign in all its suggestions. It smells to the average American of petroleum, suggests the red flag with all manner of sexual novelties, and an abusive tone toward God and religion, which in this country we can at least treat with decent respect.

Bellamy knew his public. American anarchists might protest that they were "simply unterrified Jeffersonian Democrats," and Socialists deny that they intended a violent overthrow of society. But the majority of Americans turned away from these exotic systems. One organization, the Socialist-Labor party, founded in 1877, upheld the doctrines of Karl Marx, but most of its tiny membership was foreign-born, and its effect on American reform was negligible. Under Daniel De Leon, a doctrinaire Marxian theoretician, the Socialist-Labor party entered the presidential race in 1892 but received only 21,000 votes. When De Leon attempted to disrupt the American Federation of Labor and the Knights of Labor, his authoritarian methods provoked a revolt in his party, and in 1899 a faction broke away to form the Socialist party under Eugene Debs.

ORTHODOXY CHALLENGED

The social ideas of such "underground" theorists as George and Bellamy found little support in the universities,

where orthodox economics was firmly fixed in the Gilded Age. American students learned that inequality in wealth produced the incentives without which progress was impossible; that labor's wages depended on the number of men competing for jobs who shared in a "wage fund" that no artificial regulation could modify; and that competition was the only way for free individuals to satisfy their own needs and to work for "the greatest good of the greatest number." Only in an unregulated society could the natural economic laws function properly.

These sentiments, held by the leading academic social scientists, began to be challenged in the mid-'80's by a group of younger scholars, many of whom had been trained in German universities. Economists like Richard T. Ely, John R. Commons, and Edward Bemis grew increasingly critical of laissez faire and considered far more sympathetically than had their predecessors the idea that the power of the state might legitimately be used to improve society. Under the leadership of Ely, the younger economists and some liberal clergymen founded the American Economic Association in 1885. The A.E.A. declared itself in favor of "the positive assistance of the state," and, while recognizing "the necessity of individual initiative in industrial life," it held that "the doctrine of laissez faire is unsafe in politics and unsound in morals."

Younger sociologists had also broken out of the Spencerian straitjacket by the 1890's. Whereas Spencer had seen society as composed of separate individuals each operating independently of the others, the new sociologists like Albion Small, Charles H. Cooley, and E. A. Ross argued that the individual personality was shaped by social institutions that were in turn amenable to social control. In *Sin and Society* (1907), Ross tried to show that new business conditions demanded a new code of morality, one that required the soulless corporation to take full responsibility for its anti-social acts.

The younger social scientists differed in their economic and political programs, but by and large they all distrusted a static view of the universe, absolute laws, and fixed conceptions. Society, they felt, was constantly changing and had to be examined as process and growth. Consequently, they turned to the historical past in order to understand the present and looked for relevant facts in other disciplines that would help to illuminate their own.

Foremost among the academic rebels was the economist, Thorstein Veblen (1857-1929). The son of Norwegian immigrants, the Wisconsin-born Veblen had absorbed some frontier Populism before he completed his training at Yale, where he studied under Sumner, and at The Johns Hopkins University. Always remote, always the type of renegade whom he once described as "a disturber of the intellectual peace," he concealed his feelings behind a heavily ironic and polysyllabic style, and sardonically spoofed the sacred beliefs of his society. It is not surprising, therefore, that his "predilection for shifty iconoclasm" (to use one of his own phrases), his unconventional personal life, intellectual arrogance and heretical views should have blocked his academic advancement. Veblen adopted the tone of an aloof neutral and pretended to survey society with detachment, but he was at bottom a moralist and a critic of the "kept classes" and their "pecuniary" society.

The well-to-do leisure class, according to Veblen, was not biologically the most fit. Millionaires were not, as Sumner had insisted, "a product of natural selection," nor were they socially useful. The captains of enterprise sabotaged the industrial machine, because their primary concern—unlike that of the engineer—was financial.

In his most widely read book, *The Theory of the Leisure Class* (1899), and in a

Thorstein Veblen (1857-1929), by Edwin B. Child.

number of other volumes, Veblen discussed the habits and thoughts of the upper class as if he were reporting the behavior of a primitive tribe, and introduced ethical, psychological, biological, and anthropological observations not to be found in conventional economic studies. Although he asserted that only the "is" interested him, not the "right to be," he envisaged a community of "masterless" men organized under a technical elite. Veblen's ideas seemed merely whimsical in the early 1900's, but his influence grew during the 1920's and reached its peak after the Great Crash of 1929.

II. *New Lines of Thought*

THE PHILOSOPHERS

What chiefly distinguished pre-Darwinian from post-Darwinian science, as

Veblen pointed out, was the way in which the scientist looked at his facts. The Darwinian did not care whether his observations harmonized with older formulas, with long-treasured ideals, with fixed beliefs. He accepted evolution because he was less concerned (as the philosopher John Dewey remarked) "in what or who made the world" than in "what kind of world it is anyway." This, said Dewey, was "the intellectual transformation effected by the Darwinian logic." But the transformation did not occur immediately, for the "Darwinian logic" clashed with an older one deeply embedded in the American mind.

Before the Civil War, the prevailing philosophy in the United States was known as Scottish or "common-sense" realism. The Scottish philosophy was an adaptation of some of the insights and methods of Enlightenment thought to the needs of Protestant, mainly Calvinist, religion; it was the standard philosophy taught in the denominational colleges by such men as the Reverend James McCosh of Princeton, the Reverend Noah Porter of Yale, and their followers. It supposed that man possessed a God-implanted faculty which enabled him to arrive at truth. As Newton had formulated the laws of the universe, so other men could formulate natural laws of politics, economics, and ethics. In the hands of most of the common-sense philosophers, these laws had a way of turning out to be justifications of the status quo and of conservative ways of thought.

In the 1870's and after, German idealism, particularly as developed by Hegel and his followers, made inroads upon the Scottish school. Hegel had seen the whole course of history as the working out of divine purpose according to certain general laws of change. But since Hegelians looked upon the present state of affairs as an inevitable stage in historical development, Hegelianism served as well as the Scottish philosophy to justify existing conditions. Its chief element of novelty lay in the fact that it taught reverence for the state and preached that the individual could be truly free only by subordinating himself harmoniously to the development of his national government and the institutions of his society. William T. Harris, who became United States Commis-

sioner of Education in 1889, was a leading American Hegelian.

Possibly the most influential and certainly the most readable of the American idealists was Josiah Royce, a brilliant Californian who taught at Harvard from 1882 until his death in 1916. Royce defended the idealistic belief in an absolute mind, but unlike the more orthodox Hegelians he found a larger and more active place for the individual in the universe. Royce preached a social ethic in which the greatest good was not to be found in aggregate happiness but in unification and harmony. He believed that through the principle of loyalty many individuals could be brought together into the unity of a single life, and he built a large part of his later philosophy around this theme of social cohesion.

Toward the end of the century a new school of philosophy appeared which regarded the concerns of the idealists as irrelevant. The "pragmatists," as they came to be known, repudiated all fixed systems of belief and evaluated ideas in terms of their evident consequences. The forerunners of pragmatism, Chauncey Wright and Charles Peirce, were both remarkable thinkers, but neither received much credit for pragmatism's development. Two other men, William James and John Dewey, broadened and humanized pragmatism from a method of thinking into a philosophy of action.

William James (1842-1910), the brother of the novelist Henry James, had revolted from the determinism of Herbert Spencer and from all systems of thought that left no place for chance or human will. A splendid writer, James made fun of Spencer's jaw-breaking definition of evolution, redefining it as "a change from a no-howish untalkaboutable all-alikeness to a some-howish and in general talkaboutable not-all-alikeness by continuous sticktogetherations and somethingelseifications." With wit and learning, James upheld the independence of the mind and "the right to believe at our own risk any hypothesis that is live enough to tempt our will." If he preached against absolutes, he also rejected a paralyzing skepticism, a "snarling logicality" that held men back from any impulsive or generous commitment. In the late '60's, he had gone through a profound emotional crisis and had emerged from this ordeal with an intense will to believe and with a conviction that the purpose of thinking was "to help change the world."

As a philosopher and psychologist at Harvard, James developed his case against the "awfully monotonous" Spencerian universe, wrote a brilliant exposition on the active role of the mind (*Principles of Psychology*, 1890), and later expounded his views on pragmatism. The pragmatist, James wrote,

. . . turns away from abstraction and insufficiency, from verbal solutions, from bad *a priori* reasons, from fixed principles, closed systems, and pretended absolutes and origins. He turns towards concreteness and adequacy, towards facts, towards action and towards power.

He regards theories as *"instruments, not answers to enigmas."* Pragmatism "has no dogmas, and no doctrines save its method," James said; it is a method for arriving at the truth. Pragmatism appealed to America's preference for facts over theory, but when James declared that "the true is the name of whatever proves itself to be good in the way of belief, and good, too, for definite, assignable reasons," he laid himself open to the charge that pragmatism was only a high-sounding name for vulgar expediency—anything is good that works.

The same charge was later leveled at John Dewey's "instrumentalism," another version of the pragmatic philosophy. Starting out as an idealist, Dewey (1859-1952) had been converted to pragmatism in the 1890's after reading James, but soon the disciple began to influence the master. Far more deeply than James, Dewey believed in the intelligence as a tool for social reform, and he had less interest in the private struggles of the individual mind than in the interactions between men and the community. The mind, he said, "is at least an organ of service for the control of environment," and he called upon philosophers to stop speculating on what were for him meaningless quibbles and to turn to politics, education, and ethics.

In the end, men do what they can do. They refrain from doing what they cannot do. They do what their own specific powers in conjunction with the limitations and resources of the environment permit. The effective control of their powers is not through precepts, but through the regulation of their conditions. If this regulation is to be not merely physical or coercive, but moral, it must consist of the intelligent selection and determination of the enviroments in which we act; and in an intelligent exaction of responsibility for the use of men's powers.

Like Ward, George, and other social dissenters, Dewey was an early critic of laissez faire and Social Darwinism in politics and business. More than others, he also applied his ideas to education which he felt must be intimately related to the rest of life and made into an instrument for social reform. Dewey conceived of the school as a social institution through which the child would learn to criticize the customs and beliefs of society as a whole. The child would acquire this knowledge not by absorbing the conventional "truths" of his teachers, not by having his mind "disciplined" through the traditional drills, but by developing a scientific approach to the solving of problems. Dewey wanted students to participate directly in the issues or situations that concerned them, to learn by doing. Nevertheless, he urged constantly that his own democratic values must permeate every aspect of educational training. In the early decades of the twentieth century, Dewey's "progressive" theories began to influence American education and launched a debate that still rages between his followers and pseudo-followers, and their critics.

THE LAW AND SOCIAL THEORY

The Darwinian influence also transformed old conceptions of the law. The preceding generation had commonly believed that the law was something handed down from on high, and that judicial deci-

Louis D. Brandeis (1856-1941).

sions were inevitable, logical interpretations of constitutions or statutes. The man who perhaps did most to undermine this belief was Oliver Wendell Holmes (1841-1935), son of the poet of the same name, and friend of his fellow Harvardian, William James. Holmes did his work on the bench. For twenty years he served on the Massachusetts Supreme Court before being appointed to the United States Supreme Court in 1902. By the time of his retirement in 1932, he had become one of the most celebrated judges in the world.

To Holmes, the law was part of the social process, an outcome of social views, a reflection of political compromises. Even the decisions of judges, he demonstrated in his book, *The Common Law* (1881), arose out of prejudices and preconceptions. For this reason, he boldly challenged the blind faith in precedent and warned that the law must never lag too far behind concrete experience. "It is revolting," Holmes said, "to have no better reason for a rule of law than that so it was laid down in the time of

Henry IV. It is still more revolting if the grounds upon which it was laid down have vanished long since, and the rule simply persists from blind imitation of the past."

The fact that Holmes freely criticized the law did not make him indiscriminately liberal. He retained a stubborn conservative streak throughout his life and a deep contempt for those "stinking upward and onwarders" who claimed to be "on the ground floor with God." Yet his cynicism and his acceptance of injustice and suffering as two ineradicable elements of life did not make him a pessimist. Holmes bravely faced the unknowable universe.

Holmes once confessed that he hated facts: "I have little doubt that it would be good for my immortal soul to plunge into them, good also for the performance of my duties, but I shrink from the bore." Louis Dembitz Brandeis (1856-1941), appointed to the Supreme Court by Wilson in 1916 against the concerted opposition of many eminent public figures, relied extensively on facts and felt that without them, no just legal decision was possible. Brandeis agreed with his friend and colleague Holmes that the social beliefs of judges colored their judicial decisions; all the more reason then for expecting them to support their rulings not merely with legal arguments but also with relevant objective economic and social facts. As a "people's lawyer," Brandeis had become convinced that the law lagged behind economic realities, that it needed to understand and to act upon the revolutionary social and economic changes wrought by the industrial transformation of the country.

In an epoch-making brief presented in the case of *Muller* v. *Oregon* (1908), Brandeis defended the constitutionality of a tenhour law governing the work of women in Oregon laundries, and showed with overwhelming evidence from physicians, factory inspectors, social workers, and other competent observers that the number of hours women worked affected their health and morals and hence the well-being of the entire community. The preceding generation had usually been content not to go behind the text of the laws to the texture of social reality, but Brandeis persuaded even some of the most conservative members of the Court that the facts of social life should be taken into account. By upholding the Oregon statute, the Court served notice that henceforth it would recognize the validity of these social facts in reaching its decisions.

Even the supreme law, the Constitution itself, became an object of critical study. The political scientist, Arthur F. Bentley, concluded in his book, *The Process of Government* (1908), that all law was the result of conflicts among interest groups, and that constitutions were merely a special form of law. Another writer, J. Allen Smith, argued in *The Spirit of American Government* (1907) that the framers of the Constitution of the United States had intended not to realize democracy but to check it. In *An Economic Interpretation of the Constitution* (1913), the brilliant Columbia University historian, Charles A. Beard, dared to confront the material interests of the framers of the sacrosanct document. Beard's scholarship in this book was subsequently riddled by other historians; his conclusions were questioned or rejected. But to his liberal contemporaries, Beard had stripped away the myths about the making of the Constitution and disclosed how considerations of property had shaped the fundamental law of the land. Such works released the mind from its shackles and induced a whole generation of social scientists to reexamine the precepts of their society and assess the possibilities of reform. As the progressive historian Vernon L. Parrington summed it up, "the solid results of their labor remained after the popular ferment subsided, as a foundation for later liberals to build on."

THE HISTORIANS

The analogy between Darwinian ideas of biological evolution and the development of social institutions was too obvious to be missed by historians, and by the 1880's some of them were convinced that history could be transformed into an exact science once laws of social evolution had been ascertained. The popular writer and lecturer John Fiske pursued this course of thought for a wide general audience, tracing America's political development from its earliest stages to its present complexity. Academic historians under the influence of Herbert B. Adams of The Johns Hopkins University, and John W. Burgess of Columbia University, proud of their Anglo-Saxon heritage, were led to combine biological or racial evolution with institutional change. In particular, they professed to see American democracy as an evolutionary result of political practices beginning with those of primitive tribes in Germany. Inspired by the racist views of English historians like E. A. Freeman and by the swelling expansionist sentiment, they made the Anglo-Saxon race the originators and the preservers of freedom. "By that race alone," one of them wrote in 1890, "it [freedom] had been preserved amidst a thousand perils; to that race alone is it thoroughly congenial; if we can conceive the possibility of the disappearance among peoples of that race, the chance would be small for that freedom's survival. . . ." The young politician Theodore Roosevelt and the even younger novelist Frank Norris saw expansion merely as a continuation of an Anglo-Saxon drive that had begun in ancient German forests.

To Frederick Jackson Turner, Wisconsin-born and trained at Johns Hopkins, the conquest of the American frontier was also part of an evolutionary process. But Turner argued in his immensely influential essay, "The Significance of the Frontier in American History" (1893), that American democracy originated not in the German but in the American forests. According to Turner, the European settler eventually conquered the New World wilderness, but during his long struggle the conqueror was himself transformed by his American environment, stripped of his civilized garments, and forced either to adapt to new conditions or perish. Wrote Turner:

The advance of the frontier has meant a steady movement away from the influence of Europe, a steady growth of independence on American lines. And to study this advance, the men who grew up under these conditions, and the political, economic, and social results of it, is to study the really American part of our history.

The closing of the frontier that Turner made so much of in 1893 had, he believed, dangerous implications for America. The frontier had created the American character; from it had sprung the toughness, resourcefulness, individualism, and versatility that made the country great. Turner had misgivings as he contemplated the new industrialized and urbanized civilization that now overlay the once-savage wilderness, but he remained hopeful that America, because of its frontier heritage, would escape the social evils that plagued the tired civilization of Europe.

Optimistic faith might sustain a buoyant middle-westerner like Turner, but to Henry Adams (1838-1918) and his brother, Brooks —the descendants of presidents—the future looked black. Throughout his life as political observer, journalist, professor, novelist, and traveler, Henry Adams had been fascinated by historical forces and had often lived close to the men who made history; his meticulous and often brilliant account of the Jefferson and Madison administrations and several historical biographies showed that he could write history as well.

But as he grew older, he took pleasure in demonstrating to his own satisfaction that history is not progress but degradation. Thus he could maliciously observe in his famous autobiography, *The Education of Henry Adams* (1907), that America's decline could be measured by contrasting Washington with Grant. In *Mont-Saint-Michel and Chartres* (1904), he contrasted the spiritual vitality of the Middle Ages, the age of unity symbolized by the cult of the Virgin, with the destructive violence of industrial civilization, the age of multiplicity symbolized by the dynamo. Drawing a very dubious analogy from physics, Adams concluded that the constantly accelerating dissipation of energy would ultimately end in the destruction of human civilization, and he even calculated the possible dates of this cosmic debacle.

Brooks Adams shared his brother's pessimism, but for a short time he allowed his hopes to be stirred by the possibility of America's forging ahead in the competition among nations. By 1912, however, he agreed with Henry that America could not adapt itself quickly enough to changing conditions and that its leaders lacked the will and the imagination to convert the United States into a disciplined state.

III. *Education*

THE HIGHER LEARNING

Beginning in the 1890's, American reformers complained about the alleged dictatorship of the plutocrats over the universities, about professors being tried for economic heresies and dismissed from their posts for offending conservative founders or trustees. They could cite the cases of Richard T. Ely at Wisconsin, whose books were denounced as "utopian, impracticable or pernicious" by one of the state regents who tried unsuccessfully to have him thrown out; of Edward T. Bemis, fired from the University of Chicago for attacking the railroads and the Gas Trust; of E. A. Ross, dismissed from Stanford for holding opinions offensive to the late founder's wife. In *The Theory of Social Revolutions* (1913), Brooks Adams accused the American universities of turning out narrow, half-educated specialists who lacked the breadth of mind needed to administer a complex, centralized economy. Five years later, in *The Higher Learning in America,* Veblen savagely pilloried the universities as temples of "intellectual quietism" run by "captains of erudition" for the production of salesmen.

But it was by no means true that academic freedom was stifled even during the troubled 1890's, or that university presidents (as Veblen implied) thereafter invariably knuckled under to big business. Since 1860, universities had become bigger and more bureaucratized. But more to the point, they had vastly improved in quality.

Between 1860 and 1900, public and private donations had helped finance the universities' growth. Under the terms of the Morrill Act of 1862, the federal government offered large land grants to any state that would found a college in which "agriculture and the mechanic arts" were taught. By 1868, Wisconsin, Minnesota, California, Texas, Massachusetts, and New York had established land-grant colleges, many of them co-educational. Other colleges and universities were set up through private philanthropy. Ezra Cornell, for example, who made a fortune from the electric telegraph, founded Cornell, which opened its doors in 1868. Vanderbilt (1873) and Stanford (1891) were the educational beneficiaries of two railroad millionaires, and the University of Chicago (1891) received $34 million from the oil magnate, John D. Rockefeller. The Johns Hopkins University (1876) bore the name of a wealthy Baltimore banker and railroad executive; Carnegie Institute (1896) in Pittsburgh, the name of a multimillionaire steel man.

The prewar colleges had confined themselves pretty much to non-utilitarian subjects—the classics, mathematics, and theology—but the postwar institutions responded to the demand for a business and technical education that would prepare university graduates for life in an industrial society. The prestige of science had risen so high (another result of the Darwinian revolution) that changes in the curriculum, the increasing emphasis on research, and the liberation of higher education from a narrow sectarianism had to be accepted. By the end of the century, a number of university scientists had won international reputations, among them Albert A. Michelson of the University of Chicago, who made important discoveries in molecular theory and measured the velocity of light, and Josiah Willard Gibbs of Yale, one of the great original minds of his age, whose work in theoretical physics and physical chemistry paved the way for the theory of relativity and for other scientific advances.

Thanks to men like President Charles W. Eliot of Harvard, a new kind of university emerged in which undergraduates "elected" courses from a greatly expanded curriculum instead of being "compelled to an unwelcome task." Harvard graduate schools were created, scholarly faculties were assembled, and administration was centralized. Between 1869 and 1900, Eliot also pushed through a drastic reformation of Harvard's medical and law schools. Pre-medical students, who had formerly obtained degrees with a minimum of course and clinical work, were now required to study three full years in medical school, to work in laboratories, and to take examinations. C. C. Langdell, Dean of the Harvard Law School, abolished the textbook and introduced a system whereby the law student got his knowledge by examining specific cases.

Eliot's theories—especially his "elective system," which permitted less serious undergraduates to choose an unrelated group of subjects and to avoid the difficult courses—provoked some opposition, but most universities accepted it along with the broadened curriculum and the new emphasis on commercial and scientific subjects. The founding of The Johns Hopkins University, for example, gave a strong impetus to diversified courses and furthered specialized research. Many of its faculty members had studied in Germany, and they proceeded to train a corps of teachers in the exacting methods of German university scholarship. The requirements of industry and finance were met by the technical schools that mushroomed during the last half of the century, and by institutions like the Wharton School of Finance (1881), connected with the University of Pennsylvania.

Not all the innovations that transformed the universities and colleges were intellectual. The introduction of organized sports like baseball, basketball, and football aroused an almost fanatical concern for competitive contests both inside and outside the schools, and encouraged what the poet T. S. Eliot was later to call the "decadent athleticism" of American life. By the 1890's, intercollegiate football had become a mass spectacle attended by crowds of thirty or forty thousand, and critics were already protesting against its professional emphasis.

So far as educational opportunities went, women remained "second-class citizens." Although there was much evidence to the contrary, many people continued to doubt whether women had the intellectual or the physical capacity to profit from a college education. Would not the experience of higher learning, it was asked, open the "floodgates of a torrent of evils which should sweep away the loveliness and grace and essential charm of womanhood?" The founding of Vassar College at Poughkeepsie, New York, in 1861 did much to dispel such antiquated notions. Matthew Vassar, an English-born brewer, believed that "woman having received from the Creator the same intellectual constitution as man, has the same right to intellectual culture and development." The course of study inaugurated at Vassar was as demanding as that of any male college of the day, and Vassar graduates quickly distinguished themselves as

scholars, in the professions, and in administrators. By 1880, most of the important midwestern universities were admitting women, and women's colleges like Smith, Bryn Mawr, and Wellesley—founded shortly after Vassar—were offering professional training. The diehards still insisted that women were not physically endowed to withstand the rigors of college life and grimly cited examples of breakdown and collapse, yet the number of women enrolled as undergraduates in American colleges increased from about 8,000 in 1869 to more than 20,000 in 1894. The establishment of the Association of Collegiate Alumnae in 1882—an organization composed of women graduates of a selected group of colleges and universities—gave further impetus to the movement for higher education for women.

GAINS IN PUBLIC EDUCATION

Progress in public education after 1865 was reflected in the steady lengthening of the school term, a higher dollar expenditure per pupil, a declining illiteracy rate, and compulsory school-attendance laws. The old prewar academy that had once monopolized American secondary education

College football, Cornell v. Rochester, 1889.

gave way after 1870 to the modern public high school. Curricula were widened to include history and literature, as well as vocational and commercial courses, and greater stress was laid on preparing the child to meet the challenge of his environment.

Between 1870 and 1910, the number of public high schools increased from 500 to more than 10,000, and a high-school education had begun to be what a grammar-school education once had been—the normal expectation of great numbers of young Americans, especially white youths in towns and cities. During this 40-year period, the number of pupils attending public elementary and high schools each year increased from 6,871,000 to 17,813,000. The average number of days in the school-year rose from 132 to 157, and the per capita appropriations of funds for education more than doubled. Illiteracy declined from 17 per cent of the population in 1880 to 7.7 per cent in 1910. By then the average American was getting six years of formal education. Interest had also risen in schools for the very young. The first kindergarten was established in St. Louis in 1873, and within 30 years their number had grown to 3,000.

Advances in public education were more marked in the cities than in the country areas, and were more impressive in the Northeast than in the South and West. The carpetbag governments in the South had laid the groundwork for public-school systems, but the return of the conservatives to power in the mid-1870's saw a falling off in appropriations. Even the grants of northern philanthropists like George Peabody could do little to eliminate illiteracy or overcome the prevailing apathy toward public education that was traditional in the South.

Modest in their programs, but performing an indispensable service, were the Negro vocational and normal schools that sprang up after 1865. Both white and Negro leaders had come to realize that so long as the ex-slave remained illiterate, he would remain a slave in fact if not before the law. Education would equip him for better jobs, increase his self-respect, and develop his natural aptitudes. The Hampton Normal and Agricultural Institute (1870) pioneered in vocational training for Negroes. Its most famous graduate, Booker T. Washington, became the head of a normal school at Tuskegee, Alabama, in 1881, and the educational leader of the Negroes.

Casting down your bucket among my people [he told influential whites], helping and encouraging them . . . to education of head, hand, and heart, you will find that they will buy your surplus land, make bloom the waste places in your fields, and run your factories. While doing this you can be sure in the future, as in the past, that you will be surrounded by the most patient, faithful, law-abiding and unresentful people the world has ever seen.

Such docility infuriated militant Negroes, and today Booker T. Washington's attitude toward Negro-white relations is repudiated by the majority of his race. Nevertheless, his services to his people should not be minimized. If Washington prepared his students for agriculture, domestic service, and the lower-paid factory jobs, it was simply because better jobs were not open to them.

POPULARIZING CULTURE

For those who had finished their limited schooling and still hungered for learning, a number of privately sponsored agencies came into being that provided a varied, though usually diluted fare. The men who launched these agencies were prompted by both idealistic and mercenary motives, but their efforts helped bridge the gap between the intelligentsia and the average man.

A highly successful venture in popular learning began in western New York in 1874 with the establishment of the Chautauqua Assembly by an Ohio businessman, Louis Miller, and a Methodist bishop, John H. Vincent. Its original purpose was to train Sunday-school teachers during the summer months, but like the old lyceum movement (see p. 305) the Chautauqua soon expanded into wider fields. Before long, the Chautauqua Literary and Scientific Reading Circle had become a national society with study circles and a corps of eminent lecturers, including most of the presidents of the era.

Perhaps the most successful of all Chautauqua addresses was Dr. Russell H. Conwell's inspirational talk on how to get ahead, which he called "Acres of Diamonds." Conwell gave this lecture six thousand times and his audiences never seemed to tire of his message or his spectacular oratory. "Get rich, young man," he declared, "for money is power, and power ought to be in the hands of good people. . . . I say you have *no right to be poor*. . . . You and I know that there are some things more valuable than money; nevertheless, there is not one of these things that is not greatly enhanced by the use of money. . . . Love is the grandest thing on God's earth, but fortunate is the lover who has plenty of money." Conwell never allowed his huge income from lecturing to accumulate. He gave much of it away to deserving young men and later founded Temple University in Philadelphia, whose president he remained until his death in 1925.

Other more commercial "Chautauquas" soon appeared, and entrepreneurs capitalizing on the craving for self-culture also organized correspondence schools and published "libraries" of cheap books that were sold either by subscription or distributed through department stores and mail-order houses. Middle-class women found an outlet for their cultural interests in the "literary" clubs later to be satirized by Edith Wharton in *The Custom of the Country* and by Sinclair Lewis in *Main Street*. These were united into the General Federation of Women's Clubs in 1889. Commenting on the Chautauqua's contribution to American popular culture, an observer in 1892 suggested that its "fundamental consequence in our hastily settled and heterogeneous land" was its influence on the "stagnant homes from Maine to California." If the actual product in education" was not large, "it set minds in motion" and lessened "the popular suspicion of expert knowledge."

IV. *The Writer and His World*

THE ESCAPISTS

The year 1865 was a dividing point between old and new America. Hawthorne and Thoreau were dead, Emerson was past his prime and retiring more and more into himself, and Melville was living virtually forgotten in prison-like anonymity. Of all the writers who belonged to the "Golden Day" and who wrote after Appomattox, only Walt Whitman still sounded his "barbaric yawp over the roofs of the world."

Emily Dickinson (1830-1886), the one authentic poetic genius whose work belongs to the post-Civil War period, published only a few poems during her lifetime. This spinster-recluse of Amherst, Massachusetts, had virtually retired from the world by the time she was 30, and her poetry—which she wrote for herself and her friends—dealt with the themes that had concerned her Puritan forebears: love, death, God, eternity, with the rapture of sudden illumination and the emblematic meaning of the universe. Although her verse resembles Emerson's in its terseness and wit, her view of nature and God was less benign and optimistic. Nature's garden, she observed, was filled so closely with wasps and bees and with snakes that it caused "a tighter breathing/ And zero at the bone." The "certain slant of light" she saw on winter afternoons oppressed "like the weight of cathedral tunes." Emily Dickinson's poetry was often marred by coyness and sentimentality, but her best lyrics (among the finest in our literature) are distinguished by their freshness of diction and imagery. She was able in the most remarkable way to translate the humble objects of her surroundings into symbols of eternity.

The industrialized and urbanized America that emerged in the '70's and '80's was not a congenial subject for the older American writers. Perhaps a measure of their uneasiness is the curious fact that many of them gave themselves over to recalling a pastoral America precisely at that moment when country people were flocking to the cities. Already conscious of their lost heritage, these writers tried to strengthen their spiritual ties with the past. The result was the so-called "local-color" movement in American fiction. Writers like Bret Harte, Joel Chandler Harris, Sarah Orne Jewett, and George Washington Cable sought to capture the "native element" of distinctive sections—the California mining country, the New England village, the southern plantation, the Kentucky and Tennessee mountains. Theoretically, the local colorist did not rule out the city:

The local movement will include the cities as well [wrote the local colorist, Hamlin Garland, in 1894], and St. Louis, Chicago, San Francisco, will be delineated by artists born of each city, whose work will be so true that it could not have been written by anyone from the outside. The real utterance of a city or a locality can only come when a writer is born out of its intimate heart. To such a one, nothing will be "strange" or "picturesque"; all will be familiar, and full of significance or beauty. The novel of the slums must be written by one who has played there as a child, and taken part in all its amusement; not out of curiosity, but out of pleasure seeking. It cannot be done from above nor from the outside. It must be done

Mark Twain (Samuel Clemens) (1835-1910).

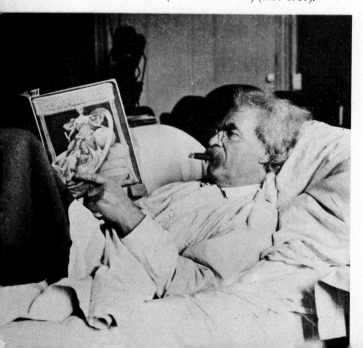

out of a full heart and without seeking for effect.

With few exceptions, however, the local colorists stuck to what they considered to be the authentic part of America—the village, the small town, the farm—and lovingly recorded the variations in dialect and the manners and customs of the past.

MARK TWAIN

Mark Twain (1835-1910)—the pen-name of Samuel L. Clemens—belonged by temperament to the local-color tradition and was regarded in his own day as a regional author. But he was a writer of far greater dimensions than the local colorists. In many respects, Mark Twain was the most revealing figure in post-Civil War American literature and the man who best combined the virtues and defects of the period he so caustically analyzed. Born in Hannibal, Missouri, he had been a reporter, river pilot, and popular lecturer before he made his first success with *The Innocents Abroad* (1869), a wild and absurdly funny account of a junket through Europe and the Near East.

Mark Twain wrote prolifically about everything from jumping frogs to Andrew Carnegie and penned historical romances and pessimistic fantasies. But his best works, *The Adventures of Tom Sawyer* (1876), *Life on the Mississippi* (1883), and *The Adventures of Huckleberry Finn* (1884), all derive from the days when he lived close to the great river. It was his loyalty to the simple republican America of his boyhood that partly accounts for his rage over the betrayal of democratic ideals in the Gilded Age. "In my youth," wrote Twain, "there was nothing resembling a worship of money or of its possessor, in our region." It took people like Jay Gould, he said, "to make a God of the money and the man":

The gospel left behind by Jay Gould is doing giant work in our days. Its message is "Get money. Get it quickly. Get it in abundance. Get it dishonestly if you can, honestly if you must."

And yet Twain shared the Philistinism and provincialism of the society he entertained, enjoyed "striking it rich," speculated reck-lessly, and always wrote with an eye on his large audience. As he put it:

I have never tried in even one single instance to help cultivate the cultivated classes. I was not equipped for it by native gifts or training. And I never had any ambition in that direction, but always hunted for bigger game—the masses.

In his own subtle way, however, Mark Twain was a moralist who looked upon mankind with exasperation because of its cruelty, credulity, and pigheadedness, and with compassion because it was not to blame. Huckleberry Finn is an ironical attack against social hypocrisy, false respectability, and the canons of success—all bound up in the "civilization" from which Huck is trying to escape. In renouncing civilization, Huck remains true to his natural goodness without denying human depravity or his kinship with the wicked. As Mark Twain wrote: "I am the whole human race without a detail lacking . . . the human race is a race of cowards; and I am not only marching in that procession but carrying a banner."

THE REALISTS
AND NATURALISTS

William Dean Howells (1837-1920), a friend of Mark Twain, was the leader of the postwar school of self-conscious "Real-ists." Born and reared in Ohio, Howells had come to literature, as so many of his con-temporaries had, through the printer's office and the newspaper. A campaign life of Lin-coln earned him a consular appointment in Venice. After his return from Italy in 1865, he became sub-editor and then editor-in-chief (1871-1881) of the *Atlantic Monthly* in Boston, and from 1886 to 1891 wrote his most influential criticism in the "Editor's Study" in *Harper's Monthly* in New York. Howells published at least 40 works of fic-tion and many plays and critical works. By 1900, many of the younger writers consid-ered him the dean of American letters.

"Realism," as Howells used the term, simply meant "the truthful treatment of commonplace material." The romanticism permeating the popular literature of his

day was immoral, in Howells' opinion, be-cause it corrupted American taste and falsi-fied life. In place of sensational tales or "lies," Howells wanted to create fiction that maintained "fidelity, not merely to the pos-sible, but to the probable and ordinary course of man's experience." Let fiction, he said,

. . . cease to lie about life; let it portray men and women as they are, actuated by the mo-tives and passions in the measure that we all know; let it leave off painting dolls and work-ing them by springs and wires; let it show the different interests in their proportions; let it forbear to teach pride and revenge, folly and insanity, egotism and prejudice, but frankly own these things for what they are, in what-ever figures and occasions they appear; let it not put on fine literary airs; let it speak the dialect, the language, that most Americans know—the language of unaffected people every-where—and there can be no doubt of an un-limited future, not only of delightfulness but of usefulness, for it.

Howells practiced what he preached in his own novels. His best known, and probably his best works, are *The Rise of Silas Lap-ham* (1885), the story of a self-made busi-nessman, and *A Hazard of New Fortunes* (1890), which reflected his first-hand experi-ence in New York of the competitive strife and extremes of social inequality that had long disturbed him. In this novel he implicitly condemned the mindless struggle for wealth, the paradox of Fifth Avenue luxury and East Side squalor, and the deg-radation of the republican dream.

Although Howells' friend, Henry James (1843-1916), could not find enough material for fiction in what he regarded as the bleak American scene, he allied himself, and properly, with Howells' camp. James was born in New York, but he spent a good deal of his youth in Europe. After a half-hearted attempt to study law at Harvard, he gave himself entirely to literature, and from 1875 until his death he did most of his writing abroad. Because he visited his native land so infrequently, and because so many of his novels and short stories have a European setting, James has been considered by many critics to be outside the main currents of American literature. Actually, his international plots deal almost exclusively with Americans, and from his foreign vantage point he discerned much about the character of his countrymen that escaped his fellow writers who remained at home.

Like Hawthorne, by whom he was profoundly influenced, James liked to place his Americans in what he called "morally interesting situations." He subjected his traveling businessmen (*The American*, 1877), his sensitive and intellectually curious heroines (*The Portrait of a Lady*, 1881), his artist heroes, hungry for culture (*Roderick Hudson*, 1876), to moral tests that they either passed or failed. America remained for him —with all its artistic sterility—a land of innocence and promise; Europe was beautiful but decadent. James was not only a superb technician and psychologist; he was also a social historian who faithfully recorded the moral cracks and strains in the upper-class society he depicted.

As a result of the realists' efforts, the young writers who came of age in the last two decades of the century could experiment even more bodly than their predecessors in literary reality. Although it no longer took courage to portray a society committed to railroads, stockyards, real estate, and Wall Street, the new literary school that evolved went much farther than the realists in describing the seamy and brutal aspects of American life. "Naturalism," as the new movement was called, derived its inspiration from French novelists like Emile Zola, who believed that literature should be governed by the same scientific laws that guided the physiologist. Man's fate was determined by heredity and environment, by inward drives and external circumstances over which he had no control. Theoretically, the naturalist writer put down objectively what he saw, no matter how disgusting or shocking.

In America, naturalists like Stephen Crane (1871-1900) and Frank Norris (1870-

1902) never matched the frankness of the French school, but they dealt with themes that Howells, who always had his eye fixed on the young girl reader, did not care to touch. In *Maggie, A Girl of the Streets* (1893), Crane wrote of the seduction and suicide of a New York slum girl; in *The Red Badge of Courage* (1895), he reproduced convincingly the animal fear of a young Civil War recruit under fire and his psychological recovery. In all his tales and sketches of derelicts and soldiers, of frightened, abandoned people, Crane suggests that men must struggle without guidance from the supernatural. Nature is like the ocean or the snowstorm.

Norris, a less able writer than Crane and more given to melodrama, disliked the kind

Henry James, with the English dramatist, James M. Barrie, on his right.

of realism Howells represented because it dealt with the commonplace, with "the tragedy of the broken tea cup." Norris had a fondness for huge supermen with "primordial" jaws, and he loved to describe the clash of titanic natural forces. Many of his books were spoiled by exaggerated violence and sensationalism, but in *McTeague* (1899), the story of a man's reversion to brutishness, he displayed a power that was new in American fiction. In his best-known novel, *The Octopus* (1901), Norris presented an epic struggle between the California wheat-growers and the railroad. The seeming radicalism of this book was considerably diluted by Norris' message that the wheat and the railroad represented natural forces, each governed by the law of supply and demand. "Men have only little to do in the whole business."

In Jack London (1876-1916), many of the themes of Frank Norris' writing were repeated, especially the tendency to exalt the brutal while at the same time offering moral judgments on the brutality of the whole social order. Born in 1876, and thrown on his own resources at an early age in the tough water-front environment of Oakland, California, London became a hobo and a seaman, among other things, before settling down to write. His literary career lasted only 18 years, but in its course he produced over 50 books. He died in 1916, burnt out by his exertions and by the rage against life that expressed itself in his work.

London embraced a naturalistic social philosophy in which he preached, at one and the same time, a despairing doctrine of the subordination of man to the impersonal forces of nature, and the hopeful teachings of socialism. He never reconciled these ideas, but his work often successfully expressed one or the other. He was one of the most widely read writers of his time and one of the few American writers to gain recognition in Europe. He remains today one of the two or three most popular American authors in Soviet Russia. London's most interesting writings are his autobiographical novel, *Martin Eden* (1909), and his social novel *The Iron Heel* (1907),

concerned with the fight to the death between the exploited classes and a plutocratic oligarchy. His greatest success, a book about pack dogs in the Yukon, *The Call of the Wild* (1903), glories in details of animal conflict.

The writings of Theodore Dreiser reflected a naturalism that was even more uncompromising than that of Crane, Norris, or London. But in Dreiser, the replacement of the good and the bad by the strong and the weak was accompanied by a deeper feeling for character and a profound, almost maternal, tenderness. Dreiser was born in Terre Haute, Indiana, of German immigrant parents, in 1871. His early life in a family of 13 children was filled with squalor and hardship. After years of drifting from one unsatisfactory job to another, Dreiser spent several years as a newspaperman in Chicago, St. Louis, Cleveland, and Pittsburgh, where he saw at first hand the hard

Theodore Dreiser (1871-1945).

side of city life. His experiences inspired him with the idea of treating a great American metropolis as realistically as Balzac had treated Paris.

Dreiser had to battle against the restrictions set by the tradition of polite literature, and his position was not secure until the 1920's. His first novel, one of his best, *Sister Carrie,* was published in 1900 and then quickly withdrawn because many persons objected to its frankness. In a style criticized for its clumsiness, it tells of a young girl who comes to Chicago from a small western town and succumbs in succession to the blandishments of a vulgar but generous salesman and then to a restaurant manager. Sister Carrie takes a grip on her own fortunes, and in the end becomes a successful actress. The greatest chapters of the book, one of the most remarkable sequences in American letters, trace the gradual deterioration of her second seducer, Hurstwood, who drifts toward complete ruin while Carrie is winning success.

Although Dreiser is always compassionate toward his characters, it is seldom clear whether he is complaining about harsh human society or about the harshness of life itself. His characterization of an adventurous business tycoon patterned after a Chicago traction magnate, Charles T. Yerkes, in *The Financier* (1912) and *The Titan* (1914) could be taken either as a naturalist's comments on the waste and immorality of life itself or as a part of the Progressive protest against rapacious business. Dreiser's hero, Frank Cowperwood, has his image of life fixed in his mind when as a boy at an aquarium he sees a lobster devour a squid:

Things lived on each other—that was it. Lobsters lived on squids and other things. What lived on lobsters? Men, of course! And what lived on men? he asked himself. Was it other men? . . . He wasn't so sure about men living on men; but men did kill each other. How about wars and street fights and mobs? He had seen a mob once. It attacked the *Public Ledger* building as he was coming home from school. His father had explained why. It was about the slaves. That was it! Sure, men lived on men. Look at the slaves.

Cowperwood grows up with the touch

of Midas in his business dealings and the touch of Don Juan in his love life. In his pursuit of money and women, he is ruined once but boldly builds a whole new career. Toward him Dreiser maintains a mixed attitude of condemnation and approval, but basically he condones Cowperwood. Like the less successful organisms—like the squid that are eaten—Cowperwood is merely a product of nature, but a more interesting product than most of the others. In a self-consciously moral period, however, like the Progressive era in which these volumes first appeared, it was impossible for many Americans to read the Cowperwood novels without finding in them an indictment of the whole order of unchecked greed that the Progressive reformers were trying to tame.

THE PERSISTENCE
OF ROMANTICISM

Although the realists and naturalists had tried to deal honestly with the political corruption, the class struggles, and the squalor of urban life, and had gained some following among the more advanced and liberal of their generation, they failed to weaken the position of the sentimental-traditional school of writers. The sentimentalists were content to hold their thousands of readers with stories of love and renunciation, cloak-and-dagger romances, tales of exotic lands. They did their best to cushion their middle-class audience, the largest in the world, from the raw and dynamic society around them. Since their reading public was largely female, they showed no disposition to "trifle with the marriage relation." A love story, thought Frances Marion Crawford, an able and talented representative of the genteel school, should be clear and sweet, should "create and foster agreeable allusions." This was precisely what Howells failed to do, an anonymous reviewer in *The Nation* complained in 1888; the heroine of his realistic school of fiction simply could not be considered a nice girl:

She talks too much, and talks in a slangy, jerky way that is odiously vulgar. She is frank, too frank, on every subject and occasion. She is contemptuous of authority, even of parental authority, and behaves in a high-handed way about her love affairs. She is alas! something of a freethinker. She rides a bicycle, and plays tennis, and rows a boat. She laughs loudly, and dresses in a manly fashion, and acts altogether in accord with an epoch that travels its sixty miles an hour. She is very smart and clever, but in her better moments she makes us sigh for the girls who thought their parents infallible and who were reverent churchwomen—the girls who were so shrinkingly modest, and yet so brave in emergencies—the girls who were so fully accomplished and so beautiful, and yet who had no higher ambition than to be the dearly-beloved wife of a noble-hearted man and the good house-mother of happy children.

The traditionalists not only ignored sex or treated it as trivial; they also shied away from any philosophy that weakened faith in a benevolent Providence or that questioned the economic and political assumptions of those in authority.

Throughout the last three decades of the nineteenth century, the romanticists and the realists carried on a kind of journalistic warfare. To the former, the realists (or "pseudo-realists," as one critic called them) had "taught pessimism in every line of their work. They taught that marriage is a failure, that home is a brothel, that courtship is lewd, that society is an aggregation of animals." The realists countered with the charge that the romanticists were writing flimsy juvenile fiction and that they avoided the vital issues of the day—divorce, strikes, women's rights, Wall Street, public education—and that their oversimplified psychology confined them to the bare classifications of villain and hero.

In practice, however, both the traditionalists and the radicals made concessions to popular taste and interests. Each tried to satisfy a reading audience that was troubled and fascinated by the threat of an impend-

ing social revolution and, at the same time, was enamored of the romantic past. It wished to be edified and informed, to have a little ethnology, archaeology, geography, ethics, history, and pseudo-science mixed into its fictional brew. Since romantic fiction outsold the realistic novels four to one and dominated the best-seller lists every year, it is hardly surprising that the realists and naturalists did not hesitate to inject a little exotic color, violence, mysticism, and pseudo-science into their work. This was especially true of the younger naturalists— Crane, Norris, Dreiser, and London—who emerged in the '90's and after. They resented the work of the genteel, but they also rebelled against Howell's cult of the ordinary and the drab. Unabashed romantics at heart, they were far more imbued with middle-class ideals and prejudices than they or their contemporaries suspected.

Dreiser, Norris, and London, for example, shared the beliefs and the prejudices of the half-educated Americans they sometimes criticized and shocked. They concocted flamboyant "Horatio Alger" stories, violent and sensational, in which their superman heroes triumphed over the "mongrel" races of the world and dominated the weak and the unfit. They simplified the great social problems—politics, finance, law, revolution—and created a set of heroes hardly differing physically or mentally from the posturing supermen of the romanticists. By 1900, romantic fiction writers and realists were appearing simultaneously in the pages of the *Saturday Evening Post,* and it was not always easy to distinguish them from one another.

Readings

* Asterisk indicates that book is available in paperback.

Post-Civil War intellectual history is discussed fully in Merle Curti, *The Growth of American Thought* (1964); R. H. Gabriel, *The Course of American Democratic Thought* (1956); H. S. Commager, *The American Mind* * (1950); and Richard Hofstadter, *Anti-Intellectualism in American Life* * (1963). More specialized treatments of ideas between 1865 and 1920 are Richard Hofstadter, *Social Darwinism in American Thought* * (1955); M. G. White, *Social Thought in America* * (1949); Daniel Aaron, *Men of Good Hope* * (1951); and Charles Page, *Class and American Sociology: From Ward to Ross* (1940). Perry Miller, *American Thought: Civil War to World War I* * (1954), is an excellent anthology prefaced by a first-rate introduction.

A. G. Keller, *Reminiscences (Mainly Personal) of William Graham Sumner* (1933), best conveys the flavor of the man, but Sumner himself must be read to be appreciated. Standard on their subjects are Samuel Chugerman, *Lester F. Ward: The American Aristotle* (1939); C. A. Barker, *Henry George* (1955); A. E. Morgan *Edward Bellamy* (1944); and Joseph Dorfman, *Thorstein Veblen and His America* (1934). David Riesman, *Thorstein Veblen, A Critical Interpretation* * (1953), is a less laudatory analysis. Veblen's own writings, beginning with *The Theory of the Leisure Class* * (1899) should be sampled. R. B. Perry, *The Thought and Character of William James* * (2 vols., 1954) is an excellent biography containing many extracts from his letters. Sidney Hook, *John Dewey* (1939), is admirable. Oliver Wendell Holmes best reveals himself in Max Lerner, ed., *The Mind and Faith of Justice Holmes* (1943), and in his remarkable correspondence: *Holmes-Pollock Letters* (2 vols., 1941), and *Holmes-Laski Letters* * (2 vols., 1953), both edited by M. D. Howe. Howe's biography of Holmes, *The Shaping Years 1870-1882* (1957), and *The Proving Years 1870-1882* (1963), admirably place the man in his times. For Brandeis, see A. T. Mason, *Brandeis: A Free Man's Life* (1946).

H. H. Bellot, *American History and American Historians* (1952), is a useful survey which may be supplemented by Michael Kraus, *A History of American History* (1937), and W. T. Hutchinson, ed., *The Marcus W. Jernegan Essays in American Historiography* (1937). W. H. Jordy's *Henry Adams: Scientific Historian* * (1952) is informative and well-written.

Richard Hofstadter and W. P. Metzger, *The Development of Academic Freedom in the United States* * (1955), is a good introduction to the history of higher learning. Hofstadter and Wilson Smith, *American Higher Education, A Documentary History* (2 vols., 1961), offers much illuminating contemporary material. G. P. Schmidt, *The Liberal Arts College* (1957) contains a short and readable section on the American college during this period. See also Henry James III, *Charles W. Eliot, President of Harvard University, 1869-1909* (2 vols., 1930); and the *Autobiography of Andrew Dickson White* (1905).

The expansion of primary and secondary schools is covered by E. P. Cubberley, *Public Education in the United States* (1934), and E. W. Knight, *Education in the United States* (1951). Other pertinent studies include C. W. Dabney, *Universal Education in the South* (2 vols., 1936); Merle Curti, *The Social Ideas of American Educators* * (1935); Thomas Woody, *A History of Women's Education in the United States* (2 vols., 1929); H. K. Beale, *Are American Teachers Free?* (1936); and Rush Welter, *Popular Education and Democratic Thought in America* (1962). L. A. Crimmin, *Progressivism in American Education* (1961) is the best account of this subject. The story of the Chautauqua movement is told in Victoria and R. O. Case, *We Called It Culture: The Story of Chautauqua* (1948).

Of the many books on the literary history of the period, these few may be mentioned here: Alfred Kazin, *On Native Grounds* * (1942); Van Wyck Brooks, *New England: Indian Summer* * (1940), and *The Confident Years, 1885-1915* (1952); Edmund Wilson,

The Shock of Recognition * (1955), a brilliantly edited anthology; Bernard De Voto, ed., *Mark Twain in Eruption* (1940), and the same author's *Mark Twain's America* (1951), a retort to Van Wyck Brooks, *The Ordeal of Mark Twain* * (1955). For Mark Twain's early years, Dixon Wecter, *Sam Clemens of Hannibal* * (1952) is indispensable. For his mature years the same may be said of Justin Kaplan, *Mr. Clemens and Mark Twain* (1966). A. B. Paine, *Mark Twain's Letters, Arranged with Comment* (2 vols., 1917), and Charles Neider, *The Autobiography of Mark Twain* (1959), present his own views. Everett Carter, *Howells and the Age of Realism* (1954), discusses Howells and his contemporaries. Howells' work is authoritatively covered by E. H. Cady, *The Road to Realism* (1956), and *The Realist at War* (1958). The best introductions to Henry James are Leon Edel, *Henry James: The Untried Years, 1843-1870* * (3 vols., 1953), and F. W. Dupee, *Henry James: His Life and Writings* (1956). Lars Åhnebrink, *Beginnings of Naturalism in American Fiction* (1955), is helpful as background for Norris, Crane, London, Sinclair, and Dreiser. Kenneth Lynn, *Dream of Success* (1955), challenges some previously held notions about the naturalists. Thomas Beer, *Stephen Crane: A Study in American Letters* (1923), admirably discusses Crane in his cultural setting. John Berryman, *Stephen Crane* * (1950), is also perceptive. A sample of London's writing is collected in P. S. Foner, *Jack London, American Rebel* * (1947). There are stimulating essays on Norris, Crane, and London in M. D. Geismar's *Rebels and Ancestors: The American Novel, 1890-1915* * (1953). The life and ideas of Dreiser are treated by a number of writers and critics in Alfred Kazin and Charles Shapiro, eds., *The Stature of Dreiser* * (1955). Informative biographies of Dreiser include R. H. Elias, *Theodore Dreiser, Apostle of Nature* (1949); and F. O. Matthiesson, *Theodore Dreiser* (1951).

CHAPTER TWENTY-THREE

For more than five hundred years before the age of space, the history of European man was the history of overseas expansion. To explain his impulse to envelop or explore new territories would be to explain his nature. Duty moved him as much as daring, the word of God as much as the spirit of adventure, power as strongly as trade, pride as strongly as profit. The quest for freedom and personal independence urged him on as irresistibly as the quest for knowledge. He was impelled to spread "civilization," but also to escape from it.

In this long history of expansion, the European discovery of America was but a

America's
Imperialist Adventure

single chapter; and for more than three centuries after this discovery, the New World was the scene of acute rivalry among the European nations. By the eighteenth century, this rivalry, especially that between Britain and France (Spain and other pretenders to world power having fallen to the status of secondary nations), had spread to India and other parts of the Orient. Britain's victory over Napoleon in 1815 put her far ahead in the contest for empire, and the progress of the Industrial Revolution in the United Kingdom kept her beyond the reach of all comers for a hundred years.

But the Industrial Revolution also spread throughout Europe, and after the worldwide fall in prices following the international Panic of 1873, competition for world markets became increasingly intense. The wealth created by the new industrialism gave a fresh impetus to imperial ambitions that had been banked since Waterloo. France, Belgium, Holland, Russia, and above all Bismarck's newly unified Germany, each now sought "a place in the sun." They were soon to be followed by Italy and westernized Japan. Latin America, the islands of the Pacific, the interior of Africa and China, indeed all the world, once again became the stage of the imperial drama. Out went western explorers, missionaries, travelers, traders, engineers, inventors, politicians, generals, and admirals, carrying with them Britain's "White Man's Burden," France's *mission civilsatrice,* and rising Germany's *Kultur.*

Like Britain, most of the late-comers, once the growth of their own industrial systems had become stable and their profits modest, sought channels for more fruitful investment in the booming railroads and industries in the United States. By the 1890's, the United States itself was ready to shoulder the "expansionist destiny" of the Anglo-Saxon race, to join "the Christian nations," as an American missionary said, who "are subduing the world, in order to make mankind free."

I. *The Renewal of Continental Aspirations*

MEXICO AND THE MONROE DOCTRINE

Expansion, of course, was hardly a new idea in the United States in the 1890's. Even before the Revolution the American colonists had resisted the mother country's policy of restricting settlement to an area east of the Appalachians. Once independent, the United States expanded westward across the continent with astonishing rapidity. Nor, since Jefferson's time, were Mexico to the south and Canada to the north ever more than momentarily beyond the horizon of America's continental ambitions.

Following her defeat by the United States in 1848 (see Chapter 12), Mexico had been torn by factional conflict out of which she emerged, ten years later, with two governments locked in a bitter civil war. One was the government of Miguel Miramón, which had the support of the Church, the army, and the rich. The other was the government of the Zapotec Indian, Benito Juarez, the government of "la reforma," covetous of church lands, republican in spirit, sufficiently friendly toward the United States to have agreed, in exchange for badly needed funds, to the McLane-Ocampo Treaty of December, 1859, making Mexico virtually a protectorate of the Republic to the north. The United States Senate, riven itself over the slavery issue in 1859, rejected the McLane-Ocampo Treaty; but when Juarez, in 1861, emerged victorious over Miramón, Lincoln welcomed him as the first civilian ruler of Mexico under a constitutional regime.

Juarez's administration promptly got into difficulties with European monarchies which had helped finance his enemies and which also made claims for damage to their property during the civil war. When Juarez, early in 1862, suspended payments on Mexico's debt and ignored the damage claims, Britain, Spain and France sent troops to collect. Britain and Spain quickly withdrew from the venture on discovering that they were merely abetting the ambitions of Napoleon III of France to take advantage of the United States' own involvement in civil war to reenter the New World mainland and establish a Catholic monarchy there. Left alone, Napoleon, as we have seen (p. 434), proceeded to do just that, defeating Juarez' forces in 1863 and placing the puppet, Maximilian of Austria, on the Mexican throne, backed by French military strength.

As the North began to look to victory in America's civil war in 1864, even Union generals considered marching into Mexico to throw the monarchists out. In April, that year, the House of Representatives resolved that the action of the French was "deplorable," and refused to "acknowledge any monarchical Government erected on the ruins of any republican Government in America under the auspices of any European power." Again, in 1866, Grant and other generals urged President Johnson to evict the French by force, but Johnson preferred the advice of Secretary of State Seward, who gently reminded Napoleon III of American interests and invited him to withdraw. Fearful of a reunited United States near Mexico and a newly aggressive Prussia on his European borders, Napoleon reluctantly consented. The last French troops left Mexico in the spring of 1867. Maximilian, by then grown enamored of his imperial role, attempted to reign without the French, but by June, 1867, Juarez' forces had overthrown, courtmartialed and executed him. Juarez then ruled until his death in 1872, which prepared the way for the long dictatorship of Porfirio Díaz, who ruled until 1911 (see p. 640).

In his contact with Napoleon, Seward never mentioned the Monroe Doctrine, but it was apparent to all Europe that the United States was now strong enough to enforce its will in the western world if sufficiently aggravated, and indeed that Latin America could look to her for protection from European aggression. In the United States itself the Monroe Doctrine, really for the first time since its enunciation, became an explicit element of policy.

THE ALASKA PURCHASE

While avoiding armed conflict with foreign enemies, Johnson's administration carried through successful negotiations with foreign friends. Among these was Russia, which had favored the Union cause from the start. In March, 1867, the Russian minister in Washington offered to unload distant and costly Alaska, hoping, among other things, in light of the new power politics in Europe and the world, to build up the United States as a counterweight to Britain. Secretary Seward, an ardent expansionist, jumped at the opportunity, and after an all-night session with the Russians completed the deal at 4 A.M. on the morning of March 30. That very day, the President astounded the Senate with a request for approval of the purchase treaty.

The opposition press quickly denounced "Seward's Folly" and "Johnson's Polar Bear Garden," while the agreement aroused instant opposition in Congress. A remarkable three-hour speech by Charles Sumner, still chairman of the Committee on Foreign Relations (see p. 474), helped carry the project through the Senate on April 9. Sumner had as little use for Alaska as most others, but he insisted that more was to be

gained by sustaining Seward and thereby maintaining Russian friendship than by rejecting the frigid property. The purchase, Sumner also pointed out, would have the effect of removing "one more monarch from this continent." The House proved a more difficult hurdle; but a vigorous "educational" campaign by Seward, and a liberal infusion of cash by the Russians, finally won House consent, on July 23, for the appropriation needed to complete the transaction. The final price was $7,200,000.

On completing the negotiations, Seward expressed the hope that Alaska would form the northern arm of a giant American pincer movement to eliminate the British monarch along with the Russian by squeezing Canada into the American fold. "I know that Nature," he said, "designs that this whole continent, not merely these thirty-six states, shall be sooner or later, within the magic circle of the American Union."

HUNGER FOR CANADA

During the Civil War, Canada had afforded Confederate soldiers escaping from Union prisons, and active Confederate agents, a sanctuary from which to mount attacks on the northern frontier, especially in Vermont and New York. These attacks, of course, had ceased with the end of the war, but in 1866 northerners were again reminded of the problems British control of Canada could raise. That year, the Fenians, or the Irish Revolutionary Brother-Republics, an organization of Irish-Americans in New York, began a series of assaults on Canada with the bizarre hope of capturing the country and holding it as a hostage until the British gave Ireland her independence. The Irish vote had become an important factor in northern politics, and how to retain it while discountenancing adventures of this sort presented a ticklish problem to Johnson's administration. But rather than yield to the temptation of supporting or even condoning Irish violence, the administration chose to give Great Britain a lesson in neutral conduct by taking stern measures against anyone who used American bases for foreign intrigues.

The failure of Secretary Seward's early postwar efforts to settle American claims against Britain arising from the depredation of such wartime sea raiders as *Alabama* (see p. 433) soon showed that the American lesson was wasted on the United Kingdom leaders. At first, Britain refused even to receive Seward's proposals, and resentful Americans began to eye the Fenian escapades as something worth joining if only to make Britain see the light. By 1869, however, Europe itself was in turmoil because of Bismarck's expansionist policies, and Britain, like others, wanted American friendship in the imminent competition with Germany. In January, 1869, Britain and the United States signed the Johnson-Clarendon Convention for arbitrating all claims they had against each other.

Although this agreement had many defects, it satisfied the administration as a peaceful solution to the issue of the Confederate cruisers. Since it made no apology, however, for Britain's release of the cruisers nor any reference to the "indirect damage" they caused in prolonging the war, the Senate, under Sumner's leadership, rejected it in April, 1869, by a vote of 54 to 1. Seward's claims, known by the overall name of the *Alabama* claims, had amounted to around $15 million. Sumner began to agitate for indirect claims of well over $2 billion addi-

tional, and he suggested that Britain's withdrawal from North America, leaving Canada ripe for American annexation, would go far toward paying the bill. Sumner's claims only deepened Britain's disenchantment caused by the rejection of the Johnson-Clarendon Convention; at the same time, the worsening of the European situation prompted her to swallow her pride. New negotiations got underway in Washington in January, 1871. On May 8, the Treaty of Washington was concluded, and before the end of the month the Senate approved it. This treaty settled other important issues, including a new dispute over the Canadian fisheries. In 1872, the arbitration tribunal set up by the treaty threw out America's indirect claims over the cruiser activity and awarded the United States $15.5 million.

The hunger for Canada was far from dead, however. In 1886, young Theodore Roosevelt, just bursting upon the American political stage, said in a Fourth of July address that he looked forward to the "day when not a foot of American soil will be held by any European power." His friend, Henry Cabot Lodge, commented at about the same time:

From the Rio Grande to the Arctic Ocean there should be but one flag and one country. . . . The tendency of modern times is toward consolidation. . . . Small states are of the past, and have no future.

In 1891, James G. Blaine said he expected that Canada would "ultimately seek . . . admission to the union."

II. *Beyond Continental Frontiers*

A NASCENT PACIFIC POWER

Nor did American ambitions end with North America or the water's edge. Commodore Matthew C. Perry in the 1850's thought it "self-evident" that the United States would have to "extend its jurisdiction beyond the limits of the western continent." At that time Cuba in particular was in the eye of many southern expansionists. In 1867, just after the Alaska purchase,

Seward, seeking naval bases in the Caribbean, made an agreement to buy the Virgin Islands of St. Thomas and St. John from Denmark. But the House refused to appropriate more money for territory, and the treaty never came up in the Senate. We may recall, too, how in 1869 President Grant's minions hungered for the annexation of Santo Domingo, again without success (see p. 473). At that time two themes were expressed which were to have considerable influence later on. "We cannot have colonies, dependencies, subjects," said the New York *Tribune,* "without renouncing the essential conception of democratic institutions." "The true interests of the American people," the Philadelphia *Press* added, "will be better served at this important period of our national history by a thorough . . . development of the immense resources of our existing territory than by any rash attempts to increase it."

Nevertheless, the construction of the transcontinental railroads after the Civil War (see p. 518), while giving added strength to the argument for concentrating on the development of domestic resources, also sharpened American appetites for Pacific outlets and islands that had first been whetted by the rapid settlement of Oregon and California in the 1840's and 1850's. Even in those early decades the United States had acquired "most-favored-nation" treaty rights in China giving her trade terms equal to those of any other country; and after Commodore Perry had forcibly opened Japan (see p. 366), Townsend Harris, the first American consul there, negotiated a treaty of friendship by which he became the chief advisor on international relations to the inexperienced Japanese government. In 1856, while a "guano craze" was sweeping American agriculture (guano was a rich fertilizer made from the excrement of sea fowl), Congress enacted the "Guano Law" permitting the president to recognize as "appertaining to the United States" any islands rich in guano that might be occupied by Americans. By 1880, some 50 small islands, most of them in the Pacific, had thus become "appurtenances" of the United States. Some of them, long after their guano was gone, attained importance in the air age. In 1867 the United States Navy took possession of uninhabited Midway Island deep in the Pacific, but inability to dredge its harbor disappointed those who sought to use it as a way station for American ships. Soon after, Samoa in the southern Pacific and Hawaii in the northern Pacific involved

the United States in epochal arrangements.

After the intensification of the China trade and the spread of Pacific whaling early in the nineteenth century, Samoa had become well known to mariners as a refuge for vessels caught in Pacific storms. By the 1830's ships of many nations had begun to make regular stops at the islands for replenishment of supplies, and various religious denominations sent missionaries there to cater to the spiritual needs of the visiting crews as well as to convert the Polynesian natives. After the completion of the first transcontinental railroad in 1869, Samoa took on new interest for American businessmen, especially those engaged in trade between San Francisco and Australia who wished to convert the fine harbor of Pago Pago into a coaling station for steamships. A treaty worked out for this purpose in 1872 failed even to be brought up for a vote in the United States Senate. But in 1878, following a friendly visit to Washington the year before by a Samoan prince, a new treaty was negotiated and approved. While denying the Samoans the privilege they sought of becoming a "protectorate" of the United States, this treaty obliged the United States to "employ its good offices" in adjusting differences between Samoa and other nations.

It was not long before this treaty was put to a stern test. In the mid-1880's, Germany, already the leading economic power in Samoa, began to expand her activities at the expense of Britain and the United States. In 1889, dissatisfied with Samoan cooperation, the Germans violently replaced the reigning "king" with a more friendly native prince under their armed protection. The United States promptly supported the faction of the deposed ruler and, together with Britain, dispatched combat ships to the islands. Talk of war was rife; but a hurricane, blowing up at the appropriate moment and making rubble of all but one of the naval vessels in the

Queen Liliuokalani (1838-1917).

"the first departure from our traditional and well established policy of avoiding entangling alliances with foreign powers in relation to objects remote from this hemisphere."

THE QUESTION OF HAWAII

The Hawaiian Islands, strategically a natural outpost of the North American continent, were much less remote from the United States than Samoa and had been engaged in relations with Americans for a longer time. New York and New England vessels in the China trade called at the islands in the 1790's, and in the following three decades Hawaiian produce as well as Hawaiian ports played a part in the fur trade (see p. 245). As early as 1820, Yankee missionaries had settled in the islands and proceeded to transform Honolulu into a pleasant replica of a New England town. After 1840, Hawaii became the center of South Pacific whaling, and by 1860, along with French, British, and other craft, about 400 American whalers had visited the islands. By then, many American citizens owned permanent homes in Hawaii, while many Hawaiians, after shipping on American vessels, found work in California and settled there.

After 1826, Hawaii became a focus of French Catholic missionary activity as well as French business enterprise—both objectionable to the entrenched Protestants, white and converted native alike. By 1840, France herself seemed on the verge of militant intervention in the islands to protect her religious and commercial interests. When nationals of other expansionist powers, also threatened to supplant the stumbling Hawaiian government with a more efficient one of their own choosing, the United States was prevailed upon to take the first official step to preserve the islands' independence. In 1842, Daniel Webster, as Secretary of State, formally declared that the United States had a greater interest in Hawaii than any other country and would look with dissatisfaction upon any European power that sought "to take possession of the islands as a conquest" or

islands' vicinity, effectively put off hostilities. In the meantime, Britain and the United States agreed to attend a meeting with Bismarck in Berlin, and there, in June, 1889, the three powers established a tripartite protectorate over Samoa. German aggression in the islands had been checked; but friction among the three protecting nations persisted until 1899 when, by a new agreement, Samoa was formally divided between the United States and Germany. The United States then acquired Pago Pago harbor and surrounding territory while Germany got the rest of the land. Britain, for withdrawing, received from Germany the Gilbert and Solomon Islands in the southern Pacific.

Small though the Samoan issue was, Cleveland's Secretary of State. Walter Q. Gresham, saw its significance when he said in 1894, with manifest distaste, that it was to exercise "any undue control over the existing Government, or any exclusive privileges or preferences in matters of commerce." Rival foreign claims to Hawaiian ports and trade continued to agitate the islands, and a growing local faction sought outright annexation to the United States. In 1854, the Pierce administration accepted an offer from the Hawaiian king to negotiate an annexation treaty; but the king's death brought a change in local policy and the treaty project fell through.

After 1850, sugar-growing supplanted whaling as Hawaii's main economic dependence, and problems of land tenure and labor supply were added to the earlier issues between the government and outside capitalists and among the rival promoters themselves. Until 1875, American sugar producers in the Louisiana area had succeeded in keeping Hawaiian sugar out of United States ports. That year, however, a reciprocity treaty between the United States and the islands (negotiated under threats by Hawaiian growers to look to Britain for markets and political support) admitted Hawaiian sugar into the United States and American commodities into Hawaii, both duty-free. Political reciprocity also was involved. In exchange for a reassertion of Webster's old promise of America's "dissatisfaction" with any other nation's tampering with Hawaii's independence, the islands pledged themselves not to alienate any territory to foreign governments or to extend to them the commercial privileges won by the United States. Under the operation of the reciprocity treaty, Hawaiian sugar-growing boomed, and with it flourished the rest of the business community engaged in financing sugar operations, hauling sugar products, supplying and maintaining machinery and tools, and in general satisfying the needs of a newly prosperous country. The native Hawaiians themselves, however, grew increasingly restive as they saw more and more of their arable land controlled by white—mainly American-descended—planters, and themselves ever more deeply submerged under an influx of uncongenial Chinese workers.

Negotiations to renew the reciprocity treaty began in 1884, but the United States Senate would not approve a new agreement until 1887 when, in recognition of the rising strategic importance of Hawaii in the imperialist contest, it won an amendment granting the United States exclusive use of Pearl Harbor as a coaling station and repair base for naval vessels. In the same year, Hawaiian-born white businessmen, fed up with the corrupt and authoritarian regime of King Kalakaua, brought off a bloodless revolution against the ruler, forced him to accept a new framework of government— the "Bayonet Constitution," Hawaiians called it—giving themselves control of the government and extending the franchise to white foreigners. Property qualifications, in turn, disfranchised most native citizens.

Strategically, politically, and economically, Hawaii was moving ever closer to the United States. But there was to be more violence before annexation itself was accomplished. In 1890, 99 per cent of Hawaiian exports consisted of sugar for the American mainland. In that year Congress admitted other foreign sugars (as well as Hawaii's) duty-free; but the Louisiana planters persuaded Congress to give United States growers a bounty of two cents a pound. Hawaii's single-staple economy was sorely wounded. At the same time, nativist Hawaiians grew more and more antagonistic toward the discriminatory new constitution. Hawaiian discontent spread after 1891, when King Kalakaua died and was succeeded by his sister, Queen Liliuokalani, a "strong and resolute" opponent of white rule. By 1893, "Queen Lil's" calculated disregard of constitutional restraints, and ultimately her efforts to throw off the constitution altogether, drove white businessmen into a second rebellion. They had the enthusiastic support of the American minister to Hawaii, John L. Stevens, who secured for them the protection of American troops landed from a cruiser.

Stevens promptly recognized the provisional government set up by the rebels, who lost no time in dispatching a five-man commission to Washington to negotiate a treaty of annexation. This treaty, sent to the Senate by the retiring President Harrison, who favored it, was held up by Democratic opposition, and was still under discussion when Grover Cleveland was inaugurated in March. Suspicious of Stevens' activities in Hawaii, Cleveland recalled the treaty from the Senate and sent a former Democratic congressman, James H. Blount of Georgia, as a special commissioner to the islands to investigate the situation there. Secretary of State Gresham, in summarizing Blount's report for Cleveland in October, 1893, charged that Stevens, by his abuse of the authority of the United States, had done a great wrong to a "feeble but independent State." The President concluded that the revolution could not have succeeded without the support of Stevens and that the majority of the natives were against annexation. Cleveland tried to restore the Queen to control under a constitutional regime, but the provisional government was adamant. In 1894, it wrote still another constitution, proclaimed a Hawaiian Republic, and confirmed Sanford B. Dole as President.

Cleveland, realizing that he would have to use force to unseat the new government, recognized it in August, 1894, but he refused to accede to its urgent wish for annexation. In 1897, under McKinley, a new annexation treaty was worked out, but the Senate, reflecting popular discontent with American imperialist adventures, rejected it. The public temper changed during the Spanish-American war (see p. 632), and in July, 1898, by a joint resolution, Congress made Hawaii, "a part of the territory of the United States,"—the first sizable part overseas. In 1959, a year after Alaska was admitted to the Union, Hawaii became the fiftieth state.

III. *Economic and Diplomatic Militancy*

BLAINE AND MAHAN

So intent were Americans after the Civil War on developing their home market for industrial products rather than their exports, with building home railroads and factories rather than overseas investments, that the United States merchant marine, for almost a century among the greatest in the world, was allowed to disappear almost entirely from the sea. Similarly, the United States navy, once as strong as the merchant marine, and in skill and spirit second to none on the oceans, was reduced by the 1880's to a small number of wooden sailing hulks which were worse than useless in an age of steel and steam.

Nevertheless, there were certain American spokesmen who willingly shouldered, even in the most discouraging times, the mantle of empire that Seward himself had inherited from the expansionist generation of the 1840's and 1850's. Among these men were James G. Blaine, who served as Secretary of State in 1881 under Garfield and again from 1889 to 1892 under Harrison; and Captain, later Admiral, A. T. Mahan, the gifted propagandist who became the mentor of Theodore Roosevelt and Henry Cabot Lodge.

As a young man, Blaine had been an ardent admirer of Henry Clay. Like Clay he was, as we have seen (Chapter 20), a perpetual aspirant for the presidency who never satisfied his ambition; and like Clay he used the power and prestige of lesser offices to push an aggressive and spirited diplomacy, especially in Latin America. Blaine strove not only to keep European governments out of this area but also to further American influence and commercial intercourse with the republics to the south.

Latin Americans still had strong religious and nationality ties with Spain and Portugal, and strong commercial ties with Britain. In the 1870's Germany began to seek Latin-American outlets for German goods and German capital. In an effort to deflect Latin-American trade and develop-

622

ment toward the "Big Sister" to the north, Blaine in 1881 issued invitations to a Pan-American conference. Acceptances were still coming in when Garfield's assassination caused the meeting to be canceled. Back in office in 1889, Blaine revived his original scheme. That year, on his invitation, delegates from 18 nations met in Washington and formed the Pan-American Union, but they accomplished little else.

Although Latin Americans persisted in buying largely from Europeans, they were selling largely in the United States, and largely items that were duty free. When the Latin-American delegates to the 1889 conference failed to grant tariff concessions to United States exports, Blaine showed his hand by threatening to retaliate with tariffs on Latin-American goods. The so-called "reciprocity" provision of the McKinley Tariff of 1890 (see p. 557), which said the United States would reciprocate for favorable treatment and meant also that we would resist unfavorable treatment, was Blaine's weapon. Few Latin-American countries, in response to Blaine's tactics, increased either their trade with or their tenderness toward the United States.

As Secretary of State, Blaine also advocated a powerful new American navy. In 1881, with his approval, Secretary of the Navy William H. Hunt persuaded Congress to set up the Naval Advisory Board to agitate for larger naval appropriations. Though Blaine was soon out of office, this first step led to others. In 1883, Congress appropriated funds for the famous "White Squadron" of four new steel ships equipped with steam power and a full rigging of white sails. But these vessels constituted only a token navy, since they had no armor. The establishment of the Naval War College at Newport in 1884 gave further impetus to "big navy" propaganda. At Newport in 1886, just before he was made President of the College, Captain Mahan gave the lectures that eventually became the heart of his series of books on sea power in history. Such was the state of American opinion at this time that Mahan's classic-to-be, *The Influence of Sea Power upon*

History, 1660-1783, went three years before finding a publisher in 1890.

During the 'nineties Mahan also published a series of magazine articles which were collected in a book entitled *The Interest of America in Sea Power* (1897). Here Mahan applied to American conditions the general principles outlined in his historical writings. Britain, he said, had grown great on sea power; the United States should profit by her example, not simply by rebuilding her merchant marine and her navy but by adding overseas colonies and naval bases throughout the world. Without colonies and bases, Mahan argued, ships of war would be "like land birds, unable to fly far from their own shores." In particular, the United States must have naval bases in the Caribbean to protect a potential isthmian canal, and in the Pacific not only to guard and assist American commerce but also to take part in the coming great struggle between Western and Oriental civilizations.

Mahan's ideas were promptly taken up by a group of influential Republican Senators, including Lodge and Albert J. Beveridge, and by Theodore Roosevelt, soon to be Assistant Secretary of the Navy. Later they shaped the strategic thinking of Franklin D. Roosevelt. British navalists also took him up, and Kaiser Wilhelm II found in his writings additional arguments for the naval challenge Germany was already issuing to the United Kingdom.

Between 1883 and 1890, largely because of the work of Blaine and Mahan, Congress authorized the building of nine cruisers, and construction began on the first modern American battleship, *Maine*. Then came the Naval Act of 1890, the result of a report from a Naval Policy Board that Secretary of the Navy Benjamin F. Tracy had set up to investigate the whole naval expansion issue. Heretofore, to calm foreign anxieties over American naval expansion and modernization, the navy had been described officially as consisting of "seagoing coastline battleships." Now the fiction of coastline defense was officially abandoned, and the idea of a "navy second to none" began to emerge. Tracy's Naval Policy Board acknowledged that the United States had "no colonies nor any apparent desire to acquire them," that its foreign trade was "carried in foreign vessels," and that its manufactures competed "with those of other nations in but few markets." But the Board also urged the construction of 200 modern warships. Although Congress did not go that far, it authorized the construction of so many battleships, cruisers, gunboats, and torpedo boats that by 1898 only Britain and France outranked the United States as a naval power.

The expansionists turned next to the resurrection of the merchant marine. In 1891, they persuaded Congress to enact the Ocean Mail Subsidy Act, which by increasing federal payments for carrying overseas mail encouraged the construction and operation of new vessels. In addition, the reciprocity provisions of the McKinley Tariff Act stimulated exports, as did the provision of an act of 1891 that empowered the president to raise tariffs against European countries that did not give most-favored-nation treatment to American meat products.

Toward the end of the century, the position of the United States in world trade was greatly improved, as Blaine had hoped. American imports, valued at $462 million in 1870, almost doubled in the next 30 years, reaching $850 million in 1900; in the same period, American exports almost tripled, rising from $530 million to approximately $1.4 billion. The Panic of 1893, which shrank markets at home, thereby greatly stimulated the quest of American businessmen for markets abroad. Summarizing business efforts during the depression, Frederick Emory, Chief of the Bureau of Foreign Commerce of the Department of State, said of the years 1896 and 1897:

The United States is no longer the "granary of the world" merely. . . . Its sales abroad of manufactured goods have continued to extend with a facility and promptitude of results which

excited the serious concern of countries that, for generations, had not only controlled their home markets, but had practically monopolized certain lines of trade in other lands. . . . Notwithstanding the fact that organized effort to reach foreign markets for our manufactures is as yet in its infancy, the ability of the United States to compete successfully with the most advanced industrial nations in any part of the world, as well as with those nations in the home markets, can no longer be seriously questioned.

Senator Beveridge put the case even more aggressively in a speech delivered in April, 1898:

American factories are making more than the American people can use; American soil is producing more than they can consume. Fate has written our policy for us; the trade of the world must and shall be ours. We will establish trading-posts throughout the world as distributing-points for American products. We will cover the ocean with our merchant marine. We will build a navy to the measure of our greatness. Great colonies governing themselves, flying our flag and trading with us, will grow about our posts of trade.

THE MARTIAL SPIRIT

While the United States was girding both her navy and her factories to serve the growth of foreign trade, a series of diplomatic incidents from time to time triggered talk of war. These incidents also did much to foster the martial spirit that some leaders had begun to desire.

One incident arose over the old problem of American fishing rights in Canadian waters. Friction over these rights had increased as a result of other issues in Canadian-American relations during and after the Civil War (see p. 617), and while the Treaty of Washington of 1871 (see p. 618) formally resolved some of the difficulties, American fishermen continued to be harrassed and exploited by local authorities in Canada and Newfoundland. After ten years, the Treaty of Washington permitted the signatories to terminate the arrangements on two years' notice. When the United States, accordingly, notified Canada in 1883 that it would terminate the treaty on July 1, 1885, Canada retaliated by taking American fishing vessels found in her waters after that date. "Wherever the American flag on an American fishing smack is touched by a foreigner," declaimed Henry Cabot Lodge, then a young congressman from Massachusetts, "the great American heart is touched." The Detroit *News* boasted in February, 1887:

We do not want to fight,
But, by jingo, if we do,
We'll scoop in all the fishing grounds
And the whole Dominion too.

Cleveland's administration proceeded to negotiate a working arrangement with Britain to end the fishing controversy in the East, but another controversy over the seal fisheries in the Bering Sea area soon worsened relations once more. In fishing for seal, Canadians used methods that threatened to exterminate the herd. To protect their own catch, American revenue cutters began to seize Canadian fishing schooners in the Bering Sea after 1886. Canadians protested vigorously, and the resulting diplomatic intercourse only heightened the ill feeling. When rumors spread in 1890 that British warships were policing the North Pacific, war talk again was heard. "The thing to do," explained the Sioux City *Journal,* is to "shoot *any* British ship which is in those waters." Cooler heads again prevailed, and an arbitration treaty was ratified in February, 1892. The arbitration court eventually decided against the United States on all disputed points.

A third episode occurred after a revolt in 1891 against the president of Chile, in which the United States had backed the president. When the rebels won, feeling against the United States ran high; and when, in October, 1891, the captain of *U.S.S. Baltimore,* then in Valparaiso, permitted his crew to go ashore unarmed, a riot broke out between them and some Chileans in which two Americans were killed and others were imprisoned. Chilean apologies were slow in coming, and President Harrison hinted that he might invite Congress to declare war. Other prominent people in the United States were bursting to take up the cudgels, among them

Theodore Roosevelt, whose intimates thereafter were to taunt him as "the Chilean Volunteer." Just in time, a full apology arrived to calm American feelings, and Chile eventually agreed to pay $75,000 to the families of the dead sailors and to the men who had been injured in the fracas.

A more serious affair brought the United States closer to war in 1895. This incident involved disputed territory between British Guiana and neighboring Venezuela on which gold was discovered in the 1880's. When Venezuela broke off diplomatic relations with Britain in 1887, the United States offered to act as mediator, but Britain rejected the proposal. The last American mediation effort was made in July, 1895, by Richard Olney, Cleveland's Secretary of State. In a note to Lord Salisbury, the British Foreign Minister, Olney reminded him of the non-colonization clauses of the Monroe Doctrine and proceeded to invite Britain to leave America altogether. "Three thousand miles of intervening ocean make any permanent political union between a European and an American state unnatural and inexpedient," Olney wrote. Then he added these provocative words:

Today, the United States is practically sovereign on this continent, and its fiat is law upon the subjects to which it confines its interposition. Why? It is not because of the pure friendship or good will felt for it. . . . It is because, in addition to all other grounds, its infinite resources combined with its isolated position render it master of the situation and practically invulnerable as against any or all other powers.

Olney closed with a suggestion of "peaceful arbitration."

Salisbury took his time in replying. When he did, in November, 1895, he rejected arbitration and proceeded to remind the United States that the Monroe Doctrine was not recognized in international law and did not apply to boundary disputes. Cleveland made the Olney-Salisbury interchange public in December, when he himself further fired opinion by a message to Congress. In it he asked for funds to finance a commission to determine the actual boundary between British Guiana and Venezuela, and then added the inflammatory assertion that "it will . . . be the duty of the United States to resist by every means in its power, as a wilful aggression upon its rights and interests" any efforts by Great Britain to grasp any territory that the United States, after investigation, found of right to be Venezuela's. He was fully aware, he said, "of all the consequences that may follow." But "there is no calamity which a great nation can invite which equals that which follows a supine submission to wrong and injustice and the consequent loss of national self-respect and honor, beneath which are defended a people's safety and greatness."

Congress cheered these fighting words and voted for the fact-finding commission. Twenty-six governors promptly pledged their support. If war came, said Theodore Roosevelt, he hoped he might "have a hand in it myself." "The bankers, brokers, and anglomaniacs generally," he moaned to his

sympathetic friend Lodge, seemed to favor "peace at any price. . . . Personally I rather hope that the fight will come soon. The clamor of the peace faction has convinced me that this country needs a war."

Since the Venezuelan boundary dispute coincided with mounting silverite aspirations for action against the alleged center of the "gold power," it was much more inflammatory than any of the earlier episodes had been. But the peace parties eventually won out both in the United States and Britain. Cleveland's proposal for a boundary commission gave Americans time to simmer down, since nothing could be done until the commission reported. Britain, meanwhile, was growing increasingly concerned over the rise and rivalry of Germany. In 1896 she was faced with a serious outbreak of violence by the Boers in South Africa, and a telegram of sympathy sent to the Boer leader on January 3 by Kaiser Wilhelm of Germany served as a reminder of more important matters at stake in Europe. British leaders thus refused to be drawn further into a dispute with the United States, which itself had become a power to be courted. In February, 1897, at

The Venezuela boundary dispute, 1896.

KEEP OFF!
The Monroe doctrine must be respected.

America's behest, Britain and Venezuela negotiated a treaty turning the boundary dispute over to international arbitration. In 1899, a final settlement was made. Cleveland and Olney had won their gamble in asserting the power of the United States

alone to decide upon the extent to which the Monroe Doctrine could be pushed.

IV. *The Spanish-American War*

THE CUBAN CRISIS

As the Venezuela issue faded, the young American inflammables found a new incident to exploit—the Cuban insurrection against Spain, which had begun in 1895.

For decades, of course, Americans had been interested in acquiring Cuba, but the isolationism of the post-Civil War generation quieted the issue. When the Cubans rebelled against Spanish rule in 1868, Americans looked on indifferently. This rebellion dragged on for ten sickening years. Then, having lost many men and spent large sums to crush the Cubans, Spain agreed to undertake serious reforms. The Cubans made two major demands: (1) emancipation of the slaves on the island, and (2) self-government for the island's inhabitants. Spain actually took another ten years before freeing the slaves, and she postponed granting autonomous government indefinitely. She made the mistake, moreover, of giving amnesty to the rebel leaders, who promptly exiled themselves to the United States and agitated for Spain's expulsion from the New World.

Spain's irresponsibility in Cuba soured her relations with the United States, but there were few inflammatory incidents before 1895. By then, however, the world, the United States, and Cuba herself had all greatly changed. The aggressive activities of Britain, France, and Germany in the Western Hemisphere had made it increasingly likely that if Cuba were lost to decadent Spain she would fall to a much more vigorous power. France's efforts, starting in 1881, to build a canal across the Isthmus of Panama heightened the rising threat from Europe in the Caribbean. In the United States, in turn, expansionism, naval-ism and empire-building, as we have seen, were being pushed and our own interest in a canal connecting the Atlantic and the Pacific as well as in coaling stations, strategic harbors and protected bases had matured.

The changes in Cuba were as great as elsewhere. After the emancipation of the slaves, large amounts of European and American capital had moved in, bringing modern methods to the island, especially in the production of sugar. At the same time, Europe had greatly enlarged its own sugar production, and the United States gradually became Cuba's main market and source of capital. An executive agreement with Spain in 1884, which removed the American duty on Cuban sugar, further stimulated production, pushing it to a record 1,050,000 tons in 1894. Events then suddenly conspired against Cuban prosperity. Europe's production of beet sugar became so great that the world price of sugar fell. The Panic of 1893 and the following depression further weakened prices. Finally, the Wilson Tariff of 1894 (see p. 563) restored a 40 per cent duty on sugar. Raw sugar brought 8 cents a pound in 1884. By 1895, the price had broken to 2 cents, and the Cuban way of life broke with it.

When insurrection started again in 1895, American interests were inevitably threatened. To quell the rebels, Spain sent over her best general and 200,000 men, but the Spaniards could not cope with the insurgent leaders and their guerilla followers, who had taken to the hills. The rebels also embarked on the widespread destruction of property in order to exhaust government resources and thereby force the withdrawal of government forces. American property naturally was lost in the holocaust, much of

"Who Destroyed the Maine?"—Hearst's front page, February 17, 1898.

it deliberately destroyed in an effort to force the United States to intervene to protect her interests, and many Americans now renewed the old demand for annexation of the island. In January, 1896, Spain placed General Valeriano Weyler in command in Cuba. Weyler did not hesitate to fight fire with fire, and soon earned the nickname "Butcher." Weyler made Cuba a country of concentration camps, into some of which he drove the guerillas and into others the rest of the population. Since few could work, few could eat, and starvation and disease soon took 200,000 lives.

During all this time a Cuban junta, which had been organized in New York, kept agitating for American intervention and Cuban autonomy. At the same time, Joseph Pulitzer of the New York *World* and William Randolph Hearst of the New York *Journal* started a spirited circulation

battle, each trying to outdo the other in printing gory stories of Spanish brutality. Mahan, Roosevelt, Lodge, Beveridge, and others also whipped up the war spirit. President Cleveland, however, refused to be stampeded. He feared, as he said in 1896, that "there were some outrages upon both sides, if the truth were known." By March, 1897, McKinley had become President on a platform calling for Cuban independence. But even he was convinced by the end of the year of Spain's good intentions in offering reforms. A change of government in Spain led to Weyler's replacement by a new general who had orders to end the concentration-camp system.

War might still have been averted had not a chance series of events occurred. On February 9, 1898, a letter stolen by a rebel sympathizer in Havana from the Havana post office fell into the hands of Hearst's New York *Journal*. In it, Dupuy de Lôme, the Spanish minister to the United States, characterized McKinley, after his first message to Congress in December, 1897, as "weak and a bidder for the admiration of the crowd, besides being a would-be politician who tries to leave a door open behind himself while keeping on good terms with the jingoes of his party." This was a private letter, but Hearst made it as public as possible. Spain disavowed any evil intent on her minister's part, and de Lôme himself resigned as soon as the letter was published. The *Maine* tragedy followed in less than a week.

The new battleship *Maine,* had been sent to Havana in January, 1898, when the American consul-general there cabled that American property and persons were in danger. Spain was assured that the ship's visit had no aggressive purpose, and when *Maine* arrived later in January her officers and men were entertained by the Spanish General Blanco. Then on February 15, *Maine* apparently hit a submarine mine, and two officers and 258 members of the crew were lost. An immediate official inquiry left the causes of the explosion uncertain, but Congress appropriated $50 million for national defense just the same. *Maine's*

Captain Sigsbee had wired right after the disaster that "Public opinion should be suspended until further report." But it was not long before the cry, "Remember the *Maine!,*" was whipping up the country.

THE "SPLENDID LITTLE WAR"

At the head of the war party stood Theodore Roosevelt, who, as Assistant Secretary of the Navy, as early as February 25, 1898, seized on the temporary absence of his chief to cable Commodore George Dewey at Hong Kong, in command in the Pacific: "In the event of declaration of war Spain, your duty will be to see that the Spanish squadron does not leave the Asiatic coast, and then offensive operations in Philippine Islands." In the meantime, sympathetic politicians, intellectuals, and publicists kept the pressure on McKinley.

But peace still had many strong and well placed partisans in the Cabinet, in Congress, in the Republican party, and among substantial business groups, and these men prevailed upon the wavering President to make every effort to avoid war. Accordingly, the State Department cabled a series of demands to Spain on March 27, of which the most important was the one for an armistice in Cuba until October 1, leading to American mediation there. Within four days, the Spanish government, fearful of its own people in case of war, made many concessions, but stated it would agree to an armistice only if the rebels themselves requested it. Hopeful of eventual American intervention on their behalf, the rebels made no such request. Spain, in the meantime, scrambled to find support and allies in Europe; but the German Foreign Minister, on April 5, conveyed the attitude of most other nations when he told the Spanish ambassador: "You are isolated, because everybody wants to be pleasant to the United States, or, at any rate, nobody wants to arouse America's anger; the United States is a rich country, against which you simply cannot sustain a war." When the Pope agreed to suggest an armistice, thereby saving Spain the humiliation of yielding to an American ultimatum,

Spain, on April 5, grasped the offer and conveyed her acquiescence to McKinley. Not until April 9, however, would she consent to American mediation in Cuba; and her delay was disastrous.

Prodded by the press and the war enthusiasts, McKinley was already at work on a militant message to Congress, which he delivered on April 11. The President was obliged, in this message, to take notice of Spain's last-minute capitulation on American mediation, of which he had been aware for two days. But he buried his remarks on this embarrassing reversal of Spanish policy near the end of his message. Clearly the Spanish surrender to American demands warranted a wholly new message, but McKinley was by now too thoroughly intimidated by the war cry to seize the reins of leadership for peace. His evasiveness made it easier for Congress to interpret his message as a demand for war. The formal declaration of war came on April 25, effective as of April 21.

On April 27, duly alerted by the Presi-

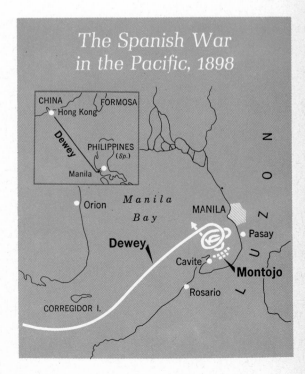

The Spanish War in the Pacific, 1898

dent now, as well as by T.R., Commodore Dewey in Hong Kong raised steam and on the night of the 30th sailed into Manila Bay. The next morning, after giving the famous order, "You may fire when you are ready, Gridley," Dewey blasted the antiquated Spanish fleet that was sitting there. Admiral Montojo, the Spanish commander, lost all his ships and 381 men; American casualties were 7 wounded sailors. News of the victory arrived in Washington May 7.

Dewey lacked the necessary men for further "offensive operations in Philippine Islands," and by the time the first reinforcements of 2,500 arrived on June 30, British, French, Japanese, and German men-of-war were swarming around the Philippines seeking to protect their nationals. The German force was much the strongest, and Dewey was suspicious of it. But it had no aggressive designs, though stories of its supposed threats began to circulate in the United States. By July 25, about 11,000 American troops had landed in the Philippines, under General Wesley Merritt. Supported by Filipino insurrectionists under Emilio Aguinaldo, whom Dewey had helped arm, Merritt took Manila on August 13.

By then, indeed, the "splendid little war," as Hay called it, had already come to a close in the West Indies. On April 29, a Spanish fleet under Admiral Cervera had sailed west from the Cape Verde Islands, destination unknown. American coastal cities panicked and demanded naval protection. A patrol fleet was established to satisfy eastern politicians, and the main American fleet under Admiral William T. Sampson and Commodore Winfield Scott Schley tried to find Cervera before he got to Cuba, where they decided he was headed. They could not locate him, however, until he was safely in Santiago harbor, where Sampson bottled him up. A military expedition was now planned to capture Santiago overland and force Cervera out under the American fleet's waiting guns.

On June 14, a poorly equipped expeditionary force of 17,000 men under General William R. Shafter finally left Tampa, Florida. Typical of this army was the First Volunteer Cavalry Regiment, the "Rough Riders," which had no horses. Shafter and his men reached the Cuban coast in the vicinity of Santiago on June 20 and took six days to disembark. A few more days passed before this army moved on toward the Cuban port. The Spaniards had 200,000 men in Cuba, but only 13,000 in Santiago. And of these, because of problems of transport and supply, only 1,700 could be mobilized to meet the Americans. The Spaniards were well trained and well armed, however. After a two-day battle, which saw Roosevelt lead the Rough Riders up San Juan Hill on July 1, the American attack petered out. "We are within measurable distance of a terrible military disaster," Roosevelt admitted in a letter to Lodge.

Luckily for Shafter, the Spaniards were even more spent, and on July 3 Cervera decided to escape if he could. Sampson's fleet was awaiting this move, but expected Cervera to try to sail away at night. When the Spaniard left in broad daylight instead, the surprised American ships became so snarled in their own tracks that Cervera almost got free. Overwhelming American firepower, however, finally destroyed his wooden ships. Of Cervera's men, 744 were killed or wounded. The American fleet suffered little damage and had but one man killed and one wounded. On July 16, General Linares surrendered Santiago to the Americans. On July 25, a second American expeditionary force, commanded by General Nelson A. Miles, made a triumphant if belated march through Puerto Rico. By July 13, the Spanish government had already begun to seek a peace treaty, and on August 12 hostilities were declared over. The next day, Manila fell.

All told, the United States lost 5,462 men in the four-months' war, of whom only 379 fell in combat. The rest died from disease and other causes. Spain's losses in the fighting were much higher, and in addition she lost the remnants of her once-imposing New World empire. Confirmation of her loss was to be found in the peace treaty, on which formal meetings began in Paris on October 1. In December, the treaty was signed. Ratification by the Senate, however, was another matter.

AN IMPERIAL PEACE

Every excuse was offered for America's plunging into war with Spain because no clear justification could be found. The war opened the mysterious vessel that was the American heart and mind. No question of American security or American honor was involved; and if there had been, Spain had cleared the way to satisfaction two weeks before war started. It was (various spokesmen said) America's duty to liberate Cuba, America's destiny to grasp new markets and new lands, America's obligation to bring western culture to the dark places of the earth, America's mission to Christianize the heathen. But why in 1898?

Perhaps an editorial in the *Washington Post*, read into the *Congressional Record* just before the start of the war, touched close to the heart of the matter:

A new consciousness seems to have come upon us—the consciousness of strength—and with it a new appetite, the yearning to show our strength. . . .

Ambition, interest, land hunger, pride, the mere joy of fighting, whatever it may be, we are animated by a new sensation. We are face to face with a strange destiny.

The taste of Empire is in the mouth of the people even as the taste of blood in the jungle. It means an Imperial policy, the Republic, renascent, taking her place with the armed nations.

Shortly after the war began, "Marse" Henry Watterson, editor of the influential

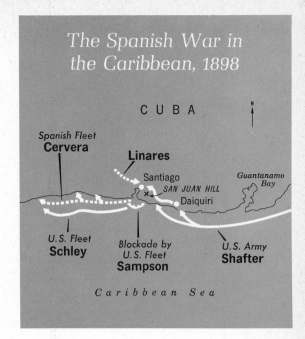

The Spanish War in the Caribbean, 1898

CUBA

Spanish Fleet **Cervera**

Linares

Santiago

SAN JUAN HILL

Daiquiri

Guantanamo Bay

U.S. Fleet **Schley**

Blockade by U.S. Fleet **Sampson**

U.S. Army **Shafter**

Caribbean Sea

"Charge of San Juan Hill," by Frederick Remington.

Louisville *Courier-Journal,* had told a New York reporter:

From a nation of shopkeepers we become a nation of warriors. . . . From a provincial huddle of petty sovereignties held together by a rope of sand we rise to the dignity and prowess of an imperial republic incomparably greater than Rome. . . . We risk Caesarism, certainly; but even Caesarism is preferable to anarchism. We risk wars; but a man has but one time to die, and either in peace or war, he is not likely to die until his time comes. . . . In short, anything is better than the pace we were going before these present forces were started into life. Already the young manhood of the country is as a goodly brand snatched from the burning, and given a perspective replete with noble deeds and elevating ideas.

America's leading political wit, Finley Peter Dunne, put it perhaps more simply:

"We're a gr-reat people," said Mr. Hennessy earnestly. "We ar-re," said Mr. Dooley, "We ar-re that. An' th' best iv it is, we know we ar-re."

American ambiguity about the precipitating causes of hostilities no doubt helped muddle the nation's peace aims. The United States clearly had no territorial ambitions at the outbreak of the war. Congress' war resolution had stated that Cuba ought to be free and independent, and if Spain failed to grant independence instantly McKinley might use the armed forces of the United States to win Cuba's freedom. Then followed a fateful amendment, offered by Senator Henry M. Teller of Colorado, that the United States pledge herself to leave Cuba in control of the Cuban people.

But even while the war with Spain was in progress, American policy toward the acquisition of territory began to change. On July 6, 1898, Congress adopted a joint resolution annexing Hawaii to the United States. Two weeks later, in stating terms for an armistice in the war, McKinley demanded the cession of Puerto Rico and of Guam. He stipulated, moreover, that the United States was to occupy the "city, bay, and harbor of Manila pending the conclu-

sion of a treaty of peace." "By our code of morality," McKinley had said earlier, annexation of territory "would be criminal aggression." By July he had become less abstemious. "We must keep all we get," he said; "when the war is over, we must keep what we want."

While America's negotiators were preparing to make the treaty with Spain, American hunger for the Philippines kept growing. First it was only Manila; then, on September 16, the negotiators were instructed by McKinley to take nothing less than the island of Luzon. By October 26, the whole archipelago was being demanded. When Spain demurred, an ultimatum was issued on November 21, to which Spain capitulated. The continuing fear that Germany would seize the Philippines in her bid to become a Pacific power no doubt fed America's own expansive demands. McKinley also had a more palatable explanation ready. "There was nothing left for us to do," the President explained to a group of Methodist ministers after the United States had annexed the islands, "but to take them all, and to educate the Filipinos, and to uplift and civilize and Christianize them, and by God's grace do the very best we could by them as our fellow men for whom Christ also died."

The final treaty, insuring the freedom of Cuba and granting to the United States the Philippines (for a payment of $20 million), Puerto Rico, and Guam, was signed on December 10. In the debate on ratification in the Senate, the annexation of the Philippines became the main issue. Many people in the country had opposed the war from the start; and in November, 1898, they mobilized in the Anti-Imperialist League and employed every available propaganda technique to defeat annexation even if it meant defeating the treaty. Opposed to them were the brash young men of the war party, flushed with victory and determined to enjoy its fruits.

On February 6, 1899, the Senate narrowly ratified the treaty by 57-27—only two votes above the required two-thirds. The decision was influenced by the reaction of the Filipinos themselves. On December 21, 1898, while the debate in the Senate was at its peak, McKinley had ordered the War Department to extend the military occupation of Manila to the entire archipelago. This move touched off armed Filipino resistance, which promptly took the lives of American soldiers and no doubt swayed Senate votes. The movement that had started as an effort to liberate the Cubans quickly became a war to subjugate the Filipinos. The islanders, led by Aguinaldo, held off the Americans for three years in a conflict that cost more than the war with Spain itself and found the United States forced to employ the same concentration-camp methods that the Spanish had used to combat the Cuban guerrillas.

Nor, indeed, were the Cubans liberated. Despite the Teller Amendment, General Leonard Wood remained in Cuba as military governor until May 20, 1902, when Cuba was forced to accept the restraints of the so-called Platt Amendment. This amendment to an army appropriation bill limited Cuba's treaty-making powers, her right to borrow money, and other prerogatives of sovereignty. Moreover, Cuba could not withhold lands wanted by the United States for coaling or naval stations, nor yield territory to any other power. Finally, the amendment permitted the United States at its own discretion to intervene in Cuba "for the protection of life, property, and individual liberty." The United States required the incorporation of the Platt Amendment in any constitution drawn up by Cuba, and also stipulated that Cuba make a permanent treaty with the United States restating the amendment's terms. The Platt Amendment remained in force until 1934, when it and related treaties were abrogated by agreement. At that time the United States retained Guantánamo Bay and its shore area as a naval base.

THE PUBLIC
AND THE COURT CONCUR

The war with Spain had ushered the people of the United States into a new era. The conflict itself, the problems of the

peace treaty, the pacification of Aguinaldo's rebels, and the shackling of free Cuba all kept the issue of the new imperialism constantly before the public. In the midst of the discussion and debate, the election of 1900 took place (see p. 567). William Jennings Bryan, the Democratic candidate, had been instrumental in securing some Democratic votes for the treaty of peace in the Senate. Unsympathetic to the treaty himself, he urged its support partly to protect his party from the imputation of wanting the war renewed, and partly to get the whole issue of imperial expansion into the campaign. McKinley's substantial victory was interpreted by many as a victory for the new course. When McKinley was assasinated a few months after his inauguration in 1901 and Theodore Roosevelt became President, the imperialist camp had reason to expect that expansionism would be further encouraged.

In May, 1901, in the so-called *Insular Cases,* the Supreme Court added its sanction to the assent of the executive and the people. In these cases, the Court held, essentially, that the Constitution did not follow the flag, that the rights of United States citizens did not automatically belong to the people of the territories. The *Insular Cases* arose over the Foraker Act of 1900, under which the territorial government of Puerto Rico was set up. According to this act, Puerto Rican goods entering the United States were to pay duties for two years equivalent to 15 per cent of the duties levied on similar products of *foreign* countries under the Dingley Tariff of 1897 (see p. 566). If Puerto Rico was in fact part of the United States, duties on her goods, like duties on goods crossing state boundaries, were unconstitutional. The Court saved the duties by deciding, in language "not easily understood," as one constitutional historian put it, that Puerto Rico was "territory appurtenant . . . but not part of the United States," and that Congress could determine how much of the Constitution applied to the "native inhabitants." The Court's stand carried beyond mere duties on goods into the whole area of civil rights.

In 1903, even though Hawaii had been made a regular territory of the United States in 1900, the Supreme Court also held that these islands had not been "incorporated" into the Union and that the native citizens thus had not become regular citizens of the United States. The case in question arose out of the denial of trial by jury to the Hawaiian people. The Court decided that it was lawful to follow the existing criminal procedure in the islands instead of substituting that laid down for Americans by the federal Constitution. In reaching this decision, the Court differentiated arbitrarily between "fundamental rights" which could not be abridged, and "procedural rights" which could be. Trial by jury,

it held, was a "procedural right" only.

These early imperial distinctions, however, were soon swept aside. Americans were not comfortable in the role of colonizers and empire-builders, and even the Philippines were quickly put on the road toward self-government. The foundations were laid by the Philippine Commission appointed in 1900 with William Howard Taft as chief. By 1907, the Filipinos had gained the right to elect the lower house of the legislature, and in 1916 the Jones Act gave them virtual autonomy over their domestic affairs. Some of this ground was lost during the 1920's, but in 1934 the Tydings-McDuffie Act provided for independence after ten years. The Filipinos agreed to the ten-year provision in 1936. When the islands were recovered from Japan during World War II, the Filipinos finally achieved their independence, as originally planned, on July 4, 1946.

v. *A World Power*

THE "OPEN DOOR"
IN CHINA

With a new empire in the Pacific, the United States became more interested than ever before in affairs in the Far East. The great prize there was the relatively impotent and passive country of China, where, at the turn of the century, many imperial powers, including Japan, France, Germany, Britain and Russia, were staking out exclusive "spheres of influence." If China were to become dismembered, American hopes for further trade with that country clearly would be disappointed. The problem posed to the United States was to find a way of achieving and maintaining equal trading rights in China without risking war and without becoming a party to further partition. The situation became particularly acute in 1898, when it appeared that the British were about to use some newly leased territory on the mainland opposite Hong Kong to smuggle imports into China without paying the Chinese tariff. If the other imperial powers were to follow this example, the Chinese government would lose all

its tariff revenues, and political as well as commercial chaos would result.

To meet this situation, McKinley's Secretary of State, John Hay, in September, 1899, sent his memorable "Open Door" notes to Britain, Germany, and Russia, and later to Japan, Italy, and France, inviting them to agree to three points: (1) No nation was to interfere with the trading rights or privileges of other nations within its sphere of influence. (2) Chinese officials were to be permitted to collect duties under the existing tariffs, which granted the United States most-favored-nation privileges. (3) No nation was to discriminate against nationals of other countries in levying port duties and railroad rates.

It is noteworthy that Hay's notes made only the most circumspect proposals. He had not asked the great powers to cease partitioning China. He simply tried to persuade them to declare that they would respect the trade rights of others within their own spheres. None, however, was prepared to make even such a nominal concession. Yet Hay himself was not ready to accept their vague rejections. He saved himself from a fiasco by calmly announcing on March 20, 1900, that the powers had all granted "final and definitive" consent to his request. The only power that cared to challenge this audacious bluff was Japan.

Hardly had negotiations over the "Open Door" notes been concluded when a group of fanatical Chinese nationalists, organized as the Order of Literary Patriotic Harmonious Fists and hence called by Westerners the "Boxers," rose up against foreigners in their country. Before they were put down by an international force to which the United States contributed 2,500 men, they had killed hundreds of persons and destroyed much property. Only swift action by Britain and the United States now restrained the partitioning powers from retaliating by subjugating more territory.

Hay advised the imperial rivals that the policy of the United States was to seek a solution that would "preserve Chinese territorial and administrative entity" and "safeguard for the world the principle of equal and impartial trade with all parts of the Chinese Empire." This announcement

went farther than the Open Door notes and also had more effect. Eventually, the nations participating in the suppression of the Boxers accepted a money indemnity from China rather than new grants of territory. The United States' share of almost $25 million was larger than necessary to meet the losses she suffered, and she later returned the balance to China where it was used to help educate Chinese students in the United States.

Americans felt that Hay had achieved a major diplomatic victory in preventing further partition. The New York *Nation* called it "a splendid instance of American sagacity winning a peaceful victory." What had made the settlement possible, however, was the unwillingness of the European powers at this time to enter into a scramble in China that might touch off a general war.

RELATIONS WITH JAPAN

The succession of Theodore Roosevelt to the presidency in September, 1901,

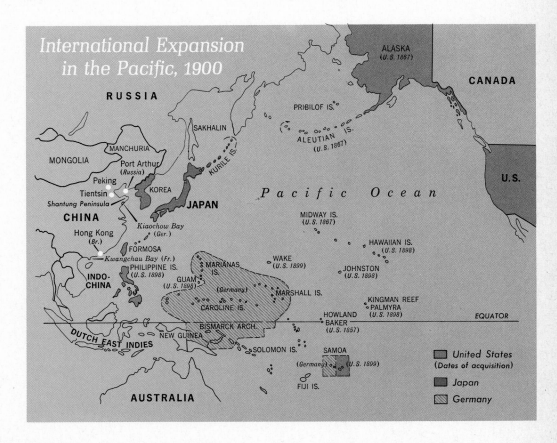

International Expansion in the Pacific, 1900

seemed to promise a period of aggressive foreign policy. A robust 43 at the time he took office, Roosevelt had built his reputation partly on his Spanish war service. For some years previously, he had preached the importance of what he called "the soldierly virtues." "No triumph of peace," he had told the Naval War College in 1897, "is quite so great as the supreme triumphs of war. . . . The men who have dared greatly in war, or the work which is akin to war, are those who deserve best of the country." Roosevelt felt that American interests could be maintained only if the nation increased its strength and actively extended its influence throughout the world. But except for his aggressive conduct in acquiring the Panama Canal territory (see p. 638), his policies were more moderate than his pronouncements.

Roosevelt's first major move was prompted by the Russo-Japanese War of 1904-1905. Encouraged by a treaty of alliance with Britain, signed in 1902, Japan felt free to try to drive the Russians out of Manchuria, where the two nations had become rivals. Her adventure won some sympathy in the United States which traditionally feared the power of the czars and now looked to Japan as a possible counterweight to it in the Far East. Japan's easy victory over Russia, however, persuaded Roosevelt that Japan's own expansion was a greater threat than had been imagined. And when the small nation, at a great military advantage but exhausted by her efforts in attaining it, secretly asked Roosevelt, in the spring of 1905, to mediate the conflict, he grasped the opportunity to impose his own constraints. Before he would agree to intervene, Roosevelt insisted that Japan respect the principles of the Open Door policy. When she agreed, the President invited her delegates and the Russians to meet at Portsmouth, New Hampshire, in August. Here, among other claims, the Japanese demanded a huge money indemnity to offset their war costs. When the Russians balked, Roosevelt warned the Japanese against pressing their demand, and they accepted some small territorial grants instead.

T.R.'s "balance of power" aspirations in the Far East may have slowed down Japan's rise, but Japan nevertheless emerged from this war as the dominant power in Asia. The Japanese people, in turn, had counted on an indemnity from Russia for tax relief and did not quickly forget that Roosevelt seemed responsible for robbing them of it.

Americans had their own reactions to Japan's victory. Prejudice against the Japanese had long existed on the West coast in particular and Japan's emergence as a great power now heightened American anxiety about the "yellow peril." In October, 1906, the Board of Education of San Francisco ordered the segregation of the 93 Japanese children in the city in a separate school. News of this action stung Japanese racial pride and led a number of Japanese newspapers to call for drastic action. Roosevelt was furious over California's provocation, but the American federal system gave him no jurisdiction over the California public schools. Only after denouncing the San Francisco action in his annual message of 1906 as a "wicked absurdity" and bringing a great deal of pressure on local authorities, did Roosevelt succeed in getting the action reversed. At the same time, he promised the Californians that the Japanese immigration that had alarmed them would be curbed. A series of notes in 1907 and 1908 made up the Gentleman's Agreement by which Japan promised to issue no more passports to workers seeking to emigrate to the United States.

Having mollified the Japanese, Roosevelt was anxious, as he wrote to a friend, "that they should realize that I am not afraid of them." In 1907, as a demonstration of American strength, he decided to send the American fleet around the world on a practice cruise. Remarkably enough, Japan welcomed the visit of the fleet as a friendly gesture and for a time Japanese-American relations improved. The Root-Takahira Agreement of November, 1908, reflected the better feeling. An executive agreement not a treaty, the terms bound only T.R.'s administration and that then serving in Japan. Both powers agreed to maintain the status quo in the Pacific area, to uphold the Open Door in China, and to support by peaceful means that country's "independence and integrity." By saying nothing of Manchuria, however, the agreement seemed to concede Japan's special interest there. Indeed Roosevelt was courting Japan at the cost of retreating from Hay's Open Door principle. It was in the American interest, he wrote in 1910, "not to take any steps as regards Manchuria which will give the Japanese cause to feel . . . that we are hostile to them, or a menace—in however slight a degree— to their interests."

Roosevelt's Far Eastern policy was upset by his successor as President, William Howard Taft, and Taft's Secretary of State, the corporation lawyer, Philander C. Knox. They favored in particular a policy of encouraging American investment and trade abroad, a policy that became known as "Dollar Diplomacy." Taft had an imposing explanation of it: "This policy has been characterized as substituting dollars for bullets. It is one that appeals alike to idealists of humanitarian sentiments, to the dictates of sound policy and strategy and to legitimate commercial aims." One of the troubles with "Dollar Diplomacy" was that those Americans who controlled investment dollars were as yet reluctant to invest them in far-off places. One of Taft's pet projects was to have American bankers finance China's purchase of Manchurian railroads in which Russia and Japan both were interested. His effort only aroused the suspicion and animosity of Russia and Japan, driving together the two nations T.R. had sought to keep apart.

THE PANAMA CANAL

The extension of American interests in the Pacific and the Caribbean seemed to make all the more urgent the construction of a canal to link these great waters, a project that as early as 1850 had led the United States and Great Britain to agree on the Clayton-Bulwer Treaty. This treaty stipulated that the two nations would enjoy equal rights in any canal constructed across Central America. Now, the United

States pressed Britain to permit her to build the canal alone, and in 1901 Britain yielded. She was at this time deeply involved in the Boer War in South Africa and felt disposed to court American friendship—all the more so since her rivals, Germany and Japan, equally aware of America's new world role, were taking the same course.

After one false start that foundered on a clause prohibiting the United States to fortify the projected canal, Britain and the United States agreed on the Hay-Pauncefote treaty of 1901 which gave the United States a free hand to build, control, and, by implication, to fortify the canal. In return, the United States promised that the canal would be open without discrimination to the commercial and fighting vessels of all nations.

Two routes were possible for the canal, one through Panama, in the Republic of Colombia, the other through Nicaragua. Years before, a French canal company, led by Ferdinand de Lesseps, had gone bankrupt trying to dig a waterway through Panama; but a successor corporation, the

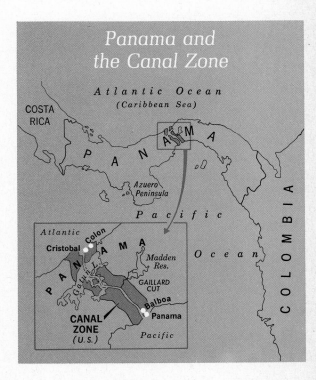

Panama and the Canal Zone

New Panama Canal Company, had acquired its assets as well as an extension of its concession of canal rights from Colombia until 1904. A rival canal enterprise, the Maritime Canal Company of Nicaragua, meanwhile, had entered the field, but had made little progress. By 1898 the New Panama Canal Company was ready to sell out to the United States if it could get Colombia's consent, and the Nicaraguan government was eager to interest the United States in rescuing the Maritime Canal Company and its enterprise. Both routes and both companies had their American enthusiasts; in June, 1902, after much maneuvering and debate, the Panama route won. This was a signal triumph for the French company—and its persuasive counsel, the New York law firm of Sullivan and Cromwell—for had it not been able to sell its rights before they reverted to Colombia in 1904 it would have lost everything. Colombia itself, however, had still to be heard from.

By holding the alternative of a Nicaraguan canal over the heads of Colombia's negotiators, John Hay was able to drive a hard bargain with Tomás Herrán of Colombia in a treaty approved by the United States Senate in March, 1903. Forty million dollars had been earmarked earlier for the New Panama Canal Company, which was empowered by the treaty to transfer to the United States all its rights in Colombia. The treaty stipulated that $10 million cash and $250,000 annually were to be paid to Colombia itself for the rights to a canal zone six miles wide across the Isthmus of Panama. Colombia, torn by revolution during the years of conflict over the canal route, had a new government in 1903 which suddenly expressed resentment over some of the treaty terms, including what it considered inadequate monetary compensation and inadequate safeguards of its national sovereignty. When the government tried to revise some of the terms Herrán had subscribed to, Hay responded with such threats that, to preserve its own dignity, the Colombian Senate was obliged to reject the treaty in August, 1903, by a vote of 24 to 0. Many believed that the new gov-

"Construction of Panama Canal Lock," lithograph by Pedro Miguel, 1912.

ernment was holding out until 1904 so that it and not the French concessionaires would receive the $40 million supposed to go to the New Panama Canal Company. President Roosevelt lost no time in announcing that the "black-mailers of Bogotá" must not be allowed "permanently to bar one of the future highways of civilization." The Indianapolis *Sentinel* marked out the course that would be followed to break this impasse when it calmly observed in August, 1903: "The simplest plan of coercing Colombia would be inciting a revolution in Panama . . . and supporting the insurrectionary government." Such thoughts also stirred in Roosevelt's fertile brain.

Roosevelt was determined to have the canal site on whatever terms, and the French company naturally was anxious to close the deal. Furthermore, the people of Panama were growing restless, fearing that if the United States did not soon construct the canal on their soil she would turn to Nicaragua instead. Several parties concerned thus arrived at the conclusion that a revolution in Panama would be extraordinarily convenient both for those in the United States who wanted a Panama site and for the French company as well. So, under the leadership of its ingenious adventurer-lobbyist, Philippe Bunau-Varilla, the French company fomented a revolution in Panama against the Colombian government—but only after Bunau-Varilla had sounded out Roosevelt and Hay to be sure that the United States would prevent Colombia from suppressing it. The revolution could not have succeeded without the cooperation of the American navy. On October 30, 1903, *U.S.S. Nashville* was ordered, in case of rebellion, to seize the Panama railroad and to prevent the landing of any armed force within 50 miles of Panama. This order cut the Colombian troops off from the revolutionary area, and the revolution took place quietly. Washington promptly recognized a minister from the new republic of Panama and a treaty was signed giving the United States the desired strip for $10 million and $250,000 a year.

Roosevelt has been much criticized for his complicity in the Panamanian revolution. He defended himself by remarking: "If I had followed traditional conservative methods I should have submitted a dignified state paper of probably 200 pages to Congress and the debate would be going on yet; but I took the Canal Zone and let Congress debate; and while the debate goes on the canal does also." Roosevelt's high-handed behavior and remarks created many enemies for the United States throughout Latin America, and probably did not speed up completion of the canal significantly. Within a decade of the Panamanian revolution, however, under the direction of Colonel George W. Goethals, an army engineer, and thanks to the feats of sanitation achieved by Colonel W. C. Gorgas, an army medical officer, the canal was finished. On August 15, 1914, the first ocean steamer passed through it.

In 1914, the Wilson administration, desiring to placate Colombia and win good will in Latin America, concluded a treaty with Colombia that apologized for the part played by the United States in the Panamanian revolution and set aside $25 million to be paid to Colombia to soothe her wounded feelings. Roosevelt's friends in the Senate would not abide this slur upon his conduct and the treaty was shelved. In 1921, after Roosevelt's death, the treaty minus the apology at last passed the Senate by a vote of 69 to 19, and Colombia received its indemnity in full.

IN THE CARIBBEAN SPHERE

The Panama Canal, by giving the United States a great new enterprise to protect, deepened American involvement in the Caribbean. The political and financial instability of the smaller Caribbean republics posed an especially touchy problem. If any one of them failed to pay interest due on its bonds, which were largely held by European financiers, some European state itching for imperialist expansion, like France in Mexico in 1863 (see p. 616), might simply move in with the idea of staying indefinitely. To avert this danger, President Roosevelt in his message to Congress on December 6, 1904, set forth what is known as the Roosevelt Corollary to the Monroe Doctrine: "Chronic wrong-doing . . . may in America, as elsewhere, ultimately require intervention by some civilized nation, and in the Western Hemisphere the adherence of the United States to the Monroe Doctrine may force the United States, however reluctantly, in flagrant cases of such wrong-doing or impotence, to the exercise of an international police power."

The first application of the Roosevelt Corollary came in 1905, when the Dominican Republic found itself unable to pay its debts. After a show of force by the United States, the Dominican government had to invite the United States to step in and take

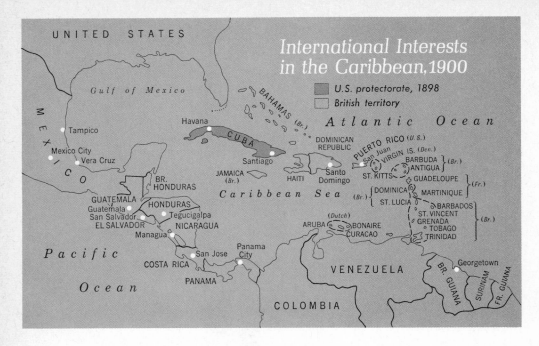

■ U.S. protectorate, 1898
☐ British territory

control. The foreign debt was scaled down and transferred from European to American bankers, and a certain percentage of customs collections was allocated to pay Dominican debts. Cuba also drew the attention of the Roosevelt administration in 1906, when revolutionary disturbances prompted the administration to land troops to restore order. They were not withdrawn until 1909.

Intervention in Latin America continued under President Taft. Taft and Knox hoped that the financial administration set up for the Dominican Republic might become the model for further intervention in the Caribbean and hoped that the pursuit of Dollar Diplomacy would enable American bankers not merely to protect the Panama Canal, but also to build up a financial empire. To this end, Secretary Knox persuaded American bankers to increase their interest in the debt of Honduras and to put capital into the National Bank of the Republic of Haiti.

The outstanding instance of Dollar Diplomacy took place in 1911, when a revolution broke out in Nicaragua and American bankers took charge of the country's finances. In 1912, American marines were landed to prevent further upheavals here.

United States intervention in the affairs of Caribbean neighbors aroused great hos-

tility throughout Latin America, and when Woodrow Wilson succeeded Taft in 1913, he promised that the United States would "never again seek one additional foot of territory by conquest." The outbreak of World War I in 1914, however, made the American government more vigilant than ever in the Caribbean, and while President Wilson busied himself with more important problems of foreign policy the State Department and the Navy Department continued to intervene. In 1915, American marines entered Haiti in response to violent revolutionary disturbances and did not leave until 1934, when a new constitution was imposed on the Haitian Republic by the Navy Department. The Wilson administration occupied the Dominican Republic again in 1916, and also intervened in Cuba in 1917. By then Wilson had also become deeply embroiled in his painful adventure in Mexico.

WILSON IN MEXICO

In May, 1911, President Porfirio Díaz, dictator of Mexico since 1877, was overthrown by a revolutionary coalition led by the liberal idealist, Francisco Madero. Unable to organize a new regime rapidly enough, the revolutionaries were themselves suppressed in February, 1913, by General Victoriano Huerta, who coldly arranged the assassination of Madero. Most European governments now recognized the Huerta regime, and American business interests, with large investments in Mexican industry, urged Wilson to do likewise. But Wilson, shocked by this official murder, refused on the ground that the Mexican regime was not a free government resting on the consent of the governed. "We can have no sympathy," he said, "for those who seek to seize the power of government to advance their own personal interests or ambition."

Wilson's departure from the historic American policy of recognizing all governments in power involved serious practical difficulties. It threw upon the United States the dubious responsibility of deciding which foreign governments were pure and which were not. When an "immoral" foreign regime survived, the United States was faced with the unpalatable alternatives of losing prestige by being forced to retreat from its non-recognition policy or of intervening actively to uphold that policy, even at the risk of war. Attempting to decide on the morality of a foreign government involves meddling in its domestic affairs. Wilson justified his efforts to unseat Huerta when he said to a group of visiting Mexican newspapermen: "Our sincere desire was nothing else than to assist you to get rid of a man who was making the settlement of your affairs for the time being impossible." Wilson himself made such settlement all the more impossible by persuading the British government which had a strong interest in Mexican oil, to abandon Huerta in return for a rash American promise to protect Britain's Mexican concessions and for adjustments in Panama canal tolls.

When Huerta's government failed to collapse as Wilson hoped it would, he offered to help the anti-Huerta Constitutionalist forces in Mexico under Venustiano Carranza. Carranza wanted no support from unpopular Yankees, but Wilson nevertheless revoked an embargo on arms to Mexico that had been established by President Taft, hoping that this move would help the Constitutionalists get the weapons they needed to overthrow Huerta. When Hu-

erta's regime withstood the challenge, Wilson found himself unable to redeem the pledge he had made to Mexico and to the world that he would guarantee constitutional government in that country.

On April 9, 1914, an incident occurred that gave Wilson an excuse for intervention. One of Huerta's officers arrested the crew of an American vessel that had landed behind the government's lines at Tampico. Although the Mexicans promptly released the Americans with expressions of regret, the commander of the American squadron demanded a more formal apology, which Huerta refused. Wilson took Huerta's action as an insult to the nation and asked Congress for authority to win redress by arms. Even before Congress could act, Wilson learned of a German steamer that was about to arrive at Vera Cruz with a load of ammunition for the Huerta government. In order to keep armaments that might be used against American forces out of the country, Wilson at once (April 21) ordered the Navy to occupy the port, which it did in an action that cost 126 Mexican lives. Even Carranza's Constitutionalists were angered by Wilson's occupation of Mexican territory and threatened war.

At this critical point, the "A.B.C." powers—Argentina, Brazil, and Chile—offered to mediate, and Wilson welcomed this chance to crawl away from his difficulties. Mediation failed, but Huerta's regime, unable to secure arms from European nations busy strengthening their own forces, soon collapsed nevertheless. Carranza took over the presidency in August, 1914, and a year later Huerta's best general, Francisco "Pancho" Villa, took command of the opposition forces. Disorders spread, and in March, 1916, Wilson sent General John J. Pershing across the border on a "punitive expedition" against Villa, who had repeatedly raided American territory and killed American citizens. Carranza himself replied to this "invasion" by mobilizing his own army.

Preoccupied as he was with the war in Europe, Wilson at last withdrew Pershing's forces and in March, 1917, recognized Carranza's regime. Peace was maintained, but only after Wilson had aroused the lasting distrust of a people he meant to help.

Readings
Asterisk indicates that book is available in paperback.

P. T. Moon, *Imperialism and World Politics* (1926), is a comprehensive work that places the problem of imperialism in a world setting. Up-to-date American accounts may be found in the general diplomatic histories by Leopold, DeConde, and Pratt cited in our general bibliography. B. H. Williams, *Economic Foreign Policy of the United States* (1929), is a useful supplement to other general works. This theme is stressed by Walter LaFeber, *The New Empire, An Interpretation of American Expansion 1860-1898* (1963); and J. W. Pratt, *Expansionists of 1898* * (1936). A. K. Weinberg, *Manifest Destiny* * (1935), is a penetrating study of other impulses behind America's expansionist urge. See also Richard Hofstadter, *Social Darwinism in American Thought* * (1955). D. W. Pletcher, *The Awkward Years: American Foreign Relations under Garfield and Arthur* (1962), is the definitive account, which may be supplemented by A. F. Tyler, *The Foreign Policy of James G. Blaine* (1927). Outstanding general accounts of foreign relations under succeeding administrations include F. R. Dulles, *The Imperial Years* (1956); E. R. May, *Imperial Democracy, The Emergence of America as a Great Power* (1961); H. K. Beale, *Theodore Roosevelt and the Rise of America to World Power* * (1956); and G. F. Kennan, *American Diplomacy 1900-1950* * (1951).

A. T. Mahan, *The Influence of Sea Power upon History 1660-1783* * (1890), was the first of this influential writer's long list of books. W. D. Puleston, *Mahan* (1939), is an informative biography. Harold and Margaret Sprout, *The Rise of American Naval Power 1776-1918* (1939); and G. T. Davis, *A Navy Second to None* (1940), are excellent on American naval policy. On American policy in different regions, see S. F. Bemis, *The Latin American Policy of the United States* (1943); Dexter Perkins, *A History of the Monroe Doctrine* * (1955); D. G. Munro, *Intervention and Dollar Diplomacy in the Caribbean 1900-1921* (1964); J. F. Rippy, *The United States and Mexico* (1931); Tyler Dennett, *Americans in Eastern Asia* (1922); A. W. Griswold, *The Far Eastern Policy of the United States* * (1938); and Charles Vevier, *The United States and China 1906-1913* (1955). Theodore Morgan, *Hawaii, A Century of Economic Change 1778-1876* (1948); and S. K. Stevens, *American Expansion in Hawaii 1842-1898* (1945), cover the background of the fiftieth state. C. C. Tansill, *Canadian-American Relations 1875-1911* (1943), is a sound scholarly monograph. On the changing relations with Britain, see L. M. Gelber, *The Rise of Anglo-American Friendship: A Study in World Politics 1898-1906* (1938); and C. S. Campbell, Jr., *Anglo-American Understanding 1898-1903* (1957).

A good, short introduction to the Spanish-American conflict is H. W. Morgan, *America's Road to Empire* * (1965); see also, Morgan's, *William McKinley and His America* (1963); and Margaret Leech, *In the Days of McKinley* (1959). Relevant biographies of expansionists include J. A. Garraty, *Henry Cabot Lodge* (1953); C. G. Bowers, *Beveridge and the Progressive Era* (1932); and H. F. Pringle, *Theodore Roosevelt* * (rev. ed., 1956). Walter Millis, *The Martial Spirit* (1931), captures the spirit of the age and of the war itself. Frank Freidel, *The Splendid Little War* * (1958), is excellent. Orestes Ferara, *The Last Spanish War* (1937), conveys the Spanish point of view. J. E. Wisan, *The Cuban Crisis as Reflected in the New York Press 1895-1898* (1934), is illuminating. Theodore Roosevelt, *The Rough Riders* * (1899), is the classic account.

A comprehensive study of America's postwar empire is J. W. Pratt, *America's Colonial*

Experiment (1950). D. F. Healy, *The United States in Cuba 1898-1902* (1963), is definitive on the background of the Platt Amendment. Richard Hofstadter, "Manifest Destiny and the Philippines" in Daniel Aaron, ed, *America in Crisis* (1952), is a valuable essay on making the peace treaty. On Aguinaldo's uprising, see Leon Wolff, *Little Brown Brothers* (1961). Two books tell the story of the Panama Canal: Gerstle Mack, *The Land Divided* (1944); and D. C. Miner, *The Fight for the Panama Route* (1940). In addition to general works cited above on Far Eastern policy, see Tyler Dennett, *John Hay* (1933); and P. C. Jessup, *Elihu Root* (2 vols., 1938). Many of the works cited for Wilson in Chapter 24 deal with the Mexican intervention. Here we may note A. S. Link, *Wilson the Diplomatist* * (1957); Harley Notter, *The Origins of the Foreign Policy of Woodrow Wilson* (1937), and H. F. Cline, *The United States and Mexico* * (1953).

CHAPTER TWENTY-FOUR

While many Americans around the turn of the century felt, as Walter Hines Page, the editor of the *Atlantic Monthly* said in 1898, that "the adventurous spirit of our Anglo-Saxon forefathers" must plant American institutions in "every part of the world," many others felt even more strongly that these institutions themselves were in dire need of overhauling. The preceding generation of Americans had devoted its energies to settling the continent, developing its resources, building a mighty industrial system, making money. The new generation set out to reform what it considered the gravest abuses of the society it had inherited.

As its name implies, the Progressive

The Progressive
Movement

Movement fed on the belief that further progress toward social justice was not only possible but urgent. Different Progressives pointed out different roads to reform, but most of them shared the same goals: (1) to make political life more democratic, 2) to make economic life fairer and more competitive, (3) to make social life more moral and more just. They hoped to eliminate privilege and favoritism, to level out the distribution of income, to broaden opportunities for the common man. If these goals were not won, they feared American society would fall victim to plutocracy or socialism, and in either case that its traditional forms of democratic government would wither.

From the 1870's to the 1890's, as we have seen (Chapter 20), various voices had been raised on behalf of reform. But Progressive criticism of American society became at once more comprehensive and more penetrating than that which had earlier been heard. The Progressives, moreover, went much farther along the path from criticism to action. The Progressive Movement fathered both the Republican "Square Deal" of Theodore Roosevelt and the Democratic "New Freedom" of Woodrow Wilson. A host of other reforms that were not, strictly speaking, a part of either program won the backing of men in both major parties and of the majority of voters.

I. *The Progessive Mind*

The Progressives were an inquisitive, energetic, and optimistic breed. Sophisticated enough to know that things were not always what they seemed on the surface, the reformers pried into the hidden crannies of American society. Sometimes horrified by what they found, they were rarely discouraged about the correctives to be applied. Since they made the whole of American society their concern, their movement was exceedingly diverse and their programs are hard to summarize. But the following generalizations seem valid.

(1) Progressives were deeply tinged with the message of social Christianity; to save the individual, they felt they must save society. By the early twentieth century, to be sure (see Chapter 22), the thinking of most intellectually sophisticated Americans had been deeply affected by Darwinism, by materialism, by the secular outlook generally. And yet they had by no means forgotten their Christian heritage nor the call of their religion for concern over the condition of their fellow men. This was what the evangelical Progressive, William Allen White, saw when he declared in 1910 that "in the soul of the people there is a conviction of their past unrighteousness." It was no accident that the Progressive sociologist, E. A. Ross, should have entitled one of his most widely read books (admired, among others, by Theodore Roosevelt) *Sin and Society.*

(2) Since their whole purpose was to effect changes in society, the Progressives naturally looked for philosophic support among those willing to question fixed systems of belief. Nor did they have far to look. One of their most gifted mentors was the Harvard philosopher and psychologist, William James, who so dearly embraced "the will to believe," yet whose "pragmatism" as we have seen (p. 597), marked a turning away from unverified and often unverifiable abstractions about nature and man. Pragma-tists and Progressives, as James' confrere, John Dewey emphasized (see p. 598), regarded theories not as answers but as instruments of investigation, and judged their value by their consequences when applied.

(3) In keeping with their pragmatic philosophy, the Progressives had a passion for facts. Who actually benefited from an unregulated economy? How did existing institutions really work under alleged economic laws? Did competition insure an open society with equal opportunity for all? Did government intervention produce evil results? Who really exerted power through the state? What ideas influenced judges when they passed on the validity of laws? Who put up the money for elections? How much did the construction of the city hall really cost? Earlier thinkers such as Henry George and Edward Bellamy had already raised many of these questions and supplied philosophical answers. The Progressives sought a solid basis in information for practical social improvements.

(4) The Progressives particularly condemned the entrenched conservative belief in passive government. Conservatives had argued that in the long run the economy would work best if left to economic laws alone. But the Progressives, on the evidence of the recent Panic of 1893 and the ensuing depression, saw economic conditions under the laws of economics going only from bad to worse. They felt free to call upon federal and state governments not only to investigate the facts of labor conditions, monopoly, banking, and farm credit, but to do something about them.

(5) Their view of positive government naturally confronted them with the necessity of strengthening the democratic process and making it work more effectively. The surrender of community rights to corporations and bosses they attributed to public apathy. Once the people roused themselves, the Progressives believed, they would stamp out corruption and exploitation and return

to the American heritage of self-government lost sight of in the age of plutocracy.

(6) Many Progressives feared the plutocrats as much for their uncontrolled Philistinism as for their uncontrolled power, as much for their corruption of taste as for their corruption of business and politics. The reformer, Henry Demarest Lloyd, anticipated their attitude when he wrote in *Wealth Against Commonwealth* (1894):

If our civilization is destroyed as Macaulay predicted, it will not be by his barbarians from below. Our barbarians come from above. Our great money-makers have sprung in one generation into seats of power kings do not know. The forces and the wealth are new, and have been the opportunity of new men. Without restraints of culture, experience, the pride, or even the inherited caution of class or rank, these men, intoxicated, think they are the wave instead of the float, and that they have created the business which has created them. To them science is but a never-ending repertoire of investments stored up by nature for the syndicates, government but a fountain of franchises, the nations but customers in squads, and a million the unit of a new arithmetic of wealth written for them. They claim a power without control, exercised through forms which make it secret, anonymous, and perpetual. The possibilities of its gratification have been widening before them without interruption since they began, and even at a thousand millions they will feel no satisfaction and will see no place to stop.

The mere existence of "robber barons," whether or not they made others poor and themselves rich, was a provocation to the rest of society. Their swollen fortunes made men of more modest means feel small and insignificant. Their lack of scruples put men of principle at a disadvantage. Even their charities and philanthropies—for they were sometimes generous—seemed pretentious, as though designed to throw other men's generosity into the shade. The follies in which they and their families indulged were in keeping with their immense means. They built huge and ugly houses, employed armies of servants, permitted themselves fantastic extravagances. The doings of the rich made piquant newspaper copy. At one party the guests, all on horseback, rode their mounts into a luxurious hotel. At a great dinner, cigarettes rolled in hundred-dollar-bills were passed out to the guests and smoked after the coffee. At another, each guest found in one of his oysters a magnificent black pearl. Perhaps the most irritating single event was the notorious Bradley Martin ball, given at a cost of $369,000 during the severe depression winter of 1896-1897. The hostess appeared as Mary Queen of Scots, displaying among her ornaments a massive ruby necklace once worn by Marie Antoinette, and one of the guests, August Belmont, wore a $10,000 suit of steel armor inlaid with gold. Theodore Roosevelt, then police commissioner, saw all too well how this unthinking extravagance would arouse the poor of New York, and growled, "I shall have to protect it by as many police as if it were a strike."

"From the Depths," an illustration in John A. Mitchell's The Silent War, *1906.*

(7) The corruption and open callousness of the new rich only made the Progressives the more deeply aware, and the more deeply fearful, of the social distress of the vast underlying population. According to a Census Bureau estimate made in 1893, the wealthiest 9 per cent of American families owned about 71 per cent of the national wealth. But the problem went deeper than such general statistics. Industrial accidents brought tragedy, and then poverty, to an extraordinary large portion of the working class; even in 1913, after safety measures had been adopted by many industries, 25,000 workers were estimated to have been killed on their jobs and 700,000 gravely injured. Women and children worked long hours in factories, fields, and mills, most of them unprotected by legislation or by unions. Immigrants in the cities lived under the most trying conditions, with little chance of becoming first-class citizens. The Negro, victimized by his heritage of slavery, terrorized and voteless in the South and segregated and neglected in the North, challenged the conscience of every informed and humane American. The Progressives were on the whole more sensitive than Americans had ever been to the persistence of social inequality and social problems apparently arising from it, and to the urgent need for correcting them. They felt that they stood at a great watershed in American history: they might spill down the side of decay and disaster; or they might, of their own free will, find their way to the development of a society more creative, and more comfortable than America had ever known.

THE "WISCONSIN WAY"
AND THE MUCKRAKERS

The Progressives, obviously, were thinkers and readers. Men like Roosevelt and Wilson were only the topmost figures of the most intellectual political generation since that of the Founding Fathers. One of their problems was to find the right things to read. This they resolved by writing many of the right things themselves. The years from 1900 to 1914 saw the publication of such novel approaches to American politics as Walter Weyl's *The New Democracy*, Herbert Croly's *The Promise of American Life*, and Walter Lippmann's *Drift and Mastery*, all recalling the democratic values of the agrarian past and proposing ways for sustaining them in the urban, industrial present. The caustic analysis of the Constitution by such scholars as J. Allen Smith and Charles A. Beard (see Chapter 22) were written in the same reform spirit; they strove to make the fundamental law itself less sacrosanct and therefore more amenable to Progressive alteration. More specific issues were dealt with in such influential books as Louis D. Brandeis' study of the "Money Trust," *Other People's Money*, and C. R. Van Hise's *The Conservation of Natural Resources in the United States*. William Allen White's *The Old Order Changeth: A View of American Democracy*, although a short book, dealt comprehensively with the Progressive program and spirit.

A significant Progressive innovation was the publication of extensive government reports on social issues. If trust and tariff problems were to be tackled head-on, if railroads were to be effectively regulated, if long hours of work were to be reduced, if other hazards of employment and urban living were to be ameliorated, expert testimony in depth was required. There were precedents, to be sure, for taking such testimony by legislative committees, the most productive one being the Hepburn investigation of the railroads in New York State in 1879. But the Progressives enlarged and institutionalized the practice.

The first great federal investigation of this sort began in 1898, when Congress set up the Industrial Commission to study the relation of the burgeoning trusts to labor, immigration, agriculture, technology, and related subjects. Its report, in nineteen thick volumes, remains a mine of information; in the Progressive era it supplied much of the basic information for such social critics as Veblen and John R. Commons. The most intensive use of the legislative investigating function was made in Wisconsin under the governorship of Robert M. La Follette from 1901 to 1906. La Follette also introduced the employment by the state government of the faculty of the state university as a "brains trust." Reform governors in other states eagerly copied the "Wisconsin Way."

Serious works in political philosophy and detailed government reports on social conditions greatly assisted Progressive leaders, but they hardly met the popular craving for facts. The sensational novels of the newly realistic generation of American writers—London, Norris, Dreiser, and others (see Chapter 22)—no doubt satisfied many. But many more turned hungrily to the new "muckraking" magazines and books.

'Muckraking" got its name from a speech made by T.R. in 1906 about the work of the journalists who were exposing the sordid aspects of American society. "In Bunyan's *Pilgrim's Progress*," he said, "you may recall the description of . . . the man who . . . was offered the celestial crown for his muck-rake . . . but continued to rake the filth on the floor." Even though he agreed that many of their charges were true, Roosevelt condemned the muckrakers because he feared their widely read exposures would arouse dangerous discontent. But the muckrakers insisted that the American people would not fight for reforms until they had been fired with indignation. And the way to create indignation was to report every ugly fact that could be uncovered.

Muckraking was a creation of the new magazines. Before the 1890's, there were no mass-circulation magazines in the United States. Limited audiences—usually about 130,000—bought the staid and respectable old family magazines such as the *Century, Harper's, Scribner's,* and the *Atlantic.* During the 1890's a group of enterprising businessmen brought out a wholly new kind of popular magazine patterned after newspapers. The new magazines sold for half the price of the older journals, contained livelier stories and articles, and were heavily illustrated. The new conservative magazines such as the revitalized *Saturday Evening Post* and the *Ladies' Home Journal* soon reached audiences of a million and more. The muckrake magazines such as

McClure's, Everybody's, Cosmopolitan, Collier's, and the *American* did not do quite as well as that but far outsold the old journals and created a greater stir even than the more widely read conservative ones.

The muckrake publishers recruited a band of extremely able reporters and supplied them with funds and facilities such as no reporters ever enjoyed before, thereby enabling them to probe deeply into obscure court records, to locate and interview witnesses, and by other means to dig up mountains of facts. Very little that seemed wrong in America escaped the muckrakers. Perhaps their most famous accomplishment was a series by Lincoln Steffens, who investigated Philadelphia, Pittsburgh, and other American cities and found them all suffering from the same ills: bribery by businessmen, corrupt and shrewd party bosses, political collusion, special privilege, organized vice, venal police, and apathetic citizens. Ida Tarbell's almost equally famous exposé of Standard Oil retold the story of the pitiless methods by which that huge combine had been built. Charles Edward Russell threw a searching light on the beef trust. Thomas Lawson, a reformed speculator, exposed Amalgamated Copper, which he said had been "responsible for more hell than any other trust or financial thing since the world began." The novelist David Graham Phillips wrote a series called "The Treason of the Senate."

Muckraking articles were followed by many muckraking books. John Spargo's *The Bitter Cry of the Children* described the appalling conditions of child labor in the United States; George Kibbe Turner exposed prostitution and the white slave traffic in his *Daughters of the Poor;* Ray Stannard Baker discussed the treatment of the Negro in his *Following the Color Line.*

In a few cases, muckraking had direct and distinctly wholesome effects. Upton Sinclair's novel *The Jungle,* a nauseatingly realistic exposure of Chicago's food-packing methods, spurred the passage of pure-food legislation by Congress. Burton J. Hendrick's *The Story of Life Insurance* stimulated the regulation of the large New York life insurance companies during the governorship of Charles Evans Hughes. Other disclosures led to important local reforms. Confronted with the shocking revelations of the muckrakers, the average citizen could no longer imagine that American life was pure and innocent. The main question was, what would he do about it?

II. *Progressivism in the Cities and the States*

REFORMING LOCAL POLITICS

The Progressive movement originated on the local level and spread from the cities to the states and ultimately to the federal government. The movement for municipal reform as we have seen (Chapter 21), began in the 1870's but was given a strong impetus during the 1890's, with Chicago in the lead following the World's Fair of 1893. In 1894 New York City reformers overthrew Tammany Hall. In 1901 Tom Johnson, a rich railway operator and manufacturer who had been converted to reform by reading Henry George, was elected mayor of Cleveland, an office he held until 1910. His work and that of another Ohioan, Samuel ("Golden Rule") Jones of Toledo, set examples for local reformers elsewhere.

By their municipal reforms many Progressives hoped to take control of public affairs from the corrupt political bosses and turn it over not to political reformers but to distinterested experts more or less responsible to the people themselves. To improve municipal government, they proposed that the mayor and council, usually creatures of corrupt machines, be replaced by independent administrative commissions. This idea was first tested in Galveston, Texas, in 1901 after the city council proved unequal to the emergency caused by a flood. Galveston's five-man commission worked so well that by 1914, 400 cities had adopted a system of local management by popularly elected commissioners. Other cities soon empowered such commissioners to appoint an expert city manager responsible to the commissioners, to run the city's departments. By 1923 more than 300 cities had adopted this method of government.

Legally, the cities were the creatures of the state legislatures, where the work of municipal reformers often was undone by the allies of unseated city bosses. Thus municipal reformers often were forced to extend their attack to the state machines. Governor LaFollette of Wisconsin was perhaps the greatest of the state reformers. Besides creating the "Wisconsin Way," he made many innovations in regulating railroads and utilities and improving the tax system of the state. In California Governor Hiram Johnson fought an epic battle with the railways and eventually brought them under state supervision. The election of Charles Evans Hughes as governor of New York State in 1906 was his reward for exposing unscrupulous insurance practices.

More specifically democratic reforms were sought through the state legislatures. Perhaps the innovation expected to be most salutary was the *direct primary.* Reformers hoped the direct primary would insure the selection of abler and more independent officeholders by leaving the choice of candidates to the people themselves, rather than to the party machines. By 1916 some form of the direct primary had been adopted by all the states except Rhode Island, Connecticut, and New Mexico. The *initiative*—a reform that permitted the public to propose legislation—was adopted in several states, as was the *referendum,* which enabled the voters to approve or reject measures passed by the legislatures. Such devices were especially popular in the western states.

The *recall* of public officers through popular votes, another reform device, received widespread support as a means of getting rid of unsatisfactory officials before their terms expired. The proposal to recall judges and thereby expose the judiciary to popular feeling especially aroused the ire of conservatives. But many judges were in bad odor for having invalidated social legislation and seven states, all west of the Mississippi, actually passed laws providing for their recall. Nowhere, however, were these laws invoked. During the 1912 campaign Theodore Roosevelt boldly suggested as an alternative to the recall of the judges, the recall of judicial decisions. Only Colorado adopted such a measure, and it was declared unconstitutional in 1921.

Short-ballot laws, intended to simplify the voter's problems when he went to the polls, were adopted in many cities; and corrupt practices acts, intended to prevent graft and the excessive use of money in elections, were adopted in most of the states. The Seventeenth Amendment provided for one of the changes most in demand among reformers. This amendment, passed by Congress in 1912 and ratified by May 31, 1913, took from state legislatures the privilege of electing United States senators and gave it directly to the voters.

Although the reformers put a great many of their political reforms into law, the direct primary, the initiative, referendum and recall, and the other devices often misfired, frequently because of the people's inability to sustain their interest in politics. The bursts of reform usually ended in public apathy and the return of the old guard.

PROGRESSIVE
SOCIAL LEGISLATION
The Progressives had greater success with social than with political reforms. Some progress in legislating against child labor had already been made in almost half the states by 1900. In 1914, after a concerted drive by child-labor reformers, every state but one had set a minimum age, usually 14, at which a child could work in industry. Enforcement was made simpler in many of these states by laws requiring school attendance until the minimum working age. Other measures prohibited the employment of children at night and in dangerous occupations. In 1916 Congress passed the Keating-Owen Act, which prohibited the

shipment in interstate commerce of goods made in factories, mines, and quarries that employed children under specified ages. Two years later, in *Hammer* v. *Dagenhart,* the Supreme Court declared this act unconstitutional on the ground that it invaded the police powers of the states and attempted to use federal control of interstate commerce to attain other ends. The states responded so well to this setback that by 1930, 41 of them had child-labor laws.

Between 1896 and 1908 a number of states, led by New York and Massachusetts, had limited the work-day and work-week for women. In 1908 the Supreme Court decided the case of *Muller* v. *Oregon,* in which an employer had challenged a state law establishing a ten-hour day for women workers. The Court was impressed by the arguments of the rising lawyer, Louis D. Brandeis, who had marshaled strong social and medical data to support the constitutionality of the disputed law. By upholding this law, the Court not only justified Brandeis' confidence in his unconventional brief but also opened the way to additional legislation in this area. Of special significance was legislation establishing minimum wages for women. Between 1912 and 1923, 15 states adopted such legislation. Congress also passed a law to regulate the wages of women in the District of Columbia. In 1923, however, the Supreme Court, speaking through Justice George Sutherland in the case of *Adkins* v. *Children's Hospital,* found this law unconstitutional. Justice Sutherland argued that there was no proved relationship between hours of work and health or morals and that prescribing minimum wages for grown women deprived them of freedom of contract. Since this decision affected state laws as well, it put an end for a time to any further state reform along these lines.

Insurance against industrial accidents was another objective of reformers that occasioned a considerable amount of legislation. Traditional common-law practice had left unprotected the families of workers who were injured or killed at their jobs. In order to collect compensation from employers, dependents or survivors had to go to court—in itself a costly undertaking—and prove that the victim of the accident had not willingly assumed the risks of his job, that neither he nor any fellow-worker had contributed to the negligence that caused the accident, and that the accident was the sole fault of the employer. In short, the burden of all the risks of industry had been thrown onto the workingmen and their families. After 1909, states began to adopt accident insurance systems, and by 1920 all but five had taken such action.

The Progressives also succeeded in establishing a certain amount of public responsibility for the support of children and old people. States had always provided public almshouses and had occasionally extended home relief, but not until 1911 did they begin to accept the idea that it would be better to aid dependent children in their own homes than to place them in institutions. Now the states began to pass mothers' assistance acts which set up public agencies to grant relief or financial help to working mothers with dependent children. By 1913 eight states, and by 1930 all but four, adopted such measures. These acts helped widows with dependent children, as well as families left destitute by divorce, desertion, or the incapacity of the breadwinner.

In 1914, the states started to pass legislation to provide help for the aged poor in their own homes. Arizona led the way, though its supreme court found this first law unconstitutional. Urged on by the American Association for Old Age Security, however, 13 states passed such measures during the 1920's. In most cases, persons 65 and over were made eligible for pensions amounting to as much as $30 a month.

WOMAN'S SUFFRAGE

By the start of the twentieth century, the working woman had become a common figure in American life. In 1910, about 8,000,000 women were working in factories, offices, and schools, and a few had entered the professions. These contacts with life outside the home gave women a better understanding of the country's social problems and a glimpse of their own potential as citizens. Since the 1840's, a small advance guard under the leadership of Lucretia C. Mott, a graduate of Miss Willard's famous Female Seminary in Troy, New York (see p. 305), had argued that women as well as men deserved the right to vote. Gradually other educated women were drawn to the cause. In 1869, stung by their failure to win the franchise under the Fourteenth Amendment, suffrage groups formed the American Woman Suffrage Association, with Lucy Stone and Julia Ward Howe of Boston at its head. A more radical contingent—favoring easy divorce laws and other social reforms as well as woman's suffrage—soon split off. This group, led by Susan B. Anthony and Elizabeth Cady Stanton, then organized the National Woman Suffrage Association. Efforts at reconciliation led to the formation of a Union Woman Suffrage Association, but this soon collapsed and the American and the National associations carried on separately.

By 1898, Wyoming, Colorado, Utah, and Idaho had given women full suffrage rights, and other states permitted them to vote for certain offices, such as school board members; but no federal amendment was passed, despite the nation-wide agitation. Progressivism, which had already effected reforms in many areas of special concern to women, such as child labor, newly encouraged women to demand their political rights. "We have no platform," said the president of the General Federation of Women's Clubs in 1910, "unless it is the care of women and children and the home, the latter meaning the four walls of the city as well as the four walls of brick and mortar." Although Taft and Wilson, the candidates of the major parties, evaded it, woman's suffrage became an issue in the presidential election of 1912. Roosevelt, who had hitherto opposed it, and the Progressive party (see p. 660), endorsed it. Wilson's election brought to the White

House a man of conservative southern views on women in society, but women went right on agitating and by 1914 eleven states had granted them the vote.

This small number dissatisfied many partisans who now decided to concentrate on a federal amendment. They prepared a huge petition with 400,000 signatures for Congress and opened a lobby in Washington. Some women, like Mrs. Carrie Chapman Catt and Dr. Anna Howard Shaw, preferred the quiet techniques of gradual education and propaganda. Others, following the lead of Alice Paul, patterned their strategy after the English suffragists and engaged in dramatic demonstrations and picketing. Eventually, even Wilson was persuaded to give woman's suffrage a faint-hearted endorsement. Women's role in World War I won the suffragists many new male supporters and in June, 1919, Congress, by a narrow margin, passed the Nineteenth Amendment giving them the vote. The amendment was ratified in August, 1920, and women throughout the country took part in the presidential election that fall.

PROHIBITION

While the fight for ratification of the Nineteenth Amendment was in progress, another proposed amendment came before the public. This was the prohibition amendment. Political agitation for the prohibition of the manufacture and sale of alcoholic liquors had been going on in the United States for a long time, but after more than a half-century of campaigning, only five states—Kansas, Maine, North Dakota, New Hampshire, and Vermont—were legally dry in 1898. Many women favored prohibition. Opposing them were the saloon and liquor interests, which had long been connected with machine politics. The Progressive assault on the machines encouraged many "temperance" advocates to feel that their hour had also struck.

In the early years prohibitionists had tried unsuccessfully to develop an independent Prohibition party. Later on the Women's Christian Temperance Union and the Temperance Society of the Methodist Episcopal Church took up the fight. Only with the organization of the Anti-Saloon League in 1893, however, did the "drys" at last have an agency powerful enough to carry them to victory. The Anti-Saloon League lobby kept the pressure on both major parties on the state and local levels, and after 1907, state after state in the West and South fell into the prohibition ranks. Then, in March, 1913, Congress passed the Webb-Kenyon Act over President Taft's veto. This act prohibited the shipment of intoxicating liquors into any state, territory, or district where they were intended to be used in violation of the local laws.

Encouraged by this success, the prohibitionists introduced a national prohibition amendment in Congress in December, 1913. Wartime conditions, popular resentment against German brewers, and the need to conserve the materials used in distilling soon gave prohibitionists their long-awaited opportunity to make prohibition a part of the Constitution. The Eighteenth Amendment, passed by Congress in December, 1917, was ratified in January, 1919, and went into effect in January, 1920.

III. *Progressivism in the G.O.P.*

THE REPUBLICAN ROOSEVELT

Not since the days of Jackson had the White House been occupied by a president who played the role of chief executive with the vigor of Theodore Roosevelt. A Republican by family tradition, T.R. had been mortified in youth by the bumptiousness of the "robber barons," the coarse materialism of the rising millionaires, the concentration of wealth and power in the new trusts. In his political salad days he had flirted with Mugwumpery (see p. 545), but he remained "regular" enough for Mc-Kinley himself to appoint him Assistant Secretary of the Navy just before the Spanish War. His feats as the "Rough Rider" added to his popularity, and in 1898 he was elected governor of New York. He soon showed himself to be so indepedent of the Republican machine that New York State boss, "Tom" Platt, determined that in the election of 1900 he would bury Roosevelt in the vice-presidency under McKinley. This strategy worried Mark Hanna. "Don't you realize," he cried, "that there's only one life between this madman and the White House?" In September, 1901, when an assassin shot McKinley at Buffalo, the "one life" was removed from Roosevelt's path.

T.R.'s outstanding quality was his energy. Hunter, rancher, warrior, and historian, as well as politician, he possessed an uncommon desire to leave his mark upon the world. His conception of the presidency and of executive leadership was, like his personality, aggressive. He believed that American democracy needed to be invigorated and that politics could be made honest only by strong, responsible leadership. Roosevelt once referred to the White House as a "bully pulpit." His resounding speeches on behalf of Progressivism were among his principal contributions to the movement, for he persistently whipped up Progressive sentiment even when he was not sure how to realize Progressive objectives.

BAD TRUSTS
AND BIG UNIONS

Roosevelt doubted the wisdom of attempting to break up the great corporations that seemed to run the country, as many Progressives were demanding. But he took seriously the widespread fear of the trusts and the yearning for their regulation by public agencies. To dramatize the power of Washington over that of Wall Street, T.R. in 1902 made his first positive advance on the corporations by ordering Attorney-General Philander C. Knox to bring suit under the Sherman Act (see p. 557) to dissolve the Northern Securities Company. This company, as we have seen (p. 522),

had been created by the country's greatest bankers to combine the holdings of the country's greatest railroad barons. So stunning was Roosevelt's attack upon it that J. P. Morgan himself journeyed down to Washington to find out what the President had in mind. Two years later, in 1904, the Supreme Court by a 5 to 4 vote gave its verdict. The Northern Securities Company must be broken up. The Northern Securities Company rulers soon gained their consolidation goals by other means, but this did not tarnish T.R.'s public or self image. The decision he said, was "one of the great achievements of my administration. The most powerful men in this country were held to accountability before the law."

The *Northern Securities* verdict was followed in 1905 by that in *Swift & Company* v. *United States* breaking up the "beef trust." In this case the Court reversed its decision of ten years before in *U.S.* v. *E. C. Knight Company* disallowing the application of the Sherman Act to manufacturing companies. The "beef trust" prosecution was one of the earliest outcomes of T.R.'s success in getting Congress, in 1903, to establish a Bureau of Corporations in the new Department of Commerce and Labor. In keeping with the characteristic Progressive belief in publicity as a deterrent to antisocial action, this Bureau was authorized to investigate and disclose the affairs of interstate corporations. The "beef trust" litigation had been started on the basis of the Bureau's information; and its success led the way to further prosecutions of such "evil" combinations as the "oil trust" and the "tobacco trust." These actions had indecisive results; they did not halt the wave of consolidations, but they kept alive the threat that ruthless combinations would have to face up to the President.

Another display of Roosevelt's vigor came in 1902 on the labor front. In May the United Mine Workers led by John Mitchell struck the anthracite coal fields. The workers won public sympathy, partly because of the stubbornness of the mine-owners and the arrogance of their spokesmen. George F. Baer, the President of the Reading Railroad, announced that the interests of the miners would be protected "not by the labor agitators but by the Christian men to whom God in His infinite wisdom, has given control of the property interests of the country." As the strike ran on into October, however, and it appeared that eastern cities would face serious coal shortages during the coming winter, public pressure for a settlement grew. T.R. responded by calling Mitchell and the mine-operators to the White House. Mitchell agreed to arbitrate the dispute. When the operators refused to go along, Roosevelt made secret plans to have the army work the mines for the government. He also persuaded J. P. Morgan to try to get the operators to agree to arbitration before the army moved in. Morgan won the operators over, except for one condition: They would not arbitrate if any labor official were named to the arbitration commission. Roosevelt cleverly obliged both parties by appointing a former president of one of the railroad unions to the commission as an "eminent sociologist." The mine-operators accepted the dodge and the commission went to work.

Although the union failed to gain recognition as labor's bargaining agency in the coal industry, the mine-workers won a nine-hour day, a 10 per cent wage increase, a permanent board of conciliation, and the right to select checkweighmen. Roosevelt's intervention added greatly to his prestige.

THE "SQUARE DEAL"

After he had ordered the prosecution of the Northern Securities Company in 1902, Roosevelt made his first tour of the states as President. On this trip the theme of his speeches was a "square deal" for all. The settlement of the coal strike in the workers' favor and the outcome of the *Northern Securities* case in the public's interest went far toward proving that Roosevelt meant what he promised. Thus, when the time came for the 1904 presidential campaign, T.R. was more popular than ever and won the Republican nomination at the national convention in Chicago in June without opposition. Such big capitalists as Harriman,

Morgan, and the Rockefellers, moreover, finding Roosevelt's actions more discreet than his words, made such generous contributions to the Republican party that the Democratic charge of "blackmail" became the leading campaign issue. Judge Alton B. Parker, the Democratic candidate, proved uninspiring and colorless, and Roosevelt's huge majority—7,623,000 popular votes to 5,077,000—took even him by surprise.

President at last in his own right, Roosevelt now pursued a more comprehensive reform program on the national level. His major achievements lay in railroad regulation, protection of consumers, and conservation of natural resources.

By 1904 the Interstate Commerce Act of 1887 regulating the railroads had become virtually a dead letter largely because of the Supreme Court's narrow interpretation of the Interstate Commerce Commission's powers (see p. 554). In 1903, in response

Theodore Roosevelt in the White House, 1902.

to pressure from the railroads themselves, Congress had passed the Elkins Act, making it illegal for the roads to depart in practice from their published freight rates, and making shippers as well as the roads liable for punishment for infractions. This measure struck at the practice of rebating, which the railroad companies had come to regard as a major nuisance. The Elkins Act, however, failed to give the Interstate Commerce Commission any power to fix rates, which was what farmers and businessmen wanted most. Roosevelt now prodded Congress to strengthen and enlarge the commission's powers in this respect, and in 1906, Congress passed the Hepburn Act, which began really effective federal regulation.

Heretofore, the commission could order alterations in railroad rates, but the roads did not have to comply until the courts ordered them to do so. Under the Hepburn Act, the commission was authorized to set maximum rates when complaints from shippers were received and to order the roads to comply within thirty days. The roads might still go to court, but in the interim the new rates, not the old, were to be in force. The Hepburn Act also extended the I.C.C.'s power to storage, refrigeration, and terminal facilities, and to sleeping-car, express, and pipeline companies. Within two years, shippers made more than 9,000 appeals to the commission, and a great many rates were revised downward.

In his annual message to Congress in December, 1905, Roosevelt asked for an act to protect consumers from undesirable adulterants and preservatives used in the food-packaging industry. His request was made on the basis of another characteristically progressive action—investigations conducted by Dr. Harvey W. Wiley, a chemist in the Department of Agriculture, and other scientists, which had shown that undesirable adulterants and preservatives were being widely used in canned foods.

The packing interests naturally fought T.R.'s proposal. They could not, however, withstand the force of public indignation aroused by Upton Sinclair's shocking novel of Chicago's meat-packing industry, *The*

Jungle, published in 1906. In June that year, Congress passed the first federal meat-inspection law. In the same year, Congress responded to Samuel Hopkins Adams' muckraking exposure of the patent medicine industry and its misleading advertising by enacting a Pure Food and Drugs Act. This law did not insure full protection to consumers, but it struck at some of the worst abuses and prepared the way for stricter regulation later on.

As an amateur naturalist and an outdoor man with a taste for natural beauty, Roosevelt took an early and intelligent interest in conservation. Under the Forest Reserve Act, which had been passed in 1891, he set aside almost 150 million acres of unsold government timber land in various parts of the country as a forest reserve. He also closed to public entry about 85 million additional acres in Alaska and the Northwest in order to give the United States Geological Survey a chance to study mineral and water resources in these areas before they were given away. He turned over the supervision of the national forests to the Secretary of Agriculture, who put a professional conservationist, Gifford Pinchot, in charge. In 1907, Roosevelt called federal and state officials and many interested private persons, to a national conservation conference. This conference became a center from which information about the conservation problem flowed out to the American public, and a National Conservation Association was established to carry on its work. All these activities checked some of the despoiling of the public domain, but they were not enough to do the job effectively.

At home in tilting with capitalists for public favor, Roosevelt was less well equipped for grasping the economic implications of the capitalists' wars among themselves. One such war helped bring about the financial panic of 1907, during which a number of New York banks went to the wall. Roosevelt naturally was eager to do something to forestall a long depression, not least because of his consciousness of the reputation of his own regime. When industrialists and Wall-Streeters thus advised him

656

that the worst of the panic would be averted if he let the United States Steel Corporation acquire control of the Tennessee Iron and Coal Company, a firm whose shaky securities were held by many precariously situated brokerage houses, Roosevelt nervously approved the combination. His act implied that at least during his administration the Steel Corporation would be immune from anti-trust prosecution. Whether it implied, too, that he had saved the country from a business collapse is now doubtful. At any rate, business continued good and T.R. evaded a blot on his record.

The Panic of 1907 and Roosevelt's effort to check it had two important consequences for American politics: (1) Financial authorities began to search for ways to strengthen national finance, a search that led to the Aldrich-Vreeland Act of 1908, and the Federal Reserve Act of 1913 (see p. 662). (2) Groundwork was laid for the later breach between Roosevelt and Taft, for in 1911, when Roosevelt's successor opened anti-trust proceedings against the United States Steel Corporation, T.R. took it as a personal rebuke, and the gulf between him and Taft widened.

TAFT AS PRESIDENT

In 1908 Roosevelt bowed to the tradition that no president should seek a third term. He stood well enough with the party to choose his friend and Secretary of War, William Howard Taft, to succeed him, and well enough with the people to put Taft over. A member of an old and well-to-do Cincinnati family, Taft had been a circuit-court judge, an unusually able governor of the Philippines, and administrator of the Canal Zone before he joined Roosevelt's cabinet. The Democrats, having fared worse with a conservative candidate in 1904 than they had earlier with Bryan, returned once more in 1908 to the "Great Commoner." But Progressive reforms made under Roosevelt left Bryan issueless and Taft won by a vote of 7,679,000 to 6,409,000. His margin in the electoral college was 321 to 162.

Although Roosevelt and Taft had imagined that their views were in harmony,

Taft tended to be more conservative than his predecessor and less willing to tussle with the Old Guard Republicans in Congress, with whom Roosevelt had had to bargain for Progressive measures. Shorn of T.R.'s leadership, many other Republicans also now began to drift comfortably back toward conservatism, thereby making all the more apparent an active and able minority in Congress, chiefly among its western members, who struck out on the road to insurgency. The result was that Taft, who inherited a powerful and united party, left it after four years weakened and divided.

One means used by Roosevelt to hold the Republican party together while winning Progressive reforms was to evade the "Great Issue" of Protection, dear to conservative hearts. He evaded it so successfully, indeed, that by 1908 the demand for downward revision, especially among western farmers and middle-class consumers struggling with the rising cost of living, impelled Taft and the Republican platform writers in 1908 to promise early action. To fulfill this promise, Taft called a special session of Congress for March, 1909, and that is when his four-year ordeal began. Taft was genuinely interested in lowering the duties on many consumer items. When proposals for downward revision were made in Congress, however, the Old Guard immediately opposed them. Moderate reductions were adopted by the House; but when Senator Aldrich and his stalwart friends in the Senate finished with the measure, as usual it not only failed to reduce duties but actually raised them slightly. Taft had done nothing to check Aldrich's emasculation of the measure, and a group of Republican insurgents in the Senate now rallied to fight against this betrayal of the party's campaign pledge. Their work was thorough and their speeches brilliant, but in the end the Payne-Aldrich Tariff reflected almost nothing of their efforts. "President Taft," said Senator Dolliver of Iowa, one of the leading insurgents, "is an amiable man, completely surrounded by men who know exactly what they want." As if signing the measure were not enough, Taft soon made a speech at Winona, Minnesota, in which he called the Payne-Aldrich Tariff "the best tariff bill that the Republican party has ever passed, and therefore the best that has been passed at all."

Taft further outraged the Progressives by submitting to the tyranny of Joseph G. ('Uncle Joe") Cannon, an earthy, uncouth old man who had been elected Speaker of the House in 1905. Believing profoundly in the success of the American system as it had been run in the past, Cannon had absolutely no patience with "all this babble for reform." By the longstanding House rules, his speakership gave him the right to appoint a majority of the Committee on Rules, which dictated what legislation would (and would not) be presented for consideration. The Speaker also had sweeping powers of appointment over other committees, powers Cannon never hesitated to use to reward his friends and punish his enemies. The Senate itself soon learned that it was futile to buck Cannon's decisions, so his tyranny extended to the whole Congress. The White House, moreover, took Cannon's views into serious consideration before proposing legislation.

T.R. found the speaker trying, but feared to challenge him. Taft disliked Cannon, whom he thought "dirty and vulgar." Characteristically, he first gave encouragement to the insurgents who wanted to dump the Speaker, and then ignominiously deserted them. In March, 1910, however, Republican insurgents, led by George W. Norris of Nebraska, took advantage of a parliamentary technicality in the House, caught Cannon by surprise, and in a 36-hour session joined with the Democrats in adopting new rules. Henceforth, the entire House would *elect* the Rules Committee, from which the Speaker was now excluded. "The clock has struck for Uncle Joe," wrote the *Wall Street Journal.* "He has stood between the people and too many things that they wanted and ought to have, and the fact that he has stood off some things that they ought not to have won't save him." Cannon's de-

feat only increased the insurgents' resentment against Taft, whose conduct had seemed devious to them.

The insurgents followed up this victory with further railroad legislation which went well beyond Taft's wishes. The Hepburn Act of 1906 had enabled the Interstate Commerce Commission to deal effectively with shippers' complaints, but nothing prevented railroads from making over-all rate increases. As finally passed, the Mann-Elkins Act of 1910 empowered the commission to suspend general rate increases, and to take the initiative in revising rates. A Commerce Court was established to speed up the judicial process by hearing appeals directly from the commission. These terms were substantially in line with Taft's desires. But the insurgents also pushed through a provision forbidding railroads from acquiring competing lines, and added another that put telephone, telegraph, cable, and wireless companies under the commission's control. Furthermore the physical evaluation of railroad property as a basis for rate-making, which was considered vital by the Progressives, and which they had not been able to get into the 1910 bill, was enacted in 1913 during the last months of the Taft administration. The Physical Evaluation Act required the I.C.C. to assess the value of all property owned by every company under its jurisdiction, and specified the manner in which this assessment was to be made. Such valuations were to be taken as prima-facie evidence of the value of the property. Now the commission could fix rates not on the basis of watered stock, but on the true value of operating assets.

What now remained of Republican unity was almost wholly destroyed by the conservation issue involved in the Pinchot-Ballinger affair. The trouble here began when the Chief Forester of the Department of Agriculture, Gifford Pinchot, heard from Louis Glavis, an investigator for the Interior Department, that Secretary of the Interior Richard A. Ballinger had agreed to let private interests take over the reserved coal lands in Alaska. Pinchot encouraged Glavis to appeal to Taft and himself issued a statement denouncing Ballinger. Taft chose to believe Ballinger's denials rather than Glavis' story and authorized Glavis' dismissal from the Interior Department. Pinchot carried on with the attack until he, too, was removed. Progressives in Congress now investigated the Interior Department and showed that Ballinger, though not found guilty of misconduct, had no sympathy with conservation policies. Taft himself, although he believed in conservation and through executive action had extended Roosevelt's policies on timber, oil, and coal lands, was tarred with the same brush.

Taft did not disappoint the Progressives at every turn. Important Progressive measures adopted during Taft's tenure included the Sixteenth Amendment, which made the federal income tax constitutional, and the Seventeenth Amendment, providing for the direct election of United States Senators, both ratified in 1913; the creation of postal savings bank and parcel post service; the establishment of separate Departments of Commerce and Labor (by dividing Roosevelt's Department of Commerce and Labor); and the establishment of a Federal Children's Bureau. Two new states, with Progressive leanings, also were admitted: New Mexico and Arizona. In his one administration, moreover, Taft initiated about twice as many prosecutions under the Sherman Act as Roosevelt did in two. His two leading cases, against International Harvester and United States Steel, however, turned out to be worse than failures. The Steel prosecution, as we have seen (p. 657), dashed all hope for reconciliation between Taft and T.R., while the Harvester action alienated its promoter and director, George W. Perkins, one of Roosevelt's prominent backers. No doubt prosecutions like these, together with the natural reluctance to invest in an apparent loser, explains some of the difficulties of Taft's supporters in raising campaign funds for 1912.

INSURGENCY

At the start of Taft's administration, Roosevelt had gone off on a hunting trip to Africa, presumably a gracious gesture to remove himself from the scene. After a triumphal tour through Europe, he returned to New York in June, 1910, where he was greeted enthusiastically. He had been keeping in touch with the Taft Administration from a distance and had grown increasingly displeased with the way things were going. To Henry Cabot Lodge he wrote: "Taft, Cannon, Aldrich and the others have totally misestimated the character of the movement which we now have to face in American life."

Almost at the moment of Roosevelt's return, the growing split in Republican ranks broke into open warfare when the Progressives learned that Taft, in anticipation of the congressional elections that year, was using the full power of presidential patronage to build up conservative strength in the Midwest, where the Progressives themselves were strongest. At first, Roosevelt refrained from any move that would publicize his estrangement from Taft. But as the campaign warmed up, he grew restive and in August he set out on a swing through the West where he gave the rousing series of speeches on the "welfare state" known as *The New Nationalism*. On August 31, 1910, at Osawatomie, Kansas he delivered his most striking address in which he came out for a number of Progressive reforms that everyone knew the administration opposed. His espousal of the popular recall of state-court decisions nullifying social legislation, and his accusation that the federal judiciary was obstructing the popular will, shocked conservatives everywhere. He said many other stirring things as well: "The object of government is the welfare of the people." "'This New Nationalism . . . demands of the judiciary that it shall be interested primarily in human welfare rather than in property." "Property shall be the servant not the master of the commonwealth." "The . . . essence of any struggle for healthy liberty has always been, and must always be, to take from one man or class of men the right to enjoy power, or wealth, or position, or immunity, which has not been earned by service to his or their fellows." By mid-September Taft was convinced that T.R. was already campaigning for the presidency in 1912. In any case, his speeches did Taft and the party no good in the congressional elections of 1910, when the House went Democratic for the first time since 1893 and many Democratic governors were elected. After a long spell out of power, it seemed that the Democrats would have an excellent chance to recapture the presidency in 1912, and also that the insurgents might capture the Republican party and repudiate Taft.

The most obvious man to lead the insurgents' challenge was La Follette of Wisconsin, who had moved from the state governorship to the United States Senate in 1906. Other Progressives, however, looked upon T.R. as a "natural," and hesitated to support La Follette until they were certain Roosevelt would not run. Roosevelt himself seems to have believed that 1912 would be a Democratic year, and that he might well wait until 1916 to lead a rejuvenated Republican party to victory while La Follette made the race in 1912. However, on February 2, 1912, Senator La Follette, tired, ill, and troubled by the serious illness of one of his daughters, collapsed while delivering a major speech. The many Progressive Republicans who had been waiting to switch to the more formidable Roosevelt took this as an occasion to desert La Follette. In February, 1912, at Roosevelt's instigation, seven Republican governors publicly wrote the ex-President, urging him to announce his candidacy. Less than two weeks later he asserted, "My hat is in the ring." A savage fight followed, and by the time of the Republican convention in Chicago in June, 1912, La Follette's support had dwindled to a small group of bitter-enders. Taft's supporters, in turn, captured the convention and nominated him for a second term on the first ballot, after Roosevelt and his followers, claiming Taft had gained his delegates by fraudulent means, stormed out.

In response to questions about his own physical energies, Roosevelt on arriving in Chicago, said that he felt "fit as a bull moose," and his supporters now hastily organized a convention of their own in that city, hoping to speed the Bull Moose back to the White House. This convention of the Progressive party, as the "Bull Moose" party was formally called, was one of the most enthusiastic in party annals. William Allen White, the Progressive Kansas journalist, described his own and the crowd's frenzy by saying, "Roosevelt bit me and I went mad." The delegates nevertheless adopted a sane enough Progressive platform calling, on the national level, for the initiative, referendum, and recall, woman's suffrage, workmen's compensation and social insurance, minimum wages for women, child-labor legislation, and federal trade and tariff commissions to regulate business.

Although heartened by the Republican crack-up, the Democrats had to mend internal divisions of their own. Bryan, still a great power in Democratic ranks, helped matters by announcing that he would not run again. When he found that the Democratic convention, meeting in Baltimore in June, 1912, leaned toward Champ Clark, the Speaker of the House, who he felt was too conservative for the times, Bryan bent his support toward Woodrow Wilson, the Democratic governor of New Jersey. Even so, Wilson could not be nominated until the 46th ballot. His platform was neither as advanced nor as comprehensive as Roosevelt's; but it was Progressive enough especially in demanding tariff reform and the restriction of trusts.

IV. *Democratic Progressivism*

THE 1912 CAMPAIGN
Woodrow Wilson was a 55-year-old Virginian who had first shown his mettle as an academic reformer while President of Princeton University in New Jersey, from 1902 to 1910. His high moral tone made him

attractive to Democratic bosses of the state, who in 1910 were seeking a respectable candidate for governor, preferably one they themselves could govern. When they offered Wilson the nomination, he acccepted. When he won the governorship, he repudiated the bosses and promoted a variety of reforms that earned him Progressive support.

As a person, Wilson was a bundle of paradoxes. Outwardly cold and forbidding, he was in fact extraordinarily intense. His great reputation in domestic politics was based upon his achievements as a reformer, yet his ideas displayed a deep sense of tradition and great reverence for the past. He was an innovator who sought to restore a social order that had long been dead, a southerner raised on English doctrines of laissez faire who lived to advance the welfare state, a man of essentially aristocratic temperament who became a spokesman of world democracy.

That Wilson should have been successful in politics is indeed remarkable, for though he had personal and intellectual distinction he lacked the equally necessary practical qualities. He was an excellent speaker, but offstage he was ill suited to the give and take of party government. His intense personality expressed itself largely in terms of ideals and principles, not in personal loyalties. He was too rigid to be compromising. The story of his political friendships is a story of misunderstanding. Colonel House wrote of him in 1915, ". . . his prejudices are many and often unjust. He finds great difficulty in conferring with men against whom, for some reason, he has a prejudice and in whom he can find nothing good."

Wilson's greatest asset in the 1912 campaign was the Republican split. Taft, however, soon lagged and the battle narrowed down to Wilson *versus* Roosevelt. Since both campaigned as Progressives, the campaign ultimately turned on the trust issue, the one issue on which they seemed clearly to disagree. As Louis D. Brandeis put it, Wilson was for regulated competition, Roosevelt for regulated monopoly. Wilson held that the business combinations were too powerful to be regulated, that salutary

Woodrow Wilson addressing crowd at Union Square, New York City, September 9, 1912.

competition could be restored to business by breaking up the monopolies, that a "new freedom" for the individual was more important than a "square deal" from the government. Roosevelt replied that Wilson's conception of economic life was archaic. To restore competition as it had once existed in America would be to deprive the country of the advantages of large-scale organization and reverse the natural processes of economic evolution. Roosevelt wanted the government to differentiate between good and bad trusts and to expose and extinguish only the bad ones.

Probably not many voters followed all these arguments, nor did they need to with two such colorful personalities in the field. Taft was altogether humiliated, winning only 8 electoral votes. Roosevelt won 88, Wilson 435. Wilson's popular vote of 6,293,000, however, was slightly less than 42 per cent of the electorate. Yet the Democrats also captured the House and Senate, and Wilson, with the additional support of

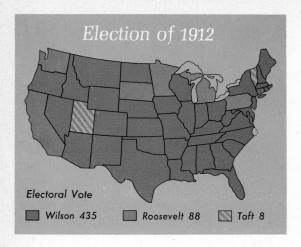

Election of 1912

Electoral Vote

■ Wilson 435   ■ Roosevelt 88   ▨ Taft 8

a bloc of Progressive Republicans, took office with excellent prospects for a constructive administration.

THE "NEW FREEDOM"

Wilson's two administrations, running from 1913 to 1921, were extraordinarily fruitful in reform legislation. First on the docket was the tariff, the demand for reduction of duties rising with the continuing rise in the cost of living. To effect downward revision, Wilson called a special session of Congress before which he appeared in person to read his tariff message. This was the first time since Jefferson abandoned the practice that a president had gone directly before the legislature.

A bill sponsored by Representative Oscar Underwood proposed to cut the Payne-Aldrich duties 10 per cent on the average. Underwood's bill passed the House, but in the Senate it ran into the usual combination of special interests. Washington swarmed with tariff lobbyists, who had their way for a time. Then Wilson took an unusual step. On May 26, 1913, he issued a public statement denouncing the lobbyists working to defeat the bill—the "great bodies of astute men [who] seek to create an artificial opinion and to overcome the interests of the public for their private profit." His declaration sounded the signal for a general attack on lobbyists which made it easier for the measure to pass in September, 1913, with essential Progressive support. The Underwood Tariff effected the first satisfactory

downward revision since the Civil War. It also included an income tax, which was intended to supply the revenue lost through tariff reduction. A tax of 1 per cent was levied on personal and corporate incomes of over $4,000, and an additional graduated surtax ranging from 1 to 6 per cent was levied on higher incomes.

The Underwood Act was hardly passed before the disruption of trade brought by World War I made it inoperative. After the war Republican regimes restored protection, but the Democrats had shown how to beat the lobbyists, and the income tax had great significance for the future.

Financial reform came next. Conservatives and reformers alike recognized the need for changes in the banking system to make money more mobile, credit more elastic, in relation to regional and seasonal requirements. Following the Panic of 1907, Congress in 1908 had adopted the emergency Aldrich-Vreeland Act which allowed banks for 6 years to issue currency against state and city bonds and commercial paper. More important, the Act set up a National Monetary Commission to study banking at home and abroad and recommend permanent reforms. This commission, with Senator Aldrich as chairman, made its report in January, 1912, proposing the creation of a great central bank with branches dominated by private banking interests. The Democrats denounced this proposal in their 1912 platform, but they were divided on an alternative to relieve the "unhealthy congestion of loanable funds in great centers," especially in New York City. The more conservative among them wanted a decentralized national system, free from Wall Street but still owned and run by private interests. Supporters of Bryan, now Secretary of State, wanted a national system owned and controlled by the government.

As it was finally passed on December 23, 1913, the Federal Reserve Act renovating the banking system set up 12 regional banking districts, each with a Federal Reserve Bank. The Federal Reserve Banks were owned by the member banks of the Federal Reserve System. All national banks were re-

662

quired to join the system, and state banks also were eligible. Member banks were required to subscribe 6 per cent of their capital to the Federal Reserve Bank in their region. On the security of this subscription and commercial and agricultural paper, the Federal Reserve Banks would create a new currency, Federal Reserve notes, issued by the Reserve Banks to member banks and circulated by them to borrowers. The Federal Reserve System was placed under the direction of the Federal Reserve Board, consisting of the Secretary of the Treasury, the Comptroller, and six other persons appointed by the President. By 1923, the Federal Reserve System embraced 70 per cent of the banking resources of the country.

Even those who denounced the new setup as one politically "as dangerous as the old United States Bank of Jackson's time," came around to admit its value. The Federal Reserve System created a currency flexible and sound and made it available to all sections of the country through the regional Reserve Banks. It also left banking a private business, under federal supervision.

Further to improve the farmer's access to funds, Congress, in May, 1916, passed the Federal Farm Loan Act creating a Federal Farm Loan Board and 12 regional Farm Loan banks patterned after the Federal Reserve System. The banks were authorized to lend sums to cooperative farm-loan associations on the security of farm lands, buildings, and improvements, up to 70 per cent of the value of these assets. Loans were to be on a long-range basis, interest was not to be more than 6 per cent, and profits were to be distributed to the members of the subscribing farm-loan associations. Within 14 years, over 4,000 farm-loan associations had been established, and over $1 billion in farm mortgages was outstanding. In 1916, another bill was passed for the benefit of farmers—the Warehouse Act—which authorized licensed warehouse operators to issue warehouse receipts against farm products deposited with them. Farmers could use these warehouse receipts as negotiable paper. This measure embodied the essential features of the sub-treasury

scheme proposed by the Populists in 1892.

The initial Wilsonian anti-trust legislation was the Federal Trade Commission Act of September, 1914, aimed at the prevention rather than the punishment of unfair trade practices. This act created a five-man Federal Trade Commission to replace Roosevelt's Bureau of Corporations. The new commission was authorized to investigate corporations engaged in interstate commerce, to look into alleged violations of anti-trust laws, and to issue "cease and desist" orders against corporations found guilty of unfair competitive methods. If that recourse failed, the commission could bring the accused corporations to court. During Wilson's administration 379 cease and desist orders were issued, and a few dissolutions of trusts were initiated in cooperation with the Department of Justice. Even so, Progressives soon came to feel that the commission was not using its powers vigorously enough. In the 1920's, moreover, business turned the commission into an instrument of corporate consolidation.

A second anti-trust law passed in October, 1914, was the Clayton Act. This act prohibited a number of business practices: price discrimination that might lessen competition or create monopoly; tying contracts —that is, contracts that forced purchasers to refrain from buying the products of competitors; the acquisition by corporations of stock in competing concerns; and the creation of interlocking directorates in corporations and banks over a specified size as measured by capitalization. Officers of corporations were made liable for prosecution if they violated these provisions. Labor unions as such were not to be construed as illegal combinations or conspiracies in restraint of trade, and labor injunctions were forbidden except when necessary to prevent "irreparable injury to property, or to a property right."

But the Clayton Act was passed on the eve of World War I, during which anti-trust action was greatly curtailed. During the conservative regimes of the 1920's, moreover, a series of Supreme Court decisions nullified the labor provisions of the act.

A few other measures completed the domestic accomplishments of the Wilson administrations. The La Follette Seaman's Act of 1915 raised the safety requirements on American ships and, by abolishing the crime of desertion released American merchant seamen from bondage to labor contracts upon their return to American ports. The Adamson Act of 1916 established an eight-hour day for workers on interstate railways. The Keating-Owen Child Labor Act, passed the same year, barred products of child labor from interstate commerce; but it was declared unconstitutional two years later. The Smith-Hughes Act of 1917 subsidized vocational and agricultural education and rounded out the program that was begun during the Civil War with the land-grant colleges. When Wilson entered the presidential campaign of 1916, he could point to a substantial record of legislative achievement and to hopes for more of the same in the future. The legislative program of the New Freedom, however, was largely ended by the participation of the United States in the World War in 1917, and after the war its measures were largely nullified by administrative negligence.

Readings
* Asterisk indicates that book is available in paperback.

G. E. Mowry, *The Era of Theodore Roosevelt 1900-1912* * (1958), and *Theodore Roosevelt and the Progressive Movement* * (1947), and A. S. Link, *Woodrow Wilson and the Progressive Era 1910-1917* * (1954), together provide a modern scholarly survey of of the period. See also H. U. Faulkner, *The Quest for Social Justice 1898-1914* (1931); two short books by J. M. Blum, *The Republican Roosevelt* * (1954), and *Woodrow Wilson and the Politics of Morality* * (1956); E. F. Goldman, *Rendezvous with Destiny* * (1952); Richard Hofstadter, *The Age of Reform* * (1955); John Chamberlain, *Farewell to Reform* * (1932); and Matthew Josephson, *The President Makers 1896-1919* (1940). R. B. Nye, *Midwestern Progressive Politics* (1951); G. E. Mowry, *The California Progressives* * (1951); and C. V. Woodward, *Origins of the New South* (1951), are outstanding sectional studies. Mark Sullivan, *Our Times: The United States 1900-1925* (6 vols. 1920-1935), is a panoramic yet penetrating account by an ex-muckraker.

Charles Forcey, *The Crossroads of Liberalism* (1961), examines Croly, Weyl, and Lippman. See also the early chapters of Christopher Lasch, *The New Radicalism in America 1889-1963* (1965). Important aspects of Progressive thought are discussed in Samuel Haber, *Efficiency and Uplift: Scientific Management in the Progressive Era 1890-1920* (1964), and D. W. Noble, *The Paradox of Progressive Thought* (1958). In the same spirit is the important monograph, S. P. Hays, *Conservation and the Gospel of Efficiency* (1959). See also E. R. Richardson, *The Politics of Conservation* (1962). R. H. Wiebe, *Businessman and Reform* (1962) contains useful information on management attitudes. R. S. Maxwell, *LaFollette and the Rise of the Progressives in Wisconsin* (1956) is useful for the "Wisconsin Way." Louis Filler, *Crusaders for American Liberalism* * (1939), and C. C. Regier, *The Era of the Muckrakers* (1932), cover the magazine writers. An outstanding anthology is Harvey Swados, *Years of Conscience, The Muckrakers* * (1962).

Among writings of contemporaries, Herbert Croly, *The Promise of American Life* * (1909); W. A. White, *The Old Order Changeth* (1910); Walter Weyl, *The New Democracy* * (1912); Walter Lippmann, *Drift and Mastery* * (1914); Lincoln Steffens, *The Shame of the Cities* * (1904); and R. S. Baker, *Following the Color Line: American Negro Citizenship in the Progressive Era* * (1908), are important. See also *The Autobiography of Lincoln Steffens* (2 vols., 1931), and *The Autobiography of William Allen White* (1946).

Illuminating studies of local problems and the Progressive attack upon them include

Robert Hunter, *Poverty* * (1904); Jane Addams, *Twenty Years at Hull House* * (1910); Rheta Dorr, *What Eight Million Women Want* (1910); J. A. Riis, *How the Other Half Lives* * (1890); Roy Lubove, *The Progressives and the Slums . . . 1890-1917* (1962); and R. H. Bremner, *From the Depths: The Discovery of Poverty in the United States* * (1956). On woman's rights see I. H. Irwin, *Angels and Amazons* (1933); and Andrew Sinclair, *The Better Half* (1965). Sinclair's *Era of Excess: A Social History of the Prohibition Movement* * (1962), is outstanding. See also P. H. Odegard, *Pressure Politics, The Story of the Anti-Saloon League* (1928). F. L. Allen, *The Lords of Creation* (1935), offers a breezy introduction to the big business background; this may be supplemented by H. U. Faulkner, *The Decline of Laissez Faire 1897-1915* (1951). O. E. Anderson, Jr., *The Health of a Nation* (1958), is useful on the fight for pure food.

The autobiographies of both Theodore Roosevelt (1914) and Robert M. La Follette (1913) are well worth reading. H. F. Pringle's *Theodore Roosevelt* * (1931) is outstanding, but may be supplemented by two more recent works: W. H. Harbaugh, *Power and Responsibility: The Life and Times of Theodore Roosevelt* * (1961), and Carlton Putnam, *Theodore Roosevelt* (1958), of which only volume I, to 1886, has yet been published. An illuminating source is *The Letters of Theodore Roosevelt* (8 vols., 1951-1954), admirably edited by E. E. Morison, and others. The standard biography of Taft is H. F. Pringle, *Life and Times of William Howard Taft* (2 vols., 1939). La Follette's story is well told by Belle Case and Fola La Follette (2 vols., 1953). The deterioration of the Roosevelt-Taft relationship can be traced in A. W. Butt, *The Intimate Letters of Archie Butt* (2 vols., 1930). K. W. Hechler, *Insurgency: Personalities of the Taft Era* (1940), is excellent on Cannon's downfall. A. S. Link, *Wilson*, a scholarly biography of which five volumes have been published (1947-1965), brings his life into the period of World War I. R. S. Baker, *Woodrow Wilson, Life and Letters* (6 vols., 1927-1937), is the most comprehensive completed biography. Others of value include A. C. Walworth, *Woodrow Wilson* (2 vols., 1958); J. A. Garraty, *Woodrow Wilson* (1956); and H. C. F. Bell, *Woodrow Wilson and the People* (1945). Theodore Roosevelt, *The New Nationalism* * (1910); Woodrow Wilson, *The New Freedom* * (1913); and J. W. Davidson, ed., *A Crossroads of Freedom, The 1912 Campaign Speeches of Woodrow Wilson* (1956), are extraordinarily illuminating on the two leading figures. Helpful biographies of others of the era, Progressives and conservatives, include A. T. Mason, *Brandeis* (1946); P. C. Jessup, *Elihu Root* (2 vols., 1938); and J. A. Garraty, *Henry Cabot Lodge* (1953), and *Right Hand Man, The Life of George W. Perkins* (1960). The autobiography of Gifford Pinchot, *Breaking New Ground* (1947), is excellent on the conservationists; C. G. Bowers, *Beveridge and the Progressive Era* (1932), good on the Senate Progressives; N. W. Stephenson, *Nelson W. Aldrich* (1930), outstanding on the conservatives. Champ Clark, *My Quarter Century of American Politics* (2 vols., 1920), and Oscar Underwood, *Drifting Sands of Party Politics* (1928), shed light on the Democratic party.

CHAPTER TWENTY-FIVE

On June 28, 1914, the Archduke Franz Ferdinand, heir to the Austro-Hungarian throne, was shot and killed by a revolutionary Slav at Sarajevo in the Austrian province of Bosnia. Austria, aroused by the chronic agitations of her Slavic peoples for self-rule, claimed that the Serbian government, itself committed to the Slavic cause, had known of the impending assassination and had done little to prevent it. Austria now presented Serbia with a series of demands that involved the surrender of her independence. When Serbia refused to meet one of these demands, Austria, assured of the backing of her German ally, declared

The First
World War

war. Russia, the leader of the Slavic world, felt that she could not stand by while Serbia was crushed. When Russia began to mobilize her army on her German as well as her Austrian frontier, it seemed to signalize to all Europe that a general conflict was about to begin.

There was good reason for this European reaction. For a generation and more the European nations had been living in fear of one another, and as their suspicions grew so did their arms (see p. 572). They also began to seek allies. By 1914 Europe was divided roughly into two camps. One was the Triple Alliance, comprising Austria-Hungary, Germany and Italy—although Italy was soon to break with the two Central Powers, while Turkey was to join them. The second was the Triple Entente, comprising France, Russia, and Great Britain. Each of the nations in these camps also had commitments to smaller nations outside them. The United States, already feeling the strains of a quarter of a century of overseas expansionism and imperialism, had commitments to none.

When Russia refused to check her mobilization on the German frontier, Germany declared war on her on August 1, 1914. In the event of such a war German military leaders had long planned to move first against Russia's ally, France, in the hope of crushing her even before Russia could ready her unwieldy forces. Thus on August 3, 1914, Germany declared war on France. When she struck at France through Belgium, Britain on August 4 declared war on Germany. Italy, meanwhile, remained neutral until May, 1915, when the western Allies in a secret treaty promised her after the war, in exchange for intervention on their side, more territory than she could refuse. Both the Central Powers and the western Allies also lost no time in flooding the United States with propaganda in their efforts to win American support.

In the war of words between the western Allies and the Central Powers the advantage lay with the Allies whose language, both literally and philosophically, Americans better understood. The United States, moreover, had a president, in Woodrow Wilson, who seemed peculiarly fond of words and peculiarly vulnerable to them, especially high-sounding ones. And when the United States eventually did join the Allies in the European conflict, which itself then became a world war, Wilson embraced the opportunity to explain the American action in the most elevated language:

This is the People's War, a war for freedom and justice and self-government amongst all the nations of the world, a war to make the world safe for the peoples who live upon it, . . . the German peoples themselves included.

Wilson made a convenient distinction between the "military masters of Germany" and their subjects, and avowed that the United States entered the war against the former, "not as a partisan," but as everybody's friend.

Yet it was to be acts rather than words that would bring an end to America's long abstention from the fighting itself, and especially aggressive acts on the part of the Central Powers in the war at sea that finally committed the United States to the Allied cause. As late as 1916, Wilson campaigned for re-election on the slogan, "He kept us out of war," and won. When the United States at last entered the war against the Central Powers, there were widespread misgivings about Wilson's step, not least among Progressives. Once Wilson committed the country to fighting on the side of the western Allies, however, enthusiasm for "the war to make the world safe for democracy" touched the hearts of the great majority. And once victory was won, hopes for the attainment of the American purpose in the war were high.

These hopes soon were dashed by the bitter legacy of Europe's long history of national jealousies and by Wilson's own self-righteousness. Among those who participated in the actual fighting, moreover, the slaughter in the trenches had crushed the thought of any higher purpose than killing. "I was embarrassed," says Lieutenant Henry in Ernest Hemingway's *A Farewell to Arms,* "by the words sacred, glorious, and sacrifice . . . We had . . . read them, on proclamations, now for a long time, and I had seen nothing sacred, and the things that were glorious had no glory and the sacrifices were like the stockyards in Chicago, if nothing was done with the meat except to bury it. . . . Abstract words such as glory, honor, courage, were obscene."

I. *America's Road to War*

THE PROPAGANDA CAMPAIGN

Although the United States had occupied a place of some prominence in world affairs since the Spanish-American War, it was still a provincial nation in 1914, poorly informed about the transactions of Europe's chancelleries. Americans were surprised by the coming of the war and, even more, relieved not to be involved. "Our isolated position and freedom from entangling alliances," said the *Literary Digest,* "inspire our press with the cheering assurance that we are in no peril of being drawn into the European quarrel." President Wilson himself appealed to the people in the early days of the war to be "impartial in thought as well as in action."

It was not long, however, before the loyalties of the more than 30 million Americans of European birth or parentage became engaged with one side or the other, while Wilson himself shared the sympathy of the majority with the Allied cause. Since the turn of the century, as we have seen (p. 637), Britain had made conscientious efforts to woo American friendship in anticipation of the German threat in Europe, and elsewhere in the world. Ties of language and literature bound the cultivated classes of both countries; bonds of trade and finance united parts of their business communities. For France there was a somewhat more vague enthusiasm that dated back to the days of Lafayette, an enthusiasm soon extended to "poor little Belgium," Germany's first victim. Many Americans, at least since the accession in 1888 of Kaiser Wilhelm II, who was given to grandiose and alarming pronouncements about Germany's imperial ambitions, had come to regard Germany with deepening suspicion. The martyrdom of Belgium confirmed them in believing that the German government was ruthless and unprincipled, a belief further strengthened by mounting evidence early in the war of violence by German and Austrian agents in America directed toward crippling industrial production that might assist the Allied cause.

As the propaganda campaign developed, therefore, Germany was in the unenviable position of having to counter widespread hostility, while the British and the French had only to intensify friendly sentiments. British control of the Atlantic cables gave the Allies an additional advantage, enabling them to censor all war news emanating from Europe except for wireless dispatches. The British, moreover, missed few tricks in putting their language advantage to work. American newspaper publishers and editors, movie-makers, prominent writers, teachers, and college presidents all were mobilized for the cause. As Sir Gilbert Parker, the Canadian novelist who took

charge of British propaganda, later explained: "We asked our friends and correspondents to arrange for speeches, debates, and lectures by American citizens, but we did not encourage Britishers to go to America and preach the doctrine of entrance into the war."

Allied propagandists conjured up a terrible picture of German rapine, plunder, and cruelty in Belgium, most of which was later proved false, but much of which was readily accepted in America. The war at sea also favored the public-relations work of the Allies. By 1916, their blockade of Central Europe brought hunger and malnutrition to women and children, but such slow cruelty was hard to dramatize, while German submarine warfare caused shocking sinkings at sea which struck horror into the hearts of everyone.

FREEDOM OF THE SEAS
The rivalry between the Allied blockade and the German submarine offensive dominated the war at sea from the start, and naturally involved the United

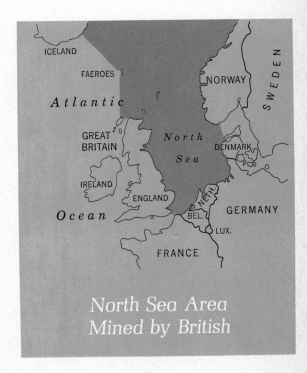

North Sea Area
Mined by British

States in conflicts with both parties over the traditional rights of neutral carriers.

One of the earliest disputes between Britain and the United States arose over the definition of contraband—that is, goods which in international law may not be supplied by a neutral to one belligerent without risk of lawful seizure by another. Early in the war, the British arbitrarily redefined contraband to embrace *all* articles of importance—including foodstuffs, hitherto not designated—that might give direct or indirect aid to the enemy. In the beginning they exempted cotton to conciliate the South and to avoid building up pressures on Wilson's administration from that quarter.

The liberties the British were taking with the traditional right of visit and search caused additional friction. It had always been permissible under international law for a belligerent vessel to stop and visit a neutral merchantman to search for contraband, and either to release it if none was found, or to send it to a prize court for legal action if contraband was aboard. The British insisted that the task of searching a large modern vessel had become too complicated for them to observe the usual procedure any longer. Instead, they often insisted on conducting neutral vessels to port for a thorough examination, a procedure that caused long delays and imposed great economic losses on American shippers. Although wartime shipping remained profitable, and although the British paid for many of the cargoes they confiscated, their behavior was widely resented in American shipping circles and within the Wilson administration.

A third source of trouble stemmed from the way the British conducted their blockade. The British intercepted not only American ships bound for Germany, but also those destined for neutral countries near enough to act as entry points to German markets. A system of rationing imports for neutral countries was worked out by the Allies under which these countries were forbidden to import substantially more than they had before the war.

In November, 1914, the British government declared the North Sea a military area and mined it so thoroughly that no neutral vessel could pass through without first stopping to receive British direction on how to navigate in the mined zones. This was a radical departure from earlier international practice, but to all complaints Britain replied that she was fighting for her life and could not be bound by maritime laws framed under conditions now obsolete.

The Wilson administration sent numerous sharp protests to London which forcefully argued the case against British practices from the standpoint of tradition. When in the summer of 1916 the British government forbade British subjects to trade with any of a blacklist of 85 persons or firms in the United States suspected of giving aid to Germany, American tempers were sorely tried. Wilson professed himself "about at the end of my patience with Great Britain and the Allies. This blacklist business is the last straw. . . . Can we any longer endure their intolerable course?"

In spite of the irritation produced by such conflicts, there seems no reason to believe that the United States ever really considered going to war against the Allies. American grievances were not pressed to the breaking point. "England is fighting our fight," Wilson declared at one point to his secretary, Joseph Tumulty. When members of his Cabinet urged him to embargo exports to Britain early in 1915, Wilson replied, even that early: "Gentlemen, the Allies are standing with their backs to the wall fighting wild beasts. I will permit nothing to be done by our country to hinder or embarrass them in the prosecution of the war unless admitted rights are grossly violated." If the Germans should succeed, he once told the British ambassador, "we shall be forced to take such measures of defense here which would be fatal to our form of Government and American ideals." Many thoughtful men throughout the country agreed. As the former Secretary of State, Elihu Root, wrote to an English friend, "The principle of Anglo-Saxon liberty seems to have met the irreconcilable conception of the German State, and the two ideas are battling for control of the world."

Certain non-ideological considerations also constrained Wilson's administration. The United States, for example, might after all decide at some time to enter the war against Germany and, once in it, to employ the same maritime practices against which it was now arguing. This possibility added a note of obscurity to American notes. "Short and emphatic notes were dangerous," Secretary Lansing later recalled. "Everything was submerged in verbosity. It was done with deliberate purpose. It insured continuance of the controversies and left the questions unsettled, which was necessary in order to leave this country free to act and even to act illegally when it entered the war."

Profitable trade supplied a second reason for American restraint. True, the Allied blockade so interfered with American commerce with the Central Powers that this commerce fell from a value of almost $170 million in 1914 to hardly more than $1 million in 1916. But American commerce with Britain, France, Russia, and Italy in the same period rose from $825 million almost to $3.25 billion. This gain so much more than offset the loss of trade with Germany and her friends that the United States, in the throes of a business depression when the war in Europe began, was soon enjoying a boom that lasted until 1919.

The surge in Allied trade quickly transformed the United States from a debtor to a creditor nation and confronted Wilson with a vital decision. Old American debts to the Allied powers had been paid off by the sale of war goods. Now the Allies, no longer the suppliers of capital for American industrial development, had to call for loans from America to finance further buying. If these loans were denied, it seemed clear that the Allies might be defeated, Americans would lose their profitable war business, and the United States would lapse back into depression that might endanger the Democratic administration. "Our prosperity," wrote Secretary of the Treasury William G. McAdoo to Wilson on August 21, 1915, "is dependent on our continued and enlarged foreign trade. To preserve that we must do everything we can to assist our customers to buy. . . . To maintain our prosperity, we must finance it. Otherwise it may stop and that would be disastrous." The State Department, under Secretary William Jennings Bryan's urging, had originally discouraged American bankers from making private loans to the Allied governments. The administration now substantially reversed its position and permitted war lending to go on.

As time passed, the United States came to have a tremendous economic stake in the Allies' ability to pay back what they borrowed, and many years later a Senate Committee headed by Gerald P. Nye charged that the United States finally entered the war simply to assure the safety of bankers' loans and munitions-makers' profits. This charge underlay the neutrality laws of the 1930's which may have strengthened Hitler's own aggressive resolves (see chapter 29). It distorts the facts of the situation in World War I, largely by omitting all the other elements of sympathy and policy that impelled Wilson to act as he did and most of Americans to back him.

SUBMARINE WARFARE

The more deeply the United States became involved with the Allies, the less constraint she felt in dealing with the Central Powers. The latter's submarine warfare, in turn, tended only to justify the administration's mounting hostility.

A frail craft, the submarine, once it surfaced, could easily be sunk even by the light deck guns of armed merchant vessels. Submarine commanders therefore could not follow the established practice of halting an enemy merchant ship, ascertaining its identity, and providing for the safety of its passengers and crew before sending it to the bottom. To operate a submarine at maximum effect and in least danger, its captain had to hit and run. British practices

German Submarine
Zone, Feb. 15, 1915

ICELAND

Atlantic

Scapa Flow

GREAT
BRITAIN

North

Sea

NORWAY

SWEDEN

DENMARK

IRELAND

ENGLAND

NETH.

Ocean

BEL.

LUX.

GERMANY

FRANCE

on the high seas, Wilson said, involved only property damages, which could be adjusted at the end of the war; submarine tactics involved "the fundamental rights of humanity. . . . The loss of life is irreparable." When the German government announced on February 4, 1915, that it was setting up a war area around the British Isles in which all enemy ships would be destroyed without warning, and in which it was clear that neutral vessels would not be safe, the stage was set for the prolonged controversy that eventually carried the United States into the fighting. Submarine warfare, the Germans argued, was no more inhuman than the Allied food blockade that starved innocent civilians; they offered to change their submarine tactics if the blockade were lifted, but there was no hope of altering Allied policy in that direction. Early in 1915, when more and more Allied merchant vessels were being sunk, it became evident that the lives of Americans traveling on belligerent ships were in grave danger. The German government issued warnings about that danger, and Secretary of State Bryan urged the President to forbid Americans to take this risk. Wilson refused, insisting that American travelers were simply exercising a traditional right.

On May 7, 1915, a German submarine sank the unarmed British liner *Lusitania* with the loss of 1,198 passengers, 128 of them Americans. Although the ship was carrying rifle cartridges and other contraband, and thus invited attack, the shocking toll of lives dramatized the submarine issue. "The torpedo that sank the *Lusitania*," declared *The Nation*, "also sank Germany in the opinion of mankind." Some Americans demanded that the United States go to war at once, but Wilson opposed this step. "There is," he said in a public address, "such a thing as a man being too proud to fight. There is such a thing as a nation being so right that it does not need to convince others by force that it is right." Militant Americans called Wilson's caution cowardice, but the administration refused to do more than send three vigorously worded notes of protest to Germany. The second of these came so close to being a threat of war that Secretary of State Bryan, who wanted peace at any reasonable cost, resigned rather than sign it. He was replaced by the ardent Anglophile, Robert Lansing. Nine months after the sinking, Germany acknowledged responsibility for the loss of American lives and agreed to pay an indemnity. But nothing had been settled when the United States went to war.

After the *Lusitania* tragedy, more sinkings occurred, and American protests elicited German promises that submarine methods would be modified. When in March, 1916, however, a submarine torpedoed the unarmed French ship, *Sussex,* injuring Americans aboard, Wilson considered the promises broken and warned Germany that if she did not immediately abandon her murderous tactics, "the United States can have no choice but to sever diplomatic relations." This threat drew from the Germans the so-called *Sussex* pledge of May 4, 1916, declaring that no more merchant vessels would be sunk without warning, *provided* that the United States held Britain accountable for *her* violations of international law. By ignoring this proviso but accepting the pledge, Wilson succeeded in forcing Germany to place crippling restrictions on her principal maritime weapon.

Wilson was convinced soon after the start of hostilities that the best way of keeping the United States at peace was to end the war. Thus, in January, 1915, and again a year later, he sent his personal adviser, Colonel Edward M. House, on peace missions to Europe, but these visits came to nothing. Discouraged by House's failures, Wilson gave way to the strong agitation for preparedness led, among others, by Theodore Roosevelt, and ordered the enlargement of the army, the navy, and the merchant marine. Peace-minded Progressives were horrified, but in espousing preparedness, Wilson appropriated what might have been a useful Republican issue in the 1916 presidential campaign.

German self-justification for the sinking of the Lusitania. *This medallion shows, left: Death selling tickets at the Cunard office; a German holding up a cautioning finger; an inscription proclaiming "business first"—right: the sinking* Lusitania, *laden with war supplies.*

Four years earlier, Wilson had been elected only because normal Republican strength was split between Roosevelt and Taft (see p. 660). Now the Republicans spurned Roosevelt, who eagerly sought the nomination, and united behind an attractive candidate, Justice Charles Evans Hughes of the Supreme Court. It was hard to see how Wilson could be re-elected, especially since T.R. willingly abandoned the Progressive party, hoping thereby to end the disastrous Republican split, and campaigned vigorously for Hughes. Hughes, however, missed his chance. He so straddled

the whole issue of war and peace that the Democrats dubbed him Charles "Evasive" Hughes. Wilson, at the same time, could boast of the *Sussex* pledge which he had wrung from the Germans while keeping America "out of war." Wilson's domestic reforms (see Chapter 24) also helped him, swaying the votes of a great many supporters of the Progressive and Socialist parties, as well as of labor, farmer, and antiwar groups. In the end, the election hung on the Far West. Wilson carried California by a mere 4,000 votes and with it enough states in the electoral college to give him a majority. In the popular vote he led 9,129,000 to 8,538,000. The fact that Wilson carried all but four states west of the Mississippi as well as the entire South, is evidence of the surviving Progressive strength and of the demand for peace in those regions.

THE DECISION TO FIGHT

A few weeks after his election victory Wilson made a new effort to arrange a peace, dispatching a note to all belligerent powers asking them to state acceptable terms. At this moment, soured by the Allies' cool reception of House's proposals and the British blacklisting practices, Wilson was perhaps more genuinely neutral in feeling than at any time since the start of the war. Unfortunately for him, Germany's military fortunes then were at a peak and a week earlier she had expressed her own willingness to talk peace. The timing of Wilson's note, apparently an echo of the German feelers, deeply offended the Allies and nothing came of it.

Wilson followed this gesture with another which only deepened Allied suspicions. In a speech before the Senate on January 22, 1917, he announced to the world his own conception of a just and lasting peace and outlined ideas for a League of Nations to maintain it. "It must be a peace without victory," he asserted, adding prophetically,

Victory would mean peace forced upon the loser, a victor's terms imposed upon the vanquished. It would be accepted in humiliation, under duress, at an intolerable sacrifice, and would leave a sting, a resentment, a bitter memory upon which terms of peace would rest, not permanently, but only as upon quicksand. Only a peace between equals can last.

Most Americans greeted this speech with enthusiasm, but to the Allies it seemed to be a withdrawal of the informal sympathy and accord they had come to expect from the United States. They were especially distressed because of their own deteriorating position in the fighting which itself, within ten days of Wilson's speech, led the German's boldly to revoke the *Sussex* pledge and strike for complete victory. On January 31, 1917, they announced that their submarines would again sink all vessels on sight, armed or unarmed, within a specified zone around the British Isles and in the Mediterranean. The Germans knew that they now risked almost certain war with the United States, but they hoped to knock Britain out of the war by cutting off her food supply before United States forces reached the battlefields. They almost won their desperate gamble.

As he had promised, Wilson broke off diplomatic relations with Germany. He next called upon Congress to authorize the arming of American merchant vessels. When a filibuster led by Senator La Follette blocked this proposal, Wilson angrily charged in the press: "A little group of wilful men, representing no opinion but their own, have rendered the great Government of the United States helpless and contemptible." Wilson's aides soon uncovered an old statute authorizing the president to arm vessels without congressional sanction and on March 12 he issued the appropriate order. Wilson thought he might still avoid war, but two events, one a small incident, the other a world-shaking revolution, killed his and the country's hopes.

In January, 1917, British naval intelligence intercepted a message in code from German Foreign Secretary Alfred Zimmermann to the German minister in Mexico, informing him of the German decision to resume unrestricted submarine warfare. The message instructed Zimmermann to propose to Mexico that if war came between the United States and Germany, the Mexicans and Germans should make an alliance (which Mexico should try to persuade Japan to join) and fight together, and that Germany would support Mexico in an effort to recover "her lost territory in New Mexico, Texas, and Arizona." In February the British passed this message along to Washington. After holding it for almost a week for fear of its effect on American opinion, Wilson decided to make it public on March 1 to create further support for his armed-ship bill. American sentiment for drastic measures against Germany rose to fever pitch. The New York *Post* thought the note was "the final proof that the German government has gone stark mad," and that it argued "the existence of an international madman, whom it is becoming increasingly an international duty to place under restraint."

Within two weeks, the March revolution in Russia replaced the tyrannical czarist regime with a provisional republican government, and thereby made it easier to describe the Allied war against the Central Powers as a war of democracies against autocracies. This change in the Allied setup removed one of the last brakes on the United States' joining the Allied cause. The liberal Walter Weyl wrote: "The final impelling reason for this declaration of war was the Russian Revolution which cast the influence of a great nation in favor of true democratization of the war and against merely imperialistic use of victory." At the same time, sinkings of American ships began in the Atlantic, with five going down in March alone.

To declare war was hateful to a man of conscience like Wilson. More than once during the closing days of March, 1917, he asked his close associates, "What else can I do? Is there anything else I can do?" He foresaw that waging a great war would tax to the utmost, perhaps even destroy, American tolerance for dissent and the American system of constitutional government. To Frank Cobb of the New York *World,* he confessed what was on his mind:

He said that when a war got going it was just war and there weren't two kinds of it. It required illiberalism at home to reinforce the men at the front. We couldn't fight Germany and maintain the ideals of Government that all thinking men shared. He said we would try it but it would be too much for us.

"Once lead this people into war," he said, "and they'll forget there ever was such a thing as tolerance. To fight you must be brutal and ruthless, and the spirit of ruthless brutality will enter into the very fibre of our national life, infecting Congress, the courts, the policeman on the beat, the man in the street." Conformity would be the only virtue, said the President, and every man who refused to conform would have to pay the penalty.

He thought the Constitution would not survive it; that free speech and the right of assembly would go. He said a nation couldn't put its strength into war and keep its head level; it had never been done.

"If there is any alternative, for God's sake, let's take it," he exclaimed.

But Wilson could see no alternative, and on the following day, April 2, 1917, he went before Congress to read the war message that had been lying on his desk as he spoke

to Cobb. He reviewed the history of the submarine controversy and asserted that the United States was fighting for the rights of neutrals, for international law, and for security from ruthless autocracy. "The world must be made safe for democracy." This was not a quarrel with the German people but with their imperial government. He urged the American people to fight "without rancor and without selfish object":

It is a fearful thing to lead this great peaceful people into war, into the most terrible and disastrous of all wars, civilization itself seeming to be in the balance. But the right is more precious than peace, and we shall fight for the things which we have always carried nearest our hearts,—for democracy, for the right of those who submit to authority to have a voice in their own Governments, for the rights and liberties of small nations, for a universal domination of right by such a concert of free peoples as shall bring peace and safety to all nations and make the world itself at last free.

On April 4 the Senate adopted the war resolution, 82 to 6; on April 6 the House voted for it, 373 to 6.

II. *Embattled at Home and Overseas*

THE ALLIES' CRISIS

America's decision to join in the fighting against the Central Powers came when the Allied cause was faring badly almost everywhere. After their courageous stand at Verdun early in 1916, which made "they shall not pass" the heroic slogan of the day, the French had suffered such terrible losses on the Western Front that some of their leaders were engaging in independent peace talks with the Austrians, who themselves were ready to desert the Germans. In the French army, moreover, defeatism had reached the point where ten divisions had mutinied. In the Balkans a carefully prepared Allied offensive had failed. In 1916 alone, the Russian armies

lost a million men, and the Russian people were ready to oppose any government that would not call a halt to the slaughter.

Worst of all, the new German submarine campaign had proved a great success. Sinkings of Allied merchant vessels averaged almost 570,000 tons per month in February and March, 1917, and reached 881,000 tons in April, when Britain had grain enough for only six to eight weeks. One ship in every four that tried to enter or leave Britain went down. At this time, Admiral Jellicoe, Britain's naval chief, told the American Admiral, William S. Sims, "it is impossible for us to go on, if losses like this continue. . . . The Germans . . . will win unless we can stop these losses—and stop them soon."

Although it was to be many months before the United States could put sufficient numbers of men in the field to influence the course of the war on land, the navy could help cope with the emergency at once. Heretofore, Allied merchantman captains had preferred to go it alone at sea, relying on speed and maneuverability to dodge torpedoes. Obviously this was a poor reliance, and many naval officers had been urging the convoy system in which whole fleets of merchant vessels would sail together under cruiser and destroyer escorts. Merchant captains doubted that their ships could hold fixed stations in a convoy. But under Admiral Sims' urging, the convoy system was adopted with impressive results. Allied monthly shipping losses fell from 881,000 tons in April to 289,000 tons in November. Moreover, not one American troop-transport ship was sunk, although two British transports were lost with Americans aboard. Before the war's end, the United States had also launched more than a hundred sub-chasers and had put 500 airplanes to work spotting enemy U-boats. She had also taken the initiative in laying a tremendous mine barrier across the North Sea which eventually closed that area as an exit for submarines. In all, more than 2,000 American vessels of all sizes had been thrown into the conflict.

AMERICAN MOBILIZATION

America's participation in the war demanded of her two things she had never done before: Vast numbers of men had to be transported across the ocean to fight against a great power 3,000 miles away; and the entire continental economy had to be mobilized to back them up.

Even before Congress declared war, thousands of American youth had volunteered their services to the Allies, and many of them saw the four full years of fighting. The combined strength of the Regular Army and the National Guard at this time was about 378,000 men, trained or partially trained. These men furnished the officers and non-coms of the new army created by a national draft. On May 18, 1917, Congress passed a Selective Service Act, requiring all men between the ages of 21 and 30 (it was extended later to 18 and 45) to register for military service. Registrants were placed in five classes, headed by able-bodied unmarried men without dependents. From this group alone the nation drew all the 2,810,000 men actually drafted for service in the army, although by the end of the war, as many as 4,800,000 American men and women were enrolled in the army, navy, and marine corps. To train these recruits, 32 military camps were hastily built, most of them in the South.

Although some experts recommended that the United States finance its immense war effort on a pay-as-you-go basis, with wartime profits and earnings taxed to the utmost, the government resorted to borrowing on a large scale. The total cost of the war from April, 1917, to June, 1920, is estimated at $32.8 billion, of which about a half was raised by four Liberty loan drives in 1917-1918 and the rest by taxes. Rather than sell bonds through bankers, as Lincoln's government had done during the Civil War, Wilson's administration chose to sell them directly to small as well as large buyers, enlisting volunteers to hawk them to every household and backing their efforts with rallies and entertainments, and posters spread across the land. Unresponsive citizens were scorned as slackers or German sympathizers, and each loan was over-subscribed. New taxes on luxuries and corporations, and higher income taxes, paid for most of the rest of the war costs.

To mobilize the nation's other resources, Wilson created the Council of National Defense, consisting of six Cabinet members and an advisory commission of seven additional civilians. Under the council's supervision, six huge wartime agencies devoted themselves to specific tasks of economic mobilization. One of these agencies, the Emergency Fleet Corporation, had been created as early as April, 1916, to enlarge the United States merchant marine. Another, the Food Administration, ably headed by Herbert Hoover, undertook to supply civilians and combatants. Hoover set such a high government price for wheat and other crops that American farmers greatly enlarged the acreage under cultivation. The Fuel Administration doled out coal and oil. The Railroad Administration consolidated the nation's railroads and, without removing them from private ownership, operated them as a single system.

In March, 1918, the Council of National Defense placed the War Industries Board under the direction of Bernard Baruch and gave him dictatorial powers over American business in wartime. Great savings were effected by minute regulations covering everything from the number of trunks traveling salesmen could carry to the styles of pocket knives that could be produced and the number of stops elevators could make. Immense strides were made through standardization. For instance, the number of sizes and styles of plows was reduced from 376 to 76, the number of colors of typewriter ribbons from 150 to 5. As a result of some 1,200 such economies, Americans conserved labor and material for the war effort, and also learned a great deal about the advantages of standardization and planning.

Samuel Gompers, President of the American Federation of Labor, on becoming one of the civilian advisers of the Council of National Defense, declared that the American worker backed the war but hoped that the government would prevent exploitation and profiteering at his expense. In March, 1918, the War Labor Conference Board, which had been set up by the Secretary of Labor as an advisory agency, drew up a set of guiding principles for the administration. In return for its pledge not to strike, labor was assured of the right of collective bargaining, of the maintenance of the 8-hour day where it existed, and other privileges. A National War Labor Board was set up to mediate labor disputes and a War Labor Policies Board to deal with labor grievances. Between 1915 and 1917, the number of strikes had tripled and the number of persons involved more than doubled. Strikes fell off thereafter, while the A.F.L. pushed its membership from 1,950,000 in 1915 to 2,800,000 in 1918.

Actually, labor shared in the wartime prosperity, though not so spectacularly as farmers and businessmen. The demand for labor was great, and in some industries wages rose even faster than prices. In the most favored industries, like manufacturing, mining, and transportation, it is estimated that workers were enjoying real earnings as much as 20 per cent higher in 1918 than in 1914. For all wage-earners, however, the rise in real earnings was closer to 4 per cent. As is usual in periods of rapid price rises, salaried employees had a bad time, losing perhaps as much as one-third of their pre-war purchasing power.

Neither businessmen nor farmers neglected the opportunities opened up by wartime demand. The War Industries Board, unwilling to delay production by lengthy negotiations, gave up the traditional practice of competitive bidding and made war purchases on the basis of cost-plus contracts. These contracts guaranteed sellers profits ranging from $2\frac{1}{2}$ to 15 per cent of production costs. By padding costs, some contractors made enough to increase dividend payments and executive salaries substantially and still pile up profits despite high taxes. Large personal fortunes increased. In 1914 only 5,000 persons, and in 1918, 13,000, reported annual incomes in the $50,000 to $100,000 tax brackets. Progressive tax policies cut deeply into these incomes and those of corporations, so that a sizable proportion of the tax burden was shifted from lower income to higher income families. The modern policy of graduated income taxes placing upon the wealthy a progressively higher share of tax burdens may be said to have begun during the war.

Encouraged by the government and lured by high prices, farmers stretched their resources to the utmost in order to acquire more land. From 1916 to 1919, harvested wheat acreage, for example, rose from 53,510,000 to 73,700,000 acres, the total crop from 634,572,000 to 952,097,000 bushels.

Farmers helped to feed the country and its Allies and lined their pockets in the process. The real income of farm operators was 29 per cent higher in 1918 than it had been in 1915. But soon after the wartime demand ended, the farmers found themselves in deeper financial trouble than ever before.

Wilson's administration attempted to mobilize the American mind as well as American resources. Something in this direction probably had to be done to offset the strong feeling against fighting in Europe. "We are going into war at the command of gold," Senator George W. Norris of Nebraska had charged in a popular speech against the declaration of war. Many Americans continued to sympathize with the Central powers, others had mixed loyalties, still others remained indifferent. Evidence of widespread opposition appeared in the strong showing of the Socialist party in municipal elections in 1917. In some communities Socialists won as much as 30 or 40 per cent of the vote.

Within two weeks after the declaration of war, Congress established the Committee on Public Information to keep the fires of patriotism burning brightly. Wilson named George Creel, once a prominent muckraker, to head this committee and Creel, in turn, conscripted journalists, scholars and clergymen to convince the country of German depravity as ingrained in the enemy's very culture and history.

Creel's committee and other propaganda agencies seem to have been all too successful. As Wilson himself had forecast (see p. 675), intolerance soon spread across the land. In some places, superpatriots beat up pacifists, broke up their meetings and those of socialists and liberals, and tarred and feathered left-wing labor leaders. In Butte, Montana, masked men dragged a crippled IWW organizer from his bed and hanged him. Although the vast majority of German-Americans accepted the necessity of war once the United States had entered it, they became the most obvious targets of abuse. Libraries removed German books, which were sometimes publicly burned. Schools dropped the German language from the curriculum. A peak in silliness was reached by restaurants that renamed sauerkraut "liberty cabbage," and kennels that rechristened dachshunds "liberty pups."

Congress made intolerance official by adopting the Espionage Act of June, 1917, and the Sedition Act of May, 1918. The Espionage Act prescribed a fine of up to $10,000 and a prison term of 20 years for anyone who interfered with the draft or attempted to encourage disloyalty. The Sedition Act set the same penalty for anyone who obstructed the sale of United States bonds, incited insubordination, discouraged recruiting, or who would "wilfully utter, print, write or publish any disloyal, profane, scurrilous, or abusive language" about the American form of government, the flag, the uniforms of the services, or the Constitution, or "advocate any curtailment of production . . . of anything necessary or essential to the prosecution of the war." Over 1,500 persons were imprisoned under these laws, including the socialist leader, Eugene V. Debs, and more than 450 conscientious objectors. Only a few Americans protested that this was a strange way to conduct a war for liberty and democracy.

The first American troops, under Major-General John J. Pershing, arrived in France in June, 1917, and were fed into the sagging Allied lines largely to bolster morale. As the American build-up continued, certain contingents began to see independent action, the first major force of the American army entering battle in October, 1917, near Toul, east of Verdun. When in March, 1918, the Germans launched their massive spring offensive, hoping to end the war, about 300,000 American soldiers had reached France and more were arriving every day. By the war's end, more than 2 million men had been carried to Europe, of whom about 1,400,000 saw fighting service, all but a few on the Western Front. In April, 1918, the Germans enjoyed a numerical superiority on this front of perhaps 320,-000. By November, fresh American troops had given the Allies a preponderance of 600,000.

Despite all the mobilization efforts at home, American artillery units were equipped largely with French 75 mm. field guns. The American program for airplane production developed so slowly that American aviators were forced to fly foreign-made craft. Ill-prepared to meet the problems of armored tank production, American industry made negligible contributions in this area. British transports, moreover, carried more American soldiers to Europe than did American vessels.

Of necessity, large numbers of Americans were thrown into battle inadequately trained, but they played a decisive role in the last eight months of the war. The Allies hoped to continue to use American troops as replacements, and to brigade them with French or British units. Pershing, however, fought this policy, feeling that the Allies had grown too defensive-minded and that the Americans would be more successful conducting independent offensive operations. Hence the greater part of the American army soon took its place in the lines as a separate force under Pershing's command,

subject, after April, 1918, to the over-all supreme command of Marshal Foch of France.

Pershing's men faced their first major test when assigned to help repulse a menacing German thrust toward Paris. By May 30, 1918, the Germans had reached Château-Thierry on the Marne, only 50 miles from the French capital. The French commander called on Pershing for help, and on May 31 the 2nd and 3rd American Divisions and a brigade of marines went into action in support of French colonial troops. Certain German contingents had actually crossed the Marne. The Americans drove them back and from June 6 to 25 cleared nearby Belleau Wood of enemy forces. In July, when the German General Staff made its last great effort to break through to Paris between Rheims and Soissons, 85,000 Americans helped check the assault.

In its first major offensive assignment, September, 1918, the American army launched an attack on the St. Mihiel salient, a German bulge protruding sharply into the Allied lines across the Meuse River

The 33rd Division in a front-line trench near Gorges, October 3, 1918.

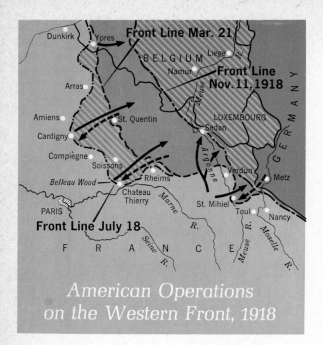

American Operations on the Western Front, 1918

The Meuse-Argonne offensive, which lasted from late September to early November, was one of the fiercest battles in American military history. Together with the French forces on that front, the Americans captured more than 25,000 prisoners and a great deal of equipment, but at a high cost in casualties. This offensive, part of a co-ordinated drive against the Central Powers all along the Western Front, in Italy, in Greece, and in Palestine, helped bring Germany and her allies to their knees. At the end of September, Bulgaria surrendered. Turkey followed in October and Austria in November. Finally, on November 11, Germany with her armies everywhere in retreat, her navy on the verge of general mutiny, and her civilian populaton hungry, exhausted, and dangerously discontented, gave up resistance and signed an armistice.

The war was not over, since terms of peace had yet to be worked out, but the fighting was at an end. American losses— 48,000 killed in battle, 2,900 missing in action, 56,000 dead of disease—were light in comparison with the losses the other great powers had suffered since 1914. Russia counted 1,700,000 battle deaths, Germany 1,800,000, France 1,385,000, Britain 947,000, and Austria-Hungary 1,200,000. But America's losses were heavy in proportion to the length of time she had been in the war and the number of her troops engaged. Americans had had more than a mere glimpse of the horrors of the gigantic struggle.

southeast of Verdun. Pershing sent American troops against both flanks of the salient, and with some French support reduced it in two days. An American army of half a million troops was engaged. At the cost of 7,000 casualties, it captured 16,000 German prisoners and over 400 guns, and established a new threat to the fortified center of Metz. By Foch's orders, however, the American army was not sent on toward Metz but was shifted westward and down the Meuse River, through the Argonne Woods toward Sedan, with the object of taking that city and cutting the strategically important Sedan-Metz railroad.

III. *Losing the Peace*

THE FOURTEEN POINTS

While his administration was waging a zealous propaganda campaign on the home front, Wilson himself was sending propaganda messages to enemy peoples urging them to give up the struggle. When the United States still was neutral, his appeal for "peace without victory" had brought hope to a world already war weary. When the United States went to war, he kept asserting that hostilities were directed not against the German people but against their government. Neither punitive damages nor territorial gains were the Allies' real objectives, he said, but rather the end of autocratic government and a settlement that would insure permanent peace. On January 8, 1918, he set forth in a speech to Congress his famous Fourteen Points, which he called "the only possible program." Briefly summarized, these were his proposals:

I. Open covenants of peace, openly arrived at.
II. Absolute freedom of navigation upon the seas in peace and in war.
III. The removal, so far as possible, of all economic barriers among the nations consenting to the peace.
IV. Guarantees that national armaments will be reduced to the lowest point consistent with domestic safety.
V. An impartial adjustment of colonial claims giving equal weight to the interests of the populations concerned and to the government whose title is to be determined.
VI. The evacuation of all Russian territory.
VII. The evacuation and restoration of Belgium.
VIII. All French territory should be freed, the invaded portions restored, and the wrong done to France in 1871 in the matter of Alsace-Lorraine should be righted.
IX. Readjustment of Italian frontiers along clearly recognizable lines of nationality.
X. The peoples of Austria-Hungary should be accorded opportunity for autonomous development.
XI. Rumania, Serbia, and Montenegro should be evacuated, occupied territories restored, Serbia accorded free and secure access to the sea. The Balkan States should be constituted along historically established lines of nationality.
XII. The Turkish portions of the Ottoman Empire should be assured a secure sovereignty, the other nationalities under Turkish rule should have autonomous development. The Dardanelles should be open to the commerce of all nations under international guarantees.
XIII. An independent Polish state should be erected and should be assured a free and secure access to the sea.
XIV. A general association of nations must be formed under specific covenants for the purpose of affording mutual guarantees of political independence and territorial integrity to great and small states alike.

His Fourteen Points made Wilson a hero to people everywhere. Those struggling for national freedom and self-determination were heartened. Liberals were pleased with his espousal of open diplomacy and lower trade barriers. Nations heavily taxed for war purposes rallied behind the idea of a reduction of armaments. Even the Germans,

who distrusted British sea power, found merit in the proposal for freedom of the seas. The League of Nations idea raised hopes for the prevention of all the horrors of the battlefield. Throughout the world, men of good will toasted the health and worshipped the image of the American President. On a visit to Italy, George Creel found in a peasant's mountain cabin a shrine with a wax figure of a patron saint on one side and a picture of Wilson on the other.

Lofty though they were, Wilson's ideals found competing ones in Russia, and Wilson himself found a challenger in Lenin who as recently as November, 1917, had led the Bolsheviks in overthrowing the Provisional Government of Alexander Kerensky which had earlier overthrown the czar (see p. 674). In March, 1918, after failing to get the Allies to end the war on Wilson's terms, the Bolsheviks signed the Treaty of Brest-Litovsk with the Central Powers, thereby freeing the Germans on the Eastern Front. To keep the Germans occupied there, the Allies quickly made their fateful decision to send troops to Russia to fight the Germans and the Bolsheviks alike. Japanese and American forces also landed in Vladivostok in Siberia. Allied troops remained in Russia until 1919 and the Japanese were still in Vladivostok in 1922, but their efforts won them nothing but the lasting suspicion of the communists whose own success deepened Allied fears that the whole order of western capitalism might go down if peace were not soon made and reconstruction begun on hopeful terms.

The communist ideal, enlivened by Lenin's success, spread to other parts of Europe, but in the West, Wilson's ideal of a revitalized liberal democracy survived even though its chances were significantly weakened by Wilson's mounting difficulties with the democracy at home. Those who believed that the United States never should have entered the war could hardly be expected to rally behind him. Many others who had favored fighting nevertheless resented being dragged into Europe's quarrels by German aggression and favored a vengeful settlement. Political jealousies fed on these discontents and deepened the opposition to the President. Republicans in particular had been listening for years to Theodore Roosevelt denouncing him as a weakling, a coward and a fraud. "Let us," preached Roosevelt, "dictate peace by the hammering guns and not chat about peace to the accompaniment of the clicking of typewriters."

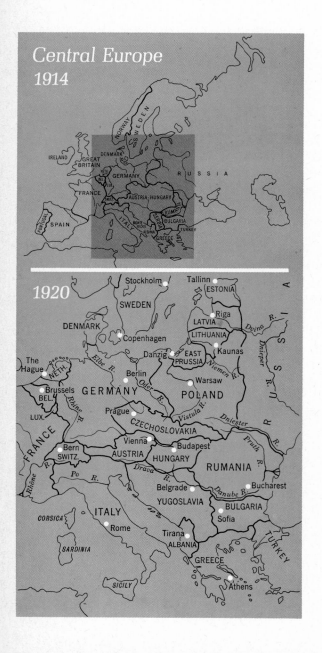

Central Europe
1914

1920

In October, 1918, facing the off-year congressional elections, Wilson was troubled by the thought that his role as peacemaker would be greatly weakened if the American people repudiated his party at the polls. Accordingly, he issued a fatal appeal to the voters, asking them to express their approval of his leadership by voting for Democratic representatives and senators. Not only did Wilson's appeal fail, it also embittered those many Republicans who had loyally supported his war policies. At the polls the voters elected Republican majorities to both houses and Wilson journeyed to meet his fate at Paris in December, 1918, apparently as the repudiated leader of his country.

Wilson further angered the members of the opposition party when he failed to appoint a single Republican leader, or indeed a single senator from either party, as a member of the Peace Commission to accompany him to Paris. Eminent Republicans, men like William H. Taft or Charles Evans Hughes or Elihu Root, could have been counted on to support internationalist views. But the only Republican appointed to the Peace Commission was the able career diplomat, Henry White, who had retired from active political life almost a decade before. The composition of the Peace Commission encouraged the suspicion that Wilson did not want to be accompanied by a strong and independent delegation.

THE VERSAILLES TREATY

The Paris Peace Conference, a conference of victors to decide the fate of the vanquished, sat from January to June, 1919. The Big Four—Britain, France, Italy, and the United States—made the important decisions. Britain was represented by her Prime Minister, David Lloyd George, who had won a general election the preceding December on a campaign calling for the severe punishment of Germany. France was represented by her Premier, Georges Clemenceau, a determined promoter of French interests and French security who cared about little else. Vittorio Orlando, the Italian Prime Minister, was at Paris to see that Allied territorial promises to Italy were met. When it became clear that they would not be, Orlando went home and the Big Four became the Big Three.

Wilson came to Paris with three cardinal goals: political self-determination for the peoples of Europe, and to some extent for the peoples of colonial countries, to foster democracy; free trade to foster prosperity; and a League of Nations to insure a lasting peace. Wilson knew that the wartime sufferings of the Allies would make it difficult to persuade them to forget purely national grievances and aspirations. He told one of the experts who accompanied him to Paris that "we would be the only disinterested men at the Peace Conference, and that the men whom we were about to deal with did not represent their own people." The second part of this assertion typified the kind of miscalculation to which Wilson was prone, for the Allied peoples shared only too fully in Clemenceau's single-minded concern for security and in Lloyd George's demand for vengeance. Wilson left Paris with his disinterested goals only partially attained; unfortunately, his concessions were made largely to secure the League of Nations, which the United States Senate was to strip of power by forbidding the United States to join. Wilson also succeeded in moderating the onerous Allied demands on Germany; but here, too, he was far from attaining his humane goal of "peace without victory." By secret wartime treaties, France had been promised Alsace-Lorraine and the rich Saar Basin; Britain, most German colonies and a free hand in Egypt, Persia, and Mesopotamia; Italy, the recovery of Trentino, the southern Tyrol, and control of the Adriatic Sea. Other territories had been promised to Japan, Rumania, and the Russia of the czars, and all together, they made the final treaty terms harsh enough almost to insure that the Germans would make every effort to break the peace when they felt strong enough once more to do so.

The Treaty of Versailles, signed by Germany on June 28, 1919, stripped her of all

her colonies in Africa and the Far East, and of Alsace-Lorraine and the Saar Basin north of Lorraine. France won all rights in the coal-rich Saar for 15 years, after which its future was to be decided by a plebiscite. On the east, German territory was given to Poland to form the "Polish Corridor" to the Baltic Sea, a provision that split Germany in two and was a bitter pill for the people. The huge and in fact unpayable indemnity of $5 billion levied on the Germans and the provision for additional "reparations" later on made them look upon the Allies as vultures. Perhaps most distressing to them was the "war guilt" article in the Versailles Treaty which attempted to justify the indemnity and reparations by forcing Germany to acknowledge responsibility for starting the war. In an effort to avert future aggression by a vengeful people, the treaty deprived Germany of her navy and her merchant marine and forbade her to have an army of more than 100,000 men. Other treaties in conjunction with the Versailles Treaty established new states such as Czechoslovakia and Yugoslavia by virtually dismantling the Austro-Hungarian empire.

For all its harshness, the Versailles Treaty was no more punitive than the terms Germany would have imposed on the Allies had she been victorious. "It is a very severe settlement with Germany," Wilson said in September, 1919, "but there is not anything in it that she did not earn." A year earlier, at Brest-Litovsk, the Germans had dictated exorbitant terms to Russia, grasping tremendous territories inhabited by millions.

The Versailles Treaty, nevertheless, failed to satisfy Clemenceau who refused to sign until Britain and the United States promised in a separate agreement to come to the aid of France in the event of a future attack upon her. Wilson no doubt suspected that the United States Senate would reject such an "entangling alliance," which it did. His own expectation was that the League of Nations would perform the role given to this alliance, and he strove successfully to get the Allies to include the League Covenant in the treaty. "It is a definite guarantee against the things which have just come near bringing the whole structure of civilization to ruin," Wilson said of the League. The covenant set up a permanent Secretariat with headquarters at Geneva, a Council of nine members, and an Assembly. The Council consisted of one representative each from the United States, Great Britain, France, Italy, and Japan, and four others chosen by the Assembly. The Assembly had a voting representative from every member nation. A Permanent Court of International Justice was also set up at the Hague.

All nations and self-governing dominions were welcomed as members of the League. Members pledged themselves "to respect and preserve as against external aggression the territorial integrity and . . . political independence of other members"; to give publicity to treaties and armaments; to recognize the right of each member to bring any threat to peace to the League's attention, and to submit dangerous disputes to arbitration; to refrain from war until three months after the decision of the arbiters; to refrain from war with nations complying with League decisions; and to employ military and economic sanctions against nations resorting to war in violation of League agreements.

The League Council in particular was to make plans to reduce armaments and to mitigate the dangers arising from their private manufacture. It was also to set up agencies "to secure and maintain fair and humane conditions of labor," to supervise "traffic in opium and other dangerous drugs" and "in women and children," and "as a sacred trust of civilization" to look after the peoples of "colonies and territories which as a consequence of the late war" no longer were governed by their former rulers.

Since the Treaty of Versailles covered only the settlement with Germany, other treaties had to be made with her allies. The Treaty of St. Germain with Austria attempted to insure that she would not initiate or consent to union with Germany. The Treaty of Trianon, signed by Hungary in 1920, drastically reduced the borders of the old Magyar kingdom. The Treaty of Neuilly, governing the Bulgarian settlement, trimmed that country's pre-war borders. The Treaty of Sèvres with Turkey stripped her of almost all her non-Turkish territory. Turkish nationals prevented its ratification, and in the Treaty of Lausanne, in 1923, Turkey won substantially better terms.

THE LEAGUE IN THE SENATE

When Wilson returned to the United States from Paris for a few weeks in February, 1919, certain senators immediately made clear to him their discontent with the League covenant. When he formally presented the Versailles Treaty, including the League covenant, to the Senate on July 10, two days after his final return from Paris, he was confronted by the ominous Republican majority elected in 1918 and especially by his sworn foe, Henry Cabot Lodge of Massachusetts, now Chairman of the Senate Foreign Relations Committee. Backing Lodge was a strong group of "irreconcilables," including such old Progressives as William E. Borah, Hiram Johnson, and Robert M. La Follette. Borah set the uncompromising tone when he cried, "No entangling alliances!" thereby raising the barrier of intransigent isolationism. The League was undemocratic, Borah said; it was based upon force. "You cannot yoke a government whose fundamental maxim is liberty to a government whose first law is force and hope to preserve the former. . . . We may become one of the four dictators of the world, but we shall no longer be master of our own spirit."

Nevertheless, more than the needed two-thirds of the Senate appeared ready to vote for some form of League membership, and there is every evidence that the majority of the people would have backed them—despite the opposition of German-Americans because of the harshness of the treaty, of Italian-Americans because of the frustration of their homeland's demands, and of

Irish-Americans who were bitter over Wilson's failure to secure Irish independence.

Through the summer of 1919, as the Senate and the people debated the League, Wilson himself grew ever more adamant against even minor modifications in the covenant and more tactless about his all-or-nothing stand. When the French Ambassador, Jusserand, assured him that the Allies would gladly accept American membership with reservations that would satisfy the doubts of an influential group of Republican senators, Wilson said flatly: "Mr. Ambassador, I shall consent to nothing. The Senate must take its medicine." When the irreconcilables, lavishly financed, then opened a tremendous propaganda barrage, the President decided to take his own case to the country. Although exhausted by work and illness, Wilson set forth early in September on a nation-wide speaking tour covering 8,000 miles and involving 37 lengthy speeches in 22 days. While he was gone, Lodge proposed a series of reservations to the covenant which he knew Wilson would reject and over which the Senate might talk the whole treaty to death.

Lodge's strategy worked. By the time his reservations were introduced in the Senate, Wilson had suffered a physical breakdown forcing him to cancel the rest of his trip. Early in October he suffered a stroke that left him half-paralyzed. His sick-bed appeal to "all true friends of the treaty" to spurn the Lodge reservations helped defeat them in the Senate in November. But a resolution to ratify the treaty and hence the League without any reservations also failed, by a vote of 55-38, with all but one of the Republicans lined up against it. Enough sentiment for the League remained even in the Senate for the treaty to be brought up again in March, 1920. This time it won a small majority, 49 to 35, one far short of the needed two-thirds, and it and the League were dead. The war with Germany thus did not officially end for the United States until July 2, 1921, when Congress passed a joint resolution declaring that hostilities were over and reserving the rights and privileges of a victorious power.

THE ELECTION OF 1920

Even with the treaty dead in the Senate, Wilson did not give up hope. The election of 1920, he announced, must be "a great and solemn referendum." The people themselves would now vote directly on the issue. But it has rarely been possible to make an American presidential election a clear referendum on any issue of foreign policy, and 1920 was no exception.

Deprived of their most popular leader by Theodore Roosevelt's death early in 1919, the Republicans, at their national convention in Chicago in June, split so badly over the candidacy of T.R.'s friends, General Leonard Wood and Governor Frank O. Lowden of Illinois, that they turned at last to an obscure Ohio senator, Warren G. Harding, as a standard-bearer they could control. A pleasant, pliable man, Harding, during his one term in the Senate, had quietly opposed the League during the fight over the treaty. Earlier he had been the editor of the Marion (Ohio) *Daily Star*. As his running mate the convention chose Calvin Coolidge, who had been even more obscure than Harding until, as Governor of Massachusetts, he suddenly gained national fame on being credited with having broken the Boston police strike of September, 1919.

To run against Harding, the Democrats, at their convention in San Francisco later in June, named another Ohioan, the popular and progressive Governor James M. Cox, who had not been closely identified with the Wilson administration. As his running-mate they chose Franklin D. Roosevelt, Wilson's Assistant Secretary of the Navy.

Cox, impressed with Wilson's personal gallantry, waged his campaign on the League issue. But the Republicans caught the mood of the public by evading this and other issues as well. "Keep Warren at home," advised the dying boss, Boies Penrose of Pennsylvania. "Don't let him make any speeches. If he goes out on a tour somebody's sure to ask him questions, and Warren's just the sort of damned fool that will try to answer them." The Republican platform condemned the covenant of the League, but Harding in speeches from his front porch promised to work for "an association of nations." Irreconcilables like Borah and Johnson supported Harding as an enemy of the League, while a group of 31 prominent pro-League Republicans signed an appeal for his election.

Cox was crushed at the polls, 16,152,000 to 9,147,000, receiving only 34 per cent of the popular vote. No major-party candidate had ever been defeated so badly. But, as a contemporary observer remarked, Cox was beaten "not by those who dislike him but by those who dislike Wilson and his group." After the strenuousness of "Teddy" Roosevelt, the sacrifices of the war years, the fatiguing moralism of Wilson himself, the American people seemed to suffer a complete revulsion from "problems" and reforms. The New York *World* wrote: "The American people wanted a change, and they have voted for a change. They did not know what kind of a change they wanted, and they do not know today what kind of a change they have voted for."

Readings

Asterisk indicates that book is available in paperback.

The definitive account of Woodrow Wilson and World War I will be found in the biography still in progress by A. S. Link (5 vols., 1947-1965). Other Wilson biographies cited in Chapter 24 also are useful here. A. S. Link, *Wilson the Diplomatist* * (1957); Harley Notter, *The Origins of the Foreign Policy of Woodrow Wilson* (1937); and Edward Buehrig, *Woodrow Wilson and the Balance of Power* (1955), deal illuminatingly with the development of Wilsons' policies. On his policies at maturity, see, in addition, Charles Seymour, *American Neutrality 1914-1917* (1935), and *American Diplomacy during the World War* (1934); and E. R. May, *The World War and American Isolation 1914-1917* (1959), as well as works cited below on peacemaking and the League of Nations. R. E. Osgood examines underlying forces in *Ideals and Self-interest in America's Foreign Relations* * (1953). G. F. Kennan, *Russia Leaves the War* (1956), and *The Decision to Intervene* (1958), are exceedingly illuminating on the American spirit in foreign affairs. See also, A. J. Mayer, *The Political Origins of the New Diplomacy* * (1959).

S. B. Fay, *Origins of the World War* (2 vols., 1930), and B. E. Schmitt, *The Coming of the War* (2 vols., 1930), thoroughly examine the European background. On the specific onset of the war, see B. W. Tuchman, *The Guns of August* * (1962). C. C. Tansill, *America Goes to War* (1938), and Walter Millis, *The Road to War* (1935), are more critical of Wilson's role than Seymour and May, cited above. F. L. Paxson, *American Democracy and the World War* (3 vols. 1936-1948), is the most thorough on its subject. See also, P. W. Slosson, *The Great Crusade and After 1914-1928* (1930). Excellent general works on the fighting from 1914 on include Cyril Falls, *The Great War* * (1959); S. L. A. Marshall, *World War I* * (1964); and H. W. Baldwin, *World War I* * (1962). Barrie Pitt, *1918: The Last Act* * (1962); and H. R. Rudin, *Armistice, 1919* (1944), are definitive on the end of the fighting.

On wartime propaganda, its truths and untruths, the following general studies are uesful: H. C. Peterson, *Propaganda for War* (1939); Harold Levine and James Wechsler, *War Propaganda and the United States* (1940); and Arthur Ponsonby, *Falsehood in Wartime* (1928). George Creel's personal account, *How We Advertised America* (1920), is revealing. See also J. R. Mock and Cedric Larson, *Words that Won the War* (1939). On wartime restraints on opinion, see Zechariah Chafee, *Free Speech in the United States* (1941 ed.); Donald Johnson, *Challenge to American Freedoms: World War I and the*

Rise of the American Civil Liberties Union (1963); William Preston, Jr., *Aliens and Dissenters: Federal Suppression of Radicals 1903-1933* (1963); and such special studies as Carl Wittke, *The German-Americans and the World War* (1936); C. J. Child, *The German-American in Politics 1914-1917* (1939); and H. C. Peterson and G. C. Fite, *Opponents of War 1917-1918* (1957).

E. E. Morison, *Admiral Sims and the Modern American Navy* (1942); and J. G. Harbord, *The American Army in France 1917-1919* (1936), afford general accounts of naval and military aspects respectively. Laurence Stallings, *The Doughboys, The Story of the AEF, 1917-1918* * (1963), is a spirited account of the American foot soldier. On the high command, see J. J. Pershing, *Final Report* (1919), *My Experiences in the World War* (2 vols., 1931), and Richard O'Connor, *Black Jack Pershing* (1961). On the home front, in addition to Paxson and Slosson, see Bernard Baruch, *American Industry in the War* (1941); W. E. Leuchtenburg, *The Perils of Prosperity* * (1958); Herbert Stein, *Government Price Policy during the World War* (1939); and D. F. Houston and Helen Basil, *Eight Years with Wilson's Cabinet* (2 vols., 1926), the personal account of the wartime Secretary of Agriculture.

Many of the works cited in the first paragraph deal with Wilson and the peace and the League. See in addition, T. A. Bailey, *Woodrow Wilson and the Lost Peace* * (1944), and *Woodrow Wilson and the Great Betrayal* * (1945), both critical. John Garraty, *Henry Cabot Lodge* (1953), makes the case for its subject; see also H. C. Lodge, *The Senate and the League of Nations* (1925); and M. C. McKenna, *Borah* (1961). J. M. Keynes, *The Economic Consequences of the Peace* (1919), is a sharp attack on the "Big Four," including Wilson. More friendly are Paul Birdsall, *Versailles Twenty Years After* (1941); and D. F. Fleming, *The United States and the League of Nations 1918-1920* (1932). See also, Robert Lansing, *The Peace Negotiations: A Personal Narrative* (1921); L. A. R. Yates, *The United States and French Security 1917-1921* (1957); S. P. Tillman, *Anglo-American Relations at the Paris Peace Conference of 1919* (1961); and Herbert Hoover, *The Ordeal of Woodrow Wilson* * (1958). On Wilson's heartbreaking last efforts, see Dexter Perkins, "Woodrow Wilson's Tour," in Daniel Aaron, ed., *America in Crisis* (1952).

Excellent on the election of 1920 are Wesley Bagby, *The Road to Normalcy* * (1962); and Andrew Sinclair, *The Available Man: Warren Gamaliel Harding* (1965). Also useful are S. H. Adams, *Incredible Era* * (1939); J. M. Cox, *Journey Through My Years* (1946); and Frank Freidel, *Franklin D. Roosevelt: The Ordeal* (1954).

CHAPTER TWENTY-SIX

In his inaugural address in March, 1921, President Harding seemed to strike the proper note when he declared, "we seek no part in directing the destinies of the Old World." To help carry the country back to the "normalcy" of isolation in politics and business he promised to bring the "best minds" to Washington. He redeemed this promise in part by making such outstanding men as Charles Evans Hughes Secretary of State, Herbert Hoover Secretary of Commerce, and Henry C. Wallace Secretary of Agriculture. But he also brought with him a group of local friends, neither scrupulous nor competent, who eventually came to be known as the "Ohio gang." Harding, like

From Normalcy
to Depression

the people, was really tired of the "best minds." With his Ohio cronies he played poker and drank in the White House while the nation found its own way home.

In the frenetic years from 1919 to 1932, the public mood zig-zagged from one extreme to the other: first, unfounded hysteria over alleged radicalism; then unfounded complacency over ephemeral good times; and finally, deepening gloom and near panic over the chilling grip of the depression. Immediately after the war, a spirit of provincialism and intolerance spread across the land and strengthened the control of stand-patters. The Progressive party, as we have seen (p. 671), disintegrated

in 1916. Wilson's own party, so firmly united during most of his administration, now split into snarling factions which rendered it helpless for two successive elections to play the role of a responsible opposition. "What we want in America," said Harding in 1920, "is less government in business and more business in government." The ultra-conservative business leaders who took over at this time pursued selfish policies during the poorly shared prosperity that soon lulled the country and only made the eventual economic crash the more disastrous. One result was that the Republicans eventually became as helpless as the Democrats so recently had been.

I. The Return to "Normalcy"

HARDING'S ORDEAL

Of the great gathering in Chicago which in June, 1920, had named Warren G. Harding as the Republican standard-bearer (see p. 685), William Allen White, a lifelong Republican, wrote: "I have never seen a convention—and I have watched most of them since McKinley's first nomination—so completely dominated by sinister predatory economic forces as was this." Not long after, the California Progressive, Hiram Johnson, said: "The war has set the people back for a generation. . . . They are docile; and they will not recover from being so for many years. The interests which control the Republican party will make the most of their docility."

Actually, the principal predators among the new leaders were not to get in their most selfish licks until postwar repression (see p. 691) and "Coolidge Prosperity" (see p. 698) had further softened the people. Harding's own administration was little more than one long betrayal of a man wholly unsuited to the high office by associates whose pleasures were not so innocent as they appeared. Harry Daugherty, a small-time lobbyist for tobacco, meat, and utility interests who first launched the Harding presidential balloon and was rewarded with the Attorney-Generalship, was dismissed by President Coolidge in 1924 when his petty improprieties were revealed. Daugherty had made a business, while in office, of selling liquor permits, pardons, and paroles to criminals at fancy prices. A year earlier, Daugherty's henchman, Jesse Smith, who conducted a sort of clearing-house for the "Ohio gang's" graft, committed suicide and fortunately for Daugherty and others, the gang's worst secrets died with him. Even so a number of administration insiders soon found their way to jail.

Charles R. Forbes, an adventurer and one-time deserter from the army, had so charmed Harding that he had been put in charge of the Veterans' Bureau. Forbes was eventually discovered to have swindled the country of no less than $250 million by demanding kick-backs from compliant contractors and suppliers. Forbes also would condemn supplies meant for veterans and sell them at knock-down prices in return for rebates to himself. In 1925, he was sent to Leavenworth Prison. Colonel Thomas W. Miller, Harding's Alien Property Custodian, in turn, was convicted of conspiracy to defraud the government. For lavish gifts Miller was found to have distributed to American firms for far less than they were worth the valuable German chemical and other patents confiscated during the war.

The most spectacular of the Harding scandals was the notorious Teapot Dome affair. Since 1909, when the conservation movement was in full swing, three tracts of oil-rich public land had been set aside under the jurisdiction of the Secretary of the Navy for navy needs. In 1921, with Navy Secretary Denby's consent, Harding transferred these lands to the custody of his Secretary of the Interior, Albert B. Fall, an intimate of private oil men to whom he had also given the power to lease the oil reserves. Within a year, with no competitive bidding, Fall secretly leased Teapot Dome Reserve in Wyoming to Harry F. Sinclair's Mammoth Oil Company, and soon after leased a second reserve at Elks Hill to a company headed by Edward F. Doheny. Under these leases the private operators were to give the government certain amounts of oil for the privilege of exploiting the fields. For his favoritism, Fall received about $225,000 in Liberty Bonds and a herd of cattle from Sinclair and a "loan" of $100,000 from Doheny, a surge of wealth that soon attracted the interest of vigilant senators. A committee headed by Senator Thomas J. Walsh of Montana gradually untangled the sordid story, the Supreme Court voided the leases, and public demand for Secretary Denby's resignation mounted. Fall, convicted of accepting a bribe, was

690

fined $100,000 and sentenced to a year in prison, though Doheny and Sinclair, oddly enough, were acquitted of having bribed him. Sinclair, nevertheless, found his own way to jail on conviction for contempt of the Senate for refusing to answer questions and contempt of court for having hired detectives to shadow the jury at his trial.

From the start, Harding had been overwhelmed by all but the ceremonial functions of the presidency. Every decision cost him endless hesitations and torments. "I knew this job would be too much for me," he once moaned to a friend. On another occasion he exclaimed to a secretary:

> John, I can't make a damn thing out of this tax problem. I listen to one side and they seem right, and then—God!—I talk to the other side and they seem just as right, and here I am where I started. I know somewhere there is a book that will give me the truth, but, hell, I couldn't read the book. I know somewhere there is an economist who knows the truth, but I don't know where to find him and haven't the sense to know him and trust him when I find him. God! What a job!

Harding had learned of some of the scandals of his administration before they became public. Exhausted by the tasks of his office, tormented by the realization that he had been betrayed by his friends and that the betrayal would forever blacken his name, he sank rapidly under his burdens. In the summer of 1923 he fell ill and on August 2 he died. Still ignorant of the worst of this worst of all administrations, the public went into mourning as deep as that for any president since Lincoln. Even when the worst came out, the public preferred to forget rather than denounce Harding. Indeed, it was the exposers who were denounced. The *New York Times* called Senator Walsh and his colleagues "assassins of character." The *Tribune* called them "scandalmongers," and a prominent patriot charged that "a gigantic international conspiracy" of socialists or communists, he was not sure which, had instigated their probe.

USES OF THE RED SCARE

The almost unshakable tolerance of "normalcy" in the immediate postwar years

was matched by the unprecedented intolerance of any departure from the norm. During the war, as we have seen (p. 678), Americans had grown accustomed to the suppression of dissent; with the war's end, intolerance that had been directed mainly against those suspected of sympathizing with Germany and the Central Powers embraced a wider variety of persons—foreigners in general, Negroes, radicals, strikers. In large part, the new wave of fear could be traced to the Bolshevik Revolution in Russia, after which communist "cells" were set up in many countries, including the United States—a practice that seemed to give credence to Soviet threats to overrun the capitalist world. In part, the scare arose out of labor violence during the immediate postwar economic cycle.

During the war, trade unions had grown enormously in numbers and militancy as workers found them a shield against rising prices. In the short postwar boom of 1919-1920, prices continued to soar and the unions, largely relieved of their wartime no-strike pledges, backed new wage demands with their traditional weapon. In 1919, there were 3,630 strikes involving some 4 million workers, but gains were few. In September, 1919, the A.F.L. struck the United States Steel Corporation, and after violence which left 18 workers dead, the strike collapsed in January, 1920. In November, 1919, the United Mine Workers struck the bituminous coal operators but were forced, a month later, to yield to a federal injunction, after which a few gains were obtained. Most of the strikers sought traditional wage and hour improvements, but some demanded certain more fundamental changes. The railroad workers, for instance, endorsed the widely discussed Plumb Plan, which called for continued government management of the railroads with labor participation. The principal result of this agitation was simply to speed up the return of the railroads to private control. This was

The Wall Street explosion, September 16, 1920, which did so much to keep the red scare alive.

effected by the Esch-Cummins Act of 1920 which enlarged the powers of the Inter-state Commerce Commission over rates and profits, but also, for the first time, author-ized and indeed encouraged the roads to plan combinations that would make their operations more efficient, and some lines did consolidate. The United Mine Workers, in turn, demanded nationalization of the coal mines, to no effect.

Business leaders genuinely feared "radi-calism" of any sort; but they also hoped to make use of the public's fear of communism and anarchism as a weapon against organ-ized labor. The avowed adherents of com-munism and anarchism came to less than 1 per cent of the adult population of the country, but business propaganda ignored this fact and in the general hysteria it was overlooked. To offset "foreign ideologies" employer associations spent large sums pro-moting the "American Plan" to inculcate anti-union attitudes. "We have," said one spokesman, "the school, the pulpit, and the press" through which to "sell" the message.

In 1919 and 1920 a "bomb scare" inten-sified the "red scare." In September, 1920, one bomb exploded in Wall Street breaking the windows in the House of Morgan and killing 38 persons. Other bombs, seemingly aimed at the great capitalists of the country, suggested a concerted "red" conspiracy. Growing fear nurtured growing repression. Preachers, professors, even movie actors who espoused unpopular causes were la-beled as Reds. The New York State Assem-bly expelled five duly elected Socialist members in January, 1920, simply because of their party affiliation.

To extinguish what he called the "prai-rie-fire" of revolution that menaced the country, Wilson's Attorney-General, the one-time reformer, A. Mitchell Palmer, on January 2, 1920, launched a series of raids to round up alien members of the Commu-nist party for deportation. In the course of these raids, federal agents arrested over 6,000 men, many of whom turned out to be neither aliens nor communists. One-third of those arrested were later released. The raids were followed by the eventual deportation of 556 aliens convicted of no crimes.

A few months after the "Palmer raids," two alien Italian anarchists, Nicola Sacco and Bartolomeo Vanzetti, were arrested for a murder that had been committed in connection with a payroll robbery in South Braintree, Massachusetts. In 1921, the two were brought to trial before Judge Webster Thayer and a jury. On the jury's finding them guilty, the Judge sentenced the two defendants to death. At first the trial attracted only slight attention, but as protests against the verdict began to be made throughout the country and the world, more and more Americans questioned its validity. The actual evidence against the men was inadequate, and the suspicion grew that they had been convicted not because they had committed the crime but because of prejudice against their political beliefs. Thayer's conduct at the trial only deepened suspicion of the verdict. An investigation committee appointed by Governor Fuller of Massachusetts concluded that the trial judge had been guilty of a "grave breach of official decorum," but nonetheless, it said, justice had been done.

Motions for appealing the verdict delayed the execution of the two men for years, and Vanzetti's dignified demeanor and his and Sacco's quiet persistence in their anarchist beliefs while their lives hung in the balance won additional sympathy for them. When they were electrocuted at last in 1927, amid a new wave of world-wide protests, millions were convinced of their innocence, and millions more were convinced that, guilty or innocent, they had not been given a fair trial. Scholarly studies almost half a century after the case tend to support the decision of the court, but the worldwide protest against it at the time did much to free the public from the prevailing mood of intolerance.

THE REPRESSION OF "MINORITIES"

Anti-foreign feeling in the wake of the war also brought to a head the anti-

immigration agitation that had been growing since the late nineteenth century (see p. 540). Yankee Brahmins and bluebloods, especially alarmed by the onset of the "new" immigration, had formed the Immigration Restriction League in 1894 to give strength to their demand for closing the gates. These xenophobes had the support of liberals and labor leaders fearful that immigration was threatening the American way of life in general and the workers' standard of living in particular. Businessmen also joined the agitation after measuring the gains of having an unrestricted supply of new workers against the costs of the radical "foreign ideas" with which all immigrants were supposed to be infected.

The agitation for immigration restriction took many forms, but Congress, before the war, appeared to have settled on some version of a literacy test by which to make restriction effective. More, in fact than restriction was aimed at. Since it was the "new" immigration that aroused the greatest apprehension, and since a large proportion of the "new" immigrants were illiterate, the literacy test would serve to bar those from southern and eastern Europe without closing the door against those from other

Sacco (second left) and Vanzetti entering the trial courthouse, Dedham, Massachusetts.

A 1920 cartoon reflecting the growing anti-immigration sentiment which led to new restrictive laws.

European lands. The sponsors of the literacy tests did not try to mask their aims. Such tests, said Senator Henry Cabot Lodge in 1896,

. . . bear most heavily upon the Italians, Russians, Poles, Hungarians, Greeks, and Asiatics, and very lightly, or not at all upon English-speaking immigrants or Germans, Scandinavians, and French.

Lodge held that "the mental and moral qualities which make what we call our race" could be protected only by preserving America from

. . . the wholesale infusion of races whose traditions and inheritances, whose thoughts and beliefs are wholly alien to ours and with whom we have never assimilated or even been associated in the past.

President Cleveland in 1897, Taft in 1913, and Wilson in 1915 and 1917, each vetoed bills requiring some evidence of ability to read or write as a condition for entry to the United States. The 1917 bill, passed over Wilson's veto, became law despite the President's insistence that its effect was simply to close off traditional American opportunity to the poor and was in no sense a test of "mental and moral qualities." By this act no alien over 16 years of age who could not read English or his own language could pass beyond Ellis Island. The ineffectiveness of the literacy test as a selective

device was shown in 1920 and 1921, when, following an almost complete stoppage of immigration during World War I, more than 300,000 Italians entered the country. Congress then embarked on its explicit "quota system" based on "national origins."

The Immigration Restriction Act of 1921, assigned each European nation a quota (most Asiatics were already barred) based on 3 per cent of the number of its nationals resident in the United States in 1910. This measure was expected to limit immigration to about 350,000 persons, largely from northwestern Europe. The National Origins Act of 1924 cut quotas to 2 per cent and made the base year 1890, when the proportion of northwestern Europeans in the American population had been much higher than in 1910. The National Origins Act also shut the door completely on Japanese immigrants, a step which Japan had warned would have "grave consequences," and which she viewed as a national humiliation. The Act of 1924 was to operate only until 1927, after which no more than 150,000 immigrants were to be admitted annually according to quotas based on the ratio of each country's nationals to the whole American population in 1920. In the depression years 1931 to 1939, immigration fell far below even this niggardly allowance, ranging from 12,000 to 63,000 Europeans annually.

Ironically, the desire to restore the "Nordic," Protestant norm in the American population was frustrated to a degree by the failure of these measures to apply to immigrants from Western Hemisphere countries. During the 1920's, almost a million Canadians, many of them French-speaking Catholics, and at least half a million Mexicans, whose enumeration was notoriously careless and whose numbers no doubt were higher, crossed their respective borders to work in the factories of New England and the fields of the South.

A larger and much more significant American migration was that of southern Negroes to northern cities. About 400,000 Negroes served in the armed forces during World War I, half of them overseas in

France, where many, indeed, stayed on. When the war ended, many others, having discovered a way of life unimagined in the cotton fields, sought work in urban industry on being discharged from the service. Here they found many Negroes who had come north during the war to take factory jobs in war production. The Negro population of the North soared from 850,000 in 1910 to 1,400,000 in 1920, and to 2,300,000 in 1930. In northern metropolises such as New York, Chicago, Detroit, Cleveland, and Buffalo, the percentage of Negroes in the population grew by 100 to 250 per cent.

This Negro surge was no more welcome to the white immigrants and other whites than the "new" immigration itself was welcome to the older segments of the population. Racial violence reached such a peak in northern cities in 1919, that that year is still remembered among Negroes as the year of the Red Summer. As Negro numbers grew, discrimination, always present, itself became harsher. Yet life in the South, as in the "old country" for the white immigrant, remained something only to escape if opportunity offered. Race riots in the north were more than matched in killings by the spread of lynching in the South. At the same time, even the most menial industrial job, which is all the Negro attained until he himself gained union strength, offered more hope than share-cropping or farm labor. Northern cities, moreover, offered Negro children education of a kind; the educated, certain white-collar opportunities; the white collar man, certain professional careers. Negroes could become teachers, journalists, doctors, lawyers, however few their number. In the 1920's, moreover, the Negro entertainer, working mainly in New York's Harlem and Chicago's South Side, neither yet a solid, segregated ghetto, became an exotic attraction to white society, a hero to Negro youth, a model of hope and success.

But, like the "new" immigrant, the northern Negro in particular, soon became the target of organized assault, beyond the cruelty of discrimination and segregation. After the red scare, the revival of the Ku

Klux Klan provided the most hateful symptom of intolerance. The Klan of Reconstruction days had died in the 1870's. The new Klan, founded in Georgia in 1915, grew rapidly after 1920 and at its peak in 1924 no less than 4,500,000 "white male persons, native-born Gentile citizens," as they said, had joined the hooded group. On its terroristic night raids, the Klan burned fiery crosses to advertise its presence. It flogged or kidnaped Negroes and whites alike, acted as a moral censor, especially as an enforcement arm for Prohibition (see p. 696), made and unmade local politicians, and cowed union organizers.

By 1924, Klan leaders decided that their favorite target, the Negro, was "not a menace to Americanism in the sense that the Jew or Roman Catholic is a menace," and thereafter, Jews and Catholics bore the brunt of Klan violence. The Klan's political influence by then had become so great that the Democratic national convention, after anguished days of debate that hopelessly split the party, dared not adopt a resolution condemning the group by name. Nor did the Democrats have a monopoly of the Klan problem. In Indiana, the group's leader, D. C. Stephenson, had built up an organization powerful enough to dominate the Republican party. When Stephenson, in November, 1925, was convicted of second-degree murder on the death of a young girl who took poison in their hotel room after he had abducted and assaulted her, he insisted that he had been framed. He took his revenge by giving the newspapers all the sordid details of state officials associated with him. Other exposés disclosed the depths of Klan corruption and soon drove most of its respectable members away.

THE DRY DECADE

The crime and corruption fostered in the 'twenties by the attempt, under the Eighteenth Amendment (see p. 653), to suppress the traditional drinking habits of the

American people made the old time saloon look like an innocent institution. In anticipation of the Amendment's becoming law in 1920, Congress in October, 1919, over President Wilson's veto, passed the Volstead Act to implement it. The act defined intoxicating liquor as any beverage containing more than one-half of 1 per cent of alcohol, and forbade any person, except for religious and medical purposes, to "manufacture, sell, barter, transport, import, export, deliver, furnish, or possess" such beverage without a license. The Commissioner of Internal Revenue was to enforce the act.

Making liquor illegal had two immediate results. The old saloon gave way to the covert "speakeasy" where drinking soon took on the glamour of a seemingly harmless conspiracy. At the same time, by putting outside the pale of the law a personal habit that millions of Americans would not give up, Prohibition opened up a new field for city gangs. Gangs had existed in American cities before Prohibition, often exercising power over local government. National Prohibition made liquor the main source of gang income, raised that income to sybaritic levels, and enlarged gang domination of local police and local politics. Congress, although forced by public pressure to play ball with the "drys," never voted enough money for more than token enforcement of the Volstead Act. The Commissioner of Internal Revenue rarely had as many as 2,000 prohibition agents to police the entire country, whereas the Capone gang alone had a private army in Chicago of at least a thousand well-armed thugs. Capone's and hundreds of other gangs quickly gained control of the undercover liquor business—bootlegging, rum-running, and speakeasy operation. At its peak, the Capone gang took in $60 million a year.

Criticism of the "noble experiment," as it was called, grew louder and louder as its fruits ripened. Much of the criticism arose within the Democratic party, which appealed more strongly than the Republicans to those elements in the population, at least in the North, for whom drinking was an immemorial social custom. It became an issue in the campaign of 1928, when Al Smith proposed to do away with national Prohibition and return the problem to the states. Herbert Hoover, his Republican opponent (see p. 705), temporized. After his election, Hoover named a commission headed by the distinguished lawyer, George W. Wickersham, to study enforcement problems. Its report, published in January, 1931, reviewed all the evils of the "experiment" in frank detail; yet a majority of the commission urged its continuance, failure though it was. As a contemporary columnist put it:

> Prohibition is an awful flop.
>   We like it.
> It can't stop what it's meant to stop.
>   We like it.
> It's left a trail of graft and slime,
> It's filled our land with vice and crime,
> It don't prohibit worth a dime,
>   Nevertheless, we're for it.

After the Democratic victory in the election of 1932, Congress, in February, 1933, adopted the Twenty-first Amendment repealing the Eighteenth, and by the end of the year the repeal amendment had been ratified. With control of liquor returned to the states only seven chose to continue Prohibition. Mississippi, in 1966, became the last of the seven to go "wet." Some states continued to give communities a "local option" on the issue.

FUNDAMENTALISM ON TRIAL

The repression of foreigners and "foreign" ideologies and habits soon carried over to the repression of free thought in general. Here, among the Klansmen and the "drys," Protestant fundamentalists, demanding a literal reading of the Bible and resisting all modifications in theology in the light of modern scientific discovery or Biblical criticism, led the assault. Their crusade against science, like the prohibitionists' crusade against drink, was simply the effort of a minority to shore up a failing scheme of values by resorting to legal compulsion.

The Darwinian theory of evolution be-

came the particular target of fundamentalist assaults. A Tennessee law forbidding the
teaching of evolution in public schools
loomed as an object of fascination to the
country when a high-school teacher, John
T. Scopes, was tried for violating it in 1925.
Reporters came from all over the nation to
cover the trial, at which William Jennings
Bryan joined the prosecution and Clarence
Darrow headed the defense. The climax
came with Darrow subjecting Bryan himself
to pitiless questioning that exposed his
ignorance and inconsistencies. Bryan died
shortly after his ordeal. Scopes, found
guilty, was fined the nominal sum of $100,
but the country's ridicule thereafter took
much of the sting from fundamentalist
attacks.

THE DEFENSE OF DISSENT

Those who cared deeply about
American traditions of freedom of expression and personal liberty found the
right-wing hysteria, ethnic intolerance, and
anti-intellectualism of the postwar years
disheartening. In 1922, when fears of radicalism had waned somewhat, Katherine
Fullerton Gerould still could write in
Harper's Magazine:

America is no longer a free country in the
old sense; and liberty is, increasingly, a mere
rhetorical figure. . . . No thinking citizen, I
venture to say, can express in freedom more
than a part of his honest convictions. . . . The
only way in which [he] . . . can preserve any
freedom of expression, is to choose the mob that
is most sympathetic to him, and abide under the
shadow of that mob.

Yet the forces of freedom would not be
silenced altogether. When the New York
Legislature expelled its five Socialist members in 1920 (see p. 692), Governor Alfred
E. Smith commented:

Although I am unalterably opposed to the
fundamental principles of the Socialist Party,
it is inconceivable that a minority party, duly
constituted and legally organized, should be
deprived of its right to expression, so long as
it has honestly, by lawful methods of education
and propaganda, succeeded in securing rep-

resentation, unless the chosen representatives
are unfit as individuals. . . .

Our faith in American democracy is confirmed not only by its results, but by its
methods and organs of free expression. They
are the safeguards against revolution. To dis-
card the methods of representative government
leads to the misdeeds of the very extremists we
denounce . . . and serves to increase the number
of the enemies of orderly free government.

True to these principles, Smith vetoed a
proposed loyalty oath for teachers, laws to
limit political freedom in New York, and
similar measures. When the legislature
wished to set up an elaborate apparatus to
hunt out and prosecute "criminal anarchy,"
Smith fought it. "The traditional abhorrence of a free people of all kinds of spies
and secret police," he said, "is valid and
justified and calls for the disapproval of
this measure."

Supreme Court Justice Oliver Wendell
Holmes was another who often cautioned
against indiscriminate attempts to suppress
unpopular ideas. In *Schenck* v. *U.S.* (1919),
Holmes upheld the Socialist Schenck's conviction for conspiracy in distributing a circular aimed to obstruct the wartime draft.
In so doing, however, he tried to draw a
line between those forms of speech that
must be protected and those to be classified
as dangerous to the state. "The character
of every act depends upon the circumstances in which it is done," he said. "The
most stringent protection of free speech
would not protect a man in falsely shouting
fire in a theatre and causing a panic. . . .
The question in every case is whether the
words used are used in such circumstances
and are of such nature as to create a clear
and present danger that they will bring
about the substantive evils that Congress
has a right to prevent." This "clear and
present danger" test for free speech was
cited in many later decisions.

Holmes himself soon found occasion to
apply his test in an eloquent dissenting
opinion in a case superficially similar to

Schenck's—the case of *Abrams* v. *U.S.* (1919), in which a majority of the Court upheld the conviction of a group of Russian emigrants for distributing leaflets opposing American intervention in Russia. Holmes held that the specific statements made by the defendants did not constitute a threat to the government or to the conduct of its war against Germany. The Court had departed, he insisted, from the reasonable line it had drawn in the Schenck case. "Congress certainly cannot forbid all effort to change the mind of the country," he said. "Only the emergency that makes it immediately dangerous to leave the correction of evil counsels to time warrants making any exception to the sweeping command, 'Congress shall make no law . . . abridging the freedom of speech.'"

A third outstanding opponent of intolerance, especially that of the Klan, was William Allen White, the popular editor from Emporia, Kansas. "The thought," White said in 1924, "that Kansas should have a government beholden to this hooded gang of masked fanatics, ignorant and tyrannical in their ruthless oppression," prompted him, in September, to announce his candidacy for governor on an independent ticket, in protest against the Republican party's nomination of a man whom the Klan strongly supported. Though defeated, as he had expected, White succeeded in securing the election of members to the State Charter Board who refused to issue the Klan a charter to operate in Kansas. Moreover, White told one friend, "The fact that I could get out and spit in the face of the Klan, and had done it, has cleared up the atmosphere." White probably was correct about that, and in any case, as the decade wore on, a certain spirited iconoclasm and shedding of taboos were to give the 'twenties a lasting lively tone (see Chapter 28).

II. *The Politics of Complacency*

THE ELECTION OF 1924

Among the most widely reported of the postwar strikes had been that of the Boston police in 1919. Governor Calvin Coolidge of Massachusetts so resoundingly proclaimed his own role in breaking that strike that he won a national reputation that earned him the nomination for vice-president the next year. When Harding died in 1923, Coolidge inherited the postwar problems of the country; but the full force of these problems was postponed for some years by the beginning of a business boom. By 1924, "Coolidge prosperity" had become so real that it was a foregone conclusion that the Republican convention in Cleveland would name him to seek the presidency in his own right. To run for vice-president the convention named Charles G. Dawes, a Chicago lawyer and banker.

A boon to the G.O.P., "Coolidge prosperity" was only one of the hurdles the Democrats faced in 1924. One faction, which backed the candidacy of William G. McAdoo, Wilson's son-in-law and Secretary of the Treasury, found its strength in the rural, Protestant, "dry" segments of the party. A second faction, whose candidate was the "Happy Warrior," New York's Catholic Governor, Alfred E. Smith, drew its support from the city machines and the "wets." After a furious convention battle in the broiling heat of a New York City summer over the question of denouncing the Klan (see p. 695), the McAdoo and Smith forces fell into a sullen deadlock that lasted 16 days. When it became clear that the party was so badly wrecked that the nomination was worthless, the delegates settled on John W. Davis, an impeccably conservative New York corporation lawyer. To conciliate the more reform-minded Democrats, the convention named as his running-mate William Jennings Bryan's brother, Charles.

A third candidate also was in the field— Robert M. La Follette, nominated at last on a Progressive party ticket. Senator Burton K. Wheeler of Montana, one of the leading investigators in the Teapot Dome affair, bolted from the Democrats to accept the Progressive vice-presidential nomination.

In the campaign, both major candidates concentrated their fire on La Follette whom they charged with encouraging the radicalism that had become such a bogy in the public mind. La Follette, nevertheless, polled nearly 5 million votes. Davis received 8,386,000 votes, and Coolidge a thumping 15,725,000. The size of Coolidge's majority, after that won by Harding in 1920, showed that the customary two-party struggle in American politics had temporarily ended and that the Republican party would have a free hand.

REPUBLICAN
ECONOMIC POLICIES

"Coolidge prosperity" seemed, by 1924, to have justified the economic measures taken by Republican leaders before their smashing success that year. Perhaps most influential among these leaders was Andrew Mellon, the immensely wealthy head of the aluminum trust, owner of oil companies, steel mills, utilities and banks, a lavish contributor to the party, who became Secretary of the Treasury in 1921. Herbert Hoover once called Mellon "the greatest Secretary of the Treasury since Alexander Hamilton." A more cynical observer remarked that Mellon was the only Secretary of the Treasury under whom three presidents had served, Hoover included.

Despite the $24 billion national debt created largely by the war, Mellon favored the prompt reduction of taxes to encourage business enterprise. "Anybody knows," he once said, "that any man of energy and initiative can get what he wants out of life. But when that initiative is crippled by legislation or a tax system which denies him the right to receive a reasonable share of his earnings, then he will no longer exert himself and the country will be deprived of the energy on which its continued greatness depends."

In accord with Mellon's philosophy, the Revenue Act of 1921 repealed the wartime excess profits tax and reduced the surtax, but a revolt of Senate progressives staved off further cuts for the time being. Then in

a series of five acts from 1924 and 1929 Congress slashed tax rates, to the delight of the wealthy. Despite the tax cuts, business prosperity made it possible to reduce the national debt to $16 billion by 1930. By leaving great untaxed sums in the hands of corporations and private individuals who could find no sound investment outlets for them, however, Mellon's tax policies probably abetted the speculation in securities and real estate that preceded the stock market crash of 1929.

As taxes went down, tariffs went up. The Fordney-McCumber Act of 1922 raised duties to record levels, thereby making repayment to war debts in goods more difficult for Allied countries. It also led other nations to adopt retaliatory tariffs against American exports. Nonetheless, protection was part of "normalcy," and it remained so popular that in 1930 the Hawley-Smoot Tariff raised many duties higher than ever. More than a thousand economists petitioned President Hoover to veto the act, but to no avail, and foreign retaliatory measures hit American exports a severe blow.

Apparently pleased to keep American enterprise from competing abroad, the Republican administrations also moved to circumscribe competition at home. To the chairmanship of the Federal Trade Commission, President Coolidge appointed W. E. Humphrey, who promised that it would no longer be, as he called it, "a publicity bureau to spread socialistic propaganda." The F.T.C. began to encourage one business conference after another for the purpose of making industry-wide agreements on trade practices.

As Secretary of Commerce under both Harding and Coolidge, Herbert Hoover encouraged corporations to cooperate with one another by sharing information, accepting codes of fair practice, and standardizing products to eliminate waste. In some respects, the codes of fair practice, some 200 of which were put into operation, anticipated the codes later adopted under Franklin D. Roosevelt's N.R.A. (see p. 717). Unhampered by the threat of anti-trust prosecution, businessmen in the 1920's went on an unprecedented merger spree. In the field of public utilities alone, 3,744 firms were swallowed up, and comparable consolidations occurred in banking, transportation, and trade.

Organized labor, by contrast, lost ground during these years. The serious strikes against the steel, coal, meat and railroad industries from 1919 to 1922 had failed. Increasingly, employers recruited workers into company unions, whose members numbered over 1.5 million by 1929. Other unions, except those of traditionally organized skilled craftsmen, were kept out of most industries by employers' open shop drives. A.F.L. membership, at a high of 4,078,000 in 1920, fell to about 3 million in 1923, where it remained until 1929.

Thirty-four states liberalized workmen's compensation laws in the 'twenties, but labor and social legislation fared badly in the courts. Two Supreme Court cases in 1921, *Duplex Printing Press* v. *Deering,* and *Truax* v. *Corrigan,* exposed strikers to injunctions thought to be illegal under the Clayton Act (see p. 663). In 1922, in *Bailey* v. *Drexel Furniture Company,* the Court held that child labor could not constitutionally be regulated by a discriminatory tax levied on products manufactured by children. The next year, in *Adkins* v. *Children's Hospital,* the Court struck down an act of Congress establishing minimum wages for women and children in the District of Columbia. Only in 1932, after the depression had created a new political mood, did the forces of labor succeed in pushing through Congress the Norris-LaGuardia Act against labor injunctions, a measure President Hoover reluctantly signed.

THE POWER ISSUE

During the war, when it became clear that something had to be done to insure the steady supply of nitrates for making explosives, the government built two nitrate plants at Muscle Shoals on the Tennessee River in Alabama, and began construction of a power dam, later named Wilson Dam. At the war's end, work on the dam ceased and the House cut off further funds for the entire development. Disturbed by this action, Senator Norris of Nebraska, chairman of the Committee on Agriculture, argued that the Tennessee River projects represented an immense wasted asset, and that steps should be taken to complete the dam and bring it and the plants' power into operation. Norris had a good case, for the idled plants and the unfinished dam so far had cost the government $145 million.

Characteristically, the government at this time decided to solve the problem by leasing the sites for private power development. Henry Ford made an offer for them that captured the public imagination, but it also raised the distressing thought that the Tennessee Valley might fall into the hands of a single millionaire noted for his personal crochets and petty tyrannies. Congress hesitated to take positive action for private power development, while the private utilities fought all efforts to keep Muscle Shoals a public project.

Finally, in 1928, Norris introduced a bill for government production and sale of power from Wilson Dam and manufacture and sale of fertilizer. Congress, with widespread support from agricultural areas, passed the bill in May, 1928, only to have Coolidge kill it by a pocket veto. In 1931, Hoover, as president, vetoed a similar measure in a message famous for its philosophical portents. "I hesitate," he wrote,

to contemplate the future of our institutions, of our country, if the preoccupation of its officials is to be no longer the promotion of justice and equal opportunity but is to be devoted to barter in the markets. That is not liberalism, it is degeneration. . . . Muscle Shoals can only be administered by the people upon the ground, responsible to their own communities, directing them solely for the benefit of their communities, and not for purposes of pursuit of social theories of national politics.

And there the matter rested until the Roosevelt administration adopted an entirely new policy with the establishment of the Tennessee Valley Authority in 1933.

THE FARMER
IN PEACETIME

The nation's most serious economic problem in the 1920's was agricultural distress, especially among growers of such staple crops as wheat, cotton and corn who remained saddled with debt from wartime overexpansion (see p. 675). Dairy, vegetable and fruit farmers prospered from nearby expanding city markets. Staple farmers had to compete in world markets where stronger competition from Canadian, Australian, and Argentine wheat, and Brazilian, Egyptian, and Indian cotton, added to their woes. When women turned from cotton to rayon fabrics, and families altered diets to include more fruits and vegetables at the expense of pork, beef, and flour, the pinch on the staple farmer tightened. Republican leaders urged higher tariffs as the sovereign remedy for farmers as for businessmen. But tariffs brought exporters no balm; indeed, they further injured the farmer by provoking foreign retaliation in the form of higher duties against American agricultural exports. Net farm income, including that of prosperous dairy and truck farmers, fell from almost $9.5 billion in 1919 to $5.3 billion in 1928.

Farm distress helped create a strong farm bloc in Congress which sponsored a complicated program for farm aid in the McNary-Haugen bill. Twice defeated earlier, this bill was passed in 1927 and again in 1928, only to be vetoed both times by the President. "Farmers have never made money," Coolidge averred. "I don't believe we can do much about it." But the farm bloc also had its successes. The Agricultural Credits Act of 1923 created 12 Intermediate Credit Banks, capitalized by the government, to make loans to farm cooperatives; it also encouraged private investors to extend agricultural credit. The Agricultural Marketing Act of 1929 set up the Federal Farm Board to stimulate the growth of cooperatives and endowed it with a revolving fund of $500 million to assist such agencies, through purchases and other means, to hold staple surpluses off the market and thereby support prices. These measures failed to improve the farmer's lot largely because of each grower's determination to maximize his own crop. Yet, in an adverse political environment, they sustained the pressure for a broad federal farm program first developed by the Grange and soon to culminate in New Deal measures (see p. 719).

III. *The "Golden Glow"*

THE GENUINENESS
OF PROSPERITY

Staple farmers were not the only Americans excluded from the general prosperity of the 'twenties. Irving Bernstein calls his outstanding history of labor in this period *The Lean Years,* and in certain specialized industries and areas, such as textile manufacturing in New England and the southern piedmont and coal mining in Kentucky, suffering was acute. Yet the economy as a whole did well. With prices holding steady, "real income" for each person in the country rose on average between 1921 and

1929, from $522 to $716; for each person gainfully employed real income rose from $1,308 to $1,716. These striking gains reflected a tremendous increase in the productivity of the individual worker, brought about by improved technology based mainly on the application of electricity to manufacturing, and by improved procedures derived in part from theories of "scientific management" popularized by Frederick Winslow Taylor and his followers. The fact that the stock market magnified even the real progress of the American economy, especially during the later phases of the boom, has caused emphasis to be placed on the speculative side of business during the 'twenties. This emphasis is proper, for Wall Street, though no longer the bellwether of the economy, remained more closely related to its operations than at any time since. Yet the stock-market surge—and the stock-market crash of 1929—have tended to obscure many of the genuine gains of the period and how they were won.

The First World War itself contributed significantly to the boom. For one thing, the Liberty and Victory bond drives had accustomed millions to investing in securities and thus made it easier for postwar corporations to finance new or expanded ventures with stocks and bonds without knuckling under to the conservative oligarchy of the old money trust. Many corporations, moreover, made so much money during the war that they could often pay for expanded or improved facilities without going to the money market at all. Wartime tax policies heightened the effect of wartime financial policies. In particular, the excess-profits tax of the war years had prompted corporations to plow back their heavy earnings into modernized, electrified low-production-cost plant and equipment which paid off in productivity and profits when the war was over. Wartime labor shortages, in turn, often made such technological advances mandatory for survival.

Many industries that came of age in the 'twenties also were created by the war or matured by its demands. In 1903, Wilbur and Orville Wright had made the first successful flight in a motor-driven heavier-than-air contraption at Kitty Hawk, North Carolina. But airplane progress languished until the war proved the practicality of the new machines for scouting and eventually for combat. After the war, flyers home from the battlefield worked up a considerable business taking enthusiasts up for two to five minute flights. Transcontinental air-mail service began in 1920 and the first regularly scheduled flights—between Chicago and Cheyenne—three years later. The Air Commerce Act of 1926 gave substantial mail subsidies to private airlines and helped make commercial flying a big business. After Charles A. Lindbergh in May, 1927, made his momentous solo flight from New York to Paris, flying became more popular than ever. By 1930, 122 American airlines were carrying almost half a million passengers over 50,000 miles of air routes. All told, airline planes that year flew about 37 million miles, a spectacular 360 per cent increase over so recent a year as 1928.

The First World War gave the American chemical industry an even greater boost than it gave flying. Before 1914, American chemical companies had produced little but the simple heavy acids and alkalies used in basic industrial processes. During the war, explosives became the principal product of the industry and many new chemical plants were built to supply the needs of the Allies. Once the war was over, two government measures effectively stimulated the growth of a great chemical industry. The first was the confiscation of German coal-tar patents and their assignment to American chemical corporations. The second, motivated by popular demand for chemical self-sufficiency in the event of another war, was the imposition of forbiddingly high duties on chemical imports. By 1929, certain beneficiaries of these measures, such as Allied Chemicals, Union Carbide, and the old DuPont company, had far outstripped all foreign chemical firms or cartels. The American chemical industry that year produced new plastics, alloys, and "allied products" as well as the older acids and alkalies valued at $3,750,000,000.

THE ELECTROCHEMICAL REVOLUTION

In conjunction with electricity, chemicals revolutionized a number of other industries. Signal advances in the production of electricity itself fostered this development. Between 1920 and 1929, the rise in the efficiency of the power industry was such that a 25 per cent increase in coal burned brought a 100 per cent increase in kilowatt hours generated. Such progress so cheapened electric power by 1929 that 70 per cent of American factory machinery was operated by electricity, compared with but 30 per cent 15 years before. The most striking gains from the combination of electrical and chemical processes were made in the petroleum industry, fortunately for the burgeoning automobile industry itself. Between 1913 and 1928, electrochemical processes tripled the quantity of gasoline that could be refined from a gallon of crude oil. Electrochemical processes in the steel industry, in the meantime, led to sharp improvements in the quality of the parts of internal-combustion engines, which thus burned with much higher efficiency the gasoline so much more efficiently produced. The combination of electricity and chemistry in metallurgy also brought marked gains in the manufacture of such commodities as floor lamps, phonographs, refrigerators, radios, washing machines, vacuum cleaners, and other adjuncts of the good life.

Besides revolutionizing industrial technology in the 1920's electricity revolutionized factory organization and procedures. By permitting the transmission of power over tremendous distances, it freed the factory from the river valley and the coal field and gave management much greater opportunity to consider proximity to markets and other "location" factors in deciding on factory sites. By permitting the even flow of power throughout huge plants, electricity added immensely to the flexibility of organization within the factory as well. Electricity made much more efficient than heretofore the "straight-line" system of production, the conveyor and the moving assembly line. It opened the way to economies in the production of interchangeable parts that would have astounded Eli Whitney. It also put a premium on the standardization of jobs and commodities.

THE AUTOMOBILE COMES
OF AGE

No industry was more firmly rooted in the technological and managerial changes of the postwar years than the automobile industry. For the rubber, glass, and alloys of which body and engine parts were made, the automobile manufacturers depended in-

creasingly on the new chemical and electrical knowledge and the new electro-chemical processes. Ultimately, the automobile manufacturers grew into the greatest users of each of the commodities that went into the automobile, and work on automobile assembly lines became more highly mechanized and repetitive than elsewhere.

American experience firmly underpinned the growth of automobile production. From the nation's earliest days men had been trained by the carriage manufacturers in the making of bodies, springs, and wheels. Since the 1820's the building of steamboats and locomotives, and since the 1850's the building of farm machinery, had developed a widespread familiarity with engines. In the last decades of the nineteenth century tricycle and bicycle manufacturers had spurred the development of pneumatic tires. The American environment, in turn, reinforced the impact of American technological experience. The United States was a country of majestic distances and of a growing middle class which was sufficiently prosperous to purchase thousand-dollar commodities in which they could traverse the wide-open spaces with satisfying speed and comfort.

Experiments to produce a "horseless carriage" had been conducted in Europe and the United States through most of the nineteenth century, with steam, electricity, alcohol, and other fuels as the motive force. In 1877 George B. Selden of Rochester, New York, built a workable vehicle employing a gasoline engine which he failed to patent until 1895. By then many other experimenters had entered the field, but not until about 1903 did the automobile become commercially feasible. By 1910 about 60 American companies were producing cars for sale, and General Motors, a combination promoted by William C. Durant to bring the chaotic competition in the industry under control, was two years old.

One of the most vulnerable aspects of the

Body drop, outdoor assembly at Ford plant, Highland Park, Michigan, 1915.

General Motors combine was Durant's failure to get Ford into it. By 1908 Henry Ford was already a prominent automobile manufacturer. The next year he introduced the renowned "tin lizzie," Model T, in "any color you choose so long as it's black," list price $950. By 1913 Model T had been brought down to $550 and Ford sold 168,000 of them—a volume representing about one-third of the whole automobile business of the country that year. In 1914, Ford opened his revolutionary plant at Highland Park, Michigan, equipped with the first electric conveyor belt, which carried the gradually assembled car at a uniform—and rapid—speed past stationary workers, each equipped with the materials and tools to perform his one simple mechanical task. In 1913 it had taken 14 hours, on the average, for workers to assemble a Model T. In the new plant they could do it in 93 minutes. In 1914, Ford produced 248,000 cars—45 per cent of the total automobile output—at a base price of $490. His profit that year exceeded $30 million. By 1925, Ford was turning out a complete car every ten seconds; but by then people were beginning to tire of the tin lizzie and the drift toward more distinctive

models with more comfortable appointments had begun in earnest.

In 1920 about 9 million automobiles were registered in the United States. By 1930 registration had risen to nearly 30 million. "We'd rather do without clothes than give up the car," said a "Middletown" housewife in the mid-1920's. "I'll go without food before I'll see us give up the car," said another.

A SMALL CLOUD HOVERS

While the new production techniques and new consumer-goods industries were giving a golden glow to "Coolidge prosperity," the older industries were contributing their share. Throughout American history the real key to the health of the economy has been the private construction industry, which, traditionally, engaged more capital and more labor than any other, including railroading. Not only did the American population grow continuously at a high rate, creating new or enlarged families that required new housing, but the mobility of the people from farm to city, from town to town, from low-paying to higher-paying jobs, all intensified the demand. In the 'twenties houses were built at a record rate, partly to compensate for the slowdown in construction during the

704

war. Records also were set in industrial building and the rebuilding of railroad facilities worn out by wartime traffic. The remarkable growth of the power industry and in home and factory electrification, in turn, stimulated the construction of new power plants and distributing facilities. Finally, there was government construction, never, since the days of the canals, a negligible factor in the economy.

In the 1920's a large new item began to appear in local, state, and federal budgets: outlays for paved-road building. As late as 1921, "Chains on all four wheels" and "a shovel with a collapsible handle" were prescribed equipment for touring by automobile. In the next ten years government expenditure for street and highway construction exceeded the capital outlay for most private industries. This was, in effect, a hidden subsidy to the automobile industry and indeed to the entire economy. When private investment slowed down in the late 'twenties and government outlays failed to compensate for this weakness, the crash and the depression loomed.

In part, this weakness could be attributed to a second imbalance in the economy which weakened it even more: the maldistribution of income and wealth (see p. 707). Still other small clouds hovered, but for all but a few, the "golden glow" of the prevailing good times obscured them. America seemed to have discovered the perpetual motion prosperity machine, and little sympathy was wasted on those who did not bask in its accomplishments. In the summer of 1929, John J. Raskob, the millionaire chairman of the Democratic National Committee, said:

If a man saves $15 a week, and invests in good common stocks, and allows the dividends and rights to accumulate, at the end of twenty years he will have at least $80,000 and an income from investments of around $400 a month. He will be rich. And because income can do that, I am firm in my belief that anyone not only can be rich, but ought to be rich.

"We in America," declared the newly elected President Hoover at this time, "are nearer to the final triumph over poverty

than ever before in the history of any land. . . . We have not reached the goal, but given a chance to go forward with the policies of the last eight years, we shall soon with the help of God be in sight of the day when poverty will be banished from this nation."

THE ELECTION OF 1928

Hoover's election in 1928 reflected the nation's mood. Gone was the lingering discontent that four years earlier caused almost 5 million Americans to vote for Robert La Follette. Calvin Coolidge had laid down the popular dictum, that "the business of the United States is business." When "Silent Cal" also let slip the announcement that he did not "choose to run" again in 1928, Republican leaders took him at his word and turned, appropriately, to his Secretary of Commerce, Herbert Hoover.

Born in modest circumstances on an Iowa farm, Hoover had enjoyed a rewarding career as an engineer and promoter farther west and in other countries before winning acclaim for relief work in Europe during World War I. After the war, he was also credited with having used American plenty to thwart the advance of communism. These activities had added to his reputation for practicality a reputation for humanitarianism. His attacks on the many unwise aspects of peacemaking, in turn, gave him standing as a statesman. The Eng-

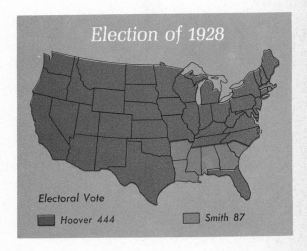

Election of 1928

Electoral Vote
Hoover 444   Smith 87

lish economist, John Maynard Keynes, wrote of him: "Mr. Hoover was the only man who emerged from the ordeal of Paris with an enhanced reputation." Hoover's long career as Secretary of Commerce provided further proof of his administrative skill. He had never run for office, but the politicians agreed that he would make a formidable candidate.

To oppose Hoover the Democrats this time united behind "Al" Smith, an engaging symbol for politically awakening immigrants of the chances of the common man to rise. As Governor of New York, as we have seen (p. 697), Smith had made an excellent record in supporting liberal legislation and liberal ideas. But this record seemed irrelevant to the nation at large. Smith was an Irishman, a Catholic, a New Yorker, and a "wet"—in short the incarnation of everything calculated to arouse the suspicions of rural and smalltown America.

Many anti-Catholics of the sort who had supported the Klan believed that Smith's election would bring the Pope himself to Washington to take over the government. A whispering campaign that gained particular influence in the South spread this idea.

In the light of Hoover's initial advantages, it seems unlikely that any Democrat could have beaten him. His popular majority exceeded 6 million votes, and he carried all but eight states, including, for the first time since Reconstruction, five in the Solid South. Smith's defeat, nevertheless, left a lasting wound among many Catholics who blamed bigotry alone for it. Other Democrats could have found some balm in Smith's performance. His vote doubled that of Davis in 1924; and in the country's 12 largest cities, strongly Republican in the two preceding presidential elections, his total vote exceeded Hoover's. The future, moreover, lay with the urban voter.

IV. *The Politics of Depression*

THE GREAT CRASH

Herbert Hoover, after taking the oath of office as President of the United States on March 4, 1929, opened his inaugural address with this statement: "If we survey the situation of our Nation at home and abroad, we find many satisfactions." In his closing paragraph, in words still brimming with euphoria, he listed some of them:

Ours is a land rich in resources; stimulating in its glorious beauty; filled with millions of happy homes; blessed with comfort and opportunity. In no nation are the institutions of progress more advanced. In no nation are the fruits of accomplishment more secure.

Less than eight months later, on October 29, 1929, as *The New York Times* said, "stock prices . . . swept downward with gigantic losses in the most disastrous trading day in the stock market's history." In a few hours more than $10 billion of America's "fruits of accomplishment" were washed away. During the next few years,

the "glorious beauty" of the American West, as an observer told Congress, had been caught by "unemployed timber workers and bankrupt farmers" who started forest fires in the State of Washington that raged all summer, "in an endeavor to earn a few honest dollars as fire fighters"; America's bankrupt "happy homes" had closed their doors on thousands of unemployed women who even in winter slept in the public parks; America's shrunken "opportunity" had drawn "more than 100,000 applications" from such heavily industrialized states as Pennsylvania, Michigan, Massachusetts, and Ohio, according to *Business Week* magazine, for 6,000 skilled jobs in Russia that had been announced by the New York office of Amtorg.

When Hoover spoke of the "many satisfactions" in the "situation of our Nation" in his inaugural, he also said, "we find some causes for concern." The "most malign" of these "is disregard and disobedience of law," largely "due to the additional burdens imposed upon our judicial system by the

President Hoover and Spelling Bee winners.

eighteenth amendment." But the "great crash" and the "great depression" soon disclosed more serious flaws than Prohibition in the American way of life. The rhetoric of business success obscured even what some men were willing to grant might be "pockets" of economic distress. The betrayal of the rhetoric by the disastrous course of events disclosed more pockets than had been acknowledged, larger ones than had been supposed, and their tendency to grow and fester.

Throughout the 'twenties, as we have seen (p. 700), the deepening distress among the staple farmers drained much of the purchasing power needed to sustain the demand for industrial goods. Among industrial workers, at the same time, unemployment remained stubbornly high, only once, in 1926, dropping under a million, and in 1924 and 1928 soaring over 2 million—a condition that further weakened commodity markets. Worse than these telltale trends was the uneven distribution of income and wealth even among those who basked in the boom. The slowly rising real wages of industrial workers were outdistanced by the

salaries, savings, and profits of those higher on the economic ladder. In 1929, the 24,000 richest families had an aggregate income more than three times as large as that of the 5.8 million poorest families, and 40 per cent of all families had incomes under $1,500. No wonder general consumer purchasing power failed to keep pace with the production potential of the modern industrial plant. During the 'twenties, advertising became a favorite panacea for stimulating sales of consumer goods. But advertising, by and large, only stimulates wants, not ability to pay. Purchasing power was stretched by the extraordinary development of installment selling and "personal credit" agencies. But these also reached their limits when it was discovered that people were paying more for interest than for goods. "Welfare capitalism," including employee stock ownership and profit-sharing, much publicized in the 'twenties, was really a union busting device and did little to spread the wealth.

Those who were getting rich, meanwhile, found their savings piling up out of all proportion to the opportunities for sound investment and soon turned to speculation in real estate and securities. Speculation, as so often in the past, turned the whole economy into a "bubble" sure to burst. The economic situation abroad only extended the disaster. European nations depended on American credit for the imports they needed to restore their battered economies and to stabilize their currencies. But credit had limits which were the more speedily reached because American tariffs kept out European goods which would have helped scale down European debts. American manufacturers, in turn, thus found it harder and harder to sell abroad. The American and European economies were so closely linked that the depression soon became world-wide.

At first, many optimists decided that the depression had been touched off merely by a failure of confidence. Hoover himself insisted that "the fundamental business of the country, the production and distribution of commodities, is on a sound and prosperous basis." "Prosperity is just around the corner," he kept saying, like a prayer that went unanswered. His political opponents soon turned these phrases into sharp-edged weapons. The Republicans had claimed as "Coolidge prosperity" a prosperity that Coolidge had done nothing to protect. Now the Democrats pinned the label "Hoover depression" to a crash that Hoover had done little to bring about.

THE SHORT REACH
OF GOVERNMENT
For all his stress on confidence, Hoover did realize that the country was sick as well as sad, and his administration took certain somatic as well as psychological measures to cure it. In 1930, when the collapse of wheat and cotton prices assumed the dimensions of a catastrophe, the Federal Farm Board, set up the year before (see p. 701), formed a Grain Stabilization Corporation and Cotton Stabilization Corporation to buy these staples in the open market in the hope of stemming the decline. For a time this policy succeeded; but when government warehouses bulged with surpluses that dealers felt might be released at any

time, staple prices felt the pressure and resumed their slide. By 1932, both corporations suspended operations. Cotton, which brought 16 cents a pound in 1929, now sold for 6 cents. Wheat fell from $1.00 to 38 cents a bushel.

The administration also took steps to help industry and labor. Early in 1930 Congress granted the President $700 million for public works. This was only the start of an unprecedented program that saw Hoover spend almost $3 billion on public construction. The President also tried to get business leaders to delay discharges and wage cuts. Many industrialists strove to comply with the President's suggestions, but they could not long keep men at work and their wages up when no markets materialized. By 1932, 12 million were unemployed and the wages of the rest plummeted. As great corporations faced bankruptcy, insurance companies and philanthropic organizations that had so confidently invested in corporate securities also were menaced. To help shore them up, Congress, in January, 1932, created the Reconstruction Finance Corporation. By the end of the year, the R.F.C. had loaned $1.5 billion to about 5,000 companies.

Hoover believed that the burden of paying inter-governmental debts was a great drag on world trade and world recovery. In June, 1931, therefore, he proposed a one-year moratorium on debt payments, a pro-

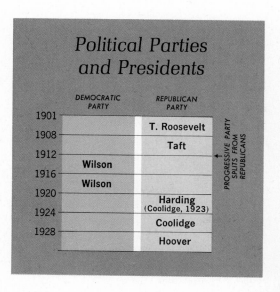

posal accepted by the 15 governments involved. A more drastic step would have been to cancel the obligations outright, which, in effect, was the outcome of Hoover's step, since, on the ending of the moratorium in 1932, only five governments made their payments to the United States. In the following year none but Finland (which paid in full) made more than token payments.

Hoover's measures, although they reflected greater government efforts than ever before to check the slide in business activity, proved wholly inadequate to the crisis. Jobless families succumbed to disease; private and voluntary hospitals were swamped; other relief agencies did yeoman work, but soon sank under the tidal wave of distress. Hoover, the "great humanitarian" of the war years, was now widely portrayed as a cold and callous leader. His own remarks gave the color of truth to such views. "Nobody is actually starving," he once told newspapermen. "The hoboes, for example, are better fed than they have ever been. One hobo in New York got ten meals in one day." Such comments did not set well with millions of unemployed forced to rummage in garbage cans for food. The picture of a harsh President became seared in the hearts of millions in the summer of 1932 when, with the November elections approaching, the "Bonus Army" of 12,000 jobless veterans marched to Washington in hopes of persuading Congress to make a veterans' bonus appropriation. On Hoover's orders, they were driven from the city with tear gas and bayonets.

THE ELECTION OF 1932

Aware that they had to name Hoover for a second term or openly acknowledge his responsibility for the country's plight, the Republicans renominated the President on the first ballot at their early June convention in Chicago. When the Democrats met in Chicago two weeks later, "Al" Smith was also once more strongly in the running for renomination in a campaign that was almost certain to bring a Democratic victory. The delegates, how-

ever, looked elsewhere. On the fourth ballot they named Smith's successor as governor of New York, Theodore Roosevelt's socialite cousin Franklin Delano Roosevelt. In the Republican sweep of 1928, F.D.R. had held New York for his party, and in 1930 he was re-elected Governor almost by acclamation. When nominated in 1932 by the Democrats, Roosevelt dramatically flew to Chicago to accept the honor in person, something no other candidate had done. "I pledge you, I pledge myself," he told the delegates, "to a new deal for the American people."

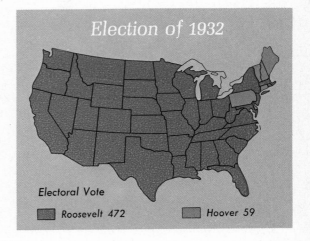

Election of 1932

Electoral Vote

Roosevelt 472   Hoover 59

The main issue in the campaign was the cause of the depression. Hoover placed the blame on World War I and on world-wide conditions that followed it. Without denying that the depression was world-wide, Roosevelt held that it also stemmed from flaws in the American economy. Hoover warned that an excess of governmental zeal would destroy liberty. Roosevelt called for novel governmental methods to meet novel conditions, although his few specific commitments were conventional. Liberals, indeed, were as much disappointed by his campaign as conservatives were frightened. Yet more voters were heartened by his promises, however vague, than were impressed by Hoover's warnings, however dire. Roosevelt received 22,821,000 votes, Hoover 15,761,000. The Democratic candidate carried all but six states, his electoral college margin soaring to 472 to 59. His party moreover, won overwhelming majorities in both houses of Congress.

Readings

Asterisk indicates that book is available in paperback.

A. M. Schlesinger, Jr., *The Crisis of the Old Order 1919-1933* * (1957), is eminently readable. Shorter general accounts of value include W. E. Leuchtenburg, *The Perils of Prosperity 1914-1932* * (1958); and J. D. Hicks, *Republican Ascendancy 1921-1933* * (1960). See also, Karl Schriftgiesser, *This Was Normalcy* (1948). F. L. Allen, *Only Yesterday* * (1931), is an admirable "informal" social history of the 'twenties. R. S. and H. M. Lynd, *Middletown* * (1929), and *Middletown in Transition* * (1937), afford intensive analyses of life in prosperity and depression. G. E. Mowry, *The Twenties, Fords, Flappers & Fanatics* * (1963); and D. A. Shannon, *The Great Depression* * (1960), are illuminating short anthologies. On Harding, see S. H. Adams, *Incredible Era* * (1939); and Andrew Sinclair, *The Available Man, Warren Gamaliel Harding* (1965).

Irving Bernstein, *The Lean Years, A History of the American Worker 1920-1933* (1960), is an excellent general account. David Brody, *The Steel Strike of 1919* (1965), is a valuable special study. R. K. Murray, *Red Scare* * (1955), is definitive. See also, Stanley Coben, *A. Mitchell Palmer* (1963). J. P. Clark, *Deportation of Aliens from the United States* (1931), is comprehensive on a neglected subject. Francis Russell, *Tragedy in Dedham* (1962), is excellent on the Sacco-Vanzetti case. See also O. K. Fraenkel, *The Sacco-Vanzetti Case* (1931); and G. L. Joughin and E. M. Morgan, *The Legacy of Sacco and Vanzetti* * (1948). R. L. Garis, *Immigration Restriction* (1927), covers the subject well. It may be supplemented by R. A. Divine, *American Immigration Policy 1924-1952* (1957); and John Higham, *Strangers in the Land* * (1955). On the surge of Negro migration northward, see Robert Weaver, *The Negro Ghetto* (1948); Gilbert Osofsky, *Harlem: The Making of a Ghetto, Negro New York 1890-1930* (1966); and the early chapters of St. Clair Drake and H. R. Cayton, *Black Metropolis* * (1945), on Chicago. A. S. Rice, *The Ku Klux Klan in American Politics* (1961); and J. M. Mecklin, *The Ku Klux Klan* (1924), tell the story of the organization. Prohibition is well presented in Charles Merz, *Dry Decade* (1931); Herbert Asbury, *The Great Illusion* (1950); and Andrew Sinclair, *Era of Excess, A Social History of the Prohibition Movement* * (1962). N. F. Furniss, *The Fundamentalist Controversy 1918-1931* (1954), is illuminating. Ray Ginger, *Six Days or Forever?* * (1958), is excellent on the Scopes Trial. See also Zechariah Chafee, *Free Speech in the United States* (1941 ed.), and Richard Hofstadter, *Anti-intellectualism in American Life* (1963).

The best study of Coolidge and his times is W. A. White, *A Puritan in Babylon* * (1938). Useful special studies of Republican rule include Malcolm Moos, *The Republicans* (1956); and M. R. Werner, *Privileged Characters* (1955). George Soule, *Prosperity Decade: From War to Depression 1917-1929* (1947), is a useful introduction to the postwar economy. More general is T. C. Cochran, *The American Business System, A Historical Perspective 1900-1955* * (1957). Two works by A. D. Chandler, Jr., offer the most penetrating accounts of big business management: *Strategy and Structure, Chapters in the History of Industrial Enterprise* * (1962); and *Giant Enterprise, Ford, General Motors, and the Automobile Industry* * (1964), an excellent anthology. A. P. Sloan, Jr., *My Years with General Motors* * (1964), is best on that company. Allan Nevins and F. E. Hill, *Ford: The Times, The Man, and The Company* (1954); *Ford: Expansion and Challenge* (1957); and *Ford: Decline and Rebirth, 1933-1962* (1963), fully cover the company and the industry. Among more critical studies of the man see, for example, Keith Sward, *The Legend of Henry Ford* (1948). On airplanes, F. C. Kelly, *The Wright Brothers* (1943); and H. L. Smith, *Airways:*

The History of Commercial Aviation in the United States (1942), are illuminating. Stuart Chase, *Men and Machines* (1929), is a well-written introduction to modern technology. The basic work on national income is Simon Kuznets, *National Income and its Composition 1919-1938,* Vol. I (1941). A. A. Berle, Jr., and G. F. Means, *The Modern Corporation and Private Property* (1932), is a classic study of business concentration. On security speculation, see W. Z. Ripley, *Main Street and Wall Street* (1927).

On the power issue, see *Fighting Liberal, The Autobiography of George W. Norris* * (1945). For farm problems, see Theodore Saloutos and J. D. Hicks, *Agricultural Discontent in the Middle West,* 1900-1939 * (1951); J. D. Black, *Agricultural Reform in the United States* (1930); R. B. Nye in *Midwestern Progressive Politics* (1951); and Grant McConnell, *The Decline of Agrarian Democracy* (1953).

Election campaigns may be studied in K. C. MacKay, *The Progressive Movement of 1924* (1947); R. V. Peel and T. C. Donnelly, *The 1928 Campaign* (1931); and the same authors' *The 1932 Campaign* (1935). Frank Freidel, *Franklin D. Roosevelt: The Triumph* (1956), has a masterly account of Roosevelt's 1932 campaign. The fullest biography of Smith is H. F. Pringle, *Alfred E. Smith: A Critical Study* (1927). Oscar Handlin, *Al Smith and His America* (1958), is excellent in setting Smith in perspective. These books may be supplemented by Smith's own *Up to Now* (1929); and by Emily Smith Warner's biography of her father, *The Happy Warrior* (1956). The religious issue in the election of 1928 is objectively studied by E. A. Moore in *A Catholic Runs for President* (1956).

The onset of the depression is ably discussed in Gilbert Seldes, *The Years of the Locust* (1933). J. K. Galbraith, *The Big Crash* * (1955), is a penetrating study of the 1929 debacle. Hoover's policies are defended by W. S. Meyers and W. H. Newton, *The Hoover Administration* (1936); and in *The Memoirs of Herbert Hoover: The Great Depression, 1929-41* (1952). Hoover gives succinct expression to the business philosophy of the 1920's in *American Individualism* (1922). An antidote to Hoover is J. W. Prothro, *The Dollar Decade, Business Ideas in the 1920's* (1954).

CHAPTER TWENTY-SEVEN

By March 4, 1933, when Franklin D. Roosevelt took the oath of office as the thirty-second President of the United States, three and a half years had passed since the Great Crash of October, 1929. Better than any array of the morbid statistics, Roosevelt, in his inaugural address, described the decline, the decay, the prostration of those years:

Values [he declared] have shrunken to fantastic levels; taxes have risen; our ability to pay has fallen; government of all kinds is faced by serious curtailment of income; the means of exchange are frozen in the currents of trade; the withered leaves of industrial enterprise lie

The New Deal

on every side; farmers find no markets for their produce; the savings of many years in thousands of families are gone. More important, a host of unemployed citizens face the grim problem of existence, and an equally great number toil with little return. Only a foolish optimist can deny the dark realities of the moment.

And yet, Roosevelt continued, "our distress comes from no failure of substance. We are stricken by no plague of locusts," but only by the mental and moral collapse of "the rulers of the exchange of mankind's goods," who "have admitted their failure and abdicated."

The money changers have fled from their high seats in the temple of our civilization. We may now restore that temple to the ancient truths. The measure of the restoration lies in the extent to which we apply social values more noble than mere monetary profit.

But "changes in ethics alone," obviously were not enough. "This Nation asks for action and action now. Our greatest primary task is to put people to work. . . . It can be accomplished in part by direct recruiting by the Government itself, treating the task as we would treat the emergency of a war." The new President continued:

Action in this image and to this end is feasible under the form of government which we have inherited from our ancestors. Our Constitution is so simple and practical that it is possible always to meet extraordinary needs by changes in emphasis and arrangement without loss of essential form. . . . But it may be that an unprecedented demand and need for undelayed action may call for temporary departure from that normal balance . . . of executive and legislative authority. I am prepared under my constitutional duty to recommend the measures that a stricken nation in the midst of a stricken world may require. . . . In the event that Congress shall fail to take [appropriate action], . . . I shall ask the Congress for the one remaining instrument to meet the crisis—broad Executive power to wage a war against the emergency, as great as the power that would be given me if we were in fact invaded by a foreign foe.

Eleanor Roosevelt found the inaugural ceremony "very, very solemn and a little terrifying." It was especially terrifying "because when Franklin got to that part of his speech when he said it might become necessary for him to assume powers ordinarily granted in war time, he received his biggest demonstration."

I. *A Bold Experiment in Government*

THE NEW BROOMS

Charming, self-assured, energetic and fearless, F.D.R. was the New Deal's greatest asset. Whatever may have lain hidden behind the famous Roosevelt smile, it was an extraordinarily effective instrument in private and public relations. The Roosevelt voice was also a great political tool. "I loved that voice," exclaimed Mary McLeod Bethune, the director of the influential Division of Negro Affairs under the New Deal's National Youth Administration (see p. 724); it made her feel, despite disappointments, that she could keep coming back to the man. Roosevelt became the first American politician to develop a radio personality. In his radio "fireside chats," he made the people feel that he was discussing important questions with them, man-to-man.

Roosevelt, Rexford G. Tugwell writes in his perceptive biography, "often covered a prayerful calculation with a pleasantry," and he chides historians who make too much of F.D.R.'s frequent flippant remarks as evidence of irresponsibility. Yet many of Roosevelt's pleasantries need not have had prayer behind them to be effective. Less

Franklin Delano Roosevelt; delivering one of his "fireside chats," 1938.

than two weeks after his inauguration, he remarked calmly after supper at the White House, "I think this would be a good time for a beer." Three days later Congress repealed the Volstead Act and permitted the sale of beer and light wines before the Eighteenth Amendment itself was repealed.

Although the nation's basic problems were economic, Roosevelt's art was not economics, but politics. In the badly divided Democratic party of the 1920's he learned how to keep friends on both sides of a political fence. When his tact failed him, as it occasionally did, it was only because he had decided to play a strong part. One of the sources of Roosevelt's strength was his ability to make decisions without undue anxiety. "You'll have to learn that public life takes a lot of sweat," he told an associate, "but it doesn't need to worry you. You won't always be right, but you mustn't suffer from being wrong. That's what kills people like us."

Though hardly a passionate person, Roosevelt was deeply moved by the plight of the destitute. He believed that every underprivileged interest had a legitimate claim on the sympathies of the government. Many people spoke of the New Deal, during its early days, as an attempt at economic planning, but it would be more accurate to call it a period of economic experimentation. No one knew of a single panacea, and the range of Roosevelt's policies proved as varied as the men around him. These included veteran politicians such as Postmaster-General James A. Farley of New York who had a card-index mind in which deserving and undeserving Democrats were sorted out; and Secretary of State Cordell Hull, a national legislator of many years service whose Tennessee background was reflected in his support of the traditional southern quest for lower tariffs and freer world trade. William H. Woodin, a conservative industrialist who enjoyed the confidence of businessmen, was made Secretary of the Treasury. When Woodin resigned after giving yeoman service during the urgent bank crisis of 1933 (see below), he was succeeded by Henry Morgenthau,

Jr., an old friend of the President's. The reform element was strongly represented by the old "Bull Mooser," Harold L. Ickes, who became Secretary of the Interior; Henry A. Wallace, the son of Harding's and Coolidge's Secretary of Agriculture, who now filled this post himself; Frances Perkins, who had worked with Roosevelt in Albany and as Secretary of Labor became the first woman Cabinet member; and Harry Hopkins, in many ways the most influential of all, although not in the Cabinet until 1939. Even less formally related to the administration than Hopkins were the members of the "brain trust," notably Raymond Moley, A. A. Berle, Jr., and Tugwell, who in the early days were perhaps closest to Roosevelt.

Hoover's approach to the problem of recovery had been largely the traditional one of allowing the deflation to run its course. The New Dealers were far less patient, far more eager to experiment with currency inflation and with heavy government spending to "prime the pump" of business. They hoped also to make the crisis an occasion for reforms. They began tentatively here, but when public pressure for change became apparent, they moved in a venturesome spirit.

RESCUING THE BANKS

One of the most serious effects of the long depression—the headlong plunge of the nation's banks toward bankruptcy—set the stage for one of the most electrifying New Deal steps. This came within a day or two of Roosevelt's inauguration and gave the public a welcome taste of leadership.

By 1933 so many unsound banks had failed that even solvent institutions were menaced by frightened depositors rushing to withdraw their money. To stem the panic, the governors of almost half the states had declared "bank holidays," and by inauguration day, March 4, most of the banks in the country were closed. By proclamation on March 6, Roosevelt suspended all banking operations and gold transactions. Three days later, called into special session, Congress passed the Emergency Banking Act, which ratified the President's actions and established procedures for getting the sound banks back in business. Roosevelt then went on the air with his first "fireside chat," a brilliant and successful effort in which he reassured the people on the soundness of the banking system that was about to emerge from the reorganization. To speed up the reorganization, the Reconstruction Finance Corporation was ordered to advance funds where needed, and before the end of March most of the sound banks were reopened and the unsound ones were on the way to being permanently closed. Within another month, more than 12,000 banks, with 90 per cent of the country's deposits, were functioning normally. "In one week," wrote Walter Lippmann of the bank crisis, "the nation, which had lost confidence in everything and everybody, has regained confidence in the government and in itself." The suspicions even of many conservatives were quieted by Roosevelt's spurning the more radical solution to which he could easily have resorted —nationalizing the banks. Moderate men saw that his aim was not to establish a new economic system but to rescue the existing one.

Bank reform followed on the heels of the banking crisis. One of the most salutary reform measures was the Glass-Steagall Act of June, 1933, which created the Federal Deposit Insurance Corporation and authorized it to guarantee bank deposits up to $5,000 per depositor, thereby making a repetition of the scares of 1932-1933 unlikely. Many banks had got into trouble by speculating in the stock market with depositor's funds through security affiliates. The Glass-Steagall Act forbade national banks to maintain such affiliates and prescribed other reforms to divorce commercial from investment banking. The simple sanity of this law did not prevent the American Bankers Association from fighting it "to the last ditch," as its president said.

While on the subject of stocks and bonds Congress, in May, 1933, passed the Securities Act, requiring much greater publicity for the details of stock promotions and closing the mails to sellers failing to provide it. This measure was followed in June, 1934, by the Securities Exchange Act creating the Securities and Exchange Commission, which was authorized to require the registration of all securities in which the stock exchanges dealt and to cooperate with the Federal Reserve Board in regulating the purchase of securities on margin. The Public Utility Holding Company Act of 1935 (see p. 727), gave the S.E.C. supervisory powers over the management of holding companies. A number of other measures further enlarged the S.E.C.'s power to provide an elaborate system of protection for the American investor. The Banking Act of 1935, meanwhile, greatly increased federal authority over the banking system by empowering the Federal Reserve Board to regulate interest rates.

PLAYING WITH MONEY

Business recovery proved more elusive than banking reform. The New Deal tried many nostrums to stimulate industrial activity, most of them without success. One of its earliest expedients was to cheapen the dollar and thereby reduce the burden of fixed debts, which were such a drag on production, and at the same time raise domestic prices to encourage output. Cheapening the dollar was also expected to stimulate exports by making the American medium of exchange more easily obtainable by those using foreign currencies. Roosevelt was skeptical of this device, but Congress, in May, 1933, pressed by urgent demands from the western wing of the Democratic party for such nostalgic inflationary measures as the printing of greenbacks and the free coinage of silver, authorized the President to issue up to $3 billion in paper money with which to pay federal obligations and even redeem United States bonds. This measure also authorized him to reduce the gold content of the dollar by as much as 50 per cent, provide for unlimited coinage of both gold and silver at a ratio that he could set, accept a limited amount of silver in debt payments from foreign governments, and issue silver certificates against the bullion thus received. In June, by a joint resolution, Congress took the further step of explicitly voiding all clauses in past or future contracts, government or private, requiring payment of obligations in gold, thereby taking the United States off the gold standard. The constitutionality of this measure was upheld by the Supreme Court in the Gold Clause Cases of 1935.

Although Congress had surrendered to the greenbackers and the silverites, the President used his new authorization with great caution. Even so, he promptly got into trouble with foreign governments whose representatives had assembled in mid-June at the London Economic Conference for the specific purpose of *stabilizing* world currencies so that importers and exporters might gain a clearer grasp of the profitability of their transactions. These governments counted on a stable dollar as the linchpin of any agreements they might make. But if the United States intended to indulge in manipulation of the value of the dollar with a free hand, the cause of renewed international trade and hence of international recovery was lost. On July 3 Roosevelt sent a radio message to the conference saying the United States would pursue its own course. This message wrecked the conference; but supporters of the New Deal defended the action on the grounds that the participating nations had themselves offered no concessions to compensate for the rigid dollar they wanted.

By October, 1933, it had become clear to the administration that, while the powers granted to it by Congress were imprudently broad, Congress' resolution simply taking the dollar off the gold standard was ineffectually narrow. In a new effort to boost commodity prices by monetary manipulation, the Treasury was now ordered to purchase gold at rising dollar rates. Purchases of domestically mined gold began in October, but presently foreign gold was bought as well. But even this expedient was given up by the end of January, 1934, when the

President, by proclamation fixed the gold content of the dollar at 59.06 cents.

Subsequently, again contrary to its will, the administration was also forced by a ruthless bloc of western senators to launch upon an extraordinary silver-purchase program. It became clear that if the administration did nothing for silver the silver bloc would sabotage its entire legislative program. Under the terms of the Silver Purchase Act of June 19, 1934, the Treasury was obliged to buy the entire output of the domestic silver mines at an artificially high price. The immense subsidy to silver producers entailed by this act cost the government almost $1.5 billion in the next fifteen years—a ghastly revenge for the specter of William Jennings Bryan. Secretary of the Treasury Morgenthau admitted in 1935: "Our silver program is the only monetary fiscal policy that I cannot explain or justify." The net result of the whole monetary experiment was that at some cost to the Treasury but with little benefit to the nation, an abnormally large portion of the world's bullion supply found its way to United States vaults.

THE N.R.A.   Currency experiments implied that under favorable monetary conditions the ordinary market mechanisms of the economy might themselves push prices up. But the New Dealers were not alone in their awareness that the market mechanisms themselves needed artificial respiration and probably a permanent iron lung. To help the economy breathe once more, Congress, in June, 1933, passed the National Industrial Recovery Act (N.I.R.A.). Roosevelt hailed it "as the most important and far-reaching legislation ever enacted by the American Congress." The labor leader, John L. Lewis, said: "We are convinced that there has been no legal instrument comparable with it since President Lincoln's Emancipation Proclamation." In fact,

NRA parade in New York City.

the act's most far-reaching consequence was to disqualify all such Rube Goldbergs in the future.

The N.I.R.A. would never have been heard of except for the depression crisis. But more specifically, in part to take advantage of the crisis, it was the outcome, on the one hand, of plans for industrial reorganization put forward by such businessmen as Bernard Baruch and Gerard Swope, President of General Electric, and by leaders of the United States Chamber of Commerce. Their aim was not so much to expand the economy as to ration the nation's business among the surviving corporations consistently with Roosevelt's goal of stabilization "for all time." On the other hand, the act was the outcome of an attempt by the administration to head off a bill that had been introduced by Senator Hugo Black of Alabama, providing for a work limit of 30 hours a week in factories. Black's measure had passed the Senate in April, 1933, and was subsequently linked with a proposal to impose a minimum wage. The package frightened conservative industrialists and aroused the disapproval of the administration as well.

Under the provisions of the N.I.R.A., the anti-trust laws were in effect suspended and trade associations and other business groups were permitted to draw up "codes of fair competition" which would include sweeping price agreements, firm production quotas, and wage scales sufficient significantly to improve the condition of the poorest-paid workers. Each type of business was given the power to draw up its own

code. The government reserved the right to accept or reject the codes, to set up its own when companies in any industry failed to agree, and to enforce them. Section 7 (a) of the N.I.R.A. guaranteed labor the right of collective bargaining. A National Recovery Administration (N.R.A.) was formed to administer the codes under the chairmanship of the ebullient and profane General Hugh Johnson, a protégé of Bernard Baruch, who had worked under Baruch on the War Industries Board (see p. 675).

In order to make the N.R.A. comparable to mobilization for war, N.R.A. administrators organized parades and mass meetings. They adopted a placard with a Blue Eagle as a symbol to be awarded for display to businessmen and even to consumers who cooperated. One of their hoped-for-effects was to stir up boycotts of firms that did not cooperate, thus presumably substituting public pressure for legal enforcement. General Johnson blared forth in his characteristically grandiloquent way: "When every American housewife understands that the Blue Eagle on everything she permits to come into her home is a symbol of its restoration to security, may God have mercy on the man or group of men who attempt to trifle with this bird." Asked what would happen to those who did not cooperate, Johnson simply replied: "They'll get a sock on the nose." In fact, violators of the codes or objectors like Henry Ford, who met code requirements but refused to sign up, were seldom prosecuted. N.R.A. administrators may have anticipated that, put to the judicial test, the entire scheme would meet the

718

fate that did in fact lie in wait for it in the Supreme Court.

No less than 746 N.R.A. codes were adopted by businessmen eager to get started again. But friction soon retarded recovery. The paper work required to supply needed information to the government quickly reached fantastic proportions and was resented. Big corporations resisted all further signs of bureaucratic interference. Small firms, in turn, complained that the codes, drawn up by the larger firms in each industry, discriminated against the little fellows. Workers, who at first rallied to the N.R.A., soon nicknamed it the "National Run Around." Code administrators, they said, characteristically sided with anti-union employers in labor disputes. Employers, on their part, detested the very existence of Section 7 (a) and the expansion of organized labor it foretold. Insofar, moreover, as the codes succeeded in reviving production by raising prices, they aroused consumer discontent.

The N.R.A. had reached a low point in popularity when the Supreme Court, in May, 1935, killed it. In the case of *Schechter Poultry Corporation* v. *United States,* the Court unanimously found that the National Industrial Recovery Act was unconstitutional on two counts: first, that it improperly delegated legislative powers to the executive; and second, that the provisions of the poultry code constituted a regulation of intrastate, not interstate, commerce. The New Deal's far-reaching plan for industry and labor lay in fragments.

The N.R.A. had not been entirely in vain. For example, at the time the codes were adopted, some of the most exploited workers in the textile industry had been receiving wages as low as $5 a week. To such workers the cotton textile code, which prescribed minimum wages of $12 to $13 a week was heaven-sent. As Arthur M. Schlesinger, Jr., has observed, N.R.A. fostered many social reforms: It established the principle of maximum hours and minimum wages on a national basis. It reduced child labor. It made collective bargaining a national policy. The cancellation of the codes brought about, in many instances, a restoration of poor working conditions to which later reform measures were addressed (see p. 728).

THE FUTURE OF AGRICULTURE

In the summer of 1932, Milo Reno of the Farmers' Holiday Association said:

We have issued an ultimatum to the other groups of society. If you continue to confiscate our property and demand that we feed your stomachs and clothe your bodies, we will refuse to function. We don't ask people to make implements, cloth, or houses at the price of degradation, bankruptcy, dissolution, and despair.

In January, 1933, before Roosevelt's inauguration, the normally conservative head of the Farm Bureau Federation, Edward A. O'Neal, told a Senate committee: "Unless something is done for the American farmer we will have revolution in the countryside within less than twelve months." Soon farmers began to take matters into their own hands. They forcibly halted eviction sales and mortgage foreclosures, intimidated and assaulted public officials and the agents of banks and insurance companies. Late in April, a mob of farmers in Le Mars, Iowa, angered by the refusal of a judge to suspend foreclosure proceedings on a neighbor's farm, dragged the offending jurist from the bench, mauled him, took him from the city in a truck (perhaps with the original purpose of lynching him), smeared him with grease and dirt, tore off his trousers, and left him on the road. Within a short time, the Governor had to put several Iowa counties under martial law and call in the National Guard. "Americans are slow to understand," commented the New York *World-Telegram,* "that actual revolution already exists in the farm belt. . . . When the local revolt springs from old native stock, conservatives fighting for the right to hold their homesteads, there is the warning of a larger explosion."

An Oklahoma farmer and his sons seek shelter from a dust storm, 1936.

The New Dealers were in fact well aware of the need for prompt action. When they took it, they approached the farm problem in the same mood with which they approached the problems of industry. The New Deal farm plan was incorporated in the Agricultural Adjustment Act of May, 1933, which set up an Agricultural Adjustment Administration (A.A.A.) to carry out its provisions.

Abandoning all hope of regaining the lost foreign market for staples (see p. 701), the A.A.A. hoped to raise farm prices by cutting back production to domestic needs and rationing the domestic market among producers. In this way it planned to bring farm prices back to "parity" with those of the prosperous prewar years, 1909-1914. Further to compensate farmers for cooperating with the government plan, A.A.A. was authorized to pay various sorts of subsidies for acreage withdrawn from production and for certain marketing practices. Funds to finance the program were to come from taxes levied on the processors of farm products, such as millers, cotton-ginners, and meat-packers. At first, the act provided for crop reduction only in cotton, wheat, corn, hogs, rice, tobacco, and milk; later, it was extended to other products.

To cut production when people were hungry was bound to invite criticism. But farm spokesmen insisted that if the profit system meant anything, the farmers had the same right to do this as businessmen. "Agriculture," said Secretary Wallace, "cannot survive in a capitalistic society as a philanthropic enterprise." To make matters worse, the A.A.A. did not begin to function until after the spring planting of 1933. To achieve its desired reduction in marketable staples that year, it was forced to supplement acreage restriction with orders to farmers to "plow under" a large part of their crops. With millions starving in the cities, the A.A.A. action seemed heartless. It also fell short of its goal. Many farmers accepted government checks for reducing acreage, and then calmly proceeded to cultivate their remaining acres more intensively. As a result, the net reduction in crops did not amount to nearly as much as the government planners had hoped.

In 1934, Congress supplemented acreage restriction with production quotas and imposed taxes on violators. The new and old laws helped double and triple farm staple prices and brought about a dramatic rise in the total net income of farm operators from $1.8 billion in 1932 to $5 billion in 1936.

720

On January 6, 1936, in the Hoosac Mills Case (*U.S.* v. *Butler, et. al.*), the Supreme Court, in an even more stunning decision than the *Schechter* ruling (p. 719), found that A.A.A. crop control methods unconstitutionally invaded powers reserved to the states. They also found the processing tax not the general revenue measure it pretended to be but an illegal means "to take money from the processor and bestow it upon farmers [simply] to help farmers attain parity prices and purchasing power."

Following the Hoosac Mills decision, Congress passed the Soil Conservation and Domestic Allotment Act which put crop restriction on a new basis, with the avowed object now to increase soil fertility and conserve resources. The A.A.A. was authorized to pay farmers for adopting soil-conservation measures and for reducing acreage used for soil-depleting crops. Congressional appropriations instead of the outlawed processing tax were relied upon to finance the program. When prices tumbled again in 1937, Congress in February, 1938, supplemented the Soil Conservation Act with a second Agricultural Adjustment Act. This law embodied Secretary Wallace's idea of the "ever-normal granary." The price fall in 1937 had come from bumper crops pro-

duced in response to the high prices of 1936. This new act aimed to keep such bumper crops off the market by compensating farmers for storing them until years of shortages made it possible to bring them on to the market without fear of undermining it. Large sums were paid to farmers under this measure, but staple growers did not really prosper until wartime demand in the 1940's again pushed crop prices up.

Of course there were millions of farm families that gained nothing from commercial-farm legislation. As the depression wore on, concern for share-croppers, farm tenants, and hired farm laborers grew. The New Deal's response in this area was the Resettlement Administration, created in April, 1935. Rural poverty was hard to ameliorate, but the R.A. made a noble effort. It withdrew a total of 9 million acres of virtual waste land from cultivation, moved the families on them to resettlement areas, extended loans to farmers who could not obtain credit elsewhere, and encouraged cooperation among farmers who had always insisted on going it alone.

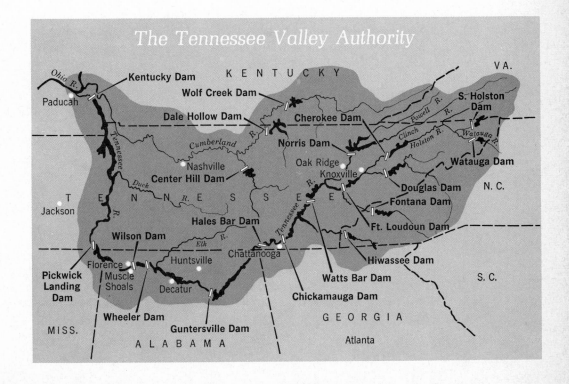

The Tennessee Valley Authority

Late in 1936, Secretary Wallace reported on a trip he had taken through the South:

I have never seen among the peasantry of Europe poverty so abject as that which exists in this favorable cotton year in the great cotton states from Arkansas to the East Coast. . . . I am tempted to say that one third of the farmers of the United States live under conditions which are so much worse than the peasantry of Europe that the city people of the United States should be thoroughly ashamed.

In response to the report of a presidential committee on rural poverty, Congress, in 1937, passed the Farm Tenancy Act to provide loans to share-croppers, tenant farmers, and farm laborers for the purchase of land, livestock, supplies, and equipment. By June, 1944, 870,000 rural families had been helped.

THE T.V.A.

One of the poorest of all American farm areas was the Tennessee Valley; and nowhere was the indictment of American farm poverty more justifiable, for the Valley was immensely rich in natural resources. Government projects to harness the mighty Tennessee River itself were begun at Muscle Shoals during World War I, but were checked later, as we have seen (p. 700), by the opposition of private power interests and vetoes of enabling legislation by Coolidge and Hoover. Roosevelt, as Governor of New York in this era, by contrast, had fostered the idea of public power and had helped set up a state power authority. In January, 1933, after his election as President, Roosevelt visited Muscle Shoals in the company of experts and soon had a grand plan in view for the whole valley. This plan came to fruition when Congress, on May 18, 1933, created the Tennessee Valley Authority and empowered it to buy, build, and operate dams in the Tennessee Valley, generate and sell electric power, plan reforestation and flood control, withdraw marginal lands from cultivation, and in general to further the well-being of the Valley's people.

Of all the New Deal's experiments in government, the T.V.A. probably was the boldest and most original. An unprece-dented independent public corporation national in scope, it was placed under the management of three directors, with Arthur E. Morgan as chairman. Its area of responsibility embraced no less than 40,000 square miles in seven states. In this region, partly with the assistance of P.W.A. (see p. 724), the T.V.A. built 16 new dams and took over five others. The first of the new ones, the Norris Dam northwest of Knoxville, Tennessee, and justly named for the Nebraska Senator, was completed in 1936. By 1940, four dams were generating electric power in the T.V.A. region and over 400,000 users, many of them farmers and most of them for the first time, were directly or indirectly served. Rates generally were low, and the T.V.A. "yardstick" forced private companies in the area also to keep rates down. Land was being redeemed and improved, and the people of the Valley were developing pride in their region and affection for the plan.

Like earlier Valley projects, T.V.A. was ceaselessly fought by the power companies. They, in turn, gained the support of many disinterested conservatives who saw in the experiment a threat to the system of private enterprise and rugged individualism. And like other New Deal measures, T.V.A. was taken to court at an early opportunity. Unlike some other measures, it survived. In 1936, in *Ashwander* v. *Tennessee Valley Authority,* the Supreme Court ruled that at no point had the Authority exceeded constitutional powers. T.V.A. became a pillar of strength in World War II.

The plan for a similar development in the Missouri Valley, the projected M.V.A., was never completed. Other New Deal hydroelectric projects—Grand Coulee and Bonneville Dams on the Columbia River, Hoover Dam on the Colorado, Fort Peck Dam on the upper Missouri—did not include T.V.A.'s broad social program.

WORK FOR THE UNEMPLOYED

When Roosevelt took office, at least 12 million American workers were unemployed; with their families they added up to about 50 million persons, many of them on the verge of starvation. The New Deal's bold experiments in economic legislation only once, in 1937, managed to bring the number of unemployed below 8 million, and in 1940 it was back above that figure, at a level five times as high as in 1929.

Heretofore the government had held hands off the problem of the unemployed. President Cleveland clearly expressed the traditional attitude during the depression of the 1890's when he said it was the people's duty to support the government, not the government's duty to support the people. President Hoover subscribed to this philosophy. He helped as much as he could to coordinate private relief efforts; but when these were overwhelmed by the unprecedented immensity of the problem as early as 1930, he clung to the harsh precedent. The writer, Martha Gellhorn, touring the country in 1933, reported to Harry Hopkins that the main problem among the unemployed was "a dangerous feeling of helplessness and dependence. . . . I find them all in the same shape—fear, fear driving them into a state of semi-collapse; cracking nerves; and an overpowering terror of the future . . . each family in its own miserable home going to pieces." But Hoover refused to "Prussianize" the poor, as he said, with public assistance.

The New Deal brought a new philosophy to the problem of relief just as it did to the problem of recovery. In 1933, the issue was no longer whether the federal government should act—this question had been settled by the 1932 election. The issue now was whether the government should simply make handouts to the poverty-stricken, which was the cheapest plan, or whether it should provide work relief, which seemed less wasteful and more humane. In accordance with suggestions made by Roosevelt in an address to Congress in March, 1933, several lines of action were adopted.

The first New Deal measure providing assistance to the unemployed was an act of March, 1933, creating the Civilian Conservation Corps (C.C.C.). This act looked to the youth of the country, not the aged. At one point the C.C.C. had 500,000 young men, 18 to 25, on its rolls, recruited from cities, sent to camps built by the War Department, and put to work on reforestation, fire-prevention projects, road and dam construction, the control of mosquitoes and other pests, and similar tasks. They were given housing and recreational facilities and were paid $30 a month, of which $22 was sent to their families. By the end of 1941, some 2,750,000 youths had spent some part of their lives in the C.C.C. camps.

The first comprehensive New Deal relief measure was the act of May, 1933, creating the Federal Emergency Relief Administration (F.E.R.A.) under Harry Hopkins and providing it with a fund of half a billion dollars to be used for direct emergency relief to states and localities. Although the federal government provided the money, the relief itself was to be administered by the states. At first, cash payments were distributed, but Hopkins believed that work relief was both psychologically and economically superior to a dole. He also was concerned with quick results. When approached with a project that needed long and detailed planning, one that he was assured would "work out in the long run," Hopkins snapped, "People don't eat in the long run—they eat every day." In time almost half of those receiving relief were put to work on jobs that presumably did not compete with private business. Pay began at 30 cents an hour. In all, the F.E.R.A. spent about $4 billion.

The Civil Works Administration, set up in November, 1933, run entirely from Washington and given wholly to work relief, supplemented F.E.R.A. for a short time. Widely criticized by opponents of the New Deal on the ground that it "made work" on leaf-raking and similar futile tasks, it in fact performed many useful services, such as repairing roads and improving schools and parks, before being absorbed in the spring of 1934 into the expanding F.E.R.A. program.

A month after F.E.R.A. had been set up,

the National Recovery Act (see p. 717) created as part of the recovery program the Public Works Administration (P.W.A.) under Secretary of the Interior Ickes. P.W.A. was more a "pump priming" than a relief agency; its duties included the planning of bridges, dams, hospitals, and similar public projects and contracting for their construction by private companies. But Ickes was so cautious in approving contracts that P.W.A. was disastrously slow in getting started. Eventually, however, the $4.25 billion it spent by 1937 on about 35,000 projects was credited with stimulating the business recovery that seemed then to be on the way. Among its achievements were the Triborough Bridge in New York City, a new sewage system for Chicago, a municipal auditorium for Kansas City, a water supply system for Denver, and two new aircraft carriers, *Yorktown* and *Enterprise*.

Many persons complained that the New Deal relief agencies, besides duplicating one another's tasks, had made no effort to distinguish between employable persons who needed relief and "unemployables" who could not have found work even in good times. Early in 1935, Roosevelt proposed a reorganization of the entire relief program, with the federal government to aid employables only, the care of others to be left to the states and municipalities. In May that year, Congress passed the Emergency Relief Act putting these proposals into effect. The C.C.C. and P.W.A. were continued. All other federal relief was brought under a new agency, the Works Progress Administration (W.P.A.), directed by Harry Hopkins. When its operations ended, in July, 1941, W.P.A. had spent no less than $11.3 billion. At its peak in November, 1938, 3,275,000 persons were on its payroll, and all told, W.P.A. provided work for 8 million individuals. Among its more than 250,000 projects were hospitals, bridges, municipal power plants, school buildings, slum clearance, and the rehabilitation of army posts and naval stations.

W.P.A. also recognized the claims of the arts, whose practitioners, like other workers, were left stranded by the depression. Its projects in the fine arts, music, and the theater gave employment to painters, writers, actors, singers, instrumentalists, stage hands, and others, and brought to thousands who had never seen a play or heard a concert many often brilliant performances. W.P.A.'s Federal Writers Project put hundreds of additional writers to work collecting documents, writing local histories, and making surveys and studies of lasting value. W.P.A.'s cultural work was supplemented by a National Youth Administration (N.Y.A.), which helped meet the needs of youths with intellectual interests. Through the N.Y.A. young people between 16 and 25 found part-time employment in high schools, colleges, and universities, chiefly at tasks that assisted these institutions in the conduct of their affairs.

No part of the New Deal drew more criticism than its relief program. The cost was truly enormous for the times, and the tax burdens had to be carried by the depressed private sector of the economy. Many critics charged, usually inaccurately, that relief was inefficiently handled. Others, often justly, accused the administration of using relief for political purposes. No part of the relief program, in turn, drew more criticism than its support of cultural activities. Many Americans had no sympathy with the idea that musicians, writers, and artists had as much claim on the community as did workers in other fields. It was said also, and often with truth, that persons with radical and unconventional views were being employed on the cultural projects. Few such critics seemed to realize that these projects might restore to such persons a sense of security and personal pride sufficient to mitigate their radicalism. Elsewhere in the world, where intellectuals and artists had been completely neglected, they often turned toward fascism or communism.

The relief program also had its eloquent defenders who pointed to the preservation of resources, the restoration of the land, the city improvements it accomplished. At the very least, they said, it saved millions for whom private charity and private enterprise had no answer.

II. *Challenge and Response*

THE REFERENDUM OF 1934

Most of the New Deal's famous "alphabetical agencies"—N.R.A., T.V.A., A.A.A., S.E.C., C.C.C., P.W.A.—had their inception in the first stirring "hundred days" of the Roosevelt administration. These were the days of the special session of the 73rd Congress, which sat from March 9 to June 16, 1933, probably the most creative congressional session since the first one in 1789. The unquenchable spirit and contagious optimism of the leader at the helm had turned a paralyzing disaster into an inspiring opportunity. Unprecedented measures of reform and relief were adopted with near unanimity. The opposition, which had shunned responsibility, appeared for the moment, shamed, shocked, or stunned into silence. When recovery itself proved elusive, however, the enemies of the New Deal took heart; such signs of recovery as there were, moreover, brought them many followers who believed, with the emergency thankfully passing, that "normalcy" should again be restored, and the sooner the better.

The New Deal fathered enemies on the left as well as the right (see p. 726), but it was those on the right who, after 18 months of Roosevelt, did most to make the congressional elections of 1934 an immensely important referendum. They grew horrified at the abandonment of the gold standard, resentful of the S.E.C. as a slur on Wall Street's morality, fearful of the implications of T.V.A. for the utilities industry, alarmed at the collectivism of the N.R.A. and A.A.A., and shocked at the break from the traditions of individualism and decentralization manifest in the relief policy.

For as long as leading businessmen could remember, even during the Progressive Era and World War I, control of affairs had never been far from their hands. As one corporation lawyer, Frederic R. Coudert, wrote to another, James M. Beck, in 1932: "When you and I first began to practice law, one hardly needed to know that there was a Federal Government until one went abroad." Now, under Roosevelt, business power was confronted by the massive and expanding power of the federal government. Looming on another side was the growing force of organized labor, whose numbers gave it new political as well as economic leverage. And at the head of the government stood the thoroughly objectionable figure of the President himself. The Republican leader Ogden Mills expressed the feelings of the Roosevelt haters when he said: "We have to turn back many centuries to the days of absolute autocrats to find so great a power over millions of men lodged in the hands of a single fallible being."

The question whether these conservative critics represented the views of the majority, or even of a very substantial minority of the people, as they surely would have a mere half-dozen years earlier, was at issue in the 1934 campaign. Walter Lippmann, warned those whom he called the "hysterical conservatives" that they had "not a ghost of a chance to win." But Roosevelt, taking no chances, made a few astute appeals to the public to support liberal-minded candidates. When the people were told that the New Deal was destroying the Constitution and tearing up the Bill of Rights, Roosevelt suggested that they read the Bill of Rights for themselves and "ask yourself whether you personally have suffered the abatement of a single jot of these great assurances." Again, when they were told that the New Deal was ruining the country, he asked them to judge by their own situations. "Are you," he asked in June, "better off than you were last year? Are your debts less burdensome? Is your bank account more secure? Are your working conditions better?"

These questions were put in full confidence that most people could answer in the affirmative. And at the polls they did. The Republicans' crushing defeats in 1932 were exceeded in 1934. In the Senate, the Democratic margin rose from 25 to 44 seats; in the House the already huge Democratic majority soared over 200. Arthur Krock, *The New York Times* commentator, called this repudiation of the New Deal's critics, "the most overwhelming victory in the history of American politics."

THE VOICE OF THE DEMAGOGUE

If the referendum of 1934 buried those who believed that the President was going too far too fast, it must also have reminded him, if he needed reminding, that the spirit of protest was still rising and that those who believed the New Deal moved too little and too slowly would be heard from. In the second half of his first term, Roosevelt became increasingly concerned with the voices on the left, and especially those of a new breed of demagogue who arose to deepen the widespread popular discontent.

Most formidable among these demagogues was Senator Huey Long, the "Kingfish" of Louisiana. A skilled rabble-rouser with a remarkable command of the popular idiom, Long had built up a national following, especially large in the Mississippi Valley and on the Pacific Coast, on the strength of his vague plan to "share the wealth." In 1935, a survey conducted by the Democratic National Committee disclosed that Long might win from 3 to 4 million votes on a third party ticket, thereby gaining the balance of power in American politics, with perhaps disastrous consequences for the Democrats in the 1936 presidential campaign. This alarming possibility was dissipated by Long's assassination in September, 1935.

Two other demagogues enjoyed large followings. One was an elderly California physician, Dr. Francis E. Townsend, who early in January, 1935, announced the "Townsend Plan" by which the government would give $200 a month to every citizen 60 years old or older, the cost to be paid by

a sales tax. Each pensioner would be required to spend his allowance within the month, thereby, according to the plausible doctor, starting such a wave of consumer buying that business would boom and make it easy for the rest of the country to bear the cost. Responsible economists dismissed the Townsend Plan as a crackpot scheme—one of them, Paul Douglas, estimated that it would require half the national income to be turned over to 8 per cent of the population—but Townsend Clubs were organized throughout the country by desperate old men and women. Their combined membership was said to be about 3 million in 1935, with perhaps as many as 7 million unaffiliated supporters. Frightened politicians began to endorse Townsend's scheme. Roosevelt had to face the fearsome possibility that a large proportion of the voters over 60 would be forged into a voting bloc in full cry for an impossible "reform."

More forceful yet more vague than Dr. Townsend was the "radio priest," Father Charles E. Coughlin. Coughlin broadcast weekly from Royal Oak, Michigan, and won an enormous audience for his assaults, in the old Populist idiom, on Wall Street and the international bankers. His spurning "hate" harangues seemed more satisfying to his frustrated followers than his conventional demands for a "living annual wage" and "nationalization of banking and currency and of national resources." Originally one of Roosevelt's supporters, Coughlin, in January, 1935, began to flay the administration for failing the people.

To those concerned over the rise of Hitler, Mussolini, and other dictators abroad, Long, Coughlin and company loomed as the "forerunners of American fascism," as the able journalist Raymond Gram Swing called them. Their popularity, coinciding as it did with organized labor's own growing discontent with the N.R.A. (see p. 719), suggested in the spring of 1935 that the mass appeal of the Roosevelt administration, so high in its earliest months, was about to dissolve. Roosevelt himself was aware of the real popular grievances underlying the demagogues' appeal and

726

privately he even spoke of doing something "to steal Long's thunder." The Wealth Tax, the Social Security Act, the National Labor Relations Act, and some others all were responses to this thunder from below. But their natural consequence, by the time of the election of 1936, was to deepen the thunder from above.

THE 1935 REFORMS

Three of the new reform measures were enacted in one fateful month, August, 1935. One of the August laws, inspired by the administration's desire to check the growth of gigantic personal fortunes, was the Revenue Act of 1935, sometimes called the Wealth Tax or the "soak the rich" law. Tax rates, which had already been raised by earlier New Deal measures, were now pushed much higher, reaching 75 per cent on individual incomes above $5 million. Holding companies used for the management of private fortunes also were heavily taxed, and corporation levies were lifted to an historic peak. Roy W. Howard, the publisher of a chain of newspapers heretofore sympathetic toward Roosevelt, now wrote the President in an open letter that businessmen believed the Wealth Tax to be simply a punitive measure inspired by revenge against political opponents. Their resentment, Howard cautioned, was growing. Roosevelt replied that the act was intended to "create broader range of opportunity" and to impose needed taxes in accordance with ability to pay. He took the caution to heart, however, and promised that business would now have a "breathing spell."

The second enactment of August, 1935, was the Public Utility Holding Company Act. Holding companies, as we have seen (p. 558), were corporations permitted to hold the securities of other corporations. Often, by holding only a tiny fraction of a great corporation's securities, but a fraction still large enough to exercise strong leverage where other holdings were scattered, the holding company could dominate policies to its own advantage. Many other technical and legal devices—such as the designation of only a small part of a corporation's

stock as "voting stock," which could then be acquired for a song, along with the full power of the voting privilege—furthered holding companies' domination of basic industries. Domination could be pushed to still broader ranges by the practice of "pyramiding"—a procedure by which holding companies, in a manner similar to that by which they gained control of operating corporations, also gained control of other holding companies and hence of the operating corporations *they* controlled.

Holding companies, and especially those engaged in the practice of pyramiding, had become especially active in the rapidly expanding electric power industry during the 1920's; and in 1932, 13 of the largest of them controlled no less than 75 per cent of all the electric power distributed across the land. The most fantastic public power pyramid of all was that created by Samuel Insull of Chicago. At his peak, Insull was board chairman of 65 corporations out of a total of 111 that made up his empire. When the whole pyramid collapsed in 1932, it was called "the biggest business failure in the history of the world." Insull himself fled the country. Efforts to extradite him to stand trial for fraudulent use of the mails, embezzlement, and other crimes, made him as much a front page story as the New Deal, and his trial in 1934 kept the glare of publicity on the whole vulnerable industry, its reputation already soured by its ceaseless battle against the T.V.A.

Consumers as well as investors had suffered from public utility holding companies, and the Act of August, 1935, required that those which could not, within five years, demonstrate that they had brought about economies in management must be dissolved. This "death sentence" clause touched off a bitter struggle in Congress, and holding companies spent large sums trying to defeat it. At length, after some compromises, the "death sentence" remained in the measure, which was signed on August 28. Its constitutionality was questioned, but the Supreme Court eventually upheld it. Every effort to impose the "death sentence," however, continued to be stubbornly resisted.

The third August enactment was the Social Security Act, to secure "the men, women, and children of the Nation against certain hazards and vicissitudes of life." This measure, for the first time, provided for federal payments, directly or through the states, for pensions for the aged and the infirm, for unemployment insurance, and for benefits to dependent mothers and children. The government was to pay pensions of up to $15 a month to the poor over 65 years of age, and the states were expected to pay an equal amount. Federal retirement funds, ranging from $10 to $85 a month, were to be paid to workers who retired at 65 and who had participated in the plan before their retirement. Agricultural workers, household servants, government employees, and those working for non-profit religious or charitable organizations, were among those excluded. The money for those included was to be raised by a payroll tax levied equally on employers and employees. Most states promptly set up old-age pension and unemployment insurance systems conforming to the provisions of the act. A worker who lost his job could collect from $5 to $15 a week for a period of about 15 weeks while he looked for work.

By 1940, about 50 million workers were protected by social security. From time to time since then, new classes of workers have been covered, money payments increased, and the period for receiving unemployment insurance extended. A non-partisan Social Security Board administers the program.

The Social Security Act passed the House and Senate with far larger majorities than the other reform measures. Its opponents, however, made up in emphasis what they lacked in numbers. Several of them asserted that it would mean the end of free government. "The lash of the dictator will be felt," said one congressman.

Those who participated in the act, as in other New Deal measures, felt otherwise. So much has been made of the bureaucratization of government under the New Deal that its democratizing tendencies, especially among those heretofore deprived of the right or impulse to participate in decisions critical to their well-being, have been lost sight of. The N.I.R.A., for example, asserted that "employees shall have the right to organize and bargain collectively *through representatives of their own choosing,* and shall be free from the interference, restraint, or coercion of employers . . . or their agents." The National Labor Relations Act of July, 1935 (see below), stated this right in even stronger terms. The A.A.A., in turn, gave thousands of Negro cotton farmers in the South who had never voted before the right to participate equally with others in the referendums by which regional crop controls were voted up or down. Under the Social Security Act, finally, millions of aged and incapacitated workers in the cities and in rural areas found a new interest in state governments made responsible by the act for state contributions to pension and other funds. "Yes ma'am," said a destitute old woman after a week of publicity for "human security" in her state, "we all know about it . . . Now that we know all the facts the legislators just can't rightly afford not to find the money."

THE LABOR MOVEMENT
IN INDUSTRY AND POLITICS

When the Supreme Court, in May, 1935, found the National Industrial Recovery Act unconstitutional, and thereby invalidated Section 7(a) guaranteeing labor the right of collective bargaining (see p. 719), Congress did little about the rest of the defunct act, but it promptly, in July, 1935, enacted the National Labor Relations Act to afford labor a more defensible framework for organizing activities. The long-run effects of this measure for the political future of the New Deal, for the Democratic party, and for the country generally, were to prove as profound and lasting as its economic consequences.

Even while Section 7(a) had been in oper-

728

ation, militant labor organizers, especially in the mass-employment industries, had gone to the workers with great success with the argument, "The President wants you to join." With this approach, immense gains were made in industries that were already partially organized, and also in new ones, like the automobile and the rubber-tire industries, where there had been no unions before. Total union membership, which had stood at 2,857,000 in 1933, rose to 3,728,000 by 1935. Collective bargaining under Section 7(a) never worked to the satisfaction of labor leaders largely because of management domination of code machinery, but it had given them a remarkable organizing weapon which was easily made into a political one as well. The National Labor Relations Act, or the Wagner Act as it is often called after Senator Robert F. Wagner of New York, a major force behind its enactment, was one of its first victories.

The Wagner Act established a National Labor Relations Board (N.L.R.B.) of three members, in place of 7(a's) National Labor Board. It also re-enacted in almost the same words the collective bargaining guarantees of 7(a), but it tightened the restrictions on "unfair labor practices" of employers who tried to coerce workers into joining company unions, to dominate outside unions, and to interfere with a worker's decision to join a union. The act provided that the representative of the majority of the employees in any plant should be the *exclusive* bargaining representative of *all* the employees, and empowered the N.L.R.B. to investigate and certify the proper representatives and to hold supervised elections among employees when there was a dispute over which union should represent them.

Business organizations led by the powerful National Association of Manufacturers, protested that the National Labor Relations Act was one-sided. But labor and government replied that its aim was to rectify the great one-sidedness of corporate power in dealing with unorganized workers. Under the new act no less than 340 company unions were broken up. Membership in free trade unions continued to grow,

until in 1941 it had reached 10.5 million. By then the N.L.R.B. had handled 33,000 cases affecting more than 7,000,000 workers. More than 90 per cent of the cases had been settled amicably, and over 75 per cent of the strikes certified to the Board had been settled peaceably.

The remarkable rise in organized labor, nevertheless was accompanied by considerable strife, not only between workers and employees, but also within labor's own ranks. The A.F.L. itself was badly split. The leaders of the old craft unions that had first come together in the Federation (see p. 537), sought to retain their own power and standing as the "aristocracy of labor." Loath to bring in the unskilled and semi-skilled workers of the mass-production industries, they also refused to permit other leaders to organize such workers in new unions. But these leaders were themselves tough men who did not brook obstruction.

The issue came to a head in the national convention of the A.F.L. in October, 1935, when a majority of the delegates stood fast for craft unionism. A month later, John L. Lewis of the United Mine Workers and seven other A.F.L. leaders met separately and organized the Committee for Industrial Organization (C.I.O.), nominally to advise the A.F.L. on how to organize the mass-production industries. Lewis became chairman of the committee. In January, 1936, the A.F.L. executive council ordered the C.I.O. to disband. On refusing, they were suspended in August, and expelled in March, 1937, taking with them unions representing 1,800,000 workers. A massive organizing campaign followed, contributing heavily to the record 4,740 strikes that year. Early in 1938, when the C.I.O. boasted nearly 4 million members, the leaders formed a new, independent organization with the same initials, the Congress of Industrial Organizations.

One of the C.I.O.'s novel weapons, outlawed by the Supreme Court in 1939, was

Overturned and broken cars line the road during strike at Newton Steel Company, Monroe, Michigan, June 11, 1937.

the "sit down" strike. Workers, instead of walking off the job and picketing went to their posts in the plants and stayed there, thus making it hard for scabs to replace them. Sit-down strikes against two giant automobile companies, General Motors in January, 1937, and Chrysler in April, won the C.I.O. recognition as bargaining agent for their workers. In March, 1937, United States Steel Corporation, once the terror of organized labor, also capitulated.

"Little Steel" proved harder to crack. On Memorial Day, 1937, Chicago police killed ten pickets during a strike against the Republic company, "Little Steel's" leader. Other strikes, like that against Republic all lost, brought violence in Youngstown, Massilon, and Cleveland, Ohio. Little Steel did not fall until 1941 when it signed contracts even conforming to the N.L.R.B. order to reinstate workers fired during the 1937 struggle.

As labor grew more aggressive and important in politics as well as business, the split in its ranks caused much irritation and many difficulties. A peace movement finally brought about a merger of the A.F.L. and C.I.O. in 1955; but lingering bitterness

over the old battles forestalled a genuine reconciliation.

THE ROOSEVELT COALITION

Toward the end of Theodore Roosevelt's administration in 1908, the New York *Tribune* commented that the lasting value of the "Square Deal" lay in its "calling public attention to social problems and bringing them into politics." The lasting value of the New Deal lay in its transforming political discussion of social justice into far-reaching legislation and administration. This transformation had been largely accomplished by the end of 1935 and helped Franklin D. Roosevelt forge an extraordinary political coalition with which to push on with the work. "We will win easily next year," he told his Cabinet in November, 1935, about the coming presidential election, "but we are going to make it a crusade."

The elements of Roosevelt's coalition were partly traditional and partly new. First among the traditional forces stood the solid Democratic South. Southerners had backed the greater part of the New Deal reforms thus far, though some of them regretted the administration's solicitude for Negroes, and industrialists thought relief payments and N.R.A. wage scales were undermining the sweatshop wages paid white factory hands. Cotton and tobacco had done well under the New Deal, moreover, and the Democratic party in the still largely agrarian South held firm.

Second among the traditional forces were the Democratic machines in northern cities. Roosevelt did not set himself up as a crusader against machines. He preferred to use, not to destroy them. True, his relations with Tammany were touchy, for as a Governor of New York with presidential aspirations he had found it necessary to avoid too close an identification with such an unsavory body. Tammany men found it hard to forgive this, or his convention victory over Smith in 1932. But Jim Farley opened new lines to New York's Democratic leaders, while Roosevelt attracted additional support from such militant independents as New York City's Mayor, Fiorello H. La Guardia, and from the American Labor party, an unaffiliated group that massed the city's labor and left-wing strength behind him. Elsewhere, Roosevelt played ball with city machines and their bosses, happy after a long dry season of Republican presidents to have a Democrat in the White House. The Hague machine in New Jersey, the Flynn machine in the Bronx, the Kelly-Nash machine in Chicago, the Pendergast machine in Kansas City, Missouri, all could be counted on to deliver the votes.

Roosevelt's success with urban voters was furthered by his strong appeal to new immigrant groups who with other minorities were especially hard hit by the depression and also had begun to play a more active role in politics. Where Smith had spoken for the religious and ethnic aspirations of these people, to their demand for respect within the American political system, Roosevelt responded to their desperate economic need. Anglo-Saxon old-fashioned America, as represented by Hoover, had turned a cold shoulder to them. Roosevelt had helped them.

Among ethnic elements, Negroes had

ample grounds to shun the administration. Virtually all N.R.A. codes, for example, discriminated against Negroes on employment, wages, and job-improvement opportunities. A.A.A. crop control payments went largely to farmers with sizable acreage, leaving the Negro share-cropper's hand empty, his market curtailed. The C.C.C., in turn, began as a "lily white" agency; less than 3 per cent of the first quarter million enrolled were Negroes. Complete segregation, moreover, remained the rule here even when Negro participation was enlarged. Aubrey Williams, a white southerner and Negro champion among New Deal aides, wrote his boss, Harry Hopkins, in 1934 about the F.E.R.A.: "Negroes don't get a fair deal; I don't know how to secure one for them." In the N.Y.A. only Mary Bethune's pertinacity won Negro students some semblance of a fair shake. New Deal agencies and New Deal funds often were administered on a state or local basis. In such instances, local patterns of discrimination ruled with little correction from above.

And yet the Negro voter responded to the New Deal with enthusiasm and formed a strong part of the Roosevelt coalition. The reasons are not hard to find. In the first place, however partial his share, he, like others, did participate in New Deal relief, where there had been little or none under Hoover. Despite almost universal second-class treatment, he, like others, did benefit from New Deal reforms. And, however circumscribed his stake, he, like others, did share in New Deal economic recovery, often through the new labor movement the New Deal fostered. The New Deal approached relief, reform, and recovery on a national and a general basis. Many of its leaders, Roosevelt often included, feared for their over-all goals if established social patterns were to be attacked. Party solidarity, not to be discounted, also suggested caution on race matters to Democratic chieftains. They did little or nothing, for example, to fight the poll tax that disqualified most Negroes of voting age in the South, or to check the lynching of others. At the same time, especially in Washington itself, Roosevelt and many of his aides showed the same warmth to Negro leaders as they did to others. In the Cabinet, Ickes and Miss Perkins always proved strong Negro champions who gave Negro spokesmen a hearing and fought discrimination where they could. The New Deal also employed numerous Negro administrators. The Negro community itself had not yet developed many leaders of its own of national stature. The concern for Negro problems shown by certain New Dealers furthered the careers of such leaders and respect for them among their people. Perhaps above all, Eleanor Roosevelt's liberality of spirit and unstinted support of Negro, as of other minority aspirations, rubbed off on the urban Negro voter and carried him from his traditional allegiance to the party of Lincoln to the Roosevelt bandwagon.

The success of the New Deal's agricultural program also brought into Democratic ranks many normally Republican westerners. Iowa, for example, had gone Republican in every election from 1916 to 1928, often overwhelmingly so. In the anguish of 1932, it had swung to Roosevelt and in 1936 was still solidly behind him.

Labor's newly organized millions also swung heavily into the Roosevelt camp during 1935 and 1936, and were made welcome. John L. Lewis and other C.I.O. leaders organized Labor's Non-partisan League to mobilize the labor vote in industrial centers. The C.I.O. gave half a million dollars to the 1936 Democratic campaign. Nor did Roosevelt suffer from the split in labor's ranks, for A.F.L. President William Green, after visiting the President, announced that 90 per cent of labor's vote would be his.

The course followed by labor paralleled that of many intellectuals throughout the country. Suspicious at first of the retrogressive features of the N.R.A. and A.A.A., and troubled by the inadequacy and inconsistency of the many New Deal measures, teachers, writers, clergymen, artists, and journalists rallied behind the New Deal after the 1935 reforms. Intellectuals were heartened by the administration's receptivity to ideas and experts, and by its readiness to assist unemployed artists, scholars, and writers. The shrillness of the conservative business attack on Roosevelt caused many a writer or teacher to give him even more cordial support. Nor, for that matter, were businessmen altogether absent from the coalition. Roosevelt counted many loyal personal friends among businessmen. Others, notably anti-tariff merchants and bankers, were traditionally Democrats. Still others represented the socially-minded rich long familiar to America. A large number also came from sectors of the economy—consumer goods manufacturers, for example, and chain and department store owners and other retailers—who benefited directly from gains in mass purchasing power brought about by New Deal reform and relief measures. From them Roosevelt won a gratifying response when the chips were down. Their contributions were feeble compared with the immense outpourings the Republicans got from the corporate and personal holders of "the big money," but Roosevelt needed fewer funds to win votes than did his opponents.

THE ELECTION OF 1936

By the time of the 1936 election, the New Deal had made most of the progress it was going to make in instituting business recovery, forwarding labor organization, ameliorating the farm problem, and supporting those on relief. The general economic statistics, moreover, confirmed the success of the program. Farm income, as we have seen (p. 720), had shot up dramatically. Average weekly earnings of workers in manufacturing had risen since 1932 from $17 to almost $22. While some 7 million remained unemployed, this figure had dropped by 4 million since Roosevelt took office, and the unemployed were now receiving enough to keep body and soul together. The rise in national income from $41.7 billion in 1932 to $64.7 billion in 1936 reflected the general advance.

The Republicans, who held their national convention in Cleveland in June, however, did not shrink from a head-on confrontation. They raked the New Deal from stem to stern. "America is in peril," their platform began. The administration had dishonored the country by repudiating sacred obligations. It had committed frightful waste and extravagance, used public funds for partisan purposes, "bred fear and hesitation" in business, thereby prolonging the depression. "We invite all Americans, irrespective of party, to join us in defense of American institutions." For president the convention nominated Governor Alfred M. Landon, of Kansas, and for vice-president, Frank Knox, a Chicago newspaper publisher.

The Democrats, meeting in Philadelphia, renominated Roosevelt and Vice-president Garner by acclamation. "These economic royalists," Roosevelt told the convention, "complain that we seek to overthrow the institutions of America. What they really complain of is that we seek to overthrow their power. Presidents do make mistakes," he added, "but the immortal Dante tells us that divine justice weighs the sins of the cold-blooded and the sins of the warm-hearted in different scales."

Coughlinites and other malcontents came together in Cleveland to form a third party, the Union party, and nominated William Lemke, a Republican congressman from North Dakota, as their standard bearer; but the ranks of the demagogues had become sadly depleted after the Social Security Act of 1935 had stolen much of Dr. Townsend's thunder and the assassination of Huey Long. Coughlin, moreover, had tired many of his own followers, and had received unmistakable evidence that the Roman Catholic hierarchy found his political behavior embarrassing. Lemke was to poll fewer than a million votes and carry not a single state.

Some disaffected Democrats, including Al Smith, went over to Landon during the campaign, but his principal support came from the Liberty League, financed by conservative millionaires. The character of their defense of liberty is suggested by

Roosevelt's remark after his victory, in which he mocked at them for having attributed to him "the worst features of Ivan the Terrible, Machiavelli, Judas Iscariot, Henry VIII, Charlotte Corday, and Jesse James." Their outcries made Landon appear far less liberal and humane than he actually was, and his campaign suffered accordingly. Roosevelt defended his policies with vigor and skill before large audiences across the country, but was also influenced by Liberty League tactics. Near the end of the campaign, before a wildly enthusiastic crowd in Madison Square Garden, he declared that the New Deal had been struggling with "business and financial monopoly, speculation, reckless banking, class antagonism, sectionalism, war profiteering." He went on: "Never before in all our history have these forces been so united against one candidate as they stand today. They are unanimous in their *hate* for *me—and I welcome their hatred.*"

It was the bitterest campaign since 1896, but the end was never in doubt. Roosevelt carried all but two states, Maine and Ver-

Rev. Gerald L. K. Smith, a follower of the late Huey Long; Dr. Francis E. Townsend, share-the-wealth advocate; Representative William Lemke, Union party candidate for president; 1936.

mont; his 27,751,000 popular votes represented 60 per cent of the total cast. In the cities his margins reached record levels. Perhaps most important, by winning even more overwhelmingly than he had in 1932, he made the Democratic party the normal majority party of the country.

The fate of the minor parties testified to the inclusiveness of the Roosevelt coalition. Lemke's showing disappointed not only his followers but also those Republicans who had hoped in the early days of the campaign that he would draw enough votes from Roosevelt to swing some states to Landon. The fact that his support came largely from isolationist counties with large Irish and German Catholic populations suggests that Lemke's strength was founded more on ethnic than on economic discontent. The record of the Socialist and Communist candidates showed that the New Deal had completely broken the forces of independent political radicalism. Four years earlier, Norman Thomas, the Socialist party nominee, had won 881,000 votes; in 1936 he had 187,000. William Z. Foster, the Communist candidate in 1932, had won 102,000 votes; his successor in 1936, Earl Browder, got only 80,000.

Roosevelt's second inauguration took place, not on the traditional date of March 4, but on January 20, 1937—the date prescribed by the Twentieth Amendment to the Constitution, the "Lame Duck" Amendment, which was ratified in 1933. This amendment pushed forward the installation of newly elected presidents and congresses, eliminating the lame duck sessions, often made up of defeated members under a defeated president, held between January and the old inauguration date.

In his second inaugural address, Roosevelt expressed no complacency over his victory or his achievements. It was in this address that he said,

> In this nation I see tens of millions of its citizens—a substantial part of its whole population—who at this very moment are denied the greater part of what the very lowest standards of today call the necessities of life.
> I see millions of families trying to live on incomes so meager that the pall of family disaster hangs over them day by day.
> I see millions whose daily lives in city and on farm continue under conditions labelled indecent by so-called polite society half a century ago.
> I see millions denied education, recreation, and the opportunity to better their lot and that of their children.
> I see millions lacking the means to buy the products of farm and factory and by their poverty denying work and productiveness to many other millions.
> I see one-third of a nation ill-housed, ill-clad, ill-nourished.

Roosevelt promised that the New Deal would continue to do everything in its power to remedy these conditions. At the start of the New Deal, he said, "we did . . . first things first." But,

> Our covenant with ourselves did not stop there. Instinctively we recognized a deeper need —the need to find through government the instrument of our united purpose to solve for the individual the ever-rising problems of a complex civilization. Repeated attempts at their solution without the aid of government had left us baffled and bewildered. . . . We refused to leave the problems of our common welfare to be solved by the winds of chance and the hurricanes of disaster.
> In this we Americans were discovering no wholly new truth; we were writing a new chapter in our book of self-government.

As it happened, the growing self-consciousness of the New Deal also helped the opposition to coalesce.

III. *The Climax of the New Deal*

THE COURT FIGHT

In some ways Roosevelt's victory in the 1936 election was too sweeping. American political parties, being loose coalitions, almost always suffer inner splits of some kind. The presence of a strong opposition tends to make party members submerge differences and close ranks. When the opposition is inordinately weak, however, internal differences come quickly to the fore, and feuds are fought out. The climax of the New Deal came when Roosevelt, trying to clear the way for further reforms, challenged the power of the Supreme Court; and when, having failed in this enterprise, he tried unsuccessfully to reshape his own party into a more consistently liberal instrument. These undertakings were costly enough, but his woes were also increased by a sharp business recession in 1937-1938, which damaged his prestige and raised once again the question of whether his administration knew where it was going. The overwhelming public endorsement of 1936 was thus followed by some of Roosevelt's most striking political defeats. Even so, he was to make progress with his promised reforms.

The President's attack on the Supreme Court came out of a clear blue sky on February 5, 1937, when, apparently having consulted no one but his Attorney-General, Homer S. Cummings, who drafted the bill for him, Roosevelt proposed to Congress what was promptly called his "court-packing bill." In it he asked that whenever a federal judge failed to retire within six months after reaching the age of 70, an additional federal judge should be appointed. Although the proposal applied to the entire federal judiciary, it was obviously aimed at the Supreme Court, where six of the judges were already over 70 and thus as many as six judges could be added, bringing the full Court to 15.

Although the announcement came as a shock, the need for some such bill seemed clear enough. The people had undeniably approved of the New Deal, but the Supreme Court had unmistakably, emphatically, and disastrously opposed its early legislation. Only in the Gold Clause and T.V.A. cases had it sustained any of the major New Deal measures. In 1935 and 1936 the Court had struck down N.R.A. (including the labor section, 7(a)) and A.A.A. It had rejected a railroad retirement plan and the Bituminous Coal Act, which was intended to reorganize a sick industry. It had invalidated congressional legislation to pro-

tect farm mortgages, and it had thrown out a municipal bankruptcy act. To those who sympathized with the New Deal social program, the Court seemed to be creating a no-man's land where neither state nor federal power could be brought to bear on critical problems. Unless the Court were reformed, it appeared unlikely that additional reform legislation could be made effective.

The number of Supreme Court justices had, in fact, been changed several times in the past, but the present array of nine had been fixed for so long it almost had the sanction of constitutional authority. A possible alternative to Roosevelt's plan would have been to enlarge the number of judges by constitutional amendment, but to pass such an amendment would have taken years. An amendment removing or limiting the Court's power to review acts of Congress would also have been difficult to pass and almost impossible to explain, though in theory it would have been a more direct and open attack upon the problem. Roosevelt's plan was a short cut, but it lacked candor. Its real purpose was to change the tenor of the judges' decisions by bringing new blood into the Supreme Court; but Roosevelt's assertion that it was intended to help the federal courts generally to catch up with their business seemed disingenuous. This aspect of the bill, even to a large number of New Dealers, gave color to the charge that Roosevelt was indeed seeking those dictatorial powers that his opponents all along had said he wanted.

Even while debate on the bill was in progress events occurred that further weakened its chances. Most important, within a few weeks of Roosevelt's bombshell, Justice Owen J. Roberts, influenced perhaps by the clamor over the Court's conservatism and by the results of the 1936 election, began to vote on the liberal side in some cases. "A switch in time saves nine," said a legal wit.

The sudden liberalism of Justice Roberts became apparent on March 29, 1937, when the Supreme Court handed down three decisions that bespoke its change of heart. In *West Coast Hotel Co.* v. *Parrish,* by 5-to-4, it sustained a state minimum wage law, thus overruling the reactionary decision in *Adkins* v. *Children's Hospital* (1923) (see p. 700) and even a very recent decision by the same justices in *Morehead* v. *New York ex. rel. Tipaldo* (1936). On the same day the Court unanimously sustained the revised Farm Mortgage Act of 1935 and the Railway Labor Act as amended in 1934. Even more important for the course of the New Deal were five decisions on April 12 upholding the National Labor Relations Act. Six weeks later, in two 5-to-4 rulings, the Court sustained the social security legislation.

In May, Justice Van Devanter, one of the most conservative men on the bench, struck another blow at the court-reform bill when he announced his intention to retire, thus making it clear that Roosevelt would have at least one appointment of his own. Then in June, the Senate Judiciary Committee gave the *coup de grâce* to the bill, reporting against it by the narrow vote of 10 to 8. It was a "needless, futile, and utterly dangerous abandonment of constitutional principle," said the report. It "should be so emphatically rejected that its parallel will never again be presented to the free representatives of the free people of America." On July 22, the Senate heeded this advice. It voted overwhelmingly, 70 to 20, to recommit the bill to the Judiciary Committee, where it was forever buried.

And yet Roosevelt had a sort of triumph after all, over and above the recent heartening decisions. In August, 1937, he appointed the liberal Hugo L. Black of Alabama to Van Devanter's place on the Court. In the next few years other aging justices also took the cue and began to retire—Cardozo and Sutherland in 1938, Butler and Brandeis in 1939, and finally Hughes and McReynolds in 1941. To five of the vacancies thus created Roosevelt appointed liberals and New Dealers—Stanley Reed, Felix Frankfurter, William O. Douglas, Robert H. Jackson, and Frank Murphy. The sixth place went to James F. Byrnes of South Carolina. Into

the Chief Justiceship vacated by Hughes, Roosevelt shifted the learned, liberal Harlan Fiske Stone, a firm advocate of ample federal powers. New Dealers thus could console themselves with the thought that they had lost the battle but won the war, even though the whole procedure had opened a lasting rift in the Democratic party and left a lingering bad taste in the mouth of the public.

STRAINING
TOWARD THE WELFARE STATE
    The hazards and hurt feelings of the Court fight did not deter the President from pushing for the amelioration of the plight of the underprivileged, which he had promised in his second inaugural and which Court reform itself was intended to speed up. Many reforms were gained or extended during F.D.R.'s second term; but once again, the political costs were high, indicating that the reform potential of the Democratic coalition was being exhausted.

Among those reforms that extended earlier programs were the Bituminous Coal Act of 1937, which set up a code of competition for the sick soft-coal industry, replacing one enacted in 1935 and outlawed by the Court; the Farm Tenancy Act of 1937 (see p. 722), which was strongly opposed by southern conservatives; the second Agricultural Adjustment Act, passed in 1938 (see p. 721); and the Food, Drug, and Cosmetic Act of 1938. The last of these, remedying serious defects in the Pure Food and Drugs Act of 1906 (see p. 656), prohibited the misbranding of products and misleading advertising.

The two most novel reforms attempted to strike more seriously at inadequate housing and low wages. As early as 1933 the administration had created the Home Owners Loan Corporation (H.O.L.C.) with huge resources to protect impoverished householders from losing their property through mortgage foreclosure. In June, 1934, it had set up the Federal Housing Administration (F.H.A.) to lend money mainly to middle-income families for repairing old houses or building new ones. The H.O.L.C. had also undertaken housing development, and had helped more than a million home-owners. But positive action in *low-income housing* came only now with the Wagner-Steagall Housing Act of September, 1937, which established the United States Housing Authority (U.S.H.A.) and authorized it to make long-term, low-interest loans to state or city public-housing agencies to clear slums and construct houses that met its standards. Tenants for these houses were to be restricted to those who evidently could not pay rents high enough to induce private builders to construct dwellings for them. By 1941, the U.S.H.A. had torn down more than 78,000 sub-standard buildings and built homes for 200,000 families. This accomplishment met only a small portion of the need, but private building interests henceforth stalled the program.

The last major New Deal reform measure was the Fair Labor Standards Act of June, 1938. The outcome of long-standing liberal agitation, this measure had failed to pass Congress on its first try. Finally, after Roosevelt gave it his support, it became law over strong opposition from southern Democrats. To those covered by this act, which included most industrial workers but conspicuously omitted farm labor on the insistence of rural congressmen, it aimed to secure a minimum wage of 40 cents an hour and a maximum work-week of 40 hours. Even these modest objectives would be attained gradually. Beginning at 44 hours, the work-week was to be lowered to 40 hours in three years. Beginning at 25 cents an hour, the minimum wage was to be raised to 40 cents after eight years. The law also called for time-and-a-half for overtime, banned the employment of children under 16, and limited workers under 18 to non-hazardous occupations.

Many Americans were shocked to discover that over 750,000 workers were so poorly paid that they received immediate wage increases when the law first went into effect in August, 1938. The hours of 1,500,000 workers were shortened at the same time. Modest as its requirements were, the law was an important step toward outlawing sweatshop conditions and abuses of child labor. Years

afterward, in 1949, when rising prices had wiped out the benefits of the minimum wage increase, President Truman persuaded Congress to raise the level to 75 cents, and it was raised still higher under each subsequent administration.

Although Congress yielded to the President's demand for housing and labor legislation, it grew even more refractory on other issues. A special session called in the fall of 1937 balked at all Roosevelt's recommendations when southern Democrats bolted to form a new coalition with Republicans. With astonishing stubbornness, Congress refused both in 1937 and 1938 to pass an innocuous executive reorganization bill overhauling executive agencies in the interests of efficiency. A modified bill was at last passed in April, 1939. The previous April, a congressional spokesman begged the White House, "For God's sake, don't send us any more controversial legislation!" That May, the southern Democratic-Republican coalition passed a bill cutting taxes on large corporations, which Roosevelt allowed to become law without his signature. General Hugh Johnson, an old associate turned foe, exulted: "The old Roosevelt magic has lost its kick."

THE CONSERVATIVE REVIVAL

Much of F.D.R.'s unwonted political difficulty arose from the fact that all the apparent New Deal gains in the matter of business recovery went aglimmering in 1937 when no less than 4,000,000 returned to the unemployment rolls. The "Roosevelt recession," so-called, seems to have come about partly because the administration, encouraged by signs of business advance, had called for a reduction of expenditures by the W.P.A. and other New Deal agencies. High tax rates, enacted in 1935 and 1936, also seem to have cut private investment, and the accumulation of funds in the Treasury under the social security laws cut purchasing power. The readiness with which retrenchment in government expenditures started the downward trend suggested that the administration still could not do without its spending policies. Early in 1938, the President and Congress put the spending program back into high gear. Once more recovery began to stir, though the mid-1937 level of business activity was not again reached until World War II.

The recession, though it had its chief effects on the government's tax and spending policies, aroused new concern over the pricing policies of American business as an obstacle to recovery. Now the administration, once responsible for the N.R.A.'s comprehensive attempt to organize industry and arrange price agreements, espoused an opposite philosophy and opened an attack on monopoly. In a message to Congress in April, 1938, Roosevelt warned that private power was growing "stronger than [the] democratic state itself." Business concentration, he said, was "seriously impairing the effectiveness of private enterprise," and added: "Big Business collectivism in industry compels ultimate collectivism in government." In June, Congress created the Temporary National Economic Committee (T.N.E.C.) to restudy the whole structure of American private enterprise. T.N.E.C.'s thorough work, collected in 37 volumes of testimony and 43 monographs, remains a landmark in government economic investigations. The administration, meanwhile, launched a vast trust-busting program. Ironically, the campaign was put in the hands of Assistant Attorney-General Thurman W. Arnold, who had poured scorn on the antitrust acts in his satiric book, *The Folklore of Capitalism.* The Antitrust Division of the Department of Justice, now greatly expanded, began a crusade against artificial price-maintenance. The theory behind the program was that the heavy industries enjoyed a semi-monopoly that enabled them to maintain their prices even in bad times, whereas the more competitive industries had to cut their prices drastically. This situation, it was alleged, contributed to the imbalance of the economy, cut purchasing power, and impeded recovery. Arnold initi-

ated many prosecutions, but the outbreak of World War II made it impossible to judge their long-range value.

These drastic steps only seemed to strengthen and spread the growing dissatisfaction with the New Deal already intensified by the persistent "recession." On the eve of the congressional elections of 1938, Roosevelt recalled his efforts to "pack" the Supreme Court by attempting to "purge" the Democratic party of conservative southerners and others who themselves were alienated by the growing prestige of labor in the New Deal. Again, he only succeeded in adding numbers to the discontented while purging almost no one. In the elections themselves, the Democrats, northern and southern, retained majorities in both houses, but the Republicans made large gains, raising their representation in the House from 89 to 164 and in the Senate from 16 to 23. Even the President now seemed ready to acknowledge that the reform urge in the New Deal was spent. In his annual message to Congress in January, 1939, he said: "We have now passed the period of internal conflict in the launching of our program of social reform. Our full energies may now be released to invigorate the processes of recovery in order to preserve our reforms." Recovery was soon to come, but by way of a new war in Europe and not the application of energy at home.

AN ASSESSMENT
Although the New Deal commanded the loyalty of the majority of Americans, as shown by the election results, it was hotly contested at every turn and is still the subject of considerable controversy.

Anti-New Dealers point out that the New Deal was an expensive experiment, that it persistently failed to balance the budget, and that from the fiscal year 1932 to 1940 the national debt increased from $19.5 billion to almost $43 billion. The New Deal, they argue, also built up a large bureaucracy; the number of civilian federal employees jumped from 588,000 in 1931 to 1,128,000 in 1940. At the same time, it had failed to restore the confidence of the business community which held the real key to recovery. In 1939, when all the experiments were over, more than 8,700,000 workers remained unemployed by private industry.

Defenders of the New Deal have strong counter arguments. New Deal policies raised the debt, but they also helped raise national income from $41.7 billion in 1932 to $70.8 billion in 1939. Furthermore, pro-New Dealers contend that if unemployment under the New Deal is measured in terms of real human suffering and social waste, it was far less burdensome than in earlier days. Finally, the New Deal had placed on the statute books a number of measures to make life more comfortable and secure, measures that would benefit not only contemporaries, but also millions of Americans yet to be born. After 1936, not even the Republicans quarreled in their party platforms with such reforms as the Social Security Act, minimum wages and hours, improved hous-

ing for low-income families, or the insuring of bank deposits.

When Roosevelt came into office in 1933, many Americans were flirting with false gods—with thoughts of violence, with doubts about democracy, with political panaceas of the extreme right and the extreme left. The New Deal restored their belief that a democratic people could cope with its own problems in a democratic way. This demonstration was significant for the whole western world. Tyranny ruled in Russia, Germany, Italy, and Japan. But in the most powerful of the western democracies, the people still moved, erratically but freely, toward the solution of their problems through constitutional and parliamentary means.

Readings
* Asterisk indicates that book is available in paperback.

The best short introduction to the New Deal is W. E. Leuchtenburg, *Franklin D. Roosevelt and the New Deal* * (1963). A. M. Schlesinger, Jr., *The Coming of the New Deal* (1959), and *The Politics of Upheaval* (1960), carry his comprehensive history of The Age of Roosevelt through the 1936 election. Frank Friedel, *Franklin D. Roosevelt* (3 vols., 1952-1956), is the definitive biography as far as it goes, which is only through the 1932 election. Outstanding comprehensive biographies include R. G. Tugwell, *The Democratic Roosevelt* (1957); and J. M. Burns, *Roosevelt; The Lion and the Fox* * (1956). Besides Tugwell's, the best "inside" narratives include Frances Perkins, *The Roosevelt I Knew* * (1946); Raymond Moley, *After Seven Years* (1939); H. L. Ickes, *The Autobiography of a Curmudgeon* (1943); and R. E. Sherwood, *Roosevelt and Hopkins* * (1948). Samuel Rosenman, ed., *The Public Papers and Addresses of Franklin D. Roosevelt* (9 vols., 1938-1941), is an exceptionally valuable collection. J. M. Blum, *From the Morgenthau Diaries, Years of Crisis 1928-1938* (1959), and *Years of Urgency 1938-1941* (1964); and *The Secret Diary of Harold L. Ickes* (3 vols., 1953-1954), disclose the inside story of the Treasury and the Interior respectively by Roosevelt's most enduring Cabinet members. R. S. and H. M. Lynd, *Middletown in Transition* * (1937); and F. L. Allen, *Since Yesterday* * (1940), deal with the social history of the period. See also C. A. and M. R. Beard, *America in Midpassage* (2 vols., 1939). Frank Freidel, *The New Deal and the American People* * (1964), is a valuable anthology of contemporary material. Harvey Swados, ed., *The American Writer and the Great Depression* * (1966), conveys the impact of the age through exceptionally well-selected examples of creative writing. See also, Daniel Aaron, *Writers on the Left* * (1961).

From a vast and often technical literature on special phases of the New Deal, the following may be recommended: Jesse Jones, *My Thirteen Years with the R.F.C., 1932-*

1945 (1951); A. W. Crawford, *Monetary Management Under the New Deal* (1940); and Milton Friedman and A. J. Schwartz, *A Monetary History of the United States 1867-1960* (1963). More discursive on finance and related subjects is M. S. Eccles, *Beckoning Frontiers* (1951). H. S. Johnson, *The Blue Eagle from Egg to Earth* (1935), is the N.R.A. from the point of view of its chief. See also L. S. Lyon and others, *The National Recovery Administation* (1935). Sidney Fine, *The Automobile under the Blue Eagle* (1963), is an illuminating special study. H. A. Wallace, *New Frontiers* (1934), suggests some of the philosophy behind the A.A.A. Other significant works on the farm problem include J. D. Black, *Parity, Parity, Parity* (1942); Gilbert Fite, *George N. Peek and the Fight for Farm Parity* (1954); E. G. Nourse and others, *Three Years of the Agricultural Adjustment Administration* (1937); and A. F. Raper and I. D. Reid, *Sharecroppers All* (1941). D. E. Lilienthal, *T.V.A.: Democracy on the March* (1938), and *Journals, The TVA Years 1939-1945* (1946), are by the one-time T.V.A. chairman. See also C. H. Pritchett, *The Tennessee Valley Authority: A Study in Public Administration* (1943). On private power, see M. L. Ramsay, *Pyramids of Power: The Story of Roosevelt, Insull, and the Utility Wars* (1937).

H. L. Ickes, *Back to Work: The Story of the P.W.A.* (1935); D. S. Howard, *The WPA and Federal Relief Policy* (1943); and J. K. Galbraith and G. G. Johnson, Jr., *Economic Effects of Federal Works Expenditures 1933-1938* (1940), deal with the attack on poverty and unemployment. On this subject, S. F. Charles, *Minister of Relief: Harry Hopkins and the Depression* (1963), supplements Sherwood's work, above. P. H. Douglas, *Social Security in the United States* (1939); and E. E. Witte, *The Development of the Social Security Act* * (1962), cover this basic reform. Labor under the New Deal is dealt with authoritatively in Selig Perlman, *Labor in the New Deal Decade* (1945); Walter Galenson, *The C.I.O. Challenge to the A.F.L., A History of the American Labor Movement 1935-1941* (1960); Philip Taft, *The A.F. of L. From the Death of Gompers to the Merger* (1959); and Edwin Young and Milton Derber, eds., *Labor and the New Deal* (1957). H. R. Cayton and G. S. Mitchell, *Black Workers and the New Unions* (1939); and H. S. Northrup, *Organized Labor and the Negro* (1944), are revealing studies. Nathan Straus, *The Seven Myths of Housing* (1944), affords an expert analysis.

Clair Wilcox, *Competition and Monopoly in American Industry* (1940), is an excellent introduction to that subject. See also, Thurman Arnold, *Bottlenecks of Business* (1940). Arnold's, *The Folklore of Capitalism* * (1937), deftly lays bare some of the pitfalls of trustbusting. David Lynch, *Concentration of Economic Power* (1946), is a useful examination of the T.N.E.C. reports and conclusions. Outstanding general economic studies of the period include Broadus Mitchell, *Depression Decade: From New Era Through New Deal 1929-1941* (1947); A. H. Hansen, *Full Recovery or Stagnation* (1938); and K. D. Roose, *Economics of Recession and Revival* (1954). See also, Daniel Fusfeld, *The Economic Thought of Franklin D. Roosevelt and the Origins of the New Deal* (1958).

In addition to the general works on Roosevelt and the New Deal, informative on politics are J. A. Farley, *Jim Farley's Story* (1948); and Charles Michelson, *The Ghost Talks* (1941), two accounts by insiders. Opposition reactions will be found in Herbert Hoover, *Addresses upon the American Road* (1938), and *Memoirs* (3 vols., 1951-1952); and A. M. Landon, *America at the Crossroads* (1936). George Wolfskill, *The Revolt of the Conservatives: A History of the American Liberty League, 1934-1940* (1962), is a scholarly account. Pressure from the left is analyzed in D. R. McCoy, *Angry-Voices: Left-of-Center Politics in the New Deal Era* (1958); and A. M. Bingham, *Challenge to the New Deal* (1934), and *Insurgent America* (1935). Irving Howe and Lewis Coser, *The American Communist Party: A Critical History 1919-1957* * (1957) and Earl Latham, *The Communist Controversy in Washington: From the New Deal to McCarthy* (1966), are authoritative. E. L. Tatum, *The Changed Political Thought of the Negro 1915-1940* (1951), is an illuminating account. R. G. Swing, *Forerunners of American Facism* (1935); and H. T. Kane, *Louisiana Hayride* (1941), tell the story of the demagogues and their leader, Huey Long. E. E. Robinson, *The Roosevelt Leadership* (1955), is an evaluation by a Hoover enthusiast. Other evaluations are available in Richard Hofstadter, *The American Political Tradition* * (1948), and *The Age of Reform* * (1955).

The story of the Court fight is well told in Joseph Alsop and Turner Catledge, *The 168 Days* (1938). E. S. Corwin, *Court over Constitution* (1938); and R. H. Jackson, *The Struggle for Judicial Supremacy* * (1941), state the case against the Court. Corwin's *Constitutional Revolution* (1941), evaluates the outcome. On this theme, see also C. H. Pritchett, *The Roosevelt Court: A Study in Judicial Politics and Values 1937-1947* (1948).

CHAPTER TWENTY-EIGHT

Early in 1929, just before the Great Crash, when the well-off could still afford to wonder about their relation to God and the Universe, and not to their fellowmen, Joseph Wood Krutch published *The Modern Temper*. In a social sense it was an optimistic book. Although its theme was the dissipation of values, the *inevitable* disintegration of the moral structure of society, well-fed, well-clothed, well-housed men, their creature comforts apparently more readily taken care of than ever before in history and likely to continue so, might "submit," as Krutch says, with the exhilarating "detachment" of the scientist to the

The

Modern Temper

tragedy he described. Such submission, indeed, would be but an intellectual coming of age, a willing surrender of "the world of poetry, mythology, and religion," which "represent the world as man would like to have it," and a gallant embracing of the "world of science," the "world as he gradually comes to discover it."

For the cozy bowl of the sky arched in a protecting curve above him he must exchange the cold immensities of space and, for the spiritual order which he has designed, the chaos of nature.

Krutch himself would set the mature example.

Krutch called *The Modern Temper,* "A Study and a Confession." Twenty-five years later he wrote what he permitted others to call a "reply" to *The Modern Temper.* To this book Krutch himself gave the title, *The Measure of Man,* and described it as "A Study and a Refutation." He insisted here that, "the most prevalent educated opinion is still that men are animals and that animals are machines." And yet he now confronted "the stubborn fact of consciousness," accepting, with William James, "the pragmatic ground that whatever we say we believe we never find it possible to act on any assumption other than that there are choices open to us." He also accepted Alfred North Whitehead's dictum that, "scientific thinking is, after all, only a *way* of thinking, rather than a description of ultimate reality." And yet the best Krutch would even now begrudge mankind was the possibility of "adjustment" to the "dismal assumptions which make Social Engineering rather than Existentialist resignation the dominant religion of today." Social Engineering itself lay in the hands of "the manipulators of the media of mass communication." They look, said Krutch, to "the creation of a Robot Utopia whose well-adjusted citizens will have comfortably forgotten that their forefathers believed themselves to be Men."

Others in America and elsewhere have usually been more sanguine. In the United States in particular, early in the twentieth century, many intellectuals saw "the masses" not as animals, but as the élan vital of a society smothered by the genteel tradition. These intellectuals called the "media of mass communication" the "lively arts," and found laughter once again in the movies of Mack Sennet and Charlie Chaplin, in comic strips like "Bringing Up Father" and "Krazy Kat," in "dixieland jazz," "ragtime," and The Follies. They saw these media and new-fangled radio as liberating not "conditioning" instrumentalities. In the 'twenties, moreover, even the most skeptical and escapist authors in the grand tradition wrote with a disenchantment that itself reflected active moral judgment not resignation, and as a group they endured more frequent personal "crack-ups" than any earlier generation of American writers.

The depression of the 'thirties dragooned many American authors back to social realism, some of them embracing the "Robot Utopia" of the U.S.S.R., which seemed to offer a viable alternative to the cruel failures of individualism and capitalism. As late as 1937, when many such authors were abandoning the cruel totalitarianism of Russia under Stalin, the playwright Albert Bein exclaimed: "When I . . . see these people looking, with microscopes, for pimples on the shining face of the Soviet Union, I wonder, am I crazy or what?" The *New Masses* of the 'thirties became the mouthpiece of the diehard American totalitarians. The original *Masses* of the 'teens was the mouthpiece of "the lyric years." Krutch's *The Modern Temper,* in its sharp, sophisticated way, serves efficiently to divide the two. The natural determinism and philosophical fatalism it celebrates helped undermine the lyricism and élan of the earlier age, helped underpin the scientism and regimentation of the later one. And yet, as such social crises as the depression at home and World War II abroad showed, the conventional values of civilization—mercy and justice, liberty and democracy, the humanistic values Krutch and others considered "childish"— were not to be shirked because of the ascribed indifference of the universe to them.

I.   *The Lyric Years*

IN QUEST
OF THE CONTEMPORARY
        The exuberant cultural interlude that ushered in Woodrow Wilson's presidency in 1912 has been called the "little renaissance"—"little," for being rudely interrupted by America's entry into World War I in 1917, but also for representing more of an accentuation than a renewal of the artistic war against gentility that had begun after the Civil War and had proceeded thereafter in fits and starts (see Chapter 22). The new writers who came of age around 1912, like their rebel predecessors, attacked the genteel tradition for its deliberate blindness to reality, its polite protective evasions. But worse than its artistic philosophy in general, now, was its particular failure, in the words of Van Wyck Brooks, "to grasp the contemporary American mind and its problems, to discover what the contemporary mind is, and what it is capable of, and how it can be best approached."

Brooks' generation and a brilliant group of younger novelists, poets, dramatists, critics, and artists proceeded to examine "the contemporary mind" and to arrive at some interesting if not always flattering conclusions about it. Many of these writers and artists came from regions and ethnic backgrounds heretofore skimpily represented in creative circles in America. Some of the most talented lived beyond the precincts of the eastern seaboard. A number had attended no university nor could they be considered "gentlemen" in the sense that the genteel understood that term. Some associated in groups and adhered to programs, artistic, cultural, or political. Others carried on their battle as lone-wolves, preferring to perfect themselves as artists rather than try to save the world. Yet they also found a solidarity with the others, especially before the war, in their informal "league of youth,"—"freely experimental," as one of their manifestoes said, "skeptical of inherited values, ready to examine old dogmas, and to submit afresh its sanctions to the test of experience."

THE "LEAGUE OF YOUTH"

The cultural program of the young radicals reaffirmed a creed that had been set forth more than a century before: the idea that America must produce a civilization that truly reflected American democracy and American life. They advocated no break with the European past, but they deplored the parochial dependence of American writers and artists on European models and European approval.

Van Wyck Brooks, an articulate spokesman for the new generation, expressed its convictions and hopes in a series of challenging books. By 1913, he had come to believe, with the Harvard philosopher and poet, George Santayana, that "all nationalities are better at home," that a transplanted culture sickens and dies. He had accepted the injunction of the Irish poet, William Butler Yeats, that "one can only reach out to the universe with a gloved hand,—that glove is one's nation." What Brooks and his friend Randolph Bourne, a promising and

dedicated member of the "league of youth," were groping for was "a socialized world culture" in which America would play a leading part. "How many drafts we have issued in the past upon European thought, unbalanced by any investment of our own!" Brooks wrote. "The younger generation have come to feel this obligation acutely." He concluded: "Certainly no true social revolution will ever be possible in this country till a race of artists, profound and sincere, have brought us face to face with our own experience."

Others, no less idealistic and dedicated, joined in this crusade. Randolph Bourne blamed college professors for failing to take advantage of the "usable past." Ezra Pound in *Patria Mia* (written before 1913 but unpublished for many years thereafter) predicted that America was preparing for an intellectual awakening, a "risorgimento"; foreshadowing the slogan of the 1912 presidential campaign, Pound declared that the "first duty of a nation is to conserve its human resources." Like Brooks, who in *America's Coming of Age* (1915) spoke of the gulf between the "highbrows" living in an abstract dream world far removed from the realities of American life and the "low brows" dedicated to practical, vulgar ends and "cynically contemptuous of ideals," Pound repudiated the "dry rot" of gentility and the "red blood" of "the school of virility," and believed then that America had more to say than both.

Across the country, in large cities and in small towns, "intellectually emancipated" Americans met in little free-thinking kingdoms where they might escape from the "bourgeois pigs" or the "apathetic, mawkishly-religious middle class." Bohemia might be a small circle of artists and writers in Chicago or St. Louis or even Davenport, Iowa, but its mecca by 1914 was a few West Side blocks in downtown New York known as Greenwich Village. Here the Revolution, in both its cultural and political phases,

John Sloan, "Greenwich Village Backyards," 1914.

was brooded over if not hatched. The wildest young rebels from all over America came to the Village to be free, to flout convention, to live vibrantly. Young women, drawn there from the small towns bobbed their hair, threw away their corsets, gave studio parties, debated the "new" ideas.

One of the gilded priestesses of the new Bohemia was Mabel Dodge (Luhan)—a wealthy lady of advanced views who opened her Fifth Avenue apartment to Village rebels of every persuasion. At her famous evenings, the guests discussed everything from penology and poetry to birth-control—anything, in short, that came under the heading of "opinions." It was generally conceded that when, in Mabel Dodge's words, "strangely penetrating intuitions rose to consciousness," they should not be repressed.

Such over-simplified Freudian notions were now beginning to be bandied about. Although Freud's influence was not to be fully felt until the 'twenties, his visit to America in 1909 and the translation before 1915 of certain of his early works—*The Interpretation of Dreams,* and *Three Contributions to a Theory of Sex,* for example—had brought him to the attention of the

Village intellectuals. For the most part they used arbitrarily selected insights of psychoanalysis to justify their private revolts against convention. "Puritan" opposition to the alleged immoralities implicit in Freud helps explain why the radicals elevated him to a symbol of protest.

To Village denizens, *The Masses,* first published in 1912 under the editorship of Max Eastman, one of the early popularizers of Freud, expressed the "correct" attitude toward art, politics, and morals. Though committed to socialism, *The Masses* reflected a peculiar anarchism and paganism—what one of its editors (the poet, novelist, and Village historian, Floyd Dell) called the "play spirit." It was both passionately reformist and refreshingly gay. "What made us so 'objectionable,'" Max Eastman later remarked "was not primarily our attack on capitalism—that question was still a trifle academic in America. But we voiced our attack in a manner that outraged patriotic, religious, and matrimonial, to say nothing of ethical and aesthetic tastes and conventions."

A distinctive feature of *The Masses* were the drawings and cartoons of the "Ashcan School." Their master, Robert Henri, a Philadelphia painter, encouraged his young disciples, William Glackens, John Sloan, George Luks, and George Bellows, to represent the life around them faithfully, even though it meant dignifying saloons and Bowery boys, prostitutes and horse-cars.

The photographer, Alfred Stieglitz, as early as 1908, had begun to exhibit in his Fifth Avenue gallery the newer experimental painting from abroad known generally as post-Impressionism and representing the work of Matisse, Braque, Picasso, and others. The new art, in its more extreme forms of Cubism and Fauvism, defied "realism" as vigorously as the "Ashcan School" embraced it. After the post-Impressionist Armory Show in New York City in 1913—it was also hung in Boston and Chicago, where thousands flocked to see it—the prestige of the "Ashcan School" declined even among the young rebels. When academic traditionalists, in particular, denounced the new art, some members of the "league of youth" gleefully leapt to its defense.

The abstract designs that bewildered or amused the uninitiated at the Armory Show in time were adopted for commercial use in architecture, advertising, and hundreds of mass-produced articles; but the antagonism between what is loosely called "modern art" and academicism continued long after the individualists of 1913 had expressed in paint and plastic forms their private visions.

THE NEW THEATER
AND THE NEW POETRY

Out of *The Masses'* circle came an exciting experiment in the theater—the Provincetown Players. A group of Greenwich Village writers had been spending their summers at Provincetown, Massachusetts. In 1913, inspired largely by the roving teacher, philosopher, and writer, George Cram Cook, the Provincetown group began to produce amateur plays. Three years later, they were operating a theater in the Village with the assistance of sympathetic artists and writers who performed as actors.

The Players' greatest gift to the theater was Eugene O'Neill (1888-1953), who among his other occupations had worked as a common seaman. O'Neill's *Bound East For Cardiff,* a one-act play produced in Cook's theater in 1916, recalled the world of tramp steamers, waterfront dives, and seaman's talk the playwright had observed at first hand. The young O'Neill also contributed poetry to *The Masses,* threatening with his verse to torpedo the "Rust-eaten, grimy galleons of commerce." But before 1920 he put aside his radicalism and began to write plays in which characters struggled against uncontrollable natural forces. *Emperor Jones* (1921), *Anna Christie* (1920), *The Hairy Ape* (1922), *Desire Under the Elms* (1924), *Strange Interlude* (1927), and *Mourning Becomes Electra* (1931) make up a partial list of plays that won O'Neill the Nobel Prize in 1936.

O'Neill's work was often marred by excessive psychological baggage and ponderous grappling with "big" themes. But in his early plays, and in at least two of his last,

The Iceman Cometh (1946) and *Long Day's Journey Into Night* (1956), O'Neill's dramatic gifts were most clearly displayed: an ability to write dialogue at once vernacular and lyrical and an emotional sincerity that distinguished his plays from the sleazy entertainment of the commercial stage.

Two *avant garde* magazines performed for the new poetry a role similar to that of Cook's Provincetown theater for the new drama—Harriet Monroe's *Poetry,* founded in 1912, and Margaret Anderson's *Little Review,* which followed in 1914. Both were published in Chicago, the home of a school of poets whose calliope yells startled the eastern seaboard.

One of them, Carl Sandburg (1878-   ), crowded into his verse much of the turbulent middle-western life he had observed in the prairie towns of Illinois and in the raw metropolis of Chicago,

> Stormy, husky brawling
> City of the Big Shoulders.

A child of Swedish immigrants, Sandburg quit school at thirteen and worked at odd jobs before becoming a journalist. *Chicago Poems* (1916), his first book of verse, incorporated the American vernacular long

Eugene O'Neill (1888-1953).

absent from American letters. In successive volumes, Sandburg continued his poetic notations on mid-America in broken free-verse rhythms. Sandburg wrote of steelworkers, of "Boxcars, clocks, steam-shovels, churns, pistons, boilers, scissors—," of towns illuminated at night by the coke ovens, of itinerant work gangs, Yiddish restaurants, and the Mayor of Gary, Indiana, with his "cream cool pants" and white shoes, of men who "had bunches of specialized muscles around their shoulders," of honkytonks in Cleveland. He studded his verse with slang: "neck-tie parties," "galoots," "chippies," "mouthpiece," "crummy." Sandburg is at his best when he captures the world of silos and cornfields, the band concerts in the small towns where girls with their "flowing and circling dresses" and the "boys driving sorrel horses" giggle

> Amid the cornet
> staccato and the tuba oompa, gigglers,
> God knows,
> gigglers daffy with life's razzle-dazzle.

Chicago Poems and *Smoke and Steel,* best convey Sandburg's urban mood.

Vachel Lindsay (1879-1931) also dealt with midwestern themes. His reputation today rests on a few poems like "The Congo" and "General Booth Enters into Heaven." But just as Whitman's self-image as a brawny, open-shirted vagabond belies the inner man, so Lindsay's medicine-man pose is less typical of him than his tender and elegiac lyrics about Governor Altgeld of Illinois, Lincoln, and Johnny Appleseed, or his poems of failure and defeat, such as "The Leaden Eyed":

> Let not young souls be smothered out before
> They do quaint deeds and fully flaunt their
>   pride.
> It is the world's one crime its babes grow
>   dull,
> Its poor are ox-eyed, limp and leaden-eyed.
>
> Not that they starve, but starve so dream-
>   lessly,
> Not that they sow, but that they seldom
>   reap,
> Not that they serve, but have no gods to
>   serve,

Not that they die, but that they die like sheep.

Even Vachel Lindsay's unsuccessful poems frequently contain startling rhythms, remarkable lines, and metaphors of astonishing freshness. This poet, artist, mystic, and democrat hoped to make his native city, Springfield, Illinois, a center for his Gospel of Beauty. If his religious upbringing made him curiously strait-laced in his tastes, he conveyed his theories irreverently, and in poems like "Factory Windows are Always Broken" jokingly embodied his revolt against the industrial age. In 1914 and for the next decade, Lindsay achieved some reputation, but he exhausted himself lecturing to audiences who wanted him to recite the verse he liked the least. When he committed suicide in 1931, Sherwood Anderson observed: "We do very well by our poets here, when they are dead."

Edgar Lee Masters (1869-1947) was the third outstanding Chicago poet. A lawyer (he was Clarence Darrow's partner), Masters wrote nothing of importance before *Spoon River Anthology,* published in 1915. Few books strip away the romantic aura of small-town life so completely. Most of the children of Spoon River—the good and the bad, the talented and the untalented, the saints and the hypocrites—die thwarted and broken. Knowlt Hoheimer, killed by a bullet at Missionary Ridge, wishes that he had been jailed for stealing hogs instead of running away to join the Union army; Editor Whedon, who crushed reputations "or bodies, if need be," to sell his papers, lies buried where the town sewage and refuse are dumped; Elliott Hawkins, who looked like Abraham Lincoln and served the railroad interests faithfully, lies comfortably under his tombstone and asks the "world-savers" what they have gained from their labors. Yet a few survive the travail of living and are toughened and purified by it. Fiddler Jones ends his life "with a broken fiddle," but with "a thousand memories" and "not a single regret." And Lucinda Matlock, dead at 96 after a strenuous life, affirms:

What is this I hear of sorrow and weariness,
Anger, discontent and drooping hopes?
Degenerate sons and daughters,
Life is too strong for you—
It takes life to love Life.

Chicago also fostered what Ezra Pound, *Poetry's* European correspondent, called the "technic and aesthetic" poets. Pound (1885- whose influence on American and British poetry is hard to exaggerate, was a westerner born in Hailey, Idaho, but from 1909 on, he held down a trans-Atlantic outpost, encouraging young poets in America (and in Britain, too), to revolt against the old clichés, the "obscure reveries," and "the classics in paraphrase." To the vigor of Whitman, whom he honored as a poetic ancestor, he wished to add the precision of Henry James and the fine hardness of the painter Whistler—men who proved the possibility of being artists and at the same time Americans. The "Imagists," led by Pound and Amy Lowell, a Bostonian lady as aggressive and as opinionated as Pound himself, advocated the kind of verse that presented hard, clear, poetic outlines in concentrated images. Pound soon abandoned imagism for new discoveries. He encouraged promising young poets like T. S. Eliot, whose now much anthologized "The Love Song of J. Alfred Prufrock" bewildered even the most advanced American critics when it appeared in *Poetry* in 1915. Pound also praised the verse of Robert Frost when that poet was still unread in America.

Frost (1875-1963) was born in San Francisco but moved to New England in his tenth year. His most distinctive poetry evokes the bleak beauty of the New Hampshire hills, and the taciturn and self-contained Yankees who speak in his monologues seem a part of the landscape. Before he went to England in 1911 so that he could write poetry "without further scandal in the family," he had worked as a bobbin boy in a textile mill,

edited a paper, and studied briefly at Dartmouth and Harvard. Frost's first two volumes of verse, *A Boy's Will* (1913) and *North of Boston* (1914), were published in England, and he was still virtually unknown when he returned to the United States in 1914, a man of 40. The American publication of *North of Boston* in 1914, however, firmly established his reputation as one of America's foremost poets.

Frost followed in the tradition of Emerson (one of his favorite poets) and Emily Dickinson (see p. 605), for he also chose to illuminate the prosaic materials of everyday life, to derive profound insights about man and eternity from a patch of snow, a bird's nest, a stone wall, a birch tree, from pastures and ax-halves. These emblems of New England were exactly named and placed with a countryman's assured knowledge. They also meant something. "A poem," Frost said, "begins in delight and ends in wisdom." Such poems as "After Apple-Picking," "Mending Wall," and "Stopping By Woods on a Snowy Evening" begin as pictures from experience and end as thought.

The popularity of Frost and other contributors to the poetry revival weakened the bastions of traditionalism, and the rebels whose work had been condemned as so much obscure fustian began to appear with increasing frequency in the older literary magazines. Young poets, whose reputations were to become well-established by the middle 'twenties, made their debuts before 1920: Wallace Stevens—now generally regarded as the peer of Eliot and Frost; Hart Crane, author of "The Bridge"; and Edward Arlington Robinson, much of whose work antedated the poetry renaissance.

II. *Years of Disenchantment*

THE WAR AND THE INTELLECTUALS

In 1917, two events occurred that blasted the buoyant hopes of Van Wyck

Brooks, Pound, and Bourne and brought the "joyous season" to a close. On April 2 the United States went to war in Europe;

six months later the October Revolution brought the Bolsheviks to power in Russia. Artists and intellectuals now found public opinion less tolerant of free thought and pacifists and radicals were shouted down (see p. 678). *The Masses,* symbol of joy and liberation, was banned after its editors had twice been brought to trial for impeding the war effort. *The Seven Arts,* edited by Paul Rosenfeld and Waldo Frank, suspended publication in 1917. "The mental . . . as well as the financial . . . strain was too great," one of the editors wrote to a subscriber. "Everything liberal (and liberating) is being hounded to death . . . from free speech to free verse."

It was now left to Randolph Bourne to make the most bitter pronouncements of the "league of youth." Many of his friends had begun to support the war, but Bourne, weak, crippled, pursued by government agents, and denied an outlet for his writing, refused to change his views. In *The Seven Arts,* he wrote in June, 1917:

> To those of us who still retain an irreconcilable animus against war, it has been a bitter experience to see the unanimity with which the American intellectuals have thrown their support to the use of war-technique. . . . And the intellectuals are not content with confirming our belligerent gesture. They are now complacently asserting that it was they who effectively willed it, against the hesitation and dim perceptions of the American democratic masses. A war made deliberately by the intellectuals! A calm moral verdict, arrived at after a penetrating study of inexorable facts! Sluggish masses, too remote from the world-conflict to be stirred, too lacking in intellect to perceive their danger! An alert intellectual class, saving the people in spite of themselves. . . !

As the war's legacy, Bourne foresaw only the most profound decline:

> The war will leave the country spiritually impoverished, because of the draining away of sentiment into the channels of war. Creative and constructive enterprises will suffer not only through the appalling waste of financial capital in the work of annihilation, but also in the loss of emotional capital in the conviction that war overshadows all other realities.

Soon other American intellectuals would share Bourne's feeling that the nation's best years and best hopes were behind it and that they were helpless to restore the spirit. Many of them took at once a more private and more professional attitude toward their work. The religion of art changed from a social gospel to a personal commitment—the last precious refuge of the individual talent.

Gertrude Stein called the postwar writers and artists the "lost generation" because in their youth the war had broken the continuity of their lives. Yet not all of them were so discouraged, fatalistic, and nihilistic as they have been pictured. Indeed, the "jazz age," if it was marked by a desperate frivolity, was also marked by a hectic and often healthful iconoclasm. "Coolidge prosperity" in a war-scarred world almost seemed a sin that drove many American artists and writers back to Europe in revulsion—itself a moral act—where they joined others who had never come home from the war. Still others, who stuck it out at home, drew corrosive satires of "Babbittry" and otherwise undermined the conventional values in preparation, perhaps, for something better.

THE EXPATRIATES

The many American writers and artists who went abroad before the war had gone to look, to compare, to criticize. America remained their homeland despite their tirades against its defects, and they believed that she would yet produce a vital culture. The expatriates of the 1920's were different. To be sure, they considered themselves, sometimes almost belligerently, as cultural representatives of their native land, but not of its standardization, Puritanism, "snooping smut-hounds" (H. L. Mencken's phrase), or machine-culture. In Paris, their Mecca, as Malcolm Cowley, the expatriates' historian explained, the artist enjoyed the "tolerance" for "indiscipline," and his work was respected. France, said Gertrude Stein, "surrounds you with a civilized atmosphere and then lets you be yourself."

The habits and attitudes of the Paris expatriates have been recounted in Ernest Hemingway's *The Sun Also Rises* (1926) and F. Scott Fitzgerald's *Tender is the Night* (1934) and more objectively assessed in Cowley's *Exile's Return* (1936). Of all the members of the lost generation they were the most profoundly disenchanted. They had a private code and a private language, wrote the novelist Kay Boyle, one of the "exiles." "Those who speak it follow no political leader and take no part in any persecution or conquest; nor have they to do with a vocabulary of the rich or the poor or any country or race; it being simply one way of communication between the lost and the lost"—an airy, groundless way of finding, sustaining, one another.

And that, I believe [wrote Cowley], was the final effect on us of the War; that was the honest emotion behind a pretentious phrase like "the lost generation." School and College had uprooted us in spirit; now we were physically uprooted, hundreds of us, millions, plucked from our own soil as if by a clamshell bucket and dumped, scattered among strange people. All our roots were dead now, even the Anglo-Saxon tradition of our literary ancestors, even the habits of slow thrift that characterized our social class. We were . . . infected with the poison of irresponsibility—the poison of travel, too, for we had learned that problems could be left behind merely by moving elsewhere—and the poison of danger, excitement, that made our old life seem intolerable.

A symptom of this intellectual disaffection was the Dadaist movement that flourished briefly in Paris during the 'twenties. It stood for the privacy of art, nihilism, absurdity. Every man rode his own hobbyhorse, his own Dada, and the ideal Dadaist production was shocking, unique, purposeless, incomprehensible. The novelist and critic Waldo Frank recognized that such a movement suited tired and battered Europe; it was, he said, "a salutary burst of laughter in a world that felt itself too old." But he criticized the young expatriates who joined the Dadaists, suggesting that America, with its Ku Klux Klan, William Jennings Bryan, and Hollywood, was zany enough for any poet.

MENCKEN AND MENCKENISM
H. L. Mencken (1880-1956), the "master of revels" of the jazz age, had al-

ready begun to practice at home what Waldo Frank preached abroad. Mencken's career began in 1899 when, as police reporter for the Baltimore *Morning Herald,* he gained his first familiarity with the underworld and the conventional superstructure of American society. His apprenticeship in literary iconoclasm began with books on Bernard Shaw in 1905 and on his idol, Nietzsche, in 1908. His contributions to *Smart Set* before 1917 set the tone for the *American Mercury,* which he founded with George Jean Nathan in 1924. Unlike the evangelical Village Bohemians, Mencken from the outset had attacked social idealists and radicals along with the Philistines. His social philosophy was anti-democratic both before and after the war, all the more devastatingly so since for Mencken the conventional middle-classes, the pillars of society, even more than the masses, consisted of boobs, yokels, or peasants, and America was their paradise.

During the prewar period Mencken's iconoclasm served a direct purpose. He defended Dreiser against charges of immorality, he lampooned American provincialism, he, like other rebels, spoke out for what he ironically called the "mongrel and inferior" Americans of European ancestry. No one, with the possible exception of Poe, had so steeped himself in popular American culture. Newspapers, magazines, religious pamphlets, advertisements—nothing escaped his attention. He loved and understood the vernacular, as his splendid *The American Language,* first published in 1919, attests. With it, and the esoteric vocabulary culled from his wide and indiscriminate reading, he developed a unique prose style, a raffish journalese all his own.

The 'twenties, especially the early 'twenties, were made for Mencken. Edmund Wilson aptly refers to his relish "for the squalid, semi-literate writing" produced by his contemporaries, not least those now in high places. The prose of President Harding, which he likened to that of a "rhinoceros liberating himself by main strength from a lake of boiling molasses," became his particular butt. Mencken's ferocious assault on all America's Public Truths delighted his followers and made him one of the most hated men in the United States. He systematically mauled every sacred conviction of the common man. Democracy was a failure, but it provided "the only really amusing form of government ever endured by mankind." The plutocracy lacked "all the essential characters of a true aristocracy: a clean tradition, culture, public spirit, honesty, honor, courage—above all, courage." Monogamy was against nature; romantic love a lie. Protestantism was "down with a wasting disease." The American farmer was "a tedious fraud and ignoramus, a cheap rogue and hypocrite" who "deserves all that he ever suffers under our economic system." Mencken reserved his deepest scorn for the "ordinary Class I Babbitt," the flower of the American "booboisie." In one of his volumes of *Prejudices,* which he began publishing in 1919 and continued every year or two for the next few years, Mencken asked of himself: "If you find so much that is unworthy of reverence in the United States, then why do you live here?" He replied with another question, "Why do men go to zoos?"

Readers eventually grew fatigued with Mencken, but as late as 1927 Walter Lippmann thought him to have been "the most powerful personal influence on this whole generation of educated people." That his influence was in fact good rather than bad, and deliberately so, Mencken himself acknowledged when he dropped his mask of cynicism and revealed himself a moralist:

The iconoclast [he wrote once] proves enough when he proves by his blasphemy that this or that idol is defectively convincing— that at least one visitor to the shrine is left full of doubts. The liberation of the human mind has best been furthered by gay fellows who heaved dead cats into sanctuaries and then went roistering down the highways of the world proving to all men that doubt, after all, was safe—that the god in the sanctuary was a

fraud. One horse-laugh is worth ten thousand syllogisms.

Mencken's *American Mercury,* moreover, was among the first to welcome with hosannas the "new" writers of the 'twenties—the O'Neills, Sinclair Lewises, Hemingways, F. Scott Fitzgeralds—and to force conservative critics to accept their work as that of the voice of America.

THE STERNER INDICTMENT

If the First World War shook the faith of so many intellectuals in society in general and in American values in particular, the October Revolution in Russia suggested to some that social redemption might yet be possible and the grounds on which to seek it. Among the hopeful were old Bohemians like Max Eastman, Robert Miner, Joseph Freeman, Michael Gold and Floyd Dell, men once affiliated with *The Masses* and its successor in 1919, *The Liberator,* who now repudiated their carefree past. The Russian experience, Dell declared in the early 'twenties,

showed us that "freedom" is a bourgeois myth. It would set up in place of "freedom" certain definite and realizable goals, of a not unfamiliar sort, and it would teach us that these are to be achieved by organizing social activities involving all of the customary personal virtues, including such dull matters as honesty, sobriety, responsibility, and even a sense of duty . . . it would offer us the possibility, in the nature at present of a religious hope, of shaping the whole world nearer to the heart's desire.

Until the Great Crash of October, 1929, brought many expatriates back from Europe broke, and the Great Depression convinced them that capitalism was as bankrupt as themselves (see p. 761), Dell and company found few converts. Those among the lost generation in Greenwich Village as in Paris who deigned at least to take a look at the Soviet Union usually came away with the suspicion that as an alternative to American materialism the USSR was simply another Babbitt society in the making, or something worse.

This second disenchantment reinforced

that of the war itself and thereby strengthened the tendency among intellectuals to take up, on the one hand, the boisterous raillery of Mencken and on the other, the sophisticated fatalism of Krutch. The latter, for this generation, had been anticipated in 1918, if not in 1907, by the publication of *The Education of Henry Adams,* which had been privately circulated since the earlier year. Adams—historian, novelist and prophet, grandson and great-grandson of presidents—confessed that he could not adjust to the civilization of the dynamo, where "order," as far as the human spirit was concerned, "was an accidental relation obnoxious to nature," and where we therefore "must accept the regime." In the 'twenties, when the civilization of the dynamo—science and technology—seemed to prove itself in America's apparently permanent prosperity, the regime grew easier to accept. Belief in Dell's "religious hope" of "shaping the world nearer to the heart's desire" was a fantasy. Wrote Krutch: "We know at least that we have discovered the trick which has been played on us and that whatever else we may be we are no longer dupes."

There remained still a third choice—one closely embraced by those as cold as Krutch to religion yet less willing to abdicate to nature's indifference to man. Their opening manifesto was *Civilization in the United States, An Inquiry by Thirty Americans,* a fat book of close to 600 pages edited by Harold E. Stearns and published in 1922. "We wished to speak the truth about American civilization as we saw it," wrote Stearns, "in order to do our share in making a real civilization possible."

The truth as they saw it and wrote of it proved more damning than Mencken's diatribes: The theater, according to George Jean Nathan, was "at once the richest theater in the world and the poorest. Financially it reaches to the stars; culturally . . . it reaches to the drains." The American city, Lewis Mumford wrote, was an index of the country's material success and spiritual failure. "The chronic state of our literature," Van Wyck Brooks said, "is that of a youthful promise which is never redeemed. . . . For half a century the American writer as a type has gone down in defeat." The universities, said Professor Joel Spingarn, seemed to have been created "for the special purpose of ignoring or destroying scholarship." Business simply showed, said Garet Garrett, "Man's acquisitive instinct acting outside of humanistic motives." The American husband, Alfred Kuttner found, "becomes everything in his business and nothing in his home. . . . The wife, on her part, either becomes hysterical or falls victim of religious reformatory charlatanism." The corrective lay deeper than Marx's dialectic: "There must be an entirely new deal of the cards in one sense," wrote Stearns; "we must change our hearts."

Two other important books written at the beginning and end of the 'twenties seemed to corroborate these conclusions without the charge to do better. Thorstein Veblen's *Absentee Ownership* (1923) reviled the country town as "the perfect flower of self-help and cupidity standardized on the American plan," and Robert S. and Helen M. Lynd exposed the cultural barrenness of their *Middletown* (1929).

III. *The Lively Arts*

THE BOGUS BARED

Few Americans of any class read Stearns, Veblen, or even the Lynds during the 'twenties; their bludgeoning of American culture made few dents on their targets. A broader disenchantment with the mainstream of American culture was implicit in the welcome given even by certain "highbrows" to the "low-brow" or the "lively" arts. The very name by which they were called served to separate the quick from the dead, the brisk from the "bogus."

As it happened, the most important of the lively arts of the 'twenties, the movies, were also the most highly mechanized, the most highly capitalized, the one closest to big business in production and distribution methods. Like the programs of their later rivals, radio and TV, movies were "mass produced" for "mass audiences" and already alarmed many about the "mass conditioning" of the "mass mind." Others, however, saw the mechanized movies, as they saw the other lively arts, as another broad avenue of escape from the horse-and-buggy sentimentalism of the cultural life. In the 'twenties, among movies themselves, the bogus was already being separated from the genuine. Serious critics also began to make distinctions among the productions of the other lively arts. No one took them more seriously, and contemporary fine art more skeptically, than Gilbert Seldes, Harvard '14, who in 1924 identified the new creative fields and gave them standing in his popular book, *The Seven Lively Arts*. What were the "seven" Seldes found? Actually, his title was a catch phrase, numerically inexact. TV, except experimentally, was still in the future. Besides the movies and radio, Seldes emphasized popular music and the dance, the musical theater, the newspaper comic strip.

"Bogus is counterfeit," Seldes wrote, "and counterfeit is bad money, . . . and unless it is discovered, bad money will drive out good. . . . The existence of the bogus is not a serious threat against the great arts, for they have an obstinate vitality and in the end—but only in the end—they prevail. It is the lively arts which are continually jeopardized by the bogus, and it is for their sake that I should like to see the bogus go sullenly down to oblivion." To speed it on, Seldes issued this "manifesto" in his book:

If there were an Academy I should nail upon its doors the following beliefs:
That Al Jolson is more interesting to the intelligent mind than John Barrymore and Fanny Brice than Ethel;
That Ring Lardner and Mr. Dooley in their best work are more entertaining and more important than James B. Cabell and Joseph Hergesheimer in their best;

That the daily comic strip of George Herriman [*Krazy Kat*] is easily the most amusing and fantastic and satisfactory work of art produced in America to-day;
That Florenz Ziegfeld is a better producer than David Belasco;
That one film by Mack Sennet or Charlie Chaplin is worth the entire *oeuvre* of Cecil de Mille;
That *Alexander's Ragtime Band* and *I Love a Piano* are musically and emotionally sounder pieces of work than *Indian Love Lyrics* and *The Rosary*;
That the circus can be and often is more artistic than the Metropolitan Opera House in New York;
That Irene Castle is worth all the pseudo-classic dancing ever seen on the American stage; and
That the civic masque is not perceptibly superior to the Elks' Parade in Atlantic City.

"All of these comparisons," Seldes wrote later, "were made, obviously, for purposes of shock. In that, they apparently succeeded."

THE MOVIES

The oldest of the modern lively arts, the motion picture, was born as a humble peep-show in a penny arcade. The viewer put a nickel in a device called a kinetoscope (invented by Thomas A. Edison about 1896) and saw tiny figures moving against blurred backgrounds. Edison, regarding his invention as little more than a childish toy, soon lost interest in it, but others took it up and soon succeeded in projecting images on a screen for the benefit of large audiences. By 1905, more than 5,000 "nickelodeons," housed in converted stores and warehouses throughout the country, were running rudimentary films for a five-cent admission.

The peep-shows had prospered by showing short, presumably comic action, such as a man sneezing. The new films, some as long as a thousand feet, introduced an array of new frenetic devices. There were endless variations on the theme of the chase, with cowboys chasing badmen, city sleuths chasing bank robbers. Comedians threw custard pies at one another and slipped on banana peels. The first picture with a recognizable plot was *The Great Train Robbery* (1903), and its instant success set every producer to turning out thrillers. But there were still no stars, no sex, no culture. It was David W. Griffith who finally liberated the movie camera from the themes of the nickelodeon and the techniques of stage filming. His *The Birth of a Nation* (1914), though a partisan and intolerant film about the Civil War and Reconstruction, was grandly received, budgeted at an unheard-of $100,000, and directed with imagination. Sweeping panoramas of massed armies, fade-outs, and close-ups of the principals showed what could be done with a camera.

By 1917, the movies had become a multi-million-dollar industry, with Hollywood as the film capital, complete with all its now familiar trappings. Luxurious movie theatres began to replace the nickelodeons in towns across the country, and Americans were spending $175 million a year on admissions. The first stars—Mary Pickford, Roscoe ("Fatty") Arbuckle, Douglas Fairbanks, Marie Dressler—earned fabulous salaries, lived glamorous lives, and attracted incredible newspaper and magazine attention, much of it promoted by movie press agents to keep the stars in the public eye. The stars themselves sometimes cooperated only too well. In 1920, "America's Sweetheart," Mary Pickford, shocked her fans by divorcing the actor Owen Moore in Nevada and promptly marrying the dashing Douglas Fairbanks. The next year, "Fatty" Arbuckle gave a fabulous party in a San Francisco hotel at which one of the feminine guests died under suspicious circumstances. The press immediately leapt on the tragedy as a "sex crime," Arbuckle himself was implicated, and though acquitted after several trials, was driven from his movie career.

Such incidents only heightened Hollywood's reputation as a Gomorrah from which unspeakable sin was being spread by movies with such titles as *Sinners in Silk* and *Women Who Give.* Although these films promised considerably more than they gave, moralists worried about their effect on the youth of the 'twenties and agitated for official censorship. In 1922, the film producers, having decided to forestall such cen-

sorship by regulating their own affairs, hired Will H. Hays, who had been chairman of the Republican National Committee and Harding's Postmaster-General, to act as their conscience. The moral code Hays devised set certain standards governing love-making, décolletage, crime, and profanity. Since Hays' day the code has been revised from time to time, becoming more or less strict as the pressures on the industry fluctuated. The larger issue of the distortions this censorship imposes on reality were seldom examined by industry authorities.

While sex, or at least the promise of sex, was not easily suppressed by the Hays office, the industry's ambivalent attitude toward it helped give a strong impulse to the production of other types of pictures, especially the grand spectacles which exploited the vast mechanical possibilities of the camera. This, after all, was in the great Griffith vein; but where Griffith dealt boldly with contemporary themes, his successors gave currency to the counterfeit. The most successful of them was de Mille, whose grandiose religious concoctions—*The Ten Commandments, The Flood, The King of Kings*—deeply offended those who had high hopes for the new art form.

Besides sex and spectacles, comedy quickly became a movie staple, in the old "nickelodeon" tradition. Arbuckle, Harold Lloyd, and Buster Keaton were among the leading "gag" men of the day, but it was Charlie Chaplin who gave movies their standing with the intellectuals. Edmund Wilson, in *The New Republic* in September, 1925, reviewed Charlie in *The Gold Rush:*

The one performer of Hollywood who has succeeded in doing anything distinguished with this primitive machinery of gags is, of course, Charlie Chaplin. In the first place, he is, I believe, the only comic star in the movies who does not employ a gag-writer; he makes everything up himself; so that, instead of the stereotyped humor of even the best of his competitors, most of whose tricks could be interchanged among them without anyone's knowing the difference, he gives us jokes that, however crude, have an unmistakable quality of personal fancy. Furthermore, he has made it a practice to use his gags as points of departure for genuine comic situations.

Wilson added that along with such earlier Chaplin productions as *The Kid* and *The Pilgrim,*

with their gags and their overtones of tragedy, their adventures half-absurd, half-realistic, their mythical hero, now a figure of poetry, now a type out of the comic strips, [*The Gold Rush*] represents the height of Chaplin's achievement. He could scarcely, in any field, surpass the best moments of these pictures.

Wilson thought *The Gold Rush,* with its "finer psychology and . . . less spectacular farce," would not be able to hold its popularity against" the cruder comedians. But he soon found that "what has happened is the reverse of what I predicted. *The Gold Rush* has had a conspicuous success; and so far from playing Chaplin off the screen, Buster Keaton and Harold Lloyd have taken to imitating him."

Wilson also found exhilaration in another aspect of the movies, the enlightening, not the "conditioning" one. "The film about Evolution which was shown in New York last summer," he wrote in November, 1925, "reminded one of the great possibilities of the cinema for scientific exposition. . . . If the picture could only, I thought, be shown in Dayton, Tennessee (see p. 696), the inhabitants of that backward region might be shaken in their literal faith in the account of creation in Genesis."

RAGTIME AND JAZZ

What the projector did for motion, the phonograph, another Edison invention, did for sound. The effort to record and reproduce the human voice and musical performances went far back into the nineteenth century. Edison became interested in the problem in the 1870's in order to develop a labor-saving device for use in conjunction with the telegraph. The best telegraph operators could send perhaps forty words a minute, a rate less than half as fast as men normally talked. Edison sought a machine that could take down message after message and then transmit each at a hundred or more words a minute. He took out his first patent on such a machine in 1877 and thereafter, with others, worked out the enormous improvement that led to the process of cutting master disks, reproducing masses of identical records from them, and spinning them on turntables where their sound would be animated by a needle and sent forth through a horn. By 1905, the phonograph had become a successful commercial device by which comedians and actors, and leading singers and musicians in opera and on the stage, could be heard in the home or in places of public entertainment. By 1914, more than half a million phonographs were being manufactured each year and soon the figure verged on a million.

Before radio (see p. 757), the phonograph gave the greatest impetus to the spread of popular music, much of it ragtime and jazz which the devotees of the lively arts in the 'twenties hastened to differentiate from the pseudo-Viennese sentimentality of composers like Victor Herbert. "Ragtime," Seldes wrote in *The Seven Lively Arts,* "is not, strictly speaking, time at all." While its composers required syncopation at precisely the right moment and employed other technical devices, the main thing was that their music "has torn to rags the sentimentality of the songs which preceded it." The first great name in ragtime was Irving Berlin, who wrote "Alexander's Ragtime Band," "simple and passionate and utterly unsentimental," thought Seldes in 1924. Then came the characteristic accolade:

What makes the first rag period important was its intense gaiety, its naïveté, its tireless curiosity about itself, its unconscious destruction of the old ballad form and the patter song. The music drove ahead; . . . led to fresh accents. . . . For half a century syncopation had existed in America, anticipating the moment when the national spirit should find in it its perfect expression; for that half century serious musicians had neglected it; they were to study it a decade later when ragtime had revealed it to them.

The second great name in ragtime was Paul Whiteman, whose exceptionally large popular band gave it currency in concerts and records. The aspirations of the new musicians are revealed most dramatically in the work of George Gershwin, who made the first and perhaps most successful efforts to write serious music in the ragtime idiom. The New York Symphony Society played his Piano Concerto in 1926, the same year in which Paul Whiteman's band presented Gershwin's opera, "135th Street," in Carnegie Hall. Gershwin had written it three years before for George White's *Scandals*. Edmund Wilson, reviewing these events, did not fail to find the Whiteman band "very fastidious and elegant, and stamped with the ideal of perfection."

Jazz presented a different problem to the critics of the lively arts who, for a long time, remained outside the Negro world, or at least the southern world, from which it sprang. Jazz spread northward, especially to Chicago's South Side and New York's Harlem, only with the accelerated migration of Negroes themselves to the great cities above the Mason-Dixon line (see p. 695). The first dixieland "jass" bands (as it was spelled), played in these cities around 1915, the year W. C. Handy wrote his epochal "St. Louis Blues." In 1922, F. Scott Fitzgerald, already a precocious celebrity (see p. 764), published *Tales of the Jazz Age,* and thereafter (though not necessarily through cause and effect) Harlem in particular became the resort of "fast" young New York socialites prowling for exotic thrills. Not until midway in the decade did jazz strike Seldes and his friends:

> The fact that jazz is our current mode of expression, has reference to our time and the way we think and talk, is interesting; but if jazz music weren't itself good the subject would be more suitable for a sociologist than an admirer of the gay arts. Fortunately, the music and the way it is played are both of great interest. . . . If—before we have produced something better— we give up jazz we shall be sacrificing nearly all there is of gaiety and liveliness and rhythmic power in our lives. Jazz, for us, isn't a last feverish excitement, a spasm of energy before death. It is the normal development of our resources,

the expected, the wonderful, arrival of America at a point of creative intensity.

Thereafter, those who could not get to Harlem obtained records instead, and the virtuosos of the trumpet, trombone, clarinet, piano, and drums became as well known to enthusiasts as Caruso to opera lovers and Babe Ruth to baseball fans.

RADIO

Unlike the movies, whose commercial possibilities were exploited from the first, the early development of radio was haphazard and accidental. In 1920, perhaps 20,000 amateur "hams" listened on home-made sets to wireless messages, sent mainly from ships at sea. That year, as an experiment, the Westinghouse Electric and Manufacturing Company in Pittsburgh began to broadcast musical programs. Amateurs in the area responded enthusiastically, and soon popular demand induced Westinghouse to put the programs on a regular basis and to introduce reports of baseball scores. A Pittsburgh department store began to advertise radio sets, and in 1920 the first commercial broadcasting station, KDKA, was set up in Pittsburgh to broadcast the results of the Harding-Cox election.

KDKA was an enormous success; overnight, radio too became big business. Within four years, 562 stations were sending out music, stock-market and news reports, bedtime stories, church services, and prizefights. By 1930, over 12 million American families had radios; by 1940 the figure passed 28 million. By then there were 765 radio stations across the land, approximately a fourth of them controlled by newspapers or newspaper chains bent on dominating competitive news outlets. Now that Americans could listen to nominating conventions and campaign speeches in their homes, their interest in politics grew. Millions followed the Smith-Hoover campaign of 1928 by radio, and millions more followed the dramatic developments of the New Deal era by listening to Franklin D. Roosevelt's "fireside chats."

As a news medium, radio continued to perform a real service. Although it gave fewer details than the newspapers, it got those details to the public more swiftly. Radio reporting, under the supervision of the Federal Communications Commission after 1937, also tended to be freer from the bias, distortion, and extravagant omissions of which so many newspapers were guilty.

Once established as a national habit, radio-listening became the object of intensive study by two groups—the advertisers, who paid for most of the entertainment, and the critics of popular culture, who were concerned about its quality. As a selling medium, radio seemed unsurpassed. The advertiser could reach into the homes of millions and repeat his message hour after hour. Most people, surveys showed, tend to accept "commercials" as the price they must pay for free entertainment. Even illiterates were corralled for the advertisers message, while the siren sound captured the more sophisticated as well.

Radio's first step toward cultural prestige, taken as early as the mid-'twenties, was the weekly nationwide broadcast of opera from the Metropolitan in New York. Symphony concerts soon followed, under such eminent conductors as Stokowski and Toscanini. From time to time, experimental poetry and drama were encouraged, and independent stations, freed from network advertising pressure, produced exciting shows whose continuity was only occasionally broken by a sponsor's message. Yet, it was time more than talent that radio had to sell; and every minute had to be put to productive use. The demand for programs put a tremendous strain on the creative community whose work soon became stereotyped. One of the first victims was popular music itself, sadly corrupted by the specialists of Tin Pan Alley in New York who made a business of supplying radio tunes, as one critic said, "about as fast as manufacturers could roll out cars or lipsticks." In the mid-1930's, a reporter wrote that "as deadlines ap-

proach for melody orders, song teams work straight through lunch and dinner and, if necessary, far into the night." Tin Pan Alley, it was said "was as hysterical as the mad market it served." The climax of stereotyping came with the "soap opera," according to Seldes, "the great invention of radio, its single notable contribution to the art of fiction."

As early as the mid-'twenties, Seldes began looking to radio largely as the means by which to reverse the tendency toward the bogus already too apparent in de Mille type big-business movies. "Ignorant and unhappy People," was his salutation in an open letter to the movie magnates in 1924:

The Lord has brought you into a narrow place—what you would call a tight corner—and you are beginning to feel the pressure. A voice is heard in the land saying that your day is over. The name of the voice is Radio. . . . It is easier to listen than to read. And it is long since you have given us anything significant to see. . . . If the historian tells you that the pictures you produced in 1910 were better than those you now lose money on, he is worthless to you. But if he fails to tell you that the pictures of 1910 were the way to the real right thing and that you have since departed from that way, discharge him as a fool.

Seldes advised them to unearth "a mechanical genius to explain the camera and the projector to you." Instead, the movies went the radio one better, bringing in the talking picture, which was perfected between 1926 and 1929.

THE LIVELY ARTS ON THE STAGE

The fragility of the lively arts is evident in the constant fears of cannibalism among its nervous practitioners. If radio was going to eat up the movies, the talking pictures were promptly looked upon as carnivores preying on the "legitimate theater." "The Legitimate Theater, usually known as Broadway," wrote Lloyd Lewis in the *New Republic* in March, 1929, "is in a panic today, with many of its temples dark and many of its priests and vestals rushing about the streets of the walled city, crying out that the movie vandals are at the gates of the citadel at last, . . . armed with new electrical catapults and strange talking devices." For once, the jeremiads had some basis. Talking pictures propelled the movies to their commercial peak even during the depression years of the 'thirties; Hollywood, moreover, dangled immense pecuniary lures before the eyes of dramatists, novelists, composers, and actors, and even the most serious succumbed. At the same time, vaudeville and musical revues, the liveliest of the theater's attractions, at least to the admirers of the lively arts, declined and eventually disappeared.

Seldes called vaudeville, "the most immediate of the minor arts," and while he recognized its long history in the United States, "nothing I have heard," he writes in *The Seven Lively Arts,*

leads me to believe that there were better days in vaudeville than those which open benignant and wide over Joe Cook and Fanny Brice and the Six Brown Brothers, over the two Briants and Van and Schenck and the four Marxes and the Rath Brothers and the team of Williams and Wolfus; over Duffy and Sweeney and Johnny Dooley and Harry Watson, Jr., as Young Kid Battling Dugan, and Messrs. Moss and Frye, who ask how high is up.

If most of these luminaries mean nothing to today's readers, it only proves how close to the end of the long tradition they were. What critics like Seldes especially admired in vaudeville, moreover, made the medium especially elusive. This was "the refinement of technique":

I am sure that the vaudeville stage makes such demands upon its artists that they are compelled to perfect everything. They have to do whatever they do swiftly, neatly, without lost motion; they must touch and leap aside. . . . The vaudeville stage . . . permits no fumbling, and there are no reparable errors. The materials they use are trivial, yes; but the treatment must be accurate to the hair's breadth; the wine they serve is light, it must fill the goblet to the very brim, and not a drop must spill over.

"It is, of course, obvious," Seldes concludes "that the responsibility in this case is exactly that of the major arts."

The revue became a staple of the Broadway stage as early as 1907, when Florenz Ziegfeld produced the first of his *Follies,* lavish "girlie" shows spiced with the humor of such vintage stars as Will Rogers, Ed Wynn, and W. C. Fields, the trick dancing of Leon Errol, the chanting of Eddie Cantor. Almost annual editions followed, and by 1923 Edmund Wilson was acclaiming the *Follies* as "a permanent institution" on which "comments . . . are always in order." Within five years the *Follies* were challenged by George White's *Scandals* and Earl Carroll's *Vanities,* and within ten years all had passed on.

Wilson's "comments" contained the usual reservations of the admirers of the lively arts:

In general, Ziegfeld's girls have not only the Anglo-Saxon straightness—straight backs, straight brows, and straight noses—but also the peculiar frigidity and purity, the frank high-school girlishness which Americans like. . . . He tries, furthermore, to represent, in the maneuvers of his well-trained choruses, not the movement and abandon of emotion, but what the American male regards as beautiful: the efficiency of mechanical movement. The ballet at the *Ziegfeld Follies* is becoming more and more like military drill; . . . it is too much like watching setting-up exercises.

But there was the obeisance and capitulation as well:

Yet there is still something wonderful about the *Follies.* It exhibits the persistent vitality as well as the stupidity of an institution. Among these green peacocks and gilded panels . . . there is realized a glittering vision which rises straight out of the soul of New York. The *Follies* is such fantasy, such harlequinade as the busy well-to-do New Yorker has been able to make of his life. . . . As I say, there is a splendor about the *Follies.* It has, in its way, both distinction and intensity.

THE COMIC STRIP

In the mid-'twenties no fewer than 20 million readers followed the fates of their favorites among the characters of the daily newspaper comic strip. During the depression the comics were the one feature which financially pressed publishers would not curtail or cut out. More people, according to the polls then popular, bought the papers for the comics than for any other reason, and their creators were earning $1,000 to $1,500 weekly for their work.

The comics, like other lively arts, had a long history in American journalism that went back at least to 1889. As competitive features, color was early lavished upon them; the saffron so generously spread over the comics during the Pulitzer-Hearst circulation war in New York just before the Spanish-American War (see p. 628) is credited with fostering the epithet, "Yellow Journalism." These early comics might be called one-shots; neither their characters nor their themes were continued from day to day. "The Katzenjammer Kids," which appeared Sundays in the New York *Journal* beginning in 1894, was the first strip with regular characters. Ten years later some dailies began to publish strips two or three times a week. The first six-day strip was H. C. ("Bud") Fisher's "A. Mutt"—later "Mutt and Jeff"—published in the *San Francisco Chronicle* starting in November, 1907. The very names of some of these early comics made permanent contributions to the American vernacular: "Let George Do It," the work of George McManus, was one. Others included "Happy Hooligan," "Hairbreadth Harry," and "Bringing Up Father," another McManus creation starting in 1912. The lasting favorite with the critics of the lively arts, George Herriman's "Krazy Kat," first appeared in 1911.

"Of all the lively arts," Seldes writes, "the Comic Strip is the most despised." One reason for this was its early commercialization.

Even in 1906, the president of the National Association of Newspaper Circulation Managers, told the members:

Whatever merits the comic supplements may have possessed in the beginning, when their creators were artists of original methods, distinctive. style, and freshness and fertility of humor, they have to a large extent departed, . . . [for] even the originators and leaders have found themselves pumped well-nigh dry of ideas in the struggle to keep up the constant output.

It was not long, moreover, before professional protectors of children's minds such as the International Kindergarten Union, the League for the Improvement of the Children's Comic Supplement, the ·League of American Penwomen, and others, assaulted the fun and fantasy of the growing medium. The admirers of the lively arts in the 'twenties could not have cared less. The comic strip, they believed was essentially adult, not child fare. "With those who hold that a comic strip cannot be a work of art I shall not traffic," Seldes declared. And warming again to his constant theme, he added:

The qualities of *Krazy Kat* are irony and fantasy—exactly the same, it would appear as distinguish *The Revolt of the Angels;* it is wholly beside the point to indicate a preference for the work of Anatole France, which is in the great line, in the major arts. It happens that in America irony and fantasy are practiced in the major arts by only one or two men, producing highclass trash; and Mr. Herriman, working in a despised medium, without an atom of pretentiousness, is day after day producing something essentially fine. . . . In the second order of the world's art it is superbly first rate—and a delight!

The comic strip, moreover, soon proved a rich recourse to those in other arts—in vaudeville, revues, comedies, songs, and ballets—for characters and ideas.

IV. *The Intellectuals Turn Left*

WRITERS DURING
THE DEPRESSION DECADE

The intellectual spokesmen for the lively arts, as we have seen, were men and women whose confidence in the masses remained strong despite the prevailing disenchantment of the postwar years. Once the prosperity of the 'twenties vanished and depression became a constant part of the American scene, intellectual disenchantment also seemed to disappear and the writers and others were drawn more closely, once again, to the common lot. Expatriates returning from Paris in 1930 and 1931 found the country stirring with new impulses. The broad, humane sympathies traditional in American liberalism began to revive. Personal and aesthetic revolt was being transformed once again into public and political revolt. Writers were thinking less about criticizing their country, more about doing something to save it from disaster. Bohemians became radicals. Business culture, formerly disdained for success and complacency, was now despised for failure and frigidity.

In the election of 1932, a number of writers supported the Communist candidate, William Z. Foster. Foster, as Edmund Wilson put it, was too uncomfortably susceptible to the "awful eye of the Third International" for some, but he seemed preferable to the candidates of the major parties, who lacked "either moral force or intellectual integrity." The writers were not entirely alone in this estimation, for in that year Foster polled 102,000 votes, a small fraction of 1 per cent of the total popular vote, yet the largest vote ever received by a presidential candidate on the Communist ticket. The writers who voted Communist in 1932, besides Wilson, included John Dos Passos, Sherwood Anderson, Malcolm Cowley, Waldo Frank, and Horace Gregory. They issued a manifesto calling "for the overthrow of the system which is responsible for all crises" and "the establishment of a workers' and farmers' government." The New Deal drew some writers back from the far left, and after the Nazi-Soviet pact of 1939 (see p. 779), only a few of the 1932 signers of the manifesto remained in the Communist camp. During the interval the "left" writers produced a considerable literary stir and a number of important novels, stories, plays, and poems.

Although Communist party officials paid little attention to writers and regarded their work as of small importance to the move- ment, communist editors in the early 'thirties made serious overtures to them. They organized writers' and artists' societies like the John Reed Clubs, and in the *New Masses* (founded in 1926) and especially in the lesser left-wing periodicals, they published the often crude work of literary unknowns. Young writers from the lower-middle or laboring classes, familiar with hobo "jungles," farm foreclosures, industrial strikes, and lynchings were encouraged to set down their experiences. Few of the so-called "proletarian" novels, stories, poems, and plays rated highly as literature, but there were powerful exceptions. Henry Roth's *Call It Sleep* (1935), a story of an immigrant childhood in New York's East Side, successfully evaded the heavy-handed editorializing that disfigured so much proletarian writing. Robert Cantwell's *Land of Plenty* (1934), was a taut and exciting account of a strike in a wood veneer factory.

By far the most widely read of all the depression novels was John Steinbeck's *The Grapes of Wrath* (1939), a chronicle of an Oklahoma farm family who, after being tractored off their land, joined the migration of "Okies" to California. Steinbeck's saga of this exodus and his account of the miseries of the fruit-and-vegetable pickers in the Salinas Valley was in no sense Marxist. Rather it was a study in human ecology, a view of mass-man victimized by intangible economic forces yet worthy of pity and compassion. Steinbeck's novel created widespread sympathy for the migratory workers and was hailed by the Left as the *Uncle Tom's Cabin* of the depression years.

As Steinbeck wrote of the rural poor, other novelists dealt with the depressed Irish, Poles, Negroes, and Jews of the cities. In his sturdy triology, *Young Lonigan* (1932-1935), James T. Farrell traced the lives of Chicago Irish who lacked moral focus despite the ministrations of the Church, who smarted over their rejection by respectable Protestant society, and who fought a losing battle with alcoholism—all their problems deepened by the depression. A similar story was told of Chicago's North Side Poles in the fiction of Nelson Algren, and of the Negro proletariat in Richard Wright's *Uncle Tom's Children* (1938) and *Native Son* (1940). Clifford Odets' play, *Awake and Sing,* dramatized the impact of the depression on a lower-middle-class Jewish family in the Bronx. Perhaps the most deeply despairing as well as most original of all the novels written in the depression decade was *Miss Lonelyhearts* (1933), Nathanael West's tragi-comic portrayal of an urban wasteland in which irremediable wrongs make life a perpetual horror.

THE NEW DEAL
AND CULTURAL NATIONALISM

When Hitler seized power in Germany in 1933, those Americans who had found Mussolini's brand of fascism defensible seemed able for a time to live with the new Nazi version. Many intellectuals, on the right as well as the left, however, grew alarmed at Nazi viciousness, especially since they feared for a time that such New Deal experiments as N.R.A. might lead the United States along a similar totalitarian road. Most of them quickly changed their minds; and when the Spanish Civil War broke out in 1936 (see p. 777), further totalitarian successes there prompted many American intellectuals to re-examine and re-evaluate their own institutions and to find unappreciated virtues in their culture. As the New Deal began to cope more effectively with the problems of the dispossessed, moreover, confidence in the recuperative powers of American society began to rise. Former critics and expatriates now found the United States full of complex and undiscovered wonders. Everything American took on a new interest and seemed worthy of reporting, recording, narrating, photographing, and understanding.

Whereas the critics of the 'twenties had focused on the businessman and the powers-that-were in American society, the enthusiasts of the late 'thirties and early 'forties turned to the common man with his sufferings, his courage, his struggles, his virtues. Photographers from the Farm Security Administration (see p. 724) went out to the American land to portray the people who worked on it, in all their native plainness and dignity. The authors of the various W.P.A. local and regional guides went back to local history lovingly and lingeringly and prepared the first composite survey of the American states.

Still other projects investigated American folklore, recorded white and Negro spirituals, Indian songs, folk tunes, and a mass of unknown music written by forgotten American composers. On post-office walls all over the country, W.P.A. artists painted regional scenes and memorable local episodes. Americans who had never been theater- or concert-goers flocked to Federal Theater performances like that of Sinclair Lewis' play, *It Can't Happen Here,* which in four months in 1936 reached an audience of 275,000. A Negro *Macbeth* played to 120,000 that year and T. S. Eliot's *Murder in the Cathedral* to 40,000. The Federal Theater charged no admission from those unable to pay and only a small amount from others.

Literary and social historians, some of whom had been America's most caustic critics, now became loving defenders. Thus Van Wyck Brooks no longer lectured tartly on the failure of the writer in America, as he had in his studies of Henry James and Mark Twain. Indeed, he dropped his critical task almost entirely and wrote in five immensely successful books, beginning with *The Flowering of New England* (1936) and ending with *The Confident Years: 1885-1915* (1952), warm appreciations of all American cultural aspirants. In these volumes, Brooks found everything about American writers important and interesting except, perhaps, the failing he had once attacked so sharply.

Other critics followed Brooks. Lewis Mumford located indigenously American elements in native architecture. Archibald MacLeish castigated his fellow intellectuals for toying irresponsibly with their own disillusionment and infecting the impressionably young with cynicism. John Dos Passos, abandoning his revolutionary views, savored the innocence and virtue of the early Republic in *The Ground We Stand On* (1941). And Charles and Mary Beard, whose *Rise of American Civilization* (1927) had provided the radicals with historical ammunition for their assault on the ruling class, now in *The Republic* (1943) praised American political practices and warned

against Old World wars and intrigues. Even H. L. Mencken settled down with his pleasantly reminiscent autobiographical volumes, *Happy Days* (1940), *Newspaper Days* (1940), and *Heathen Days* (1943).

v. *Literature: The Major Phase*

DREISER, ANDERSON, LEWIS

The literary generation of the prewar lyric years (see p. 744) produced work of such power and maturity that they gained for American literature a firmer place in world literature than it had enjoyed before. The literary generation that followed built well upon this strong foundation. In neither period, perhaps, did any single writer emerge of greater stature than Melville, Emerson, Hawthorne, Whitman, Mark Twain or Henry James, but probably more good writing and more important books were produced in these years than in any comparable period in the history of the United States. This was especially true of the novels of the postwar years—those of Anderson and Lewis, Hemingway, Fitzgerald and Dos Passos, Wolfe and Faulkner, who shared many of the values and perspectives of the critics we have examined but were not to be lured by protests, proclamations and manifestoes from the grand tradition.

These writers owed much to those of the past, Norris, Crane and London, for example (see Chapter 22), who were long dead, and to *their* contemporary, Theodore Dreiser, the "Hindenburg of the American novel," as Mencken called him, who continued to brood over the spectacle of man—weak and pitifully equipped—trying to cope with the forces of nature. Dreiser's most widely read novel, indeed, *An American Tragedy*, was published as late as 1926. Thereafter he wrote nothing of permanent value. During the 'thirties he became increasingly involved in political and social

questions and before his death joined the Communist party. As a thinker and stylist, Dreiser had probably been the most vulnerable of all the major writers in the twentieth century, but in his best fiction and non-fiction he was a superb reporter whose clumsiness did not prevent him from lifting his grubby stories above the commonplace world he loved and with which he was vitally in touch.

Dreiser's closest link with the postwar generation was through his friend, Sherwood Anderson (1878-1941). For Anderson, the great evil had been the Industrial Revolution, which had destroyed the mystery and poetry of the village and had isolated man from man. "Time and again," Anderson wrote, "I had told the story of the American man crushed and puzzled by the age of the machine." The loneliness of Americans, he thought—the reaching out for human contact and finding none—produced the aberrations of behavior and outlook he described in *Winesburg, Ohio* (1919), in his best novel, *Poor White* (1920), and in stories like "The Egg." The procession of grotesques that moved through his tales—the drunkards, keyhole peepers, bedroom mutterers—had become twisted and deformed because their emotions found no outlet. As Anderson wrote of one of his Winesburg characters, "The living force within could not find expression." Anderson's frankly confessional tone, his candor about hitherto unmentionable themes, broke the ice for Hemingway, Wolfe, and Faulkner among others who followed him.

Although Sinclair Lewis (1885-1951) was

a middle-westerner like Anderson, his picture of village America was neither so tender nor elegiac. In fact Anderson resented Lewis' sardonic view of the small town, as presented in his first successful novel *Main Street* (1920), which sold almost 400,000 copies in its first year. *Main Street's* setting, Gopher Prairie, with its "unsparing, unapologetic, ugliness," suggested to Anderson that Lewis had focused on the externals and missed "the minor beauties" and interior history of the Midwest.

Certainly Lewis never probed very deeply into his characters' minds. His greatest single creation, George Folansbee Babbitt, coined a new word for the English language, but Lewis' long list of novels, which reproduce with varying success the occupations, conversations, and customs of middle-class America, seldom cracked the surface. Even his major characters seem less real than their possessions, and his minor characters often little more than caricatures.

Yet there was a certain appropriateness in Lewis' winning the Nobel Prize for literature in 1930—the first American writer to do so. For although he did not enter into his society as deeply as Dreiser or Anderson, he had without apology or mitigation presented its brashness and vulgarity. Unlike many of his contemporaries, Lewis did not find his country depressing. On the contrary, America was to him "as strange and complex as China" and the land of "one of the most amusing, exasperating, exciting, and completely mysterious peoples in the world." Despite his sometimes savage forays into the sacred precincts of the middle class, Lewis was, at bottom, its loyal and devoted chronicler. European readers, who saw him only as an angry satirist of American materialism, mistook his real intentions. He could lash out at the frauds and bigots with Menckenian gusto, but his castigations were directed at those who betrayed the true mission of the bourgeoisie.

Lewis' work deteriorated after the middle 'twenties, when he ended up parodying himself. But in *Main Street, Babbit* (1922), and *Elmer Gantry* (1927), Lewis was the red Indian "stalking through the land of his enemies." In these books, his inventiveness, his sense of the ludicrous, and his humanitarianism were successfully blended.

FITZGERALD AND HEMINGWAY

The death of F. Scott Fitzgerald in 1940 ended the career of a writer who twenty years before had attracted almost as much attention as the author of *Main Street*. One book, *This Side of Paradise*, published in 1920 when Fitzgerald was 24, turned him into a celebrity overnight, the laureate of the glittering carnival world he told about in *Tales of the Jazz Age* (1922) and *The Beautiful and the Damned* (1922).

Even during the "perpetual Maytime" of the 'twenties, however, Fitzgerald had sniffed the air of catastrophe:

All of the stories that came into my head had a touch of disaster in them—the lovely young creatures in my novels went to ruin . . . my millionaires were as beautiful and damned as Thomas Hardy's peasants. In life these things hadn't happened yet, but I was pretty sure living wasn't the reckless, careless business these

F. Scott Fitzgerald (1896-1940).

people thought—this generation younger than me.

In his best novel, *The Great Gatsby* (1925), he managed to suggest simultaneously the glitter of American prosperity and the treacherous foundations on which it rested. Jay Gatsby, the idealistic and romantic bootlegger who believes every dream can be made real simply by wishing for it intensely enough, is betrayed by his gangster friends and by the privileged rich who "smashed up things and then retreated back into their money or their vast carelessness."

Thus before the 'thirties Fitzgerald was saying that Americans, for all their bright hopes, could not escape history, and in his last books, *Tender Is the Night* (1934) and the unfinished *The Last Tycoon,* published in 1941 after his death, he wrote skillfully and movingly of the deterioration of that world whose advent he had announced with such bravado. "America's great promise," he confessed to a friend in the 'thirties, "is that something is going to happen, and after a while you get tired of waiting because nothing happens to people except that they grow old and nothing happens to American art because America is the story of the moon that never rose. . . . The fresh strong river of America! . . . America is so decadent that its brilliant children are damned almost before they are born."

Although Ernest Hemingway survived Fitzgerald by more than two decades, his best work was also confined to the years before the second world war. Soldier, expatriate, reporter, he had perfected his style by 1924, having learned everything he could from his mentors, Sherwood Anderson, Ezra Pound, and Gertrude Stein. His language was largely monosyllabic, mechanical, concrete—drawn from many vernaculars; yet it glittered all the same. It was Hemingway's response to the world of wartime rhetoric and high-sounding abstractions, a style (as the critic John Peale Bishop put it) "that would record an American experience, and neither falsify the world without nor betray the world within."

From the outset, Hemingway wrote of war and violence and death, of sport and dissipation. *The Sun Also Rises* (1926) told of expatriates desperately amusing themselves in a postwar wasteland: drinking, watching bullfights, making love, all to no purpose. *A Farewell to Arms* (1929), the most famous of the American war novels, was followed by *To Have and To Have Not* (1937), a composite of fishing trips, sex, machine guns, booze, and literary gossip, and *For Whom the Bell Tolls* (1940), a powerful story based on the Spanish Civil War. Hemingway, in other books, wrote of bullfighting in *Death in the Afternoon* (1932), and big-game hunting in *The Green Hills of Africa* (1935).

In all these works, and in his collections of short stories (the best illustrations of Hemingway's magnificent talent), he showed a central concern with the universal problems of conduct and honor. In a world filled wtih death and disaster, he advocated

Ernest Hemingway (1898-1961) with his second wife, Martha Gellhorn.

the code of the bullfighter, the hunter, the sportsman: to accept death, the great Nada or Nothingness, with dignity and fortitude. The weak characters in Hemingway's fiction cannot bear isolation; they break down, cling to each other, or dope themselves with illusions. The strong and the brave live with style and impose some kind of order on the confusion that is life. Hemingway lived and died according to this code.

DOS PASSOS AND WOLFE

World War I made John Dos Passos (1896-   ), as it did Hemingway, suspicious of moral abstractions, but it also turned him into a rebel. Dos Passos, a child of well-to-do parents, had traveled abroad during his childhood, attended Harvard College between 1912 and 1916 (where he wrote rarified poetry and prose), and driven an ambulance in the war (where he met Hemingway). After the war, he traveled in Spain and the Near East and published two successful books—*Three Soldiers* (1921) and *Manhattan Transfer* (1925)—as well as sketches and plays. By the 'thirties, he had completed his transformation from an aesthete who lamented the absence of nymphs and ghosts in America, to a realist who in-

William Faulkner (1897-1962).

corporated the very rhythms of industry in his prose. Between 1927 and the Spanish Civil War, Dos Passos attached himself to the radical movement as a kind of independent "camp follower." He had thrown himself passionately into the defense of Sacco and Vanzetti and served on writers' committees investigating strikes. Disillusioned with communism thereafter, he became increasingly conservative and coincidentally less creative.

Dos Passos' great achievement was his trilogy, *42nd Parallel* (1930), *1919* (1932), and *The Big Money* (1936), in which he tried—as he said of another novelist—"to put the acid test to existing institutions, to strip them of their veils." *U.S.A.*, the collective title of the trilogy, covers the years 1900 to 1930 and introduces a large number of characters representing every class and a variety of occupations. The people in *U.S.A.* are moving up and down the social scale; they have no roots, no firm moral anchor, and they seem to flounder in the social maelstrom. Punctuating the narrative are snatches from newspaper headlines and popular songs; short impressionistic biographies of representative historical figures; and private interior monologues of the author himself. *U.S.A.* is a massive indictment of America. Its rich and successful characters are corrupt and unhappy; its poor people are frustrated and unhappy. Unlike the orthodox Marxist novelists almost compulsively optimistic about the coming of a new society—Dos Passos saw no grounds for optimism. His disgust with all society seemed so intense that its salvation was not only unlikely, but undesirable.

Another writer who drew on personal experience with the same intensity and candor as Dos Passos was Thomas Wolfe (1900-1938). A North Carolinian who came to New York to seek his literary fortunes, Wolfe told the story of his own life in four huge volumes of fiction that totaled more than a million words even after liberal cutting by his devoted editor, Maxwell Perkins. As Wolfe wrote to F. Scott Fitzgerald, he belonged with the "putter-inners" rather than with the "taker-outers."

In *Look Homeward, Angel* (1929), *Of Time and the River* (1935), *The Web and the Rock* (1939), and *You Can't Go Home Again* (1940), Wolfe spelled out somewhat repetitively the story of his family life, his literary hopes, and his friendships. As undisciplined as he was energetic, Wolfe had a gift for the lyrical communication of his own intensity and longings and a strong feeling for the American scene.

FAULKNER

William Faulkner (1897-1962), ranked by many critics as the foremost American literary artist of the twentieth century, continued to write after 1940, but nothing he published after that date measured up to his earlier work.

A native of Mississippi who served in the Canadian air force during World War I, Faulkner first attracted attention with a bitter book about the aftermath of the war called *Soldiers Pay* (1926). *The Sound and the Fury* (1929), *As I Lay Dying* (1930), *Light in August* (1932), and other novels written in rapid succession established him as a major writer. Although the socially conscious critics of the 'thirties underrated him, as Faulkner went on to *Absalom! Absalom!* (1936), *The Unvanquished* (1939), and *The Hamlet* (1940), his reputation as an epic commentator on the mind and spirit of the South spread in America and Europe. The Nobel Prize in literature, which Faulkner received in 1949, was a belated recognition of his genius.

It is now clear that Faulkner's complicated narratives of Indians, Negroes, planters, townspeople, yeoman farmers, and poor whites who people his imaginary Yoknapatawpha County make up a social history of the deep South. At the same time, the Yoknapatawpha saga is a private vision of ruin and decay, violence and terror, a chapter in man's tragic destiny. Faulkner's characters, whether they be aristocratic families or poor-white clans like the Snopeses, live in a land already doomed by the curse of slavery and the private exploitation of the wilderness. Their salvation, most succinctly and powerfully worked out in Faulkner's magnificent story, "The Bear," lies only in re-establishing contact with natural forces (as represented by the bear, Old Ben, and the primeval) and passively enduring them.

But that obviously, was not to be—not in the South, not in the United States, not in the world. The new world war in the offing was to present the extreme challenge of technology, not primitive nature. The new world after the war would bring, in literature and the arts, a new skepticism toward conventional values, but not so much, as in the 'twenties, merely because of disillusionment with them; rather, because of the obvious immensity of the postwar challenge and the frustrations in meeting it.

Readings
* *Asterisk indicates that book is available in paperback.*

Many essential works already cited fully in the text are not repeated in these Readings. Good general introductions to the literary history covered in this chapter are Van Wyck Brooks, *The Confident Years, 1885-1915* (1952), and Afred Kazin, *On Native Grounds* * (1942). Henry May, *The End of American Innocence* * (1959), is a comprehensive survey of American thought and culture between 1912 and 1917. Christopher Lasch, *The New Radicalism in America, 1889-1963* (1965), traces the radical progressive tradition in biographical portraits. The situation of intellectuals in the recent past is considered in Richard Hofstadter, *Anti-Intellectualism in American Life* (1963). The story of the "Little Renaissance" may be found in H. M. Jones, *The Bright Medusa* (1952); Floyd Dell,

Intellectual Vagabondage (1926); and the early chapters of Joseph Freeman, *An American Testament: A Narrative of Rebels and Romantics* (1936). George Santayana, *Winds of Doctrine* (1913), is an important contemporary record as well as entertaining reading. Daniel Aaron, *Writers on the Left* * (1961), deals with the impact of radical ideas between 1912-1940. See also W. B. Rideout, *The Radical Novel in the United States, 1900-1954* (1956), and Malcolm Cowley, ed., *After the Genteel Tradition* (1936). An important history of *avant garde* periodicals is F. J. Hoffman, C. Allen, and C. F. Ulrich, *The Little Magazines* (1946). For the influence of Freud, see F. J. Hoffman, *Freudians and the Literary Mind* (1945).

The story of literary Bohemia is told in Albert Parry, *Garrets and Pretenders* * (1933), and, out of personal experience, in Floyd Dell, *Love and Greenwich Village* (1926). Of relevant autobiographies, the following are among the best: Max Eastman, *Enjoyment of Living* (1948), and *Love and Revolution* (1965); Mabel Dodge Luhan, *Intimate Memories: Background* (1933), *European Experiences* (1935), and *Movers and Shakers* (1936); Floyd Dell, *Homecoming* (1933); and Lincoln Steffens, *The Autobiography of Lincoln Steffens* (2 vols., 1931). Granville Hicks, *John Reed, The Making of a Revolutionary* (1936), is the most detailed account, but it should be supplemented with relevant pages from Theodore Draper, *The Roots of American Communism* * (1957). Louis Filler, *Randolph Bourne* (1943), provides the essential facts. Van Wyck Brooks, ed., *The History of a Literary Radical & Other Papers by Randolph Bourne* (1956), is indispensable. Also useful are Brooks' own autobiographical essays, *Days of the Phoenix: The Nineteen-Twenties I Remember* (1957), and *Scenes and Portraits: Memories of Childhood and Youth* (1954).

Brooks' *John Sloan, A Painter's Life* (1955), is an excellent description of the "Ashcan School" of painters. See also Bruce St. John, ed., *John Sloan's New York Scene, from Diaries, Notes and Correspondence 1906-1913* (1965). Especially recommended are Meyer Shapiro's brilliant essay, "Rebellion in Art," in Daniel Aaron, ed., *America In Crisis* (1952); and M. W. Brown, *The Story of the Armory Show* (1963). Helen Deutsch and Stella Hanau, *The Provincetown Players: A Story of the Theatre* (1931), is a good account of this experiment. For the story of the insurgent theater in the '30's, see Harold Clurman, *The Fervent Years* * (1957), and H. F. Flanagan, *Arena* (1940), an account of the Federal Theater. The best life of O'Neill is Croswell Bowen, *The Curse of the Misbegotten* (1959).

The Chicago poets and writers are treated in Bernard Duffey's excellent study, *The Chicago Renaissance in American Letters* (1954). Harry Hansen, *Midwest Portraits* (1923), is a personal reminiscence of the Chicago poets. S. T. Coffman, *Imagism* (1951), deals with that poetic school, and much information of a biographical and technical interest may be found in Ezra Pound, *Letters, 1907-1941,** edited by D. D. Paige (1950).

The best introduction to the lively arts is Gilbert Seldes, *The Seven Lively Arts* (1924), which may profitably be supplemented by Seldes' later works, *The Great Audience* (1951), and *The Public Arts* (1956). On the movies, see Lewis Jacobs, *The Rise of the American Film* (1939); and Nathan Leites and Martha Wolfenstein, *Movies* (1950). Llewellyn White, *The American Radio* (1947), may be supplemented by Charles Siepmann, *Radio, Television, and Society* (1950). Sigmund Spaeth, *A History of Popular Music in America* (1948), is a general account. See also, Winthrop Sargeant, *Jazz* (1946). Bernard Rosenberg and D. M. White, *Mass Culture* (1958), offers a useful introduction to later concern over the mechanical lively arts. See also the Readings for Chapter 31.

For the '20's and '30's, F. J. Hoffman, *The Twenties* * (1955), is informative; Malcolm Cowley, *Exiles' Return* * (1951) is indispensable. Selections from Mencken's writings are available in paperback editions. William Manchester, *Disturber of the Peace: The Life of H. L. Mencken* * (1950), is a sound and informative biography. Particularly recommended as a guide to the '20's are Edmund Wilson's essays collected in *The Shores of Light* * (1952) and in *The American Earthquake* * (1958), which documents the '30's as well. For the literary history of the '30's see the previously cited *Writers on the Left;* J. W. Beach, *American Fiction: 1920-1940* (1951); the chapter on the intellectuals and the left in Irving Howe and Louis Coser, *The American Communist Party* * (1958); and

Murray Kempton, *Part of Our Time: Some Monuments and Ruins of the Thirties* (1955). Harvey Swados, ed., *The American Writer and the Great Depression* * (1966), is an invaluable anthology.

The following titles contain interesting material on the life and times of the writers mentioned in this chapter. Dreiser's autobiographical writings, extensive and illuminating, should be supplemented by R. H. Elias, *Theodore Dreiser: Apostle of Nature* (1949); W. A. Swanberg, *Dreiser* (1965); and R. H. Elias, ed., *Letters of Theodore Dreiser* (3 vols., 1959). Irving Howe, *Sherwood Anderson* (1951), is sharp and perceptive if not sympathetic; it should be supplemented by H. M. Jones, ed., *Anderson's Letters* (1953), and by Anderson's entertaining but untrustworthy books, *A Story Teller's Story* (1924), and *Sherwood Anderson's Notebook* (1926). Sinclair Lewis' non-fiction is collected in H. E. Maule and M. H. Cane, eds. *The Man from Main Street* * (1953); and Harrison Smith, ed., *From Main Street to Stockholm: Letters from Sinclair Lewis, 1919-1930* (1952). Mark Schorer, *Sinclair Lewis: An American Life* * (1961), is the definitive biography. F. Scott Fitzgerald, *The Crack-Up* * (1945), is a compilation of letters and notes edited by his friend, Edmund Wilson. It should be read in conjunction with Arthur Mizener's fine biography of Fitzgerald, *The Far Side of Paradise* * (1951), and Andrew Turnbull, *Scott Fitzgerald* * (1962). C. H. Baker, *Hemingway, the Writer as Artist* (1956); C. A. Fenton, *The Apprenticeship of Ernest Hemingway* * (1954); and Philip Young, *Ernest Hemingway* * (1954), all contain useful biographical information as well as interpretation. A. E. Hotchner, *Papa Hemingway, A Personal Memoir* (1966), deepens the story. *A Moveable Feast* * (1964) is Hemingway's posthumous memoir of his expatriate years. Thomas Wolfe, *Letters*, Elizabeth Nowell, ed. (1956), is a massive volume of self-revelation. The best introduction to Faulkner is Malcolm Cowley's long essay that prefaces *The Portable Faulkner* * (1946).

CHAPTER TWENTY-NINE

The war that began in Europe when Hitler invaded Poland on September 1, 1939, awoke the United States from the dream of continentalism and isolation into which she again had fallen after Wilson's fruitless effort to make the *world* safe for democracy twenty years earlier.

It had not been a peaceful dream for the United States. Even those expatriates who found in postwar Europe higher cultural standards and a more congenial intellectual atmosphere than at home rubbed most of their countrymen the wrong way. Europe, it was said in the 'twenties, was an arid waste-

The War
for Survival

land inhabited by quarrelsome people who would always be at one another's throats. Europeans had no character; they could not govern themselves; they did not even pay their debts.

Will Rogers, the most popular American humorist of the era, gave voice to the American attitude during his trip abroad in 1926. "A bunch of American tourists were hissed and stoned yesterday in France," Rogers gibed, "but not until they had finished buying." On his return home, Rogers remarked: "France and England think just as much of each other as two rival bands of Chicago bootleggers. Gloating over our unpopularity is the only thing they have ever agreed on perfectly." Of Old-World politics he had this to say:

I arrived in Paris late at night. The next day we had Briand Premier for breakfast; Herriot Premier for lunch; Poincaré for dinner; and woke up the next morning and Briand is back in again. This is not a Government; it's an old-fashioned Movie, where they flash on the screen: "Two minutes, please, while we change Premiers."

During the 'twenties few Americans had the foresight to condemn the virulent fascism in Italy, but most of the other European "isms"—bolshevism, anarchism, socialism, syndicalism, and many more—seemed to be poisonous infections only too easily spread. The rise of Nazism in Germany in the 'thirties, finally, only confirmed the American opinion that Europeans should be abandoned to their own devices. This movement in particular was to grow sufficiently aggressive in policy to menace American interests and sufficiently inhumane in character to trouble the American soul. Yet the United States long remained cool toward its victims.

The prevailing American attitude toward the Far East differed from that toward Europe. America's "continental destiny" had always drawn her westward toward the Pacific, and since the early nineteenth century American politicians, missionaries, businessmen, and journalists had looked beyond that ocean for further trade and future empire. Many Americans who believed that Europe was the land of the past felt, however irrationally, that the Orient was the land of the future. The trouble here was that American aspirations soon encountered the much more imperious ambitions of Japan, which the United States itself had quickened.

In the 'thirties the United States often tried to interest European nations in collective action to check Japanese expansion. At the same time the United States remained aloof from Europe's own systems of collective security. Both policies failed. Weakened by American isolation, European collective security collapsed in the face of Nazi aggression. With the Europeans sorely tried on their own continent, American efforts to involve them in the Orient were doomed. The distress of America's old allies after Hitler's Polish adventure had spread into a new general war was the signal for Japan to strike at the United States itself. What confronted Americans after the catastrophe at Pearl Harbor on December 7, 1941, then, was no longer the task of making their political institutions prevail throughout the world, but simply that of keeping them intact at home. In candid recognition of this predicament, Franklin D. Roosevelt called World War II the "War for Survival."

I. *Between-Wars Diplomacy*

THE WASHINGTON CONFERENCE: 1921-1922

The futility of trying to keep separate the European and Oriental theaters of international friction must have become manifest to the United States when Japan persisted in nibbling away at Siberia as well as China even while World War I was in progress. Once that war was over, Japan also grasped formerly German islands in the Pacific. What made her activities the more menacing was her treaty of alliance with Britain which she had renewed for ten years in 1911 and which continued in force.

This combination of two great naval powers was itself enough to compel the United States in 1916 to embark on a vast program of battleship construction which had nothing to do with the German submarine menace. When World War I ended two years later with the German navy dispersed, world naval imbalance became greater than ever, and the United States felt it must become a counterweight to Britain's dominance on the Atlantic as well as to Japan's strength on the Pacific. Rivalry with the British for Middle Eastern petroleum, which the war had made into a vital strategic resource, itself threatened to cause an Anglo-American conflict which American naval leaders felt they must urgently prepare for.

The obvious way to prepare was to build more and more capital ships—that is, battleships and cruisers. But another possibility presented itself: an agreement to check the monstrously costly naval race. In 1920 the United States began to explore the feasibility of a great-power conference to work out such an agreement. These explorations resulted in invitations by President Harding in July, 1921, to France and Italy as well as Britain and Japan to meet with the United States in Washington, beginning Armistice Day, November 11.

The delegates had hardly settled in their seats on the first business day of the Washington Conference, November 12, 1921, when United States Secretary of State Charles Evans Hughes, the presiding officer, electrified them with a blunt proposal for a ten-year holiday in the construction of capital ships. Hughes went farther. He urged that the capital-ship tonnage of the United States and Britain be limited to 500,000 and that of Japan to 300,000. This was in keeping with their current power ratio of 5-5-3; but it also meant that Britain and Japan would have to jettison no less than 66 ships and the United States no less than 30 in order to get down to their allotted strength.

Naturally, heated bargaining followed Hughes's proposal, but long before the conference ended in February, 1922, a five-power naval treaty was signed which endorsed the 5-5-3 ratio virtually at Hughes's tonnage figures and which permitted France and Italy capital ship tonnages of 175,000. Although smaller ships were not covered by the agreement, the naval race was thus at least partially suspended.

Two other important agreements made at the Washington meeting were the so-called Four-Power Pact and Nine-Power Pact. The first replaced the irritating Anglo-Japanese alliance with a new agreement which included the United States and France along with Britain and Japan, and pledged the signatories to keep the peace in the Pacific region by respecting one another's rights there, and to consult together when any of these rights seemed threatened. The second agreement, in which China, Italy, Belgium, the Netherlands, and Portugal joined the members of the Four-Power Pact, reaffirmed the "Open Door" principle in China and guaranteed her sovereignty, independence, and territorial integrity.

JAPAN IN CHINA

The Washington Conference was welcomed in most of the world as a triumph of diplomacy in the quest for enduring peace. When it was followed in 1928 by the Kellogg-Briand Pact renouncing war as an instrument of national policy (which 62 nations, including Japan, signed) a fragile world order seemed somewhat strengthened. Japan, however, was simply marking time. If anything, her hunger for a continental empire of her own to cap her extraordinarily rapid industrialization and modernization grew steadily. China remained the apple of her eye, and in September, 1931, using as an excuse a provocative incident on the Japanese-controlled South Manchurian Railway, Japanese forces stormed into China's Manchuria province.

The United States and the League of Nations promptly reminded Japan of her treaty responsibilities, but to no avail, and by January, 1932, the Japanese army had crushed all resistance in Manchuria.

When it had become clear that reminders alone would have no effect on Japan, the question was raised for Western diplomats whether Japan should be subjected to economic sanctions. Secretary of State Henry L. Stimson suggested this possibility to President Hoover, but feeling that sanctions might lead the United States once more into an unwanted war, the President firmly opposed them. His decision, and the reluctance of the powers in the League to go beyond it, had thus limited action on the part of the West to moral pressure which Japan felt free to ignore.

On January 7, 1932, Secretary Stimson stated in a note to Japan and China that the United States could not recognize any treaty or agreement in the Orient that infringed her rights. This policy—refusing to recognize territorial conquest in Asia—became known as the "Stimson Doctrine," though it had earlier been enunciated and applied by Secretary of State Bryan. The

Stimson Doctrine, however, foresaw no use of arms to back it up. Stimson had hoped that the British government would associate itself with his declaration, but the British Foreign Office, instead, issued a statement which, as Stimson later said, could be interpreted by the world, including the Japanese government, only as "a rebuff to the United States." The American people, too absorbed in their own domestic problems to care much about Manchuria, did not "give a hoot in a rain barrel" (as a Philadelphia newspaper said) who controlled North China. And the administration, to its credit, refrained from using the incident to distract the public from the woes of the depression.

The situation deteriorated on January 28, 1932, when Japan, stung by a Chinese boycott outside of Manchuria, invaded Shanghai, wiped out the Chinese force there and killed defenseless civilians. For the first time, militant sentiment against Japan began to appear in the United States, but President Hoover continued to oppose even economic coercion as an invitation to war. The administration confined itself to making protests where American interests in Shanghai were affected.

Secretary Stimson, fearing that he would only court another humiliating rebuff if he appealed to the signers of the Nine-Power Pact against Japan, decided to issue a message to the world in an informal way by expressing his views in a letter to Senator Borah, chairman of the Senate Committee on Foreign Relations. In this letter, Stimson asserted that the United States would stand on its treaty rights in the Far East, specifically those recognized in the Nine-Power Pact (see p. 773), and invited other nations to do the same. He pointedly warned that the violation of one of the Washington treaties released other parties from the other treaties. This move was greeted with strong approval in the American press, and on March 11, 1932, the League of Nations Assembly adopted a resolution using much the same language. Subsequently, the League's Lytton Commission issued a report condemning Japan's actions and refusing to recognize the validity of the puppet regime Tokyo had established in Manchuria as the state of Manchukuo. When, as a substitute, the Lytton Commission, in February, 1933, proposed an autonomous Manchurian state under face-saving Chinese sovereignty but effective Japanese control, Japan's only response was to withdraw from the League the following month. In December, 1934, she also renounced the Washington Conference naval agreement; and when the United States and Britain refused in 1936 to grant her naval parity with themselves, she embarked on a naval expansion program which the other two great naval powers felt impelled to match.

"GOOD NEIGHBORS"
IN LATIN AMERICA

For a time after World War I relations between the United States and the countries of Latin America also deteriorated. The key to our Latin American policy was the safety of the Panama Canal. But political instability in many Latin American countries brought wider United States involvement under the "Roosevelt Corollary" to the Monroe Doctrine (see p. 639) and intervention from time to time to protect American business investments.

Each of these considerations—strategic, diplomatic, and economic—resulted by 1924, in the United States actively interfering in the government of ten Latin American nations. Often United States' armed forces became involved—as in Panama in 1921, in the Dominican Republic from 1921 to 1924, and in Honduras in 1923. Since 1912, moreover, United States marines, on invitation from Nicaragua, helped to keep order in that country. When the marines were withdrawn at last in 1925, Nicaragua again became so turbulent that President Coolidge almost immediately sent them back in force, and by 1927 more than 5,000 marines were again exercising what Coolidge called our "moral responsibility" there. Early that year a special presidential envoy won over rebel and government leaders in Nicaragua to the idea of an election in 1928 under United States supervision. The results were generally satisfactory to both groups. But the followers of General Augusto César Sandino, one of the rebel leaders, refused to be pacified, retired to the hills, and harassed American marines until 1933, when the last of them were called home.

A crisis in Mexico in 1924 brought a salutary change in American tactics that led ultimately to Franklin D. Roosevelt's "Good Neighbor Policy." The Mexican Constitution of 1917 had reaffirmed the old Mexican principle violated during the long Díaz regime (see p. 640), that the Mexican government retained the ownership of all Mexican mineral and oil resources. By then, United States businessmen, encouraged by Díaz, had invested heavily in Mexican development and feared that the application of this principle might be made retroactive and their properties liable to confiscation. When President Plutarco Calles of Mexico took office in 1924, he announced his desire to make just such a change. The Mexican Congress then provided that petroleum rights acquired before 1917 would be limited to 50 years. The pressure of American oil interests and the influence of American Catholics who resented Calles' anti-clerical policy, together with the conventional interventionist tradition soon sparked talk of a new war with Mexico to force her to keep hands off. But in 1927 President Coolidge, taking his cue from a unanimous Senate resolution for peaceful arbitration, sent to Mexico his former Amherst classmate, Dwight L. Morrow, a partner in the House of Morgan, with the curt instruction: "Keep us out of war." Morrow proved an excellent diplomat, and his friendly feeling for the Mexicans was soon returned. Favored by a decision of the Mexican Supreme Court, he worked out with Calles a compromise by which American investors could retain permanently the oil properties they had held before the Constitution of 1917 went into effect. Later expropriation under the Cárdenas regime in 1938 led to a complex settlement in 1941 under which American oil properties and other claims were bought out by Mexico. American oil companies received about $42 million for their properties, and other American interests another $40 million.

Morrow's success in Mexico heralded a major change in American diplomacy in Latin America. At the Inter-American Conference at Havana in January, 1928, some of the Latin-American countries felt for the first time that they could candidly express to American diplomats their dislike of American interventionist polices. With its southern neighbors growing more proud and independent, and with its world position growing more perilous, the United States in turn began to feel that it could ill afford to make any more enemies in Latin America. The United States' retreat from past policies was made apparent at the Washington Conference on Conciliation and Arbitration in December, 1928, when we signed treaties of conciliation and arbitration with Latin American countries that amounted to a promise to refrain from any unilateral action in future relations with these nations.

In 1930, a State Department memorandum expressly repudiated the Roosevelt Corollary to the Monroe Doctrine (see p. 639). The Monroe Doctrine, it said, "states a case of the United States *vs.* Europe, and not of the United States *vs.* Latin America." Events were to show that this was not mere talk. In 1932, when El Salvador defaulted on a bond issue, the United States did not, as it had so casually done in the past, intervene to help American bankers recover their losses. In the same year, America withdrew her marines from Haiti and relaxed her supervision of that country's financial affairs.

In his first inaugural address in March, 1933, Franklin D. Roosevelt said he hoped "to dedicate this nation to the policy of the good neighbor." He did in fact continue the new policy of self-restraint in Latin America, but not before his good intentions were severely tested in Cuba. There, in August, 1933, President Gerardo Machado, iron-fisted dictator though he was, could not check civil strife brought on by depression conditions and was ousted by the army, perhaps with a push from Roosevelt's ambassador, Sumner Welles. When further revolutionary activity brought Ramón Grau San Martín to the provisional presidency of Cuba, Roosevelt withheld recognition. San Martín's military backers, led by Sergeant Fulgencio Batista, quickly took the cue and in January, 1934, conducted an election which carried the United States-backed candidate, Carlos Mendieta, the first of a string of Batista puppets, to the presidency. "I fell because Washington willed it," San Martín declared. Roosevelt did not deny that non-recognition was intervention, but prided himself, by refraining from landing troops, on the discovery, as he said, of a practical way in which the United States "could apply the doctrine of the Good Neighbor." A still more practical way was found in May, 1934, when the United States, on Sumner Welles' urging, negotiated a treaty with the Mendieta government, abrogating the Platt Amendment (see p. 633), thereby formally releasing Cuba from further liability to United States interference.

Even while the Cuban troubles were in progress, moreover, Secretary of State Hull and Latin American delegates to the Montevideo Conference of American States approved a proposal stating that "no state has the right to intervene in the internal or external affairs of another." At this Conference Hull also announced a new American plan to reduce tariffs through reciprocal trade agreements, further pleasing the delegates. In the spirit of the Montevideo agreement, the United States, in March, 1936, signed a treaty with Panama surrendering its right to interfere in Panama's affairs and increasing its annual payments for canal rights. When Panama agreed in 1939, to permit the United States, in emergencies, to defend the canal unilaterally, the Senate approved this treaty. In the same spirit, the United States, in 1941, peaceably negotiated with Mexico over the expropriation of oil properties (see p. 775).

The campaign to conquer the deep suspicion of "Yanqui imperialism" gained ground slowly and seemed destined never fully to overcome old grievances and new irritations. But as the years wore on, the United States achieved a measure of prestige in Latin America that would have seemed impossible earlier in the century; and when World War II began, she was assured of cooperation in the Southern Hemisphere.

ISOLATION FROM EUROPE

Good friends in Latin America became all the more welcome to the United States as the lack of sympathy and understanding with Europe grew. American immigration and protectionist policies in the 'twenties shut out European peoples and European goods. The acrimonious arguments over Allied war debts, which the United States refused to cancel and European nations refused to pay, reflected the breakdown of mutual respect.

As for the League of Nations, perhaps nothing bespoke American sentiment so well as Harding's remark in 1923 that the United States "does not propose to enter now by the side door, or the back door or the cellar door." True, eminent American individuals like John Bassett Moore served on the World Court, the League's judicial agency, and American observers attended sessions of the League, giving their country, as Clemenceau said, representation "by an ear but not by a mouth." By 1930, the United States had actually taken part in 40 League conferences, but even to suggest the possibility of overt cooperation with the League, as Secretary Stimson did in 1931 over the Far Eastern crisis (see p. 773), was to risk the wrath of many powerful newspapers throughout the country. Paradoxically, the public was ready to give overwhelming approval to such a grandiose but essentially empty gesture as the Kellogg-Briand Pact, first signed in Paris in August, 1928 (see p. 773). Some Americans scoffed at the pact as an "international kiss." But the Senate ratified it, 85 to 1.

Isolationism survived the 1929 crash and the depression. Nor did the coming of the New Deal at first mark a change, except for the lowering of tariff barriers in 1934. Even before his nomination in 1932, Roosevelt, once a good Wilsonian and a hardy exponent of the League, allowed himself to be pressured by the Hearst press into repudiating the League. "American participation in the League," he said then, "would not serve the highest purpose of the prevention of war and a settlement of international difficulties in accordance with fundamental American ideals." Roosevelt's disruption of the London Economic Conference of 1933 (see p. 717) seemed to commit the United States more firmly than ever to a go-it-alone policy.

Isolation was deepened in the mid-'thirties by the widespread notion that munitions-makers, profiteers, and "international bankers" had conspired to draw the United States into World War I for their own selfish purposes. This notion was given more or less official sanction by the "merchants of death" investigations of 1934, conducted by a Senate Committee headed by Gerald P. Nye of North Dakota. One of the results of this investigation was the Neutrality Act of 1935, hastily passed because of the Italian invasion of Ethiopia that year. This act provided that when the president proclaimed that foreign countries were in a state of war, Americans could not legally sell or transport munitions to them. Congress placed a six-month limit on this embargo, which did not include such basic war materials as oil, steel, and copper. Though he signed the measure, Roosevelt did not hide his feeling that it would do nothing to keep the country out of war. As he later put it, the arms embargo "played right into the hands of the aggressor nations [which] were actually encouraged by our laws to make war upon their neighbors."

In 1936, Congress prohibited loans to belligerents, and in the Neutrality Act of May 1, 1937, made civilian travel on belligerent ships illegal. This act also authorized the president to decide when a state of war existed or when civil war endangered the peace of the world, and in such situations an embargo on the export of arms and ammunition, and on credits, was to begin at once. A "cash-and-carry" plan, limited to two years, empowered the president to require belligerent nations buying non-military goods in this country to pay cash for them and to take them away in their own ships.

The neutrality acts of the mid-'thirties made no distinction between aggressors and victims in future wars. The isolationists expected to keep America out of any war simply by making it unprofitable for us to become involved. As fascism in Italy, Nazism in Germany and military tyranny in Japan grew more brutal at home, however, and more aggressive abroad, many Americans became embarrrassed by the holier-than-thou policy of aloofness. Embarrassment deepened when the League of Nations and the United States itself kept hands off after Mussolini, the fascist Premier of Italy, launched a war of conquest against Ethiopia in October, 1935.

After his quick success in Ethiopia, Mussolini turned to other adventures. In 1936, when Spanish fascists, with strong church support, rebelled against their country's republican government, he promptly sent them troops, planes, and supplies. Hitler soon followed with assistance of his own. American opinion was deeply divided over the Spanish war; many Americans sided with the Spanish government, which the United States had long since recognized, and some even volunteered to fight for it. Soviet support of the Spanish government, however, made it easier for American fascist sympathizers and Catholic supporters of General Francisco Franco's uprising to win congressional backing for a joint resolution forbidding the export of munitions to either side. Congress passed such a resolution on January 6, 1937. Naturally, this action hurt the Spanish government rather than the rebels, who already were receiving ample foreign assistance. In March, 1939, after a cruel and exhausting war, the Republican government was overwhelmed, and all

Spain fell under the control of a dictator friendly to Mussolini and Hitler. There-after isolationism had an increasingly bitter taste for more and more Americans.

II. *To the Brink of War*

As might have been expected, the first official abandonment of the neutrality spirit was provoked not by the European totalitarians but by the Japanese. After Japanese and Chinese forces clashed at Peiping near the Manchurian border in July, 1937, large Japanese detachments overran North China. President Roosevelt attacked the aggression in his famous "quarantine speech" of October 5, 1937. Ninety per cent of the people of the world wanted peace, he said, but their security was threatened by the other 10 per cent; peace-loving nations must act together to quarantine aggressors:

There is a solidarity, an interdependence about the modern world, both technically and morally, which makes it impossible for any nation completely to isolate itself from economic and political upheavals in the rest of the world, especially when such upheavals appear to be spreading and not declining. . . . We are determined to keep out of war, yet we cannot insure ourselves against the disastrous effects of war and the dangers of involvement. We are adopting such measures as will minimize our risk of involvement, but we cannot have complete protection in a world of disorder in which confidence and security have broken down.

As in the recent past, no action was taken against Japan, but in January, 1938, Roosevelt called on Congress for a billion dollars to enlarge the navy, a sum Congress voted in May. Within the year, totalitarian experiments in aggression in Europe brought on a crisis there. Hitler, who had come to power in Germany in January, 1933, and fifteen months later had renounced the Versailles Treaty terms on German disarmament (see p. 683), had long been campaigning for the return of German territory lost in World War I, where German people still lived. In March, 1936, while Mussolini's adventure in Ethiopia engaged the attention of western Europe (see p. 777), Hitler, with impunity, had actually occupied the Rhineland, adjacent to France. Now, in September, 1938, he was poised to grab the Sudetenland of Czechoslovakia. Again France, along with Britain, remained unprepared to confront a rearmed Germany in battle, and at the disastrous meeting in Munich on September 29 they let Hitler have what he wanted. We secured "peace with honor . . . peace in our time," at Munich, British Prime Minister Neville Chamberlain told his people, but his words failed to reassure them or the people of the smaller nations.

At Munich, having gained the Sudetenland, Hitler promised to leave the rest of Czechoslovakia alone; but in March, 1939, he swallowed up the remainder of the small republic. Not to be outdone, Mussolini three weeks later took Albania. Hitler's word obviously was worse than worthless. Yet the frightened world applauded President Roosevelt when in April, 1939, he wrote to Hitler and Mussolini asking them to pledge, for a period of ten years, that they would not attack any one of a list of 31 nations. Hitler replied for both with the suggestion that the danger of aggression existed only in Roosevelt's mind. The reality of the danger was brought closer in May, 1939, when a stubborn group of Senate isolationists blocked an administration request for revisions of the neutrality laws to permit economic aid to Britain and France in case of war.

Apparently safe from American industrial might on the western front, Hitler, in August, 1939, shocked the world by making a non-aggression pact with the Russian totalitarians on his eastern front. This double protection left him free to attack Poland, which with British and French encouragement, had been sturdily resisting demands for the return of territory similar to those made on Czechoslovakia. At the same time, the new pact left Russia free to satisfy her own territorial ambitions. On September 1, 1939, Hitler's legions invaded Poland while his air force rained bombs on Polish cities. Despite the discouraging stand of the United States Senate, Britain and France honored their Polish commitments by declaring war on Germany only two days later. As the law still required, Roosevelt invoked the Neutrality Act against the belligerents, but he did not repeat Woodrow Wilson's appeal for neutrality in thought as well as in deed. "Even a neutral," said Roosevelt, "cannot be asked to close his mind or his conscience."

Before Munich, according to public opinion polls, only a third of the American people favored selling arms to Britain and France in the event of war. By mid-September, 1939, when Roosevelt called a special session of Congress to revise the neutrality laws, and specifically to repeal the arms embargo so that munitions could be sold to the old Allies, he had the support of at least two-thirds of the people. In his message to Congress, Roosevelt also asked for authority to prevent American ships from sailing into danger zones so that provocative incidents on the high seas could be avoided. Belligerents must carry their own cargoes. All these requests were voted by Congress on November 3, 1939. Lifting the arms embargo pleased the interventionists; restoration of cash-and-carry pleased the still formidable isolationists.

Isolationism attracted a motley group: pacifists and socialists opposed on principle to war; Germans and Irish who hated Britain more than they feared dictatorship; and some outright fascist sympathizers. After the Russo-German pact of August, 1939, this strange set of bedfellows was joined by the American Communist party, all-out for non-intervention so long as it was in Russia's interest. The isolationists set up an organization called America First to promote their point of view. Colonel Charles A. Lindbergh expressed their sentiments when he declared: "In the future we may have to deal with a Europe dominated by Ger-

many. . . . An agreement between us could maintain peace and civilization throughout the world as far into the future as we can see."

Interventionists found their voice in the Committee to Defend America by Aiding the Allies, whose chairman was William Allen White. White replied to Lindbergh that many countries that had tried to be neutral, as Lindbergh advised, had been destroyed: "Hitler's whole philosophy, his idea of government, his economic setup, his insatiable ambitions, all make it impossible for a free country and a free people to live beside Hitler's world enslaved."

TOWARD INTERVENTION

When Hitler delayed until April, 1940, to move on the western front, many even in Europe were lulled by the seemingly "phony war." When Hitler did move, however, he did so with such terrifying speed and force that neutral Scandinavia and the Low Countries—Belgium, Holland and Luxembourg—and France herself were all brought to their knees by the "blitzkrieg" within seven weeks. When Belgium fell, Britain had to strain every resource to rescue her own expeditionary force from the Continent, a rescue effected under the pounding of German planes and guns between May 28 and June 4, when the last of her more than 335,000 men had been evacuated safely home from Dunkirk, France, on the Belgian frontier. A week later, on June 10, Mussolini sprang at France from the south, while her armies were reeling back from Hitler in the north. On June 22, completely crushed, France signed an armistice.

The British Empire now stood suddenly alone against German arms and the Berlin-Rome Axis.

The battle of France is over [Churchill told the House of Commons]. I expect that the Battle of Britain is about to begin. Upon this battle depends the survival of Christian civilization. . . . If we fail, then the whole world, including the United States, . . . will sink into the abyss of a new Dark Age. . . . Let us therefore brace ourselves to our duties, and so bear ourselves that, if the British Empire and its Commonwealth last for a thousand years, men will say "This was their finest hour."

During the summer and fall of 1940, in a tremendous effort to bring Britain to her knees, Hitler sent clouds of planes against English cities. Bombs poured down on London, Manchester, Birmingham, Plymouth, Dover, and Portsmouth. The town of Coventry became a target for saturation bombings. Tens of thousands of civilians were killed and wounded. But the Royal Air Force fought back with extraordinary courage, and by fall it was clear that Hitler's attempt to bomb Britain into defeat would fail. If Britain was to be subjugated it must be by invasion, and Churchill, at the time of Dunkirk, had promised to resist that "to the end, . . . whatever the cost may be . . . until, in God's good time, the New World, with all its power and might, steps forth to the rescue and liberation of the Old."

Churchill's effort not only to brace his own people but also, as he explained later, to assure America of their resolution, was not lost on the administration. As early as May, 1940, Roosevelt requested funds from Congress for "at least 50,000 planes a year." In June, denouncing Mussolini's attack on France he promised not to recognize infringements of her territory. In August, with the Canadian Prime Minister, Mackenzie King, he agreed to set up a joint board for the defense of the northern half of the Western Hemisphere. Throughout the summer, moreover, aid was being rushed overseas. Military equipment that could not be transferred directly from government to government was sold to American private firms, which then resold it to Britain.

By September, 1940, almost 60 per cent of those in the United States responding to a public opinion poll felt that it was more important to help Britain then to stay out of the war. At that time, on September 3, Roosevelt took his most daring step. By executive agreement, which did not require Senate concurrence, he made the famous deal with Britain transferring to her 50 over-age but still effective destroyers desperately needed to stave off German submarines. In exchange, Britain gave the United States sites for naval bases in Newfoundland and Bermuda and rent-free leases for six additional sites in the Caribbean and South Atlantic. As outraged as many senators by this high-handed trade was Hitler himself, who had every right to consider it an act of war. As Churchill later observed, "it marked the passage of the United States from being neutral to being non-belligerent." But Hitler did nothing to stir the United States to join the Allies, and some of the senators, two weeks later, helped enact the first peacetime draft in American history. By then, too, Congress had appropriated about $16 billion for airplanes, warships, and other "defense" needs.

The climax of the isolationist-interventionist debate came at about the same time as the presidential election of 1940. The Democrats, at their convention in Chicago in mid-July, boldly broke the two-term tradition and renominated Roosevelt, naming Secretary of Agriculture, Wallace as his running mate. The Republicans leaned heavily toward two eminent, outspoken isolationist senators, Arthur H. Vandenberg of Michigan and Robert A. Taft of Ohio. Their own strength tinged with isolationism the stand of a third aspirant, the flashy young District Attorney of New York, Thomas E. Dewey. But the drift of the times became abundantly clear when the bright young men in the party rallied so strongly behind a newcomer to politics, Wendell L. Willkie of New York, that they put him across on the sixth ballot at the Philadelphia convention at the end of June. Willkie was a magnetic public-utilities executive who first came into prominence as a leader in the fight of private power interests against the T.V.A. His charm, apparent then, grew with his own growing liberalism; and by 1940 his stand on the war in Europe was close to Roosevelt's own. This similarity probably hurt him more than it helped him in the campaign, because while it left him with a popular position it also deprived him of an issue on which to set himself off from his veteran opponent. Willkie lost by a popular vote of 22,305,000 to 27,244,000 and an electoral vote of 82 to 449, but he restored the Republican party to a position of vigorous opposition without accepting the views of its isolationist wing—an outstanding personal success. His premature death in 1944 was a blow to this party.

The election hardly over, Roosevelt renewed the debate over foreign policy in a "fireside chat" to the people on December 29, 1940. "There will be no 'bottlenecks' in our determination to aid Great Britain," he said then; "all our present efforts are not enough. We must have more . . . of everything, . . . We must be the great arsenal of democracy." One week later, in his annual message to Congress on January 6, 1941, he went further: "The time is near when . . . those nations which are now in actual war with aggressor nations . . . will not be able to pay . . . in ready cash. We cannot, and will not, tell them they must surrender, merely because of inability to pay for the weapons we know they must have." He then proposed "lend-lease" as the most practical means by which the United States, while remaining at peace herself, could help arm Britain and her allies not only to defeat the totalitarian menace, but in the future to build a better world in which the "four essential human freedoms" —freedom of speech, freedom of worship, freedom from want, and freedom from fear —might animate all nations.

The lend-lease bill—to supply Britain and her allies with arms carried in their own ships to be returned or replaced when the war was over—was fiercely opposed in Congress as a step toward American involvement in the fighting. Senator Wheeler of Montana called it the "New Deal's 'triple A' foreign policy—to plow under every fourth American boy"—a remark that Roosevelt branded "the most untruthful, the most dastardly, unpatriotic thing that has been said in public life in my generation." But public opinion favored lend-lease, and on March 11, 1941, Congress at last approving it, the President signed the

measure. Churchill referred to it as "the most unsordid act in the history of any nation." Lend-lease had a salutary effect on British finances and British morale even before the massive flow of arms began. It also gave a strong impulse to American intervention despite official disclaimers. Indeed, Admiral Harold R. Stark, United States Chief of Naval operations, promptly wrote his fleet commanders: "The question as to our entry into the war now seems to be *when,* and not *whether.*"

THE AMERICAN COMMITMENT

To insure that American lend-lease ended up at its destination and not at the bottom of the sea, Roosevelt, once the measure had become law, immediately took steps to help Britain fight the "wolf-packs" of German submarines that infested the Atlantic, and soon extended American "defense" lines all the way to Greenland and Iceland. In a more aggressive move still, on March 31, 1941, he ordered the coast guard to seize 65 German or German-controlled ships then in American ports. On May 15 a German torpedo sank the American merchantman, *Robin Moor,* in the South Atlantic. Roosevelt responded by proclaiming an unlimited national emergency, and on June 16 he requested Germany and Italy to close their consulates in the United States. These Axis countries replied by ordering

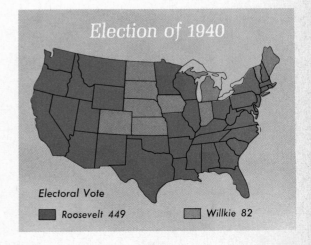

Election of 1940

Electoral Vote

■ Roosevelt 449   □ Willkie 82

American consulates in their countries closed also.

Thereafter the United States edged ever closer to war in the Atlantic. In July, the President announced that the United States by agreement with the Icelandic government, was taking over the defense of Iceland, hitherto in the hands of the British, for the duration of the war; and that the United States navy would keep convoy lines open as far as Iceland. In August, he dramatically met Winston Churchill on a British battleship at sea, where the two statesmen drew up an eight-point declaration, the Atlantic Charter, in which they professed what amounted to common war aims (see below). In September, when a German submarine near Iceland fired two torpedoes at the United States destroyer, *Greer,* and when two American-owned merchantmen were sunk, Roosevelt delivered a radio talk in which he declared that United States patrols would henceforth defend the seas against German "piracy" by striking the first blow at any Axis raiders they encountered. In October, when the American destroyer, *Kearney,* was damaged near Iceland in a battle with German submarines, Roosevelt issued a statement in which he asserted, "America has been attacked. . . . The shooting has started." At the end of October, the destroyer, *Reuben James,* was sunk off Iceland while engaged in convoy duty, and Congress responded in November by removing the restriction in the Lend-Lease Act prohibiting American vessels from sailing "into a combat area in violation of . . . the Neutrality Act of 1939" (see p. 779). Henceforth, American merchant ships were to be allowed to sail well-armed, and were to be permitted to carry lend-lease supplies direct to Britain.

Thus, by the fall of 1941, the United States had become an open ally of Britain without actually being in a state of war. What held the country back was not so much the agitations of the isolationists, now a distinctly small minority of the public, but the ultimate reluctance of the average American, even when he was heart and soul for the destruction of Nazi tyranny, to take the final step into another monstrous conflict. Nonetheless, a public opinion poll taken as early as June, 1941, showed that four out of five Americans believed that the nation was already in the war for all practical purposes.

While the United States and the Axis nations approached their fateful confrontation, Hitler, on June 22, 1941, had altered the entire pattern of the war by his astounding invasion of Russia, so recently his partner in their non-aggression pact. What led him to take this momentous step is uncertain. Perhaps he hoped, with a few well-calculated blows, to win the wheat of the Ukraine, the oil of the Caucasus, and the greater part of Russia's industrial resources. Then the British would recognize that they were at war with an invincible continental empire and would have to come to terms. Whatever his calculations, Hitler obviously underestimated by a wide margin Russia's potential for resistance. Others did likewise. In June, 1941, for example, immediately after the Nazi attack on Russia, Henry L. Stimson, now Roosevelt's Secretary of War, estimated that it would take Hitler from one to three months to conquer the Soviets. Secretary of the Navy Knox thought it would take "anywhere from six weeks to two months." They were soon proved wrong, of course. When winter came, the German armies were still outside Moscow and Leningrad, and Russia was still mustering her strength.

Churchill, an inveterate foe of bolshevism, nevertheless welcomed the Russians as comrades in arms, just as he had welcomed the American "arsenal." "I have only one purpose, the destruction of Hitler," he told his secretary. "If Hitler invaded Hell I would make at least a favorable reference to the Devil in the House of Commons." Alone and battered at the end of 1940, Britain, six months later thus found herself with two powerful allies, in a formidable if strange coalition.

In the Atlantic Charter of August, 1941, Roosevelt and Churchill had endorsed generously broad goals in the war against the Axis: no territorial aggrandizement, no changes of territory against the wishes of the people concerned, self-government for all peoples, free access to trade and raw materials, freedom from war, from fear, and from want, freedom of the seas, and the abandonment of war as an instrument of of international relations. The Atlantic Charter goals were disturbingly reminiscent of Wilson's Fourteen Points (see p. 680). Russia's qualified endorsement of the goals of the Charter early in November, when the United States extended lend-lease to her, was more disturbing still. Russia's endorse-

ment contained the ominous proviso: "Considering that the practical application of" the principles of the Charter "will necessarily adapt itself to the circumstances, needs, and historic peculiarities of particular countries." This was a threat as well as a caution. But the problems of the present had become too urgent to allow much time for worrying about future difficulties.

III. *Engaging the Axis*

PEARL HARBOR

When Churchill agreed to the Atlantic Charter's principles for the postwar world, he also stated the Charter's more immediate objectives: "to cause our enemies concern," to "cheer our friends," and to "make Japan ponder." Japan, her appetite whetted by the Indo-China possessions of fallen France and the East Indian colonies of occupied Holland, had joined Italy and Germany in the Axis back in September, 1940. Now, even if she pondered the Allies growing strength, she would not on that account put aside her grandest ambitions. Early in the afternoon of December 7, 1941, a strong carrier-borne force of Japanese planes swooped down on the American naval base at Pearl Harbor in Hawaii. Although the American naval and military commanders there had been warned by the administration that a Japanese attack was likely, they had failed to prepare for such an eventuality and were caught by surprise. Most of the American aircraft were destroyed on the ground, and the unprotected naval vessels suffered frightful damage. Five battleships and three cruisers were sunk or put out of action and other ships were hit hard. In this one assault, 2,335 American servicemen and 68 civilians were killed; 1,178 were wounded. The next day, a shocked Congress voted to declare war on Japan, and when Germany and Italy on December 11 declared war on

the United States, Congress responded immediately with similar declarations against them.

Since his 1937 "quarantine" speech (see p. 778), Roosevelt had been cautious in dealing with continuing Japanese aggression. As early as December, 1937, when Japanese planes sank the American gunboat, *Panay,* in the Yangtze River, war had seemed possible; but Japan quickly apologized for the attack and paid reparations for the lives lost. From then on, the United States followed an ambiguous line. On the one hand, Roosevelt refused to invoke the Neutrality Act lest it halt the movement of supplies over the tortuous Burma Road to Chinese forces opposing Japan. Yet Americans continued to sell large quantities of scrap iron and steel, copper, oil, lead, and machinery to the Nipponese. It would have been possible, after January, 1940, to end this traffic by imposing embargoes on it. But Roosevelt hesitated at first to make this move because he thought it would only cause Japan to seek these commodities by further conquest in Asia. In May, 1940, as a deterrent to Japan, Roosevelt ordered the transfer of the United States Pacific fleet base from San Diego, California, to Pearl Harbor.

As a further deterrent, after the fall of France in June, 1940, Congress in July passed a law requiring Americans henceforth to obtain federal licenses for the ex-

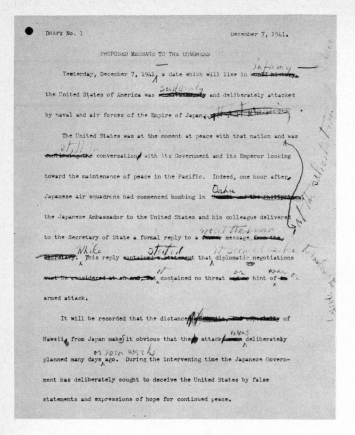

First draft of page 1 of Roosevelt's "date which will live in infamy" war message to Congress the day after Pearl Harbor.

port of oil and scrap metal. Under this law, Roosevelt, on July 26, ordered critical aviation gasoline withheld from Japan, a step which drew a strong but futile Japanese protest. The next month Japan forced the helpless Vichy government in France to surrender bases in *northern* Indo-China, a move which prompted Roosevelt, on September 25, to extend the embargo to iron and steel scrap, and to grant a large new loan to Chiang Kai-shek in China. Two days later Japan joined the German-Italian coalition.

The formation of the Berlin-Rome-Tokyo Axis, ostensibly to promote Hitler's "New Order" in Europe and the prosperity of "Greater East Asia" under Japan, was explicitly intended to warn the United States to keep hands off both. If she attacked any of the signatories, the other two agreed to come to the assistance of the vic-

tim. The first major change in the Pacific thereafter followed the Nazi invasion of Russia in June, 1941, which removed the last possibility that sizable Soviet forces could be deployed against Japan. That July, Tokyo compelled the Vichy government to yield new French bases, this time in *southern* Indo-China. Roosevelt retaliated promptly by freezing all Japanese assets in the United States, a move Japan as promptly reciprocated, thereby all but paralyzing trade between the two countries. On August 17, 1941, Roosevelt warned the Japanese that if they made any further moves to impose military domination on neighboring countries, the United States would take "all steps which it may deem necessary toward safeguarding [its] legitimate right and interest."

The previous December, United States Naval Intelligence cryptographers had broken Japan's secret diplomatic code, "Magic," and Washington was enabled to listen in on messages from Tokyo to its emissaries in the American capital. One thing seemed certain from these messages— Japan had no intention to forego the annihilation of Chiang Kai-shek. At the same time, the United States had no intention of sacrificing him to Japan's ambition. Further negotiations between the two countries foundered principally on this issue. In Japan itself in mid-October, 1941, the relatively conciliatory Konoye government was forced to resign in favor of General Hideki Tojo, who feared for his army's morale if, after years of sacrifice, it must yield its Chinese goal under American pressure. "If a hundred million people merge into one iron solidarity to go forward," Tojo declared, "nothing can stop us." He would have been glad to have China without war with the United States; but on October 23 his Cabinet agreed to speed up military preparations, and by November 3 had decided on the attack on Pearl Harbor. At the same time, negotiations at Washington were to continue—after November 17 under the direction of Saburo Kurusu, a special envoy dispatched by air.

From the secret code, Washington knew

that if satisfactory negotiations were not completed by November 29, "things are automatically going to happen." On November 20, Kurusu and the Japanese ambassador presented Secretary of State Hull with proposals which seemed no less than a demand that the United States approve and abet Japan's conquests in Asia. On November 26, the State Department presented counter-proposals offering Tokyo favorable trade relations in exchange for the withdrawal of her forces from China and Indo-China, and her joining a non-aggression pact with other nations that had interests in the Far East. Japan obviously would not accept such terms. "I have washed my hands of it," said Hull to Secretary of War Stimson that day, "and it is now in the hands of you and Knox, the Army and Navy." Hull did not realize how right he was. Unknown to the American negotiators, a Japanese carrier force had just set out from its base in the Kurile Islands on its fatal errand. On December 1, dismissing the American demands as "fantastic," Kurusu nevertheless asked that discussions continue, a gesture that can be construed only as a blind for the impending raid. Washington knew then of Japanese troop movements which Roosevelt thought foreshadowed an attack in the Southwest Pacific—on Thailand, Malaya, and the Dutch East Indies, which were, in fact, the main Japanese objectives. On December 6, he sent a hasty peace appeal to the Japanese emperor which was answered on December 7 by the bombs at Pearl Harbor.

As one consequence of the disaster, Roosevelt's most bitter critics later accused him of having provoked Japan to attack in order to bring the United States into the war in Europe, and of having deliberately exposed the navy to disaster at Pearl Harbor in order to create a situation that would unite Americans behind his war. That Roosevelt wanted to enter the war by November, and that he knew that a firm stand against Japan might bring about drastic action on her part, seems beyond doubt. However, had the alternative policy been adopted, and had the United States stood quietly by

while Japan conquered an immensely rich empire, Roosevelt would have been criticized for his inaction. The notion that Roosevelt conspired to defeat and destroy a substantial part of the navy he had served and lovingly built up, and that his administration and high military authorities were involved in the plot, may be left to those who find such notions plausible. The fact remains that there was slackness both in Washington and at Pearl Harbor, and that the full advantage of the naval intelligence coup in deciphering the Japanese code was thrown away—a ghastly mistake and missed opportunity not uncharacteristic of war emergencies everywhere.

The sequel to Pearl Harbor was immediate and unmitigated disaster. Japan followed up her startling triumph with attacks on the Philippines, Wake Island, Guam, Hong Kong, British Malaya, and Thailand. Thailand surrendered immediately, Guam on December 13, Wake Island on December 20, and Hong Kong on December 25. American troops in the Philippines under General Douglas MacArthur made brave stands on the Bataan Peninsula and on the fortress island of Corregidor, but after MacArthur managed to escape to take command in Australia, Bataan surrendered in April, 1942, Corregidor in May.

In the Southwest Pacific on December 10, the Japanese paralyzed British striking power by sinking the battle cruiser *Repulse* and the battleship *Prince of Wales*. They then captured Singapore, the center of British authority in Asia, and pushed the defenders out of the Netherlands Indies. By March, 1942, they had conquered Burma and closed the Burma Road, thereby reducing aid to China to a trickle.

The only offsetting Allied gains came in Latin America, where within a few days of the assault on Pearl Harbor twelve countries—with Argentina a conspicuous exception—either declared war on the Axis or broke relations with its members. "We are now to gather the fruits," Hull wrote later, "of our innumerable measures to apply and solidify the doctrine of the Good Neighbor."

THE BALANCE OF FORCES

The anti-Axis powers, in the spring of 1942, had little reason to expect they could win the war quickly, if indeed they could win at all. To be sure, they outnumbered the Axis powers, but the latter could draw on enormous labor resources in Central Europe, the occupied part of Russia, and the Southwest Pacific. Occupied France and friendly Spain could add materially to the German war potential, not least by helping to make the Atlantic and the western Mediterranean hazardous for Allied shipping. Axis forces also occupied North Africa from Tunis to the Egyptian border, and Germany's formidable Africa Corps, under General Erwin Rommel, seemed on the verge of smashing eastward to Alexandria, closing the Suez Canal, and forcing Turkey to join the dictators. When the eastern Mediterranean became impassable on this account, Allied ships had to take the long route around the Cape of Good Hope to supply British forces in the Middle East. In southern Russia, the Germans were hammering, too, at the Caucasus, and threatened to drive through to Iraq and Iran and complete the conquest of the routes to the East, cutting Britain off from her empire.

At best, a war lasting 7 to 15 years seemed in the offing for the Allies. But such a pessimistic forecast neglected some Allied assets, notably American resources and American industrial capacity. Moreover, Allied planning and administration proved vastly superior to vaunted centralization of authority in the dictatorships both in individual countries and in the coordination of national efforts. Coordination presented a special challenge after January 1, 1942, when at a meeting in Washington, 26 nations, the first of the United Nations (see p. 806), pledged the full employment of their resources to defeat the Axis.

The United States and Britain in particular, through their combined Chiefs of Staff and the intimate collaboration of Roosevelt and Churchill, worked together with remarkable harmony during most of the war. At an early point in their joint effort, their military planners made an important overall decision. They would conduct a holding operation in the Pacific until the United States could mobilize enough aid for Britain and Russia to take the offensive in Europe. After the Axis had been defeated in Europe, Japan's turn would come. Those in the United States who wanted to concentrate all effort immediately on the Oriental challenger hotly criticized this decision, but it was vindicated by events.

In the spring of 1942, two important naval victories strengthened Allied hopes that Japan could be held at bay. One was the battle of the Coral Sea, in which a Japanese assault on Port Moresby in New Guinea, an important site in American-Australian communications, was turned back. The United States lost the carrier *Lexington* in the engagement; but when the Japanese retired on May 11, 15 of their capital ships had been sunk and 20 damaged. The second was the battle of Midway Island, June 3-6. Japanese capture of Midway would have made Pearl Harbor unusable. To save the island, Admiral Chester Nimitz sailed out to meet a much larger Japanese force and after sustaining heavy losses sent the enemy reeling homeward.

AMERICAN MOBILIZATION

The attack on Pearl Harbor closed the debate over isolation. Even Senator Wheeler admitted, "The only thing now to do is to lick hell out of them." Differences of opinion continued over the conduct of the war, but public support for participation was complete.

Since almost no one doubted the necessity for war, there was much less intolerance than in World War I. The harsh exception was the expulsion of loyal Japanese-Americans from their homes and their incarceration in relocation centers. Supreme Court Justice Murphy found in this act "a melancholy resemblance" to the Nazi treatment of the Jews, and the American Civil Liberties Union called it "the worst single whole-sale violation of civil rights of American citizens in our history." Even such panic-inspired repression, however, did not deter many Nisei units—made up of Americans of Japanese descent—from performing heroic-ally in the United States armed forces. Their work, along with the growing reali-zation of how unfairly their and other Japanese families had been treated, led the federal government to pay more than $35 million to the evacuees for property losses.

An American army of 1,600,000 men was already in existence at the time of Pearl Harbor, most of them recruited through the first peace-time draft (see p. 780). Eventu-ally, all men between 18 and 45 were made subject to military service, and for the first time, women were permitted to volunteer in the armed forces. By the war's end, 15 million men and more than 200,000 women had served in the army, navy, marines and coast guard.

Behind these men and women stood American industry, agriculture, labor, and science. Critics of the President had dis-missed as wishful thinking his call for 50,000 planes a year in 1940. In 1942 over 47,000 aircraft were built; for 1944 the figure rose above 96,000. By 1945 no less than 55 million tons of merchant shipping and 71,000 naval vessels had been launched by American yards. Because Malayan and East Indian rubber supplies had been cut off early in the war, an entire synthetic rub-ber industry had to be established; by 1944, this industry was producing no less than 762,000 tons a year.

In other American industries, first lend-lease and then American war production ended the dreary saga of unemployment. Negroes, who were called equally with whites to serve in the armed forces, also re-sumed their migration to the factories which had been checked by the depression. Many Americans sensed the hypocrisy of waging a war against racism abroad while full rights were denied millions at home, and for the first time, in 1941, a federal Fair Employment Practices Committee (F.E.P.C.) was created to protect minorities from job

discrimination on grounds of race, color or creed. During the war millions of women joined or replaced men on the assembly lines and kept war plants going day and night. A War Manpower Commission shifted workers into areas where they were most needed, and made other arrangements to insure the most efficient use of the labor force.

The inducement to work in war plants grew as average weekly earnings rose from $23.86 in 1939 to $46.08 in 1944. After the Japanese attack on Pearl Harbor, the A.F.L. and the C.I.O. made no-strike pledges. But later, as prices rose and as the most des-perate period of war passed, strikes became quite frequent, though almost entirely in industries not contributing directly to the war effort. Workers were widely criticized for the strikes. But the slogan, "There are no strikes in foxholes," was met with the retort, "There are no profits either." In fact, America was waging war with a sizable sec-tor of the economy still operating free of wartime controls. Profits were piling up, and workers were demanding a greater share in them. Corporate profits after taxes rose from $5 billion in 1939 to almost $10 billion in 1944, and many new fortunes were made.

Although the farm population fell dur-ing the war (despite draft exemptions for many agricultural workers), farm produc-tion soared. In 1945, output per farm worker, responding to favorable weather and scientific aids, almost doubled the level that had been reached during 1910 to 1914, agriculture's golden years. Farm income also doubled. The war showed, too, that a small farm laboring force, working with improved agricultural techniques, could meet the nor-mal needs of the domestic market, a dem-onstration that soon influenced farm and financial policies. To protect farmers from a postwar collapse such as that following the wartime expansion in 1917-1918, the Price Stabilization Act of 1942 contained some special agricultural concessions. Some commodity prices were to be supported at 90 per cent of parity for two years after the end of hostilities. No price ceilings were to be set on agricultural products until their prices had reached either 110 per cent of parity or the level that existed from 1919 to 1929, whichever might be higher. These arrangements were in effect continued in the Stabilization Extension Act of 1944. The farmers had driven a hard bargain with the government. Some farm prices rose above the ceiling prices paid by consumers, and the government itself was forced to make up the difference. Roosevelt protested, but members of the agricultural bloc in Congress exerted all their influence to make sure that the practice continued.

A concerted effort was made during the war by the Office of Price Administration, under the chairmanship of Leon Henderson, to control inflation elsewhere in the economy. Price ceilings were set on a wide variety of consumers' goods, and a few products, such as sugar, coffee, and meat, especially in demand in the armed services, were rationed without causing undue hardship. Prices had already risen about 25 per cent when controls were first authorized in January, 1942, and they continued to rise slightly. But serious inflation was avoided.

Wartime science in the United States came under the direction of the Office of Scientific Research and Development, headed by Vannevar Bush and President James Conant of Harvard. Their work profited greatly from the contributions of refugee scientists from Axis countries and the cooperation of British scientists as well. Among their major developments was "radar," a form of microwave detection which made it possible for planes to locate and bomb submarines trying to make speed by running surfaced in fog or darkness. But their most lethal development was the atomic bomb. Refugee scientists knew that the Nazis were at work on atomic fission and shuddered at the thought of their perfecting a bomb before the Allies could do so. As early as January, 1939, three refugees, Albert Einstein, Leo Szilard, and Eugene Wigner, warned President Roosevelt of this danger, but not until the spring of 1941 was the long and complicated Allied bomb project seriously launched. The following year a nuclear laboratory was set up under the direction of Professor J. Robert Oppenheimer, at Los Alamos, New Mexico, where some of the world's greatest scientists set to work to translate preliminary experiments into a deliverable weapon. On July 16, 1945, the first experimental bomb was successfully exploded at the Alamogordo air base in New Mexico.

By mid-1943, American war costs were running at $8 billion a month, as high as the *yearly* budgets of the peacetime New Deal. In 1945, for the first time in history, the federal government spent over $100 billion. The total cost of the war to the United States was about $350 billion—ten times that of World War I.

After July 1, 1943, employers began to collect income taxes for the government from employees by deducting them from payrolls, an innovation that continued to be used after the war, and one that assured the government of its revenues and kept the workers abreast of their tax liabilities from month to month. Income and other taxes paid for two-fifth of the war's huge cost. Yet between 1941 and 1945, the national debt rose from about $48 billion to $247 billion.

Politics were not suspended in the war years. In the congressional elections of 1942, the Republicans gained considerable ground by capitalizing on public discontent with military defeats. But by 1944, the military situation had completely changed, and the Republicans had to contend once again with Roosevelt's popularity. Thomas E. Dewey, now risen to governor of New York, became their candidate. The Democrats, with the third-term tradition shattered ("There is a law against bigamy," quipped a commentator, "but whoever heard of a law against trigamy?"), nominated Roosevelt with little ado. The convention spotlight, since Roosevelt's health was already an issue, centered on the choice for vice-president. After a stormy session, Henry Wallace, who was unpopular with city bosses and southern conservatives, was

788

dropped in favor of Senator Harry S. Truman of Missouri, who had commanded attention as chairman of a Senate committee investigating wartime contracts. Dewey had no sound issue on which to campaign, since he and his party had accepted most of the administration's program, including the commitment to a new international organization (see p. 786). Roosevelt won by a

vote of 25,602,000 to 22,006,000 and by 432 to 99 in the electoral college. The Democrats' choice of a vice-president proved fateful, indeed, for Roosevelt was to serve less than four months of his fourth term.

IV. *Toward Victory*

AT WAR IN EUROPE AND AFRICA

To win the war, it was vital for the Western powers to gain mastery of the sea and the air. For months after the United States entered the war, U-boats wreaked havoc along the Atlantic and Gulf coasts, and in the Caribbean, thereby carrying the war directly to American shores. The rate of sinkings ran extremely high, while the toll of U-boats was relatively low until a new system of convoys was worked out, using a host of light ships on the deep and patrolling coastal waters with bombers and blimps. Still, the cost in tonnage and lives continued to run at extravagant levels, and it was only the tremendous rate of American merchant-ship production that chiefly offset the submarine plague.

In the air, supremacy had passed to Britain's RAF during the great clashes over England in 1940. By 1941, when British aircraft production alone surpassed Germany's, the RAF went on the offensive, returning in kind the terrible attacks that Germany had inflicted on British cities. Sustained RAF bombing reached a peak during July, 1943, when night raids over Hamburg destroyed more than a third of the port and killed over 60,000 persons. In August, 1942, American airmen joined the British in raids over the Continent, supplementing RAF saturation bombings after dark with precision bombing of specific targets by day. Between them, the two air forces dropped more than 2,600,000 bombs on enemy sites. At one point, there was talk among the Allies of trying to bring Germany down through air attacks alone, thus avoiding the

immense casualties that an invasion of Hitler's "Fortress Europe" on the Continent would almost surely entail. But this notion had to be abandoned. Air attacks never succeeded in biting deeply enough into the production of such essentials as planes, submarines, or synthetic rubber. On the other hand, air assaults were devastating in the long run to two major targets: transportation and refineries. When the time came for the Allies to invade the Continent, Germany was gravely hampered by the disruption of her transport at home and in France, and by shortages of fuel for her planes and tanks.

Any invasion of the Continent was still some time off. In June, 1942, when Russian cries for a second front had become importunate, Churchill and Roosevelt, meeting in Washington, learned that General Rommel's army, now sweeping over Egypt (see p. 786), was to be reinforced. Disaster thus faced the thin line of defenders of the Middle East, and this predicament settled all argument over Churchill's eagerness to strike first at "Fortress Europe" in the presumed "soft under-belly" of the Balkans (chiefly to keep the Russians out), and the Americans' enthusiasm for a limited assault in France in anticipation of an all-out attack in the future. Instead, plans were promptly made for Allied reinforcement of the British troops confronting Rommel, which included the assignment of the imperious General Bernard L. Montgomery to the command of the key Eighth Army. The over-all North African operation was placed under General Dwight D. Eisenhower, who

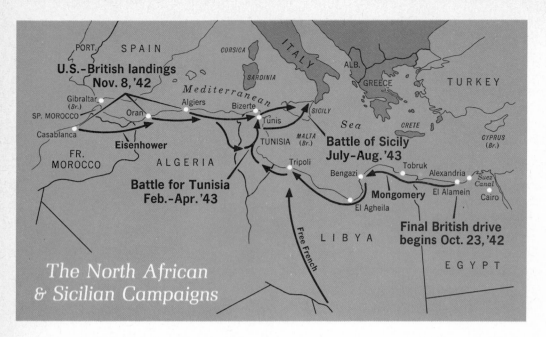

U.S.–British landings
Nov. 8, '42

Eisenhower

Battle for Tunisia
Feb.–Apr. '43

Battle of Sicily
July–Aug. '43

Final British drive
begins Oct. 23, '42

Mongomery

Free French

The North African
& Sicilian Campaigns

had just been named Supreme Allied Commander in the Mediterranean theater.

Rommel's frightening course across Egypt had halted, spent, at El Alamein, on the Mediterranean, and there, on October 23, 1942, the first great Allied land offensive of the war began. In twelve days Montgomery's army sent Rommel's tanks and his Italian contingents streaming back toward Libya and Tripoli. "Up to Alamein," crowed Churchill, "we survived. After Alamein we conquered." Quickly broadening the conquest was the Allied assault from the West which began on November 8, 1942. On that date, three Allied armies, 185,000 strong, under Eisenhower, two starting from England and one from the United States, began landing at Algiers, Oran, and Casablanca in French North Africa. The landings were as tricky politically as tactically. The politics of Torch, the code name for the offensive, revolved around the touchy relations of the Allies with leaders both of the collaborators and the devoted underground (often dominated by trained and disciplined communists) in Hitler's Europe.

The Allies hoped in French North Africa to land their troops as expeditiously and safely as possible. But it was difficult to keep Torch secret from the Germans and thereby gain all the advantages of surprise while at the same time informing the French there that friendly forces were approaching. Moreover, most of the French administrators and the French navy in North Africa (largely out of hatred for the British) had remained loyal to Vichy, so the invaders were not necessarily friends. The landings at Algiers met little resistance; those at Casablanca and Oran encountered heavy fire and heavy fighting from the French fleet, parts of which were sunk. French land forces, in turn, would have nothing to do with General Henri Giraud, a hero of the fall of France who had escaped from prison in Germany and was brought to North Africa by Eisenhower. The troops proved more responsive to Admiral Jean Darlan, chief of all Vichy forces, who was visiting a sick son in Algiers (perhaps a pretext) and became impressed with Eisenhower's strength. Darlan imposed a cease-fire on Vichy-oriented French troops in North Africa on November 11.

Conveniently for the Allies, this political chameleon was assassinated on Christmas Eve, 1942. A tussle for French African leadership followed between Giraud and General Charles de Gaulle, the uncompromising foe of Vichy. De Gaulle won; and while he personally became a thorn to Churchill and Roosevelt, his work and that of his Free French forces contributed to victory and to the subsequent French revival.

Rommel, now under severe pressure from the West as well as from the East, managed to frustrate both Montgomery and Eisenhower for months. Nevertheless, the momentum of El Alamein in October, strengthened by the Russians' own remarkable check to the German assault at Stalingrad in November (see p. 795), gave hope and flair to Allied planning; and when Churchill and Roosevelt met once more at Casablanca in January, 1943, they confidently made plans for victory on all fronts.

At Casablanca the Allied leaders decided to invade Sicily and Italy after the Axis had been cleared out of North Africa, agreed to send sufficient forces to the Pacific to take the offensive there, and promised to ease pressure on the Russians by setting up another front in Europe that would engage enemy armies "as heavily as possible." They also announced that they would accept only the "unconditional surrender" of the Axis.

North Africa was completely liberated when General Von Arnim surrendered Rommel's army of 350,000 men (the "Fox" himself having evaded capture) in Tunisia on May 13, 1943. The liquidation of Nazi North African submarine and air bases was soon completed. Franco Spain was deterred from intervening on the Axis side. The southern Mediterranean again became available to the Allies at normal wartime risk, and pressure on the Middle East was eased. Two months before the capitulation of Rommel's army, General Giraud had restored representative government in French North Africa, voided all legislation there under the Vichy regime, and, with Algiers as his base, promoted the liberation of mainland France.

The projected attack on Italy began on July 10, which was as early as sufficient landing craft could be assembled; and by August 17, when Sicily was cleared, 100,000 German prisoners had been taken. Meanwhile, King Victor Emmanuel and members of the Fascist Grand Council had deposed Mussolini and had set up a new government under Marshal Pietro Badoglio, who immediately sued for peace. On September 8, 1943, the Italian government

signed an unconditional surrender, but Italy herself was still occupied by strong German forces which Hitler, on learning of the perfidy of his Axis partner, promptly strengthened. The Allies objective was to wipe out these forces, or at least so occupy them that they could not be used against the Russians. At the same time, the Western powers had another objective. Control of Italy would permit them to move eastward into the Balkans and forestall the Soviets from overrunning southern Europe when the final push against Hitler came.

Unfortunately for them, the Italian campaign, in the words of British General Maitland Wilson, deteriorated into a "slow painful advance through difficult terrain against a determined and resourceful enemy." The Allies had taken Naples on September 28, 1943. Rome lay but 100 miles north, but could not be captured until June 4, 1944, only two days before the cross-channel invasion of France was to begin (see p. 793). On April 28, 1945, Italian partisans captured Mussolini, murdered him, and mutilated his body. But the Nazis in Italy fought on until May 2, a mere five days before the Reich itself collapsed.

CONFERENCE DIPLOMACY

Following the Casablanca Conference of January, 1943, Roosevelt and Churchill had met in Washington in May, 1943, and agreed tentatively on starting the invasion of France by way of Normandy within twelve months. In August, 1943, they met again in Quebec to firm up and elaborate the invasion plans. They also officially recognized the French Committee of National Liberation as the government of Algeria and of French overseas territories that acknowledged its authority. In October in Moscow, the Foreign Ministers of the Big Three—Hull for the United States, Eden for Britain, and Molotov for the U.S.S.R.—drew up the first general understanding among themselves. The Western spokesmen prom-

Panoramic view of the invasion beach at Normandy, June, 1944, gives a vivid picture of the magnitude of the Allied landing operation.

ised the Russians to open the invasion of France in 1944. All three declared their intention to establish as soon as possible a general international organization "for the maintenance of international peace and security." They also proposed to foster a democratic future for Italy. The future of Poland, where Russia's interest was more immediate, however, proved a snare.

"Conference diplomacy" was continued at Cairo in November, 1943, when Roosevelt and Churchill agreed on Eisenhower as the supreme commander of the forces to invade the Continent. They also conferred with Chiang Kai-shek on the Pacific war and planned to aid him by intensifying air operations in Japan-held Burma to insure an increased flow of supplies to China "over the hump" of the Himalayas. They promised to fight until Japan surrendered unconditionally and to see to it that she returned certain territories, including Manchuria and Formosa, to China. The three powers stated that they were "determined that . . . Korea shall become free and independent."

The next month Roosevelt and Churchill met with Stalin for the first time in

Teheran, the capital of Iran. Here D-Day for the Normandy invasion, under the code name "Overlord," was definitely set for May or June, 1944, when it was to synchronize with a Russian offensive against Hitler from the East. Stalin also confirmed the promise made at the Moscow Conference to enter the war against Japan as soon as Germany was defeated. The Grand Alliance agreed to aid Marshal Tito and the Yugoslav "partisans" in ridding their country of Hitler's forces. They also decided on Polish borders, with Russia taking part of the much-divided country on the East, and Poland to be compensated on the West at Germany's expense. Germany, in turn, was to be destroyed as a military power.

Although these important decisions were in general harmoniously reached, Churchill left Teheran with deep misgivings. Roosevelt, he felt, gave too much credence to Russian assertions of cooperation in the long future. At the close of the meeting the Big Three announced: "We came here with hope and determination. We leave here, friends in fact, in spirit, and in purpose." Roosevelt's sanguinity was apparent when

792

he told Congress on his return that he "got along fine with Stalin," and predicted: "We are going to get along with him and the Russian people—very well indeed."

THE END OF HITLER

Everything abetted Operation Overlord except the weather. Victory in the Battle of Britain had won the Allies command in the air. Victory in the Battle of the Atlantic and in North Africa had secured command of the seas. The amphibious landings and the establishment of beachheads at Casablanca, Oran, Sicily, and Salerno had yielded invaluable experience. Even the awful, disappointing stalemate in Italy which engaged needed Allied manpower, tied down enemy troops and equipment that Hitler needed much more desperately in France. Above all else, victory depended on success in the Battle of Production, and in the very first weeks following D-Day American production met the severest test.

For four years Hitler had concentrated on making northern France the most impregnable wall of his fortress. For six weeks Allied air attacks pulverized this wall and the communication lines leading to it. Then, on June 4, 1944, 2,876,000 men—supported by 2,500,000 tons of supplies, 11,000 airplanes, and a vast fleet of ships—stood straining in England for the takeoff. Tension mounted unbearably when a storm over the Channel forced Eisenhower to withhold the signal twenty-four hours. The next night's weather was scarcely better, but Overlord was on. The first troop carriers with 176,000 men anchored off the Normandy beaches at 3 a.m., June 6. Two weeks later, almost half a million Allied soldiers were fighting in Normandy when a mighty hurricane ripped up the shore. The havoc it left was terrifying, and only the prior success of the air arm in sealing off the ravaged zone from enemy reinforcements averted a dreaded German counterattack. The ultimate effect, however, was heartening:

There was no sight in the war [writes General Eisenhower] that so impressed me with the industrial might of America as the wreckage on

the landing beaches. To any other nation the disaster would have been almost decisive; but so great was America's productive capacity that the great storm occasioned little more than a ripple in the development of our build-up.

There were other checks in Normandy. The landings there—as against obviously more suitable places—had caught the Nazis by surprise; but so intensive had been their preparation, they were able to mobilize resistance quickly. Then came their V-1's and V-2's whose rain of terror on London was not stemmed until their very launching sites were captured. The V-1 was a pilotless airplane, loaded with explosives, whose mechanism enabled it to hold a predetermined course until it blew up with terrible force on contact with its target. The V-2 was a rocket which descended from the immense height of its arc with such speed that "the first warning of its coming was the explosion. During flight it could not be heard, seen, or intercepted." The first V-1 struck London on June 12, 1944, six days *after* D-Day, the first V-2 early in August.

"The effect of the new German weapons," Eisenhower writes in *Crusade in Europe,*

was very noticeable upon morale. Great Britain had withstood terrific bombing experiences. But when in June the Allies landed successfully on the Normandy coast the citizens unquestionably experienced a great sense of relief. . . . When the new weapons began to come over London in considerable numbers their hopes were dashed. Indeed, the depressing effect of the bombs was not confined to the civilian population; soldiers at the front began again to worry about friends and loved ones at home.

General Eisenhower continues:

It seemed likely that, if the German had succeeded in perfecting and using these new weapons six months earlier than he did, our invasion of Europe would have proved exceedingly difficult, perhaps impossible. I feel sure that if he had succeeded in using these weapons over a six-month period . . . Overlord might have been written off.

Nevertheless the build-up continued and Overlord progressed. By July 24, more than a million Allied troops had subdued 1,500 square miles of Normandy and Brittany. The next day, General George S. Patton, Jr.'s magnificent Third Army swept after the Germans and turned their retreat into a rout. On August 25, assisted by a Free French division under General Leclerc, Patton liberated Paris, where, two days later, de Gaulle installed himself as President of a provisional government. Patton himself kept going, with Omar Bradley's First Army moving more slowly on his left. Farther north, Montgomery, with Canadian and British forces, was hurtling through Belgium, where they liberated the key port of Antwerp on September 4.

The Germans, having lost half a million men and virtually all of France, had decided to take refuge behind their long neglected West Wall in the homeland across the Rhine. Patton hungered to burst after them. At the same time, Montgomery was straining for permission to make "one powerful and full-blooded thrust towards Berlin." But the speedy Allied offensives had so stretched supply lines that only one of the two could safely be turned loose. In one of his most difficult decisions, Eisenhower leaned toward Montgomery in whose path lay the Nazi access roads to Antwerp and the bases of the V-weapons. Patton judged this "the most momentous error of the war," and with Bradley's backing acted as though it were not final. Eisenhower, whose overall strategy had favored blunting both Patton's and Montgomery's epic thrusts in order to gain "the whole length of the Rhine before launching a final assault on interior Germany," failed to resolve the conflict over priorities of supply. Montgomery's momentum was dissipated; Patton's progress slowed.

Hitler used the lucky respite to rally his forces. On December 16, 1944, he startled the Allies with his breakout in the thinly defended Ardennes forest in southern Bel-

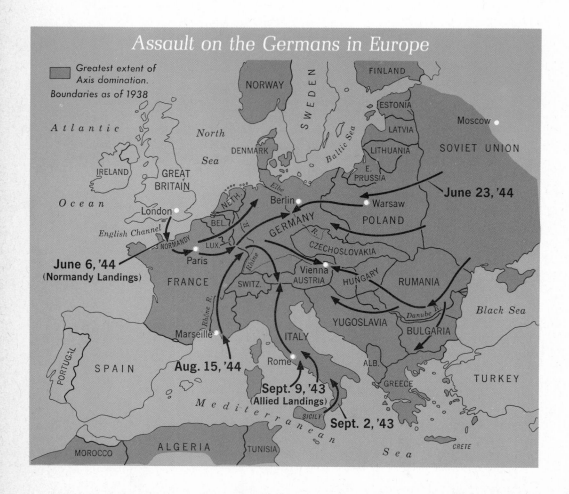

Assault on the Germans in Europe

Greatest extent of Axis domination.
Boundaries as of 1938

June 23, '44

June 6, '44
(Normandy Landings)

Aug. 15, '44

Sept. 9, '43
(Allied Landings)

Sept. 2, '43

gium. In ten days his armies advanced fifty miles until checked by the heroic American stand at the cross-roads town of Bastogne. By mid-January, 1945, in the famous "Battle of the Bulge," the Germans had been pushed back to their old line with the satisfaction, such as it was, of having delayed Eisenhower's grand push another month.

In the meantime, the Russians had taken every advantage of Hitler's preoccupation with the second front. The apex of the Nazi invasion of the U.S.S.R. had been reached in the Crimea in the summer of 1942 at the approaches to the industrial city of Stalingrad on the River Volga. The battle for Stalingrad opened in July. In November, Marshal Zhukov grasped the initiative, and on January 31, 1943, after one of the "dourest, bloodiest, and most prolonged" battles, the German armies capitulated.

Soviet reclamation of the Crimea began that spring and was completed when the signal for Overlord was given. Elimination of Nazi forces in the Balkans started in the summer of 1944. Only in Greece, where Churchill in October at last got in his Balkan licks by dispatching troops to bend the civil war there to the conservative side, were the communists thwarted in establishing subservient regimes. By February, 1945, Finland also had yielded again to Russian arms, Poland had been organized as a communist state, Hungary had fallen, Czechoslovakia had been penetrated, and Vienna's collapse was imminent. At the time of the Yalta Conference, February 4-11, 1945, Soviet armies stood only fifty miles from Berlin. No people besides the Jews had suffered more from Nazi atrocities than the Russians; none of the Western Allies had sacrificed as much as they in the fighting itself. Soviet claims on the sympathy of the free world were immense. Few Americans foresaw what use she would make of it.

Russia had begun compensating herself long before Yalta. Here she made verbal concessions—to the establishment of the United Nations Organization in April, 1945, and to "holding free and unfettered elections as soon as possible" in Poland and elsewhere—in exchange for promises of even

greater territorial gains. Most of these were to be at the expense of Japan, with whom Russia was still at peace, so the promises, as well as other Yalta terms (see p. 805), were kept secret. The Soviet was also given, along with reparations in goods, the privilege of the "use of German labor" in her own reconstruction. Tentative decisions were also made at Yalta—and more or less confirmed at the Potsdam Conference in July and August 1945 (see p. 807)—for the multiple administration of Berlin and the partitioning of Germany, for the trial of "war criminals," and the planning of a general peace conference that never was held.

To Churchill the vagueness of the Yalta understandings was ominous. By the time of the meeting he had learned—to his fright —of America's determination to withdraw her entire force from Europe within two years of V-E day. To offset the resulting preponderance of Soviet strength on the Continent, he insisted that France be included among the "Great Powers" who would share control of Germany and the emergent world organization. In Roosevelt's eyes, Russian concessions on the prompt establishment of the world organization, and Russian agreement to participate in "liberating China from the Japanese yoke" in "two or three months" after the European war ended, justified everything.

The European war ended soon, but not without more tough and costly fighting. On March 7, 1945, the Allies at last plunged across the Rhine over the railroad bridge at Remagen, the only bridge still standing. On April 25, American and Russian troops made contact at the Elbe. On May 1, Hitler committed suicide in Berlin. On May 2, the flaming capital capitulated. On May 7, General Jodl, Hitler's heir in authority, signed the unconditional surrender at Eisenhower's headquarters.

Two of the Axis partners had succumbed. Within a week half the American air force in Europe was bound for the Pacific and the demobilization of the massive American Army had begun. "Meanwhile," Churchill asked in anguish on May 12, "what is to happen about Russia? . . . An iron curtain is drawn down upon their front. We do not know what is going on behind."

Exactly one month earlier, on April 12, 1945, Roosevelt had died suddenly of a cerebral hemorrhage in Warm Springs, Georgia. At Teheran, at the end of 1943, he had presumably suffered a slight stroke, but this became the second best kept secret of the war. Not since the assassination of Lincoln did the removal of a president so move the American people. Men and women wept openly in the streets. Most appalled of all, perhaps, was F.D.R.'s modest successor, Harry S. Truman, who even as Vice-President had been kept in ignorance of the war's best kept secret, the imminent perfection of the atomic bomb (see p. 788).

THE DOWNFALL OF JAPAN

Postwar Russia became President Truman's problem, but embattled Japan required attention first. On April 18, 1942, Japan received a foretaste of the future when army B-25's led by Colonel James H. Doolittle took off from "Shangri La" and dropped a load of bombs on Tokyo. "Shangri La," the name F.D.R. jokingly gave to the bombers' base, turned out to be a group of American aircraft carriers commanded by Vice-Admiral William F. Halsey. All the bombers were lost in China where their crews had to bail out; and the sortie did little damage to Tokyo. Nevertheless it had momentous consequences.

Doolittle's raid is credited with infecting the Japanese with what one of their admirals called "victory disease." To regain face, the Japanese war lords mounted a sudden new offensive even before they had begun to digest the immense fruits of their initial thrust. This offensive was aimed at nailing down a naval and air line of defense from Attu, the westernmost of the Arctic Aleutians, to Port Moresby, the best harbor in New Guinea on the far side of the Equator. Anchor points were to be at Japanese-held Wake and American-held

Midway. Inside this line Japan expected to chew up China at her pleasure and perhaps India as well. These plans, as we have seen (p. 786), were checked by Japanese fleet losses in the Coral Sea in May, 1942, and at the disastrous Battle of Midway, June 3-6.

Following their failure at Midway, the Japanese had consoled themselves by grasping Attu and Kiska in the Aleutians. For the moment Alaska seemed on the verge of doom and Seattle itself threatened by attack. Men and materials needed elsewhere were rushed to the Territory; the "Alcan Highway" across Canada was begun; and operations were planned which retrieved Attu in May and Kiska in August, 1943.

The Japanese were even less successful in a second attack on Port Moresby, this one begun over land in July, 1942. To protect this attack, they had begun to clear an air strip on Guadalcanal, one of the near-by (as South Pacific distances go) Solomon Islands. The United States at the same time was eyeing Guadalcanal for the starting point of its own first offensive on Japan's more exposed bastions, especially the island fortress of Rabaul off New Britain.

On August 7, 1942, the first combined American and Australian landings on Guadalcanal were begun against sharp resistance. Two days later a Japanese cruiser force swooped down on the half-unloaded Allied transports in the Solomons' Savo Sea and in "the worst defeat ever suffered by the United States navy" (the words are Admiral Morison's) sank virtually all the protective fighting ships. The transports ran, and the Japanese force, its mission accomplished, moved off. For six months ill-equipped, half-starved Marines clung to Guadalcanal's air strip at Henderson Field while huge naval actions covering reinforcement attempts by both sides raged in the surrounding waters. The turning point came in mid-November, and in January the Japanese were ordered by Tokyo to evacuate the island, which they did successfully on February 9, 1943.

Before the end of the year the Japanese had also been cleared out of most of New Guinea. In addition, they had been forced to yield enough of Bougainville, the north-ernmost of the Solomons, for the Allies to maintain air operations there. Bougainville lay only 235 miles from Rabaul—near enough for Allied bombers to neutralize that fortress.

Guadalcanal was the Pacific theater's El Alamein. The Japanese never succeeded in establishing the line behind which they could exploit their "co-prosperity" sphere on the Asian mainland. After Guadalcanal they became fully occupied with defending the Pacific and mainland redoubts they did hold as a screen for their home islands. This defense was fanatical. The Japanese navy continued strong and ably led. The Japanese army and air force, much underrated by prewar commentators, was recruited from the impoverished peasantry and treated by the war lords like fatted calves. The soldiers' devotion to their leaders and their cause was beyond reason. Allied leaders like Douglas MacArthur, chief of Southwest Pa-

cific operations, learned this lesson early and built their strategy upon it. The military Chiefs of Staff in Washington became so impressed with Japanese fortitude that even at the time of the Yalta Conference, when the brilliance of Allied strategy had been well demonstrated, they advised Roosevelt that the Pacific war had at least two years to run with full Russian assistance and considerably longer without.

Allied success in the South Pacific—their establishment in the Solomons, the neutralizing of Rabaul, the clearing of New Guinea —greatly augmented the security of Australia where MacArthur was preparing for his dramatic return to the Philippines as the last step but one to the taking of Tokyo. The prospect was tempting, but the way bristled with snares. North and east of the

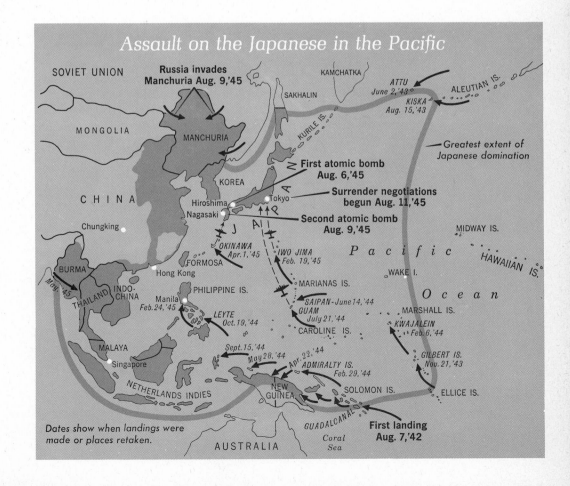

Assault on the Japanese in the Pacific

Dates show when landings were made or places retaken.

Victims of A-bomb explosion await aid in Hiroshima, August 6, 1945. The first bomb killed an estimated 160,000 persons.

Solomons lay the Gilbert Islands; north of them, the Marshalls, and farther north still, Wake. Together they marked the easternmost advance of Japanese power; and even the barren atolls of each configuration had been armed with air strip, artillery, and adamant men. To the west of this arc, ranging once more from south to north, lay the Palau Islands, the Carolines, Guam, and the Marianas, all, as befit their greater proximity to Japan, even more intensely armed than the outermost line. Farther north and west lay formidable Iwo Jima; and in the shadow of Honshu itself, Okinawa. This defense in depth extending more than 3,000 miles, shielded Tokyo and exposed any invasion from the Philippines to murderous flanking fire.

To roll back this defense island by island, atoll by atoll, fanatic by fanatic would occupy a generation and still offer scant hope of success. MacArthur's command devised the bold alternative of "island hopping," a strategy designed to open quickly a viable path to the heart of Japan while leaving to highly mobile air power the task of neutralizing the uncleared rear. Even so, hundreds of unsung battles were waged by armies as large as those that once decided the fate of nations for atolls where there "had probably never been twenty white men assembled together at any one time." The burden of this offensive was placed in the hands of Admiral Nimitz and his Central Pacific fleet. But every assault involved unprecedented co-ordination of the forces of sea, land, and air. None was easy. Tarawa established the Allied hold on the Gilberts in November, 1943; Kwajalein, control of the Marshalls in February, 1944. In May, Wake was taken. On June 19-20, in the immense naval Battle of the Philippine Sea, Admiral Raymond Spruance thwarted a Japanese effort to reinforce the Marianas, and by August 1 Saipan and Tinian there, as well as adjacent Guam, all had succumbed. In September, after some costly hand-to-hand fighting for armed caves, Peleliu in the Palaus was cleaned out.

Three heartening results were earned by this savage surge. First, Truk in the Carolines, Japan's main Central Pacific naval station, was made innocuous without costly frontal assault by the control established over the surrounding island groups. Second, from Saipan and the other Marianas giant superfortresses could reach Tokyo, and the capital and other home island cities hence-

798

forth were systematically assaulted with fire bombs that consumed their wooden buildings and decimated the civilian population. Third, the path from New Guinea to the Philippines was opened. On October 19, 1944, a grand armada carrying MacArthur and 250,000 men set out for the Philippine island of Leyte. Four days later virtually the entire Japanese navy converged on Allied transports in Leyte Gulf, and from October 23 to 25 the greatest sea battle in history was fought. At its end the United States emerged in complete command of the Pacific. Manila fell to MacArthur's forces on February 23, 1945, but not until July 5 were the last of the Japanese rooted out.

By then, Iwo Jima and Okinawa had been taken at a sickening cost of 70,000 men. *Kamikaze* attacks by Japanese suicide fliers who plunged their bomb-laden planes into American fighting ships accounted for many of the American casualties at Okinawa. Both campaigns—Iwo had been gained by March 16, 1945, and Okinawa by June 21—wiped out any lingering doubt that the Japanese would resist invaders to the last knife or bullet or breath.

Their power to resist by means of the instruments of modern warfare had by then been sorely depleted. The island-hopping campaign had finished all but the remnants of their navy and their air force. American submarines, the silent service, had sunk more than half of their once proud merchant marine which kept them supplied with the oil, rubber, tin, and grain of their mainland conquests. These conquests themselves, moreover, had been under strong attack since the winter of 1943-1944 by British and American forces. The Allies struggled to get Chiang Kai-shek to fight harder for China—the British for the protection of India, the Americans for the eviction of Japan—but Chiang was nursing his arms for a future showdown with the communists who were gathering their forces in the Chinese North. Most progress was made against the Japanese in Burma where Rangoon, the principal port, was retaken in

May, 1945. But Japan did not yield her other mainland territories until her total collapse at home had been brought about by extraordinary means.

On July 26, 1945, three weeks after the reconquest of the Philippines, ten days after the first successful detonation of the A-bomb, Allied leaders assembled at Potsdam sent an ultimatum to the enemy: "The alternative to surrender is prompt and utter destruction." No surrender came. On August 6 the first atomic bomb to be used in warfare was dropped on Hiroshima. Still no word from Japan, but Russia, intent on being in on the imminent kill, declared war on August 8, the very deadline of her "two to three months after V-E day" promise at Yalta, and overran the Japanese forces in Manchuria. On August 9, a second bomb was dropped on Nagasaki. At last, on August 10, Tokyo sued for peace—but made a condition: that Emperor Hirohito be permitted to retain his throne. This condition was accepted by the Allies and on September 2, 1945, formal surrender ceremonies were conducted in Tokyo Bay on the battleship *Missouri*, with General MacArthur accepting for the United States.

The most terrible war in history had ended in the most terrible display of force. After the bombing of Nagasaki, President Truman said, "We have spent two billion dollars on the greatest scientific gamble in history—and won." A few days later he added, "The atomic bomb is too dangerous to be let loose in a lawless world. That is why Great Britain, Canada, and the United States, who have the secret of its production, do not intend to reveal that secret until means have been found to control the bomb." While Russia had retired behind the "iron curtain," the West had retired, or thought it had retired, behind a scientific curtain of its own, one that was to prove more penetrable.

Readings

* Asterisk indicates that book is available in paperback.

Allan Nevins, *The United States in a Chaotic World: A Chronicle of International Affairs 1918-1933* (1950), affords a short scholarly survey of diplomacy between World War I and the New Deal. This may be supplemented by W. S. Myers, *The Foreign Policy of Herbert Hoover* (1940); R. H. Ferrell, *American Diplomacy and the Great Depression* (1957); and Dexter Perkins, *The New Age of Franklin Roosevelt* * (1957). Hajo Holborn, *The Political Collapse of Europe* (1951), is outstanding on the changing diplomatic environment on the Continent. On this subject, see also E. H. Carr, *The Twenty-Years' Crisis 1919-1939* * (1942). On the American environment, see Selig Adler, *The Isolationist Impulse, Its Twentieth Century Reaction* * (1957); R. E. Osgood, *Ideals and Self- Interest in America's Foreign Relations* * (1953); and Alexander De Conde, ed., *Isolation and Security: Ideas and Interests in Twentieth Century American Foreign Policy* (1957).

Special subjects on between-wars diplomacy are dealt with authoritatively in the following: on the Washington Conference, J. C. Vinson, *The Parchment Peace* (1950); on the Kellogg-Briand Pact, R. H. Ferrell, *Peace in Their Time* (1952); on the Stimson Doctrine, H. L. Stimson and McGeorge Bundy, *On Active Service in Peace and War* (1948); and E. E. Morison, *Turmoil and Tradition, A Study of the Life and Times of Henry L. Stimson* * (1960); on other aspects of Far Eastern relations, F. R. Dulles, *Forty Years of American-Japanese Relations* (1937); and A. W. Griswold, *The Far Eastern Policy of the United States* * (1938); on Latin America, Alexander De Conde, *Herbert Hoover's Latin American Policy* (1951); Bryce Wood, *The Making of the Good Neighbor Policy* (1961); and H. F. Cline, *The United States and Mexico* * (1953); on "merchants of death," W. S. Cole, *Senator Gerald P. Nye and American Foreign Relations* (1962). F. J. Taylor, *The United States and the Spanish Civil War 1936-1939* (1956); and W. A. Williams, *American Russian Relations 1781-1947* (1952), are valuable specialized works. Herbert Feis, *The Diplomacy of the Dollar: First Era 1919-1932* (1950); and R. L. Buell, *The Hull Trade Program* (1938), cover aspects of international economic relations. These are elaborated in J. W. Pratt, *Cordell Hull* (1964); and Cordell Hull, *Memoirs* (2 vols., 1948).

Comprehensive accounts of American diplomacy in the immediate prewar years will be found in two works by W. L. Langer and S. E. Gleason, *The Challenge to Isolation 1937-1940* * (1952), and *Undeclared War 1940-1941* (1953). These may be supplemented by Donald Drummond, *The Passing of American Neutrality* (1955); and R. A. Divine, *The Illusion of Neutrality* (1962), and *The Reluctant Belligerent* * (1965). Basil Rauch, *Roosevelt: From Munich to Pearl Harbor* (1950); Herbert Feis, *The Road to Pearl Harbor* * (1950); and Roberta Wohlstetter, *Pearl Harbor, Warning and Decision* (1962), all defend American policy. H. D. Hall, *North American Supply* (1955), is excellent on aid to Britain. H. L. Trefousse, *Germany and American Neutrality 1939-1941* (1951), is a scholarly study. W. S. Cole, *America First, The Battle Against Intervention 1940-1941* (1953), covers the hostility to Roosevelt's pro-Allied course. See also, T. A. Bailey, *The Man in the Street* (1948); and Walter Johnson, *The Battle Against Isolation* (1944), on public sentiment and foreign policy. Hostile views of Roosevelt's diplomacy include C. A. Beard, *American Foreign Policy in the Making 1932-1940* (1946), and *President Roosevelt and the Coming of the War* (1948); C. C. Tansill, *Backdoor to War* (1952); and G. E. Morgenstern, *Pearl Harbor, The Secret History of the War* (1947).

Eliot Janeway, *The Struggle for Survival* (1951), is a good short account of wartime mobilization and its conflicts. An excellent "inside" account is D. M. Nelson, *Arsenal for Democracy* (1944). See also, E. R. Stettinius, Jr., *Lend-Lease, Weapon for Victory* (1944). More general but informative is R. E. Sherwood, *Roosevelt and Hopkins* * (1950). Joel

801

The War for Survival

Seidman, *American Labor from Defense to Reconversion* (1953); and W. W. Wilcox, *The Farmer in the Second World War* (1947), cover their subjects well. Bruce Catton, *War Lords of Washington* (1948), is a critical account of the War Production Board. A valuable special study is R. H. Connery, *The Navy and the Industrial Mobilization in World War II* (1951). On other aspects of economic mobilization, see L. V. Chandler, *Inflation in the United States 1940-1948* (1951); R. E. Paul, *Taxation for Prosperity* (1947); and Herbert Feis, *Seen from E. A., Three International Episodes* (1947). Morton Grodzins, *Americans Betrayed: Politics and Japanese Evacuation* (1949), is excellent on the Japanese-American incident. W. F. Ogburn, ed., *American Society in Wartime* (1943); and Jack Goodman, ed., *While You Were Gone: A Report on Wartime Life in the United States* (1946), are useful general accounts. On the mobilization of American science, see J. P. Baxter, III, *Scientists Against Time* (1946); on the development of the bomb, the best account is R. G. Hewlett and O. E. Anderson, Jr., *The New World* (1962).

A. R. Buchanan, *The United States and World War II* * (Vol. I, 1964), offers a good introduction to many phases of the first three years of American involvement, including the military side. Winston Churchill, *The Second World War* * (6 vols., 1948-1953), is indispensable on the conduct of the war, especially the military side. On the naval side, equally authoritative is S. E. Morison, *History of United States Naval Operations in World War II* (15 vols., 1947-1958). Morison, *The Two-Ocean War* (1963), is, as its subtitle says, "A short history of the United States Navy in the Second World War." His *Strategy and Compromise* (1958), is a short penetrating essay on important phases of military and naval action. See also, K. R. Greenfield, ed., *Command Decisions* (1959). Walter Millis, *This is Pearl!* (1947), is a dramatic account of the assault. On Japan's fall see Herbert Feis, *Japan Subdued, The Atomic Bomb and the End of the War in the Pacific* (1961). Chester Wilmot, *The Struggle for Europe* * (1952), is a critical account of the war there. See also, H. W. Baldwin, *Great Mistakes of the War* (1950). Useful short narratives of the fighting include Fletcher Pratt, *War for the World* (1950); and R. W. Shugg and H. A. DeWeerd, *World War II* (1946). D. D. Eisenhower, *Crusade in Europe* * (1948); and O. N. Bradley, *A Soldier's Story* * (1951), are good examples of first-hand accounts by outstanding generals. Outstanding first-hand naval accounts include W. F. Halsey, *Admiral Halsey's Story* (1947); and W. D. Leahy, *I Was There* (1950). H. H. Arnold, *Global Mission* (1949), is by the American air commander. Ernie Pyle, *The Story of G.I. Joe* (1945); and Bill Mauldin, *Up Front* * (1945), are illuminating on the ordinary soldier. S. A. Stouffer, and others, *The American Soldier* * (2 vols., 1949), presents the results of a sociological investigation.

Herbert Feis, *Churchill, Roosevelt, Stalin* (1957), is outstanding on conference diplomacy. See also his *The China Tangle* * (1953), and *Between War and Peace* (1960). From the extensive literature on the Yalta Conference, see R. F. Fenno, Jr., ed., *The Yalta Conference* * (1953); and J. L. Snell, ed., *The Meaning of Yalta* (1956).

CHAPTER THIRTY

World War II tipped the earth on its axis more violently than any event since the discovery of America almost five hundred years before, and probably more violently than any event in recorded history. The harnessing of atomic energy and the maturation of the science of rocketry—making possible both the annihilation of man's planet and the exploration of outer space—no doubt were the most explosive developments of all. Closer to everyday life were the political explosions, especially in Asia and Africa, that really marked the burning out of long fuses ignited in World War I. Colonial and other economically exploited peoples, made aware by 1918 of the weak-

A World
in Continuous Crisis

ness of the imperial powers and their dependence on the products and labor of exotic lands, had been ripening for rebellion a long time before World War II offered them strategic opportunities to strike.

Closer still to life even in the United States were the world-wide technological, social, and medical detonations of the war years. Virtually everywhere, including the United States, unprecedented quantities of non-atomic power were applied to production during the hostilities, and the power surge attained revolutionary velocity once the fighting ended. The new wealth thus produced helped beget a massive population boom. In the more highly developed indus-

trial countries, especially in the Western Hemisphere, where the persistent prewar depression had imposed a degree of birth control, the birth rate soared. In typical underdeveloped countries in both hemispheres, where birth rates had always been exceedingly high, the new medicine and medical hygiene, growing largely out of wartime "crash" programs in research and application, helped keep alive a revolutionary proportion of the newly born.

The "overwhelming and unprecedented" population explosion, to use the words of an outstanding population expert, Kingsley Davis, quickly dissipated any smiling sentimentality about the enrichment children might bring to family life. In countries like India and Egypt, where families struggled over the centuries to extract subsistence from tiny plots of overworked soil, the population explosion simply meant that many more mouths had to be fed from the same poor land. Many wartime and postwar developments made the feeding of the extra mouths possible. As in western and central Europe in the nineteenth century, and to a lesser degree in Russia, so in agrarian countries of our own time brutal reforms in landholding often increased the land's bounty. In combination with improved farm implements and improved husbandry, widespread irrigation projects closely related to the revolutionary spread of power facilities, also helped. Yet, as one economist put it after a study of the population burst in Ceylon, "the problem of development was . . . that of keeping the standard of living from falling—not of raising it."

The challenge of poverty in an age of massive gains in productivity was well described by Kingsley Davis when he wrote in September, 1957:

Poor people are more numerous today than ever before, because population is sky-rocketing in the poorer countries. If two-thirds of the earth's population was impoverished a century ago and one-third today, there would still be more poor people now than there were then. With many countries multiplying at a rate near 3 per cent per year, their economies must somehow move ahead at 4 or 5 per cent per year if poverty is to be reduced. This is no easy task when the ratio of people to resources is already excessive and the poverty so great that capital can hardly be accumulated for long-run industrial development.

The "one world" into which we have all been crowded and jostled since the war, Davis observed, was filled with "the youngest population ever known." The persistence of poverty in this world—and the fact that its highest incidence has been in countries where the proportion of clamorous youth is greatest—added ominously to postwar political instability. The extraordinary performance of the American economy in the postwar years in some ways only aggravated world-wide political unrest. American affluence became a goal and a goad to destitute nations, new and old alike. And the elusiveness of the goal, despite lavish American financial and technical aid, only deepened the prick of the goad. The even more extraordinary gains of the communist economies of Russia and China, despite some later checks, also made the mouths of hungry youths in hungry lands water.

The revolutionary nature of the postwar years was manifest in the continuing challenge of totalitarianism to democracy, inside as well as outside the United Nations. But it was more profoundly manifest in the shattering of old empires, especially in Asia and Africa; in the creation since World War II of a large number of new and hopeful nations; in the aspirations of the downtrodden and oppressed in rich and poor lands alike for a better life in every way; in the world-wide "population explosion" which itself most deeply menaced these aspirations; and in the progress of science, which possessed within itself the double power to remove this menace either by making man wholly extinct or by making his labor infinitely more fruitful.

I. *The Complex Legacy of World War II*

THE YALTA REVELATIONS

The conflict between the revolutionary postwar future and the persistence of prewar and wartime thought was nowhere more apparent than at the Yalta Conference of February, 1945 (see p. 795), which came, as Churchill wrote to President Roosevelt in a somber mood on the eve of the

meeting, "when the Great Allies are so divided and the shadow of war lengthens out before us."

The wartime unity of the Grand Alliance among the United States, Britain, and the U.S.S.R. had, as we have seen (p. 782), been forced upon them by their powerful enemies. As the strength of these enemies waned toward the close of the war, differences among the Allies rose nearer the surface. At the time of the Yalta Conference, when the Russians were already pressing into Germany and the Western Allies had liberated France, these differences were brought into the open although the terms by which certain of them were settled were kept secret (see p. 795). Those made public largely concerned the future of Germany, Poland, and Yugoslavia, where Russian occupying forces made Roosevelt-Churchill bargaining difficult. Those kept secret largely concerned territory to be granted to Russia at Japan's expense.

The concessions made to Russia in the Far East rested on the assumption that Soviet intervention against Japan, which was offered in return, would be of great military value to the Allies. As it happened, Russia's intervention was unnecessary. The atomic bomb had not yet been successfully tested, but Japan had already been brought to the verge of collapse by aerial bombardment and naval blockade. Intelligence reports available in Washington made this clear but were never put before the President. On the basis of obsolete information, the Chiefs of Staff at Yalta urged the importance of Soviet cooperation against Japan. Thus advised, Roosevelt and Churchill made their concessions.

When, with the fall of Japan, the secret provisions of the Yalta agreement were revealed, Roosevelt, already in his grave (see p. 796), was subjected to a vast amount of criticism in the United States on all counts. His defenders replied that his critics failed to bear in mind the military situation at the time, not only in the Pacific but also in eastern Europe, almost all of which Russian armies had overrun. To effect the liberation of any of this territory, the Western Allies would have had to use force. Presumably this recourse would have led speedily to a third world war, a prospect even more offensive to public opinion in Britain and America than the Yalta agreements themselves. There can be little doubt, moreover, that, even without the concurrence of Roosevelt and Churchill at Yalta,

Stalin would have seized what he wanted in Asia as he had in Europe, and might have seized even more than he had been granted by agreement.

Of course, as we have seen (p. 792), Roosevelt, if not Churchill, had an additional long-term goal in insisting on pleasing Stalin—the creation of the United Nations. On returning from Yalta on March 1, 1945, Roosevelt declared that the agreement there, "spells the end of the system of unilateral action and exclusive alliances and balances of power and all the other expedients which had been tried for centuries—and have failed. We propose to substitute for all that a universal organization in which all peace-loving nations will finally have a chance to join"—including the U.S.S.R.

The old League of Nations had failed at least as badly as the traditional balance of power arrangements in attempting to keep the world's peace. But this did not deter F.D.R. Even he, however, grew disillusioned very quickly. On April 1, 1945, only 11 days before his death, Roosevelt sent Stalin a sharp message decrying "the lack of progress made in carrying out . . . the political decisions which we reached at Yalta, particularly those relating to the Polish question," which so deeply concerned the millions of Polish-American voters. Stalin on his part, a few weeks before V-E day, had grown suspicious of western actions which he interpreted as attempts to make a separate peace with Germany, a move forbidden by the United Nations Declaration of 1942 (see p. 786). Piqued, Stalin held off until the last moment before sending his delegation to San Francisco where work began on the United Nations charter on April 25, 1945. Stalin's delay only deepened Western suspicions of him.

THE U.N. UNDERWAY

Certain U.N. instrumentalities had been created even before the charter was written. As early as November, 1943, 44 nations had set up the United Nations Relief and Rehabilitation Administration (UNRRA) to assist areas liberated from Germany, Italy, and Japan. The following July the first of two conferences that year to plan the postwar world was held at Bretton Woods, New Hampshire, with representatives of 44 nations in attendance. This conference created an International Monetary Fund to stabilize national currencies, and an International Bank for Reconstruction and Development to extend loans to nations for rehabilitation. The second conference, beginning in August at Dumbarton Oaks near Washington, D.C., drafted plans for the United Nations charter. At Yalta the following February, the Big Three agreed to meet at San Francisco in April, 1945, to launch the international organization itself, and also ironed out certain issues which might have wrecked the San Francisco meeting before it was even under way. The principal issue presumably settled here involved voting procedure in the Security Council of the United Nations Organization. The Big Three, as they revealed the following month, specified at Yalta that the permanent members of the Security Council would have veto power over all major decisions of that body. They also agreed that the Soviet Union would have three votes in the General Assembly of the United Nations, since the Ukraine and Byelo-Russia were to be recognized for voting purposes as independent nations. The Russians had begun by demanding 16 votes for the various associated republics of the Soviet Union, arguing that only this arrangement would give them comparable influence with what they felt would be an American and British Commonwealth bloc. Roosevelt replied that by the same reckoning the United States should have 48 votes. Of course, it was membership and voting procedure in the Security Council, not in the General Assembly, that mattered. Still, Roosevelt's critics harped on this minor concession.

The delegates at San Francisco, representing 50 nations, witnessed a continuous and usually sharp dispute between the Russians and the Western powers that sometimes threatened the meeting. By June 26, 1945, however, the work of the conference was completed and the charter signed.

As agreed earlier, the charter provided for two major U.N. agencies: (1) The General Assembly, in which all member nations have one vote—except Russia which has the two additional ones for two of its republics. The General Assembly has the power to discuss all questions falling within the scope of the United Nations charter and to recommend suitable action to the Security Council. Failing Security Council action, the Assembly, according to a resolution adopted in 1950, may itself recommend action to member nations. (2) The Security Council, composed of 11 members, remains in continuous session in order to settle international disputes as they arise. On this body, the Big Five—the Big Three plus France and Nationalist China—have permanent seats; the other seats rotate for two-year terms among other members. The decision on voting procedure in the Security Council gave the veto power to any permanent member. This decision indicated that the Council would be unable to oppose aggression by any of the major powers. Whether it could oppose aggression even by minor powers remained doubtful. The U.N. charter provided that, on the call of the Security Council, the members make armed contingents available to the organization. It was expected that such contingents would be largely supplied by the five great powers on the Council itself. Four of these powers, recognizing differences in their ability to conform to this expectation, promptly agreed that their contributions be "comparable." The U.S.S.R., openly scornful of the "great power" status of some of her colleagues on the Council, insisted that contributions be "equal." Equal contributions would have resulted merely in a token army. The issue was resolved by leaving U.N. forces to later "agreement or agreements," thereby, as the Russians intended, at least temporarily drawing the teeth from the organization.

Four other agencies complete the permanent U.N. structure: an International Court of Justice; a Secretariat to coordinate the work of the U.N.; an Economic and Social Council; and a Trusteeship Council to handle colonies taken from Japan and Italy. From time to time additional U.N. commissions and agencies have been set up for special purposes.

The United States Senate had debated the Covenant of the League of Nations for eight months before rejecting it. The Senate debated U.N. membership for only six days, and approved it by a vote of 89 to 2. A Gallup poll conducted at the time showed only 3 per cent of the American people against membership, 31 per cent undecided, and 66 per cent in favor. The U.N. held its first meetings in London in 1946, and then moved to New York City, its permanent home. At the end of 1966 this home housed the delegations of 122 countries, many of them new nations as well as new members, but still absent were such "great powers" as West Germany and Red China.

One of the first and most ominous issues confronting the new organization, and one still unresolved 20 years later, was that of nuclear war. In June, 1946, Bernard M. Baruch submitted to the recently created U.N. Atomic Energy Commission recommendations for control of atomic weapons. His plan called for the creation of an international agency to which the United States would turn over her atomic secrets provided that this agency be given the power to inspect atomic installations in any country to see that atomic weapons were not being manufactured. As soon as the system of inspection was working, the United States would destroy its stock of atomic weapons and join in the prohibition of their manufacture. But the U.S.S.R., still far behind the United States in atomic research and suspicious of international agencies, countered by proposing an international agreement to abandon atomic warfare and prohibit the making of atomic weapons, but with no provision for inspection. This was unacceptable to the United States. In the following decades immense progress was made in employing atomic energy for

peaceful as well as wartime purposes, but progress toward the regulation of atomic weapons was slow. Progress became all the more urgent after September, 1949, when the U.S.S.R., after years of intense scientific espionage as well as scientific research, detonated its own first atomic bomb—a blow as much to Truman's archaic policy of scientific secrecy (see p. 799) as to western security, which rested so heavily upon it.

THE CONQUERED NATIONS

The problem of settling the fate of the conquered nations also disclosed the growing tension between the communists and the West. In July, 1945, President Truman, Clement Attlee, Churchill's successor as British Prime Minister, and Stalin, met at Potsdam, Germany, to deal with the future of the old Axis members. Here they reaffirmed the four-power occupation of Germany, worked out details of German reparations payments, and tentatively settled the Polish-German frontier. Finally, the Potsdam Conference set up a Council of Foreign Ministers of the United States, Britain, Russia, and China to draw up peace treaties with Italy, Bulgaria, Rumania, Hungary, and Finland. These treaties were signed in February, 1947, and, except in Italy and Finland, virtually sanctioned Soviet control over, and United States recognition of, communist regimes.

During 1945 and 1946, the leading Nazis were tried at Nuremberg before an international military court on charges of having started the war and conducting it in ways that violated fundamental human decency. The trial revealed the full story of Nazi barbarity. Ten leading "war criminals" were executed. In all, over 500,000 Nazis were found guilty in the American zone and received sentences of varying severity. Similar trials in Japan led to the execution of former Premier Tojo and six other war leaders, and lighter sentences for about 4,000 other "war criminals."

In 1948 the Russians, irked by friction arising from the administration of Germany, ordered a blockade of the city of Berlin, which, though situated deep in their zone, was jointly administered by the U.S.S.R. and the West. By threatening the Germans in the Western zone of Berlin with starvation, the Soviets hoped to force the Allies to evacuate Berlin altogether. The Allies met the challenge by developing the "air lift," an ingenious technique by which food and supplies were delivered to the city by continuously shuttling cargo planes. In the end, it was the U.S.S.R. that gave in and lifted the blockade in May, 1949.

Frustrated by their failure to reach agreement with the Soviets on Germany, the Western powers met in June, 1948, and consented to the creation of an unarmed German Federal Republic, embracing the three Western zones. The new state was launched in September, 1949. In October, 1949, the Soviets established the rival east German state called the German Democratic Republic.

The administration of conquered Japan was left to General Douglas MacArthur. Under American direction, a new constitution went into effect in May, 1947, turning the fundamental powers of government over to representatives elected by the people. The Emperor renounced his claim to divinity, and the constitution renounced war as a right of the nation. Many social reforms were carried out, including the dissolution of the great industrial and commercial monopolies and the restoration of large tracts of land to the peasants. In September, 1951, following the fall of China to the communists in 1949 (see p. 819) and the outbreak of the Korean war in 1950 (see p. 820), 49 nations—the U.S.S.R. not among them—signed a general peace treaty with Japan restoring her "full sovereignty," including her right to redevelop her armaments industry and her armed services. This treaty was negotiated at the instigation of the United States to rebuild Japan into a military power to offset communism in Asia as Germany was soon to be strengthened to

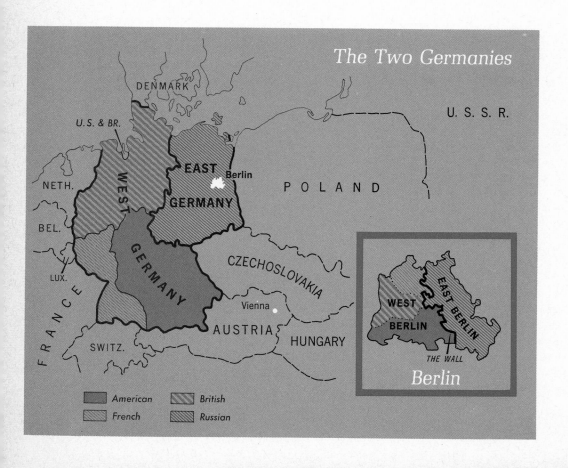

The Two Germanies

DENMARK

U.S. & BR.

NETH.

BEL.

LUX.

FRANCE

SWITZ.

WEST GERMANY

EAST GERMANY

Berlin

POLAND

U.S.S.R.

CZECHOSLOVAKIA

Vienna

AUSTRIA

HUNGARY

WEST BERLIN

EAST BERLIN

THE WALL

Berlin

American   British
French   Russian

Harry S Truman takes the oath of office from Chief Justice Harlan Fiske Stone.

offset communism in Europe (see p. 833). At this time mutual security agreements were also made with the Philippines, Australia, and New Zealand.

II. *The Truman Administration at Home*

DEMOBILIZATION
AND DOMESTIC PROSPERITY

With Roosevelt's death in April, 1945, the presidency, as we have seen, had fallen to a Midwesterner with no experience in world affairs other than service in World War I. A small businessman before he entered politics in his home state of Missouri, Harry S. Truman had done well during World War II as chairman of a Senate committee investigating wartime contracts. At first overawed by the office he had inherited ("Boys, if you ever pray, pray for me now," he told reporters), he grew increasingly confident in the White House.

Truman's sudden ascent to the presidency at the very climax of the war had prompted him to leave the major responsibility for American war-end policy overseas to the armed services chiefs in the field. Their training, as it happened, stressed the traditional American distinction between "military" and "political" objectives, unfortunately to the detriment of the latter, and as the fighting drew toward a successful close their main goal seemed to be, "getting the

boys back home." Once the fighting ended, in September, 1945, "the boys" themselves began agitating for their quick release while their families pressed the administration to "bring daddy back." By mid-summer, 1946, the army had been cut from over 8 million to under 2 million men, the navy from 3.3 million to 980,000. "I termed this," Truman wrote in his *Memoirs,* " 'the most remarkable demobilization in the history of the world, or "disintegration," if you want to call it that.' " Disintegration reached a low point in 1948, when the army had only 550,000 men and all the armed services together numbered 1,446,000.

The discharged servicemen, meanwhile, rushed back to their homes to enjoy the benefits of the "G.I. Bill of Rights." Formally known as the Servicemen's Readjustment Act, passed in June, 1944, this "bill" entitled veterans to medical treatment in new veterans' hospitals, vocational rehabilitation for the crippled, unemployment insurance for a year, government loans for building homes or establishing businesses, and education in colleges or vocational

809

schools proportionate to the length of their military service. Between 1945 and 1952 over $13.5 billion was spent for education alone under this program, including that of Korean War veterans (see p. 821).

Economic demobilization was carried out as swiftly as military demobilization. During the four war years the federal government had built about 85 per cent of the new facilities needed for war production. When the war ended, the government found itself in possession of the most advanced and efficient industrial facilities in the world. Most government plants were run during the war by private corporations under contracts with liberal options for purchase. After the war private corporations bought the majority of such plants for a small fraction of their cost. On this foundation, the business community itself went on a spree of private expenditure for plant construction that dwarfed any similar movement in the nation's history and provided one of the most explosive features of the postwar boom.

Looking toward still further modernization, Congress, in August, 1946, created the Atomic Energy Commission, placing it under civilian control after defeating a proposal to give the armed services chiefs a veto on its actions. The commission was to promote private and government research into the peaceful as well as military uses of atomic energy and to develop facilities for its production.

The 1944 Democratic platform, moving beyond the goals of the New Deal itself, pledged to "guarantee full employment" when the war was over. After a long debate on the relative roles of business and government, Congress, in February, 1946, passed the landmark Maximum Employment Act to redeem this pledge. This act for the first time committed the federal government fully to utilize the nation's economic resources to insure "maximum employment, production and purchasing power." The act created a Council of Economic Advisers to keep the president informed on economic trends and on proper public measures to soften business downswings and sustain business prosperity.

To stimulate postwar business with an eye on full employment, Congress, in November, 1945, cut wartime taxes an estimated $6 billion. In November, 1946, despite Truman's veto of such a measure the previous July as too hasty, Congress swept away all wartime price controls under the OPA (see p. 788), except those on rents, sugar and rice. With these further incentives, industrial production soared. So strong was the pent up demand, however, that shortages soon intensified the already sharp inflation. Indeed, the hunger for consumer goods in particular was phenomenal, reflecting the new middle-class aspirations of the American working people. "Rosie the Riveter," Maurice O'Connell of the C.I.O. told the Los Angeles Chamber of Commerce soon after V-J day, "isn't going back to emptying slop jars. . . . Times have changed. People have become accustomed to new conditions, new wage scales, new ways of being treated."

Inflation naturally helped broaden the wave of strikes that swept the country after the removal of wartime restrictions. Labor, like other segments of the economy, had a lot of catching up to do. One of the most far-reaching strikes was that of the United Mine Workers in April, 1946. Although Truman ordered government seizure of the coal pits, the mineworkers eventually made important wage gains. A nation-wide railroad strike, followed by fruitless labor-management negotiations, prompted Truman to seize the railroads in May, 1946. Only a last-minute settlement halted passage at this time of stern anti-union legislation.

The postwar inflation and labor conflicts hurt the Democratic party, especially in the cities which had supplied so much strength to the earlier Roosevelt coalition (see p. 730). The party was also hurt by revelations of successful Soviet espionage. The most unnerving exposé occurred in Canada, not in the United States, in February, 1946, when 23 persons, one a member of the Canadian parliament, another an atomic scientist, and the rest in high "positions of trust," were cited as members of an *atomic* spy ring attached to the Canadian Communist party.

Questions were instantly raised in the United States by those who for a decade or more had harped on the New Deal's "softness" on communism, about the possible implication of highly-placed Americans in this episode and perhaps in others still secret. Strengthened by such spots on the Democratic record, the Republicans, in the elections of 1946, won a majority in both houses of the Eightieth Congress.

Once this Congress convened in January, 1947, the Republican leadership resuscitated the House Un-American Activities Committee which had been formed as a temporary investigation unit in 1938 largely to advance the personal political fortunes of its chairman, the Democrat, Martin Dies of Texas. Now, with a strong push from the freshman California Congressman, Richard M. Nixon, the committee proceeded to hunt out communists and alleged communists to advance the fortunes of the Republican party generally. Its most resounding coup was the Hiss case which opened in August, 1948, on the eve of the presidential campaign (see p. 823). With his own eye on this campaign, Truman proposed many progressive measures to the new legislature aimed especially at rebuilding Democratic urban strength. Among his proposals were comprehensive medicare and civil rights bills. On such domestic issues, however, Congress reflected the general conservative reaction to the New Deal era that had set in before the war (see p. 737). Truman's program languished, the civil rights part of it largely because of southern opposition in his own party.

The Eightieth Congress' most controversial measure, adopted over Truman's veto in June, 1947, was the Taft-Hartley Act, which outlawed the closed shop, forced unions to accept a 60-day "cooling-off period" before striking, required them to make public financial statements, forbade them to contribute to political campaigns, put an end to the checkoff system in which employers help collect union dues, and required union leaders to file affidavits that they were not communists before their unions could enjoy privileges under the

National Labor Relations Board. Labor leaders denounced the Taft-Hartley Act as a "slave-bill," but it did not prevent them from making substantial gains. From 1945 to 1952, union membership rose from 14,600,000 to 17,000,000.

In March, 1947, the new Congress passed the Twenty-second Amendment to the Constitution, limiting the president to two terms, a back-handed slap at F.D.R. This amendment was declared ratified in February, 1951. As the incumbent, Truman was explicitly exempted from its provisions. In July, 1947, Congress also adopted a Presidential Succession Act revising the statute of 1886 which had made the *appointive* Secretary of State the successor to a president serving without a vice-president. The new measure designated the *elective* Speaker of the House as first in line, with the president *pro tempore* of the Senate next and the Secretary of State and other Cabinet members only then becoming eligible.

REMOBILIZATION
AND DOMESTIC FEARS

Republican success with the communist issue in 1946 showed that the country could not fall peaceably asleep with sweet dreams of domestic prosperity to be enjoyed in isolation, as it wished to do. The Russian menace was real enough, as the Canadian revelations demonstrated. The fall of Czechoslovakia to a local communist coup in February, 1948, only underscored what subversion and treachery beyond the borders of the U.S.S.R. could accomplish if not checked. The Berlin blockade in June, 1948 (see p. 808), directly challenged western intentions in Europe. With the failure of the U.N. to develop its own conventional peace-keeping military force or to control the spread of nuclear weapons, in turn (see pp. 806, 807), the United States was compelled to realert its own defenses.

The whole question of the confrontation with the U.S.S.R. around the world, occupied the Truman administration from the moment it gained its bearings. We shall discuss administration foreign policy in the next section in detail (see p. 814). Before the memorable 1948 presidential campaign, the administration also took steps at home that amounted to a rapid remobilization once the hopes on which the hasty postwar demobilization rested were shattered.

In an effort to reassure the country on the one hand and to offset the ardor of the Republican-dominated House Un-American Activities Committee, on the other, Truman, in March, 1947, ordered a full-scale "loyalty investigation" of all present and prospective federal employees, those under the merit system to be examined by the Civil Service Commission, others by the heads of their departments or agencies. No source of information was to be ignored however questionable, including F.B.I. and other police files and those of the Un-American Activities Committee itself. Moreover, all information garnered, along with any "loyalty" data worked up by government bureaus since 1939, was to become part of a "central master index." Among the "standards for refusal of employment or removal from employment" was "sympathetic association" with any foreign or domestic organization designated by the Attorney-General as "subversive." In compliance with the President's order, Attorney-General Clark, in December, 1947, issued a list of 90 organizations deemed disloyal to the United States.

Henry Wallace, who had been forced to resign as Truman's Secretary of Commerce late in 1946 after publicly rejecting the President's "get tough" policy with Russia, was only one among thousands who now denounced Truman's order as a "red hunt." The President himself realized that the investigation might quickly poison the very freedom it was supposed to protect, and took steps to guard against this. He could not check the proliferation of similar probes in state and local governments and "sensitive" industries, where even the few federal safeguards often were omitted.

When the federal investigation was completed in April, 1951, the records of no less than 3,225,000 civil servants had been scrutinized. Under pressure of the inquiry, 2,900 had resigned, and a mere 300 had been dismissed. The investigation's broad criteria of what constituted subversion made it possible that none of these individuals was a communist, although no doubt some had been. In any case, so thorough was the screening, the Republicans could not uncover a single communist holdover from the long Democratic regime after they took office in 1953.

The Truman administration quickly followed reassurance with rearming. In July, 1947, the Eightieth Congress passed the momentous National Security Act centralizing the administration of the armed services and enlarging their duties. The act created a new National Military Establishment, soon to be renamed the Department of Defense, under a single new civilian Secretary of Defense on the Cabinet level. Within the new structure, it provided for the first time for a distinct Department of the Air Force, whose uniformed Chief of Staff, together with the uniformed chiefs in the Department of the Army and Department of the Navy, were to make up the Joint Chiefs of Staff, "the principal military advisers to the President." The act also created the National Security Council to be presided over by the president. Under this council, the act set up a Central Intelligence Agency to coordinate all government "intelligence activities." Secretary of the Navy Forrestal became the first Secretary of Defense.

In June, 1948, Congress passed a new selective service act to replace the wartime draft which had been permitted to expire the previous March. In July, to effect on the executive level at least a part of the civil rights program that the legislature let die, Truman issued this far-reaching order: "that there shall be equality of treatment and opportunity for all persons in the armed services without regard to race, color, religion or national origin," allowing "the time required to effectuate any necessary changes without impairing efficiency or morale."

812

Their victories in the 1946 elections gave the Republicans high hopes of regaining the presidency in 1948 after 16 years. Truman's remobilization policies, by promoting serious splits in Democratic ranks on the left and the right, seemed only to have enhanced Republican prospects. In December, 1947, Henry Wallace, still brooding over the administration's firm resistance to communist infiltration at home and Russian aggression abroad (see p. 814), announced that he would run for president on a third-party ticket. Some analysts thought he might win 5 to 8 million votes, enough to sink any Democratic candidate. At the same time, conservative southerners simmered over the liberal Democrats' growing attention to Negro equality. Buoyed up by their good fortune, the Republicans at their Philadelphia convention in June rejected the conservative isolationist, Senator Robert A. Taft, renominated Thomas E. Dewey of New York, and adopted a platform that was internationalist on foreign policy and moderate on domestic issues.

For months before the Democrats convened in Philadelphia on July 12, leaders of all persuasions tried feverishly to hold the party together. Liberals led by Mayor Hubert Humphrey of Minneapolis early in 1948 formed Americans for Democratic Action (ADA) to help keep the Wallaceites in tow. They won the support of many big-city bosses with well-organized Negro and other ethnic minorities to satisfy. Southerners by and large, certain that a victory for the liberals would alienate millions in their section, fought them. When a broad-based movement to draft the immensely popular General Eisenhower failed, the Truman regulars closed ranks and put him over on July 15. The ADA group, meanwhile, had carried through a liberal platform defending the F.D.R.-Truman tradition, denouncing Taft-Hartley, and promising anti-lynching and anti-poll tax laws. As a sop to southerners, the convention named acting-President of the Senate, Alben W. Barkley of Kentucky, for vice-president.

The sop failed. On July 17, the so-called Dixiecrats, meeting in Birmingham, Alabama, formed the States' Rights Democratic party and nominated Governor J. Strom Thurmond of South Carolina for president. Five days later, the Wallace liberals formed the Progressive party and named their favorite as standard-bearer.

The total failure of the unity efforts made Truman's cause seem hopeless. The defection of the southerners, however, enhanced his appeal to the strategically important Negro voters of the North; and Wallace's campaign, which was quietly manipulated by a small group of communists and their sympathizers, served to dramatize the fact that Truman was no friend of the extreme left. While Dewey conducted a self-confident but extraordinarily vague campaign, Truman stormed up and down the land denouncing "the no good, good-for-nothing Eightieth Congress" —one that, as we have seen, did pass momentous legislation, but did little to extend the welfare state. Truman's hard-hitting tactics scored with the voters. To the surprise of the world, he pulled off the greatest upset in American political history. When the ballots were counted, Truman had 24,105,000 popular and 303 electoral votes to Dewey's 21,969,000 and 189. Thurmond carried only four deep-South states, while Wallace, whose appeal faded from week to week, failed to carry a single one.

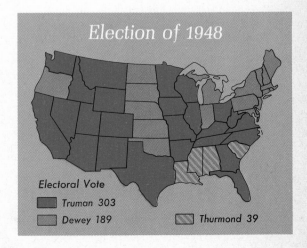

Election of 1948

Electoral Vote

Truman 303

Dewey 189

Thurmond 39

Convinced that he had received a popular mandate to carry on what he now called his Fair Deal, Truman drew up a program of legislation designed to go the New Deal one better. At vital points a newly influential coalition of Republicans and conservative Democrats blocked him, but he made headway despite it. In 1949 he secured an amendment to the New Deal's Fair Labor Standards Act (see p. 737) which raised the minimum wage from 40 to 75 cents an hour. A new Social Security Act, passed in August, 1950, added almost 10 million to those eligible for benefits. A National Housing Act, passed in July, 1949, provided large sums to cities for aid in slum clearance and for the construction of over 800,000 units for low-income families. Congress, however, defeated the Brannan Plan (an ambitious program for stabilizing farm income), turned down a strong civil-rights program for Negroes, and refused to repeal the Taft-Hartley Act although it did amend the act along lines desired by labor.

III. *The Truman Administration and Foreign Affairs*

THE "COLD WAR"
AND "CONTAINMENT" IN EUROPE

The rapidity with which the United States, in Churchill's words, "had chosen to scuttle their military might" once World War II had been won proved as welcome to the Soviets as to the American people. While Americans attempted to resume politics as usual, the Russians undertook to consolidate their recent territorial gains (see p. 795) and resume their expansive tendencies. In March, 1946, speaking at Fulton, Missouri, Churchill, enlarging the scope of a term he had used a year earlier, observed that from the Baltic to the Adriatic, "an iron curtain has descended across the Continent" behind which Stalin was doing as he pleased.

Stalin's first new target actually was oil-rich Iran in the strategic Middle East, but his reach soon extended to her European neighbor, Turkey, and to Turkey's neighbor, Greece, both keys to the equally strategic Mediterranean.

During the war, Stalin's forces had helped promote a communist separatist movement in Azerbaijan, Iran's northernmost province on the Soviet border. Now, in November, 1945, they supported a communist revolt there looking toward the province's autonomy. According to the Big Three agreement at Teheran, Iran's capital, in 1943 (see p. 792), all Allied troops were to be removed from Iran by March 2, 1946, but instead of removing his, Stalin only increased them.

Iran had already complained to the U.N. of Soviet interference, and on March 5 Truman backed Security Council efforts to protect Iran by sending a strong note to Stalin demanding his adherence to the Teheran accord. Stalin took this message to heart and by May, 1946, had removed his troops. But he had also forced Iran into a bipartisan agreement for participation in Iranian oil production, thus weakening Britain's long-standing interests there, and for the autonomy of Azerbaijan. With American aid, Iran, in December, 1946, regained hegemony over Azerbaijan, but the Soviet threat persisted in the entire area.

For centuries the Russians had sought access to the Mediterranean by way of the Turkish straits leading out from the Black Sea. In March, 1945, they renewed their ancient demands for Turkish territory in this region and soon began employing troops, as in Iran, to enforce them. Stern British and American notes late in the year deterred the Russians for the time being but also impelled them to shift their assault westward to Greece. Here, until February, 1947, British forces helped the Greek government fight off communist guerrillas strengthened by bands from such adjacent Soviet satellites as Yugoslavia, Bulgaria, and Albania. Britain herself, however, was in dire financial trouble at this time (see p. 815), and on February 24, 1947, she was forced to notify the United States that she could no longer bear the burden of resisting communism in the Mediterranean theater. She planned to withdraw her troops from Greece and also to terminate her aid to Turkey.

This was implicit acknowledgment of the end of British supremacy in the Mediterranean. In March, 1946, Britain had acknowledged the independence of Transjordan (renamed Jordan in 1949), and in April, 1947, had turned over the future of Palestine to the U.N., leading, in May, 1948, to the creation, with mixed United States reactions, of the independent state of Israel. These steps hastened Britain's decline in the Middle East. France, meanwhile, had completed her promised withdrawal from Syria and Lebanon by August, 1946. It became clear, therefore, that henceforth, leadership in the defense of the free world, with all the obligations it entailed, must pass to the United States.

Truman took up the challenge. In March, 1947, he went before Congress to make a revolutionary statement known since as the Truman Doctrine:

I believe that it must be the policy of the United States to support free peoples who are resisting attempted subjugation by armed minorities or by outside pressure. . . . If we falter in our leadership, we may endanger the peace of the world—and we shall surely endanger the welfare of this nation.

Truman asked Congress for $400 million to assist Greece and Turkey, and with the help of Senator Arthur Vandenberg of Michigan, the Republican Chairman of the Senate Committee on Foreign Relations who had formerly been an isolationist, he got it in May. Between 1947 and 1950, the United States spent about $660 million on aid to Greece and Turkey, and both were saved from communist conquest.

In a speech in his native South Carolina in April, 1947, Bernard Baruch signified the reawakening of the American people and the nature of their unprecedented commitment when he said: "Let us not be deceived—today we are in the midst of a cold war." The alarming economic predicament of Western Europe, brought home by Britain's shocking retreat from her Mediterranean life line, soon led the administration to take

the initiative in this war following its effective defensive stand in Greece and Turkey. After some earlier intimations of the new approach, projecting nothing less than the reconstruction of the whole European economy as a unit in order to foster conditions favorable to democracy, Secretary of State George C. Marshall more or less formally announced it in his commencement address at Harvard on June 5. As Marshall put it:

Our policy is directed not against any country or doctrine, but against hunger, poverty, desperation, and chaos. Its purpose should be the revival of a working economy in the world so as to permit the emergence of political and social conditions in which free institutions can exist.

The U.S.S.R. and its satellites, although invited to participate in the Marshall Plan, did everything to subvert it. Western European leaders, however, took up the proposal with alacrity and at a meeting in Paris in July drew up a broad program. American isolationists presented additional hurdles, but the communist *coup* in Czechoslovakia in February, 1948, made the need for action painfully evident and isolationist opposition collapsed. In April, 1948, Congress passed a bill providing $5.3 billion for the first twelve months of Marshall Plan aid, thus launching the European Recovery Program.

Britain, almost entirely dependent upon outside food supplies and on a vigorous world trade for the wherewithal to pay for them, was economically much the worst off in Western Europe at this time. The situation in France, however, appeared more ominous because her large Communist party, capitalizing on a century of deprivation among the working classes, thwarted all efforts to revive the economy in order to hasten a general political collapse. In Italy deprivation had an even longer history than in France and communism an even stronger hold. In defeated Germany, starvation was common and chaos ruled.

"The rehabilitation of the economic structure of Europe," Marshall said, "quite evidently will require a much longer time and greater effort than had been foreseen." Actually, Western Europe's recovery, built on Marshall plan aid, was remarkably swift. Between 1948 and 1952, under the Economic Cooperation Administration, about $12 billion in Marshall Plan funds were advanced, more than half the total to Britain, France, and Germany. By 1952, having survived the economic crisis, Western Europe was launched on a long business boom, which itself was accelerated by the formation of the "Common Market" in 1957 and other economic groupings soon after, as projected by Marshall himself. Moreover, the advance of communism on the Continent had been thwarted and Communist parties in the West languished.

The Marshall Plan was supplemented in 1949 by Truman's Point Four program "for the improvement and growth of undeveloped areas," where resistance to communism would thereby be strengthened. From 1951 to 1954, Congress appropriated nearly $400 million for Point Four, thereby promoting the worldwide "revolution of rising expectations."

The animating idea behind the Truman Doctrine, the Marshall Plan, and Point Four was the concept of "containment." Under the signature, "X," George F. Kennan, a Foreign Service career man and a student of Russian life who had spent some time in the U.S.S.R. during the war, set forth the policy projected by this concept in an article, "The Source of Soviet Conduct," in *Foreign Affairs,* July, 1947.

In brief, the goal of this policy was to "contain" the Soviet Union and its satellite states within their existing boundaries, in the hope that internal divisions and failures would in time so weaken them that they could no longer threaten the security of the United States and the Western World. Kennan warned that the Soviet leaders had not junked the old communist ideology, but also that it should not be assumed that they would commit themselves to some "do-or-die program" to overthrow Western so-

ciety. Their own belief in the inevitable fall of capitalism convinced them that time was on their side and that they could afford to wait. The history of Russia and the teachings of Lenin both argued, he said, that the Soviets would move with caution, retreating when necessary "in the face of superior force." Under such circumstances, Kennan concluded:

It is clear that the main element of any United States policy toward the Soviet Union must be that of a long-term, patient but firm and vigilant containment of Russian expansive tendencies. . . . The Soviet pressure against the free institutions of the Western world is something that can be contained by the adroit and vigilant application of counter-force at a series of constantly shifting geographical and political points, corresponding to the shifts and maneuvers of Soviet policy, but which cannot be charmed or talked out of existence. The Russians look forward to a duel of infinite duration.

Kennan's counsel for a long-range policy of patience, firmness, and strength dashed all hope for a quick, spectacular victory in the Cold War. As a more dynamic alternative to "containment," a number of politicians and writers began to advocate "liberation"—that is, direct attempts to free captive peoples from the Soviet yoke. The right wing of the Republican party became infatuated with this idea (see p. 826), but it was difficult to give substance to it, short of total war. "Some voices," Truman wrote later in his *Memoirs,* "were raised in America calling for a break with the Russians" at this time. "These people did not understand that our choice was only between negotiations and war. There was no third way." The possibility of war, even with negotiations, moreover, was not lost sight of, and, as we have seen (p. 812), steps were taken on the home front to confront it if it came. Further steps were now taken on the diplomatic front as well.

Article 51 of the U.N. charter sanctioned "collective self-defense" arrangements until the Security Council could act "to maintain peace and security." In March, 1948, under the sanction of this article and of the Marshall Plan, Britain, France, the Nether-

The Iron Curtain and NATO, 1949

lands, Belgium, and Luxembourg signed a treaty of economic cooperation and military alliance. This step prompted the United States Senate, in June, 1948, to adopt the Vandenberg Resolution to the effect that the United States should seek peace through collective defense arrangements with friendly powers. The Vandenberg Resolution led to the North Atlantic Treaty, signed on April 4, 1949, by twelve Western nations. Article 5 of this treaty stated that an armed attack upon any member would be considered an attack upon all, and promised that each would go to the assistance of the party attacked by whatever action was thought necessary, "including the use of armed force." The treaty was to remain in effect for twenty years.

To build up the military strength of the members of the North Atlantic Treaty Organization (NATO), Congress passed the Mutual Defense Assistance Act in September, 1949. From October of that year to the end of 1953, the United States supplied almost $6 billion worth of arms and military material to European allies and another $1.7 billion to other countries. While the European allies also strained to make their own contributions to NATO, they failed by and large to do so, so that NATO gradually came to depend on air power as a deterrent to the Soviet, and particularly on the American Strategic Air Command (SAC), organized in 1951. SAC in turn imposed on the United States the need for air bases in many parts of the world, not all of them very friendly, and thus sometimes awkwardly influenced diplomatic decisions.

THE SECURITY
OF LATIN AMERICA

During World War II, all the Latin American countries except Argentina and Chile had cooperated readily with the Western Allies to the extent of supplying strategic materials and making bases available, and Brazil and Mexico also became active belligerents against the Axis, sending troops overseas. Argentina, herself aspiring to South American leadership in competition with both Brazil and the United States, grew especially envious of Brazil because of the United States lend-lease aid she received, including arms.

After the strongly pro-fascist military leader, Colonel Juan D. Perón, became virtual dictator of Argentina in 1944, relations between his country and the United States deteriorated to the degree that the United States' friends among Latin American nations began to fear for the peace of the hemisphere. The upshot was an inter-American conference at the Castle of Chapultepec near Mexico City early in 1945 with Argentina excluded, the United States present. On March 6, the conference adopted the Act of Chapultepec, an informal agreement declaring that an attack by any state against the territory or "the sovereignty or political independence of an American State shall . . . be considered an act of aggression against" the signers. Argentina, aware of her growing isolation, declared war on the Axis on March 27, 1945, and a few days later accepted the Chapultepec agreement. The United States, in return, over Soviet opposition, helped her win a seat at the San Francisco Conference in April, when she, like all other Latin American countries, became a charter member of the U.N.

The end of the war saw the end of the profitable markets for strategic raw materials that Latin American countries enjoyed during the conflict. It also saw the frustration of their hopes for industrialization, to which they had looked forward during the war as a springboard for future economic growth. When neglect by the United States followed hard upon the restoration of peace, suspicion grew that the Good Neighbor policy (see p. 775) had been merely a screen for wartime exploitation. When the United States, early in 1946, then apparently crudely interfered with the Argentine election that year, which saw Perón win by a landslide despite (or because of) United States opposition, the old anxieties about "Yanqui imperialism" deepened, even among Perón's Latin enemies. A crushing blow came in June, 1947, when Latin America found herself excluded from Marshall Plan aid.

The Cold War soon stirred the Truman administration to seek to mend hemispheric as well as more distant fences. At the Inter-American Conference near Rio de Janiero in August and September, 1947, the United States participated in writing the Rio Pact, sanctioned, like NATO, by the U.N. charter. This pact made the mutual defense provisions of the Act of Chapultepec into a permanent treaty and defined the area of its operation. The United States Senate quickly approved this treaty, 72 to 1. A second step was the creation at Bogotá, Colombia, in March, 1948, of the Organization of American States (OAS) to supplant the old Pan-American Union. The OAS charter confirmed the Rio Pact and created a permanent executive council with headquarters in Washington to sustain its strength and to oversee other inter-American contacts. Additional provisions were aimed mainly at countering communist infiltration; but rejection by the United States of new requests for Marshall Plan-type aid through the OAS, which might have gone further than the more militant measures to develop resistance to communism in Latin America, disenchanted many in the region. They were also hurt by Canada's aloofness from hemispheric concerns while she, more than Latin America, shared in the fruits of United States prosperity.

THE HOT WAR IN ASIA

"Containment" worked well enough in Europe, but in the Far East an entirely different situation developed with the fall of China to the communist forces there in 1949. These forces had come into existence long before World War II, and throughout the war the United States tried to get them and the Nationalists under Chiang Kai-shek to work together to defeat Japan. But this policy failed dismally. General Joseph W. Stilwell, in charge of coordinating Chinese wartime efforts against Japan, concluded that Chiang's government "is a structure based on fear and favor, in the hands of an ignorant, arbitrary, stubborn man." At the war's end the Chinese communists, encouraged by the Soviets, received the surrender of Japanese armies independently, amassed their own arms, and even engaged in skirmishes with the Nationalists.

In an attempt to stave off civil war in China and the extension of communist rule there, Truman, late in 1945, had sent General Marshall to the divided country. On his return in December, 1946, Marshall reported that he had been frustrated not only by the communists but also "by irreconcilable groups within [Chiang's] Kuomintang party interested in the preservation of their own feudal control." From 1945 to 1949, Chiang received $3 billion in American aid, most of it squandered or allowed to fall into communist hands.

By 1950, with the communists in control of most of China, Chiang had withdrawn to Taiwan (Formosa). As his American critics feared, he left behind great stores of American-made military supplies. His government was still recognized by the United States, which, unlike Britain and most other major nations, refused to recognize the (communist) People's Republic of China, although she had recognized new communist regimes in Europe (see p. 807), or to consent to the new China's admission to the U.N.

A strong faction in the United States continued to argue that anti-communist forces in China had been given too little support, and that, more liberally backed, Chiang Kai-shek might have won. Most historians believe that only massive United States military intervention could have saved Chiang's government on the continent and that the American people would not have supported the effort required.

The hot war between Chiang and the Chinese communists had a sequel in nearby

Korea that was just as hateful to Americans as Chiang's fall. At the Cairo Conference in November, 1943, it had been decided that Korea, held by the Japanese during the war, should be made independent. This decision was reaffirmed at Potsdam in July, 1945. In August that year the Russians agreed to accept the surrender of the Japanese in Korea north of the 38th parallel, leaving the United States, on the arrival of its forces in September, to accept the surrender below that line. This military decision probably kept the Russians from overrunning the entire country; but it also created the fateful division of the land which soon hardened. North of the 38th parallel the Soviets characteristically established solid communist control and thereafter resisted all efforts to unify Korea on any grounds short of communist domination. The United States referred the question of Korean unity and independence to the U.N. in September, 1947, and although opposed by the U.S.S.R., the General Assembly voted to set up a temporary commission to supervise an all-Korean election.

When the Soviets boycotted the U.N. commission, it held elections for a national assembly in May, 1948, in the United States sector alone. The elected national assembly then adopted a constitution, voted Syngman Rhee in as first president, and on August 15 proclaimed the Republic of Korea, which the United States and thirty other nations recognized. That very day, the Russians held elections above the 38th parallel leading to the formation of the rival North Korean state which they and their adherents recognized in turn. By December, leaving the North Koreans heavily armed, the U.S.S.R. recalled its troops. The U.N., in the meantime, where Russia blocked South Korea's bid for membership and continued to do so as late as 1966, made its temporary commission permanent, its object being to bring about "the complete independence and unity of Korea." At the General Assem-

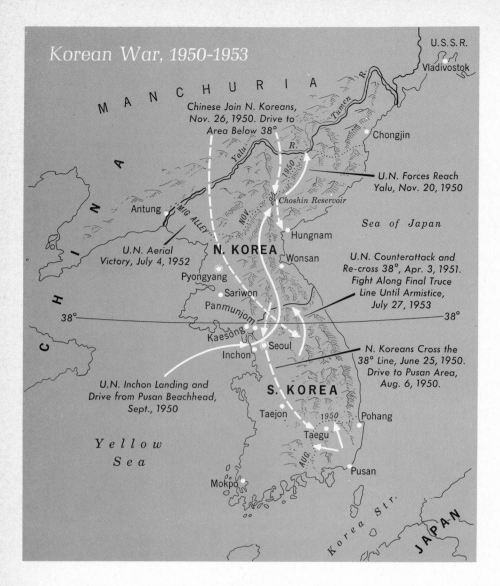

Korean War, 1950-1953

U.S.S.R.

Vladivostok

M A N C H U R I A

Chinese Join N. Koreans,
Nov. 26, 1950. Drive to
Area Below 38°

Chongjin

U.N. Forces Reach
Yalu, Nov. 20, 1950

Antung

Choshin Reservoir

Sea of Japan

C H I N A

U.N. Aerial
Victory, July 4, 1952

N. KOREA

Hungnam

Wonsan

U.N. Counterattack and
Re-cross 38°, Apr. 3, 1951.
Fight Along Final Truce
Line Until Armistice,
July 27, 1953

Pyongyang

Sariwon

Panmunjom

38°   38°

Kaesong

Inchon

Seoul

N. Koreans Cross the
38° Line, June 25, 1950.
Drive to Pusan Area,
Aug. 6, 1950.

U.N. Inchon Landing and
Drive from Pusan Beachhead,
Sept., 1950

S. KOREA

Yellow
Sea

Taejon

Taegu

Pohang

Pusan

Mokpo

Korea Str.

JAPAN

bly's suggestion, the United States recalled
its troops from South Korea in June, 1949,
leaving much military material and about
500 "advisors" behind.

North and South Korea thus faced one
another across an artificial border, each
more or less backed by a rival great power
committed to unification on its own terms.
Border raids soon threatened, in the words
of the U.N. commission, to broaden into a
"barbarous civil war." The outbreak of this
war may have been hastened by a speech on
January 12, 1950, by Secretary of State Dean
Acheson outlining United States Asia policy
following the establishment of Red China.
In this speech, Acheson described the American "defensive perimeter" in the Orient so

as to exclude South Korea. In case of attack,
he said, "the initial reliance" of nations excluded "must be on the people attacked to
resist it," and then on "the entire civilized
world under the Charter of the United Nations." In order to help South Korea resist,
Truman, in February, 1950, approved an
act providing her with $110 million in eco-
nomic aid. Military aid also was increased.
Acheson's declaration may have incited
North Korea, and the United States activity
in the south may have provoked her. In
any case, her attack on South Korea on
June 25, 1950, was not, as she claimed, a
reprisal for border raids, but, in the words
of the U.N. commission, a "well-planned,
concerted, and full-scale invasion."

The North Korean assault posed a painful problem for the democracies. If they permitted South Korea to be overrun, the door might be opened to further communist incursions from China now, as well as from the U.S.S.R. with its atomic bomb (see p. 824), thus undermining the confidence of other nations relying on the United States.

Truman responded to the emergency with decision. At his urgent request, the U.N. Security Council met on the afternoon of the invasion and by a vote of 9-0 (the Soviet delegation having walked out on another issue and remaining absent until August 1) held North Korea accountable for "a breach of the peace." The Council demanded an immediate end to hostilities and an embargo by all members on aid to North Korea. The next evening, having received a direct appeal from South Korea for assistance, Truman ordered American naval and air units to help push North Koreans back over the 38th parallel. He also ordered the fleet to keep Chiang Kai-shek from attempting to invade the continent from Formosa and thereby draw China into the war. On the following day, June 27, the Security Council urged positive action by U.N. members against North Korea. Truman then broadened his earlier military instructions and with other nations responded to the Security Council's call. American troops comprised about four-fifths of the U.N. forces in Korea. The U.N. troops in turn were more than matched in numbers by the army South Korea eventually put in the field.

The Korean fighting grew as savage as many World War II campaigns, and losses ran high. By the end of August, 1950, moreover, the outnumbered U.N. forces under the command of General Douglas MacArthur had been pushed far south and almost into the sea in the area around the port of Pusan. Fortune changed in September when, heavily reinforced, MacArthur opened a counterattack with a brilliant amphibious landing at the port of Inchon behind the North Korean line. A full-scale offensive in November drove the North Koreans back toward the 38th parallel and destroyed a considerable part of their army. Taking advantage of this moment of superiority, U.N. forces pushed across the 38th parallel on October 9, 1950, and pressed on toward the Yalu River, North Korea's Chinese boundary. Late that November, in a move almost too well remembered by Americans henceforth (see p. 835), Red China threw her own huge armies into the fray and thrust the U.N. forces back below the 38th parallel, recapturing the South Korean capital of Seoul.

Irked by restraints imposed upon him by the U.N.'s Kennan-like strategy of conducting a limited war for the limited objective of restoring South Korea's frontier, General MacArthur now publicly expressed his dissatisfaction with both the U.N. and President Truman. Even at the risk of becoming involved in open war with Red China, a development that many sober observers believed might lead to war with the Soviet Union, MacArthur urged an all-out Korean effort. General Omar N. Bradley, Chairman of the Joint Chiefs of Staff, warned that a major war against Red China would be "the wrong war at the wrong place, in the wrong time and with the wrong enemy." Mac-Arthur rejected this decision and finally caused President Truman, on April 11, 1951, to relieve him of his Korean command and of his control of the occupation forces in Japan for insubordination. MacArthur returned to the United States where he received a hero's welcome, but sympathy for his position quickly faded.

On June 23, 1951, the head of the Soviet delegation in the U.N. suggested that the Korean conflict might be settled if both parties were willing. This announcement led to armistice negotiations that began on July 10, 1951, and proceeded with exasperating delays for two whole years, during which fighting often broke out. When peace finally was restored (see p. 828), the political division of Korea was continued and it has remained a source of friction.

IV. *The Onset of McCarthyism*

The strains of the Cold War, as we have seen, did not deter the American people from taking strong measures to meet the Soviet menace in Europe; nor did the progress of communism in Asia sap their will to confront it there. Yet the inconclusiveness of results in both theaters wore on the nerves of many, causing them to seek scapegoats among their fellow citizens for the elusive finality of victory.

Scapegoats, as in the 'twenties, were not hard to find. Indeed, certain sectors of the population, especially among the descendants of old-time families, had never surrendered their belief in the reality of the "Red Scare" of the 'twenties (see p. 691), which they associated with the "new immigrant" groups (see p. 693). Their persistent fear of such groups was aggravated by the turmoil of the depression years, when communist and communist "front" organizations enjoyed their American heyday while unaffiliated writers, ministers, teachers, and other spokesmen also veered to the left.

The turmoil of the war years, in turn, put a great strain on what *Fortune* magazine in 1942 called the "petrified nationalisms from over there" of the "new immigrant" groups themselves and their offspring. The war placed the heaviest burdens on Italian-Americans who, with many German-Americans and anti-British Irish-Americans, felt impelled to be pro-fascist (although the Axis was the enemy) and indiscriminately "anti-communist" (although the Soviets were allies). Once the war ended, the ranks of the "red" haters were filled out by millions of other "new immigrant" families—those who had roots in countries behind the Iron Curtain where, according to the Republican party platform of 1952, "the negative, futile and immoral policy of 'containment' abandons countless human beings to despotism and godless terrorism."

To all such Americans, and to those who played upon their fears for partisan pur-poses, Roosevelt's formal recognition of the Soviet Union in 1933 stood out ever more clearly as a tell-tale act. His wartime aid to Russia beginning in 1941, his "Asia last" military strategy in contrast to Stalin's alleged "Asia first" policy during the fighting, his concessions at Yalta in 1945, and his half-surrender of United States sovereignty to the U.N. soon after apparently confirmed the perfidiousness of his character and that of his associates, so that it was easy for many to believe Senator Joseph McCarthy of Wisconsin in 1950, when he branded "the whole group of twisted-thinking New Dealers" as communists who "have led America near to ruin at home and abroad."

Before Senator McCarthy made this accusation, much additional background for it, as we have seen (p. 811), had been developed by the revived House Un-American Activities Committee (HUAC) following the Republican success in the elections of 1946. The committee's yeastiest adventure in this period was a two-week foray into Hollywood in October, 1947, "to expose those elements that are insidiously trying to . . . poison the minds of your children, distort the history of our country, and discredit Christianity." According to the New York *Herald-Tribune,* itself a Republican paper, the Hollywood investigation soon "dissolved into the ludicrous." Nevertheless, it did frighten movie moguls into an indiscriminate house-cleaning which spread to radio and nascent TV, and the blacklisting of actors, writers, directors, and others, some of whom remained barred from employment twenty years later.

The Hollywood adventure had been preceded by the committee's haling before it in Washington, starting in February, 1947, of hard-core Communist party functionaries, many of whom preferred citations for contempt to answering the summons. Eugene Dennis, then the General Secretary of the Communist party in the United States, was one of these. At Congressman Nixon's suggestion, the committee agreed not only to ask the House to bring contempt charges against Dennis but also to ask the Justice Department to investigate the communist "conspiracy" to violate the Smith Act of 1940, in which he played a part. The Smith Act made it illegal for a person to advocate "overthrowing . . . any government in the United States by force," or to "affiliate" with groups teaching this doctrine. In July, 1948, the Justice Department did procure the indictment of Dennis and ten other high-ranking communist leaders under this act. In October, 1949, in the federal district court in New York, they were convicted and sentenced to heavy fines and jail terms. The United States Supreme Court, 6 to 2, upheld the convictions in June, 1951.

Validation of the Smith Act by the Supreme Court majority seemed to diminish the value Justice Holmes in 1919 had put on "the free trade in ideas" under the guarantees of the First Amendment (see p. 697). "Certain kinds of speech are so undesirable," said Chief Justice Vinson for the Court in the *Dennis* case, "as to warrant criminal prosecution." Holmes had denied the justice of such prosecution unless advocacy led to *acts* portending a "clear and present danger" to the nation. Justice William O. Douglas, in his dissent in the *Dennis* case, held that no such acts were proven imminent, and that the communist "conspiracy" was in fact a waning menace which the F.B.I. and other accredited agencies could easily control. But the times had outstripped this view. The *Dennis* ruling encouraged many states and municipalities, under local acts and ordinances similar to the Smith Act, to pursue thousands of alleged subversives, sometimes on the basis of mere hearsay or invention offered by frightened or vindictive individuals.

The Hiss case, the HUAC's most far-reaching triumph, began on August 3, 1948, on the heels of the Dennis indictment in July. On that day, Whittaker Chambers, admittedly a long-time Soviet agent in the United States who said he quit the Communist party in 1937, was brought before the committee to help corroborate earlier testi-

mony about the communist "apparatus" in Washington, D.C. Chambers, an editor of *Time* magazine, told a sensational story, one made no less provocative by his report, later verified, that he had told the same story to the State Department at the time of the Berlin-Moscow pact of 1939 (see p. 778), with no result. In his story, Chambers named members of the Washington apparatus of the 'thirties, persons who might still be communists, he said, whose main objective was to infiltrate the uppermost places in the government with party men. Espionage was secondary.

Alger Hiss, in government service in the mid-'thirties and early 'forties but since 1947 president of the private Carnegie Endowment for International Peace, was one of those named. On learning of Chambers' accusation he promptly telegraphed a full denial to the committee and asked for a hearing, which was granted on August 5. This and subsequent hearings, interspersed with re-examinations of Chambers, elicited more and more details of Hiss' activities in the 'thirties, including espionage. When Hiss persisted in his denials, Chairman J. Parnell Thomas warned, "Certainly one of you will be tried for perjury." Neither could be prosecuted for his other admitted or alleged crimes since these had taken place more than seven years before and thus, under the statute of limitations, were beyond legal reach.

On the day of Hiss' first hearing, President Truman had replied to questions about the "spy investigations": "They are simply a red herring. They [the Republicans] are using this as a red herring." The 1948 presidential campaign was then in full-swing, and many thought the Democratic victory in this campaign (see p. 813) might weaken the HUAC and sidetrack the Hiss issue. In December, 1948, however, a federal grand jury in New York indicted Hiss for perjury. His trial began in May, 1949, and when, at the end of it, the jury disagreed, a second trial opened in November. In January, 1950, he was found guilty and sentenced to a $10,000 fine and five years in prison. After appeals to higher courts confirmed the validity of this verdict, Hiss went to prison in March, 1951.

In his earliest denial of Chambers' "complete fabrications," Hiss boldly told the HUAC: "I think my record in the Government service speaks for itself." It did, but not in his favor. Hiss had been a remarkably fat catch for the committee. A Harvard Law School graduate and secretary to no less a personage than Justice Holmes, he then served as one of the early New Dealers in the AAA. After switching to the State Department, he became involved in planning the U.N. at Dumbarton Oaks and San Francisco. He was a member, but only a subordinate one, of Roosevelt's Yalta delegation, and finally, before leaving the government in 1946, served as director of the State Department's Office of Special Political Affairs. All in all, he loomed as a shining example to the "ethnics" of the penetration of communism even among the country's best people, and to best people as a traitor to his class as well as his country.

While the Hiss case was in progress, the HUAC made other striking accusations and the FBI bestirred itself to uncover additional Soviet agents, so that Truman's "red herring" charge soon came back to haunt him. The news of the first successful Soviet atomic bomb explosion late in September, 1949, deepened the shock of the red scare. When this news was followed within ten days by the official proclamation of the communist People's Republic of China (and within a few months by this Republic's treaty of "Friendship, Alliance and Mutual Assistance" with the U.S.S.R.), Truman's "containment" policy seemed as bankrupt as the Republican Asia Firsters had claimed all along. Their anger grew uncontrollable when, in January, 1950, Dean Acheson made his "defensive perimeter" speech (see p. 820) announcing the United States' newly narrowed Asia policy in the face of the Soviet's dramatically broadened one.

Truman had named Acheson to succeed

General Marshall as Secretary of State in January, 1949, even though Acheson had insisted from the first that he would not turn his back on his friend Alger Hiss, "whatever the outcome." After hearing Acheson's presentation of the new Asia policy, the Asia Firsters led by "Mr. Republican" himself, Senator Robert A. Taft, shattered the bipartisanship in foreign policy so painstakingly constructed by Senator Vandenberg and launched their assault on the State Department and the Secretary, from which neither soon recovered. The Department, Taft said, was filled with communists and fellow travelers who had "surrendered to every demand of Russia . . . and promoted at every opportunity the Communist cause in China." Acheson himself "must go." Taft's brutal colleague, Senator McCarthy, as hungry for a partisan issue as Taft, pounced on this theme.

THE WISCONSIN SENATOR
AND HIS FRIENDS
In his "Lincoln-day week-end" speech in West Virginia on February 9,

Senator McCarthy, with his aide, Roy Cohn, at Congressional hearing, May, 1954.

1950, Senator McCarthy declared that the United States, the strongest nation on earth on V-J day, had been shorn of her strength, "because of the traitorous actions of those who have been treated so well by this nation. . . . The bright young men [in the State Department] who are born with silver spoons in their mouths are the ones who have been the worst." None was worse than their chief, Secretary Acheson, "this pompous diplomat in striped pants, with a phony British accent," who "could vouch for Hiss absolutely." McCarthy then added: "I have here in my hand," the names of "two hundred and five men that were known to the Secretary of State as being members of the Communist party and who nevertheless are still working and shaping the policy of the State Department."

McCarthy gradually backed away from this figure, keeping in the limelight with new ones until, in the end, he was unable to substantiate a single name. A subcommittee of the Senate Foreign Relations Committee, set up under the conservative Democrat, Millard E. Tydings of Maryland, to investigate McCarthy's charges, found them "the most nefarious campaign of half-truths and untruth in the history of the Republic." But nothing was done to check the accuser. On the contrary, Taft gave him the full benefit of his own prestige. "McCarthy should keep talking," he said, "and if one case doesn't work he should proceed with another."

Senator Tydings himself was up for re-election in November, 1950. In retaliation for his investigation, McCarthy's staff, which he made available to Tydings' opponent, helped doctor a photograph in order to show Tydings in friendly conversation with a Communist party leader. This forgery helped defeat Tydings and McCarthy's power to intimidate waxed stronger.

Events also played into his hands. While he was engaging in what became known as "the numbers game" in February, 1950, British authorities arrested for atomic espionage Dr. Klaus Fuchs, a German-born nuclear physicist and naturalized British subject who had worked on the American

bomb at Los Alamos in 1944. Fuchs admitted the charges and on March 1 was sentenced to 14 years in prison. He also implicated certain American communists in his work, which certainly speeded up Russian success with the bomb. Acting on Fuchs' information, the FBI in the summer of 1950 arrested Ethel and Julius Rosenberg and their friend, Morton Sobell. For a crime "worse than murder," in the words of the trial judge, the Rosenbergs, in March, 1951, were sentenced to death, Sobell to 30 years. After many appeals failed, the Rosenbergs were executed on June 19, 1953.

Such cases helped validate the red scare and lend credence to McCarthy's charges, which grew in reach and recklessness as the "limited" Korean War eroded American morale. A low point was touched on June 14, 1951, when, after General MacArthur's recall from Korea (see p. 821), McCarthy made a bid to retrieve the headlines with a 60,000-word attack in the Senate on MacArthur's rivals, General Marshall and General Eisenhower. Marshall, he said, "with great stubbornness and skill, always and invariably [was] serving the world policy of the Kremlin." Deeply involved with him, "in a conspiracy so immense and an infamy so black as to dwarf any previous such venture in the history of man," was his "firm supporter" and "fast-rising protege, 'Ike' Eisenhower."

"McCarthyism" by then had passed into the language as an expression for wild charges of disloyalty. More and more Americans, however, came to believe, as the Senator himself told his home following in Wisconsin, that "McCarthyism is Americanism with its sleeves rolled." Money began to pour in on McCarthy, at first in small denominations from a multitude of alarmed neurotics, then in big bundles from economic royalists. Superpatriot secular societies like the Daughters of the American Revolution, organizations of professional veterans like the American Legion, and authoritarian "hyphenate" clubs and churches, meanwhile, took up the cudgels. Public opinion polls showed more people fearful of communism "creeping in in places" than of civil liberties being thrown out. The Supreme Court's decision in the *Dennis* case in June, 1951 (see p. 823), openly reflected the strength of the McCarthyite spirit.

Congress naturally responded to such grass roots sentiment. On September 23, 1950, over Truman's vigorous veto, it passed the McCarran Internal Security Act incorporating a drastic new sedition provision making it "unlawful . . . knowingly to . . . conspire . . . to perform any act which would substantially contribute to the establishment within the United States of a totalitarian dictatorship." All "communist-action" and "communist front" organizations were assumed to be such conspiracies and required to register with the Attorney General. In case of an "Internal Security Emergency," the act authorized the President, "to apprehend and . . . detain . . . each person as to whom there is reasonable ground to believe that such person probably will engage in, or . . . conspire with others to engage in, acts of espionage or sabotage." Any alien, moreover, with the slightest "subversive" taint on his record was to be "excluded from admission to the United States." In his veto message, Truman characterized parts of the Internal Security Act as "the greatest danger to freedom of speech, press, and assembly since the alien and sedition laws of 1798."

On June 30, 1952, Congress supplemented the Internal Security Act with the McCarran-Walter Immigration Act, passed again after a resounding Truman veto. The act up-dated but hardly liberalized the widely attacked quota system (see p. 694) which worked particular hardship on displaced persons and refugees from communist countries. More to the point, it required the Attorney General to screen out "subversives" within the permitted quotas and empowered him to deport such persons even after they had become naturalized Ameri-

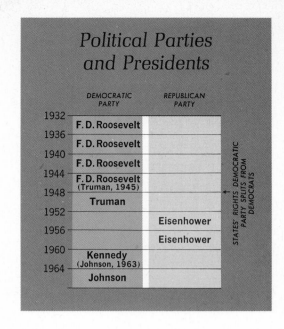

Political Parties and Presidents

	DEMOCRATIC PARTY	REPUBLICAN PARTY	
1932	F. D. Roosevelt		
1936	F. D. Roosevelt		
1940	F. D. Roosevelt		
1944	F. D. Roosevelt (Truman, 1945)		
1948	Truman		← STATES' RIGHTS DEMOCRATIC PARTY SPLITS FROM DEMOCRATS
1952		Eisenhower	
1956		Eisenhower	
1960	Kennedy (Johnson, 1963)		
1964	Johnson		

can citizens. "Seldom," said Truman, "has a bill exhibited the distrust evidenced here for citizens and aliens alike—at a time when we need unity at home and the confidence of our friends abroad." Yet worse was to come following the frustration of the McCarthyites in the election of 1952.

THE ELECTION OF 1952

It seemed at first to many shocked Republicans that the press reports not the public had snatched away a victory already won in the presidential campaign of 1948 (see p. 813). Once they recovered from their shock, those Republican leaders who had opposed the nomination of the internationalist easterner Thomas E. Dewey, and had favored Taft, blamed the defeat on bipartisanship in foreign policy. Looking to the rehabilitation of the party in 1952, these leaders, as we have seen (p. 824), helped smash bipartisanship following the Russian bomb explosion and the fall of Chiang Kai-shek. Following the Truman administration's decision in 1951 to constrain MacArthur and "contain" the Korean War, they accelerated their program to enlist behind their new policy of "liberation" the millions of "ethnics"—some hopefully put their number at nearly 30 million in 17 key industrial states—distressed by the communist menace at home and abroad. At this time, the Republican National Committee set up an Ethnic Origins Division and under it a Foreign Language Group Activities section. At the head of this section they placed Arthur Bliss Lane, a former Ambassador to Poland who had become one of McCarthy's stanchest backers. Lane struck especially hard at "appeasement" at Yalta and urged the party explicitly to repudiate the agreements made there.

The success of Lane's campaign was evident in the 1952 platform adopted by the party at its national convention in Chicago in July. This platform promised to "repudiate all commitments . . . such as those of Yalta which aid Communist enslavement," and castigated, as we have seen (p. 822), the "containment" policy which "abandoned" so many millions to it. Two years before the convention, John Foster Dulles, the leading Republican advisor to Truman's State Department on bipartisan foreign policy, had written: "If at a time of national peril, two presidential candidates should compete in making novel and unseasoned proposals, designed primarily to win votes, the end of that campaign would leave our foreign relations in a shambles." Now, for practical vote-winning purposes, Dulles became the captive of the "new look," and helped put the appropriate platform planks across.

Yet too many Republicans, rank-and-filers as well as leaders who had backed Dewey, were committed to bipartisanship in principle and to the Truman version of it in practice to yield further to the Asia Firsters. Many of them also loathed McCarthy as deeply as most Democrats, a feeling they found it ever easier to transfer to his misguided friend Taft, again the Asia Firsters' favorite. Their own choice, largely because they believed he alone could stand up to the Wisconsin mudslinger, was Eisenhower, who had turned down the Democrats four years earlier.

At the very start of the convention, the Eisenhower managers forced the National Committee leaders to recall the credentials they had approved for contested Taft dele-

gates from the rubber-stamp southern states. They then seated their own southern delegates by the vote of the whole assemblage. From there they went on to put "Ike" across on the first ballot. The Taft men took what solace they could from the nomination for vice-president of Congressman Nixon, the HUAC luminary from the rapidly growing state of California.

The Republicans' snaring Eisenhower only deepened the pessimism with which the Democrats approached their national convention two weeks later. Many voters believed the McCarthyite charge that their reign had been "twenty years of treason." The inconclusive Korean War and the inflation it created also weakened the Democrats. The inflation was dramatized by the steel strike in 1952, which Truman failed to arbitrate and which resulted in both higher wages and higher steel prices. Moreover, beginning in 1951, certain petty scandals came to light involving the use of influence by persons close to Truman himself. The fact that it was the Democrats who made most of these revelations did not prevent the administration from being branded as corrupt by many.

After Truman announced in March, 1952, that he would not be a candidate, the leading Democratic aspirant became Senator Estes Kefauver of Tennessee, who had gained a national reputation as head of the special Senate Committee that had in fact uncovered so much Democratic graft. When Kefauver failed to win on the first two ballots at the Chicago convention, the delegates drafted Truman's choice, the eloquent but unwilling Governor of Illinois, Adlai E. Stevenson. Senator John J. Sparkman of Alabama became his running-mate.

Once named, Stevenson conducted a vigorous and unusually eloquent campaign that won him many enduring supporters among intellectuals, often caricatured as "egg heads." He particularly denounced the "liberation" promises of his opponents as a "cynical . . . attempt . . . to play upon the anxieties of foreign nationality groups in this country." Truman himself, foreseeing the actual consequences of the "liberation" line (see pp. 832, 839), declared that, "Nothing could be worse than to incite uprisings that can only end by giving a new crop of victims to the Soviet executioners."

To the surprise of no one, Eisenhower's vast appeal, enhanced by his campaign pledge to fly to Korea and end the stalemate there, carried him to a striking triumph. He received 33,824,000 popular votes to Stevenson's 27,314,000. In the electoral college, his margin was 442 to 89, with the Solid South for the first time since 1928 contributing to the Republican total. Yet the Republicans had reason for misgivings. Even "Ike's" tremendous popularity brought the party a mere majority of eight in the House and,

worse, a standoff in the Senate. The Taft wing should have been especially troubled. Eisenhower, for example, carried Wisconsin by over 350,000 votes; McCarthy won reelection there by less than 140,000. In numerous Polish-, German-, and Czech-American wards in such key industrial cities as Chicago, Akron, Baltimore and Cleveland, moreover, the "ethnics" combined with the "egg heads" to give Stevenson majorities of over 60 per cent. They voted as Americans not as "hyphenates."

The appeal to "ethnic" blocs, nevertheless, reached a new level of intensity and was heightened thereafter. The strong movement of Negroes to the cities in this period, added a new inflammatory element which may have thrown all white groups, in fact, ever more closely together in defense of their own gains.

v.   *The Republicans in Power*

MODERATION

ON THE HOME FRONT

A month after his victory at the polls, Eisenhower flew to Korea; but many more months passed before the touchy armistice there was resolved by the agreement of July 27, 1953, to return to the prewar setup. By then, the three-year war had cost the United States over $15 billion and more than 140,000 casualties. The United Nations had not won a united Korea but then neither did the communists, and the primary purpose for which their aggression had been met—to show that it would be forcibly withstood—had been accomplished.

While Korean negotiations dragged out, the new President faced up to the issues at home. His most significant decision, reflecting his party's stand in rejecting Taft's candidacy, was to go along with the moderates at the cost of disappointing the extreme right wing. Far from attempting any drastic reversal of Democratic policies, Eisenhower embraced many of them. The Republicans even overreached the Democrats in certain respects. On April 1, 1953, the new Congress created the Department of Health, Educa-

tion and Welfare. Congress also showed its commitment to the welfare state by adding 10 million persons to the number entitled to receive social security benefits.

At the same time, the Eisenhower administration limited the Democrats' long-term public housing program to one year, and in order to cut taxes it drastically reduced the budget, especially the military and foreign aid items. To slow down the accumulation of farm surpluses in government warehouses under the price support program (see p. 788), Secretary of Agriculture Benson first reduced the point at which payments were to begin from Truman's 90 per cent of parity to 75 per cent, and then secured congressional authorization for a flexible scale ranging from 82.5 to 90 per cent.

President Eisenhower, seeking to improve party unity, often sought Taft's advice and support for legislation, and the Senator usually gave his blessing to administration measures. After Taft died in July, 1953, the Republican right wing grew increasingly rebellious. Right-wingers strongly backed an amendment proposed by Senator Bricker of Ohio to limit the treaty-making powers of the president, a measure only narrowly defeated in the Senate. Under right-wing influence, Congress refused further to revise the Taft-Hartley Act, and rejected administration plans for national health insurance, aid to schools, and aid to states for highways. A more constructive action in May, 1954, authorized the joint building with Canada of a St. Lawrence seaway, opened in 1959, which made it possible for ocean-going vessels, by way of Montreal, to dock at Great Lakes ports.

THE CLIMAX OF MCCARTHYISM

One thing Taft failed to do for the new administration was to muzzle McCarthy. The Republican victory in 1952 naturally opened congressional committee chairmanships to party leaders and McCarthy got his. Taft, a dominant figure in the Senate, averred they had put McCarthy "where he can't do any harm" by giving him the obscure Government Operations Committee; but any committee affording funds and staff would have served McCarthy's purpose, and he soon found occasion to renew his assault on his favorite target, the State Department.

In February, 1953, Eisenhower nominated Charles E. Bohlen as ambassador to the U.S.S.R. Bohlen was a veteran Foreign Service officer who unfortunately had served as Roosevelt's interpreter at Yalta. No choice could have stung the Senator and his friends more sharply. After vicious condemnations of the nominee they permitted the Senate to approve him; but their pound of flesh was the appointment of their own man as the State Department's new "security" officer, and henceforth few worked there without McCarthyite consent. Having cleansed the stables at home, as he thought, McCarthy next turned to operations abroad. His first target here was the Voice of America, the overseas broadcasting unit of the United States Information Agency, where, after the most demoralizing search, he failed to uncover a single party man. On the heels of this venture came another, the victim this time being the State Department's International Information Administration, which disseminated printed materials

through libraries in many parts of the world. Much of this material, McCarthy's agents declared, proved to be as "subversive" as the workers who had shelved it. Many books by eminent American writers, one of them Secretary Dulles' cousin, were ordered withdrawn, and to the shock of the world, some were publicly burned.

To placate the man his election was supposed to spirit away, the President himself, on April 27, 1953, issued his own "loyalty order" instituting a probe of government employees to outdo Truman's. The categories for "security risks" were made broader and vaguer than ever, the safeguards fewer and weaker. Not one communist could be found; but in a short time more than half a million civil servants, almost a fifth of the total, resigned in protest. In December, 1953, Eisenhower dismayed the whole scientific community by ordering a "blank wall" to be placed between J. Robert Oppenheimer, the great nuclear physicist who had directed the making of the first atomic bomb (see p. 788), and all secret atomic data. Oppenheimer, at this time head of the Institute for Advanced Study in Princeton, also served as chairman of the General Advisory Committee of the Atomic Energy Commission. The administration learned that McCarthy had him in view as another victim for having associated with communist friends in the 'thirties, and wanted to get to him first. Oppenheimer soon was cleared of any taint of disloyalty, but in the eyes of AEC he remained unemployable in the future because of "fundamental defects in his character."

The legislature as well as the executive knuckled under to McCarthy's pressure, Congress enacting new security legislation in 1953 and 1954 extending the range of the McCarran Act (see p. 826), and enlarging the vulnerability of naturalized citizens as well as aliens to penalties for alleged subversive activities. McCarthy's star began to fade with his attack in the summer of 1954 on the army's own "coddling" of communists. After the elections that year returned Democratic majorities to both houses, a move to expel or at least to censure him gained headway. In December, 1954, by a vote of 67 to 22, he was "condemned" by the Senate for "conduct unbecoming a member." McCarthy died unsung in May, 1957, but McCarthyism, a far deeper malady than the Red Scare of the 'twenties, continued to alienate creative men from government service.

TOWARD NEGRO EQUALITY

Negro recognition and respect under the New Deal (see p. 731) and Negro progress during World War II (see p. 787) laid the groundwork for further Negro gains under the Truman administration and in the early years of Eisenhower's first term. In February, 1946, a Senate filibuster killed an administration measure for a permanent federal Fair Employment Practices Committee, but before the end of the year five states—New York, New Jersey, Massachusetts, Connecticut and Washington—had set up their own FEPC's and many more were to follow. In December, 1946, Truman named a distinguished Committee on Civil Rights, composed of leaders of both races. This committee's report, *To Secure These Rights,* published in 1947 and widely circulated before the presidential election the next year, recommended a broad program for the repeal of Jim Crow legislation and the advancement of Negro equality. New threats of southern filibusters frustrated administration efforts to implement this program, but Truman took important steps on the executive level, the major one being his order of July, 1948, to desegregate the armed forces (see p. 812). President Eisenhower continued the implementation of this order on taking office early in 1953. He also promoted the desegregation of public places in the District of Columbia and of public housing there.

Before its momentous decision in May, 1954, in *Oliver Brown et al.* v. *Board of Education of Topeka, Kansas,* ordering the end of public school segregation (see p. 831),

the Supreme Court had also taken significant steps toward raising the Negro's status under law.

The nadir of Supreme Court action had come in *Plessy* v. *Ferguson* in 1896, when seven justices, against one, decided that separate, if equal, facilities provided by a state satisfied the requirement of the Fourteenth Amendment that no state deprive a citizen of the United States of "the equal protection of the laws." The *Plessy* decision upheld the constitutionality of a Louisiana statute requiring Negroes and whites to ride in separate railroad cars, but it soon spawned many new Jim Crow laws segregating housing on entire city blocks, and in hospitals, parks, schools, and other public facilities. The "equality" of the separate Negro facilities under these laws, moreover, was rarely maintained.

The Supreme Court began eroding the *Plessy* ruling in 1917 when it declared a Louisville, Kentucky, Jim Crow housing ordinance unconstitutional. In the 1930's, the National Association for the Advancement of Colored People (NAACP) began attacking the inequality of Negro educational facilities and especially of Negro teacher salaries in the courts. A turning point came in the Supreme Court decision in 1938 in *Missouri* ex rel *Gaines* v. *Canada,* one of a series of cases in *higher education* through which the idea of the inherent inequality of separate facilities was developed. The University of Missouri Law School, in the absence of a Negro law school in the state, attempted to meet the "equal" requirement by offering to pay the Negro, Lloyd Gaines', tuition in an out-of-state school. The Court, 7 to 2, held that he must be trained in Missouri in whose courts he would practice, and not in some jurisdiction foreign to them. In the absence of a Negro law school there, he must be admitted equally with whites to the one at the University.

Similar decisions covering medical as well as law schools led the NAACP, and others, to fight not inequality but segregation itself. At the time of the epochal *Brown* ruling in May, 1954, cases were pending from South

Carolina, Virginia, Delaware, and the District of Columbia, as well as from Kansas, all of which were covered by the decision.

In September, 1953, the Chief Justice of the Supreme Court, Fred M. Vinson, died and in his place Eisenhower named Governor Earl Warren of California. Some observers believe that Vinson's court would have continued its earlier tendency merely to strengthen the necessity for real "equality" in separate facilities, at least until Congress explicitly made segregation illegal. Warren's court, including three southern justices, decided unanimously to embrace Justice John Marshall Harlan's bold dissent in the *Plessy* case. The doctrine of separate but equal, Harlan had said, "would stimulate aggressions, more or less brutal and irritating, upon the admitted rights of colored citizens." The "thin disguise of 'equal' accommodations . . . will not mislead anyone, or atone for the wrong this day done." Speaking for his court, Warren undertook to right this wrong:

> In approaching . . . the effect of segregation itself on public education . . . we . . . must consider public education in the light of its full development and its present place in American life throughout the Nation. . . . Today, education is perhaps the most important function of state and local governments. . . . It is the very foundation of good citizenship. Today it is a principal instrument in awakening the child to cultural values, in preparing him for later professional training, and in helping him to adjust normally to his environment. . . . In the field of public education the doctrine of "separate but equal" has no place. Separate educational facilities are inherently unequal.

Much has been made of the sudden and shocking character of the Supreme Court's ruling. No doubt it shocked millions, North and South, who had heretofore given little thought to the issue. It probably stunned the President himself. Yet the particular cases had been before the courts for years before their final resolution, which itself had the concurrence of briefs from the Justice Department. Great care, moreover, was taken in its implementation, which was placed in the hands of local courts permitted to employ guidelines reflecting local

situations, provided only that they require "a prompt and reasonable start toward full compliance," which then should proceed "with all deliberate speed."

In border states and in the North, considerable progress was made toward compliance within two years. In the deep South, however, it became clear that compliance would take time and might involve violence. In September, 1957, Little Rock, Arkansas, became the focal point of southern resistance when Governor Orval E. Faubus used the National Guard to prevent nine Negro children from entering that city's Central High School. President Eisenhower countered by providing the children with federal military protection, and they were subsequently enrolled.

Faubus' overwhelming victory in winning a third term as Arkansas' governor in August, 1958, was also an endorsement of his segregation stand and a signal to the rest of the South. When the election returns were in, Harry Ashmore, liberal editor of the Little Rock *Gazette*, gloomily predicted that the moderate position would now be "clearly untenable for any man in public life anywhere in the region. A period of struggle and turmoil lies ahead."

The handful of Negro students in Little Rock were subjected to such harassment by extremist white students that the local school board soon asked for a $2\frac{1}{2}$-year suspension of the integration program. The request came to the Supreme Court in September, 1958, when attorneys for the school board argued that it could not at present put integration into effect because of "the total opposition of the people and of the State Governor of Arkansas." Over a reasonable length of time, perhaps, the situation would change. Attorneys for the NAACP, led by their chief counsel, Thurgood Marshall, replied: "There can be no equality of justice for our people if the law steps aside, even for a moment, at the command of force and violence." The Supreme Court agreed and on September 12, 1958, unanimously denied the request. Seventeen days later it delivered an unprecedented written opinion on the case, in which, to underline their unanimity, all nine justices were listed as co-authors. This opinion declared:

The constitutional rights of respondents [Negro children] are not to be sacrificed or yielded to . . . violence and disorder. . . . The constitutional rights of children not to be discriminated against in school admissions on grounds of race or color declared by this court can neither be nullified openly and directly by state legislators or state executives or judicial officers, nor nullified by them through any evasive scheme for segregation.

The outlook, however, remained bleak. During the first integration year, 1955-1956, 450 school districts in the South had been integrated; in the following year, another 270 had been added; in the third, only 60 more; in the fourth, 1958-1959, only another dozen. Thus out of the 2,985 bi-racial school districts in the South, only 792 had been integrated, none in the deep South nor Virginia. A distinguished southern lawyer described the situation in these words: "It is like an army advancing. It first overruns the outposts. In the first two hours, it may advance two miles. Then it may hit the hard core of resistance and in the next two days, advance two yards. Now it means advancing from the beachhead, hedgerow by hedgerow, school district by school district, with a bitter fight . . . for each district."

Those in the fight, however, did not flag, least of all the Negroes themselves. Indeed, while concentrating first on the school issue, they soon broadened their campaign for equality until it encompassed every phase of life, just as repression and segregation did. In 1957 and in 1960, conforming to the Negro's rising militancy, Congress passed the first federal civil rights acts in almost a century (see p. 477). Broad at the outset, these acts, as adopted, were largely confined to the Negro's right to vote, and they made the procedure for federal intervention in this critical field so tortuous that even the nominal gains were nullified. Nevertheless, these two measures revived

dormant federal commitments. "I don't believe you can change the hearts of men with laws or decisions," President Eisenhower had said, urging caution in implementing the *Brown* ruling. A few years later, Martin Luther King, Jr., observed, "the law may not change the heart—but it can restrain the heartless." That much and more, sometimes to be sure with disheartening consequences, the law was to undertake (see pp. 857, 860).

THE "NEW LOOK"
IN FOREIGN POLICY

The Republicans, as we have seen (p. 827), took office promising a dynamic alternative to the "negative, futile and immoral policy of 'containment.'" They would "liberate" central Europe from communism's grip, "rollback" Soviet power in eastern Europe, and "unleash" Chiang Kai-shek in Asia. The architect of this ambitious program was to be John Foster Dulles who, as Eisenhower's Secretary of State, enjoyed extraordinary freedom of action. But Dulles soon proved to be more a man of words than acts.

An early test for the "new look" in Europe came suddenly in March, 1953, when Stalin died. The U.S.S.R. was in such turmoil over his successor that Malenkov, who emerged as the new premier but was obliged to share power with other aspirants, tried to abate outside pressure by talk of "peaceful coexistence" with capitalist countries. He also relaxed certain controls over Russian satellite peoples, a step which, in June, 1953, led to an uprising in East Berlin that quickly spread across all East Germany. This revolt, a precursor of others in 1956 (see p. 839), had to be suppressed by Soviet troops and only subsided when all hope had gone for "liberation" help from the Western occupied parts of Germany, or elsewhere.

"Rollback" soon followed "liberation" to the dustbin, with even costlier consequences. As early as 1950, in order to spread the cost of creating the proposed 96 NATO divisions (see p. 817), the French government, despite the profound anxieties of the people, had itself suggested the creation of a European Defense Community (EDC) tied to NATO, with non-member West German units merged into its joint force. An EDC treaty for this purpose, drawn up in May, 1952, was still being debated in France in December, 1953, when Dulles, in an effort to speed things along, threatened her with an "agonizing reappraisal" of American troop commitments on the Continent, leading to their ultimate withdrawal. The only practical outcome of this threat was the French Assembly's outright rejection of the EDC treaty in August, 1954. Following this "shattering blow," as Dulles called it, an alternative British plan was accepted by the United States, France and others in October. Under this plan, which went into effect in May, 1955, West Germany was granted full sovereignty as Japan had been earlier (see p. 808), admitted to NATO with full equality, and permitted to raise her own army of 12 divisions to become part of the NATO force.

West Germany's membership may have raised American hopes for NATO to a peak. The new German divisions, however, proved discouragingly slow in materializing, while economic and other factors, such as the yearning for the relaxation of tensions encouraged by the Russians' "peaceful coexistence" line, prompted the older European members gradually to curtail their own contributions. The overweening economizing of the Eisenhower administration, in turn, which in fact had given a touch of credibility to Dulles' "agonizing reappraisal" threat, hastened NATO's deterioration.

Eisenhower's personal pet goal was balancing the budget. This could only be accomplished by cutting massive military spending. Thus, in October, 1953, conforming to the President's guidelines, the National Security Council had announced a new addition to the "new look" which phrasemaker Dulles soon called "massive retaliation," and which others justified by one more phrase, "more bang for a buck."

"Rollback" had lost its urgency and its punch. Under the new "basic decision," dependence on costly ground forces would everywhere be reduced or eliminated. Nor would the United States be lured into any

more hateful little wars like that in Korea. Instead, the administration would simply let the communists in Moscow and Peking know that any new menaces to American security from those quarters would be met by American nuclear and thermonuclear assaults on their cities and civilians.

Since the United States had already loosed two nuclear bombs, her allies shuddered at the thought that she might become hardened to the practice. The Russians and the Chinese, however, refused to be bluffed. "Massive retaliation" simply informed them that they could do what they wished short of inciting total war. Aggression by infiltration, subversion, nationalist "fronts" and guerrilla "civil wars"—by intensive *political* means, in short—would now find the United States handcuffed by having narrowed the area of her own response to her traditional massive *military* rejoinder. Under the new policy, George Kennan wrote, the communists would now outdo themselves to fill "every nook and cranny in the basin of world power." They did, in fact, do so. Moreover, by the end of 1954, they had developed delivery systems for their own nuclear weapons, thereby confronting the Eisenhower administration, as Churchill put it, with a "balance of terror," and frightening later administrations with the "missile gap" (see p. 854). This confrontation gave Dulles ground for another empty verbal triumph—"brinksmanship," the art of going "to the brink of war," as he put it, without "being scared."

THE NEW NATIONALISM IN ASIA

An early test for the new "new look" in the Far East arose in the first months of 1954. Earlier, the nascent nationalism of colonial peoples in Asia, as in North Africa and the Middle East, had been inflamed by their commitment to World War II by such imperial powers as Britain, France, and Holland, with little or no consultation with "native" leaders. The wartime difficulties of the imperial powers sorely damaged their prestige and, as it turned out, sapped their power to withstand postwar nationalist movements.

Britain, the greatest of the imperial powers, was the first to yield to the inevitable in Asia as she had in the Middle East and in the Mediterranean theater (see p. 815). This step was made easier by her broader preparation for self-government, such as it was, of the native populations of many of her imperial lands. The victory of the Labor party in the British home elections of 1945 (see p. 807) also brought into office leaders more responsive to native claims than the Conservatives might have been. Thus, one after another in 1947 and 1948, such former British colonies as India (and newly created Pakistan), Ceylon, and Burma were granted independence, all but Burma choosing to remain in the British Commonwealth. A fifth British colony made up of the Malay States and neighboring settlements had gained a more limited degree of self-government by February, 1948, when a communist uprising, fomented by veteran party leaders in the local Chinese population, precipitated a long guerrilla war involving British forces. By 1957, the communist threat was sufficiently reduced for the Federation of Malaya to become a self-governing member of the Commonwealth, one that in 1963, with the addition of certain adjacent areas, was renamed the Federation of Malaysia.

The Dutch, less well equipped than the British to retain, or rather regain, their prewar Asian empire, proved less ready as well to let it go—to the embarrassment of United States policy in Europe and the Far East. During their wartime occupation of the Dutch East Indies (see p. 785), the Japanese had encouraged an anti-Dutch nationalist movement culminating in the creation of a puppet state, the Indonesian Republic. With Japan's fall, this republic had become virtually independent and when the Dutch, in an effort to regain their hold there, sent troops to the East Indies, they encountered strong resistance. During the fighting, the Dutch looked to the United States for help, and the Truman administration, aware of the need of the Dutch in NATO in Europe, felt impelled to give it. On the other hand, the administration was constrained by its effort to establish an anticolonial posture in the world. In the end, American pressure forced the Dutch, in 1949, reluctantly to yield self-government to Indonesia within a hastily formed Dutch-Indonesian Union. When this Union collapsed in 1954, the Republic of Indonesia, under the continuing leadership of Achmed Sokarno, became entirely independent. As unhappy over American dallying with the Dutch as the Dutch were over what they considered American interference in their internal affairs, Sokarno promptly assumed a "neutralist" position in the Cold War.

The French proved even more determined than the Dutch to retain their valuable Southeast Asia possessions centered in Indochina, a mid-nineteenth century creation including three old troubled kingdoms, Laos, Cambodia and Vietnam. With Britain and Holland on their way out as Asian powers, the United States wished to help the French, especially after the Red Chinese intervention in Korea in 1950 seemed to emphasize their aggressive intent.

THE VIETNAM TEST

The situation in Indochina differed in one major way from that in other European imperial domains overrun by Japan. Elsewhere, as in the Dutch East Indies, the Japanese had found it advantageous to employ Western-educated native leaders as their occupation administrators, rather than the more questionably loyal European colonial civil servants who had remained in Asia. They also sought to strengthen the allegiance of these native leaders by catering to their political and cultural nationalism. In Indochina, the Japanese had less need of native leaders because the pro-Vichy French there were Axis-oriented. Thus the nationalist Indochinese natives, more profoundly hostile to repressive French imperialism than the natives of the British Empire, were driven underground. Here, like the "partisans" in Nazi-occupied countries of Europe during the war, they soon fell under the domination of highly trained communists who had begun to work underground against French rule long before World War II. The principal nationalist group in Indochina was the Vietminh in Vietnam. By 1945, it had become little more than the nationalist front for the Vietnamese communist party under the veteran Russian-trained Ho Chi Minh.

By V-J day, the Vietminh itself had liberated part of northern Vietnam from the Japanese and in September, 1945, had proclaimed the Democratic Republic of Vietnam, with Hanoi its capital and Ho Chi Minh its President. In March, 1946, during the struggle for power in postwar France between the Gaullists and others, the new Vietnam administration was recognized as a "free state" within a French Union hastily established like that of the Dutch (see p. 834) in imitation of the British Commonwealth, but hardly so liberal. In June, Ho was invited to Paris to consult on the future of the new state under this ad hoc arrangement, a mission from which he returned in September wholly disenchanted with the French attitude toward real independence.

By then, local French commanders striving to set up a separatist regime in Cochin China, Vietnam's southernmost province, had clashed repeatedly with Vietminh terrorists seeking to make good Hanoi's claim to over-all control. By December, other clashes in the north had grown into a general war. The rivalry grew more intense after June, 1949, when the French, having successfully set up former native rulers as puppets in Cambodia and Laos, now officially tried the same tactic in Vietnam. Their puppet here was Bao Dai, scion of an old ruling family, who had no popular following and preferred Paris to Saigon, his new capital.

The proclamation of the communist Chinese Republic in October, 1949, gave a tremendous boost to Vietminh morale and soon to Vietminh strength as well. Early in 1950, Red China formally recognized the Vietminh regime in Hanoi, making it, in effect, more a captive of communism than ever and less able to sustain its avowed na-

tionalist stance. The United States and Britain, especially concerned this time about French support for NATO in Europe, responded by recognizing the Saigon regime of Bao Dai. More than that, the Truman administration began to offset Red Chinese aid to Ho with American aid to Bao.

The Chinese military intervention in the Korean War in October, 1950, gave the United States almost as much concern about the future of Vietnam as of Korea; and once this war ended, the United States greatly enlarged its assistance to the beleaguered French. By the end of 1953, the Eisenhower administration found itself paying two-thirds of the cost of the French military effort, or about $1 billion per year. But it could not save the French after their main army, early in 1954, allowed itself to be trapped in the untenable fortress of Dienbienphu, near the Laotian border.

Eisenhower had already stated that the fall of Indochina "would be of a most terrible significance to the United States of America." Southeast Asia, he added, was of "transcendent importance" to American security; a communist victory in Vietnam, with Red China support, might find all free governments in the Far East soon toppling like a row of dominoes, a phrase to become famous later on. Did he order Dulles, then, to warn Moscow and Peking of "massive retaliation"? Did he order the bombs to rain upon them? He did not. Dulles, with Admiral Arthur R. Radford, Chairman of the Joint Chiefs of Staff, instead, went to Congress with a request for authority to order an American air-strike on Dienbienphu from navy carriers. But Congressional leaders warned them that another Korea, let alone a war with Red China, would be more unpalatable than ever to the American people and their representatives. Eisenhower, on his part, refused to sanction unilateral American military action. On April 10, Dulles flew to London to seek British support, but was sternly rebuffed.

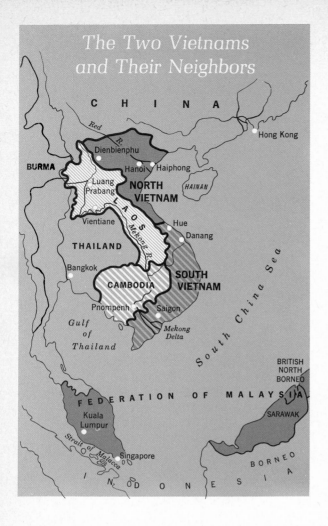

The Two Vietnams and Their Neighbors

certain to end with something less than complete victory over the communists.

The Geneva armistice agreement, adopted on July 20, provided for a military truce between the Vietminh and the French military command, the latter openly acting for its Saigon puppet regime. The truce assigned to the Vietminh the land north of the 17th parallel, to the French the land south of it. Like the Korean division at the 38th parallel, the one in Vietnam was explicitly "provisional"; but like the former, and like the earlier one in Germany, it soon hardened. One element favoring Vietminh acceptance of the agreement was the proposal for Vietnam-wide elections to unify the country, a proposal independently supported by the United States the next day, provided such elections were "supervised by the United Nations to insure that they are conducted fairly." The "final declaration" at Geneva, signed by no one, stipulated that the elections should take place by July, 1956. It also recognized the independence of Cambodia and Laos.

Not until January, 1955, did the French turn back the Saigon regime to Bao Dai and his "strong man," Prime Minister Ngo Dinh Diem. Fearful of a regimented communist victory in the 1956 elections, Diem found reasons for putting off his approval, not least that, after all, his government had not been a party to the agreement. Ten years later the elections seemed more distant than ever. Meanwhile, the Red Chinese had begun to assist in the further "communization" of North Vietnam, while the United States gradually increased its own aid to Diem's authoritarian regime in the South.

On the day after the Geneva agreements, July 21, 1954, President Eisenhower had stated that the Geneva armistice "contains features which we do not like," but "in compliance with the obligations and principles . . . of the United Nations Charter, the United States will not use force to disturb the settlement." He added: "The renewal of Communist aggression would be viewed by us as a matter of grave concern." In October, 1954, he added further, in a letter

When an administration trial balloon about "putting our boys in" only resoundingly confirmed congressional opinion of the people's attitude, the "new look" grew paler than ever.

By the time Dienbienphu, and the French with it, capitulated to Ho Chi Minh on May 7, 1954, the representatives of nine powers, including France, Red China, the U.S.S.R., Britain, and the United States, and the two Vietnams and their neighbors, had already convened at Geneva to work out some arrangements in the light of the inevitable collapse. Korea was also on the agenda, perhaps simply to justify Secretary Dulles' presence. In any case, at a time when McCarthyism was at its very crest and the State Department most demoralized by it (see p. 829), Dulles, fearful of "Asia First" opinion at home, absented himself from the Geneva discussions on Vietnam which were

to Diem, his willingness "to examine" with him "how an intelligent program of American aid given directly to your government can assist Vietnam . . . in developing and maintaining a strong, viable state, capable of resisting attempted subversion or aggression through military means." But such aid must be founded upon "performance on the part of the Government of Vietnam in undertaking needed reforms." Diem's government proved slow in undertaking reforms, but the United States, at the same time, was reluctant to cast him adrift.

The Geneva agreements had promised that civilians, north or south, would be permitted to move freely to whichever "regrouping zone" they wished. Within two years almost a million people had fled southward from the terrors of North Vietnam communization, and half a million more were forcibly restrained from joining them. It was in this period that the "Viet Cong" first became heard of in the South as a terrorist group. No doubt Diem's suppression of local government, his installation of cruel favorites to rule the countryside, his political executions and other acts, served to arouse many South Vietnamese themselves to violent retaliation. No doubt, too, certain of the "refugees" from North Vietnam had come to organize favorably disposed South Vietnamese into communist, or Viet Cong, cadres. By 1958, the Viet Cong had begun guerrilla attacks against the Diem regime, soon leading to assassinations of village chiefs. By the next year it was openly receiving assistance from the north, and in September, 1960, was formally acknoweldged by Ho as the National Front for the Liberation of South Vietnam. Ho now stepped up his assistance to the Viet Cong, much of it coming over the Ho Chi Minh Trail, the natural route through northern Laos, a region dominated by the Pathet Lao, the Hanoi-backed communist force in that neighboring land. The Eisenhower administration, meanwhile, accelerated the pace of its own intervention in Laos as well as in South Vietnam, a policy it bequeathed to later administrations (see Chapter 31).

A WALL OF WORDS

After the Geneva conference, whose results were widely criticized in the United States and elsewhere as a second Munich, Dulles sought to retrieve American standing by forming a collective organization in Southeast Asia that he hoped would serve as a counterpart to NATO in Europe. But he was promptly rebuffed by such significant new South Asia countries as India, Burma, Indonesia and Ceylon which resented American intrusion and feared that United States efforts to lock in Red China on the south might simply provoke her to new aggressive acts. Two mainland countries, Pakistan and Thailand, along with the Philippines and Australia and New Zealand, proved somewhat more receptive. At Manila in September, 1954, they met with the United States, Britain and France and signed the Manila Pact creating the Southeast Asia Treaty Organization (SEATO). Laos, Cambodia and South Vietnam, unable under the Geneva agreements to make alliances, were nevertheless included in the SEATO arrangements by a special protocol. These arrangements, however, were far weaker than NATO's (see p. 816). They merely committed the signatory powers to meet any common danger in accordance with its constitutional system.

Dulles continued to pretend that the "massive retaliation" policy remained meaningful. "The deterrent power we thus create," he said after the Manila meeting, "can protect many as effectively as it protects one." But the Philippines were not convinced and Dulles gave them a verbal promise that the United States would respond immediately in the islands if they were attacked.

On his way home from Manila, Dulles visited Chiang Kai-shek on Taiwan and on December 2 made a SEATO-type pact with him. Both parties agreed, however, to try first to settle peacefully any disputes they became involved in with other countries. By this provision Chiang was only the more securely "leashed," not "unleashed." Dulles' visit to Taiwan had been prompted by Red China's bombing of Quemoy and Matsu, two Free China islands just off her shore, during the Manila meeting. His pact with Chiang led the Red Chinese, in January, 1955, to talk of actually seizing these islands, and Congress hastened to affirm the President's authority to use American troops to repel them. On January 18, Red China did seize the island of Yikiang somewhat to the north; but the administration decided that Yikiang's protection did not come under the agreement with Chiang.

Between the SEATO countries in the Far East and the NATO countries in the West lay the strategic Middle East, where Arab nationalism, already inflamed by the creation of Israel in 1948 (see p. 815), was aggravated after 1952 by the overthrow of King Farouk in Egypt. A new Egyptian republic emerged in place of the monarchy, and Colonel Gamel Abdel Nasser emerged as its strong man with ambitions to unite the neighboring Arab lands under Egyptian leadership. An elementary first step was the elimination of remaining vestiges of colonialism, most provokingly evident in Britain's continuing control of a powerful military base at the Suez canal. Dulles hoped to draw Nasser's growing strength toward the West by pressing the British to yield the base, which they reluctantly did in October, 1954.

Dulles by then, for more than a year, had been promoting a Middle East defense organization to close the gap between SEATO and NATO. Greece and Turkey had been admitted to NATO in 1952; and in April, 1954, Turkey and Pakistan, a SEATO member, had signed a mutual defense treaty. In February, 1955, Turkey and her neighbor, Iraq, meeting at Baghdad, Iraq's capital, signed a similar treaty, to which, at Dulles' behest, Britain, Pakistan and Iran also subscribed in October. These arrangements became known as the Baghdad Pact, under which the Middle East Treaty Organization (METO) was formed, one more in keeping with SEATO's weaknesses than NATO's relative strengths.

President Eisenhower with Dag Hammarskjold and John Foster Dulles at Geneva, July, 1955.

To the confusion of all parties, Dulles kept the United States out of this organization. Widespread American sympathy for Israel, especially among Jews who contributed heavily to the urban vote, constrained the administration from appearing to huddle too closely with Arab powers who had sworn to destroy the Jewish state. A second reason for Dulles' action was the fear that overt American participation in METO, which ran across Russia's southern frontier the way SEATO ran across Red China's, might be the more provocative of Soviet retaliation.

Dulles was not the only one to abstain from METO. Nasser himself, who was particularly to be lured into the organization, also stayed out, to Dulles' great discomfiture. Nasser resented the inclusion of Iraq, a fellow Arab state which preferred American aid to Arab unity. He also wished freedom of action in playing off the U.S.S.R. and the West against one another to Egypt's national advantage. India represented an even more important rift in Dulles' verbal cordon. Her position had become clear in April, 1955, at the Bandung conference in Indonesia. Indonesia's President Sokarno called this meeting of 29 African as well as Asian nations, most of them newly independent, "the first international conference of colored peoples in the history of mankind." Here India's Prime Minister Nehru denounced NATO as the shield of colonialism, and with his colleagues joined Premier Chou En-lai of Red China in endorsing "neutrality" *against* the West.

While Dulles was heightening tensions in exotic lands, the U.S.S.R. and even Red China seemed bent for the moment on relaxing them. In May, 1955, the Soviets agreed to end the four-power occupation of Austria and accept her independence despite her Western leanings. They next acknowledged the independence of the communist regime Marshal Tito had set up in Yugoslavia in 1948. As though acting by arrangement with Moscow, Red China now began to release American airmen whom it had been holding in prison as spies for a year.

In June, 1955, the heads of the Big Four powers—the United States, Britain, France and the U.S.S.R.—met at their first "Summit Conference" at Geneva. President Eisenhower tried to make the most of the meeting by boldly proposing that the Soviets and the United States agree to permit aerial reconnaissance of each other's military installations. The Soviets rejected this plan, but it did mark the start of continuous efforts to check the arms race, which bore fruit in the treaty of July 25, 1963, limiting the testing of nuclear weapons (see p. 854).

The hopeful meeting at Geneva was followed in February, 1956, by the denunciation of Stalin as a tyrant and a monster by the Russian Communist party head, Nikita Khrushchev. Khrushchev especially stigmatized Stalin's "unrealistic appreciation" of western determination to defend Korea by arms, and he deplored the Soviet involvement in the whole "risky" business. Such words clearly burned the ears of Chou En-

lai in Red China, following his own successful intervention in Korea (see p. 821). Chou was quick to assert Red China's "legitimacy" as against Khrushchev's "bourgeois revisionism" in the monolithic Leninist-Stalinist succession, and the rift between the two communist giants widened thereafter.

The dramatic split in communist ranks itself hastened the end of the East-West "thaw." The Chinese challenge made Khrushchev feel increasingly obliged to accommodate the nostalgic Stalinists in the U.S.S.R., even at the risk of alienating larger segments of his own crisis-weary population. Thus, when, in the wake of the "de-Stalinization" foray, some Soviet satellite leaders hoped for greater freedom in managing their countries' affairs, they were rudely disillusioned. It is true that Poland, under Wladyslaw Gomulka, was permitted to soften somewhat the repressions of the police state. But in Hungary, resistance to Russian authority was crushed by the Red Army in November, 1956; and in June, 1958, the Hungarian Reds announced that Imre Nagy, the resistance chief who had been abducted during the uprising after a promise of safe conduct, had been sentenced to death and executed for treason. "I cannot think," said President Eisenhower, "of any incident that could have, and has, more shocked the civilized world." But the opportunity Nagy had given the administration to implement Dulles' policy of "liberation" in Europe again had been allowed to slip by.

The futility of METO, with dire consequences for the future of NATO as well, had by then also been disclosed. In February, 1955, Israeli forces invaded the Gaza strip, a contested area on their Egyptian border. Nasser's difficulty in dislodging them underscored his military weakness and in September he made a deal with the Soviets to exchange Egyptian cotton for communist arms and training. Still hoping for Egyptian friendship, the United States rebuffed Israel's bid for offsetting military assistance. Instead, in cooperation with Britain, Dulles tried to woo Nasser with economic aid in the construction of the Aswan Dam to harness the power of the Nile. Continuing anti-Western gestures by the Egyptians, however, persuaded Dulles to cancel this offer on July 19, 1956. One week later, Egypt, in retaliation, boldly announced the nationalization of the Suez Canal and her intention of using canal tolls to build the dam herself.

In October, 1956, Israel launched an invasion of Egypt with the announced objective of destroying the bases from which Egyptian raids had been made on Israeli territory. This action was followed by a sudden Anglo-French invasion of the Suez area. But Eisenhower and Dulles opposed their allies' use of force and, to their consternation, at the U.N. the United States joined the Soviet Union in condemning it. The General Assembly then voted to organize a U.N. police force to supervise a cease-fire, but only the threat of unilateral Soviet intervention through "volunteers" induced the British and French to accept the U.N. call for peace on November 6. After American and Soviet warnings, Israel also agreed to withdraw from Egyptian territory, and on November 15, the first detachments of a U.N. Emergency Force arrived in Egypt to oversee the settlement. Nothing was solved in the Middle East by these steps and the Western alliance itself was badly shaken.

When the Soviets continued to arm Arab nations, METO members, in turn, called on the United States to join the Baghdad Pact. This the administration refused to do lest Soviet intervention be accelerated. Instead, in a special message to Congress in January, 1957, the President asked for endorsement of the "Eisenhower Doctrine," a unilateral warning to the U.S.S.R. that the United States would defend the whole Middle East against Soviet attack. Congress foresaw no direct Soviet attack, only increased Soviet subversion as Kennan had forecast (see p. 833). It withheld approval until March when, by a joint resolution, it gave the President, at his discretion, the power to use American forces to help any Middle East

nation, at its request, to resist "armed attack from any country controlled by international communism."

THE ELECTION OF 1956

Although there had been widespread anticipation of a business depression following the end of intensive wartime demand in 1945, the first postwar decade saw only two minor recessions, and in 1956, as in 1928, the Republicans were able to campaign on the slogan of "Peace, Progress and Prosperity." Failures in foreign affairs only seemed to inspire public sympathy for "Ike"; and his heart attack of 1955 and serious surgery in 1956 brought him closer still to the common lot. Inordinately dependent on Eisenhower's personal appeal, Republican leaders thus urged him to run again despite his questionable health, and at the San Francisco convention in August they renominated him by acclamation, along with Vice-president Nixon.

The President's illnesses and Nixon's controversial reputation made many Democrats feel that they had a chance to re-enter the White House. Despite Truman's opposition this time, Adlai E. Stevenson easily won renomination at the Democratic convention in Chicago, with Senator Kefauver becoming his running-mate. The Democrats tried to exploit economic discontent, notably in the farm belt, to criticize the failures in foreign policy, and to capitalize on the President's ill health by dwelling on the threat of a Nixon succession. But "Ike's" personal appeal overcame all issues and helped him win even more decisively than in 1952. Polling 34,751,000 votes to 25,427,000 for Stevenson, "Ike" received 58 per cent of the popular vote. In the electoral college, he won by 457 to 73. The Democrats, nevertheless, maintained their 49-to-47 margin in the Senate and increased by two seats their comfortable majority in the House. Not since the time of Zachary Taylor, had a president been elected without carrying at least one house of Congress for his party.

THE SHOCK OF THE SPUTNIK

In his second inaugural address, on January 21, 1957, Eisenhower said: "We

840

honor, no less in this divided world than in a less tormented time, the people of Russia. We do not dread, rather do we welcome, their progress in education and industry." Only a few months later the American people suffered a shock which suggested that they would not, after all, welcome Soviet progress quite so heartily. On August 26, 1957, the Russians reported the first successful tests of an intercontinental ballistic missile (ICBM). Within six weeks, on October 4, they electrified the world by using the missile's rocket engine to launch man's first space satellite, Sputnik I. On November 3, the Soviets sent up Sputnik II, carrying a small dog.

During the course of the next year, the successful launching of four American satellites brought some comfort, which again was dissipated by the Russian success on January 2, 1959, with Lunik I, the first space vehicle to traverse the full distance of about 250,000 miles to the moon. Lunik did not hit the moon but roared into space to become the first artificial planet in orbit around the sun. Two months later, on March 10, the United States successfully put a planet of its own in orbit. The next stage in space exploration involved putting a man in orbit around the earth. This feat, and even more spectacular ones, were accomplished in the 'sixties.

The shock of the Sputniks led Congress in September, 1958, to pass the National Defense Education Act. To stimulate scientific education, this act offered loans and scholarships to qualified high school and college students and grants to educational institutions for laboratories and equipment. At the same time, borrowers and assisted scholars were required to disclaim any communist sympathies and to take an exceptional oath of allegiance to the United States. Certain schools and colleges refused to participate in the program because of this element of thought control, which also alienated many outstanding students. Campus unrest was aggravated by the greatly enlarged contributions of government agencies and business corporations to university scientific research which drew faculty members from

the classroom and left students with a feeling of neglect.

REPUBLICANISM UNDER STRESS

During Eisenhower's second administration, the communists made much of their manifest successes in the space race which helped impress many of the new nations to whom the United States often seemed to be shuffling along with a slowdown in business expansion, a disturbing level of unemployment, and serious racial strife. Their new standing in the world prompted the Russians, as Kennan had foretold, to promote new crises in Asia, in the Middle East, in divided Germany, and in Cuba and Latin America generally. In July, 1958, the United States and Britain were impelled to send troops to Lebanon and Jordan to offset Soviet and Egyptian pressure on pro-Western governments there. In August the Chinese Reds renewed their systematic bombing of Quemoy and Matsu. In October Khrushchev created a new storm over the flow of refugees from East to West Berlin and demanded the latter's demilitarization. The administration held firm, but the issue remained hot.

Still nearer home, meanwhile, Latin America had begun to boil. In April and May, 1958, Vice-president Nixon visited a number of Latin-American countries in an effort to revive friendly feeling (see p. 818). Nixon was hostilely received, and in Venezuela and Peru he was stoned. When on January 1, 1959, Fidel Castro established his government in Cuba after his five-year struggle to overthrow the hateful Batista, many Americans saluted his success. But it was not long before Castro began using Cuba as a base for exploiting the deep antipathy toward the United States in the rest of Latin America and Khrushchev began using Castro for his own ends.

The Eisenhower administration had come into office crusading against Democratic corruption. In mid-1958 it was itself besmirched by corruption even more far-reaching than that it had denounced. Revelations of scandals soon forced the resignation of high administration and Republican party officials including no less a personage than Sherman Adams, the confidential and powerful Assistant to the President. The depth of the party's trouble was soon disclosed in the 1958 congressional elections, when it suffered a disaster comparable only to those of early New Deal years. In the Senate the Democrats widened their two-vote margin to an overwhelming 64 to 34. In the House their already substantial lead of 235 to 200 was broadened to 283 to 153.

The shadow cast by the 1958 elections was only deepened by the last two years of the Eisenhower administration during which, with the resignation of Sherman Adams in September, 1958, and the death of Dulles in May, 1959, the President was largely on his own. On the domestic front, unemployment and inadequate economic growth persisted. In certain states, such as the coal regions of Pennsylvania, West Virginia, and Kentucky, and the old industrial regions of New England, hard times had become a permanent part of the way of life, and little was done to bring the people in these "distressed areas" into the mainstream of American progress. In other parts of the country, unemployment was especially acute among Negroes, who were discriminated against by unions and management alike, and in any case, because of the lack of educational opportunities, were prevented from seeking jobs on white-collar levels where personnel was most in demand. While industrial employment remained slack, conditions in agriculture drove many from the farms. The continued rapid mechanization of agriculture and the operation of the price supports for staples both favored the large-farm corporation, which needed relatively few hands to produce massive crops. Farm employment and farm-family income thus tended to fall off and add to the drag on the economy.

While such general tendencies hurt the Republican administration, more specific acts also cost them dearly. One of the most abrasive of these was the Landrum-Griffin Act for stricter control of unions, passed in September, 1959. This federal measure was supplemented in many states by so-called "right-to-work" laws eliminating the closed or union shop. While these measures cost the Republicans much of the support "Ike" had won for them among the rank and file of American workers, the President's own handling of the longest steel strike in American history in 1959, which resulted in significant union gains and significant rises in steel prices, angered the growing middle classes.

The administration was also hurt by new crises in foreign affairs. Late in 1959, Nixon visited a jovial Khrushchev in Russia and the ground was prepared for a new summit conference subsequently scheduled for May 16, 1960, in Paris. On May 5, however, came news of the shooting down of an American U-2 reconnaissance plane over Soviet territory. Before acknowledging the truth of Soviet protests that the plane was on a regular spying mission, the administration trapped itself in a web of denials, and half truths. Khrushchev arrived in Paris for the scheduled meeting, demanding American apologies and punishment of those responsible for the flight. Eisenhower declined to apologize, took full responsibility himself, indicated that such flights might well continue, and stayed away from Paris.

While East-West relations thus deteriorated, relations among the anti-communist powers also worsened. Many Japanese resented the continuing United States occupation of Okinawa and continuing United States stress on the militarization of their homeland. When Eisenhower visited the Far East in June, 1960, anti-American demonstrations in Tokyo became so militant he was officially advised to omit Japan from his itinerary since his personal security could not be assured. France, meanwhile, bled white in her interminable struggle to retain Algeria in North Africa, was saved from civil war at home only by the ascent of the imperious Charles de Gaulle as Premier in June, 1958. In December, de Gaulle was elected president of the Fifth French Republic, virtually with dictatorial powers. In love with himself and the traditions of his country, he was to prove intractable, once more, as an ally. The violence that broke out in the Congo when Belgium reluctantly agreed to the formation of the Republic of the Congo in June, 1960, further weakened Western unity and raised the curtain on a new region for "East-West" conflict.

THE
ELECTION OF 1960

Eight years in office proved a great strain on the Republican party, especially since it had failed to balance the budget, reduce the national debt, end the upward wage-price spiral, restore farm income, and significantly cut taxes—all goals dear to the heart of the conservative wing. It had also failed to roll back the communists and restore the good old days of continental security for which Dulles himself often expressed a strong nostalgia. The Republican moderates had had their chance and had failed. When the time came to choose a candidate at the 1960 convention in Chicago, the conservatives were so fully in command of the party machinery that the liberal Republican Governor of New York, Nelson A. Rockefeller, who won such a brilliant victory in 1958 when most other Republicans were going down to crashing defeats, had already been warned to stand aside. On the first ballot the convention named Richard M. Nixon for president. As his running mate it chose Henry Cabot Lodge, American delegate to the United Nations.

The Democrats, heartened by the Twenty-second Amendment which kept the still popular "Ike" from seeking a third term, had begun to look to 1960 even before the 1956 campaign. Many hats were in the ring; but after his extraordinary performance in a series of primaries, Senator John F. Kennedy of Massachusetts clearly overshadowed the opposition (see p. 851). At the party convention in Los Angeles he won on the first ballot. Fearful of the effects of the

strong civil rights stand of the northern wing of the party, and of Kennedy's Catholicism, the Democrats, in an attempt to hold the South, prevailed upon Senator Lyndon B. Johnson of Texas to run for vice-president.

The campaign was highlighted by the first TV debates between presidential candidates, from which Kennedy seemed to have gained more than his opponent. Nixon suffered from the luke-warm support of "Ike" himself and from his own checkered past. Kennedy's winning margin was a mere 113,000, out of a record 68.8 million votes cast. What probably saved him from defeat

Election of 1960

ALASKA
HAWAII
Electoral Vote
Kennedy 303   Nixon 219
Byrd 15

(when as popular a Protestant might have won an easy victory) was the solid support he received from Catholics and Negroes. At least 70 per cent of such voters, according to reliable estimates, endorsed him. The first Catholic president, Kennedy, at 43, was also the youngest man ever to be elected. He soon surrounded himself with young advisers pledged, like himself, to get the country moving again across "new frontiers."

Readings

Asterisk indicates that book is available in paperback.

O. T. Barck, Jr., *A History of the United States Since 1945* * (1965), affords a useful survey. See also E. F. Goldman, *The Crucial Decade—and After, America 1945-1960* * (1960); and John Brooks, *The Great Leap, The Past Twenty-Five Years in America* (1966).

H. S. Truman, *Memoirs* * (2 vols., 1955); Cabell Phillips, *The Truman Presidency* (1966); and two biographies, Jonathan Daniels, *The Man From Independence* (1950), and Alfred Steinberg, *The Man From Missouri* (1962), tell Truman's story. D. D. Eisenhower, *The White House Years, Mandate for Change 1953-1956* * (1963), and *Waging Peace 1956-1961* (1965), are the General's own account. See also R. J. Donovan, *Eisenhower, The Inside Story* (1956); E. J. Hughes, *The Ordeal of Power, A Political Memoir of the Eisenhower Years* * (1963); and E. L. Dale, Jr., *Conservatives in Power, a Study in Frustration* (1960), an economic memoir. On other political aspirants in the early postwar years see S. G. Brown, *Conscience in Politics: Adlai E. Stevenson in the 1950's* (1961); W. S. White, *The Taft Story* (1954), and K. M. Schmidt, *Henry Wallace: Quixotic Crusader* (1960). Useful analyses of voter habits include V. O. Key, Jr., *The Responsible Electorate, Rationality in Presidential Voting 1936-1960* (1966); Samuel Lubell, *The Future of American Politics* * (1952), and *Revolt of the Moderates* (1956); Heinz Eulau, *Class and Party in the Eisenhower Years* (1962); and C. W. Mills, *White Collar* * (1951). L. L. Gerson, *The Hyphenate in Recent American Politics and Diplomacy* (1964), is an illuminating special study. On the far right and related issues, see Richard Hofstadter, *The Paranoid Style in American Politics and Other Essays* (1965). On the far left, see Earl Latham, *The Communist Controversy in Washington: From the New Deal to McCarthy* (1966); and D. A. Shannon, *The Decline of American Communism: A History of the Communist Party of the United States Since 1945* (1959).

Useful introductions to foreign affairs include John Spanier, *American Foreign Policy Since World War II* * (1962); C. V. Crabb, Jr., *American Foreign Policy in The Nuclear Age* (1965); and W. G. Carleton, *The Revolution in American Foreign Policy* * (1964). See also M. F. Herz, *Beginnings of the Cold War* (1966), and N. A. Graebner, *Cold War Diplomacy 1945-1960* * (1962), which includes documents. On wartime conferences see Herbert Feis, *Churchill, Roosevelt, Stalin* (1957), and *Between War and Peace; The Potsdam Conference* (1960); and J. L. Snell, ed., *The Meaning of Yalta* (1956). Walter Millis, ed., *The Forrestal Diaries* (1951), is illuminating. See also N. A. Graebner, *The New Isolationism* (1956), presenting Senator Taft's views. G. F. Kennan, *Russia and the West Under Lenin and Stalin* * (1961); and D. J. Dallin, *Soviet Foreign Policy after Stalin* (1961), illuminate the Russian side. L. M. Goodrich and E. I. Hambro, *Charter of the United Nations: Commentary and Documents* (1949), is standard. See also F. O. Wilcox and H. F. Haviland, Jr., *The United States and the United Nations* (1961). *Everyman's United Nations* (1964 ed.) is the official "basic history." T. R. Fehrenbach, *This Kind of Peace* (1966), is a sharp critique of the U.N.

Hajo Holborn, *American Military Government* (1947), is good on the occupation of Germany. E. O. Reischauer, *The United States and Japan* * (1957) deals with the occupation of that country. Herbert Feis, *Foreign Aid and Foreign Policy* (1964), affords a useful survey. R. E. Osgood, *NATO: The Entangling Alliance* (1962), is basic. Herbert Feis, *The China Tangle* * (1953); and Tang Tsou, *America's Failure in China 1941-1950* (1963), help unravel that subject. See also, A. D. Barnett, *Communist China and Asia: Challenge to American Policy* * (1960), and Robert Blum, *The United States and China in World Affairs* (1966). David Rees, *Korea, The Limited War* (1964); and Robert Leckie,

Conflict, The History of the Korean War * (1962), are two good accounts. J. W. Spanier, *The Truman-MacArthur Controversy and the Korean War* * (1959), is excellent.

The loyalty question is discussed from different points of view in R. K. Carr, *The House Un-American Activities Committee 1945-1950* (1952); Walter Gellhorn, *Security, Loyalty, and Science* (1950), and *The States and Subversion* (1952); and J. W. Caughey, *In Clear and Present Danger* (1958). James Rorty and Moshe Decter make a close examination of the evidence in *McCarthy and the Communists* (1954). Richard Rovere, *Senator Joe McCarthy* * (1959), places the accuser in context. Alistair Cooke, *A Generation on Trial* (1950), is illuminating on the Hiss case. Whittaker Chambers, *Witness* (1952), is an extraordinary personal document. Alger Hiss, *In the Court of Public Opinion* (1957), is a weaker attempt at defense. C. P. Curtis, *The Oppenheimer Case, The Trial of a Security System* (1955), affords an able legal analysis.

J. R. Beal, *John Foster Dulles* (1959); and Richard Goold-Adams, *John Foster Dulles: A Reappraisal* (1962), are helpful. J. C. Campbell, *Defense of the Middle East* * (1960), is informative. From the vast and largely controversial literature on the Vietnam war, the following may be suggested; Ellen Hammer, *The Struggle for Indochina* (1954); R. H. Fifield, *The Diplomacy of Southeast Asia* (1958); B. B. Fall, *The Two Viet-Nams* (1963); Robert Shaplen, *The Lost Revolution* (1965); and American Friends Service Committee, *Peace in Vietnam, A New Approach to Southeast Asia* * (1966). Theodore Draper, *Castro's Revolution: Myths and Realities* * (1962), is outstanding. On other phases of Latin American relations see, D. M. Dozer, *Are We Good Neighbors? Three Decades of Inter-American Relations 1930-1960* (1959).

Domestic issues under Truman and Eisenhower are well covered in the general works cited above. Useful special studies include, Joel Seidman, *American Labor from Defense to Reconversion* (1953); H. C. Millis and E. C. Brown, *From the Wagner Act to Taft-Hartley* (1950); Murray Benedict and O. C. Stine, *The Agricultural Commodity Programs: Two Decades of Experience* (1956); Lauren Soth, *Farm Trouble in an Age of Plenty* (1957); the Editors of *Fortune*, *The Changing American Market* (1955); A. A. Berle, *The 20th Century Capitalist Revolution* * (1954); and J. K. Galbraith, *American Capitalism* * (1952), and *The Affluent Society* * (1958).

The basic introduction to the Negro Revolution is Gunnar Myrdal, *An American Dilemma* * (2 vols., 1944). Talcott Parsons and K. B. Clark, eds., *The American Negro* (1966), is an indispensable deepening and updating of Myrdal and much more besides. D. R. Matthews and J. W. Prothro, *Negroes and the New Southern Politics* (1966), places the Negro voter in the social setting. J. H. Franklin, *From Slavery to Freedom, A History of American Negroes* (1956 ed.), and Loren Miller, *The Petitioners, The Story of the Supreme Court of the United States and the Negro* (1966) supply essential background. The 1954 desegregation decision and other Warren decisions may be found in H. M. Christman, ed., *The Public Papers of Chief Justice Earl Warren* * (1966 ed.). Anthony Lewis, *Portrait of a Decade, The Second American Revolution* (1964), is an outstanding "first-hand account of the struggle for Civil Rights from 1954-1964." Also excellent on this decade is L. E. Lomax, *The Negro Revolt* * (1962). M. R. Konvitz, *Expanding Liberties, Freedom's Gains in Postwar America* (1966), is authoritative on the new legal environment. T. D. Clark, *The Emerging South* (1961), presents that section's own conflicts illuminatingly. Martin Luther King, Jr., *Stride Toward Freedom* * (1958), and *Why We Can't Wait* * (1964), are parts of the testament of the Negro leader. R. P. Warren, *Who Speaks for the Negro?* * (1966), is a superb anthology of the rank and file's own words.

T. H. White, *The Making of the President* * (1960), is excellent on the election of 1960. See also, T. C. Sorensen, *Kennedy* (1965); and R. M. Nixon, *Six Crises* (1962).

CHAPTER THIRTY-ONE

Writing in *The New York Times Magazine* in August, 1966, less than ten years after the first man-made satellite, Sputnik I, rose a short distance into space (see p. 840), Walter Sullivan, the *Times'* science editor, raised the question, "What Earthly Use is the Moon?" His answers were very earthly, in terms commonplace to us:

"The moon has virtually no atmosphere. . . . Its surface materials have therefore not been oxydized in the manner of earth rocks. . . . The moon may thus open new vistas in chemistry and mineralogy.

"What if the lunar rocks prove rich in material useful to our technology? Can it be

The New World
of the 'Sixties

shipped to earth to augment our depleting resources?

"Some . . . believe such shipments will be feasible and economical. They note that the difficulty of lifting heavy payloads from the earth to the moon is no indication of what it would cost to reverse the process. . . . The moon . . . has no air and much less gravity" than the earth; thus "escape velocity" there is but one-sixth of that required here. A moon vehicle bound for earth could be launched by "a power plant on the moon. . . . The only fuel needed en route would be for guidance."

Sullivan continued:

There are other possible uses of the lunar environment, based either on its low gravity or its absence of air. As our knowledge of chemistry, metallurgy, and solid-state electronic devices becomes more advanced it is likely that many industrial processes will emerge that must be carried out in a deep vacuum. On the moon [where the natural] vacuum is more nearly complete than any achievable in ordinary laboratories, . . . that would mean out-of-doors and some have proposed that the moon may therefore become the home of specialized industries.

"A lunar colony," moreover, "could be largely self-sustaining," for "studies of meteorites and observations of stellar spectra (which indicate the chemical composition

847

of the stars) show that essentially the same elements, with the same properties, abound everywhere." Thus on the moon as on earth we may expect to find even those elements "required to generate nuclear energy," and others "that combine to form organic molecules—carbon, nitrogen, hydrogen, oxygen, sulphur and phosphorus—" from which, "with improved knowledge of chemical synthesis," could be made "proteins, carbohydrates and fats in special food factories."

All this may lie in the far distance, may even be visionary, Sullivan conceded: "The moon's chief immediate resource is knowledge. Written upon the face of the moon is much of the history of the solar system—a record steadily erased from the surface of

Moon shot, taken November 23, 1966, from Lunar Orbiter II, shows floor of crater, Copernicus.

the earth. . . . For a true understanding of the past—and some glimpse of the future—we must look to the moon."

By 1966, the United States alone was looking to the moon to the tune of over $5 billion annually, an outlay that had quadrupled in four years and was exceeded in the federal budget, aside from such fixed commitments as interest payments and disbursements for social security, only by that for "National Defense"—to which, indeed, it might justifiably have been added.

Nothing could be more rational, more intellectually orderly, than celestial exploration looking to moon landings and the light they may throw on the universe, past and future. Yet the terrestrial creature engaged in it remained simultaneously as irrational as he was rational, spontaneously as instinctive as he was intellectual, a being as likely as not, under any momentary provocation, to forego his future, to forget his past. No age knew better than our own that knowledge is power as well as understanding, that the instinct of curiosity, so strong in science, feeds the instinct of aggression, so strong in society, and in turn is fed by it. Would moon landings and moon settlements, then, transform this natural earth satellite into a *rational* extension of its planet, its vacuum filled with mankind intellectually modified for survival there—and here? Or would the earth itself revert to the condition of the moon, its precarious life and fertility the more thoroughly destroyed for mankind's moon research?

Many scientists in the 'sixties professed an extraordinary optimism about man and his chances. In an age of cascading scientific, man-made change, they said, man himself must also change, even, according to the biophysicist, John R. Platt, in "emotional reactions and social behavior." His new knowledge of life need not necessarily be abused for power's sake, nor his new power over life thoughtlessly unloosed. The eminent "behavioral physiologist," Konrad Lorenz, observed in 1966 in his book, *On Aggression:*

We know that, in the evolution of vertebrates, the bond of personal love and friendship was the epoch-making invention created by the great constructors when it became necessary for two or more individuals of an aggressive species to live peacefully together and to work for a common end.

Lorenz then confidently conjectured that space might inspire a similar invention for societies of the aggressive species:

Above all, the exploration of space . . . give[s] scope for militant enthusiasm, allowing nations to fight each other in hard and dangerous competition without engendering national or political hatred. . . . I believe that the tremendous and otherwise not quite explicable public interest in space flight arises from the subconscious realization that it helps to preserve peace. May it continue to do so!

Ranging still farther afield, Lorenz added:

I agree with Dr. [J.] Marmor's assertion that modern war has become an institution, and I share his optimism in believing that, being an institution, war can be abolished.

Others perhaps too close to war, too removed from science and space, found it harder, in the 'sixties, to yield to what William James before both world wars called, "the will to believe." They found it hardest to build hopes on what James also called war's "moral equivalents," celestial or terrestrial. U Thant, the Secretary-General of the United Nations, still in the 'sixties mankind's best hope short of the moon for the "bond of love and friendship" among societies, was one of the least sanguine. In the introduction to his annual report for 1965-1966, U Thant wrote: "This has been a year in which, to all those looking and working towards larger international cooperation for the peace and well-being of mankind, the disappointments will seem to have outweighed once more the modest gains made in some directions." U Thant, by no means a lugubrious man, continued:

Generally speaking and as reflected by positions taken in the United Nations, the powerful nations have not during this period shown themselves able to rise above the suspicions, fears and mistrust that springs from their different ideologies and from their different conceptions of the best interests of the rest of the world; nor the rich nations above their concern for the con-

tinuation of their own prosperity; nor the poor nations above the dead weight of their chronic poverty and their anachronistic social structures.

But U Thant's pessimism may have been as excessive as the scientists' optimism. In the 'sixties war did not seem on the verge of being abolished; yet the concept of "limited war," which had helped keep the world generally at peace for a hundred years after the fall of Napoleon in 1815 (see p. 452), again offered a distinct alternative to the total wars of the recent past. "Economic development," in turn, had encountered discouraging setbacks—in the assisting countries largely because of its subordination to primarily military objectives; in the assisted countries largely because of the disheartening corruption characteristic of "anachronistic social structures." By 1966, in fact, a "development weariness" had set in. Yet the concept of "development" for the poorer countries, one of the new experts in the field pointed out in *Fortune* in October, 1966, was first articulated "a mere seventeen years ago," in Truman's Point Four program of 1949 (see p. 816). In that year, "the Harvard University libraries contained not a single book on economic development that by present standards would be considered even remotely adequate. . . . No body of knowledge or theory" existed. There were "few experienced people, a meager organizational structure." Today, he said,

when the World Bank opens development talks with a new country, it supplies a reading list of 400 books. . . . The grand total of professional developers . . . is on the order of 100,000. . . . Their constructive and hopeful voices are heard in every one of the poorer countries. They are the magnets drawing developing-country energy toward the priority of development, and away from the political ratholes into which it would otherwise go. . . . The past several years have brought a great accumulation of experience, knowledge and organization in the development field. They have also brought a great improvement in relations between developing countries and private capital.

"In our prevailing pessimism," this developer concluded, "we are letting the past obscure the future."

In the developed countries themselves, moreover, while much remained to be done to bring the underlying populations out of the slough of poverty and alienation, much also was being done on an unprecedented scale. In the mid-'sixties, the "democracy of the automobile" and of consumer credit in Europe, the democracy of desegregation and of higher education in America each encountered "backlash" resistance. Many Europeans feared the growing mechanization of their society—or "Americanization," as they often called it; many Americans feared the growing "socialization" of theirs. Yet the instrumentalities for individual self-determination on a mass scale multiplied, and the will to employ them deepened, especially among the articulate spokesmen for the underlying populations and their new supporters among the world's youth.

Finally, even the treaty of "love and friendship" in space, promulgated by the United Nations on December 9, 1966, after long-standing Soviet-American differences had been resolved, was found, as the *New York Times* put it, to have been "perhaps a symbolic preparatory step toward curbing the arms race on earth." This treaty prohibited the placing of weapons of "mass destruction" in orbit around the planet or installing them on the moon, and precluded claims of national sovereignty over any celstial body. Like the nuclear test ban treaty of 1963 (see p. 854), the space treaty was less comprehensive than it sounded and its punitive sections were weak. The *Times* remained skeptical that it had more than symbolic value. But, as President Kennedy said in his first state of the Union message almost at the outset of the 'sixties, "Where nature makes natural allies of us all, we can demonstrate that beneficial relations are possible even with those with whom we most deeply disagree, and this must someday be the basis of world peace and world law."

I. *"The New Frontier Is Here"*

KENNEDY WITHOUT TEARS

Young as he was when he delivered his first state of the Union message in January, 1961, John F. Kennedy had already served 14 years in Congress, the last eight of them in the Senate. Judged by the standards of his presidential years, Kennedy's congressional record was in some respects worse than undistinguished. "There is an old saying in Boston," he once recalled, "that 'we get our religion from Rome and our politics at home.'" In the home of his father, Ambassador Joseph P. Kennedy, young Jack in the early 'forties had found "America Firsters" (see p. 779) highly in favor, in the early 'fifties McCarthyites most welcome. It took some time for the home environment, congenial as it was to his Irish Catholic constituency, to rub off the political aspirant.

In the late 'forties, the young Congressman consorted with the most malignant critics of his party's China policy. In 1950, in a talk at Harvard, his *alma mater,* he declared about the alleged communists in government who presumably sold Chiang out: "McCarthy may have something." Later that year he helped carry the McCarran Internal Security Act through the House over Truman's resounding veto (see p. 826). After his election to the Senate in November, 1952, over Henry Cabot Lodge, an open target for the Massachusetts McCarthyite press, Kennedy did nothing to check his Wisconsin colleague. The Senate's condemnation of McCarthy in December, 1954 (see p. 830), found Kennedy in a hospital fighting for his life after spinal surgery. His absence absolved him from having to decide whether to vote for condemnation or not; and ever after, although under heavy liberal pressure to do so, he manfully refrained from indicating how his vote might have gone. Perhaps he did not know.

It was during his long convalescence from this operation that Kennedy wrote his book, *Profiles in Courage,* a series of sympathetic studies of federal legislators who, in challenging situations, put their consciences above their constituencies and voted as their concern for the right rather than for reelection dictated. Kennedy's liberal supporters took what solace they could from the implications of this popular work and from his outstanding pro-labor record, which was less disinterested since he represented a district with many wage earners.

Yet liberals had trouble with still other aspects of Kennedy's congressional behavior, with his willingness, for example, to economize on appropriations for TVA and REA (the Rural Electrification Administration) and, as late as 1957, to expose civil rights workers to the mercies of all white southern juries. When, the next year, Massachusetts sent Kennedy back to the Senate with a majority of 873,000 votes—by far the largest majority ever polled in any Massachusetts campaign—his illiberal record seemed to justify itself. Kennedy's election showing, oddly enough, also justified power-hungry liberals in jumping on the bandwagon. Their course was made easier, as Tom Wicker of the *Times* Washington office said in *Kennedy Without Tears,* by the Senator's "undue regard for Harvard and a craving for its approval." Few defeated candidates for Harvard's Board of Overseers presumed to try a second time, and few Catholics ever gained consideration. But Kennedy, after his rejection in 1955, "grimly ran again," Wicker writes, "and his election to the Board was a cherished triumph."

In 1956 Kennedy also had made an unsuccessful bid for the Democratic vice-presidential nomination, a setback that similarly strengthened his resolve to seek the presidency, his real goal, in 1960. His dallying with southerners on civil rights legislation in 1957 has been excused as a quest for party unity on behalf of his candidacy. In his overwhelming senatorial campaign of 1958, politics first felt the full force of Kennedy money and clan loyalty translated into an organized assault on the citadels of complacency and prejudice. It was really the proud family that was running Jack, with the goal of stunning recalcitrant party leaders into submission. That objective gained in spectacular fashion in Massachusetts, there remained the rest of the country to conquer. Despite all those congressional years, the Senator still lacked a national reputation. How was he to combat the profound public antipathy to his religion and the selfish resistance of party hacks? His chief asset, perhaps, was the emerging senatorial personality on which so much of the late President's reputation rests.

On January 2, 1960, Kennedy announced his candidacy for the topmost place on the party ticket, challenging any other Democratic aspirant to "submit to the voters his views, record and competence in a series of primary contests." If the nomination "ever goes into a back room," he said, "my name will never emerge." The results we know (see p. 843). In the first half of 1960, usually in his wife's company, the Senator traveled over 65,000 miles in some 25 states and made more than 350 speeches. His aim was to see and hear as well as to be seen and heard, especially in the great agricultural heartland of the nation, the citadel most foreign to him and most alien to his urban, Irish past. "Whatever other qualifications I may have had when I became President," Kennedy said later of his primaries experience, "one of them at least was that I knew Wisconsin better than any other President. My foot tracks are in every house in this state. . . . I know the difference between the kind of farms they have in the Seventh District and the First District." Kennedy "outsmarted all the pros," said Tammany boss Carmine De Sapio. Stuart Symington, the pros' early favorite, acknowledged that Kennedy "had just a little more courage, . . . stamina, wisdom and character than any of the rest of us." No one was more willing than the victor to admit that he also had more money; yet he knew that many even richer men had tried the same course only to fail before the starting gun.

Kennedy's long contact with politics had

been shallow enough to leave the glow of youth undimmed, the candor credible, the humor fresh, the modesty unfeigned. His infectious zest for life seemed only to have been heightened by a long history of personal sorrow that continued into the White House—by the violent deaths of young relatives and friends, the mental illness of a sister, his own questionable health and close brushes with eternity. He did not expect to live forever. "If someone is going to kill me," he would say in discussing security precautions with his aides, "they're going to kill me." Such fatalism, for him, only reinforced a native skepticism of absolutes, an eager acceptance of growth and change. Nixon, although as young as himself, Kennedy said at the outset of the final campaign, "has the courage of our old convictions." But "the New Frontier is here, whether we seek it or not." Some time after his victory, the President observed: "Our progress as a nation can be no swifter than our progress in education. The human mind is our fundamental resource."

During the 1960 campaign, as his aide T. C. Sorensen tells the story, Kennedy learned that the father of the Negro leader, Martin Luther King, Jr., had announced his support after having earlier decided to vote against Kennedy on religious grounds. " 'That was a hell of an intolerant statement, wasn't it?' said Kennedy. 'Imagine Martin Luther King having a father like that.' Then a pause, a grin and a final word: 'Well, we all have fathers, don't we.' " Kennedy really was unprepared for the presidency, but perhaps no more than most other successful bidders. As late as December, 1962, on reviewing his first two years in office, he acknowledged to the electorate on nationwide TV: "The responsibilities placed on the United States are greater than I imagined them to be and there are greater limitations upon our ability to bring about a favorable result than I had imagined them to be. . . . It is much easier to make the speeches than it is finally to make the judgments." Yet he had come far from "my father's house," and would come farther still.

852

THE ISSUES
OF THE THOUSAND DAYS

"Anybody who would spend $40 billion in a race to the moon for national prestige is nuts," said General Eisenhower after he had retired from the presidency. The new President had other ideas. In May, 1961, under the heading "Urgent National Needs," he told Congress: "No single space project in this period will be more impressive to mankind" than that of "landing a man on the moon and returning him safely to earth." The following year, in a speech in Houston, Kennedy said: "The exploration of space will go ahead whether we join in it or not. . . . We mean to be a part of it —we mean to lead it." It was during Kennedy's administration that annual space appropriations soared over $5 billion.

The new administration, nevertheless, was soon brought down to earth by persistent world and domestic problems. The very first of these, an exceedingly critical one since the McCarthyite destruction of government morale and the resignations following the Eisenhower loyalty order (see p. 829), was manning the administration. Between his election and his inauguration Kennedy searched far for the executive team he finally brought together. The dynastic heir apparent, Robert F. Kennedy, became Attorney-General with perhaps broader powers than any previous holder of that office. Other leaders included Secretary of Defense, Robert S. McNamara; Secretary of State, Dean Rusk; and Chairman of the Council of Economic Advisors, Walter W. Heller. Below these luminaries the President sought for an able civil service. "Let it be clear," he stated at the outset, "that this Administration recognizes the value of dissent and daring, that we greet healthy controversy as the hallmark of healthy change. Let the public service be a proud and lively career."

Kennedy's victory, essentially one for northern cities, religious and racial minorities, big government, and internationalism, seemed to draw dissident conservatives more firmly together and more decidedly to the "right." Both major parties had taken formal notice of the burgeoning Klan, the rising John Birch societies and similar "hate" organizations which flooded Congress and the private mails with blood-curdling reports of the sell-out of Americanism by such respected figures as Eisenhower and Chief Justice Warren. Having overcome these elements in the campaign, Kennedy meant to keep them in their place.

Other domestic issues—the "clutter" of "unfinished and neglected tasks"—faced by the Kennedy administration had, by the early 1960's, assumed a familiar ring. Kennedy noted them in his first state of the Union message: the "squalor" of our cities; the vast overcrowding of our classrooms; the termination because of financial need of the education of "one-third of our most promising high school graduates"; persistent recession and unemployment, especially in long-term "distressed areas"; automation in industry and its intensification of the job shortage, especially among "blue shirt" workers; the drain of American gold abroad, largely for economic and military assistance, and the menace this held for the stability of the dollar; the unbalanced budgets and the national debt, and their relation to the care of growing numbers of old people, of the indigent sick, and of others in need; the waste of natural resources as basic as our threatened water supply.

But all these issues paled before that of Negro equality, which Kennedy in 1961 failed to mention, but which by the summer of 1963 rightfully dominated the headlines. The year 1963 marked the hundredth anniversary of the Emancipation Proclamation. Largely because thousands of Negroes had by then risen from their heritage of slavery to become part of the American middle class, the mass of the American Negro population found the inspiration, the leadership, and even the economic leverage to seek first-class citizenship for themselves and education for their children to prepare them for better jobs and social equality.

In February, 1963, Kennedy proposed his first civil rights legislation to Congress, which liberals branded as "thin." A few weeks later mass Negro demonstrations be-

gan in Birmingham, Alabama, and before the summer was over more than 800 cities and towns had seen peaceful Negro protests, often in the face of dogs and fire hoses employed by police. The climax of the Negro campaign came on August 28, when over 200,000 Negroes and sympathetic whites marched on Washington "for Jobs and Freedom Now." In June the administration had beefed up its proposed civil rights legislation, but the measure languished in committee until 1964 (see p. 857).

To the embarrassment of American foreign policy, the headlines of 1963 made known around the world the brutality with which Negro demonstrations often were suppressed. Yet the most remarkable feature of the equality movement continued to be the restraint of whites and Negroes alike. Leadership in the Negro nonviolence movement rested with Martin Luther King, Jr., a young minister barely in his thirties. As the movement spread, others shared leadership with him while still others sought their selfish advancement on the wings of rank and file aspirations. White resistance, moreover, as President Kennedy had feared, began to grow with the Negro's forward steps (see p. 861).

Kennedy's efforts to enlarge federal aid to education and to extend federal "medicare" to the aged also failed. Congress remained cold as well to his proposal for a department of urban affairs on the Cabinet level. The President's urgent pushing of these measures nevertheless helped set the stage for their adoption under his successor (see pp. 859, 860).

The strength of the United States in foreign affairs depended very largely on the strength of the domestic economy. Many avenues were explored for stimulating American economic growth. Early in 1962 Kennedy proposed a broad tax cut for consumers as a means to stimulate the demand for goods. A general business revival in 1962 and 1963 seemed to make the proposed cuts irrelevant, but most observers agree that the reductions actually voted in 1964 kept the revival going and pushed the economy to record heights (see p. 857).

By the early 1960's Americans had also acquired a certain familiarity with the world's trouble spots where tensions failed to be eased by the new administration's own new military look. In July, 1961, Kennedy declared that "we intend to have a wider choice than humiliation or all-out nuclear action." He ordered a considerable build-up in conventional arms, manpower and air power, and a modernization of procedures to improve the nation's ability to strike at the right place at the right time. "Massive retaliation" (see p. 833) gave way to "flexible response." At the same time, the nuclear missile potential was also increased, so that the possibility of real massive retaliation would gain in "credibility," thereby reducing the likelihood of extreme provocation.

An unfortunate legacy from the previous administration caught the Kennedy "team" off balance before its new look materialized and precipitated the most extreme provocation of the decade. In one of his last acts as President, Eisenhower had broken off diplomatic relations with Castro's Cuba in protest against "a long series of harassments, baseless accusations, and vilifications." One of the accusations was far from baseless. For nine months about 1,500 anti-Castro Cuban exiles had been secretly in training under C.I.A. men for an invasion of their island with the intention of overthrowing the regime by fomenting internal uprisings. Assured of the success of this misguided adventure in "rollback" by the team he had inherited, the new President allowed it to proceed. In April, 1961, in anticipation of American air support, the trainees attempted to land at the Bay of Pigs, 90 miles from Havana. Air support, never clearly promised, was not forthcoming, and the invasion instantly failed amidst recriminations that persisted years later. Over 1,200 of the invaders were taken prisoner and held for almost two years.

From this triumph Castro moved forward in his plan to make Cuba a solid outpost of the Soviet regime, complete with missile bases set up by the U.S.S.R. On October 22, 1962, Kennedy warned Russia that he would not tolerate this "clandestine, reckless and provocative threat to world peace." War was never nearer; but the Soviets, recognizing the gravity of Kennedy's stand, promptly agreed to recall their ships on the high seas carrying more supplies for Cuba and to remove the offending bases.

On October 20, 1962, the Chinese communists invaded India at many points and a general Asian war seemed to be in the offing just when the Cuban missile crisis was aflame in the West. One month later, although meeting little effective opposition, the Chinese called off the war, but the menace to India continued. The most striking feature of this conflict was the support the Soviets gave, not to their fellow communists, but to neutralist India. This policy dramatized the profound split in the communist camp which first became public knowledge in 1956 (see p. 839) and which now raised new hopes for a "detente" between the Soviets and the West. These hopes were strengthened when, in July, 1963, the three nuclear powers, the United States, Britain and the U.S.S.R. signed a fairly innocuous treaty pledging themselves to end nuclear testing which "causes radioactive debris" outside their own borders. They recognized that this was only a first step, as the preamble to the treaty said, toward "the speediest possible achievement of an agreement on general and complete disarmament under strict international control in accordance with the objectives of the United Nations." The three powers invited all others to sign the treaty. In the West, Germany had misgivings and France was openly hostile. In the East, Red China denounced the Soviets and the Western powers alike.

The growing multiplicity of voices in the communist sphere complicated the dangerous situation in Southeast Asia without improving it. In Laos, while the United States continued its support of the conservative Boun Oum regime, the Soviets supported the claims of the exiled neutralist government of Souvanna Phouma, and Red China secretly backed the communist Pathet Lao. By May, 1962, the Pathet Lao controlled almost two-thirds of Laos and had forced the Boun Oum government to flee to Thailand where Kennedy quickly dispatched naval and military contingents to thwart any possible invasion. This show of force helped bring about an agreement in July, 1962, on a coalition government in Laos composed of the three claimant groups; but the Pathet Lao kept up its harassment of its partners and also kept open the path of North Vietnamese aid to the Viet Cong in South Vietnam (see p. 837).

Here, beginning in October, 1961, following a survey on the scene by General Maxwell Taylor, Kennedy gradually enlarged American military aid to the Diem regime in Saigon (see p. 836), even though Diem's program of repression across the countryside grew more violent while his militancy against the Viet Cong declined. By November, 1963, American military personnel in South Vietnam exceeded 17,000 and casualties grew with the size of the commitment. Two months earlier, Kennedy declared of the South Vietnamese:

In the final analysis, it's their war. They're the ones who have to win it or lose it. We can help them as advisers but they have to win it.

To improve the prospects of winning, the South Vietnam General Duong Van Minh, on November 1, 1963, overthrew the Diem regime (probably with American encouragement) and shortly after executed Diem and his brother. The new government won prompt United States recognition, but by the time of Kennedy's assassination it had won few military laurels.

In Europe meanwhile, the wall the communists had built in August, 1961, separating East from West Berlin, was still standing and was the scene of intermittent conflict. In Africa, the U.N. troops in the Congo (see p. 842) succeeded in bringing about a precarious truce in December, 1962, which they continued to maintain for months thereafter, awaiting the Republic of the Congo's own growth in strength and stability. The U.N., in financial straits

largely because of the failure to receive payment of peace-keeping levies from the U.S.S.R. and France, gingerly withdrew its forces in June, 1964, but not without warning of the still dangerous situation, which again almost immediately deteriorated.

The Kennedy administration's activities abroad also included certain peaceful enterprises. One experiment was the establishment of the Peace Corps, "a pool of trained men and women," as the President described it, "sent overseas . . . to help foreign countries meet their most urgent needs for skilled manpower." Created on a pilot basis by executive order in March, 1961, the Peace Corps had done so well by September that Congress made it permanent. In March, 1961, Kennedy also outlined his plan for an Alliance of Progress with Latin American nations, on the model of the Marshall Plan from which, with much resulting bitterness, as we have seen (p. 818), they had been excluded. In August, at a general conference at Punta del Este in Uruguay, all but Cuba subscribed to it. By 1963, Latin America was proving characteristically slow in imple-

J.F.K. and Konrad Adenauer, 1962.

menting reforms at home that would have speeded American assistance for building broadly based economies. But the question of Latin American progress had begun to engage the interest of less formal American enterprises as well, with hope for the future which, by 1966, seemed on the verge of being realized. Finally, in October, 1962, Kennedy signed the Trade Expansion Act under which Congress gave the president enlarged powers to reduce tariffs and otherwise liberalize trade terms with already highly skilled nations.

Such remained the hopeful but ambiguous state of the world and the nation in the summer of 1963. In the previous November, 51 million Americans, the largest ever in a non-presidential year, went to the polls and broke tradition by fully supporting the administration in power. The Republicans were surprised, as well, by the defeat of Richard M. Nixon for the governorship of California. But they found some balm in gaining the governorships of three heavily industrial states, Ohio, Pennsylvania, and Michigan. In Pennsylvania, moreover, they found in William W. Scranton, and in Michigan, in George Romney, two new aspirants for the 1964 presidential sweepstakes. Senator Barry Goldwater of Arizona

and the liberal Governor Rockefeller of New York, as well as Nixon himself, however, remained the leaders in the contest to face the Democratic candidate. The shocking assassination of President Kennedy in Dallas, Texas, Friday, November 22, 1963, obscured for the time being who this candidate might be. The new President, Lyndon Baines Johnson of Texas, however, took office with a show of firmness that foretold for 1964 his own likely quest for the candidacy which he had vainly sought in 1960.

Kennedy's assassination threw not only the United States, but the entire world outside of Red China, into deepest mourning. If there had been any question earlier about the place of the United States as the leader of the free world, the free world's response to his passing answered this question resoundingly in the affirmative. But perhaps Fidel Castro put it best, when on learning the dreadful news, he blurted out in his excitable fashion to the French journalist, Jean Daniel: "Everything is changed. The United States occupies such a position in world affairs that the death of its President affects millions of people in every country of the globe. . . . I'll tell you one thing; at least Kennedy was an enemy to whom we had become accustomed."

II. *L.B.J.*

THE SUCCESSION YEAR

John F. Kennedy took criticism from the press and public far more calmly than most presidents, but he did become annoyed when his lack of emotion was taken for a lack of commitment. One writer who drew his irritation was James McGregor Burns, an early Kennedy biographer. "Burns seems to feel," Kennedy told "Ted" Sorensen, "that unless somebody . . . shouts at the top of their voice they are not concerned about a matter." There was little chance of making this mistake about L.B.J. During the 1964 campaign, James Reston of the *New York Times* wrote of him:

When he is unleashed in a crowd, striding ahead

of a battalion of Secret Service fullbacks, he is an elemental and awesome figure.

On the platform, . . . when he is at his shouting best, arms waving like a helicopter, he not only commands but almost stuns his audience.

There is something contradictory about Lyndon Johnson's pacifying role on the one hand and his appearance and manner on the other. He is a healer in the garb of warrior. He tells us to "reason together" at the top of his voice. He is a whirlwind who wants to calm the waves.

Although he had difficulties with the bereaved Kennedy family on the day of the assassination, Johnson swiftly made the transition from Vice-President to President. In this he was aided by the loyalty of the top Kennedy men, all of whom stayed on. Little time elapsed before L.B.J. began working his old magic with Congress, speeding the progress of strong Kennedy bills for the prosperity tax cut and civil rights.

At his last news conference, Kennedy said of the coming session of the 88th Congress: "I am looking forward to the record of this Congress, but . . . this is going to be an 18-month delivery." It was only a few months after that, on February 26, 1964, that President Johnson signed the tax bill providing cuts of $11.5 billion, and significantly reducing the withholding rate from 18 to 14 per cent. Only a few months later, on July 2, he signed the Civil Rights Act. James Farmer, the militant Negro leader of the Congress of Racial Equality (CORE), said this measure was an "act of goodwill and reconciliation" between Negroes and the white community," following the cruel summer of 1963. But Farmer warned that "there will be no breathing spell on demonstrations. . . . We will continue to use our body and spirit to secure . . . the reality of equality."

The most sweeping civil rights act in American history, the new law enlarged *federal* power to protect voting rights, to provide open access for all races to public facilities, to sue to speed up lagging school desegregation, to insure equal job opportunities in businesses and unions with more than 25 persons.

In promoting the civil rights act in his first state of the Union message in January, 1964, Johnson said: "Unfortunately, many Americans live on the outskirts of hope, some because of their poverty and some because of their color, and all too many because of both." To raise the hopes of such people, he proposed a new measure of his own, an "unconditional" declaration of "war on poverty in America." This war Congress also endorsed, in August, 1964, when it appropriated almost $950 million for ten separate anti-poverty programs to be supervised by the Office of Economic Opportunity set up by the bill. Key features included a Job Corps to train underprivileged youths for the labor market; a work-training program to employ them; an adult education program; and a "domestic peace

corps" to enlist the privileged on behalf of the poor.

The rapid tempo of far-reaching change under the new administration was kept up by the "Warren Court." In June, 1964, in a 6 to 3 decision believed by many to be of equal importance with the school desegregation ruling ten years before (see p. 831), the Court, with the Chief Justice speaking for the majority, declared that both houses of state legislatures "must be apportioned on a population basis" in order that citizens gain the constitutional guarantee of "equal protection of the law." This decision was a blow to rural areas which dominated state Senates. At the same time it gave cities and the fast-growing suburbs the potential of unchecked legislative power. By 1966 most states had reapportioned their legislatures in conformity to the Court's ruling.

On October 16, 1964, Nikita Khrushchev suddenly was ousted from power, to be succeeded as premier by Alexei Kosygin and as party secretary by Leonid Brezhnev. That Khrushchev was not disgraced or executed showed that the Russians had made some little progress of their own in achieving peaceful successions. Yet the U.S.S.R. remained for some time thereafter ridden by uncertainty. The "thaw" that Khrushchev fostered at home had been in part responsible for his removal, not least because of the new opportunity it gave the Red Chinese to claim the legitimate leadership in the Leninist-Stalinist revolutionary tradition. Those Russians who had benefited from the thaw looked with misgivings on the new leaders, who nevertheless failed altogether to close the breach with the Asians. The conflicts in the communist camp may have increased the likelihood that one or the other of the great Red countries would embark on new foreign military adventures. But their domestic problems and their strained relations may also have held them back. In any case, the communists' dilemmas underlay in part President Johnson's willingness to risk "escalating" the Vietnam war after his landslide victory in the November elections.

THE JOHNSON LANDSLIDE

Kennedy's assassination while on a party fence-mending mission in Dallas rocked the Republican party as much as it did the world and the country. The election campaign of 1964 had in fact already begun, with the assumption by both parties that Kennedy would be the Democratic candidate. His removal left the Republicans without a clear target. It did not faze Barry Goldwater and his backers, however. As early as June, 1963, Goldwater spoke confidently of winning the Republican nomination. "You see," he said then, "I have one advantage. I've done my political homework. I've spent the last 5½ years traipsing around the country helping precinct chairmen elect candidates and raise money." Goldwater's determination to end Republican "me-tooism" did not frighten the many party veterans who secretly shared his views. He was for liberty, against big government. The Democrats, he said, were for big government, which curtailed liberty. In announcing his candidacy in January, 1964, he added, "I will offer a choice, not an echo. This will not be an engagement of personalities. It will be an engagement of principles." Goldwater soon lost a whole series of primaries, but he held his delegates.

A frantic "stop Goldwater" movement was launched on the eve of the Republican convention in San Francisco in July. On the very day the voting was to begin, liberal Governor Scranton was thrust forward as a forlorn hope, but Goldwater delegates carried their champion to victory on the first ballot. He himself then named the reactionary New Yorker, William E. Miller, as his running mate, because, he explained, "he drives Johnson nuts." Goldwater's acceptance speech brought only "amazement and shock," in Governor Rockefeller's words, to his liberal Republican opponents: "Let our Republicanism, so focused and so dedicated," said the candidate, "not be made fuzzy by any unthinking and stupid labels. I would remind you that extremism in the defense of liberty is no vice. And let me remind you also that moderation in the pursuit of justice is no virtue."

In June, 1964, segregationist Governor George Wallace of Alabama entered the presidential race by running in a number of Democratic party primaries. He did well enough to frighten many already worried by Goldwater; but the latter's nomination deprived Wallace of the conservative support he sought. When the Democrats met at their convention in Atlantic City in August, Johnson's nomination was a foregone conclusion and after a spirited contest, with much political in-fighting, Senator Hubert H. Humphrey won the ticket's second place.

The campaign itself gradually deteriorated into a conflict of personalities rather than of principles despite Goldwater's boast. When it was all over, the Fair Campaign Practices Committee declared: "Rarely have the reputations of two opponents for the Presidency been pried by so many into the stereotypes of maniac and thief." At the end, Johnson won an overwhelming victory. Goldwater scored in Alabama, Georgia, Louisiana, Mississippi and South Carolina—George Wallace country—and in his home state of Arizona, but nowhere else. His popular vote was 27,176,873, his electoral vote 52. Johnson's popular vote of 43,128,918 gave him 61 per cent of the total, surpassing even F.D.R.'s record percentage in 1936. His electoral vote was 486. The Republican party seemed finished; yet it was to have a significant revival in 1966, far sooner than its most optimistic adherents anticipated.

THE GREAT SOCIETY
AND THE "ESCALATED" WAR

"There has been a growing recognition," President Kennedy wrote in November, 1961, "that we must fit our power to our responsibilities." A year later, as we have seen (p. 852), he acknowledged that it might perhaps be the other way around, that we must fit our responsibilities to our power. As President, Johnson's experience seemed to work the opposite way. In his first state of the Union message as an elected

Commander-in-Chief, in January, 1965, he said, "We will not, and should not, assume it is the task of Americans alone to settle all the conflicts of a torn and troubled world." Yet, a year later, on the same occasion, he said, "This nation is mighty enough —its society is healthy enough—its people are strong enough—to pursue our goals in the rest of the world while still building a great society here at home."

The "Great Society" was the central theme of L.B.J.'s first new message to the 89th Congress that convened in January, 1965. When that Congress terminated its business in the fall of 1966, it had made one of the most constructive records in history —too constructive, indeed, for many Americans who, in the by-elections of November, 1966, shocked the Democrats by undermining their domination of House and Senate and the governorships of the states. One of the most extraordinary Republican victories was that of the movie actor, Ronald Reagan, a conservative political neophyte, over the veteran liberal Democrat, "Pat" Brown, for the governorship of the new number one state in the Union, California. Reagan's campaign was based mainly on the administration's excessive "interventionism," with interventionism on behalf of the Negro an important "backlash" factor but not necessarily the predominant one. Governor Romney in Michigan, and the resurgent Governor Rockefeller in New York, also won smashing victories, theirs on behalf of the Republican liberal wing.

The first of the striking new measures of the 89th Congress, adopted in April, 1965, was the Elementary and Secondary Education Act, which provided $1.3 billion in federal aid to all pupils in school districts. By earmarking these funds for pupils instead of for schools directly, Congress was able to include those who attended parochial as well as public institutions, thereby circumventing constitutional issues on the separation of church and state and neutralizing the powerful parochial-school lobby which had helped defeat Kennedy's education bill. Later in 1965, Congress also appropriated $2.3 billion to enlarge federal loans to college students and other assistance to higher education.

A second far-reaching congressional achievement was the adoption of the "medicare" amendments to the Social Security Act, which the President approved on July 30, 1965. The "medicare" amendments, a victory for the aged over the relentless lobbying of the American Medical Association, provided hospital insurance and certain post-hospital care for virtually all Americans on reaching the age of 65, although in anticipation of the expanded coverage of the Social Security Act itself, the new laws stipulated that after 1968 only those under social security would receive the hospital insurance. This insurance was to be paid for out of compulsory increases in social security taxes. A second part of the new program provided a voluntary system of medical insurance covering doctors' bills, diagnosis procedures, and other medical services and supplies. This insurance was to be available to all over 65 who agreed to pay $3 per month for it.

L.B.J. at the Texas White House, 1965.

The failure of certain southern states to enforce the voting registration provisions of the Civil Rights Act of 1964 brought the resumption of Negro demonstrations that James Farmer had promised (see p. 857). These took place first in Alabama, particularly in the town of Selma where, on February 1, 1965, Martin Luther King, Jr., and 770 other Negroes were arrested. Early in March, Alabama state troopers and auxiliaries, using tear gas and whips, frustrated an attempted civil rights march from Selma to Montgomery, the state capital. After President Johnson, on March 20, federalized the Alabama National Guard and ordered it to protect the marchers (Governor Wallace having earlier refused to protect them), the procession of some 25,000 Negroes and sympathetic whites from all over the country began. The night the march ended, one white woman participant was killed by Klan gunfire and soon after a Boston minister was slain.

Congress responded to the evident need by enacting the third of its important measures, the Voting Rights Act, signed by the President August 6, 1965. This act suspended all literacy tests and other devices still used in certain southern states and in districts in a few others from Alaska to Maine to keep voting lily white (see p. 484), and empowered "federal examiners" in effect to register all who qualified simply under age, residence, and objective educational requirements. The act also directed the Attorney-General to start suits to test the constitutionality of the poll tax in states where it survived. Such suits began the day after the act was signed, and by April, 1966, the last of the poll tax laws, that of Mississippi, had been outlawed. Two months earlier a new drive to register 2 million eligible Negroes in 11 southern states had begun.

Other notable domestic legislation of the 89th Congress included a new immigration act terminating the discriminatory national-origins quota system (see p. 694); special assistance legislation for the redevelopment of the 11 depressed states in "Appalachia"; acts to promote the beautification of high-ways, the purification of smog-laden air, and the restoration of polluted waterways; a constitutional amendment covering the presidency during the incumbent's disability (see Appendix); and acts creating two new departments on the Cabinet level, one for Housing and Urban Affairs (September 9, 1965); the second for Transportation (October 15, 1966). In addition, massive new appropriations were made for older "Great Society" measures, including the war on poverty (see p. 857) and the regeneration of cities.

When the 89th Congress adjourned on October 22, 1966, the American economy had enjoyed six solid years of extraordinary economic expansion, pushing the annual gross national product almost to $740 billion, employment almost to 73 million persons. Thus, its brilliant legislative record was underpinned by a record-smashing prosperity. Yet young persons and colored persons still found it hard to get jobs or to take satisfaction in other aspects of American domestic success. Life on family farms, moreover, remained dreary while city dwellers were exposed to unprecedented violence and fears, augmented by the easy access to guns and other weapons and the mobility afforded by the automobile to the underworld and its fringes among the repressed.

Most Americans never lived better than in the 'sixties, especially those in the suburbs distant from the urban blight. Educational performance and aspirations had never been higher. Far fewer books than in the 'fifties dealt with the poverty of American culture. A much healthier sign were the books on the culture of poverty—books deepening the understanding and enlivening programs of improvement. The general tone of science, philosophy, and religion, if not of literature, had taken on a hopeful optimism about the relation of man and his universe (see p. 862). Yet, for the time being at any rate, deep social dissatisfactions seemed to darken the hue of good times and good prospects.

Two situations in particular intensely aggravated the general malaise made evident in the 1966 elections. One was the spread of large-scale Negro demonstrations to northern metropolises, starting with the murderous riots in the Watts ghetto of Los Angeles in mid-August, 1965, during which 35 persons were killed and property damage soared to $100 million. Later that year and in 1966, rioting spread to Harlem in New York, and to Chicago, San Francisco, and other northern cities, exposing the deprivation and desperation of the Negro slums and slum dwellers as well as the savage prejudice and hate of urban whites in attempting to defend their own recent social gains. The cry for "black power," once heard only on the fringes of the Negro Revolution, now threatened to overwhelm the nonviolent camp, and in any case it alienated many liberal white supporters of the Negro cause and sharply shrank their contributions to it. Among those alienated were many northern legislators who allowed the administration bill for mandatory open housing to die with the close of the 89th Congress in October, 1966. This defeat for a "Great Society" project was also a setback for desegregation in housing and hence in neighborhood schooling—so sharp a one, in-

deed, that efforts were now addressed largely to improving rather than eliminating ghetto life.

The second unsettling situation, overshadowing all other foreign affairs, was the Johnson administration's huge "escalation" of the war in Vietnam. Discontent over this policy was aggravated by the often contradictory official pronouncements, especially about employing new means of killing and reaching for new targets.

By the end of 1966, Americans in Vietnam had soared from the 17,000 of 1963 to over 380,000, exceeding the peak of 350,000 in Korea. Starting in June, 1965, American ground troops had begun to engage the Viet Cong in direct fighting. The South Vietnamese also promised to step up their efforts after Vice Marshal Nguyen Cao Ky took over as Premier of the eighth South Vietnam government since the end of Diem (see p. 855). In November, 1965, some 30,000 persons took part in a "March on Washing-

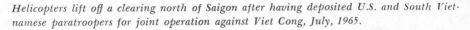

Helicopters lift off a clearing north of Saigon after having deposited U.S. and South Vietnamese paratroopers for joint operation against Viet Cong, July, 1965.

ton for Peace in Vietnam," evidence of the widespread unpopularity of the war there. And yet the continuing "escalation" of appropriations for the war by congressmen sensitive to constituent opinion seemed to indicate the willingness of most Americans to support the administration's aims.

These aims were well stated in Richard Rovere's "Letter from Washington" in the *New Yorker* magazine, in August, 1965, when he reported the story of the President's turning to Robert McNamara and saying "that he was counting on the Secretary of Defense to keep us in the war," and then turning to Dean Rusk and saying "that he was counting on the Secretary of State to get us out of the war." Johnson "had concluded," writes Rovere, "—or rather he had reaffirmed his earlier conclusion—that the only way he could get to the peace table was by shooting his way there. The end he seeks is disengagement; the only available means to that end is further engagement."

Yet the administration's terms for "disengagement" remained unclear, and its Southeast Asia goals thereafter remained uncertain. Following the President's extraordinary Asian tour in October, 1966, culminating in the "summit conference" in Manila among Asian supporters of his policy, the administration seemed to rest its case for the long-term victory over communism on victory, not disengagement, in Vietnam. Indeed, Johnson proposed to extend the "Great Society" not only to Southeast Asia but to all other underdeveloped regions. At the same time, there was no let up in "peace feelers" by the U.N., the Pope, the Italians, and many other parties, including the United States; and no let up in bombing North Vietnam, presumably to improve Hanoi's receptivity to "peace" moves and Ho Chi Minh's willingness to communicate them to the Viet Cong. If Johnson was, as Reston said, "a healer in the garb of a warrior," he had perhaps no option but to pursue his warlike course. His decline in popularity at home in 1966 would perhaps be reversed if the healing came before his administration's end.

III. *The New Universe of Man*

"Many of our most sensitive spirits today," wrote John R. Platt in 1966, "still see man as the anti-hero, the helpless victim of weapons and wars, of governments and mechanisms and soul-destroying organizations and computers. As indeed he is. But . . . there grows up even in the laboratories the realization that man is also mysterious and elusive, hedged about with indeterminacies, self-determining and perpetual, a lighthouse of complexity and the organizing child of the universe. . . . Yes, we die; but mankind lives."

The optimistic scientists of the 'sixties themselves had a heavy heritage of guilt and horror to forget or suppress after their wartime and related experiences in the 'forties and 'fifties. The initial outcome of their incredibly illuminating nuclear research brought lasting traumatic shocks which were only deepened by the subsequent revelations of the complicity of for-

mer colleagues in the unspeakable scientific barbarism of death camps and genocide. Reason seemed to offer small resistance to primitive instincts that defied understanding and warped and depressed the spirit. But scientists, probing ever more deeply into the nature of man and of the universe around him, employing in their work for constructive purposes the very instrumentalities of mass killing and mass regimentation and oppression, seemed to have found the path to hope. Man's precarious existence in his world seemed to have become a challenge and an inspiration.

Perhaps, in the 'sixties, scientists had become "our most sensitive spirits." But the ones Platt and his fellow-scientists complained of under that rubric were those in the more traditional "creative" fields, in music and art and architecture, and especially in literature. Many writers, like the many scientists, had probed the depravities of war and society in the 'forties and 'fifties, the monstrous acts of friends and enemies alike. Their shock was at least as deep; their ultimate response quite different—and in scientific eyes, quite unjustified.

Out of World War II came a few powerful books—Norman Mailer's *The Naked and the Dead* (1948) and James Jones' *From Here to Eternity* (1951) are among the most celebrated—and a number of works in the stunned Ernest Hemingway manner. But most young American writers seemed impelled to repress the war, to resume normal life, complete their education, marry. They found much to criticize, to be sure; national smugness, self-righteousness, and materialism offended them as it had their elders in 1918. Their antipathies, however, were less passionate and less specific, and their hunger for the kind of secure life of which they had been so long deprived made them passive. A grateful government enabled the veterans to complete their education on the GI bill. Universities provided havens for young poets, novelists, and playwrights; foundations paid for their European sojourns; and writers' "conferences" in many parts of the country gave them pleasant employment tutoring literary novices in their craft.

The young writers, disciplined, serious, well-educated, right-minded, had gained, as one of them put it, "an unearned maturity." Some reveled in it. Others found the very ease of their progress disquieting, as though their capacity for vision and originality scarcely stirred people in an age of television and movies, commercialized sports and comic books. What chance did the liberal arts have when the cultural leaders themselves seemed to be losing faith in the importance of literacy and the intellect? What future was there for the creative artist in an age of conformism? Or in an age of science?—which they still looked upon with the fatalism of a Joseph Wood Krutch (see p. 743) or a young Bertrand Russell: "Brief and powerless is Man's life. . . . Blind to good and evil, reckless of destruction, omnipotent matter rolls on its relentless way."

An answer of sorts to these questions and

to the conforming writers who asked them came in the mid-'fifties from a raucous company subsequently stigmatized as the "Beat Generation." Soon the "Beatnik" (a term coined by a San Francisco columnist) became a subject of sermons and editorials. With his unkempt beard, disheveled dress, and curious argot ("cool," "square," "hip") he stood as the antithesis of his "square" counterpart. The code of the "Beats," as reflected, for example, in the verse of their poet-laureate, Allen Ginsburg, and in the fiction of Jack Kerouac, advised nose-thumbing at the "rat race." In principle, the Beat, living in obscurity, achieved a mystical transcendence through Zen Buddhism, drugs, jazz, action painting, bongo drums, or sex.

Future literary historians may come to see these self-styled "Holy Barbarians" as a continuation of the war between the "heart" and the "head" that had started with the wilder transcendental radicals of Emerson's day. Their vogue might also be seen as one phase of youth's world-wide revolt against the "phony," dramatized so poignantly in J. D. Salinger's *Catcher in the Rye* (1951). Yet in the process of defending themselves and explaining their movement, many Beats took on the "Madison Avenue" values they ostensibly condemned. The best known among them cashed in on their notoriety lecturing at schools and colleges and even to women's groups.

The Beats could be dismissed by their critics as loafers and hooligans, more ludicrous than fearful. Viewers-with-alarm had greater difficulty in understanding apparently respectable writers whose work seemed so out of keeping with national power and prosperity. According to an editorial in *Life* magazine, Sept. 12, 1955, our writers were

still producing a literature which sounds sometimes as if it were written by an unemployed homosexual living in a packing-box shanty on the city dump while awaiting admission to the county poorhouse.

Behind this rather simple-minded view that a prosperous and dynamic society deserved an optimistic literature lay the fear that American writers, having lost touch with their audience, were distorting the national "image" for foreign readers. But the writers who came of age during the war years seemed unable to shape the amorphous post-war society into meaningful or familiar patterns. Traditional beliefs and loyalties had altered. People seemed to float even more freely in the social flux than they had before the war, and rising standards of living, while benefitting a substantial portion of the population, had not removed the feelings of anxiety and helplessness, the sense of being acted upon rather than acting. The atrocities of every-day life, the novelist Philip Roth observed, seemed to dwarf the writer's "meager imagination." At mid-century, he had "his hands full in trying to understand, and then describe, and then make *credible* much of American reality."

The new writers' vision of his everyday terror was often projected in the form of grotesque comedy, as if the only way to convey the unspeakable was to envelop it in a horrible joke. This was a far cry from the humorless despair of a T. S. Eliot or the tight-lipped restraint of a Hemingway or the rage of a Steinbeck, but may have been foreshadowed in some of Sherwood Anderson's stories or the novels of Nathanael West. The new work, however, was more jaunty in style. The degree of experimentation, to be sure, varied enormously. Novelists like Saul Bellow or Ralph Ellison did not depart from the older realism so drastically as Truman Capote or John Hawkes, nor did such playwrights as Arthur Miller so drastically as Tennessee Williams and Edward Albee.

The altered appearance of the American scene in the new literature reflected in part the private experiences and backgrounds of the writers themselves. Before 1920, American writers had been very largely white Anglo-Saxon Protestants who hailed from the Northeast and Middle West. An occasional "hyphenate" like the German-American Theodore Dreiser proved the ex-

ception, but few writers of any importance came from recent immigrant stock or from the rural hinterlands of the South. By 1960, however, a significant portion of the most interesting American literature was being written by men and women connected in some way with minorities—racial, ethnic, and cultural. The so-called "Southern renaissance" was the work of writers who were simultaneously the products and articulators of a society outside the main currents of urban industrial America, a society as remote to the average northern reader as China.

Nor could it be argued any longer that a foreign-sounding name or a colored skin was inevitably a professional handicap. Saul Bellow, Bernard Malamud, Norman Mailer, Philip Roth, to name only a few, were of Jewish origin; Ralph Ellison and James Baldwin were Negroes; Vance Bourjaily and Jack Kerouac added Lebanese and French-Canadian ingredients. None of these men wrote as an outsider; each spoke out uninhibitedly as an American, a deserving beneficiary of his country's intellectual heritage. Yet detached as they were from their ancestral culture, they somehow retained a marginal outlook. And without renouncing their ethnic or racial past, they translated their own and their minority's experiences into the province of the imagination.

The pain of these experiences may have been sufficient to justify the writers' private and parochial outlook. President Johnson as well as President Kennedy in the 'sixties tried unusually hard to involve the nation's creative talent in their political and social goals, but with small reward. American society, wrote the novelist Norman Mailer after Kennedy's election, was a "vast central swamp of tasteless, toneless authority whose dependable heroes were drawn from F.B.I. men, doctors, television entertainers, corporation executives, and athletes who would cooperate with public relations." It was his hope that Kennedy, glamorous and attractive, might redeem it, a hope surrendered before the President's tragic death. The poet, Robert Lowell, in turn, on declining an invitation to one of President Johnson's

White House parties in the summer of 1965, probably expressed the views of the literary opposition when he wrote: "Although I am very enthusiastic about most of your domestic legislation and intentions, I nevertheless can only follow our present foreign policy with the greatest dismay and distrust. . . . We are in danger of imperceptibly becoming an explosive and suddenly chauvinistic nation, and we may even be drifting on our way to the last nuclear ruin."

Scientists were at least as deeply aware as poets of the possibilities of "nuclear ruin," but no longer allowed this cliche of doom to crush all aspiration or crowd out all hope. The biophysicist John R. Platt, again, spoke for many when he wrote in *The Step to Man* (1966):

We used to think of ourselves as orphans in the world. Now we discover that we are children of the universe, that it has been creating and supporting us for a long time and can go on doing so. We were meant to be here, so to speak.

We thought we were insignificant. Now we discover that we are the most complicated thing in creation, as far as we know.

We thought we were disinherited. Now we discover that we have been given power and resources beyond imagining—the power of the sun itself—to do with what we want.

We thought we were helpless, bound by our animal inheritance, or by the darkness of our twisted subconscious, to irredeemable social organizations or to irrational follies and wars. Now we discover that it is culture that shapes our minds and actions, and . . . that consequently we are free to make of ourselves and our children what we choose. . . .

I think this revolution in philosophical attitudes that is coming out of the laboratories has not been widely appreciated but is even more important than the great technological revolutions of this century. This new position of intellectual man, in astronomy, in biology, and in psychology and the other sciences, opens the door to a new sense of human freedom.

Readings

Asterisk indicates the book is available in paperback.

Many books listed for Chapter 30, including those on the Negro Revolution and the Vietnam war are also recommended for the 'sixties. R. J. Whalen, *The Founding Father, The Story of Joseph P. Kennedy* * (1964), is a revealing introduction to "the family he raised to power." See also T. C. Sorensen, *Kennedy* * (1965); A. M. Schlesinger, Jr., *A Thousand Days, John F. Kennedy in the White House* (1965), and Tom Wicker, *Kennedy without Tears, the Man beneath the Myth* (1964). J. W. Gardner, ed., *To Turn the Tide* * (1962), presents Kennedy's words during his first presidential year. On the assassination, see *A Concise Compendium of the Warren Commission Report on the Assassination of John F. Kennedy* * (1964). Critical books on the Warren Report, include Mark Lane, *Rush to Judgement* (1966), and E. J. Epstein, *Inquest, The Warren Commission and the Establishment of Truth* (1966). William Manchester, *Death of a President* (1967), is a tour de force on the assassination which supports the Warren findings. Robert Novak and Rowland Evans, *Lyndon B. Johnson, The Exercise of Power* (1966), takes the President back to his congressional years. Philip Geyelin, *Lyndon B. Johnson and the World* (1966), is illuminating on his approach to foreign affairs. Harold Faber, ed., *The Road to the White House: The Story of the 1964 Election by the Staff of the New York Times* (1965), is outstanding.

Roger Hilsman and R. C. Good, eds., *Foreign Policy in the Sixties* (1965), is a collection of penetrating essays on world-wide relationships. On major phases of American involvement see, for example, M. D. Irish, ed., *World Pressures on American Foreign Policy* * (1964). Edmund Stillman and William Pfaff, *Power and Impotence, The Failure of America's Foreign Policy* (1966), is a stimulating if unconstructive critique. The *An-*

nual Report of the Secretary-General is indispensable for the current work of the United Nations.

The modern relationship of military power and diplomacy is explored in Urs Schwarz, *American Strategy: A New Perspective, The Growth of Politico-Military Thinking in the United States* (1966). More detailed studies in this vein include T. C. Schelling, *Arms and Influence* (1966); Herman Kahn, *On Thermonuclear War* (1960); and W. W. Kaufmann, *The McNamara Strategy* (1964). Walter Millis, *American Military Thought* (1966), is an historical anthology relevant to today's thinking. I. L. Horowitz, *The War Game, Studies of the New Civilian Militarists* * (1963), is a useful critique.

Three of the many facets of the new military-diplomatic world are discussed in R. N. Rosencranz, ed., *The Dispersion of Nuclear Weapons* (1964); Morris Janowitz, *The Military in the Political Development of New Nations* * (1964); and N. W. Chamberlain, *The West in a World Without War* * (1963). Paul Douglas, *America in the Market Place, Trade, Tariffs and the Balance of Payments* (1966), is an analysis of conventional relationships by the expert Illinois Senator. T. W. Schultz, *Transforming Traditional Agriculture* * (1964), gets at the roots of world hunger. Barrington Moore, Jr., *Social Origins of Dictatorship and Democracy, Lord and Peasant in the Making of the Modern World* (1966); and C. E. Black, *The Dynamics of Modernization: A Study in Comparative History* (1967), offer broader perspectives.

B. J. Wattenberg and R. M. Scammon, *This U.S.A., An Unexpected Family Portrait . . . Drawn from the Census* (1965), affords an exceptional survey based on the 1960 census returns. Suggestive books on varied domestic subjects include W. W. Heller, *New Dimensions of Political Economy* (1966), by Kennedy's Chairman of the Council of Economic Advisors; Michael Harrington, *The Other America, Poverty in the United States* (1962); Oscar Lewis, *La Vida, A Puerto Rican Family in the Culture of Poverty—San Juan and New York* (1966); Edward Higbee, *Farms and Farmers in an Urban Age* (1963); "Cities," in *Scientific American*, September, 1965; Kenneth Keniston, *The Uncommitted: Alienated Youth in American Society* (1965); Fritz Machlup, *The Production and Distribution of Knowledge in the United States* (1962); "Information," in the entire issue of *Scientific American* on Computers, September, 1966; and W. J. Baumol and W. G. Bowen, *Performing Arts; the Economic Dilemma* (1966).

Far out books on space exploration include Walter Sullivan, *We Are Not Alone, The Search for Intelligent Life on Other Worlds* (1964); and I. S. Shklovskii and Carl Sagan, *Intelligent Life in the Universe* (1966). J. R. Platt, *The Step to Man* (1966), is a collection of "visionary essays" on scientific intelligence on earth. Konrad Lorenz, *On Aggression* (1966), is hopeful on mind over instincts. D. K. Price, *The Scientific Estate* (1965), is a good introduction to the ramifying relations of science and government.

Marshall McLuhan, *Understanding Media, The Extensions of Man* (1964), is an imaginative interpretation of the popular media. J. J. Waldmeir, *Recent American Fiction, Some Critical Reviews* * (1963); and Richard Kostelanetz, ed., *On Contemporary Literature* * (1964), offer critical essays on creative writing. Nineteen American poets express their views in Howard Nemerov, *Poets on Poetry* (1966).

Appendix

General Readings

Asterisk indicates that book is available in paperback.

The works cited below are provided first, to acquaint the student with the nature of the historical discipline and related fields; and second, to direct him to useful general histories, reference and source books, and periodicals, in American History.

HISTORY AND RELATED DISCIPLINES

A. S. Eisenstadt, *The Craft of American History* * (2 vols., 1966), is an outstanding collection of essays on interpreting the American past. John Higham, ed., *The Reconstruction of American History* * (1962), presents critical assessments of the treatment of major topics. Economics, Political Science and Sociology rank high among the social sciences most useful in the study of history. Penetrating introductions to them will be found in the short, scholarly volumes in the following: Otto Eckstein, ed., *Foundations of Modern Economics Series* * (1964-1967); R. A. Dahl, ed., *Foundations of Modern Political Science Series* * (1963-   ); and Alex Inkeles, ed., *Foundations of Modern Sociology Series* * (1964-   ). E. R. A. Seligman and Alvin Johnson, eds., *Encyclopaedia of the Social Sciences* (15 vols., 1930-1935), remains invaluable. On the relation of other sciences to history, see, for example, W. T. Jones, *The Sciences and the Humanities; Conflict and Reconciliation* (1965); and Gerald Holton, ed., *Science and Culture, A Study of Cohesive and Disjunctive Forces* (1965).

REFERENCE WORKS AND PERIODICALS

Oscar Handlin and others, eds., *The Harvard Guide to American History* * (1954), is the most comprehensive bibliographic source. *Paperbacks in Print*, published quarterly, offers a complete listing.

Allen Johnson and Dumas Malone, eds., *Dictionary of American Biography* (21 vols., 1928-1944); and J. T. Adams and R. V. Coleman, eds., *Dictionary of American History* (6 vols., 1940), are comprehensive works on the lives of outstanding Americans and the stories of leading events. T. C. Cochran and Wayne Andrews, eds., *Concise Dictionary of American History* (1962), is a one-volume abridgement of Adams and Coleman. R. B. Morris, ed., *Encyclopedia of American History* (1965), is a dependable summary, with a supplement of 400 biographies. W. L. Langer, ed., *Encyclopedia of World History* (1952), is superb. United States Department of Commerce, *Historical Statistics of the United States* (1957), with *Continuation to 1962* (1965), is immensely useful for quantitative information. For maps, see C. O. Paullin, *Atlas of the Historical Geography of the United States* (1932), and, by the editors of *American Heritage*, *The American Heritage Atlas of United States History* (1966). Invaluable for its fine text as well as for its excellent military maps is Brig.-Gen. V. J. Esposito, ed., *The West Point Atlas of American Wars 1689-1953* (2 vols., 1959). R. H. Brown, *Historical Geography of the United States* (1948), is outstanding for the physical environment.

The American Historical Review, although devoted to all fields of history, gives much space to research and reviews in American History. Strictly American History periodicals include: *The Journal of American History* (until 1964, *The Mississippi Valley Historical Review*), *The Journal of Southern History*, *The William and Mary Quarterly*, and *The Pacific Historical Review*. *The American Quarterly* is published by the American Studies Association. The following journals often carry articles and reviews important for American History: *The Journal of Economic History; Political Science Quarterly; American Political Science Review; American Sociological Review;* and *American Journal of Sociology*. Important for recent history are *Foreign Affairs; Scientific American; Fortune; Daedalus;* and *Yale Review*.

COLLECTIONS OF SOURCES

H. S. Commager, ed., *Documents of American History* * (1963), is a massive collection of public documents, invaluable for its coverage. William Miller, ed., *Readings in American Values, Selected* and *Edited from Public Documents of the American Past* * (1964), is more selective. Richard Hofstadter, ed., *Great Issues in American History* * (2 vols., 1958), focuses on major controversies, beginning in 1765. The following series offer a wide selection of contemporary materials in short well-edited paperbacks: *Spectrum* (Prentice-Hall); *Anvil* (Van Nostrand); and *Documents in American Civilization* (Anchor). The Amherst series, *Problems in American Civilization* (Heath), are well-edited paperbacks, presenting opposing scholarly treatments of major issues. Sidney Fine and G. S. Brown, eds., *The American Past, Conflicting Interpretations of Great Issues* (2 vols., 1965), is a useful anthology of journal articles.

Substantial collections of materials in more specialized fields include: K. H. Porter and D. B. Johnson, eds., *National Party Platforms 1840-1960* (1961); W. A. Williams, ed., *The Shaping of American Diplomacy* (1956); Armin Rappaport, *Sources in American Diplomacy* * (1966); J. R. Commons and others, eds., *Documentary History of American Industrial Society* (10 vols., 1910-1911); and A. D. Chandler, Jr., *The Forces in American Economic Growth Series* * (5 vols., 1964-1967). Moses Rischin, ed., *The American Gospel of Success* (1965), is an excellent collection on ascent and aspiration. Herbert Aptheker, *A Documentary History of the Negro People in the United States* * (1951) affords valuable testimony to 1910. Staughton Lynd, *Nonviolence in America: A Documentary History* * (1966), breaks new ground. Oscar Handlin, ed., *This Was America* * (1949), is an illuminating collection of foreign commentary. Richard Hofstadter and Wilson Smith, eds., *American Higher Education* (2 vols., 1961), is comprehensive. F. O. Matthiessen, *The Oxford Book of American Verse* (1950), is a fine anthology.

COMPREHENSIVE GENERAL WORKS

H. S. Commager and R. B. Morris, eds., *The New American Nation Series* * (1954-   ), on its completion, will afford the most comprehensive modern treatment of American history. By 1966, twenty volumes, each with full bibliographies, had been issued. Other useful multi-author series include A. M. Schlesinger and D. R. Fox, eds., *A History of American Life* (13 vols., 1927-1948); Allen Johnson, ed., *Chronicles of America* (50 vols., 1918-1921, with 6 additional volumes edited by Allan Nevins, 1950-1951); and D. J. Boorstin, ed., *The Chicago History of American Civilization* * (1956-   ), offering short works on special periods and topics.

C. A. and M. R. Beard, *The Rise of American Civilization* (1927), *America in Midpassage* (1939), and *The American Spirit* (1942), although somewhat dated, remain valuable for their sweep and insight. D. J. Boorstin, *The Americans: The Colonial Experience* * (1958), and *The Americans: The National Experience* * (1965), are the first two volumes of a history in progress. Older comprehensive works by single authors, still of value, include George Bancroft, *History of the United States* (10 vols., 1834-1875), to the end of the Revolution; and Edward Channing, *History of the United States* (6 vols., 1905-1925), to the end of the Civil War. For the Middle Period, see J. F. Rhodes, *History of the United States From . . . 1850 to . . . 1877* (7 vols., 1906), and Allan Nevins' 10-volume work in progress, of which 6 volumes from 1847 to 1863 had been published by 1966. For the later period, see E. P. Oberholtzer, *A History of the United States Since the Civil War* (5 vols., 1917-1937), and A. M. Schlesinger, Jr., *The Age of Roosevelt* (1957-   ), of which three volumes covering 1919 to 1936 had been published by 1966.

POLITICAL AND CONSTITUTIONAL HISTORY

A. H. Kelly and W. A. Harbison, *The American Constitution, Its Origins and Development* (1963), is an outstanding history from the early English background through the civil rights controversies of the 1960's, rich in bibliography. Charles Warren, *The Supreme Court in United States History* (2 vols., 1937), is standard for the nineteenth century. R. G. McCloskey, *The American Supreme Court* (1960), is a short modern history. E. S. Corwin, ed., *The Constitution of the United States of America, Analysis and Interpretation* * (1953), is an invaluable annotated edition that traces Supreme Court decisions on every section.

On the executive, see E. S. Corwin, *The President, Office and Powers* * (1957). G. B. Galloway, *History of the House of Representatives* (1962), and G. H. Haynes, *The Senate of the United States* (2 vols., 1938), cover the legislature. Leonard White, *The Federalists* (1948), *The Jeffersonians* (1951), *The Jacksonians* (1954), and *The Republican Era 1869-1901* (1958), are excellent on administrative history. See also, J. J. Corson and J. P. Harris, *Public Administration in Modern Society* * (1963). W. E. Binkley, *American Political Parties: Their Natural History* (1963), is standard. Richard Hofstadter, *The American Political Tradition* * (1948), and Louis Hartz, *The Liberal Tradition in America* * (1955), offer modern interpretations.

DIPLOMATIC AND MILITARY HISTORY

Alexander DeConde, *A History of American Foreign Policy* (1963), is an outstanding text. J. W. Pratt, *A History of United States Foreign Policy* (1965); and R. W. Leopold, *The Growth of American Foreign Policy* (1962), are also useful. S. F. Bemis, ed., *American Secretaries of State and Their Diplomacy* (10 vols., 1927-1929), may be supplemented by N. A. Graebner, ed., *An Uncertain Tradition: American Secretaries of State in the Twentieth Century* (1961).

The West Point Atlas of American Wars (see under Reference Works, above) is outstanding for military engagements. Department of the Army ROTC Manual, *American Military History 1607-1953* (1956), is an authoritative short account. Walter Millis, *Arms and Men, A Study of American Military History* * (1956), is a critical survey. Walter Millis, ed., *American Military Thought* (1966), is a panoramic anthology. W. A. Ganoe, *The History of the United States Army* (1942), and Harold and Margaret Sprout, *The Rise of American Naval Power* (1942), are standard. The role of the military in American democracy is discussed historically in A. A. Ekirch, Jr., *The Civilian and the Military*

(1956). S. P. Huntington, *The Soldier and the State, The Theory and Politics of Civil-Military Relations* * (1957), is more analytical.

THE FRONTIER, THE WEST, AND THE SOUTH

R. A. Billington, *Westward Expansion* (1967), is a well organized history of the moving frontier, with an up-to-date bibliography. F. J. Turner, *The Frontier in American History* * (1920), and *The Significance of Sections in American History* (1932), are classic studies. R. M. Robbins, *Our Landed Heritage* * (1942), affords a good general account of the disposal of the public domain. On the Indians and related subjects, see *Readings* for Chapter 18. W. D. Wyman and C. B. Kroeber, *The Frontier in Perspective* * (1957), is made up of essays on frontiers from Roman times onward, as well as the American frontier.

Many works on the distinctive South are cited in chapter *Readings,* especially Chapters 13 and 17. W. H. Stephenson and E. M. Coulter, *A History of the South* (10 vols., 1947—   ) is an outstanding series. Valuable one-volume books covering the range of southern history include F. B. Simkins, *History of the South* (1953); W. B. Hesseltine, *The South in American History* (1960); W. J. Cash, *The Mind of the South* * (1941); E. Q. Hawk, *Economic History of the South* (1934); and J. B. Hubbell, *The South in American Literature 1607-1900* (1954).

ECONOMIC HISTORY

Of the numerous general surveys, the following may be suggested: E. C. Kirkland, *A History of American Economic Life* (1951), in the narrative tradition; and R. M. Robertson, *History of the American Economy* (1964), in the analytic tradition. Henry David and others, eds., *The Economic History of the United States* (1945-   ), is a projected 10-volume work by leading scholars, of which all but the first and last volumes had been published by 1966. D. R. Dewey, *Financial History of the United States* (1934), remains a standard work. Milton Friedman and A. J. Schwartz, *A Monetary History of the United States 1867-1960* (1963), is illuminating on the last century. The standard work on labor history is J. R. Commons and others, *History of Labor in the United States* (4 vols., 1918-1935). J. G. Rayback, *A History of American Labor* * (1959), is a sound one-volume work.

E. E. Edwards, "American Agriculture: The First Three Hundred Years," in the *1940 Yearbook of Agriculture,* published by the Department of Agriculture, is an excellent short account. M. R. Benedict, *Farm Policies of the United States 1790-1950* (1953), is good on issues and legislation. V. S. Clark, *History of Manufactures in the United States* (3 vols., 1929), is standard. On modern tendencies, see, for example, C. R. Hall, *History of American Industrial Science* (1954); and A. D. Chandler, Jr., *Strategy and Structure, Chapters in the History of Industrial Enterprise* * (1962). Roger Burlingame, *March of the Iron Men* * (1938), *Engines of Democracy* (1940), and *Backgrounds of Power* (1949), comprise a highly readable history of American technology.

T. C. Cochran and William Miller, *The Age of Enterprise* * (1942), is a general interpretation from 1800 to the New Deal. Joseph Dorfman, *The Economic Mind in American Civilization* (5 vols., 1946-1959) is a wide-ranging history of American political-economic thought. Simon Kuznets, *National Income and Its Composition 1919-1938* (1941), is a landmark in statistical research, one of many National Bureau of Economic Research publications of lasting value for American History.

SOCIAL AND URBAN HISTORY

M. R. Davie, *World Immigration* (1949), is a history of the movement of peoples since colonial times. Carl Wittke, *We Who Built America* * (1940), is a general survey of the immigrant in the United States. M. L. Hansen, *The Atlantic Migration 1607-1860* * (1940), is a valuable study of the "old" newcomers. On the "new" immigration, Oscar Handlin, *The Uprooted* (1951) is outstanding. See also, Oscar Handlin, *Immigration as a Factor in American History* * (1959). The leading general history of the Negro in Africa and America is J. H. Franklin, *From Slavery to Freedom: A History of American Negroes* (1956). See also, Benjamin Quarles, *The Negro in the Making of America* * (1964). Anti-immigrant prejudice and its consequences are traced in R. A. Billington, *The Protestant Crusade 1800-1860* * (1938), and John Higham, *Strangers in the Land, Patterns of American Nativism 1860-1925* * (1955). On more recent tendencies, see, for example, Nathan Glazer and D. P. Moynihan, *Beyond the Melting Pot, The Negroes, Puerto Ricans, Jews, Italians, and Irish of New York City* * (1963).

For general and interpretive histories of urbanization, see the *Readings* for Chapter 21. To these may be added Charles Abrams, *The City is the Frontier* (1965), and R. C. Weaver, *The Urban Complex* * (1966). R. C. Wood, *Suburbia* * (1959) is a good introduction. A. W. Calhoun, *A Social History of the American Family* (3 vols., 1917-1919), is the only comprehensive book on this subject. D. P. Moynihan, *The Negro Family, The Case for National Action* * (1965), is a short penetrating analysis. On high society, Dixon Wecter, *The Saga of American Society* (1937), is excellent. See also, E. D. Baltzell, *The Protestant Establishment, Aristocracy and Caste in America* * (1964). I. G. Wyllie, *The Self-Made Man in America* * (1954), is an excellent historical account. See also, S. M. Lipset and Reinhard Bendix, *Social Mobility in Industrial Society* (1959), and C. W. Mills, *White Collar* * (1952). On selected special subjects, see, F. R. Packard, *History of Medicine in the United States* (2 vols., 1931); Blake McKelvey, *American Prisons* (1936); and F. R. Dulles, *America Learns to Play* (1940).

INTELLECTUAL AND CULTURAL HISTORY

V. L. Parrington, *Main Currents in American Thought* * (3 vols., 1927-1930), though much criticized, remains a standard work. Merle Curti, *The Growth of American Thought* (1964), is comprehensive. R. H. Gabriel, *The Course of American Democratic Thought* (1956), covers the period since 1815. H. W. Schneider, *A History of American Philosophy* (1946), is the standard work. Richard Hofstadter, *Anti-intellectualism in American Life* * (1963), is a history of the obstacles to the realm of the mind. R. E. Spiller and others, *Literary History of the United States* (3 vols., 1943), is an exhaustive survey. The third volume, a valuable bibliography, should be supplemented by H. M. Jones, *Guide to American Literature and Its Backgrounds Since 1890* (1953). Van Wyck Brooks, *Makers and Finders* (5 vols., 1936-1952), on writers from 1800 to 1915, is rich in background. Marcus Cunliffe, *The Literature of the United States* * (1954), is a sound one-volume account. Constance Rourke, *American Humor* * (1931), is a brilliant study of national character.

Leading books in special fields of art include, O. W. Larkin, *Art and Life in America* (1949); E. P. Richardson, *Painting in America, the Story of 450 Years* * (1956); James Burchard and Albert Bush-Brown, *The Architecture of America, A Social and Cultural History* (1966); and J. M. Fitch, *American Building* (1948).

The standard works on journalism are F. L. Mott, *American Journalism* (1950), and *A History of American Magazines* (4 vols., 1930-1957). Merle Curti, *Social Ideas of American Educators* (1935), is a thoughtful introduction. E. P. Cubberley, *Public Education in the United States* (1934), is an excellent older work, to be supplemented, for example, by A. E. Bestor, *The Restoration of Learning* (1955), and J. B. Conant, *The American High School Today* * (1959). On the higher learning, see Richard Hofstadter and Walter Metzger, *Academic Freedom in the United States* * (1955), which goes well beyond the scope of its title, and Laurence Veysey, *The Emergence of the American University* (1965). Winthrop Hudson, *Religion in America* * (1965), is a leading general work. S. E. Mead, *The Lively Experiment, The Shaping of Christianity in America* (1963), is a penetrating short analysis. E. B. Greene, *Religion and the State* * (1941), and J. F. Wilson, *Church and State in American History* * (1965), afford good introductions to that issue.

The Declaration of Independence

When in the course of human events, it becomes necessary for one people to dissolve the political bands which have connected them with another, and to assume, among the powers of the earth, the separate and equal station to which the laws of nature and of nature's God entitle them, a decent respect to the opinions of mankind requires that they should declare the causes which impel them to the separation.

We hold these truths to be self-evident, that all men are created equal; that they are endowed by their Creator with certain unalienable rights; that among these, are life, liberty, and the pursuit of happiness. That, to secure these rights, governments are instituted among men, deriving their just powers from the consent of the governed; that, whenever any form of government becomes destructive of these ends, it is the right of the people to alter or to abolish it, and to institute a new government, laying its foundation on such principles, and organizing its powers in such form, as to them shall seem most likely to effect their safety and happiness. Prudence, indeed, will dictate that governments long established, should not be changed for light and transient causes; and, accordingly, all experience hath shown, that mankind are more disposed to suffer, while evils are sufferable, than to right themselves by abolishing the forms to which they are accustomed. But, when a long train of abuses and usurpations, pursuing invariably the same object, evinces a design to reduce them under absolute despotism, it is their right, it is their duty, to throw off such government and to provide new guards for their future security. Such has been the patient sufferance of these colonies, and such is now the necessity which constrains them to alter their former systems of government. The history of the present King of Great Britain is a history of repeated injuries and usurpations, all having, in direct object, the establishment of an absolute tyranny over these States. To prove this, let facts be submitted to a candid world:—

He has refused his assent to laws the most wholesome and necessary for the public good.

He has forbidden his governors to pass laws of immediate and pressing importance, unless suspended in their operation till his assent should be obtained; and, when so suspended, he has utterly neglected to attend to them.

He has refused to pass other laws for the accommodation of large districts of people, unless those people would relinquish the right of representation in the legislature; a right inestimable to them, and formidable to tyrants only.

He has called together legislative bodies at places unusual, uncomfortable, and distant from the depository of their public records, for the sole purpose of fatiguing them into compliance with his measures.

He has dissolved representative houses, repeatedly for opposing, with manly firmness, his invasions on the rights of the people.

He has refused, for a long time after such dissolutions, to cause others to be elected; whereby the legislative powers, incapable of annihilation, have returned to the people at large for their exercise; the state remaining, in the meantime, exposed to all the danger of invasion from without, and convulsions within.

He has endeavored to prevent the population of these States; for that purpose, obstructing the laws for naturalization of foreigners, refusing to pass others to encourage their migration hither, and raising the conditions of new appropriations of lands.

He has obstructed the administration of justice, by refusing his assent to laws for establishing judiciary powers.

He has made judges dependent on his will alone, for the tenure of their offices, and the amount and payment of their salaries.

He has erected a multitude of new offices, and sent hither swarms of officers to harass our people, and eat out their substance.

He has kept among us, in time of peace, standing armies, without the consent of our legislatures.

He has affected to render the military independent of, and superior to, the civil power.

He has combined, with others, to subject us to a jurisdiction foreign to our Constitution, and unacknowledged by our laws; giving his assent to their acts of pretended legislation:

For quartering large bodies of armed troops among us:

For protecting them by a mock trial, from punishment, for any murders which they should commit on the inhabitants of these States:

For cutting off our trade with all parts of the world:

For imposing taxes on us without our consent:

For depriving us, in many cases, of the benefit of trial by jury:

For transporting us beyond seas to be tried for pretended offences:

For abolishing the free system of English laws in a neighboring province, establishing therein an arbitrary government, and enlarging its boundaries, so as to render it at once an example and fit instrument for introducing the same absolute rule into these colonies:

For taking away our charters, abolishing our most valuable laws, and altering, fundamentally, the powers of our governments:

For suspending our own legislatures, and declaring themselves invested with power to legislate for us in all cases whatsoever.

He has abdicated government here, by declaring us out of his protection, and waging war against us.

He has plundered our seas, ravaged our coasts, burnt our towns, and destroyed the lives of our people.

He is, at this time, transporting large armies of foreign mercenaries to complete the works of death, desolation, and tyranny, already begun, with circumstances of cruelty and perfidy scarcely paralleled

in the most barbarous ages, and totally unworthy the head of a civilized nation.

He has constrained our fellow citizens, taken captive on the high seas, to bear arms against their country, to become the executioners of their friends, and brethren, or to fall themselves by their hands.

He has excited domestic insurrections amongst us, and has endeavored to bring on the inhabitants of our frontiers, the merciless Indian savages, whose known rule of warfare is an undistinguished destruction of all ages, sexes, and conditions.

In every stage of these oppressions, we have petitioned for redress, in the most humble terms; our repeated petitions have been answered only by repeated injury. A prince, whose character is thus marked by every act which may define a tyrant, is unfit to be the ruler of a free people.

Nor have we been wanting in attention to our British brethren. We have warned them, from time to time, of attempts made by their legislature to extend an unwarrantable jurisdiction over us. We have reminded them of the circumstances of our emigration and settlement here. We have appealed to their native justice and magnanimity, and we have conjured them, by the ties of our common kindred, to disavow these usurpations, which would inevitably interrupt our connections and correspondence. They, too, have been deaf to the voice of justice and consanguinity. We must, therefore, acquiesce in the necessity which denounces our separation, and hold them, as we hold the rest of mankind, enemies in war, in peace, friends.

We, therefore, the representatives of the United States of America, in general Congress assembled, appealing to the Supreme Judge of the world for the rectitude of our intentions, do, in the name, and by the authority of the good people of these colonies, solemnly publish and declare, that these united colonies are, and of right ought to be, free and independent states: that they are absolved from all allegiance to the British Crown, and that all political connection between them and the state of Great Britain is, and ought to be, totally dissolved; and that, as free and independent states, they have full power to levy war, conclude peace, contract alliances, establish commerce, and to do all other acts and things which independent states may of right do. And, for the support of this declaration, with a firm reliance on the protection of Divine Providence, we mutually pledge to each other our lives, our fortunes, and our sacred honor.

The Constitution of the United States of America

We the people of the United States, in order to form a more perfect union, establish justice, insure domestic tranquillity, provide for the common defense, promote the general welfare, and secure the blessings of liberty to ourselves and our posterity, do ordain and establish this Constitution for the United States of America.

ARTICLE I

Section 1. All legislative powers herein granted shall be vested in a Congress of the United States, which shall consist of a Senate and House of Representatives.

Section 2. 1. The House of Representatives shall be composed of members chosen every second year by the people of the several States, and the electors in each State shall have the qualifications requisite for electors of the most numerous branch of the State legislature.

2. No person shall be a representative who shall not have attained to the age of twenty-five years, and been seven years a citizen of the United States, and who shall not, when elected, be an inhabitant of that State in which he shall be chosen.

3. Representatives and direct taxes [1] shall be apportioned among the several States which may be included within this Union, according to their respective numbers, which shall be determined by adding to the whole number of free persons, including those bound to service for a term of years, and excluding Indians not taxed, three fifths of all other persons.[2] The actual enumeration shall be made within three years after the first meeting of the Congress of the United States, and within every subsequent term of ten years, in such manner as they shall by law direct. The number of representatives shall not exceed one for every thirty thousand, but each State shall have at least one representative; and until such enumeration shall be made, the State of New Hampshire shall be entitled to choose three, Massachusetts eight, Rhode Island and Providence Plantations one, Connecticut five, New York six, New Jersey four, Pennsylvania eight, Delaware one, Maryland six, Virginia ten, North Carolina five, South Carolina five, and Georgia three.

4. When vacancies happen in the representation from any State, the executive authority thereof shall issue writs of election to fill such vacancies.

5. The House of Representatives shall choose their speaker and other officers; and shall have the sole power of impeachment.

Section 3. 1. The Senate of the United States shall be composed of two senators from each State, chosen by the legislature thereof,[3] for six years; and each senator shall have one vote.

2. Immediately after they shall be assembled in consequence of the first election, they shall be divided as equally as may be into three classes. The seats of the senators of the first class shall be vacated at the expiration of the second year, of the second class at the expiration of the fourth year, and of the third class at the expiration of the sixth year, so that one third may be chosen every second year; and if vacancies happen by resignation, or otherwise, during the recess of the legislature of any State, the executive thereof may make temporary appointments until the next meeting of the legislature, which shall then fill such vacancies.[4]

3. No person shall be a senator who shall not have attained to the age of thirty years, and been nine years a citizen of the United States, and who shall not, when elected, be an inhabitant of that State for which he shall be chosen.

4. The Vice President of the United States shall be President of the Senate, but shall have no vote, unless they be equally divided.

5. The Senate shall choose their other officers, and also a president pro tempore, in the absence of the Vice President, or when he shall exercise the office of the President of the United States.

6. The Senate shall have the sole power to try all impeachments. When sitting for that purpose, they shall be on oath or affirmation. When the President of the United States is tried, the chief justice shall preside: and no person shall be convicted without the concurrence of two thirds of the members present.

7. Judgment in cases of impeachment shall not extend further than to removal from office, and disqualifications to hold and enjoy any office of honor, trust or profit under the United States: but the party convicted shall nevertheless be liable and subject to indictment, trial, judgment and punishment, according to law.

Section 4. 1. The times, places, and manner of holding elections for senators and representatives, shall be prescribed in each State by the legislature thereof; but the Congress may at any time by law make or alter such regulations, except as to the places of choosing senators.

2. The Congress shall assemble at least once in every year, and such meeting shall be on the first Monday in December, unless they shall by law appoint a different day.

Section 5. 1. Each House shall be the judge of the elections, returns and qualifications of its own members, and a majority of each shall constitute a quorum to do business; but a smaller number may adjourn from day to day, and may be authorized to compel the attendance of absent members, in such manner, and under such penalties as each House may provide.

2. Each House may determine the rules of its proceedings, punish its members for disorderly behav-

[1] See the 16th Amendment.
[2] See the 14th Amendment.
[3] See the 17th Amendment.

[4] See the 17th Amendment.

ior, and, with the concurrence of two thirds, expel a member.

3. Each House shall keep a journal of its proceedings, and from time to time publish the same, excepting such parts as may in their judgment require secrecy; and the yeas and nays of the members of either House on any question shall, at the desire of one fifth of those present, be entered on the journal.

4. Neither House, during the session of Congress, shall, without the consent of the other, adjourn for more than three days, nor to any other place than that in which the two Houses shall be sitting.

Section 6. 1. The senators and representatives shall receive a compensation for their services, to be ascertained by law, and paid out of the Treasury of the United States. They shall in all cases, except treason, felony, and breach of the peace, be privileged from arrest during their attendance at the session of their respective Houses, and in going to and returning from the same; and for any speech or debate in either House, they shall not be questioned in any other place.

2. No senator or representative shall, during the time for which he was elected, be appointed to any civil office under the authority of the United States, which shall have been created, or the emoluments whereof shall have been increased, during such time; and no person holding any office under the United States shall be a member of either House during his continuance in office.

Section 7. 1. All bills for raising revenue shall originate in the House of Representatives; but the Senate may propose or concur with amendments as on other bills.

2. Every bill which shall have passed the House of Representatives and the Senate, shall, before it become a law, be presented to the President of the United States; If he approves he shall sign it, but if not he shall return it, with his objections, to that House in which it shall have originated, who shall enter the objections at large on their journal, and proceed to reconsider it. If after such reconsideration two thirds of that House shall agree to pass the bill, it shall be sent, together with the objections, to the other House, by which it shall likewise be reconsidered, and if approved by two thirds of that House, it shall become a law. But in all such cases the votes of both Houses shall be determined by yeas and nays, and the names of the persons voting for and against the bill shall be entered on the journal of each House respectively. If any bill shall not be returned by the President within ten days (Sundays excepted) after it shall have been presented to him, the same shall be a law, in like manner as if he had signed it, unless the Congress by their adjournment prevent its return, in which case it shall not be a law.

3. Every order, resolution, or vote to which the concurrence of the Senate and the House of Representatives may be necessary (except on a question of adjournment) shall be presented to the President of the United States; and before the same shall take effect, shall be approved by him, or being disapproved by him, shall be repassed by two thirds of the Senate and House of Representatives, according to the rules and limitations prescribed in the case of a bill.

Section 8. The Congress shall have the power

1. To lay and collect taxes, duties, imposts, and excises, to pay the debts and provide for the common defense and general welfare of the United States; but all duties, imposts, and excises shall be uniform throughout the United States;

2. To borrow money on the credit of the United States;

3. To regulate commerce with foreign nations, and among the several States, and with the Indian tribes;

4. To establish an uniform rule of naturalization, and uniform laws on the subject of bankruptcies throughout the United States;

5. To coin money, regulate the value thereof, and of foreign coin, and fix the standard of weights and measures;

6. To provide for the punishment of counterfeiting the securities and current coin of the United States;

7. To establish post offices and post roads;

8. To promote the progress of science and useful arts, by securing for limited times to authors and inventors the exclusive right to their respective writings and discoveries;

9. To constitute tribunals inferior to the Supreme Court;

10. To define and punish piracies and felonies committed on the high seas, and offenses against the law of nations;

11. To declare war, grant letters of marque and reprisal, and make rules concerning captures on land and water;

12. To raise and support armies, but no appropriation of money to that use shall be for a longer term than two years;

13. To provide and maintain a navy;

14. To make rules for the government and regulation of the land and naval forces;

15. To provide for calling forth the militia to execute the laws of the Union, suppress insurrections and repel invasions;

16. To provide for organizing, arming, and disciplining the militia, and for governing such part of them as may be employed in the service of the United States, reserving to the States respectively, the appointment of the officers, and the authority of training the militia according to the discipline prescribed by Congress;

17. To exercise exclusive legislation in all cases whatsoever, over such district (not exceeding ten miles square) as may, by cession of particular States, and the acceptance of Congress, become the seat of the government of the United States, and to exercise like authority over all places purchased by the consent of the legislature of the State in which the same shall be, for the erection of forts, magazines, arsenals, dockyards, and other needful buildings; and

18. To make all laws which shall be necessary and proper for carrying into execution the foregoing powers, and all other powers vested by this Constitution in the government of the United States, or any department or officer thereof.

Section 9. 1. The migration or importation of such persons as any of the States now existing shall think proper to admit, shall not be prohibited by the Congress prior to the year one thousand eight hundred and eight, but a tax or duty may be imposed on such importation, not exceeding ten dollars for each person.

2. The privilege of the writ of habeas corpus shall not be suspended, unless when in cases of rebellion or invasion the public safety may require it.

3. No bill of attainder or ex post facto law shall be passed.

4. No capitation, or other direct, tax shall be laid, unless in proportion to the census or enumeration hereinbefore directed to be taken.[5]

5. No tax or duty shall be laid on articles exported from any State.

6. No preference shall be given by any regulation of commerce or revenue to the ports of one State over those of another: nor shall vessels bound to, or from, one State be obliged to enter, clear, or pay duties in another.

7. No money shall be drawn from the treasury, but in consequence of appropriations made by law; and a regular statement and account of the receipts and expenditures of all public money shall be published from time to time.

8. No title of nobility shall be granted by the United States: and no person holding any office of profit or trust under them, shall, without the consent of the Congress, accept of any present, emolument, office, or title, of any kind whatever, from any king, prince, or foreign State.

Section 10. 1. No State shall enter into any treaty, alliance, or confederation; grant letters of marque and reprisal; coin money; emit bills of credit; make any thing but gold and silver coin a tender in payment of debts; pass any bill of attainder, ex post facto law, or law impairing the obligation of contracts, or grant any title of nobility.

2. No State shall, without the consent of the Congress, lay any imposts or duties on imports or exports, except what may be absolutely necessary for executing its inspection laws: and the net produce of all duties and imposts laid by any State on imports or exports, shall be for the use of the treasury of the United States; and all such laws shall be subject to the revision and control of the Congress.

3. No State shall, without the consent of the Congress, lay any duty of tonnage, keep troops, or ships of war in time of peace, enter into any agreement or compact with another State, or with a foreign power, or engage in war, unless actually invaded, or in such imminent danger as will not admit of delay.

ARTICLE II

Section 1. 1. The executive power shall be vested in a President of the United States of America. He shall hold his office during the term of four years, and, together with the Vice President, chosen for the same term, be elected, as follows:

2. Each State shall appoint, in such manner as the legislature thereof may direct, a number of electors, equal to the whole number of senators and representatives to which the State may be entitled in the Congress: but no senator or representative, or person holding an office of trust or profit under the United States, shall be appointed an elector.

The electors shall meet in their respective States, and vote by ballot for two persons, of whom one at least shall not be an inhabitant of the same State with themselves. And they shall make a list of all the persons voted for, and of the number of votes for each; which list they shall sign and certify, and transmit sealed to the seat of the government of the United States, directed to the president of the Senate. The president of the Senate shall, in the presence of the Senate and House of Representatives, open all the certificates, and the votes shall then be counted. The person having the greatest number of votes shall be the President, if such number be a majority of the whole number of electors appointed; and if there be more than one who have such majority, and have an equal number of votes, then the House of Representatives shall immediately choose by ballot one of them for President; and if no person have a majority, then from the five highest on the list the said House shall in like manner choose the President. But in choosing the President, the votes shall be taken by States, the representation from each State having one vote; a quorum for this purpose shall consist of a member or members from two thirds of the States, and a majority of all the States shall be necessary to a choice. In every case, after the choice of the President, the person having the greatest number of votes of the electors shall be the Vice President. But if there should remain two or more who have equal votes, the Senate shall choose from them by ballot the Vice President.[6]

3. The Congress may determine the time of choosing the electors, and the day on which they shall give their votes; which day shall be the same throughout the United States.

4. No person except a natural born citizen, or a citizen of the United States, at the time of the adoption of this Constitution, shall be eligible to the office of President; neither shall any person be eligible to that office who shall not have attained to the age of thirty-five years, and been fourteen years a resident within the United States.

5. In case of the removal of the President from office, or of his death, resignation, or inability to discharge the powers and duties of the said office, the same shall devolve on the Vice President, and the Congress may by law provide for the case of removal, death, resignation or inability, both of the President and Vice President, declaring what officer shall then act as President, and such officer shall act accordingly, until the disability be removed, or a President shall be elected.

6. The President shall, at stated times, receive for his services a compensation, which shall neither be increased nor diminished during the period for which he shall have been elected, and he shall not receive within that period any other emolument from the United States, or any of them.

7. Before he enter on the execution of his office, he shall take the following oath or affirmation:— "I do solemnly swear (or affirm) that I will faithfully execute the office of President of the United States, and will to the best of my ability, preserve, protect and defend the Constitution of the United States."

Section 2. 1. The President shall be commander in chief of the army and navy of the United States, and of the militia of the several States, when called into the actual service of the United States; he may require the opinion, in writing, of the principal officer in each of the executive departments, upon any subject relating to the duties of their respective offices, and he shall have power to grant reprieves and pardons for offenses against the United States, except in cases of impeachment.

2. He shall have power, by and with the advice and consent of the Senate, to make treaties, provided two thirds of the senators present concur; and he shall nominate, and by and with the advice and consent of the Senate, shall appoint ambassadors, other public ministers and consuls, judges of the Supreme Court, and all other officers of the United States, whose appointments are not herein otherwise provided for, and which shall be established by law: but the Congress may by law vest the appointment of such inferior officers, as they think

[5] See the 16th Amendment.

[6] Superseded by the 12th Amendment.

proper, in the President alone, in the courts of law, or in the heads of departments.

3. The President shall have power to fill up all vacancies that may happen during the recess of the Senate, by granting commissions which shall expire at the end of their next session.

Section 3. He shall from time to time give to the Congress information of the state of the Union, and recommend to their consideration such measures as he shall judge necessary and expedient; he may, on extraordinary occasions, convene both Houses, or either of them, and in case of disagreement between them with respect to the time of adjournment, he may adjourn them to such time as he shall think proper; he shall receive ambassadors and other public ministers; he shall take care that the laws be faithfully executed, and shall commission all the officers of the United States.

Section 4. The President, Vice President, and all civil officers of the United States, shall be removed from office on impeachment for, and conviction of, treason, bribery, or other high crimes and misdemeanors.

ARTICLE III

Section 1. The judicial power of the United States shall be vested in one Supreme Court, and in such inferior courts as the Congress may from time to time ordain and establish. The judges, both of the Supreme and inferior courts, shall hold their offices during good behavior, and shall, at stated times, receive for their services, a compensation, which shall not be diminished during their continuance in office.

Section 2. 1. The judicial power shall extend to all cases, in law and equity, arising under this Constitution, the laws of the United States, and treaties made, or which shall be made, under their authority;—to all cases affecting ambassadors, other public ministers and consuls;—to all cases of admiralty and maritime jurisdiction;—to controversies to which the United States shall be a party;—to controversies between two or more States;—between a State and citizens of another State;—between citizens of different States;—between citizens of the same State claiming lands under grants of different States, and between a State, or the citizens thereof, and foreign States, citizens or subjects.

2. In all cases affecting ambassadors, other public ministers and consuls, and those in which a State shall be party, the Supreme Court shall have original jurisdiction. In all the other cases before mentioned, the Supreme Court shall have appellate jurisdiction, both as to law and fact, with such exceptions, and under such regulations as the Congress shall make.

3. The trial of all crimes, except in cases of impeachment, shall be by jury; and such trial shall be held in the State where the said crimes shall have been committed; but when not committed within any State, the trial shall be at such place or places as the Congress may by law have directed.

Section 3. 1. Treason against the United States shall consist only in levying war against them, or in adhering to their enemies, giving them aid and comfort. No person shall be convicted of treason unless on the testimony of two witnesses to the same overt act, or on confession in open court.

2. The Congress shall have power to declare the punishment of treason, but no attainder of treason shall work corruption of blood, or forfeiture except during the life of the person attainted.

7 See the 11th Amendment.

ARTICLE IV

Section 1. Full faith and credit shall be given in each State to the public acts, records, and judicial proceedings of every other State. And the Congress may by general laws prescribe the manner in which such acts, records and proceedings shall be proved, and the effect thereof.

Section 2. 1. The citizens of each State shall be entitled to all privileges and immunities of citizens in the several States.8

2. A person charged in any State with treason, felony, or other crime, who shall flee from justice, and be found in another State, shall on demand of the executive authority of the State from which he fled, be delivered up to be removed to the State having jurisdiction of the crime.

3. No person held to service or labor in one State under the laws thereof, escaping into another, shall, in consequence of any law or regulation therein, be discharged from such service or labor, but shall be delivered up on claim of the party to whom such service or labor may be due.9

Section 3. 1. New States may be admitted by the Congress into this Union; but no new State shall be formed or erected within the jurisdiction of any other State; nor any State be formed by the junction of two or more States, or parts of States, without the consent of the legislatures of the States concerned as well as of the Congress.

2. The Congress shall have power to dispose of and make all needful rules and regulations respecting the territory or other property belonging to the United States; and nothing in this Constitution shall be so construed as to prejudice any claims of the United States, or of any particular State.

Section 4. The United States shall guarantee to every State in this Union a republican form of government, and shall protect each of them against invasion; and on application of the legislature, or of the executive (when the legislature cannot be convened) against domestic violence.

ARTICLE V

The Congress, whenever two thirds of both Houses shall deem it necessary, shall propose amendments to this Constitution, or, on the application of the legislatures of two thirds of the several States, shall call a convention for proposing amendments, which in either case, shall be valid to all intents and purposes, as part of this Constitution, when ratified by the legislatures of three fourths of the several States, or by conventions in three fourths thereof, as the one or the other mode of ratification may be proposed by the Congress; Provided that no amendment which may be made prior to the year one thousand eight hundred and eight shall in any manner affect the first and fourth clauses in the ninth section of the first article; and that no State, without its consent, shall be deprived of its equal suffrage in the Senate.

ARTICLE VI

1. All debts contracted and engagements entered into, before the adoption of this Constitution, shall

8 See the 14th Amendment, Sec. 1.
9 See the 13th Amendment.

be as valid against the United States under this Constitution, as under the Confederation.[10]

2. This Constitution, and the laws of the United States which shall be made in pursuance thereof; and all treaties made, or which shall be made, under the authority of the United States, shall be the supreme law of the land; and the Judges in every State shall be bound thereby, any thing in the Constitution or laws of any State to the contrary notwithstanding.

3. The senators and representatives before mentioned, and the members of the several State legislatures, and all executive and judicial officers, both of the United States and of the several States, shall be bound by oath or affirmation to support this Constitution; but no religious test shall ever be required as a qualification to any office or public trust under the United States.

ARTICLE VII

The ratification of the conventions of nine States shall be sufficient for the establishment of this Constitution between the States so ratifying the same.

Done in Convention by the unanimous consent of the States present the seventeenth day of September in the year of our Lord one thousand seven hundred and eighty-seven, and of the independence of the United States of America the twelfth. In witness whereof we have hereunto subscribed our names.

[Names omitted]

*   *   *

Articles in addition to, and amendment of, the Constitution of the United States of America, proposed by Congress, and ratified by the legislatures of the several States, pursuant to the fifth article of the original Constitution.

AMENDMENT I [First ten amendments ratified December 15, 1791]

Congress shall make no law respecting an establishment of religion, or prohibiting the free exercise thereof; or abridging the freedom of speech, or of the press; or the right of the people peaceably to assemble, and to petition the government for a redress of grievances.

AMENDMENT II

A well regulated militia, being necessary to the security of a free State, the right of the people to keep and bear arms, shall not be infringed.

AMENDMENT III

No soldier shall, in time of peace be quartered in any house, without the consent of the owner, nor in time of war, but in a manner to be prescribed by law.

AMENDMENT IV

The right of the people to secure in their persons, houses, papers, and effects, against unreasonable searches and seizures, shall not be violated, and no warrants shall issue, but upon probable cause, supported by oath or affirmation, and particularly describing the place to be searched, and the persons or things to be seized.

[10] See the 14th Amendment, Sec. 4.

AMENDMENT V

No person shall be held to answer for a capital, or otherwise infamous crime, unless on a presentment or indictment of a grand jury, except in cases arising in the land or naval forces, or in the militia, when in actual service in time of war or public danger; nor shall any person be subject for the same offense to be twice put in jeopardy of life or limb; nor shall be compelled in any criminal case to be a witness against himself, nor be deprived of life, liberty, or property, without due process of law; nor shall private property be taken for public use, without just compensation.

AMENDMENT VI

In all criminal prosecutions, the accused shall enjoy the right to a speedy and public trial, by an impartial jury of the State and district wherein the crime shall have been committed, which district shall have been previously ascertained by law, and to be informed of the nature and cause of the accusation; to be confronted with the witnesses against him; to have compulsory process for obtaining witnesses in his favor, and to have the assistance of counsel for his defense.

AMENDMENT VII

In suits at common law, where the value in controversy shall exceed twenty dollars, the right of trial by jury shall be preserved, and no fact tried by a jury shall be otherwise reëxamined in any court of the United States, than according to the rules of the common law.

AMENDMENT VIII

Excessive bail shall not be required, nor excessive fines imposed, nor cruel and unusual punishments inflicted.

AMENDMENT IX

The enumeration in the Constitution of certain rights shall not be construed to deny or disparage others retained by the people.

AMENDMENT X

The powers not delegated to the United States by the Constitution, nor prohibited by it to the States, are reserved to the States respectively, or to the people.

AMENDMENT XI [January 8, 1798]

The judicial power of the United States shall not be construed to extend to any suit in law or equity, commenced or prosecuted against one of the United States by citizens of another State, or by citizens or subjects of any foreign State.

AMENDMENT XII [September 25, 1804]

The electors shall meet in their respective States, and vote by ballot for President and Vice President, one of whom, at least, shall not be an inhabitant of the same State with themselves; they shall name in their ballots the person voted for as President, and in distinct ballots, the person voted for as Vice President, and they shall make distinct lists of all persons voted for as President and of all persons voted for as Vice President, and of the number of

votes for each, which lists they shall sign and certify, and transmit sealed to the seat of the government of the United States, directed to the President of the Senate;—The President of the Senate shall, in the presence of the Senate and House of Representatives, open all the certificates and the votes shall then be counted;—The person having the greatest number of votes for President, shall be the President, if such number be a majority of the whole number of electors appointed; and if no person have such majority, then from the persons having the highest numbers not exceeding three on the list of those voted for as President, the House of Representatives shall choose immediately, by ballot, the President. But in choosing the President, the votes shall be taken by States, the representation from each State having one vote; a quorum for this purpose shall consist of a member or members from two thirds of the States, and a majority of all the States shall be necessary to a choice. And if the House of Representatives shall not choose a President whenever the right of choice shall devolve upon them, before the fourth day of March next following, then the Vice President shall act as President, as in the case of the death or other constitutional disability of the President. The person having the greatest number of votes as Vice President shall be the Vice President, if such number be a majority of the whole number of electors appointed, and if no person have a majority, then from the two highest numbers on the list, the Senate shall choose the Vice President; a quorum for the purpose shall consist of two thirds of the whole number of Senators, and a majority of the whole number shall be necessary to a choice. But no person constitutionally ineligible to the office of President shall be eligible to that of Vice President of the United States.

AMENDMENT XIII [December 18, 1865]

Section 1. Neither slavery nor involuntary servitude, except as a punishment for crime whereof the party shall have been duly convicted, shall exist within the United States, or any place subject to their jurisdiction.

Section 2. Congress shall have power to enforce this article by appropriate legislation.

AMENDMENT XIV [July 28, 1868]

Section 1. All persons born or naturalized in the United States, and subject to the jurisdiction thereof, are citizens of the United States and of the State wherein they reside. No State shall make or enforce any law which shall abridge the privileges or immunities of citizens of the United States; nor shall any State deprive any person of life, liberty, or property, without due process of law; nor deny to any person within its jurisdiction the equal protection of the laws.

Section 2. Representatives shall be apportioned among the several States according to their respective numbers, counting the whole number of persons in each State, excluding Indians not taxed. But when the right to vote at any election for the choice of electors for President and Vice President of the United States, representatives in Congress, the executive and judicial officers of a State, or the members of the legislature thereof, is denied to any of the male inhabitants of such State, being twenty-one years of age, and citizens of the United States, or in any way abridged, except for participating in rebellion, or other crime, the basis of representation therein shall be reduced in the proportion which the number of such male citizens shall bear to the whole number of male citizens twenty-one years of age in such State.

Section 3. No person shall be a senator or representative in Congress, or elector of President and Vice President, or hold any office, civil or military, under the United States, or under any State, who having previously taken an oath, as a member of Congress, or as an officer of the United States, or as a member of any State legislature, or as an executive or judicial officer of any State, to support the Constitution of the United States, shall have engaged in insurrection or rebellion against the same, or given aid or comfort to the enemies thereof. But Congress may by a vote of two thirds of each House, remove such disability.

Section 4. The validity of the public debt of the United States, authorized by law, including debts incurred for payment of pensions and bounties for services in suppressing insurrection or rebellion, shall not be questioned. But neither the United States nor any State shall assume or pay any debt or obligation incurred in aid of insurrection or rebellion against the United States, or any claim for the loss or emancipation of any slave; but all such debts, obligations, and claims shall be held illegal and void.

Section 5. The Congress shall have power to enforce, by appropriate legislation, the provisions of this article.

AMENDMENT XV [March 30, 1870]

Section 1. The right of citizens of the United States to vote shall not be denied or abridged by the United States or by any State on account of race, color, or previous condition of servitude.

Section 2. The Congress shall have power to enforce this article by appropriate legislation.

AMENDMENT XVI [February 25, 1913]

The Congress shall have power to lay and collect taxes on incomes, from whatever source derived, without apportionment among the several States, and without regard to any census or enumeration.

AMENDMENT XVII [May 31, 1913]

The Senate of the United States shall be composed of two senators from each State, elected by the people thereof, for six years; and each senator shall have one vote. The electors in each State shall have the qualifications requisite for electors of the most numerous branch of the State legislature.

When vacancies happen in the representation of any State in the Senate, the executive authority of such State shall issue writs of election to fill such vacancies: *Provided,* That the legislature of any State may empower the executive thereof to make temporary appointments until the people fill the vacancies by election as the legislature may direct.

This amendment shall not be so construed as to affect the election or term of any senator chosen before it becomes valid as part of the Constitution.

AMENDMENT XVIII [January 29, 1919][11]

After one year from the ratification of this article, the manufacture, sale, or transportation of intoxicating liquors within, the importation thereof into, or the exportation thereof from the United States and all territory subject to the jurisdiction thereof for beverage purposes is hereby prohibited.

The Congress and the several States shall have concurrent power to enforce this article by appropriate legislation.

This article shall be inoperative unless it shall have been ratified as an amendment to the Constitution by the legislatures of the several States, as provided in the Constitution, within seven years from the date of the submission hereof to the States by Congress.

[11] Repealed by the 21st Amendment.

AMENDMENT XIX [August 26, 1920]

The right of citizens of the United States to vote shall not be denied or abridged by the United States or by any State on account of sex.

Congress shall have the power to enforce this article by appropriate legislation.

AMENDMENT XX [January 23, 1933]

Section 1. The terms of the President and Vice President shall end at noon on the 20th day of January, and the terms of Senators and Representatives at noon on the 3d day of January, of the years in which such terms would have ended if this article had not been ratified; and the terms of their successors shall then begin.

Section 2. The Congress shall assemble at least once in every year, and such meeting shall begin at noon on the 3d day of January, unless they shall by law appoint a different day.

Section 3. If, at the time fixed for the beginning of the term of President, the President-elect shall have died, the Vice President-elect shall become President. If a President shall not have been chosen before the time fixed for the beginning of his term, or if the President-elect shall have failed to qualify, then the Vice President-elect shall act as President until a President shall have qualified; and the Congress may by law provide for the case wherein neither a President-elect nor a Vice President-elect shall have qualified, declaring who shall then act as President, or the manner in which one who is to act shall be selected, and such person shall act accordingly until a President or Vice-President shall have qualified.

Section 4. The Congress may by law provide for the case of the death of any of the persons from whom the House of Representatives may choose a President whenever the right of choice shall have devolved upon them, and for the case of the death of any of the persons from whom the Senate may choose a Vice President whenever the right of choice shall have devolved upon them.

Section 5. Sections 1 and 2 shall take effect on the 15th day of October following the ratification of this article.

Section 6. This article shall be inoperative unless it shall have been ratified as an amendment to the Constitution by the legislatures of three-fourths of the several States within seven years from the date of its submission.

AMENDMENT XXI [December 5, 1933]

Section 1. The Eighteenth Article of amendment to the Constitution of the United States is hereby repealed.

Section 2. The transportation or importation into any State, Territory, or possession of the United States for delivery or use therein of intoxicating liquors in violation of the laws thereof, is hereby prohibited.

Section 3. This article shall be inoperative unless it shall have been ratified as an amendment to the Constitution by conventions in the several States, as provided in the Constitution, within seven years from the date of the submission thereof to the States by the Congress.

AMENDMENT XXII [March 1, 1951]

No person shall be elected to the office of the President more than twice, and no person who has held the office of President, or acted as President, for more than two years of a term to which some other person was elected President shall be elected to the office of the President more than once.

But this article shall not apply to any person holding the office of President when this article was proposed by the Congress, and shall not prevent any person who may be holding the office of President, or acting as President, during the term within which this article becomes operative from holding the office of President or acting as President during the remainder of such term.

This article shall be inoperative unless it shall have been ratified as an amendment to the Constitution by the legislatures of three-fourths of the several States within seven years from the date of its submission to the States by the Congress.

AMENDMENT XXIII [March 29, 1961]

Section 1. The District constituting the seat of Government of the United States shall appoint in such manner as the Congress may direct:

A number of electors of President and Vice President equal to the whole number of Senators and Representatives in Congress to which the District would be entitled if it were a State, but in no event more than the least populous State; they shall be in addition to those appointed by the States, but they shall be considered, for the purposes of the election of President and Vice President, to be electors appointed by a State; and they shall meet in the District and perform such duties as provided by the twelfth article of amendment.

Section 2. The Congress shall have power to enforce this article by appropriate legislation.

AMENDMENT XXIV [January 23, 1964]

Section 1. The right of citizens of the United States to vote in any primary or other election for President or Vice President, for electors for President or Vice President, or for Senator or Representative in Congress, shall not be denied or abridged by the United States or any State by reason of failure to pay any poll tax or other tax.

Section 2. The Congress shall have power to enforce this article by appropriate legislation.

AMENDMENT XXV [February 10, 1967]

Section 1. In case of the removal of the President from office or of his death or resignation, the Vice President shall become President.

Section 2. Whenever there is a vacancy in the office of the Vice President, the President shall nominate a Vice President who shall take office

upon confirmation by a majority vote of both Houses of Congress.

Section 3. Whenever the President transmits to the President pro tempore of the Senate and the Speaker of the House of Representatives his written declaration that he is unable to discharge the powers and duties of his office, and until he transmits to them a written declaration to the contrary, such powers and duties shall be discharged by the Vice President as Acting President.

Section 4. Whenever the Vice President and a majority of either the principal officers of the executive departments or of such other body as Congress may by law provide, transmit to the President pro tempore of the Senate and the Speaker of the House of Representatives their written declaration that the President is unable to discharge the powers and duties of his office, the Vice President shall immediately assume the powers and duties of the office as Acting President.

Thereafter, when the President transmits to the President pro tempore of the Senate and the Speaker of the House of Representatives his written declaration that no inability exists, he shall resume the powers and duties of his office unless the Vice Presi-

dent and a majority of either the principal officers of the executive departments or of such other body as Congress may by law provide, transmit within four days to the President pro tempore of the Senate and the Speaker of the House of Representatives their written declaration that the President is unable to discharge the powers and duties of his office. Thereupon Congress shall decide the issue, assembling within forty-eight hours for that purpose if not in session. If the Congress, within twenty-one days after receipt of the latter written declaration, or, if Congress is not in session, within twenty-one days after Congress is required to assemble, determines by two-thirds vote of both Houses that the President is unable to discharge the powers and duties of his office, the Vice President shall continue to discharge the same as Acting President; otherwise, the President shall resume the powers and duties of his office.

Admission of States to the Union

1.	Delaware	Dec. 1, 1787	26.	Michigan	Jan. 26, 1837
2.	Pennsylvania	Dec. 12, 1787	27.	Florida	Mar. 3, 1845
3.	New Jersey	Dec. 18, 1787	28.	Texas	Dec. 29, 1845
4.	Georgia	Jan. 2, 1788	29.	Iowa	Dec. 28, 1846
5.	Connecticut	Jan. 9, 1788	30.	Wisconsin	May 29, 1848
6.	Massachusetts	Feb. 6, 1788	31.	California	Sept. 9, 1850
7.	Maryland	Apr. 28, 1788	32.	Minnesota	May 11, 1858
8.	South Carolina	May 23, 1788	33.	Oregon	Feb. 14, 1859
9.	New Hampshire	June 21, 1788	34.	Kansas	Jan. 29, 1861
10.	Virginia	June 25, 1788	35.	West Virginia	June 19, 1863
11.	New York	July 26, 1788	36.	Nevada	Oct. 31, 1864
12.	North Carolina	Nov. 21, 1789	37.	Nebraska	Mar. 1, 1867
13.	Rhode Island	May 29, 1790	38.	Colorado	July 1, 1876
14.	Vermont	Mar. 4, 1791	39.	North Dakota	Nov. 2, 1889
15.	Kentucky	June 1, 1792	40.	South Dakota	Nov. 2, 1889
16.	Tennessee	June 1, 1796	41.	Montana	Nov. 8, 1889
17.	Ohio	Mar. 1, 1803	42.	Washington	Nov. 11, 1889
18.	Louisiana	Apr. 30, 1812	43.	Idaho	July 3, 1890
19.	Indiana	Dec. 11, 1816	44.	Wyoming	July 10, 1890
20.	Mississippi	Dec. 10, 1817	45.	Utah	Jan. 4, 1896
21.	Illinois	Dec. 3, 1818	46.	Oklahoma	Nov. 16, 1907
22.	Alabama	Dec. 14, 1819	47.	New Mexico	Jan. 6, 1912
23.	Maine	Mar. 15, 1820	48.	Arizona	Feb. 14, 1912
24.	Missouri	Aug. 10, 1821	49.	Alaska	Jan. 3, 1959
25.	Arkansas	June 15, 1836	50.	Hawaii	Aug. 21, 1959

Presidents, Vice-Presidents, and Cabinet Members

President	Vice-President	Secretary of State	Secretary of Treasury
1. George Washington — Federalist — 1789	John Adams — Federalist — 1789	T. Jefferson 1789; E. Randolph 1794; T. Pickering 1795	Alex. Hamilton 1789; Oliver Wolcott 1795
2. John Adams — Federalist — 1797	Thomas Jefferson — Democratic-Republican — 1797	T. Pickering 1797; John Marshall 1800	Oliver Wolcott 1797; Samuel Dexter 1801
3. Thomas Jefferson — Democratic-Republican — 1801	Aaron Burr — Democratic-Republican — 1801; George Clinton — Democratic-Republican — 1805	James Madison 1801	Samuel Dexter 1801; Albert Gallatin 1801
4. James Madison — Republican — 1809	George Clinton — Independent-Republican — 1809; Elbridge Gerry — Democratic-Republican — 1813	Robert Smith 1809; James Monroe 1811	Albert Gallatin 1809; H. W. Campbell 1814; A. J. Dallas 1814; W. H. Crawford 1816
5. James Monroe — Republican — 1817	D. D. Thompkins — Democratic-Republican — 1817	J. Q. Adams 1817	W. H. Crawford 1817
6. John Q. Adams* — 1825	John C. Calhoun* — 1825	Henry Clay 1825	Richard Rush 1825
7. Andrew Jackson — Democrat — 1829	John C. Calhoun — Democrat — 1829; Martin Van Buren — Democrat — 1833	M. Van Buren 1829; E. Livingston 1831; Louis McLane 1833; John Forsyth 1834	Sam. D. Ingham 1829; Louis McLane 1831; W. J. Duane 1833; Roger B. Taney 1833; Levi Woodbury 1834
8. Martin Van Buren — Democrat — 1837	Richard M. Johnson — Democrat — 1837	John Forsyth 1837	Levi Woodbury 1837
9. William H. Harrison — Whig — 1841	John Tyler — Whig — 1841	Daniel Webster 1841	Thos. Ewing 1841
10. John Tyler — Whig and Democrat — 1841		Daniel Webster 1841; Hugh S. Legare 1843; Abel P. Upshur 1843; John C. Calhoun 1844	Thos. Ewing 1841; Walter Forward 1841; John C. Spencer 1843; Geo. M. Bibb 1844
11. James K. Polk — Democrat — 1845	George M. Dallas — Democrat — 1845	James Buchanan 1845	Robt. J. Walker 1845
12. Zachary Taylor — Whig — 1849	Millard Fillmore — Whig — 1849	John M. Clayton 1849	Wm. M. Meredith 1849
13. Millard Fillmore — Whig — 1850		Daniel Webster 1850; Edward Everett 1852	Thomas Corwin 1850
14. Franklin Pierce — Democrat — 1853	William R. D. King — Democrat — 1853	W. L. Marcy 1853	James Guthrie 1853
15. James Buchanan — Democrat — 1857	John C. Breckinridge — Democrat — 1857	Lewis Cass 1857; J. S. Black 1860	Howell Cobb 1857; Philip F. Thomas 1860; John A. Dix 1861
16. Abraham Lincoln — Republican — 1861	Hannibal Hamlin — Republican — 1861; Andrew Johnson — Unionist — 1865	W. H. Seward 1861	Salmon P. Chase 1861; W. P. Fessenden 1864; Hugh McCulloch 1865
17. Andrew Johnson — Unionist — 1865		W. H. Seward 1865	Hugh McCulloch 1865

* No distinct party designations.

Secretary of War		Attorney-General		Postmaster-General †		Secretary of Navy		Secretary of Interior	
Henry Knox	1789	E. Randolph	1789	Samuel Osgood	1789	Established		Established	
T. Pickering	1795	Wm. Bradford	1794	Tim. Pickering	1791	April 30, 1798.		March 3, 1849.	
Jas. McHenry	1796	Charles Lee	1795	Jos. Habersham	1795				
Jas. McHenry	1797	Charles Lee	1797	Jos. Habersham	1797	Benj. Stoddert	1798		
John Marshall	1800	Theo. Parsons	1801						
Sam'l Dexter	1800								
R. Griswold	1801								
H. Dearborn	1801	Levi Lincoln	1801	Jos. Habersham	1801	Benj. Stoddert	1801		
		Robert Smith	1805	Gideon Granger	1801	Robert Smith	1801		
		J. Breckinridge	1805			J. Crowninshield	1805		
		C. A. Rodney	1807						
Wm. Eustis	1809	C. A. Rodney	1809	Gideon Granger	1809	Paul Hamilton	1809		
J. Armstrong	1813	Wm. Pinkney	1811	R. J. Meigs, Jr.	1814	William Jones	1813		
James Monroe	1814	Richard Rush	1814			B. W. Crownin-			
W. H. Crawford	1815					shield	1814		
Isaac Shelby	1817	Richard Rush	1817	R. J. Meigs, Jr.	1817	B. W. Crownin-			
Geo. Graham	1817	William Wirt	1817	John McLean	1823	shield	1817		
J. C. Calhoun	1817					Smith Thompson	1818		
						S. L. Southard	1823		
Jas. Barbour	1825	William Wirt	1825	John McLean	1825	S. L. Southard	1825		
Peter B. Porter	1828								
John H. Eaton	1829	John M. Berrien	1829	Wm. T. Barry	1829	John Branch	1829		
Lewis Cass	1831	Roger B. Taney	1831	Amos Kendall	1835	Levi Woodbury	1831		
B. F. Butler	1837	B. F. Butler	1833			Mahlon Dickerson	1834		
Joel R. Poinsett	1837	B. F. Butler	1837	Amos Kendall	1837	Mahlon Dickerson	1837		
		Felix Grundy	1838	John M. Niles	1840	Jas. K. Paulding	1838		
		H. D. Gilpin	1840						
John Bell	1841	J. J. Crittenden	1841	Francis Granger	1841	George E. Badger	1841		
John Bell	1841	J. J. Crittenden	1841	Francis Granger	1841	George E. Badger	1841		
John McLean	1841	Hugh S. Legare	1841	C. A. Wickliffe	1841	Abel P. Upshur	1841		
J. C. Spencer	1841	John Nelson	1843			David Henshaw	1843		
Jas. M. Porter	1843					Thos. W. Gilmer	1844		
Wm. Wilkins	1844					John Y. Mason	1844		
Wm. L. Marcy	1845	John Y. Mason	1845	Cave Johnson	1845	George Bancroft	1845		
		Nathan Clifford	1846			John Y. Mason	1846		
		Isaac Toucey	1848						
G. W. Crawford	1849	Reverdy Johnson	1849	Jacob Collamer	1849	Wm. B. Preston	1849	Thomas Ewing	1849
C. M. Conrad	1850	J. J. Crittenden	1850	Nathan K. Hall	1850	Wm. A. Graham	1850	A. H. Stuart	1850
				Sam D. Hubbard	1852	John P. Kennedy	1852		
Jefferson Davis	1853	Caleb Cushing	1853	James Campbell	1853	James C. Dobbin	1853	Robert McClelland	1853
John B. Floyd	1857	J. S. Black	1857	Aaron V. Brown	1857	Isaac Toucey	1857	Jacob Thompson	1857
Joseph Holt	1861	Edw. M. Stanton	1860	Joseph Holt	1859				
S. Cameron	1861	Edward Bates	1861	Horatio King	1861	Gideon Welles	1861	Caleb B. Smith	1861
E. M. Stanton	1862	Titian J. Coffey	1863	M'tgomery Blair	1861			John P. Usher	1863
		James Speed	1864	Wm. Dennison	1864				
E. M. Stanton	1865	James Speed	1865	Wm. Dennison	1865	Gideon Welles	1865	John P. Usher	1865
U. S. Grant	1867	Henry Stanbery	1866	A. W. Randall	1866			James Harlan	1865
L. Thomas	1868	Wm. M. Evarts	1868					O. H. Browning	1866
J. M. Schofield	1868								

† Not in Cabinet until 1829.

President	Vice-President	Secretary of State	Secretary of Treasury	Secretary of War
18. Ulysses S. Grant 1869 Republican	Schuyler Colfax 1869 Republican Henry Wilson 1873 Republican	E. B. Washburne 1869 Hamilton Fish 1869	Geo. S. Boutwell 1869 W. A. Richardson 1873 Benj. H. Bristow 1874 Lot M. Morrill 1876	J. A. Rawlins 1869 W. T. Sherman 1869 W. W. Belknap 1869 Alphonso Taft 1876 J. D. Cameron 1876
19. Rutherford B. Hayes 1877 Republican	William A. Wheeler 1877 Republican	W. M. Evarts 1877	John Sherman 1877	G. W. McCrary 1877 Alex. Ramsey 1879
20. J. A. Garfield 1881 Republican	C. A. Arthur 1881 Republican	James G. Blaine 1881	Wm. Windom 1881	R. T. Lincoln 1881
21. Chester A. Arthur 1881 Republican		F. T. Freling-huysen 1881	Chas. J. Folger 1881 W. Q. Gresham 1884 Hugh McCulloch 1884	R. T. Lincoln 1881
22. G. Cleveland 1885 Democrat	T. A. Hendricks 1885 Democrat	Thos. F. Bayard 1885	Daniel Manning 1885 Chas. S. Fairchild 1887	W. C. Endicott 1885
23. Benj. Harrison 1889 Republican	Levi P. Morton 1889 Republican	James G. Blaine 1889 John W. Foster 1892	Wm. Windom 1889 Charles Foster 1891	R. Proctor 1889 S. B. Elkins 1891
24. G. Cleveland 1893 Democrat	A. E. Stevenson 1893 Democrat	W. Q. Gresham 1893 Richard Olney 1895	John G. Carlisle 1893	D. S. Lamont 1893
25. William Mc-Kinley 1897 Republican	Garret A. Hobart 1897 Republican Theo. Roosevelt 1901 Republican	John Sherman 1897 Wm. R. Day 1897 John Hay 1898	Lyman J. Gage 1897	R. A. Alger 1897 Elihu Root 1899
26. Theodore Roose-velt 1901 Republican	Chas. W. Fair-banks 1905 Republican	John Hay 1901 Elihu Root 1905 Robert Bacon 1909	Lyman J. Gage 1901 Leslie M. Shaw 1902 G. B. Cortelyou 1907	Elihu Root 1901 Wm. H. Taft 1904 Luke E. Wright 1908
27. W. H. Taft 1909 Republican	J. S. Sherman 1909 Republican	P. C. Knox 1909	F. MacVeagh 1909	J. M. Dickinson 1909 H. L. Stimson 1911
28. Woodrow Wil-son 1913 Democrat	Thomas R. Marshall 1913 Democrat	Wm. J. Bryan 1913 Robert Lansing 1915 Bainbridge Colby 1920	W. G. McAdoo 1913 Carter Glass 1918 D. F. Houston 1920	L. M. Garrison 1913 N. D. Baker 1916
29. Warren G. Harding 1921 Republican	Calvin Coolidge 1921 Republican	Chas. E. Hughes 1921	Andrew W. Mellon 1921	John W. Weeks 1921
30. Calvin Cool-idge 1923 Republican	Charles G. Dawes 1925 Republican	Chas. E. Hughes 1923 Frank B. Kellogg 1925	Andrew W. Mellon 1923	John W. Weeks 1923 Dwight F. Davis 1925
31. Herb. Hoover 1929 Republican	Charles Curtis 1929 Republican	Henry L. Stimson 1929	Andrew W. Mellon 1929 Ogden L. Mills 1932	James W. Good 1929 Pat. J. Hurley 1929
32. Franklin D. Roosevelt 1933 Democrat	J. Nance Garner 1933 Democrat H. A. Wallace 1941 Democrat H. S. Truman 1945 Democrat	Cordell Hull 1933 E. R. Stettinius, Jr. 1944	Wm. H. Woodin 1933 Henry Morgenthau, Jr. 1934	Geo. H. Dern 1933 H. A. Woodring 1936 H. L. Stimson 1940
33. Harry S. Truman 1945 Democrat	Alben W. Barkley 1949 Democrat	James F. Byrnes 1945 Geo. C. Marshall 1947 Dean G. Acheson 1949	Fred M. Vinson 1945 John W. Snyder 1946	R. H. Patterson 1945 K. C. Royall 1947 **
34. Dwight D. Eisenhower 1953 Republican	Richard M. Nixon 1953 Republican	J. Foster Dulles 1953 Christian A. Herter 1959	George C. Humphrey 1953 Robert B. Anderson 1957	*Sec'y of Defense* Est. July 26, 1947 J. V. Forrestal 1947 L. A. Johnson 1949 G. C. Marshall 1950 R. A. Lovett 1951 C. E. Wilson 1953
35. John F. Kennedy 1961 Democrat	Lyndon B. Johnson 1961 Democrat	Dean Rusk 1961	C. Douglas Dillon 1961	N. H. McElroy 1957 T. S. Gates, Jr. 1959 R. S. McNamara 1961
36. Lyndon B. Johnson 1963 Democrat	Hubert H. Humphrey 1963 Democrat	Dean Rusk 1963	C. Douglas Dillon 1963 Henry W. Fowler 1965	

** Lost cabinet status in 1947.

Attorney-General	Postmaster-General	Secretary of Navy	Secretary of Interior	Secretary of Agriculture	Other Members
E. R. Hoar 1869 A. T. Ackerman 1870 Geo. H. Williams 1871 Edw. Pierrepont 1875 Alphonso Taft 1876	J. A. J. Creswell 1869 Jas. W. Marshall 1874 Marshall Jewell 1874 James N. Tyner 1876	Adolph E. Borie 1869 Geo. M. Robeson 1869	Jacob D. Cox 1869 C. Delano 1870 Zach. Chandler 1875	Cabinet status since 1889.	*Sec'y of Commerce and Labor* Est. Feb. 14, 1903 G. B. Cortelyou 1903 V. H. Metcalf 1904 O. S. Straus 1907 Chas. Nagel 1909 (Dept. divided, 1913)
Chas. Devens 1877	David M. Key 1877 Horace Maynard 1880	R. W. Thompson 1877 Nathan Goff, Jr. 1881	Carl Schurz 1877		
W. MacVeagh 1881	T. L. James 1881	W. H. Hunt 1881	S. J. Kirkwood 1881		*Sec'y of Commerce* Est. March 4, 1913 W. C. Redfield 1913 J. W. Alexander 1919 H. C. Hoover 1921 H. C. Hoover 1925 W. F. Whiting 1928 R. P. Lamont 1929 R. D. Chapin 1932 D. C. Roper 1933 H. L. Hopkins 1939 Jesse Jones 1940 Henry A. Wallace 1945 W. A. Harriman 1946 C. W. Sawyer 1948 S. Weeks 1953 L. L. Strauss 1958 F. H. Mueller 1959 L. H. Hodges 1961 L. H. Hodges 1963 John T. Conner 1965
B. H. Brewster 1881	T. O. Howe 1881 W. Q. Gresham 1883 Frank Hatton 1884	W. E. Chandler 1881	Henry M. Teller 1881		
A. H. Garland 1885	Wm. F. Vilas 1885 D. M. Dickinson 1888	W. C. Whitney 1885	L.Q.C. Lamar 1885 Wm. F. Vilas 1888	N. J. Colman 1889	
W. H. H. Miller 1889	J. Wanamaker 1889	Benj. F. Tracy 1889	John W. Noble 1889	J. M. Rusk 1889	
R. Olney 1893 J. Harmon 1895	W. S. Bissell 1893 W. L. Wilson 1895	Hilary A. Herbert 1893	Hoke Smith 1893 D. R. Francis 1896	J. S. Morton 1893	
J. McKenna 1897 J. W. Griggs 1897 P. C. Knox 1901	James A. Gary 1897 Chas. E. Smith 1898	John D. Long 1897	C. N. Bliss 1897 E. A. Hitchcock 1899	James Wilson 1897	
P. C. Knox 1901 W. H. Moody 1904 C. J. Bonaparte 1907	Chas. E. Smith 1901 Henry C. Payne 1902 Robt. J. Wynne 1904 G. B. Cortelyou 1905 G. von L. Meyeh 1907	John D. Long 1901 Wm. H. Moody 1902 Paul Morton 1904 C. J. Bonaparte 1905 V. H. Metcalf 1907 T. H. Newberry 1908	E. A. Hitchcock 1901 J. R. Garfield 1907	James Wilson 1901	
G. W. Wickersham 1909	F. H. Hitchcock 1909	G. von L. Meyer 1909	R. A. Ballinger 1909 W. L. Fisher 1911	James Wilson 1909	
J. C. McReynolds 1913 Thos. W. Gregory 1914 A. M. Palmer 1919	A. S. Burleson 1913	Josephus Daniels 1913	F. K. Lane 1913 J. B. Payne 1920	D. F. Houston 1913 E. T. Meredith 1920	*Sec'y of Labor* Est. March 4, 1913 W. B. Wilson 1913 J. J. Davis 1921 W. N. Doak 1930 Frances Perkins '33 L. B. Schwellenbach 1945 M. J. Tobin 1948 M. P. Durkin 1953 J. P. Mitchell 1953 A. J. Goldberg 1961 W. Willard Wirtz 1962
H. M. Daugherty 1921	Will H. Hays 1921 Hubert Work 1922 Harry S. New 1923	Edwin Denby 1921	Albert B. Fall 1921 Hubert Work 1923	H. C. Wallace 1921	
H. M. Daugherty 1923 Harlan F. Stone 1924 John G. Sargent 1925	Harry S. New 1923	Edwin Denby 1923 Curtis W. Wilbur 1924	Hubert Work 1923 Roy O. West 1928	H. M. Gore 1924 W. M. Jardine 1925	
Wm. D. Mitchell 1929	Walter F. Brown 1929	Chas. F. Adams 1929	Ray L. Wilbur 1929	Arthur M. Hyde 1929	
H. S. Cummings 1933 Frank Murphy 1939 Robt. H. Jackson 1940 Francis Biddle 1941	James A. Farley 1933 Frank C. Walker 1940	Claude A. Swanson 1933 Chas. Edison 1940 Frank Knox 1940 James V. Forrestal 1944	Harold L. Ickes 1933	H. A. Wallace 1933 C. R. Wickard 1940	*Sec'y of Housing and Urban Development* Est. Sept. 9, 1965 Robt. C. Weaver 1966
Tom C. Clark 1945 J. H. McGrath 1949 J. P. McGranery 1952	R. E. Hannegan 1945 J. L. Donaldson 1947	James V. Forrestal 1945 ††	H. L. Ickes 1945 Julius A. Krug 1946 O. L. Chapman 1951	C. P. Anderson 1945 C. F. Brannan 1948	
Herbert Brownell, Jr. 1953 W. P. Rogers 1957	Arthur E. Summerfield 1953	*Sec'y of Health Educ. & Welfare* Est. April 1, 1953 O. C. Hobby 1953 M. B. Folsom 1955 A. S. Flemming 1958	Douglas McKay 1953 Fred Seaton 1956	Ezra T. Benson 1953	*Sec'y of Transportation* Est. Oct. 15, 1966 Alan S. Boyo 1966
Robt. F. Kennedy 1961	J. Edward Day 1961 John Gronouski 1963	Abraham A. Ribicoff 1961 A. Celebreeze 1962	Steward L. Udall 1961	Orville L. Freeman 1961	
Robt. F. Kennedy 1963 Nicholas deB. Katzenbach 1965	John Gronouski 1963 Lawrence F. O'Brien 1965	A. Celebreeze 1963 John W. Gardner 1965	Steward L. Udall 1963	Orville L. Freeman 1963	

†† Lost cabinet status in 1947.

Justices of the United States Supreme Court

Name (Chief Justices in Italics)	Service (Term)	(Years)	Name (Chief Justices in Italics)	Service (Term)	(Years)
John Jay (N.Y.)	1789-1795	6	*Melville W. Fuller* (Ill.)	1888-1910	22
John Rutledge (S.C.)	1789-1791	2	David J. Brewer (Kans.)	1889-1910	21
William Cushing (Mass.)	1789-1810	21	Henry B. Brown (Mich.)	1890-1906	16
James Wilson (Pa.)	1789-1798	9	George Shiras, Jr. (Pa.)	1892-1903	11
John Blair (Va.)	1789-1796	7	Howell E. Jackson (Tenn.)	1893-1895	2
James Iredell (N.C.)	1790-1799	9	Edward D. White (La.)	1894-1910	16
Thomas Johnson (Md.)	1792-1793	½	Rufus W. Peckham (N.Y.)	1895-1909	14
William Paterson (N.J.)	1793-1806	13	Joseph McKenna (Calif.)	1898-1925	27
John Rutledge (S.C.) [1]	1795-1795		Oliver W. Holmes (Mass.)	1902-1932	30
Samuel Chase (Md.)	1796-1811	15	William R. Day (Ohio)	1903-1922	19
Oliver Ellsworth (Conn.)	1796-1800	4	William H. Moody (Mass.)	1906-1910	4
Bushrod Washington (Va.)	1798-1829	31	Horace H. Lurton (Tenn.)	1909-1914	5
Alfred Moore (N.C.)	1800-1804	4	*Edward D. White* (La.)	1910-1921	11
John Marshall (Va.)	1801-1835	34	Charles E. Hughes (N.Y.)	1910-1916	6
William Johnson (S.C.)	1804-1834	30	Willis Van Devanter (Wyo.)	1910-1937	26
Brock. Livingston (N.Y.)	1806-1823	17	Joseph R. Lamar (Ga.)	1910-1916	6
Thomas Todd (Ky.)	1807-1826	19	Mahlon Pitney (N.J.)	1912-1923	11
Joseph Story (Mass.)	1811-1845	34	James C. McReynolds (Tenn.)	1914-1941	27
Gabriel Duval (Md.)	1811-1835	24	Louis D. Brandeis (Mass.)	1916-1939	23
Smith Thompson (N.Y.)	1823-1843	20	John H. Clarke (Ohio)	1916-1922	6
Robert Trimble (Ky.)	1826-1828	2	*William H. Taft* (Conn.)	1921-1930	9
John McLean (Ohio)	1829-1861	32	George Sutherland (Utah)	1922-1938	16
Henry Baldwin (Pa.)	1830-1844	14	Pierce Butler (Minn.)	1922-1939	17
James M. Wayne (Ga.)	1835-1867	32	Edward T. Sanford (Tenn.)	1923-1930	7
Roger B. Taney (Md.)	1836-1864	28	Harlan F. Stone (N.Y.)	1925-1941	16
Philip P. Barbour (Va.)	1836-1841	5	*Charles E. Hughes* (N.Y.)	1930-1941	11
John Catron (Tenn.)	1837-1865	28	Owen J. Roberts (Pa.)	1930-1945	15
John McKinley (Ala.)	1837-1852	15	Benjamin N. Cardozo (N.Y.)	1932-1938	6
Peter V. Daniel (Va.)	1841-1860	19	Hugo L. Black (Ala.)	1937-	
Samuel Nelson (N.Y.)	1845-1872	27	Stanley F. Reed (Ky.)	1938-1957	19
Levi Woodbury (N.H.)	1845-1851	6	Felix Frankfurter (Mass.)	1939-1962	23
Robert C. Grier (Pa.)	1846-1870	24	William O. Douglas (Conn.)	1939-	
Benjamin R. Curtis (Mass.)	1851-1857	6	Frank Murphy (Mich.)	1940-1949	9
John A. Campbell (Ala.)	1853-1861	8	*Harlan F. Stone* (N.Y.)	1941-1946	5
Nathan Clifford (Maine)	1858-1881	23	James F. Byrnes (S.C.)	1941-1942	1
Noah H. Swayne (Ohio)	1862-1881	19	Robert H. Jackson (N.Y.)	1941-1954	13
Samuel F. Miller (Iowa)	1862-1890	28	Wiley B. Rutledge (Iowa)	1943-1949	6
David Davis (Ill.)	1862-1877	15	Harold H. Burton (Ohio)	1945-1958	13
Stephen J. Field (Calif.)	1863-1897	34	*Fred M. Vinson* (Ky.)	1946-1953	7
Salmon P. Chase (Ohio)	1864-1873	9	Tom C. Clark (Tex.)	1949-	
William Strong (Pa.)	1870-1880	10	Sherman Minton (Ind.)	1949-1956	7
Joseph P. Bradley (N.J.)	1870-1892	22	*Earl Warren* (Calif.)	1953-	
Ward Hunt (N.Y.)	1872-1882	10	John M. Harlan (N.Y.)	1955-	
Morrison R. Waite (Ohio)	1874-1888	14	William J. Brennan (N.J.)	1956-	
John M. Harlan (Ky.)	1877-1911	34	Charles E. Whittaker (Mo.)	1957-1962	5
William B. Woods (Ga.)	1880-1887	7	Potter Stewart (Ohio)	1958-	
Stanley Matthews (Ohio)	1881-1889	8	Byron R. White (Colo.)	1962-	
Horace Gray (Mass.)	1881-1902	21	Arthur J. Goldberg (Ill.)	1962-1965	3
Samuel Blatchford (N.Y.)	1882-1893	11	Abe Fortas (Tenn.)	1965-	
Lucius Q. Lamar (Miss.)	1888-1893	5			

[1] Appointed and served one term, but not confirmed by the Senate.

Presidential Elections, 1789–1964

Year	Number of States	Candidates	Party	Popular vote	Electoral vote	Percentage of popular vote
1789	11	GEORGE WASHINGTON	No party designations		69	
		John Adams			34	
		Other Candidates			35	
1792	15	GEORGE WASHINGTON	No party designations		132	
		John Adams			77	
		George Clinton			50	
		Other Candidates			5	
1796	16	JOHN ADAMS	Federalist		71	
		Thomas Jefferson	Democratic-Republican		68	
		Thomas Pinckney	Federalist		59	
		Aaron Burr	Democratic-Republican		30	
		Other Candidates			48	
1800	16	THOMAS JEFFERSON	Democratic-Republican		73	
		Aaron Burr	Democratic-Republican		73	
		John Adams	Federalist		65	
		Charles C. Pinckney	Federalist		64	
		John Jay	Federalist		1	
1804	17	THOMAS JEFFERSON	Democratic-Republican		162	
		Charles C. Pinckney	Federalist		14	
1808	17	JAMES MADISON	Democratic-Republican		122	
		Charles C. Pinckney	Federalist		47	
		George Clinton	Democratic-Republican		6	
1812	18	JAMES MADISON	Democratic-Republican		128	
		DeWitt Clinton	Federalist		89	
1816	19	JAMES MONROE	Democratic-Republican		183	
		Rufus King	Federalist		34	
1820	24	JAMES MONROE	Democratic-Republican		231	
		John Quincy Adams	Independent Republican		1	
1824	24	JOHN QUINCY ADAMS	Democratic-Republican	108,740	84	30.5
		Andrew Jackson	Democratic-Republican	153,544	99	43.1
		William H. Crawford	Democratic-Republican	46,618	41	13.1
		Henry Clay	Democratic-Republican	47,136	37	13.2
1828	24	ANDREW JACKSON	Democrat	647,286	178	56.0
		John Quincy Adams	National Republican	508,064	83	44.0
1832	24	ANDREW JACKSON	Democrat	687,502	219	55.0
		Henry Clay	National Republican	530,189	49	42.4
		William Wirt	Anti-Masonic	} 33,108	7	} 2.6
		John Floyd	National Republican		11	
1836	26	MARTIN VAN BUREN	Democrat	765,483	170	50.9
		William H. Harrison	Whig		73	
		Hugh L. White	Whig	} 739,795	26	} 49.1
		Daniel Webster	Whig		14	
		W. P. Mangum	Whig		11	

Percentage of popular vote given for any election year may not total 100 per cent because candidates receiving less than 1 per cent of the popular vote have been omitted.

Prior to the passage of the Twelfth Amendment in 1804, the electoral college voted for two presidential candidates; the runner-up became Vice-President. Data from *Historical Statistics of the United States, Colonial Times to 1957* (1961), pp. 682–683, and *The World Almanac*.

Presidential Elections, 1789–1964 (Cont.)

Year	Number of States	Candidates	Party	Popular vote	Electoral vote	Percentage of popular vote
1840	26	WILLIAM H. HARRISON	Whig	1,274,624	234	53.1
		Martin Van Buren	Democrat	1,127,781	60	46.9
1844	26	JAMES K. POLK	Democrat	1,338,464	170	49.6
		Henry Clay	Whig	1,300,097	105	48.1
		James G. Birney	Liberty	62,300		2.3
1848	30	ZACHARY TAYLOR	Whig	1,360,967	163	47.4
		Lewis Cass	Democrat	1,222,342	127	42.5
		Martin Van Buren	Free Soil	291,263		10.1
1852	31	FRANKLIN PIERCE	Democrat	1,601,117	254	50.9
		Winfield Scott	Whig	1,385,453	42	44.1
		John P. Hale	Free Soil	155,825		5.0
1856	31	JAMES BUCHANAN	Democrat	1,832,955	174	45.3
		John C. Frémont	Republican	1,339,932	114	33.1
		Millard Fillmore	American	871,731	8	21.6
1860	33	ABRAHAM LINCOLN	Republican	1,865,593	180	39.8
		Stephen A. Douglas	Democrat	1,382,713	12	29.5
		John C. Breckinridge	Democrat	848,356	72	18.1
		John Bell	Constitutional Union	592,906	39	12.6
1864	36	ABRAHAM LINCOLN	Republican	2,206,938	212	55.0
		George B. McClellan	Democrat	1,803,787	21	45.0
1868	37	ULYSSES S. GRANT	Republican	3,013,421	214	52.7
		Horatio Seymour	Democrat	2,706,829	80	47.3
1872	37	ULYSSES S. GRANT	Republican	3,596,745	286	55.6
		Horace Greeley	Democrat	2,843,446	*	43.9
1876	38	RUTHERFORD B. HAYES	Republican	4,036,572	185	48.0
		Samuel J. Tilden	Democrat	4,284,020	184	51.0
1880	38	JAMES A. GARFIELD	Republican	4,453,295	214	48.5
		Winfield S. Hancock	Democrat	4,414,082	155	48.1
		James B. Weaver	Greenback-Labor	308,578		3.4
1884	38	GROVER CLEVELAND	Democrat	4,879,507	219	48.5
		James G. Blaine	Republican	4,850,293	182	48.2
		Benjamin F. Butler	Greenback-Labor	175,370		1.8
		John P. St. John	Prohibition	150,369		1.5
1888	38	BENJAMIN HARRISON	Republican	5,447,129	233	47.9
		Grover Cleveland	Democrat	5,537,857	168	48.6
		Clinton B. Fisk	Prohibition	249,506		2.2
		Anson J. Streeter	Union Labor	146,935		1.3
1892	44	GROVER CLEVELAND	Democrat	5,555,426	277	46.1
		Benjamin Harrison	Republican	5,182,690	145	43.0
		James B. Weaver	People's	1,029,846	22	8.5
		John Bidwell	Prohibition	264,133		2.2
1896	45	WILLIAM MCKINLEY	Republican	7,102,246	271	51.1
		William J. Bryan	Democrat	6,492,559	176	47.7
1900	45	WILLIAM MCKINLEY	Republican	7,218,491	292	51.7
		William J. Bryan	Democrat; Populist	6,356,734	155	45.5
		John C. Woolley	Prohibition	208,914		1.5

* Because of the death of Greeley, Democratic electors scattered their votes.

886

Year	Number of States	Candidates	Party	Popular vote	Electoral vote	Percentage of popular vote
1904	45	THEODORE ROOSEVELT	Republican	7,628,461	336	57.4
		Alton B. Parker	Democrat	5,084,223	140	37.6
		Eugene V. Debs	Socialist	402,283		3.0
		Silas C. Swallow	Prohibition	258,536		1.9
1908	46	WILLIAM H. TAFT	Republican	7,675,320	321	51.6
		William J. Bryan	Democrat	6,412,294	162	43.1
		Eugene V. Debs	Socialist	420,793		2.8
		Eugene W. Chafin	Prohibition	253,840		1.7
1912	48	WOODROW WILSON	Democrat	6,296,547	435	41.9
		Theodore Roosevelt	Progressive	4,118,571	88	27.4
		William H. Taft	Republican	3,486,720	8	23.2
		Eugene V. Debs	Socialist	900,672		6.0
		Eugene W. Chafin	Prohibition	206,275		1.4
1916	48	WOODROW WILSON	Democrat	9,127,695	277	49.4
		Charles E. Hughes	Republican	8,533,507	254	46.2
		A. L. Benson	Socialist	585,113		3.2
		J. Frank Hanly	Prohibition	220,506		1.2
1920	48	WARREN G. HARDING	Republican	16,143,407	404	60.4
		James M. Cox	Democrat	9,130,328	127	34.2
		Eugene V. Debs	Socialist	919,799		3.4
		P. P. Christensen	Farmer-Labor	265,411		1.0
1924	48	CALVIN COOLIDGE	Republican	15,718,211	382	54.0
		John W. Davis	Democrat	8,385,283	136	28.8
		Robert M. La Follette	Progressive	4,831,289	13	16.6
1928	48	HERBERT C. HOOVER	Republican	21,391,993	444	58.2
		Alfred E. Smith	Democrat	15,016,169	87	40.9
1932	48	FRANKLIN D. ROOSEVELT	Democrat	22,809,638	472	57.4
		Herbert C. Hoover	Republican	15,758,901	59	39.7
		Norman Thomas	Socialist	881,951		2.2
1936	48	FRANKLIN D. ROOSEVELT	Democrat	27,752,869	523	60.8
		Alfred M. Landon	Republican	16,674,665	8	36.5
		William Lemke	Union	882,479		1.9
1940	48	FRANKLIN D. ROOSEVELT	Democrat	27,307,819	449	54.8
		Wendell L. Willkie	Republican	22,321,018	82	44.8
1944	48	FRANKLIN D. ROOSEVELT	Democrat	25,606,585	432	53.5
		Thomas E. Dewey	Republican	22,014,745	99	46.0
1948	48	HARRY S. TRUMAN	Democrat	24,105,812	303	49.5
		Thomas E. Dewey	Republican	21,970,065	189	45.1
		J. Strom Thurmond	States' Rights	1,169,063	39	2.4
		Henry A. Wallace	Progressive	1,157,172		2.4
1952	48	DWIGHT D. EISENHOWER	Republican	33,936,234	442	55.1
		Adlai E. Stevenson	Democrat	27,314,992	89	44.4
1956	48	DWIGHT D. EISENHOWER	Republican	35,590,472	457†	57.6
		Adlai E. Stevenson	Democrat	26,022,752	73	42.1
1960	50	JOHN F. KENNEDY	Democrat	34,227,096	303**	49.9
		Richard M. Nixon	Republican	34,108,546	219	49.6
1964	50	LYNDON B. JOHNSON	Democrat	42,676,220	486	61.3
		Barry M. Goldwater	Republican	26,860,314	52	38.5

† Walter B. Jones received 1 electoral vote.   ** Harry F. Byrd received 15 electoral votes.

Illustrations

Index

A

Aberdeen, Lord, 317, 321-322
Abilene, Kansas, 503
Abolitionism (*see also* Negroes; Slavery): colonial era, 140-141; organization, 308-310; Republican party, 397; Kansas free-soilers, 396-397; John Brown, 397, 401-402; Copperheads, 419-420; Civil War agitation, 419-420
Abrams v. U.S., 698
Absalom! Absalom! (Faulkner), 767
Acadia, 98
Acheson, Dean, 820, 824-825
Adams, Brooks, 545, 601
Adams, Charles Francis, 433, 475, 584
Adams, Charles Francis, Jr., 445
Adams, Henry, 220, 353, 472, 542, 545, 584, 601
Adams, Herbert B., 600
Adams, John: religious attitudes, 112; revolutionary activity, 126, 134-135, 139-140; on slavery, 139, 158; peace commissioner, 151; Massachusetts constitution, 157; Vice-president, 183-184, 191; President, 196-201; Supreme Court, 201-202
Adams, John Quincy: War of 1812, 122, 226-227; Secretary of State, 230-232; Monroe Doctrine, 232-233; 1824 campaign, 265-266; on executive power, 266-267; President, 266-268; Indian policy, 267; economic thought, 267
Adams, Samuel, 179, 183, 213; "Caucus Club," 93; Boston Massacre, 134; Committees of Correspondence, 135; Boston Tea Party, 136; constitutional debate, 179
Adams, Samuel Hopkins, 656
Adams, Sherman, 841
Adams-Onis Treaty, 230
Adamson Act, 664
Addams, Jane, 581
Adet, Pierre A., 198
Adkins v. Children's Hospital, 651, 700
Adventures of Huckleberry Finn, The (Twain), 606
Adventures of Tom Sawyer, The (Twain), 606
Agriculture: Indian, 6, 8; colonial, 19, 48-49, 60-61, 78, 82, 85, 88; early nineteenth century, 234, 242-243; mechanization, 368-369; western plains, 365-370; industrial

growth and, 380; Homestead Act, *1862*, 434; sharecropping and crop-lien, 480-483; World War I effect, 677-678; federal credit assistance, *1920s*, 701; New Deal reforms, 719-722; World War II effect, 787-788; price supports, 828, 842
Agricultural Adjustment Act, *1933*, 720-721
Agricultural Adjustment Act, *1938*, 721, 725, 728, 736
Agricultural Credits Act, *1923*, 701
Agricultural Marketing Act, *1929*, 701
Aguinaldo, Emilio, 630, 633
Air Commerce Act, *1926*, 702
Airplane, in 1920s, 702
Aix-la-Chapelle, Peace of, 98-99
Al Aaraaf (Poe), 295
Alabama, 205, 237
Alabama claims, 618
Alabama Letters, 324
Alaska: Monroe Doctrine, 232; annexation, 617; conservation, 656-658; World War II, 796
Albany Congress, 99
Albee, Edward, 864
Albion, Robert G., 372
Alden, John, 53
Aldrich, Nelson W., 657
Aldrich, Thomas Bailey, 554, 575
Aldrich-Vreeland Act, *1908*, 657, 662
Alexander I (Russia), 232, 268
Algren, Nelson, 762
Alien and Sedition Acts, *1798*, 198-199, 203
Allan, John, 295
Allegheny Mountains, 77
Allen, Ethan, 138, 167
Allen, Levi, 167
Alliance for Progress, 855-856
Allison, William, 555
Altgeld, John, 536, 538, 563
Ambrister, Robert, 230
America First, 779
American, The (James), 608, 649
American Association for the Advancement of Education, 304-305
American Civil Liberties Union, 786-787
American Colonization Society, 309, 355
American Commonwealth, The (Bryce), 576
American Crisis, The (Paine), 154
American Democrat, The (Cooper), 204
American Economic Association, 595
American Federation of Labor (*see also* Labor; Labor unions): collective bargaining efforts, 537-538;

Homestead strike, 538; Pullman strike, 538; socialist influence, 595; membership, 677, 700; red scares, 691; C.I.O. split, 729; New Deal support, 732
Americans for Democratic Action, 813
American Fur Company, 244-245
American Journal of Education, 305
American Labor party, 731
American Legion, 826
American Mercury, 751-752
American party (*see* Know Nothings)
American Philosophical Society, 117
American Protective Association, 584
American Railway Union, 537-538
American Revolution: background, 126-137; First Continental Congress, 136-137; Second Continental Congrses, 138; military action, 138-139, 144-151; Declaration of Independence, 139-141; Tories, 141-142, 164; army organization, 142-143; French assistance, 146-147, 149-151; Treaty of Paris, 151
American Slavery as It Is (Weld), 359
American society and culture (*see also* Education; Literature; Religion): colonial, 76, 78-82, 85, 89-91, 109, 111; free Negroes, 264; early nineteenth century, 288-311; southern, 338-345, 352-360, 456, 458; materialism, *1800's*, 514-515; Chautauqua, 604-605; twentieth century, 742-745, 753-760, 762, 850, 863-865
American Speaking Telephone Company, 528
"American System," 215, 265
American Telephone and Telegraph Company, 528
American Temperance Society, 306-307
American Tragedy, The (Dreiser), 763
American Union Company, 528
American Woman Suffrage Association, 652
America's Coming of Age (Brooks), 745
Ames, Fisher, 183
Ames, Oakes, 474, 518
Amiens, Peace of, 206
Anderson, Major Robert, 408
Anderson, Margaret, 747
Anderson, Sherwood, 761, 763-764
André, Major John, 148
Andrews, Samuel, 524
Andros, Sir Edmund, 68-70
Anglicanism, 21, 56, 69, 84, 88, 105-106, 108-111, 141
Anna Christie (O'Neill), 747

Cooper, Thomas, 357
Copernicus, Nicholas, 114
Coral Sea, battle of, 796
Cornell, Ezra, 602
Cornell University, 602
Corning, Erastus, 376
Cornwallis, Lord Charles, 148-150
Coronado, Francisco de, 18
Corporations (see individual names; Industry)
Corruption: carpetbaggers, 469-471; Grantism, 474-477; 1876 election, 478; railroad promoters, 517-518, 520, 523; civil service, 544, 549-550; Tweed ring, 545; nineteenth-century urban, 576-577; journalist attacks, 584-585; Harding administration, 689-691
Cortez, Hernando, 7, 17
Cosmopolitan, 649
Cotton (see also Slavery; Textile industry): 1812 production, 214; Western lands, 247-248; northern manufacture, 254-256, 382-383; plantation system, 349-351; factor system, 352; post-Civil War production, 458; sharecropping and crop lien, 481-482; Cotton Stabilization Corporation, 707-708
Cotton Stabilization Corporation, 707-708
Coudert, Frederic R., 725
Coughlin, Father Charles E., 726, 733
Council of Economic Advisers, 810
Council of National Defense, 677
Council of New England, 52, 54
Coureurs de bois, 24
Court of High Commission, 35, 38, 41
Court of Star Chamber, 34, 41
Courtship of Miles Standish, The (Longfellow), 295
Cowley, Malcolm, 750-751, 761
Cox, Jacob D., 473, 475
Cox, James M., 685-686
Coxey, General Jacob S., 562
Crane, Hart, 749
Crane, Stephen, 608-609
Crane, Verner W., 83
Crawford, Frances Marion, 610
Crawford, William H., 233, 265
Crédit Mobilier, 474, 476, 518
Creek Indians, 128, 272
Creel, George, 678, 681
Creole incident, 316-317
Crittenden, John J., 406
Crittenden Resolution, 458
Crocker, Charles, 518
Crockett, David, 321
Croker, Richard, 577
Croly, Herbert, 648
Cromwell, Oliver, 42, 56, 67
Cromwell, Thomas, 32
Crown Point, battle of, 100
Cuba, 101, 618: Ostend Manifesto, 391; Spanish-American War, 627-633; Platt Amendment, 633; Batista, 775-776; Castro, 841; Bay of Pigs, 854; missile crisis, 854-855
Cullom Committee, 553
Culture (see American society and culture)
Cumberland Gap, 128
Cummings, Homer S., 735
Currency (see Banks; Money)
Currency Act of 1751, 93
Currency Act of 1764, 129, 132
Curtis, Cyrus H. K., 585
Curtis, George W., 475, 545
Curtis, General Samuel R., 426, 494
Custer, George A., 494-495, 501
Custom of the Country, The (Wharton), 605
Czechoslovakia, 683

Dabney, Thomas S. G., 344
Dadaists, 751
Da Gama, Vasco, 15
Dairy farming, 370
Dallas, Alexander, 234
Dalton brothers, 502
Dan, Adam, 575
Dana, Richard Henry, Jr., 328
Darlan, Admiral Jean, 790
Darrow, Clarence, 697
Dartmouth College, 109
Dartmouth v. Woodward, 235
Darwin, Charles, 514-515, 591-592, 593
Daugherty, Harry, 690
Daughters of the American Revolution, 825
Davenport, James, 109
Davenport, Reverend John, 58
Davis, David, 479
Davis, Jefferson: Compromise of 1850, 335; Civil War military strategist, 416, 423-424, 439; early career, 417; Confederate leader, 418; economic problems, 432-433; surrender, 447; imprisonment, 448
Davis, John, 11
Davis, John W., 698-699
Davis, Kingsley, 803-804
Davy, Sir Humphrey, 116
Dawes, Charles G., 698
Dawes, William, 137
Dawes Act, 496-497
Day, Benjamin, 302
Deane, Silas, 146
Dearborn, General Henry, 221-222
Death in the Afternoon (Hemingway), 765
De Bow, J. D. B., 363
Debs, Eugene V., 537-538, 595, 678
Declaration of Independence, 102, 139-141
Declaration of Rights and Grievances, 133
Declaratory Act, 1776, 133
Deere, John, 368, 508
Deerslayer, The (Cooper), 295
De Forest, John, 342
De Gaulle, Charles, 790, 794, 842
De Grasse, Admiral, 150
Deism, 105, 107, 113-114
Delaware, 26, 64-66, 162, 172, 178, 410, 465
De Leon, Daniel, 595
De Lesseps, Ferdinand, 637
Dell, Floyd, 746, 752-753
De Mille, Cecil B., 755
Democratic party, 283, 285-286, 332-333, 336, 394, 397-398, 403-404, 419-420, 446, 468-469, 476, 478-479, 484-485, 544-546, 563-565, 813, 826-828
Democratic Republicans, 268
Democratic Vistas (Whitman), 300
Denmark, 195, 618
Dennis, Eugene, 822-823
De Ojeda, Alonzo, 17
Depew, Chauncey M., 483
Depressions (see Economy)
De Sapio, Carmine, 851
Desert Land Act, 1877, 506
Desire Under the Elms (O'Neill), 747
De Smet, Father, 323
De Soto, Hernando, 18
Despotism in America (Hildreth), 340
Dewey, Commodore George, 629-630
Dewey, John, 597-598, 646
Dewey, Thomas E., 780, 788-789, 813, 826
Dial, The, 308

Díaz, Adolfo, 775
Díaz, Bartholomew, 115
Díaz, Porfirio, 640
Díaz del Castillo, Bernal, 7
Dickens, Charles, 294, 314-315
Dickinson, Emily, 605
Dickinson, John, 161
Diem, Premier Ngo Dinh, 855, 861
Dies, Martin, 811
Dingley Tariff, 565, 633
Dinwiddie, Robert, 99
Discourse on the Constitution and Government of the United States, A (Calhoun), 359
Discovery and exploration: Columbus, 2-5; pre-Columbian, 6-11; motivators, 11-14; Portugal, 14-16; Spain, 16-19; France, 23-25, 96-97; Holland, 25-26; England, 27-28; Lewis and Clark expedition, 244-245
Disquisition on Government, A (Calhoun), 359
District of Columbia, 334, 436
Dix, Dorothea Lynde, 307, 354
Dixon, Jeremiah, 341
Dodge, Mabel, 746
Doheny, Edward F., 690-691
Dole, Sanford B., 622
Dollar Diplomacy, 637, 640
Dominican Republic, 639-640, 774
Dongan, Colonel Thomas, 64
Doolittle, James H., 796
Dorr, Thomas W., 263-264
Dos Passos, John, 761-763, 766
Doughty, Thomas, 301
Douglas, Paul, 726
Douglas, Stephen A.: squatter sovereignty issue, 332; Compromise of 1850, 335; railroad promotion, 377; Kansas-Nebraska Act, 392-394; Dred Scott decision, 399; Lincoln-Douglas debates, 400-401; 1860 election, 403-404
Douglas, William O., 736, 823
Douglass, Frederick, 336
Downer, Samuel, 526
Drake, E. L., 524
Drake, Francis, 21, 27, 33
Drama (see Theater)
Dred Scott v. Sandford, 398-399
Dreiser, Theodore, 609-610, 649, 763-764
Dressler, Marie, 755
Drew, Daniel, 516, 582
Drexel, Morgan and Company, 521
Drift and Mastery (Lippmann), 648
Drum Taps (Whitman), 409
Dulles, John F., 827, 832-833, 835, 837-839, 841
Dumbarton Oaks Conference, 806
Dunne, Finley Peter, 557, 631
Duplex Printing Press v. Deering, 700
Du Pont, Victor, 198
Durand, Asher, 301
Durant, William C., 704
Dutch Reformed Church, 108-109
Dwight, Timothy, 242, 294
Dynamic Sociology (Ward), 593

E

East India Company, 135-136
Eastman, Max, 746, 752
Eaton, Dorman B., 545

Eaton, John H., 275
Eaton, Theophilus, 58
Economic Cooperation Administration, 716
Economic Interpretation of the Constitution, An (Beard), 600
Economy (*see also* Agriculture; Banks; Industry): colonial, 44-45, 48-49, 60, 63, 66-67, 78, 95; plantation, 79-82; American Revolution, 142; Articles of Confederation, 165-166; early nineteenth century, 234-235, 242-245, 247; Clay's American System, 265; *1837* depression, 280-282, 315, 326; *1855* depression, 362; *1857* depression, 384-385; Civil War, 433-435; post-Civil War southern, 480-482; academic theories, 514-515, 591-596, 646-648; *1893* depression, 531, 562; Mugwumps, 545; populist demands, 558-559; Progressive era, 646-648, 654-657; *1920s*, 699, 701-702, 704-705; *1929* depression, 706-709; New Deal reforms, 717-719, 732; *1937* recession, 737-738; World War II, 787-788; post-World War II, 810, 840, 853-854
Eddy, Mary Baker, 583
Eden, Anthony, 791
Edison, Thomas A., 528, 578
Education: colonial, 56, 79-80, 85, 93, 109, 117-119, 158; Land Ordinance, *1785*, 167, 205; Catholic, 293; early nineteenth century, 303-306; South, 356; Middle West, 370; Morrill Land Grant Act, 434; southern Negro, 470, 477; John Dewey's theory, 598; higher learning, *1870-1900*, 601-603; public, *1870-1900*, 603-604; Chautauquas, 604-605; Smith-Hughes Act (land grant colleges), 664; G.I. Bill, 809-810; school desegregation, 830-832; sputnik reaction, 841; *1965* Elementary and Secondary Education Act, 859
Education of Henry Adams, The, 353, 542, 601
Edwards, Haden, 320
Edwards, Jonathan, 106-109
Egypt, 837, 839-840
Einstein, Albert, 788
Eisenhower, Dwight D.: World War II, 789-791, 793; *1952* election, 827-828; Korean War, 828; party politics, 828-829; McCarthyism, 829-830; civil rights, 830-832; massive retaliation policy, 833; foreign policy, 835, 837-839; *1956* election, 840; Eisenhower Doctrine, 840; economic policy, 842
Eisenhower Doctrine, 840
El Alamein, battle of, 790
Elections (*see* Politics)
Eliot, Charles W., 550, 602
Eliot, Sir John, 42
Eliot, T. S., 603, 749, 762
Elizabeth I, 21, 33-36
Elkins Act, *1903*, 656
Elliott, William, 357
Ellison, Ralph, 864
Elmer Gantry (Lewis), 764
El Salvador, 775
Elssler, Fanny, 302
Ely, Richard T., 595, 601
Emancipation Proclamation, 433, 435, 456, 458-460
Embargo Act, *1807*, 209
Emergency Banking Act, *1933*, 716
Emergency Fleet Corporation, 676
Emergency Relief Act, *1935*, 724
Emerson, Ralph Waldo, 288, 292, 295, 296-298, 300-301, 306, 309, 329, 332, 358

Emmett, Daniel, 341
Emperor Jones (O'Neill), 747
Enclosure movement, 32
Encomienda, 18-19
Endecott, John, 54
England: medieval, 21, 32-33, 36-42; colonizing role, 27-28, 46-48, 51-54, 57, 64-67; law, 34-36; Navigation Acts, 67-68; Glorious Revolution, 69-70; French and Indian War, 97-102; colonial financial policy, 126-138; American Revolution, 144-151; Treaty of Paris, *1783*, 151, 163-164; Northwest territories, 189, 193-194; French wars, 191-195, 208-209; Jay's Treaty, 193-195; Barbary pirates, 203; impressment and embargo, 209-210, 228; War of 1812, 215-228; Rush-Bagot settlement, 228-229; Spanish Florida, 230; Latin-American revolts, 231-233; *Caroline* affair, 315-316; Aroostook War, 316; *Creole* case, 316-317; Webster-Ashburton Treaty, 317-318; Texas question, 321-332; Oregon question, 322-325; Civil War policy, 433-434; and U.S. expansion, 617-620, 625-627, 637; World War I, 667-668, 670, 675, 682-683; Washington Conference, 772-773; World War II, 779-781, 786, 789-791, 807; Cold War policy, 814-816; colonial liquidation, 833-834
English Traits (Emerson), 296
Enlightenment, 114-116
Episcopalians, 293, 357
Ericsson, John, 429
Ericsson, Leif, 11
Erie Canal, 251-252, 374-375, 379
Erie Railroad, 376, 516-517, 535
Erik the Red, 11
Errol, Leon, 759
Erskine, David, 216
Esch-Cummins Transportation Act, *1920*, 692
Espionage Act, *1917*, 678
Essays on Domestic Industry (Gregg), 351
"Ethnic" groups, modern (*see also* Politics; Immigration): and World War I, 669; World War II, 779; and McCarthyism, 822; and Republican party, 826-827
European Defense Community, 832-833
European Recovery Program, 815
Evangeline (Longfellow), 295
Evans, Oliver, 165-166
Everybody's, 649
Ewell, General Richard S., 439-440
Executive: Washington's appointments, 185-186; Navy Department establishment, 197; two-term precedent, 210; Madison's concept, 215, 220; Hartford Convention, 226; J. Q. Adam's concept, 226; Jacksonian concept, 269-271, 275, 282-283; impeachment attempt, 467-468; Department of Defense establishment, 812; Twenty-second Amendment, 811; Department of Health, Education, and Welfare establishment, 828; Department of Housing and Urban Affairs, 860; Department of Transportation, 860; Presidential Succession Act, 811
Exile's Return (Cowley), 751
Expansion (*see also* Boundaries): Louisiana Purchase, 206-208; Oregon, 229; fur trade impetus, 234-235; Texas annexation, 318-322; California annexation, 327-331; Gadsden Purchase, 332, 393; Mon-

roe Doctrine, 616-617, 625-627; Alaska purchase, 617; Pacific, 618-620; naval role, 622-624; Pan-American Union, 623; Spanish-American War, 627-633; public opinion, 631-632; Platt Amendment, 633; Dollar Diplomacy, 637, 640; Panama Canal, 637-639; Roosevelt Corollary, 639-640; in Caribbean, 639-640
Explorers of North America, The (Bartlett), 76

F

Fair Employment Practices Commission, 787
Fair Labor Standards Act, *1938*, 737
Fairbanks, Douglas, 755
Fall, Albert B., 690
Farewell to Arms, A (Hemingway), 668, 765
Farley, James A., 715, 731
Farm Bureau Federation, 719
Farm Tenancy Act, *1937*, 722, 736
Farmer, James, 857, 860
Farming (*see* Agriculture)
Farquier, Francis, 81
Farragut, Captain David G., 428
Farrell, James T., 761
Faubus, Orval E., 831
Faulkner, William, 767
Fawkes, Guy, 38
Federal Communications Commission, 758
Federal Deposit Insurance Corporation, 716
Federal Emergency Relief Administration, 723
Federal Farm Board, 701, 707
Federal Farm Loan Act, 663
Federal Housing Administration, 736
Federal Reserve Act, *1913*, 662-663
Federal Reserve Board, 716
Federal Trade Commission, 663, 699
Federal Writers Project, 724
Federalist, The, 179
Federalist party, 179-180, 187, 189-191, 193, 195-196, 198-201, 222, 233
Feke, Robert, 87
Fenians, 617-618
Fenno, John, 190
Ferdinand, King, 3, 5, 16-17
Fetterman, Captain W. J., 493-494
Field, Marshall, 586
Fields, W. C., 759
Fillmore, Millard: Compromise of 1850, 336; accedes to presidency, 336; American party candidate, 398
Finance (*see* Banks; Taxation)
Financier, The (Dreiser), 610
Fine Arts (*see* Architecture; Painting; Sculpture)
Finland, 795, 807
Fish, Hamilton, 473-474
Fishing: colonial era, 60, 87, 101; Canada-U.S. disputes, 227, 229, 618, 624-625; Pacific Northwest, 232; New England, 242-243
Fisk College, 470
Fisk, Jim, 473, 516
Fiske, John, 166
Fithian, Philip, 80
Fitzgerald, F. Scott, 751, 757, 764-766
Fitzhugh, George, 355-356
Flagler, Henry M., 524, 526
Fletcher v. Peck, 205
Fleury, Jean, 23
Flint, Timothy, 308
Florida, 63, 83, 101, 128, 163, 189,

898

Morison, Samuel Eliot, 16
Mormons, 325-327
Morrill Land Grant Act, *1862*, 434, 507, 602
Morris, Gouverneur, 163, 184
Morris, Robert, 143, 164-165, 213
Morrow, Dwight L., 775
Morse, Samuel F. B., 381-382
Morton, Oliver, 468-469
Motion pictures, 754-756
Mott, Lucretia C., 652
Mount Holyoke College, 305
Mountjoy, Lord, 34
Mourning Becomes Electra (O'Neill), 747
Muckrakers, 649-650
Mugwumps, 545, 550-551
Muller v. Oregon, 651
Mumford, Lewis, 753, 762
Munich Conference, 778-779
Munn v. Illinois, 552-553
Murder in the Cathedral (Eliot), 762
Murphy, Frank, 736
Muscle Shoals, 700, 722
Music: early nineteenth century, 302; jazz and ragtime, 756-757
Mussolini, Benito, 778-779, 791
Mutual Defense Assistance Act, 817

N

Nagy, Imre, 839
Naked and the Dead, The (Mailer), 863
Nantes, Edict of, 22
Napoleon I, 208-209, 216, 223, 231
Napoleon III, 434, 616-617
Nashville, battle of, 446
Nasser, Gamal Abdel, 837-839
Nast, Thomas, 475, 477, 577, 584
Nathan, George Jean, 751, 753
Nation, The, 475
National Association for the Advancement of Colored People, 830
National Association of Manufacturers, 729
National Conservation Association, 656
National Defense Education Act, 841
National Economist, 559-560
National Farmer's Alliance, 559
National Gazette, 190-191 198
"National Highway," 249
National Housing Act, 814
National Industrial Recovery Act, *1933*, 717-718, 728
National Labor Relations Act, *1935*, 728
National Labor Relations Board, 729, 811
National Labor Union, 536
National Municipal League, 577
National Origins Act, *1924*, 694
National Recovery Administration, 718-719, 725
National Republican party (*see also* Whig party), 268, 278
National Security Council, 812
National Trades Union, 258
National Woman Suffrage Association, 652
National Youth Administration, 714, 724
Native Son (Wright), 762
Naturalization (*see* Citizenship; Immigration)
Nature (Emerson), 296
Naval Act, *1890*, 623
Naval War College, 623
Navigation Acts, 67-68, 70-71, 84
Navy (*see also* World War I; World War II): American Revolution, 146-147; *1798* expansion, 197;

Jefferson de-emphasizes, 203; War of 1812, 218, 220-222; Civil War, 428-429; expansionist role, 622-624; Washington Conference, *1921*, 772-773; *1938* expansion, 778; Department of Defense structure, 812
Navy Department, 197
Nebraska, 364, 367, 391-396, 509
Negroes (*see also* Civil rights; Slavery): Portuguese trade in, 15; and *conquistadores*, 19; in Lesser Antilles, 26; new to Virginia, 45; Virginia laws on, 49; in Carolina, 62; in Georgia, 63; in colonial population, 76, 125; free, 158-159, 264, 345-346; southern caste system, 345-347; Civil War population, 345-346, 353; Civil War, 448; colonization attempts, 454, 460, 462; Reconstruction era, 456-457, 462, 470; Force Act, *1870*, 471-472; Mississippi Plan, 477; education, 477, 604; plantation system, 481; northern migration, 574, 694-695; muckrakers, 648-649; New Deal, 731-732; jazz, 757; World War II, 787; *1948* election, 813; Truman's civil rights program, 814, 830; school desegregation, 830-832; Kennedy's civil rights proposals, 853; Civil Rights Act, *1964*, 857; rights demonstrations, 1960's, 860-861
Nelson, William, 421-422
Netherlands, 25-26, 58-59, 63-64, 85, 94, 97, 147, 165, 816-817, 833-834
Neutrality: Neutrality Proclamation, *1793*, 192; late eighteenth century, 192-194, 196-198; Napoleonic wars, 208-210; violations and War of 1812, 215-216, 219; Neutrality Act, *1818*, 231; Civil War and English, 433-434; World War I violations, 474, 669-672; Neutrality Act, *1935*, 777; Neutrality Act, *1937*, 777
Neutrality Act, *1935*, 777
Neutrality Act, 1937, 777
Neutrality Proclamation, *1793*, 192
New Deal (*see also* Roosevelt, Franklin D.): bank reforms, 715-716; monetary reforms, 716-717; National Recovery Administration, 717-719; agriculture, 719-722; Tennessee Valley Authority, 722; relief measures, 722-724; *1934* election, 725-726; opposition, 726-727, 738; public utilities, 727-728; Social Security Act, *1935*, 728; politics, 730-734; Court fight, 734-736; housing, 736-737; labor, 737; recession, 737-738; assessment, 738-739
New Democracy, The (Weyl), 648
New England Emigrant Company, 395
New Hampshire, 58, 166-167, 170
New Harmony, 307-308
New Jersey, 64-65, 84-85, 158, 160, 162, 178, 263
New Mexico, 98, 334, 336, 392, 495, 500, 659
New Orleans, 96-97, 101, 164, 189, 192, 195, 206, 224-226, 247, 428
New Republic, The, 758
New York, 63-64, 70, 84-86, 92, 134, 144, 147-149, 159-160, 162, 167, 171-173, 179, 263-264, 367, 376
New York City, 85, 118, 142, 252-253, 376, 578-579
New York and Harlem Railroad, 375
New York Central Railroad, 516-517, 535

Newfoundland, 46, 60, 87
Newport, Captain Christopher, 43-44
Newton, R. Heber, 582
New Zealand, 809, 837
Nevada, 499-500
Niagara, battle of, 224, 227
Nicaragua, 37, 373, 637-640, 774
Nicholson, Francis, 70
Nimitz, Admiral Chester, 786, 798
Nine-Power Pact, 773-774
Nixon, Richard M., 811, 822, 827, 840-843, 852, 856
Non-Intercourse Act, *1809*, 209, 215
Norris, Frank, 608
Norris, George W., 658, 678, 700
Norris-LaGuardia Act, *1932*, 700
North, Lord, 134, 136, 138-139, 146, 150
North American Review, The, 233, 300, 303, 584
North Atlantic Treaty Organization, 816-817, 832-833
North Carolina, 61-62, 128, 133, 141, 149, 162, 167, 180, 264, 353, 410, 484
North of Boston (Frost), 749
North West Company, 244
Northern Pacific Railroad, 519, 521-522
Northern Securities Company, 522, 531, 654
Northwest Ordinance, *1787*, 168-169, 207, 332
Northwest passage, 27, 33
Northwest Territory: Land Ordinance of 1785, 167-168, 205, 237; British in, 189, 193-194
Notes on Virginia (Jefferson), 351
Nullification, 274-276
Nullification Proclamation, 276
Nye, Gerald P., 671, 777

O

Oberlin College, 305
Ocean Mail Subsidy Act, 621
Ochs, Adolph S., 585
O'Connell, Maurice, 810
Octopus, The (Norris), 609
Odets, Clifford, 762
Of Plymouth Plantation (Bradford), 21, 53
Of Time and the River (Wolfe), 767
Ogden, Aaron, 236
Ogden v. Saunders, 235
Oglethorpe, James, 62
O'Higgins, Bernardo, 231
Ohio, 167, 189, 205, 367, 377
Ohio Company, 99, 127, 168-169
Ohio Oil Company, 526
Oil (*see* Petroleum industry)
Okinawa, 798-799
Old Order Changeth: A View of American Democracy, The (White), 648
"Olive Branch Petition," 138
Oliver, James, 508
Olmsted, Frederick Law, 344, 347, 580, 587
Olney, Richard, 538, 553-554, 625, 627
Omoo (Melville), 300
O'Neal, Edward A., 719
O'Neill, Eugene, 747
Onis, Luis de, 230
Open Door policy, 634-637, 773
Oppenheimer, J. Robert, 788, 829
Orders-in-Council, 216, 219
Oregon, 205, 229, 244, 322-325, 495
Organization of American States, 818
Origin of Species (Darwin), 514, 591, 593